BUTTERFLIES OF BRITAIN AND WESTERN EUROPE AND THEIR CATERPILLARS

Published by Princeton University Press in 2026
41 William Street, Princeton, NJ 08540, USA
99 Banbury Road, Oxford, OX2 6JX, UK
press.princeton.edu

The original edition of this book has been published in French language
under the title *Papillons de jour d'Europe occidentale. Identifier tous les Papilionoidea et leurs
chenilles*, Copyright © Delachaux et Niestlé, Paris, 2024

English language translation copyright © 2026 by Jean-Pierre Moussus

Requests for permission to reproduce material from this work
should be sent to delachaux@lamartiniere.fr

GPSR Authorized Representative: Easy Access System Europe - Mustamäe tee 50, 10621
Tallinn, Estonia, gpsr.requests@easproject.com

ISBN 978-0-691-27179-8
Ebook ISBN 978-0-691-27191-0
Library of Congress Control Number: 2025931522
British Library Cataloging-in-Publication Data is available

Cover image by Richard Garvey-Williams / Alamy Stock Photo
Cover designer: Ben Higgins

Printed in Spain
10 9 8 7 6 5 4 3 2 1

JEAN-PIERRE **MOUSSUS**

BUTTERFLIES OF BRITAIN AND WESTERN EUROPE AND THEIR CATERPILLARS

An Identification Guide

PRINCETON UNIVERSITY PRESS
PRINCETON AND OXFORD

Contents

GEOGRAPHICAL AND SYSTEMATIC LIMITS OF THE GUIDE

Geographical coverage

This book deals with all the recognized butterfly species present in Europe, but Europe is not a geographically defined space with clear environmental boundaries that are consensually agreed upon. I have opted for a delineation that combines political and geographical units, encompassing all countries whose entire territory is located west of the eastern limit of the European Union, north of its southern limit, and south of its northern limit (excluding Greenland), adding the archipelagos of the Canary Islands, Madeira, and the Azores, and the island of Cyprus. This choice includes the following 42 countries: Albania, Andorra, Austria, Belgium, Bosnia and Herzegovina, Bulgaria, Croatia, Cyprus, the Czech Republic, Denmark, Spain, Estonia, Finland, France, Germany, Greece, Hungary, Iceland, Ireland, Italy, Kosovo, Latvia, Liechtenstein, Lithuania, Luxembourg, Malta, Monaco, Montenegro, North Macedonia, the Netherlands, Norway, Poland, Portugal, Romania, the United Kingdom, San Marino, Serbia, Slovakia, Slovenia, Sweden, Switzerland, and Vatican City. Ukraine, Belarus, the western part of Russia (excluding the Kaliningrad enclave), Moldova, and the western part of Turkey are excluded.

Species included and systematic choices

This guide presents a monograph for 474 species. To define this list, I relied

The geographical area covered by this field guide.

on the website www.lepiforum.org, which I consider to be the most up-to-date and well-argued in many respects, especially in terms of European butterfly taxonomy and systematics. The last list officially published by Martin Wiemers *et al.* dates back to 2018 and, in addition to being debated, does not take some more recently published works into account. The species list presented here is identical to the one available on Lepiforum, for which I activated the geographical filter "Europe" for the Papilionoidea superfamily. Europe is broadly interpreted on Lepiforum to include the western part of Russia up to the Urals and Ukraine, as well as the western part of Turkey. I thus excluded the following species from the 552 species list resulting from the activated filter, as they are absent from the selected area:

HESPERIIDAE

Pyrgus melotis

LYCAENIDAE

Callophrys butlerovi, Callophrys chalybeitincta, Glabroculus cyane, Glaucopsyche laetifica, Lycaena japhetica, Lysandra corydonius, Neolycaena rhymnus, Palaeophilotes panope, Plebejus maracandica, Polyommatus budashkini, Polyommatus damocles, Polyommatus damone, Polyommatus elena, Polyommatus icadius, Polyommatus menalcas, Polyommatus pljushtchi, Praephilotes anthracias, Tomares callimachus, and *Tongeia fischeri*

NYMPHALIDAE

Boloria alaskensis, Boloria angarensis, Boloria oscarus, Boloria selenis, Boloria tritonia, Chazara persephone, Coenonympha amaryllis, Coenonympha phryne, Erebia callias, Erebia cyclopius, Erebia dabanensis, Erebia discoidalis, Erebia edda, Erebia jeniseiensis, Erebia rossii, Erebia zaitsevi, Hipparchia autonoe, Hipparchia pellucida (after the work by Coutsis *et al.*, published in 2018, showed that those specimens, usually considered to belong to this species, actually belonged to the *Hipparchia christenseni–Hipparchia volgensis* species complex), *Hyponephele huebneri, Issoria eugenia, Lasiommata deidamia, Oeneis ammon, Oeneis magna, Oeneis melissa, Oeneis polixenes, Pseudochazara beroe, Pseudochazara euxina, Pseudochazara hippolyte, Satyrus bryce,* and *Satyrus virbius*

I have also excluded from this list species that are mentioned very rarely (often only once). Their occurrences are clearly linked to accidental human transport, as these species exhibit a low tendency to undertake long dispersal journeys in the wild. Their arrival is often associated with the maritime transport of their commercially exploited host plant (*e.g.*, the banana) along with larval stages. Butterfly exhibition farms can also be the source of tropical butterflies escaping into the wild. However, they cannot establish themselves there due to the lack of available host plants and their inability to survive Europe's winters, which are relatively cold compared with those in their natural habitats.

HESPERIIDAE

Hylephila phyleus and *Saliana longirostris*

LYCAENIDAE

Strymon melinus

*The Lime Butterfly (*Papilio demoleus*) is a migratory Asian species that undertakes dispersal journeys of several hundred kilometres, potentially leading it to accidentally reach Europe.*

NYMPHALIDAE
Caligo illioneus, Colobura dirce, Hypanartia lethe, Junonia oenone, Opsiphanes cassiae, Opsiphanes tamarindi, Speyeria cybele, and *Vanessa indica*

I also don't present three species whose presence in Europe has occurred only a few times and most likely resulted from an exceptional deviation during the very long dispersal or migration journeys they can carry out. One of them, the Lime Butterfly (*Papilio demoleus,* Papilionidae), appears to be expanding westward from South Asia and the Middle East. This is a species to keep an eye on, as its arrival in Cyprus in 2021 and its survival through a harsh winter could indicate the beginning of a permanent settlement in Europe.

The Caper White (*Belenois aurota*) is an Afro-tropical migratory Pierid species. It is known from a single European record, in Malta. The Ionian Emperor (*Thaleropis ionia*) is a Near Eastern Nymphalid species with only one recorded occurrence on the Aegean island Kastellórizo.

Furthermore, the past records of the Papilionid *Papilio glaucus,* native to North America, and the Nymphalid *Vanessa braziliensis,* native to South America, are highly doubtful. These species are consequently not presented in this book.

Eventually, a number of species whose validity is currently debated are not explicitly covered but are grouped with those of which they are often considered subspecies or ecotypes.

LYCAENIDAE
Phengaris rebeli (ecotype of *P. alcon*); *Polyommatus abdon* (status very uncertain regarding *P. icarus*); *P. eleniae* (considered one of the European subspecies of *P. orphicus*); *Polyommatus exuberans, P. galloi,* and *P. pelopi* (all three considered lineages of *P. ripartii,* whose diversity has likely been oversplit into as many species in the past); and *Polyommatus virgilia* (considered a subspecies of *P. dolus*).

NYMPHALIDAE
Coenonympha elbana (considered a subspecies of *C. corinna*)

I have added the Lura Anomalous Blue (*Polyommatus lurae*) to the list established by Lepiforum, since I was informed in November 2022 about the publication of an article describing the taxon by the authors themselves. The compelling data produced by these researchers justifies treating populations of this blue, closely related to *P. aroaniensis* and *P. orphicus,* as a separate species. The Vosges Ringlet (*Erebia vogesiaca*) is also considered here as a separate species (and not a subspecies of the Yellow-spotted Ringlet, *E. manto*) following the very recent and convincing work by Jospin *et al.* published in 2023.

The reader should keep in mind that the definition of a species remains a matter of convention (even if it can be scientifically argued), and what I propose in this guide is just one of many ways to present this diversity at a given time. There is no doubt that subsequent research will at least partially question these choices.

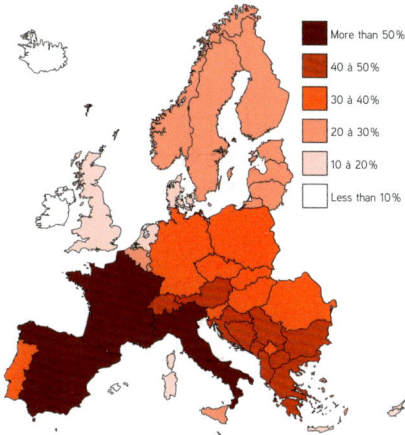

Butterfly diversity across European countries. For each country, the colour shows the percentage range of the total number of species (474).

The legend on the map reads:

- More than 50%
- 40 à 50%
- 30 à 40%
- 20 à 30%
- 10 à 20%
- Less than 10%

A PRIMER OF EUROPEAN BUTTERFLY BIOGEOGRAPHY AND DIVERSITY

Europe is a continent with fewer butterflies than one might expect

This section provides some concepts and figures to help the reader better understand and grasp Europe's butterfly diversity – what it represents in comparison with the global diversity of this superfamily, and how and why it is spatially structured within the geographical area covered by this guide. That area has an approximate surface of 5 million square kilometres, which represents roughly 3.4% of the emerged lands (around 148 million sq km), or 3.7% if the Antarctic continent, with an area of 13 million square kilometres and devoid of any butterflies, is excluded from the calculation. Today, there are approximately 19,000 described butterfly species worldwide.

The 474 species presented here thus encompass 2.5% of this considerable diversity. That 2.5% of the species inhabit 3.4% of the area means that Europe is, on average, slightly impoverished in butterflies compared with an assumed equitable species distribution across the globe, which would result in 3.4% of diversity on 3.4% of the world's land surface. For comparison, Peru alone is home to around 4,000 species of butterflies, representing nearly 20% of this group's diversity on less than 1% of the world's area (approximately 1.3 million sq km). To better understand the factors controlling the distribution of butterfly diversity in Europe, it can be useful to consider the geography in some detail, such as by examining a map showing the percentage of the 474 included species that occurs in each European country.

Mediterranean regions show high butterfly diversities

Several observations can be drawn from the study of this rough map. First and foremost, there is a growing latitudinal biodiversity gradient towards the south. In the four champions of butterfly diversity in Europe – Italy, France, Spain, and Greece – a significant portion of the country is located in the Mediterranean region. The Mediterranean domain is considered a biodiversity hotspot on a global scale. Wherever climatic conditions similar to those around *Mare Nostrum* (the Roman name for the Mediterranean Sea) are found – namely, at the southern tip of South Africa, southern and southwestern Australia, a large part of the Chilean Pacific coast, and along the Pacific coast of California – botanical diversity is remarkable, and many plant species are endemic. This botanical diversity is likely to be the fundamental factor explaining the great number of primary consumers – the herbivores, to which butterflies belong – that live there. Moreover, the Mediterranean climate is the one in the studied area that offers the longest growing season. This may have led, through character displacement, to phenological shifts between closely related species exploiting the same host plants during their larval stages or the same flowers as adults. For example, many Lycaenids exploit clovers, while many Pierid species use as host plants common Brassicaceae, which bloom for an extended period throughout the year.

These shifts now perhaps enable the coexistence of these species in environments where resource availability is prolonged by favourable climatic conditions, thus mitigating the intensity of interspecific competition. Mediterranean winters are also less harsh, especially along the coasts. Among the numerous species that live there, some manage to reproduce nearly year-round and, more importantly, to survive the winter without entering diapause. This remarkable metabolic slowdown, however, is present in all species inhabiting the temperate, mountainous, and arctic regions of Europe and can be considered an adaptation to the onset of the harsh season, marked by winter months, during which frost might occur. Negative temperatures below freezing can be fatal to ectothermic (cold-blooded) animals, which lack resistance mechanisms to coldness, such as partial body dehydration, the production of antifreezing compounds, or the

accumulation of organic solutes in extracellular fluids, that would lead to a lowering of the temperature at which they will freeze. These challenging conditions mean that such areas are not likely to host species from the tropical biome, despite its being a considerable biodiversity reservoir. These species, lacking the physiological mechanisms of diapause, often breed year-round at lower latitudes.

Among examples of species originating from the tropics that endure the adverse season without diapause are Lang's Short-tailed Blue (*Leptotes pirithous*) and the Long-tailed Blue (*Lampides boeticus*), as well as the Mediterranean Skipper (*Gegenes nostrodamus*), the Millet Skipper (*Pelopidas thrax*), and Zeller's Skipper (*Borbo borbonica*). The magnificent Two-tailed Pasha (*Charaxes jasius*), the Monarch (*Danaus plexippus*), and the Plain Tiger (*Danaus chrysippus*) are also part of this group. The case of the Geranium Bronze (*Cacyreus marshalli*) is interesting in this regard. Originally breeding in South Africa and introduced to Europe through the importation of its widely used decorative host plants, it quickly spread and is now visible throughout many European countries. Breeding studies indicate that the development cycle occurs without diapause. However, as it likely benefits from less severe winter conditions in urban areas where its host plants are protected by their owners, it has been able to move away from the Mediterranean region, unlike other species dependent on wild host plants that are more exposed to winter cold. The Mediterranean region, as a transitional domain between the tropical and temperate biomes, therefore remains relatively permeable to species from lower latitudes.

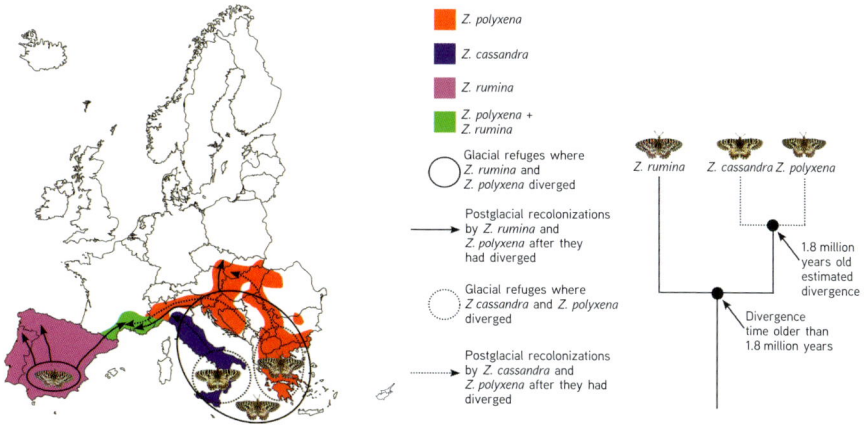

Speciation in the genus Zerynthia *during the Pleistocene glaciations. The map illustrates the various glacial refuges that successively sheltered populations of the Southern Festoon and the Spanish Festoon's common ancestor, as well as different populations of Southern Festoons. Geographical isolation over tens of thousands of years led to the genetic divergence of these populations, which prevented further hybridization events and justified their species status. The phylogeny of these three species helps in dating these divergence events. The current observed geographic distributions result from a recolonization of the northern Mediterranean region during the present interglacial period. According to Zinetti* et al. *2013 and Dapporto 2010.*

The legacy of Pleistocene glaciations

The geography of the Mediterranean basin features three major peninsulas that extend southward: the Iberian, Italian, and Balkan Peninsulas. The southern tips of these three regions currently enjoy a very mild Mediterranean climate, even in winter. During the successions of glacial and interglacial periods that marked the Quaternary era, these areas served as glacial refuges for cold periods when glaciers from the Alps covered a significant part of the temperate zone, while the rest of it looked like today's arctic tundra. The particular geographical arrangement of these peninsulas (elongated along a north-to-south axis) led to the isolation of species populations widely distributed throughout temperate Europe during the previous interglacial

period. Fragmented into two or three separate populations, their geographical distribution was restricted to refuges located in the peninsulas during the ice age. This geographical isolation gave rise to the diversification of temperate or Mediterranean butterflies during glacial periods and makes a significant contribution to the latitudinal gradient of butterfly diversity.

Species such as the Southern Festoon (*Zerynthia polyxena*) and the Spanish Festoon (*Z. rumina*) differentiated in this way. The former is found in the Balkans and Italy, reaching the western end of its range in southern France. The latter is Iberian and reaches the eastern and northern ends of its range in southern France. In the contact zone between the two species, hybridization is rare, and the offspring of such crosses suffer from low fitness, as experimental results confirm. The most plausible explanation for this biogeographical pattern is that the common ancestor of these two species once flew across the entire Mediterranean region and part of the temperate zone, retreating into two distinct populations during a glaciation in some Iberian and Balkan and/or Italian refuges. The two isolated populations have become sufficiently differentiated that the possibilities of hybridization between the two species are limited today. This scenario likely repeated within the populations of Southern Festoons, as suggested by the work of Zinetti *et al.* (2013). The Italian Festoon (*Z. cassandra*) is likely to have emerged through the isolation, during a more recent glaciation, of two populations of Southern Festoons: one persisted in the southern Italian peninsula, while the other occupied the Balkan refuge. With the postglacial warming following this period of genetic divergence, the former recolonized the Italian territory from its southern tip to the Po Valley, while the latter reinvaded the Balkans and the area from northern Italy to southern France, where it coexists with the Spanish Festoon, from which it had separated during a previous glaciation.

The Mediterranean region is both a welcoming land for new species from the South and the East and a cradle for the emergence of new species whose populations were fragmented during glacial periods. The glacial refuges for most species found today in the European temperate regions were also located in the Mediterranean peninsulas. However, unlike the most thermophilic species, whose recolonization has been limited so far to the Mediterranean region, these species have been able to reestablish themselves well beyond, some reaching as far north as the southern part of Fennoscandia. The relatively low diversification of these lineages means that, unlike Mediterranean species, their populations maintained genetic flows during the last glacial maximum, likely because they did not exclusively occupy the southernmost regions of the three peninsulas.

However, the glacial legacy extends beyond Mediterranean species. In fact, it shapes a significant portion of today's European butterfly communities, especially in mountainous and boreal/arctic zones. For example, why do more butterflies breed in Switzerland and Austria compared with Hungary and Romania, although the latter are about the same size or slightly bigger and located at similar latitudes? The second major factor contributing to butterfly diversity is topography.

For instance, the mountainous regions of Europe, like the Mediterranean regions (especially if they are both mountainous and Mediterranean), are high-biodiversity areas shaped by the succession of glacial and interglacial episodes over the last few million years. Chorological (concerning species' ranges) and, more recently, genetic data help us understand the history of non-Mediterranean butterflies during glaciations.

Studies by Thomas Schmitt and others provide evidence that, for several species – notably, the ringlets, like the Scotch Argus (*Erebia aethiops*) and the Large Ringlet (*E. euryale*) – the genetic differentiation patterns observed today between populations inhabiting different regions of the arc of the Alps (*e.g.*, the eastern and western parts) indicate the existence of two or three distinct glacial refuges at the piedmont of the Alps during the last glaciation.

This differentiation, however, has not been so significant that these populations can now be considered distinct species, but these lineages now have subspecies status. In the case of the Common Brassy Ringlet species complex (*Erebia cassioides*), the divergence process went a step further, resulting in a group of species that includes the Western Brassy Ringlet (*E. arvernensis*), Freyer's Brassy Ringlet (*E. neleus*), the Swiss Brassy Ringlet (*E. tyndarus*), Lorkovic's Brassy Ringlet (*E. calcarius*), De Lesse's Brassy Ringlet (*E. nivalis*), and the Ottoman Brassy Ringlet (*E. ottomana*), all flying in the Alps.

These data show that, during glacial episodes, many species found today at higher altitudes occupied glacial refuges located not in the Mediterranean region but in the foothills of mountain ranges whose peaks were largely covered by glaciers. They could also survive in landscapes that may have resembled arctic nunataks – continental areas emerging like islands amidst glaciers. With the climatic warming that followed the glacial maximum, populations of these cold-adapted species colonized high-altitude environments, where they found suitable breeding conditions.

While the Alps are by far the highest and most extensive mountain range in Europe, similar genetic differentiation processes have also occurred around other European mountain ranges. The Pyrenees, the Carpathians, the western

Balkan mountain chains along the Adriatic coast, the eastern Balkan mountain chains in Bulgaria and northern Greece, the Cantabrian Mountains, the Sudetes, and the French Massif Central – all of these mountain chains served as places of geographic isolation within non-Mediterranean glacial refuges, thus leading to the emergence of genetic lineages that are sources of today's diversity.

Austrian and Swiss butterfly communities, located at the heart of the Alpine arc, receive more of this glacial legacy than neighbouring Hungary, which is less mountainous and hosts less diversity. At a similar latitude, Romania also has fewer species. Although the Carpathians played a role similar to the Alps, that massif is lower and more restricted, thus also resulting in less diversity.

The relative positions of different mountain masses in the European mountainous archipelago are also crucial to understanding the spatial structure of butterfly diversity in Europe. The ranges of some mountain-dwelling species were coupled during glacial episodes; populations from one glacial refuge reconquered two different chains because the refuge was located between them.

For instance, while the Pyrenees host a few endemic species like the Pyrenean Ringlet (*Erebia gorgone*) and the Gavarnie Blue (*Agriades pyrenaica*), the latter shared with the Cantabrian massif, it is interesting to note that species like Shepherd's Fritillary (*Boloria pales*), the Mountain Dappled White (*Euchloe simplonia*), and the Glandon Blue (*Agriades glandon*) inhabit both the Alps and the eastern part of the Pyrenees. The genetic similarities between these Alpine and Pyrenean populations suggests that they have been separated only since the current interglacial period and that they probably occupied the same refuge located in southern France during the last glacial maximum.

Similar connections exist between the French Massif Central and the Pyrenees, which share the *constans* subspecies of the Yellow-spotted Ringlet (*Erebia manto*), and between the eastern part of the Alps and the western mountain masses of the Balkans along the Adriatic coast.

This same process also explains the existence of a set of species with largely disjointed ranges between the Alpine arc and the boreal/arctic zones. Examined closely, this type of distribution actually encompasses two subcategories: those called boreo-montane, found in the mountainous and subalpine parts of mountain ranges (mainly the Alps) and in the domain of boreal forests, and those called arctic-alpine, which fly in alpine meadows and the tundra of the far north of Scandinavia.

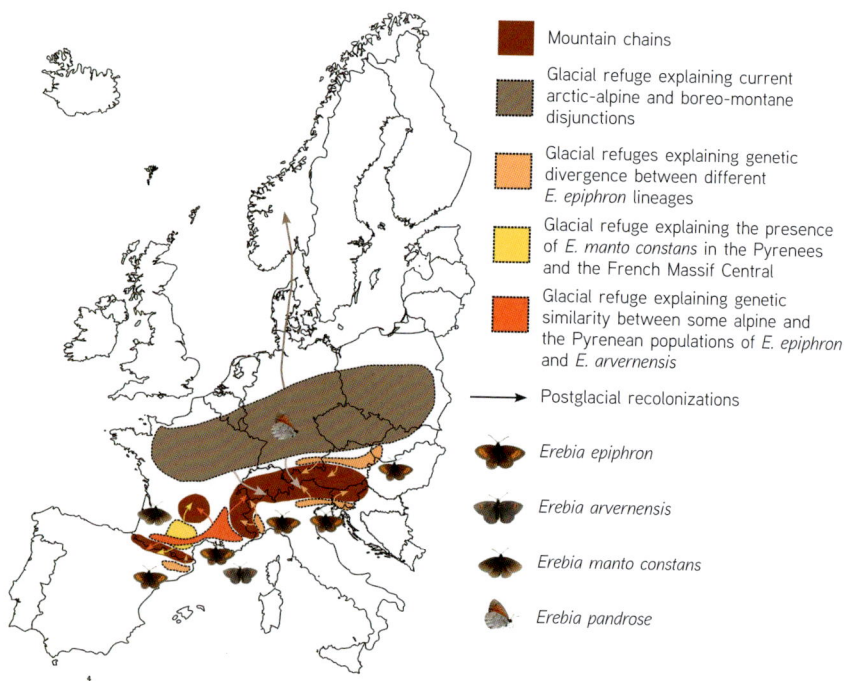

Legend:
- Mountain chains
- Glacial refuge explaining current arctic-alpine and boreo-montane disjunctions
- Glacial refuges explaining genetic divergence between different *E. epiphron* lineages
- Glacial refuge explaining the presence of *E. manto constans* in the Pyrenees and the French Massif Central
- Glacial refuge explaining genetic similarity between some alpine and the Pyrenean populations of *E. epiphron* and *E. arvernensis*
- Postglacial recolonizations
- *Erebia epiphron*
- *Erebia arvernensis*
- *Erebia manto constans*
- *Erebia pandrose*

Non-Mediterranean glacial refuges occupied by different ringlet species currently flying in mountainous (Erebia manto), subalpine, and alpine regions (E. epiphron, E. arvernensis, and E. pandrose) of the Alpine and Pyrenean massifs, as well as in arctic regions (E. pandrose). The same species may have spent the glacial period in distinct refuges at the foothills of the chains, thus diverging into multiple lineages; an example is E. epiphron in the Alps. Conversely, current populations from different massifs can be genetically very close if they have recolonized them from the same glacial refuge, as seen with E. arvernensis in the Alps, the Pyrenees, and the Massif Central, and E. pandrose in the Alps and Scandinavian regions (according to Schmitt 2007 and 2009, and Schmitt et al. 2012).

The first group of species includes, for example, the Moorland Clouded Yellow (*Colias palaeno*), the Apollo (*Parnassius apollo*), the Silvery Argus (*Aricia nicias*), and the Thor's, Titania's, and Bog Fritillaries (*Boloria thore*, *B. titania*, and *B. eunomia*, respectively). The second group includes species such as the Glandon Blue (*Agriades glandon*), the Alpine Blue (*A. orbitulus*), the Dewy Ringlet (*Erebia pandrose*), and the Alpine Grizzled Skipper (*Pyrgus andromedae*).

Genetic studies on some of these species, such as the Dewy Ringlet, show that Scandinavian populations are genetically close to Alpine populations. This result is consistent with the hypothesis of a broad lowland distribution between the Alps and the front of the Scandinavian glaciers during the last glacial maximum and a retraction in altitude to the south and towards high latitudes to the north during the interglacial period we are currently experiencing, which has been too short for a significant genetic divergence to occur.

The same result has been published for Scottish and boreal populations of the Northern Brown Argus (*Aricia artaxerxes*), whose genetic resemblance suggests a similar distribution during the last glacial maximum.

Island butterfly communities are differentiated but impoverished

Europe is rich in islands and archipelagos whose distribution spans the continent's entire latitudinal and longitudinal gradient. This allows for an informative comparison of the richness and specificity of butterfly communities. The latitudinal gradient discussed earlier is also evident in the case of islands. Iceland is certainly not the most relevant destination for observing butterflies, as only species that recolonize the island each year from the continent, such as the Painted Lady (*Vanessa cardui*) and the Red Admiral (*V. atalanta*), can be found there. In total, fewer than five butterfly species can be recorded there during the warm season.

At the other end of the gradient, Cyprus and Sardinia each host several dozen species that complete their entire developmental cycle there. These islands also serve as arrival points for strays and tropical and Near Eastern colonizers, in the case of Cyprus. England is located at an intermediate latitude and has about 60 breeding species, nearly ten more than Cyprus and almost as many as Corsica. This apparent positive diversity anomaly is explained by the island's larger size compared with others. *The Theory of Island Biogeography*, published by Robert H. MacArthur and Edward O. Wilson in 1967, provides the conceptual framework for understanding differences in diversity among islands. Two fundamental parameters add to the latitude factor – namely, the distance from the nearest continent capable of sending colonizing migrants and the island's surface area that is proportional to its habitat diversity and potential for hosting species.

The age of the island is also positively correlated with its richness because time has allowed species to arrive and perhaps even differentiate on-site. In the case of England, the latitude is temperate, but the surface area is large, and the distance separating this country from the rest of the European continent is small, particularly as the level of the Channel has often been greatly reduced during recent glacial periods. Ireland, located at the same latitude, is much poorer in butterflies, and the community is a subset of the English assemblage. This suggests that colonization occurred mostly from England rather than from the more distant continent. The initial species pool was therefore reduced, and the island's surface area is much smaller than that of its neighbour.

Beyond the latitude effect, Iceland's case is also illustrative of the impact of an island's distance from the nearest continent. Norway and Finland have species capable of living at latitudes similar to those of Iceland, such as the Dusky-winged and Polar Fritillaries (*Boloria improba* and *B. polaris*, respectively) or the Northern and Pale Arctic Clouded Yellows (*Colias hecla* and *C. tyche*). Nevertheless, they likely never managed to colonize Iceland, located over 1,000 kilometres away from the Norwegian coast, and appeared only about 15 million years ago. Island communities are thus impoverished compared with their continental counterparts, especially when they are distant and small. Nevertheless, they often harbour lineages that are unique to them; these are the so-called endemic species or subspecies.

To understand the emergence of an endemic species, it is necessary to examine the colonization scenario of an island by a butterfly species. This event is rare, especially when the distance between the island and the continent is significant. It typically involves a fertilized female or, exceptionally, a few butterflies. If these strays manage to find favourable

breeding conditions where they arrive, their very small numbers can establish a new population. However, due to sampling effects, these few founders may not exactly match the norm of the population they come from. If there is a genetic basis for this difference, what was exceptional in the continental population can become the norm in the island population. Moreover, the demographic bottleneck experienced by this population in its early stages increases the intensity of genetic drift – that is, the sampling effects occurring with each breeding event. This can lead to considerable variation in the population's average features (morphological, biochemical, behavioural).

The combination of the founder effect and intense genetic drift often leads to rapid differentiation of island lineages compared with continental lineages. The colonization of Mediterranean and Aegean islands by graylings provides a good example of an evolutionary radiation related to insularity. The Italian Grayling (*Hipparchia neapolitana*), the Sicilian Grayling (*H. blachieri*), the Ponza Grayling (*H. sbordonii*), and the Madeiran Grayling (*H. maderensis*) are all closely related to the Southern Grayling (*H. aristaeus*), which inhabits Corsica and Sardinia. The Karpathos Grayling (*H. christenseni*), the Cyprus Grayling (*H. cypriensis*), and the Cretan Grayling (*H. cretica*) are related to the Grayling (*H. semele*), a species that is widespread on the continent. Very subtle differences in male genitalia or their androconial scales allow differentiation, while wing patterns are usually indistinguishable from one another.

Moreover, Europe has several islands or archipelagos that are located in peripheral positions, providing a touch of exoticism to their butterfly communities. Cyprus hosts, for example, the majority of the European populations of the African Ringlet (*Ypthima asterope*), a species widespread in the Near and Middle East. This also holds true for the Levantine Leopard (*Cigaritis acamas*) and the Small Desert Blue (*Luthrodes galba*). A similar observation can be made regarding communities in the eastern Aegean Islands archipelago, on which a few species otherwise widespread in Turkey fly. The Aegean Meadow Brown (*Maniola telmessia*), the Orange-banded Hairstreak (*Satyrium ledereri*), and the False Marbled Skipper (*Muschampia stauderi*) belong to this category.

The archipelagos of the Canary Islands, the Azores, and Madeira are also covered in this guide. They are politically linked to Spain, for the former, and to Portugal, for the latter two. The communities populating these islands are mainly composed of species originating in the Western Palaearctic. For the Canary Islands, which are home to about 30 species, Wiemers (1995) indicates that 75% are of Palaearctic origin, 16% of Ethiopian origin, 6% of Nearctic origin, and 3% of Oriental origin. The Canary Islands and the Azores are volcanic islands. The former are about 20 million years old, while the latter emerged over the last 5 million years. Their butterfly communities have built up through colonization events by continental species that crossed the ocean separating these islands from more or less nearby continents. The greater distance to travel explains, for example, why few Nearctic species are found there. Only some

naturally migratory species, like the Monarch (*Danaus plexippus*), could have strayed there and thus founded populations (thereby fortunately losing their migratory character).

Depending on the time that has elapsed since these chance events, island lineages may have given rise to subspecies or endemic species for these archipelagos, or even for certain islands only. These communities have also been somewhat modified during historical periods by human-driven introductions. For example, the Large White (*Pieris brassicae*) and the Small White (*P. rapae*) arrived on these islands a few decades ago, for the former, and probably a bit longer ago, for the latter. Island communities are therefore peculiar in that they are a subset of continental assemblages sowing their species at random, which can then evolve into distinct lineages over time.

MAJOR THREATS TO EUROPEAN BUTTERFLIES

For a change, I begin this ominous section by examining a map: it shows the conservation status for butterfly species across European countries. In most, inventories, known as red lists, aim to assess the status of species populations within a taxonomic group. Typically, national experts decide, based on various data, to assign every species a status in the country selecting from the following: least concern, near threatened, vulnerable, endangered, critically endangered, data deficient, not applicable, and not evaluated.

The map presented to the right results from a synthesis and standardization of European countries' red lists. The authors of this work (Maes *et al.* 2019) assigned a score to each species based on its conservation status on the national red list. For instance, a score of 100 was given to a species gone extinct in that country, 80 to the critically endangered status, 50 to an endangered species, 30 to the vulnerable category, 20 to a near-threatened species, and 1 to a species with a least-concern status. The map below shows the average species scores on red lists for every European country.

The European geography of butterfly conservation first reveals that Mediterranean countries have relatively well-preserved populations with averages below 10, or even 5 for Italy and Spain. This means that a species randomly chosen from these countries is likely to have a least-concern status. In contrast, in Western and Central Europe, there are regions where butterfly populations are particularly threatened: Benelux, Denmark, and the Czech Republic. An average score above 30 means that a randomly chosen species in these countries' red lists is vulnerable.

No less than 15% of historically breeding species in the Netherlands have now gone extinct. This figure rises to 20% for Belgian Flanders. How can these alarming numbers be explained? First, it should be noted that the United Kingdom has lost 97% of its abundantly flowered meadows, 80% of its limestone grasslands, 50% of its mature forests, and 40% of its wild heaths. This is a true environmental massacre. I here wish to heavily emphasize a crucial point. While

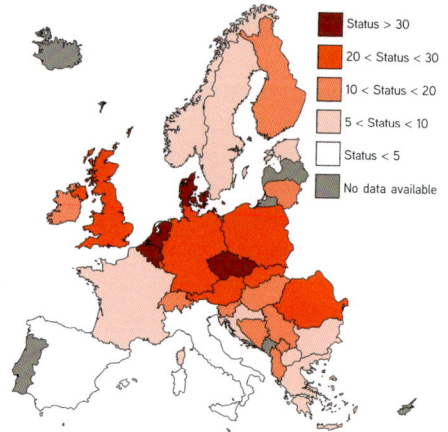

Legend:
- Status > 30
- 20 < Status < 30
- 10 < Status < 20
- 5 < Status < 10
- Status < 5
- No data available

Butterflies' conservation status in European countries. *The status indicator presented here has been calculated based on the species from each country's red list, to which a score has been assigned according to their conservation status (higher when the species is more threatened), according to Maes* et al. *(2019).*

intense media coverage daily alerts us to the problem of climate change, we often think that the current biodiversity crisis in our countries finds its main causes there. This is a serious mistake. There is no doubt that climate change will have tremendous consequences on living organisms in the coming years and decades, and the intensity of its effects will increase. However, the map presented here, showing such variable butterfly conservation status at small spatial scales, almost rules out climate change. How could climate change be responsible for a calamitous conservation status in Belgian Flanders when it is, on average, much better in France and Luxembourg?

This very alarming situation originates from habitat degradation due to human activities, with agriculture leading the way. In their 2006 study, Van Swaay *et al.* analyzed the various decline causes of 71 threatened species of European butterflies to prioritize them. Their results show that the two main threats to these species are wetland drainage, affecting almost half of them, and the conversion of natural areas into intensively used farmland, accounting for about 80% of the declines. Our agriculture is thus primarily responsible for this crisis, and the drainage of natural wetlands often aims to use them for agricultural purposes. According to this publication, climate change ranked second to last among the 14 proposed threat types to explain the 2006 conservation status, just ahead of specimen collection by collectors. Among the five most important causes of declines is also the abandonment of agricultural land to ecological succession, which leads to open habitat loss in a large part of the temperate European territory, first by shrub cover and then by forest. Grassland habitats, which harbour particularly high floral diversity, are among the richest in butterflies. These habitats are not incompatible with low-intensity agriculture, especially low-density grazing, which has the merit of blocking or slowing down ecological succession. The abandonment of low-density grazing in a large part of temperate Europe, because it is unprofitable, leads to the widespread loss of open habitats, especially dry grasslands in limestone environments. Species of Mediterranean origin, which find favourable habitat islands at higher latitudes, are particularly affected, and this pattern is partly responsible for the lower average conservation status of temperate countries compared with those in the Mediterranean region.

However alarming it may be, I do not find this overview of the threats to our butterflies to be hopeless. I would have been much more pessimistic if climate change had emerged as the first decline cause, as acting on this global disturbance appears complex (since, for now, little effective action is being taken). Acting on the quality of our environment at the scale of a region, a country, or even a continent seems less difficult. Making our agricultural land compatible with biodiversity again is possible. This landscape revolution has two strong advantages. The first is its short-term effectiveness. Given the relatively short generation time of butterflies and other insects, demographic responses to agri-environmental measures designed with conservation biologists will be quick and therefore almost immediately visible (a few years are often enough) to everyone who has implemented them as well as to their detractors, which seems to me at least as important. The second advantage is the long-term facilitation of species adaptation to climate change. Creating or preserving a dense network of favourable environments across a national territory provides those species dependent on these habitats with a means of dispersing to patches located, for example, farther north or at higher altitudes. Favouring dispersal will indeed be a key challenge in conserving biodiversity in the context of climate change. Habitats are going to be disrupted much more than they already are today. Some territories that were once able to host a particular rare species will no longer be able to do so. Conversely, other plots that were previously unfavourable to these same species will become potential breeding grounds. If the environmental matrices that separate these two areas are incompatible with butterfly dispersal, the favourable areas will unfortunately remain out of reach, and populations will simply go extinct. Most individual butterflies have a dispersal distance of about a kilometre to a few kilometres. It is with this type of data in mind (which also concerns many more taxonomic groups) that territorial management should be carried out. This is the challenge that we all should take on: giving an almost immediate second breath to biodiversity while preparing it for a future that will undoubtedly profoundly alter it, despite our efforts to prevent that. Some may find it incongruous to read such statements in an identification guide. I think, on the contrary, that purely contemplative and recreational naturalism must now be supplemented by some proactive form of naturalism that proves useful when it comes to environmental management. The knowledge disseminated by this book – accumulated during observation sessions, readings, or in discussions among friends who share a passion for wildlife – has a role to play in the immense task that lies ahead of us. It can be used to propose, argue, and disseminate or simply to understand the problems and act with knowledge when asked to cast a vote.

HOW TO USE THIS FIELD GUIDE

Identification keys

This book is designed to enable the identification of all butterfly species that may be observed in the selected geographical area. The keys provided here are the fundamental elements of an identification process that relies on a scientific approach. The reader will find a complete key based on the upperside and another comprehensive key to the underside. These two identification keys are entirely independent, but it is obviously better to have pictures of both sides to ensure a result with certainty. However, the independence of the two keys also offers the advantage of going as far as possible – meaning identifying the species, in most cases – based on a picture of a single side.

In cases where the only available side is not sufficient, result uncertainty is explicitly integrated into the key. Indeed, indistinguishable species are included in the same block, and their names are grouped in a unique box leading to their monographic pages. This structure is also intended to allow readers who have practised identification multiple times to understand that, for a particular species, the upper or the underside alone is not enough. Aware of this, they will know that, in the field, they need to observe both sides to refine their identifications.

The use of an identification key is undoubtedly the best way to improve one's skills because it relies on a rigorous and scientific method based on the observation of morphological and biogeographic criteria. The keys presented here do not work exactly like those found in most books. They are based on the visual comparison of similar species grouped into blocks. This allows the observer to see species that may be confused side by side and to avoid flipping extensively through the book while trying to identify a specimen. The structure is designed to straightforwardly guide the reader to a block of comparable species.

The entry criteria into a block are generally easy to observe and unambiguous. However, within a block of similar species, it is sometimes necessary to have precise wing pattern details or other morphological characteristics; otherwise, the identification will remain within a range of possibilities, including all or part of the species in the block that have been reached during the process.

The key begins with blocks that help navigate towards one of the six families of European butterflies. Five of these six families have a dedicated key. Our unique European Riodinid, the Duke of Burgundy (*Hamearis lucina*), is identified in this introductory key to families. The Nymphalids are divided into two keys, one for the Satyrines and the other for the rest of the species. Identification is carried out by going through the blocks in the order they are presented in the book. The entry criteria into a block are listed at the beginning of the block. If any of these criteria are not met by the butterfly in question, one must move to the next block. The total number of blocks in the section is indicated. For example, the mention of "1/4" at the beginning of a block means that it may be necessary to continue to the fourth block to find a set of criteria that successfully match the specimen to be identified.

To begin, it is essential to spend time reading the criteria indicated at the block level and not fall into the trap of comparison "by looking at the pictures", which will inevitably lead to mistakes. With experience and learning, the reader will directly know which block of species they are dealing with and will no longer have to go through this step-by-step process (although they will unconsciously use the process when they observe the butterfly). In my opinion, the best identification guide is one that gradually becomes useless through practice because its content has been fixed in the mind.

Wing patterns and morphological features are not the only useful elements during identification. Biogeography can also lead to certain conclusions.

Block number (the first among 7 blocks that should be examined respectively)

Criteria to be checked to match this family block

A few sample species to exemplify the block criteria

Page redirection to continue the identification process

1/7 [GC brown, grey, or orange] AND [antennae hooking backwards with widely spaced insertions] AND [eyes uniformly dark not ringed with white] AND [3 pairs of legs]

Antennae hooking backwards

Dark eyes not ringed with white

Antennae hooking backwards

Antennae point slightly backwards

GC brown with yellowish spots

Antennae insertions widely spaced

GC brown

GC greyish-brown with variable tints, some pearly spots

GC grey with white spots

GC orange

GC brown

KEY TO HESPERIIDAE

→ Page 34

Sample of the introductory key to butterfly families. It is very important to read the block criteria in order to avoid making mistakes.

The first among 3 blocks to examine after having reached this page

The names of species that are hard to distinguish using wing patterns share the same inset. The pictogram between the two names indicates that they are sympatric in a restricted part of their ranges.

The first sub-block with its associated criteria. Three species can here be compared in detail using the captions pointing at the pictures.

The second sub-block, with its associated criteria

1/3 On FW: [GC pale yellow or yellow] AND [3 or 4 rectangular black spots along leading edge]

1.1 On FW: Black spots all over the wing

Many red spots on FW

Thick black crescents

This black spot not streaked with yellow

Spanish Festoon
p. 124

Black spots not very thick

No more than 1 or 2 red spots on FW

Narrow yellow crescents

Black spot streaked with yellow

Southern Festoon
p. 125

Thick black spots

No more than 1 or 2 red spots on FW

Narrow yellow crescents

Black spot streaked with yellow

Italian Festoon
p. 126

⚠ The 2 species are difficult to distinguish without genitalia examination

1.2 On FW: black spots concentrated near leading and outer edges

♀ Marked black spots at HW base

Black markings here

Short tail on HW

Eastern Festoon
p. 127

♂ Black marks absent from HW base

Sparse black markings here

Short tail on HW

Eastern Festoon
p. 127

Sparse or absent black markings here

No tail on HW

Cretan Festoon
p. 128

Page redirection to the species monograph

This pictogram means that both species, although very similar, are entirely allopatric and can therefore not be confused.

Structure and functioning of a key block.

Biogeographical information is integrated into the key when possible and relevant. Within a block, when two similar species with non-overlapping ranges are encountered, a pictogram placed between the two page references specifies this feature. Greenish black-tips (*Euchloe bazae*, *E. charlonia*, and *E. penia*) are difficult to differentiate using morphological criteria only, but they are entirely allopatric, making their identification obvious based on the specimen's record location. For other species pairs, ranges slightly overlap at a contact zone, which is also indicated by a slightly different pictogram. The Scarce Swallowtail (*Iphiclides podalirius*) and the Iberian Scarce Swallowtail (*I. feisthamelii*) are an example of this case. The former flies in much of Europe, while the latter breeds in the Iberian Peninsula. Their ranges overlap in the Eastern Pyrenees.

Within a block displaying similar species, the conclusion is drawn from the comparison of criteria mentioned directly on the pictures. Sometimes, based on a photograph, it is simply impossible to reach an identification with only one side, as the similarities between the two species are too high (as in the case of the *Melitaea* and *Hipparchia* genera). This is generally indicated by an explanatory text associated with a "caution" sign.

In the keys, only the morphological criteria distinguishing a species from those closely resembling it within the same block are indicated. A more accurate morphological description is provided in the monograph dedicated to each species.

It is important to keep in mind that all living populations are variable, and butterflies are no exception to this rule. Therefore, the encounter of an individual

Pictures showing a male Lesser-spotted Fritillary (Melitaea trivia) on the left and a Purple-edged Copper (Lycaena hippothoe) on the right. Both individuals are aberrant, with wing patterns resulting from genetic or developmental anomalies. The use of the present identification keys on these individuals is impossible, but experience allows for diagnosis.

butterfly with wing patterns not matching the key criteria is not unlikely, although it will be rare. The identification key cannot account for all this individual variability – that is, it cannot provide a complete set of subspecies, forms, or individual aberrations. This will thus lead to occasional identification dead ends. I advise, at least initially, that you practise identification on several individuals, when possible, to reduce the risk of error or failure due to this intraspecific variability. I also refer the reader to other publications emphasizing this polymorphism on a European scale, such as that of Patrice Leraut (2016).

The monographs

Each species is the subject of a brief monograph presenting the main elements of its biology, ecology, and taxonomy, along with a range map and a detailed morphological description based on captioned pictures. The following pages are dedicated to explaining the information provided in each monograph. The top banner shows the

species' English vernacular and scientific names. Below the section displaying the species pictures, the following information is provided:

Distribution maps: The data used for these range maps mostly come from the LepiDiv project led by Martin Wiemers, Alexander Harpke, Oliver Schweiger, Josef Settele, and collaborators. Thousands of data points are centralized here to produce the ranges of European butterflies (excluding the Canary Islands, Madeira, and the Azores archipelagos). I have supplemented or specified this data with information from publications about specific species, especially to clarify the distribution of certain subspecies or recently described species. At such continental scale, a map, of course, cannot account for reality in every detail, especially considering that ranges are variable over time and are, unfortunately, decreasing for many species. Therefore, I ask the reader to consider them for what they are – representations of overall patterns – and to refer

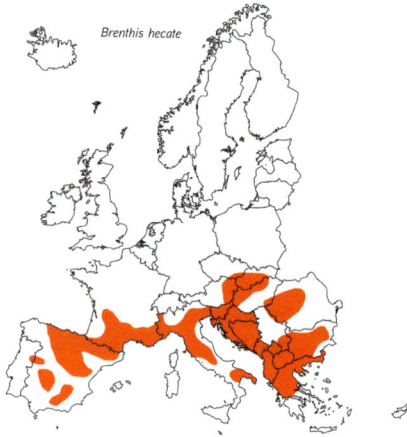

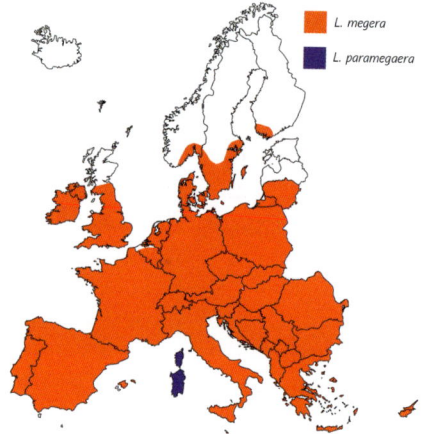

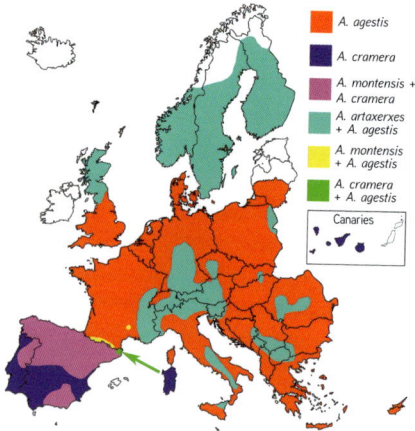

Examples of distribution maps representing various cases occurring in this guide. The map of the Twin-spot Fritillary (Brenthis hecate) depicts only this species, making understanding it straightforward. The map of the Wall Brown (Lasiommata megera) and Corsican Wall Brown (L. paramegaera) illustrates the ranges of the two species in allopatry, with colours indicating disjointed areas for these species with very similar wing patterns. The map featuring four species of the Aricia genus shows both the regions where a species might occur alone (such as southern Spain or the Canary Islands for A. cramera) and different sympatric zones (e.g., Scandinavia for A. agestis and A. artaxerxes). This supplementary information alerts the reader to the available possibilities during the identification of an individual in a given location. When the coloured area is very small, an arrow of the same colour is added to facilitate locating the region and matching it with the colour indicated in the map caption. However, it is important to bear in mind that every map's accuracy at such a scale is relative, especially regarding sympatric zones.

to regional atlases for more accurate data. Moreover, nearly 90 range maps present the ranges of multiple species together. These composite maps allow us, in cases where similar species have disjointed or partially overlapping ranges, to display them on a single map and thus highlight allopatric and sympatric regions. In this way, these maps provide additional assistance in species identification. For example, the record of a Lycaenid butterfly that looks like *Pseudophilotes baton* or *P. vicrama*

in the Balkans can only correspond to the latter, while in France, it is necessarily the former. However, in the contact zone between the two species, located in northeastern Italy, both are possible, and a more detailed examination will be necessary. These composite maps explicitly show this and are replicated in the monographs of all the concerned species, along with explanatory captions.

The following pieces of information are provided to the right of the map:

Conservation status in Europe: The pictograms follow the typical abbreviations of the International Union for the Conservation of Nature (IUCN) – namely LC (Least Concern), NT (Near Threatened), VU (Vulnerable), EN (Endangered), CR (Critically Endangered), DD (Data Deficient), NA (Not Applicable), and NE (Not Evaluated). These statuses are derived from the European butterfly red list (Van Swaay *et al.* 2010).

Climate threat level: Given the rapid climatic changes that are occurring, mainly due to anthropogenic activities, this section assesses the climate threat to the species during the 21st century. Current butterfly distributions are evolving rapidly due to these changes. Ecologists have the means to predict (with varying degrees of error) distribution shifts under a given climate scenario. These predictions rely on ecological niche modelling, which implies associating the current known presence or absence of a species with various environmental parameters (*e.g.*, temperature or moisture). The Intergovernmental Panel on Climate Change (IPCC) also provides different climate change scenarios presented as climatic parameters per geographic pixel in huge grids. When we know what the studied species needs at present to maintain its populations, it is possible to predict, with an error margin, the future suitable distribution area (by 2080) of current species considering expected climate change scenarios. Comparing the current distribution area with that predicted under a climate scenario allows us to estimate the risk of the species disappearing from the considered range. This has been done

Pictograms indicating the degree of climate threat to the focal species. The red, yellow, and green pictograms denote a high, moderate, and low extinction risk, respectively, by the year 2080 due to climate change. The grey pictogram means that this risk has not been estimated for this species or that its current range is poorly influenced by climatic factors.

by Settele *et al.* (2008) and published as a climate risk atlas of European butterflies. The authors identified six levels of climatic threat: huge risk, very large risk, large risk, moderate risk, low risk, and potential risk but not assessable for now due to data shortage or the limited role played by climate in explaining the current distribution. I propose a simplified version of these statuses by grouping the two most severe ones into one, as well as the categories large risk and moderate risk. It is important to specify that these statuses derive from a relatively pessimistic modelling in which butterfly dispersal is considered negligible, meaning that a species cannot colonize new favourable environments caused by climate changes. Therefore, the red, sun-shaped pictogram indicates two things: that the current distribution area of the butterfly is strongly influenced by climate and that the predicted distribution area in 2080 is considerably reduced compared with the current distribution area. The grey, sun-shaped pictogram indicates either that climate threat has not been evaluated for the considered species (many island species have not been integrated into this work) or that the current distribution area is poorly influenced by climate. Many widespread European species fall into this category.

Voltinism: This refers to the number of generations that the species produces in a calendar year. The number often varies over its range, in relation to the duration of the growing season that allows the development cycle to occur more or fewer times within 12 months. In some species, partial generations also occur, meaning that generally smaller numbers than a complete generation emerge subsequently to the latter. This happens, for example, in late summer or early autumn. Most often, these partial generations concern only a fraction of a species' populations, especially those living at low latitude or low altitude. They are intimately linked to food availability, which allows caterpillars to continue their development rather than entering diapause. The existence of a partial generation is noted by the addition of 0.5 to the number of complete generations produced by the species. The caterpillars of several arctic or high-altitude butterflies spread their development over two calendar years. They hatch from eggs laid during summer, spend a first winter as young caterpillars in diapause (frequently inside the eggshell), and resume their development in spring and during the following summer. They enter diapause again as caterpillars in the penultimate or last larval instar and complete their development during the following spring. This biennial development is symbolized by the 0.5 pictogram. However, I want to emphasize that such species do indeed produce one generation per year since butterflies will actually be observed every year. However, the numbers are highly variable and are often abundant every two years.

1	1–3	1–1.5	0.5

Examples of pictograms used to describe a species' voltinism. From left to right, the pictograms indicate that the species produces one generation per year; between one and three generations, depending on populations; one generation followed by a partial generation in certain populations; and one generation per year, but with a biennial larval development.

At the bottom of each monograph is a table presenting the biology of adults and that of larvae and pupae. This information is provided in the form of very visual and explicit pictograms, allowing for easier comparison between species. Most life-history traits are drawn from a publication by Middleton-Welling *et al.* (2020). I have sometimes supplemented the missing data from this outstanding and titanic synthesis with other information drawn from personal observations, specific publications, books like *La Vie des papillons* by Tristan Lafranchis *et al.* (2015), and websites like www.pyrgus.de by Wolfgang Wagner or www.lepiforum.org. Here are some clarifications on the information provided in the column dedicated to adult biology.

- *A series of pictograms provides information on the butterflies' feeding behaviour.* Although the stereotypical image of a butterfly feeding on nectar from a flower suits a majority of species, there is great variability in butterflies' feeding habits. Some adults that mainly inhabit woodland canopies or riparian areas are rarely or never encountered on flowers; an example is the Purple Emperor (*Apatura iris*). It finds sugars on rotting fruits, in sap flowing from wounded trunks, and

Series of pictograms specifying butterflies' feeding behaviours. A flower indicates nectar feeding; a fruit means that the species regularly extracts sugars from very ripe or rotting fruits. A golden drop signifies that the species consumes sap flowing from tree wounds, and an aphid indicates that it collects honeydew from these insects, just as ants would do. The excrement icon stands for the search for mineral salts and organic molecules on faeces, and the water droplet symbolizes butterflies that often drink from damp soils.

sometimes in the honeydew produced by aphid colonies (as in some Theclinae). In summer, butterflies sometimes gather by the hundreds on damp ground, such as sandy riverbanks. They find water and mineral salts here. In search of the same substances, they may even take advantage of a sweaty naturalist who comes to photograph them. This behaviour is more frequently adopted by some species than others (and more often by males than females), as indicated by the corresponding pictogram. Finally, it is not uncommon to observe a gathering of fritillaries or ringlets around a mammal dropping. Here, they are looking for mineral salts but also for organic nitrogen. The dedicated pictogram is quite explicit.

- A series of pictograms describes how males behave in their environment. Male behaviour when seeking females and whether they claim a territory or not is an important feature of a butterfly species. Some males (e.g., ringlets) spend most of their time feeding and patrolling their environment in search of females. Conversely, a male of the Brown Argus

(Aricia agestis) will remain perched on one of its favourite perches for a long time, guarding a few square metres. It will take off to chase any conspecific or heterospecific intruder entering this space or to follow a female detected from its perch. It thus typically exhibits territorial behaviour. Eventually, it is possible to observe groups of males on rocky ridges (as in the Scarce Swallowtail Iphiclides podalirius or the Southern Swallowtail Papilio alexanor) or side by side in a few square metres of grassland (as in the Small Heath Coenonympha pamphilus). These are lekking behaviours, competitive male gatherings that can be assessed by passing females the males will not fail to pursue. Some species' males show essentially one behavioural type, but many others can alternate between one and the other and are therefore assigned all the dedicated pictograms.

Series of pictograms specifying the behaviours of male butterflies. From left to right, they indicate patrolling behaviour, territorial perching with marked aggression towards conspecifics, non-territorial perching (without pursuing other butterflies), and lekking, in which males gather in specific areas. Hill-topping is also described by the use of the final pictogram.

- One of the pictogram series reflects the butterflies' dispersal abilities. These pictograms rely on the publication by Essens et al. (2017), "Ecological Determinants of Butterfly Vulnerability Across the European Continent". The first axis of the principal component analysis carried out by the authors is highly correlated to a species' dispersal distance as evaluated by experts in a non-quantitative way. Therefore, I considered the values of this first axis as a good index of a species' dispersal abilities. I cut the distribution into quartiles. The lower quartile indicates a species that is considered mainly resident (few movements exceeding 1 km around the emergence site); the two middle quartiles indicate moderate dispersers (frequent movements of a few km, especially for females looking for oviposition sites); and the upper quartile indicates large dispersers (regular movements of several tens or even hundreds of kilometres possible for the focal species). Butterflies that exhibit a marked migratory

Series of pictograms specifying the dispersal abilities of European butterflies. From left to right, they indicate low dispersal (residency); moderate dispersal of a few kilometres at most for the majority of individuals; and very strong dispersal over distances often exceeding a dozen kilometres and sometimes reaching hundreds of kilometres. The last pictogram indicates that, in addition to strong dispersal, the species exhibits marked migratory behaviours with predictable seasonal latitudinal or altitudinal movements throughout the year.

behaviour in terms of regular latitudinal or altitudinal annual movements have a large disperser pictogram associated with a double arrow indicating a round trip.

The column dedicated to larvae and pupae biology provides some information on these developmental stages.

Series of pictograms specifying the caterpillar's feeding habits. From left to right, they mean that caterpillars consume the leaves, stems, buds, or flowers and fruits of their host plant.

- *The food of the caterpillars is indicated in the form of pictograms.* While the majority feed on the vegetative parts of the plant (leaves and stems), some also or exclusively consume the flowers and fruits of the host plant or the buds.
- *The location of caterpillars and pupae accounts for the behaviours of these fundamental stages to ensure survival.* Many caterpillars whose host plants are herbaceous feed at night by climbing onto the vegetative parts of the plant, while they spend the day concealed at its base, near the ground. This behaviour is indicated by the use of the pictogram showing the caterpillar on the ground associated with the one indicating its presence in herbaceous vegetation. The pictogram showing a caterpillar or pupa on a brown background means that it spends most of its time sheltered in the litter or that metamorphosis takes place a few centimetres below the ground.
- *Finally, many Lycaenid species maintain relationships, ranging from symbiosis to parasitism, with ants.* For these butterflies, called myrmecophiles, their caterpillars are often guarded by ants that they frequently feed with carbohydrate- and amino-acid-rich secretions produced by specific glands. The caterpillars may even complete all or part of their development within the

Series of pictograms related to the location of caterpillars and pupae. From left to right, the pictograms indicate that caterpillars and pupae are, respectively, underground for the brown-background pictograms (e.g., in an ant nest); on the ground at the base of the host plant; on or under a stone for pictograms resting on a brown substrate; or in herbaceous, shrubby, or canopy vegetation for pictograms representing grass, a bush, and a tree, respectively. The ant-shaped pictogram means that the caterpillar or pupa is attended by ants or even that these developmental stages take place inside the ant nest.

ant nest. The taxonomic specificity of these relationships is highly variable; some species are known to be associated with only one ant species, while others can be maintained by ants of many species in different genera.

The meaning of all the pictograms used in the monographs and identification keys is summarized on the book's cover flaps.

The "Did You Know?" inset reports an additional element of the species' natural history. This can be a behavioural anecdote, such as an adult preference for the nectar of a particular plant, a physiological curiosity that has been the subject of a scientific study, or a controversy regarding the taxonomy or systematics of the species. This small addition aims at associating the species with something slightly less conventional than the information provided elsewhere. I have learned from my teaching experience that people remember species better if the name has been presented along with something to associate it with!

The information provided in the main monograph text includes a description of the habitat, the species' altitudinal range, and a short account of the female's oviposition behaviour. The comprehensive host plants list is mainly drawn from Clarke's provisional checklist (2022), supplemented by timely information from specific publications.

The "Systematics and Diversity" section presents the most important information regarding the focal species' infraspecific diversity or its phylogenetic relationships with other species. The subspecies list presented in this inset is rarely comprehensive and includes only the most consensual and/or widely distributed taxa. For some species, several dozen subspecies have been described, some of them questionable. Some authors consider subspecies as simple forms or simply do not recognize them. I draw most of this information from Leraut (2016), the https://ftp.funet.fi/index/Tree_of_life/insecta/lepidoptera/ditrysia/papilionoidea/ site by Markku Savela, and the www.lepiforum.org site. They are supplemented by data directly extracted from scientific articles concerning one species or another.

KEY TO BUTTERFLY FAMILIES

1/7 [GC brown, grey, or orange] AND [antennae hooking backwards with widely spaced insertions] AND [eyes uniformly dark not ringed with white] AND [3 pairs of legs]

Antennae hooking backwards

Dark eyes not ringed with white

Antennae hooking backwards

Antennae point slightly backwards

GC brown with yellowish spots

Antennae insertions widely spaced

GC brown

GC greyish-brown with variable tints, some pearly spots

GC grey with white spots

GC orange

GC brown

KEY TO HESPERIIDAE → Page 34

2/7 [[GC white or cream with transparent wing margins and large black spots on FW] OR [GC yellow with black and red spots without a long posterior tail] OR [GC yellow with a conspicuous tail on HW]] AND [3 pairs of legs]

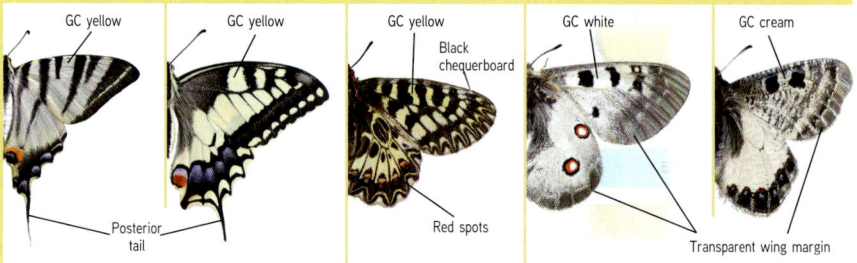

GC yellow

GC yellow

GC yellow

Black chequerboard

GC white

GC cream

Posterior tail

Red spots

Transparent wing margin

KEY TO PAPILIONIDAE → Page 40

3/7 [GC white (sometimes sprinkled with grey, but never chequered with black), yellow, orange, or orange-red] AND [no WPBS] AND [no conspicuous posterior tail on HW] AND [3 pairs of legs]

GC white; large apical orange spot

GC white

GC white

Black wing tip

GC white or pale yellow sprinkled with grey

White spots within black wing tip

Black wing tip

GC white

GC orange-red

Black wing margin

GC sulphur-yellow

Black wing margin

HW pointing backwards

GC yellow

HW pointing backwards

KEY TO PIERIDAE → Page 43

30

KEY TO BUTTERFLY FAMILIES

4/7 [Eyes black, ringed with white] AND [wing pattern exactly like the picture]

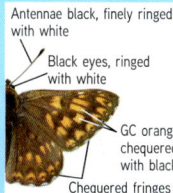

Antennae black, finely ringed with white

Black eyes, ringed with white

GC orange, chequered with black

Chequered fringes

DUKE OF BURGUNDY (RIODINIDAE) → Page 350

5/7 [Eyes black or grey, ringed with white (rarely red)] AND [antennae black, finely ringed with white] AND [GC blue, brown, grey, or orange] AND [3 pairs of legs]

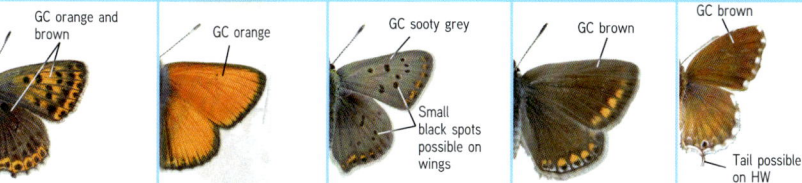

Antennae black, finely ringed with white

GC blue   GC light blue   GC purple-blue

GC very light blue

Black eyes, ringed with white

GC orange and brown   GC orange   GC sooty grey   GC brown   GC brown

Small black spots possible on wings

Tail possible on HW

KEY TO LYCAENIDAE → Page 54

6/7 [2 pairs of legs] AND [outer FW edge convex (rarely straight)] AND [[at least 1 WPBS or BPWS or series of orange spots, sometimes containing black dots or several yellow-circled black spots] OR [FW uniformly brown, grey, or black] OR [GC chequered with white and black, with no orange spot]]

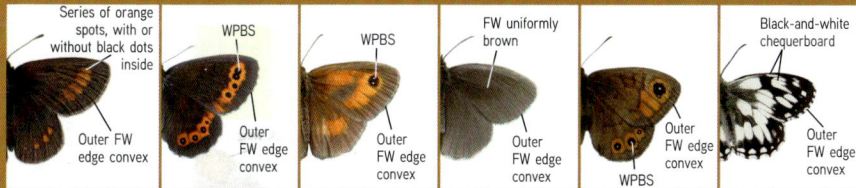

Series of orange spots, with or without black dots inside

WPBS   WPBS   FW uniformly brown   Black-and-white chequerboard

Outer FW edge convex   Outer FW edge convex   Outer FW edge convex   Outer FW edge convex   WPBS   Outer FW edge convex   Outer FW edge convex

KEY TO NYMPHALIDAE (SATYRINAE) → Page 92

7/7 [2 pairs of legs] AND [FW outer edge scalloped, concave, straight, or convex] AND [no WPBS or BPBS; no black dots in orange spots on a dark GC; no yellow-circled black spots] AND [FW GC not uniformly brown, grey, or black]

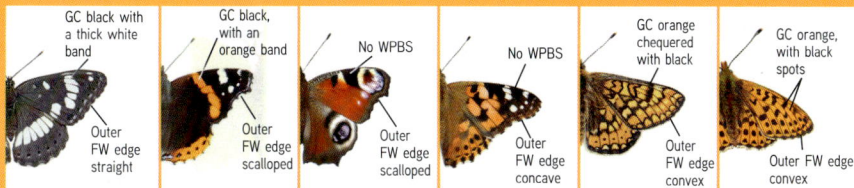

GC black with a thick white band   GC black, with an orange band   No WPBS   No WPBS   GC orange chequered with black   GC orange, with black spots

Outer FW edge straight   Outer FW edge scalloped   Outer FW edge scalloped   Outer FW edge concave   Outer FW edge convex   Outer FW edge convex

KEY TO NYMPHALIDAE (EXCEPT SATYRINAE) → Page 79

KEY TO BUTTERFLY FAMILIES

1/7 [GC brown, grey, orange, or whitish] AND [hooked antennae, with widely spaced insertions] AND [uniformly dark eyes, not white-ringed] AND [3 pairs of legs]

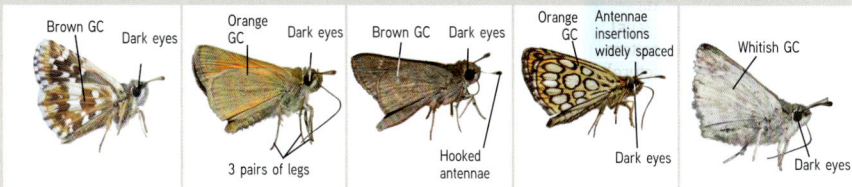

Brown GC — Dark eyes

Orange GC — Dark eyes

Brown GC — Dark eyes

Orange GC — Antennae insertions widely spaced

Whitish GC

3 pairs of legs

Hooked antennae

Dark eyes

Dark eyes

KEY TO HESPERIIDAE　　　　　　　　　　　　　　　　　→ Page 37

2/7 [[GC yellow, with long tail on HW] OR [background speckled red and black] OR [GC white or cream, with thick black spots and part of wings transparent]] AND [3 pairs of legs]

Yellow GC

Background speckled with red and black

Transparent wing margin — White GC

Transparent wing margin — White GC Thick black spots under FW

Transparent wing margin — Cream GC

Posterior tail

3 pairs of legs

KEY TO PAPILIONIDAE　　　　　　　　　　　　　　　　　→ Page 42

3/7 [GC yellow, mottled with green, sprinkled with grey or orange] AND [eyes green, grey, or brown, not ringed with white] AND [3 pairs of legs]

White GC — Grey eyes

White GC — Grey eyes — Wing veins sprinkled with grey

Grey eyes

GC white, sprinkled with grey — Grey eyes

Yellow GC — Brown eyes

GC mottled with green — Green eyes

GC mottled with green — Green eyes

GC mottled with green — Green eyes

GC orange — Green eyes

Green eyes — 3 pairs of legs

KEY TO PIERIDAE　　　　　　　　　　　　　　　　　→ Page 49

4/7 [Eyes black, ringed with white] AND [antennae black, finely ringed with white] AND [3 pairs of legs] AND [underside pattern exactly like the picture]

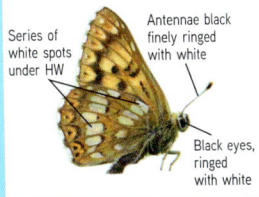

Series of white spots under HW

Antennae black finely ringed with white

Black eyes, ringed with white

DUKE OF BURGUNDY (RIODINIDAE) Page 350

5/7 [Black (rarely greyish-brown) eyes, ringed with white (rarely red)] AND [antennae black, finely ringed with white] AND [3 pairs of legs] AND [UNS different from that in block 4/7]

Antennae black, finely ringed with white

Eyes black (sometimes greyish-brown), ringed with white (rarely red)

The pictures presented on these 2 lines illustrate the diversity of Lycaenids' underside patterns.

KEY TO LYCAENIDAE → **Page 68**

6/7 [2 pairs of legs] AND [FW outer edge convex (rarely straight)] AND [[at least 1 WPBS or BPBS] OR [GC very dark with orange spots sometimes containing black dots] OR [FW GC orange with a grey margin]]

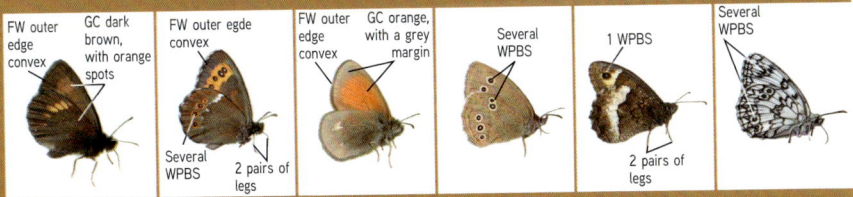

FW outer edge convex | GC dark brown, with orange spots | Several WPBS

FW outer edge convex

FW outer edge convex | GC orange, with a grey margin

Several WPBS

1 WPBS | 2 pairs of legs

Several WPBS

2 pairs of legs

KEY TO NYMPHALIDAE (SATYRINAE) → **Page 103**

7/7 [2 pairs of legs] AND [no WPBS] AND [outer FW edge scalloped, concave, straight, or convex]

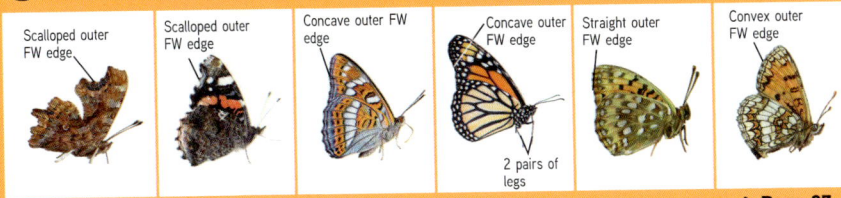

Scalloped outer FW edge

Scalloped outer FW edge

Concave outer FW edge

Concave outer FW edge | 2 pairs of legs

Straight outer FW edge

Convex outer FW edge

KEY TO NYMPHALIDAE (EXCEPT SATYRINAE) → **Page 87**

KEY TO HESPERIIDAE

1/6 FW angled upwards and above HW when the butterfly is at rest

1.1 On FW : [GC orange] AND [several light spots sometimes barely visible]

Antennae barely hooked

Pale spots (especially the outermost ones) in sharp contrast with GC

Antennae sharply hooked

Pale spots weakly contrasting with GC

Antennae barely hooked

Front of the antennal club tips orange

Pale spots aligned along a curve

Silver-spotted Skipper
p. 144

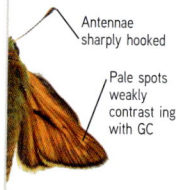

Large Skipper
p. 143

Lulworth Skipper
p. 141

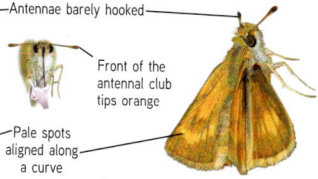

Canarian Skipper
p. 142

1.2 On FW: [GC orange] AND [no light spots]

Short and interrupted black streak in males

Front of the antennal club tips black

Long and slightly curved black streak in males

Front of the antennal club tips orange

Rectangular orange area paler than GC on FW

Short and interrupted black streak in males

Essex Skipper
p. 139

Small Skipper
p. 140

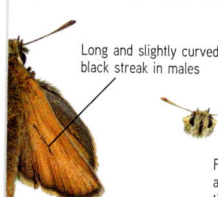

Levantine Skipper
p. 138

1.3 On FW : GC brown

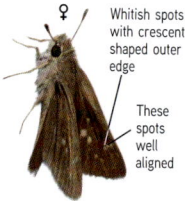

♀ Whitish spots with crescent shaped outer edge

These spots well aligned

♀ Whitish spots with a rather straight outer edge

These spots not well aligned

Well marked pearly spots

These spots not well aligned

GC brown without any pale spots in the Pygmy Skipper

These spots well aligned

♂ Dense tuft of long hairy scales on the HW costa (Mediterranean Skipper) versus sparse short (Pygmy Skipper)

Pygmy Skipper
p. 147

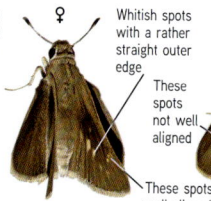

Mediterranean Skipper
p. 148

Millet Skipper
p. 150

Zeller's Skipper
p. 149

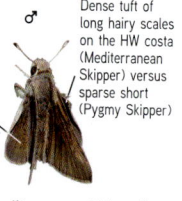

Mediterranean Skipper/ Pygmy Skipper
p. 148 et 147

2/6 [FW not angled upwards above HW when the butterfly is at rest]; On FW : [GC yellow-orange with brown spots] OR [GC chequered with yellow-orange and brown]

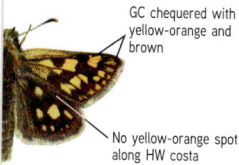

GC chequered with yellow-orange and brown

No yellow-orange spot along HW costa

♀ GC chequered with yellow-orange and brown

Yellow-orange spot along HW costa

♂ GC yellow-orange with a few brown spots

Chequered Skipper
p. 135

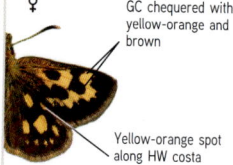

Northern Chequered Skipper
p. 136

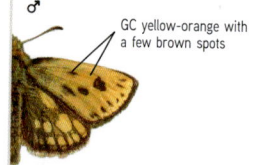

Northern Chequered Skipper
p. 136

(3/6) FW and HW in the same plane when the butterfly is at rest
On FW : [brown GC with variable tints] AND [no clear white spots in the middle of the wing]

3.1 On FW : several pearly spots

Small pearly spots
Large pearly spots
Small pearly spots
Small pearly spots

Pale but not pure white spots
Series of pure white spots
Series of large triangular pure white spots
Series of pure white spots
Series of pale regularly undulated drawings
Series of pure white spots (only 1 or 2 in the Tufted Marbled Skipper)
Series of pale irregularly curved markings

Mallow Skipper p. 151
False Mallow Skipper p. 152
Marbled Skipper p. 157
Southern Marbled Skipper p. 155
False Marbled Skipper p. 156
Oriental Marbled Skipper p. 154
Tufted Marbled Skipper p. 153

3.2 On FW : no pearly spots

Grey and brown sharply contrasting bands on FW
Grey and brown weakly contrasting bands on FW
2 very dark bands on FW

Series of small white dots along wing edges
Series of small white dots along wing edges
No white spots along wing edges

Dingy Skipper p. 145
Dingy Skipper p. 145
Inky Skipper p. 146

(4/6) [FW and HW in the same plane] AND [numerous well marked white spots on both wings]
On FW : [GC uniformly grey-brown] AND [1 or 2 missing white spots in the middle wing series]

Leading edge sprinkled with ochre
Leading edge sprinkled with ochre
Leading edge sprinkled with light grey
White spots usually ill-defined or absent here
One "equal sign" at the rear of FW

GC with pronounced copper highlights
This spot narrow
GC with pronounced copper highlights
This spot narrow
This spot thick
Small black and white spots matching those of the fringes
Complete series of white spots
Series of elongated white spots at the rear of HW

Red-underwing Skipper, Corsican and Iberian Red-underwing Skippers / Hungarian Skipper
p. 161 et 163 / p. 162
Persian Skipper p. 164
Sage Skipper p. 158
Tessellated Skipper p. 159

(5/6) [FW and HW in the same plane] AND [GC uniformly grey or brown] AND [no clear pale spots on HW]; On FW : some small white or yellow spots

Very small white spots
Very small white spots
This white spot with irregular contours
A few yellow spots

FW narrow and rather pointed
FW wide and rather rounded
Small white spots
GC chocolate brown

A few faint pale markings often absent
A few faint pale markings often absent
A few faint pale markings often absent
Sometimes a few posterior yellowish marks on HW

Warren's Skipper p. 170
Dusky Grizzled Skipper p. 168
Olive Skipper p. 172
Large Chequered Skipper p. 137

35

KEY TO HESPERIIDAE

[FW and HW in same plane] AND [GC dark brown] AND [some pale or white spots on wings]
On FW: complete series of white spots, 2 shifted outwards

Identifying species within genus *Pyrgus* is often challenging based on just 1 of the 2 sides. For some species, a detailed examination of the dissected genitalia is strongly recommended. In this block, one should proceed by elimination from left to right and from top to bottom of the page. Identification reliability decreases towards the end of the block, as illustrated with males. Females are generally darker and less sprinkled with light grey.

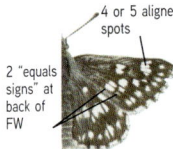

2 white spots shifted outwards

4 or 5 aligned white spots

2 "equals signs" at back of FW

3 white spots here (2 in other species)

Sigma-shaped white spot

Complete series of well-elongated pale spots

Sigma-shaped white spot

Complete series of barely elongated pale spots

Spinose Skipper p. 160

Alpine Grizzled Skipper p. 167

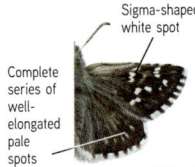

Safflower Skipper p. 165 **Yellow-banded Skipper** p. 166

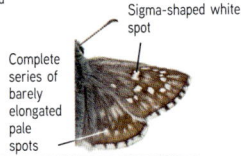

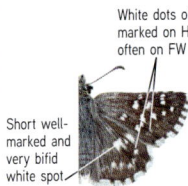

White dots often well marked on HW and also often on FW (less here)

Hourglass-shaped large white spot

Almost rectangular white spot

Thick white spots on FW

C-shaped white spot

Short well-marked and very bifid white spot

Very thick white spots on FW

Adjacent white spots form a Z

White spots rather narrow on FW

Grizzled Skipper Southern Grizzled Skipper pp. 175 and 176

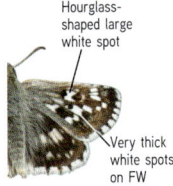

Sandy Grizzled Skipper p. 179

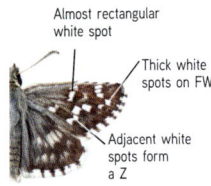

Cinquefoil Skipper p. 178

Carline Skipper p. 177

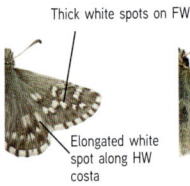

Thick white spots on FW

White spot of irregular width

Hourglass-shaped white spot

White spots leak outwards along veins

Rather small white spots on FW

Elongated white spot along HW costa

Most external white spot well marked on HW costa (hidden here)

White spots rather narrow on FW

Well-marked pale spots on HW

2 large hair tufts beneath abdomen tip (males) ♂♂

Ill-defined pale spots on HW

Northern Grizzled Skipper p. 169

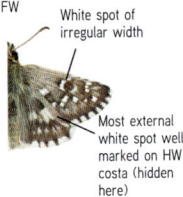

Rosy Grizzled Skipper p. 180

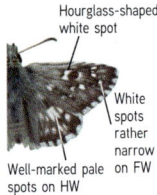

Oberthür's Grizzled Skipper p. 171

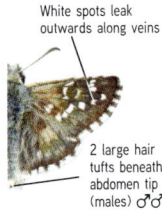

Foulquier's Grizzled Skipper p. 174

Large Grizzled Skipper p. 173

KEY TO HESPERIIDAE

1/6 [2 vivid orange bands on HW] OR [GC of FW orange]

1.1 On HW: large white spots rimmed with white or grey

2 vivid orange bands on HW

White spot often rounded or oval

This white spot elongated and often pointing forwards

Posterior series of large oval white spots on HW

Series of white spots with a straight posterior edge

Series of white spots with a straight posterior edge

Yellow-banded Skipper
p. 166

Large Chequered Skipper
p. 137

Chequered Skipper
p. 135

Northern Chequered Skipper
p. 136

1.2 On FW: small pale or white spots (may be barely visible)

Pale spots shifted forwards

Pale spots sharply contrasting with GC

Pale spots shifted forwards

Pale spots not sharply contrasting with GC

Barely visible pale spots aligned in a curve

Barely visible pale spots aligned in a curve

Pointed, long FW

Small white spots, ringed with black

No readily visible pale spots on HW

No readily visible pale spots on HW

Pure white, aligned spots

Silver-spotted Skipper
p. 144

Large Skipper
p. 143

Lulworth Skipper
p. 141

Canarian Skipper
p. 142

Zeller's Skipper
p. 149

1.3 On FW: no pale or white spots

No brighter orange area along FW leading edge

FW apex greyish

Front of antennal club tips orange

Front of antennal club tips orange

Front of antennal club tips black

Orange GC of HW has a greenish tint

Essex Skipper
p. 139

Small Skipper
p. 140

Levantine Skipper
p. 138

2/6 [GC brown or grey-brown] AND [FW narrow and pointed]

No pale spots under FW apex

A few aligned pale spots under FW apex

White spots not well-aligned under FW apex

A few well-aligned white spots under FW apex

No pale spots on HW

A few faint pale spots on HW

A few well-defined white spots on HW (absent in males)

A few well-defined white spots, ringed with black

Mediterranean Skipper
p. 148

Pygmy Skipper
p. 147

Millet Skipper
p. 150

Zeller's Skipper
p. 149

3/6 [GC of both wings brown or dark brown] AND [FW wide and rounded]

Series of white dots on edges of wings

No white dots on wing edges

Dingy Skipper
p. 145

Inky Skipper
p. 146

4/6 On HW: GC light brown or whitish, with white or pale spots sometimes barely visible
On FW and HW: shredded outer and trailing edges

4.1 On HW: [GC light brown] AND [posterior series of white or pale round spots or undulations]

3 series of ill-defined pale spots

⚠ Differ only by their genitalia

3 series of ill-defined pale spots

3 series of marks

3 series of ill-defined pale spots

Ill-defined pale spots

Ill-defined pale spots

Pale undulations

Undulating pale markings

Mallow Skipper | **False Mallow Skipper**
p. 151 | p. 152

Southern Marbled Skipper
p. 155

False Marbled Skipper
p. 156

4.2 On HW: [GC light brown or whitish] AND [posterior series of pale or white elongated spots, often barely visible]

Series of elongated white spots on FW

HW GC light brown

⚠ Uncertain identification without genitalia examination

Series of elongated white spots on FW

Elongated white spots on FW

Series of elongated white spots on HW

HW GC whitish, with series of barely visible posterior long white spots

Long posterior white spots barely visible against whitish background

Tufted Marbled Skipper | **Oriental Marbled Skipper**
p. 153 | p. 154

Marbled Skipper
p. 157

5/6 FW and HW: [fringes black and white] AND [wing edges not shredded]
On HW: [continuous white band along trailing edge] OR [1 complete series of round or ovoid white spots along trailing edge]

Bifid white spot

Series of ovoid white spots along trailing edge

Series of ovoid white spots along trailing edge (one longer)

Pale veins contrast with GC

Series of round white spots along trailing edge (one larger)

GC oval surrounded by white spots

Contiguous white spots along HW trailing edge

Continuous white band along HW edge

GC greyish

GC ochre brown

Safflower Skipper
p. 165

Spinose Skipper
p. 160

Tessellated Skipper
p. 159

Northern Grizzled Skipper
p. 169

Hungarian Sipper
p. 162

KEY TO HESPERIIDAE

6/6 FW and HW: [fringes black and white] AND [wing edges not shredded]
On HW: [no continuous white band along trailing edge] AND [1 incomplete series of white or pale spots along trailing edge]

⚠ In this block, one should proceed by elimination from left to right and from top to bottom of the page, always checking the distinctive criteria. Identification reliability decreases towards the end of the block without genitalia examination.

Series of barely visible pale dots (no large white spots) along the trailing edge

GC light brown

Sage Skipper and associated cryptic species
p. 158

White spot rimmed with black

Anvil-shaped white spot

Rosy Grizzled Skipper
p. 180

Deeply notched white spot

GC ochre (more reddish in summer)

Grizzled Skipper/ Southern Grizzled Skipper
pp. 175 and 176

Narrow, not rectangular white spot

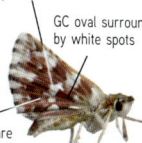

GC oval surrounded by white spots

GC reddish in summer, ochre in spring

Red-underwing Skipper/ Corsican Red-underwing Skipper/ Iberian Red-underwing Skipper/ Hungarian Skipper
pp. 161, 162, and 163

Series of white spots along FW edge

White spots align in a regular mid-wing white band

GC ochre

Persian Skipper
p. 164

White spot

The 2 white spots form an exclamation mark

Alpine Grizzled Skipper
p. 167

No white spot here (although hairy scales might look like one)

The 2 white spots form an unclear exclamation mark

Dusky Grizzled Skipper
p. 168

GC greenish-yellow

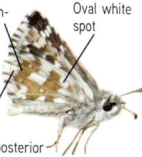

Oval white spot

Very short posterior white spot

Olive Skipper
p. 172

White spot notched on its posterior edge

HW GC reddish-brown

White spot clearly pointing forwards

Cinquefoil Skipper
p. 178

White spot notched on its posterior edge

HW GC reddish-brown

Carline Skipper
p. 177

Large, almost rectangular white spot

Large white spot with a flattened top

Sandy Grizzled Skipper
p. 179

Pale veins contrasting against GC

White spot often notched on its posterior edge

2 arrowhead-shaped anal white spots

GC ochre

Oberthür's Grizzled Skipper
p. 171

GC yellowish-brown

Rectangular white spot

Rather rectangular white spot

1 or 2 shapeless anal white spots

Large Grizzled Skipper
p. 173

White spots align in a band

GC greenish-grey

Warren's Skipper
p. 170

GC yellowish-brown

White spot often notched on its posterior edge

2 conspicuous hairy tufts beneath abdomen tip in males ♂♂

Foulquier's Grizzled Skipper
p. 174

KEY TO PAPILIONIDAE

1/3 On FW: [GC pale yellow or yellow] AND [3 or 4 rectangular black spots along leading edge]

1.1 On FW: Black spots all over the wing

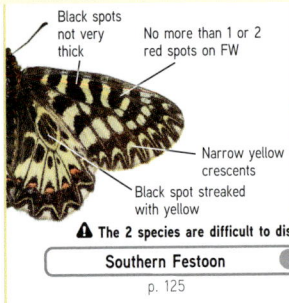

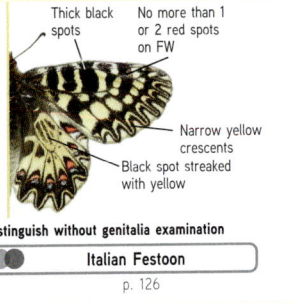

Many red spots on FW

Thick black crescents

This black spot not streaked with yellow

Spanish Festoon
p. 124

Black spots not very thick

No more than 1 or 2 red spots on FW

Narrow yellow crescents

Black spot streaked with yellow

Thick black spots

No more than 1 or 2 red spots on FW

Narrow yellow crescents

Black spot streaked with yellow

⚠ The 2 species are difficult to distinguish without genitalia examination

Southern Festoon	⬤⬤	Italian Festoon
p. 125		p. 126

1.2 On FW: black spots concentrated near leading and outer edges

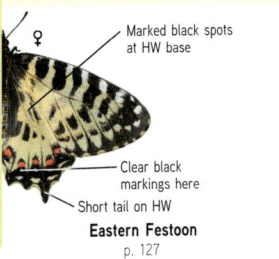

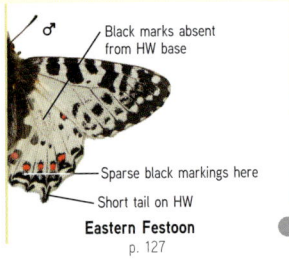

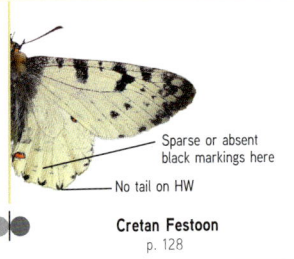

♀ Marked black spots at HW base

Clear black markings here

Short tail on HW

Eastern Festoon
p. 127

♂ Black marks absent from HW base

Sparse black markings here

Short tail on HW

Eastern Festoon
p. 127

⬤⬤

Sparse or absent black markings here

No tail on HW

Cretan Festoon
p. 128

2/3 On FW: [GC pure white or cream] AND [wing margin transparent]

2.1 On HW : GC pure white

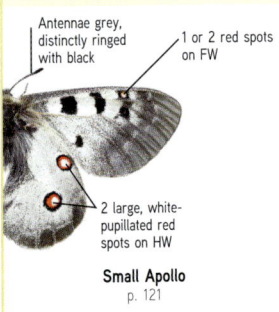

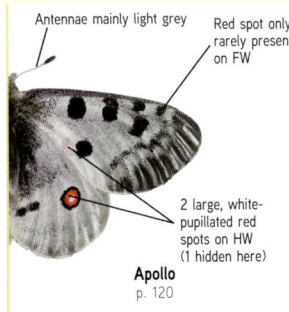

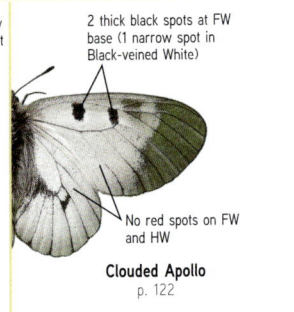

Antennae grey, distinctly ringed with black

1 or 2 red spots on FW

2 large, white-pupillated red spots on HW

Small Apollo
p. 121

Antennae mainly light grey

Red spot only rarely present on FW

2 large, white-pupillated red spots on HW (1 hidden here)

Apollo
p. 120

2 thick black spots at FW base (1 narrow spot in Black-veined White)

No red spots on FW and HW

Clouded Apollo
p. 122

2.2 On HW: GC cream

♂ Red spots faint or absent on FW

HW almost entirely cream

False Apollo
p. 123

♀ Conspicuous red spots

HW GC cream, sprinkled with grey

False Apollo
p. 123

(3/3) On FW: GC pale yellow to yellow
On HW: [conspicuous tail] AND [blue spot along with vivid orange spot]

3.1 On FW: veins not highlighted in black

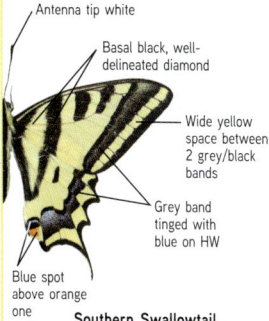

Antenna tip white

Basal black, well-delineated diamond

Wide yellow space between 2 grey/black bands

Grey band tinged with blue on HW

Blue spot above orange one

Southern Swallowtail
p. 129

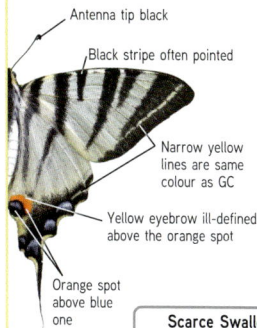

Antenna tip black

Black stripe often pointed

Narrow yellow lines are same colour as GC

Yellow eyebrow ill-defined above the orange spot

Orange spot above blue one

Antenna tip black

Black stripe often truncated

Narrow yellow lines darker yellow than GC

Yellow eyebrow well-defined above orange spot located above blue spot

Scarce Swallowtail ●● **Iberian Scarce Swallowtail**
p. 130 p. 131

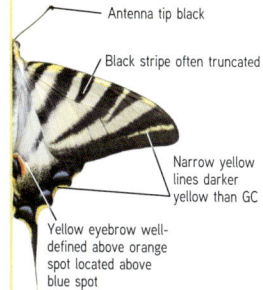

3.2 On FW: veins highlighted with black

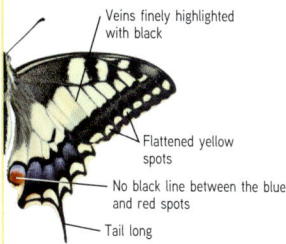

Veins finely highlighted with black

Flattened yellow spots

No black line between the blue and red spots

Tail long

Swallowtail
p. 132

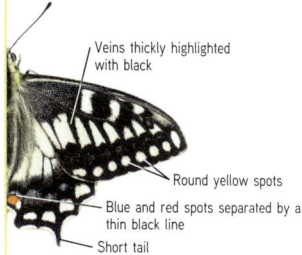

Veins thickly highlighted with black

Round yellow spots

Blue and red spots separated by a thin black line

Short tail

Corsican Swallowtail
p. 133

KEY TO PAPILIONIDAE

1/3 On HW: [GC yellow] AND [conspicuous tail]

1.1 On HW: [black stripes] AND [veins not highlighted with black]

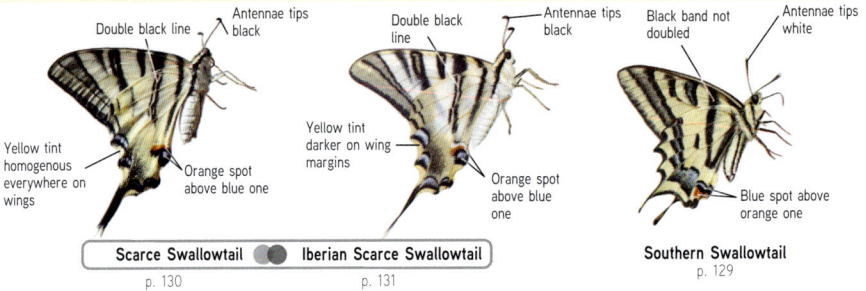

Double black line — Antennae tips black

Double black line — Antennae tips black

Black band not doubled — Antennae tips white

Yellow tint homogenous everywhere on wings

Orange spot above blue one

Yellow tint darker on wing margins

Orange spot above blue one

Blue spot above orange one

Scarce Swallowtail ⬤⬤ **Iberian Scarce Swallowtail**
p. 130　　　　　　　　　　p. 131

Southern Swallowtail
p. 129

1.2 On HW: veins highlighted with black

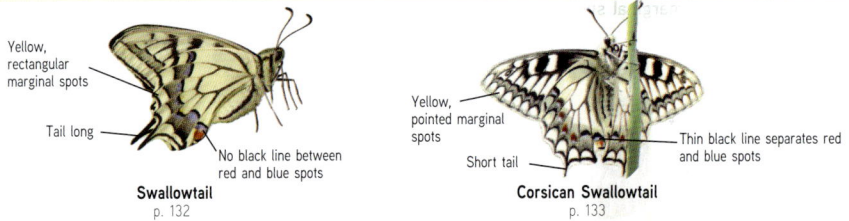

Yellow, rectangular marginal spots

Tail long

No black line between red and blue spots

Yellow, pointed marginal spots

Short tail

Thin black line separates red and blue spots

Swallowtail
p. 132

Corsican Swallowtail
p. 133

2/3 On FW: wing margin transparent

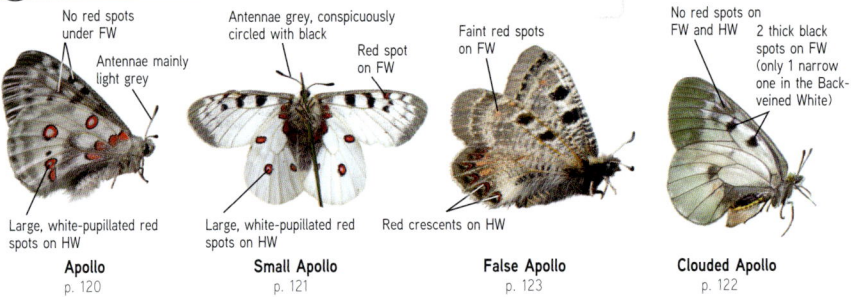

No red spots under FW

Antennae mainly light grey

Antennae grey, conspicuously circled with black

Red spot on FW

Faint red spots on FW

No red spots on FW and HW

2 thick black spots on FW (only 1 narrow one in the Back-veined White)

Large, white-pupillated red spots on HW

Large, white-pupillated red spots on HW

Red crescents on HW

Apollo
p. 120

Small Apollo
p. 121

False Apollo
p. 123

Clouded Apollo
p. 122

3/3 On HW: [GC whitish to pale yellow] AND [GC variegated with red, black, and yellow]

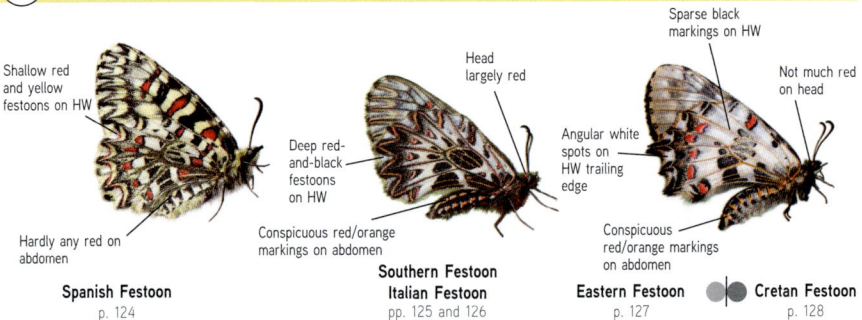

Shallow red and yellow festoons on HW

Head largely red

Sparse black markings on HW

Not much red on head

Deep red-and-black festoons on HW

Angular white spots on HW trailing edge

Hardly any red on abdomen

Conspicuous red/orange markings on abdomen

Conspicuous red/orange markings on abdomen

Spanish Festoon
p. 124

Southern Festoon
Italian Festoon
pp. 125 and 126

Eastern Festoon ⬤⬤ **Cretan Festoon**
p. 127　　　　　　　p. 128

1/9 On FW: [GC white] AND [1 long black spot in the middle of the costa]

1.1 On FW: Wing tip black, with several white spots; 1 is much larger

Black spot not connected to the costa

Black spot not connected to the costa

Outer FW edge slightly convex

Black spot not connected to the costa

Outer FW edge straight

Thick black spot containing a white line

Black spot connected to the costa

Eastern Dappled White	Western Dappled White Portuguese Dappled White	Corsican Dappled White	Green-striped White/ Canarian Green-striped Whites	Mountain Dappled White
p. 215	pp. 214 and 217	p. 213	pp. 218 and 219	p. 216

1.2 On FW: wing tip black with several white spots of similar size
On HW: black marginal spots

Narrow black spot with no white line

Drop-shaped marginal white spots

♀

Thick black spot contains white line

⚠ Differ only by their genitalia

Large black spots on HW

♀

Thick black spot contains white line

Large black spots on HW

♀

Thick black spot contains white line

Elongated white spots

Reduced black spots on HW

♀

Peak White	Bath White	Eastern Bath White	Small Bath White
p. 209	p. 206	p. 207	p. 208

1.3 On FW: wing tip black, with several white spots of similar size
On HW: no black marginal spots

Narrow black spot with no white line

Hardly any black on wing tip

♂

Thick black spot contains a white line

⚠ Differ only by their genitalia

Continuous black apical band

♂

Thick black spot contains white line

Continuous black apical band

♂

Narrow black spot contains thick white line

Wing tip discontinuously black

♂

Peak White	Bath White	Eastern Bath White	Small Bath White
p. 209	p. 206	p. 207	p. 208

1.4 On FW: wing tip black, indented with white on outer edge

♀ Narrow rectangular black spot

Reduced white indentations

Weak pale yellowish tint on HW

Narrow rectangular black spot

♀

Large white indentations

Pronounced yellowish tint on HW

Thick rectangular grey spot

♀

Reduced white indentations

Orange-tip	Eastern Orange-tip	Grüner's Orange-tip
p. 182	p. 185	p. 183

2/9 On FW: [GC sulphur yellow] AND [1 large black spot close to the middle of the costa]

Greenish Black-tip
p. 212

Spanish Greenish Black-tip
p. 211

Eastern Greenish Black-tip
p. 210

3/9 On FW: [GC white, pale yellow, or yellow] AND [wing tip orange or with an orange spot]

3.1 On FW: GC white

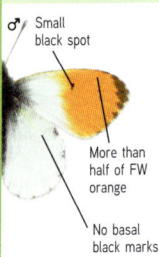

♂ Small black spot

More than half of FW orange

No basal black marks

Orange-tip
p. 182

♀ Large black spot

Only wing tip orange

No basal black marks

Provence Orange-tip
p. 184

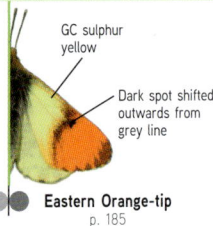

♀ No black spot

Orange wing tip, indented with black

Basal black area on both wings

Posterior black spots on HW

♂ No black spot

Orange wing tip, indented with black

Desert Orange-tip
p. 186

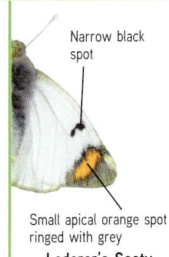

Narrow black spot

Small apical orange spot ringed with grey

Lederer's Sooty Orange-tip
p. 187

3.2 On FW: GC pale or sulphur yellow

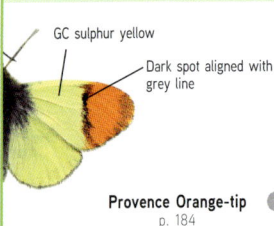

GC sulphur yellow

Dark spot aligned with grey line

Provence Orange-tip
p. 184

GC sulphur yellow

Dark spot shifted outwards from grey line

Eastern Orange-tip
p. 185

GC pale yellow

Grüner's Orange-tip
p. 183

4/9 On FW: [GC white] AND [wing tip very rounded, with a dark spot]

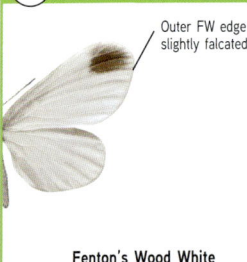

Outer FW edge slightly falcated

Fenton's Wood White
p. 230

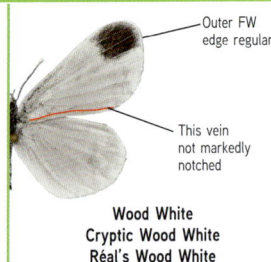

Outer FW edge regular

This vein not markedly notched

Wood White
Cryptic Wood White
Réal's Wood White
p. 229

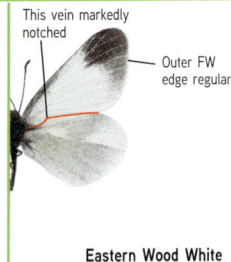

This vein markedly notched

Outer FW edge regular

Eastern Wood White
p. 228

(5/9) Head top, antennae, and legs tinged with pink
On FW and HW: GC orange

5.1 On FW: black band along outer edge that contains no pale spots

GC yellow-orange
Black band not streaked with yellow veins
GC dark orange
Short pale and marked spot
Series of spots along black band paler than GC

Thick black spot
Black band entirely streaked with yellow veins
GC dark orange
GC yellow-orange
Thick black spot
Pale elongated and marked spot (hidden on right picture)
No paler than GC spots along black band
Black band streaked with yellow veins near apex

Danube Clouded Yellow
p. 199

Balkan Clouded Yellow
p. 200

Greek Clouded Yellow
p. 198

Clouded Yellow
p. 196

GC yellow-orange
Thick black spot
Black band entirely streaked with yellow veins
No paler than GC spots along black band

GC orange
Narrow black spot
Yellow veins sometimes streak black band
No paler than GC spots along black band

Lesser Clouded Yellow
p. 197

Northern Clouded Yellow
p. 201

5.2 On FW : a black band containing pale spots

Thick black spot
FW costa orange
FW basal area largely sprinkled with grey
A few pale spots rimmed with black on interior edge

FW costa orange
Thick black spot
A few pale spots rimmed with black on interior edge

FW costa greenish
Very thick black spot

FW costa orange
Thick black spot
FW base barely sprinkled with grey
A few pale spots rimmed with black on interior edge

Danube Clouded Yellow
p. 199

Greek Clouded Yellow
p. 198

Lesser Clouded Yellow
p. 197

Northern Clouded Yellow
p. 201

FW base barely sprinkled with grey
Thick black spot
Complete series of pale spots rimmed with black on inner edge

FW base hardly sprinkled with grey
Thick black spot
Maximum of 2 pale spots rimmed with black on inner edge

Balkan Clouded Yellow
p. 200

Clouded Yellow
p. 196

45

6/9 [FW and HW edged with pink] AND [GC white, grey, pale yellow, or yellow]

6.1 On FW: black or grey band with no pale spots

GC sulphur yellow

♂

Vivid orange spot

Eastern Pale Clouded Yellow
p. 192

GC sulphur yellow

♂

Pure white spot

Moorland Clouded Yellow
p. 193

GC whitish, sprinkled with grey

Thin grey band

Faint pale orange spot

Pale Arctic Clouded Yellow
p. 195

GC white   Wide black band

♀

Pure white spot

Moorland Clouded Yellow
p. 193

6.2 On FW : [GC pale yellow or yellow] AND [a black band with pale spots inside]

GC sulphur yellow

FW base barely sprinkled with grey

♀

Vivid orange spot

HW largely sprinkled with grey

Eastern Pale Clouded Yellow
p. 192

GC sulphur yellow

Outer FW edge slightly rounded

FW base markedly sprinkled with grey

Vivid orange spot

♂

Grey streak on HW

GC pale yellow

Outer FW edge straight

FW base markedly sprinkled with grey

Faint orange spot

♂

Grey streak on HW

Berger's Clouded Yellow   **Pale Clouded Yellow**
p. 190   p. 191

6.3 On FW: [GC white or grey] AND [black band with pale spots]

♀

GC white

Vivid orange spot

HW largely sprinkled with grey

Extensive black marks on HW

Clouded Yellow
p. 196

♀

GC white

Vivid orange spot

Reduced black marks on HW

HW largely sprinkled with grey

Eastern Pale Clouded Yellow
p. 192

Outer FW edge slightly rounded

♀ GC white

Vivid orange spot

Reduced black marks on HW

Berger's Clouded Yellow
p. 190

GC white

Outer FW edge straight

♀

Faint orange spot

Grey streak on HW

Reduced black marks on HW

Pale Clouded Yellow
p. 191

GC whitish, sprinkled with grey

Mountain Clouded Yellow
p. 194

KEY TO PIERIDAE

7/9 On FW: [GC whitish, pale yellow, or yellow and orange] AND [wing tip pointed, hooking backwards]
On HW: [1 small orange spot in middle of wing] AND [trailing edge variably pointing backwards]

7.1 On FW: [GC whitish, pale yellow, or yellow] AND [tiny orange spot in middle of wing]

FW costa slightly concave

FW costa slightly convex

GC yellow

♂

GC yellow in males, ♂♂ whitish in females ♀♀

♂

FW costa slightly concave ♀

GC whitish

Long tooth points backwards

FW costa slightly concave

GC whitish

Short tooth pointing backwards

♀

Brimstone	Powdered Brimstone
p. 202	p. 203

Brimstone	Cleopatra
p. 202	p. 204

7.2 On FW: [GC pale yellow or yellow] AND [very large orange area in middle of wing]

♂

Orange area surrounded by a yellow margin

Short tooth points backwards

♂

Orange area barely (Madeiran Brimstone) or not (Canarian Brimstones) surrounded by yellow margin

HW minimally indented on posterior edge

♀

Orange area hardly surrounded by a yellow margin

HW minimally indented on posterior edge

Cleopatra	⬤⬤ Canarian Brimstones Madeiran Brimstone
p. 204	p. 205

Canarian Brimstones
p. 205

8/9 On FW: [GC white or pale yellow] AND [veins black or sprinkled with grey]

8.1 On FW: Veins abundantly sprinkled with grey

♀

GC pale yellow

Veins more or less intensively sprinkled with grey

♀

GC pale yellow

⚠ **Subspecies *adalwinda* and *flavescens* of Green-veined White also have pale yellow GC**

♀

GC white

Mountain Green-veined White
p. 227

**Green-veined White
Balkan Green-veined White**
p. 226

8.2 On FW: veins highlighted in black

♂

No black streak

Veins minimally highlighted with black on HW

⚠ **Identification difficult without genitalia examination. The Mountain Green-veined White is a mountain species. The Green-veined White can fly as high as 2,000 m.**

♂

No black streak

Veins highlighted in black only at distal end

Black streak

Veins entirely black

Green-veined White Balkan Green-veined White	Mountain Green-veined White
p. 226	p. 227

Black-veined White
p. 189

9/9 On FW: [GC white] AND [black apical mark variably extends along wing's leading and outer edges]

9.1 On FW: no black spot in middle of wing

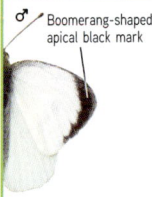

♂ Boomerang-shaped apical black mark

Apical black mark made of small triangles ♂

♂

♂ Rectangular apical black mark

⚠ **Identification difficult without genitalia examination. The Mountain Green-veined White is a mountain species. The Green-veined White can fly as high as 2,000 m.**

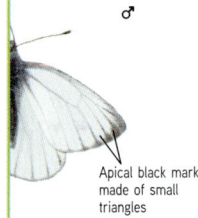

Apical black mark made of small triangles

Large White
p. 222

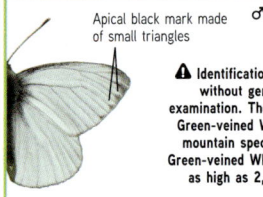

**Green-veined White
Balkan Green-veined White**
p. 226

Mountain Green-veined White
p. 227

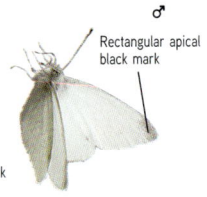

Mountain Small White
p. 225

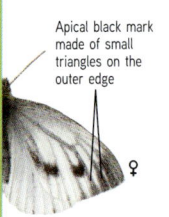

9.2 On FW: black spot in middle of wing

Apical black mark doesn't reach level of mid-wing black spot on outer edge

Apical black mark reaches level of mid-wing black spot on outer edge

Apical black mark made of small triangles

Black comma in front of apical black mark

Boomerang-shaped apical black mark

Huge central black spot

♂

♂

♂

Small White
p. 223

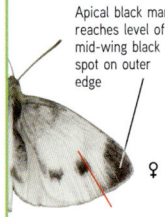

Southern Small White
p. 224

**Green-veined White
Balkan Green-veined White**
p. 226

Krueper's Small White
p. 220

Canary Islands Large White
p. 221

9.3 On FW: [round black spot in middle of wing] AND [comma-shaped black spot at back of wing]

Apical black mark doesn't reach level of mid-wing black spot on outer edge

Apical black mark reaches level of mid-wing black spot on outer edge

Boomerang-shaped apical black mark

Rectangular apical black mark

Apical black mark made of small triangles on the outer edge

♀

♀

♀

♀

♀

Small White
p. 223

Southern Small White
p. 224

Large White
p. 222

Mountain Small White
p. 225

**Green-veined White
Balkan Green-veined White**
p. 226

KEY TO PIERIDAE

FW and HW edged with pink

1.1 On FW: GC pale or vivid orange
On HW: GC greenish

Posterior band paler than GC

No black spots

Incomplete series of faint dark spots

Conspicuous comma-shaped dark spot

GC yellowish-green

Incomplete series of faint dark spots

Comma-shaped dark spot, often faint

Complete series of dark spots

GC green sprinkled with grey

♀

No brown spots

Greenish GC abundantly sprinkled with grey

Series of faint brown spots

GC glaucous green

♀

Comma-shaped dark spot rather conspicuous

♀

Northern Clouded Yellow ● ●○
p. 201

Balkan Clouded Yellow ●○ ● **Greek Clouded Yellow**
p. 200   p. 198

Lesser Clouded Yellow
p. 197

1.2 On FW: GC pale or vivid orange
On HW: GC yellowish

Marked dark spots

Large orange area

A few faint dark spots

Reduced orange area

♂

A few faint dark spots

Large orange area

♂

Dark spots, if any, hardly visible

Large orange area

Marked brown spots

Marked brown spots

Series of faint brown spots

Series of faint brown spots

Clouded Yellow
p. 196

Greek Clouded Yellow
p. 198

Balkan Clouded Yellow ● ●
p. 200

Danube Clouded Yellow ●○ ●
p. 199

1.3 On FW: [GC pale or vivid yellow] AND [pale spots in outer dark band visible via transparency]

FW outer edge straight

♀

FW outer edge slightly rounded

♂

FW outer edge usually straight

♂

HW entirely sprinkled with grey

HW only partially sprinkled with grey

HW only partially sprinkled with grey

Eastern Pale Clouded Yellow
p. 192

Berger's Clouded Yellow
p. 190

Pale Clouded Yellow
p. 191

1.4 On FW: [GC pale or vivid yellow] AND [no pale spots in outer dark band visible via transparency]

Series of dark spots

FW costa sprinkled with grey

FW costa barely sprinkled with grey or not at all

Series of dark spots

No dark spots

White spot surrounded by a double brown ring

♂

White spot surrounded by a double brown ring

♂

White spot ringed with black

♂

Eastern Pale Clouded Yellow
p. 192

Lesser Clouded Yellow
p. 197

●○ ● **Moorland Clouded Yellow**
p. 193

1/8 FW and HW edged with pink

**1.5 On FW: [GC white] AND [wing tip yellow or darker than GC]
On HW: no marginal brown spots**

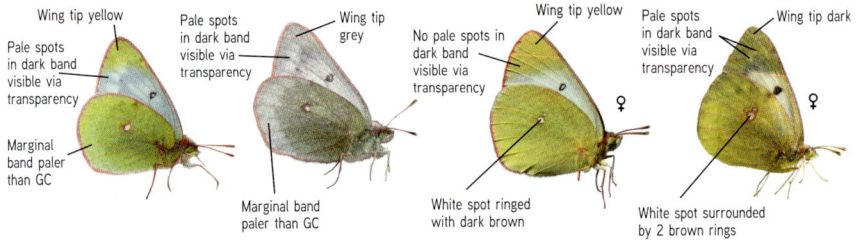

Wing tip yellow

Pale spots in dark band visible via transparency

Pale spots in dark band visible via transparency

Marginal band paler than GC

Wing tip grey

Pale spots in dark band visible via transparency

Marginal band paler than GC

Wing tip yellow

No pale spots in dark band visible via transparency

White spot ringed with dark brown

Wing tip yellow

Pale spots in dark band visible via transparency

Wing tip dark

White spot surrounded by 2 brown rings

Mountain Clouded Yellow p. 194   **Pale Arctic Clouded Yellow** p. 195   **Moorland Clouded Yellow** p. 193   **Danube Clouded Yellow** p. 199

**1.6 On FW: [GC white] AND [wing tip yellow]
On HW: 1 series of marginal brown spots**

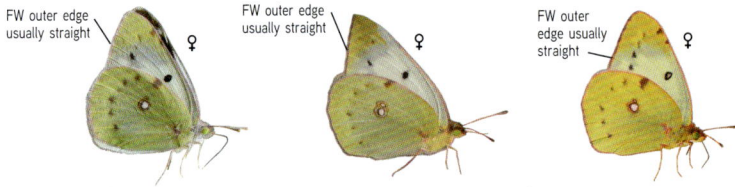

FW outer edge usually straight

FW outer edge usually straight

FW outer edge usually straight

Eastern Pale Clouded Yellow p. 192   **Greek Clouded Yellow** p. 198   **Pale Clouded Yellow** p. 191

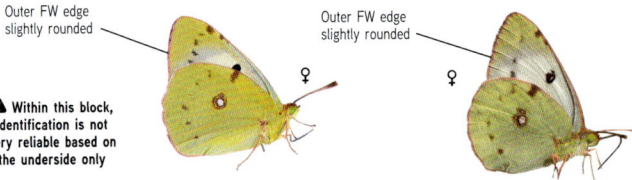

Outer FW edge slightly rounded

Outer FW edge slightly rounded

⚠ Within this block, identification is not very reliable based on the underside only

Clouded Yellow p. 196   **Berger's Clouded Yellow** p. 190

2/8 Both wings GC pale greenish-white or pale yellow with small brown spots

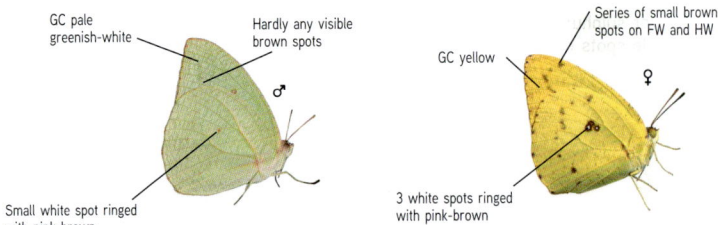

GC pale greenish-white

Hardly any visible brown spots

Small white spot ringed with pink-brown

Series of small brown spots on FW and HW

GC yellow

3 white spots ringed with pink-brown

African Migrant p. 188   **African Migrant** p. 188

50

KEY TO PIERIDAE

3/8 On FW: 1 conspicuous large orange spot at or below wing tip

Narrow marbled line above the orange area

White wing tip

GC white

HW finely marbled

♂

Orange-tip
p. 182

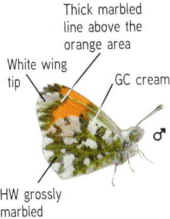

Thick marbled line above the orange area

White wing tip

GC cream

HW grossly marbled

♂

Grüner's Orange-tip
p. 183

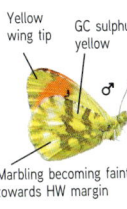

Yellow wing tip

GC sulphur yellow

Marbling becoming faint towards HW margin

♂

Provence Orange-tip
p. 184

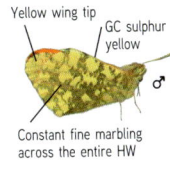

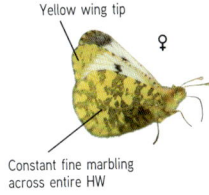

Yellow wing tip

GC sulphur yellow

Constant fine marbling across the entire HW

♂

Eastern Orange-tip
p. 185

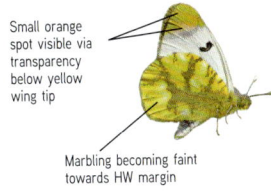

Pale orange wing tip

GC white

HW with a cream GC slightly sprinkled with grey

Desert Orange-tip
p. 186

4/8 On HW: [greenish-yellow marbling] AND [rounded pale spots between marbled areas]

4.1 On FW: GC white
On HW: rounded spaces between marbled areas are yellow

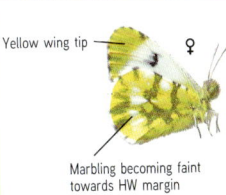

Yellow wing tip

♀

Marbling becoming faint towards HW margin

Provence Orange-tip
p. 184

Yellow wing tip

♀

Constant fine marbling across entire HW

Eastern Orange-tip
p. 185

Small orange spot visible via transparency below yellow wing tip

♀

Marbling becoming faint towards HW margin

Lederer's Sooty Orange-tip
p. 187

4.2 On FW: GC white
On HW: rounded spaces between marbled areas are white

White-striped, greenish-yellow wing tip

HW leading edge round

HW finely marbled

♀

Orange-tip
p. 182

Marbled wing tip containing white spots

HW edge angular here

HW grossly marbled

HW grossly marbled

Mountain Dappled White
p. 216

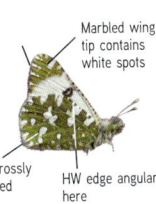

Marbled wing tip contains white spots

HW edge angular here

Western Dappled White
Corsican Dappled White
pp. 214 and 213

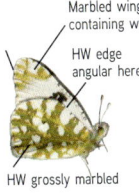

Marbled wing tip containing white spots

HW edge angular here

HW grossly marbled

Eastern Dappled White
p. 215

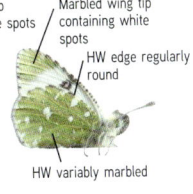

Marbled wing tip containing white spots

HW edge regularly round

HW variably marbled

Portuguese Dappled White
p. 217

4.3 On FW: GC pale or sulphur yellow
On HW: a few pale spots on a greenish marbled background

Greenish Black-tip
p. 212

Eastern Greenish Black-tip
p. 210

Spanish Greenish Black-tip
p. 211

KEY TO PIERIDAE

5/8 On HW: a white band or long white spots between yellowish-green marbled areas

Green-marbled wing tip — Thick black spot
Short white stripes

⚠ Differ only by their genitalia
Green-marbled wing tip — Thick black spot
Regular FW outer edge
Short white stripes

FW outer edge slightly angular

Green-marbled wing tip — Thick black spot
Long white stripes

Green-striped wing tip — Thick black spot
Crosswise white stripes

Apex veins sprinkled with greyish-green — Narrow black spot
Arrowhead-shaped pale spots

Bath White ⬤ Eastern Bath White
p. 206   p. 207

Small Bath White
p. 208

Green-striped White
Canarian Green-striped Whites
pp. 218 and 219

Peak White
p. 209

6/8 On FW: [wing tip hooking backwards] AND [GC white, yellow, or yellow and orange]
On HW: a more or less marked tooth on trailing edge

6.1 On HW: GC pale yellow or yellow

♂ No orange — Costa slightly convex — Long tooth points from undulated edge

♂ Costa slightly concave — Long tooth pointing from regular edge

♂ Large orange area in middle of FW — Short tooth

♂ Large orange area in middle of FW — Barely any tooth pointing from undulated edge

Powdered Brimstone p. 203

Brimstone p. 202

Cleopatra Madeiran Brimstone pp. 204 and 205

Canarian Brimstones p. 205

6.2 On HW: GC pale green

♀ Costa slightly concave — Long tooth points from regular edge

♀ Narrow pale orange streak — Costa slightly concave — Short tooth

♀ Pale FW middle (hidden here) contrasts with greenish costal area — Costa slightly convex — Long tooth points from undulated edge

♀ Large orange area in middle of FW — Barely any tooth points from undulated edge

Brimstone p. 202

Cleopatra p. 204

Powdered Brimstone p. 203

Canarian Brimstones p. 205

7/8 On FW: [GC white, with an apical, rounded dark spot] AND [wing tip very rounded]

Outer FW edge regularly rounded — Short pale spot

Outer FW edge regularly rounded — Long pale spot reaching HW base

Outer FW edge regularly rounded

⚠ Summer-generation females are difficult to distinguish
Conspicuous white area below antennal clubs in ♂♂

Outer FW edge regularly rounded
No conspicuous white area below antennal clubs in ♂♂ and ♀♀

Outer FW edge slightly falcated

Eastern Wood White p. 228

Wood White Réal's Wood White Cryptic Wood White p. 229

Wood White Réal's Wood White Cryptic Wood White p. 229

Eastern Wood White p. 228

Fenton's Wood White p. 230

KEY TO PIERIDAE

8/8 On FW: [GC white or tinged with pale yellow] AND [wing tip pointed or slightly rounded]

8.1 On HW: veins intensively sprinkled with grey or highlighted in black

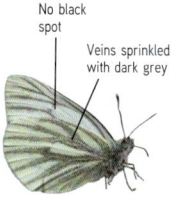

No black spot

Veins sprinkled with dark grey

⚠ **Identification reliable only by genitalia examination**

Veins sprinkled with dark grey (more diffusely in Balkan Green-veined White)

No black spot

Mountain Green-veined White	Green-veined White Balkan Green-veined White
p. 227	p. 226

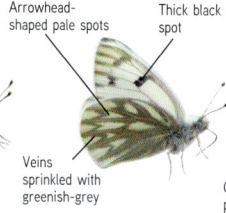

Arrowhead-shaped pale spots

Thick black spot

Veins sprinkled with greenish-grey

Peak White
p. 209

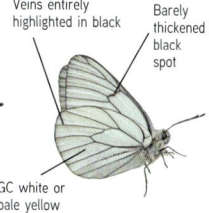

Veins entirely highlighted in black

Barely thickened black spot

GC white or pale yellow

Black-veined White
p. 189

8.2 On HW: [conspicuous grey spots or areas] OR [veins slightly sprinkled with grey]

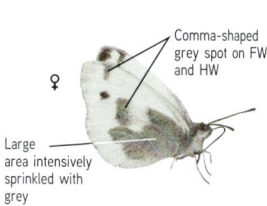

♀

Comma-shaped grey spot on FW and HW

Large area intensively sprinkled with grey

Krueper's Small White
p. 220

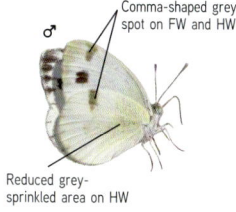

♂

Comma-shaped grey spot on FW and HW

Reduced grey-sprinkled area on HW

Krueper's Small White
p. 220

No comma-shaped grey spot on FW

Veins hardly sprinkled grey (less intensively in Balkan Green-veined White)

Green-veined White Balkan Green-veined White
p. 226

8.3 On HW: [GC whitish or pale yellow] AND [grey sprinkling between veins variably intense]

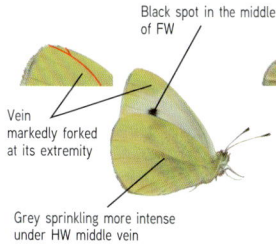

Black spot in the middle of FW

Vein markedly forked at its extremity

Grey sprinkling more intense under HW middle vein

Small White
p. 223

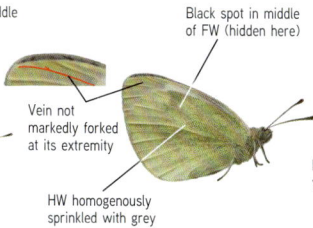

Black spot in middle of FW (hidden here)

Vein not markedly forked at its extremity

HW homogenously sprinkled with grey

Southern Small White
p. 224

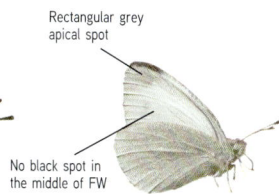

Rectangular grey apical spot

No black spot in the middle of FW

Mountain Small White
p. 225

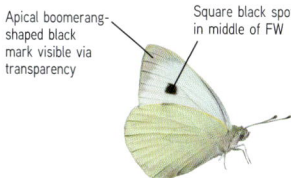

Apical boomerang-shaped black mark visible via transparency

Square black spot in middle of FW

Large White
p. 222

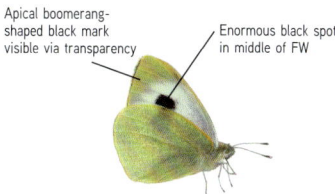

Apical boomerang-shaped black mark visible via transparency

Enormous black spot in middle of FW

Canary Islands Large White
p. 221

KEY TO LYCAENIDAE

1/3 On FW: GC blue with various tints (greyish-blue, light blue, azure blue, royal blue, purple-blue, or dull blue)

➜ **Page 55**

2/3 On FW: GC orange (black spots or purple reflections possible)

➜ **Page 61**

3/3 On FW: GC brown with various tints, sometimes a reduced basal blue area

➜ **Page 63**

1/8 On HW: at least 1 posterior tail (beware of worn butterflies)

1.1 On HW: [long posterior tail] AND [no dark lines across wing]

♂

Narrow black line

Black spots ringed with white

Single tail

♀

Thick dark band

Black spots ringed with white

Single tail

Long-tailed Blue
p. 263

♂

Narrow black line

Black spots not ringed with white

Single tail

♀

Thick dark band

Black spots not ringed with white

Single tail

Lang's Short-tailed Blue
p. 264

⚠ Extremely rare vagrant

Thick dark band

Black spots ringed with white

1 long and 1 short tail

Pomegranate Playboy
p. 250

1.2 On HW: [posterior tail] AND [dark lines across wing]

♂

Linear black spot

♂

Several thick black spots on FW

Common Tiger Blue
p. 272

Small Tiger Blue
p. 271

1.3 On HW: 1 short posterior tail

♂

GC dull blue

Narrow black band along FW and HW outer edges

Short tail

Purple Hairstreak
p. 252

♂

GC royal blue

Small black spot in middle of FW

Thick black line along FW and HW outer edges

Conspicuous tail

Short-tailed Blue
p. 292

♂

GC blue

Small black spot in middle of FW

Veins diffusely sprinkled with black near outer edge

Tail hardly visible

Eastern Short-tailed Blue
p. 288

♂

GC blue

No black spot in middle of FW

Veins finely sprinkled with black near outer edge

Tail hardly visible

Provençal Short-tailed Blue
p. 287

2/8 On FW and HW: GC purple with iridescent reflections

♂

Narrow black line

No well-defined orange band on HW

Purple-shot Copper
p. 240

♂

Thick black line

Well-defined orange band on HW

Violet Copper
p. 241

3/8 On FW (and often HW): fringes chequered

3.1 On HW: [GC greyish-blue, light or very light blue] AND [white-ringed black spots along the posterior edge]

♂ GC very light blue

Dark grey band containing more or less visible dark spots

Provence Chalkhill Blue
p. 314

♂ GC very light blue

Almost uniform dark grey band

⚠ 2 species that are difficult to distinguish. Provence Chalkhill Blue can fly in late April; late May for Chalkhill Blue

Chalkhill Blue
p. 313

♂ GC light blue

Thickened black line

Azure Chalkhill Blue
p. 312

♂ GC pale greyish blue

Grey band containing visible dark spots

Spanish Chalkhill Blue
p. 315

3.2 On FW: several oval black spots

♂ Black spots rather small

Scarce Large Blue
p. 294

♂ Large oval black spots

Large Blue
p. 293

3.3 On FW (and sometimes HW): [GC azure blue or purple-blue] AND [series of orange spots along posterior edge]

♀ Orange spots often present on FW

Azure, blue basal area

Conspicuous orange spots paired with small black spots

Adonis Blue
p. 311

♂ GC purple-blue

No orange on FW

Large black spots paired with a few orange spots

Bavius Blue
p. 279

3.4 On FW and HW: [GC azure, blue or light blue] AND [no orange]

♂ Black line thickened near wing tip

No black spot

Fringes finely chequered

GC azure blue

Holly Blue
p. 297

♂ No black spot

Black line not thickened at wing tip

GC azure blue

Fringes finely chequered

Adonis Blue
p. 311

♂ GC light blue

Fringes thickly chequered

1 black spot on each wing

Eastern Baton Blue **Baton Blue**
p. 278 p. 277

♂ GC light blue

Fringes thickly chequered

1 black spot on each wing

♂ GC light blue

Fringes thickly chequered

One black spot on each wing

Panoptes Blue
p. 276

⚠ Differ only by their genitalia

3.5 On FW and HW: [GC blue, purple-blue, lilac blue, or dull blue] AND [no orange]

♂ GC purple-blue

Series of purple-blue ringed black spots

Chequered Blue
p. 280

♂ GC dull blue

Thick black line

Fringes thickly chequered

Black and pale spots

False Baton Blue
p. 275

♀ GC dull blue

Wide dark band

Fringes thickly chequered

Pale crescents with black spots

Panoptes Blue
False Baton Blue
pp. 276 and 275

♂ GC lilac blue

Thin black line

Fringes rather finely chequered

African Babul Blue
p. 265

♂ GC purple-blue

Thick black line

Fringes thickly chequered

Canary Blue
p. 261

KEY TO LYCAENIDAE

4/8 On FW and HW: [fringes white and not chequered] AND [GC azure or light blue]

4.1 On FW and HW: thin black line along wings' outer and posterior edges

♂

♂   GC azure blue

♂   GC very reflective light blue

♂   GC turquoise blue

GC azure blue

Usually some small black spots at the back of HW

Diffuse black line on FW

Black line on HW

Turquoise Blue
p. 335

Nevada Blue
Sagra Blue
p. 336

Eros Blue
p. 333

Chelmos Blue
p. 338

4.2 On FW (sometimes HW): thick black line with clean inner edge

♂ GC very reflective light blue

♂ GC very reflective light blue

♂   GC azure blue

♂

♂

No black spots on FW

No black spots on FW

No black spots on FW

Rather small black spots on FW

Large, oval black spots on FW

Paphos blue
p. 283

Black-eyed Blue
p. 282

Green-underside Blue
p. 281

Scarce Large Blue
p. 294

Large Blue
p. 293

4.3 On FW (and sometimes HW): thick, diffuse dark band along outer edge

♂ GC azure blue

♂ GC azure blue

♂ GC light blue

♂ GC azure blue

♀ Large dark area on FW and along the HW costa

Thick dark band on 2 wings

Veins highlighted in dark

Small black spot on 2 wings

Thick dark band only on FW

Anal HW edge slightly undulated

Anal HW edge not undulated

Anal HW edge not undulated

Veins highlighted in dark grey on FW

GC azure blue

Meleager's Blue
p. 328

Damon Blue
p. 341

Silvery Argus
p. 304

Amanda's Blue
p. 334

5/8 On FW and HW: [fringes white, not chequered] AND [GC greyish-blue or very light blue]

5.1 On FW and HW: 1 black spot in middle of wing, sometimes hardly visible on HW

♂ GC very light blue

♂ GC light greyish-blue

♂ GC light greyish-blue

♂ GC very light blue

No marked black spots at back of HW

No marked black spots at back of HW

Black spots, some topped with small orange spots

Arctic Blue
p. 301

Bosnian Blue
p. 302

Gavarnie Blue
p. 299

Blue Argus
p. 310

KEY TO LYCAENIDAE

5/8 On FW and HW : [fringes white not chequered]
AND [GC greyish-blue or very light blue]

5.2 On FW and HW: no black spot in middle of wing

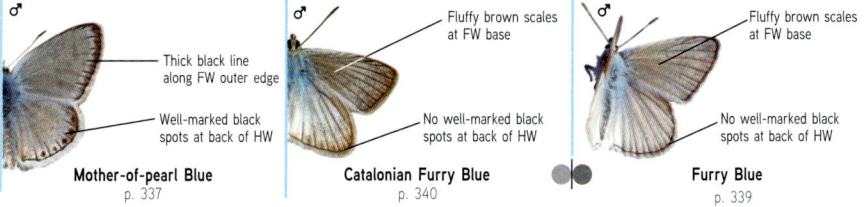

♂ — Thick black line along FW outer edge

— Well-marked black spots at back of HW

♂ Fluffy brown scales at FW base

No well-marked black spots at back of HW

♂ Fluffy brown scales at FW base

No well-marked black spots at back of HW

Mother-of-pearl Blue p. 337

Catalonian Furry Blue p. 340

Furry Blue p. 339

6/8 On FW and HW: [fringes white, not chequered, and lined with black] AND
[GC blue, purple-blue, or dull blue]

⚠ Within this block, identification is difficult using upperside only

6.1 On FW and HW: GC blue or purple-blue
On HW: no small black spots along trailing edge

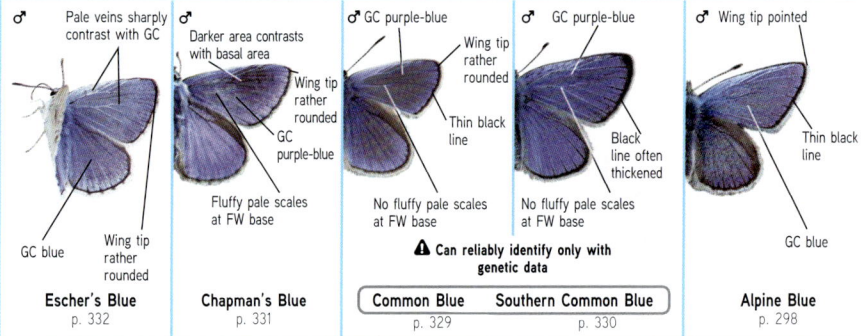

♂ Pale veins sharply contrast with GC

GC blue — Wing tip rather rounded

♂ Darker area contrasts with basal area

Wing tip rather rounded

GC purple-blue

Fluffy pale scales at FW base

♂ GC purple-blue

Wing tip rather rounded

Thin black line

No fluffy pale scales at FW base

♂ GC purple-blue

Black line often thickened

No fluffy pale scales at FW base

⚠ Can reliably identify only with genetic data

♂ Wing tip pointed

Thin black line

GC blue

Escher's Blue p. 332

Chapman's Blue p. 331

Common Blue p. 329 | **Southern Common Blue** p. 330

Alpine Blue p. 298

6.2 On FW and HW: GC royal blue or dull blue
On HW: no small black spots along trailing edge

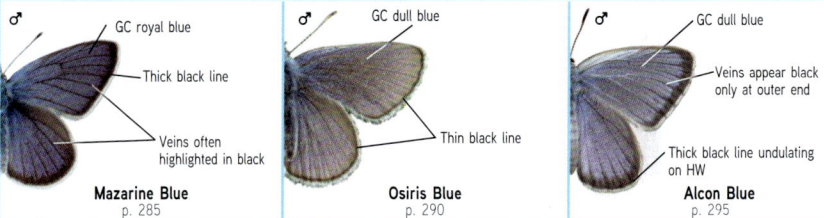

♂ GC royal blue

Thick black line

Veins often highlighted in black

♂ GC dull blue

Thin black line

♂ GC dull blue

Veins appear black only at outer end

Thick black line undulating on HW

Mazarine Blue p. 285

Osiris Blue p. 290

Alcon Blue p. 295

6.3 On FW and HW: GC blue
On HW: small black spots along trailing edge

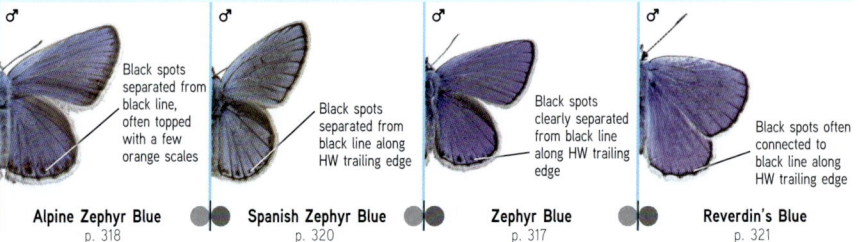

♂ Black spots separated from black line, often topped with a few orange scales

♂ Black spots separated from black line along HW trailing edge

♂ Black spots clearly separated from black line along HW trailing edge

♂ Black spots often connected to black line along HW trailing edge

Alpine Zephyr Blue p. 318

Spanish Zephyr Blue p. 320

Zephyr Blue p. 317

Reverdin's Blue p. 321

7/8 On HW and FW: [fringes white, not chequered, bordered by thick black line]
AND [GC royal blue, purple-blue, or dull blue]

⚠ **Identification is difficult within this block using upperside only**

7.1 On FW: no black spot in middle of wing
On HW: small spots or an undulated black line along trailing edge

♂ GC light purple-blue — 1 or 2 more visible black spots
Bright Babul Blue p. 266

♂ GC royal blue — Series of well-separated black spots
Alpine Zephyr Blue p. 318

♂ GC blue — Series of well-separated black spots
Loew's Blue p. 326

♂ GC royal blue — Series of black spots connected to black line
Idas Blue p. 323

♂ GC royal blue — Series of black spots connected to black line
Silver-studded Blue p. 322

7.2 On FW: no black spot in middle of wing
On HW: thick, regular black border along trailing edge

♂ Black eyes — GC dull blue — Black border not very thick
Alcon Blue p. 295

♂ Black eyes — GC royal blue — Pure white, very thick fringes — Very thick black line
Silver-studded Blue p. 322

♂ Black eyes — GC dark blue — Very thick black line
Lorquin's Blue p. 291

♂ Brown eyes — GC dark blue — Very thick black line
Dark Grass Blue p. 268

♂ Brown eyes — GC dark blue — Very thick black line
African Grass Blue p. 267

7.3 On FW : 1 linear black spot in the middle of the wing

♂ GC dark purple-blue — Thick black line on FW and HW
Small Desert Blue p. 269

♂ GC royal blue — Thick black band on FW and HW
Silver-studded Blue p. 322

♂ GC royal blue — Thick black line on FW and HW
Bellier's Blue p. 324

♂ GC dark blue — Thick black band on FW and HW
Odd-spot Blue p. 273

♂ GC dull blue — Black line, rather thin, on FW and HW
Alcon Blue p. 295

♂ GC royal blue — Thick black line on HW — Black line, rather thin, on HW
Pontic Blue p. 286

KEY TO LYCAENIDAE

8/8 On FW and HW: [fringes not chequered and bordered by thick dark band] AND [GC royal blue, purple-blue, or dull blue]

⚠ **Within this block, identification is difficult using upperside only**

8.1 On FW (and sometimes on HW): [several round or oval black spots in blue area] AND [no orange]

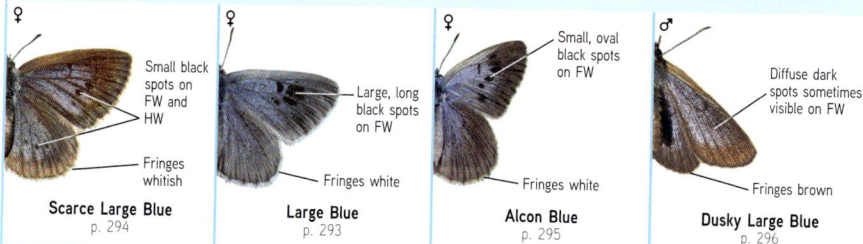

♀ Small black spots on FW and HW — Fringes whitish
Scarce Large Blue p. 294

♀ Large, long black spots on FW — Fringes white
Large Blue p. 293

♀ Small, oval black spots on FW — Fringes white
Alcon Blue p. 295

♂ Diffuse dark spots sometimes visible on FW — Fringes brown
Dusky Large Blue p. 296

8.2 On FW (and sometimes HW) : [no more than 1 black spot in the middle of the wing] AND [no orange]
On HW : a series of small black or blue spots near the trailing edge

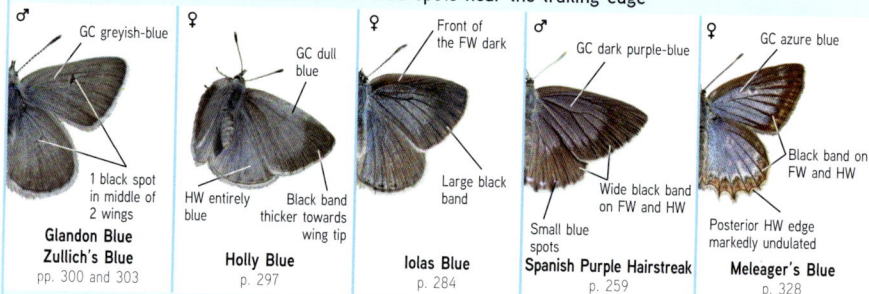

♂ GC greyish-blue — 1 black spot in middle of 2 wings
Glandon Blue Zullich's Blue pp. 300 and 303

♀ GC dull blue — HW entirely blue — Black band thicker towards wing tip
Holly Blue p. 297

♀ Front of the FW dark — Large black band
Iolas Blue p. 284

♂ GC dark purple-blue — Wide black band on FW and HW — Small blue spots
Spanish Purple Hairstreak p. 259

♀ GC azure blue — Black band on FW and HW — Posterior HW edge markedly undulated
Meleager's Blue p. 328

8.3 On FW (sometimes HW): [no more than 1 black spot in middle of wing] AND [no orange]
On HW: no small black or blue spots near trailing edge

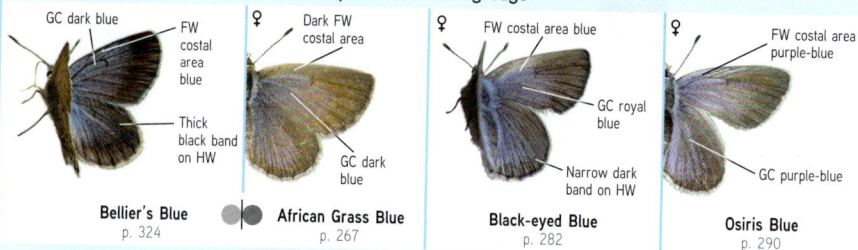

GC dark blue — FW costal area blue — Thick black band on HW
Bellier's Blue p. 324

♀ Dark FW costal area — GC dark blue
African Grass Blue p. 267

♀ FW costal area blue — GC royal blue — Narrow dark band on HW
Black-eyed Blue p. 282

♀ FW costal area purple-blue — GC purple-blue
Osiris Blue p. 290

8.4 On FW (and often on the HW): several marginal orange spots

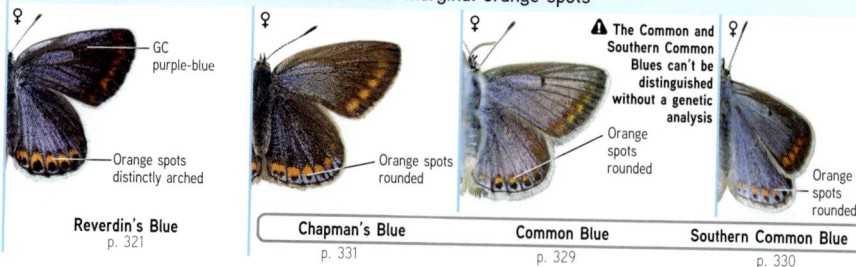

♀ GC purple-blue — Orange spots distinctly arched
Reverdin's Blue p. 321

♀ Orange spots rounded
Chapman's Blue p. 331

♀ ⚠ The Common and Southern Common Blues can't be distinguished without a genetic analysis — Orange spots rounded
Common Blue p. 329

♀ Orange spots rounded
Southern Common Blue p. 330

60

KEY TO LYCAENIDAE

1/3 On HW: GC pure orange
On FW: numerous black spots

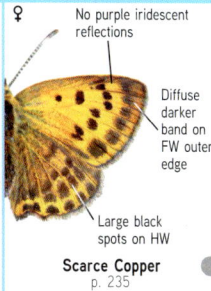

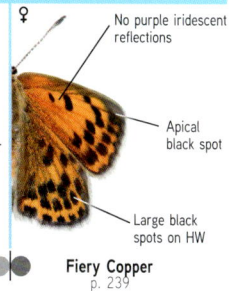

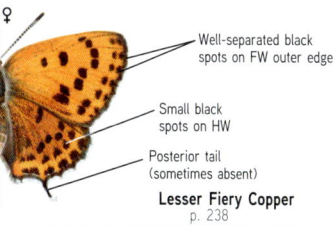

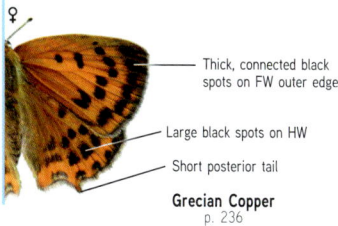

♂ Purple iridescent reflections

Small black spots on HW

Purple-shot Copper
p. 240

♀ No purple iridescent reflections

Diffuse darker band along FW outer edge

Small black spots on HW

Purple-shot Copper
p. 240

♀ No purple iridescent reflections

Diffuse darker band on FW outer edge

Large black spots on HW

Scarce Copper
p. 235

♀ No purple iridescent reflections

Apical black spot

Large black spots on HW

Fiery Copper
p. 239

♀ Well-separated black spots on FW outer edge

Small black spots on HW

Posterior tail (sometimes absent)

Lesser Fiery Copper
p. 238

♀ Thick, connected black spots on FW outer edge

Large black spots on HW

Short posterior tail

Grecian Copper
p. 236

2/3 On HW: GC dark brown or rufous brown
On FW: many black spots

2.1 On FW: 2 series of black spots on outer half of wing

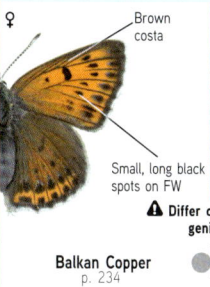

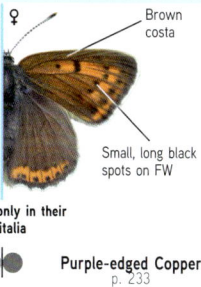

♀ Brown costa

Small, long black spots on FW

Balkan Copper
p. 234

♀ Brown costa

Small, long black spots on FW

⚠ Differ only in their genitalia

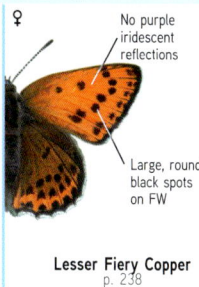

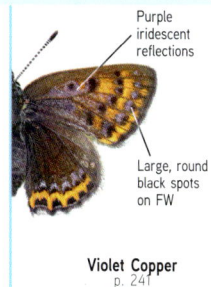

Purple-edged Copper
p. 233

♀ No purple iridescent reflections

Large, round black spots on FW

Lesser Fiery Copper
p. 238

Purple iridescent reflections

Large, round black spots on FW

Violet Copper
p. 241

2.2 On FW: 1 or 3 series of black spots on outer half of wing

1 series of shifted black spot pairs

FW GC orange

HW trailing edge undulated

Small Copper
p. 242

FW GC orange with large brown basal area

1 series of shifted black spot pairs

HW trailing edge undulated

Small Copper
p. 242

♀ 1 series of aligned black spots

Orange veins on HW

HW trailing edge not undulated

Large Copper
p. 237

♀ 3 series of black spots

HW trailing edge undulated

Sooty Copper
p. 243

3 series of black spots

Tail often present on HW

Iberian Sooty Copper p. 244

3/3 On FW: no more than 2 black spots or a few tiny black dots

3.1 On FW: no more than 2 black spots
On HW: GC pure orange

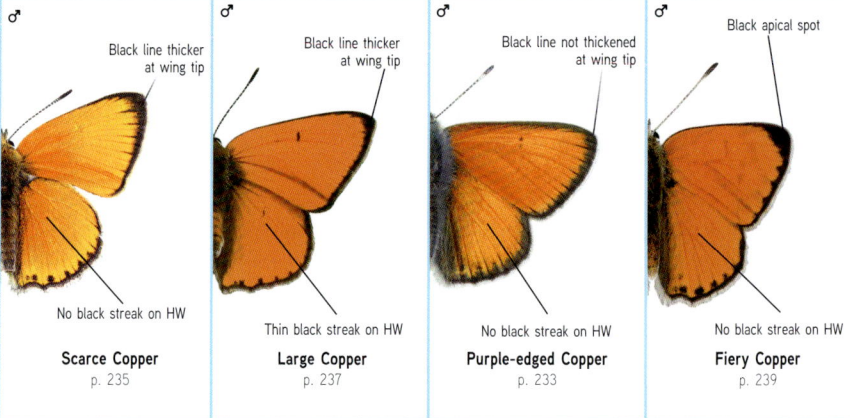

Black line thicker at wing tip

Black line thicker at wing tip

Black line not thickened at wing tip

Black apical spot

No black streak on HW

Thin black streak on HW

No black streak on HW

No black streak on HW

Scarce Copper
p. 235

Large Copper
p. 237

Purple-edged Copper
p. 233

Fiery Copper
p. 239

3.2 On FW: a few small black dots on outer half of wing
On HW: GC pure orange

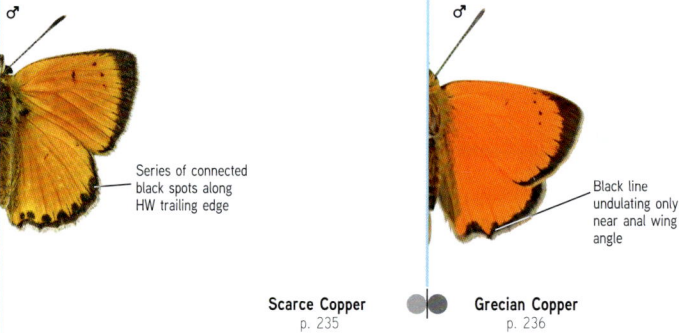

Series of connected black spots along HW trailing edge

Black line undulating only near anal wing angle

Scarce Copper
p. 235

Grecian Copper
p. 236

3.3 On FW: no more than 1 long black spot in middle of wing
On HW: extensive brown areas (sometimes with purple reflections) on inner half of wing

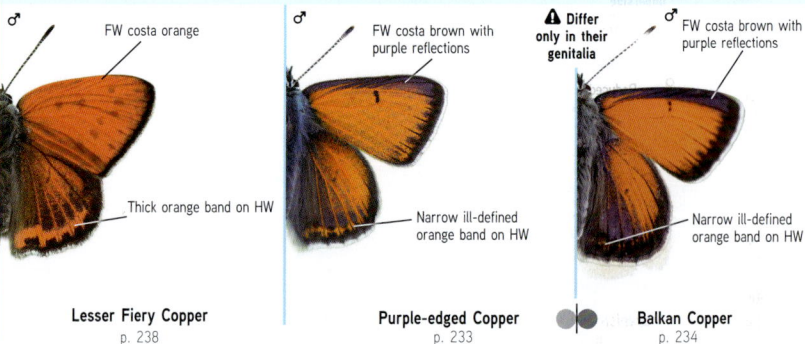

FW costa orange

FW costa brown with purple reflections

⚠ Differ only in their genitalia

FW costa brown with purple reflections

Thick orange band on HW

Narrow ill-defined orange band on HW

Narrow ill-defined orange band on HW

Lesser Fiery Copper
p. 238

Purple-edged Copper
p. 233

Balkan Copper
p. 234

KEY TO LYCAENIDAE

1/7 On HW: [a posterior tail] OR [trailing edge markedly undulated]

1.1 On FW: GC not uniform (black spots or different colours present)

♀ No orange

HW trailing edge markedly undulated

Black spots topped with whitish crescents

Meleager's Blue
p. 328

♀ Orange area on FW (larger in ♀♀)

Posterior orange tail

Brown Hairstreak
p. 251

♀ No orange

1 or 2 more visible black spots

Posterior tail

Little Tiger Blue
p. 271

♀ No orange

1 or 2 more visible black spots

Posterior tail

Common Tiger Blue
p. 272

♀ No orange

No black spot

Posterior tail

Purple Hairstreak
p. 252

1.2 On FW : GC uniformly brown

♀ GC dark greyish-brown

White fringes

Very short posterior tail

Eastern Short-tailed Blue
p. 288

♀ GC dark greyish-brown

White fringes

Very short posterior tail

Provençal Short-tailed Blue
p. 287

♀ GC dark greyish-brown

White fringes

Black spot sometimes topped with an orange spot

Long posterior tail

Short-tailed Blue
p. 292

♀ GC warm brown

Chequered fringes

White-ringed black spot

Long posterior tail

Geranium Bronze
p. 262

2/7 On FW and HW: [white fringes not chequered] AND [1 series of orange spots along wing edge, sometimes incomplete on FW]

2.1 On HW: orange spots not arched

⚠ **Within this block, identification is difficult using only the upperside**

2.2 On HW: orange spots markedly arched

♀ Often pronounced basal blue sprinkling

Well-separated orange spots

⚠ **Almost impossible to distinguish using only the upperside**

Chapman's Blue
p. 331

♀ Basal wing area often slightly sprinkled with blue

Well-separated orange spots

⚠ **Identification impossible without genetic data**

Common Blue
p. 329

♀ Basal wing area often slightly sprinkled with blue

Well-separated orange spots

Southern Common Blue
p. 330

♀ Basal wing area often slightly sprinkled with blue

Silver-studded Blue
p. 322

⚠ **Very difficult to distinguish using only the upperside**

♀ Orange spots tend to connect in a diffuse band on FW

No basal blue sprinkling

**Escher's Blue
Cretan Argus**
pp. 332 and 316

♀ Reduced orange spots on FW

No basal blue sprinkling

Spanish Zephyr Blue
p. 320

♀ No basal blue sprinkling

Incomplete series of wide orange spots

Mother-of-pearl Blue
p. 337

♀ Often pronounced basal blue sprinkling

Idas Blue
p. 323

KEY TO LYCAENIDAE

On HW: 1 series of orange spots (often incomplete)
On FW: orange spots reduced or absent

⚠ **Within this block, identification is difficult using only the upperside**

3.1 On HW: complete or almost complete series of orange spots along trailing edge

♀
Often pronounced basal blue sprinkling
Orange spots markedly arched
Reverdin's Blue
p. 321

♀
No basal blue sprinkling
Round orange spots
Mother-of-pearl Blue
p. 337

♂
No basal blue sprinkling
Round black spots on FW
Reduced orange spots on HW
Sooty Copper
p. 243

♀
No basal blue sprinkling
Round black spots on FW
Conspicuous orange band on HW
Purple-shot Copper
p. 240

3.2 On HW: 1 incomplete series of orange spots paired with white-ringed black spots along trailing edge

♀
GC dark brown
Usually a few faint orange marks on FW
Amanda's Blue
p. 334

♀
No orange on FW
GC dark brown
Zephyr Blue
p. 317

♀
GC dark brown
No orange on FW
Alpine Zephyr Blue
p. 318

♀
GC grey-brown
A few marginal dark spots
Pale spot on HW
Eros Blue
p. 333

3.3 On HW: 1 incomplete series of orange spots not paired with white-ringed black spots along trailing edge

♀
GC chocolate brown
Outer FW edge straight
Brown fringes
Reduced orange spots
Anomalous Blue
p. 342

♀
GC dark brown
Outer FW edge convex
White fringes
Reduced orange spots
Geranium Argus
p. 327

♀
GC dark brown
Outer FW edge convex
White fringes
Reduced orange spots
Turquoise Blue
p. 335

♀
GC dark brown
Outer FW edge convex
White fringes
Reduced orange spots
Nevada and Sagra Blues
p. 336

GC dark brown
Outer FW edge convex
White fringes
Reduced orange spots
Eastern Brown Argus
p. 319

♀
Outer FW edge slightly rounded
GC brown with bronze reflections
White fringes
Reduced orange spots, if any
Silvery Argus
p. 304

♀
GC brown with bronze reflections
Outer FW edge convex
White fringes
Reduced orange spots
Pontic Blue
p. 286

♀
Outer FW edge very convex
Large orange spots atop small black spots
Loew's Blue
p. 326

Outer FW edge very convex
Large orange spots atop large black spots
Grass Jewel
p. 270

KEY TO LYCAENIDAE

On FW (and sometimes HW): fringes chequered

4.1 **On HW: 1 series of orange spots atop white-ringed black spots**

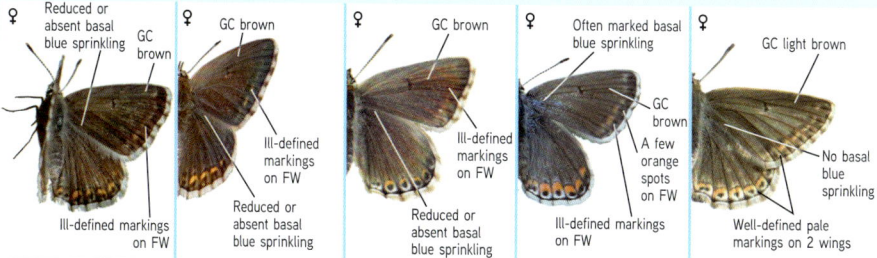

♀ Reduced or absent basal blue sprinkling — GC brown

♀ GC brown

♀ GC brown

♀ Often marked basal blue sprinkling — GC brown — A few orange spots on FW

♀ GC light brown — No basal blue sprinkling

Ill-defined markings on FW

Ill-defined markings on FW

Reduced or absent basal blue sprinkling

Reduced or absent basal blue sprinkling

Ill-defined markings on FW

Ill-defined markings on FW

Well-defined pale markings on 2 wings

Provence Chalkhill Blue	Azure Chalkhill Blue	Chalkhill Blue	Adonis Blue	Spanish Chalkhill Blue
p. 314	p. 312	p. 313	p. 311	p. 315

4.2 **On HW: complete or almost complete series of orange spots along with black spots without white ring**

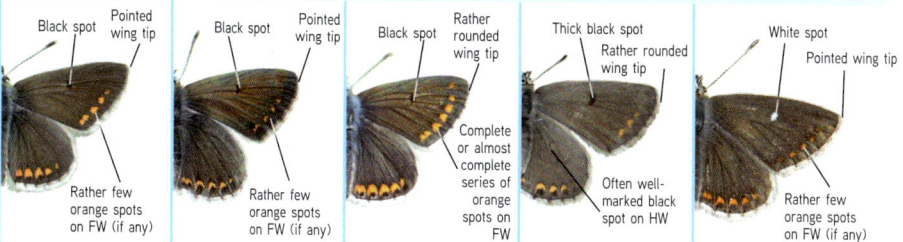

Black spot — Pointed wing tip

Black spot — Pointed wing tip

Black spot — Rather rounded wing tip

Thick black spot — Rather rounded wing tip — Often well-marked black spot on HW

White spot — Pointed wing tip

Rather few orange spots on FW (if any)

Rather few orange spots on FW (if any)

Complete or almost complete series of orange spots on FW

Rather few orange spots on FW (if any)

Northern Brown Argus	Southern Mountain Argus	Brown Argus / Southern Brown Argus	Blue Argus	Northern Brown Argus
p. 307	p. 308	pp. 305 and 306	p. 310	p. 307

4.3 **On HW: [hardly any or no orange] AND [no basal blue sprinkling]**

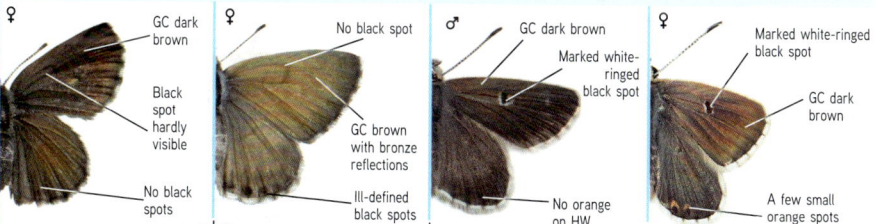

♀ GC dark brown — Black spot hardly visible — No black spots

♀ No black spot — GC brown with bronze reflections — Ill-defined black spots

♂ GC dark brown — Marked white-ringed black spot — No orange on HW

♀ Marked white-ringed black spot — GC dark brown — A few small orange spots on HW

Sardinian Blue	Canary Blue		Spanish Argus
p. 274	p. 261		p. 309

4.4 **On FW and HW: [no orange] AND [a basal blue area]**

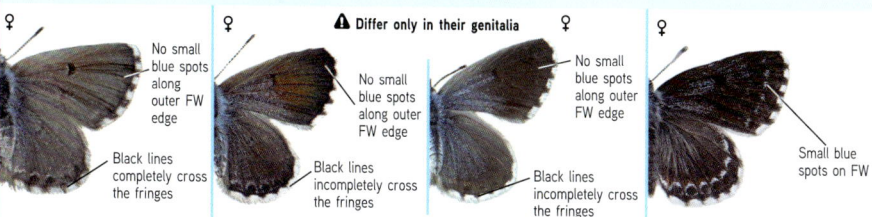

♀ No small blue spots along outer FW edge — Black lines completely cross the fringes

♀ ⚠ Differ only in their genitalia — No small blue spots along outer FW edge — Black lines incompletely cross the fringes

♀ No small blue spots along outer FW edge — Black lines incompletely cross the fringes

♀ Small blue spots on FW

False Baton Blue	Baton Blue		Eastern Baton Blue	Chequered Blue
p. 275	p. 277		p. 278	p. 280

5/7 On FW and HW: [fringes white, not chequered] AND [no orange] AND [no blue]

5.1 On FW and HW: 1 black spot, often ringed with white, in middle of wing
On HW: small, pale-ringed black spots along trailing edge

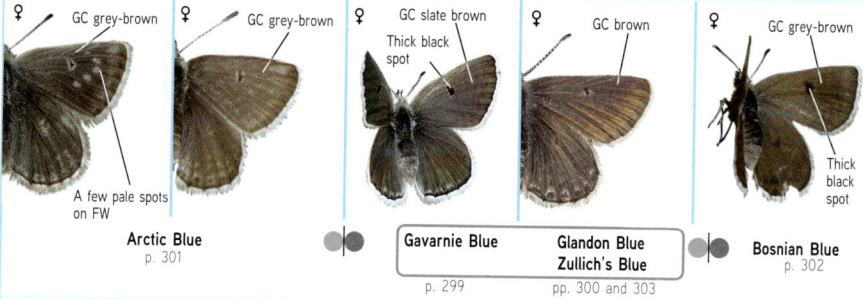

♀ GC grey-brown — A few pale spots on FW

♀ GC grey-brown

♀ GC slate brown — Thick black spot

♀ GC brown

♀ GC grey-brown — Thick black spot

Arctic Blue
p. 301

Gavarnie Blue
p. 299

**Glandon Blue
Zullich's Blue**
pp. 300 and 303

Bosnian Blue
p. 302

5.2 On FW and HW: GC light brown or brown
On FW: 1 small, long black spot in middle of wing

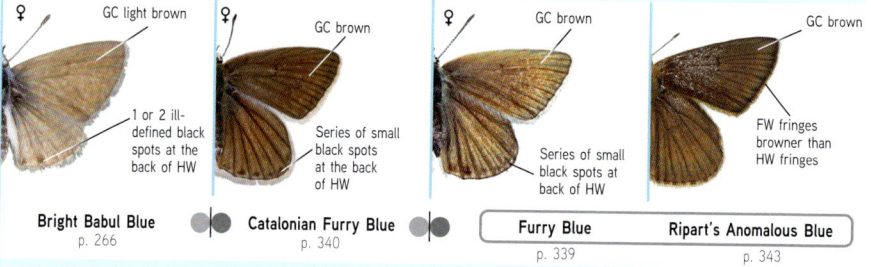

♀ GC light brown — 1 or 2 ill-defined black spots at the back of HW

♀ GC brown — Series of small black spots at the back of HW

♀ GC brown — Series of small black spots at back of HW

♀ GC brown — FW fringes browner than HW fringes

Bright Babul Blue
p. 266

Catalonian Furry Blue
p. 340

Furry Blue
p. 339

Ripart's Anomalous Blue
p. 343

5.3 On FW and HW: GC dark brown or sooty
On FW: 1 small black spot or many black spots in middle of wing

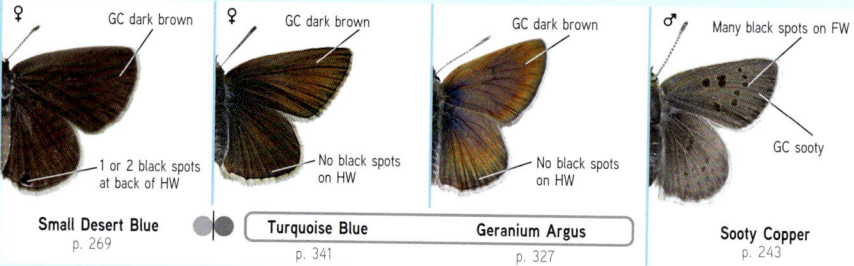

♀ GC dark brown — 1 or 2 black spots at back of HW

♀ GC dark brown — No black spots on HW

♀ GC dark brown — No black spots on HW

♂ Many black spots on FW — GC sooty

Small Desert Blue
p. 269

Turquoise Blue
p. 341

Geranium Argus
p. 327

Sooty Copper
p. 243

5.4 On FW and HW: GC brown or sooty
On FW: no black spot

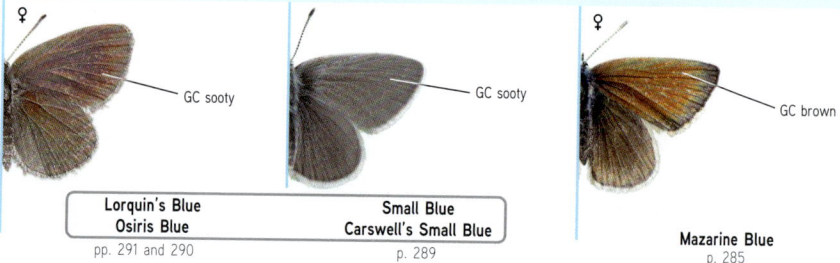

♀ GC sooty

GC sooty

♀ GC brown

**Lorquin's Blue
Osiris Blue**
pp. 291 and 290

**Small Blue
Carswell's Small Blue**
p. 289

Mazarine Blue
p. 285

6/7 On FW (sometimes HW): [brown fringes] AND [no basal blue sprinkling]

⚠ Within this block, species are particularly difficult to identify based on the upperside. They are often allopatric, but an underside view may help distinguish sympatric species.

⚠ Only in southern Spain

⚠ Only in northern Spain

⚠ Only in the Balkans and Central Europe

GC very dark brown

Fringes of 2 wings brown

HW fringe paler than FW fringe

⚠ Only in the Aoste Valley

Andalusian Anomalous Blue
p. 347

Oberthür's Anomalous Blue
p. 348

Ripart's Anomalous Blue   Anomalous
Timfristos Anomalous Blue   Blue
pp. 343 and 344   p. 342

Piedmont Anomalous Blue
p. 349

7/7 On FW (sometimes HW): [no or hardly any orange] AND [basal blue area]

7.1 On HW: 1 series of black spots near trailing edge

⚠ Only in the Balkans   ⚠ Only in the Balkans

♀ Brown eyes

♀ Black eyes

♀ Black eyes

Very dark blue basal area

Fringes of both wings brown

HW fringes white

Dark Grass Blue
p. 268

Cranberry Blue
p. 325

Odd-spot Blue
p. 273

Grecian Anomalous Blue
Kolev's Anomalous Blue   Higgins's
Lura Anomalous Blue   Anomalous Blue
pp. 344 and 346   p. 345

7.2 On HW: [a series of small black spots topped with blue] OR [a series of small blue spots along the trailing edge]

♀

♀

♀

No orange on HW

No orange on HW

Small orange spots below blue spots

Paphos Blue
p. 283

Turquoise Blue
p. 341

Spanish Purple Hairstreak
p. 259

7.3 On HW: no black spots along the trailing edge

♀

♀ Small black spots barely visible on FW

♀ Small black spot

♀

♀ Brown eyes Small black spot

GC chocolate brown

GC dull brown

GC very dark brown

Small blue spot

White fringes

GC grey-brown

Brown fringes

No blue on HW

No blue on HW

Large blue area on HW

Dusky Large Blue
p. 296

Alcon Blue
p. 295

Green-underside Blue
p. 281

Alpine Blue
p. 298

African Grass Blue
p. 267

KEY TO LYCAENIDAE

1/10 On FW: [2 basal black spots] AND [GC orange or cream]

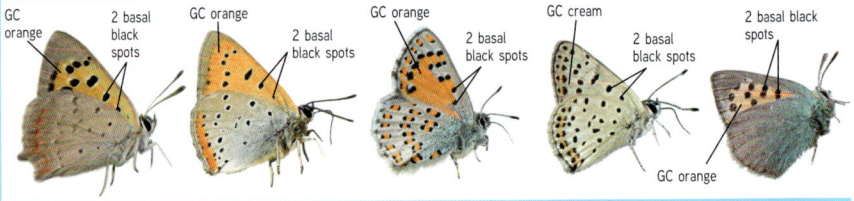

GC orange
2 basal black spots
GC orange
2 basal black spots
GC orange
2 basal black spots
GC cream
2 basal black spots
2 basal black spots
GC orange

→ **Page 70**

2/10 On HW: [GC grey-brown or ochre with no black spots in middle of wing] OR [GC beige, with white-bordered brown lines or bands, sometimes a few black spots]

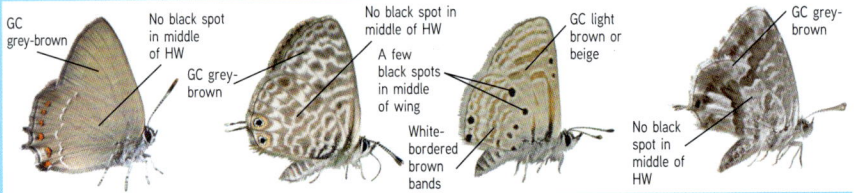

GC grey-brown
No black spot in middle of HW
No black spot in middle of HW
GC grey-brown
A few black spots in middle of wing
GC light brown or beige
GC grey-brown
White-bordered brown bands
No black spot in middle of HW

→ **Page 71**

3/10 On HW: white streak reaches at least white-ringed, mid-wing black spot

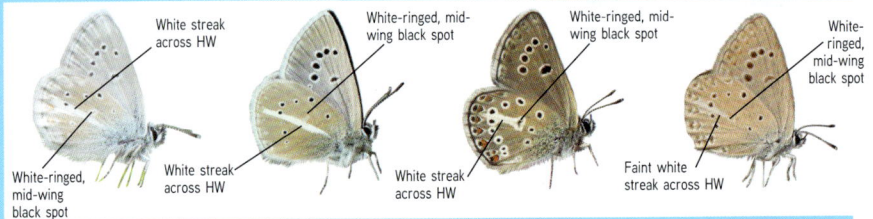

White streak across HW
White-ringed, mid-wing black spot
White-ringed, mid-wing black spot
White-ringed, mid-wing black spot
White-ringed, mid-wing black spot
White streak across HW
White streak across HW
Faint white streak across HW

→ **Page 74**

4/10 On HW: [no well-marked orange spot] AND [conspicuous marginal spots or dots]

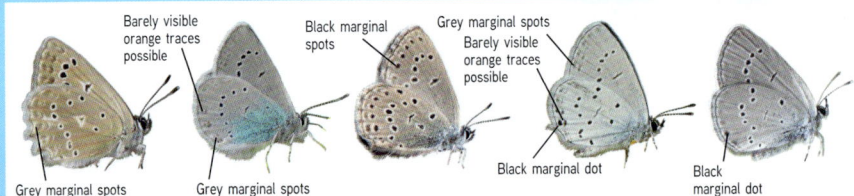

Barely visible orange traces possible
Black marginal spots
Grey marginal spots
Barely visible orange traces possible
Grey marginal spots
Grey marginal spots
Black marginal dot
Black marginal dot

→ **Page 72**

5/10 On HW: [no orange] AND [no well-marked marginal spots or dots]

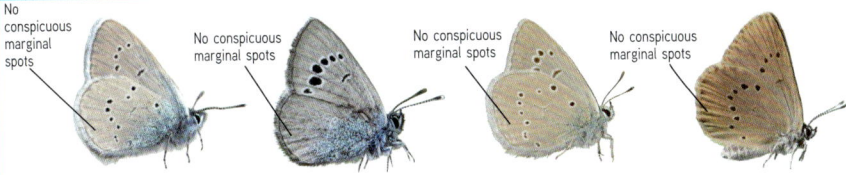

No conspicuous marginal spots

No conspicuous marginal spots

No conspicuous marginal spots

No conspicuous marginal spots

→ **Page 73**

6/10 On HW: [several marginal orange spots] OR [only oval white spots]
On FW: no orange spots

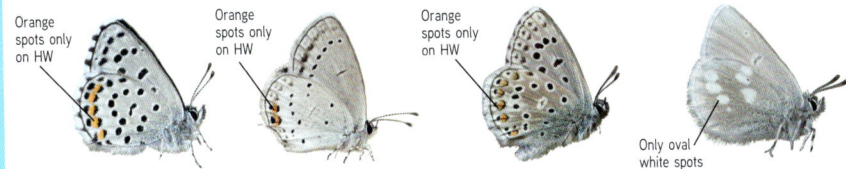

Orange spots only on HW

Orange spots only on HW

Orange spots only on HW

Only oval white spots

→ **Page 75**

7/10 On HW and FW: [several marginal orange spots]
On FW: 1 basal black spot

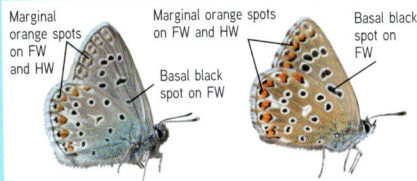

Marginal orange spots on FW and HW

Marginal orange spots on FW and HW

Basal black spot on FW

Basal black spot on FW

→ **Page 77 (blocks 1/2 and 2/2)**

8/10 On HW and FW: [several marginal orange spots]
On FW: no basal black spot

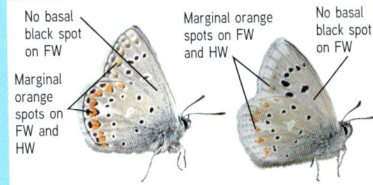

No basal black spot on FW

Marginal orange spots on FW and HW

No basal black spot on FW

Marginal orange spots on FW and HW

→ **Page 77 (block 1/5 and following ones)**

9/10 On FW and HW: GC emerald green

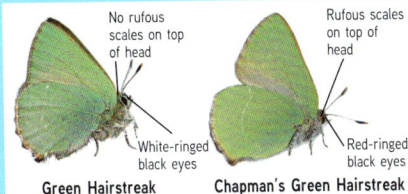

No rufous scales on top of head

Rufous scales on top of head

White-ringed black eyes

Red-ringed black eyes

Green Hairstreak

Chapman's Green Hairstreak

→ **Pages 247 and 248**

10/10 On FW and HW: [GC white] AND [sharply contrasting dark lines]

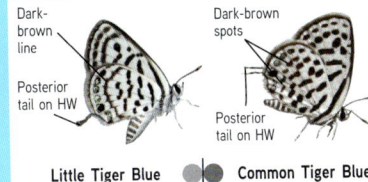

Dark-brown line

Dark-brown spots

Posterior tail on HW

Posterior tail on HW

Little Tiger Blue   **Common Tiger Blue**

→ **Pages 271 and 272**

KEY TO LYCAENIDAE

On HW: several conspicuous white spots near the wing margin

White spots of different sizes

No marginal black spots

No well-defined marginal orange line

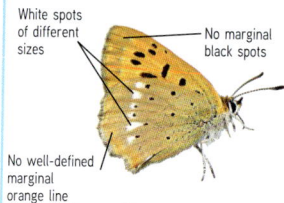

Scarce Copper
p. 235

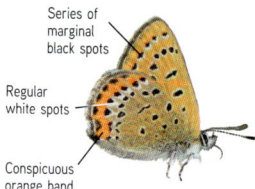

Series of marginal black spots

Regular white spots

Conspicuous orange band

Violet Copper
p. 241

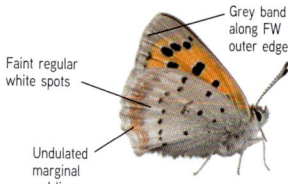

Grey band along FW outer edge

Faint regular white spots

Undulated marginal red line

Small Copper
p. 242

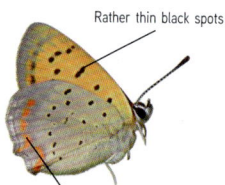

On HW: [marginal red line] OR [GC pale with faint black spots] OR [GC green]

Thick black spots

Thin undulated marginal red line

Small Copper
p. 242

Rather thin black spots

Thick undulated marginal red line

Grecian Copper
p. 236

Very faint red and black spots on HW

Fiery Copper
p. 239

Small red dots across HW

HW base emerald green (becoming blue with age)

Provence Hairstreak
p. 245

On HW: [1 orange band or incomplete series of orange spots]

Orange GC reaching FW edge

Short mid-wing black line

Marked but incomplete orange band on HW

GC bluish grey

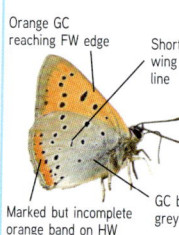

Large Copper
p. 237

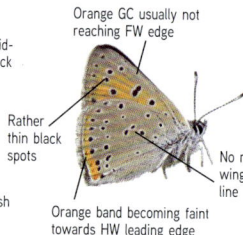

Orange GC usually not reaching FW edge

Rather thin black spots

No mid-wing short line

Orange band becoming faint towards HW leading edge

Purple-edged Copper
p. 233

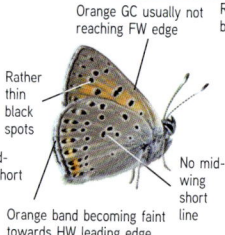

Orange GC usually not reaching FW edge

Rather thin black spots

No mid-wing short line

Orange band becoming faint towards HW leading edge

Balkan Copper
p. 234

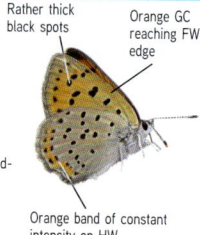

Rather thick black spots

Orange GC reaching FW edge

Orange band of constant intensity on HW

Purple-shot Copper
p. 240

On HW: [orange band or complete marginal series of orange spots]
On FW: [marginal orange spots or marginal orange area]

Thick orange band on HW and FW

GC orange

Long posterior tail

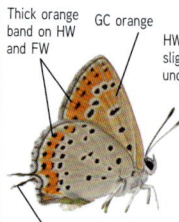

Lesser Fiery Copper
p. 238

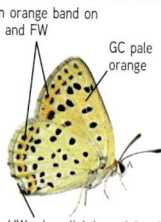

GC orange

HW edge slightly undulated

Thick orange band on HW

Thin orange band on HW and FW

GC pale orange

HW edge slightly undulated (tail sometimes present)

Sooty Copper
Iberian Sooty Copper
pp. 243 and 244

Thin orange band on HW and FW

GC cream

♂

Sooty Copper
p. 243

Large vivid orange area without any black spots

3 parallel series of orange spots

Nogel's Hairstreak
p. 246

UNS

KEY TO LYCAENIDAE

1/4 — On HW: [several white-bordered brown lines] AND [no mid-wing black spots]

White band on HW

Long tail

Black spots not entirely ringed with silvery blue scales

Long-tailed Blue
p. 263

White spots (no band) on HW

Long tail

Black spots entirely ringed with silvery blue scales

Lang's Short-tailed Blue
p. 264

Diffuse brown and whitish areas

Small black spot with no orange

Long tail

Geranium Bronze
p. 262

1 darker brown band

A short and a long tail

Thick brown bands containing silvery scales

Levantine Leopard
p. 249

FW GC orange-brown

No tail

Silver-ringed black spots with no orange

White band on HW

Canary Blue
p. 261

2/4 — On HW: [several white-bordered brown lines] AND [several mid-wing black spots]

GC light beige

Black spots bordered by a few silvery scales

Small Desert Blue
p. 269

GC light brown

No well-marked black spots

No tail

Bright Babul Blue
p. 266

GC dull brown

Well-marked black spots

No tail

African Babul Blue
p. 265

Black spot bordered with orange

1 or 2 mid-wing black spots

Long tail

Pomegranate Playboy
p. 250

3/4 — On HW: [a white line] AND [incomplete series of clearly separated marginal orange spots]

White line faint or absent on FW

Similar-sized red spots bordered with black on inner side only

False Ilex Hairstreak
p. 258

Marked white line on FW (unless worn)

Orange spots markedly increasing in size towards anal angle, bordered with black on both sides

Ilex Hairstreak
p. 257

Thick white line on both wings

Large greyish-blue spot associated with little orange

Blue-spot Hairstreak
p. 253

Very short tail

Small orange-ringed grey spot

Sloe Hairstreak
p. 254

Thick white line on both wings

GC grey-beige

Single orange-ringed black spot

Purple Hairstreak
p. 252

4/4 — On HW: [1 or 2 white lines] AND [orange band or complete series of marginal orange spots]

Vivid marginal orange band on both wings

GC ochre

Brown Hairstreak
p. 251

2 rather straight white lines on both wings

Crescent-shaped orange spots bordered with black lines

W-shaped white line on HW

White-letter Hairstreak
p. 255

Orange band bordered by series of black dots

Ill-defined, W-shaped white line on HW

Black Hairstreak
p. 256

No white line across both wings

Silvery line

Small white chevrons against black spots

Spanish Purple Hairstreak
p. 259

71

KEY TO LYCAENIDAE

1/3 On FW and HW: 1 or 2 series of well-marked marginal black spots

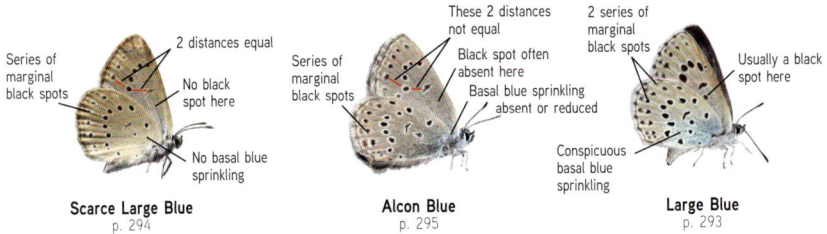

2 distances equal

Series of marginal black spots

No black spot here

No basal blue sprinkling

Scarce Large Blue
p. 294

These 2 distances not equal

Series of marginal black spots

Black spot often absent here

Basal blue sprinkling absent or reduced

Conspicuous basal blue sprinkling

Alcon Blue
p. 295

2 series of marginal black spots

Usually a black spot here

Conspicuous basal blue sprinkling

Large Blue
p. 293

2/3 On HW: [more or less complete series of faint marginal grey spots] AND [often 1 or 2 conspicuous marginal black dots]

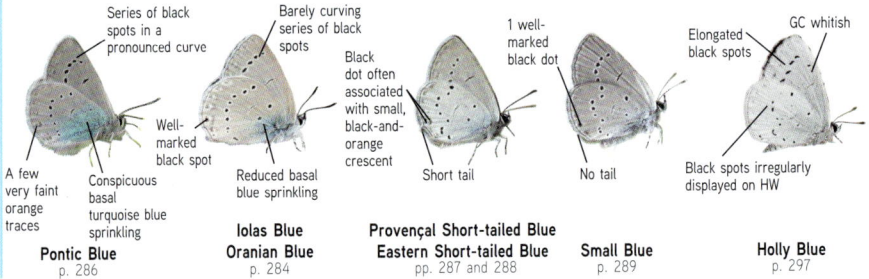

Series of black spots in a pronounced curve

Well-marked black spot

A few very faint orange traces

Conspicuous basal turquoise blue sprinkling

Pontic Blue
p. 286

Barely curving series of black spots

Black dot often associated with small, black-and-orange crescent

Reduced basal blue sprinkling

Iolas Blue
Oranian Blue
p. 284

1 well-marked black dot

Short tail

Provençal Short-tailed Blue
Eastern Short-tailed Blue
pp. 287 and 288

No tail

Small Blue
p. 289

Elongated black spots

GC whitish

Black spots irregularly displayed on HW

Holly Blue
p. 297

3/3 On FW and HW: [complete series of marginal grey spots] AND [sometimes 1 or 2 marginal black dots]

3.1 On FW: black spots of similar size or slightly larger compared with HW

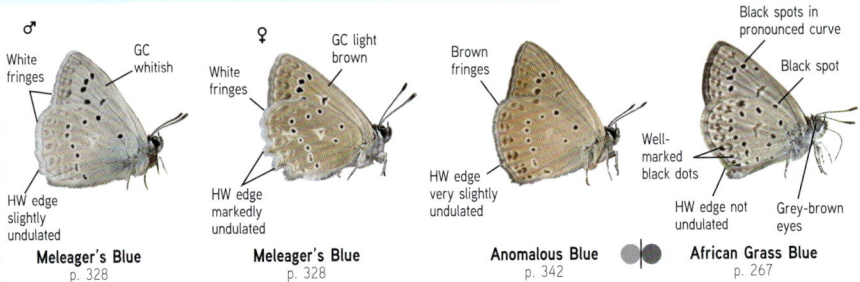

♂

White fringes

GC whitish

HW edge slightly undulated

Meleager's Blue
p. 328

♀

GC light brown

White fringes

HW edge markedly undulated

Meleager's Blue
p. 328

Brown fringes

HW edge very slightly undulated

Anomalous Blue
p. 342

Black spots in pronounced curve

Black spot

Well-marked black dots

HW edge not undulated

Grey-brown eyes

African Grass Blue
p. 267

3.2 On FW: black spots much larger than on HW

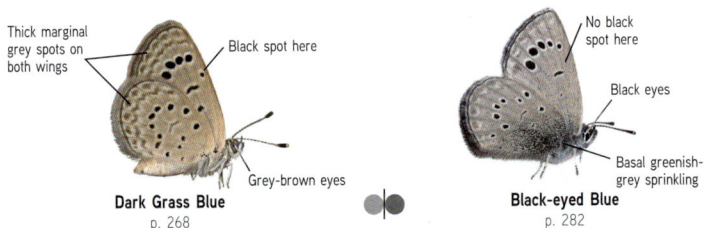

Thick marginal grey spots on both wings

Black spot here

Grey-brown eyes

Dark Grass Blue
p. 268

No black spot here

Black eyes

Basal greenish-grey sprinkling

Black-eyed Blue
p. 282

1/3 On FW: pronounced curve of black spots
On HW: wing base conspicuously sprinkled with blue

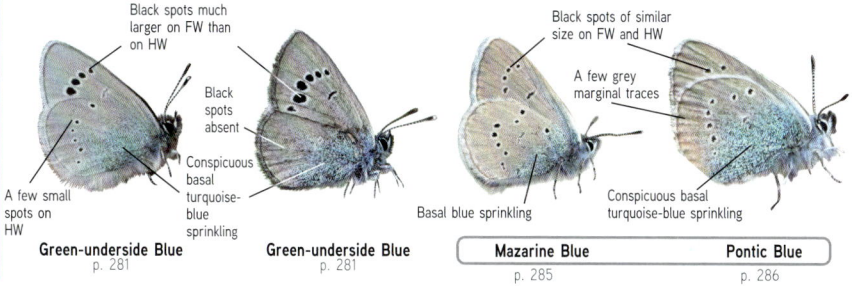

Black spots much larger on FW than on HW

Black spots absent

Conspicuous basal turquoise-blue sprinkling

A few small spots on HW

Green-underside Blue
p. 281

Green-underside Blue
p. 281

Black spots of similar size on FW and HW

A few grey marginal traces

Conspicuous basal turquoise-blue sprinkling

Basal blue sprinkling

Mazarine Blue p. 285	**Pontic Blue** p. 286

2/3 On FW: pronounced curve of black spots
On HW: wing base not sprinkled with blue

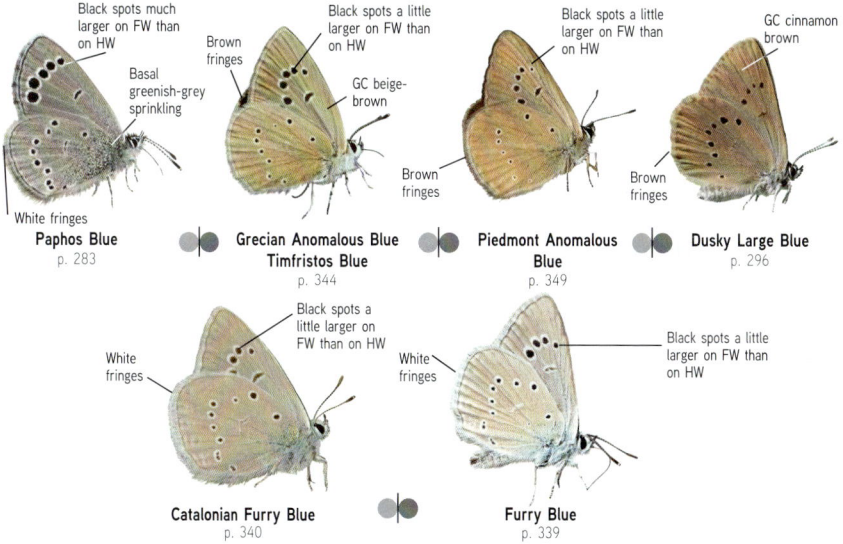

Black spots much larger on FW than on HW

Basal greenish-grey sprinkling

White fringes

Paphos Blue
p. 283

Brown fringes

Black spots a little larger on FW than on HW

GC beige-brown

Brown fringes

Grecian Anomalous Blue
Timfristos Blue
p. 344

Black spots a little larger on FW than on HW

Brown fringes

Piedmont Anomalous Blue
p. 349

GC cinnamon brown

Dusky Large Blue
p. 296

White fringes

Black spots a little larger on FW than on HW

Catalonian Furry Blue
p. 340

White fringes

Black spots a little larger on FW than on HW

Furry Blue
p. 339

3/3 On FW: almost straight series of black spots, the first shifted basally

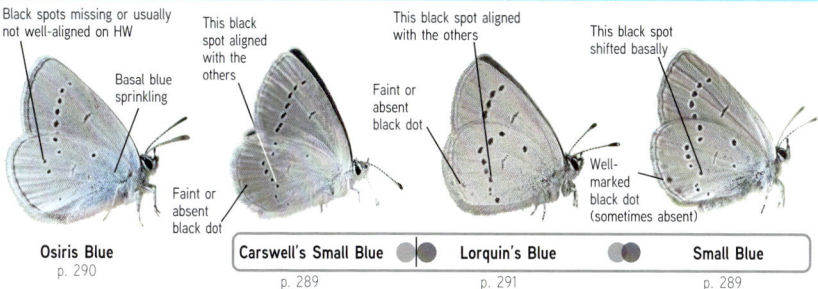

Black spots missing or usually not well-aligned on HW

Basal blue sprinkling

Faint or absent black dot

Osiris Blue
p. 290

This black spot aligned with the others

This black spot aligned with the others

Faint or absent black dot

This black spot shifted basally

Well-marked black dot (sometimes absent)

Carswell's Small Blue p. 289	**Lorquin's Blue** p. 291	**Small Blue** p. 289

1/4 On HW: conspicuous white streak across wing
On FW: white fringes

Complete series of marginal orange spots

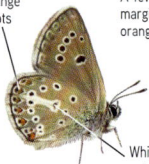

A few faint marginal orange spots

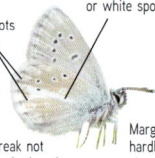

White streak extending farther than mid-wing black or white spot

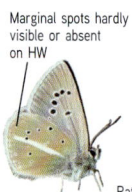

White streak extending farther than mid-wing black or white spot

Marginal spots hardly visible or absent on HW

Faint marginal dark spots on FW (darker in ♀♀)

White streak not extending farther than mid-wing black spot

Marginal spots hardly visible or absent on HW

Rather well-marked marginal spots on HW

Geranium Argus
p. 327

Silvery Argus
p. 304

Catalonian Furry Blue
p. 340

Turquoise Blue
p. 339

Chelmos Blue
p. 338

2/4 On HW: conspicuous white streak across wing
On FW: fringes tinged with brown

Thick, well-marked white streak doubled at its posterior end

⚠ These species are very difficult to distinguish. Fringes are whiter in Higgins's Anomalous Blue

Thick, well-marked white streak

White streak faint on both ends

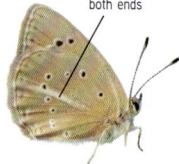

Higgins's Anomalous Blue

Ripart's Anomalous Blue
Kolev's Anomalous Blue
Lura Anomalous Blue

Andalusian Anomalous Blue
p. 347

p. 345

pp. 343 and 346

3/4 On HW: faint white streak across wing
On FW: fringes tinged with brown

Rather faint marginal spots

Rather faint marginal spots

Well-marked marginal spots

Oberthür's Anomalous Blue
p. 348

Oberthür's Anomalous Blue
p. 348

Anomalous Blue
p. 342

4/4 On HW: faint white streak across wing
On FW: white fringes

Faint white streak

Faint white streak

Catalonian Furry Blue
p. 340

Furry Blue
p. 339

KEY TO LYCAENIDAE

1/5 On HW: [1 or several white spots in middle of wing] AND [often 1 or 2 marginal orange spots]

Marked marginal black spots

Rather faint marginal black spots

Narrow but well-marked marginal black spots

Rather faint marginal black spots

No marginal spots

More white than black spots on HW

Large white spots

More white than black spots on HW

More black than white spots on HW

More black than white spots on HW

No black spot on HW

Gavarnie Blue
p. 299

Glandon Blue
Zullich's Blue
pp. 300 and 303

Bosnian Blue
p. 302

Arctic Blue
p. 301

Alpine Blue
p. 298

2/5 On HW: [no mid-wing white spot] AND [2 to 4 marginal orange spots]

2.1 On HW: [marginal black spots associated with silvery blue scales]

Well-marked marginal brown spots

Grey marginal spots

GC grey

Black spots

Black diffuse marginal spots

GC beige-grey

3 orange-ringed black spots bordered by silvery blue scales

Brown spots

Orange spot paired with an external black spot containing silvery blue scales

Orange spot paired with an external black spot containing silvery blue scales

Grass Jewel
p. 270

Cranberry Blue
p. 325

Loew's Blue
p. 326

2.2 On HW: no silvery blue scales associated with marginal black spots

Orange spots bordered with black on their inner and outer sides

Thick black spots, one of them shifted basally

Orange spots bordered with black on their inner and outer sides

Rather small black spots

Hardly any basal blue

Orange spots associated with very little black

Basal blue sprinkling

No tail

Posterior tail on HW

Conspicuous basal, turquoise blue sprinkling

Orange spots often connected on HW

Odd-spot Blue
p. 273

Short-tailed Blue
p. 292

Pontic Blue
p. 286

Mazarine Blue
p. 285

3/5 On HW: [no more than 1 mid-wing white spot] AND [complete or almost complete series of marginal orange spots]
On FW and HW: fringes not chequered

No black spots here

No black spot here

Conspicuous black spots

No black spot here

Black spot here

White triangle

No tail

Basal black spots on HW

Posterior tail on HW

No black spot here

Mid-wing black spot thickly ringed with white

Basal black spots on HW

Amanda's Blue
p. 334

Orange-banded Hairstreak
p. 260

Eros Blue
p. 333

KEY TO LYCAENIDAE

4/5 On FW and HW: [fringes chequered] AND [HW GC darker than FW GC]

FW GC grey

Marked black spots about the same size on both wings

FW GC whitish

⚠ **The 2 species are very difficult to distinguish. Provence Chalkhill Blue flies in late April, Chalkhill Blue in late May**

FW GC whitish

Well-marked black spots

FW GC whitish

Marked black spots often slightly smaller on FW

HW GC grey-brown

HW GC light brown

HW GC grey-brown

Well-marked black spots

Black spots hardly visible on HW

Adonis Blue
p. 311

Provence Chalkhill Blue	**Chalkhill Blue**
p. 314	p. 313

Spanish Chalkhill Blue
p. 315

5/5 On FW and HW: [fringes chequered] AND [HW GC same as FW GC]

5.1 On HW: complete or almost complete series of conspicuous marginal orange spots

Incomplete series of separated marginal orange spots

GC grey

Incomplete series of separated marginal orange spots

GC grey

Complete series of separated marginal orange spots

GC grey

Complete series of connected marginal orange spots

Thick marginal spots

GC whitish

⚠ **Differ only in their genitalia**

Baton Blue	**Eastern Baton Blue**
p. 277	p. 278

Bavius Blue
p. 279

Chequered Blue
p. 280

5.2 On HW: often incomplete series of narrow, hardly visible marginal orange spots

T-shaped black spots in white fringes

GC grey-brown

Thick black spots on FW

Thick black spots, not T-shaped, in fringes

Thick black spots on FW

GC grey

Black spots of similar size on FW and HW

False Baton blue	**Panoptes Blue**
p. 275	p. 276

Sardinian Blue
p. 274

KEY TO LYCAENIDAE

1/2 On FW and HW: GC rather similar

1.1 On FW and HW: GC grey

Rather well-marked orange spots on FW

Vivid orange marginal spots

Mid-wing black spot finely ringed with white

⚠ The 2 species are impossible to distinguish without genetic data

Vivid orange marginal spots

Rather well-marked orange spots on FW

♂

Orange spots reduced or absent on FW

Pale orange marginal spots

Mid-wing black spot thickly ringed with white

♂

Common Blue	Southern Common blue
p. 329	p. 330

Eros Blue
p. 333

1.2 On FW and HW: GC brown or grey-brown

Chequered fringes

Thick marginal orange spots on FW

Fringes not markedly chequered

♀

⚠ The 2 species are impossible to distinguish without genetic data

Fringes not markedly chequered

♀

Thick marginal orange spots on FW

♀

Fringes not markedly chequered

Orange spots reduced on FW

Hardly any black (if any) in this white spot

♀

Adonis Blue
p. 311

Common Blue	Southern Common Blue
p. 329	p. 330

Eros Blue
p. 333

2/2 On FW and HW: [HW GC browner than FW GC, which is greyer or whiter]

FW GC grey

Narrow orange spots on FW

FW GC light brown with a whitish area

Orange spots rather thick on FW

FW GC light brown with a whitish area

Narrow orange spots on FW

FW GC light brown with a whitish area

Thick black spots on FW

FW GC light brown with a whitish area

Black spots usually slightly smaller on HW than on FW

♂

Black spots of similar size on FW and HW

♀

Black spots usually slightly smaller on HW than on FW

♀

Thin black spots with HW marginal orange spots

♀

Adonis Blue
p. 311

Azure Chalkhill Blue	Provence Chalkhill Blue	Chalkhill Blue
p. 312	p. 314	p. 313

Spanish Chalkhill Blue
p. 315

1/5 On FW and HW: [continuous white band along fringes] AND [white fringes]

♂

FW GC grey-brown

♀

Both wings' GC light brown

♂

Series of large black spots in a pronounced curve on FW

♀

HW GC light brown

Black spots smaller on HW than on FW

Turquoise Blue/Nevada Blue/Sagra Blue
pp. 335 and 336

Rather thick black spots on HW

Mother-of-pearl Blue
p. 337

Mother-of-pearl Blue
p. 337

KEY TO LYCAENIDAE

2/5 On FW and HW: fringes chequered
On HW: [3 black spots defining a right-angled triangle] AND [white triangle]

Little white here

Complete series of large marginal orange spots (especially in ♀♀)

Little white here

3 spots defining a triangle

White band along the fringes

Black spots markedly larger on FW than on HW

3 spots defining a triangle

3 spots defining a triangle

3 spots defining a triangle

White spots on HW

Hindmost marginal orange spot missing

⚠ 4 species almost impossible to distinguish from their undersides

Brown Argus Southern Mountain Argus Northern Brown Argus	Southern Brown Argus
pp. 305, 308, and 307	p. 306

Spanish Argus
p. 309

Northern Brown Argus
p. 307

Blue Argus
p. 310

3/5 On FW and HW: white fringes
On HW: [3 black spots do not make a right-angled triangle] AND [white triangle]

Hardly any orange associated with the black spot

White triangle

This black spot paired with a marked orange spot

White triangle

3 well-aligned black spots

This black spot paired with a marked orange spot

3 black spots not well-aligned

White triangle

Escher's Blue
p. 332

Common Blue
p. 329

Chapman's Blue
p. 331

4/5 On FW and HW: white fringes
On HW: [several marginal orange spots associated with some silvery blue scales] AND [no white triangle]

Grey spots

Black spots

Reduced orange spots on FW

Small tibial spine

Reduced orange spots on FW

Rather fine, pointed black chevrons

Thick orange spots on FW

Tibial spine absent

Rather blunt black chevrons

Corsican Silver-studded Blue
p. 322

Bellier's Blue
p. 324

Silver-studded Blue
p. 322

Idas Blue
p. 323

Reverdin's Blue
p. 321

5/5 On FW and HW: white fringes
On HW: [no more than 1 marginal orange spot associated with some silvery blue scales] AND [no white triangle]

Small faint dark spots

Rather narrow orange spots on FW

A few silvery blue scales possible here

Rather thick orange spots on FW

Usually 1 silvery blue spot here

Rather narrow orange spots on FW

No silvery blue scales

Rather narrow orange spots on FW

No silvery blue scales

Cretan Argus
p. 316

Zephyr Blue
p. 317

Eastern Brown Argus
p. 319

Spanish Zephyr Blue
p. 320

Alpine Zephyr Blue
p. 318

UPS

KEY TO NON-SATYRINE NYMPHALIDAE

1/4 [GC dark with scalloped wing edges] OR [a white band crossing the HW] AND/OR [blue iridescent reflections on the wings]

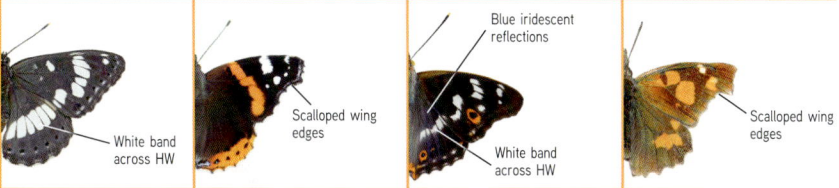

White band across HW

Scalloped wing edges

Blue iridescent reflections

White band across HW

Scalloped wing edges

→ **Page 80**

2/4 [GC red, orange, or cinnamon brown] AND [[wing edges scalloped] OR [FW with apical white spots and a concave outer edge]]

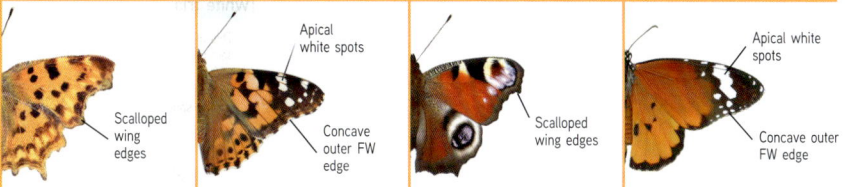

Scalloped wing edges

Apical white spots

Concave outer FW edge

Scalloped wing edges

Apical white spots

Concave outer FW edge

→ **Page 81 (block 1/4 and the following ones)**

3/4 [GC orange or greyish-green] AND [outer FW edge convex, straight, or slightly concave] AND [many black spots, but no black chequerboard on 2 wings]

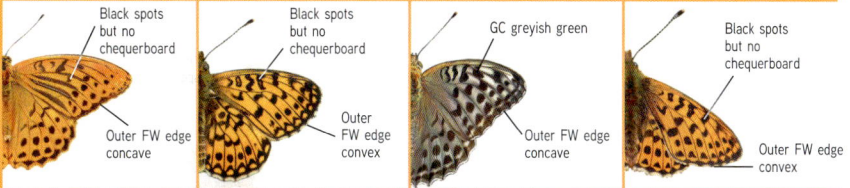

Black spots but no chequerboard

Outer FW edge concave

Black spots but no chequerboard

Outer FW edge convex

GC greyish green

Outer FW edge concave

Black spots but no chequerboard

Outer FW edge convex

→ **Page 82 (block 1/4 and the following ones)**

4/4 [GC orange, white, or pale yellow] AND [outer FW edge convex] AND [a more or less thick black chequerboard at least on HW]

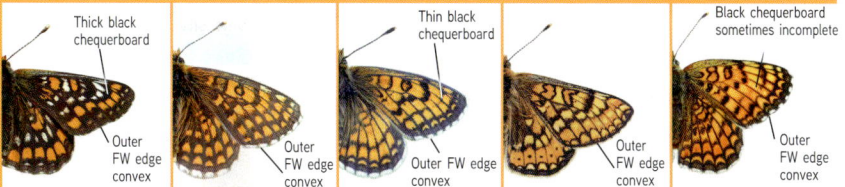

Thick black chequerboard

Outer FW edge convex

Outer FW edge convex

Thin black chequerboard

Outer FW edge convex

Outer FW edge convex

Black chequerboard sometimes incomplete

Outer FW edge convex

→ **Page 85**

79

1/3 No orange on wings

1.1 White HW band made of separate white spots

GC black with blue iridescent reflections

1 series of black dots at the back of HW

Southern White Admiral p. 370

GC dark brown without any iridescent reflections

2 series of black spots at back of HW

White Admiral p. 369

GC black

No white or black spots at back of HW

Hungarian Glider p. 371

GC black

Series of white spots at back of HW

Common Glider p. 372

1.2 HW band continuously white or pale yellow

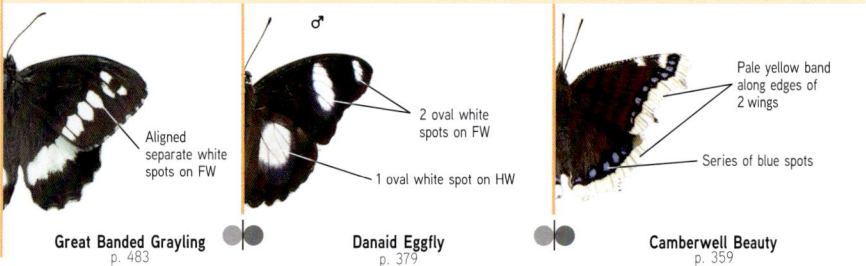

Aligned separate white spots on FW

Great Banded Grayling p. 483

♂

2 oval white spots on FW

1 oval white spot on HW

Danaid Eggfly p. 379

Pale yellow band along edges of 2 wings

Series of blue spots

Camberwell Beauty p. 359

2/3 [At least some small orange spots on the wings] AND [wing edges not scalloped]

2.1 No conspicuous iridescent blue mid-wing reflections

♀

GC dark brown

Orange-ringed black spot on FW

White band without a backwards-pointing tooth

Lesser Purple Emperor p. 375

♀

GC dark brown

Black spot barely or not ringed with orange on FW

White band with a backwards-pointing tooth

Purple Emperor p. 374

GC black

No orange-ringed black spot on HW

Map p. 368

♀

GC black with some marginal iridescent blue reflections

Series of orange spots on HW

Poplar Admiral p. 373

2.2 Conspicuous blue or purple middle wing iridescent reflections

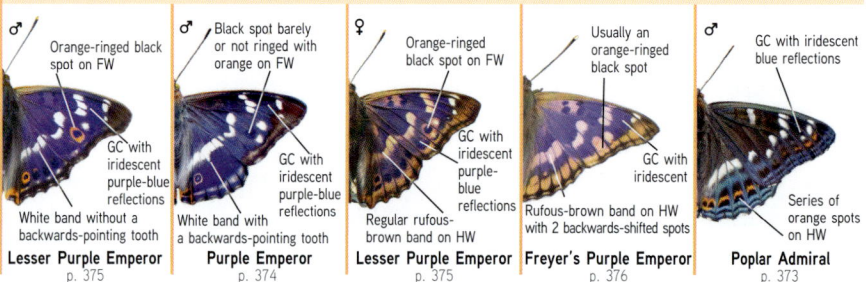

♂

Orange-ringed black spot on FW

GC with iridescent purple-blue reflections

White band without a backwards-pointing tooth

Lesser Purple Emperor p. 375

♂

Black spot barely or not ringed with orange on FW

GC with iridescent purple-blue reflections

White band with a backwards-pointing tooth

Purple Emperor p. 374

♀

Orange-ringed black spot on FW

GC with iridescent purple-blue reflections

Regular rufous-brown band on HW

Lesser Purple Emperor p. 375

Usually an orange-ringed black spot

GC with iridescent

Rufous-brown band on HW with 2 backwards-shifted spots

Freyer's Purple Emperor p. 376

♂

GC with iridescent blue reflections

Series of orange spots on HW

Poplar Admiral p. 373

UPS

KEY TO NON-SATYRINE NYMPHALIDAE

3/3 [Some large orange spots or a vivid yellow, orange, or red band on wings] AND [outer FW or HW edge scalloped]

Vivid yellow band on edges of both wings	Large red band across FW	Narrow vivid orange band across FW	Large, rounded orange spots on FW	
Series of blue spots	Red band along HW edge	Orange band along HW edge	Vivid orange band along edges of both wings	No orange band on HW
Camberwell Beauty p. 359	**Canary Red Admiral** p. 358	**Red Admiral** p. 357	**Two-tailed Pasha** p. 354	**Nettle-tree Butterfly** p. 353

1/4 [Wing edges deeply scalloped] AND [no blue on wings]

Wing tip with little brown	Wing tip with little brown	White spot on FW / Large dark area at wing tip
Usually thick black spots on FW	Reduced black spots on FW	White spot on HW
Usually at least 3 black spots on HW	Usually no more than 2 black spots on HW	No dark spot in middle of HW
Comma p. 365	**Southern Comma** p. 366	**False Comma** p. 367

2/4 [Wing edges scalloped] AND [large purple-blue spot or series of small blue spots along wing edges]

GC dark red	Yellow spots same length as black ones	Yellow spots same length as the black ones	1 black spot / Yellow spots shorter than black ones	2 black spots / Yellow spots shorter than black ones
	2 black spots here	No black spots here	3 rather round black spots	Thick black line
Large, purple-tinged spot on each wing	GC orange-red	GC orange-red	Rather thin black line / GC tawny orange	GC tawny orange / 3 rather angular black spots
Peacock p. 360	**Small Tortoiseshell** p. 361	**Corsican Small Tortoiseshell** p. 362	**Large Tortoiseshell** p. 363	**Yellow-legged T.shell** p. 364

3/4 [Wing edges not scalloped and without small white spots] On FW: [outer edge concave] AND [several small apical white spots]

♀ Dark areas; perhaps faint purple-blue reflections	Dark areas; perhaps faint purple-blue reflections	Finely yellow-striped black wing base	White spots in the black wing tip	White spots in black wing tip
Usually an orange-ringed black spot	Orange-ringed black spot			
2 backwards-shifted spots		White spots in black wing tip	Black-ringed blue spots	Series of black spots on HW
Freyer's Purple Emperor p. 376	**Lesser Purple Emperor** p. 375	**Map** p. 368	**American Painted Lady** p. 356	**Painted Lady** p. 355

81

4/4 On FW: [outer edge concave with small white spots] AND [wing tip black with white spots]

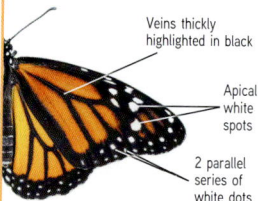

Veins thickly highlighted in black

Apical white spots

2 parallel series of white dots

Monarch p. 377

♀

Apical white band

2 parallel series of long white spots

Veins finely highlighted in black

Danaid Eggfly p. 379

Apical white band

Veins not highlighted in black

Black spots on HW

Plain Tiger p. 378

1/4 Outer wing edge slightly concave or straight, but not convex

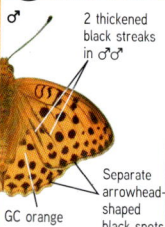

♂ 2 thickened black streaks in ♂♂

Separate arrowhead-shaped black spots

GC orange

Pallas' Fritillary p. 383

♂ Black spots connected

4 thickened black streaks in ♂♂

GC orange

Silver-washed Fritillary p. 381

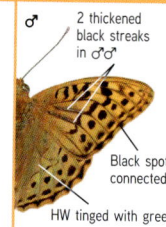

♂ 2 thickened black streaks in ♂♂

Black spots connected

HW tinged with green

Cardinal p. 382

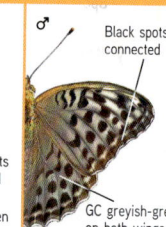

♂ Black spots connected

GC greyish-green on both wings

Silver-washed Fritillary p. 381

GC orange

3 series of black spots on HW

Queen of Spain Fritillary p. 380

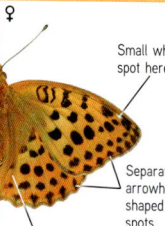

♀ Small white spot here

Separate arrowhead-shaped black spots

GC orange

Pallas' Fritillary p. 383

♂ 2 thickened black streaks in ♂♂

Outer edge slightly concave

Rather thick black crescents

GC orange

High Brown Fritillary p. 386

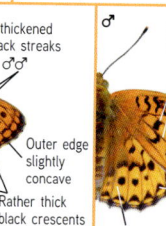

♂ 2 thin black streaks in ♂♂

Outer edge straight

Black triangles

GC orange

Dark Green Fritillary p. 385

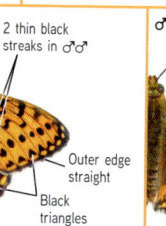

♂ 2 thin black streaks in ♂♂

Outer edge straight

Rather thin black lines

Thin black crescents

Niobe Fritillary p. 387

2/4 On FW: [outer edge convex]
On HW: [2 parallel series of rounded black spots] OR [very few small black spots]

Very few tiny black spots

Corsican Fritillary p. 384

Separate black spots along edges of both wings

Marbled Fritillary p. 388

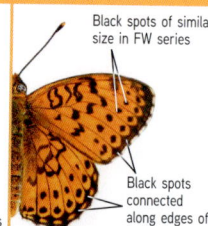

Black spots of similar size in FW series

Black spots connected along edges of both wings

Twin-spot Fritillary p. 389

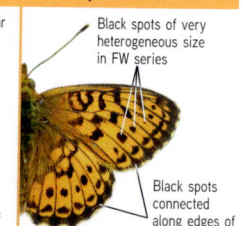

Black spots of very heterogeneous size in FW series

Black spots connected along edges of both wings

Lesser Marbled Fritillary p. 390

KEY TO NON-SATYRINE NYMPHALIDAE

3/4 On FW: [outer edge convex] AND [series of arched marginal black spots]
On HW: no round black spots near trailing edge

3.1 On FW: GC orange

♂ Reduced, faint black spots in middle of HW

Thin black crescents

Aetherie Fritillary
p. 424

♂ Thick, well-marked black spots in middle of HW

Thick black crescents

Spotted Fritillary
p. 422

♂ Thick, well-marked black spots in middle of HW

Thin black crescents

Lesser Spotted Fritillary
Sagarra's Fritillary
p. 423

♀ Diffuse black markings on FW

Thick, well-marked black spots in middle of HW

Thin black crescents

Lesser Spotted Fritillary
Sagarra's Fritillary
p. 423

3.2 On FW: GC greyish or yellow-orange (much lighter than HW GC)

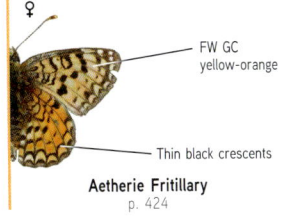

♀ FW GC greyish

Thick black crescents

Spotted Fritillary
p. 422

♀ FW GC yellow-orange

Thick black crescents

Spotted Fritillary
p. 422

♀ FW GC yellow-orange

Thin black crescents

Aetherie Fritillary
p. 424

4/4 On FW: outer edge convex
On HW: series of round black spots near trailing edge

4.1 On FW: thin or very thin black markings

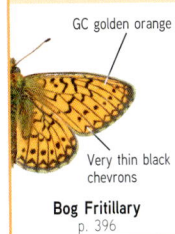

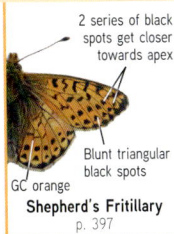

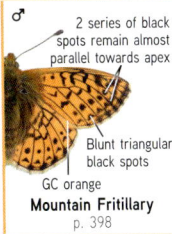

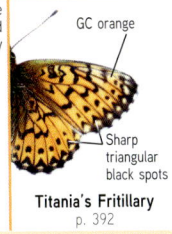

GC golden orange

Very thin black chevrons

Bog Fritillary
p. 396

2 series of black spots get closer towards apex

Blunt triangular black spots

GC orange

Shepherd's Fritillary
p. 397

♂ 2 series of black spots remain almost parallel towards apex

Blunt triangular black spots

GC orange

Mountain Fritillary
p. 398

♀ GC orange intensely sprinkled with grey

Blunt triangular black spots

Mountain Fritillary
p. 398

GC orange

Sharp triangular black spots

Titania's Fritillary
p. 392

4.2 On FW: thick black markings with diffuse contours

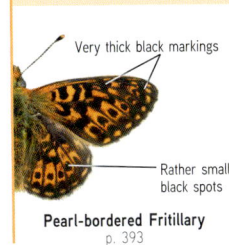

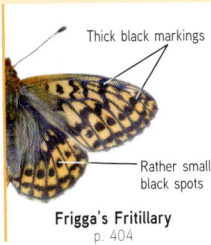

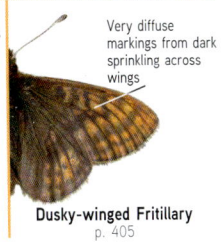

Very thick black markings

Rather small black spots

Pearl-bordered Fritillary
p. 393

Thick black markings

Rather small black spots

Frigga's Fritillary
p. 404

Thick black markings

Rather large black spots

Thor's Fritillary
p. 395

Very diffuse markings from dark sprinkling across wings

Dusky-winged Fritillary
p. 405

KEY TO NON-SATYRINE NYMPHALIDAE

4/4 On FW: outer edge convex
On HW: series of round black spots near trailing edge

4.3 On FW: [thick black markings with neat contours] AND [series of mid-wing black spots align in a zigzag line]

Thick round black spot

Thin black chevrons on FW and HW

Densely haired basal wing area

Freija's Fritillary
p. 403

Few basal brown hairs

Sharp black triangles

Titania's Fritillary
p. 392

Sharp triangles on FW and HW

Densely haired basal wing area

Arctic Fritillary
p. 402

Flattened black spots along FW outer edge

Few basal brown hairs

Thick chevrons on HW

Thick, round black spots

Weaver's Fritillary
p. 391

2 sharp chevrons facing each other

Series of blunt triangles on FW and HW

Densely haired basal wing area

Cranberry Fritillary
p. 400

Short black lines paired with rounded black spots along FW outer edge

Densely haired basal wing area

Polar Fritillary
p. 401

Black triangles along edges of 2 wings

Densely haired basal wing area

Shepherd's Fritillary
p. 397

Short black lines along edges of 2 wings

Densely haired basal wing area

Frigga's Fritillary
p. 404

4.4 On FW: [thick black drawings with neat contours] AND [series of mid-wing black spots that do not form a zigzag]

This black spot clearly shifted towards the black chevron within this orange space

Series of black chevrons connected with black wing border

Chevron-shaped black spots

Small Pearl-bordered Fritillary
p. 394

Black spot more or less in the middle of orange space

Black triangular spots

Black triangles not connected with black wing border

Pearl-bordered Fritillary
p. 393

Black triangular spots

Black triangles not connected with the black wing border

Sparse black markings at HW base

Balkan Fritillary
p. 399

Flattened black spots along FW outer edge

Thick black chevrons or triangles connected with black wing border

Thick basal black markings

Weaver's Fritillary
p. 391

UPS

KEY TO NON-SATYRINE NYMPHALIDAE

(1/3) On FW: [a thick black chequerboard] AND [series of white, yellow, and orange spots]
On HW: black dots in the orange spots hardly visible or absent

1.1 On FW: wing base orange

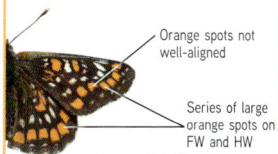

Orange spots not well-aligned

Series of large orange spots on FW and HW

Scarce Fritillary
Italian Scarce Fritillary
p. 411

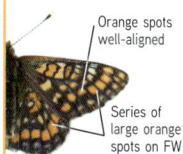

Orange spots well-aligned

Series of large orange spots on FW and HW

⚠ These 3 fritillaries are almost identical but do not fly together. Scarce and Italian Scarce Fritillaries don't fly higher than 1,000 m; Asian Fritillary flies above 1,500 m.

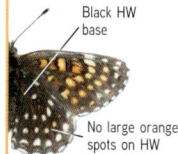

Asian Fritillary
p. 412

Black HW base

No large orange spots on HW

False Heath Fritillary
p. 418

1.2 On FW: wing base white

♂

Wings not bordered by an orange line

Cynthia's Fritillary
p. 409

Wings bordered by an orange line

Lapland Fritillary
p. 410

(2/3) On FW: black chequerboard variably thick
On HW: some conspicuous black dots in the posterior orange spots series

2.1 On FW: series of yellow, orange, and red spots

Yellow-orange spots barely contrast with adjacent rectangular spots

Marsh Fritillary
p. 406

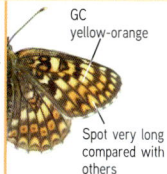

Pale spots sharply contrast with adjacent rectangular reddish spots

Spanish Fritillary
p. 408

Spots of same reddish colour as adjacent rectangular spots

Becker's Fritillary
p. 407

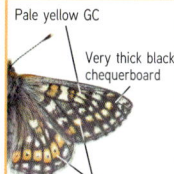

Pale yellow GC

Very thick black chequerboard

Series of pale orange spots across wings

Marsh Fritillary
p. 406

GC yellow-orange

Spot very long compared with others

Knapweed Fritillary
Eastern Knapweed Fritillary
Iberian Knapweed Fritillary
p. 427

2.2 On FW: GC homogenously orange

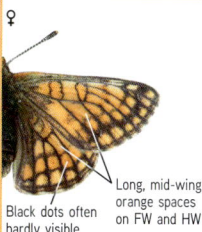

♀

Black dots often hardly visible

Long, mid-wing orange spaces on FW and HW

Cynthia's Fritillary
p. 409

Very regular chequerboard on HW

Glanville Fritillary
p. 425

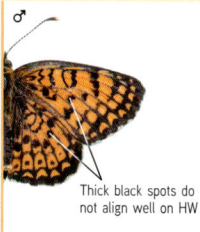

♂

Thick black spots do not align well on HW

Freyer's Fritillary
p. 426

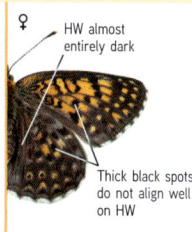

♀

HW almost entirely dark

Thick black spots do not align well on HW

85

KEY TO NON-SATYRINE NYMPHALIDAE

3/3 On FW and HW: variably complete black chequerboard
On HW: no black dots in posterior series of orange spots

3.1 On FW: [very regular chequerboard] OR [basal wing half black]
On HW: [very regular chequerboard] OR [basal wing half black]

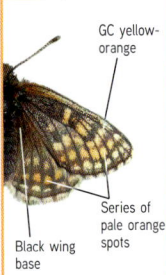

GC yellow-orange

Series of pale orange spots

Black wing base

Little Fritillary
p. 421

GC orange

Thick black spot here

Wing base orange chequered with black

Assmann's Fritillary
p. 417

Thick black spot here

GC orange

Wing base orange chequered with black

Nickerl's Fritillary
p. 416

Thick black spot here

GC orange

Black wing base

False Heath Fritillary
p. 418

Black spot perpendicular to FW trailing edge

GC orange

Black wing base

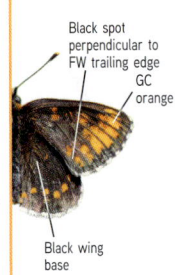

Grisons Fritillary
p. 420

3.2 On FW: more or less regular chequerboard
On HW: no long orange spaces on mid-wing

⚠ These 3 species are difficult to distinguish without examining the genitalia

Variably shaped thick black spot here

Chequerboard usually incomplete here

Heath Fritillary
Southern Heath Fritillary
pp. 413 and 414

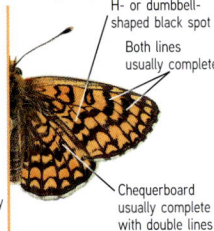

H- or dumbbell-shaped black spot here

Both lines usually complete

Chequerboard usually complete with double lines here

Provençal Fritillary
p. 415

⚠ These 3 species cannot be distinguished by their wing patterns and barely by their genitalia

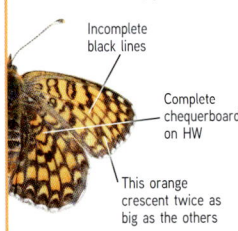

Incomplete black lines

Complete chequerboard on HW

This orange crescent twice as big as the others

Eastern Knapweed Fritillary
Iberian Knapweed Fritillary
p. 428

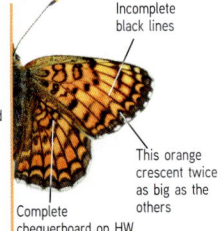

Incomplete black lines

This orange crescent twice as big as the others

Complete chequerboard on HW

Knapweed Fritillary
p. 427

3.3 On FW: more or less regular chequerboard
On HW: a mid-wing series of long orange spaces

Oblique black spot

Meadow Fritillary
p. 419

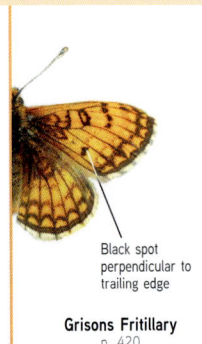

Black spot perpendicular to trailing edge

Grisons Fritillary
p. 420

♀

Usually very large, faint black spot

Cynthia's Fritillary
p. 409

Thick black spot

False Heath Fritillary
p. 418

KEY TO NON-SATYRINE NYMPHALIDAE

1/9 Body GC black, dotted with white

Series of black-rimmed white spots on edges of 2 wings

Plain Tiger
p. 378

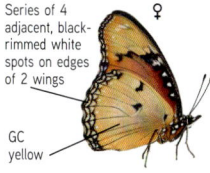

Series of 4 adjacent, black-rimmed white spots on edges of 2 wings

♀

GC yellow

Series of 4 adjacent, black-rimmed white spots along edges of 2 wings

Danaid Eggfly
p. 379

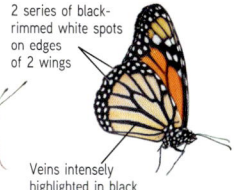

GC cinnamon brown with conspicuous white band

♂

2 series of black-rimmed white spots on edges of 2 wings

Veins intensely highlighted in black

Monarch
p. 377

2/9 [Both wings deeply scalloped] AND [FW GC not orange]

2.1 On HW: a C-, L-, V-, or comma-shaped white spot in the middle of the wing

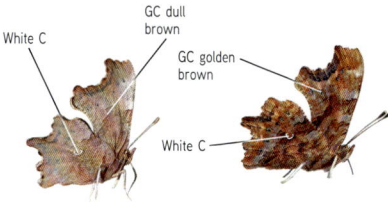

White C

GC dull brown

GC golden brown

White C

Comma
p. 365

Fine black streaks on a brown GC

White V or L

Southern Comma
p. 366

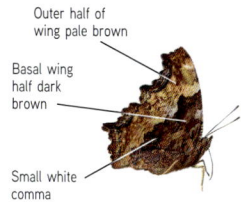

Outer half of wing pale brown

Basal wing half dark brown

Small white comma

False Comma
p. 367

2.2 On HW: a small pale dot in the middle of the wing

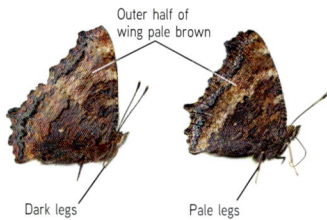

Outer half of wing pale brown

Dark legs

Large Tortoiseshell
p. 363

Pale legs

Yellow-legged Tortoiseshell
p. 364

GC of wings uniformly blackish

Peacock
p. 360

Yellow FW stripes in sharp contrast with dark ones

Small Tortoiseshell
Corsican Small Tortoiseshell
pp. 361 and 362

Pale yellow band along edges of 2 wings

Camberwell Beauty
p. 359

3/9 On FW: [outer edge scalloped or concave] AND [orange or red mid-wing area]
On HW: GC light brown, dark brown, or grey

Large red band

Dark spots finely rimmed with yellow

Canary Red Admiral
p. 358

Narrow red band

Red Admiral
p. 357

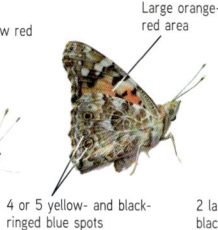

Large orange-red area

4 or 5 yellow- and black-ringed blue spots

Painted Lady
p. 355

Large red area

2 large yellow- and black-ringed blue spots

American Painted Lady
p. 356

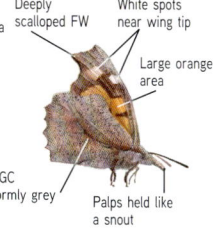

Deeply scalloped FW

White spots near wing tip

Large orange area

HW GC uniformly grey

Palps held like a snout

Nettle-tree Butterfly
p. 353

KEY TO NON-SATYRINE NYMPHALIDAE

**FW: [outer edge concave or convex] AND [GC not orange, with black spots only]
HW: 1 or more white bands across wing]**

4.1 On HW: continuous white band

White band; backwards-pointing tooth

Large, orange-ringed black spot

White band; no backwards-pointing tooth

Undulated white band; no backwards-pointing tooth

Small, orange-ringed black spot sometimes absent

Orange band along edges of 2 wings

GC reddish with many green-blue spots

2 tails

GC reddish-brown

Pale lines across wing base

Purple Emperor p. 374

Lesser Purple Emperor p. 375 — **Freyer's Purple Emperor** p. 376

Two-tailed Pasha p. 354

Map p. 368

4.2 On HW: white band made of adjacent dark-ringed white spots

GC reddish-brown

1 series of black dots

GC reddish-brown

2 series of black dots

GC orange

Iridescent blue band borders 2 wings

Series of black dots

GC reddish-brown

1 thick white band

No black dots

GC reddish-brown

2 thick white bands

No black dots

Southern White Admiral p. 370

White Admiral p. 369

Poplar Admiral p. 373

Hungarian Glider p. 371

Common Glider p. 372

On FW: [outer edge slightly concave or straight] AND [GC orange or red with black spots]

5.1 On HW: [several pearly or white spots] AND [GC largely sprinkled with green]

Veins not highlighted in black

Series of red spots

Series of red spots

Black veins

Pale or black dot here

Series of red spots

HW spots finely bordered with black

Rather reduced pearly spots

Series of red spots

Pearly spots paired with dark, crescent-shaped spots

Veins not highlighted in black

No red spots

High Brown Fritillary p. 386

Niobe Fritillary p. 387

Corsican Fritillary p. 384

Dark Green Fritillary p. 385

Series of small white dots

GC orange

White stripes on HW

Series of small white dots

GC carmine red

Silver-washed Fritillary p. 381

Cardinal p. 382

5.2 On HW: no green sprinkling

Purple area

Brown lines

Series of red spots within a rufous band

Pale spots bordered with black

Pale or black dot in Niobe Fritillary

Series of red spots

Large pearly spots

Series of red spots

Pallas' Fritillary p. 383

High Brown Fritillary **Niobe Fritillary** pp. 386 and 387

Queen of Spain Fritillary p. 380

6/9 On FW: [outer edge convex] AND [no round black spots on orange GC]
On HW: no conspicuous black dots in orange spots

Series of black-bordered white spots

Black line within white spots

⚠ These 3 fritillaries are almost identical but do not fly together. Scarce and Italian Scarce Fritillaries fly no higher than 1,000 m; Asian Fritillary flies above 1,500 m.

Black line within white spots

Marginal series of white spots on FW

Well-marked posterior series of white spots

Reduced series of white spots

Well-marked posterior series of white spots

Black line within white spots

Well-marked posterior series of white spots

Cynthia's Fritillary
p. 409

Scarce Fritillary
Italian Scarce Fritillary
p. 411

Asian Fritillary
p. 412

Lapland Fritillary
p. 410

7/9 On FW: [outer edge convex] AND [several round black spots on orange GC]
On HW: series of round orange spots in some large, pale yellow, crescent-shaped spots

7.1 On HW: 4 black dots at wing base

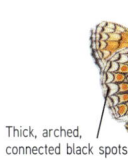

Arched black spots rather blunt

Thick, arched black spots, usually separate

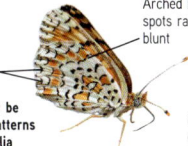

Arched black spots rather blunt

Arched black spots sharply point backwards

Thick, arched, connected black spots

⚠ These 3 species cannot be distinguished by their wing patterns and barely by their genitalia

Narrow, arched, connected black spots

Knapweed Fritillary
p. 427

Eastern Knapweed Fritillary
Iberian Knapweed Fritillary
p. 428

Aetherie Fritillary
p. 424

7.2 On HW: [no basal black dots] AND [series of long spots bordering fringes coloured like the adjacent pale, thick, crescent-shaped spots]

Arched black spots slightly thicker than the others

Oblique black spot

Black arched spots of constant thickness

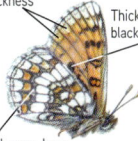

Thick black spot

Club- or dumbbell-shaped black spot

Arched black spots much thicker than the others

Rather pale zone here

Rather pale zone here

Rather dark zone here

Arched black spots slightly thicker than the others

⚠ These 3 species are difficult to distinguish without examining the genitalia

Thick black spot

Meadow Fritillary
p. 419

Grisons Fritillary
p. 420

Provençal Fritillary
p. 415

Heath Fritillary
Southern Heath Fritillary
pp. 413 and 414

7.3 On HW: [no basal black dots] AND [series of long spots bordering the fringes darker than adjacent pale, thick, crescent-shaped spots] OR [no long spots bordering fringes]

Long spots slightly darker than adjacent pale, crescent-shaped spots

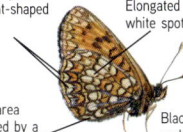

Long spots slightly darker than adjacent pale, crescent-shaped spots

Long spots slightly darker than adjacent pale, crescent-shaped spots

Elongated white spots

No long, pale spots against fringes

Anal area not crossed by a black line

Anal area crossed by a black line

Black dots in arched, crescent-shaped spots

Series of rounded white spots

Little Fritillary
p. 421

Nickerl's Fritillary
p. 416

Assmann's Fritillary
p. 417

False Heath Fritillary
p. 418

8/9
On FW: [outer edge convex] AND [several rounded black spots on orange GC]
On HW: [no well-marked black dots (some faint dark spots possible)]

8.1 On HW: some purple areas

This spot entirely pale

Spot partly sprinkled with red

3 large pearly spots

2 large white spots

2 large white spots

Dark red chevrons

No dark red chevrons

Complete series of pale spots

Complete series of pale spots

No dark red chevrons

Dark red chevrons

Series of black mid-wing chevrons

No black chevrons

Lesser Marbled Fritillary
p. 390

Marbled Fritillary
p. 388

Weaver's Fritillary
p. 391

Titania's Fritillary
p. 392

Frigga's Fritillary
p. 404

8.2 On HW: [some large red areas] AND [1 triangular mid-wing white or pearly spot]

Basal black dot

White spots along HW edge point basally

Faint black drawings on FW

Elongated white spots along HW edge

Black zigzag markings

No white spots along HW edge

Pearl-bordered Fritillary
p. 393

Arctic Fritillary
p. 402

Freija's Fritillary
p. 403

Dusky-winged Fritillary
p. 405

8.3 On HW: [some large red areas] AND [[a flattened triangular white or pearly mid-wing spot] OR [no triangular white or pearly mid-wing spot]]

Red spots do not sharply contrast with reddish GC

Well-marked black spots on FW

Faint black spots on FW (hidden here)

Faint black spots on FW

This pale spot basally invaded with red

Well-marked black spots on FW (hidden here)

Purple-red spots sharply contrast with GC

Pale spot basally invaded with red

Pale spot barely basally invaded with red

Cranberry Fritillary
p. 400

Balkan Fritillary
p. 399

Shepherd's Fritillary
p. 397

Mountain Fritillary
p. 398

Thick black spots on FW

No pure white spots in middle of HW

Basal pale dot

Black chevrons

Some purple traces across HW in fresh butterflies

Series of black-ringed, round pale spots

Thor's Fritillary
p. 395

Bog Fritillary
p. 396

KEY TO NON-SATYRINE NYMPHALIDAE

9/9 On FW: [outer edge convex] AND [GC orange or orange-red]
On HW: at least 1 series of black dots across wing

9.1 On HW: 4 basal black spots

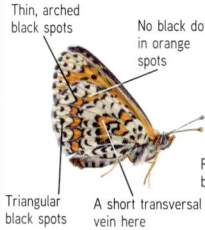

Thin, arched black spots

No black dots in orange spots

Triangular black spots

A short transversal vein here

No black dots in orange spots

No short transversal vein here

Rounded black spots

Thick, barely arched black spots

Orange spots surrounded with yellow, pointing backwards

Small, rounded black spots

Black dots in the orange spots

Entirely orange spots pointing forwards

Large triangular black spots

Black dots in the orange spots

Lesser Spotted Fritillary
Sagarra's Fritillary
p. 423

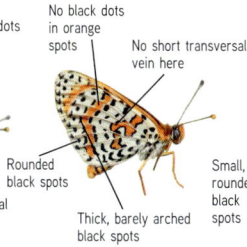

Spotted Fritillary
p. 422

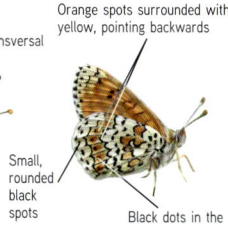

Glanville Fritillary
p. 425

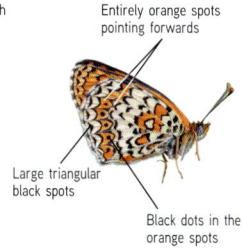

Freyer's Fritillary
p. 426

9.2 On HW: [no basal black spots] AND [series of orange, red, or brown spots containing black dots]

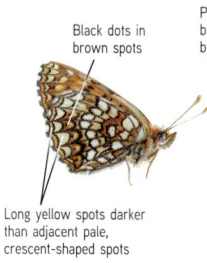

Black dots in brown spots

Pale crescent-shaped black spots bordered by a black line

Red band across HW

Long yellow spots darker than adjacent pale, crescent-shaped spots

Black dots thickly ringed with yellow

Well-marked black spots

Pale crescent-shaped black spots bordered by a red line

Red band across HW

Rather pointed pale spots

Faint dark spots here

Black dots finely ringed with yellow

Pale, crescent-shaped black spots, bordered by a red line

Red band across HW

Faint dark spots here

Pale spots rather flattened

False Heath Fritillary
p. 418

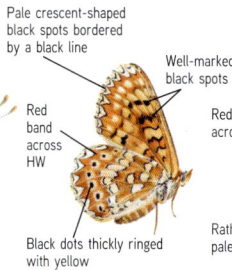

Spanish Fritillary
p. 408

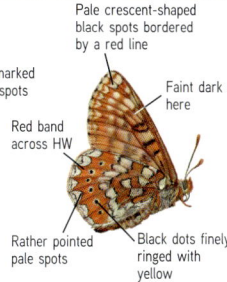

Becker's Fritillary
p. 407

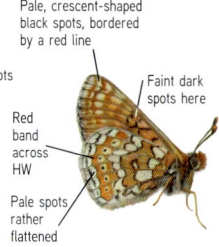

Marsh Fritillary
p. 406

9.3 On HW: [no basal black spots] AND [at least 1 series of black dots inside a series of yellow, red, and orange spots]

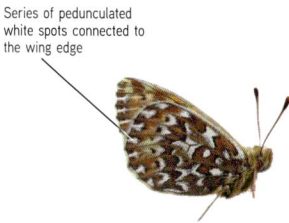

Series of pedunculated white spots connected to the wing edge

Series of black dots on FW and HW

Elongated mid-wing white spot

Black or grey dot inside this basal red spot

2 parallel series of black spots

Polar Fritillary
p. 401

Small Pearl-bordered Fritillary
p. 394

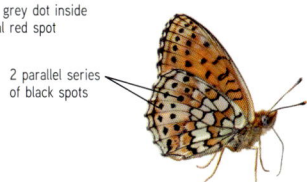

Twin-spot Fritillary
p. 389

1/5 On FW: [GC dark brown or black] AND [an orange area or a series of orange spots without WPBS but sometimes with black dots inside]

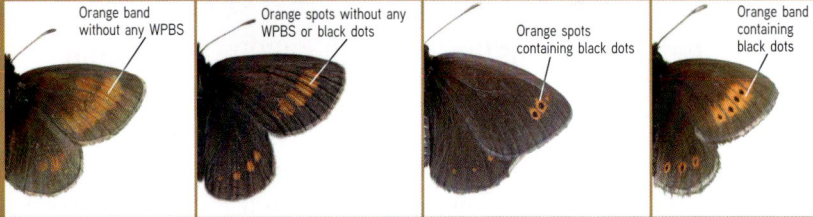

Orange band without any WPBS

Orange spots without any WPBS or black dots

Orange spots containing black dots

Orange band containing black dots

→ **Page 93**

2/5 On FW: [GC brown, grey-brown, dark brown, or black] AND [an orange area or a series of orange spots containing at least 1 WPBS]

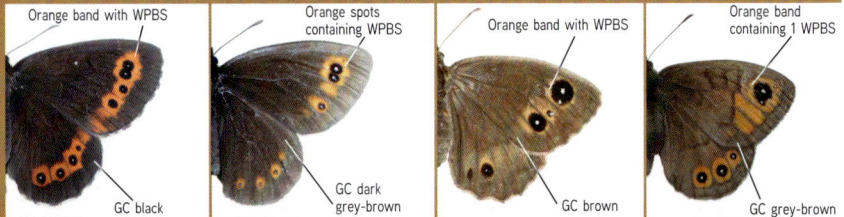

Orange band with WPBS

GC black

Orange spots containing WPBS

GC dark grey-brown

Orange band with WPBS

GC brown

Orange band containing 1 WPBS

GC grey-brown

→ **Page 94**

3/5 On FW: [GC orange or pale yellow, sometimes thickly bordered with grey-brown] AND [1 WPBS or 1 apical black spot with a double white pupil inside]

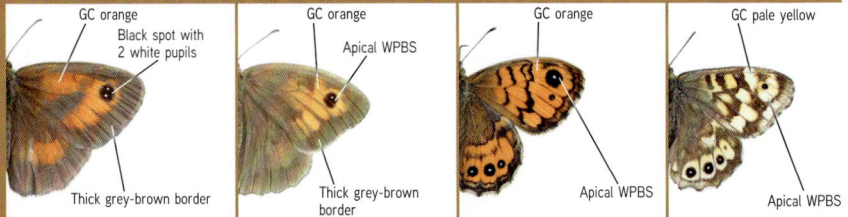

GC orange

Black spot with 2 white pupils

Thick grey-brown border

GC orange

Apical WPBS

Thick grey-brown border

GC orange

Apical WPBS

GC pale yellow

Apical WPBS

→ **Page 99**

4/5 On FW: [GC brown without orange] AND [[no WPBS] OR [several WPBS or BPBS not ringed] OR [several yellow- or orange-ringed black spots or WPBS]]

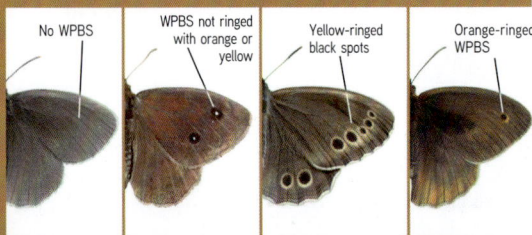

No WPBS

WPBS not ringed with orange or yellow

Yellow-ringed black spots

Orange-ringed WPBS

→ **Page 101**

5/5 On FW: [[GC dark brown or black] AND [a white band across the wing]] OR [GC chequered in white and black]

Pure white or whitish band

GC chequered in white and black

→ **Page 102**

1/4   On FW: some orange spots or an orange band without WPBS or black dots

Large orange area on FW
Large orange spots on HW
Silky Ringlet p. 499

Large orange area on FW
Reduced orange spots on HW
Mnestra's Ringlet p.496

Faint orange area on FW
Rather faint orange spots on HW
Sooty Ringlet p. 498

Series of long orange spots of different sizes on FW and HW
Yellow-spotted Ringlets p. 490

Very regular series of orange spots on FW
Series of rounded orange spots on HW
Blind Ringlet p. 493

2/4   On FW: a series of orange spots or a thick orange band with 2 apical black dots

Long orange spots of different sizes on FW and HW
Black dots (if any) barely visible
Yellow-spotted Ringlets p. 490

Orange spots almost fused in a band extending basally on its anterior half
Conspicuous black dots on HW
Bulgarian Ringlet p. 526

Large orange band covers outer half of wing
No black dots on HW
Mnestra's Ringlet p. 496

Series of long orange spots on HW
3rd black spot possible here
No black dots in HW orange spots
Eriphyle Ringlet p. 491

Series of rather faint, short orange spots on FW
Series of white spots on HW
White Speck Ringlet p. 494

3/4   On FW: a regular series of rectangular orange spots with more than 2 black dots

Dark lines across FW (absent in False Dewy Ringlet)
4 thick black dots on FW
Dewy Ringlet
False Dewy Ringlet p. 495

No black dot in apical orange spot
4 thick black dots on FW
Mountain Ringlet p. 486

Black dot in the apical orange spot
Rätzer's Ringlet p. 487

Very regular series of orange spots
Similar-sized orange spots on HW
Sudeten Ringlet p. 489

Very regular series of orange spots
This orange spot longer than the others
Lesser Mountain Ringlet p. 488

Thick black spots
Chequered fringes
Large Ringlet p. 521

4/4   On FW: [several round orange spots with black dots] OR [an irregular series of elongated orange spots with more than 2 black dots]

Rounded orange spots
Fringes uniformly grey
Arctic Woodland Ringlet p. 524

Rounded orange spots
Chequered fringes
Arctic Ringlet p. 528

Elongated orange spots on FW and HW
Yellow-spotted Ringlets p. 490

Orange spots elongated on FW, rounded on HW
Yellow-banded Ringlet p. 492

1/4 On FW: a series of orange spots, some containing WPBS

1.1 On FW: many WPBS in elongated or almond-shaped orange spots

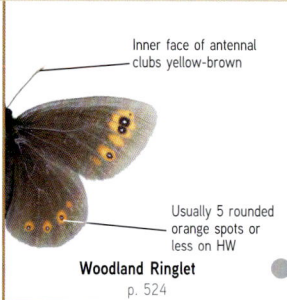

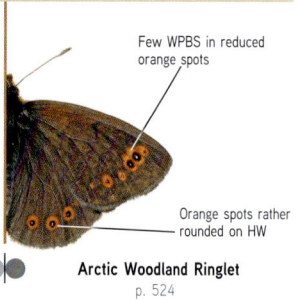

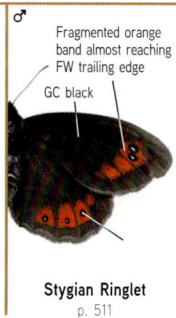

Inner face of antennal clubs black

5 orange spots or more on HW

Very bright white pupils in the black spots

Bright-eyed Ringlet
p. 525

Inner face of antennal clubs yellow-brown

Usually 5 rounded orange spots or less on HW

Woodland Ringlet
p. 524

Few WPBS in reduced orange spots

Orange spots rather rounded on HW

Arctic Woodland Ringlet
p. 524

Numerous WPBS in rather large orange spots

Orange spots rather rounded on HW

Arctic Woodland Ringlet
p. 524

No small shifted WPBS beside both big ones

Almond-shaped orange spots on HW

Almond-eyed Ringlet
p. 527

Small shifted WPBS in front of the bigger ones

Almond-shaped orange spots on HW

Piedmont Ringlet
p. 508

♂ Fragmented orange band almost reaching FW trailing edge

GC black

Stygian Ringlet
p. 511

♂ ⚠ The Styrian and Stygian Ringlets are very hard to distinguish by their uppersides

Fragmented orange band slightly shorter than in Stygian Ringlet

GC black

Styrian Ringlet
p. 510

1.2 On FW: numerous WPBS inside round orange spots

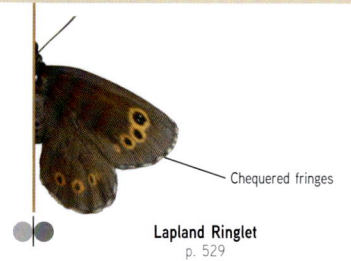

External light grey area on both wings

Fringes homogenously grey

Dalmatian Ringlet
p. 485

Chequered fringes

Lapland Ringlet
p. 529

1.3 On FW: 1 large apical orange area with 2 WPBS and another, more posterior orange spot with 1 WPBS

♂ White pupils barely visible

Water Ringlet
p. 501

♀ White pupils barely visible

Water Ringlet
p. 501

Very bright white pupils in black spots

Lefèbvre's Ringlet
p. 522

On FW: only 2 apical WPBS

2.1 On FW: conspicuous iridescent reflections on dark GC (unless worn)

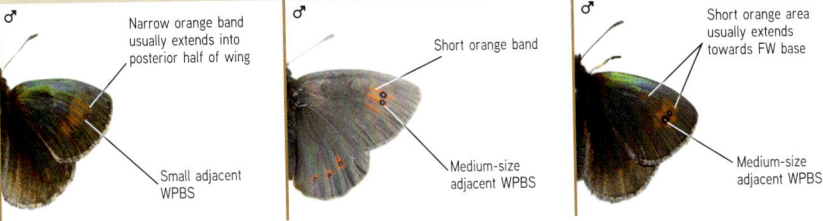

♂ Narrow orange band usually extends into posterior half of wing

Small adjacent WPBS

♂ Short orange band

Medium-size adjacent WPBS

♂ Short orange area usually extends towards FW base

Medium-size adjacent WPBS

Swiss Brassy Ringlet	Common Brassy Ringlet/Western Brassy Ringlet	De Lesse's Brassy Ringlet
p. 505	p. 502	p. 504

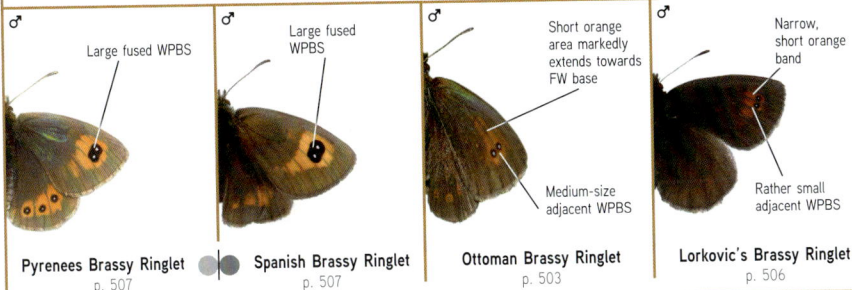

♂ Large fused WPBS

♂ Large fused WPBS

♂ Short orange area markedly extends towards FW base

Medium-size adjacent WPBS

♂ Narrow, short orange band

Rather small adjacent WPBS

Pyrenees Brassy Ringlet p. 507   Spanish Brassy Ringlet p. 507   Ottoman Brassy Ringlet p. 503   Lorkovic's Brassy Ringlet p. 506

2.2 On FW: [no iridescent reflections] AND [an orange band becoming faint towards the trailing edge]
On HW: [small WPBS often within reduced orange spots] OR [no WPBS]

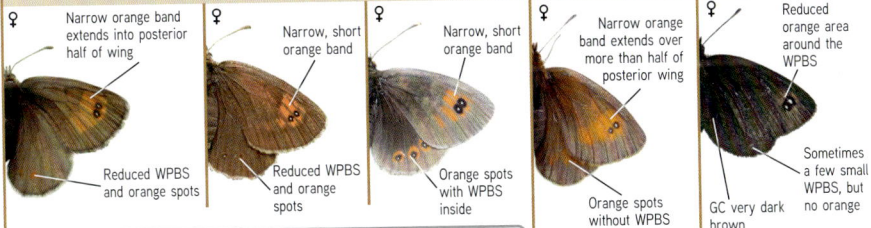

♀ Narrow orange band extends into posterior half of wing

Reduced WPBS and orange spots

♀ Narrow, short orange band

Reduced WPBS and orange spots

♀ Narrow, short orange band

Orange spots with WPBS inside

♀ Narrow orange band extends over more than half of posterior wing

Orange spots without WPBS

♀ Reduced orange area around the WPBS

Sometimes a few small WPBS, but no orange

GC very dark brown

Swiss Brassy Ringlet	Lorkovic's Brassy Ringlet	Western Brassy Ringlet / Common Brassy Ringlet	False Mnestra's Ringlet	Black Ringlet
p. 505	p. 506	p. 502	p. 497	p. 523

2.3 On FW: [no iridescent reflections] AND [narrow orange band reaching posterior half of wing]
On HW: [no orange] OR [several orange spots without WPBS]

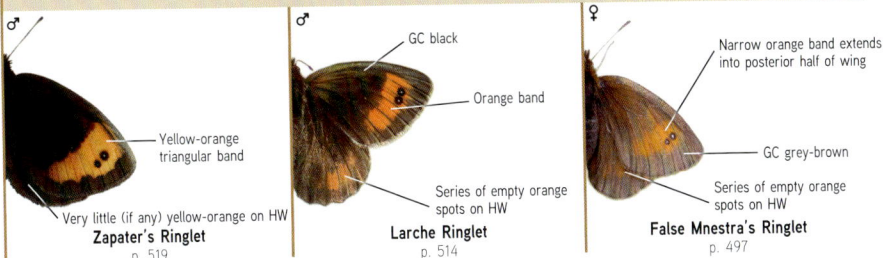

♂ Yellow-orange triangular band

Very little (if any) yellow-orange on HW
Zapater's Ringlet p. 519

♂ GC black

Orange band

Series of empty orange spots on HW
Larche Ringlet p. 514

♀ Narrow orange band extends into posterior half of wing

GC grey-brown

Series of empty orange spots on HW
False Mnestra's Ringlet p. 497

2/4 On FW: only 2 WPBS

2.4 On FW: [no iridescent reflections] AND [an orange band with its anterior end extending basally]
On HW: conspicuous orange spots with or without any WPBS inside

♂ Orange-veined black FW basal area
Very small adjacent WPBS
Large empty orange spots on HW
False Mnestra's Ringlet
p. 497

FW black basal area not orange-veined
Adjacent WPBS
Large WPBS contains orange spots on HW
Silky Ringlet
p. 499

♀ Large fused WPBS
WPBS containing orange spots on HW
Spanish Brassy Ringlet Pyrenees Brassy Ringlet
p. 507

♀ Yellow-orange triangular FW band
Reduced orange spots on HW
Zapater's Ringlet
p. 519

2.5 On FW: [no iridescent reflections] AND [rather narrow orange band almost reaches FW trailing edge] AND [GC dark brown or black]
On HW: well-marked orange spots containing WPBS

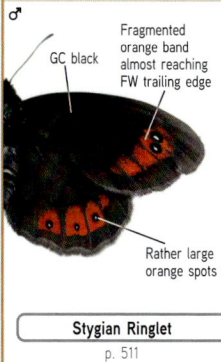

♂ GC black
Fragmented orange band almost reaching FW trailing edge
Rather large orange spots
Stygian Ringlet
p. 511

♂ ⚠ The Styrian and Stygian Ringlets are very hard to distinguish by their uppersides
Fragmented orange band slightly shorter than in Stygian Ringlet
GC black
Styrian Ringlet
p. 510

♀ GC dark brown
Fragmented orange band almost reaching FW trailing edge
Styrian Ringlet
p. 510

♂ GC black
Rather small WPBS parallel to the orange band edges
Fragmented orange band almost reaching FW trailing edge
Marbled Ringlet
p. 512

2.6 On FW: [no iridescent reflections] AND [a narrow orange band becoming faint well before reaching the trailing edge] AND [GC grey-brown]
On HW: well-marked orange spots containing WPBS

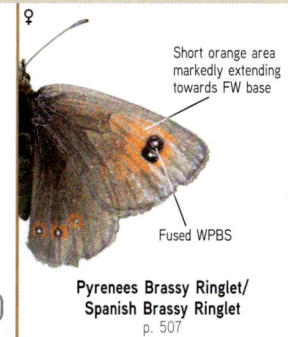

♀ Short orange area markedly extending towards FW base
Adjacent WPBS
Ottoman Brassy Ringlet
p. 503

♀ Orange band not markedly extending basally
Adjacent WPBS
Common Brassy Ringlet/Western Brassy Ringlet
p. 502

♀ Short orange area markedly extending towards FW base
Fused WPBS
Pyrenees Brassy Ringlet/ Spanish Brassy Ringlet
p. 507

3/4 On FW: more than 2 WPBS

3.1 On FW: [2 apical WPBS] AND [WPBS of very different sizes]
On HW: several rather large WPBS in orange spots

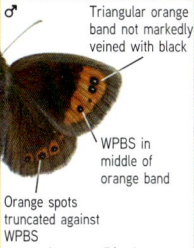

♂ Triangular orange band not markedly veined with black

WPBS in middle of orange band

Orange spots truncated against WPBS

Autumn Ringlet
p. 515

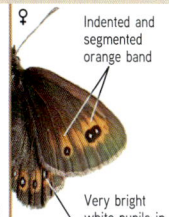

♀ Black-veined orange band

Outer edge of orange band very undulated

Marbled Ringlet
p. 512

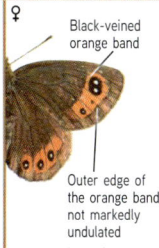

♀ Black-veined orange band

Outer edge of the orange band not markedly undulated

Stygian Ringlet
p. 511

♀ Small, shifted WPBS in front of bigger ones

Piedmont Ringlet
p. 508

♀ Apical WPBS close to orange band edge

WPBS on posterior edge of orange spots

Silky Ringlet
p. 499

3.2 On FW: [2 apical WPBS] AND [WPBS of very different sizes]
On HW: [several very small WPBS in orange spots] OR [a series of empty orange spots]

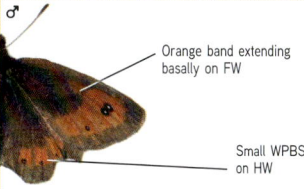

♂ Orange band extending basally on FW

Small WPBS on HW

Nicholl's Ringlet
p. 500

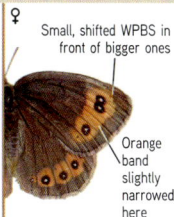

♀ Orange band extending basally on FW

Usually no WPBS on HW

Larche Ringlet
p. 514

3.3 On FW: [2 apical WPBS] AND [a 3rd WPBS of similar size] AND [GC dark brown or black]

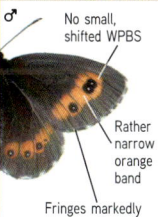

♂ No small, shifted WPBS

Rather narrow orange band

Fringes markedly chequered

Large Ringlet
p. 521

♂ No small, shifted WPBS

Orange band narrowed here

Fringes not markedly chequered

Scotch Argus
p. 513

♂ Large WPBS in reduced orange area or small orange spots

Lefèbvre's Ringlet
p. 522

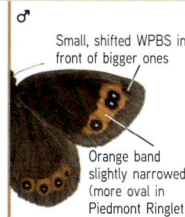

♂ Small, shifted WPBS in front of bigger ones

Orange band slightly narrowed (more oval in Piedmont Ringlet)

Chapman's Ringlet
p. 509

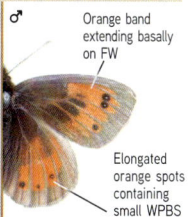

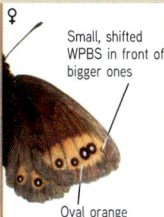

♂ Orange band extending basally on FW

Elongated orange spots containing small WPBS

Gavarnie Ringlet
p. 518

3.4 On FW: [2 apical WPBS] AND [a 3rd WPBS of similar size] AND [GC brown]

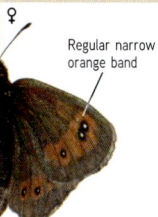

♀ Regular narrow orange band

Nicholl's Ringlet
p. 500

♀ Small, shifted WPBS in front of bigger ones

Orange band slightly narrowed here

Chapman's Ringlet
p. 509

♀ Small, shifted WPBS in front of bigger ones

Oval orange band

Piedmont Ringlet
p. 508

♀ Triangular orange band

Orange spots truncated against WPBS

Autumn Ringlet
p. 515

♀ Indented and segmented orange band

Very bright white pupils in black spots

Bright-eyed Ringlet
p. 525

97

KEY TO SATYRINAE

On FW: more than 2 WPBS

3.5 On FW: [2 apical WPBS] AND [2 other WPBS of similar size]

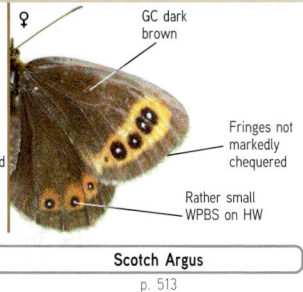

♂ GC black

Fringes markedly chequered

Arran Brown
p. 520

♀ GC dark brown

Fringes markedly chequered

Rather large WPBS on HW

♀ GC dark brown

Fringes not markedly chequered

Rather small WPBS on HW

Arran Brown — p. 520

Scotch Argus — p. 513

3.6 On FW: 3 apical WPBS

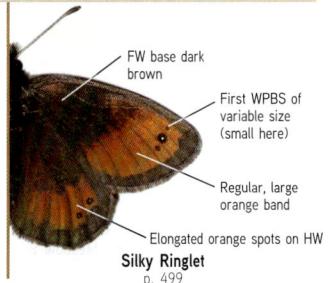

Tawny basal FW area

Spring Ringlet
p. 516

FW base dark brown

Orange band notched here

Outer orange band edge markedly undulated

de Prunner's Ringlet
p. 517

FW base dark brown

First WPBS of variable size (small here)

Regular, large orange band

Elongated orange spots on HW

Silky Ringlet
p. 499

On FW: large orange band containing 1 apical WPBS or 2 separate WPBS

4.1 On FW: 2 white dots in orange band behind apical WPBS

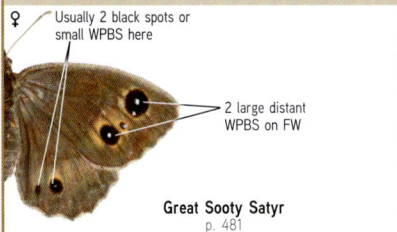

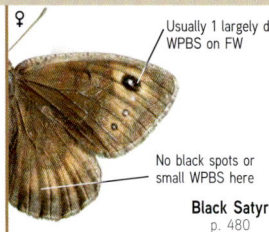

♀ Usually 2 black spots or small WPBS here

2 large distant WPBS on FW

Great Sooty Satyr
p. 481

♀ Usually 1 largely dominant WPBS on FW

No black spots or small WPBS here

⚠ In the Balkans, the Macedonian, Dark, Dils', and Brown's Graylings, as well as Balkan Grayling females, can suit this block's criteria. But they very rarely display their uppersides.

Black Satyr
p. 480

4.2 On FW: no white dot in orange band (except pupils)

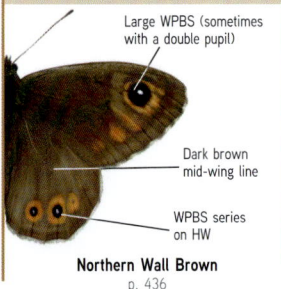

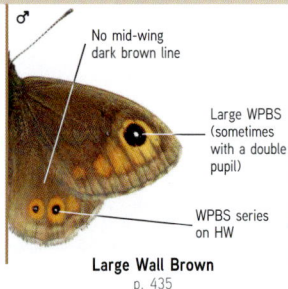

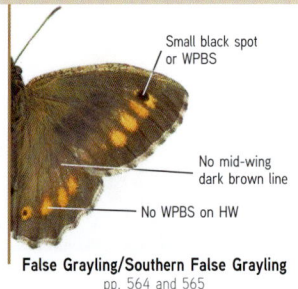

Large WPBS (sometimes with a double pupil)

Dark brown mid-wing line

WPBS series on HW

Northern Wall Brown
p. 436

♂ No mid-wing dark brown line

Large WPBS (sometimes with a double pupil)

WPBS series on HW

Large Wall Brown
p. 435

Small black spot or WPBS

No mid-wing dark brown line

No WPBS on HW

False Grayling/Southern False Grayling
pp. 564 and 565

KEY TO SATYRINAE

On FW: a diffuse or irregular brown border along the outer edge

1.1 On FW: a dark, oval basal area

♂

♂

♂

Rather large orange areas on FW and HW, unlike in Meadow Brown male

Cyprus Meadow Brown p. 447

Aegean Meadow Brown p. 448
Turkish Meadow Brown p. 449
Thomson's Meadow Brown p. 449

Sardinian Meadow Brown p. 446

⚠ All meadow brown species have very similar wing patterns, yet most have allopatric ranges. Aegean and Turkish Meadow Browns fly together on Lesbos, where they are difficult to distinguish. Thomson's Meadow Brown flies alone on Nissiros.

1.2 On FW : no basal oval-shaped dark area

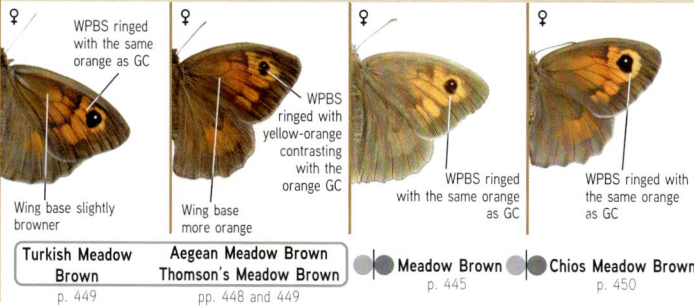

♀ WPBS ringed with the same orange as GC

♀ WPBS ringed with yellow-orange contrasting with the orange GC

♀ WPBS ringed with the same orange as GC

♀ WPBS ringed with the same orange as GC

Wing base slightly browner

Wing base more orange

Turkish Meadow Brown p. 449

Aegean Meadow Brown **Thomson's Meadow Brown** pp. 448 and 449

Meadow Brown p. 445

Chios Meadow Brown p. 450

On FW: a well-defined, regular brown border along the outer edge

2.1 On FW: brown basal area

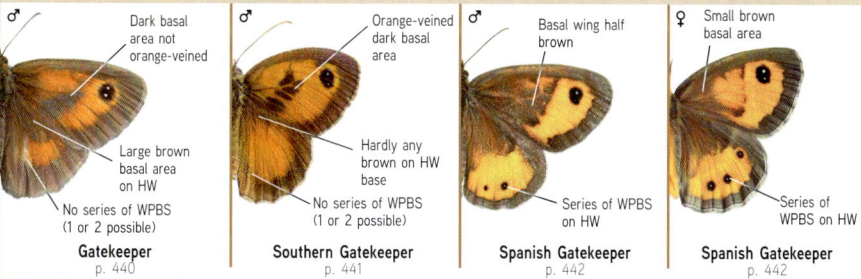

♂ Dark basal area not orange-veined

♂ Orange-veined dark basal area

♂ Basal wing half brown

♀ Small brown basal area

Large brown basal area on HW

Hardly any brown on HW base

No series of WPBS (1 or 2 possible)

No series of WPBS (1 or 2 possible)

Series of WPBS on HW

Series of WPBS on HW

Gatekeeper p. 440

Southern Gatekeeper p. 441

Spanish Gatekeeper p. 442

Spanish Gatekeeper p. 442

2.2 On FW: no brown basal area

♀ Hardly any brown on HW base

♀ Large brown basal area on HW

Southern Gatekeeper p. 441

Gatekeeper p. 440

3/4 On FW: GC pale yellow or orange chequered with brown

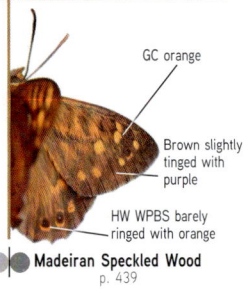

GC pale yellow

GC orange

GC orange

GC orange

Brown slightly tinged with purple

Large orange spots on HW

Small orange spots on HW

HW WPBS barely ringed with orange

Speckled Wood
p. 438

Speckled Wood
p. 438

Canary Speckled Wood
p. 437

Madeiran Speckled Wood
p. 439

4/4 On FW: [GC orange] AND [several anterior brown lines]

4.1 On FW: a conspicuous dark band across the wing

♂

No thick and diffuse dark line here

♂

Thick and diffuse dark line here

Corsican Wall Brown
p. 434

Wall Brown
p. 433

4.2 On FW: no conspicuous dark band

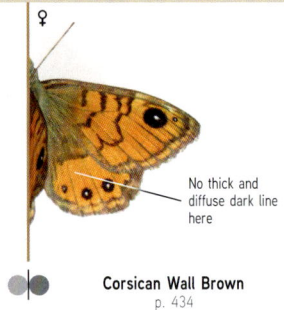

♀

Series of orange spots; rest of wing is grey-brown

♀

2 orange bands separated by diffuse, thick dark line

♀

No thick and diffuse dark line here

Large Wall Brown
p. 435

Wall Brown
p. 433

Corsican Wall Brown
p. 434

1/4   On FW: some WPBS not ringed with yellow or orange

♂ Usually 2 WPBS on FW

1 or 2 black spots or WPBS on HW

Great Sooty Satyr
p. 481

♂ Usually only 1 WPBS

No black spot or WPBS on HW

Black Satyr
p. 480

2 distant BPBS on FW

Dryad
p. 482

2 adjacent WPBS on FW

Other WPBS possible on FW and HW

Lefèbvre's Ringlet
p. 522

♂ 2 adjacent WPBS on FW

Other WPBS possible on FW and HW

Black Ringlet
p. 523

2/4   On FW: some finely yellow-ringed WPBS, BPBS, or black spots

2 blue pupils in the black spot

1 or 2 BPBS

African Ringlet
p. 484

Series of yellow-ringed black spots

2 brown lines along wing edges

Woodland Brown
p. 467

Series of WPBS on HW

Sometimes a light brown line on wing edge

False Ringlet
p. 465

♀ Series of WPBS on HW

No paler line along the wing edges

Ringlet
p. 466

3/4   On FW: WPBS or black spots finely ringed with orange

♂

Chios Meadow Brown
p. 450

♂

Meadow Brown
p. 445

♂

Turkish Meadow Brown
Aegean Meadow Brown
Thomson's Meadow Brown
pp. 449, 448, and 449

⚠ All meadow brown species have very similar wing patterns, yet most have allopatric ranges. Aegean and Turkish Meadow Browns fly together on Lesbos, where they are difficult to distinguish. Thomson's Meadow Brown flies alone on Nissiros.

4/4   On FW: no WPBS or black spots

♂ GC grey-brown

Fringes white

Ringlet
p. 466

GC dark brown

Fringes grey-brown

Yellow-spotted Ringlet
p. 490

GC black

Fringes grey

Sooty Ringlet
p. 498

KEY TO SATYRINAE

1/2 On FW: [a white or beige band across the wing] AND [1 apical WPBS or black spot]

1.1 On FW: [a pure white band] OR [a beige band becoming faint towards wing tip]

GC black

♂ GC dark brown

Wing tip rather rounded

Beige band, slightly dirty-looking

Beige band on HW

♂ GC dark brown

Wing tip rather pointed

Rather dirty-looking beige band

Beige band on HW

Pure white band on HW

⚠ **Distinguishing Woodland, Rock, and Lesser Rock Graylings without examining their genitalia is often unreliable; the ranges and some wing features help.**

Great Banded Grayling
p. 483

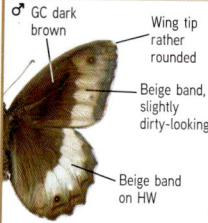

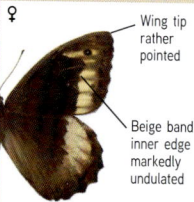

Woodland Grayling **Eastern Rock Grayling**
p. 560   p. 561

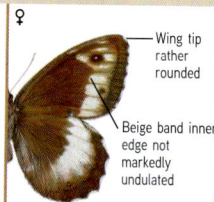

1.2 On FW: a beige band veined with black near the wing tip

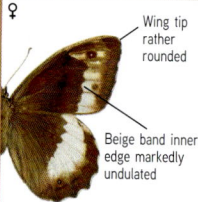

♀ Wing tip rather rounded

Beige band inner edge markedly undulated

♀ Wing tip rather pointed

Beige band inner edge markedly undulated

♀ Wing tip rather rounded

Beige band inner edge not markedly undulated

♀ Wing tip rather rounded

Beige band inner edge not markedly undulated

Woodland Grayling **Eastern Rock Grayling**
p. 560   p. 561

Rock Grayling   **Lesser Rock Grayling**
p. 562   p. 563

2/2 On FW: GC white chequered with black

2.1 On HW: pronounced thin or thicker black markings around pale or grey wing base

No black streak across this white area

Pure white basal area

Thick black mark here

Thin black streak across the outer half of this white area

White basal area sprinkled with grey

Thick black mark here

Thick, zigzag streak across middle of white area

Pure white basal area

Thick black mark here

Straight thick black streak across the middle of this white area

Pure white basal area

Fine, doubled line here

Marbled White
p. 468

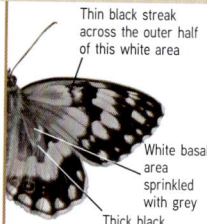

Balkan Marbled White
p. 469

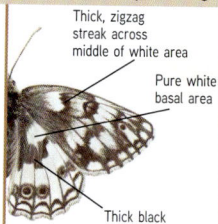

Esper's Marbled White
p. 471

Spanish Marbled White
p. 474

2.2 On HW: no black markings around basal white area

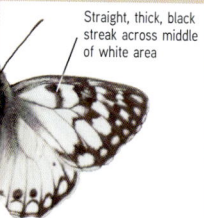

Straight, thick, black streak across middle of white area

No black streak across this white area

Thin, often incomplete black streak across basal white area

BPBS on FW

Thin black streak across outer half of white area

BPBS or black spots on FW

Sicilian Marbled White
p. 475

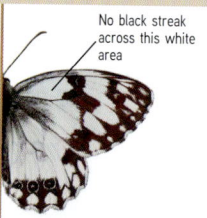

Iberian Marbled White
p. 470

Italian Marbled White
p. 473

Western Marbled White
p. 472

KEY TO SATYRINAE

1/4 On FW: [several empty orange spots or an empty orange band] OR [some black dots inside orange spots or an orange band] OR [at least 2 apical adjacent or fused WPBS]

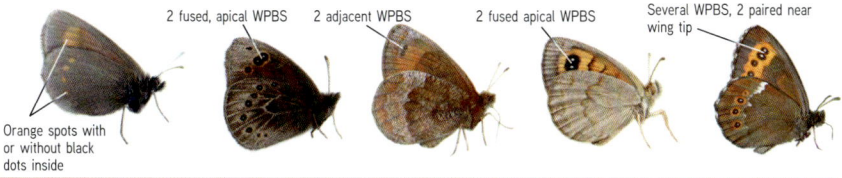

2 fused, apical WPBS

2 adjacent WPBS

2 fused apical WPBS

Several WPBS, 2 paired near wing tip

Orange spots with or without black dots inside

→ **Page 104**

2/4 On FW: [GC orange or yellow-orange] AND [at least 1 black spot with 1 or 2 white pupils inside] AND [never 2 adjacent WPBS]
Medium-sized butterflies

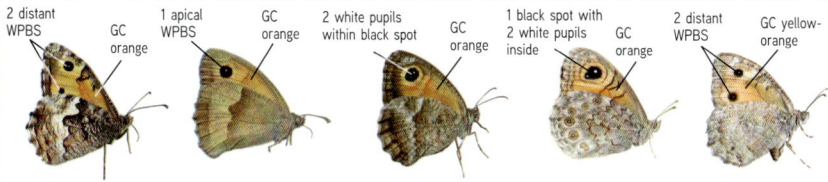

2 distant WPBS   GC orange

1 apical WPBS   GC orange

2 white pupils within black spot   GC orange

1 black spot with 2 white pupils inside   GC orange

2 distant WPBS   GC yellow-orange

→ **Page 110**

3/4 On FW: [GC orange or yellow-orange] AND [1 apical WPBS (rarely absent)]
Small butterflies

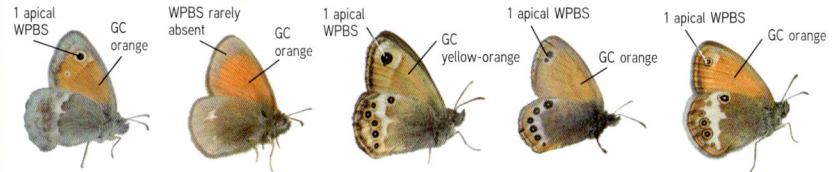

1 apical WPBS   GC orange

WPBS rarely absent   GC orange

1 apical WPBS   GC yellow-orange

1 apical WPBS   GC orange

1 apical WPBS   GC orange

→ **Page 113 (block 1/3 and the following ones)**

4/4 On FW: [GC black, brown, pale yellow, grey, or white] AND [at least 1 apical WPBS or black spot] AND [never 2 apical adjacent WPBS]

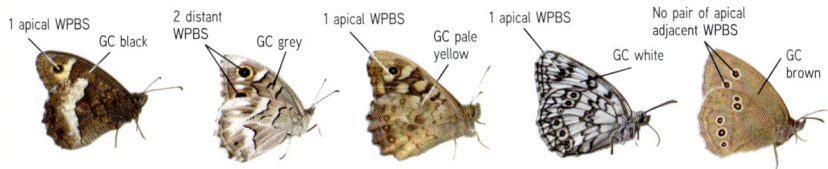

1 apical WPBS   GC black

2 distant WPBS   GC grey

1 apical WPBS   GC pale yellow

1 apical WPBS   GC white

No pair of apical adjacent WPBS   GC brown

→ **Page 115**

KEY TO SATYRINAE

1/5 On FW and HW: no WPBS (black dots possible)

1.1 On FW and HW: no black dots

Large orange area on FW

Irregular series of orange spots on FW ♂

Large orange area on FW

Large orange area on FW ♀

Faint orange band on FW (hidden here) ♂

Very regular series of orange spots on HW

Irregular series of orange spots on HW

Series of small white dots on HW

No orange spots or white dots on HW

No orange spots or white dots on HW

Blind Ringlet
p. 493

Yellow-spotted Ringlets
p. 490

White Speck Ringlet
p. 494

Sooty Ringlet
p. 498

1.2 On FW: small black dots within some orange spots
On HW: some orange, pale yellow, or whitish spots, sometimes containing black dots

Series of empty orange spots on HW

A few orange, pale yellow, or whitish spots, larger than the others, on anterior half of wing ♀

This orange spot similar to the others

This orange spot longer than the others ♀

This orange spot longer than the others

Orange spots containing black dots (sometimes hardly visible)

Series of orange spots containing black dots

Eriphyle Ringlet
p. 491

Yellow-spotted Ringlet Vosges Ringlet
p. 490

Yellow-spotted Ringlet White-spotted Ringlet
p. 490

Sudeten Ringlet
p. 489

Lesser Mountain Ringlet
p. 488

1.3 On HW: [a series of black dots in a pale yellow band] OR [several barely visible black dots in a pale band basally bordered by a brown zigzag line]

4 black dots on FW ♀

Barely visible black dots

GC grey-brown

4 black dots on FW ♂

Barely visible black dots

GC ash grey

Pale yellow band on HW

Brown zigzag lines

Brown zigzag lines

Yellow-banded Ringlet
p. 492

Dewy Ringlet
False Dewy Ringlet
p. 495

1.4 On HW: [several black dots on reduced orange spots] OR [several black dots in an outer band slightly paler than the GC]

Fringes markedly chequered

Small white tooth in middle of HW

No black dot in forwardmost orange space

GC dark grey

GC light grey

Black dot in forwardmost orange space ♀

GC light grey

Black dot in forwardmost orange space ♀

GC light grey

Black dot in forwardmost orange space

GC dark grey ♂

Fringes uniformly grey

Fringes uniformly grey

Fringes uniformly grey

Fringes uniformly grey

Large Ringlet
p. 521

Mountain Ringlet
p. 486

Rätzer's Ringlet
p. 487

2/5 On FW: 2 adjacent or fused WPBS
On HW: [GC ash grey, grey-brown, or light brown] AND [no WPBS]

2.1 On FW: 2 adjacent apical WPBS (hidden in the pictures)   ⚠ The species in this block are very difficult to
On HW: GC ash grey   distinguish by their undersides only

GC rather speckled grey	GC barely mottled grey	GC grey with slight bluish reflections	GC grey with slight bluish reflections	GC barely mottled grey
Lorkovic's Brassy Ringlet	Common Brassy Ringlet Western Brassy Ringlet	De Lesse's Brassy Ringlet	Swiss Brassy Ringlet	Ottoman Brassy Ringlet
p. 506	p. 502	p. 504	p. 505	p. 503

2.2 On FW: 2 adjacent WPBS
On HW: GC grey-brown or light brown

   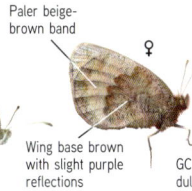 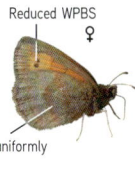

Paler beige-brown band

Reduced WPBS

Wing base brown with slight purple reflections

GC uniformly dull

Ottoman Brassy Ringlet ⬤◖ Lorkovic's Brassy Ringlet Swiss Brassy Ringlet			Water Ringlet	Mnestra's Ringlet
p. 503	p. 506	p. 505	p. 501	p. 496

2.3 On FW: 2 large fused WPBS (sometimes a 3rd, more distant one]
On HW: GC grey, grey-brown, or light brown

Usually 1 WPBS (hidden here) in addition to both apical ones

Dark wing base

Dark wing base

Orange wing base

No additional WPBS on FW

Orange wing base

No additional WPBS on FW

HW base mottled light brown

HW base mottled grey

HW base mottled grey

   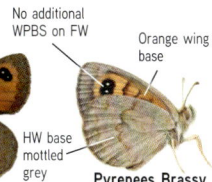

Autumn Ringlet	Spanish Brassy Ringlet	Spanish Brassy Ringlet ⬤◖	Pyrenees Brassy Ringlet
p. 515	p. 507	p. 507	p. 507

2.4 On FW: 2 medium-size fused WPBS
On HW: GC ash grey or light brown

Yellow-orange band

Orange wing base

Dark brown wing base

3rd WPBS sometimes present

GC ash grey

GC light brown

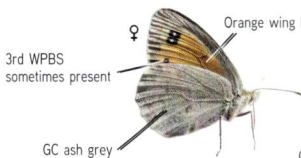 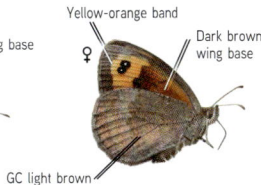

Larche Ringlet	⬤◖	Zapater's Ringlet
p. 514		p. 519

3/5 On FW: several WPBS in an orange area, orange band, or some orange spots]
On HW: [GC dark brown] AND [no WPBS]

3.1 On FW: several WPBS on round, rather separate orange spots

♂   ♀

Poorly contrasting bands across HW

Sharply contrasting bands across HW

Arctic Ringlet
p. 528

Arctic Ringlet
p. 528

3.2 On FW: 2 WPBS in an orange band
On HW: 2 or 3 sharply contrasting bands across the wing

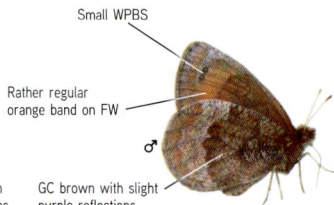

Medium-size WPBS

Small WPBS

Triangular orange band (tip hidden here)

Rather regular orange band on FW

♂   ♂

GC dull brown with no purple reflections

GC brown with slight purple reflections

Autumn Ringlet
p. 515

Water Ringlet
p. 501

3.3 On FW: several WPBS in an orange (sometimes faint) band
On HW: no sharply contrasting band across the wing

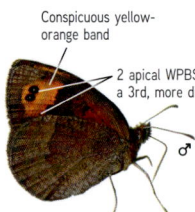
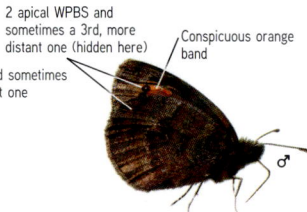
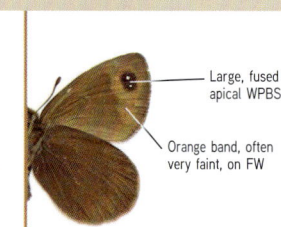

Conspicuous yellow-orange band

2 apical WPBS and sometimes a 3rd, more distant one (hidden here)

Conspicuous orange band

Large, fused apical WPBS

2 apical WPBS and sometimes a 3rd, more distant one

Orange band, often very faint, on FW

♂   ♂

Zapater's Ringlet
p. 519

Nicholl's Ringlet
p. 500

Lefèbvre's Ringlet
p. 522

3.4 On FW: WPBS in a large orange area
On HW: GC uniform, without a sharply contrasting band

Reduced WPBS

Reduced WPBS

Medium-size WPBS

♂   ♂

Posterior band very slightly paler than dark brown GC of wing base

Posterior band slightly paler than dark brown, finely mottled wing base

HW GC homogenously dark brown

Mnestra's Ringlet
p. 496

False Mnestra Ringlet
p. 497

Larche Ringlet
p. 514

4/5 On FW: WPBS in an orange area, orange band, or some orange spots
On HW: WPBS in orange spots (sometimes reduced)

4.1 On FW: several medium-size WPBS
On HW: no white spots (except for white pupils in black spots)

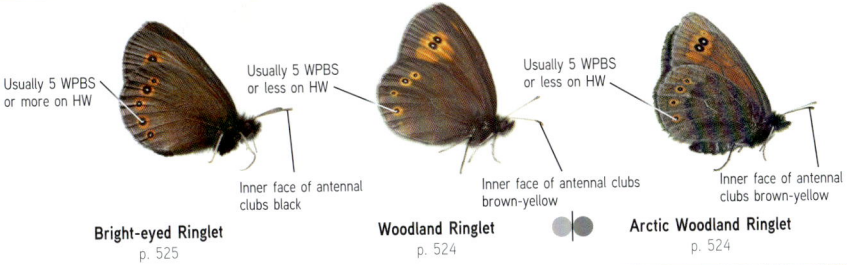

Usually 5 WPBS or more on HW

Usually 5 WPBS or less on HW

Usually 5 WPBS or less on HW

Inner face of antennal clubs black

Inner face of antennal clubs brown-yellow

Inner face of antennal clubs brown-yellow

Bright-eyed Ringlet
p. 525

Woodland Ringlet
p. 524

Arctic Woodland Ringlet
p. 524

4.2 On FW: [several medium-size WPBS] AND [fringes markedly chequered]
On HW: a white streak or some white spots

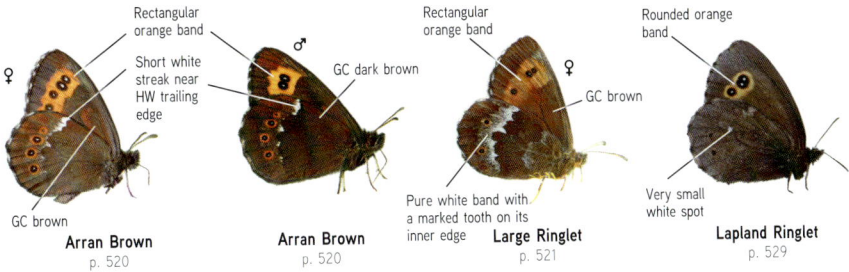

♀

Rectangular orange band

Short white streak near HW trailing edge

GC brown

Arran Brown
p. 520

♂

GC dark brown

Arran Brown
p. 520

Rectangular orange band

GC brown

Pure white band with a marked tooth on its inner edge

♀

Large Ringlet
p. 521

Rounded orange band

Very small white spot

Lapland Ringlet
p. 529

4.3 On FW: several small WPBS
On HW: no white spots (except for white pupils in black spots)

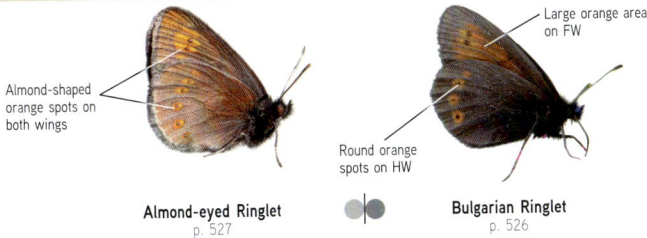

Almond-shaped orange spots on both wings

Large orange area on FW

Round orange spots on HW

Almond-eyed Ringlet
p. 527

Bulgarian Ringlet
p. 526

KEY TO SATYRINAE

On FW: WPBS in an orange area, orange band, or some orange spots
On HW: several WPBS, but no orange

5.1 On HW: [GC dark and markedly mottled] AND [veins sharply contrasting with GC]

WPBS finely ringed with orange on FW

Diffuse pale grey area surrounding the WPBS

2 adjacent apical WPBS on FW

Large orange area on FW

3 adjacent, aligned apical WPBS on FW (hidden in this picture)

Rectangular orange band on FW (hidden here)

♂

♀

Dalmatian Ringlet
p. 485

Marbled Ringlet
p. 512

de Prunner's Ringlet
p. 517

5.2 On HW: [GC light brown, markedly mottled] AND [very pale veins, sharply contrasting with GC]

3 adjacent, aligned apical WPBS on FW

Rectangular orange band on FW

2 adjacent apical WPBS on FW

Large orange area on FW

2 adjacent apical WPBS on FW

Large orange area on FW

♀

♀

Spring Ringlet
p. 516

Marbled Ringlet
p. 512

Gavarnie Ringlet
p. 518

5.3 On HW: [GC grey or light brown, not markedly mottled] AND [veins not contrasting with GC]

Rectangular orange band on FW

Basal wing half dark brown

Rectangular orange band on FW

Basal wing half dark brown

Basal wing half darker than outer orange band

Reduced, faint orange band on FW (hidden here)

♀

♀

♀

HW GC barely mottled

HW GC hardly mottled

Conspicuous brown line separating outer and inner wing halves

Barely visible line separating outer and inner wing halves

| **Chapman's Ringlet** | **Piedmont Ringlet** |
| p. 509 | p. 508 |

Styrian Ringlet
p. 510

Lefèbvre's Ringlet p. 522
Black Ringlet p. 523

5.4 On HW: [GC chocolate brown, hardly mottled] AND [veins not contrasting with GC] AND [an outer grey band containing barely visible WPBS]

Orange band narrowed here

♂

Orange band narrowed here

♀

Basal wing area not sharply contrasting with brown GC

Grey basal wing area, sharply contrasting with brown GC

Scotch Argus
p. 513

Scotch Argus
p. 513

KEY TO SATYRINAE

5/5 On FW: WPBS in an orange area, orange band, or some orange spots
On HW: several WPBS, but no orange

5.5 On HW: [GC very dark brown] AND [veins not sharply contrasting with GC]
On FW: orange band containing some WPBS

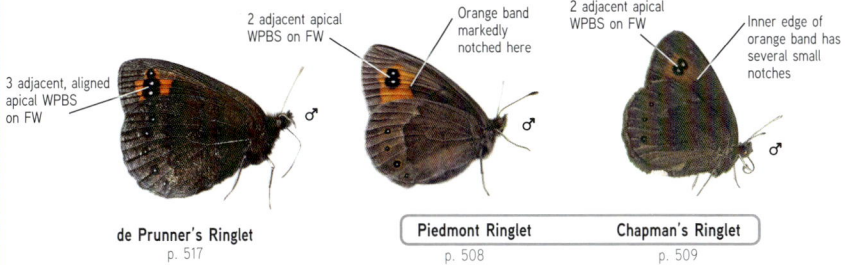

2 adjacent apical WPBS on FW

Orange band markedly notched here

2 adjacent apical WPBS on FW

Inner edge of orange band has several small notches

3 adjacent, aligned apical WPBS on FW

♂ ♂ ♂

de Prunner's Ringlet
p. 517

Piedmont Ringlet
p. 508

Chapman's Ringlet
p. 509

5.6 On HW: [GC very dark brown] AND [veins not sharply contrasting with GC]
On FW: some WPBS in a large orange area

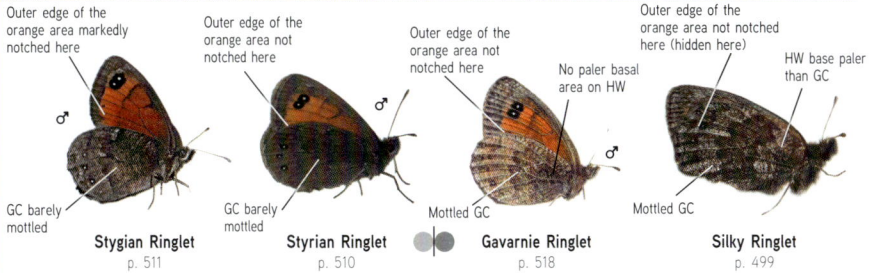

Outer edge of the orange area markedly notched here

Outer edge of the orange area not notched here

Outer edge of the orange area not notched here

No paler basal area on HW

Outer edge of the orange area not notched here (hidden here)

HW base paler than GC

♂ ♂ ♂ ♂

GC barely mottled

GC barely mottled

Mottled GC

Mottled GC

Stygian Ringlet
p. 511

Styrian Ringlet
p. 510

Gavarnie Ringlet
p. 518

Silky Ringlet
p. 499

5.7 On HW: [GC brown or light brown] AND [veins not sharply contrasting with GC] AND [some WPBS in an outer band paler than GC]
On FW: some WPBS in a large orange area

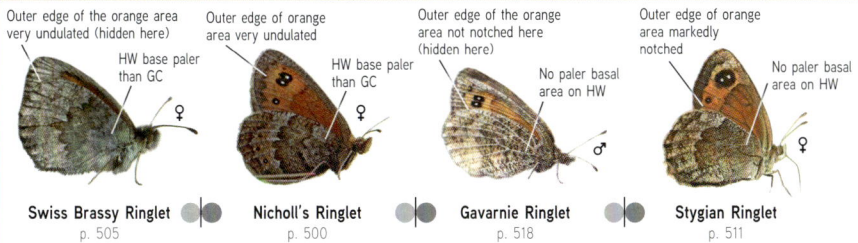

Outer edge of the orange area very undulated (hidden here)

HW base paler than GC

Outer edge of orange area very undulated

HW base paler than GC

Outer edge of the orange area not notched here (hidden here)

No paler basal area on HW

Outer edge of orange area markedly notched

No paler basal area on HW

♀ ♀ ♂ ♀

Swiss Brassy Ringlet
p. 505

Nicholl's Ringlet
p. 500

Gavarnie Ringlet
p. 518

Stygian Ringlet
p. 511

5.8 On HW: [GC very dark brown or black] AND [veins not sharply contrasting with GC]
On FW: some WPBS in a very reduced orange band (sometimes absent)

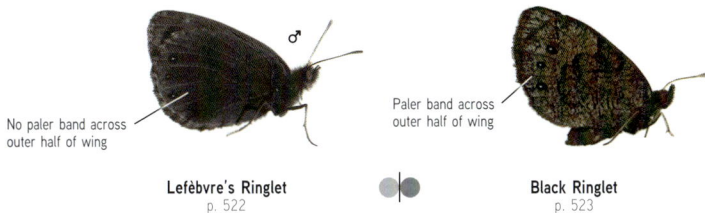

♂

No paler band across outer half of wing

Paler band across outer half of wing

Lefèbvre's Ringlet
p. 522

Black Ringlet
p. 523

1/5 On FW: [1 apical WPBS (sometimes doubly pupillated) and often a more distant one] AND [no white dot below apical WPBS]
On HW: a pale or pure white stripe (sometimes diffuse) across the wing

1.1 On HW: pale or white stripe; very sinuous, with a conspicuous notch on its inner edge

⚠ Identifying these grayling species requires genitalia examination when they are sympatric. The geographic information provided here refines the possibilities. The main identification issues arise in the Balkans and some Aegean islands. The Eolian Grayling (not illustrated here) is endemic to the Aeolian Islands, where it is the only grayling. Grayling males usually display a more sinuous and conspicuous white HW stripe than females, except for the Samos Grayling; in that species, both sexes have a rather faint, pale HW stripe.

⚠ Widely distributed in Europe

⚠ Only in the Balkans and the Aegean Islands

⚠ Only in the Balkans and the Ionian Islands

⚠ Only grayling on the Italian Pontine Islands

Grayling
p. 541

Balkan Grayling
p. 542

Delattin's Grayling
p. 543

Ponza Grayling
p. 552

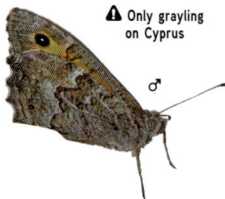

⚠ Only grayling on Cyprus

⚠ Only in Campania

⚠ The Southern Grayling is the only grayling with an orange FW in Corsica, Sardinia, and other islands in the Tyrrhenian Sea

⚠ Only in Sicily and southern Italy

Cyprus Grayling
p. 547

Italian Grayling
p. 550

Southern Grayling
Madeiran Grayling
pp. 549 and 548

Sicilian Grayling
p. 551

⚠ Only on Samos and Lesbos

⚠ Only grayling on Crete

⚠ Only grayling on Karpathos

⚠ Only graylings in the Azores

Samos Grayling
p. 545

Cretan Grayling
p. 546

Karpathos Grayling
p. 544

Azores Grayling
Le Cerf's Grayling
p. 555

1.2 On HW: white stripe rather regular and not very sinuous

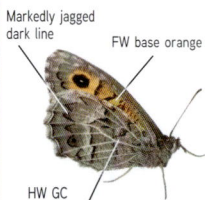

Markedly jagged dark line
FW base orange

Undulated brown line
FW base orange

FW base dark brown

Pure white band
WPBS doubly pupillated

HW GC grey-brown
Southern False Grayling
p. 565

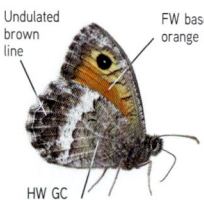

HW GC grey-brown
False Grayling
p. 564

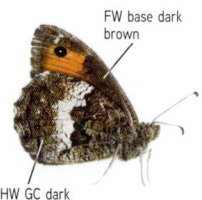

HW GC dark brown
Corsican Grayling
p. 554

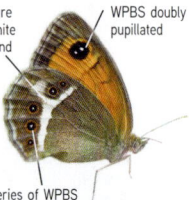

Series of WPBS on HW
Spanish Gatekeeper
p. 442

2/5 On HW: [a pale but not pure white stripe across the wing] AND [no more than 1 WPBS not ringed with yellow]

2.1 On FW: 1 reduced apical WPBS or black spot (sometimes absent)
On HW: GC brown or grey-brown, very mottled

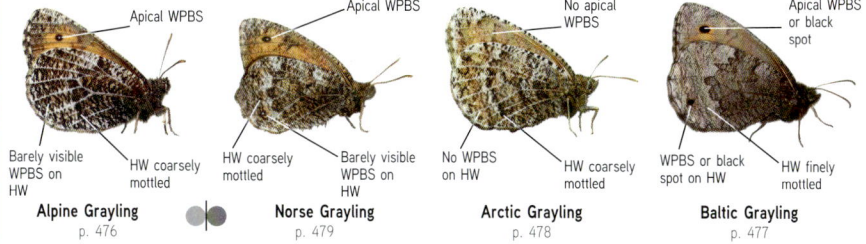

Apical WPBS

Apical WPBS

No apical WPBS

Apical WPBS or black spot

Barely visible WPBS on HW

HW coarsely mottled

HW coarsely mottled

Barely visible WPBS on HW

No WPBS on HW

HW coarsely mottled

WPBS or black spot on HW

HW finely mottled

Alpine Grayling
p. 476

Norse Grayling
p. 479

Arctic Grayling
p. 478

Baltic Grayling
p. 477

2.2 On FW: [a medium-size or large apical WPBS] AND [another posterior WPBS in females]
On HW: GC rather uniformly grey-brown (slightly paler posterior band possible)

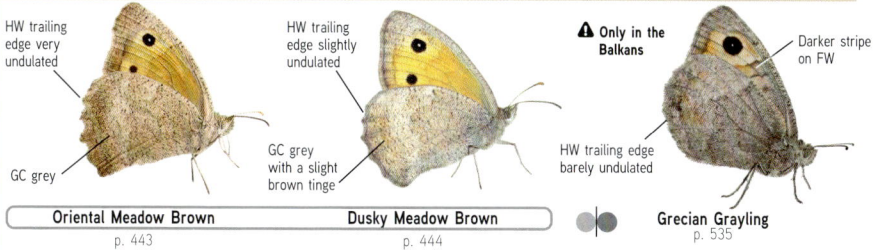

HW trailing edge very undulated

HW trailing edge slightly undulated

⚠ Only in the Balkans

Darker stripe on FW

GC grey

GC grey with a slight brown tinge

HW trailing edge barely undulated

Oriental Meadow Brown	**Dusky Meadow Brown**
p. 443	p. 444

Grecian Grayling
p. 535

2.3 On FW: 1 apical medium-size or large WPBS (sometimes doubly pupillated)
On HW: [GC grey-brown] AND [a conspicuously paler posterior band]

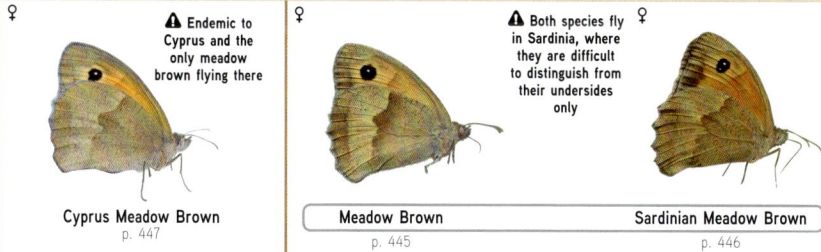

♀

⚠ Endemic to Cyprus and the only meadow brown flying there

♀

⚠ Both species fly in Sardinia, where they are difficult to distinguish from their undersides only ♀

Cyprus Meadow Brown
p. 447

Meadow Brown	**Sardinian Meadow Brown**
p. 445	p. 446

2.4 On FW: 1 apical medium-size or large WPBS (sometimes doubly pupillated)
On HW: [GC grey-brown] AND [a red-underlined, yellowish posterior band]

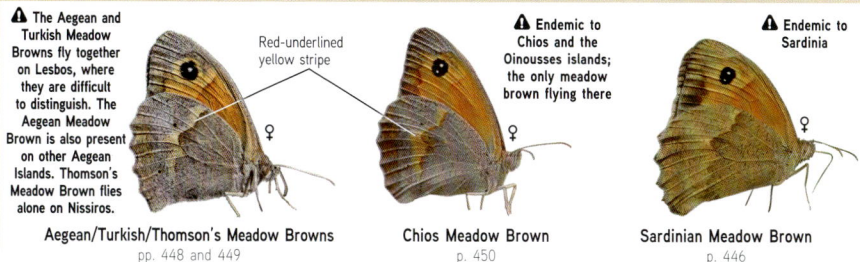

⚠ The Aegean and Turkish Meadow Browns fly together on Lesbos, where they are difficult to distinguish. The Aegean Meadow Brown is also present on other Aegean Islands. Thomson's Meadow Brown flies alone on Nissiros.

Red-underlined yellow stripe

♀

⚠ Endemic to Chios and the Oinousses islands; the only meadow brown flying there

♀

⚠ Endemic to Sardinia

♀

Aegean/Turkish/Thomson's Meadow Browns
pp. 448 and 449

Chios Meadow Brown
p. 450

Sardinian Meadow Brown
p. 446

KEY TO SATYRINAE

2/5 On HW: [a pale but not pure white stripe across the wing] AND [no more than 1 WPBS not ringed with yellow]

2.5 On FW: 1 apical, doubly pupillated black spot
On HW: a whitish, sinuous stripe on a rather mottled GC

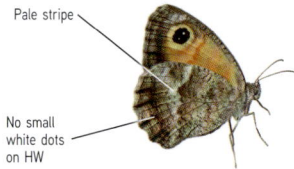

Pale stripe

Pale stripe

No small white dots on HW

Several small white dots on HW

Southern Gatekeeper
p. 441

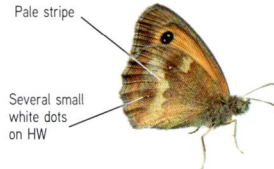

Gatekeeper
p. 440

3/5 On FW: 1 apical WPBS (sometimes doubly pupillated)
On HW: [GC uniformly grey, with a slightly paler posterior band] AND [some yellow-ringed WPBS or black spots]

3.1 On HW: few, small WPBS or black spots

⚠ Endemic to Cyprus; the only meadow brown flying there

⚠ Both species fly in Sardinia, where they are difficult to distinguish from their undersides only

⚠ Endemic to Chios and the Oinousses islands; the only meadow brown flying there

Cyprus Meadow Brown
p. 447

Meadow Brown
p. 445

Sardinian Meadow Brown
p. 446

Chios Meadow Brown
p. 450

3.2 On HW: many WPBS or conspicuous black spots

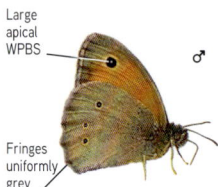

Large apical WPBS

⚠ The Aegean and Turkish Meadow Browns fly together on Lesbos, where they are difficult to distinguish. The Aegean Meadow Brown is also present on other Aegean islands. Thomson's Meadow Brown flies alone on Nissiros.

Large apical WPBS

Small apical WPBS

Fringes uniformly grey

Fringes uniformly grey

Chequered fringes

Aegean Meadow Brown/Thomson's Meadow Brown
pp. 448 and 449

Turkish Meadow Brown
p. 449

Lesser Lattice Brown
p. 432

4/5 On FW: [2 large and distant WPBS] AND [2 white spots between the 2 WPBS]

4.1 On FW: GC orange

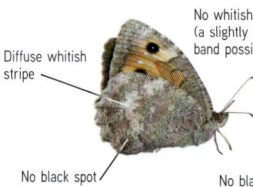

Diffuse whitish stripe

No whitish stripe (a slightly paler band possible)

Basal FW half yellow-orange

HW base darker than outer half

Whitish stripe with a well-marked inner edge

No black spot here

No black spot here

Often a small WPBS here

Usually 2 black spots here

Dils' Grayling
p. 534

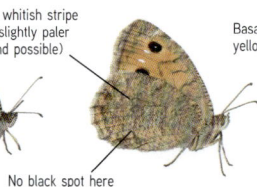

Dark Grayling
p. 533

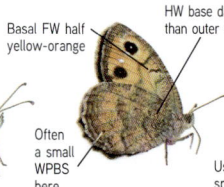

Brown's Grayling
p. 532

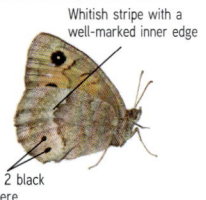

Great Sooty Satyr
p. 481

112

4/5 On FW: [2 large, distant WPBS] AND [2 white points between these WPBS]

4.2 On FW: GC yellow-orange

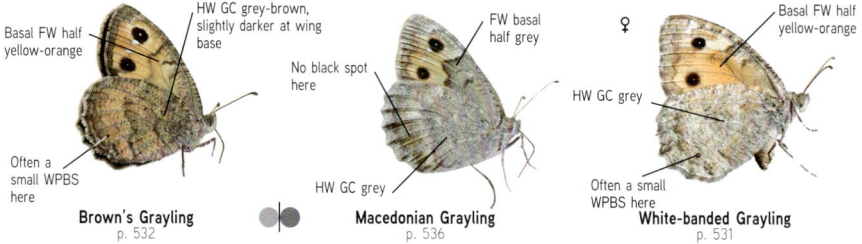

Basal FW half yellow-orange

HW GC grey-brown, slightly darker at wing base

No black spot here

Often a small WPBS here

Brown's Grayling
p. 532

FW basal half grey

HW GC grey

Macedonian Grayling
p. 536

♀

Basal FW half yellow-orange

HW GC grey

Often a small WPBS here

White-banded Grayling
p. 531

5/5 On FW: 1 apical yellow-circled WPBS (sometimes fused with a very small one)
On HW: a series of yellow- and brown-circled WPBS

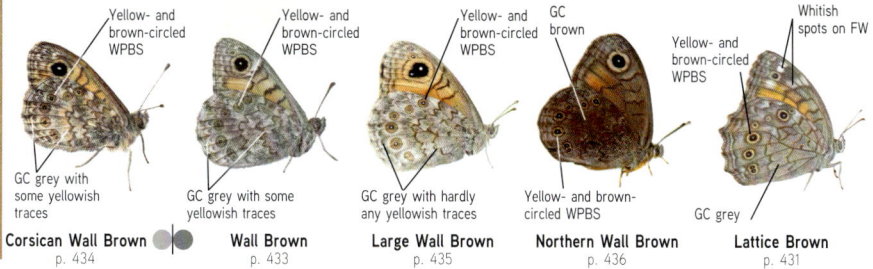

Yellow- and brown-circled WPBS

GC grey with some yellowish traces

Corsican Wall Brown
p. 434

Yellow- and brown-circled WPBS

GC grey with some yellowish traces

Wall Brown
p. 433

Yellow- and brown-circled WPBS

GC grey with hardly any yellowish traces

Large Wall Brown
p. 435

GC brown

Yellow- and brown-circled WPBS

Northern Wall Brown
p. 436

Whitish spots on FW

Yellow- and brown-circled WPBS

GC grey

Lattice Brown
p. 431

1/3 On HW: [pale or white stripe across wing] AND [series of WPBS] AND
[1 orange and 1 silver line along trailing edge]

1.1 On HW: yellow-ringed WPBS

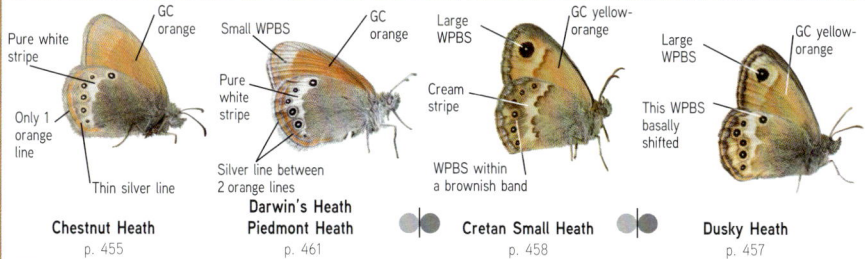

Pure white stripe

GC orange

Only 1 orange line

Thin silver line

Chestnut Heath
p. 455

Small WPBS

GC orange

Pure white stripe

Silver line between 2 orange lines

Darwin's Heath
Piedmont Heath
p. 461

Large WPBS

GC yellow-orange

Cream stripe

WPBS within a brownish band

Cretan Small Heath
p. 458

Large WPBS

GC yellow-orange

This WPBS basally shifted

Dusky Heath
p. 457

1.2 On HW: [orange-ringed WPBS] OR [WPBS not ringed]

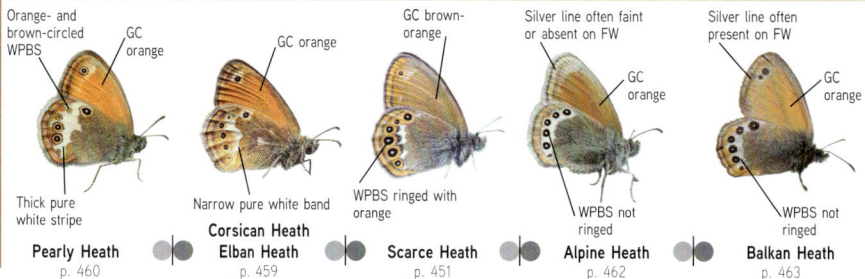

Orange- and brown-circled WPBS

GC orange

Thick pure white stripe

Pearly Heath
p. 460

GC orange

Narrow pure white band

Corsican Heath
Elban Heath
p. 459

GC brown-orange

WPBS ringed with orange

Scarce Heath
p. 451

Silver line often faint or absent on FW

GC orange

WPBS not ringed

Alpine Heath
p. 462

Silver line often present on FW

GC orange

WPBS not ringed

Balkan Heath
p. 463

113

KEY TO SATYRINAE

2/3 On HW: [at most a few separate white spots] AND [posterior orange line]

2.1 On HW: some conspicuous white spots

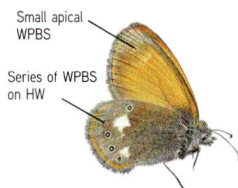

Small apical WPBS

Series of WPBS on HW

No apical WPBS

No apical WPBS

No WPBS on HW

Series of WPBS on HW

Chestnut Heath
p. 455

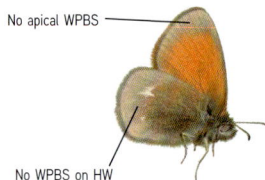

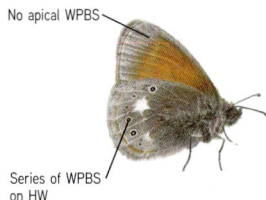

Chestnut Heath
p. 455

Chestnut Heath
p. 455

2.2 On HW: [no white spots] OR [small white spot between some WPBS]

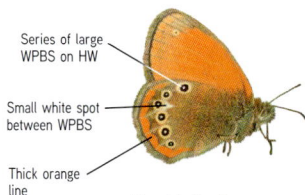

Series of large WPBS on HW

Small white spot between WPBS

Thick orange line

Series of rather small WPBS

No white spot on HW

Silver line between 2 orange lines

Spanish Heath
p. 456

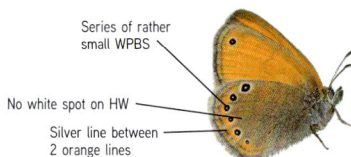

Russian Heath
p. 464

3/3 On HW: [white stripe or series of pale spots across wing] AND [no silver or orange lines along trailing edge]

3.1 On HW: no WPBS or yellow-ringed black spots (some small white dots possible)

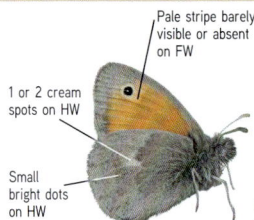

Pale stripe barely visible or absent on FW

1 or 2 cream spots on HW

Small bright dots on HW

Pale stripe barely visible or absent on FW

Small bright dots on HW

Irregular cream stripe on HW

Conspicuous pale stripe on FW

Irregular cream stripe on HW

Small, yellow-ringed dots on HW

Small Heath
p. 452

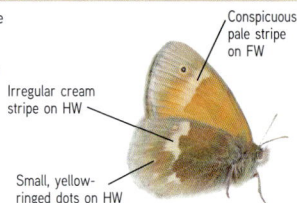

Small Heath
p. 452

Large Heath
p. 453

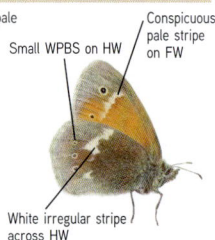

3.2 On HW: series of yellow-ringed WPBS or black spots

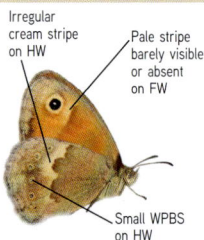

Irregular cream stripe on HW

Pale stripe barely visible or absent on FW

Small WPBS on HW

Ill-defined pale spot on HW

Small, yellow-ringed black spots on HW

Large WPBS on HW

White irregular stripe across HW

Conspicuous pale stripe on FW

Small WPBS on HW

Conspicuous pale stripe on FW

White irregular stripe across HW

Small Heath
p. 452

Eastern Large Heath
p. 454

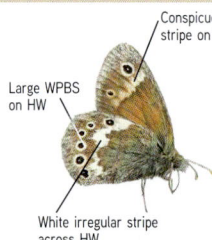

Large Heath
p. 453

Large Heath
p. 453

KEY TO SATYRINAE

UNS

1/7 On FW: [GC very dark brown] AND [1 or 2 WPBS in pale yellow band or large area]
On HW: a white and sometimes very sinuous stripe across wing

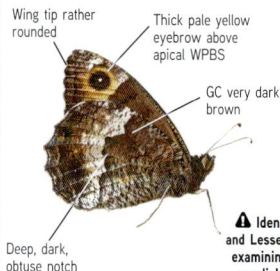

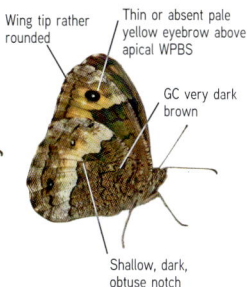

Wing tip rather rounded

Thick pale yellow eyebrow above apical WPBS

GC very dark brown

Deep, dark, obtuse notch

Wing tip rather pointed

Thin or absent pale yellow eyebrow above apical WPBS

GC very dark brown

⚠ Identifying Woodland, Rock, and Lesser Rock Graylings without examining their genitalia is often unreliable, although the ranges and some wing features help.

Shallow, dark, obtuse notch

Wing tip rather rounded

Thin or absent pale yellow eyebrow above apical WPBS

GC very dark brown

Shallow, dark, obtuse notch

Lesser Rock Grayling	Eastern Rock Grayling	Woodland Grayling
p. 563	p. 561	p. 560

Thick, pale yellow eyebrow above apical WPBS

Wing tip rather rounded

GC very dark brown

2 large WPBS on FW

♀

GC grey

Basal FW half pale yellow

Deep, dark, acute notch

Ill-defined white stripe

Very sinuous, well-defined white stripe

Rock Grayling
p. 562

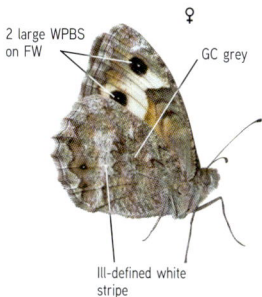

Balkan White-banded Grayling
p. 531

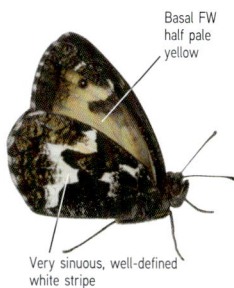

**Azores Grayling
Le Cerf's Grayling**
p. 555

2/7 On FW: [GC very dark brown or dark grey] AND [1 or 2 WPBS within or beside pure white area]
On HW: a sometimes very sinuous white stripe across wing

Thick white band across entire wing

No basal white stripe on HW

♂

No basal white stripe on HW

♂

No basal white stripe on HW

Short basal white band on HW

White band thickened in the middle

White band thickened in the middle

Thin, very sinuous white stripe across HW

Great Banded Grayling
p. 483

Balkan White-banded Grayling
p. 531

White-banded Grayling
p. 531

Tilos Grayling
p. 559

115

3/7   On FW: [GC grey] AND [2 yellow-ringed WPBS] AND [2 white dots between these WPBS]

3.1   On HW: no pure white stripe (posterior paler band possible)

♂   Basal dark line hardly visible

♀   Ill-defined posterior paler band

Dark, well-marked basal line

♀

Conspicuous, pale posterior band

Tree Grayling
p. 556

Barely visible basal dark line

Tree Grayling
p. 556

Pale, ill-defined posterior band

Freyer's Grayling
p. 557

Pale band variably defined

Canarian Tree Graylings
p. 559

3.2   On HW: pure white, black-underlined, sinuous stripe

Conspicuous black-and-white chevron

Large white spots on HW

Rather blunt, shallow, white-and-black chevron

♂

Striped Grayling
p. 558

Canarian Tree Graylings
p. 559

4/7   On FW: [GC pale yellow] AND [some basal brown lines or spots] AND [at least 1 apical WPBS]

Brown line not deeply undulated

Thick basal dark spots

♀

Rather uniform greyish GC

Hermit
p. 538

Brown line not deeply undulated

Thick basal dark spots

♂

GC pale yellow, with some large, sharply contrasting, dark spots

Hermit
p. 538

Brown line deeply undulated

Thick basal dark spots

Southern Hermit
p. 539

Basal brown lines

Brown line deeply undulated

Grey Asian Grayling
p. 537

Basal brown lines

Brown line not deeply undulated

Nevada Grayling
p. 530

5/7   On FW: [GC brown] AND [some orange or pale yellow spots]

Orange and pale yellow spots

Small white streak on HW

Canary Speckled Wood
p. 437

Slightly convex FW edge

Orange spots

GC brown with a slight purple tint

Madeiran Speckled Wood
p. 439

Orange spots

GC light brown

Speckled Wood
p. 438

Pale yellow spots

GC light brown

Speckled Wood
p. 438

6/7 On FW: [GC white] AND [some black spots and black lines]

6.1 On HW: [several thickly yellow-ringed WPBS] AND [GC pale yellow]

Thick black streak on FW base (hidden here)

Thin black streak here

Faint black spots here

No black streak here

Marked black spots here

No black streak here

Uninterrupted greyish-yellow band ♀

Uninterrupted greyish-yellow band ♀

Series of greyish-yellow spots interrupted here ♀

Series of greyish-yellow spots interrupted here ♀

Esper's Marbled White
p. 471

Balkan Marbled White
p. 469

Iberian Marbled White
p. 470

Marbled White
p. 468

6.2 On HW: [several thickly yellow-ringed WPBS] AND [GC white]

Uninterrupted greyish band

Faint black spots here

Series of greyish spots interrupted here

Thin black streak here

No black streak here

Uninterrupted greyish band

Thick black streak on FW base

Series of greyish spots interrupted here

Marked black spots here

No black streak here

♂ ♂ ♂ ♂

Balkan Marbled White
p. 469

Iberian Marbled White
p. 470

Esper's Marbled White
p. 471

Marbled White
p. 468

6.3 On HW: [series of BPBS] OR [no WPBS or BPBS]

No blue spots on HW

Brown- and yellow-ringed blue spots on HW

Brown- and yellow-ringed blue spots on HW

Brown- and yellow-ringed blue spots on HW

Grey veins

Thick brown veins

Black veins

Black veins

Sicilian Marbled White
p. 475

Western Marbled White
p. 472

Italian Marbled White
p. 473

Spanish Marbled White
p. 474

7/7 On FW and HW: [GC uniformly brown] OR [GC finely mottled with grey]

7.1 On HW: [GC brown] AND [no WPBS (but 2 small black spots possible in anal angle)]

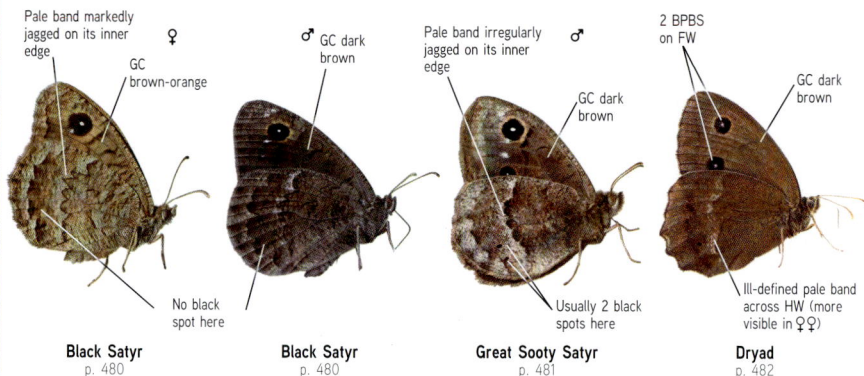

Pale band markedly jagged on its inner edge ♀

GC brown-orange

♂ GC dark brown

Pale band irregularly jagged on its inner edge ♂

GC dark brown

2 BPBS on FW

GC dark brown

No black spot here

Usually 2 black spots here

Ill-defined pale band across HW (more visible in ♀♀)

Black Satyr
p. 480

Black Satyr
p. 480

Great Sooty Satyr
p. 481

Dryad
p. 482

7.2 On HW: [GC brown] AND [series of yellow-ringed WPBS]

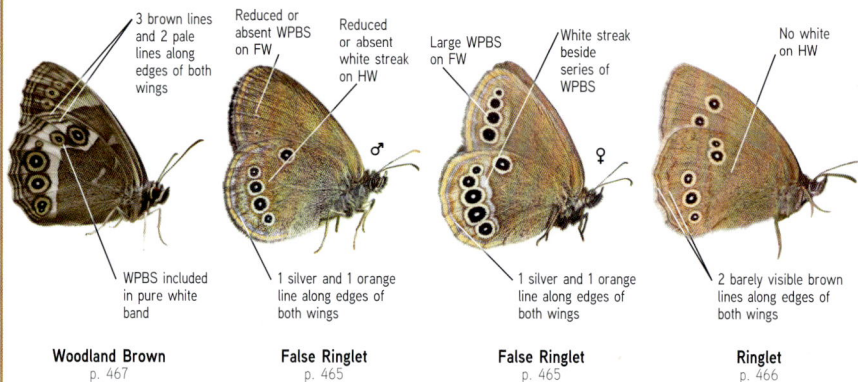

3 brown lines and 2 pale lines along edges of both wings

Reduced or absent WPBS on FW

Reduced or absent white streak on HW

Large WPBS on FW

White streak beside series of WPBS

No white on HW

WPBS included in pure white band

1 silver and 1 orange line along edges of both wings

1 silver and 1 orange line along edges of both wings

2 barely visible brown lines along edges of both wings

Woodland Brown
p. 467

False Ringlet
p. 465

False Ringlet
p. 465

Ringlet
p. 466

7.3 On HW: [GC finely mottled with grey] AND [a few yellow-ringed BPBS]

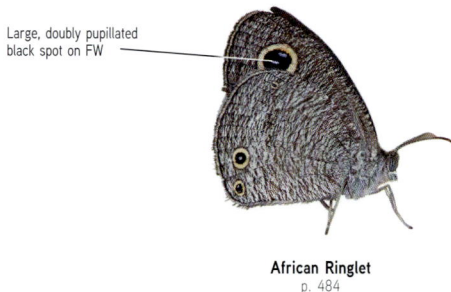

Large, doubly pupillated black spot on FW

African Ringlet
p. 484

THE PAPILIONIDS (14 SPECIES)

SUBFAMILIES	GENERA	NUMBER OF SPECIES	MAIN LARVAL HOST-PLANT FAMILIES
Parnassiinae	*Archon, Parnassius,* and *Zerynthia*	9	Crassulaceae, Saxifragaceae, Aristolochiaceae, and Fumariaceae
Papilioninae	*Iphiclides* and *Papilio*	5	Apiaceae, Rutaceae, and Rosaceae

The Papilionids comprise about 570 species worldwide. The majority inhabit low latitudes, but some have colonized Mediterranean and temperate regions. Many are large butterflies capable of covering significant flight distances. Several species engage in hill-topping, where males gather on rocky ridges awaiting females. In Europe, their colours tend to be in the yellow and white spectrum, often adorned with black and red markings. Papilionid caterpillars may exhibit vibrant colours, which can signal the accumulation of toxic compounds extracted from their host plants. They can also mimic leaves or bird droppings. When disturbed, they evert a fleshy bifid organ, called an osmeterium, above their head that emits noxious volatile compounds, such as butyric acid or terpenoids.

Parnassius apollo

Zerynthia rumina

Papilio alexanor

Archon apollinus

Papilio machaon

PAPILIONIDAE

APOLLO *PARNASSIUS APOLLO*

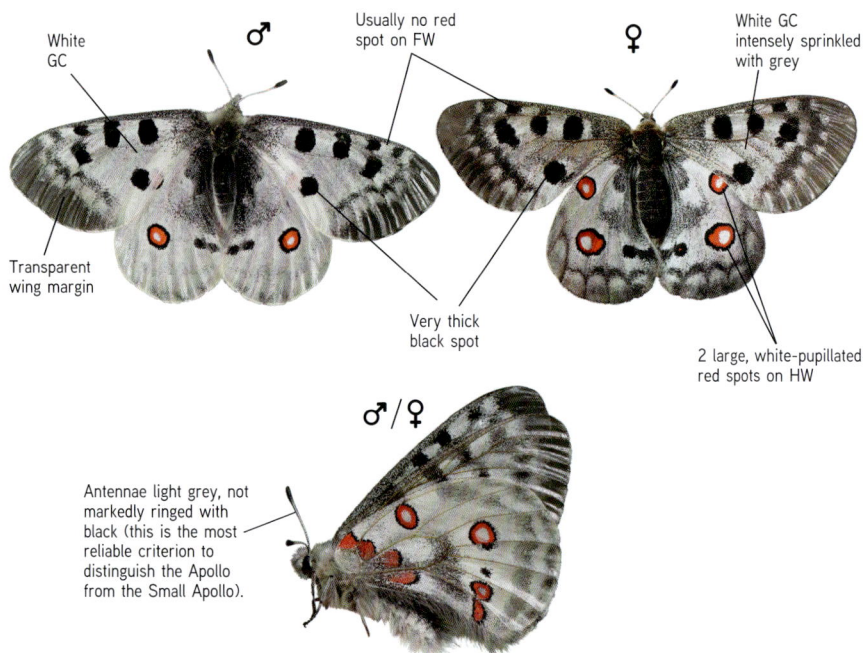

♂

White GC

Usually no red spot on FW

♀

White GC intensely sprinkled with grey

Transparent wing margin

Very thick black spot

2 large, white-pupillated red spots on HW

♂/♀

Antennae light grey, not markedly ringed with black (this is the most reliable criterion to distinguish the Apollo from the Small Apollo).

Wingspan: 62–95 mm

Habitat: Sunny, open, and often rocky, flower-rich mountain slopes.

Hibernating stage: Young caterpillar inside the egg.

Elevational range: Up to 2,500 m (rarely below 1,000 m).

Egg-laying: Eggs are laid singly on stems and leaves of the LHP.

Flight period: From May to September.

Host plants: Crassulaceae, including *Hylotelephium anacampseros, H. maximum, H. telephium, Petrosedum amplexicaule, P. forsterianum, P. montanum,* *P. ochroleucum, P. rupestre, P. sediforme, Rhodiola rosea, Sedum acre, S. album, S. annuum, S. atratum, S. brevifolium, S. dasyphyllum, S. hispanicum, S. sexangulare, S. villosum, Sempervivum arachnoideum, S. montanum,* and *S. tectorum.*

Diversity and systematics: Dozens of subspecies have been described (often several within each massif where the Apollo flies). This high diversity reflects the complex glacial legacy of this mountain species.

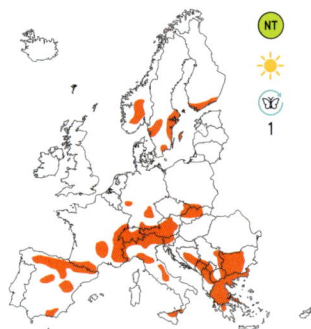

NT

1

Did you know?

The Apollo is an emblematic mountain species. It is currently threatened by habitat loss and climate change, especially at its lowest-elevation boundaries.

IMAGOS		LARVAE	
Food	🌼	Food	🍃🍃
Behaviour of males	🦋	Caterpillar location	▨
Dispersion	🦋	Chrysalis location	▨ 🌿

PAPILIONIDAE

SMALL APOLLO *PARNASSIUS PHOEBUS*

Antennae light grey, markedly ringed with black (this is the most reliable criterion to distinguish the Small Apollo from the Apollo)

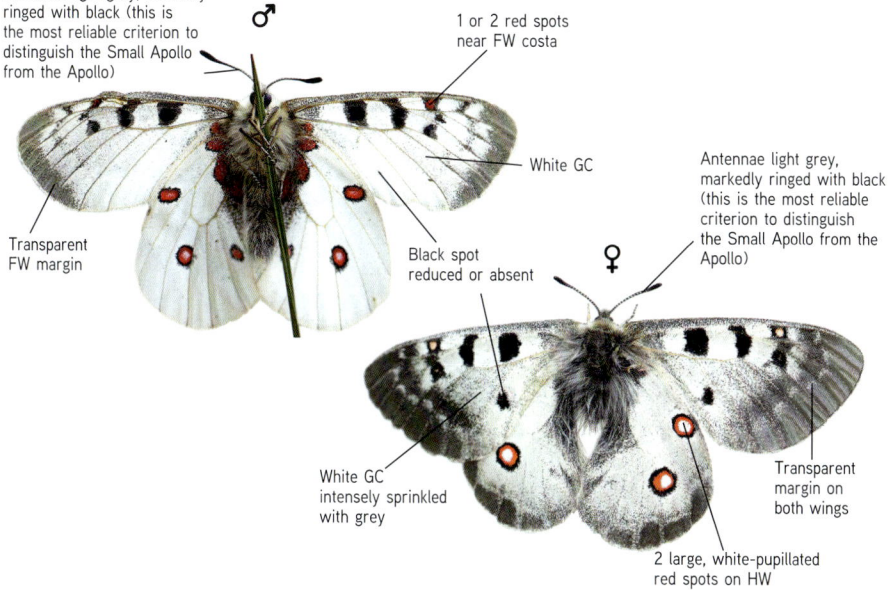

♂

1 or 2 red spots near FW costa

White GC

Antennae light grey, markedly ringed with black (this is the most reliable criterion to distinguish the Small Apollo from the Apollo)

Transparent FW margin

Black spot reduced or absent

♀

White GC intensely sprinkled with grey

Transparent margin on both wings

2 large, white-pupillated red spots on HW

Wingspan: 50–80 mm

Habitat: Alpine and subalpine grasslands and scree, especially along gullies and streams.

Hibernating stage: Young caterpillar inside the egg.

Elevational range: Between 1,500 and 2,800 m.

Egg-laying: Eggs are laid singly on stems of the LHP.

Flight period: From June to August.

Host plants: Mainly *Saxifraga aizoides* and, more rarely, *Rhodiola rosea*.

Diversity and systematics: Europe has several subspecies, including *sacerdos* (Central and French Alps), *gazeli* (southeastern French Alps), *cervinicolus* (Valais), *styriacus* (Styria), and *hansi* (Carinthia).

NT

1

Did you know?

Although morphologically similar to the Apollo, the Small Apollo differs in behaviour, spending a significant amount of time flying in the vicinity of mountain streams where its main LHP grows.

IMAGOS		LARVAE	
Food	✿	Food	🍃
Behaviour of males	🦋	Caterpillar location	🥚 🌿
Dispersion	◉	Chrysalis location	🐛 🌿

PAPILIONIDAE

CLOUDED APOLLO *PARNASSIUS MNEMOSYNE*

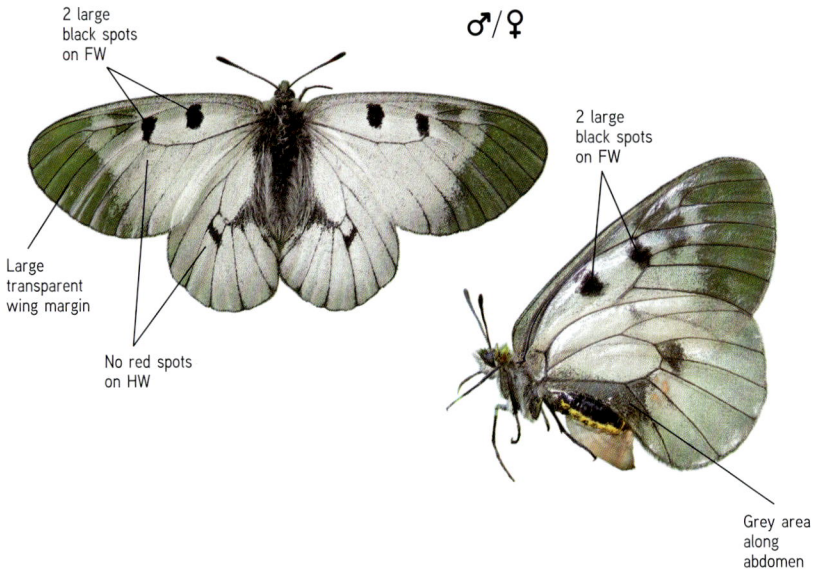

2 large
black spots
on FW

♂/♀

2 large
black spots
on FW

Large
transparent
wing margin

No red spots
on HW

Grey area
along
abdomen

Wingspan: 50–64 mm

Habitat: Flower-rich forest clearings and edges (especially beech woods where the host plants grow), mostly in mountainous and subalpine areas.

Hibernating stage: Young caterpillar inside the egg.

Elevational range: Up to 2,000 m (rare below 1,000 m).

Egg-laying: Eggs are laid singly on dry vegetation in places favourable to the host plants.

Flight period: From April to August.

Host plants: Papaveraceae in genus *Corydalis*, including *C. blanda*, *C. capnoides*, *C. caucasica*, *C. cava*, *C. intermedia*, *C. pumilla*, and *C. solida*, as well as *Pseudofumaria lutea*.

Diversity and systematics: Numerous subspecies have been described. Genetic data suggest the existence of three distinct lineages: in the western Mediterranean region (subspecies *turatii* in Italy, Sicily, the Pyrenees, and southwestern France), in central Europe (nominate subspecies), and in Anatolia (subspecies *adolphi*).

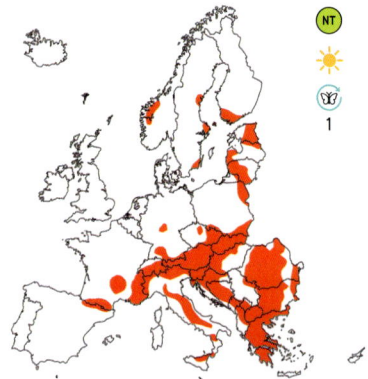

NT

1

IMAGOS		LARVAE	
Food	☆	Food	🍃
Behaviour of males		Caterpillar location	
Dispersion		Chrysalis location	

Did you know?

The Clouded Apollo caterpillars are adapted to the short growing period of their *Corydalis* host plants. They grow rapidly and undergo only three moults.

122

PAPILIONIDAE

FALSE APOLLO *ARCHON APOLLINUS*

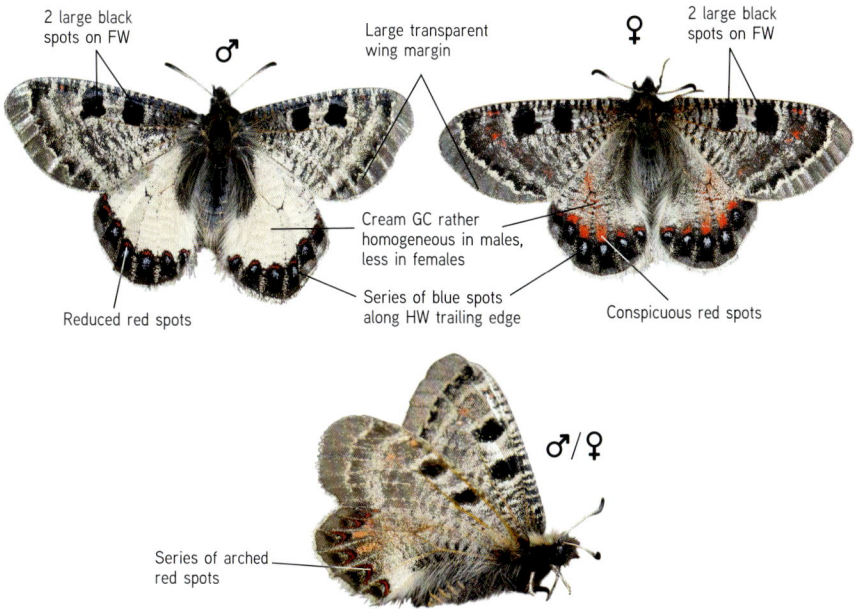

2 large black spots on FW

♂

Large transparent wing margin

♀

2 large black spots on FW

Cream GC rather homogeneous in males, less in females

Reduced red spots

Series of blue spots along HW trailing edge

Conspicuous red spots

♂/♀

Series of arched red spots

Wingspan: 54–60 mm

Habitat: Grassy and extensive agricultural environments (grass-covered vineyards, olive groves, and orchards). Also along roads.

Hibernating stage: Pupa.

Elevational range: Up to 2,000 m, but mainly below 1,000 m in Europe.

Egg-laying: Eggs are laid in small batches of fewer than 15 eggs, most often on ground elements surrounding the host plant, sometimes on its leaves.

Flight period: From late February to early June.

Host plants: Birthworts, mainly *Aristolochia rotunda*, *A. hirta*, *A. pallida*, *A. parviflora*, and *A. clematitis*.

Diversity and systematics: European populations belong to the nominate subspecies.

NT

1

Did you know?

Agricultural intensification is the main threat to the False Apollo. Its LHPs often suffer from herbicide spraying.

IMAGOS			LARVAE		
Food	🌼		Food	🌼 🍃	
Behaviour of males	🌸 🦋		Caterpillar location	🌿	
Dispersion	🦋		Chrysalis location	🐚	

PAPILIONIDAE

SPANISH FESTOON *ZERYNTHIA RUMINA*

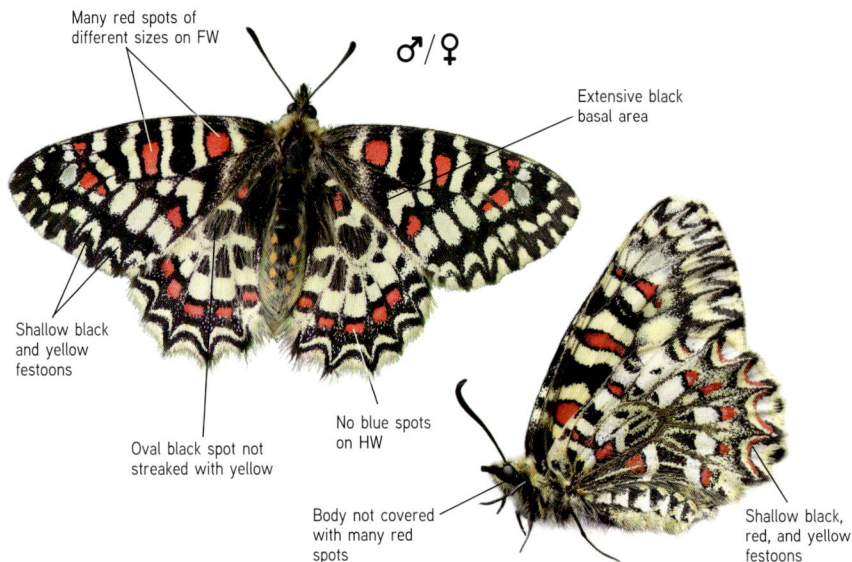

Many red spots of
different sizes on FW

♂/♀

Extensive black
basal area

Shallow black
and yellow
festoons

Oval black spot not
streaked with yellow

No blue spots
on HW

Body not covered
with many red
spots

Shallow black,
red, and yellow
festoons

Wingspan: 44–46 mm

Habitat: Dry, flower-rich grasslands, Mediterranean scrubland, and sunny woodland edges.

Hibernating stage: Pupa.

Elevational range: Up to 1,500 m.

Egg-laying: Eggs are laid singly or in very small batches (a few units) on any aerial part of the LHP.

Flight period: From February to November (when a single generation occurs, only until June).

Host plants: Birthworts, mainly *Aristolochia pistolochia*. Also *A. baetica* in southern Spain. Rarely *A. clematitis, A. rotunda, A. pallida*, and *A. paucinervis*.

Diversity and systematics: Several subspecies have been described, including *rumina* (southwestern part of the Iberian Peninsula), *medesicaste* (northwestern Spain, southern France, and northern Italy), *castiliana* (central Spain), and *petheri* (Sierra Nevada).

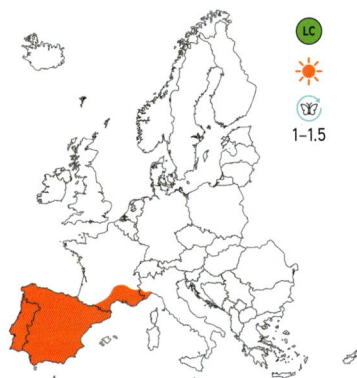

LC

1–1.5

IMAGOS		LARVAE	
Food	✿	Food	✿ 🌿
Behaviour of males	🦋	Caterpillar location	🐛 🌱
Dispersion	✲	Chrysalis location	🛡 🌱

Did you know?

To some extent, Mediterranean fires favour the Spanish Festoon because they keep habitats open in the form of grasslands; in the past, grazing sheep performed this function.

PAPILIONIDAE

SOUTHERN FESTOON *ZERYNTHIA POLYXENA*

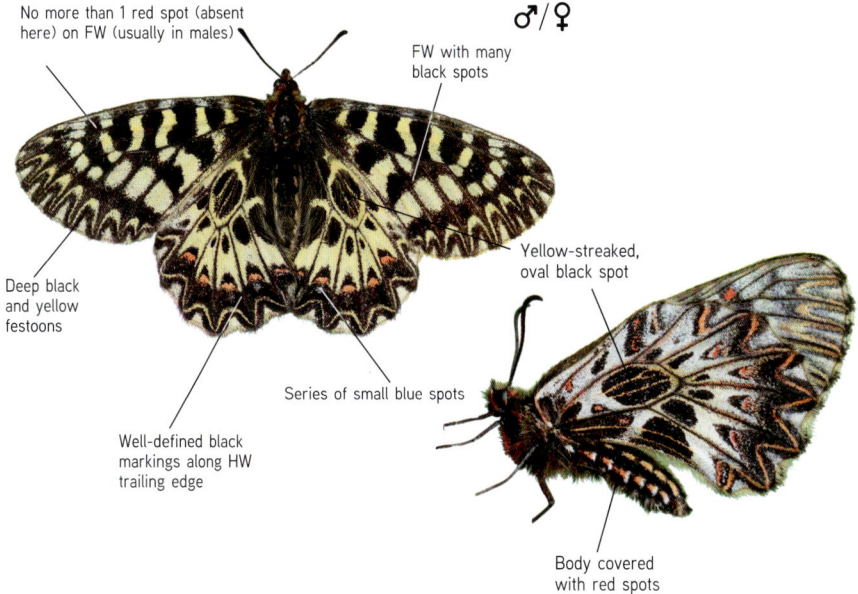

♂/♀

No more than 1 red spot (absent here) on FW (usually in males)

FW with many black spots

Deep black and yellow festoons

Yellow-streaked, oval black spot

Series of small blue spots

Well-defined black markings along HW trailing edge

Body covered with red spots

Wingspan: 46–52 mm

Habitat: A large variety of Mediterranean habitats, including grasslands, grassy garrigue, cultivated land surroundings, damp ditches, and woodland edges.

Hibernating stage: Pupa.

Elevational range: Up to 1,500 m, but mostly at low elevations.

Egg-laying: Eggs are laid singly or in very small batches (a few units), mainly on the LHP leaves.

Flight period: From March to June.

Host plants: Birthworts, especially *Aristolochia clematitis* and *A. rotunda*; more rarely, *A. pistolochia, A. pallida, A. microstoma, A. nardiana, A. paucinervis,* and *A. sempervirens.*

Diversity and systematics: The nominate subspecies *polyxena* populates the majority of the focal area, while subspecies *deminuta* is found in western Mediterranean Europe, especially in the south of France.

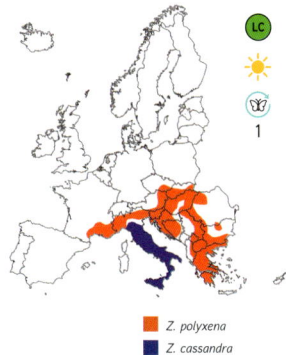

LC

1

■ *Z. polyxena*
■ *Z. cassandra*

Did you know?

The caterpillars of the Southern Festoon die if fed with another birthwort species than that on which they have started growing. The toxins produced by these plants may indeed be slightly different.

IMAGOS		LARVAE	
Food	☆	Food	☆ 🌿
Behaviour of males	🦋	Caterpillar location	🌿
Dispersion		Chrysalis location	🌿

PAPILIONIDAE

ITALIAN FESTOON *ZERYNTHIA CASSANDRA*

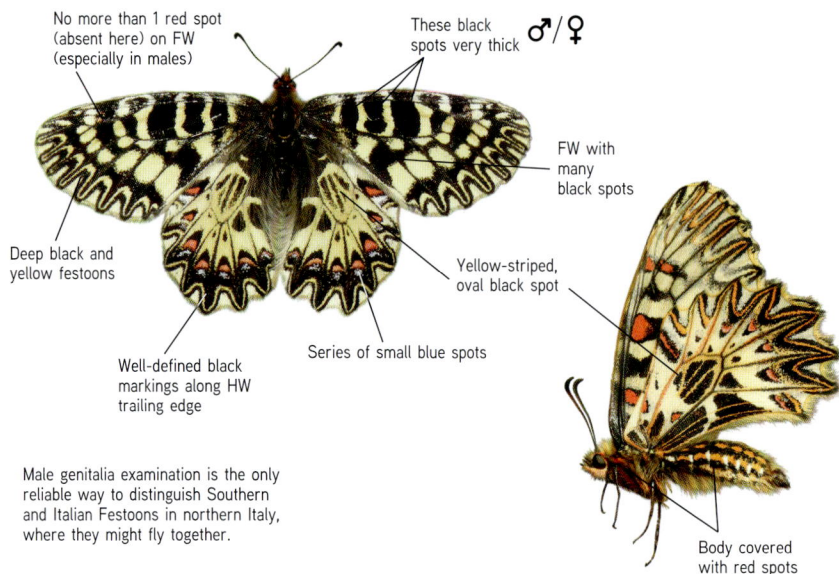

No more than 1 red spot (absent here) on FW (especially in males)

These black spots very thick ♂/♀

FW with many black spots

Deep black and yellow festoons

Yellow-striped, oval black spot

Well-defined black markings along HW trailing edge

Series of small blue spots

Male genitalia examination is the only reliable way to distinguish Southern and Italian Festoons in northern Italy, where they might fly together.

Body covered with red spots

Wingspan: 46–52 mm

Habitat: Farmland surroundings, wet ditches, and riverine areas where the LHP grows.

Hibernating stage: Pupa.

Elevational range: Up to 1,500 m, but mostly at low elevations.

Egg-laying: Eggs are laid singly or in very small batches (a few units), mainly on the LHP leaves.

Flight period: From March to June.

Host plants: Birthworts, including *Aristolochia rotunda*, *A. lutea*, *A. pallida*, *A. pistolochia*, and *A. clematitis*.

Diversity and systematics: The Italian Festoon has long been considered a subspecies of the Southern Festoon. However, despite slightly overlapping ranges, the genitalia are different, supporting the status of *Z. cassandra* as a distinct species.

LC

1

■ *Z. polyxena*
■ *Z. cassandra*

Did you know?

Its strong dispersal abilities (several km) are crucial to the survival of the Italian Festoon because it breeds in highly fragmented microhabitats where its LHPs grow.

IMAGOS		LARVAE	
Food	🌸	Food	🍃
Behaviour of males		Caterpillar location	🌿
Dispersion		Chrysalis location	🌿

PAPILIONIDAE

EASTERN FESTOON   *ZERYNTHIA CERISY*

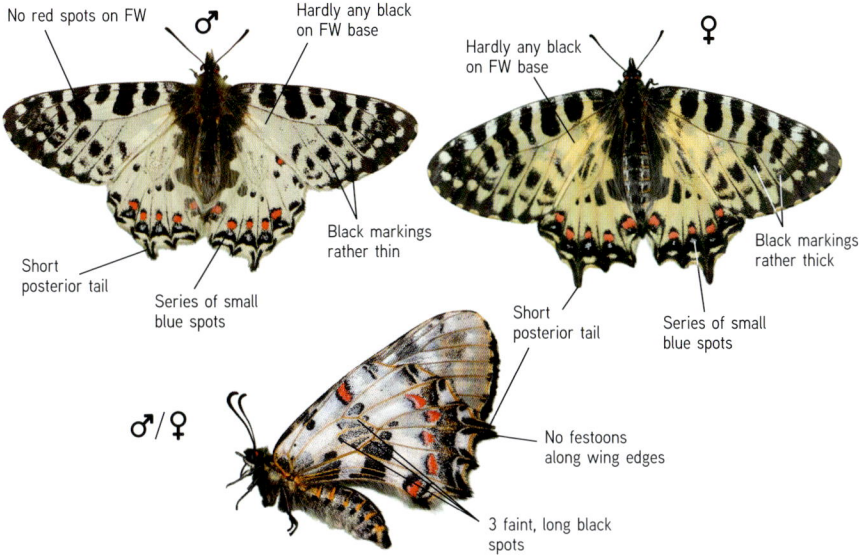

No red spots on FW

♂

Hardly any black
on FW base

Hardly any black
on FW base

♀

Black markings
rather thin

Short
posterior tail

Series of small
blue spots

Black markings
rather thick

Short
posterior tail

Series of small
blue spots

♂/♀

No festoons
along wing edges

3 faint, long black
spots

Wingspan: 52–62 mm

Habitat: Dry grasslands, extensively cultivated lands such as olive groves or vineyards, roadsides, and riverine habitats.

Hibernating stage: Pupa.

Elevational range: Up to 1,500 m (mostly at low elevations).

Egg-laying: Eggs are laid singly or in very small batches (a few units), mainly under LHP leaves.

Flight period: From March to July.

Host plants: Birthworts, mainly *Aristolochia clematitis*, *A. hirta*, *A. rotunda*, *A. guichardii*, *A. parvifolia*, and *A. sempervirens*.

Diversity and systematics: Most European populations belong to subspecies *ferdinandi*. Subspecies *cypria* and *martini* fly in Cyprus and Rhodes, respectively.

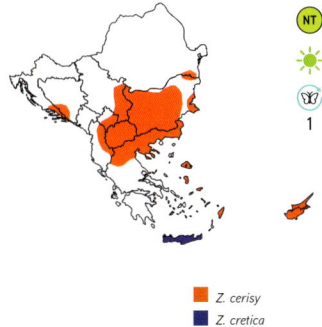

NT

1

■ Z. cerisy
■ Z. cretica

Did you know?

As with other European festoons, the Eastern Festoon's caterpillars are highly aposematic. Their vivid colours warn their predators about their toxicity due to the aristolochic acids they get from their LHPs.

IMAGOS		LARVAE	
Food	✿	Food	🍃
Behaviour of males	🦋	Caterpillar location	🌱
Dispersion	✵	Chrysalis location	🌿

PAPILIONIDAE

CRETAN FESTOON *ZERYNTHIA CRETICA*

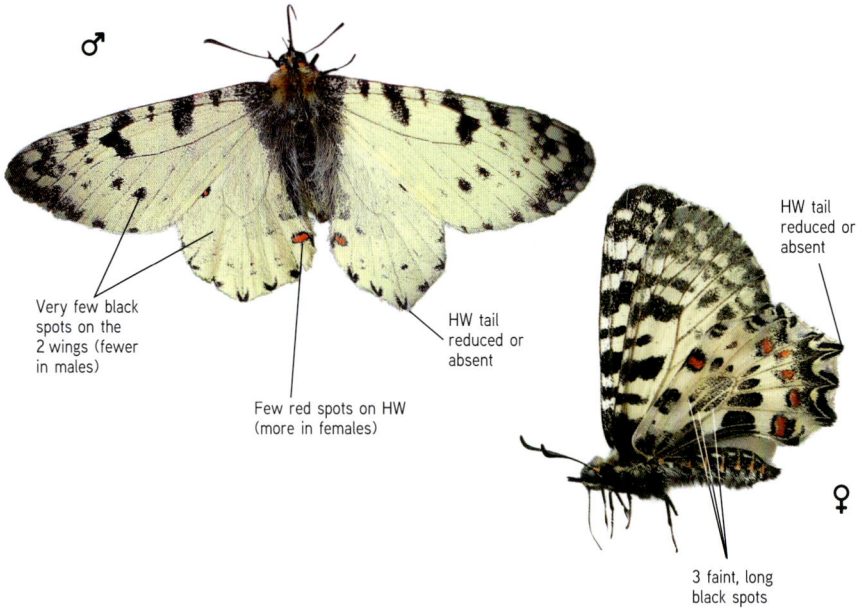

♂

Very few black spots on the 2 wings (fewer in males)

HW tail reduced or absent

Few red spots on HW (more in females)

HW tail reduced or absent

3 faint, long black spots

♀

Wingspan: 50–55 mm

Habitat: Mediterranean scrubland (garrigue and maquis), as well as rocky dry grasslands.

Hibernating stage: Pupa.

Elevational range: Up to 1,500 m.

Egg-laying: Eggs are laid singly or in very small batches (a few units), mainly on the LHP leaves.

Flight period: From February to June.

Host plants: Birthworts, mainly *Aristolochia sempervirens* and *A. cretica*.

Diversity and systematics: The Cretan Festoon was once considered a subspecies of the very similar Eastern Festoon (*Z. cerisy*). There is no notable subspecies for this Cretan endemic species.

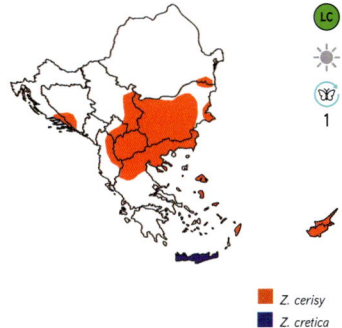

LC

1

■ *Z. cerisy*
■ *Z. cretica*

IMAGOS		LARVAE	
Food	✿	Food	✿ 🍃 🌿
Behaviour of males	🦋	Caterpillar location	🌿
Dispersion	🦋	Chrysalis location	🌿

Did you know?

Cretan Festoons are far more active in the morning before the temperature rises to unbearable levels. They then seek shelter and are much trickier to locate.

PAPILIONIDAE

SOUTHERN SWALLOWTAIL *PAPILIO ALEXANOR*

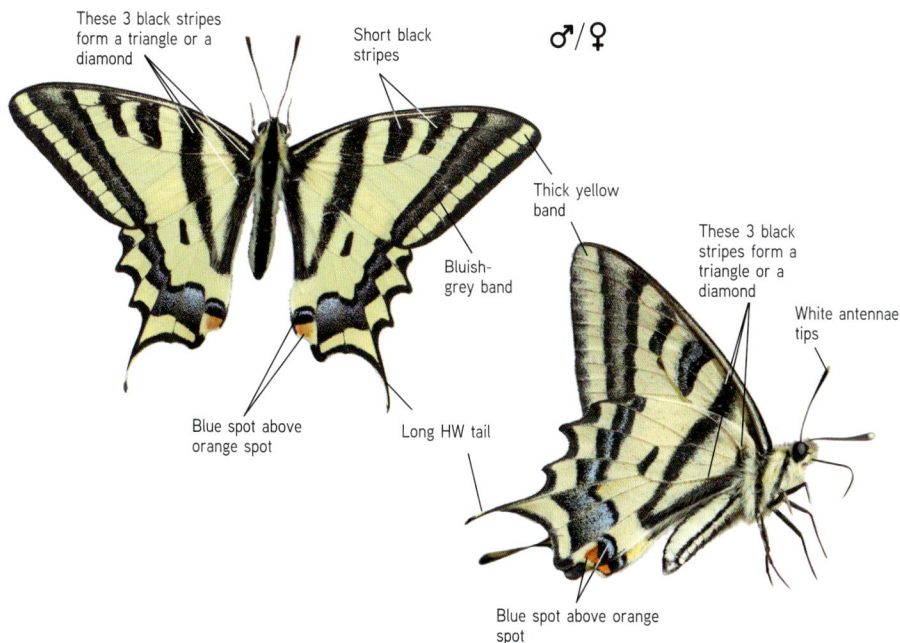

These 3 black stripes form a triangle or a diamond

Short black stripes

♂/♀

Thick yellow band

Bluish-grey band

These 3 black stripes form a triangle or a diamond

White antennae tips

Blue spot above orange spot

Long HW tail

Blue spot above orange spot

Wingspan: 62–66 mm

Habitat: Sunny, rocky slopes and poorly vegetated roadsides at early successional stages.

Hibernating stage: Pupa.

Elevational range: Up to 1,500 m (mostly at lower elevations).

Egg-laying: Eggs are laid singly on LHP leaves or inflorescences.

Flight period: From April to July.

Host plants: Apiaceae, mainly *Ptychotis saxifraga, Opopanax chironium,* and *O. hispidus.* Sometimes also *Ferula communis, Foeniculum vulgare, Falcaria vulgaris, Pastinaca sativa, Scaligeria napiformis, Seseli montanum,* and *Trinia glauca.*

Diversity and systematics: Most European populations belong to the nominate subspecies. The very rare *destelensis* subspecies might still fly near Toulon, France. Subspecies *eitschbergeri* is endemic to Samos and Lesbos.

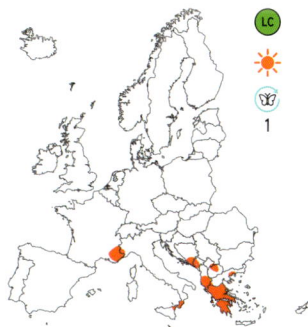

LC

1

IMAGOS		LARVAE	
Food	☆	Food	☆ 🌿
Behaviour of males		Caterpillar location	
Dispersion		Chrysalis location	

Did you know?

The Southern Swallowtails spend the night in small groups perched on flowers with their wings wide open. A real delight for photographers arriving at the end of the afternoon!

PAPILIONIDAE

SCARCE SWALLOWTAIL *IPHICLIDES PODALIRIUS*

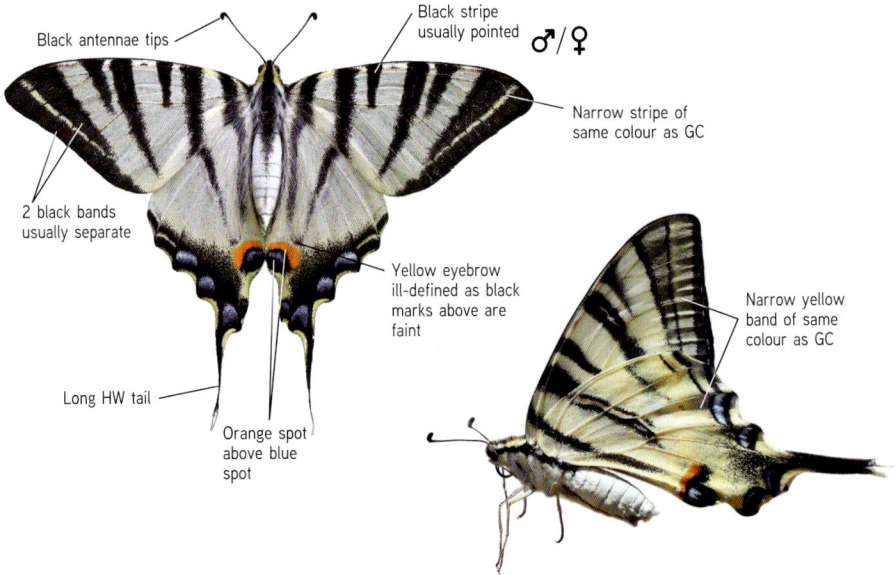

Black antennae tips

Black stripe usually pointed

♂/♀

Narrow stripe of same colour as GC

2 black bands usually separate

Yellow eyebrow ill-defined as black marks above are faint

Narrow yellow band of same colour as GC

Long HW tail

Orange spot above blue spot

Wingspan: 60–90 mm

Habitat: Scrubland, bushy grasslands, bocage, orchards, and gardens.

Hibernating stage: Pupa.

Elevational range: Up to 2,000 m (far more abundant at lower elevations).

Egg-laying: Eggs are laid singly on LHP leaves.

Flight period: From March to October.

Host plants: Numerous woody Rosaceae, including *Prunus mahaleb, P. spinosa, P. amygdalus, P. armeniaca, P. avium, P. cerasifera, P. cocomilia, P. domestica, P. padus, P. persica, P. serotina, Crataegus monogyna, C. laevigata, C. rhipidophylla, Cotoneaster horizontalis, Pyrus communis, P. bourgaeana, P. cordata, P. spinosa,* and *Sorbus aucuparia.*

Diversity and systematics: The nominate subspecies flies across Europe, although many forms have been described.

LC

1–3

■ *I. podalirius*   ■ *I. feisthamelii*   ■ *I. podalirius + I. feisthamelii*

IMAGOS		LARVAE	
Food	🌼🐌💧	Food	🍃
Behaviour of males		Caterpillar location	
Dispersion		Chrysalis location	

Did you know?

Male Scarce Swallowtails often gather at hill-topping sites like sunny ridges, where they squabble while waiting for passing females.

PAPILIONIDAE

IBERIAN SCARCE SWALLOWTAIL *IPHICLIDES FEISTHAMELII*

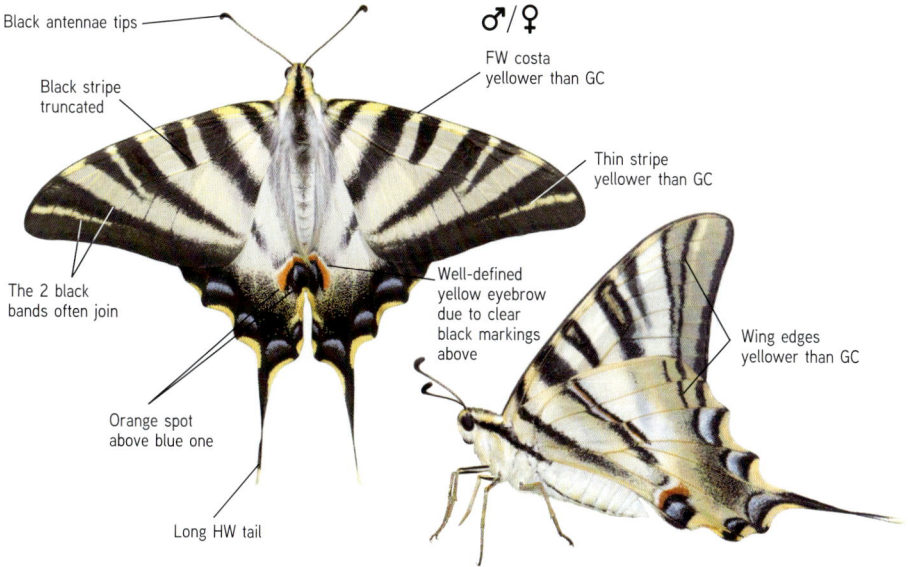

♂/♀

Black antennae tips

FW costa yellower than GC

Black stripe truncated

Thin stripe yellower than GC

The 2 black bands often join

Well-defined yellow eyebrow due to clear black markings above

Wing edges yellower than GC

Orange spot above blue one

Long HW tail

Wingspan: 60–90 mm

Habitat: Sunny and flower-rich Mediterranean scrubland, like garrigue, rocky slopes, and orchards.

Hibernating stage: Pupa

Elevational range: Up to 2,500 m (more abundant below 1,500 m).

Egg-laying: Eggs are laid singly on LHP leaves.

Flight period: From March to October.

Host plants: Woody Rosaceae, including *Prunus mahaleb, P. spinosa, P. amygdalus, P. armeniaca, P. avium, P. cerasifera, P. domestica, P. padus, P. persica, P. spinosa, Crataegus monogyna, C. laevigata, Pyrus communis, P. bourgaeana, P. cordata, P. spinosa,* and *Sorbus aucuparia.*

Diversity and systematics: The nominate subspecies flies across the Iberian Peninsula, reaching the French Oriental Pyrenees and Aude. Once considered a subspecies of the Scarce Swallowtail, the Iberian Scarce Swallowtail is now treated as a distinct species. The genitalia differ, and the two species fly together at a few French sites, where they don't appear to hybridize.

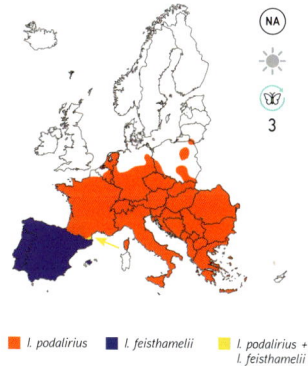

NA

3

■ *I. podalirius* ■ *I. feisthamelii* ■ *I. podalirius + I. feisthamelii*

Did you know?

The mature caterpillars of both the Scarce Swallowtail and the Iberian Scarce Swallowtail are remarkably cryptic. They look like the leaves of the LHP, mimicking their ribs and even their small, orange rust spots.

IMAGOS		LARVAE	
Food		Food	
Behaviour of males		Caterpillar location	
Dispersion		Chrysalis location	

PAPILIONIDAE

SWALLOWTAIL *PAPILIO MACHAON*

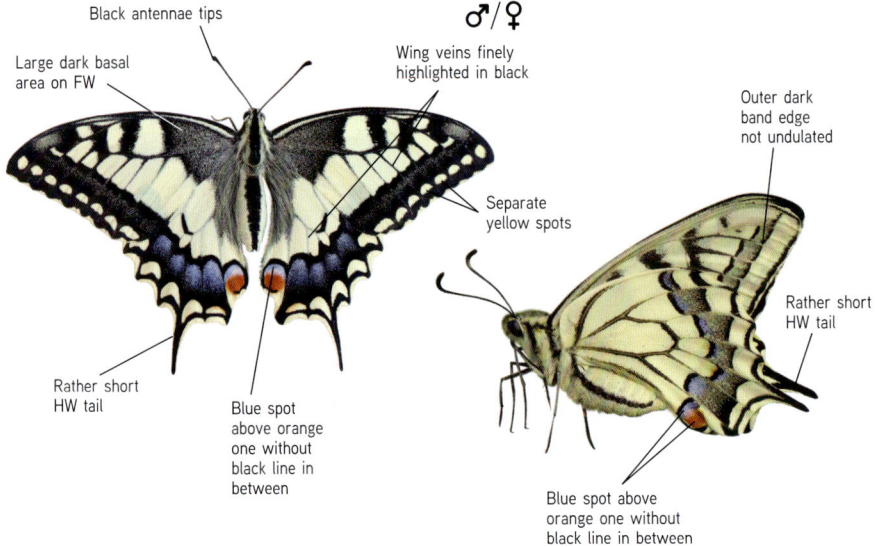

♂/♀

Black antennae tips

Large dark basal area on FW

Wing veins finely highlighted in black

Outer dark band edge not undulated

Separate yellow spots

Rather short HW tail

Rather short HW tail

Blue spot above orange one without black line in between

Blue spot above orange one without black line in between

Wingspan: 60–90 mm

Habitat: A wide variety of open or bushy habitats, including grasslands, scrublands, parks, and gardens.

Hibernating stage: Pupa.

Elevational range: Up to 3,000 m for the adults (but mostly at lower elevations).

Egg-laying: Eggs are laid singly on LHP leaves.

Flight period: From February to October.

Host plants: Most Apiaceae, including species of genera *Aegopodium, Ammi, Anethum, Angelica, Apium, Athamanta, Berula, Bupleurum, Carum, Conium, Coriandrum, Crithmum, Daucus, Dichoropetalum, Eryngium, Ferula, Foeniculum, Glaucosciadium,* *Heracleum, Kadenia, Laserpitium, Levisticum, Ligusticum, Meum, Oenanthe, Opopanax, Orlaya, Pastinaca, Petroselinum, Peucedanum, Pimpinella, Ridolfia, Scaligeria, Seseli, Silaum, Siler,* and *Sison.* Also some Rutaceae, like *Dichtamnus albus, Ruta angustifolia, R. graveolens, R. chalepensis,* and *R. montana.*

Diversity and systematics: Most European populations belong to the nominate subspecies, although many others have been described. Subspecies *britannicus* flies in the northeastern UK, while subspecies *phyrus* is found in Sicily, where the presence of *P. saharae* (differing from *P. machaon* only by the genitalia) is debated.

LC

1–3

■ *P. machaon* ■ *P. machaon + P. hospiton*

Did you know?

Young Swallowtail caterpillars resemble small bird droppings before they change to aposematic colours. This mimicry holds true for other swallowtail species.

IMAGOS			LARVAE		
Food			Food		
Behaviour of males			Caterpillar location		
Dispersion			Chrysalis location		

PAPILIONIDAE

CORSICAN SWALLOWTAIL *PAPILIO HOSPITON*

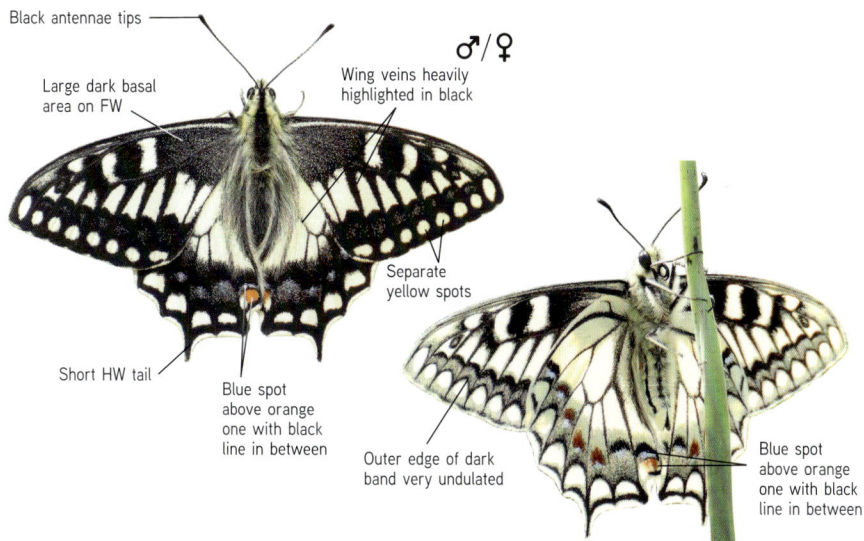

Black antennae tips

Large dark basal area on FW

Wing veins heavily highlighted in black

♂/♀

Separate yellow spots

Short HW tail

Blue spot above orange one with black line in between

Outer edge of dark band very undulated

Blue spot above orange one with black line in between

Wingspan: 58–68 mm

Habitat: Dry and rocky Mediterranean habitats, such as stony slopes, garrigues, and maquis.

Hibernating stage: Pupa.

Elevational range: Up to 2,000 m (only rarely above 1,500 m).

Egg-laying: Eggs are laid singly on LHP leaves.

Flight period: From May to July.

Host plants: Tall Apiaceae, such as *Ferula communis, Peucedanum paniculatum,* and *Pastinaca sativa.* Also *Ruta corsica* (Rutaceae).

Diversity and systematics: There are no notable subspecies for this Corsican and Sardinian endemic species. It can hybridize with the Swallowtail. Such hybrids count for a few percent of the *Papilio* butterflies encountered in Corsica.

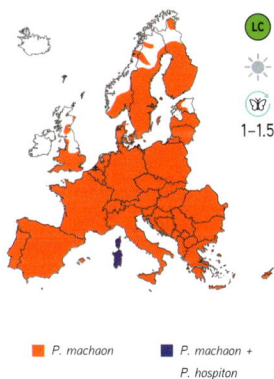

LC

1–1.5

■ *P. machaon*   ■ *P. machaon + P. hospiton*

Did you know?

Because it is toxic, sheep avoid eating Giant Fennel, which is the main Corsican Swallowtail LHP. Nevertheless, its local eradication by herbicide use or weeding can threaten this wonderful butterfly.

IMAGOS			LARVAE		
Food			Food		
Behaviour of males			Caterpillar location		
Dispersion			Chrysalis location		

THE SKIPPERS (49 SPECIES)

SUBFAMILIES	GENERA	NUMBER OF SPECIES	MAIN LARVAL HOST-PLANT FAMILIES
Heteropterinae	*Heteropterus* and *Carterocephalus*	3	Poaceae
Hesperiinae	*Borbo, Gegenes, Hesperia, Ochlodes, Pelopidas,* and *Thymelicus*	11	Poaceae, Cyperaceae, and Juncaceae
Pyrginae	*Carcharodus, Erynnis, Favria, Muschampia, Pyrgus,* and *Spialia*	35	Malvaceae, Rosaceae, Fabaceae, Lamiaceae, Convolvulaceae, and Cistaceae

Skippers are small butterflies usually with hooked antennal clubs. The Hesperids comprise approximately 3,500 species worldwide, with the highest diversity found at lower latitudes. While the background colours of European skippers are grey, brown, or orange, some tropical species display truly remarkable and often iridescent markings. The flight of these butterflies is often fast and close to the ground. Males typically exhibit a marked territorial behaviour. Skipper caterpillars are usually inconspicuous. The distinctive constriction of the body between the head and thorax gives the impression of a well-developed cephalic capsule. Most of them build a shelter to rest and pupate, using spun leaves from their host plant.

Pyrgus cirsii

Carcharodus alceae

Thymelicus sylvestris

Carterocephalus silvicola

Gegenes pumilio

HESPERIIDAE

CHEQUERED SKIPPER *CARTEROCEPHALUS PALAEMON*

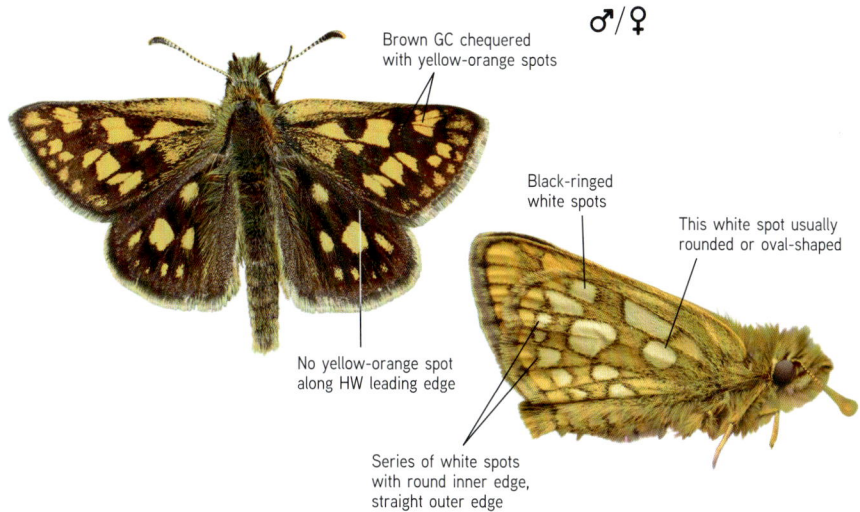

♂/♀

Brown GC chequered
with yellow-orange spots

Black-ringed
white spots

This white spot usually
rounded or oval-shaped

No yellow-orange spot
along HW leading edge

Series of white spots
with round inner edge,
straight outer edge

Wingspan: 23–30 mm

Habitat: Grassy and often damp habitats mostly within woodlands (clearings, forest edges, moorland surroundings).

Hibernating stage: Caterpillar.

Elevational range: Up to 2,000 m (mostly below 1,500 m).

Egg-laying: Eggs are laid singly on the LHP leaves.

Flight period: From April to July.

Host plants: A wide range of grasses, including *Molinia caerulea, M. arundinacea, Calamagrostis canescens, C. epigejos, C. villosa, Cynosurus cristatus, Dactylis glomerata, Digitaria sanguinalis, Elymus repens, Holcus lanatus, Bromus ramosus, Alopecurus pratensis, Brachypodium sylvaticum, B. pinnatum, Lolium giganteum, L. pratense, Milium effusum, Phalaris arundinacea, Phleum pratense, Phragmites australis,* and *Poa pratensis.*

Diversity and systematics: European populations belong to the nominate subspecies. Many forms have been described that attest to significant intraspecific variability.

LC

1

IMAGOS		LARVAE	
Food	✿	Food	🍃
Behaviour of males		Caterpillar location	🌾
Dispersion		Chrysalis location	🌱

Did you know?

Forty years after disappearing from England due to unfavourable forest management, the Chequered Skipper was successfully reintroduced in 2018.

HESPERIIDAE

NORTHERN CHEQUERED SKIPPER *CARTEROCEPHALUS SILVICOLA*

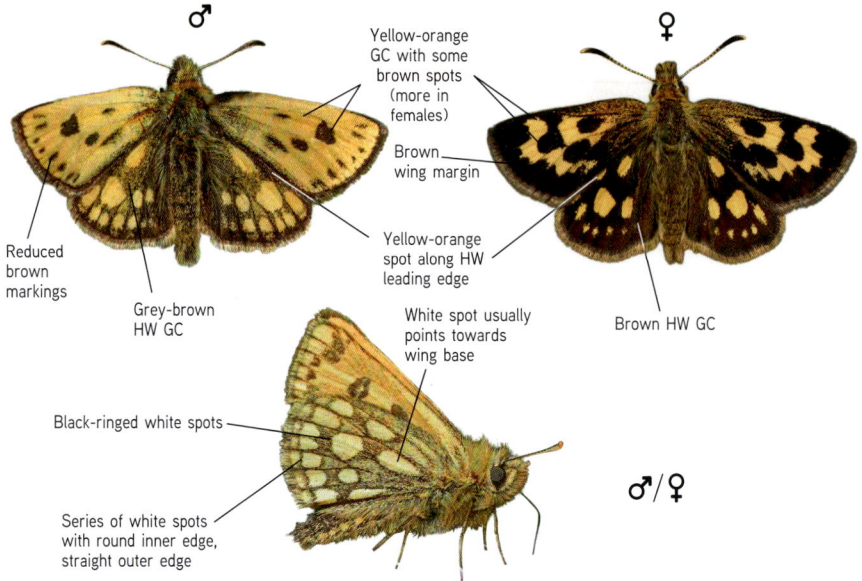

♂

Yellow-orange GC with some brown spots (more in females)

Brown wing margin

Yellow-orange spot along HW leading edge

♀

Reduced brown markings

Grey-brown HW GC

White spot usually points towards wing base

Brown HW GC

Black-ringed white spots

Series of white spots with round inner edge, straight outer edge

♂/♀

Wingspan: 22–28 mm

Habitat: Swamp forest edges, clearings, and pathsides.

Hibernating stage: Caterpillar.

Elevational range: Up to 500 m.

Egg-laying: Eggs are laid singly on the LHP leaves.

Flight period: From May to August.

Host plants: Forest grasses, such as *Calamagrostis canescens, C. arundinacea, Cynosurus cristatus, Phalaris arundinacea, Dactylis glomerata, Brachypodium pinnatum, B. sylvaticum, Milium effusum, Molinia caerulea*, and *Phalaris arundinacea*.

Diversity and systematics: This northern European species has no notable subspecies.

LC

1

IMAGOS		LARVAE	
Food		Food	
Behaviour of males		Caterpillar location	
Dispersion		Chrysalis location	

Did you know?

Adult Northern Chequered Skippers are very keen on the nectar of forest cranesbills, such as the Woodland Geranium.

HESPERIIDAE

LARGE CHEQUERED SKIPPER *HETEROPTERUS MORPHEUS*

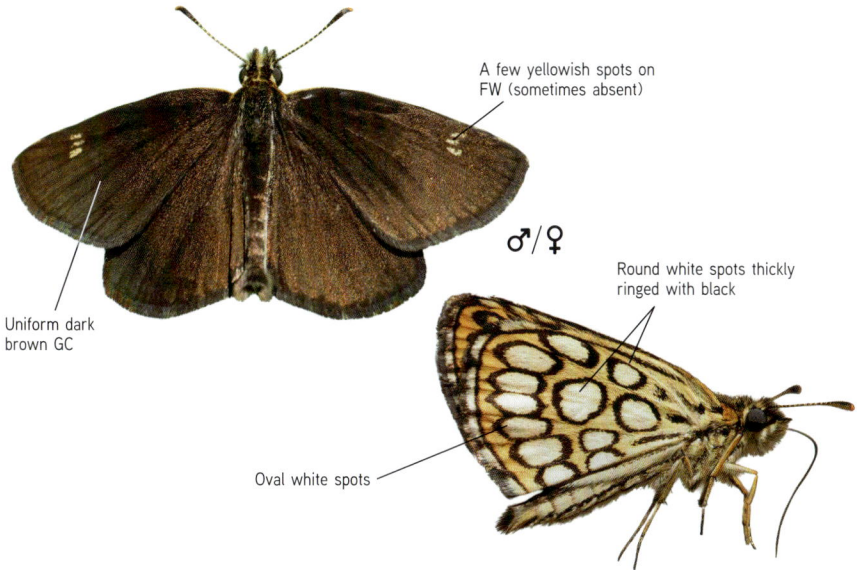

A few yellowish spots on FW (sometimes absent)

♂/♀

Round white spots thickly ringed with black

Uniform dark brown GC

Oval white spots

Wingspan: 30–37 mm

Habitat: Sheltered mesophilic or more humid grassy habitats, edges, clearings, and borders of roads and grassy paths. Extensively grazed meadows and peat bogs.

Hibernating stage: Caterpillar.

Elevational range: Up to 1,500 m (mostly at lower elevations).

Egg-laying: Eggs are laid singly or in very small batches (a few units) on the LHP leaves.

Flight period: From May to August.

Host plants: Grasses, mainly *Molinia caerulea* and *Calamagrostis canescens*. Sometimes also *Brachypodium sylvaticum*, *Phragmites australis*, and *Phalaris arundinacea*.

Diversity and systematics: Despite a disjunct range, European populations belong to the nominate subspecies. The described forms mainly correspond to more or less marked yellowish spots on the wings.

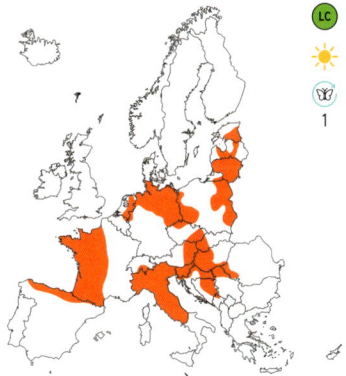

LC

1

IMAGOS		LARVAE	
Food	🌼 💧	Food	🍃
Behaviour of males		Caterpillar location	🌾
Dispersion		Chrysalis location	🌾

Did you know?

The French vernacular name, Mirror, comes from the hopping flight of the Large Chequered Skipper, whose wingbeats reveal, alternately, its dark side and its underside, which appears bright.

HESPERIIDAE

LEVANTINE SKIPPER *THYMELICUS HYRAX*

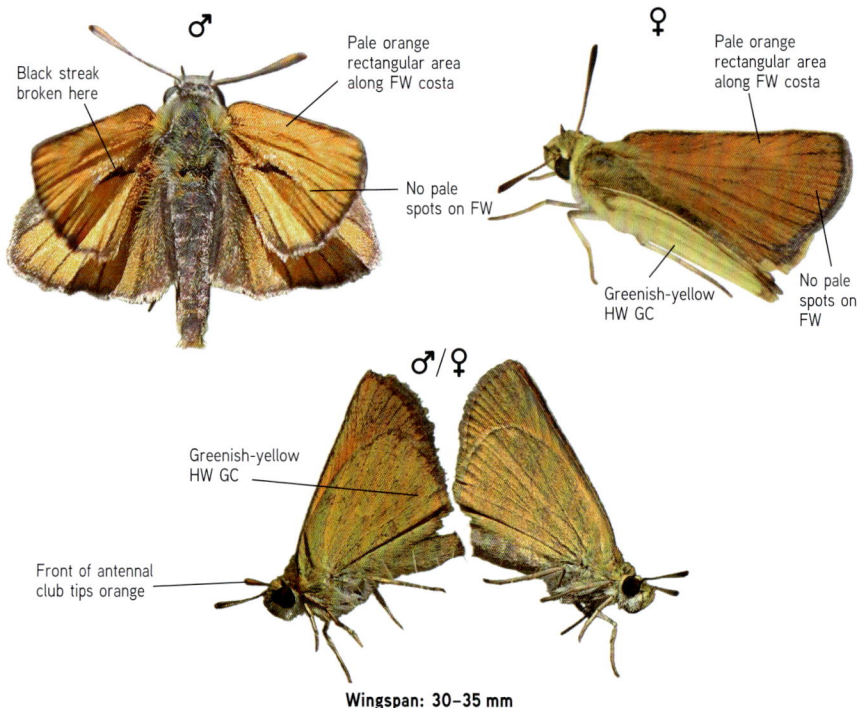

♂

Black streak broken here

Pale orange rectangular area along FW costa

No pale spots on FW

♀

Pale orange rectangular area along FW costa

Greenish-yellow HW GC

No pale spots on FW

♂/♀

Greenish-yellow HW GC

Front of antennal club tips orange

Wingspan: 30–35 mm

Habitat: Dry grasslands, garrigue, maquis, and open, stony Mediterranean woodlands.

Hibernating stage: Caterpillar.

Elevational range: Up to 2,000 m.

Egg-laying: Eggs are laid singly on the LHP leaves.

Flight period: From May to July.

Host plants: Grasses, including *Achnatherum bromoides* and *Oloptum miliaceum*.

Diversity and systematics: There are no notable subspecies for this Middle Eastern skipper.

IMAGOS		LARVAE	
Food	☆	Food	🍃
Behaviour of males		Caterpillar location	🌿
Dispersion		Chrysalis location	🌿

Did you know?

Males usually perch conspicuously in sunny places to watch over their territory, while females favour sheltered places to lay their eggs.

HESPERIIDAE

ESSEX SKIPPER *THYMELICUS LINEOLA*

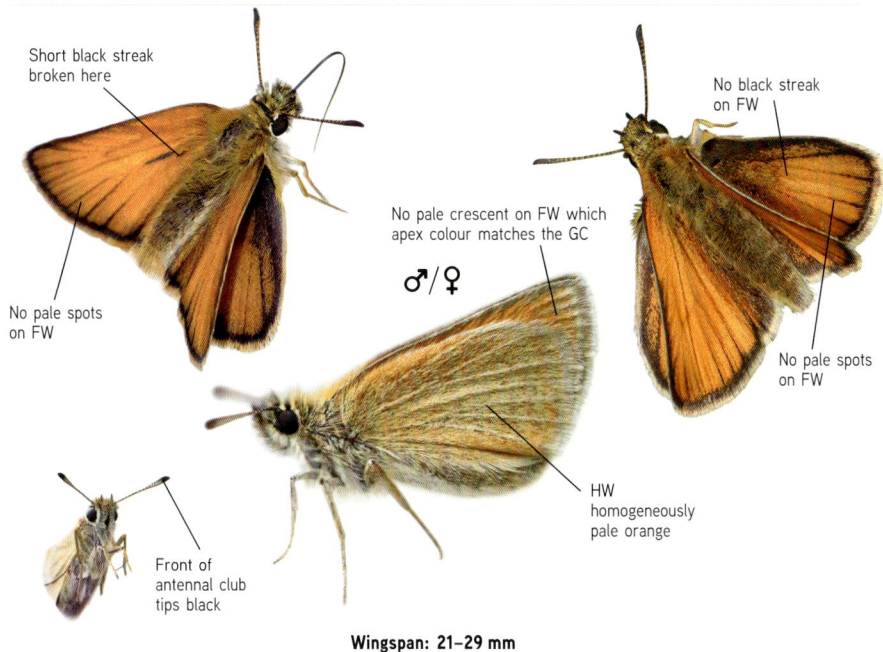

Short black streak
broken here

No black streak
on FW

No pale crescent on FW which
apex colour matches the GC

♂/♀

No pale spots
on FW

No pale spots
on FW

HW
homogeneously
pale orange

Front of
antennal club
tips black

Wingspan: 21–29 mm

Habitat: Hay and subalpine meadows, fallow lands, grassy edges and clearings.

Hibernating stage: Caterpillar inside the egg.

Elevational range: Up to 2,500 m.

Egg-laying: Eggs are laid in small batches along LHP leaves.

Flight period: From May to September.

Host plants: Numerous grasses, including *Agrostis capillaris, Alopecurus pratensis, Anthoxanthum odoratum, Arrhenatherum elatius, Avenella flexuosa, Brachypodium phoenicoides, B. pinnatum, B. sylvaticum, Bromus erectus, B. hordeaceus, B. racemosus, B. sterilis, Calamagrostis epigejos, Cynosurus cristatus, Dactylis glomerata, Festuca ovina, Lolium perenne, L. pratense, Phleum pratense, Poa pratensis, Elymus repens, Holcus lanatus, H. mollis,* and *Thinopyrum intermedium.* Also *Carex acutiformis* (Cyperaceae).

Diversity and systematics: European populations belong to the nominate subspecies.

LC

1

IMAGOS		LARVAE	
Food	🌼 💧	Food	🍃
Behaviour of males		Caterpillar location	🌿
Dispersion		Chrysalis location	🌿

Did you know?

The Essex Skipper was introduced in North America in 1910. Its caterpillars cause damage to hay-producing meadows.

HESPERIIDAE

SMALL SKIPPER *THYMELICUS SYLVESTRIS*

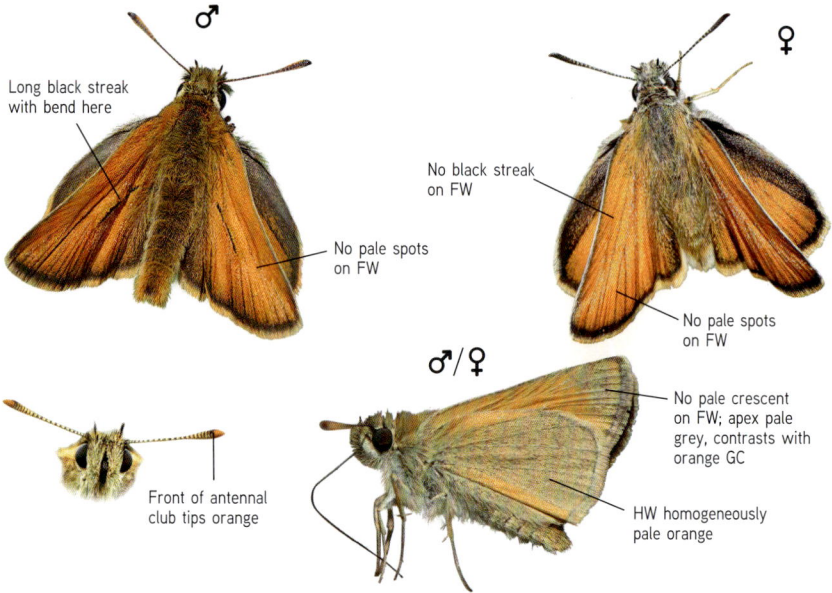

♂

Long black streak with bend here

No pale spots on FW

♀

No black streak on FW

No pale spots on FW

♂/♀

Front of antennal club tips orange

No pale crescent on FW; apex pale grey, contrasts with orange GC

HW homogeneously pale orange

Wingspan: 24–29 mm

Habitat: Meadows, grassy woodland clearings, forest edges, and roadsides.

Hibernating stage: Caterpillar.

Elevational range: Up to 2,000 m.

Egg-laying: Eggs are laid in small batches along LHP leaves.

Flight period: From April to September.

Host plants: Many grasses, including *Alopecurus pratensis, Anthoxanthum odoratum, Avena barbata, Avenella flexuosa, Brachypodium phoenicoides, B. pinnatum, B. sylvaticum, Bromus erectus, Dactylis glomerata,* *Deschampsia cespitosa, Holcus lanatus, H. mollis, Calamagrostis canescens, Cynosurus cristatus, C. echinatus, Lolium pratense, Melica ciliata, Molinia caerulea, Oloptum miliaceum, Phalaris brachystachys, P. canariensis, Phleum pratense, P. alpinum,* and *P. pheoides.*

Diversity and systematics: Most European populations belong to the nominate subspecies. Subspecies *iberica* flies in the Iberian Peninsula and southern France. Subspecies *syriaca* has been described from Greece.

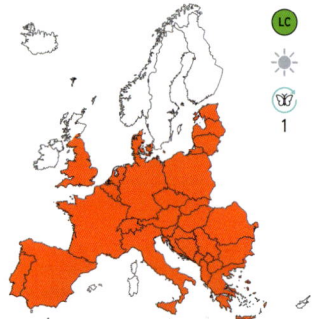

LC

1

Did you know?

The Small Skipper was the subject of an assisted colonization experiment in England in the context of climate change. Populations introduced in 2000 to sites located 35 km north of its natural distribution boundary are thriving.

IMAGOS		LARVAE	
Food		Food	
Behaviour of males		Caterpillar location	
Dispersion		Chrysalis location	

HESPERIIDAE

LULWORTH SKIPPER *THYMELICUS ACTEON*

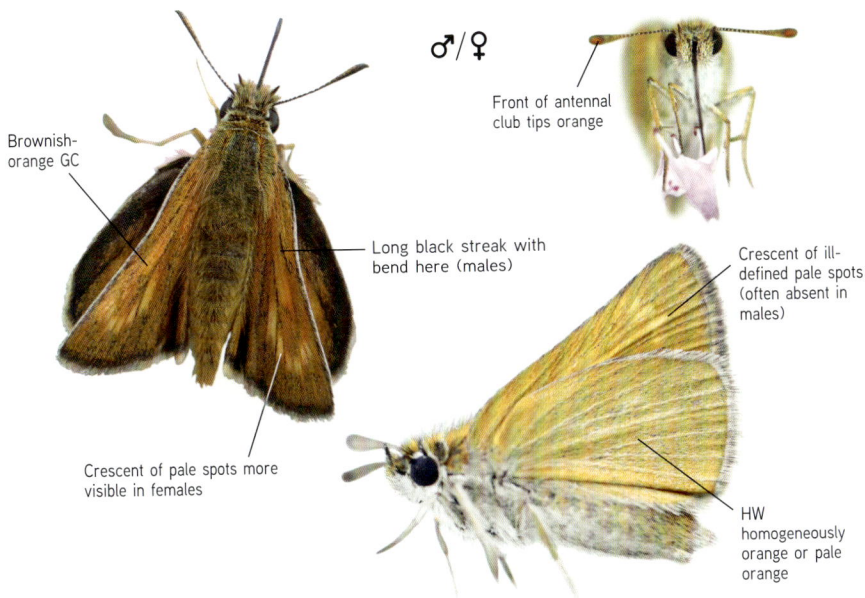

♂/♀

Front of antennal club tips orange

Brownish-orange GC

Long black streak with bend here (males)

Crescent of ill-defined pale spots (often absent in males)

Crescent of pale spots more visible in females

HW homogeneously orange or pale orange

Wingspan: 22–26 mm

Habitat: Dry and warm meadows and grasslands, often with scrubby areas.

Hibernating stage: Caterpillar.

Elevational range: Up to 1,500 m.

Egg-laying: Eggs are laid in small batches along LHP leaves.

Flight period: From April to September.

Host plants: Grasses, particularly *Brachypodium pinnatum*, *B. phoenicoides*, *B. sylvaticum*, *B. phoenicoides*, *Bromus erectus*, *Calamagrostis epigejos*, *C. villosa*, *Elytrigia repens*, *Hyparrhenia hirta*, *Achnatherum calamagrostis*, *Arrhenaterum elatius*, *Poa annua*, *Setaria verticillata*, and *Stipa pennata*. Also *Carex caryophyllea* (Cyperaceae).

Diversity and systematics: European populations of the Lulworth Skipper belong to the nominate subspecies.

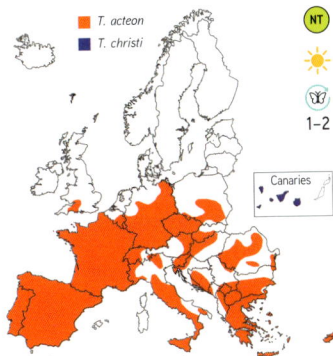

■ *T. acteon*
■ *T. christi*

NT

1–2

Canaries

Did you know?

The pronounced decline of the Lulworth Skipper outside the Mediterranean region is primarily driven by the abandonment of agropastoral activities, leading to the loss of dry grasslands.

IMAGOS		LARVAE	
Food		Food	
Behaviour of males		Caterpillar location	
Dispersion		Chrysalis location	

HESPERIIDAE

CANARIAN SKIPPER *THYMELICUS CHRISTI*

Crescent of pale spots more or less visible on FW

Brownish-orange GC

♂/♀

Front of antennal club tips orange

Crescent of ill-defined pale spots on FW

HW homogeneously orange or pale orange

Wingspan: 22–26 mm

Habitat: Bushy grasslands on sunny, rocky, volcanic slopes.

Hibernating stage: Caterpillar.

Elevational range: Up to 1,000 m.

Egg-laying: Eggs are laid on the LHP leaves.

Flight period: From February to October.

Host plants: Grasses, including *Brachypodium arbusculum*.

Diversity and systematics: The Canary Skipper is sometimes considered a subspecies of the Lulworth Skipper. The genitalia show little difference, but the geographical situation argues in favour of the species status.

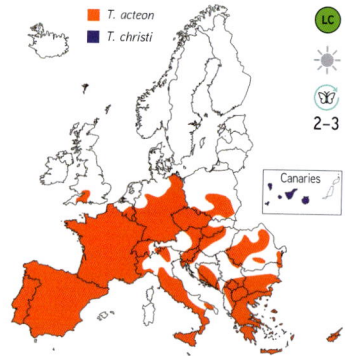

T. acteon
T. christi

LC

2–3

Canaries

IMAGOS		LARVAE	
Food	☆	Food	🍃
Behaviour of males		Caterpillar location	
Dispersion: unknown		Chrysalis location	

Did you know?

The Canary Skipper is typically found in rocky volcanic ravines. The biology of its caterpillar is poorly understood. The only known host plant was identified as such as recently as 2013!

HESPERIIDAE

LARGE SKIPPER   OCHLODES SYLVANUS

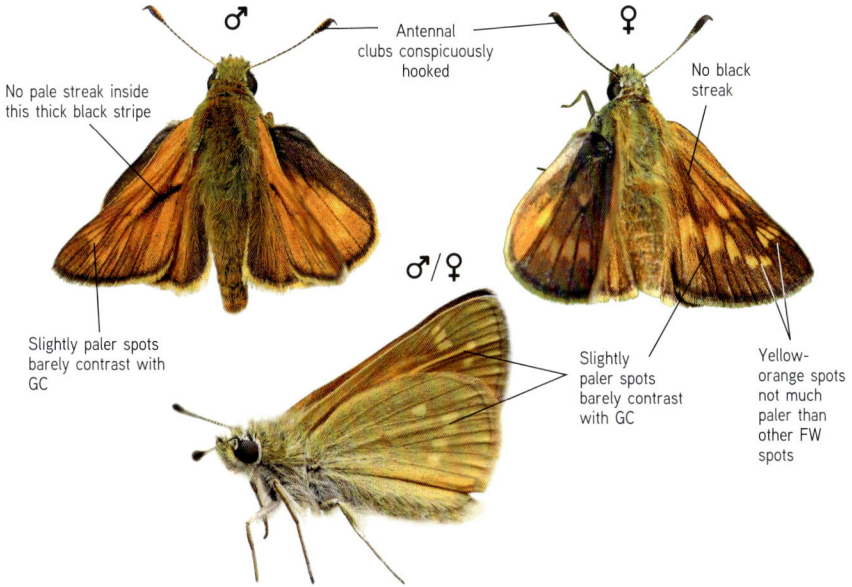

♂

Antennal clubs conspicuously hooked

♀

No pale streak inside this thick black stripe

No black streak

♂/♀

Slightly paler spots barely contrast with GC

Slightly paler spots barely contrast with GC

Yellow-orange spots not much paler than other FW spots

Wingspan: 23–33 mm

Habitat: Hedgerows, edges, and clearings; also in parks and gardens with overgrown areas.

Hibernating stage: Caterpillar.

Elevational range: Up to 2,000 m (mostly at lower elevations).

Egg-laying: Eggs are laid singly on the LHP leaves.

Flight period: From May to August.

Host plants: A wide variety of grasses, including *Agrostis capillaris*, *A. stolonifera*, *Alopecurus pratensis*, *Brachypodium pinnatum*, *B. sylvaticum*, *Bromus erectus*, *B. sterilis*, *Calamagrostis canescens*, *C. epigejos*, *Cynodon dactylon*, *Lolium arundinaceum*, *L. giganteum*, *L. perenne*, *L. pratense*, *Dactylis glomerata*, *Danthonia decumbens*, *Deschampsia cespitosa*, *Elymus repens*, *Glyceria fluitans*, *Holcus lanatus*, *Phalaris arundinacea*, *Phleum pratense*, *Poa annua*, *P. compressa*, *P. nemoralis*, *P. pratensis*, and *Molinia caerulea*. Also some Juncaceae, like *Luzula pilosa* and *Juncus effusus*, and some Cyperaceae, like *Carex diandra*.

Diversity and systematics: Most European populations belong to the nominate subspecies. However, several subspecies are described, including *nicaeensis*, which flies from southeastern France to the Iberian Peninsula.

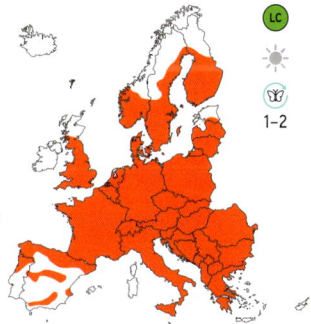

LC

1–2

Did you know?

The Large Skipper caterpillar propels its droppings far from its retreat using the comb-like structure located at the end of its abdomen. This likely makes it less detectable by predators.

IMAGOS			LARVAE	
Food			Food	
Behaviour of males			Caterpillar location	
Dispersion			Chrysalis location	

HESPERIIDAE

SILVER-SPOTTED SKIPPER *HESPERIA COMMA*

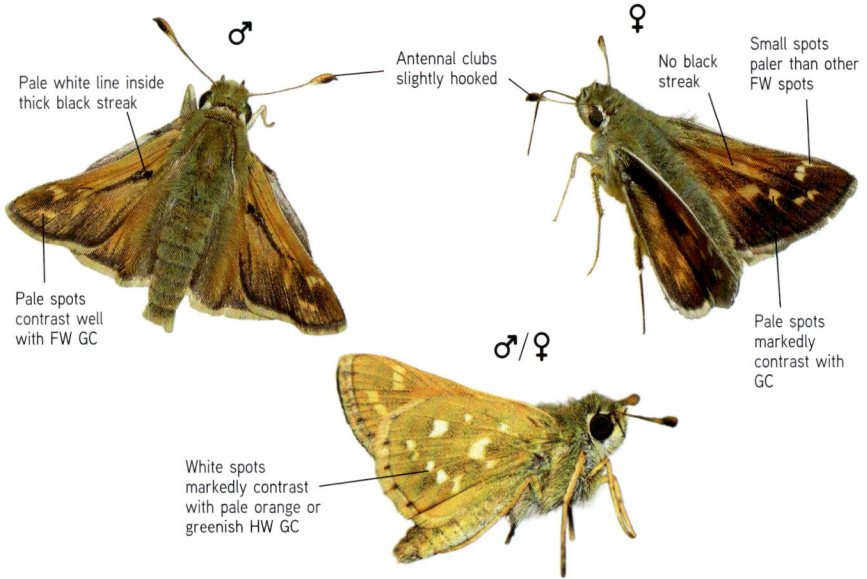

♂

Pale white line inside thick black streak

Antennal clubs slightly hooked

♀

No black streak

Small spots paler than other FW spots

Pale spots contrast well with FW GC

♂/♀

Pale spots markedly contrast with GC

White spots markedly contrast with pale orange or greenish HW GC

Wingspan: 24–34 mm

Habitat: Low-growing grasslands and grazed meadows.

Hibernating stage: Egg (and caterpillar at high-elevation sites, where the development is biennial).

Elevational range: Up to 3,000 m.

Egg-laying: Eggs are laid singly on the stems and leaves of the LHP or in its neighbourhood.

Flight period: From June to October.

Host plants: Low-growing grasses, including *Festuca ovina*, *F. rubra*, *F. liviensis*, *Agrostis vinealis*, *Avenella flexuosa*, *Corynephorus canescens*, *Deschampsia cespitosa*, *Elymus repens*, *Nardus stricta*, *Poa annua*, and *Lolium perenne*.

Diversity and systematics: Most European populations belong to the nominate subspecies. Subspecies *catena*, which flies in northern Scandinavia, is protected. Subspecies *hibera* is found in the Iberian Peninsula and southern France.

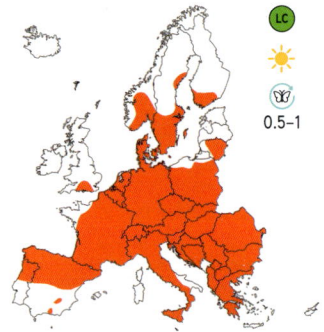

LC

0.5–1

Did you know?

In England, where the Silver-spotted Skipper declined significantly until the 1980s, its numbers have benefited from increased rabbit grazing and climate change (warmer summers).

IMAGOS			LARVAE		
Food	🌼		Food	🌿	
Behaviour of males	🦋 🌱 🌼		Caterpillar location	▬ 🌿	
Dispersion	🦋		Chrysalis location	◀▬	

HESPERIIDAE

DINGY SKIPPER ERYNNIS TAGES

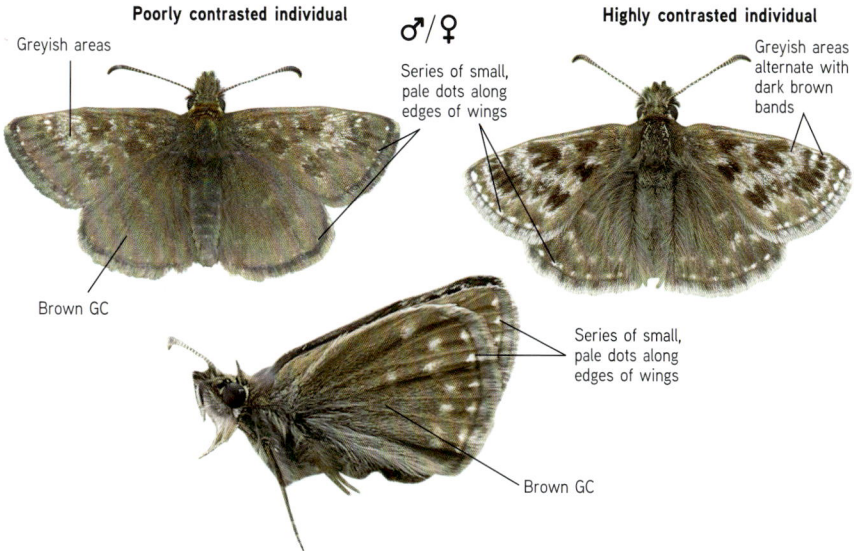

Poorly contrasted individual ♂/♀ **Highly contrasted individual**

Greyish areas

Series of small, pale dots along edges of wings

Greyish areas alternate with dark brown bands

Brown GC

Series of small, pale dots along edges of wings

Brown GC

Wingspan: 28–32 mm

Habitat: Dry grasslands, low-growing meadows, roadsides, parks, and gardens.

Hibernating stage: Caterpillar.

Elevational range: Up to 2,200 m.

Egg-laying: Eggs are laid singly on LHP leaves.

Flight period: From April to September.

Host plants: Legumes, including *Lotus corniculatus*, *L. pedunculatus*, *L. dorycnium*, *L. uliginosus*, *Securigera varia*, *Hippocrepis comosa*, *H. glauca*, *Dorycnopsis gerardi*, and *Medicago lupulina*. Also reported on *Eryngium campestre* (Apiaceae).

Diversity and systematics: Most European populations belong to the nominate subspecies. Subspecies *cervantes* flies in southern Spain, and subspecies *baynesi* in Ireland.

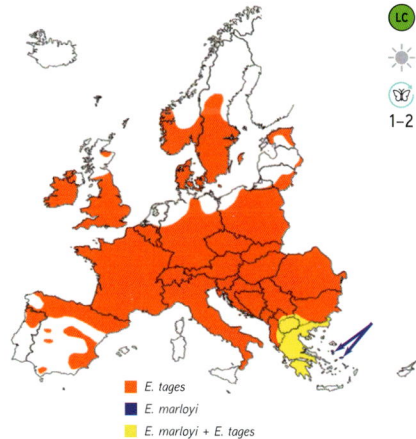

LC

1–2

■ *E. tages*
■ *E. marloyi*
■ *E. marloyi + E. tages*

IMAGOS			LARVAE		
Food			Food		
Behaviour of males			Caterpillar location		
Dispersion			Chrysalis location		

Did you know?

Adults frequently forage on bugle (genus *Ajuga*) flowers. Females lay eggs on LHPs growing near bareground areas.

HESPERIIDAE

INKY SKIPPER *ERYNNIS MARLOYI*

♂/♀

2 very dark
stripes across FW

Grey-brown GC

Small pale spots here

No series of pale dots
along wing edges

Dark brown GC

HW GC usually darker
than FW GC

No series of
pale dots along
wing edges

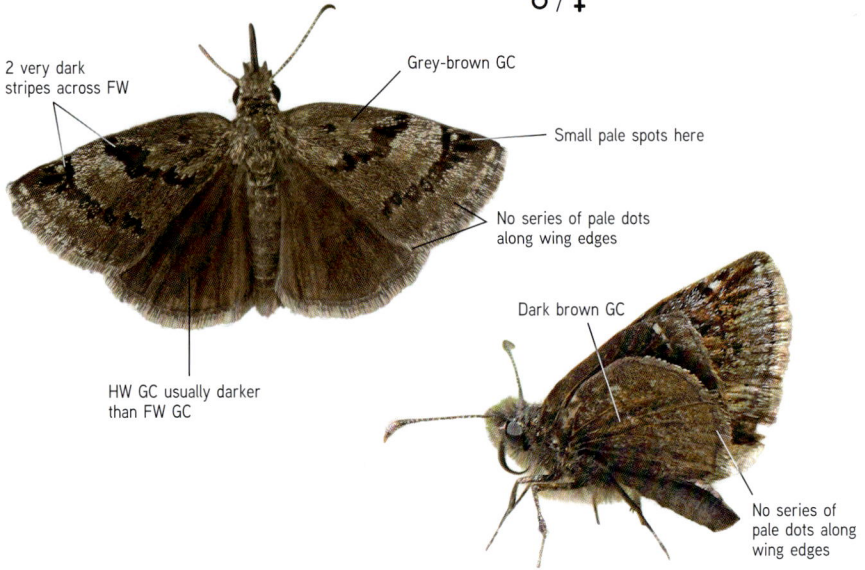

Wingspan: 28–34 mm

Habitat: Dry grasslands with bushes (including the LHP), low-growing garrigue.

Hibernating stage: Caterpillar.

Elevational range: Up to 2,000 m (mainly between 500 and 1,200 m).

Egg-laying: Eggs are laid singly on LHP stems.

Flight period: From March to October.

Host plants: Woody Rosaceae, mainly *Pyrus spinosa* and *Prunus cocomilia*.

Diversity and systematics: There are no notable subspecies for this skipper, whose European range is localized in the Balkans and a few Aegean islands.

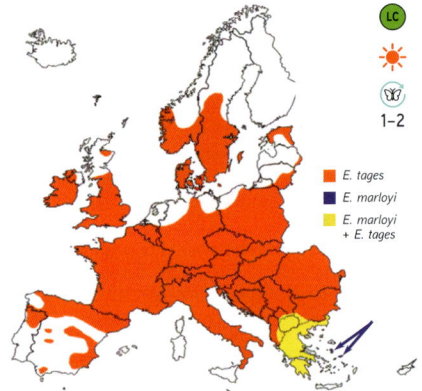

LC

1–2

■ E. tages
■ E. marloyi
■ E. marloyi
  + E. tages

IMAGOS		LARVAE	
Food	✶	Food	🍃
Behaviour of males		Caterpillar location	🌳
Dispersion		Chrysalis location	

Did you know?

Males gather on ridges, where they await the passage of females, pursuing and chasing each other as well as butterflies of other species.

146

HESPERIIDAE

PYGMY SKIPPER *GEGENES PUMILIO*

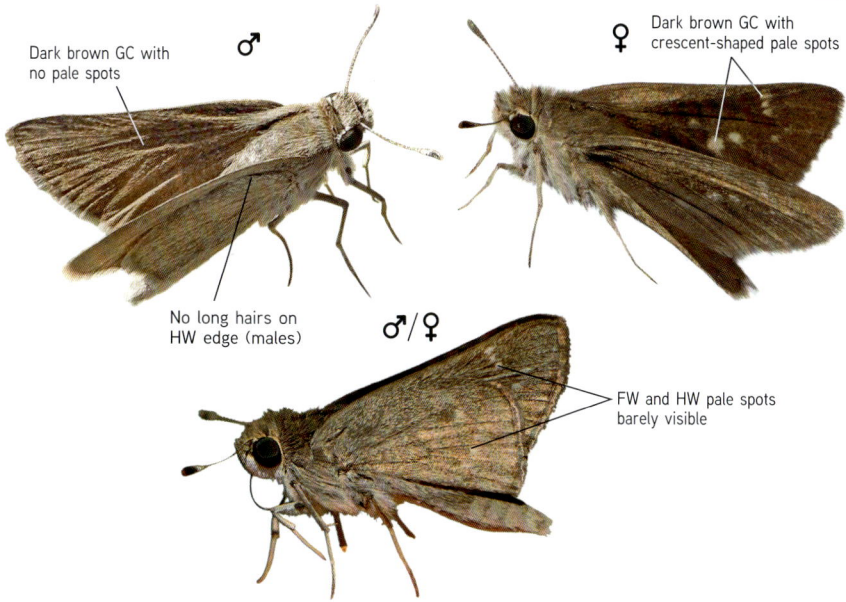

♂ Dark brown GC with no pale spots

♀ Dark brown GC with crescent-shaped pale spots

No long hairs on HW edge (males)

♂/♀

FW and HW pale spots barely visible

Wingspan: 30–34 mm

Habitat: Warm and dry stony habitats, paths, and roadsides. More abundant near the coast.

Hibernating stage: Caterpillar.

Elevational range: Up to 1,200 m (mostly at low elevations).

Egg-laying: Eggs are laid singly on LHP leaves.

Flight period: From March to November.

Host plants: Xerophilous grasses, mainly *Hyparrhenia hirta*, *Imperata cylindrica*, *Cynodon dactylon*, *Setaria verticillata*, and *Sorghum halepense*.

Diversity and systematics: European populations belong to the nominate subspecies.

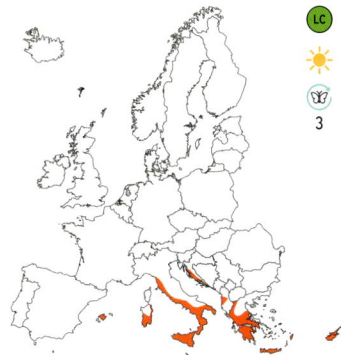

LC

3

Did you know?

It is very likely that the Pygmy Skipper has now gone extinct in France. This victim of unreasonable urbanization along the Mediterranean coasts hasn't been observed there since 1997.

IMAGOS		LARVAE	
Food		Food	
Behaviour of males		Caterpillar location	
Dispersion		Chrysalis location	

HESPERIIDAE

MEDITERRANEAN SKIPPER   *GEGENES NOSTRODAMUS*

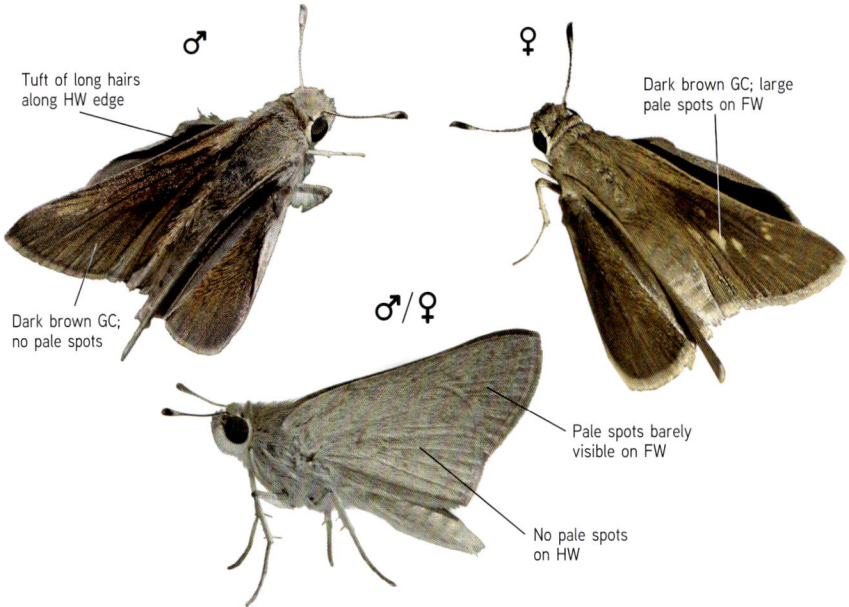

♂

Tuft of long hairs
along HW edge

♀

Dark brown GC; large
pale spots on FW

Dark brown GC;
no pale spots

♂/♀

Pale spots barely
visible on FW

No pale spots
on HW

Wingspan: 30–34 mm

Habitat: Hot and dry grassy environments, most often near the coasts. Crop surroundings, back dunes, and dried riverbeds.

Hibernating stage: Egg, caterpillar, pupa, or adult without diapause.

Elevational range: From sea level to 1,500 m (mostly at low elevations).

Egg-laying: Eggs are laid singly on LHP leaves.

Flight period: Year-round.

Host plants: Grasses, including *Sorghum halepense*, *Botriochloa ischaemum*, *Digitaria sanguinalis*, *Phragmites australis*, *Setaria verticillata*, *S. viridis*, and *Tripidium ravennae*.

Diversity and systematics: There are no notable subspecies for this peri-Mediterranean skipper.

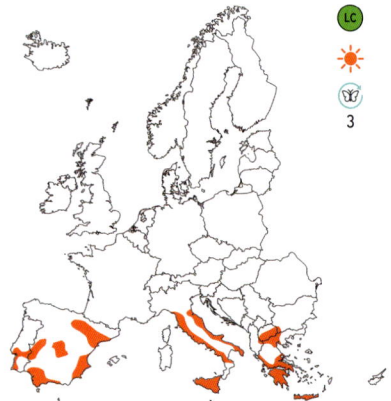

LC

3

IMAGOS		LARVAE	
Food	🌸 💧	Food	🍃
Behaviour of males		Caterpillar location	
Dispersion		Chrysalis location	

Did you know?

Coastal urbanization and agricultural intensification both threaten the habitats of the Mediterranean Skipper.

HESPERIIDAE

ZELLER'S SKIPPER *BORBO BORBONICA*

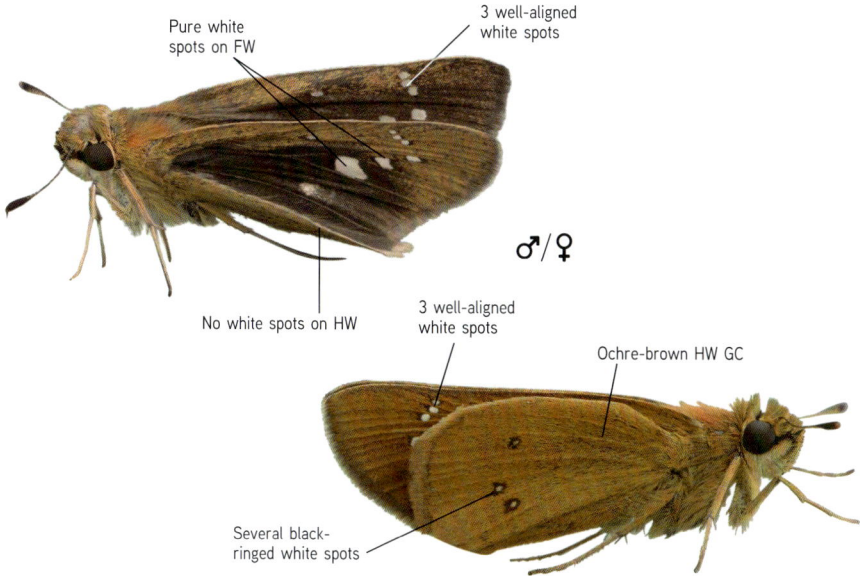

Pure white
spots on FW

3 well-aligned
white spots

No white spots on HW

♂/♀

3 well-aligned
white spots

Ochre-brown HW GC

Several black-
ringed white spots

Wingspan: 28–30 mm

Habitat: Surroundings of ponds, lakes, and rivers with overgrown vegetation.

Hibernating stage: Caterpillar.

Elevational range: Up to 500 m.

Egg-laying: Eggs are laid singly on LHP leaves.

Flight period: From May to November.

Host plants: Grasses, mainly *Polypogon viridis* in Europe. *Panicum repens* is also used in North Africa.

Diversity and systematics: The few European populations belong to the nominate subspecies.

NA

3

4

IMAGOS		LARVAE	
Food		Food	
Behaviour of males		Caterpillar location	
Dispersion		Chrysalis location	

Did you know?

Zeller's Skipper is widespread on the African continent and could extend its European range, benefiting from climate warming.

HESPERIIDAE

MILLET SKIPPER *PELOPIDAS THRAX*

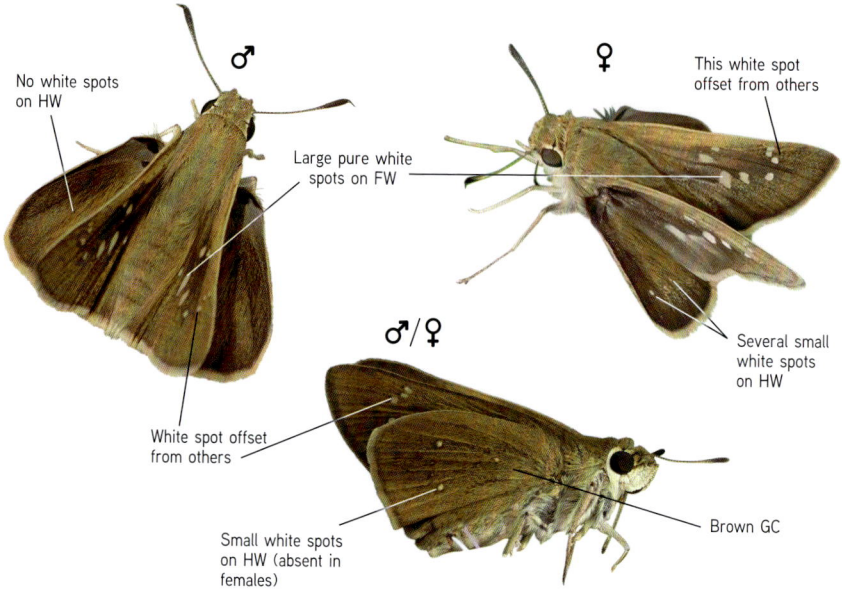

♂

No white spots on HW

Large pure white spots on FW

♀

This white spot offset from others

Several small white spots on HW

♂/♀

White spot offset from others

Small white spots on HW (absent in females)

Brown GC

Wingspan: 33–42 mm

Habitat: River and pond edges, dried streambeds, coastal wetlands, and dunes.

Hibernating stage: Caterpillar or pupa without entering diapause.

Elevational range: Up to 500 m.

Egg-laying: Eggs are laid singly on LHP leaves.

Flight period: Almost year-round.

Host plants: Grasses, including *Arundo donax*, *Phragmites australis*, *Oloptum miliaceum*, and *Oryza sativa*.

Diversity and systematics: European populations of this skipper, widespread on the African continent and Asia, belong to the nominate subspecies.

NA

3

IMAGOS		LARVAE	
Food		Food	
Behaviour of males		Caterpillar location	
Dispersion		Chrysalis location	

Did you know?

Caterpillars of the Millet Skipper are known to cause damage in Asian and African rice plantations.

HESPERIIDAE

MALLOW SKIPPER *CARCHARODUS ALCEAE*

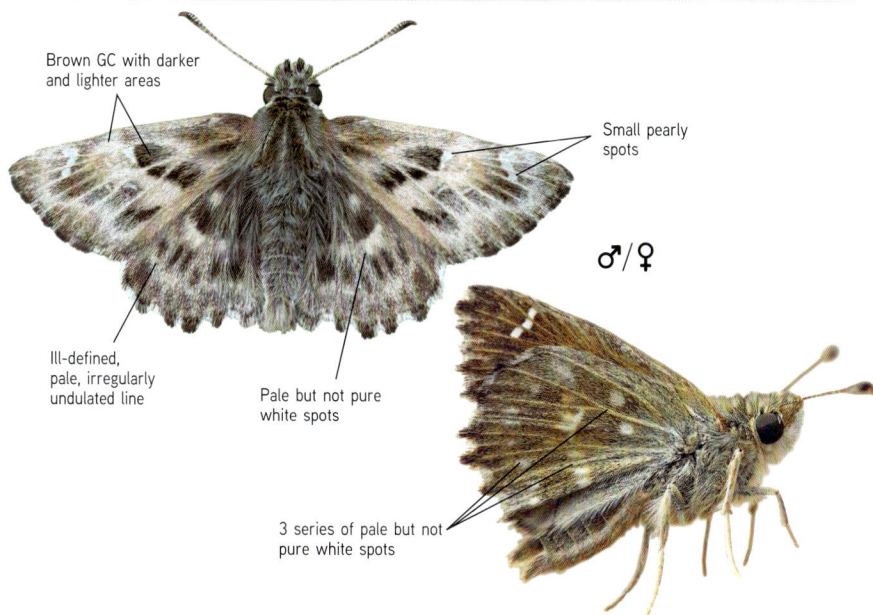

Brown GC with darker and lighter areas

Small pearly spots

♂/♀

Ill-defined, pale, irregularly undulated line

Pale but not pure white spots

3 series of pale but not pure white spots

Wingspan: 26–34 mm

Habitat: Wastelands, grasslands, parks, gardens, grassy road verges.

Hibernating stage: Caterpillar.

Elevational range: Up to 3,000 m.

Egg-laying: Eggs are laid singly on LHP leaves.

Flight period: From February to November.

Host plants: Malvaceae, including *Malva sylvestris, M. alcea, M. moschata, M. neglecta, M. multiflora, M. arborea, M. parviflora, M. punctata, M. pusilla, M. subovata, M. thuringiaca, M. trimestris, Alcea rosea, A. biennis, Althaea officinalis, A. cannabina,* and *Abutilon theophrasti.*

Diversity and systematics: Most European populations belong to the nominate subspecies. Subspecies *corsicus* flies in Corsica.

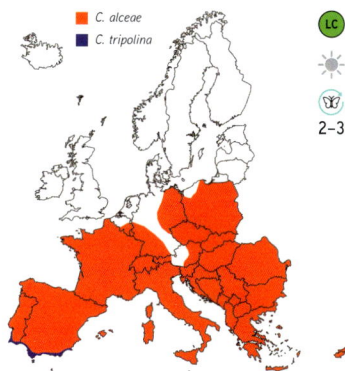

■ *C. alceae*
■ *C. tripolina*

LC

2–3

IMAGOS		LARVAE	
Food	☆	Food	🌿
Behaviour of males		Caterpillar location	🌱
Dispersion		Chrysalis location	🌱

Did you know?

The Mallow Skipper is the most common and widespread species in genus *Carcharodus*. It is also the least sensitive to habitat anthropization.

HESPERIIDAE

FALSE MALLOW SKIPPER
CARCHARODUS TRIPOLINA

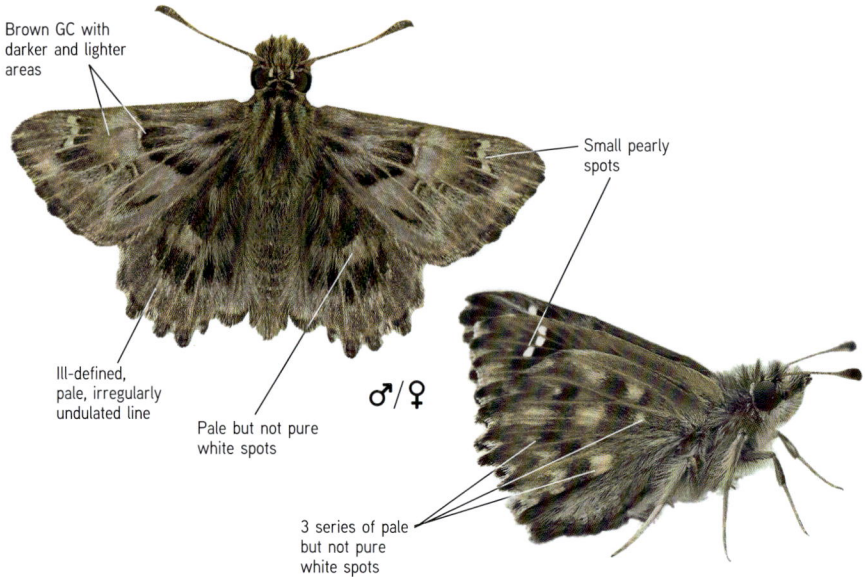

Brown GC with darker and lighter areas

Small pearly spots

Ill-defined, pale, irregularly undulated line

Pale but not pure white spots

♂/♀

3 series of pale but not pure white spots

Wingspan: 26–34 mm

Habitat: Dry meadows, fallow lands, path and road edges.

Hibernating stage: Caterpillar.

Elevational range: Up to 2,500 m (mostly at low elevations in Europe).

Egg-laying: Eggs are laid singly on LHP leaves.

Flight period: From March to September.

Host plants: Malvaceae, including *Lavatera arborea* and *Malva sylvestris*.

Diversity and systematics: There are no notable subspecies for this North African skipper, which reaches the northern limit of its range in the southern Iberian Peninsula. It can be distinguished from *Carcharodus alceae* only through genitalia dissection.

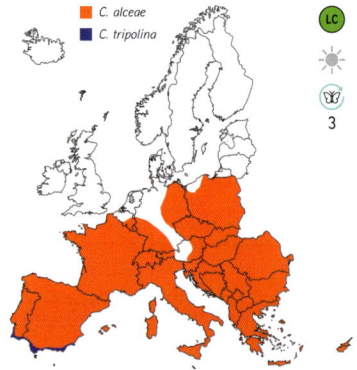

■ C. alceae
■ C. tripolina

LC

3

IMAGOS		LARVAE	
Food	🌸	Food	🍃
Behaviour of males	🌿	Caterpillar location	🌿
Dispersion : unknown		Chrysalis location	🌿

Did you know?

Genus name *Carcharodus* means "with pointed teeth", referring to the serrated appearance of these skippers' wing edges.

HESPERIIDAE

TUFTED MARBLED SKIPPER
MUSCHAMPIA FLOCCIFERA

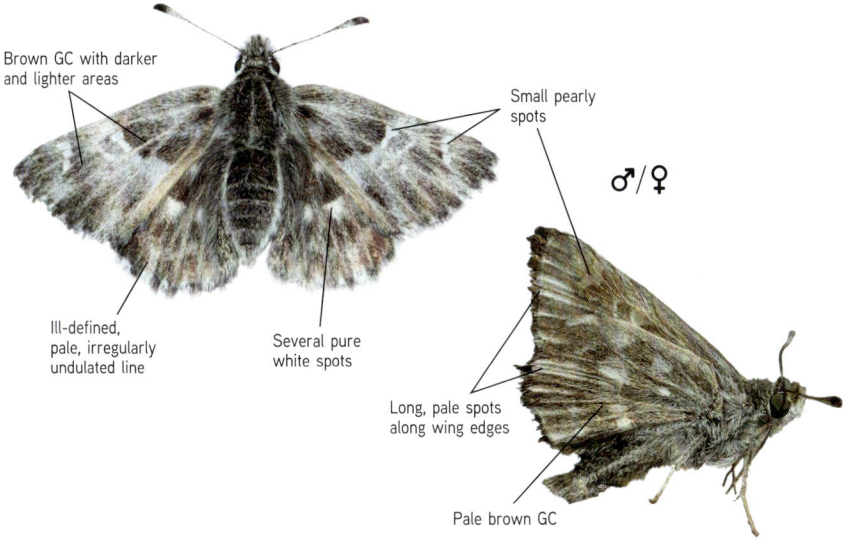

Brown GC with darker
and lighter areas

Small pearly
spots

♂/♀

Ill-defined,
pale, irregularly
undulated line

Several pure
white spots

Long, pale spots
along wing edges

Pale brown GC

Wingspan: 28–32 mm

Habitat: Moist and mesophilic flower-rich meadows, forest clearings, and subalpine meadows.

Hibernating stage: Caterpillar.

Elevational range: Up to 2,200 m.

Egg-laying: Eggs are laid singly on LHP leaves.

Flight period: From April to August.

Host plants: Lamiaceae, including *Betonica officinalis, B. hirsuta,* *B. scardica, Stachys pradica, S. recta* (in the southern part of its range), *S. palustris, S. germanica, S. alpina, Marrubium vulgare, M. peregrinum, Leonurus cardiaca,* and *Malva neglecta* (Malvaceae).

Diversity and systematics: European populations belong to the nominate subspecies.

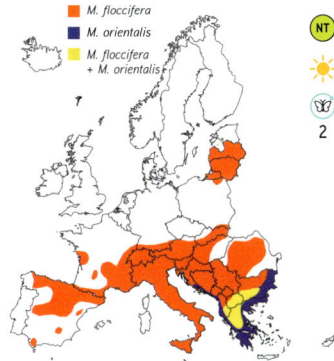

- M. floccifera
- M. orientalis
- M. floccifera + M. orientalis

NT

2

Did you know?

The Tufted Marbled Skipper has significantly declined due to unfavourable forest management (conifer plantations) and agricultural intensification (*e.g.,* more frequent mowing of meadows).

IMAGOS			LARVAE		
Food			Food		
Behaviour of males			Caterpillar location		
Dispersion			Chrysalis location		

ORIENTAL MARBLED SKIPPER *MUSCHAMPIA ORIENTALIS*

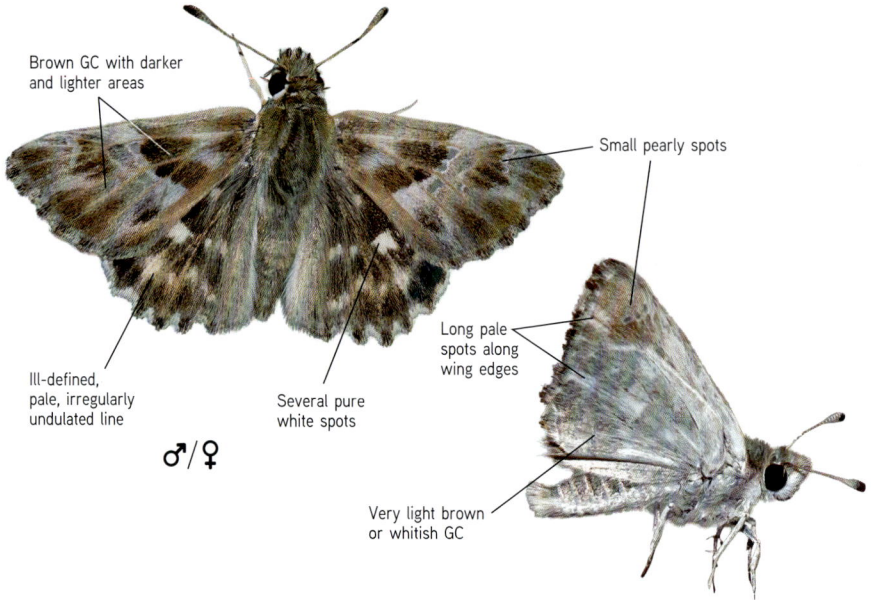

Brown GC with darker and lighter areas

Small pearly spots

Long pale spots along wing edges

Ill-defined, pale, irregularly undulated line

Several pure white spots

♂/♀

Very light brown or whitish GC

Wingspan: 28–30 mm

Habitat: Flower-rich meadows, dry or steppic grasslands. Tolerates grazing.

Hibernating stage: Caterpillar.

Elevational range: Up to 3,000 m (rarely above 2,000 m).

Egg-laying: Eggs are laid singly on LHP leaves.

Flight period: From May to August.

Host plants: Lamiaceae, including *Stachys sylvatica*, *S. cretica*, *S. germanica*, *S. iva*, *Ballota nigra*, *Marrubium velutinum*, and *Pseudodictamnus acetabulosus*.

Diversity and systematics: European populations belong to the nominate subspecies. They can be reliably distinguished from *Muschampia floccifera* only through genitalia examination.

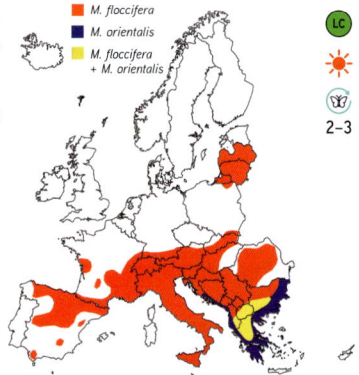

■ M. floccifera
■ M. orientalis
■ M. floccifera + M. orientalis

LC

2–3

Did you know?

At rest, Levantine Skippers and Tufted Marbled Skippers assume a distinctive posture, with the abdomen raised and wings lowered.

IMAGOS		LARVAE	
Food		Food	
Behaviour of males		Caterpillar location	
Dispersion		Chrysalis location	

HESPERIIDAE

SOUTHERN MARBLED SKIPPER *MUSCHAMPIA BAETICUS*

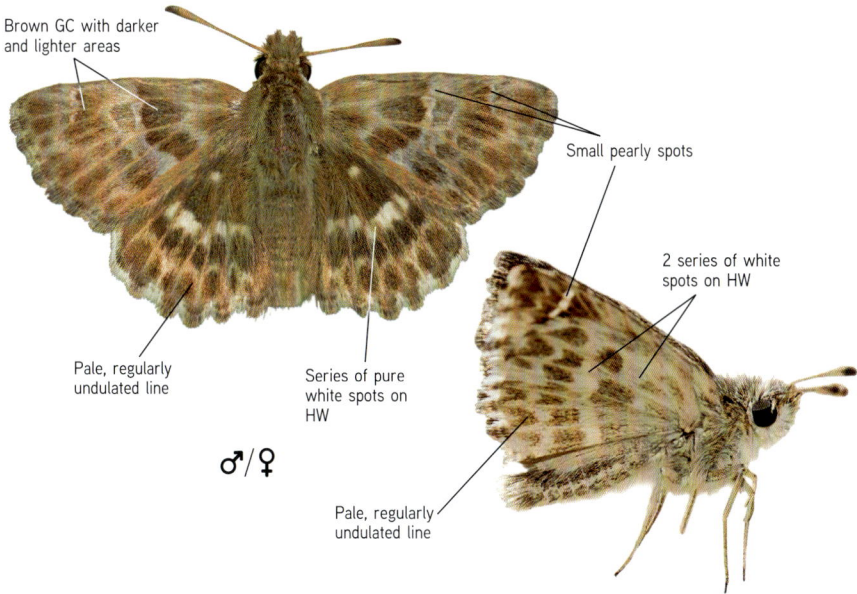

Brown GC with darker and lighter areas

Small pearly spots

2 series of white spots on HW

Pale, regularly undulated line

Series of pure white spots on HW

♂/♀

Pale, regularly undulated line

Wingspan: 28–32 mm

Habitat: Dry grasslands, rocky slopes, and flowery fallow lands. Strongly associated with sheep grazing.

Hibernating stage: Caterpillar.

Elevational range: Up to 1,500 m.

Egg-laying: Eggs are laid singly on LHP leaves.

Flight period: From May to October.

Host plants: Lamiaceae, mainly *Marrubium vulgare* and *M. incanum*; sometimes also *Ballota nigra* and *B. hirsuta*.

Diversity and systematics: Most European populations belong to the nominate subspecies. Subspecies *octodurensis* formerly flew in Switzerland before becoming extinct.

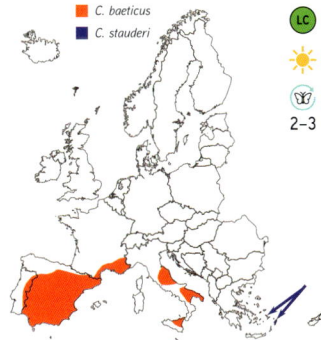

■ C. baeticus
■ C. stauderi

LC

2–3

IMAGOS		LARVAE	
Food		Food	
Behaviour of males		Caterpillar location	
Dispersion		Chrysalis location	

Did you know?

The species name, *baeticus*, refers to the Roman region of Baetica, located in Spain, where most Southern Marbled Skipper populations reside.

155

HESPERIIDAE

FALSE MARBLED SKIPPER *MUSCHAMPIA STAUDERI*

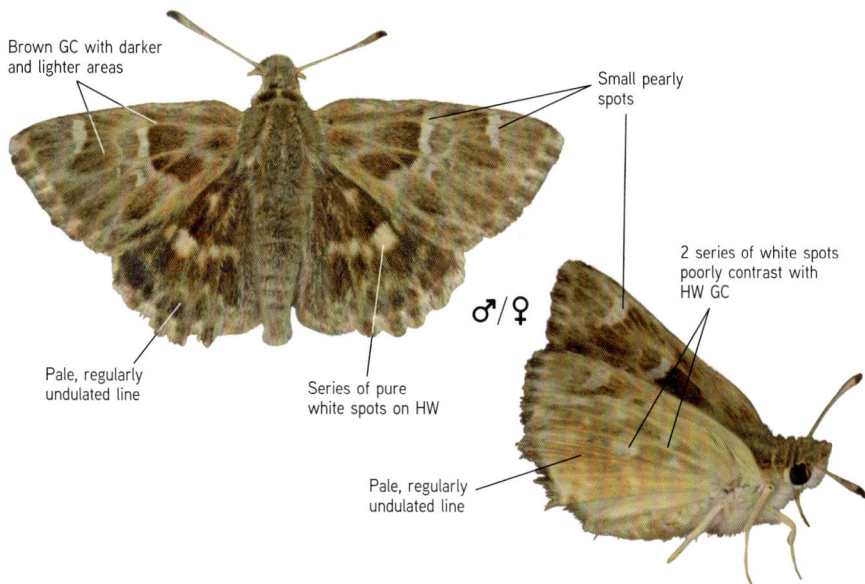

Brown GC with darker
and lighter areas

Small pearly
spots

2 series of white spots
poorly contrast with
HW GC

Pale, regularly
undulated line

Series of pure
white spots on HW

♂/♀

Pale, regularly
undulated line

Wingspan: 28–32 mm

Habitat: Stony dry and warm, flower-rich grasslands, often grazed by sheep.

Hibernating stage: Caterpillar.

Elevational range: Up to 500 m in Europe.

Egg-laying: Eggs are laid singly on LHP leaves.

Flight period: From March to October.

Host plants: Lamiaceae, including *Pseudodictamnus acetabulosus, Ballota nigra, Marrubium vulgare, Phlomis aurea,* and *P. floccosa.*

Diversity and systematics: European populations belong to the nominate subspecies. It flies only on the islands of Samos, Kos, Simi, and Rhodes.

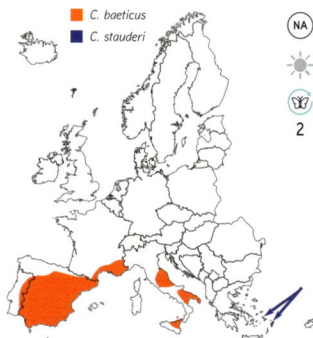

C. baeticus
C. stauderi

NA

2

Did you know?

Caterpillars enter aestivation in a shelter that allows them to endure the intense summer drought, which halts the growth of their LHPs. They resume their development in the fall.

IMAGOS		LARVAE	
Food		Food	
Behaviour of males		Caterpillar location	
Dispersion		Chrysalis location	

HESPERIIDAE

MARBLED SKIPPER   *MUSCHAMPIA LAVATHERAE*

Brown GC with
darker and lighter
areas

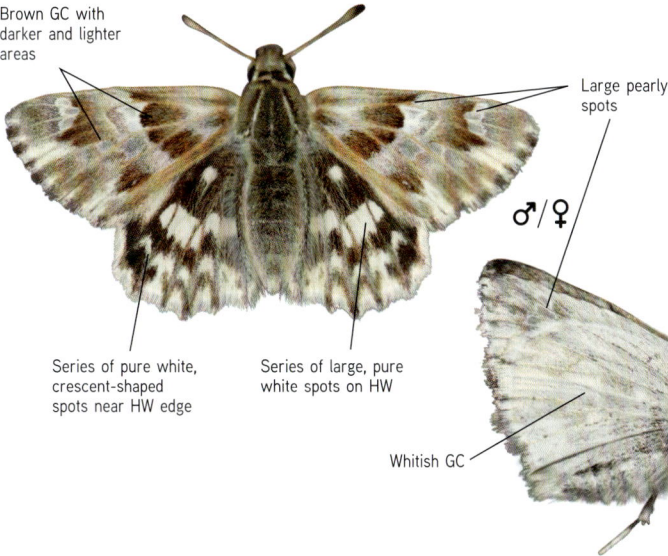

Large pearly
spots

♂/♀

Series of pure white,
crescent-shaped
spots near HW edge

Series of large, pure
white spots on HW

Whitish GC

Wingspan: 28–34 mm

Habitat: Warm and sunny stony slopes, dry grasslands, and garrigue.

Hibernating stage: Caterpillar.

Elevational range: Up to 2,000 m.

Egg-laying: Eggs are laid singly, usually on the dried calyx of past LHP inflorescences.

Flight period: From May to September.

Host plants: Lamiaceae, including *Stachys recta*, *S. germanica*, *Sideritis hyssopifolia*, and *S. hirsuta*.

Diversity and systematics: Most populations belong to the nominate subspecies. Subspecies *tauricus* flies from the Balkans to the Caucasus. Subspecies *pyrenaicus* inhabits the Central Pyrenees.

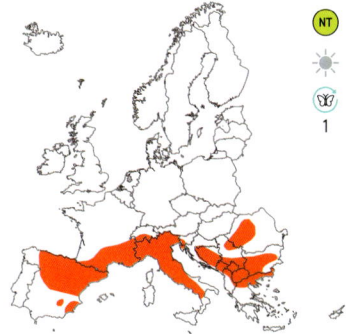

NT

1

Did you know?

Agropastoral abandonment, leading to the disappearance of dry meadows, and the development of vineyards in well-exposed favourable habitats both pose significant threats to the Marbled Skipper.

IMAGOS		LARVAE		
Food	🌼 💧	Food	🌼 🍃 🌿	
Behaviour of males		Caterpillar location	🐛 🌿	
Dispersion		Chrysalis location	🌿	

HESPERIIDAE

SAGE SKIPPERS
MUSCHAMPIA PROTO, M. ALTA AND *M. PROTEIDES*

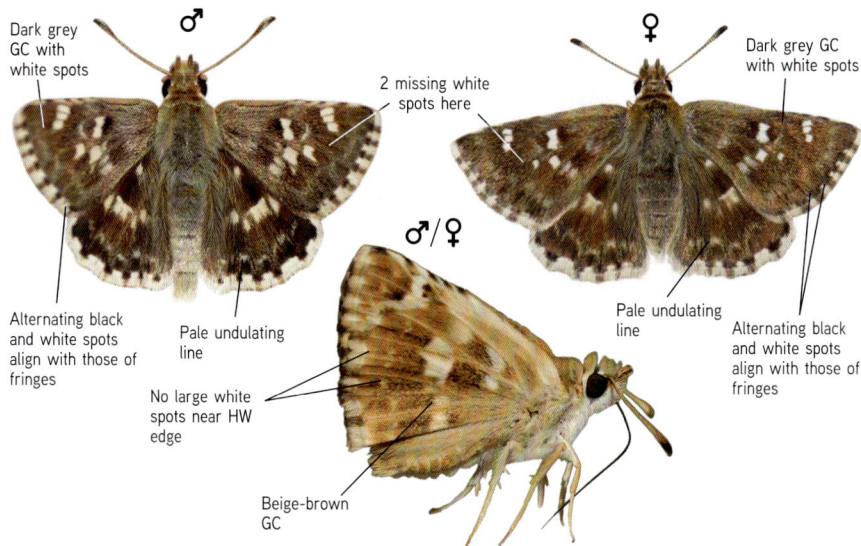

♂

Dark grey GC with white spots

2 missing white spots here

♀

Dark grey GC with white spots

Alternating black and white spots align with those of fringes

Pale undulating line

♂/♀

Pale undulating line

Alternating black and white spots align with those of fringes

No large white spots near HW edge

Beige-brown GC

Wingspan: 30–39 mm

Habitat: Dry and steppic grasslands, garrigue and maquis, often grazed.

Hibernating stage: Caterpillar inside the egg.

Elevational range: Up to 1,500 m (mostly below 1,000 m).

Egg-laying: Eggs are laid singly at the base of LHP stems or on the ground nearby.

Flight period: From May to September.

Host plants: Lamiaceae of genus *Phlomis*, including *P. herba-venti, P. fruticosa, P. lychnitis, P. purpurea,* and *P. samia.*

Diversity and systematics: A recent genetic study (2021) has revealed that *Muschampia proto* actually encompasses a complex of three cryptic species. *M. proto* represents the westernmost species, *M. alta* inhabits the Italian and Balkan peninsulas, and *M. proteides* extends from the eastern Aegean Islands to Crimea.

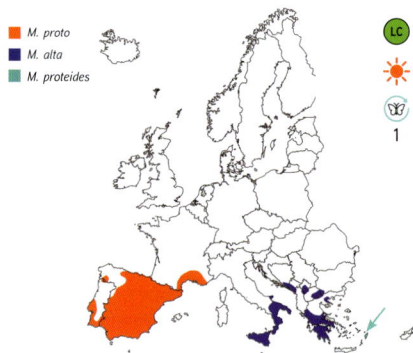

■ M. proto
■ M. alta
■ M. proteides

LC

1

Did you know?

The observed late emergence in certain populations results from the aestivation of older caterpillars within a cocoon that they will reuse in the pupal stage. This slowed-down life allows them to avoid the effects of summer drought.

IMAGOS			LARVAE		
Food			Food		
Behaviour of males			Caterpillar location		
Dispersion			Chrysalis location		

158

HESPERIIDAE

TESSELLATED SKIPPER *MUSCHAMPIA TESSELLUM*

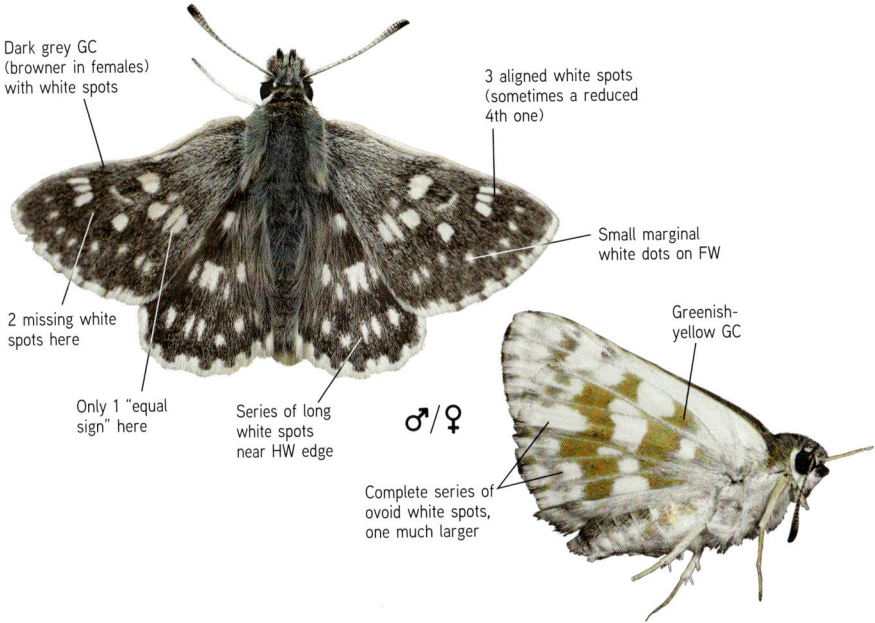

Dark grey GC
(browner in females)
with white spots

3 aligned white spots
(sometimes a reduced
4th one)

Small marginal
white dots on FW

Greenish-
yellow GC

2 missing white
spots here

Only 1 "equal
sign" here

Series of long
white spots
near HW edge

♂/♀

Complete series of
ovoid white spots,
one much larger

Wingspan: 31–36 mm

Habitat: Dry or mesophilic and often bushy grasslands on sunny slopes.

Hibernating stage: Caterpillar.

Elevational range: Up to 2,000 m (mostly below 1,500 m).

Egg-laying: Eggs are laid singly on LHP leaves.

Flight period: From April to August.

Host plants: Lamiaceae of genus *Phlomis*, including *P. samia*, *P. herba-venti*, and *Phlomoides tuberosa*.

Diversity and systematics: European populations belong to the nominate subspecies.

LC

1–2

IMAGOS		LARVAE	
Food	☆	Food	🍃
Behaviour of males		Caterpillar location	🌱
Dispersion	🦋	Chrysalis location	🌱

Did you know?

The Tessellated Skipper is locally threatened, either by pastoral abandonment or by agricultural intensification such as overgrazing.

HESPERIIDAE

SPINOSE SKIPPER *FAVRIA CRIBRELLUM*

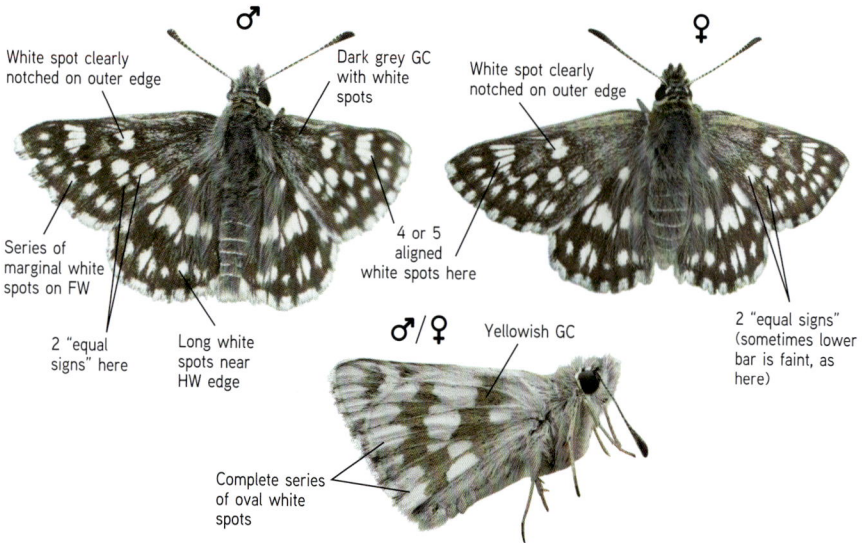

♂

White spot clearly notched on outer edge

Dark grey GC with white spots

Series of marginal white spots on FW

4 or 5 aligned white spots here

2 "equal signs" here

Long white spots near HW edge

♀

White spot clearly notched on outer edge

2 "equal signs" (sometimes lower bar is faint, as here)

♂/♀

Yellowish GC

Complete series of oval white spots

Wingspan: 26–32 mm

Habitat: Dry and stony steppic grasslands, often grazed.

Hibernating stage: Caterpillar.

Elevational range: Up to 1,000 m.

Egg-laying: Eggs are laid singly on the petioles and leaflets of the LHP leaves.

Flight period: From May to July.

Host plants: Small Rosaceae, including *Fragaria viridis*, *Potentilla deorum*, and *P. kionaea*.

Diversity and systematics: The few European populations belong to the nominate subspecies.

NT

1

IMAGOS		LARVAE	
Food	🌼 💧	Food	🌿
Behaviour of males		Caterpillar location	🌱
Dispersion		Chrysalis location	🌿

Did you know?

Only the males come to absorb mineral salts from the ground. As in other species, they likely transfer some of these to the females, who use them when producing their eggs.

HESPERIIDAE

RED-UNDERWING SKIPPER/SPANISH RED-UNDERWING SKIPPER
SPIALIA SERTORIUS/S. ROSAE

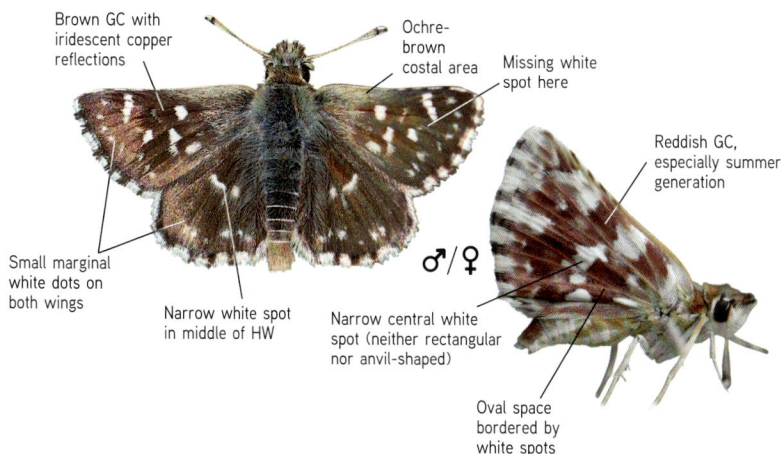

Brown GC with iridescent copper reflections

Ochre-brown costal area

Missing white spot here

Reddish GC, especially summer generation

Small marginal white dots on both wings

♂/♀

Narrow white spot in middle of HW

Narrow central white spot (neither rectangular nor anvil-shaped)

Oval space bordered by white spots

Wingspan: 22–26 mm

Habitat: Dry grasslands, nutrient-poor meadows, and wasteland.

Hibernating stage: Caterpillar.

Elevational range: Up to 1,800 m for *sertorius*, above 1,500 m for *rosae*.

Egg-laying: Eggs are laid singly on LHP inflorescences and leaflets for *sertorius*, and on the leaflets for *rosae*.

Flight period: From February to October for *sertorius*, and from April to October for *rosae*.

Host plants: Mainly *Sanguisorba minor* and *S. officinalis for sertorius*, and different *Rosa* species (*R. canina, R. pendulina, R. micrantha, R. tomentosa, R. corymbifera, R. sicula, R. elliptica, R. pouzinii*, and *R. squarrosa*) for *rosae*.

Diversity and systematics: Most European populations of *Spialia sertorius* belong to the nominate subspecies (although poorly distinct subspecies have been described). *S. rosae* is more closely related to *S. orbifer*, which replaces *S. sertorius* in the Balkans.

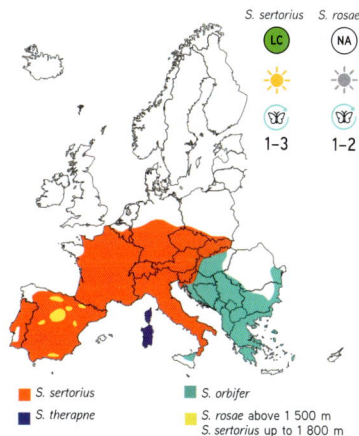

S. sertorius   *S. rosae*

LC   NA

1-3   1-2

■ *S. sertorius*   ■ *S. orbifer*
■ *S. therapne*   ■ *S. rosae* above 1 500 m
                  S. sertorius up to 1 800 m

Did you know?

The discovery of *Spialia rosae* was published only in 2016 and is based on genetic and ecological differences. European biodiversity is thus still far from having revealed all its secrets!

IMAGOS		LARVAE	
Food	☆ ◌	Food	◌
Behaviour of males		Caterpillar location	
Dispersion		Chrysalis location	

HESPERIIDAE

HUNGARIAN SKIPPER *SPIALIA ORBIFER*

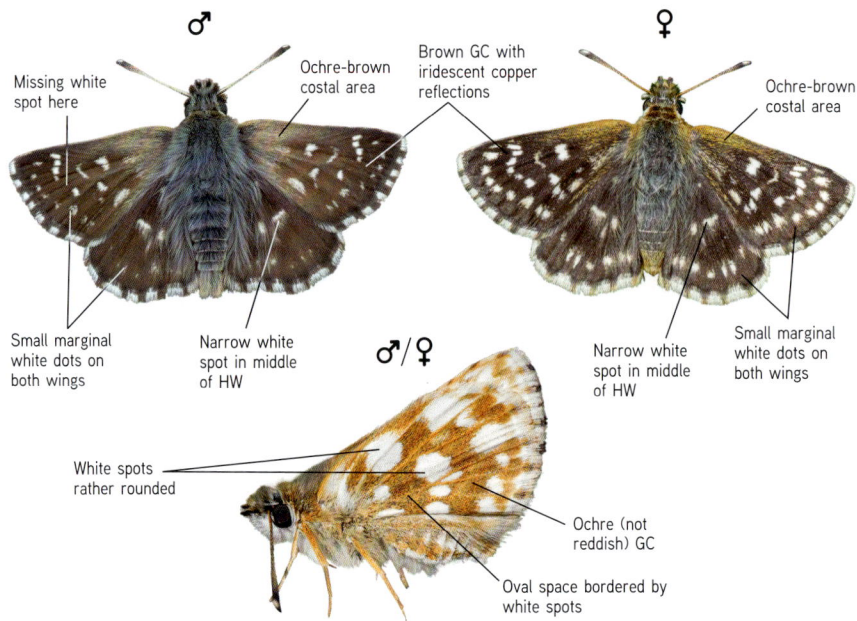

♂

Missing white spot here

Ochre-brown costal area

Brown GC with iridescent copper reflections

♀

Ochre-brown costal area

Small marginal white dots on both wings

Narrow white spot in middle of HW

♂/♀

Narrow white spot in middle of HW

Small marginal white dots on both wings

White spots rather rounded

Ochre (not reddish) GC

Oval space bordered by white spots

Wingspan: 22–28 mm

Habitat: Grasslands, low-growing meadows and garrigue, sunny grassy pathsides.

Hibernating stage: Caterpillar.

Elevational range: Up to 2,500 m.

Egg-laying: Eggs are laid singly on LHP inflorescences and leaflets.

Flight period: From April to October.

Host plants: Small Rosaceae, including *Sanguisorba minor*, *S. officinalis*, *Poterium sanguisorba*, *Sarcopoterium spinosum*, *Potentilla crantzii*, and *Rubus idaeus*.

Diversity and systematics: European populations belong to the nominate subspecies.

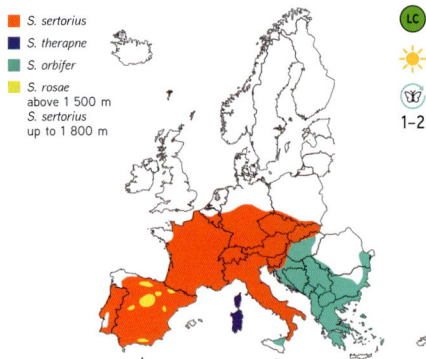

S. sertorius
S. therapne
S. orbifer
S. rosae above 1 500 m
S. sertorius up to 1 800 m

LC

1–2

	IMAGOS			LARVAE	
Food			Food		
Behaviour of males			Caterpillar location		
Dispersion			Chrysalis location		

Did you know?

Males like to land on the ground in bare spots, such as rocks, to guard their territory.

CORSICAN RED-UNDERWING SKIPPER *SPIALIA THERAPNE*

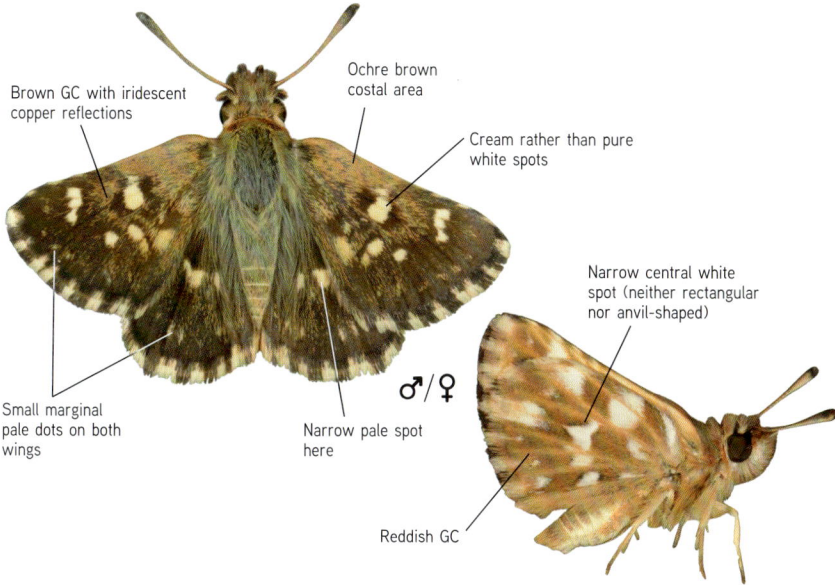

Brown GC with iridescent copper reflections

Ochre brown costal area

Cream rather than pure white spots

Narrow central white spot (neither rectangular nor anvil-shaped)

Small marginal pale dots on both wings

Narrow pale spot here

♂/♀

Reddish GC

Wingspan: 22–26 mm

Habitat: Dry, open, and sunny environments, such as garrigue-covered rocky slopes and bushy grasslands.

Hibernating stage: Pupa.

Elevational range: Up to 1,500 m.

Egg-laying: Eggs are laid singly on LHP inflorescences.

Flight period: From April to September.

Host plants: *Sanguisorba minor.*

Diversity and systematics: *Spialia therapne* was previously considered a subspecies of *S. sertorius.* However, a 2016 phylogenetic study, which evidences the existence of *S. rosae,* presents the phylogeny of the *S. sertorius* and *S. orbifer* species complex. According to these results, *S. therapne* should inevitably be elevated to the species level.

S. sertorius
S. therapne
S. orbifer
S. rosae
above 1 500 m
S. sertorius
up to 1 800 m

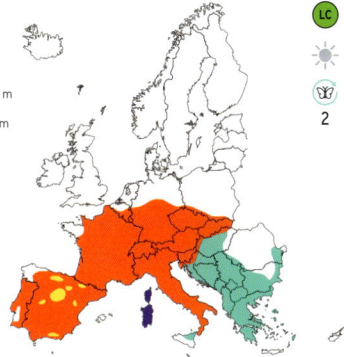

LC

2

	IMAGOS		LARVAE	
Food		Food		
Behaviour of males		Caterpillar location		
Dispersion		Chrysalis location		

Did you know?

Males of the *Spialia* genus are particularly agile at chasing any intruder entering their territory, whether it belongs to their species or not!

HESPERIIDAE

PERSIAN SKIPPER *SPIALIA PHLOMIDIS*

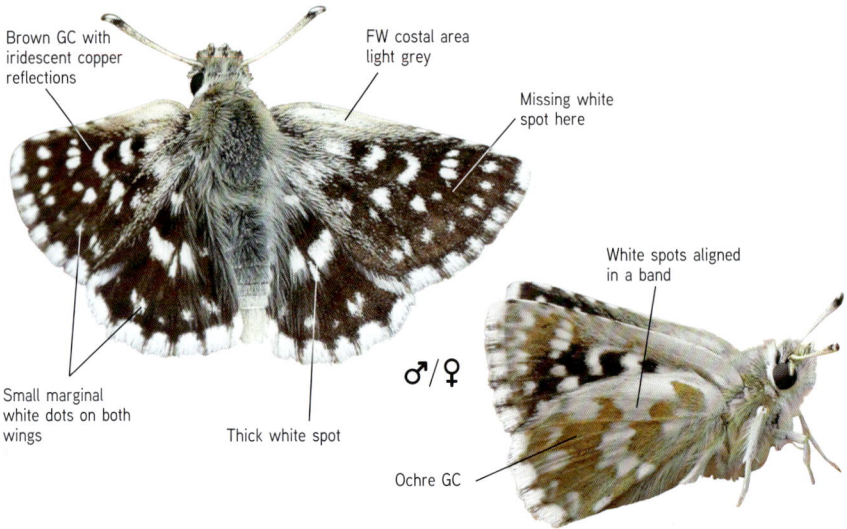

Brown GC with iridescent copper reflections

FW costal area light grey

Missing white spot here

White spots aligned in a band

Small marginal white dots on both wings

Thick white spot

♂/♀

Ochre GC

Wingspan: 24–30 mm

Habitat: Dry or steppic, stony, flower-rich grasslands.

Hibernating stage: Caterpillar.

Elevational range: Up to 2,500 m.

Egg-laying: Eggs are laid singly on LHP leaves.

Flight period: From June to September.

Host plants: Convolvulaceae, including *Convolvulus boissieri*, *C. cantabrica*, and *C. lineatus*.

Diversity and systematics: European populations belong to the nominate subspecies.

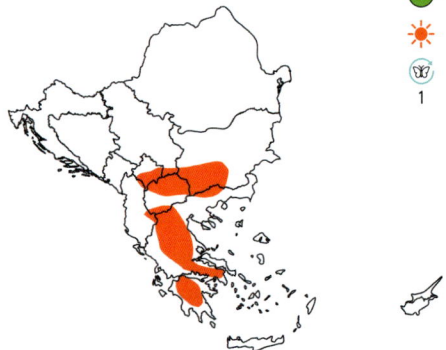

LC

1

	IMAGOS		LARVAE	
Food		Food		
Behaviour of males		Caterpillar location		
Dispersion		Chrysalis location		

Did you know?

Male Persian Skippers spend significantly more time patrolling than those of other *Spialia* species.

164

HESPERIIDAE

SAFFLOWER SKIPPER *PYRGUS CARTHAMI*

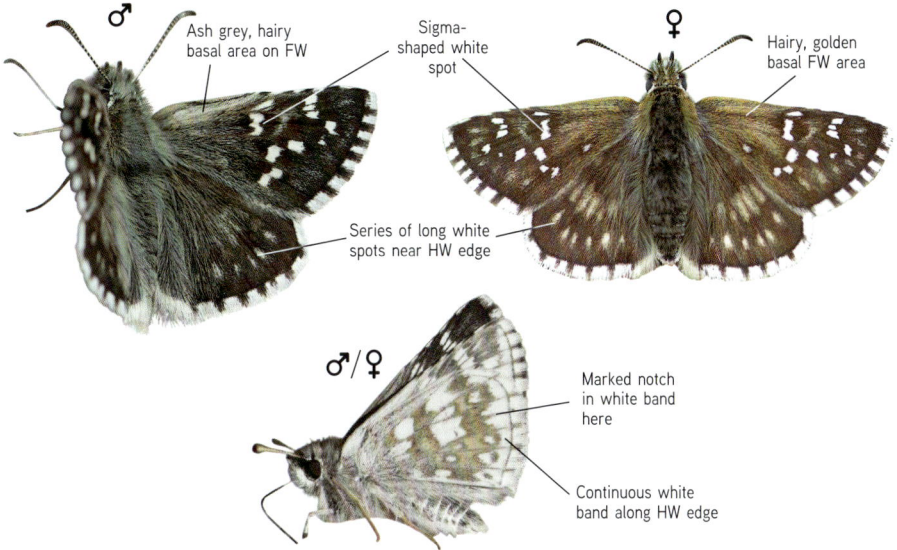

♂

Ash grey, hairy basal area on FW

Sigma-shaped white spot

♀

Hairy, golden basal FW area

Series of long white spots near HW edge

♂/♀

Marked notch in white band here

Continuous white band along HW edge

Wingspan: 30–34 mm

Habitat: Dry grasslands and flower-rich meadows, usually with bushes.

Hibernating stage: Caterpillar.

Elevational range: Up to 2,000 m.

Egg-laying: Eggs are laid singly on LHP leaflets.

Flight period: From May to September.

Host plants: Rosaceae of genus *Potentilla*, especially *P. verna*, *P. pusilla*, *P. hirta*, *P. heptaphylla*, *P. incana*, *P. reptans*, *P. crantzii*, and *P. cinerea*.

Diversity and systematics: Several subspecies have been described: *carthami* (Central and Eastern Europe, north of the Alps and east to France), *moeschleri* (southeastern Europe), *nevadensis* (the Iberian Peninsula and the majority of French and Italian populations), *valaisiacus* (northern Italy, southern Switzerland, and southeast of the Alps), and *septentrionalis* (northern Europe).

LC
1

IMAGOS			LARVAE		
Food			Food		
Behaviour of males			Caterpillar location		
Dispersion			Chrysalis location		

Did you know?

The Safflower Skipper is declining significantly outside the Alps and the Mediterranean region due to agricultural intensification and the loss of calcareous grasslands.

HESPERIIDAE

YELLOW-BANDED SKIPPER   *PYRGUS SIDAE*

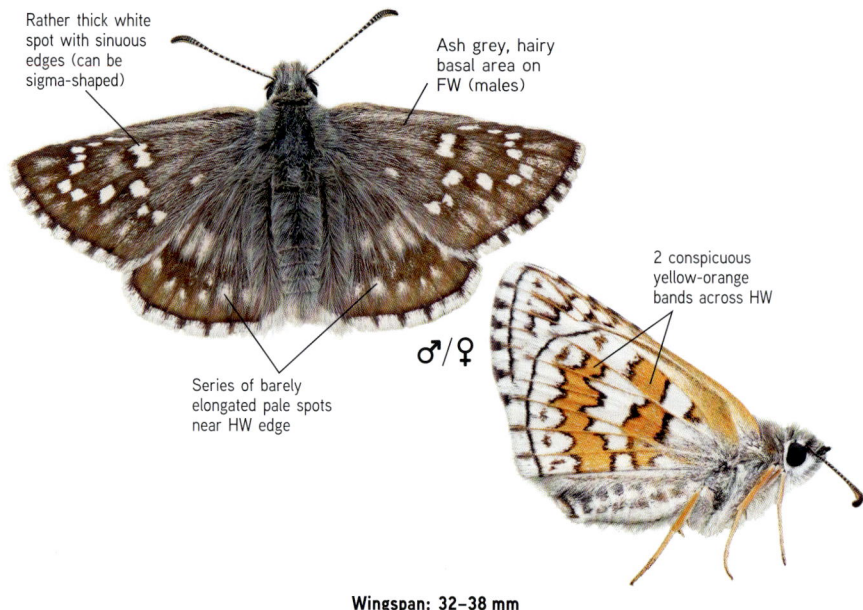

Rather thick white spot with sinuous edges (can be sigma-shaped)

Ash grey, hairy basal area on FW (males)

2 conspicuous yellow-orange bands across HW

Series of barely elongated pale spots near HW edge

♂/♀

Wingspan: 32–38 mm

Habitat: Grassy clearings, pathsides in bushy or Mediterranean forest contexts (especially pubescent oak forests), abandoned agricultural terraces.

Hibernating stage: Caterpillar.

Elevational range: Up to 1,500 m.

Egg-laying: Eggs are laid singly on LHP leaflets or flowers.

Flight period: From April to August.

Host plants: Rosaceae of genus *Potentilla*, especially *P. recta*, *P. pedata*, and *P. hirta*. Also *Abutilon theophrasti* (Malvaceae).

Diversity and systematics: Balkan populations belong to the nominate subspecies, while those from the western Mediterranean basin belong to subspecies *occiduus*.

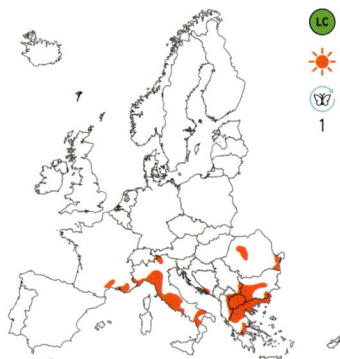

LC

1

Did you know?

Genus *Sida*, which gives its scientific name to this skipper, comprises plants in the Malvaceae family to which the LHP *Abutilon theophrasti* used to belong before its generic name changed.

IMAGOS		LARVAE	
Food		Food	
Behaviour of males		Caterpillar location	
Dispersion		Chrysalis location	

HESPERIIDAE

ALPINE GRIZZLED SKIPPER *PYRGUS ANDROMEDAE*

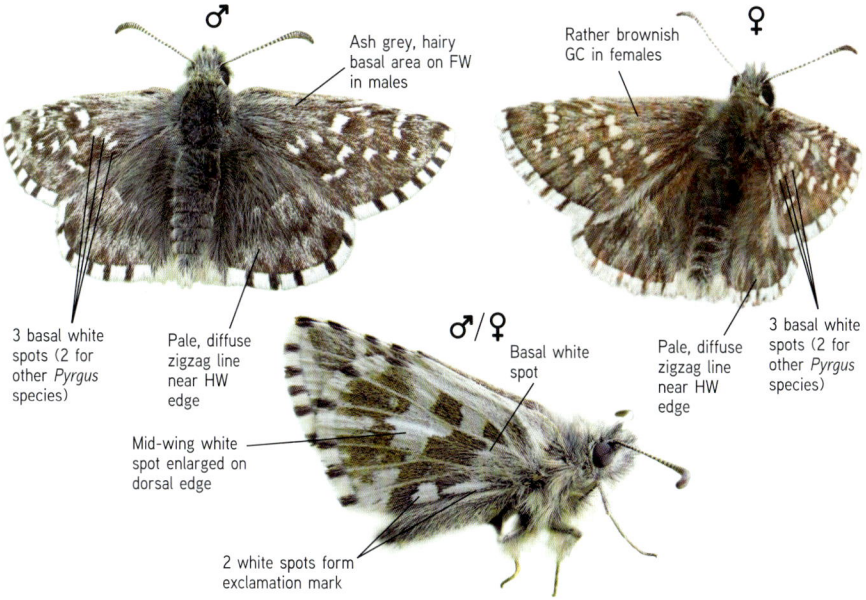

♂

Ash grey, hairy
basal area on FW
in males

Rather brownish
GC in females

♀

3 basal white
spots (2 for
other *Pyrgus*
species)

Pale, diffuse
zigzag line
near HW
edge

♂/♀

Basal white
spot

Pale, diffuse
zigzag line
near HW
edge

3 basal white
spots (2 for
other *Pyrgus*
species)

Mid-wing white
spot enlarged on
dorsal edge

2 white spots form
exclamation mark

Wingspan: 26–31 mm

Habitat: Flower-rich grasslands and low subalpine and alpine heathland.

Hibernating stage: Caterpillar for the first winter, and pupa for the second.

Elevational range: Up to 1,000 m in Scandinavia, from 1,500 to 3,000 m in temperate massifs.

Egg-laying: Eggs are laid singly on LHP leaves.

Flight period: From May to August.

Host plants: *Dryas octopetala* (Rosaceae).

Diversity and systematics: There are no notable subspecies for this arctic-alpine skipper. However, the Pyrenean, Alpine, and Scandinavian populations are genetically differentiated.

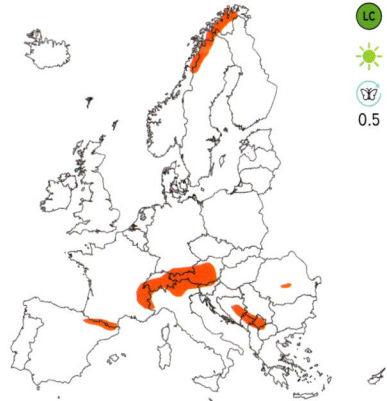

LC

0.5

IMAGOS		LARVAE	
Food		Food	
Behaviour of males		Caterpillar location	
Dispersion		Chrysalis location	

Did you know?

The Alpine Grizzled Skipper, like its main host plant, is typically a glacial relict species.

167

DUSKY GRIZZLED SKIPPER *PYRGUS CACALIAE*

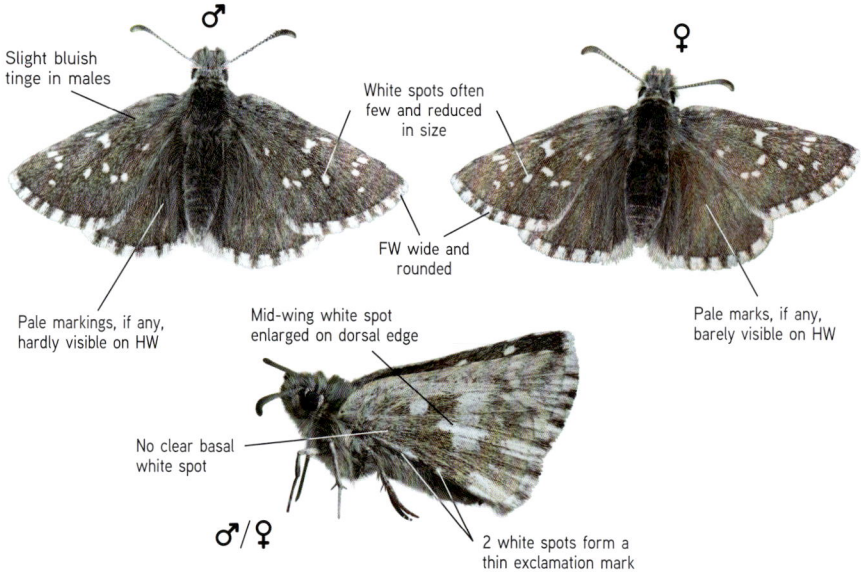

♂

Slight bluish tinge in males

White spots often few and reduced in size

♀

FW wide and rounded

Pale markings, if any, hardly visible on HW

Mid-wing white spot enlarged on dorsal edge

Pale marks, if any, barely visible on HW

No clear basal white spot

♂/♀

2 white spots form a thin exclamation mark

Wingspan: 26–31 mm

Habitat: Subalpine and alpine grasslands and meadows, especially in the vicinity of streams or other damp environments.

Hibernating stage: Caterpillar for the first winter, and pupa for the second.

Elevational range: From 1,500 to 3,000 m.

Egg-laying: Eggs are laid singly on LHP leaflets.

Flight period: From June to August.

Host plants: Rosaceae within genus *Potentilla*, especially *P. aurea, P. crantzii,* and *P. erecta.* Also *Geum montanum* and *G. rivale.*

Diversity and systematics: There are no notable subspecies for this skipper with a disjunct range across European mountains. However, genetic studies show some level of divergence among the Pyrenean, Alpine, and Central European populations.

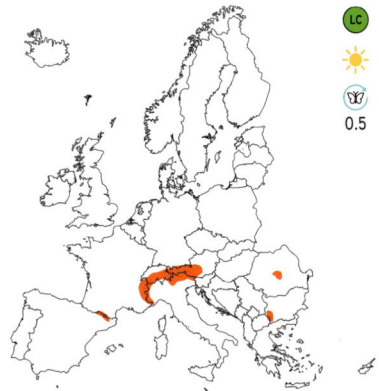

LC

0.5

IMAGOS		LARVAE	
Food	🌸💧	Food	🌸🌿
Behaviour of males		Caterpillar location	
Dispersion		Chrysalis location	

Did you know?

Biennial larval development leads to significant variations in numbers from one year to another.

HESPERIIDAE

NORTHERN GRIZZLED SKIPPER *PYRGUS CENTAUREAE*

♂/♀

White spots
rather thick

Large white spot
along outer HW
edge

Series of rounded
white spots near
HW edge

Conspicuous pale
veins contrast
with GC

White spots
aligned in a
band

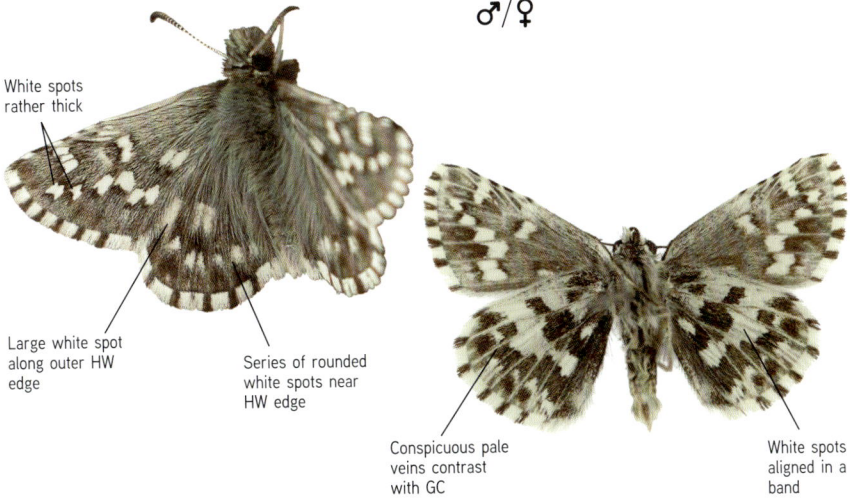

Wingspan: 26–32 mm

Habitat: Wet heaths and peat bogs, often within woodlands.

Hibernating stage: Caterpillar or pupa.

Elevational range: Up to 1,000 m.

Egg-laying: Eggs are laid singly on LHP leaves.

Flight period: From June to August.

Host plants: Rosaceae, including *Rubus chamaemorus, Potentilla canadensis, P. diversifolia,* and *Fragaria virginiana.* Also cited on *Betula nana* (Betulaceae).

Diversity and systematics: European populations belong to the nominate subspecies.

LC

1

IMAGOS	LARVAE
Food	Food
Behaviour of males	Caterpillar location
Dispersion	Chrysalis location

Did you know?

The Northern Grizzled Skipper is present throughout the boreal region, from Europe to North America and Asia.

HESPERIIDAE

WARREN'S SKIPPER *PYRGUS WARRENENSIS*

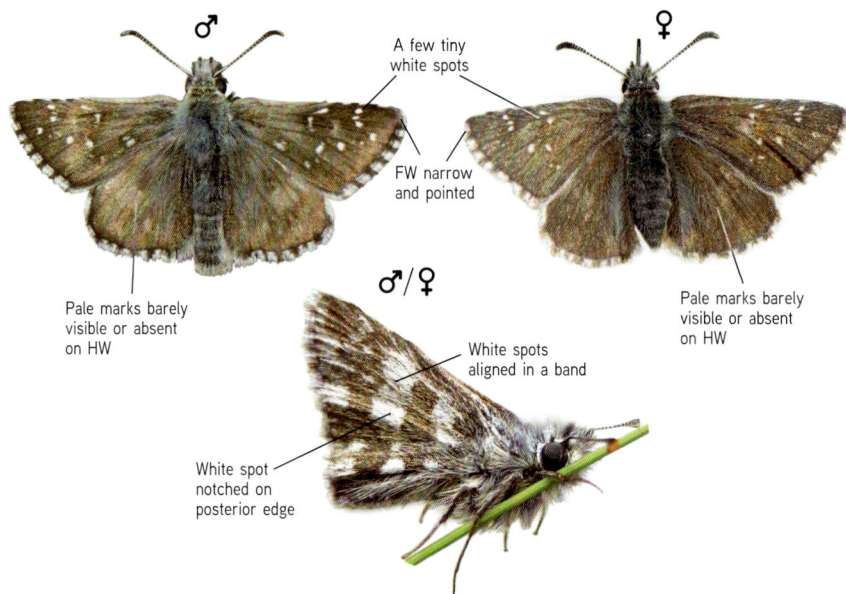

♂

A few tiny
white spots

FW narrow
and pointed

♀

Pale marks barely
visible or absent
on HW

♂/♀

White spots
aligned in a band

Pale marks barely
visible or absent
on HW

White spot
notched on
posterior edge

Wingspan: 23–26 mm

Habitat: Low-growing subalpine and alpine grasslands and meadows.

Hibernating stage: Caterpillar (twice).

Elevational range: From 1,800 to 2,600 m.

Egg-laying: Eggs are laid singly on LHP leaves.

Flight period: July and August.

Host plants: Small Cistaceae, like *Helianthemum canum*, *H. nummularium*, and *H. oelandicum*.

Diversity and systematics: There are no notable subspecies for this skipper, which is endemic to the Alpine arc. Its phylogenetic relationship with *Pyrgus alveus* remains to be ascertained.

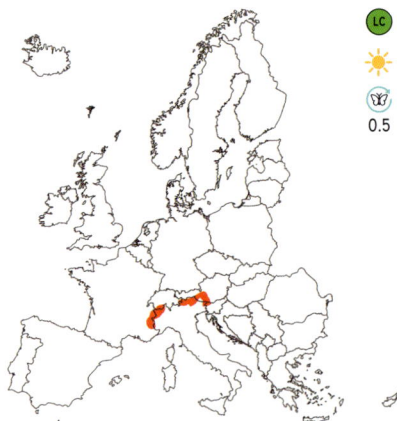

LC

0.5

IMAGOS		LARVAE	
Food	✿ 💧	Food	🍃
Behaviour of males	🦋 🦋	Caterpillar location	🌿
Dispersion	🕸	Chrysalis location	🌱

Did you know?

Adults forage primarily on thyme, small legumes, and asters.

170

HESPERIIDAE

OBERTHÜR'S GRIZZLED SKIPPER   *PYRGUS ARMORICANUS*

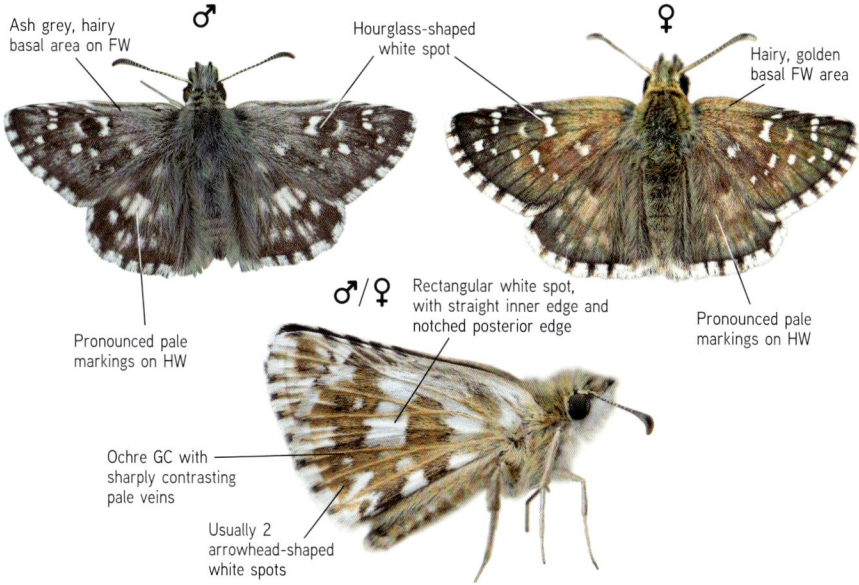

♂

Ash grey, hairy basal area on FW

Hourglass-shaped white spot

♀

Hairy, golden basal FW area

Pronounced pale markings on HW

♂/♀

Rectangular white spot, with straight inner edge and notched posterior edge

Pronounced pale markings on HW

Ochre GC with sharply contrasting pale veins

Usually 2 arrowhead-shaped white spots

Wingspan: 24–28 mm

Habitat: Dry grasslands, lean pastures, fallow lands, forest edges, and roadside embankments.

Hibernating stage: Caterpillar.

Elevational range: Up to 2,000 m (mostly at lower elevations).

Egg-laying: Eggs are laid singly on LHP leaflets.

Flight period: From March to October.

Host plants: Numerous cinquefoils, including *Potentilla neumanniana, P. reptans, P. argentea, P. recta, P. hirta, P. sterilis, P. erecta, P. pusilla, P. verna, P. pedata,* and *P. pyrenaica.* Also cited on other Rosaceae like *Fragaria vesca* and *Filipendula vulgaris* as well as on *Helianthemum nummularium* (Cistaceae).

Diversity and systematics: European populations belong to the nominate subspecies.

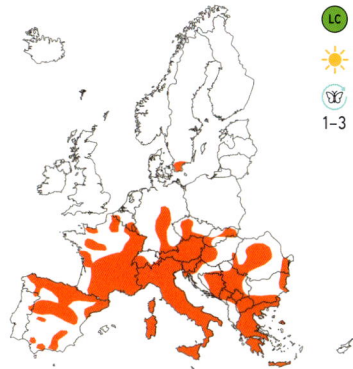

LC

1–3

IMAGOS			LARVAE	
Food			Food	
Behaviour of males			Caterpillar location	
Dispersion			Chrysalis location	

Did you know?

Like several other species in the *Pyrgus* genus, Oberthür's Grizzled Skipper benefits from extensive sheep grazing and late mowing.

HESPERIIDAE

OLIVE SKIPPER *PYRGUS SERRATULAE*

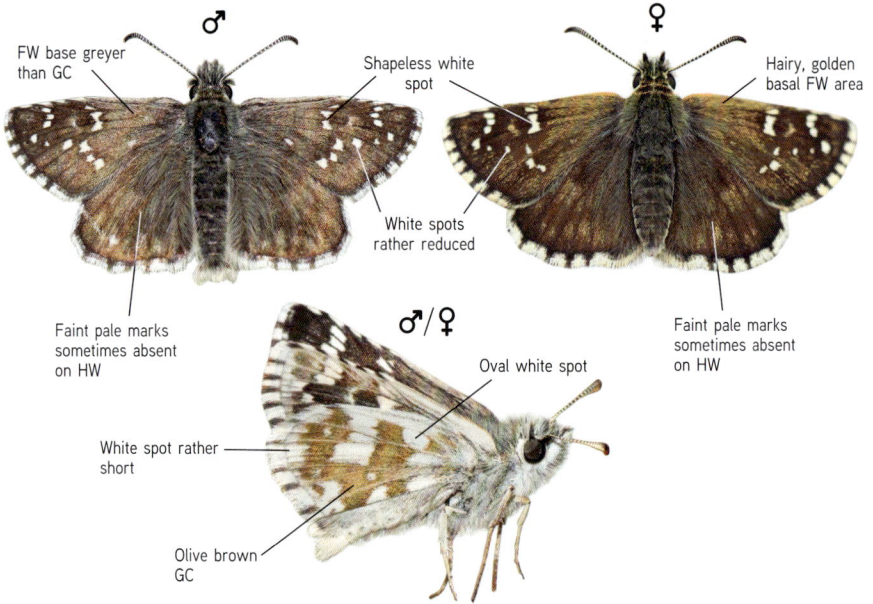

♂

FW base greyer than GC

Shapeless white spot

♀

Hairy, golden basal FW area

White spots rather reduced

Faint pale marks sometimes absent on HW

♂/♀

Oval white spot

Faint pale marks sometimes absent on HW

White spot rather short

Olive brown GC

Wingspan: 24–32 mm

Habitat: Meadows, grasslands, and pastures. Sometimes in parks and gardens.

Hibernating stage: Caterpillar.

Elevational range: Up to 2,500 m.

Egg-laying: Eggs are laid singly on LHP leaflets.

Flight period: From May to August.

Host plants: Rosaceae in genus *Potentilla*, including *P. recta, P. verna, P. heptaphylla, P. crantzii, P. aurea, P. reptans, P. pusilla, P. pedata,* and *P. frigida.* Females have also been seen laying on *Alchemilla pentaphyllea, Geum montanum, G. reptans,* and *Sibbaldia procumbens.*

Diversity and systematics: Most European populations belong to the nominate subspecies. The presence of subspecies *major* in Southern Europe is controversial. Subspecies *balcanica* is also described from Montenegro.

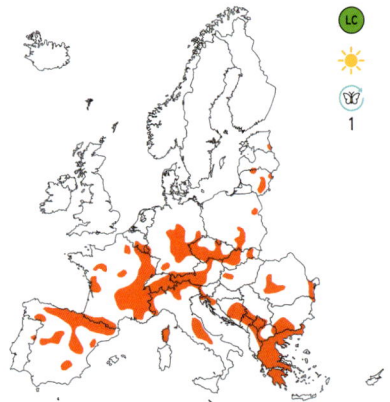

LC

1

IMAGOS		LARVAE	
Food		Food	
Behaviour of males		Caterpillar location	
Dispersion		Chrysalis location	

Did you know?

The species name, *serratulae*, refers to an aster that adults can forage on, but it is definitely not a larval host plant.

HESPERIIDAE

LARGE GRIZZLED SKIPPER *PYRGUS ALVEUS*

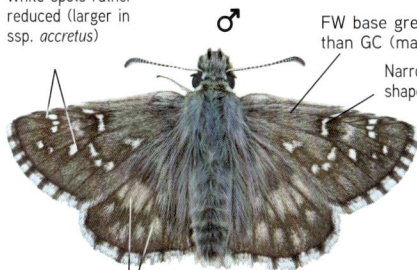

White spots rather reduced (larger in ssp. *accretus*)

♂

FW base greyer than GC (males)

Narrow, often shapeless white spot

♀

Brown GC

Faint, pale marks on HW (more visible in ssp. *accretus*)

♂/♀

Rectangular white spot

Faint pale marks on HW (more visible in ssp. *accretus*)

Rectangular white spot with straight inner edge and notched posterior edge

Greenish-yellow GC

Wingspan: 22–32 mm

Habitat: Sunny meadows and grasslands, often with bare areas.

Hibernating stage: Caterpillar.

Elevational range: Up to 2,500 m.

Egg-laying: Eggs are laid singly on LHP leaves.

Flight period: From May to September.

Host plants: Cistaceae, like *Helianthemum nummularium*, *H. hirtum, H. oelandicum*, and *Cistus lasianthus*. Small Rosaceae within genus *Potentilla*, including *P. argentea, P. reptans, P. neumanniana, P. sterilis, P. verna*, and *P. erecta*.

Diversity and systematics: The systematics of *Pyrgus alveus* is very complicated and not yet fully resolved. It is likely a complex of young species. The nominate subspecies flies from France to the Urals. *Scandinavicus* flies in southern Scandinavia, *centralhispaniae* in Spain, *trebevicensis* from southern Germany to the Balkans, and *accretus* in the Pyrenees, Western Alps, and Switzerland, sometimes in sympatry with *alveus*, which explains why it can be considered a distinct species.

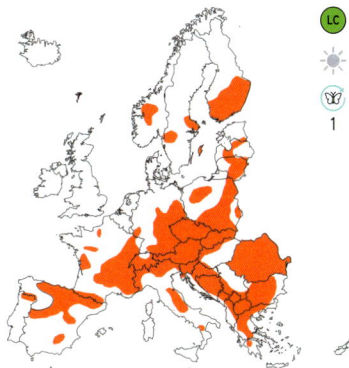

LC

1

Did you know?

Successional grassland loss due to the abandonment of extensive grazing adversely affects the Large Grizzled Skipper in the northern part of its range.

IMAGOS		LARVAE	
Food		Food	
Behaviour of males		Caterpillar location	
Dispersion		Chrysalis location	

HESPERIIDAE

FOULQUIER'S GRIZZLED SKIPPER *PYRGUS BELLIERI (= FOULQUIERI)*

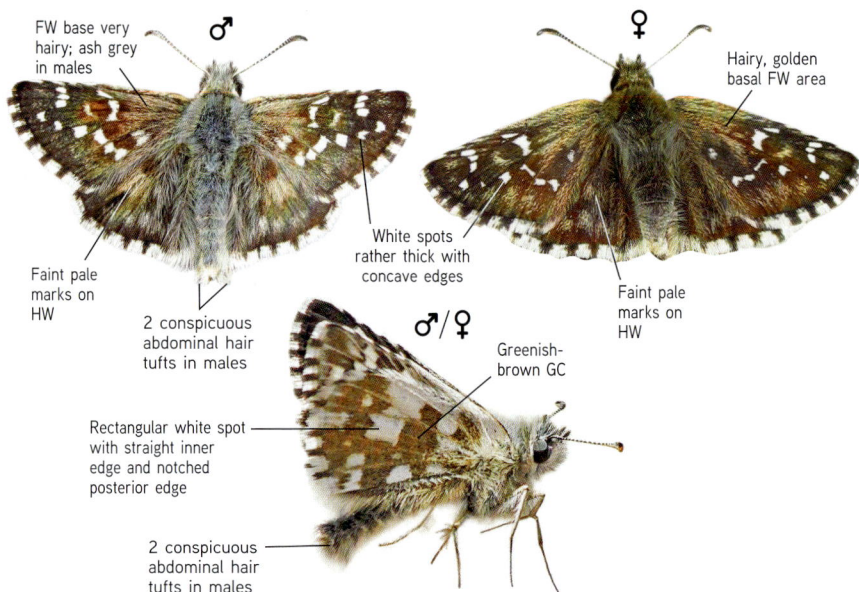

FW base very hairy; ash grey in males

♂

♀

Hairy, golden basal FW area

White spots rather thick with concave edges

Faint pale marks on HW

2 conspicuous abdominal hair tufts in males

♂/♀

Greenish-brown GC

Faint pale marks on HW

Rectangular white spot with straight inner edge and notched posterior edge

2 conspicuous abdominal hair tufts in males

Wingspan: 26–30 mm

Habitat: Dry grasslands within a forest context at low elevations; more open habitats at higher altitudes.

Hibernating stage: Caterpillar.

Elevational range: Up to 2,000 m.

Egg-laying: Eggs are laid singly on LHP leaves.

Flight period: From June to September.

Host plants: Sunroses, including *Helianthemum nummularium, H. hirtum, H. apenninum,* and *H. oelandicum.*

Diversity and systematics: The nominate subspecies flies from southern France to Spanish Catalonia. Subspecies *picenus* flies in central Italy.

LC

1

Did you know?

The Foulquier's Grizzled Skipper is difficult to identify. It can be confused with the Large Grizzled Skipper, to which it is also closely related.

IMAGOS		LARVAE	
Food		Food	
Behaviour of males		Caterpillar location	
Dispersion		Chrysalis location	

HESPERIIDAE

GRIZZLED SKIPPER *PYRGUS MALVAE*

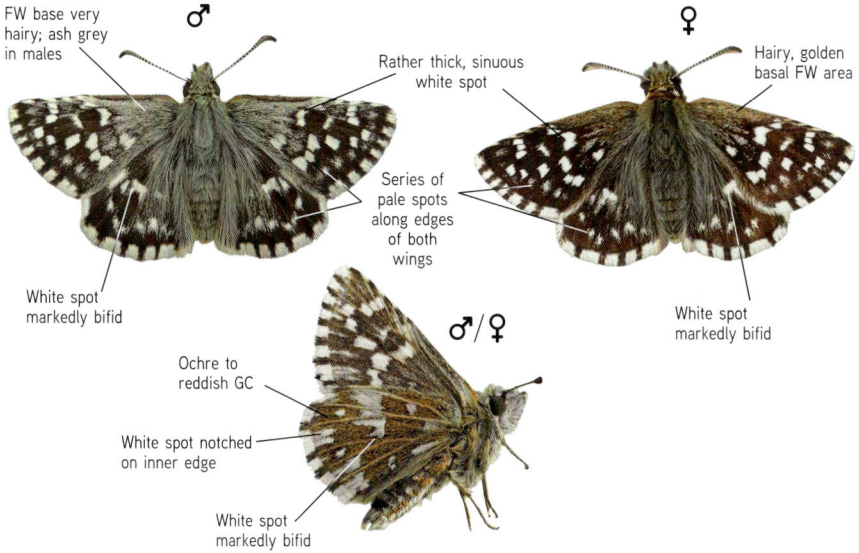

FW base very hairy; ash grey in males ♂

Rather thick, sinuous white spot

♀ Hairy, golden basal FW area

Series of pale spots along edges of both wings

White spot markedly bifid

White spot markedly bifid

♂/♀

Ochre to reddish GC

White spot notched on inner edge

White spot markedly bifid

Wingspan: 20–26 mm

Habitat: Grasslands, low-growing meadows with bare areas, forest clearings and edges.

Hibernating stage: Pupa.

Elevational range: Up to 2,500 m.

Egg-laying: Eggs are laid singly on LHP leaves.

Flight period: From March to September.

Host plants: A wide range of Rosaceae, including *Potentilla verna, P. reptans, P. heptaphylla, P. argentea, P. anglica, P. erecta, P. sterilis, P. palustris, Fragaria vesca, F. viridis, F. moschata, Geum urbanum, Comarum palustre, Agrimonia eupatoria, Rubus fruticosus, R. caesius, R. idaeus, R. aetnicus, R. canescens, Sanguisorba minor,* and *Filipendula ulmaria.* Also cited on *Helianthemum nummularium* and *H. apenninum* (Cistaceae).

Diversity and systematics: European populations belong to the nominate subspecies, although various forms have been described.

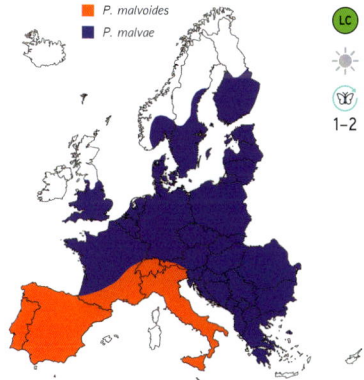

■ P. malvoides
■ P. malvae

LC

1–2

IMAGOS		LARVAE	
Food		Food	
Behaviour of males		Caterpillar location	
Dispersion		Chrysalis location	

Did you know?

The scientific name *malvae* refers to mallow plants, which the Grizzled Skipper doesn't use in either the larval or adult stage!

HESPERIIDAE

SOUTHERN GRIZZLED SKIPPER *PYRGUS MALVOIDES*

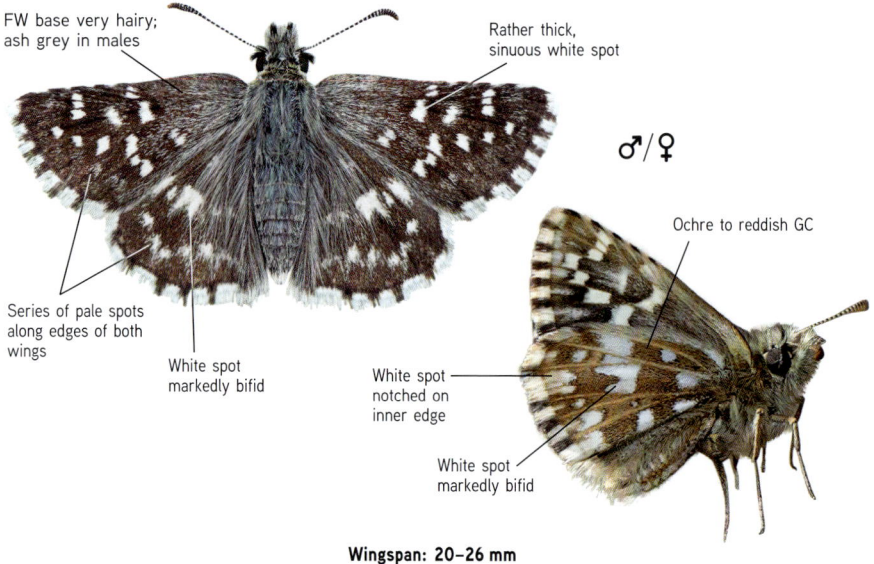

FW base very hairy; ash grey in males

Rather thick, sinuous white spot

♂/♀

Ochre to reddish GC

Series of pale spots along edges of both wings

White spot markedly bifid

White spot notched on inner edge

White spot markedly bifid

Wingspan: 20–26 mm

Habitat: Grasslands, garrigue, forest clearings and edges.

Hibernating stage: Caterpillar.

Elevational range: Up to 2,500 m.

Egg-laying: Eggs are laid singly on LHP leaves.

Flight period: From April to August.

Host plants: A wide range of Rosaceae, including *Potentilla verna, P. pusilla, P. erecta, P. reptans, P. aurea, P. argentea, P. grandiflora, P. hirta, P. crantzii, P. pensylvanica, Agrimonia eupatoria, Alchemilla glaucescens, A. hybrida, Geum montanum, Filipendula ulmaria, F. vulgaris, Rubus idaeus, R. caesius, R. fruticosus,* and *Sanguisorba minor.*

Diversity and systematics: The Spanish and French populations (excluding in the southeast) belong to the nominate subspecies. Subspecies *modestior* flies from southeastern France to Italy.

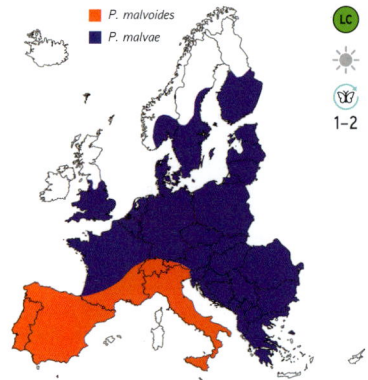

- P. malvoides
- P. malvae

LC

1–2

Did you know?

The Southern Grizzled Skipper replaces the Grizzled Skipper in the southern part of Western Europe. It is very similar to it and cannot be reliably distinguished in the narrow sympatric zone without genitalia examination.

IMAGOS		LARVAE	
Food	🌸 💧	Food	🍃
Behaviour of males		Caterpillar location	
Dispersion		Chrysalis location	

HESPERIIDAE

CARLINE SKIPPER *PYRGUS CARLINAE*

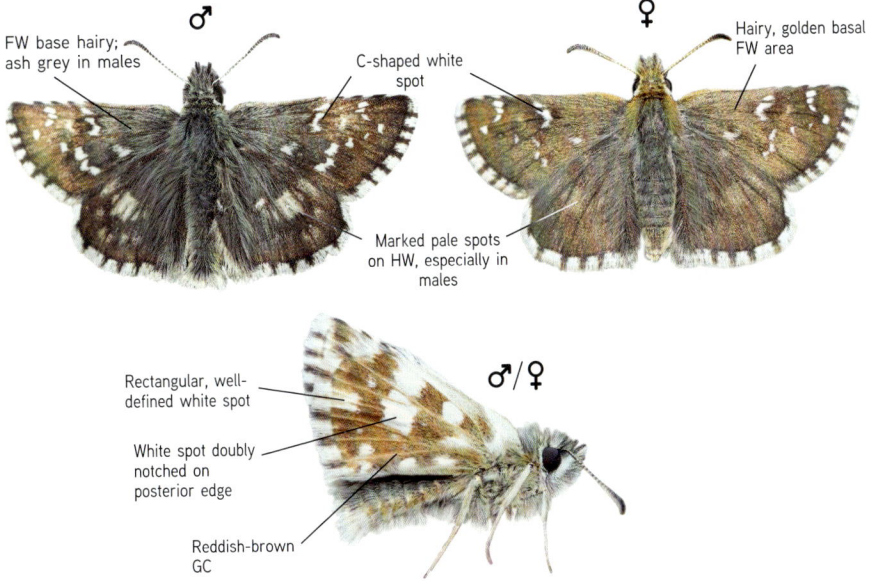

♂

FW base hairy; ash grey in males

C-shaped white spot

♀

Hairy, golden basal FW area

Marked pale spots on HW, especially in males

♂/♀

Rectangular, well-defined white spot

White spot doubly notched on posterior edge

Reddish-brown GC

Wingspan: 26–32 mm

Habitat: Montane, subalpine, and alpine sunny grasslands.

Hibernating stage: Caterpillar inside the egg.

Elevational range: From 1,000 to 3,000 m.

Egg-laying: Eggs are laid singly on LHP leaflets.

Flight period: July and August.

Host plants: Rosaceae in genus *Potentilla*, mainly *P. verna*, *P. pusilla*, and *P. grandiflora*. Also cited are *P. crantzii*, *P. reptans*, and *P. hirta*. Also *Helianthemum nummularium* (Cistaceae).

Diversity and systematics: There are no notable subspecies for this skipper that is endemic to the Alpine arc.

LC

1

IMAGOS	LARVAE
Food	Food
Behaviour of males	Caterpillar location
Dispersion	Chrysalis location

Did you know?

Females lay eggs on host plants surrounded by bareground areas, which likely provide a microclimate for the caterpillar's development.

HESPERIIDAE

CINQUEFOIL SKIPPER *PYRGUS CIRSII*

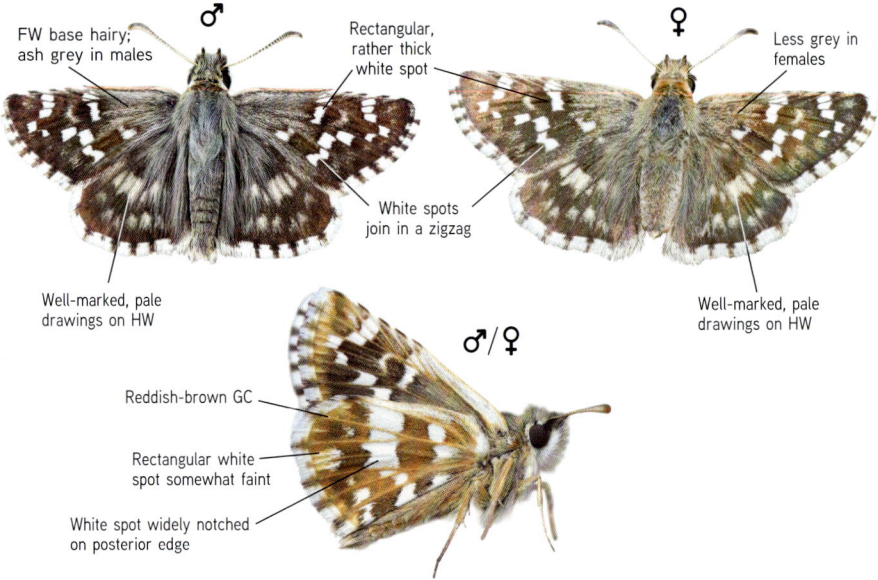

♂
FW base hairy; ash grey in males

Rectangular, rather thick white spot

♀
Less grey in females

White spots join in a zigzag

Well-marked, pale drawings on HW

Well-marked, pale drawings on HW

♂/♀

Reddish-brown GC

Rectangular white spot somewhat faint

White spot widely notched on posterior edge

Wingspan: 26–28 mm

Habitat: Dry grasslands with stones or bare areas.

Hibernating stage: Caterpillar inside the egg.

Elevational range: Up to 1,500 m.

Egg-laying: Eggs are laid singly on LHP leaflets.

Flight period: From May to August.

Host plants: Rosaceae in genus *Potentilla*, mainly *P. verna, P. pusilla, P. cinerea, P. incana, P. hirta, P. reptans,* and *P. heptaphylla.*

Diversity and systematics: Spanish and southwestern French populations belong to the *iberica* subspecies. The nominate subspecies flies in the rest of the range. The Cinquefoil Skipper was once considered a subspecies of the Carline Skipper.

VU

1

Did you know?

To develop well, larvae of the Cinquefoil Skipper need an environment devoid of vegetation around the LHP, which is facilitated by regular sheep grazing. This dependence significantly undermines this species in areas of pastoral abandonment.

IMAGOS		LARVAE		
Food		Food		
Behaviour of males		Caterpillar location		
Dispersion		Chrysalis location		

HESPERIIDAE

SANDY GRIZZLED SKIPPER *PYRGUS CINARAE*

♂/♀

FW base hairy and ash grey in males

Very thick, hourglass-shaped white spot

Very thick white spots

Yellowish-brown GC

White spot short, rectangular

Conspicuous pale markings on HW

White spot slightly notched on posterior edge

White spot points rather forwards

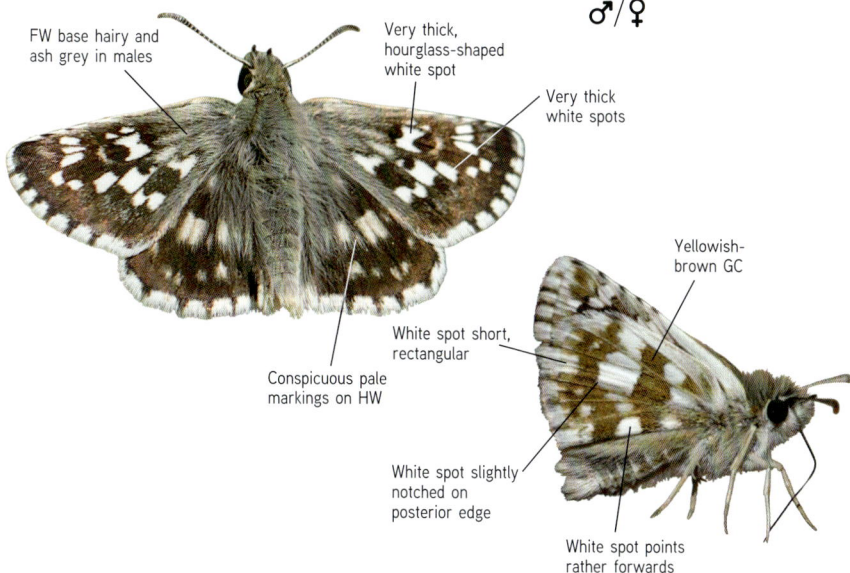

Wingspan: 30–32 mm

Habitat: Dry or steppic grasslands in the supra-Mediterranean domain, often grazed by sheep in the Balkans. Grasslands with *Filipendula vulgaris* in Spain.

Hibernating stage: Caterpillar inside the egg.

Elevational range: From 900 to 1,500 m.

Egg-laying: Eggs are laid singly on LHP calices and flower-bearing stems.

Flight period: From May to September.

Host plants: *Potentilla recta* and *P. hirta*. In Spain, also on *Filipendula vulgaris*.

Diversity and systematics: The nominate subspecies flies in the Balkans. Spanish populations belong to subspecies *chlorinda*.

LC

1

IMAGOS		LARVAE	
Food		Food	
Behaviour of males		Caterpillar location	
Dispersion		Chrysalis location	

Did you know?

The presence of this skipper in Spain is very localized. All the populations are found in less than 15,000 sq km.

HESPERIIDAE

ROSY GRIZZLED SKIPPER *PYRGUS ONOPORDI*

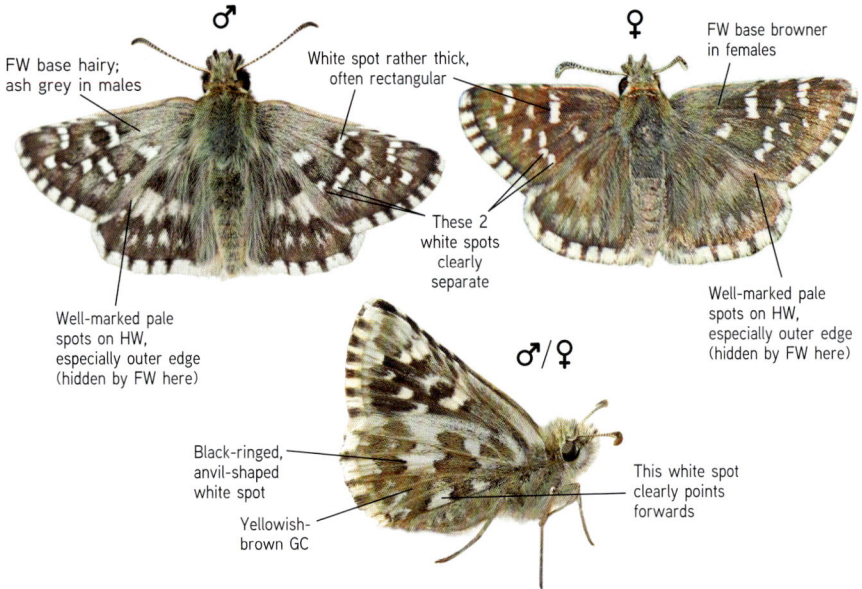

♂

FW base hairy; ash grey in males

White spot rather thick, often rectangular

♀

FW base browner in females

These 2 white spots clearly separate

Well-marked pale spots on HW, especially outer edge (hidden by FW here)

Well-marked pale spots on HW, especially outer edge (hidden by FW here)

♂/♀

Black-ringed, anvil-shaped white spot

Yellowish-brown GC

This white spot clearly points forwards

Wingspan: 22–28 mm

Habitat: Dry grasslands, meadows, edges of bushy environments, fallow lands.

Hibernating stage: Caterpillar.

Elevational range: Up to 2,500 m (mostly below 1,500 m).

Egg-laying: Eggs are laid singly on LHP leaves.

Flight period: From April to October.

Host plants: Rosaceae within genus *Potentilla*, including *P. pusilla*, *P. hirta*, *P. recta*, and *P. reptans*. Sunroses, such as *Helianthemum apenninum*, *H. nummularium*, and *H. hirtum*. Malvaceae like *Malva neglecta* and *M. parviflora*.

Diversity and systematics: There are no notable subspecies for this Western Mediterranean skipper.

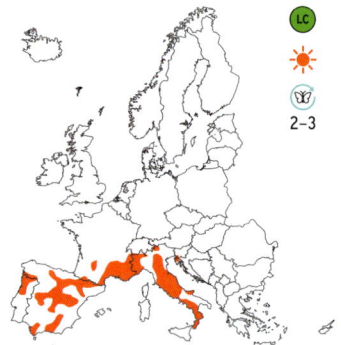

LC

2–3

IMAGOS		LARVAE	
Food	🌼💧	Food	🌿
Behaviour of males		Caterpillar location	
Dispersion		Chrysalis location	

Did you know?

The use of Malvaceae as larval host plants in the *Pyrgus* genus in Europe is known only for the Rosy Grizzled Skipper and the Yellow-banded Skipper. However, it is observed for American Grizzled Skippers.

THE PIERIDS (57 SPECIES)

SUBFAMILIES	GENERA	NUMBER OF SPECIES	MAIN LARVAL HOST-PLANT FAMILIES
Pierinae	Anthocharis, Aporia, Colotis, Euchloe, Iberochloe, Pieris, Pontia, and Zegris	32	Brassicaceae, Resedaceae, Rosaceae, Capparaceae, Cleomaceae, and Tropaeolaceae
Coliadinae	Catospilia, Colias, and Gonepteryx	20	Fabaceae, Rhamnaceae, Ericaceae, and Cesalpiniaceae
Dismorphiinae	Leptidea	5	Fabaceae

The Pierids comprise about 1,200 species worldwide. Most are found in equatorial and tropical regions. Subfamilies Pierinae and Coliadinae are medium-sized butterflies with fast and direct flight. Some of them, such as the Cabbage White or the Clouded Yellow, undertake migratory or dispersal journeys covering several hundred kilometres. Dismorphiines are smaller and move more slowly, with a leisurely flight rather close to the ground. Pierid caterpillars are often well camouflaged on their host plants, on which they feed despite the plants' toxicity (typically Brassicaceae). Some whites of genus *Pieris* are among the most widely distributed and common species in Europe, and they thrive in cabbage and rapeseed crops.

Anthocharis euphenoides

Colias alfacariensis

Pontia daplidice

Pieris brassicae

Gonepteryx rhamni

181

PIERIDAE

ORANGE-TIP *ANTHOCHARIS CARDAMINES*

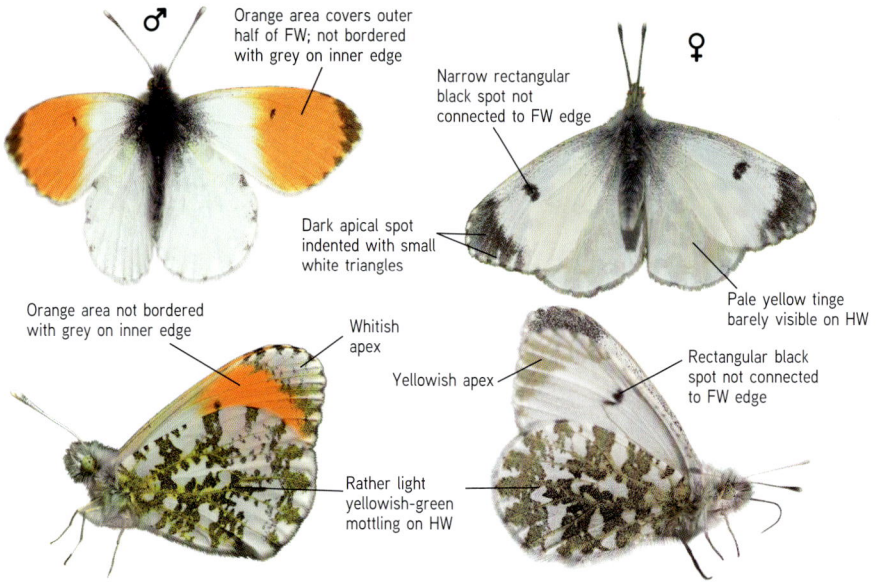

♂

Orange area covers outer half of FW; not bordered with grey on inner edge

♀

Narrow rectangular black spot not connected to FW edge

Dark apical spot indented with small white triangles

Pale yellow tinge barely visible on HW

Orange area not bordered with grey on inner edge

Whitish apex

Yellowish apex

Rectangular black spot not connected to FW edge

Rather light yellowish-green mottling on HW

Wingspan: 33–48 mm

Habitat: Mesophilic and moist meadows, forest edges and clearings, parks and gardens.

■ A. cardamines
■ A. gruneri + A. cardamines

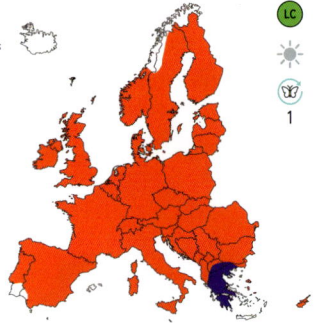

LC

Hibernating stage: Pupa.

Elevational range: Up to 2,000 m.

Egg-laying: Eggs are laid singly on LHP flower peduncles.

Flight period: From April to August.

Host plants: A wide range of Brassicaceae, mainly *Cardamine pratensis*, *Alliaria petiolata*, *Biscutella laevigata*, *Arabis hirsuta*, but also species in genera *Diplotaxis*, *Draba*, *Erucastrum*, *Hesperis*, *Hirschfeldia*, *Isatis*, *Lepidium*, *Lunaria*, *Nasturtium*, *Noccaea*, *Pseudoturritis*, *Rorippa*, *Sinapis*, *Sisymbrium*, *Teesdalia*, *Thlaspi*, and *Turritis*.

Diversity and systematics: Several subspecies and numerous forms are described. Subspecies *phoenissa* flies in Cyprus, *britannica* in England and Scotland, *hibernica* in Ireland, *meridionalis* in the western Mediterranean, *turritis* in Italy, and *montivaga* in the Southern Alps.

1

Did you know?

The Orange-tip is a species for which it is very easy to find whitish (and later orange) eggs that can be used in caterpillar rearing. However, witnessing the emergence will require exposing the pupa to winter cold and patiently waiting until the following spring.

IMAGOS		LARVAE		
Food	✿	Food	✿ 🌿 🌱	
Behaviour of males	🦋	Caterpillar location	🌾	
Dispersion		Chrysalis location	🌾	

GRÜNER'S ORANGE-TIP *ANTHOCHARIS GRUNERI*

Orange area covers outer half of FW; bordered with grey on inner edge

♂

Thick, rectangular dark spot almost connected to FW edge

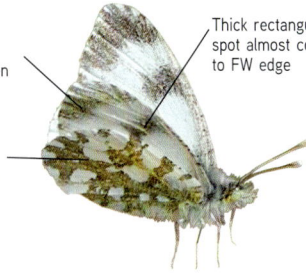

♀

Dark apical spot indented with small white triangles

Pale yellow GC

Pale yellow tinge barely visible on HW

White apex mottled with yellowish-green

Thick rectangular dark spot almost connected to FW edge

Rather light yellowish-green mottling on HW

Wingspan: 30–36 mm

Habitat: Dry rocky embankments and areas with sparse vegetation, olive groves interspersed with old stone walls.

Hibernating stage: Pupa.

Elevational range: Up to 2,000 m.

Egg-laying: Eggs are laid singly on LHP inflorescences.

Flight period: From February to July.

Host plants: Brassicaceae, including *Aethionema saxatile*, *Isatis tinctoria*, and *Thlaspi umbellatum*.

Diversity and systematics: The nominate subspecies flies in Greece, while subspecies *macedonica* has been described from Macedonia and has also been found in Bulgaria. The relevance of the latter is controversial.

A. cardamines
A. gruneri
+ A cardamines

LC

1

Did you know?

Encounters between males and females take place primarily on hilltops, where adults gather. The females then descend to lay eggs in favourable habitats.

IMAGOS		LARVAE	
Food		Food	
Behaviour of males		Caterpillar location	
Dispersion		Chrysalis location	

PIERIDAE

PROVENCE ORANGE-TIP *ANTHOCHARIS EUPHENOIDES*

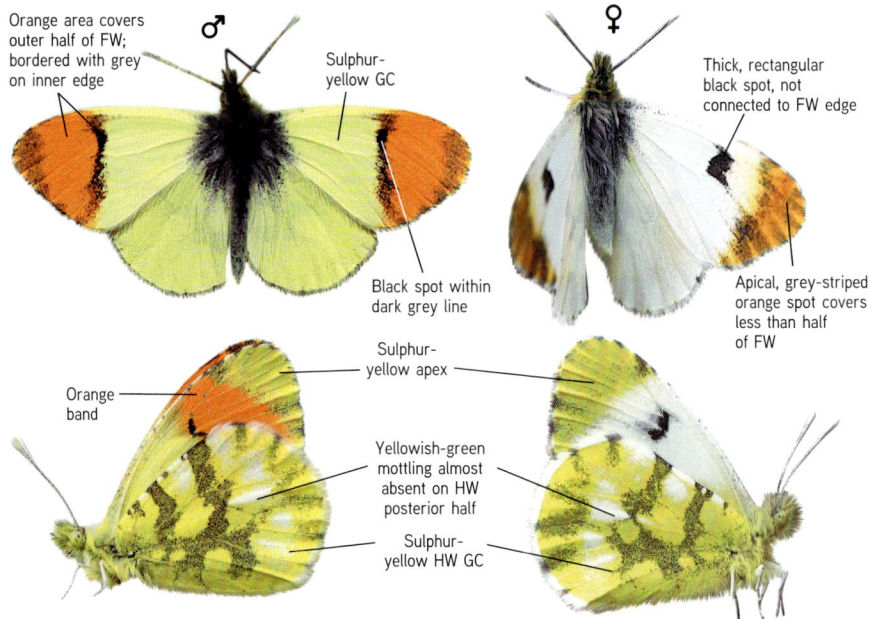

♂

Orange area covers outer half of FW; bordered with grey on inner edge

Sulphur-yellow GC

♀

Thick, rectangular black spot, not connected to FW edge

Black spot within dark grey line

Apical, grey-striped orange spot covers less than half of FW

Sulphur-yellow apex

Orange band

Yellowish-green mottling almost absent on HW posterior half

Sulphur-yellow HW GC

Wingspan: 34–40 mm

Habitat: Mediterranean forest edges and clearings, scrubland with open areas.

Hibernating stage: Pupa.

Elevational range: Up to 1,800 m.

Egg-laying: Eggs are laid singly on LHP inflorescences.

Flight period: From March to June.

Host plants: Brassicaceae, mainly in genus *Biscutella*, especially *B. laevigata*, but also *B. ambigua*, *B. auriculata*, *B. cichoriifolia*, *B. didyma*, *B. flexuosa*, *B. sempervirens*, *B. valentina*, *Erucastrum nasturtiifolium*, and *Hirschfeldia incana*.

Diversity and systematics: Most European populations belong to the nominate subspecies. Subspecies *alpium* flies in the southeast of France.

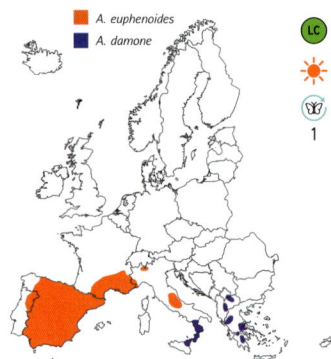

■ A. euphenoides
■ A. damone

LC

1

Did you know?

Similar to Orange-tip males, those of the Provence Orange-tip tirelessly roam edges with fast flight, often stopping only briefly to feed, mainly on Brassicaceae.

IMAGOS		LARVAE	
Food	✿	Food	✿ 🍃
Behaviour of males	🦋	Caterpillar location	🌿
Dispersion	🔛	Chrysalis location	🌱

PIERIDAE

EASTERN ORANGE-TIP *ANTHOCHARIS DAMONE*

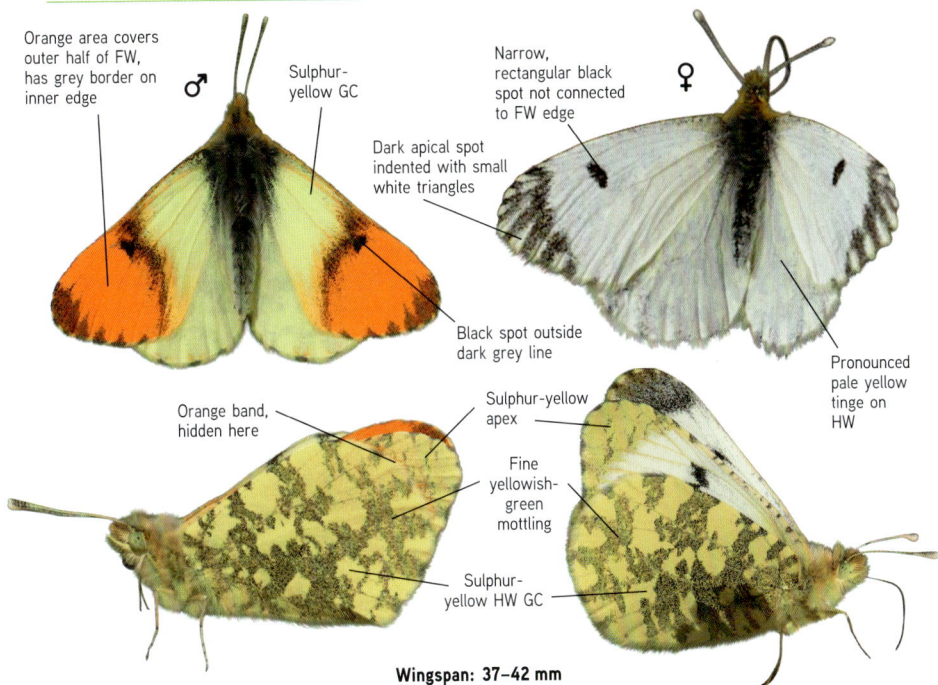

Orange area covers outer half of FW, has grey border on inner edge ♂

Sulphur-yellow GC

Narrow, rectangular black spot not connected to FW edge ♀

Dark apical spot indented with small white triangles

Black spot outside dark grey line

Pronounced pale yellow tinge on HW

Orange band, hidden here

Sulphur-yellow apex

Fine yellowish-green mottling

Sulphur-yellow HW GC

Wingspan: 37–42 mm

Habitat: Sparsely vegetated stony slopes and clear Mediterranean woodlands.

Hibernating stage: Pupa.

Elevational range: From 300 to 1,500 m.

Egg-laying: Eggs are laid singly on LHP inflorescences.

Flight period: From March to June.

Host plants: Brassicaceae, mainly *Isatis tinctoria*, *I. tomentella*, and *Aethionema saxatile*.

Diversity and systematics: The nominate subspecies flies in southern Italy and Sicily. Subspecies *eunomia* constitutes Balkan populations.

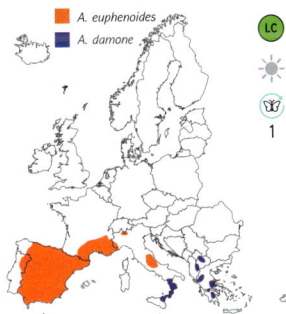

■ A. euphenoides
■ A. damone

LC

1

Did you know?

Like all Orange-tips, the pointed pupa of the Sicilian Orange-tip changes colour during its development, transitioning from a green, resembling a young leaf, to a brown, mimicking a thorn.

IMAGOS		LARVAE	
Food		Food	
Behaviour of males		Caterpillar location	
Dispersion		Chrysalis location	

PIERIDAE

DESERT ORANGE-TIP *COLOTIS EVAGORE*

♂

♀

Apical orange spot, indented with black on outer edge

Large black areas on both wings

Series of small black spots along HW edge

Conspicuous orange area on FW

Faint orange area on FW

Cream HW GC slightly sprinkled with grey

Wingspan: 30–36 mm

Habitat: Rocky slopes and dry, stony road embankments, especially in coastal areas.

Hibernating stage: Pupa without entering diapause.

Elevational range: Up to 500 m.

Egg-laying: Eggs are laid singly on stems or dry leaves of the LHP or on nearby vegetation.

Flight period: From February to October.

Host plants: *Capparis spinosa* (Capparaceae).

Diversity and systematics: European populations of this orange-tip, which is widespread in Africa, belong to subspecies *nouna*.

NA

3

Did you know?

The current restriction of the species to the coastal or warmest regions of southern Spain is due to the absence of winter diapause, making the Desert Orange-tip sensitive to cold. Climate warming is likely to promote its northward expansion.

IMAGOS		LARVAE	
Food		Food	
Behaviour of males		Caterpillar location	
Dispersion		Chrysalis location	

PIERIDAE

LEDERER'S SOOTY ORANGE-TIP *ZEGRIS MERIDIONALIS*

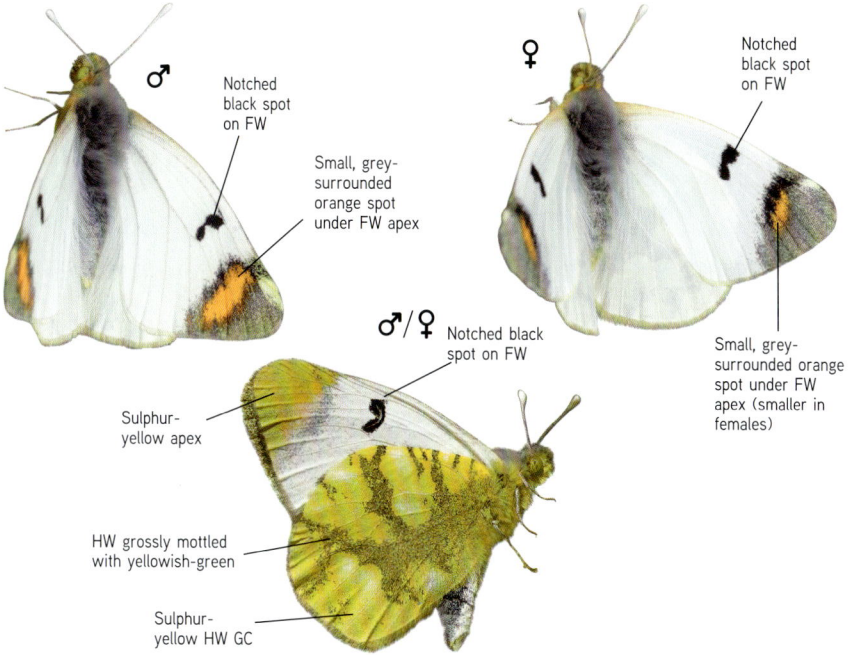

♂

Notched black spot on FW

Small, grey-surrounded orange spot under FW apex

♀

Notched black spot on FW

Small, grey-surrounded orange spot under FW apex (smaller in females)

♂/♀ Notched black spot on FW

Sulphur-yellow apex

HW grossly mottled with yellowish-green

Sulphur-yellow HW GC

Wingspan: 46–51 mm

Habitat: Open, stony, flower-rich areas, and agricultural wastelands.
Hibernating stage: Pupa.
Elevational range: Up to 1,200 m (mostly at lower elevations).
Egg-laying: Eggs are laid singly.
Flight period: From March to June.
Host plants: Brassicaceae, mainly *Isatis tinctoria*, *Hirschfeldia incana*, *Rapistrum rugosum*, and *Sisymbrium austriacum*.
Diversity and systematics: Lederer's Sooty Orange-tip is sometimes considered a subspecies of the Sooty Orange-tip, *Zegris eupheme*, which flies in Turkey and the Middle East. Differences in the genitalia argue for species status, as does the considerable distance separating the two ranges.

NT

1

IMAGOS		LARVAE	
Food	✿	Food	✿
Behaviour of males		Caterpillar location	
Dispersion		Chrysalis location	

Did you know?

Unlike other orange-tips, the caterpillar of Lederer's Sooty Orange-tip pupates in a loose silk shelter on the ground or in herbaceous vegetation.

PIERIDAE

AFRICAN MIGRANT *CATOPSILIA FLORELLA*

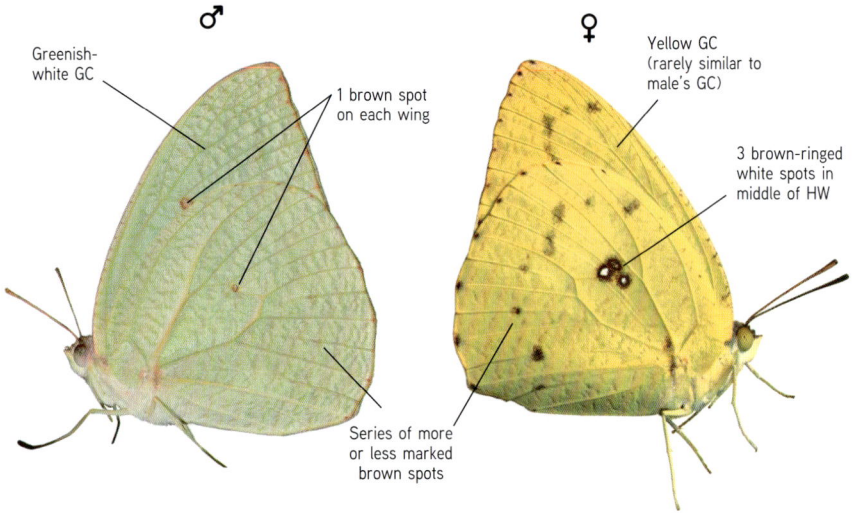

♂

Greenish-white GC

1 brown spot on each wing

♀

Yellow GC (rarely similar to male's GC)

3 brown-ringed white spots in middle of HW

Series of more or less marked brown spots

Wingspan: 45–55 mm

Habitat: Anthropized environments, such as parks and gardens or vegetated roadsides.

Hibernating stage: Egg, caterpillar, pupa, or adult without entering diapause.

Elevational range: Up to 500 m.

Egg-laying: Eggs are laid singly or in small batches on LHP leaves and flower buds.

Flight period: Year-round.

Host plants: Cesalpiniaceae in genera *Cassia* and *Senna* (including *S. didymobotrya*), introduced to the Canary Islands as ornamental plants.

Diversity and systematics: There are no notable subspecies for this Pierid, whose range extends across sub-Saharan Africa and southern Asia.

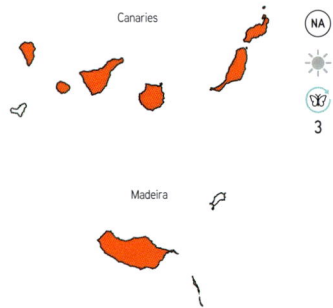

Canaries

NA

3

Madeira

Did you know?

The African Migrant is capable of long migratory movements and has regularly colonized the Canary Islands and Madeira. Its expansion to the north is currently limited by the availability of host plants and by winter cold, as it does not enter diapause.

IMAGOS		LARVAE	
Food		Food	
Behaviour of males		Caterpillar location	
Dispersion		Chrysalis location	

PIERIDAE

BLACK-VEINED WHITE *APORIA CRATAEGI*

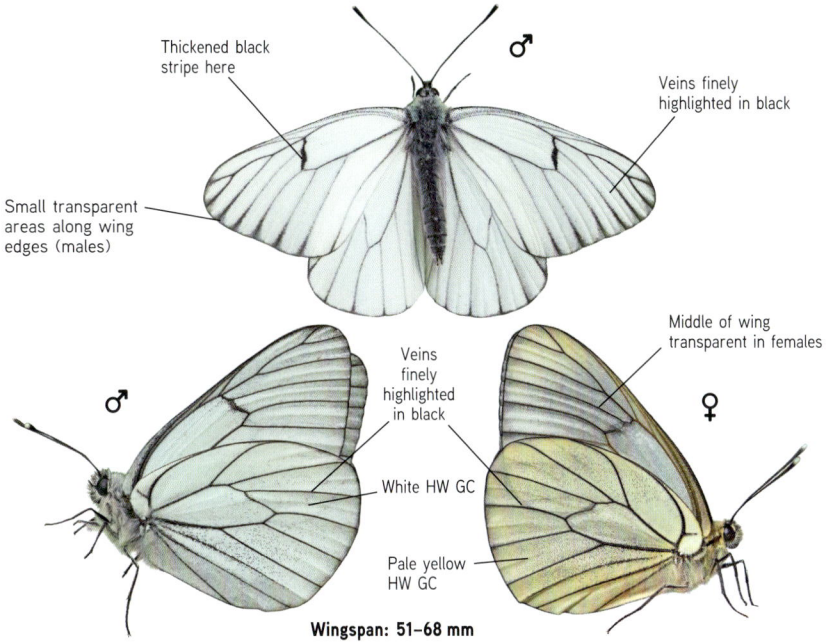

Thickened black stripe here

♂

Veins finely highlighted in black

Small transparent areas along wing edges (males)

Middle of wing transparent in females

Veins finely highlighted in black

♂

White HW GC

♀

Pale yellow HW GC

Wingspan: 51–68 mm

Habitat: Flower-rich meadows and grasslands in the vicinity of bushy areas, hedgerows, forest edges and clearings, orchards.

Hibernating stage: Caterpillar.

Elevational range: Up to 2,000 m.

Egg-laying: Eggs are laid in large batches (a few dozens) under LHP leaves.

Flight period: From April to August.

Host plants: Numerous woody Rosaceae, inluding *Crataegus monogyna*, *C. laevigata*, *C. azarolus*, *C. laciniata*, *C. pycnoloba*, *C. rhipidophylla*,

Prunus spinosa, *P. mahaleb*, *P. avium*, *P. amygdalis*, *P. armeniaca*, *P. cerasifera*, *P. cerasus*, *P. cocomilia*, *P. domestica*, *P. padus*, *P. persica*, *P. webbii*, *Pyrus communis*, *P. spinosa*, *Malus* spp. (including cultivated varieties), *Rosa canina*, *Sorbus aucuparia*, and *Amelanchier ovalis*. Also reported on *Cornus sanguinea* (Cornaceae) and *Frangula alnus* (Rhamnaceae).

Diversity and systematics: Several subspecies are described in Europe, but they differ little from the nominate subspecies.

LC

1

Did you know?

Males are extremely persistent towards females, even as the latter are just emerging. Adults can gather in groups of several hundred individuals on moist ground to drink.

IMAGOS		LARVAE	
Food	🌼💧🐛	Food	🍃
Behaviour of males	🦋	Caterpillar location	🌿
Dispersion	✳	Chrysalis location	🌾🌿

189

BERGER'S CLOUDED YELLOW *COLIAS ALFACARIENSIS*

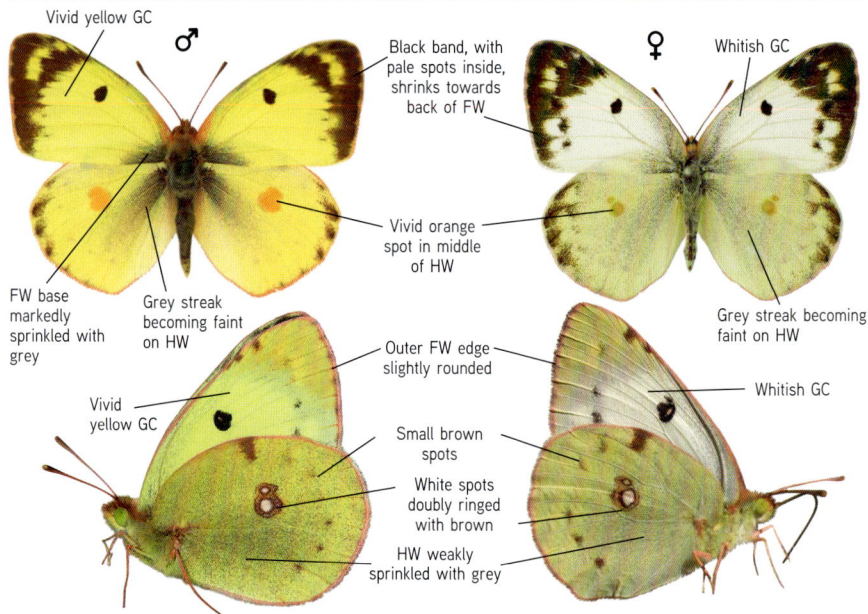

Vivid yellow GC ♂

Black band, with pale spots inside, shrinks towards back of FW

♀ Whitish GC

Vivid orange spot in middle of HW

FW base markedly sprinkled with grey

Grey streak becoming faint on HW

Grey streak becoming faint on HW

Vivid yellow GC

Outer FW edge slightly rounded

Whitish GC

Small brown spots

White spots doubly ringed with brown

HW weakly sprinkled with grey

Wingspan: 42–45 mm

Habitat: Dry calcareous grasslands and low-growing meadows.

Hibernating stage: Caterpillar.

Elevational range: Up to 2,000 m, but far more abundant below 1,500 m.

Egg-laying: Eggs are laid singly on LHP leaflets.

Flight period: From April to October.

Host plants: Legumes, mainly *Hippocrepis comosa*

and sometimes *H. emerus*, *H. glauca*, *Securigera varia*, *Coronilla securidaca*, *Astragalus monspessulanus*, and *Dorycnopsis gerardi*.

Diversity and systematics: There are no notable subspecies for this species, which is widespread across Europe and has very significant dispersal abilities that probably limit population divergences.

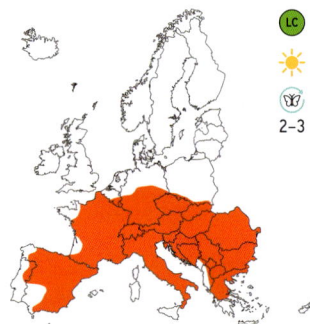

LC

2–3

Did you know?

Berger's Clouded Yellow is favoured by extensive grazing, which prevents the loss of the calcareous dry grasslands where it breeds. Its powerful and swift flight is characteristic in this environment, making the species challenging to approach!

IMAGOS		LARVAE	
Food		Food	
Behaviour of males		Caterpillar location	
Dispersion		Chrysalis location	

PIERIDAE

PALE CLOUDED YELLOW *COLIAS HYALE*

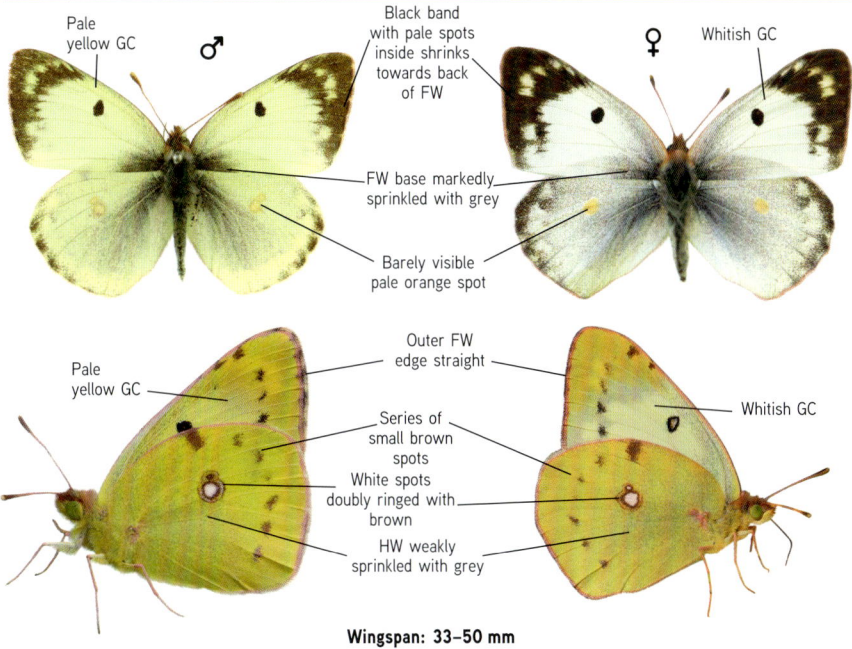

Pale yellow GC

♂

Black band with pale spots inside shrinks towards back of FW

♀ Whitish GC

FW base markedly sprinkled with grey

Barely visible pale orange spot

Outer FW edge straight

Pale yellow GC

Whitish GC

Series of small brown spots

White spots doubly ringed with brown

HW weakly sprinkled with grey

Wingspan: 33–50 mm

Habitat: Flower-rich mesophilic meadows, alfalfa crops.

Hibernating stage: Caterpillar.

Elevational range: Up to 2,000 m.

Egg-laying: Eggs are laid singly on LHP leaflets.

Flight period: From April to October.

Host plants: Legumes, including *Trifolium repens*, *T. pratense*, *T. subterraneum*, *Medicago*

sativa, *M. lupulina*, *M. falcata*, *Melilotus officinalis*, *M. albus*, *Securigera varia*, *Hippocrepis comosa*, *Onobrychis viciifolia*, *Lotus corniculatus*, *Vicia cracca*, *V. sativa*, *V. hirsuta*, and *V. tetrasperma*.

Diversity and systematics: There are numerous forms, but no notable subspecies for this species, which is widespread across Europe.

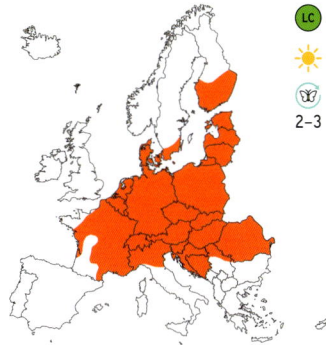

LC

2–3

Did you know?

Caterpillars are particularly sensitive to winter cold, which causes significant annual fluctuations in populations. Alfalfa crops can act as ecological traps for them when mowing is done too early.

IMAGOS		LARVAE	
Food	🌼 💧	Food	🍃
Behaviour of males	🦋	Caterpillar location	🌿
Dispersion		Chrysalis location	🌿

PIERIDAE

EASTERN PALE CLOUDED YELLOW *COLIAS ERATE*

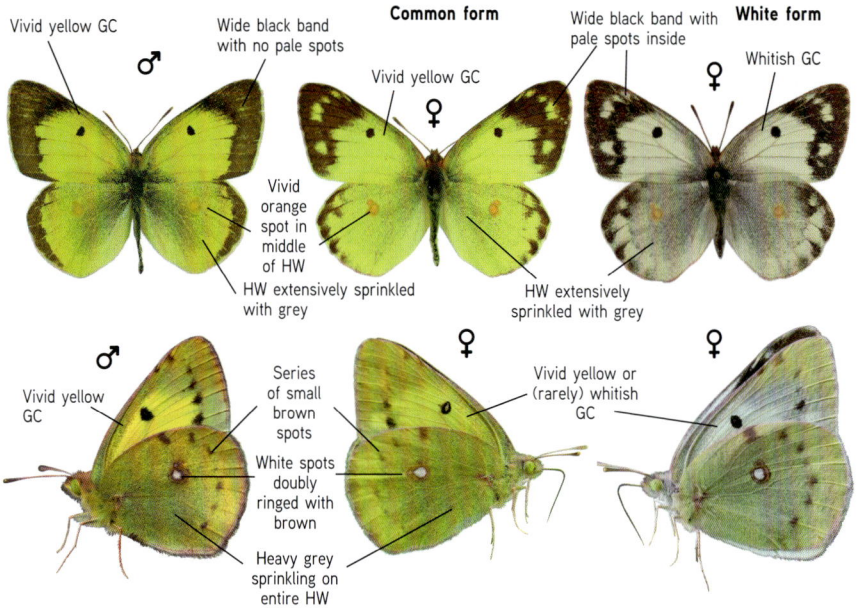

Common form

White form

Vivid yellow GC

♂

Wide black band with no pale spots

Vivid yellow GC

♀

Wide black band with pale spots inside

Whitish GC

♀

Vivid orange spot in middle of HW

HW extensively sprinkled with grey

HW extensively sprinkled with grey

♂

Vivid yellow GC

Series of small brown spots

♀

White spots doubly ringed with brown

Vivid yellow or (rarely) whitish GC

♀

Heavy grey sprinkling on entire HW

Wingspan: 46–52 mm

Habitat: Steppic grasslands, meadows, and alfalfa crops.

Hibernating stage: Caterpillar.

Elevational range: Up to 1,700 m.

Egg-laying: Eggs are laid singly on LHP leaflets.

Flight period: From May to September.

Host plants: Legumes, mainly *Medicago sativa*, *Securigera varia*, *Onobrychis* spp., and *Trifolium* spp.

Diversity and systematics: About ten subspecies are described for this Coliadine, which is widely distributed in Asia. European populations belong to the nominate subspecies, for which numerous forms are also known.

LC

2–3

Did you know?

The arrival of the Pale Clouded Yellow in Central Europe dates back to the 1980s. It continued its expansion westward until the 2000s, reaching as far as Germany and then receding in areas to the east.

IMAGOS		LARVAE	
Food		Food	
Behaviour of males		Caterpillar location	
Dispersion		Chrysalis location	

PIERIDAE

MOORLAND CLOUDED YELLOW   *COLIAS PALAENO*

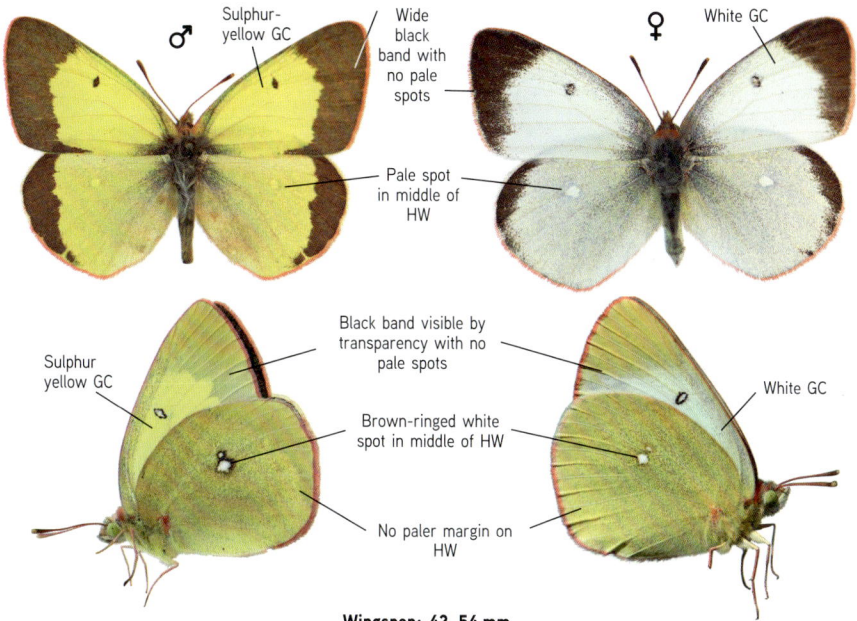

♂ Sulphur-yellow GC

Wide black band with no pale spots

♀ White GC

Pale spot in middle of HW

Sulphur yellow GC

Black band visible by transparency with no pale spots

White GC

Brown-ringed white spot in middle of HW

No paler margin on HW

Wingspan: 42–54 mm

Habitat: Bogs and montane/subalpine bog bilberry heaths.

Hibernating stage: Caterpillar.

Elevational range: From 500 to 2,500 m.

Egg-laying: Eggs are laid singly on LHP leaves.

Flight period: From June to August.

Host plants: Mainly *Vaccinium uliginosum*; sometimes also *V. myrtillus* (Ericaceae).

Diversity and systematics: Most Scandinavian populations belong to the nominate subspecies. Subspecies *europome* flies from the French Jura to Eastern Europe. Subspecies *europomene* is found in the high-altitude Alps, and the *synonyma* subspecies flies in Denmark and southern Sweden.

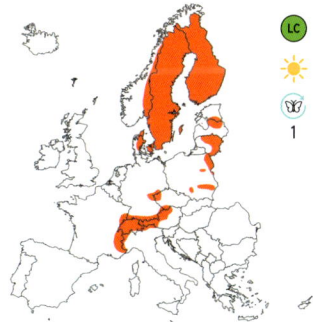

LC

1

Did you know?

The Moorland Clouded Yellow is undergoing the loss of its preferred habitats, such as bogs and other wetlands. Climate warming, the planting of conifers, and the conversion of these environments into pastures are the main threats to its populations.

IMAGOS		LARVAE	
Food		Food	
Behaviour of males		Caterpillar location	
Dispersion		Chrysalis location	

193

MOUNTAIN CLOUDED YELLOW *COLIAS PHICOMONE*

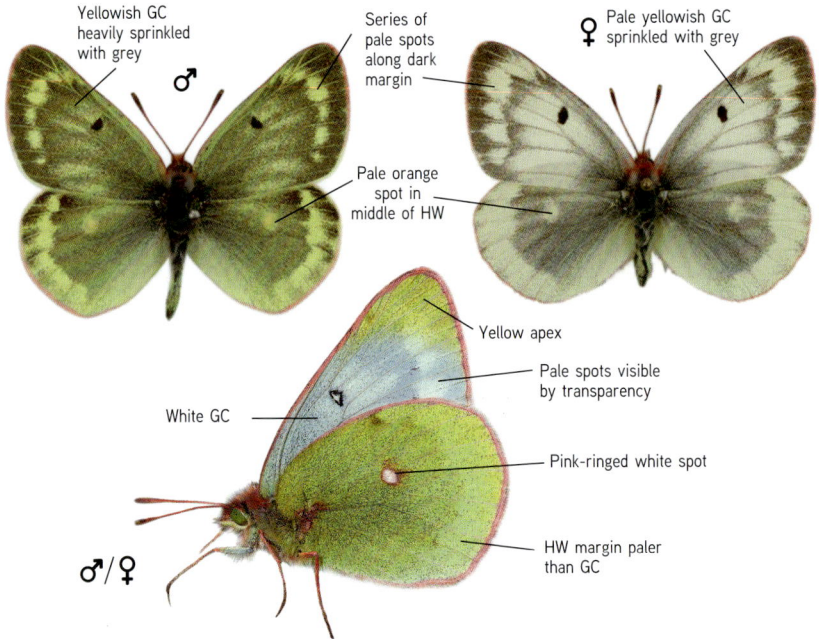

Yellowish GC
heavily sprinkled
with grey

♂

Series of
pale spots
along dark
margin

♀ Pale yellowish GC
sprinkled with grey

Pale orange
spot in
middle of HW

Yellow apex

Pale spots visible
by transparency

White GC

Pink-ringed white spot

♂/♀

HW margin paler
than GC

Wingspan: 40–50 mm

Habitat: Subalpine and alpine grasslands and meadows.

Hibernating stage: Caterpillar.

Elevational range: From 1,300 to 2,800 m (mainly above 1,500 m).

Egg-laying: Eggs are laid singly on LHP leaflets.

Flight period: From May to August.

Host plants: Legumes, including *Hippocrepis comosa, Lotus corniculatus, L. alpinus, Trifolium repens, T. pallescens*, and *Securigera varia*.

Diversity and systematics: Alpine populations belong to the nominate subspecies. The subspecies *oberthueri* and *juliani* are, respectively, described from the Pyrenees and the Cantabrian Mountains.

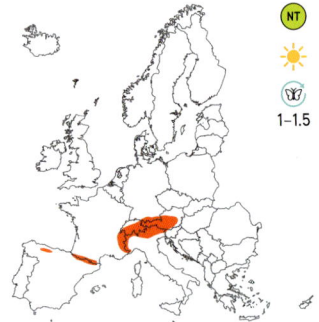

NT

1–1.5

	IMAGOS		LARVAE	
Food		Food		
Behaviour of males		Caterpillar location		
Dispersion		Chrysalis location		

Did you know?

Mountain Clouded Yellows are generalist flower feeders at high altitudes. They seldom linger for long on a flower before resuming their fast patrolling or dispersal flights.

PIERIDAE

PALE ARCTIC CLOUDED YELLOW *COLIAS TYCHE*

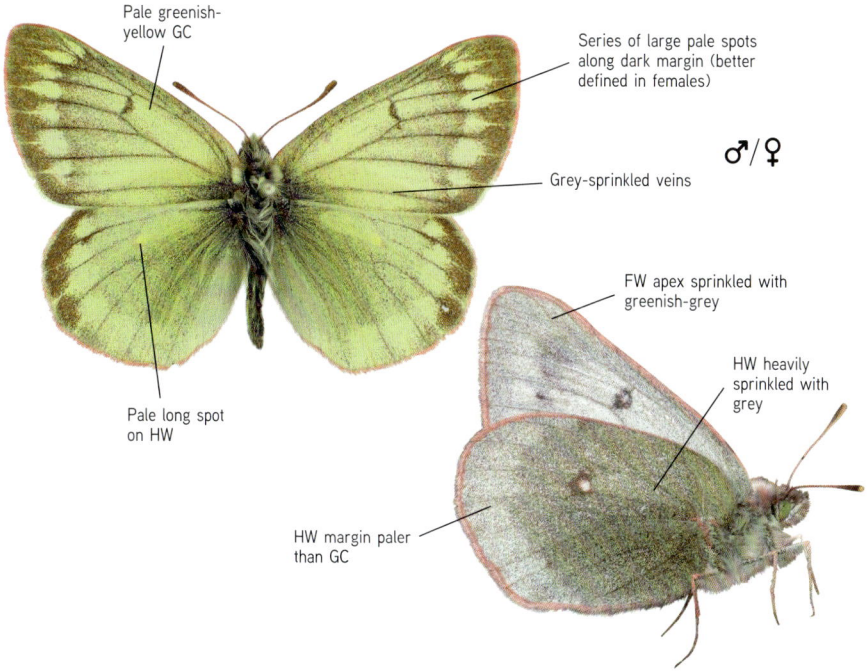

Pale greenish-yellow GC

Series of large pale spots along dark margin (better defined in females)

♂ / ♀

Grey-sprinkled veins

FW apex sprinkled with greenish-grey

HW heavily sprinkled with grey

Pale long spot on HW

HW margin paler than GC

Wingspan: 40–50 mm

Habitat: Arctic heaths and clear birch forests.

Hibernating stage: Caterpillar for the first winter, pupa for the second.

Elevational range: Up to 1,000 m.

Egg-laying: Eggs are laid singly.

Flight period: From May to July.

Host plants: Ericaceae, especially *Vaccinium uliginosum* and *V. myrtillus*. Also cited on the legumes *Astragalus alpinus*, *A. frigidus*, and *Oxytropis nigrescens*.

Diversity and systematics: European populations of this species, widely distributed around the Arctic, belong to subspecies *werdandi*.

LC

0.5

IMAGOS		LARVAE	
Food	☆	Food	🍃
Behaviour of males		Caterpillar location	
Dispersion		Chrysalis location	

PIERIDAE

CLOUDED YELLOW *COLIAS CROCEA*

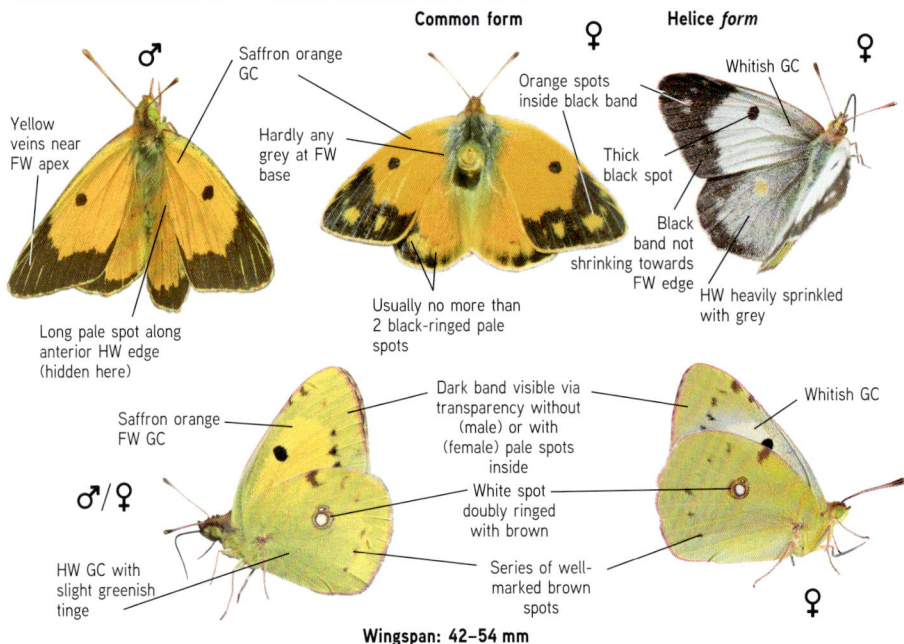

Common form ♀   **Helice** *form* ♀

♂

Saffron orange GC

Yellow veins near FW apex

Hardly any grey at FW base

Orange spots inside black band

Whitish GC

Thick black spot

Black band not shrinking towards FW edge

HW heavily sprinkled with grey

Long pale spot along anterior HW edge (hidden here)

Usually no more than 2 black-ringed pale spots

Dark band visible via transparency without (male) or with (female) pale spots inside

Whitish GC

Saffron orange FW GC

♂/♀

White spot doubly ringed with brown

HW GC with slight greenish tinge

Series of well-marked brown spots

♀

Wingspan: 42–54 mm

Habitat: A wide variety of open habitats, including grasslands, meadows, crop surroundings, parks, and gardens.

Hibernating stage: Caterpillar without entering diapause.

Elevational range: Up to 3,000 m.

Egg-laying: Eggs are laid singly on LHP leaflets.

Flight period: From March to November.

Host plants: More than 50 legume species, including *Medicago sativa, M. arabica, M. lupulina, M. falcata, M. minima, M. orbicularis, M. truncatula, Melilotus officinalis, M. albus, M. indicus,* *M. neapolitanus, Trifolium pratense, T. repens, T. dubium, T. fragiferum, T. physodes, Hippocrepis comosa, H. glauca, Lotus corniculatus, L. pedunculatus, Onobrychis viciifolia, O. alba, O. ebenoides, O. montana, O. supina, Astragalus monspessulanus, A. glycyphyllos, A. alopecurus, Lupinus luteus, Colutea arborescens,* and *Securigera varia.*

Diversity and systematics: There are no notable subspecies for this polymorphic species, which is present throughout Europe. However, numerous forms have been described.

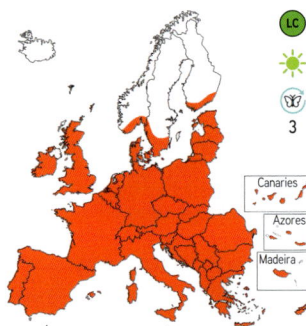

LC

3

Canaries

Azores

Madeira

Did you know?

The caterpillars' low resistance to winter frost leads to heavy losses. The recolonization of the European continent occurs every year, thanks to the marked migratory behaviour of Clouded Yellows originating from their southernmost populations.

IMAGOS		LARVAE	
Food	🔶 💧	Food	🍃
Behaviour of males	🦋	Caterpillar location	🌿
Dispersion		Chrysalis location	🌿

PIERIDAE

LESSER CLOUDED YELLOW *COLIAS CHRYSOTHEME*

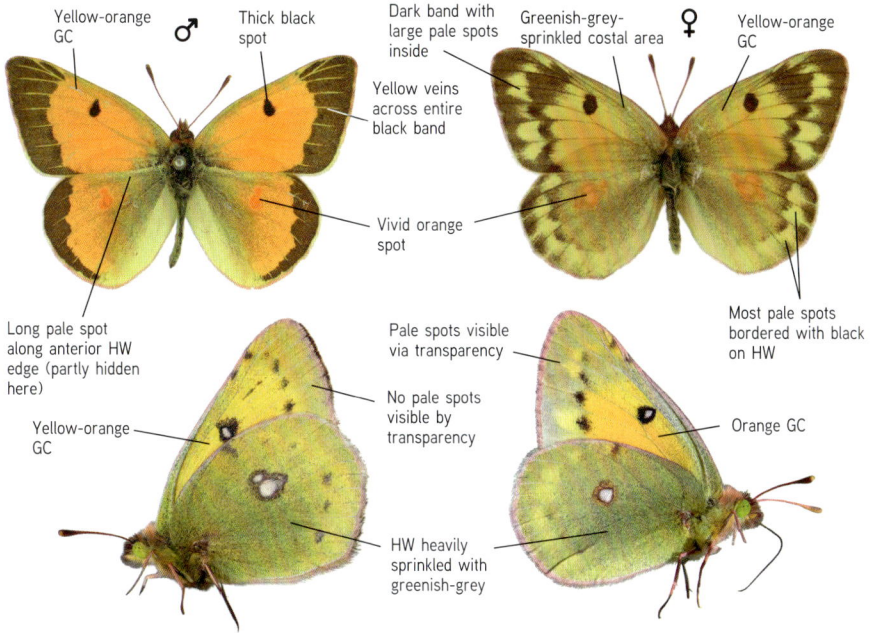

Yellow-orange GC ♂

Thick black spot

Dark band with large pale spots inside

Greenish-grey-sprinkled costal area ♀

Yellow-orange GC

Yellow veins across entire black band

Vivid orange spot

Most pale spots bordered with black on HW

Long pale spot along anterior HW edge (partly hidden here)

Pale spots visible via transparency

Yellow-orange GC

No pale spots visible by transparency

Orange GC

HW heavily sprinkled with greenish-grey

Wingspan: 40–48 mm

Habitat: Steppic grasslands.

Hibernating stage: Caterpillar.

Elevational range: Below 500 m.

Egg-laying: Eggs are laid singly on LHP leaflets.

Flight period: From April to October.

Host plants: Legumes, including *Astragalus austriacus, A. glycyphyllos, A. onobrychis, Vicia hirsuta, V. cracca,* and *V. lathyroides.*

Diversity and systematics: European populations of this Coliadine, whose range extends to Mongolia, belong to the nominate subspecies. Some females are white (form *alba*).

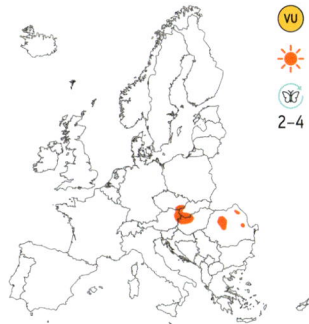

VU

2–4

IMAGOS		LARVAE	
Food		Food	
Behaviour of males		Caterpillar location	
Dispersion		Chrysalis location	

Did you know?

Favourable habitats for the Lesser Clouded Yellow are dwindling rapidly due to anthropization, particularly in Austria, where only a few populations remain.

PIERIDAE

GREEK CLOUDED YELLOW   *COLIAS AURORINA*

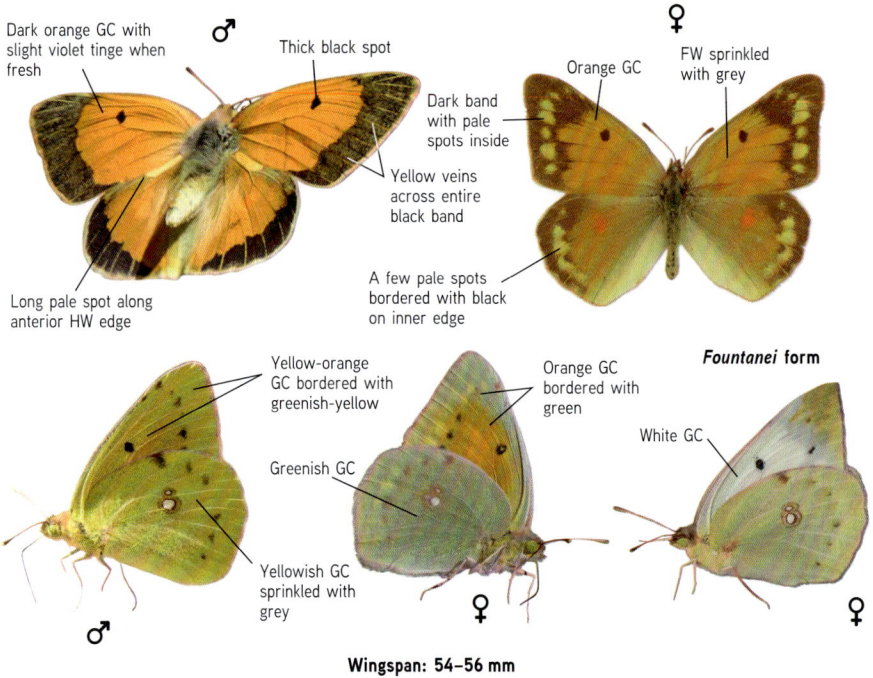

♂

Dark orange GC with slight violet tinge when fresh

Thick black spot

Dark band with pale spots inside

Yellow veins across entire black band

Long pale spot along anterior HW edge

A few pale spots bordered with black on inner edge

♀

Orange GC

FW sprinkled with grey

Yellow-orange GC bordered with greenish-yellow

Greenish GC

Yellowish GC sprinkled with grey

♂

Orange GC bordered with green

Fountanei form

White GC

♀

♀

Wingspan: 54–56 mm

Habitat: Dry, stony montane and subalpine slopes with grassy and bushy vegetation.

Hibernating stage: Caterpillar.

Elevational range: From 500 to 2,200 m.

Egg-laying: Eggs are laid singly on LHP leaflets.

Flight period: From April to August.

Host plants: Legumes, including *Astracantha rumelica*, *A. cyllenea*, *A. echinus*, *A. cruentiflora*, and *Astragalus caucasicus*.

Diversity and systematics: European populations belong to the *heldreichi* subspecies. Some females are white (form *fountanei*).

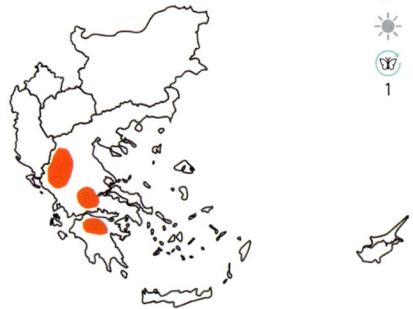

LC

1

IMAGOS		LARVAE	
Food	✿	Food	🍃
Behaviour of males		Caterpillar location	
Dispersion		Chrysalis location	

Did you know?

The Greek Clouded Yellow is called *Colias libanotica* by some authors. The *libanotica* subspecies of *C. aurorina* flies, however, in the Middle East.

PIERIDAE

DANUBE CLOUDED YELLOW *COLIAS MYRMIDONE*

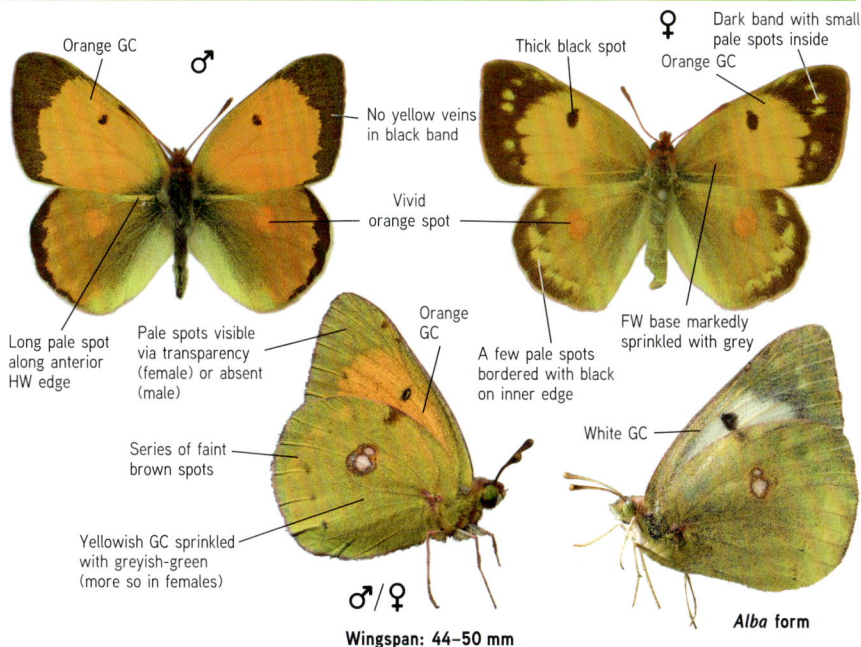

Orange GC

♂

No yellow veins in black band

Vivid orange spot

♀

Thick black spot

Dark band with small pale spots inside

Orange GC

FW base markedly sprinkled with grey

Long pale spot along anterior HW edge

Pale spots visible via transparency (female) or absent (male)

Orange GC

A few pale spots bordered with black on inner edge

White GC

Series of faint brown spots

Yellowish GC sprinkled with greyish-green (more so in females)

♂/♀

Wingspan: 44–50 mm

Alba form

Habitat: Sunny steppic forest clearings within gappy forest systems.

Hibernating stage: Caterpillar.

Elevational range: Up to 700 m.

Egg-laying: Eggs are laid singly on the LHP.

Flight period: From April to September.

Host plants: Small, woody legumes, especially *Chamaecytisus ratisbonensis*, *C. ruthenicus*, *C. austriacus*, *C. supinus*, and *Cytisus nigricans*.

Diversity and systematics: European populations belong to the nominate subspecies. Several forms are also described.

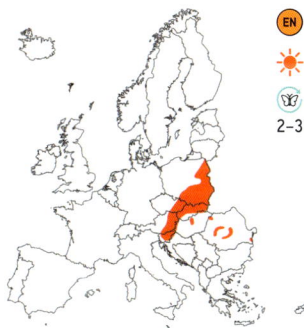

EN

2-3

Did you know?

The Danube Clouded Yellow disperses less than other Coliadine species like the Clouded Yellow. The scarcity and limited extent of its preferred habitats are related to this tendency towards philopatry.

IMAGOS		LARVAE	
Food		Food	
Behaviour of males		Caterpillar location	
Dispersion		Chrysalis location	

PIERIDAE

BALKAN CLOUDED YELLOW *COLIAS CAUCASICA*

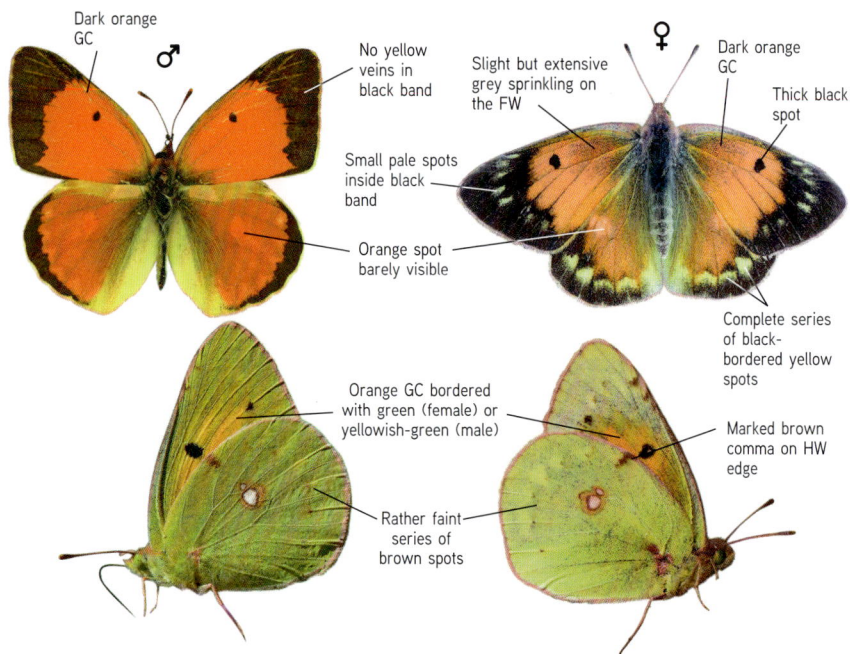

Dark orange GC

♂

No yellow veins in black band

Slight but extensive grey sprinkling on the FW

♀

Dark orange GC

Thick black spot

Small pale spots inside black band

Orange spot barely visible

Complete series of black-bordered yellow spots

Orange GC bordered with green (female) or yellowish-green (male)

Marked brown comma on HW edge

Rather faint series of brown spots

Wingspan: 50–54 mm

Habitat: Stony grasslands at the treeline; bushy grasslands and clearings at lower elevations.

Hibernating stage: Caterpillar.

Elevational range: From 600 to 2,200 m.

Egg-laying: Eggs are laid singly on the LHP.

Flight period: From June to August.

Host plants: Small, woody legumes, especially *Chamaecytisus hirsutus*, *C. eriocarpus*, and *C. supinus*.

Diversity and systematics: European populations belong to subspecies *balcanica*.

LC

1

IMAGOS		LARVAE	
Food	☆	Food	🍃
Behaviour of males		Caterpillar location	
Dispersion		Chrysalis location	

Did you know?

As with most species in genus *Colias*, females can rarely be white (*rebeli* form).

200

PIERIDAE

NORTHERN CLOUDED YELLOW   *COLIAS HECLA*

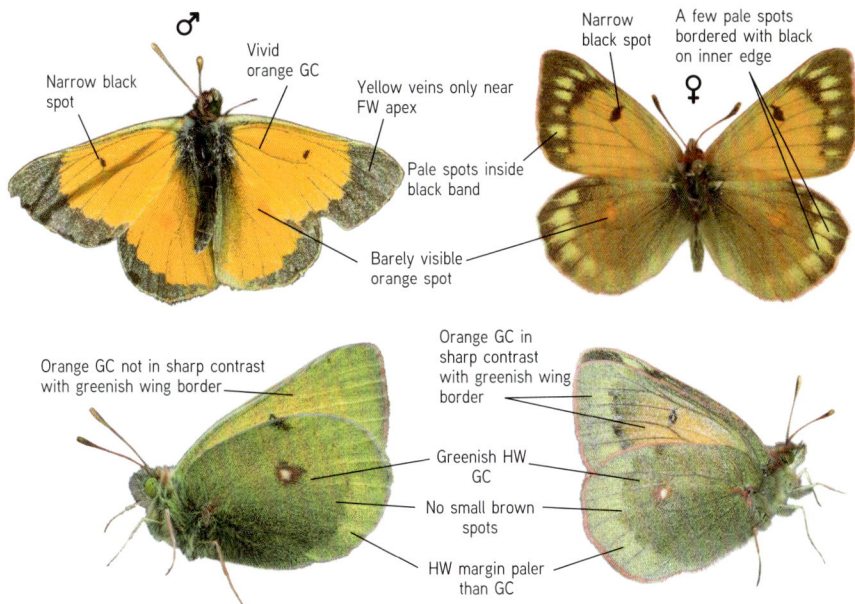

♂

Narrow black spot

Vivid orange GC

Yellow veins only near FW apex

Pale spots inside black band

Barely visible orange spot

Narrow black spot

A few pale spots bordered with black on inner edge

♀

Orange GC not in sharp contrast with greenish wing border

Orange GC in sharp contrast with greenish wing border

Greenish HW GC

No small brown spots

HW margin paler than GC

Wingspan: 35–47 mm

Habitat: Sunny grasslands and heaths of the arctic tundra.

Hibernating stage: Overwinters usually twice as a caterpillar. Sometimes a third overwintering occurs at the pupal stage.

Elevational range: Up to 1,000 m.

Egg-laying: Eggs are laid singly or in very small batches on LHP leaflets, stems, and inflorescences.

Flight period: From June to August.

Host plants: *Astragalus alpinus* (Fabaceae).

Diversity and systematics: European populations belong to subspecies *sulitelma*.

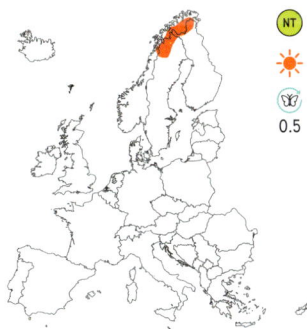

NT

0.5

IMAGOS		LARVAE	
Food		Food	
Behaviour of males		Caterpillar location	
Dispersion		Chrysalis location	

Did you know?

The Northern Clouded Yellow is widely distributed around the Arctic Circle. It is found in North America, Europe, Greenland, and Asia.

BRIMSTONE *GONEPTERYX RHAMNI*

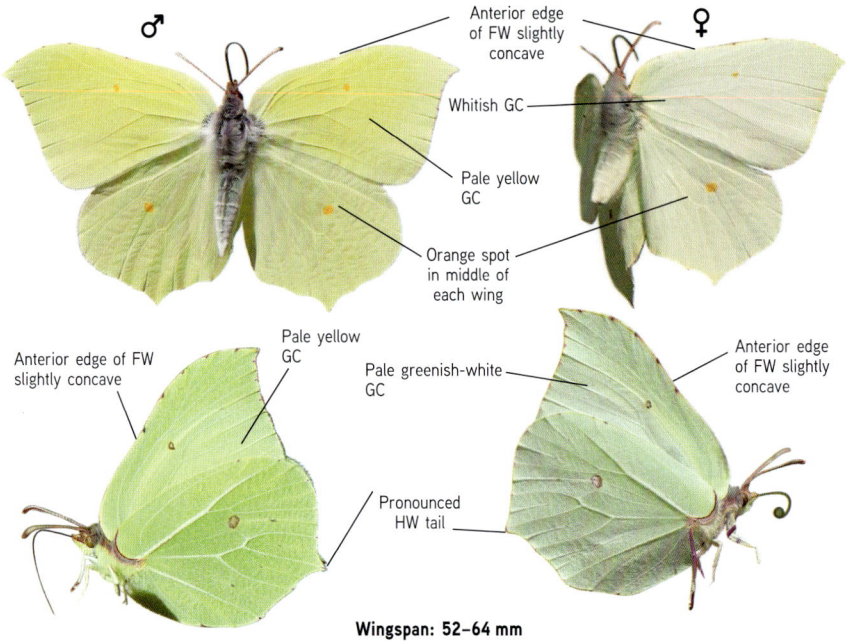

♂ ♀

Anterior edge of FW slightly concave

Whitish GC

Pale yellow GC

Orange spot in middle of each wing

Anterior edge of FW slightly concave

Pale yellow GC

Pale greenish-white GC

Anterior edge of FW slightly concave

Pronounced HW tail

Wingspan: 52–64 mm

Habitat: Clear woodlands, forest edges, woodland paths, hedges. Common in parks and gardens.

Hibernating stage: Adult.

Elevational range: Up to 2,000 m (rarely above 1,300 m).

Egg-laying: Eggs are laid singly on LHP stems and leaf buds.

Flight period: From January to September.

Host plants: Several bushes in the Rhamnaceae family, such as *Rhamnus cathartica*, *R. alaternus*, *R. alpina*, *R. lycioides*, and *Frangula alnus*.

Diversity and systematics: The nominate subspecies flies in the northern half and the centre of Europe. Subspecies *transiens* populates Southern Europe. Subspecies *gravesi* is found in Ireland.

LC

1

Did you know?

The Brimstone undertakes annual altitudinal migratory movements, allowing it to breed at higher elevations. Butterflies born from this generation descend to spend the winter at lower-elevation sites.

IMAGOS		LARVAE	
Food	✿	Food	🍃
Behaviour of males		Caterpillar location	
Dispersion		Chrysalis location	

PIERIDAE

POWDERED BRIMSTONE   *GONEPTERYX FARINOSA*

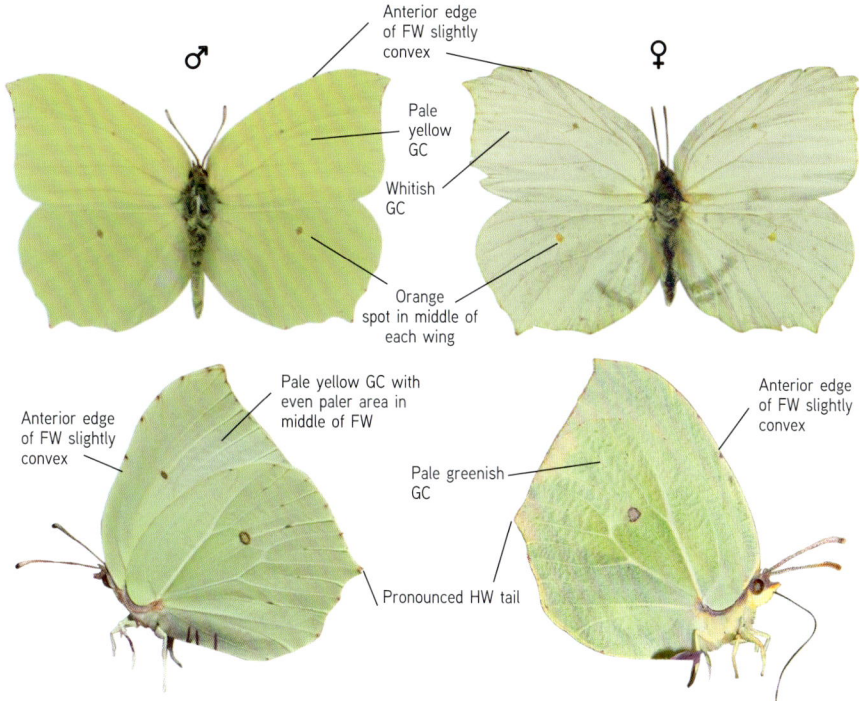

♂   ♀

Anterior edge of FW slightly convex

Pale yellow GC

Whitish GC

Orange spot in middle of each wing

Pale yellow GC with even paler area in middle of FW

Anterior edge of FW slightly convex

Anterior edge of FW slightly convex

Pale greenish GC

Pronounced HW tail

Wingspan: 56–64 mm

Habitat: Stony garrigue and maquis (at higher elevations during summer).

Hibernating stage: Adult.

Elevational range: Up to 2,500 m (breeding occurs mainly below 1,500 m).

Egg-laying: Eggs are laid singly on LHP stems and leaf buds.

Flight period: From January to November.

Host plants: Rhamnaceae, including *Rhamnus alaternus*, *R. alpina*, *R. sibthorpiana*, *R. lycioides*, *Paliurus spina-christi*, and *Ziziphus jujuba*. Also reported on other bushy species in other families (*Buxus*, *Rhus coriaria*, and *Pistacia terebinthus*).

Diversity and systematics: European populations belong to the nominate subspecies.

LC

1

IMAGOS		LARVAE	
Food	☆	Food	🍃
Behaviour of males	🦋	Caterpillar location	
Dispersion		Chrysalis location	

Did you know?

Adults can enter diapause twice during their lives: in midsummer, allowing them to avoid the intense heat, and during the winter.

PIERIDAE

CLEOPATRA *GONEPTERYX CLEOPATRA*

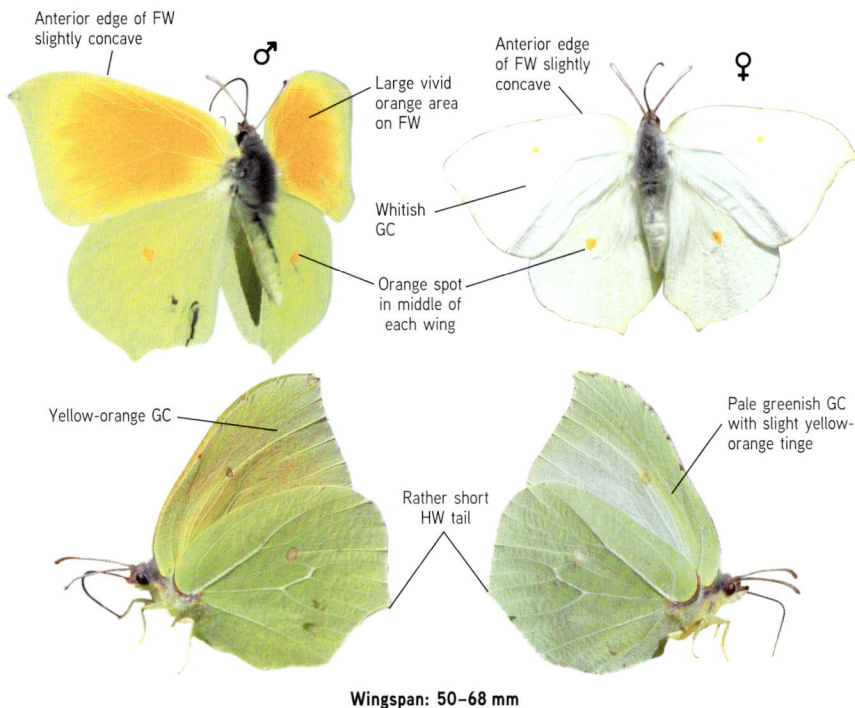

♂

Anterior edge of FW slightly concave

Large vivid orange area on FW

♀

Anterior edge of FW slightly concave

Whitish GC

Orange spot in middle of each wing

Yellow-orange GC

Rather short HW tail

Pale greenish GC with slight yellow-orange tinge

Wingspan: 50–68 mm

Habitat: Garrigue, maquis, and Mediterranean forest clearings.

Hibernating stage: Adult.

Elevational range: Up to 2,000 m.

Egg-laying: Eggs are laid singly on LHP leaves and stems.

Flight period: From February to September.

Host plants: Rhamnaceae, including *Rhamnus alaternus*,

R. alpina, R. lycioides, R. cathartica, R. infectoria, R. myrtifolia, R. oleoides, and *R. sibthorpiana.*

Diversity and systematics: Most European populations belong to subspecies *italica*. Insular subspecies *taurica, fiorii,* and *insularis* fly in Cyprus, Rhodes, and Crete, respectively.

LC

1–2

	IMAGOS			LARVAE	
Food	☆		Food	🍃	
Behaviour of males	🦋		Caterpillar location	🌿	
Dispersion			Chrysalis location	🌿	

Did you know?

The great dispersal abilities of the Cleopatra sometimes take it far beyond the limit of its breeding range.

PIERIDAE

CANARIAN BRIMSTONES/MADEIRAN BRIMSTONE
GONEPTERYX CLEOBULE, G. EVERSI, G. PALMAE/G. MADERENSIS

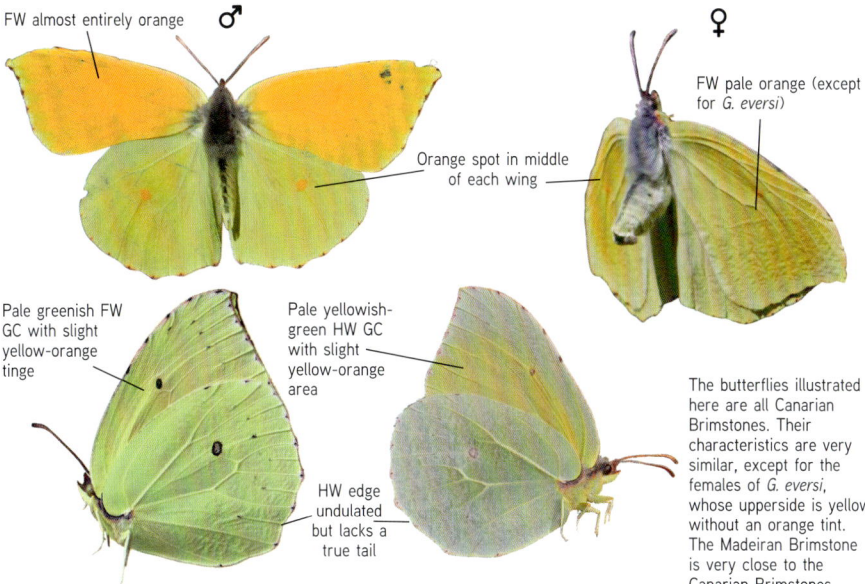

FW almost entirely orange ♂

♀

FW pale orange (except for G. eversi)

Orange spot in middle of each wing

Pale greenish FW GC with slight yellow-orange tinge

Pale yellowish-green HW GC with slight yellow-orange area

HW edge undulated but lacks a true tail

The butterflies illustrated here are all Canarian Brimstones. Their characteristics are very similar, except for the females of G. eversi, whose upperside is yellow without an orange tint. The Madeiran Brimstone is very close to the Canarian Brimstones.

Wingspan: 55–68 mm

Habitat: Laurel forest in summer, more varied habitats at lower elevations during winter for the Canarian Brimstones; laurel forest for the Madeiran Brimstone, which spends most of its time in the canopy.

Hibernating stage: Egg, caterpillar, pupa, and adult for the Canarian Brimstones; pupa for the Madeiran Brimstone.

Elevational range: Between 500 and 2,000 m for the Canarian Brimstones; below 1,700 m for the Madeiran Brimstone.

Egg-laying: Eggs are laid singly on LHP leaves.

Flight period: Year-round.

Host plants: Rhamnaceae, including *Rhamnus glandulosa* and *R. crenulata* for the Canarian Brimstones. Only *R. glandulosa* for the Madeiran Brimstone.

Diversity and systematics: *Gonepteryx eversi* and *G. palmae* are sometimes considered subspecies of *G. cleobule*.

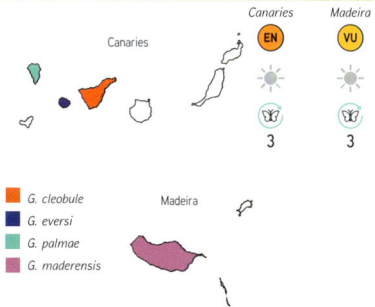

Canaries

Canaries	Madeira
EN	VU
☀	☀
🦋	🦋
3	3

- G. cleobule
- G. eversi
- G. palmae
- G. maderensis

Madeira

IMAGOS		LARVAE	
Food	✿	Food	🍃
Behaviour of males	🦋	Caterpillar location	
Dispersion		Chrysalis location	

Did you know?

These four brimstone species are related to the Cleopatra, which independently colonized the Canary Islands and Madeira, highlighting its exceptional dispersal abilities.

PIERIDAE

BATH WHITE *PONTIA DAPLIDICE*

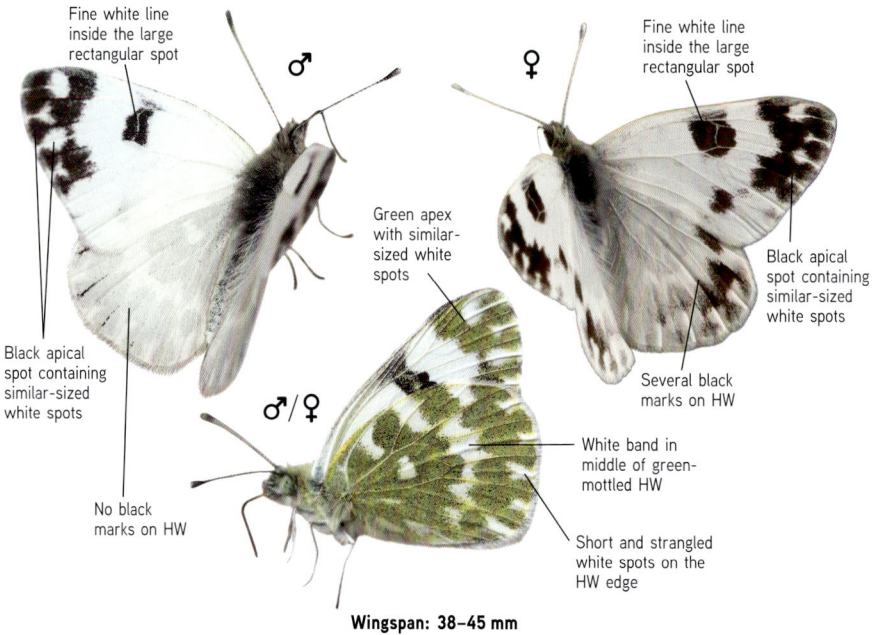

Fine white line inside the large rectangular spot

♂

♀

Fine white line inside the large rectangular spot

Green apex with similar-sized white spots

Black apical spot containing similar-sized white spots

Black apical spot containing similar-sized white spots

Several black marks on HW

♂/♀

No black marks on HW

White band in middle of green-mottled HW

Short and strangled white spots on the HW edge

Wingspan: 38–45 mm

Habitat: Open and rather dry environments, such as grasslands, roadside edges, fallow lands, rocky slopes, and dunes.

Hibernating stage: Pupa.

Elevational range: Up to 2,000 m.

Egg-laying: Eggs are laid singly on LHP stems and inflorescences.

Flight period: From February to October; year-round in the Canary Islands.

Host plants: Numerous Brassicaceae, including *Arabis hirsuta, Cakile maritima, Descurainia sophia, Diplotaxis erucoides, D. tenuifolia,* *Eruca vesicaria, Erucaria hispanica, Erucastrum gallicum, E. nasturtiifolium, Hirschfeldia incana, Iberis contracta, Lepidium campestre, L. draba, L. graminifolium, L. ruderale, Lobularia maritima, Noccaea perfoliata, Raphanus raphanistrum, Rapistrum rugosum, Sinapis alba, Sisymbrium irio, S. officinale, S. orientale,* and *Thlaspi arvense.* Also on some Resedaceae, like *Reseda alba, R. lutea, R. luteola, R. odorata, R. phyteuma,* and *Sesamoides spathulifolia.*

Diversity and systematics: European populations belong to the nominate subspecies.

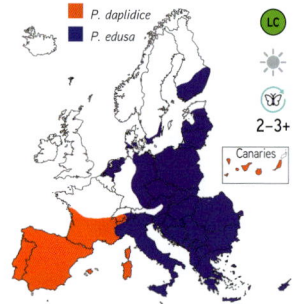

■ *P. daplidice*
■ *P. edusa*

LC

2–3+

Canaries

Did you know?

Bath Whites regularly migrate north during summer. These large-scale movements allow them to colonize new habitats, often in vain due to winter cold. However, this tendency might enable the species to adapt to climate change.

IMAGOS		LARVAE	
Food	✿	Food	✿ 🌱
Behaviour of males	🦋	Caterpillar location	🌿
Dispersion		Chrysalis location	🌿

PIERIDAE

EASTERN BATH WHITE *PONTIA EDUSA*

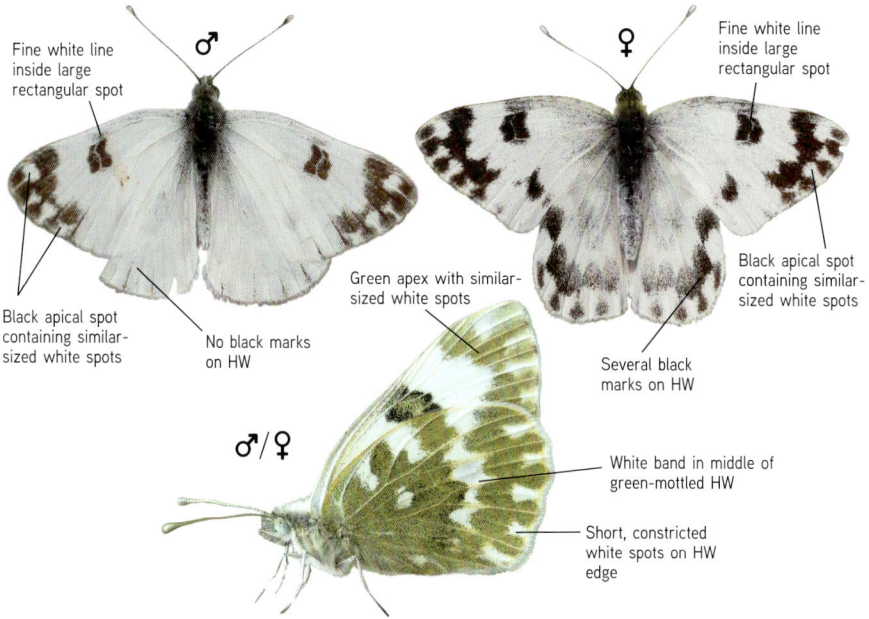

Fine white line inside large rectangular spot

♂

Fine white line inside large rectangular spot

♀

Green apex with similar-sized white spots

Black apical spot containing similar-sized white spots

Black apical spot containing similar-sized white spots

No black marks on HW

Several black marks on HW

♂/♀

White band in middle of green-mottled HW

Short, constricted white spots on HW edge

Wingspan: 38–45 mm

Habitat: Open, dry, and warm environments, dry grasslands, the vicinity of cultivated areas, roadside edges, rocky slopes, and dunes.

Hibernating stage: Pupa.

Elevational range: Up to 1,500 m (vagrants can be recorded at higher elevations).

Egg-laying: Eggs are laid singly on LHP stems and inflorescences.

Flight period: From February to October.

Host plants: Numerous Brassicaceae, including *Alliaria petiolata, Arabidopsis thaliana, Berteroa incana, B. obliqua, Brassica napus, B. nigra, Bunias erucago, Descurainia sophia, Diplotaxis tenuifolia, Erysimum cheiranthoides, Hirschfeldia incana, Lepidium draba, L. graminifolium, L. hirtum, L. ruderale, Pseudoturritis turrita, Raphanus raphanistrum, Rapistrum rugosum, Rorippa palustris, Sinapis arvensis, Sisymbrium altissimum, S. officinale, S. orientale,* and *Teesdalia nudicaulis.* Also on some Resedaceae, like *Reseda lutea, R. luteola, R. odorata,* and *R. alba,* and on *Cleome ornithopodioides* (Cleomaceae).

Diversity and systematics: European populations belong to the nominate subspecies.

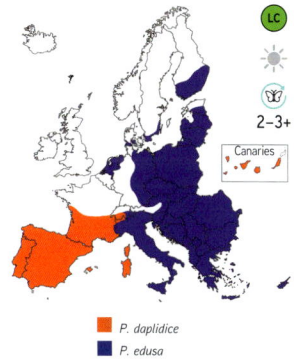

LC

2–3+

Canaries

■ *P. daplidice*
■ *P. edusa*

Did you know?

Pontia edusa cannot be separated from *P. daplidice* except through genitalia examination. As a result, their geographical ranges and respective biologies are not yet well distinguished.

IMAGOS		LARVAE	
Food	✿	Food	✿ 🌱
Behaviour of males	🦋	Caterpillar location	🌿
Dispersion	✺	Chrysalis location	🌿

PIERIDAE

SMALL BATH WHITE *PONTIA CHLORIDICE*

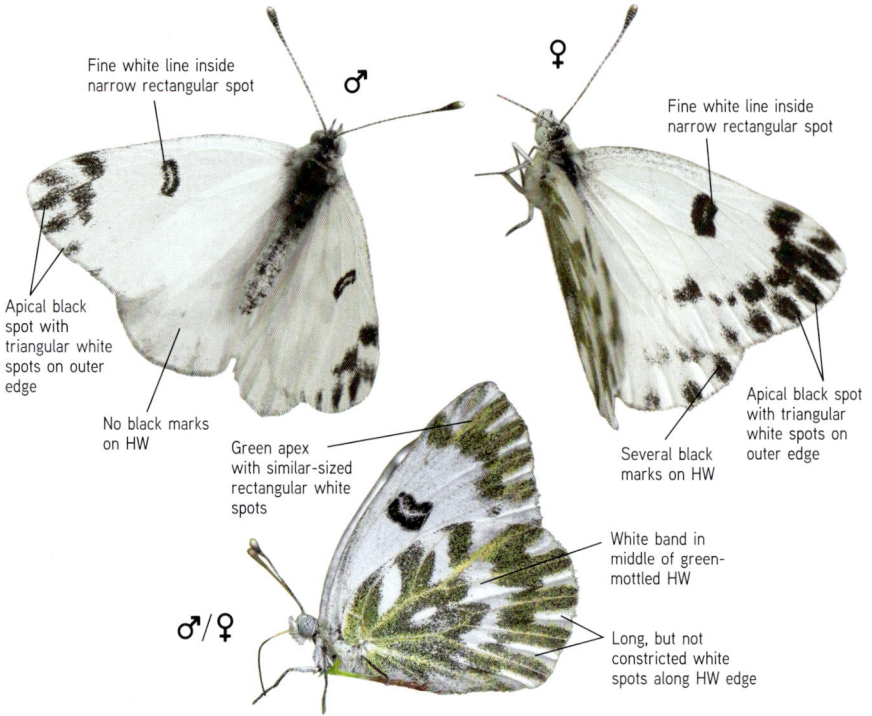

♂

♀

Fine white line inside narrow rectangular spot

Fine white line inside narrow rectangular spot

Apical black spot with triangular white spots on outer edge

No black marks on HW

Green apex with similar-sized rectangular white spots

Several black marks on HW

Apical black spot with triangular white spots on outer edge

White band in middle of green-mottled HW

♂/♀

Long, but not constricted white spots along HW edge

Wingspan: 37–40 mm

Habitat: Stony environments with very sparse vegetation, including riverbeds, recently constructed road edges, and other environments at early successional stages.

Hibernating stage: Pupa.

Elevational range: Usually below 500 m in Europe.

Egg-laying: Eggs are laid singly on LHP leaves.

Flight period: From March to November.

Host plants: Primarily *Cleome ornithopodioides* and *C. iberica* (Cleomaceae). Also *Descurainia sophia* and *Sisymbrium polymorphum* (Brassicaceae).

Diversity and systematics: European populations belong to the nominate subspecies.

LC

2–3+

IMAGOS		LARVAE	
Food		Food	
Behaviour of males		Caterpillar location	
Dispersion		Chrysalis location	

Did you know?

The caterpillar of the Small Bath White is brightly coloured compared with other marbled whites, suggesting aposematism. In contrast, the brown pupa with a light band imitates bird droppings.

PIERIDAE

PEAK WHITE *PONTIA CALLIDICE*

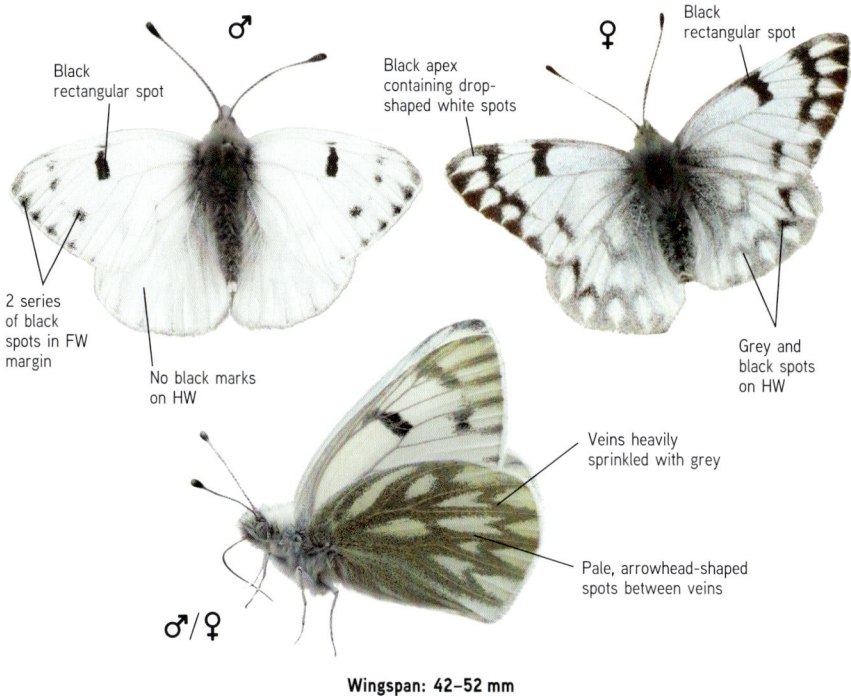

♂

Black rectangular spot

2 series of black spots in FW margin

No black marks on HW

♀

Black rectangular spot

Black apex containing drop-shaped white spots

Grey and black spots on HW

♂/♀

Veins heavily sprinkled with grey

Pale, arrowhead-shaped spots between veins

Wingspan: 42–52 mm

Habitat: Subalpine and alpine grasslands, meadows, and vegetated scree.

Hibernating stage: Pupa.

Elevational range: From 2,000 to 3,000 m (rarely below).

Egg-laying: Eggs are laid singly on LHP leaves.

Flight period: From May to August.

Host plants: Brassicaceae, including *Hornungia alpina*, *Erysimum jugicola*, *E. olympicum*, *E. sylvestre*, *Cardamine bellidifolia*, *C. pratensis*, *C. resedifolia*, *Arabis alpina*, *A. caerulea*, and *Murbeckiella pinnatifida*. Also cited on some Resedaceae, like *Reseda glauca*.

Diversity and systematics: European populations belong to the nominate subspecies.

LC

1–1.5

IMAGOS		LARVAE	
Food	✿	Food	🍃🌱
Behaviour of males	🦋	Caterpillar location	🐛 🌿
Dispersion	✳	Chrysalis location	🛡

Did you know?

The Peak White can live at very high altitudes. In the Asian part of its range, it is seen at elevations exceeding 5,000 m!

PIERIDAE

EASTERN GREENISH BLACK-TIP *EUCHLOE PENIA*

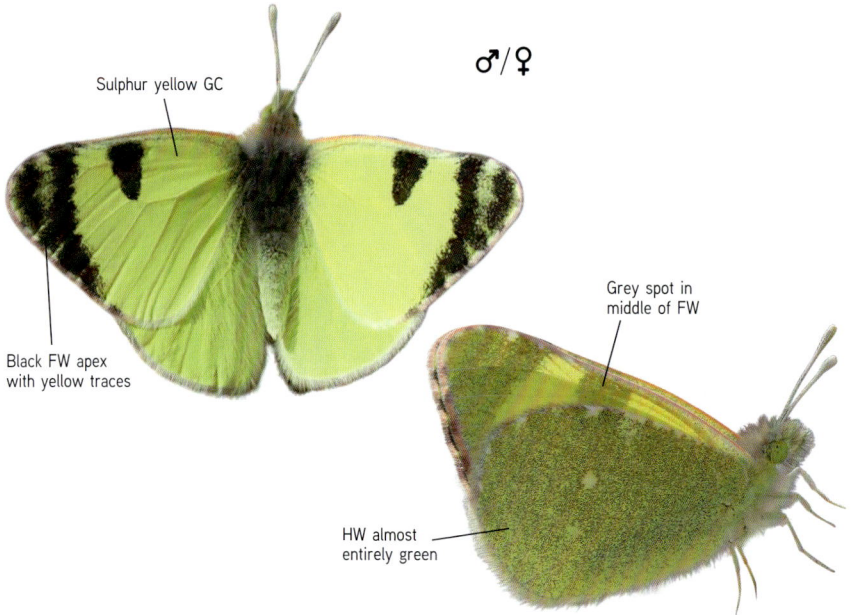

♂/♀

Sulphur yellow GC

Black FW apex
with yellow traces

Grey spot in
middle of FW

HW almost
entirely green

Wingspan: 32–36 mm

Habitat: Stony steppic grasslands.

Hibernating stage: Pupa.

Elevational range: Up to 2,000 m.

Egg-laying: Eggs are laid singly on LHP
stems and leaves.

Flight period: From March to July.

Host plants: *Matthiola fruticulosa*
(Brassicaceae).

Diversity and systematics: European
populations belong to the nominate
subspecies.

- ■ *E. penia*
- ■ *E. bazae*
- ■ *E. charlonia*

LC

1–2

Canaries

IMAGOS			LARVAE		
Food			Food		
Behaviour of males			Caterpillar location		
Dispersion			Chrysalis location		

Did you know?

Males tend to gather on hilltops,
thus practising a kind of
hill-topping.

210

PIERIDAE

SPANISH GREENISH BLACK-TIP *EUCHLOE BAZAE*

♂/♀

Conspicuous pink hairs behind head

Sulphur yellow GC

Black FW apex with yellow traces

Black spot in middle of FW

HW almost entirely green

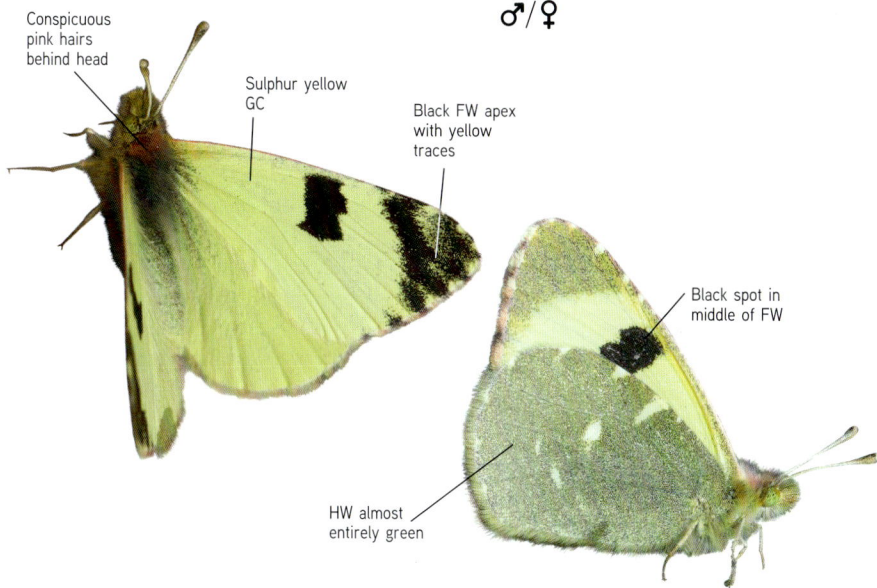

Wingspan: 32–36 mm

Habitat: Arid steppic and semi-desert environments.

Hibernating stage: Pupa.

Elevational range: Up to 1,000 m.

Egg-laying: Eggs are laid singly on the LHP.

Flight period: From March to June.

Host plants: Brassicaceae, mainly *Eruca vesicaria* (especially the nominate subspecies) and *Vella aspera* (for subspecies *iberae*). Also on *Reseda phyteuma* (Resedaceae).

Diversity and systematics: The nominate subspecies flies in the area northeast of Granada (Hoya de Baza), while subspecies *iberae* forms a small population in the area northeast of Zaragoza.

- E. penia
- E. bazae
- E. charlonia

VU

1–2

Canaries

Did you know?

Like those of the Eastern Greenish Black-tip, males of the Iberian Greenish Black-tip gather on hilltops and engage in hilltopping, while females lay their eggs in the valleys where the LHP grows.

IMAGOS		LARVAE	
Food		Food	
Behaviour of males		Caterpillar location	
Dispersion		Chrysalis location	

PIERIDAE

GREENISH BLACK-TIP *EUCHLOE CHARLONIA*

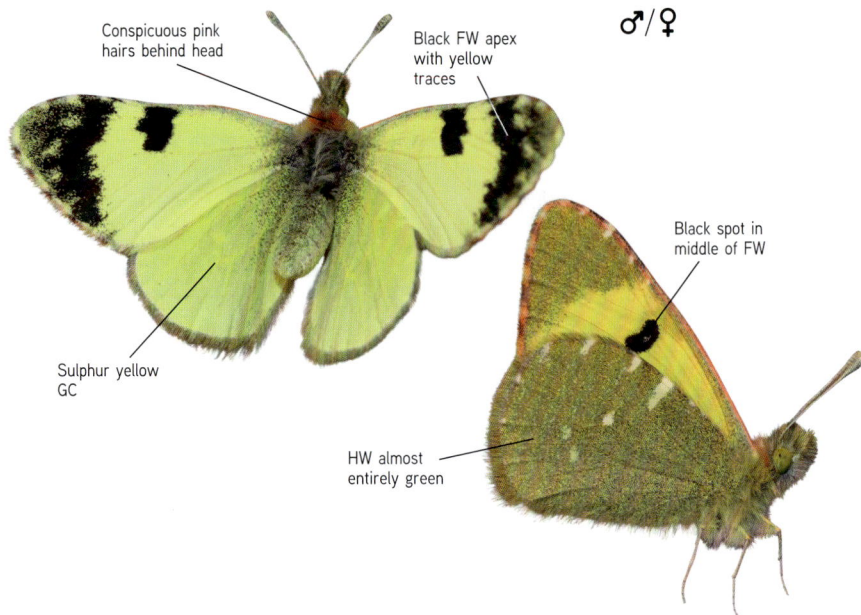

♂/♀

Conspicuous pink
hairs behind head

Black FW apex
with yellow
traces

Black spot in
middle of FW

Sulphur yellow
GC

HW almost
entirely green

Wingspan: 32–36 mm

Habitat: Arid and rocky slopes with sparse vegetation on the easternmost islands of the Canarian archipelago. Has been recorded on the eastern coast of Gran Canaria in 2018 and some following years but permanent establishment is not certain.

Hibernating stage: Pupa.

Elevational range: Up to 800 m.

Egg-laying: Eggs are laid singly on the LHP.

Flight period: Almost year-round.

Host plants: *Carrichtera annua* and *Hirschfeldia incana* (Brassicaceae), as well as *Reseda lancerotae* (Resedaceae).

Diversity and systematics: Canarian populations belong to the nominate subspecies.

■ E. penia
■ E. bazae
■ E. charlonia

LC

2

Canaries

	IMAGOS		LARVAE	
Food	🌸	Food	🌸 🍃 🌿	
Behaviour of males		Caterpillar location		
Dispersion		Chrysalis location		

Did you know?

The Greenish Black-tip is widely distributed in North Africa and has colonized the Canary Islands from this continent. The Iberian populations (*Euchloe bazae*) were formerly considered to belong to *E. charlonia*.

PIERIDAE

CORSICAN DAPPLED WHITE *EUCHLOE INSULARIS*

♂/♀

Apical black spot with white spots inside, the foremost much larger

Narrow, often sinuous black spot not connected to FW leading edge

Narrow, often sinuous black spot not connected to FW leading edge

Greenish-grey FW apex with white spots

HW with heavy greenish mottling, many white spots

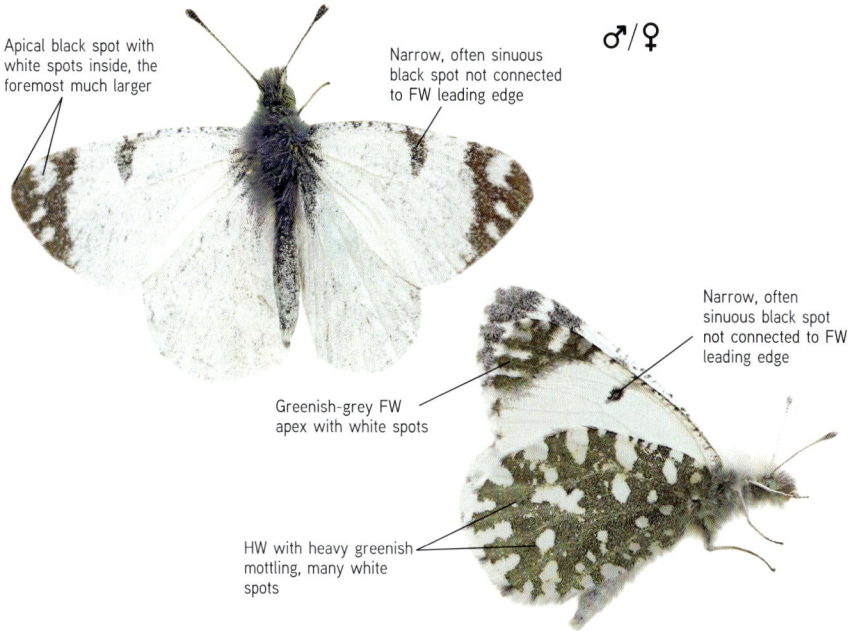

Wingspan: 33–36 mm

Habitat: Dry grasslands, wastelands, thickets, roadside verges, and flowered field margins.

Hibernating stage: Pupa.

Elevational range: Up to 1,400 m.

Egg-laying: Eggs are laid singly on LHP inflorescences.

Flight period: From February to June.

Host plants: Brassicaceae, including *Brassica nigra*, *Hirschfeldia incana*, *Sinapis* spp., *Sisymbrium officinale*, *Iberis pinnata*, *Isatis tinctoria*, and *Raphanus raphanistrum*.

Diversity and systematics: There are no notable subspecies for this Dappled White species, which is endemic to Corsica and Sardinia.

■ E. crameri
■ E. insularis
■ E. ausonia
■ E. ausonia
  + E. crameri

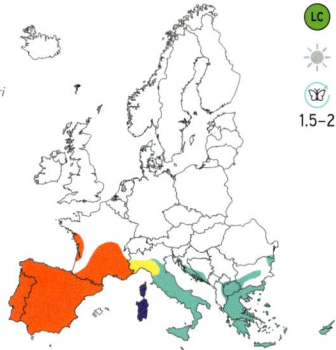

LC

1.5–2

IMAGOS		LARVAE	
Food	☆	Food	☆
Behaviour of males	🦋	Caterpillar location	🌿
Dispersion	✺	Chrysalis location	🌿

Did you know?

Adults forage extensively on Brassicaceae but do not refuse other flowers, such as Asteraceae, Scabious, and Cistaceae.

WESTERN DAPPLED WHITE *EUCHLOE CRAMERI*

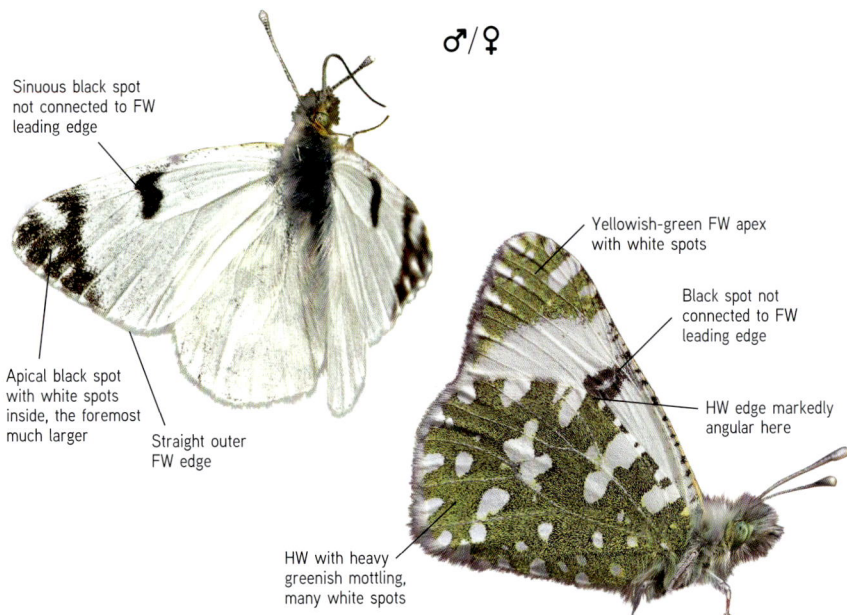

♂/♀

Sinuous black spot not connected to FW leading edge

Apical black spot with white spots inside, the foremost much larger

Straight outer FW edge

Yellowish-green FW apex with white spots

Black spot not connected to FW leading edge

HW edge markedly angular here

HW with heavy greenish mottling, many white spots

Wingspan: 40–48 mm

Habitat: Dry and bushy grasslands, garrigues, maquis, wastelands, sunny rocky slopes, and dunes.

Hibernating stage: Pupa.

Elevational range: Up to 2,000 m.

Egg-laying: Eggs are laid singly on LHP inflorescences.

Flight period: From February to June.

Host plants: Brassicaceae, including *Biscutella laevigata*, *B. auriculata*, *B. coronopifolia*, *B. valentina*, *Brassica barrelieri*, *B. fruticulosa*, *B. nigra*, *B. oleracea*, *Bunias erucago*, *Coincya monensis*, *Diplotaxis tenuifolia*, *D. virgata*, *Eruca vesicaria*, *Hirschfeldia incana*, *Isatis tinctoria*, *Iberis sempervirens*, *I. pinnata*, *I. saxatilis*, *Moricandia arvensis*, *M. moricandioides*, *Raphanus raphanistrum*, *Rapistrum rugosum*, *Sinapis alba*, *S. arvensis*, *Sysimbrium austriacum*, *S. irio*, and *S. officinale*.

Diversity and systematics: European populations belong to the nominate subspecies.

- ■ *E. crameri*
- ■ *E. insularis*
- ■ *E. ausonia*
- ▢ *E. ausonia + E. crameri*

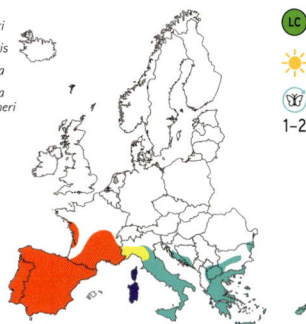

LC

1–2

IMAGOS		LARVAE	
Food	✿	Food	✿
Behaviour of males	🦋	Caterpillar location	🌱
Dispersion		Chrysalis location	🌱

Did you know?

Caterpillars of the Western Dappled White are sometimes carnivorous and do not hesitate to attack other conspecific larvae.

PIERIDAE

EASTERN DAPPLED WHITE *EUCHLOE AUSONIA*

♂/♀

Sinuous black spot not connected to FW leading edge

Yellowish-green FW apex with white spots

Black spot not connected to FW leading edge

HW edge markedly angular here

Slightly convex outer FW edge

Apical black spot with white spots inside, the foremost much larger

HW with heavy greenish mottling, many white spots

Wingspan: 40–48 mm

Habitat: Dry bushy grasslands, agricultural wastelands, forest edges, and olive groves.

Hibernating stage: Pupa.

Elevational range: Up to 2,000 m.

Egg-laying: Eggs are laid singly on LHP inflorescences.

Flight period: From February to July.

Host plants: Brassicaceae, including *Biscutella mollis*, *Brassica nigra*, *Bunias erucago*, *Eruca vesicaria*, *Erucaria hispanica*, *Hirschfeldia incana*, *Isatis tinctoria*, *Raphanus raphanistrum*, *Sinapis alba*, *S. arvensis*, *Sisymbrium officinale*, *S. orientale*, and *Turritis glabra*.

Diversity and systematics: *Euchloe ausonia* is part of a cryptic species complex with *E. crameri*, *E. simplonia*, and *E. insularis*. The nominate subspecies flies in Greece and Italy. Subspecies *taurica* inhabits the Balkans.

■ *E. crameri*
■ *E. insularis*
■ *E. ausonia*
□ *E. ausonia* + *E. crameri*

LC

1–2

Did you know?

Male Eastern Dappled Whites tend to gather and patrol hilltops, where they await the passage of females (hill-topping).

IMAGOS		LARVAE	
Food	✿	Food	✿ 🍃 🍃
Behaviour of males	🦋 ⊛	Caterpillar location	🌿
Dispersion	⊗	Chrysalis location	🌿

MOUNTAIN DAPPLED WHITE *EUCHLOE SIMPLONIA*

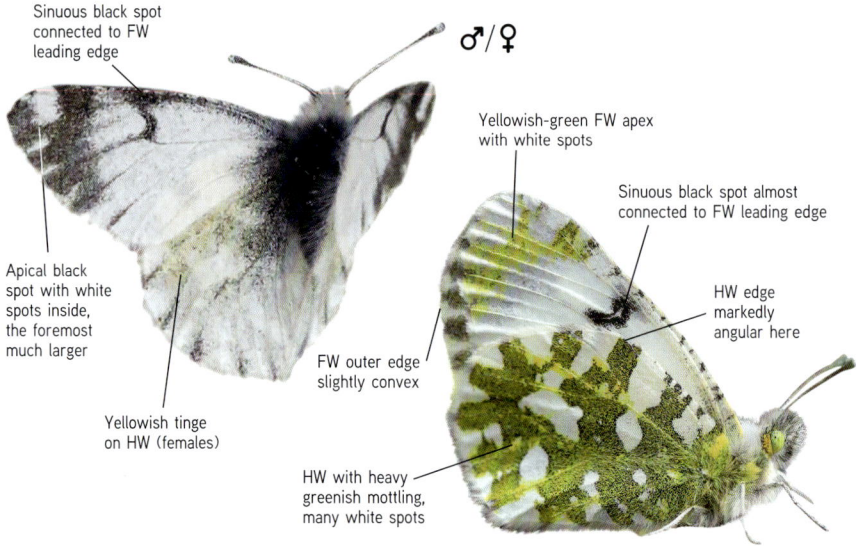

Sinuous black spot connected to FW leading edge

♂/♀

Yellowish-green FW apex with white spots

Sinuous black spot almost connected to FW leading edge

Apical black spot with white spots inside, the foremost much larger

HW edge markedly angular here

Yellowish tinge on HW (females)

FW outer edge slightly convex

HW with heavy greenish mottling, many white spots

Wingspan: 40–46 mm

Habitat: Subalpine and alpine grasslands and meadows, rocky slopes.

Hibernating stage: Pupa.

Elevational range: From 600 to 2,600 m (mainly above 1,000 m).

Egg-laying: Eggs are laid singly on LHP inflorescences.

Flight period: From April to August.

Host plants: Brassicaceae, including *Arabis sagittata*,

Barbarea vulgaris, Biscutella laevigata, Descurainia tanacetifolia, Iberis spathulata, Isatis tinctoria, Erucastrum nasturtiifolium, Sinapis arvensis, and *Sisymbrium austriacum.*

Diversity and systematics: The nominate subspecies flies in the Alps. Pyrenean populations constitute subspecies *oberthueri*. Cantabrian populations have uncertain affiliation.

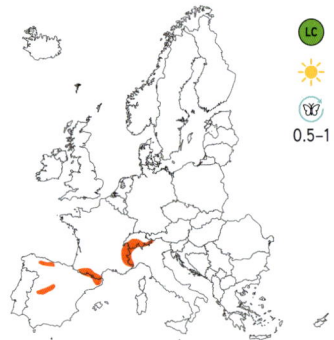

LC

0.5–1

Did you know?

Cannibalism is a common life history trait among Dappled White caterpillars, which otherwise feed exclusively on the flowers and fruits of host plants. This resource is sometimes insufficient and compensated for by consuming conspecifics sharing the same LHP.

IMAGOS			LARVAE	
Food	🌼		Food	🌼
Behaviour of males			Caterpillar location	
Dispersion			Chrysalis location	

PIERIDAE

PORTUGUESE DAPPLED WHITE   *IBEROCHLOE TAGIS*

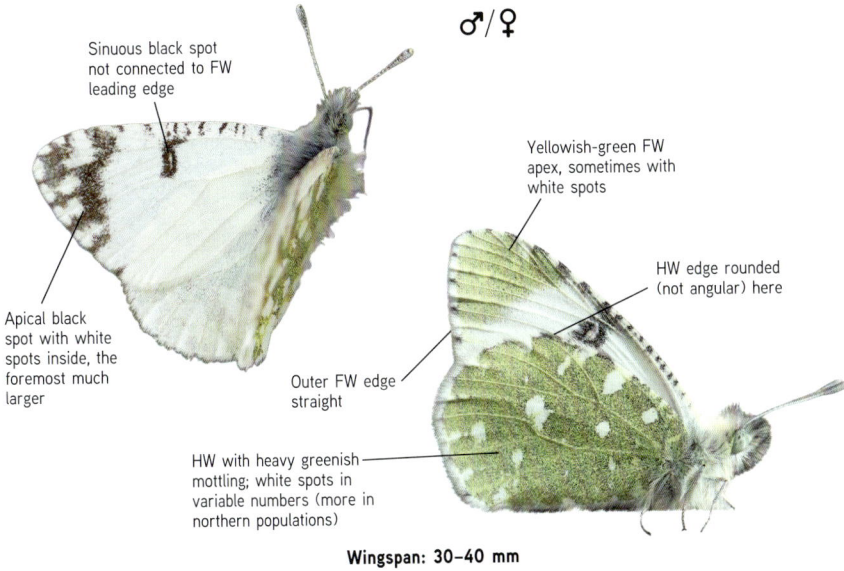

♂/♀

Sinuous black spot not connected to FW leading edge

Yellowish-green FW apex, sometimes with white spots

HW edge rounded (not angular) here

Apical black spot with white spots inside, the foremost much larger

Outer FW edge straight

HW with heavy greenish mottling; white spots in variable numbers (more in northern populations)

Wingspan: 30–40 mm

Habitat: Bushy dry grasslands, steppic grasslands, sunny rocky slopes.

Hibernating stage: Pupa.

Elevational range: Up to 1,500 m (mainly below 1,000 m).

Egg-laying: Eggs are laid singly on LHP inflorescences.

Flight period: From February to May.

Host plants: Brassicaceae in genus *Iberis*, especially *I. pinnata*, *I. sempervirens*, *I. saxatilis*, *I. ciliata*, *I. amara*, *I. fontqueri*, *I. nazarita*, *I. procumbens*, and *I. umbellata*.

Diversity and systematics: The nominate subspecies flies in Portugal. Subspecies *davidi* is present in Andalusia. Subspecies *granadensis* flies in northern Andalusia. Subspecies *castellana* inhabits central and eastern Spain. Subspecies *bellezina* makes up the French populations, and *piemonti* flies in northwestern Italy.

LC

1

Did you know?

Populations of the Portuguese Dappled White are often highly localized and rather separate, reducing genetic mixing. It is not surprising, therefore, that several subspecies are described, even though the overall distribution range isn't very extensive.

IMAGOS		LARVAE	
Food	☆	Food	☆ 🌿
Behaviour of males	🦋	Caterpillar location	🌿
Dispersion	🦋	Chrysalis location	🌿

GREEN-STRIPED WHITE *EUCHLOE BELEMIA*

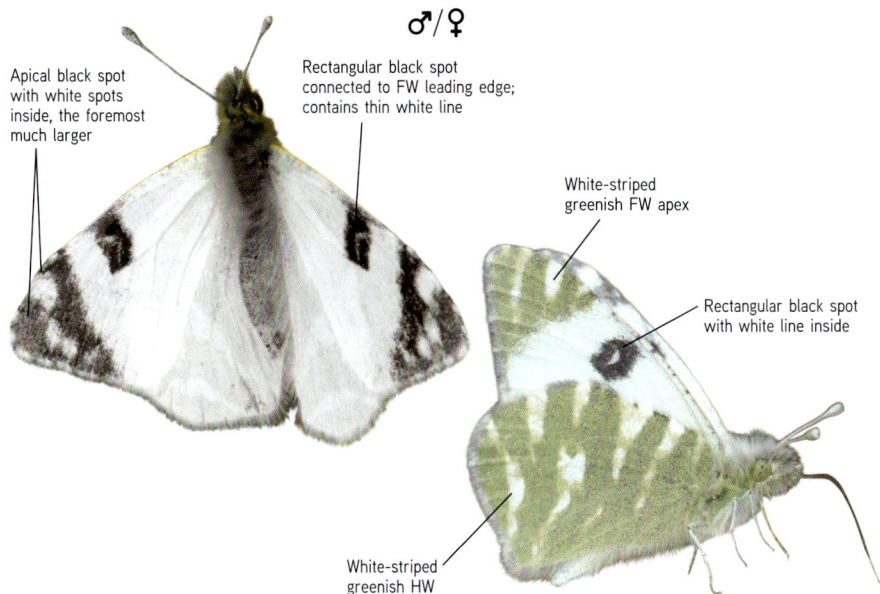

♂/♀

Apical black spot with white spots inside, the foremost much larger

Rectangular black spot connected to FW leading edge; contains thin white line

White-striped greenish FW apex

Rectangular black spot with white line inside

White-striped greenish HW

Wingspan: 36–44 mm

Habitat: Wastelands, backdunes, abandoned croplands, clear Mediterranean woodlands.

Hibernating stage: Pupa.

Elevational range: Up to 1,000 m.

Egg-laying: Eggs are laid singly on LHP inflorescences and leaves.

Flight period: From February to June.

Host plants: Brassicaceae, including *Hirschfeldia incana*, *Moricandia moricandioides*, *Raphanus raphanistrum*, *Rapistrum rugosum*, and *Diplotaxis siifolia*.

Diversity and systematics: European populations belong to the nominate subspecies. Canarian green-striped whites are now often considered separate species, rather than subspecies of *Euchloe belemia*.

- ■ *E. belemia*
- ■ *E. hesperidum*
- ■ *E. eversi*
- ■ *E. grancanariensis*

LC

2

Canaries

Did you know?

The Green-striped White reaches the northern part of its extensive North African and Near Eastern range in the Iberian Peninsula.

IMAGOS		LARVAE	
Food	✿	Food	✿
Behaviour of males		Caterpillar location	
Dispersion		Chrysalis location	

PIERIDAE

CANARIAN GREEN-STRIPED WHITES
EUCHLOE EVERSI/E. GRANCANARIENSIS/E. HESPERIDUM

♂/♀

White-striped greenish FW apex

Rectangular black spot connected to FW leading edge; contains thin white line

Rectangular black spot with white line inside

Apical black spot with white spots inside, the foremost much larger

White-striped greenish HW

The 3 Canarian Green-striped Whites have very similar wing patterns. The upperside picture is *E. grancanariensis*; the underside picture is *E. eversi*.

Wingspan: 36–44 mm

Habitat: Rocky and semiarid slopes and gullies, roadside edges, and other ruderal environments.

Hibernating stage: Pupa.

Elevational range: Up to 700 m for *Euchloe hesperidum*, 1,500 m for *E. grancanariensis*, and mainly above 1,500 m for *E. eversi*.

Egg-laying: Eggs are laid singly on LHP inflorescences, stems, and leaves.

Flight period: From December to June.

Host plants: Brassicaceae, including *Descurainia bourgaeana*, *Erucastrum canariense*, *Carrichtera annua*, *Sisymbrium erysimoides*, and *Hirschfeldia incana*.

Diversity and systematics: These three Canarian species were once considered subspecies of the Green-striped White, *Euchloe belemia*. The split of the three Canarian taxa into three different species remains debated.

- ■ *E. belemia*
- ■ *E. hesperidum*
- ■ *E. eversi*
- ■ *E. grancanariensis*

LC

2–3

Canaries

IMAGOS		LARVAE	
Food		Food	
Behaviour of males		Caterpillar location	
Dispersion: unknown		Chrysalis location	

Did you know?

Due to the heat and drought, the summer season is unfavourable for Canarian butterflies. Canarian Green-striped Whites breed before this adverse period.

PIERIDAE

KRUEPER'S SMALL WHITE *PIERIS KRUEPERI*

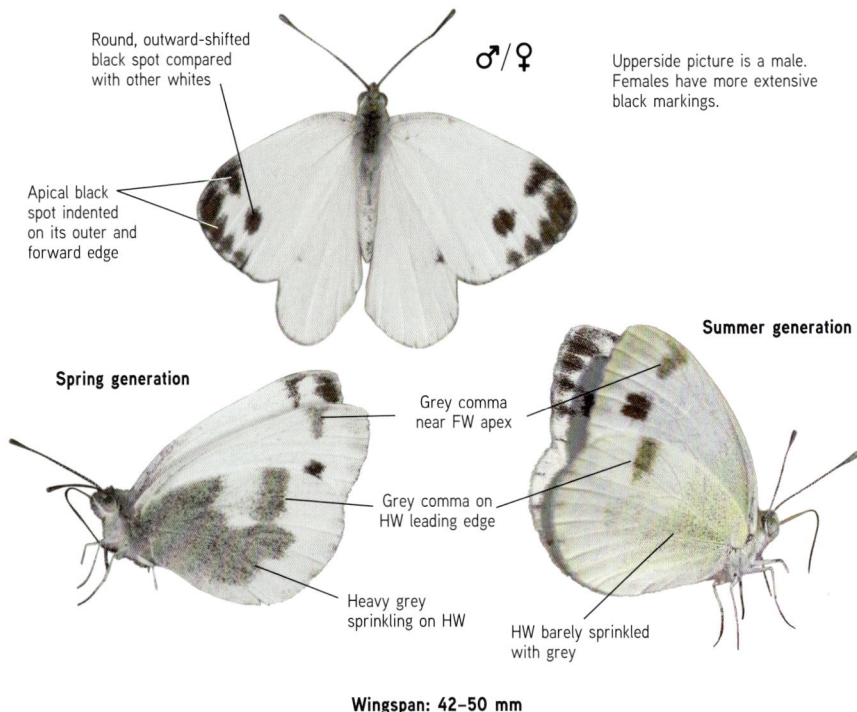

Round, outward-shifted black spot compared with other whites

♂/♀

Upperside picture is a male. Females have more extensive black markings.

Apical black spot indented on its outer and forward edge

Spring generation

Summer generation

Grey comma near FW apex

Grey comma on HW leading edge

Heavy grey sprinkling on HW

HW barely sprinkled with grey

Wingspan: 42–50 mm

Habitat: Rocky environments, such as cliffs, quarries, stony slopes, and ruins.

Hibernating stage: Pupa.

Elevational range: Up to 1,500 m.

Egg-laying: Eggs are laid singly on LHP leaves.

Flight period: From March to October.

Host plants: Brassicaceae, mainly *Alyssum saxatile* and *A. montanum*.

Diversity and systematics: European populations belong to the nominate subspecies.

LC

1–3+

Did you know?

Although they breed in particularly dry, rocky environments, adults are fond of moist soils, from which they extract water and minerals.

IMAGOS		LARVAE	
Food		Food	
Behaviour of males		Caterpillar location	
Dispersion		Chrysalis location	

220

PIERIDAE

CANARY ISLANDS LARGE WHITE *PIERIS CHEIRANTHI*

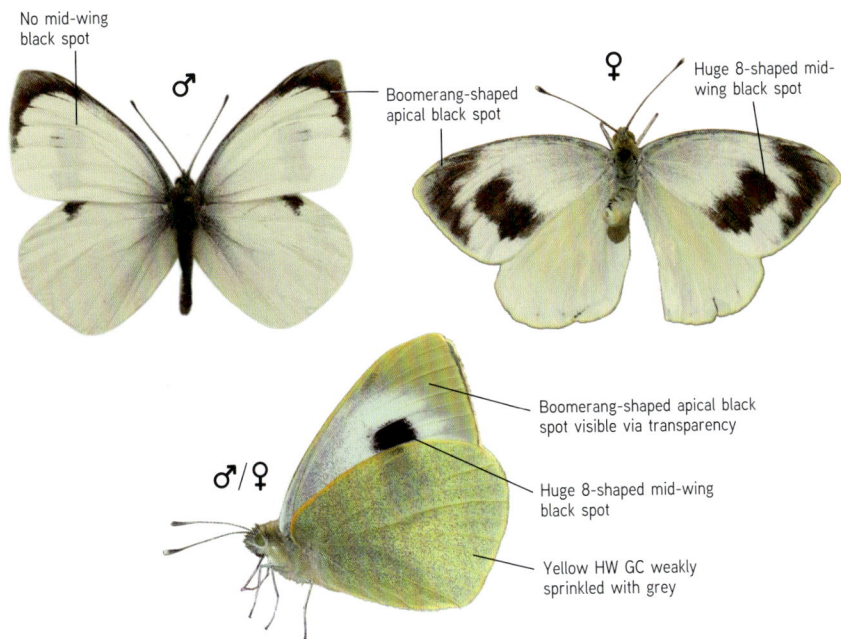

No mid-wing black spot

♂

Boomerang-shaped apical black spot

♀

Huge 8-shaped mid-wing black spot

♂/♀

Boomerang-shaped apical black spot visible via transparency

Huge 8-shaped mid-wing black spot

Yellow HW GC weakly sprinkled with grey

Wingspan: 60–65 mm

Habitat: Rocky and bushy gullies; laurel forests. Can tolerate slight anthropization.

Hibernating stage: Egg, caterpillar, pupa, or adult without entering diapause.

Elevational range: Up to 1,400 m (mainly below 1,000 m).

Egg-laying: Eggs are laid in large batches of several dozens on LHP leaves.

Flight period: Year-round.

Host plants: Brassicaceae, including *Descurainia millefolia*, *Lobularia canariensis*, *Brassica oleracea*, and *Crambe strigosa*. Also on Tropaeolaceae, like *Tropaeolum majus*, *T. minus*, and *T. peregrinum*.

Diversity and systematics: The nominate subspecies inhabits Tenerife Island. Subspecies *benchoavensis* flies on La Palma. Some authors consider *Pieris wollastoni* a subspecies (most likely extinct from Madeira) of *P. cheiranthi*.

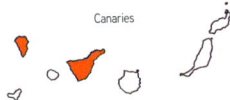

Canaries

EN

3+

Did you know?

The Canary Islands Large White is arguably the most threatened Pierid in Europe due to the destruction of its favourable habitats caused by agricultural intensification and urbanization.

IMAGOS		LARVAE	
Food		Food	
Behaviour of males		Caterpillar location	
Dispersion		Chrysalis location	

PIERIDAE

LARGE WHITE *PIERIS BRASSICAE*

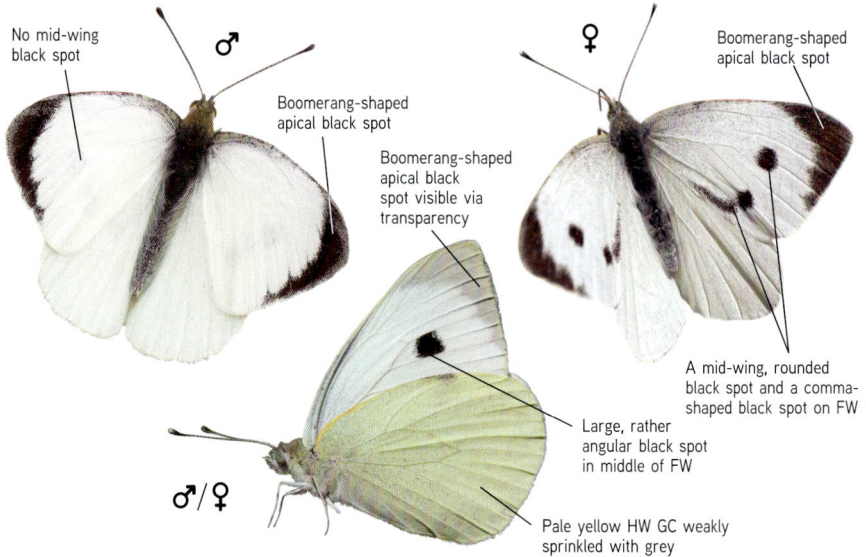

No mid-wing black spot

♂

♀

Boomerang-shaped apical black spot

Boomerang-shaped apical black spot

Boomerang-shaped apical black spot visible via transparency

A mid-wing, rounded black spot and a comma-shaped black spot on FW

Large, rather angular black spot in middle of FW

♂/♀

Pale yellow HW GC weakly sprinkled with grey

Wingspan: 49–63 mm

Habitat: Surroundings of cabbages and oilseed rape crops, flower-rich meadows, wastelands, parks, gardens, and woodland edges.

Hibernating stage: Pupa.

Elevational range: Up to 3,000 m.

Egg-laying: Eggs are laid in large batches of several dozens on LHP leaves.

Flight period: From February to November.

Host plants: A large variety of Brassicaceae in genera *Alliaria, Arabis, Armoracia, Aurinia, Barbarea, Biscutella, Brassica, Bunias, Cakile, Cardamine, Coincya, Conringia, Crambe, Descurainia, Diplotaxis, Draba, Eruca, Erysimum, Hesperis, Hirschfeldia, Hornungia, Iberis, Isatis, Kernera, Lepidium, Lobularia,* *Lunaria, Matthiola, Moricandia, Nasturtium, Raphanus, Rapistrum, Rorippa, Sinapis, Sisymbrium,* and *Thlaspi*. Also on *Capparis spinosa* (Capparaceae), *Reseda lutea* and *R. luteola* (Resedaceae), *Tropaeolum majus* (Tropaeolaceae), and a few legumes like *Cytisus multiflorus, Genista tinctoria, Medicago sativa,* and *Vicia cracca*.

Diversity and systematics: Most European populations belong to the nominate subspecies. Subspecies *cypriensis* inhabits Cyprus, while *azorensis* is found in the Azores. *Pieris wollastoni*, sometimes regarded as a subspecies of *P. brassicae*, formerly flew in Madeira, where it has not been recorded since 1977 and is likely to have gone extinct.

LC

2–3+

Azores

Did you know?

Adult Large Whites exhibit pronounced latitudinal migratory behaviour. They are often observed foraging on the inflorescences of *Buddleia*, a genus also known as butterfly bushes. The caterpillars incur a significant toll from parasitoid Hymenoptera, especially *Cotesia glomerata*.

IMAGOS		LARVAE	
Food	🌸	Food	🍃
Behaviour of males		Caterpillar location	
Dispersion		Chrysalis location	

PIERIDAE

SMALL WHITE *PIERIS RAPAE*

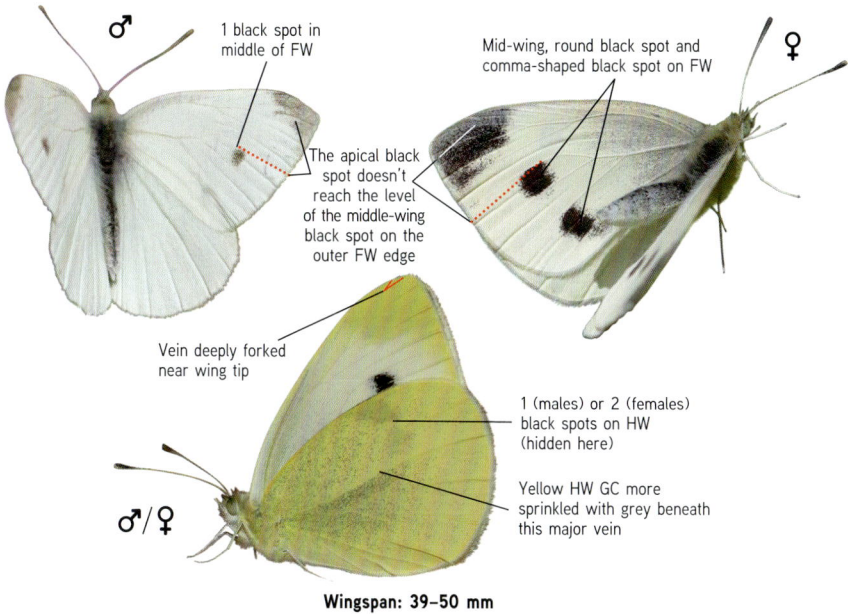

♂

1 black spot in middle of FW

Mid-wing, round black spot and comma-shaped black spot on FW

♀

The apical black spot doesn't reach the level of the middle-wing black spot on the outer FW edge

Vein deeply forked near wing tip

1 (males) or 2 (females) black spots on HW (hidden here)

Yellow HW GC more sprinkled with grey beneath this major vein

♂/♀

Wingspan: 39–50 mm

Habitat: Cabbage and oilseed rape crops, meadows, wastelands, roadside verges, parks and gardens.

Hibernating stage: Pupa.

Elevational range: Up to 2,300 m.

Egg-laying: Eggs are laid singly on LHP leaves.

Flight period: From February to November.

Host plants: Brassicaceae, including some cultivated species like *Brassica oleracea*, *B. napus*, *Raphanus sativus*, *Sinapis arvensis*. Also on large variety of wild species in genera *Alliaria*, *Alyssum*, *Arabidopsis*, *Arabis*, *Armoracia*, *Aubrieta*, *Aurinia*,

Barbarea, *Berteroa*, *Biscutella*, *Bunias*, *Cakile*, *Calepina*, *Capsella*, *Cardamine*, *Cochlearia*, *Coincya*, *Crambe*, *Diplotaxis*, *Eruca*, *Erucastrum*, *Erysimum*, *Hesperis*, *Hirschfeldia*, *Iberis*, *Isatis*, *Lepidium*, *Lobularia*, *Lunaria*, *Moricandia*, *Nasturtium*, *Noccaea*, *Pseudoturritis*, *Raphanus*, *Rapistrum*, *Rorripa*, *Rapistrum*, *Sisymbrium*, *Thlaspi*, and *Turritis*. Feeds also on *Tropaeolum majus* (Tropaeolaceae), *Reseda alba*, *R. lutea*, *R. luteola*, and *R. phyteuma* (Resedaceae).

Diversity and systematics: European populations of this widespread white belong to the nominate subspecies.

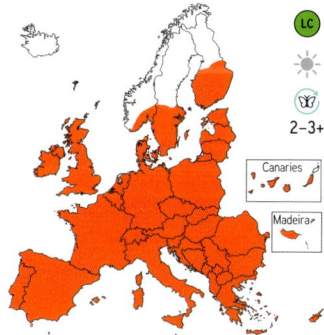

LC

2–3+

Canaries

Madeira

Did you know?

The Small White was accidentally introduced to the American continent in the 19th century and rapidly spread across it within a few decades. During the 20th century, it also successfully invaded Hawaii, New Zealand, and Australia.

IMAGOS	LARVAE
Food	Food
Behaviour of males	Caterpillar location
Dispersion	Chrysalis location

PIERIDAE

SOUTHERN SMALL WHITE *PIERIS MANNII*

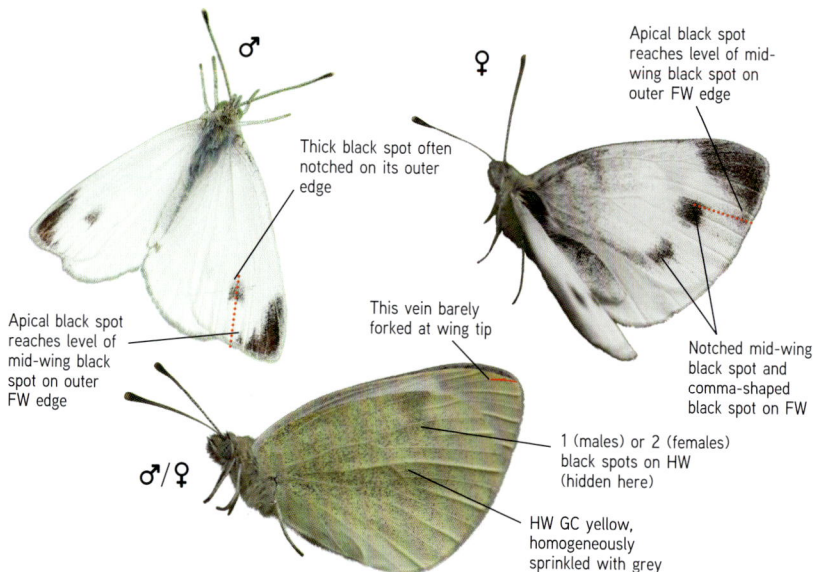

♂

♀

Apical black spot reaches level of mid-wing black spot on outer FW edge

Thick black spot often notched on its outer edge

Apical black spot reaches level of mid-wing black spot on outer FW edge

This vein barely forked at wing tip

Notched mid-wing black spot and comma-shaped black spot on FW

♂/♀

1 (males) or 2 (females) black spots on HW (hidden here)

HW GC yellow, homogeneously sprinkled with grey

Wingspan: 40–46 mm

Habitat: Dry and sunny, open environments, wastelands, rocky slopes, bushy grasslands, parks, and gardens.

Hibernating stage: Pupa.

Elevational range: Up to 1,600 m.

Egg-laying: Eggs are laid singly on LHP leaves.

Flight period: From February to November.

Host plants: A large variety of Brassiceae, including *Iberis pinnata, I. amara, I. umbellata, I. linifolia, I. sempervirens, I. saxatilis, Aethionema saxatile, Alyssoides utriculata, Aubrieta deltoidea, Aurinia saxatilis, Cardamine impatiens, Hormathophylla spinosa, Kernera saxatilis, Lepidium campestre, L. coronopus, L. graminifolium, L. ruderale, Diplotaxis erucoides, D. muralis, D. tenuifolia, Lobularia maritima, Peltaria alliacea,* and *Sinapis arvensis.* Also on *Reseda luteola* (Resedaceae).

Diversity and systematics: The nominate subspecies flies in the Balkans. In Western Europe, subspecies *andegava* is found in the northern part of the distribution area (including France), *alpigena* in the Swiss and French Alps, *roberti* in Spain, and *hemiandegava, antetodaroana,* and *cisalpina* in Italy. Due to the adult's strong dispersal abilities, the geographical boundaries of these subspecies are poorly understood.

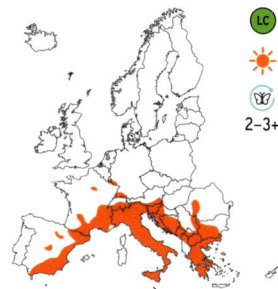

LC

2–3+

Did you know?

The Southern Small White has been expanding northward since the late 2000s. Its westward progression appears to be much slower.

IMAGOS		LARVAE	
Food	🌸💧	Food	🍃
Behaviour of males	🦋	Caterpillar location	🌿
Dispersion		Chrysalis location	

PIERIDAE

MOUNTAIN SMALL WHITE *PIERIS ERGANE*

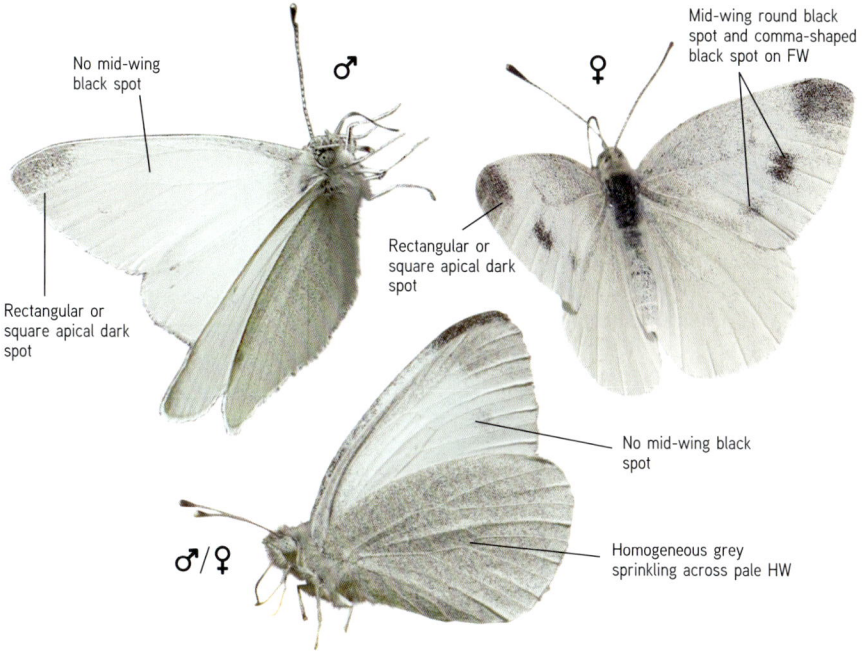

♂

♀

♂/♀

No mid-wing black spot

Rectangular or square apical dark spot

Rectangular or square apical dark spot

Mid-wing round black spot and comma-shaped black spot on FW

No mid-wing black spot

Homogeneous grey sprinkling across pale HW

Wingspan: 36–48 mm

Habitat: Bushy dry grasslands and garrigue, sunny rocky slopes and quarries.

Hibernating stage: Pupa.

Elevational range: Up to 2,000 m.

Egg-laying: Eggs are laid singly on LHP leaves.

Flight period: From February to November.

Host plants: Brassicaceae in genus *Aethionema*, like *A. saxatile*, *A. orbiculatum*, and *A. thomasianum*. Also on *Isatis tinctoria*.

Diversity and systematics: The nominate subspecies flies in Italy. Balkan populations belong to subspecies *detersa*. Subspecies *lucieni* is very localized in the French Alps. Populations in the Pyrenees belong to subspecies *gallia*.

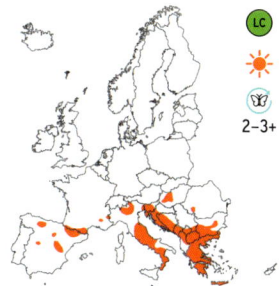

LC

2–3+

Did you know?

The Mountain Small White is a highly localized species in the western part of its range, encompassing France and Spain. However, it can be abundant in its typical habitats.

IMAGOS		LARVAE	
Food	🌸 💧	Food	🍃
Behaviour of males	🦋	Caterpillar location	🌿
Dispersion		Chrysalis location	🌿

PIERIDAE

GREEN-VEINED WHITE/BALKAN GREEN-VEINED WHITE
PIERIS NAPI/PIERIS BALCANA

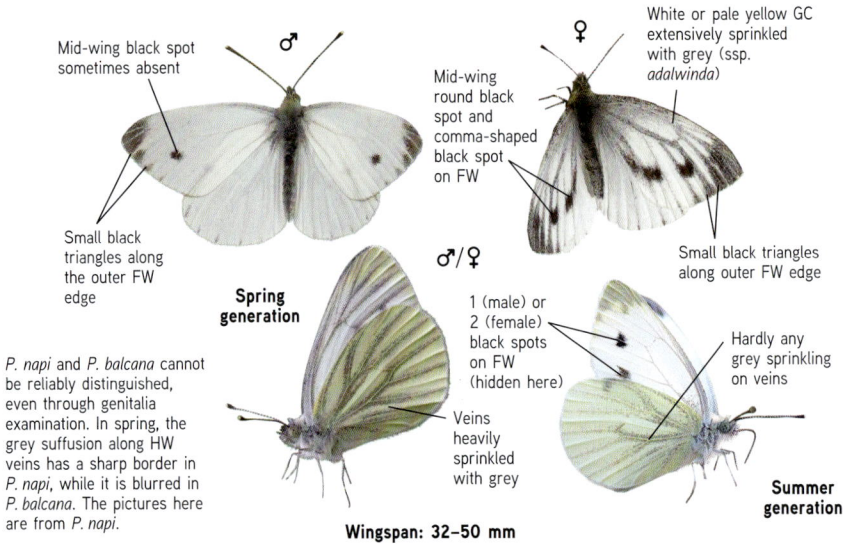

Mid-wing black spot sometimes absent

♂

♀

White or pale yellow GC extensively sprinkled with grey (ssp. *adalwinda*)

Mid-wing round black spot and comma-shaped black spot on FW

Small black triangles along the outer FW edge

Small black triangles along outer FW edge

Spring generation

♂/♀

1 (male) or 2 (female) black spots on FW (hidden here)

Hardly any grey sprinkling on veins

P. napi and *P. balcana* cannot be reliably distinguished, even through genitalia examination. In spring, the grey suffusion along HW veins has a sharp border in *P. napi*, while it is blurred in *P. balcana*. The pictures here are from *P. napi*.

Veins heavily sprinkled with grey

Summer generation

Wingspan: 32–50 mm

Habitat: Clearings, forest edges and pathsides, surroundings of Brassicaceae crops, parks, and gardens.

Hibernating stage: Pupa.

Elevational range: Up to 2,000 m for *Pieris napi*, 1,200 m for *P. balcana*.

Egg-laying: Eggs are laid singly on LHP leaves.

Flight period: From March to November for *Pieris napi*, April to October for *P. balcana*.

Host plants: A very large variety of Brassicaceae (around 60 species), mainly *Alliaria petiolata*, *Cardamine pratensis*, *Sisymbrium* spp., *Arabis* spp., *Nasturtium officinale*, *Aurinia saxatilis*. Doesn't use cultivated species as often as other whites. Also on species

in genera *Arabidopsis*, *Barbarea*, *Berteroa*, *Biscutella*, *Cakile*, *Diplotaxis*, *Draba*, *Erucastrum*, *Erysimum*, *Hesperis*, *Iberis*, *Isatis*, *Lepidium*, *Lobularia*, *Lunaria*, *Noccaea*, *Pseudoturritis*, *Raphanus*, *Rorippa*, *Sinapis*, *Sisymbrium*, *Thlaspi*, and *Turritis*. Feeds also on *Reseda lutea* (Resedaceae) and *Tropaeolum majus* (Tropaeolaceae).

Diversity and systematics: For *Pieris napi*, most European populations belong to the nominate subspecies. Subspecies *adalwinda* inhabits the northern Scandinavian regions. Subspecies *britannica* is found in Ireland. Subspecies *meridionalis* flies in Southern Europe, and subspecies *lusitanica* and *mirabilis* are described from Portugal.

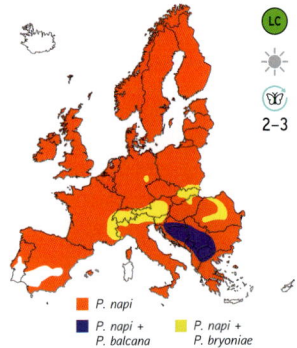

LC

2–3

■ *P. napi*
■ *P. napi* + *P. balcana*
■ *P. napi* + *P. bryoniae*

Did you know?

The systematics of *Pieris napi* are still a subject of debate. *P. balcana* has long been regarded as a subspecies of *P. napi* although a very recent genetic study (2025) has shown that it is more closely related to *P. bryoniae* than to *P. napi*.

IMAGOS		LARVAE	
Food	🌸 💧	Food	🍃
Behaviour of males	🦋	Caterpillar location	🌿
Dispersion	↗↘↙	Chrysalis location	🐛 🌿

MOUNTAIN GREEN-VEINED WHITE *PIERIS BRYONIAE*

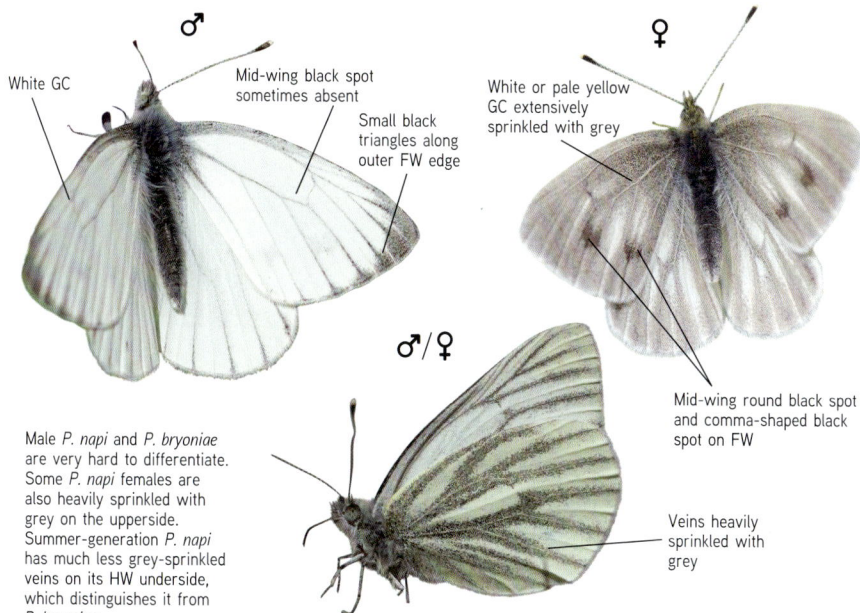

♂

White GC

Mid-wing black spot sometimes absent

Small black triangles along outer FW edge

♀

White or pale yellow GC extensively sprinkled with grey

Mid-wing round black spot and comma-shaped black spot on FW

♂/♀

Male *P. napi* and *P. bryoniae* are very hard to differentiate. Some *P. napi* females are also heavily sprinkled with grey on the upperside. Summer-generation *P. napi* has much less grey-sprinkled veins on its HW underside, which distinguishes it from *P. bryoniae*.

Veins heavily sprinkled with grey

Wingspan: 32–47 mm

Habitat: High-altitude meadows, damp clearings, and streamside megaphorbs in montane areas.

Hibernating stage: Pupa.

Elevational range: Between 500 and 2,400 m.

Egg-laying: Eggs are laid singly on LHP leaves.

Flight period: From May to September.

Host plants: Brassicaceae, including *Alliaria petiolata, Arabidopsis arenosa, A. halleri, Arabis alpina, A. ciliata, A. hirsuta, A. soyeri, Barbarea intermedia, Biscutella laevigata, Cardamine heptaphylla, C. bulbifera,* *C. pratensis, C. pentaphyllos, C. trifolia, Draba aizoides, Erucastrum gallicum, Hesperis matronalis, Hornungia alpina, Lunaria rediviva, Nasturtium officinale, Noccaea montana, N. rotundifolia, Sinapis arvensis, Thlaspi* spp., and *Turritis brassica.*

Diversity and systematics: The nominate subspecies flies in the Western Alps. Populations in the Jura mountains belong to subspecies *debrosi*. Subspecies *lorkovici* is found in the Central Alps, while subspecies *marani* inhabits the Carpathians. Subspecies *wolfsbergeri* is described from Italy.

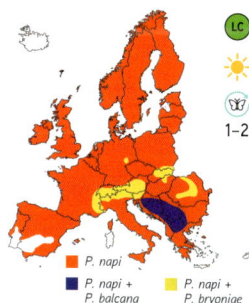

LC

1–2

■ *P. napi*
■ *P. napi + P. balcana*
■ *P. napi + P. bryoniae*

Did you know?

The Mountain Green-veined White was once considered a subspecies of the Green-veined White. The two species hybridize in the Eastern Alps, but most offspring are sterile.

IMAGOS		LARVAE	
Food		Food	
Behaviour of males		Caterpillar location	
Dispersion		Chrysalis location	

PIERIDAE

EASTERN WOOD WHITE *LEPTIDEA DUPONCHELI*

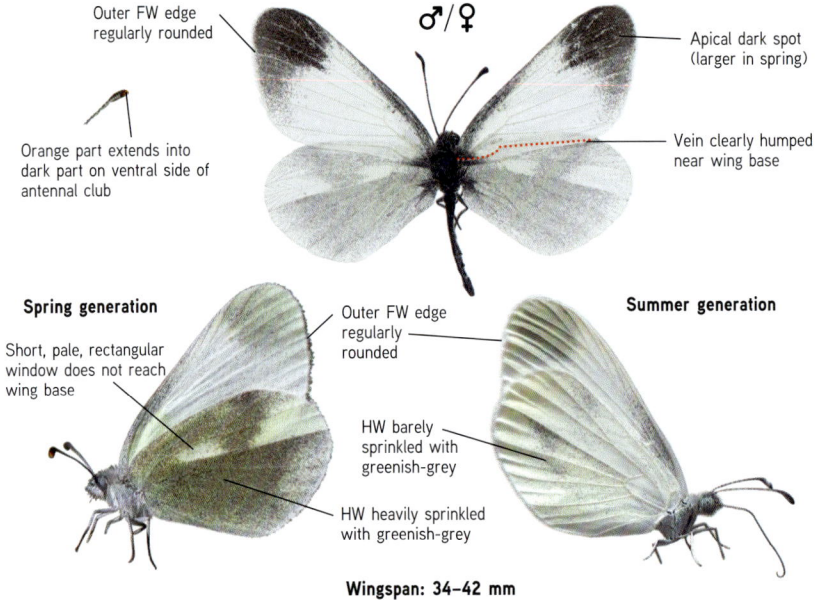

♂/♀

Outer FW edge regularly rounded

Apical dark spot (larger in spring)

Orange part extends into dark part on ventral side of antennal club

Vein clearly humped near wing base

Spring generation

Short, pale, rectangular window does not reach wing base

Outer FW edge regularly rounded

Summer generation

HW barely sprinkled with greenish-grey

HW heavily sprinkled with greenish-grey

Wingspan: 34–42 mm

Habitat: Bushy grasslands, dry clearings and forest edges.

Hibernating stage: Pupa.

Elevational range: Up to 1,200 m.

Egg-laying: Eggs are laid singly on LHP leaflets.

Flight period: From April to August.

Host plants: Herbaceous legumes, such as *Onobrychis alba*, *O. arenaria*, *O. saxatilis*, *O. supina*, *Lotus* spp., and *Lathyrus* spp.

Diversity and systematics: Southeastern French populations belong to the nominate subspecies. Those in the Balkans form subspecies *lorkovici*.

LC

2

Did you know?

The Eastern Wood White was described by Philogène Auguste Joseph Duponchel, a former Bonapartist military figure who was sidelined after the fall of the Empire. He also named the Pierid family.

IMAGOS		LARVAE	
Food	✿	Food	🌿
Behaviour of males		Caterpillar location	🌿
Dispersion		Chrysalis location	🌿

PIERIDAE

WOOD WHITE/CRYPTIC WOOD WHITE/RÉAL'S WOOD WHITE
LEPTIDEA SINAPIS/L. JUVERNICA/L. REALI

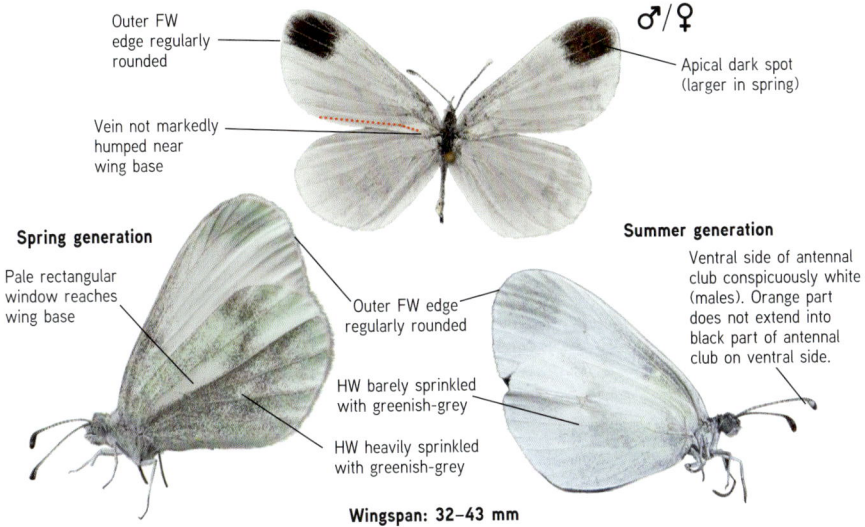

Outer FW edge regularly rounded

♂/♀

Apical dark spot (larger in spring)

Vein not markedly humped near wing base

Spring generation

Pale rectangular window reaches wing base

Outer FW edge regularly rounded

HW barely sprinkled with greenish-grey

HW heavily sprinkled with greenish-grey

Summer generation

Ventral side of antennal club conspicuously white (males). Orange part does not extend into black part of antennal club on ventral side.

Wingspan: 32–43 mm

Habitat: Meadows, bushy grasslands, forest edges and pathsides, grassy parks and gardens.

Hibernating stage: Pupa.

Elevational range: Up to 2,000 m for *Leptidea sinapis* and *L. reali*, 1,200 m for *L. juvernica*.

Egg-laying: Eggs are laid singly on LHP leaflets.

Flight period: From March to October for *Leptidea sinapis* and *L. reali*. Between April and June for *L. juvernica*.

Host plants: Mostly herbaceous legumes, including *Lotus corniculatus, L. pedunculatus, L. dorycnium, L. angustissimus, L. hirsutus, L. uliginosus, Vicia cracca, V. sepium, V. sativa, V. tenuifolia, Lathyrus pratensis,* *L. linifolius, L. aphaca, L. grandiflorus, L. laxiflorus, L. niger, L. sylvestris, L. tuberosus, L. vernus, Medicago falcata, Securigera varia, Hippocrepis emerus, Trifolium repens, T. pratensis,* and *T. dubium.*

Diversity and systematics: For *Leptidea sinapis*, most European populations belong to the nominate subspecies. Subspecies *diniensis* flies in the south of France, northern Spain, the north of Italy, and Corsica. Subspecies *colladoi* is found in the rest of Spain. For *L. reali*, there are no notable subspecies. European populations of *L. juvernica* belong to subspecies *melanogyna.*

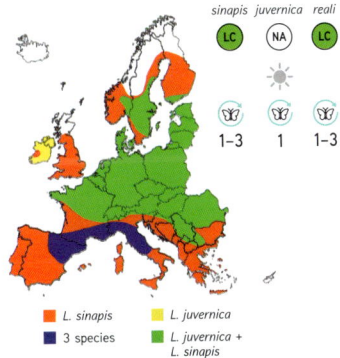

sinapis juvernica reali

LC | NA | LC

1–3 | 1 | 1–3

- L. sinapis
- 3 species
- L. juvernica
- L. juvernica + L. sinapis

Did you know?

The Cryptic Wood White was described only in 2011 and resulted from a genetic comparison (it does not have the same number of chromosomes as its two sister species). Slight statistical differences also exist at the genitalia level. Réal's Wood White differs from the other two in its genitalia.

	IMAGOS		LARVAE	
Food		Food		
Behaviour of males		Caterpillar location		
Dispersion		Chrysalis location		

PIERIDAE

FENTON'S WOOD WHITE *LEPTIDEA MORSEI*

♂ / ♀

FW slightly falcated on outer edge beneath wing tip

Apical dark spot

Spring generation

Pale rectangular window reaches wing base

FW slightly falcated on outer edge beneath wing tip

HW heavily sprinkled with greenish-grey

Summer generation

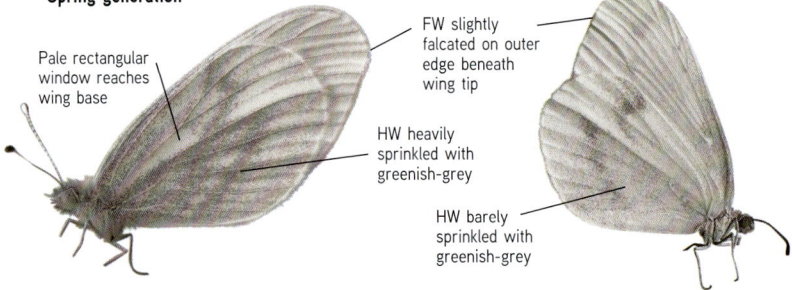

HW barely sprinkled with greenish-grey

Wingspan: 37–46 mm

Habitat: Deciduous woodland understorey, clearings, and edges (especially oak forests).

Hibernating stage: Pupa.

Elevational range: Up to 1,500 m.

Egg-laying: Eggs are laid singly on LHP leaflets.

Flight period: From April to August.

Host plants: Legumes of genus *Lathyrus*, especially *L. niger* and *L. vernus*.

Diversity and systematics: European populations belong to subspecies *major*.

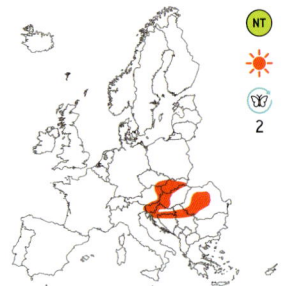

NT

2

Did you know?

Males of Fenton's Wood White sometimes exhibit a flight pattern that alternates between flapping and gliding phases, which isn't generally common among Pieridae.

IMAGOS		LARVAE	
Food		Food	
Behaviour of males		Caterpillar location	
Dispersion		Chrysalis location	

THE LYCAENIDS (125 SPECIES) AND RIODINIDS (1 SPECIES)

SUBFAMILIES	GENERA	NUMBER OF SPECIES	MAIN LARVAL HOST-PLANT FAMILIES
Theclinae	Callophrys, Deudorix, Favonius, Laeosopis, Satyrium, Thecla, and Tomares	15	Fabaceae, Fagaceae, Oleaceae, Ulmaceae, Rosaceae, Rhamnaceae, Ericaceae, Cistaceae, Arecaceae, Punicaceae, and Polygonaceae
Aphaeinae	Cigaritis	1	
Lycaeninae	Lycaena	12	Polygonaceae and Plumbaginaceae
Polyommatinae	Agriades, Aricia, Azanus, Cacyreus, Celastrina, Cyaniris, Cupido, Cyclyrius, Eumedonia, Freyeria, Glaucopsyche, Iolana, Kretania, Lampides, Leptotes, Luthrodes, Lysandra, Neolysandra, Phengaris, Plebejus, Plebejidea, Polyommatus, Pseudophilotes, Scolitantides, Tarucus, Turanana, and Zizeeria	97	Fabaceae, Geraniaceae, Cistaceae, Lamiaceae, Ericaceae, Plumbaginaceae, Primulaceae, Rosaceae, Crassulaceae, Gentianaceae, Lythraceae, Saxifragaceae, Amaranthaceae, and Euphorbiaceae

FAMILY	GENUS	NUMBER OF SPECIES	MAIN LARVAL HOST-PLANT FAMILY
Riodinidae	Hamearis	1	Primulaceae

The Lycaenids comprise approximately 5,200 members worldwide. These small butterflies often have black eyes circled in white and finely black- and white-ringed antennae. Hairstreaks (Theclines) are generally associated with bushy and forested environments, while other subfamilies are more commonly found in meadows and grasslands. Identifying them is usually easier from the underside. Many species display symbiotic relationships with ants during their larval development; the nature of these interactions ranges from mutualism to parasitism. The rather flat-shaped and cryptic caterpillars often possess organs that secrete solutions containing sugars and amino acids, which attract the ants. The latter, in turn, provide protection to these caterpillars against predators.

Lycaena hippothoe

Aricia agestis

Callophrys rubi

Lysandra bellargus

Satyrium pruni

Polyommatus daphnis

Hamearis lucina

LYCAENIDAE

PURPLE-EDGED COPPER *LYCAENA HIPPOTHOE*

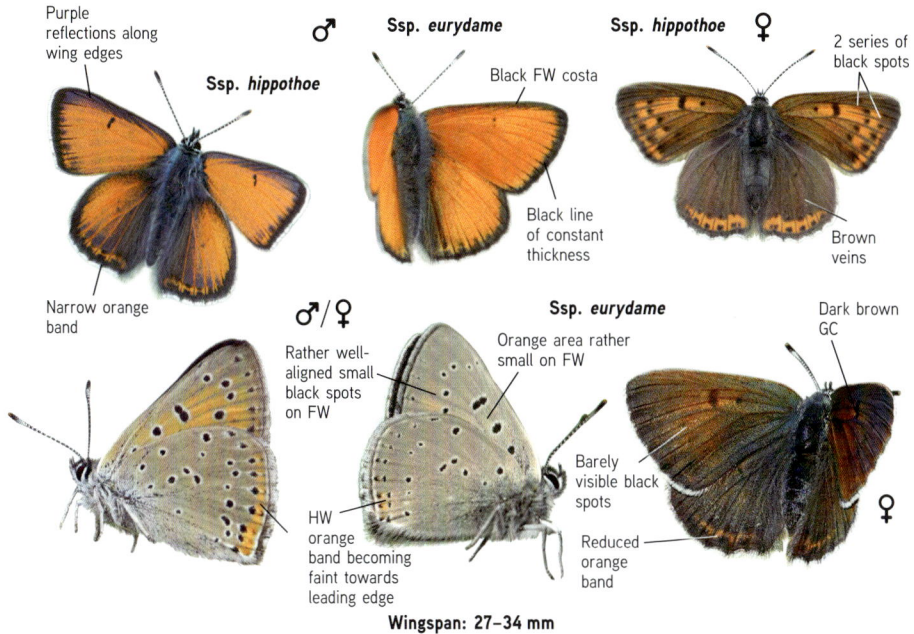

Purple reflections along wing edges

Ssp. *hippothoe*

♂ Ssp. *eurydame*

Black FW costa

Ssp. *hippothoe* ♀

2 series of black spots

Black line of constant thickness

Brown veins

Narrow orange band

♂/♀

Rather well-aligned small black spots on FW

Ssp. *eurydame*

Orange area rather small on FW

Dark brown GC

Barely visible black spots

HW orange band becoming faint towards leading edge

Reduced orange band

♀

Wingspan: 27–34 mm

Habitat: Damp or mesophilic flower-rich meadows and bogs.

Hibernating stage: Egg in Scandinavia, caterpillar elsewhere.

Elevational range: Up to 2,500 m.

Egg-laying: Eggs are laid singly on LHP stems and leaves.

Flight period: From June to August.

Host plants: Polygonaceae, including *Rumex acetosa*, *R. acetosella*, *R. confertus*, *R. crispus*, *R. hydrolapathum*, *R. lapponicus*, *R. obtusifolius*, *R. scutatus*, and *R. thysifolius*. Also on *Bistorta officinalis*.

Diversity and systematics: Most European populations belong to the nominate subspecies. Subspecies *stiberi* flies in Lapland, while subspecies *eurydame* is found at high altitudes in the Alps. Subspecies *mirus* is described from the Pyrenees, and subspecies *italica* inhabits the Apennines. Subspecies *valderiana* flies in the Maritime Alps (France).

■ L. hippothoe
■ L. candens

LC

1

Did you know?

Experiments have shown that a growing fraction of high-altitude subspecies *eurydame* caterpillars enter a second winter diapause if the temperature is low at the end of their first winter. This can be considered a physiological "gamble" on better climatic conditions the following year.

IMAGOS		LARVAE	
Food	✿	Food	✿ 🍃
Behaviour of males		Caterpillar location	🌿
Dispersion		Chrysalis location	🌿

BALKAN COPPER *LYCAENA CANDENS*

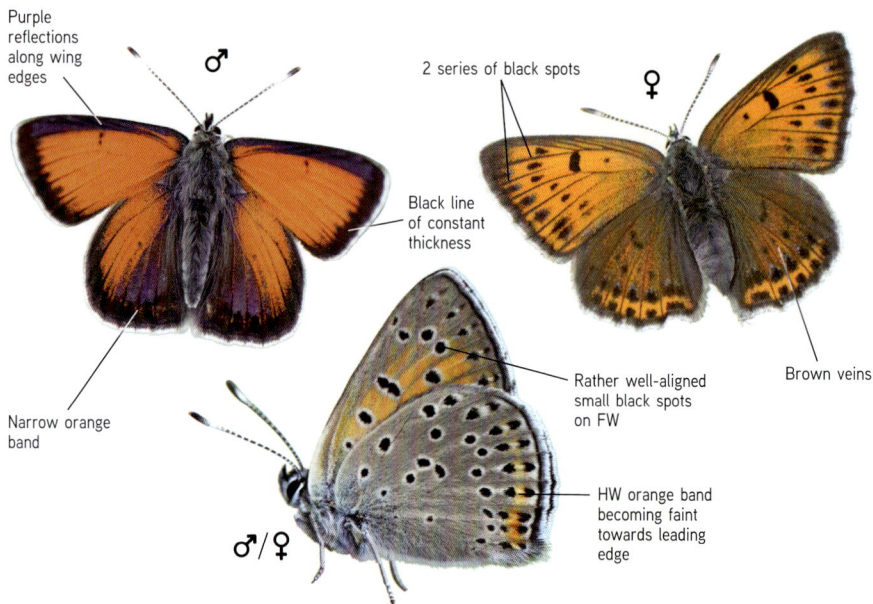

Purple reflections along wing edges

♂

2 series of black spots

♀

Black line of constant thickness

Narrow orange band

Rather well-aligned small black spots on FW

Brown veins

♂/♀

HW orange band becoming faint towards leading edge

Wingspan: 34–35 mm

Habitat: Damp and mesophilic montane and subalpine meadows, flower-rich woodland clearings.

Hibernating stage: Caterpillar.

Elevational range: Between 800 and 2,400 m.

Egg-laying: Eggs are laid singly on LHP flower stalks and leaves.

Flight period: From June to September.

Host plants: Polygonaceae in genus *Rumex*, including *R. acetosa* and *R. arifolius*.

Diversity and systematics: European populations belong to subspecies *leonhardi*.

■ *L. hippothoe*
■ *L. candens*

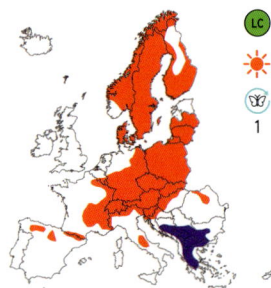

LC

1

Did you know?

The Balkan Copper was long considered a subspecies of the Purple-edged Copper. They are actually allopatric species with similar ecology; their divergence likely dates back to a recent glaciation.

IMAGOS	LARVAE
Food	Food
Behaviour of males	Caterpillar location
Dispersion: unknown	Chrysalis location

SCARCE COPPER   *LYCAENA VIRGAUREAE*

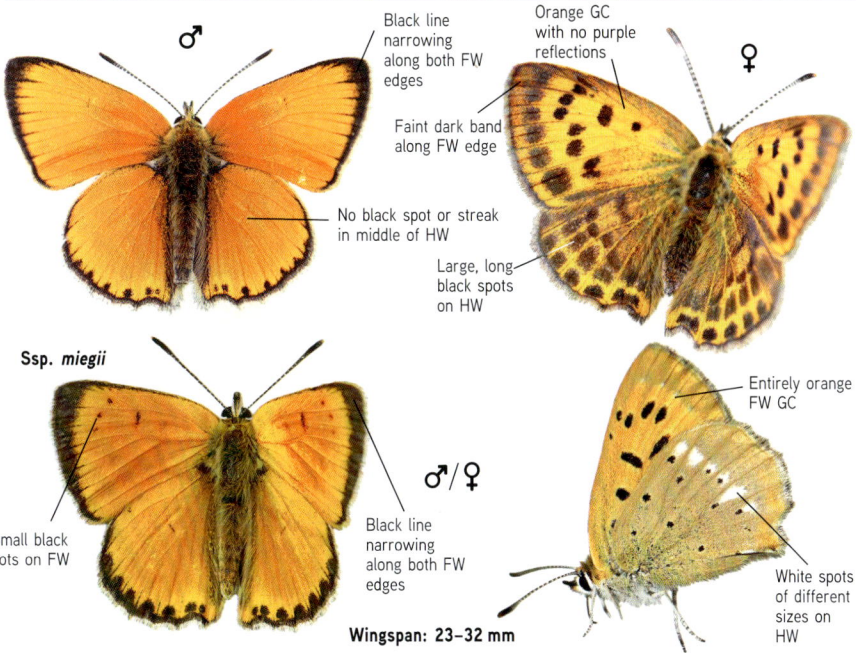

♂

Black line narrowing along both FW edges

Orange GC with no purple reflections

♀

Faint dark band along FW edge

No black spot or streak in middle of HW

Large, long black spots on HW

Ssp. *miegii*

Entirely orange FW GC

♂/♀

Small black dots on FW

Black line narrowing along both FW edges

White spots of different sizes on HW

Wingspan: 23–32 mm

Habitat: Flower-rich meadows often near forested areas, woodland clearings.

Hibernating stage: Caterpillar inside the egg.

Elevational range: Up to 2,500 m.

Egg-laying: Eggs are laid singly on dry LHP parts or leaves.

Flight period: From May to September.

Host plants: Polygonaceae in genus *Rumex*, including *R. acetosa, R. acetosella, R. crispus, R. obtusifolius, R. scutatus,* and *R. thyrsiflorus.*

Diversity and systematics: Most European populations belong to the nominate subspecies. The subspecies *miegii, montana, zermattensis,* and *pyrenaicola* fly in the centre of Spain, the Alps, the Valais in Switzerland, and the Eastern Pyrenees, respectively.

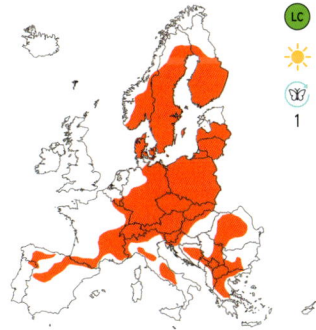

LC

1

Did you know?

Adults frequently forage on Goldenrod (*Solidago virgaurea*), which gives its French vernacular name to the species (*Le Cuivré de la Verge d'Or*, Goldenrod Copper). However, it does not constitute a larval foodplant for this copper, which is also very keen on Yarrow nectar.

IMAGOS		LARVAE	
Food	✿	Food	🍃
Behaviour of males		Caterpillar location	
Dispersion		Chrysalis location	

LYCAENIDAE

GRECIAN COPPER *LYCAENA OTTOMANA*

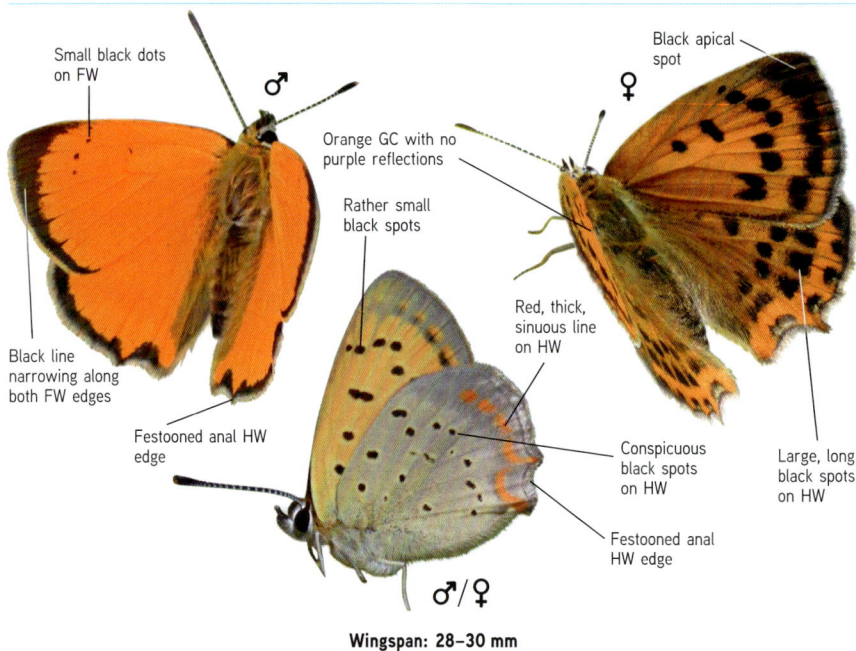

Small black dots
on FW

♂

Black apical
spot

♀

Orange GC with no
purple reflections

Rather small
black spots

Black line
narrowing along
both FW edges

Red, thick,
sinuous line
on HW

Festooned anal HW
edge

Conspicuous
black spots
on HW

Large, long
black spots
on HW

♂/♀

Festooned anal
HW edge

Wingspan: 28–30 mm

Habitat: Sunny and flower-rich, rather damp meadows, often within forested areas, coastal wetlands, grassy rocky areas.

Hibernating stage: Caterpillar.

Elevational range: Up to 1,500 m (mostly at lower elevations).

Egg-laying: Eggs are laid singly.

Flight period: From April to August.

Host plants: Polygonaceae in genus *Rumex*, including *R. acetosa* and *R. acetosella*.

Diversity and systematics: There are no notable subspecies for this copper, whose range is restricted to the Balkans and western Turkey.

LC

2

Did you know?

Disturbed Grecian Coppers do not fly very far with a determined flight, like other coppers. If an intruder persists, they display the bright colour of their wings before dropping motionless into vegetation and remaining there for a few minutes.

IMAGOS	LARVAE
Food	Food
Behaviour of males	Caterpillar location
Dispersion	Chrysalis location

LARGE COPPER *LYCAENA DISPAR*

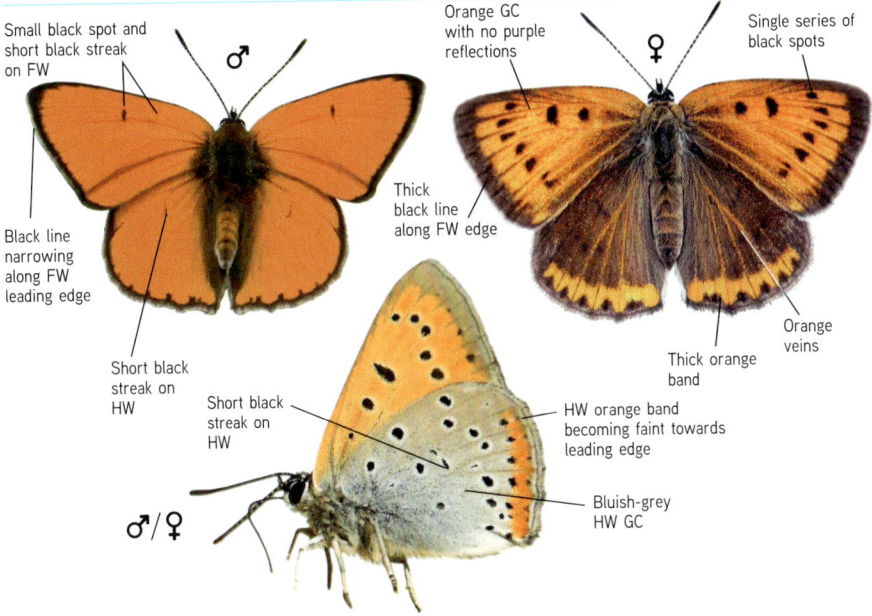

Small black spot and short black streak on FW

♂

Orange GC with no purple reflections

♀

Single series of black spots

Thick black line along FW edge

Black line narrowing along FW leading edge

Orange veins

Short black streak on HW

Thick orange band

Short black streak on HW

HW orange band becoming faint towards leading edge

♂/♀

Bluish-grey HW GC

Wingspan: 33–41 mm

Habitat: Damp meadows and ditches, bog marshes, and riparian areas.

Hibernating stage: Caterpillar.

Elevational range: Up to 1,000 m.

Egg-laying: Eggs are laid in small batches of a few units on LHP leaves.

Flight period: From May to September.

Host plants: Polygonaceae in genus *Rumex*, including *R. crispus*, *R. conglomeratus*, *R. acetosa*, *R. acetosella*, *R. obtusifolius*, *R. hydrolapathum*, *R. patientia*, *R. sanguineus*, *R. stenophyllus*, and *R. aquaticus*. Laying has also been recorded on *Iris pseudacorus* (Iridaceae).

Diversity and systematics: European populations belong to subspecies *rutilus*. Subspecies *batava* flies in Holland.

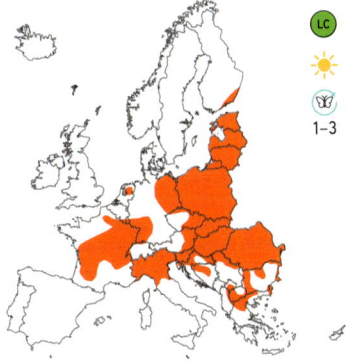

LC

1–3

Did you know?

The nominate subspecies of the Large Copper flew in England before it went extinct in the 19th century. Several reintroduction attempts, all unsuccessful, followed in the 20th century.

IMAGOS		LARVAE	
Food		Food	
Behaviour of males		Caterpillar location	
Dispersion		Chrysalis location	

LESSER FIERY COPPER *LYCAENA THERSAMON*

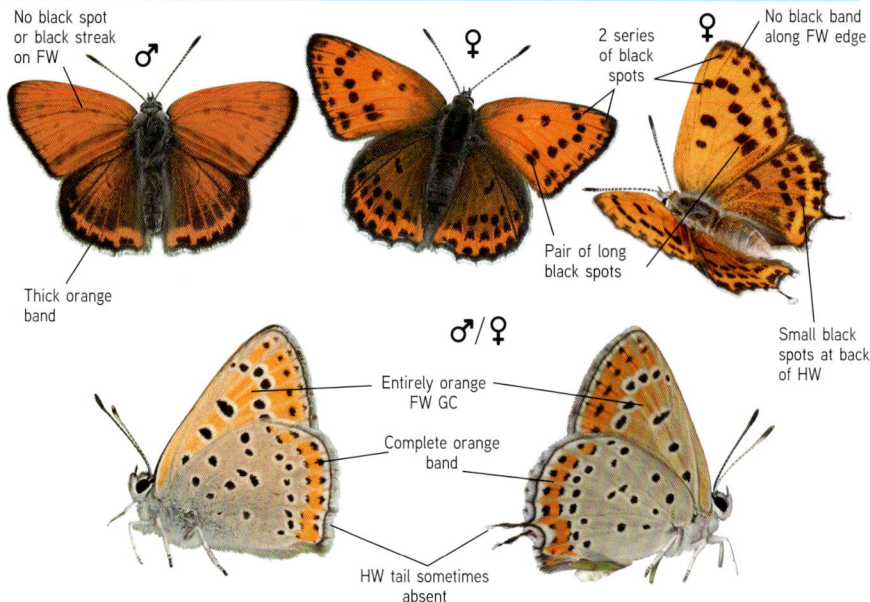

No black spot or black streak on FW ♂

♀

2 series of black spots

♀

No black band along FW edge

Pair of long black spots

Thick orange band

Small black spots at back of HW

♂/♀

Entirely orange FW GC

Complete orange band

HW tail sometimes absent

Wingspan: 28–32 mm

Habitat: Extensively grazed meadows, crop surroundings, bushy rocky grasslands, and fallow land.

Hibernating stage: Caterpillar or pupa.

Elevational range: Up to 1,500 m.

Egg-laying: Eggs are laid singly on LHP leaves, stems, and inflorescences.

Flight period: April to October.

Host plants: Polygonaceae, including *Polygonum aviculare*, *P. equisetiforme*, and *Bistorta officinalis*.

Diversity and systematics: European populations belong to the nominate subspecies.

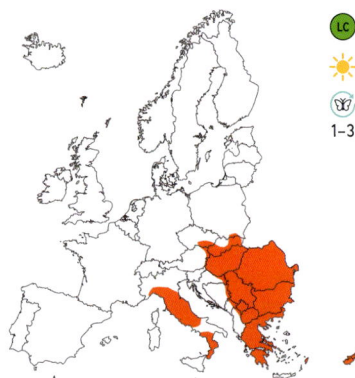

LC

1–3

IMAGOS		LARVAE	
Food	✿	Food	✿ 🌿
Behaviour of males		Caterpillar location	🌱
Dispersion		Chrysalis location	

Did you know?

Adults particularly enjoy the nectar of mint flowers. They also forage extensively on Asteraceae.

238

LYCAENIDAE

FIERY COPPER *LYCAENA THETIS*

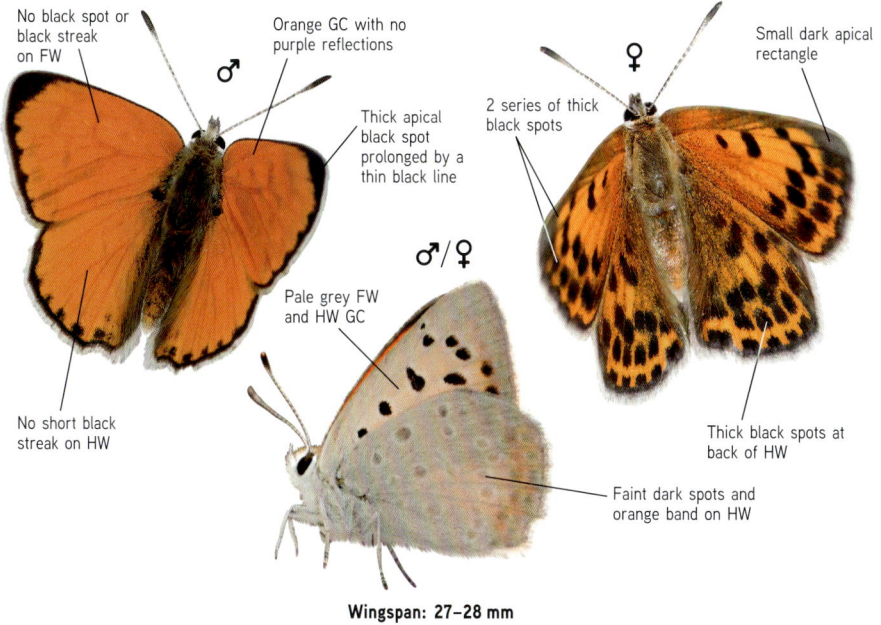

No black spot or
black streak
on FW

♂

Orange GC with no
purple reflections

♀

Small dark apical
rectangle

Thick apical
black spot
prolonged by a
thin black line

2 series of thick
black spots

♂/♀

Pale grey FW
and HW GC

No short black
streak on HW

Thick black spots at
back of HW

Faint dark spots and
orange band on HW

Wingspan: 27–28 mm

Habitat: Rocky subalpine slopes with low-growing and sparse vegetation.

Hibernating stage: Caterpillar.

Elevational range: Between 1,500 and 2,500 m.

Egg-laying: Eggs are ejected in the LHP cushion.

Flight period: July and August.

Host plants: *Acantholimon androsaceum* (Plumbaginaceae).

Diversity and systematics: European populations belong to the nominate subspecies.

NA

1

IMAGOS		LARVAE	
Food		Food	
Behaviour of males		Caterpillar location	
Dispersion		Chrysalis location	

Did you know?

The Fiery Copper is the only European copper whose caterpillars do not feed on plants in the Polygonaceae family.

239

LYCAENIDAE

PURPLE-SHOT COPPER *LYCAENA ALCIPHRON*

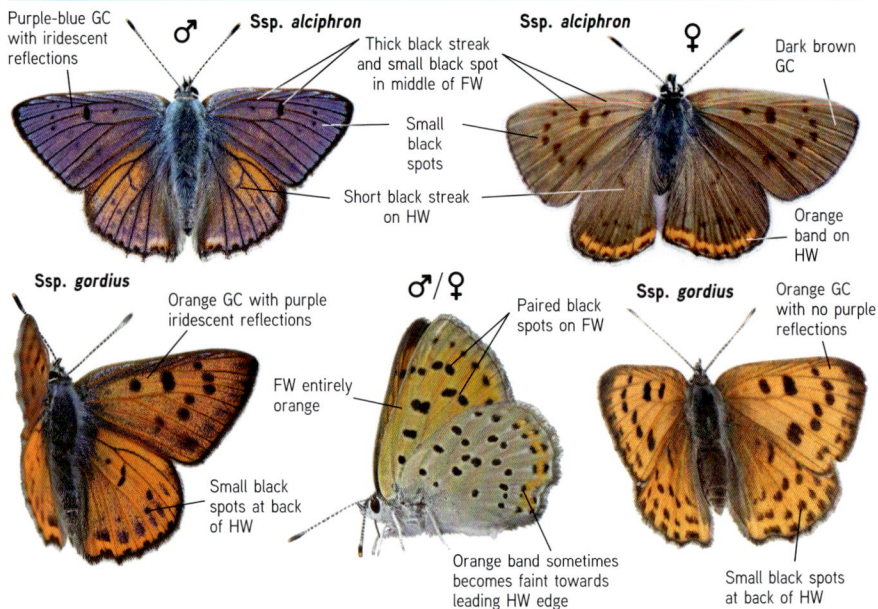

Purple-blue GC with iridescent reflections

♂

Ssp. *alciphron*

Thick black streak and small black spot in middle of FW

Ssp. *alciphron*

♀

Dark brown GC

Small black spots

Short black streak on HW

Orange band on HW

Ssp. *gordius*

Orange GC with purple iridescent reflections

♂/♀

Paired black spots on FW

Ssp. *gordius*

Orange GC with no purple reflections

FW entirely orange

Small black spots at back of HW

Orange band sometimes becomes faint towards leading HW edge

Small black spots at back of HW

Wingspan: 32–36 mm

Habitat: Dry or steppic grasslands, garrigue, bushy heaths, and scree. The nominate subspecies also flies in mesophilic meadows and flower-rich forest edges.

Hibernating stage: Young caterpillar inside the egg or just after hatching.

Elevational range: Up to 2,500 m.

Egg-laying: Eggs are laid singly or in small batches of a few units on LHP leaves and stems.

Flight period: From May to August.

Host plants: Polygonaceae in genus *Rumex*, especially

R. acetosella, R. scutatus, R. acetosa, R. pulcher, R. intermedius, and *R. thyrsiflorus.*

Diversity and systematics: More than a dozen subspecies are described for Europe. The most notable ones include the nominate subspecies, which flies in the northern half of the range, and subspecies *gordius*, which forms populations in the Iberian Peninsula, Italy, and southern France, including the Alps. Subspecies *melibaeus* populates the Balkans, and *granadensis* can be found in Andalusia.

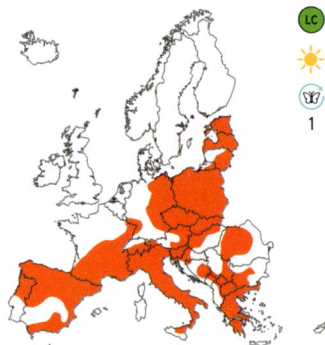

LC

1

IMAGOS		LARVAE	
Food		Food	
Behaviour of males		Caterpillar location	
Dispersion		Chrysalis location	

Did you know?

Adults are particularly attracted to thyme inflorescences. The loss of habitats due to pastoral abandonment is threatening the Purple-shot Copper.

LYCAENIDAE

VIOLET COPPER *LYCAENA HELLE*

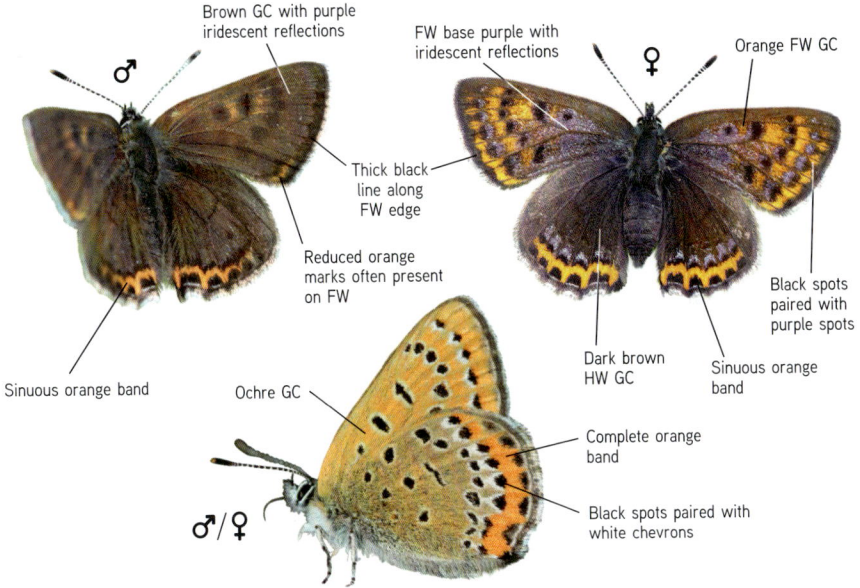

♂

Brown GC with purple iridescent reflections

FW base purple with iridescent reflections

♀

Orange FW GC

Thick black line along FW edge

Black spots paired with purple spots

Reduced orange marks often present on FW

Dark brown HW GC

Sinuous orange band

Sinuous orange band

Ochre GC

Complete orange band

♂/♀

Black spots paired with white chevrons

Wingspan: 21–27 mm

Habitat: Sheltered damp meadows where Bistort is abundant.

Hibernating stage: Pupa.

Elevational range: From 200 to 1,800 m (mainly below 1,500 m).

Egg-laying: Eggs are laid singly on LHP leaves.

Flight period: From May to August.

Host plants: Polygonaceae – above all, *Bistorta officinalis* and sometimes *B. vivipara*.

Diversity and systematics: The numerous described subspecies reflect the disjunct range due to the fragmentation of suitable habitats. Nevertheless, the subspecies are often not very distinct morphologically.

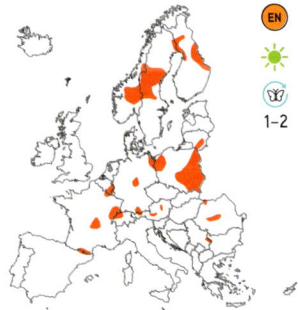

EN

1–2

Did you know?

In Poland, where the species is bivoltine, the second generation is much more abundant than the first. Males, in search of females, disperse more in spring. Females, undergoing competition for host plants, disperse more during summer.

IMAGOS		LARVAE	
Food		Food	
Behaviour of males		Caterpillar location	
Dispersion		Chrysalis location	

241

LYCAENIDAE

SMALL COPPER LYCAENA PHLAEAS

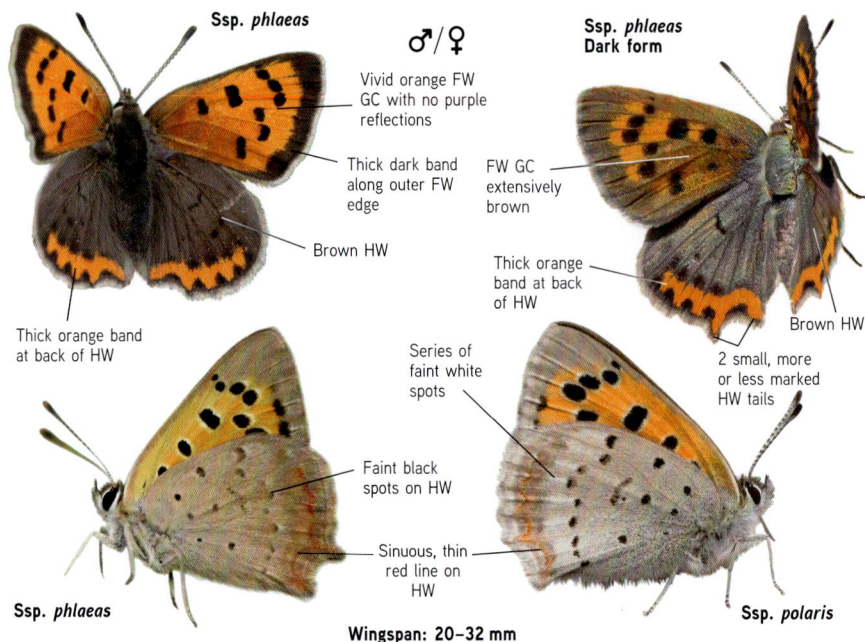

Ssp. *phlaeas*

♂/♀

Vivid orange FW GC with no purple reflections

Thick dark band along outer FW edge

Brown HW

Thick orange band at back of HW

Ssp. *phlaeas* Dark form

FW GC extensively brown

Thick orange band at back of HW

Brown HW

2 small, more or less marked HW tails

Series of faint white spots

Faint black spots on HW

Sinuous, thin red line on HW

Ssp. *phlaeas*

Ssp. *polaris*

Wingspan: 20–32 mm

Habitat: Wastelands, field edges, roadside areas, parks, gardens, forest edges, and clearings.

Hibernating stage: Caterpillar.

Elevational range: Up to 2,500 m (although it is more abundant at low elevations).

Egg-laying: Eggs are laid singly on LHP leaves.

Flight period: From February to November.

Host plants: Polygonaceae in genus *Rumex*, especially *R. acetosa*, *R. acetosella*, *R. bucephalophorus*, *R. conglomeratus*, *R. crispus*, *R. cristatus*, *R. cyprius*, *R. hydrolapathum*, *R. intermedius*, *R. obtusifolius*, *R. pulcher*, *R. sanguineus*, *R. scutatus*, and *R. thyrsiflorus*. *R. vesicarius* on the Canary Islands and *R. maderensis* on Madeira.

Diversity and systematics: Most European populations belong to the nominate subspecies. Subspecies *polaris* is found in northern Scandinavia. Subspecies *lusitanicus* and *phlaeoides* are described from continental Portugal and Madeira, respectively. Irish populations belong to subspecies *hibernica*. Additionally, numerous forms have been described.

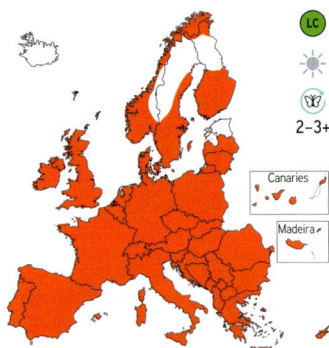

LC

2–3+

Canaries

Madeira

Did you know?

Females lay on LHPs located in microhabitats favourable to larval development. Thus, sorrels located near molehills are preferred sites.

IMAGOS		LARVAE	
Food		Food	
Behaviour of males		Caterpillar location	
Dispersion		Chrysalis location	

LYCAENIDAE

SOOTY COPPER *LYCAENA TITYRUS*

Ssp. *tityrus* ♂ **Ssp. *subalpinus*** **3 series of black spots on FW** ♀

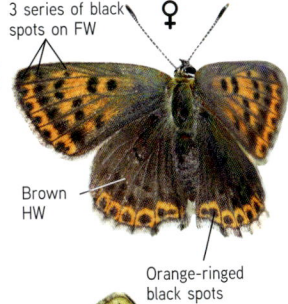

Sooty grey GC

Small orange spots on both wings

Black spots on both wings

Orange spots reduced or absent

Brown HW

Orange-ringed black spots

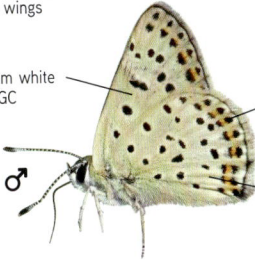
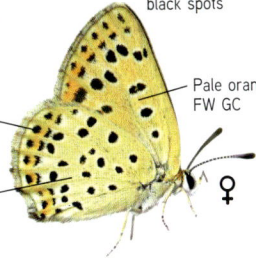

Cream white FW GC

♂

Complete series of orange spots

Cream white HW GC

Pale orange FW GC

♀

Wingspan: 28–32 mm

Habitat: Mesophilic and damp meadows, sometimes also in forest clearings and edges.

Hibernating stage: Caterpillar.

Elevational range: Up to 2,500 m.

Egg-laying: Eggs are laid singly or by two or three on LHP leaves.

Flight period: From April to October.

Host plants: Polygonaceae in genus *Rumex*, mainly *R. acetosa*, *R. acetosella*, *R. crispus*, *R. hydrolapathum*, *R. scutatus*, *R. thyrsiflorus*, and *R. tuberosus*.

Diversity and systematics: Most European populations belong to the nominate subspecies. Subspecies *subalpinus* flies at high elevations in the Alps. Subspecies *catherinei* is found in the Pyrenees. Subspecies *pallidepicta* has been described from the south of France. Numerous forms are also described.

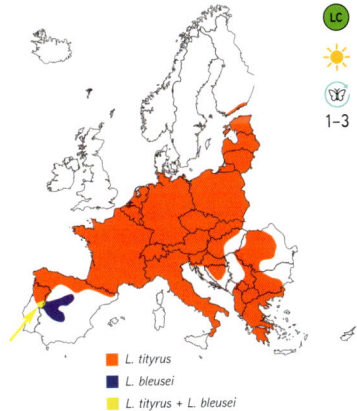

LC
1–3

■ L. tityrus
■ L. bleusei
■ L. tityrus + L. bleusei

IMAGOS		LARVAE	
Food	☆	Food	🍃
Behaviour of males		Caterpillar location	
Dispersion		Chrysalis location	

Did you know?

Males emerge before females, a result of natural selection in the context of intrasexual competition, in which the first adults to emerge claim the best territories.

LYCAENIDAE

IBERIAN SOOTY COPPER *LYCAENA BLEUSEI*

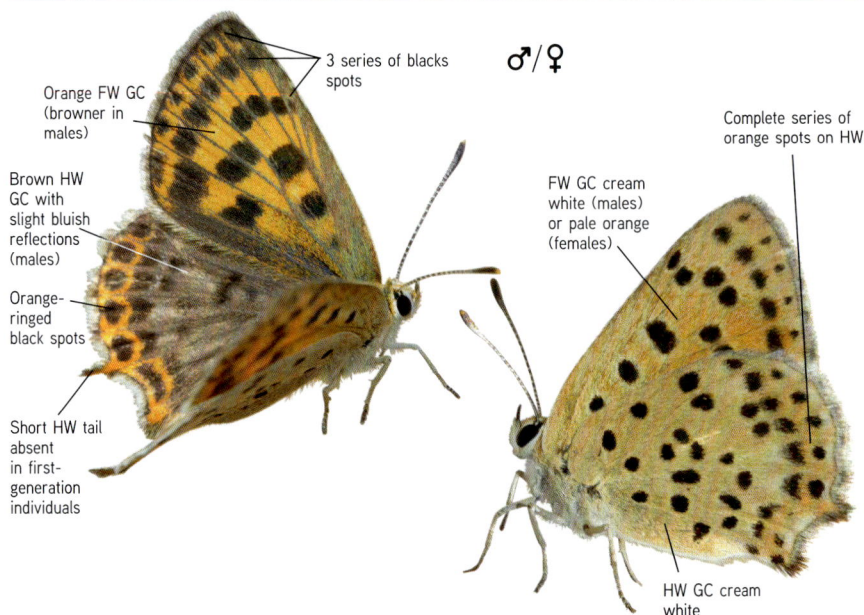

♂/♀

3 series of blacks spots

Orange FW GC (browner in males)

Brown HW GC with slight bluish reflections (males)

Orange-ringed black spots

Short HW tail absent in first-generation individuals

FW GC cream white (males) or pale orange (females)

Complete series of orange spots on HW

HW GC cream white

Wingspan: 28–32 mm

Habitat: Dry meadows, grassy pathsides, and Mediterranean clearings.

Hibernating stage: Egg.

Elevational range: Between 700 and 1,100 m.

Egg-laying: Eggs are laid singly on LHP leaves.

Flight period: From March to November.

Host plants: Polygonaceae in genus *Rumex*, including *R. acetosa*, *R. acetosella*, and *R. papillaris*.

Diversity and systematics: *Lycaena bleusei* was long considered a subspecies of *L. tityrus*. There is no notable subspecies for this copper, which is endemic to the central Iberian Peninsula.

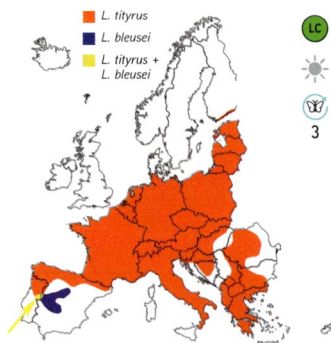

- ■ L. tityrus
- ■ L. bleusei
- ■ L. tityrus + L. bleusei

LC
3

Did you know?

In the few Spanish locations where the Iberian Sooty Copper coexists with the Sooty Copper, the former is restricted to drier habitats, while the latter is more commonly found in damper and flower-rich areas.

IMAGOS			LARVAE	
Food			Food	
Behaviour of males			Caterpillar location	
Dispersion: unknown			Chrysalis location	

LYCAENIDAE

PROVENCE HAIRSTREAK *TOMARES BALLUS*

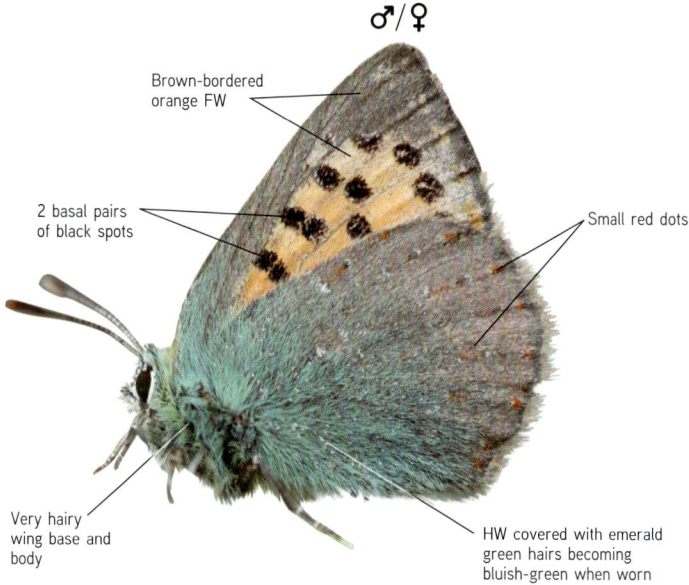

♂/♀

Brown-bordered orange FW

2 basal pairs of black spots

Small red dots

Very hairy wing base and body

HW covered with emerald green hairs becoming bluish-green when worn

Wingspan: 28–30 mm

Habitat: Recently abandoned agricultural terraces, olive groves, stony garrigue, and maquis.

Hibernating stage: Pupa.

Elevational range: Up to 1,400 m.

Egg-laying: Eggs are laid singly on LHP leaflets.

Flight period: From January to May.

Host plants: Small, mostly herbaceous legumes, such as *Astragalus glaux*, *Anthyllis vulneraria*, *A. cytisoides*, *Biserrula pelecinus*, *Erophaca baetica*, *Genista hispanica*, *Hippocrepis unisiliquosa*, *Tripodion tetraphyllum*, *Lotus dorycnium*, *L. hirsutus*, *L. ornithopodioides*, *Medicago littoralis*, *M. lupulina*, *M. minima*, *M. polymorpha*, *M. rigidula*, *M. truncatula*, *Ornithopus compressus*, and *Trifolium cherleri*.

Diversity and systematics: European populations of this species, which is also present in North Africa, belong to subspecies *catalonica*.

LC

1

IMAGOS		LARVAE	
Food	☆	Food	☆ 🌿
Behaviour of males		Caterpillar location	🌱 🐜
Dispersion		Chrysalis location	🐛 🐜

Did you know?

The Provence Hairstreak is locally threatened by the loss of its favourable open habitats due to agricultural abandonment and the decline of extensive ovine grazing.

LYCAENIDAE

NOGEL'S HAIRSTREAK *TOMARES NOGELII*

♂/♀

Single series of black-bordered orange spots on FW

Extensive orange area on FW

3 series of black-bordered orange spots on HW

Wingspan: 30–35 mm

Habitat: Steppe-forest glades, grasslands in the vicinity of forest edges where the LHP grows.

Hibernating stage: Pupa.

Elevational range: Up to 500 m in Europe.

Egg-laying: Eggs are laid singly on LHP flower buds.

Flight period: From April to July.

Host plants: *Astragalus ponticus* (Fabaceae).

Diversity and systematics: The very few European populations belong to subspecies *dobrogensis*.

VU

1

IMAGOS		LARVAE	
Food	☆	Food	☆ 🌿
Behaviour of males	🌼 🌼	Caterpillar location	🌿 🐜
Dispersion	🦋	Chrysalis location	🪵

Did you know?

Nogel's Hairstreak came close to disappearing from Europe due to the loss of its habitat. It also suffered heavily from collectors; it is one of the rarest species in the area covered by this guide.

LYCAENIDAE

GREEN HAIRSTREAK *CALLOPHRYS RUBI*

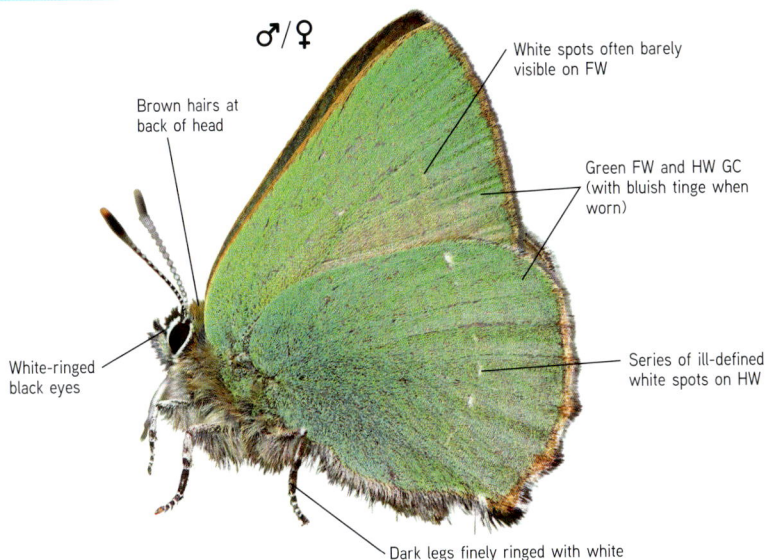

♂/♀

White spots often barely visible on FW

Brown hairs at back of head

Green FW and HW GC (with bluish tinge when worn)

White-ringed black eyes

Series of ill-defined white spots on HW

Dark legs finely ringed with white

Wingspan: 20–26 mm

Habitat: Bushy grasslands and forest edges, hedgerows, heaths, garrigue, and maquis. Also subalpine meadows.

Hibernating stage: Pupa.

Elevational range: Up to 2,500 m.

Egg-laying: Eggs are laid singly on LHP inflorescences.

Flight period: From February to July.

Host plants: More than 50 species in 11 plant families! Legumes of genera *Genista, Cytisus, Onobrychis, Chamaecytisus, Hedysarum, Ulex, Spartium, Calicotome, Dorycnium,* and *Anthyllis.* Ericaeae, including *Calluna vulgaris, Erica* spp., *Vaccinium* spp., *Empetrum nigrum,* and *Arbutus unedo.* Cistaceae, like *Helianthemum* spp. and *Cistus* spp. Rosaceae in genera *Rubus* and *Crataegus.* Rhamnaceae, including *Rhamnus cathartica* and *Frangula alnus.* Lamiaceae, like *Teucrium chamaedrys.*

Diversity and systematics: Most European populations belong to the nominate subspecies. Subspecies *fervinda* flies in the Iberian Peninsula.

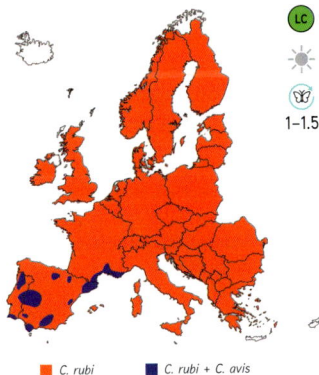

LC

1–1.5

■ *C. rubi*   ■ *C. rubi + C. avis*

IMAGOS	LARVAE
Food	Food
Behaviour of males	Caterpillar location
Dispersion	Chrysalis location

Did you know?

Males often have adjacent territories along hedges. As soon as one of them starts to fly, it is immediately pursued by its neighbours. These contests can last for several hours.

LYCAENIDAE

CHAPMAN'S GREEN HAIRSTREAK *CALLOPHRYS AVIS*

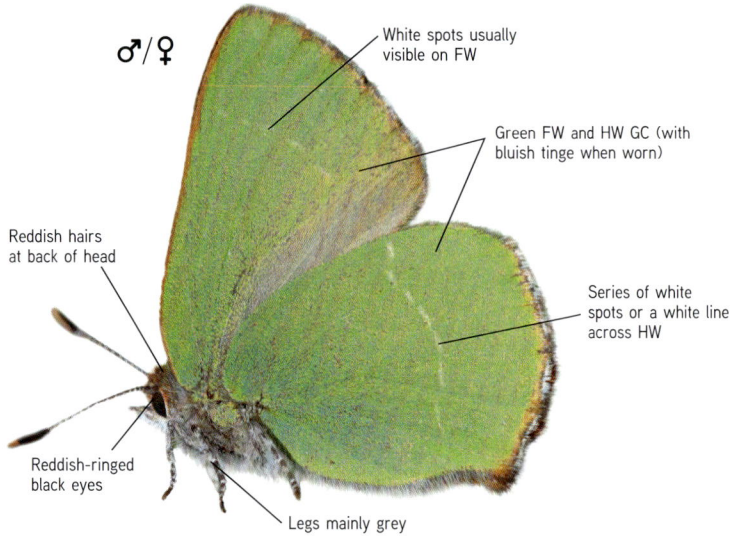

♂/♀

White spots usually visible on FW

Green FW and HW GC (with bluish tinge when worn)

Reddish hairs at back of head

Series of white spots or a white line across HW

Reddish-ringed black eyes

Legs mainly grey

Wingspan: 34–37 mm

Habitat: Maquis and high-growing garrigue.

Hibernating stage: Pupa.

Elevational range: Up to 1,000 m.

Egg-laying: Eggs are laid singly on LHP leaves and buds.

Flight period: From March to May.

Host plants: Mainly *Arbutus unedo* (Ericaeae) and sometimes *Coriaria myrtifolia* (Coriariaceae). Also cited on *Viburnum tinus* (Caprifoliaceae), *Calluna vulgaris* and *Erica arborea* (Ericaeae), and *Salvia verbenaca* (Lamiaceae), but these are used only exceptionally.

Diversity and systematics: European populations belong to the nominate subspecies.

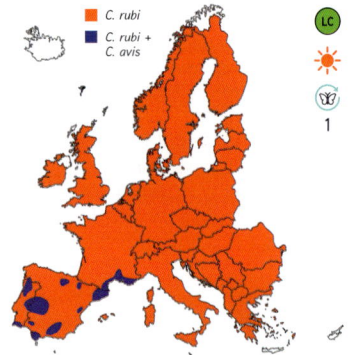

■ C. rubi
■ C. rubi + C. avis

LC

1

Did you know?

Territorial males occasionally take a short break from surveillance to feed on the flowers of the scrubland, particularly on Spanish Lavender and Rosemary. They then reposition themselves on a leaf of a Strawberry Tree (*Arbutus unedo*).

IMAGOS		LARVAE	
Food		Food	
Behaviour of males		Caterpillar location	
Dispersion		Chrysalis location	

LYCAENIDAE

LEVANTINE LEOPARD *CIGARITIS ACAMAS*

♂/♀

Brown stripes
containing silvery
streaks

1 short and 1 long
tail at back of HW

Grey eyes with
dark spots

White-and-brown-
striped abdomen

Wingspan: 24–33 mm

Habitat: Garrigue.

Hibernating stage: Caterpillar or pupa.

Elevational range: Up to 500 m.

Egg-laying: Eggs are laid singly in LHP bark crevices.

Flight period: From February to December.

Host plants: Females lay their eggs on trunks and branches of shrubs and palm trees. After hatching, the larvae are almost immediately found by ants of the *Crematogaster* genus and spend their entire development within the ant nest.

Diversity and systematics: Within the area covered by this guide, present only in Cyprus. These populations belong to subspecies *cypriaca*.

NA

1–3

IMAGOS	LARVAE
Food ☆	Food: Ant brood. Also fed by ant workers via trophallaxis.
Behaviour of males 🦋 🐜	
Dispersion: unknown	
	Caterpillar location 🐛 🐜
	Chrysalis location 🪱 🐜

Did you know?

The abdomen of the Levantine Leopard is particularly large in both females and males, reflecting the rich diet provided by their ant partners. These fat stores allow adults to cope with the shortage of nectar that occurs during certain very dry periods.

POMEGRANATE PLAYBOY *DEUDORIX LIVIA*

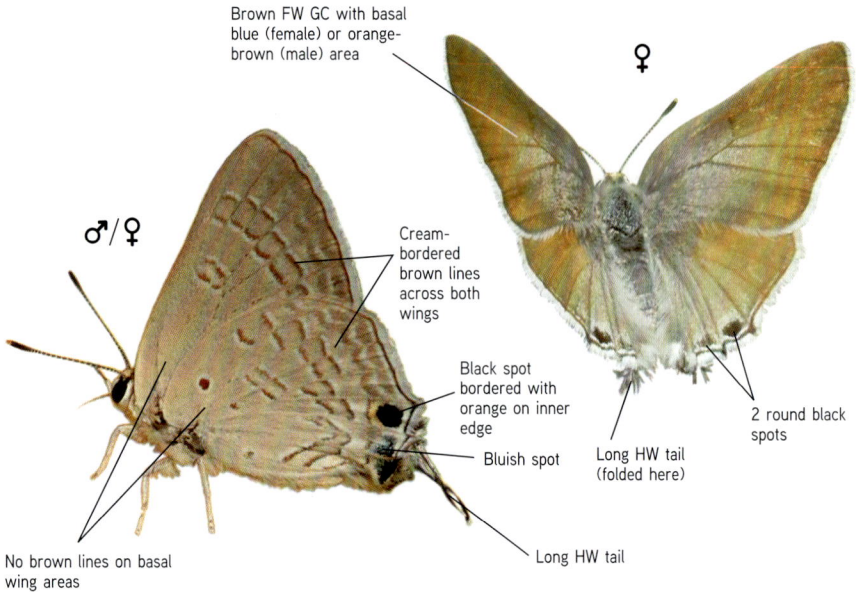

Brown FW GC with basal blue (female) or orange-brown (male) area

♀

♂/♀

Cream-bordered brown lines across both wings

Black spot bordered with orange on inner edge

Bluish spot

Long HW tail (folded here)

2 round black spots

No brown lines on basal wing areas

Long HW tail

Wingspan: 29–38 mm

Habitat: In its native range, it inhabits oases, wadis, and cultivated environments.

Hibernating stage: Caterpillar, without entering diapause.

Elevational range: Up to 500 m.

Egg-laying: Eggs are laid singly on LHP pods.

Flight period: From March to December.

Host plants: Above all, *Acacia farnesiana* (Fabaceae), *Phoenix dactylifera* (Arecaceae), and *Punica granatum* (Punicaceae).

Diversity and systematics: The few strays observed in Europe likely belong to the nominate subspecies.

(NA)

3

IMAGOS		LARVAE	
Food		Food	
Behaviour of males		Caterpillar location	
Dispersion		Chrysalis location	

Did you know?

To date, there have been only two records of this African species in Europe: one in Cyprus (a female) and the other in Greece, where the Pomegranate Playboy attempted to breed. However, the caterpillars could not withstand the winter cold.

LYCAENIDAE

BROWN HAIRSTREAK *THECLA BETULAE*

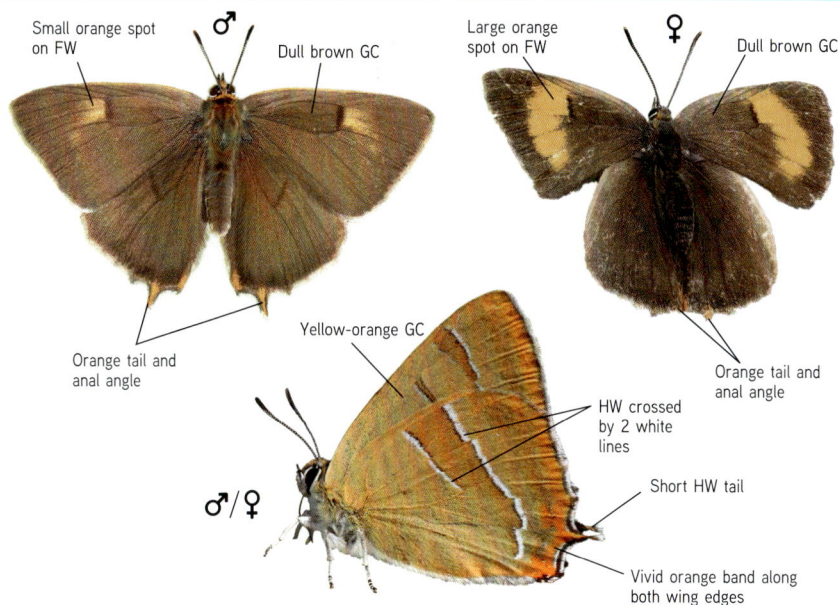

Small orange spot on FW

♂

Dull brown GC

Large orange spot on FW

♀

Dull brown GC

Orange tail and anal angle

Yellow-orange GC

Orange tail and anal angle

♂/♀

HW crossed by 2 white lines

Short HW tail

Vivid orange band along both wing edges

Wingspan: 30–40 mm

Habitat: Thorny shrubby areas, shrub edges, and sunny thickets.

Hibernating stage: Egg.

Elevational range: Up to 1,500 m.

Egg-laying: Eggs are laid singly or paired along LHP stems, usually next to a leaf bud.

Flight period: From June to October.

Host plants: Woody Rosaceae, including *Prunus spinosa*, *P. amygdalus*, *P. armeniaca*, *P. avium*, *P. cerasifera*, *P. cerasus*, *P. domestica*, *P. padus*, *P. persica*, *P. serotina*, *P. serrulata*, *P. triloba*, *Crataegus monogyna*, and *Chaenomeles japonica*. Betulaceae, like *Corylus avellana* and *Betulus pendula*.

Diversity and systematics: European populations of this hairstreak, widely distributed in Asia, belong to the nominate subspecies.

IMAGOS			LARVAE			
Food			Food			
Behaviour of males			Caterpillar location			
Dispersion			Chrysalis location			

Did you know?

The scientific name of the species associates it with the birches, although the caterpillars feed on it rather rarely.

251

LYCAENIDAE

PURPLE HAIRSTREAK *FAVONIUS QUERCUS*

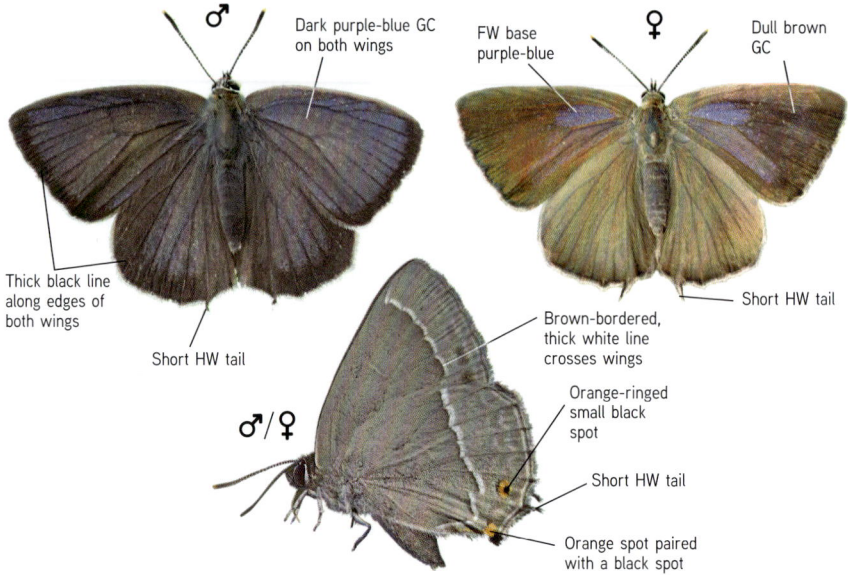

♂

Dark purple-blue GC on both wings

FW base purple-blue

♀

Dull brown GC

Thick black line along edges of both wings

Short HW tail

Short HW tail

Brown-bordered, thick white line crosses wings

♂/♀

Orange-ringed small black spot

Short HW tail

Orange spot paired with a black spot

Wingspan: 29–35 mm

Habitat: Oak forests and forest edges.

Hibernating stage: Egg.

Elevational range: Up to 2,000 m.

Egg-laying: Eggs are laid singly or by two or three on LHP leaf buds.

Flight period: From May to October.

Host plants: Fagaceae, mainly *Quercus robur*, *Q. petraea*, and *Q. pubescens*. Sometimes also *Q. alnifolia*, *Q. cerris*, *Q. coccifera*, *Q. faginea*, *Q. ilex*, *Q. infectoria*, *Q. pyrenaica*, *Q. rotundifolia*, *Q. rubra*, and *Q. suber*.

Diversity and systematics: Most European populations belong to the nominate subspecies. Subspecies *iberica* flies in the Iberian Peninsula, while subspecies *interjecta* flies from Italy to the south of France.

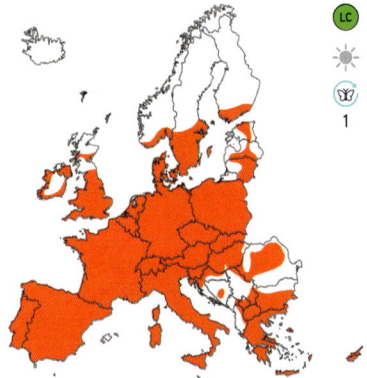

LC

1

IMAGOS		LARVAE	
Food		Food	
Behaviour of males		Caterpillar location	
Dispersion		Chrysalis location	

Did you know?

The compound eyes of the Purple Hairstreak are covered with bristles on their anterior half. Their function remains unknown.

LYCAENIDAE

BLUE-SPOT HAIRSTREAK   *SATYRIUM SPINI*

♂/♀

Brown-bordered
thick white line
crosses wings

Series of orange
spots on HW

Biggest orange spot
paired with a black spot
on its outer edge

HW tail

Large bluish-
grey spot

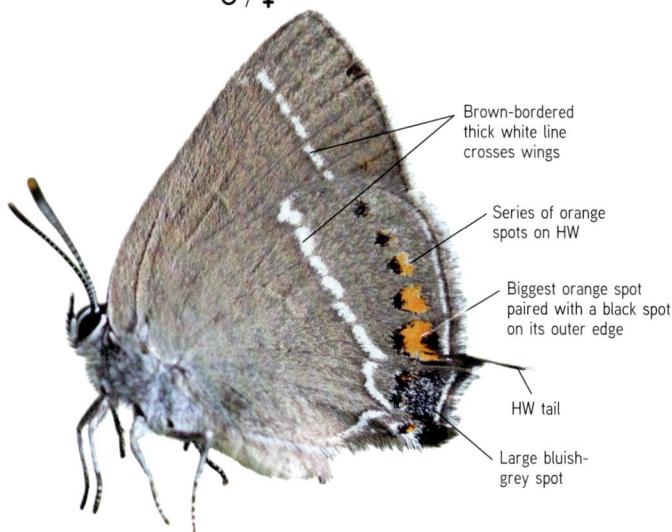

Wingspan: 28–32 mm

Habitat: Warm, bushy grasslands, meadows, and garrigues, as well as scrubby edges.

Hibernating stage: Caterpillar inside the egg.

Elevational range: Up to 2,200 m.

Egg-laying: Eggs are laid singly or by two or three on LHP leaf buds.

Flight period: From May to August.

Host plants: Rhamnaceae, mainly *Rhamnus cathartica*, *R. alaternus*, *R. alpina*, *R. saxatilis*, *R. lycioides*, *R. myrtifolia*, *R. pumila*, *R. saxatilis*, *Frangula alnus*, and *Paliurus spina-christi*.

Diversity and systematics: European populations of this hairstreak, widespread in Eurasia, belong to the nominate subspecies.

LC

1

Did you know?

Adults frequently forage on the inflorescences of thyme, blackberry, and White Stonecrop. Males engage in endless territorial skirmishes from the bushes they perch on.

IMAGOS		LARVAE	
Food	🌼 🐛	Food	🍃 🍂
Behaviour of males		Caterpillar location	🍃 🐜
Dispersion		Chrysalis location	

253

SLOE HAIRSTREAK *SATYRIUM ACACIAE*

♂/♀

Series of small, aligned, brown-bordered white streaks

Series of orange spots on HW

Biggest orange spot paired with black spot on outer edge

Very short HW tail

Small grey spot

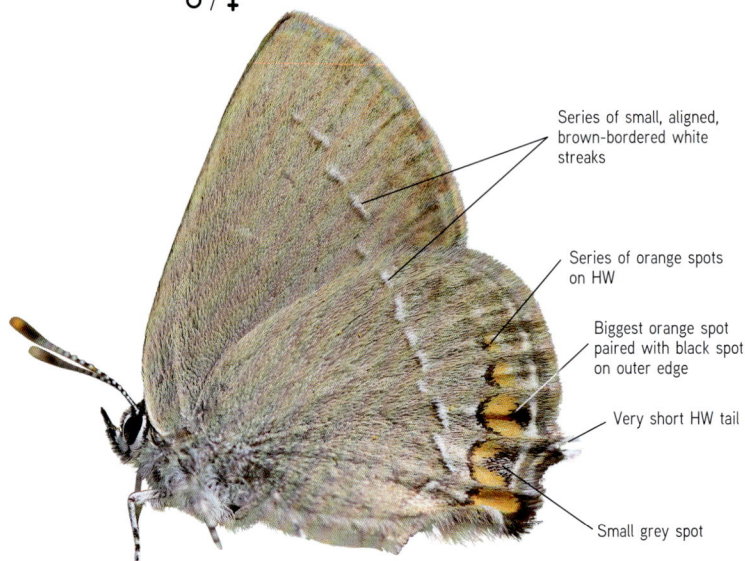

Wingspan: 28–32 mm

Habitat: Thorny shrubby areas, bushy edges, grasslands, and meadows colonized by Blackthorn bushes.

Hibernating stage: Caterpillar inside the egg.

Elevational range: Up to 2,300 m.

Egg-laying: Eggs are laid singly on LHP leaf buds.

Flight period: From May to August.

Host plants: Rosaceae in genus *Prunus* – above all, *P. spinosa*, and sometimes *P. amygdalus* and *Cotoneaster integerrimus*.

Diversity and systematics: There are no notable subspecies for this hairstreak, whose range is widespread across Asia.

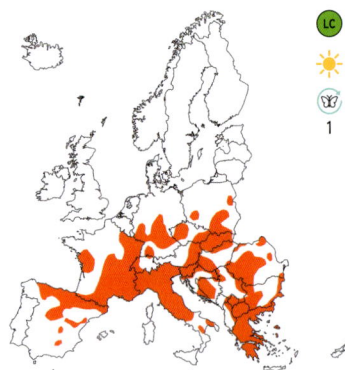

LC

1

IMAGOS			LARVAE	
Food	✿		Food	🍃
Behaviour of males	🌼 🌼		Caterpillar location	🌿
Dispersion	🌼		Chrysalis location	🪲 🌿

Did you know?

During oviposition, females sometimes lose a portion of their abdominal setae, which remain attached to the egg. This helps better conceal the egg.

LYCAENIDAE

WHITE-LETTER HAIRSTREAK *SATYRIUM W-ALBUM*

♂/♀

Thick white line, conspicuously W-shaped on HW

Continuous orange band bordered with black undulated line on inner edge

2 HW tails (a short and a longer one)

Biggest orange spot paired with black spot on outer edge

Small grey spot

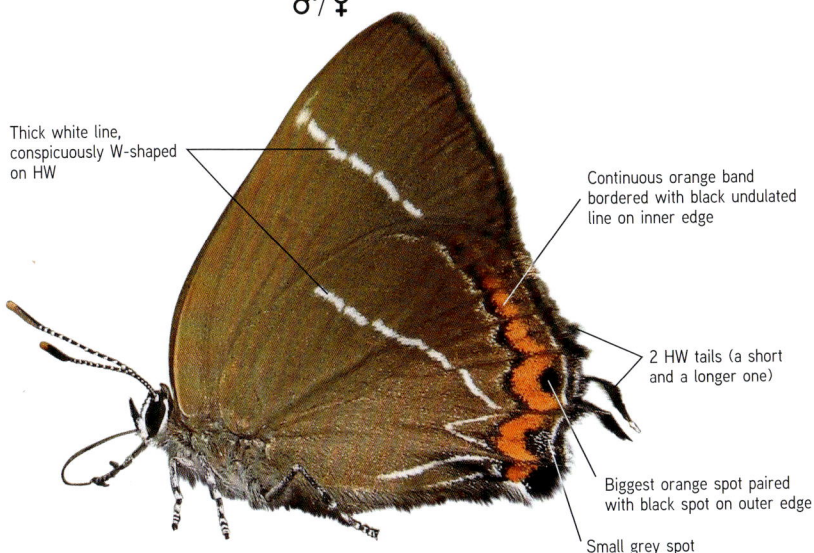

Wingspan: 28–32 mm

Habitat: Hedgerows, edges, and clearings where elms grow.

Hibernating stage: Caterpillar inside the egg.

Elevational range: Up to 1,700 m.

Egg-laying: Eggs are laid singly or in a few units at the bases of LHP leaf buds.

Flight period: From June to August.

Host plants: Ulmaceae, including *Ulmus glabra*, *U. minor*, *U. pumila*, and *U. laevis*.

Diversity and systematics: European populations belong to the nominate subspecies.

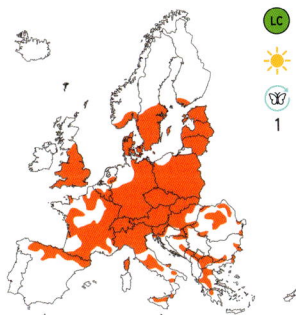

LC

1

Did you know?

White-letter Hairstreaks can sometimes breed in urban areas, taking advantage of ornamental elm plantations that serve as ecological refuges, especially when Dutch elm disease has devastated these host plants in natural environments.

IMAGOS		LARVAE	
Food		Food	
Behaviour of males		Caterpillar location	
Dispersion		Chrysalis location	

LYCAENIDAE

BLACK HAIRSTREAK *SATYRIUM PRUNI*

♂/♀

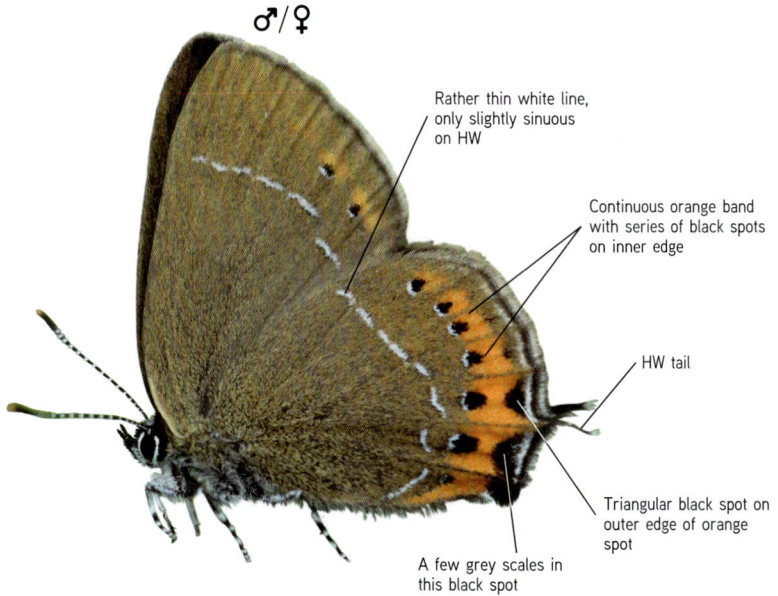

Rather thin white line, only slightly sinuous on HW

Continuous orange band with series of black spots on inner edge

HW tail

Triangular black spot on outer edge of orange spot

A few grey scales in this black spot

Wingspan: 25–36 mm

Habitat: Blackthorn-rich thickets, hedgerows, bushy clearings and edges.

Hibernating stage: Caterpillar inside the egg.

Elevational range: Up to 1,200 m.

Egg-laying: Eggs are laid singly or in a few units at the bases of and along LHP stems.

Flight period: From May to July.

Host plants: Rosaceae in genus *Prunus*, mainly *P. spinosa*, but sometimes also *P. padus*, *P. domestica*, *P. mahaleb*, *P. fruticosa*, and *P. triloba*. Also cited on *Rhamnus lycioides* (Rhamnaceae).

Diversity and systematics: European populations belong to the nominate subspecies.

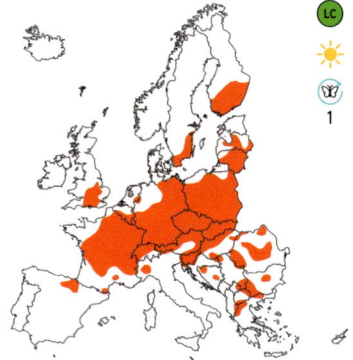

LC

1

IMAGOS		LARVAE	
Food		Food	
Behaviour of males		Caterpillar location	
Dispersion		Chrysalis location	

Did you know?

The white-spotted brown pupa of the Black Hairstreak closely resembles bird droppings. This type of mimicry is quite common among butterflies.

LYCAENIDAE

ILEX HAIRSTREAK *SATYRIUM ILICIS*

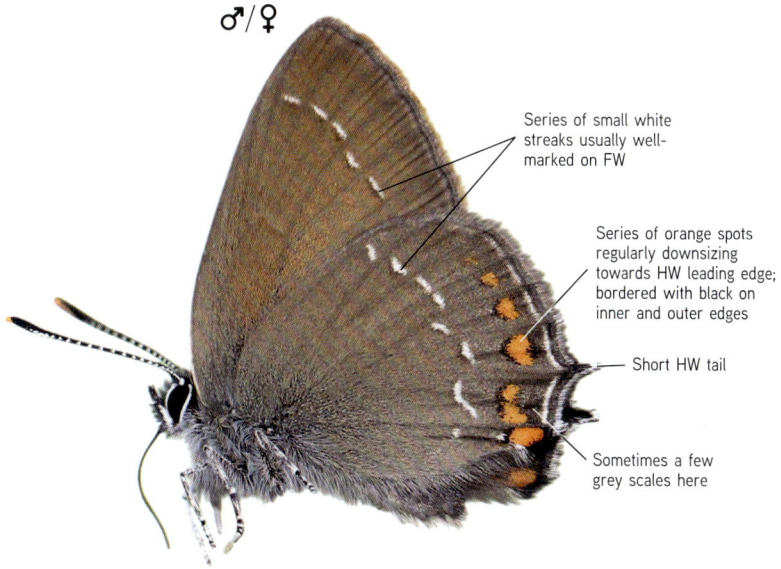

♂/♀

Series of small white streaks usually well-marked on FW

Series of orange spots regularly downsizing towards HW leading edge; bordered with black on inner and outer edges

Short HW tail

Sometimes a few grey scales here

Wingspan: 32–36 mm

Habitat: Clear oak woodlands and their edges and clearings.

Hibernating stage: Caterpillar inside the egg.

Elevational range: Up to 2,500 m.

Egg-laying: Eggs are laid singly along LHP stems.

Flight period: From May to August.

Host plants: Oaks, mainly *Quercus pubescens, Q. petraea, Q. robur, Q. ilex, Q. cerris, Q. coccifera, Q. faginea, Q. pyrenaica,* and *Q. rotundifolia.* Rarely on *Prunus spinosa* (Rosaceae) and *Ulmus minor* (Ulmaceae).

Diversity and systematics: There are no notable subspecies for this hairstreak, which is widespread across Asia and the Near East.

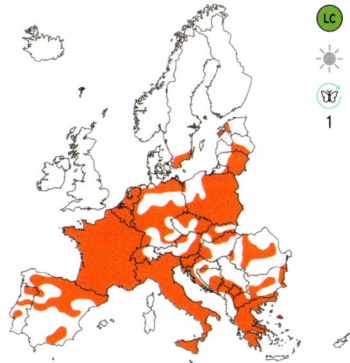

LC

1

IMAGOS		LARVAE	
Food ✿		Food 🌿	
Behaviour of males		Caterpillar location 🐜	
Dispersion		Chrysalis location	

Did you know?

Adults enjoy foraging on the flowers of White Stonecrop, Privet, and Blackberry. Softwood plantations are particularly unfavourable for the Ilex Hairstreak.

257

LYCAENIDAE

FALSE ILEX HAIRSTREAK *SATYRIUM ESCULI*

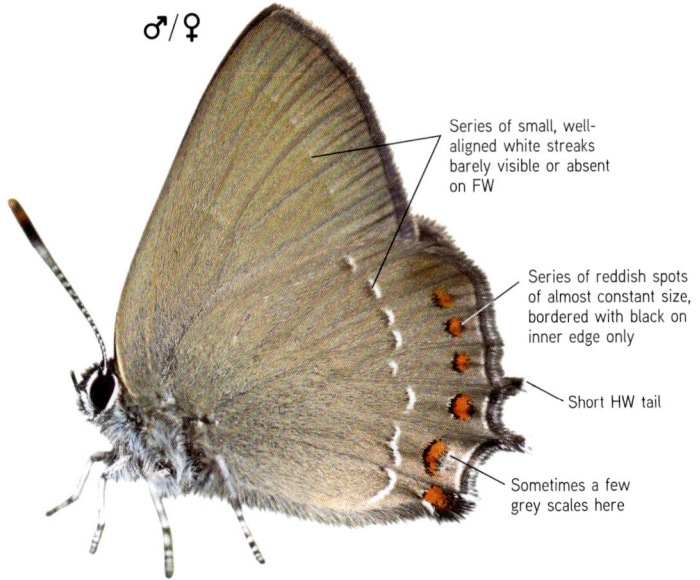

♂/♀

Series of small, well-aligned white streaks barely visible or absent on FW

Series of reddish spots of almost constant size, bordered with black on inner edge only

Short HW tail

Sometimes a few grey scales here

Wingspan: 30–34 mm

Habitat: Bushy grasslands and garrigues, oak woodland clearings and edges.

Hibernating stage: Caterpillar inside the egg.

Elevational range: Up to 1,500 m.

Egg-laying: Eggs are laid singly along LHP stems.

Flight period: From May to August.

Host plants: Oaks, mainly *Quercus coccifera* and *Q. ilex*; sometimes also *Q. pubescens*, *Q. robur*, *Q. pyrenaica*, and *Q. rotundifolia*.

Diversity and systematics: European populations belong to the nominate subspecies.

LC

1

IMAGOS		LARVAE	
Food	✿	Food	🍃 🌳 🐜
Behaviour of males		Caterpillar location	
Dispersion		Chrysalis location	

Did you know?

The nectar of thymes, lavenders, and scabiouses is on the menu for adults, who also enjoy foraging on blackberry flowers.

258

LYCAENIDAE

SPANISH PURPLE HAIRSTREAK *LAEOSOPIS ROBORIS*

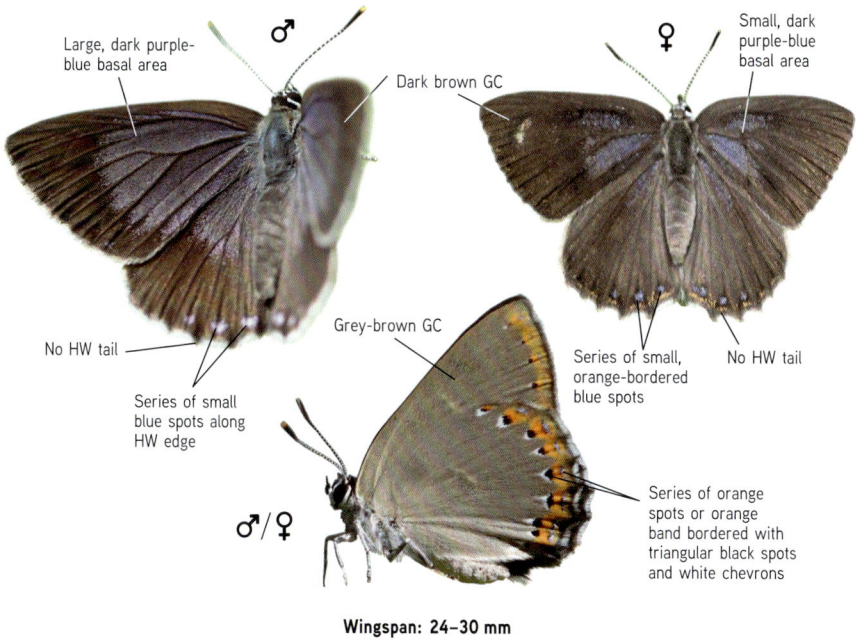

♂

Large, dark purple-blue basal area

Dark brown GC

♀

Small, dark purple-blue basal area

No HW tail

Grey-brown GC

Series of small, orange-bordered blue spots

No HW tail

Series of small blue spots along HW edge

♂/♀

Series of orange spots or orange band bordered with triangular black spots and white chevrons

Wingspan: 24–30 mm

Habitat: Mediterranean riparian areas, bushy garrigues with ashes or bushy Oleaceae.

Hibernating stage: Caterpillar inside the egg.

Elevational range: Up to 1,500 m.

Egg-laying: Eggs are laid singly along LHP stems.

Flight period: From May to July.

Host plants: Oleaceae, especially *Fraxinus excelsior*, *F. ornus*, *Ligustrum vulgare*, *Phyllirea angustifolia*, and *P. latifolia*.

Diversity and systematics: Several subspecies are described for the Iberian Peninsula, southern France, and northwestern Italy.

LC

1

Did you know?

Eggs of the Spanish Purple Hairstreak are sometimes laid quite low on the host plant leaves; a flood can submerge them for several days during winter. This prolonged exposure to water does not hinder the development of the larvae the following spring.

IMAGOS			LARVAE			
Food	✿		Food	✿	🌿	
Behaviour of males			Caterpillar location			
Dispersion			Chrysalis location			

LYCAENIDAE

ORANGE-BANDED HAIRSTREAK *SATYRIUM LEDERERI*

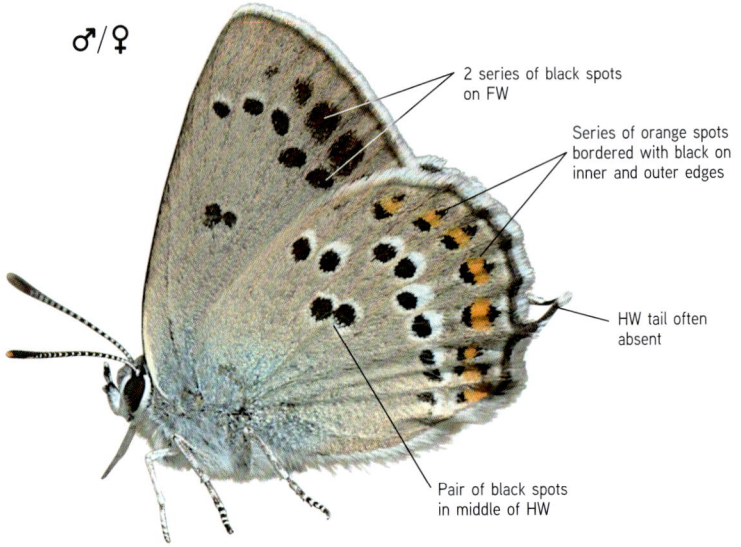

♂/♀

2 series of black spots on FW

Series of orange spots bordered with black on inner and outer edges

HW tail often absent

Pair of black spots in middle of HW

Wingspan: 26–31 mm

Habitat: Dry, rocky slopes with sparse vegetation.
Hibernating stage: Caterpillar inside the egg.
Elevational range: Between 900 and 1,300 m in Samos.
Egg-laying: Eggs are laid singly on the LHP.
Flight period: From May to July.
Host plants: *Atraphaxis billardieri* (Polygonaceae).
Diversity and systematics: Samos island populations (the only ones in Europe) belong to subspecies *christianae*.

IMAGOS	LARVAE
Food	Food
Behaviour of males	Caterpillar location
Dispersion	Chrysalis location

Did you know?

In Samos, the Orange-banded Hairstreak reaches the western limit of its range, which extends widely to the east (Turkey and the Caucasus).

LYCAENIDAE

CANARY BLUE *CYCLYRIUS WEBBIANUS*

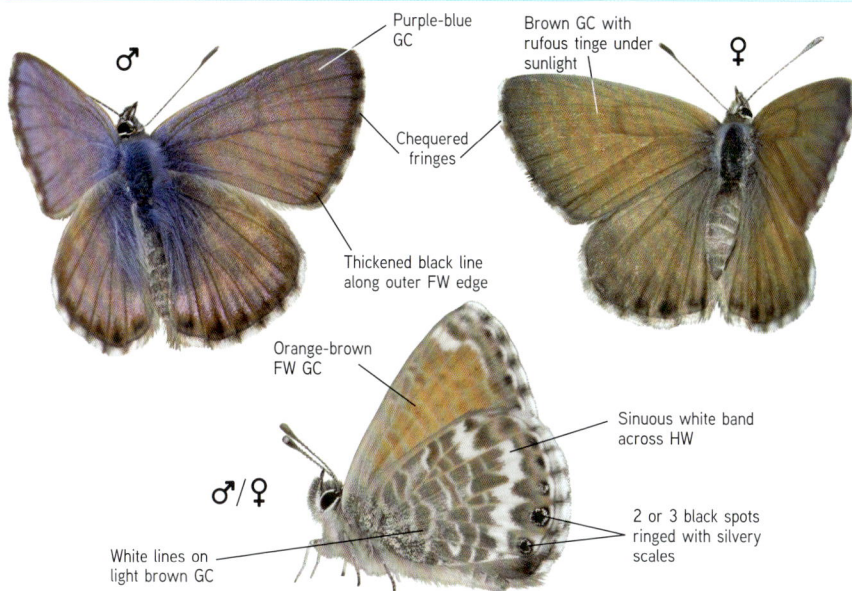

♂

Purple-blue GC

Brown GC with rufous tinge under sunlight

♀

Chequered fringes

Thickened black line along outer FW edge

Orange-brown FW GC

Sinuous white band across HW

♂/♀

2 or 3 black spots ringed with silvery scales

White lines on light brown GC

Wingspan: 25–30 mm

Habitat: A wide range of open habitats, such as volcanic slopes and gullies, cultivated and ruderal areas.

Hibernating stage: Egg, caterpillar, pupa, or adult.

Elevational range: Up to 2,500 m.

Egg-laying: Eggs are laid singly or in batches of up to a dozen on LHP flower buds.

Flight period: Year-round at lower elevations and from May to October at higher altitudes.

Host plants: Legumes, including *Lotus sessilifolius*, *L. glaucus*, *L. campylocladus*, *Adenocarpus viscosus*, *A. foliosus*, *Cytisus supranubius*, *Genista canariensis*, *G. stenopetala*, and *Telina stenopetala*.

Diversity and systematics: The nominate subspecies flies on La Gomera. The populations on La Palma and Gran Canaria form subspecies *palmae* and *grancanariensis*, respectively.

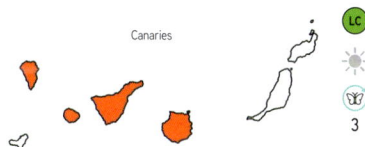

Canaries

LC

3

IMAGOS	LARVAE
Food	Food
Behaviour of males	Caterpillar location
Dispersion: unknown	Chrysalis location

Did you know?

Adults are highly attracted to flowers, making them relatively easy to observe and approach, a delight for photographers!

LYCAENIDAE

GERANIUM BRONZE *CACYREUS MARSHALLI*

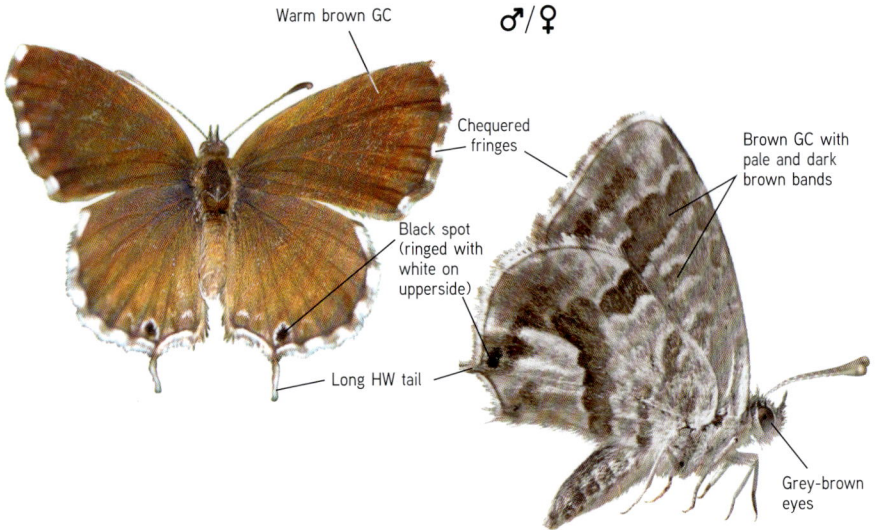

Warm brown GC

♂/♀

Chequered fringes

Brown GC with pale and dark brown bands

Black spot (ringed with white on upperside)

Long HW tail

Grey-brown eyes

Wingspan: 21–26 mm

Habitat: More or less urbanized areas, like towns and villages, but also their surroundings where the ornamental LHPs are grown.

Hibernating stage: Caterpillar and pupa.

Elevational range: Up to 2,000 m, but breeds only at lower elevations.

Egg-laying: Eggs are laid singly on LHP leaves, stems, and inflorescences.

Flight period: From March to October.

Host plants: *Pelargonium peltatum* and *P. zonale* (Geraniaceae). Now also suspected of using indigenous Geraniaceae, such as *Geranium molle*, *G. sylvaticum*, or *G. pyrenaicum*.

Diversity and systematics: There are no notable subspecies for this small Lycaenid, which originated from South Africa.

NA

3+

Canaries

Did you know?

The Geranium Bronze was introduced to Europe in the early 1990s through the importation of storksbills, its host plants, which are widely used as ornamental plants on our continent. It quickly spread in southwestern Europe.

IMAGOS		LARVAE	
Food	✿	Food	✿ 🍃 🌿 🌱
Behaviour of males		Caterpillar location	🌿
Dispersion		Chrysalis location	🌱

LYCAENIDAE

LONG-TAILED BLUE *LAMPIDES BOETICUS*

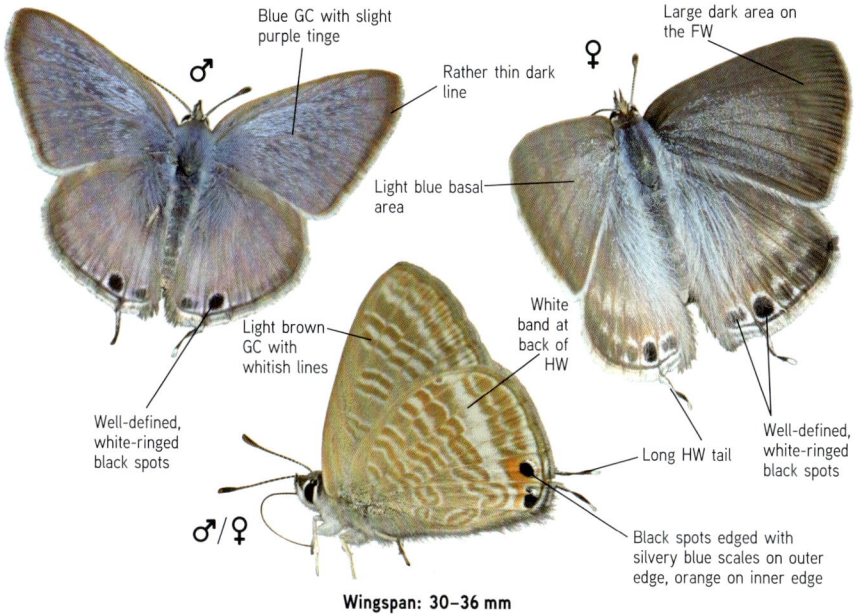

Blue GC with slight purple tinge

Rather thin dark line

Large dark area on the FW

♂

♀

Light blue basal area

Light brown GC with whitish lines

White band at back of HW

Well-defined, white-ringed black spots

Well-defined, white-ringed black spots

Long HW tail

♂/♀

Black spots edged with silvery blue scales on outer edge, orange on inner edge

Wingspan: 30–36 mm

Habitat: Rather open or bushy environments; also parks and gardens.

Hibernating stage: Egg, caterpillar, or pupa without entering diapause.

Elevational range: Up to 2,000 m (breeds mostly below 1,000 m).

Egg-laying: Eggs are laid singly on LHP flower buds.

Flight period: From March to November.

Host plants: A wide range of legumes, including *Colutea arborescens, C. atlantica, Bituminaria bituminosa, Calicotome villosa, Astragalus alopecuroides, A. glycyphyllos, Lathyrus cirrhosus, L. latifolius, L. ochrus, L. oleraceus, L. sylvestris, L. tingitanus, L. tuberosus, Lotus corniculatus, L. creticus, Lupinus luteus, L. polyphyllus, Pisum sativum, Phaseolus vulgaris, Cytisus arboreus, C. scoparius, Hippocrepis emerus, Onobrychis humilis, O. viciifolia, O. alba, Robinia hispida, R. pseudoacacia, Spartium junceum, Ulex europaeus, U. minor,* and *U. parviflorus.*

Diversity and systematics: European populations belong to the nominate subspecies.

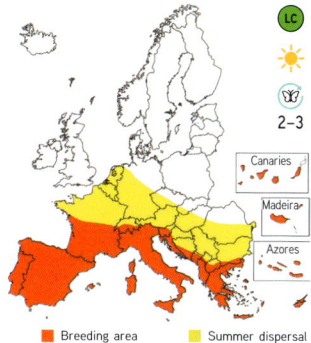

LC

2–3

Canaries

Madeira

Azores

■ Breeding area   ■ Summer dispersal

Did you know?

Every summer, Long-tailed Blues disperse to the north and attempt to breed outside their range. These attempts often prove futile due to the poor resistance to winter cold of the developmental stages, which can't enter diapause.

IMAGOS		LARVAE	
Food	✿	Food	✿ 🍃
Behaviour of males		Caterpillar location	
Dispersion		Chrysalis location	

LYCAENIDAE

LANG'S SHORT-TAILED BLUE *LEPTOTES PIRITHOUS*

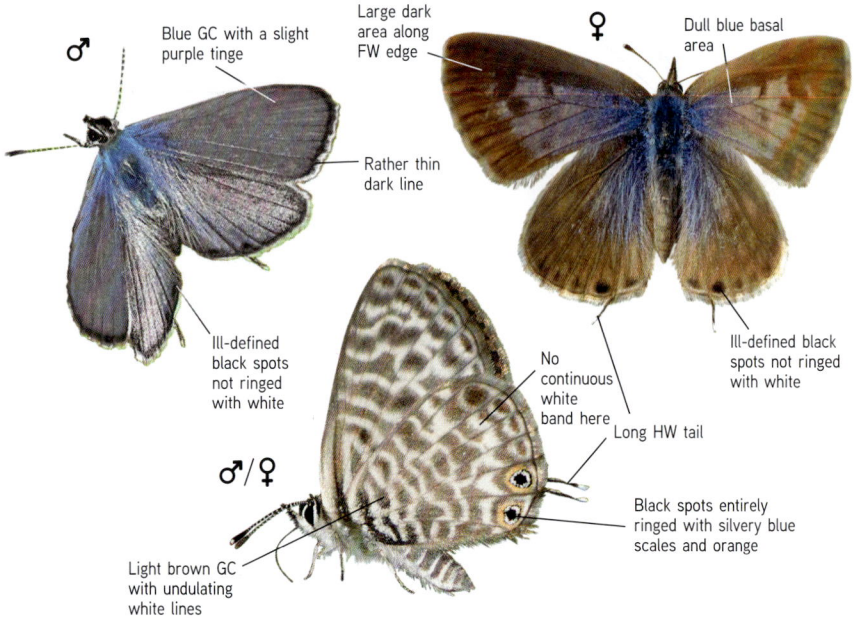

♂ Blue GC with a slight purple tinge

Large dark area along FW edge

♀ Dull blue basal area

Rather thin dark line

Ill-defined black spots not ringed with white

No continuous white band here

Long HW tail

Ill-defined black spots not ringed with white

♂/♀

Black spots entirely ringed with silvery blue scales and orange

Light brown GC with undulating white lines

Wingspan: 24–26 mm

Habitat: Wastelands, garrigue, bushy Mediterranean riverine habitats, parks, and gardens.

Hibernating stage: Caterpillar or pupa without entering diapause.

Elevational range: Up to 2,000 m (breeds successfully only at lower elevations).

Egg-laying: Eggs are laid singly on LHP inflorescences.

Flight period: From March to October.

Host plants: A wide range of legumes, including *Medicago arborea*, *M. sativa*, *M. marina*, *M. suffruticosa*, *Melilotus albus*, *M. neapolitanus*, *M. officinalis*, *Onobrychis viciifolia*, *Lotus dorycnium*, *L. creticus*, *L. hirsutus*, *Melilotus* spp., *Ulex gallii*, *U. minor*, *U. parviflorus*, and *Sophora japonica*. Also on *Lythrum salicaria* (Lythraceae), *Plumbago auriculata* (Plombaginaceae), *Polygonum aviculare* (Polygonaceae), *Sambucus ebulus* (Caprifoliaceae), *Calluna vulgaris*, and *Erica multiflora* (Ericaceae), as well as *Humulus lupulus* (Cannabaceae).

Diversity and systematics: European populations belong to the nominate subspecies.

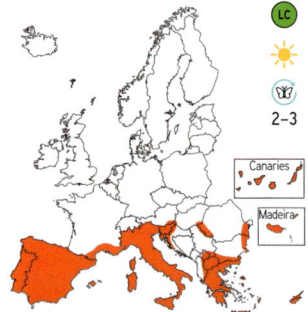

LC

2–3

Canaries

Madeira

Did you know?

This tropical species reaches the northern limit of its range in Europe and is confined to the Mediterranean region due to the lack of winter diapause. However, it can be observed far beyond this area due to marked dispersal in late summer.

IMAGOS		LARVAE	
Food	✿	Food	✿
Behaviour of males		Caterpillar location	
Dispersion		Chrysalis location	

LYCAENIDAE

AFRICAN BABUL BLUE *AZANUS JESOUS*

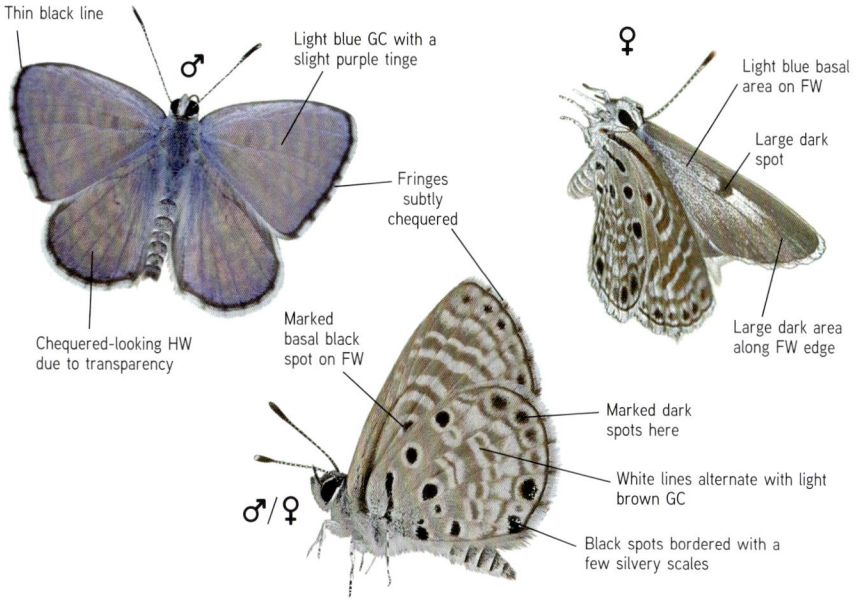

Thin black line

Light blue GC with a
slight purple tinge

♂

♀

Light blue basal
area on FW

Large dark
spot

Fringes
subtly
chequered

Marked
basal black
spot on FW

Chequered-looking HW
due to transparency

Large dark area
along FW edge

Marked dark
spots here

White lines alternate with light
brown GC

♂/♀

Black spots bordered with a
few silvery scales

Wingspan: 21–22 mm

Habitat: Dry environments where the LHPs grow and around
which adults remain most of the time.

Hibernating stage: Egg, caterpillar, pupa, or adult.

Elevational range: Up to 1,500 m.

Egg-laying: Eggs are laid singly on the LHP.

Flight period: From February to August.

Host plants: *Acacia gummifera*, *Prosopis farcta*, and *Vachellia
karroo* (Fabaceae).

Diversity and systematics: The few European populations belong
to the nominate subspecies.

NA

3+

	IMAGOS			LARVAE	
Food	☆ ⌂ ◊		Food	☆ 🌿	
Behaviour of males			Caterpillar location	🌳 🐜	
Dispersion: unknown			Chrysalis location		

Did you know?

Known in Europe only from a
single Cypriot specimen until the
early 2000s, the African Babul
Blue was later found in the
Spanish province of Cádiz, where
it forms viable populations.

BRIGHT BABUL BLUE *AZANUS UBALDUS*

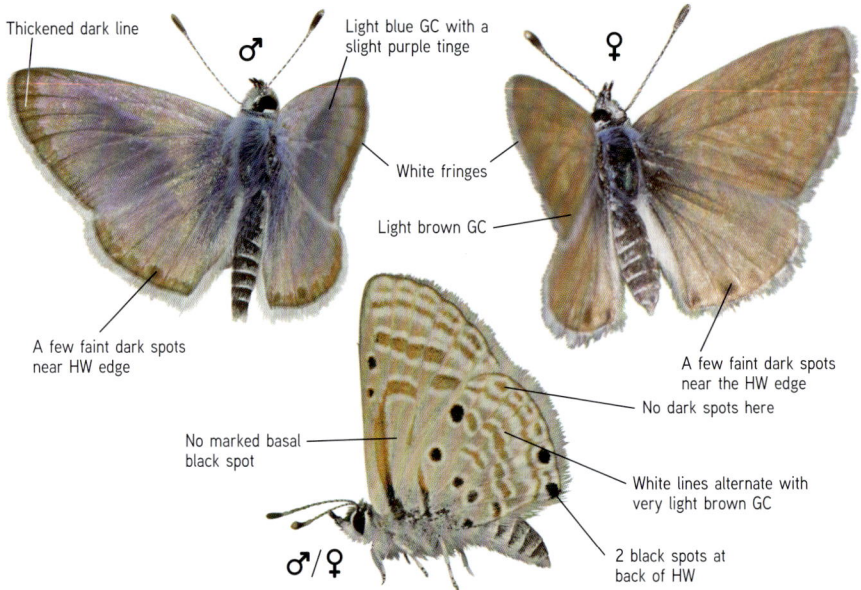

Thickened dark line

Light blue GC with a slight purple tinge

♂

♀

White fringes

Light brown GC

A few faint dark spots near HW edge

A few faint dark spots near the HW edge

No dark spots here

No marked basal black spot

White lines alternate with very light brown GC

♂/♀

2 black spots at back of HW

Wingspan: 10–15 mm

Habitat: Arid to semi-desert areas where the LHPs grow.

Hibernating stage: Egg, caterpillar, pupa, or adult.

Elevational range: Up to 1,500 m.

Egg-laying: Eggs are laid singly or in a few units on LHP flower buds.

Flight period: Year-round.

Host plants: Legumes, especially *Vachellia farnesiana*, *V. karroo* (in Malta), and *Prosopis juliflora*.

Diversity and systematics: There are no notable subspecies for this widespread blue, which is also found in Africa and South Asia.

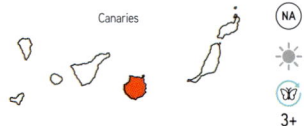

Canaries

NA

3+

Did you know?

The Bright Babul Blue has recently established itself in Malta, where it forms viable populations. An individual was also observed in 2019 in the Sierra Nevada, the first in continental Europe, likely transported by the wind.

IMAGOS			LARVAE		
Food			Food		
Behaviour of males			Caterpillar location		
Dispersion: unknown			Chrysalis location		

LYCAENIDAE

AFRICAN GRASS BLUE *ZIZEERIA KNYSNA*

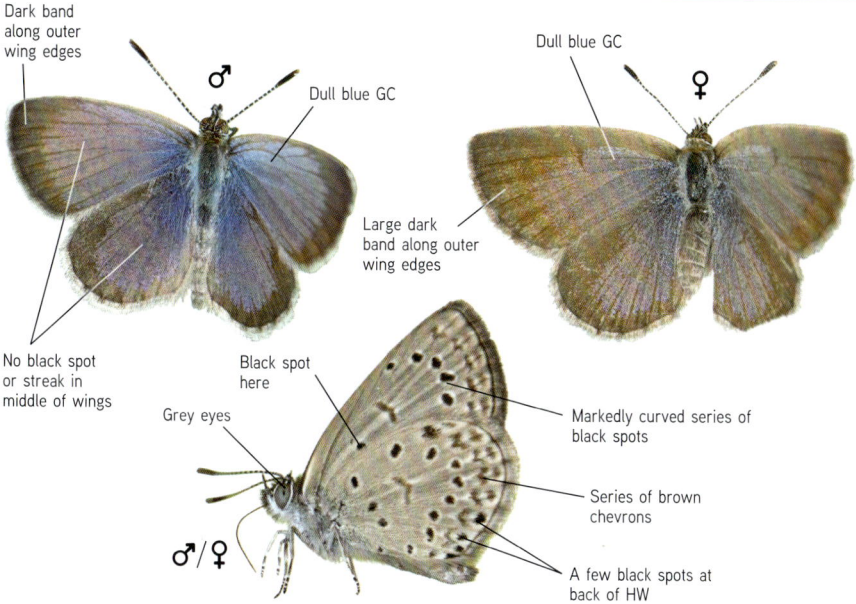

Dark band along outer wing edges

♂

Dull blue GC

Dull blue GC

♀

Large dark band along outer wing edges

No black spot or streak in middle of wings

Black spot here

Grey eyes

Markedly curved series of black spots

Series of brown chevrons

♂/♀

A few black spots at back of HW

Wingspan: 20–24 mm

Habitat: Ruderal areas, villages, parks, gardens, and crop surroundings.

Hibernating stage: Egg, caterpillar, pupa, or adult without entering diapause.

Elevational range: Up to 1,000 m.

Egg-laying: Eggs are laid singly on the LHP.

Flight period: From February to October in continental Spain, year-round in the Canaries.

Host plants: A wide variety of plants in different families, especially legumes like *Medicago lupulina*, *M. minima*, *M. polymorpha*, *M. sativa*, *Trifolium fragiferum*, and *T. repens*. Also on *Amaranthus deflexus* (Amaranthaceae), *Glinus lotoides* (Moluginaceae), and *Tribulus terrestris* (Zygophyllaceae).

Diversity and systematics: Continental Spain populations do not differ from the nominate subspecies. The populations in the Canary Islands form subspecies *corneliae*.

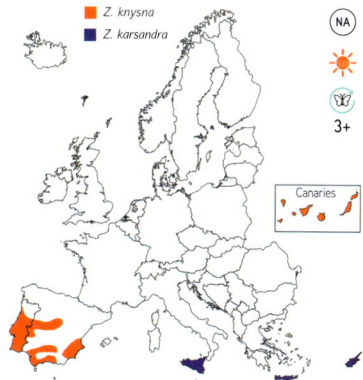

■ *Z. knysna*
■ *Z. karsandra*

NA

3+

Canaries

Did you know?

African Grass Blue adults usually fly very low. They take advantage of the irrigation of Mediterranean crops, which allows their weedy host plants to thrive.

IMAGOS		LARVAE	
Food		Food	
Behaviour of males		Caterpillar location	
Dispersion		Chrysalis location	

267

LYCAENIDAE

DARK GRASS BLUE *ZIZEERIA KARSANDRA*

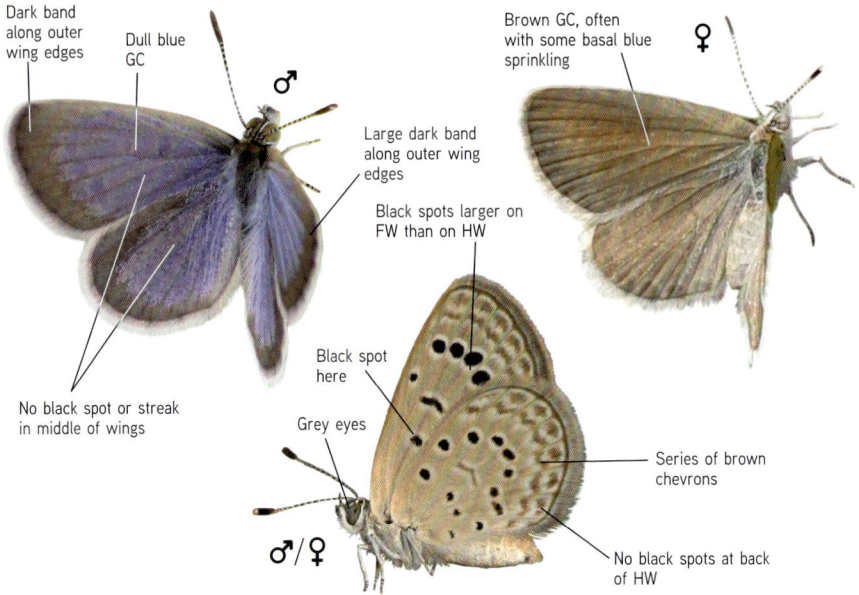

Dark band along outer wing edges

Dull blue GC

♂

Brown GC, often with some basal blue sprinkling

♀

Large dark band along outer wing edges

Black spots larger on FW than on HW

Black spot here

No black spot or streak in middle of wings

Grey eyes

♂/♀

Series of brown chevrons

No black spots at back of HW

Wingspan: 20–24 mm

Habitat: Ruderal areas, parks, gardens, and crop surroundings.

Hibernating stage: Egg, caterpillar, pupa, or adult without entering diapause.

Elevational range: Up to 500 m.

Egg-laying: Eggs are laid singly on LHP flower calyces.

Flight period: From February to November.

Host plants: *Polygonum equisetiforme* (Polygonaceae), as well as some Amaranthaceae, including *Amaranthus blitum*. Also on *Glinus lotoides* (Moluginaceae), *Trifolium fragiferum* (Fabaceae), *Andrachne telephioides* (Phyllanthaceae), and *Tribulus terrestris* (Zygophyllaceae).

Diversity and systematics: There are no notable subspecies for this blue, which is also widespread in North Africa and South Asia.

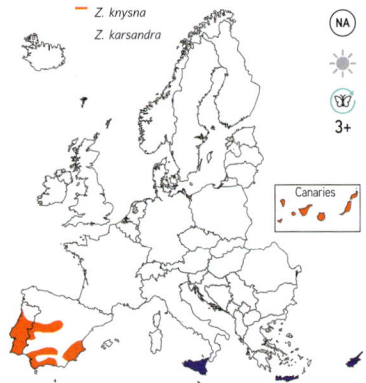

Z. knysna
Z. karsandra

NA

3+

Canaries

IMAGOS		LARVAE	
Food		Food	
Behaviour of males		Caterpillar location	
Dispersion		Chrysalis location	

Did you know?

The Dark Grass Blue was previously considered a subspecies of the African Grass Blue, from which it differs by its genitalia.

LYCAENIDAE

SMALL DESERT BLUE *LUTHRODES GALBA*

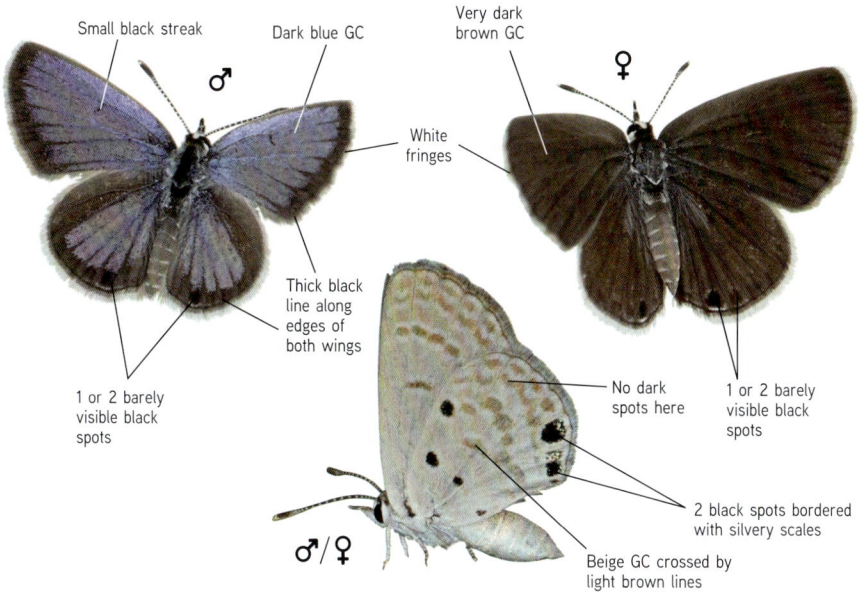

Small black streak

Dark blue GC

Very dark brown GC

♂

♀

White fringes

Thick black line along edges of both wings

1 or 2 barely visible black spots

No dark spots here

1 or 2 barely visible black spots

2 black spots bordered with silvery scales

♂/♀

Beige GC crossed by light brown lines

Wingspan: 18–22 mm

Habitat: Dry, scrubby areas.
Hibernating stage: Probably caterpillar or pupa.
Elevational range: Up to 500 m.
Egg-laying: Eggs are laid singly on the LHP.
Flight period: From April to November.
Host plants: *Prosopis farcta* (Fabaceae).
Diversity and systematics: European populations belong to the nominate subspecies.

NA

3+

IMAGOS	LARVAE
Food	Food
Behaviour of males	Caterpillar location
Dispersion: unknown	Chrysalis location: unknown

Did you know?

In Europe, the Small Desert Blue is present only in Cyprus. Adults are highly associated with the host plant and rarely leave the areas where it grows.

GRASS JEWEL *FREYERIA TROCHYLUS*

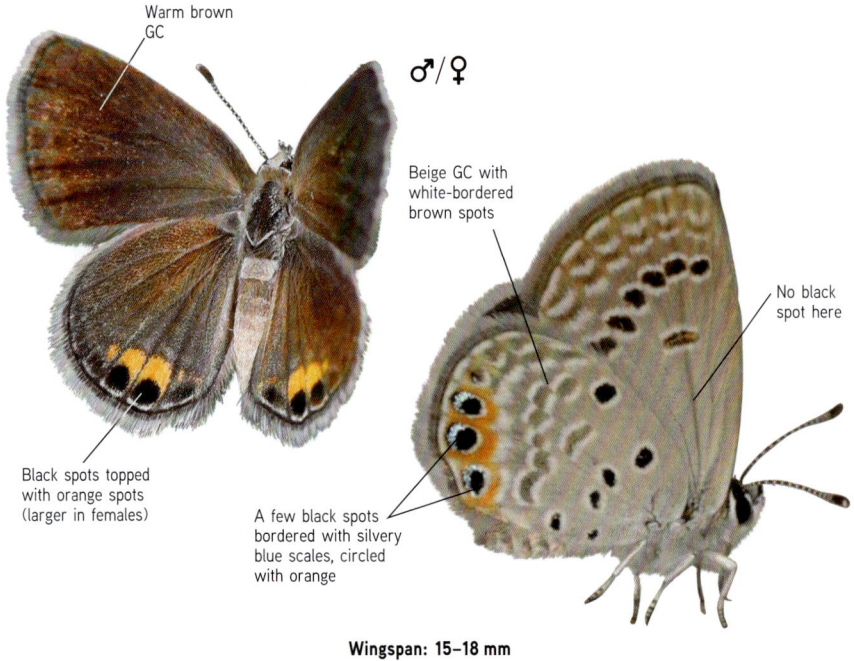

Warm brown GC

♂/♀

Beige GC with white-bordered brown spots

No black spot here

Black spots topped with orange spots (larger in females)

A few black spots bordered with silvery blue scales, circled with orange

Wingspan: 15–18 mm

Habitat: Stony dry grasslands with sparse vegetation, low-growing garrigues.

Hibernating stage: Pupa.

Elevational range: Up to 1,000 m.

Egg-laying: Eggs are laid singly on LHP leaves.

Flight period: From March to November.

Host plants: *Andrachne telephioides* (Euphorbiaceae).

Diversity and systematics: European populations belong to the nominate subspecies.

LC

3+

IMAGOS		LARVAE	
Food		Food	
Behaviour of males		Caterpillar location	
Dispersion		Chrysalis location	

Did you know?

The Grass Jewel is the smallest butterfly in Europe. Its small size and low-flying behaviour make it inconspicuous and challenging to detect.

LYCAENIDAE

LITTLE TIGER BLUE *TARUCUS BALKANICUS*

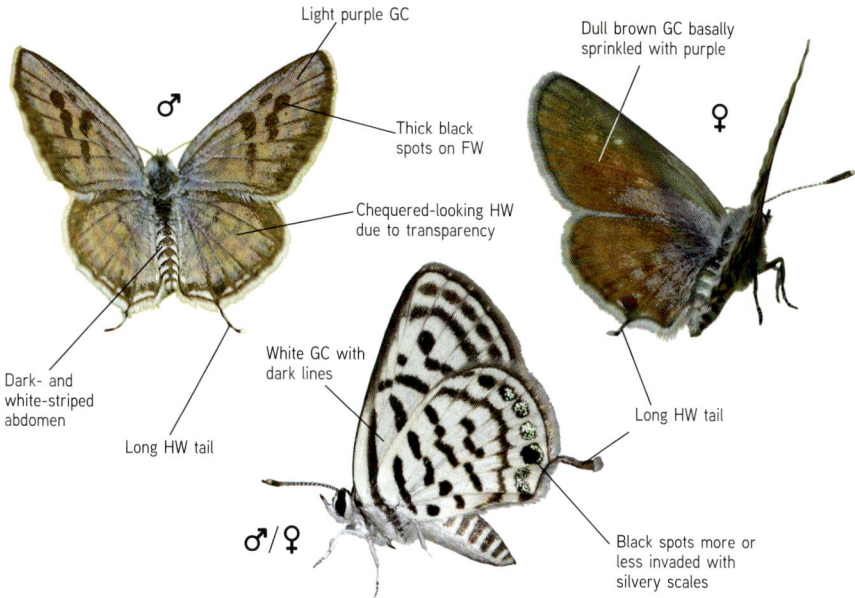

Light purple GC

Dull brown GC basally
sprinkled with purple

♂

♀

Thick black
spots on FW

Chequered-looking HW
due to transparency

White GC with
dark lines

Dark- and
white-striped
abdomen

Long HW tail

Long HW tail

♂/♀

Black spots more or
less invaded with
silvery scales

Wingspan: 18–22 mm

Habitat: Stony grasslands and meadows with sparse *Paliurus spina-christi*.

Hibernating stage: Pupa.

Elevational range: Up to 1,500 m.

Egg-laying: Eggs are laid singly at the bases of LHP spines.

Flight period: From April to October.

Host plants: Rhamnaceae, mainly *Paliurus spina-christi*, but also *Ziziphus jujuba*, *Z. leucodermis*, *Z. lotus*, and *Z. nummularia*.

Diversity and systematics: European populations belong to the nominate subspecies.

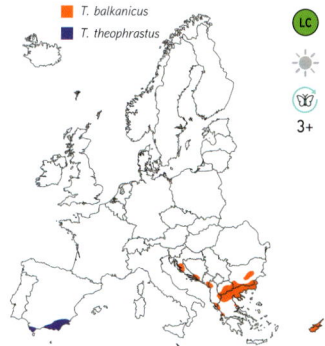

■ *T. balkanicus*
■ *T. theophrastus*

LC

3+

Did you know?

Caterpillars of the Little Tiger Blue mainly feed on the chlorophyllous parenchyma of their host plant's leaves, which are left with a typical whitened appearance.

IMAGOS		LARVAE	
Food		Food	
Behaviour of males		Caterpillar location	
Dispersion		Chrysalis location	

LYCAENIDAE

COMMON TIGER BLUE *TARUCUS THEOPHRASTUS*

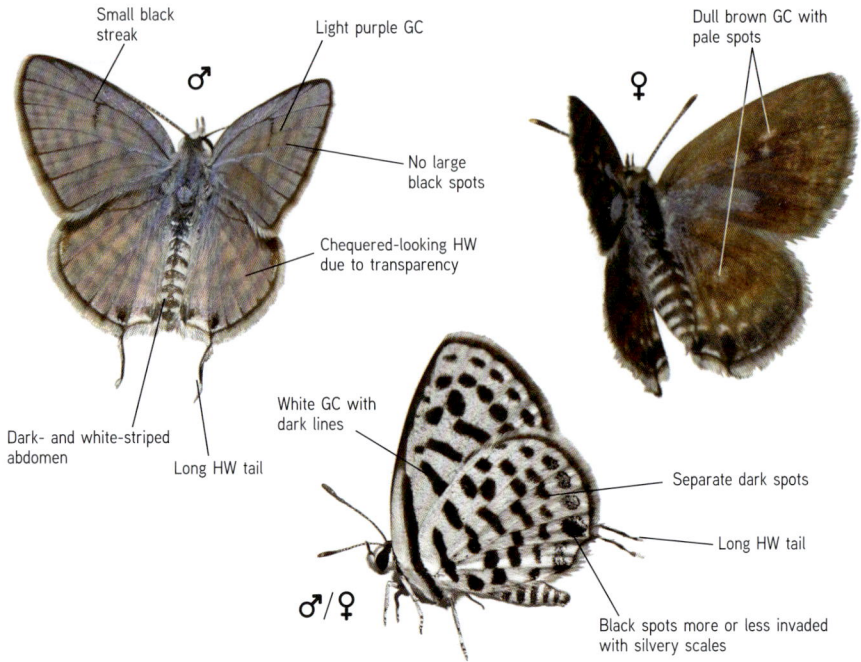

Small black streak

Light purple GC

♂

Dull brown GC with pale spots

♀

No large black spots

Chequered-looking HW due to transparency

Dark- and white-striped abdomen

Long HW tail

White GC with dark lines

♂/♀

Separate dark spots

Long HW tail

Black spots more or less invaded with silvery scales

Wingspan: 20–22 mm

Habitat: Arid and scrubby coastal areas.

Hibernating stage: Pupa.

Elevational range: Up to 500 m.

Egg-laying: Eggs are laid singly at the base of LHP stems and leaves.

Flight period: From April to September.

Host plants: Rhamnaceae, mainly *Ziziphus lotus*, *Z. jujuba*, *Z. spina-christi*, and *Paliurus spina-christi*.

Diversity and systematics: There are no notable subspecies for this blue, which is widespread across North Africa.

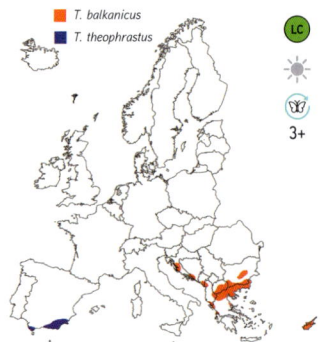

T. balkanicus
T. theophrastus

LC

3+

IMAGOS		LARVAE	
Food		Food	
Behaviour of males		Caterpillar location	
Dispersion		Chrysalis location	

Did you know?

Adults, highly dependent on their host plants, spend most of their time perching on them or flying around them.

ODD-SPOT BLUE *TURANANA TAYGETICA*

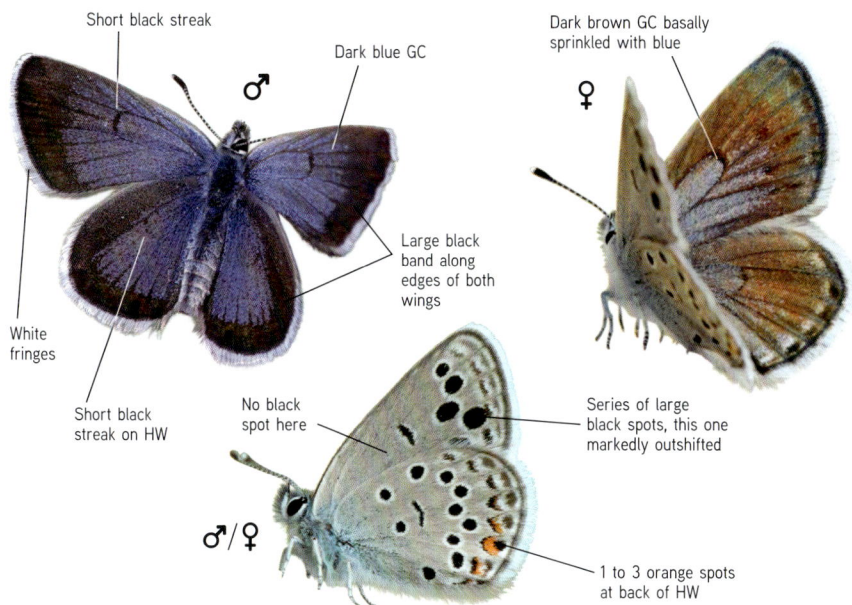

Short black streak

Dark blue GC

♂

Dark brown GC basally sprinkled with blue

♀

Large black band along edges of both wings

White fringes

Short black streak on HW

No black spot here

♂/♀

Series of large black spots, this one markedly outshifted

1 to 3 orange spots at back of HW

Wingspan: 20–22 mm

Habitat: Dry, rocky subalpine heaths, where its cushion-like LHP grows.

Hibernating stage: Pupa.

Elevational range: From 1,000 to 2,300 m.

Egg-laying: Eggs are laid singly on LHP flowers.

Flight period: From April to July.

Host plants: *Acantholimon androsaceum* (Plumbaginaceae).

Diversity and systematics: Most Greek populations belong to the nominate subspecies. Subspecies *endymionoides* is described from Mount Chelmos.

EN
1–2

IMAGOS		LARVAE	
Food	✿ 💧	Food	✿
Behaviour of males		Caterpillar location	
Dispersion		Chrysalis location	

Did you know?

Turanana taygetica was previously considered a subspecies of *T. endymion*, found in Anatolia. The distinct genitalia and allopatric situation argue in favour of the split.

LYCAENIDAE

SARDINIAN BLUE   *PSEUDOPHILOTES BARBAGIAE*

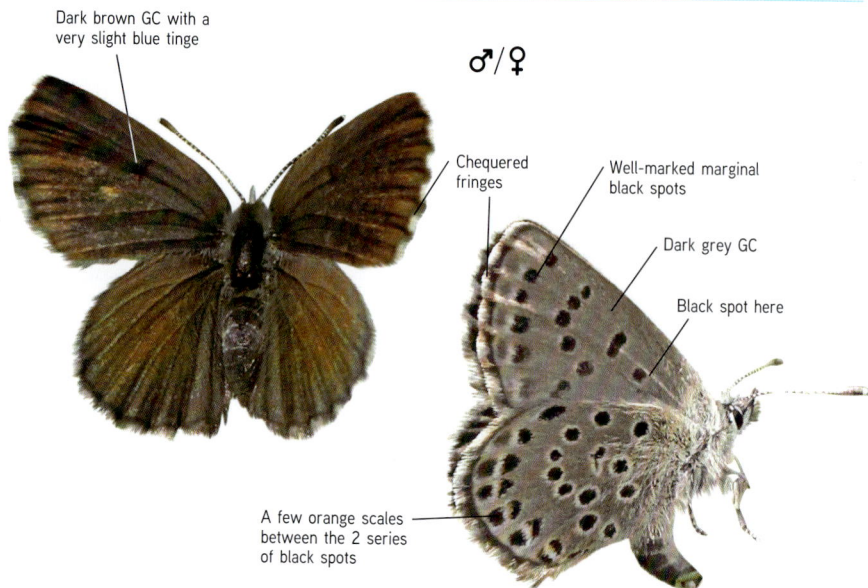

Dark brown GC with a very slight blue tinge

♂/♀

Chequered fringes

Well-marked marginal black spots

Dark grey GC

Black spot here

A few orange scales between the 2 series of black spots

Wingspan: 21–23 mm

Habitat: Dry, warm, and rocky slopes covered with bushy grasslands or garrigue.

Hibernating stage: Caterpillar.

Elevational range: Between 700 and 1,500 m.

Egg-laying: Eggs are laid singly on LHP stems, leaves, or flower buds.

Flight period: From April to July.

Host plants: *Thymus herba-barona* (Lamiaceae).

Diversity and systematics: There are no notable subspecies for this blue, which is endemic to the Gennargentu massif in Sardinia.

- P. baton
- P. vicrama
- P. baton + P. vicrama
- P. barbagiae
- P. panoptes
- P. panoptes + P. abencerragus
- P. baton + P. panoptes
- P. baton + P. abencerragus

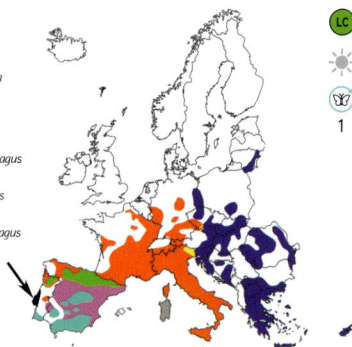

LC

1

IMAGOS		LARVAE	
Food	☆	Food	☆ 🌿
Behaviour of males	🌼	Caterpillar location	🌱
Dispersion	🦋	Chrysalis location	🐛

Did you know?

Adults forage on thyme flowers, as well as those of everlastings. Males often perch on asphodels to monitor their territory.

LYCAENIDAE

FALSE BATON BLUE *PSEUDOPHILOTES ABENCERRAGUS*

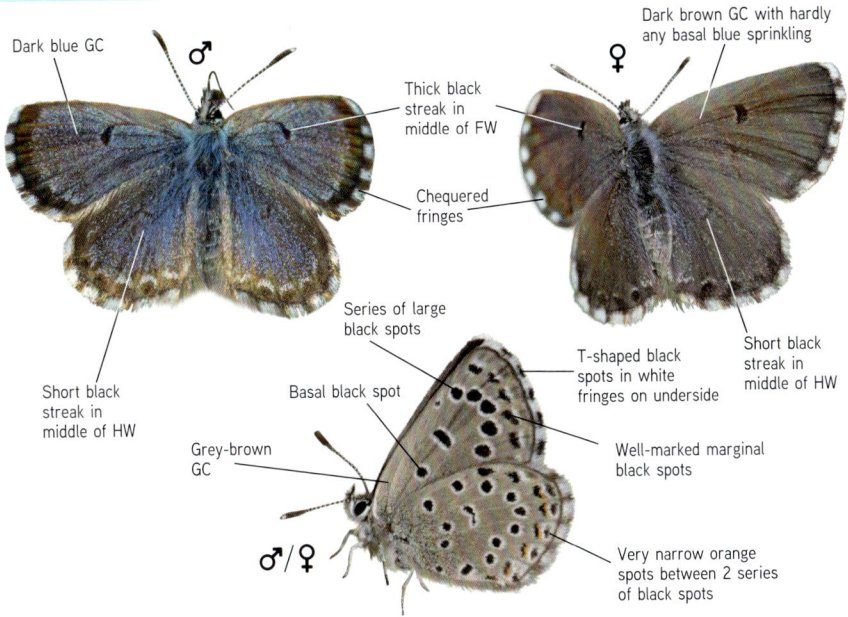

Dark blue GC

♂

Thick black streak in middle of FW

Chequered fringes

Dark brown GC with hardly any basal blue sprinkling

♀

Short black streak in middle of HW

Short black streak in middle of HW

Series of large black spots

Basal black spot

Grey-brown GC

T-shaped black spots in white fringes on underside

Well-marked marginal black spots

Very narrow orange spots between 2 series of black spots

♂/♀

Wingspan: 18–22 mm

Habitat: Dry, flower-rich grasslands and Mediterranean regeneration areas.

Hibernating stage: Pupa.

Elevational range: Up to 1,500 m.

Egg-laying: Eggs are laid singly on LHP leaves and bracts.

Flight period: April and May.

Host plants: *Cleonia lusitanica* (Lamiaceae).

Diversity and systematics: Most populations belong to the nominate subspecies. Subspecies *amelia* is described from Portugal.

P. baton
P. vicrama
P. baton + P. vicrama
P. barbagiae
P. panoptes
P. panoptes + P. abencerragus
P. baton + P. panoptes
P. baton + P. abencerragus

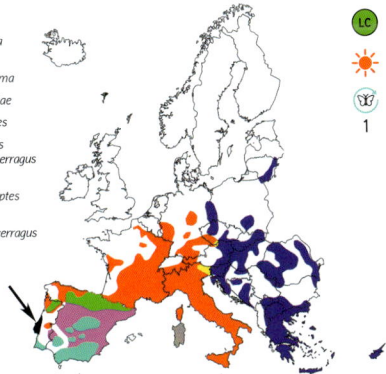

LC

1

	IMAGOS		LARVAE	
Food		Food		
Behaviour of males		Caterpillar location		
Dispersion		Chrysalis location		

Did you know?

False Baton Blue adults forage extensively on thyme and Asteraceae inflorescences.

PANOPTES BLUE *PSEUDOPHILOTES PANOPTES*

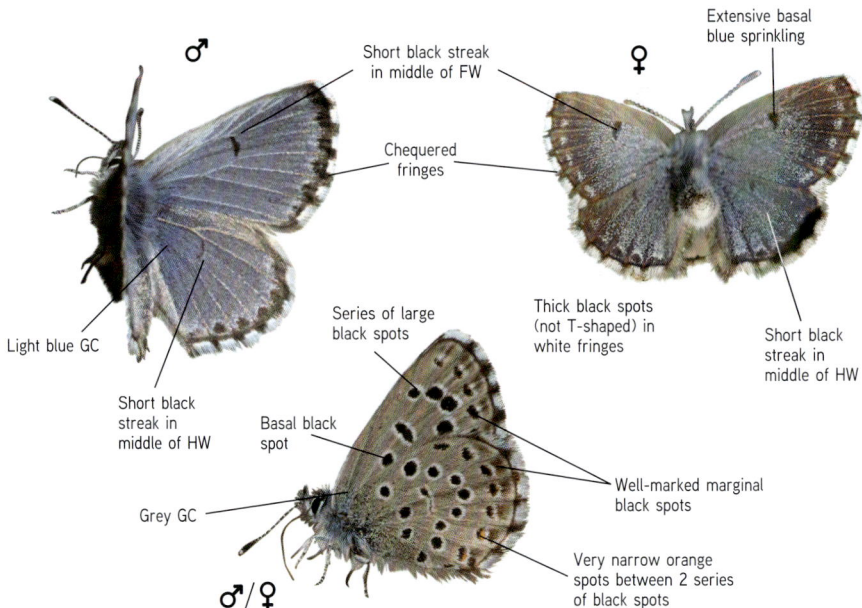

♂

Short black streak
in middle of FW

Chequered
fringes

♀

Extensive basal
blue sprinkling

Short black
streak in
middle of HW

Light blue GC

Short black
streak in
middle of HW

Basal black
spot

Series of large
black spots

Thick black spots
(not T-shaped) in
white fringes

Grey GC

♂/♀

Well-marked marginal
black spots

Very narrow orange
spots between 2 series
of black spots

Wingspan: 21–22 mm

Habitat: Sunny, rocky slopes covered with low-growing garrigue.

Hibernating stage: Pupa.

Elevational range: Between 500 and 2,000 m.

Egg-laying: Eggs are laid singly on LHP leaves.

Flight period: From March to June.

Host plants: Lamiaceae in genus *Thymus*, especially *T. mastichina*, *T. zygis*, *T. orospedanus*, *T. vulgaris*, *T. hyemalis*, and *T. granatensis*.

Diversity and systematics: There are no notable subspecies for this blue, which is endemic to the Iberian Peninsula.

P. baton
P. vicrama
P. baton
+ P. vicrama
P. barbagiae
P. panoptes
P. panoptes
+ P. abencerragus
P. baton
+ P. panoptes
P. baton
+ P. abencerragus

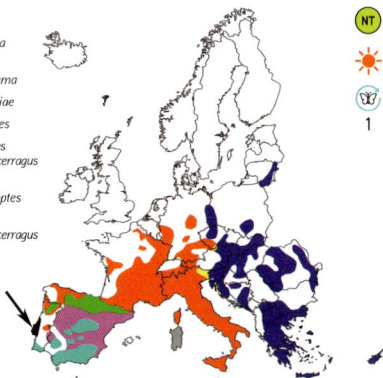

NT

1

IMAGOS		LARVAE	
Food		Food	
Behaviour of males		Caterpillar location	
Dispersion		Chrysalis location	

Did you know?

Panoptes Blue adults like to forage on lavender and LHP flowers.

LYCAENIDAE

BATON BLUE *PSEUDOPHILOTES BATON*

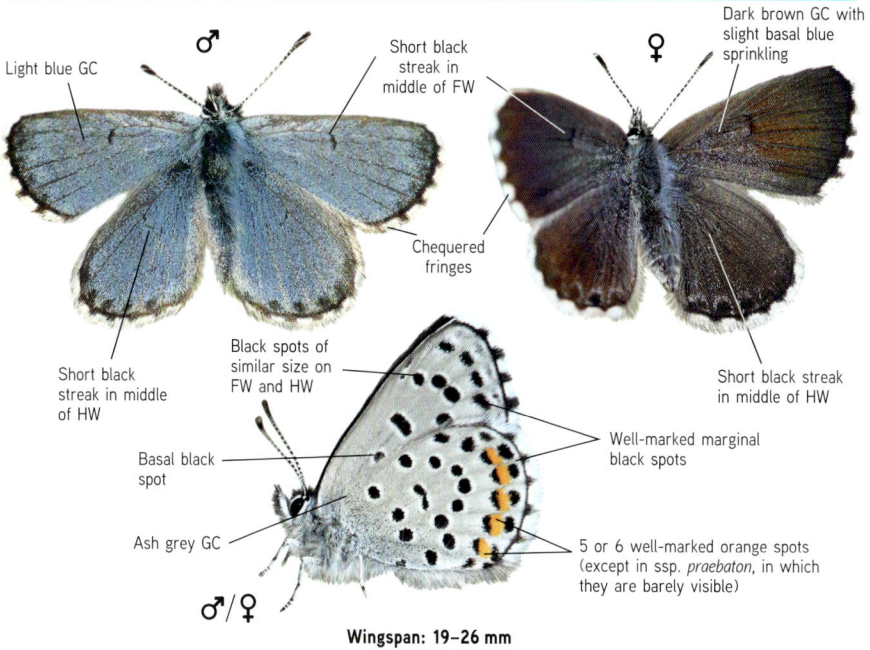

♂

Light blue GC

Short black streak in middle of FW

♀

Dark brown GC with slight basal blue sprinkling

Chequered fringes

Short black streak in middle of HW

Black spots of similar size on FW and HW

Short black streak in middle of HW

Basal black spot

Well-marked marginal black spots

Ash grey GC

5 or 6 well-marked orange spots (except in ssp. *praebaton*, in which they are barely visible)

♂/♀

Wingspan: 19–26 mm

Habitat: Dry grasslands, garrigue, heaths, and sunny, rocky slopes.

Hibernating stage: Pupa.

Elevational range: Up to 2,000 m.

Egg-laying: Eggs are laid singly on LHP inflorescences.

Flight period: From April to August.

Host plants: Lamiaceae, including *Lavandula angustifolia*, *L. latifolia*, *L. stoechas*, *Mentha arvensis*, *M. longifolia*, *M. suaveolens*, *Satureja hortensis*, *S. montana*, *Thymus nitens*, *T. serpyllum*, *T. vulgaris*, *T. pulegioides*, and *T. praecox*.

Diversity and systematics: Most populations belong to the nominate subspecies. Subspecies *occidentalis* flies in Portugal. Subspecies *albonotata* is found in Spain, while subspecies *praebaton* is present in the Eastern Pyrenees.

- ■ P. baton
- ■ P. vicrama
- ■ P. baton + P. vicrama
- ■ P. barbagiae
- ■ P. panoptes
- ■ P. panoptes + P. abencerragus
- ■ P. baton + P. panoptes
- ■ P. baton + P. abencerragus

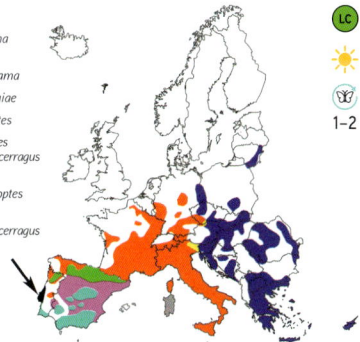

LC

1–2

Did you know?

Like many other species, the Baton Blue is a victim of the loss of dry grasslands, especially in the northern part of its range, which is severely affected by the decline of pastoral activities.

IMAGOS		LARVAE	
Food		Food	
Behaviour of males		Caterpillar location	
Dispersion		Chrysalis location	

LYCAENIDAE

EASTERN BATON BLUE *PSEUDOPHILOTES VICRAMA*

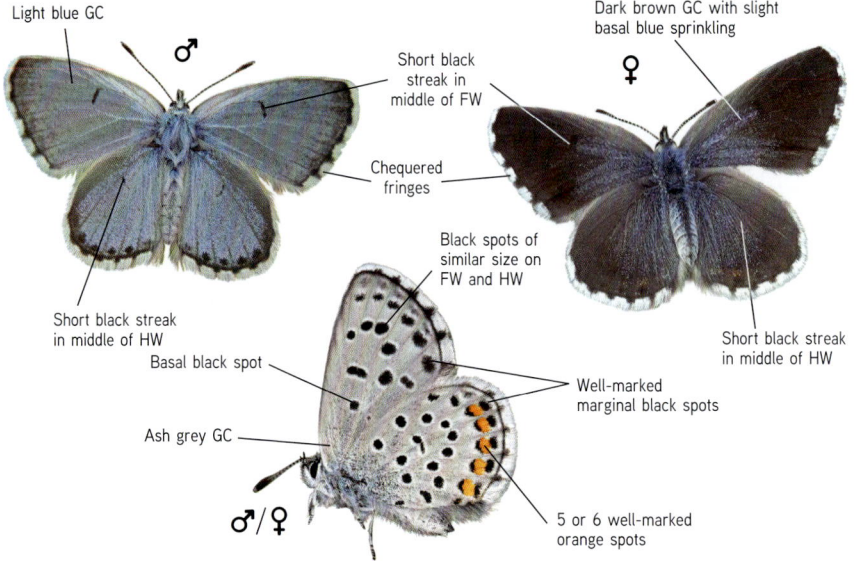

Light blue GC

♂

Short black streak in middle of FW

Dark brown GC with slight basal blue sprinkling

♀

Chequered fringes

Black spots of similar size on FW and HW

Short black streak in middle of HW

Basal black spot

Ash grey GC

Well-marked marginal black spots

Short black streak in middle of HW

♂/♀

5 or 6 well-marked orange spots

Wingspan: 19–26 mm

Habitat: Stony, dry grasslands, low-growing meadows, heaths, and maquis with vegetation-free areas.

Hibernating stage: Pupa.

Elevational range: Up to 2,000 m.

Egg-laying: Eggs are laid singly on LHP flower buds.

Flight period: From May to August.

Host plants: Lamiaceae, including *Thymus calcareus*, *T. longicaulis*, *T. pallasianus*, *T. praecox*, *T. pulegioides*, *T. serpyllum*, *T. glabrescens*, *Clinopodium nepeta*, *Hyssopus officinalis*, *Mentha spicata*, *Satureja montana*, *S. thymbra*, and *Rosmarinum officinalis*. Also reported on a few legumes, like *Melilotus officinalis* and *Securigera varia*.

Diversity and systematics: European populations belong to subspecies *schiffermuelleri*.

■ P. baton
■ P. vicrama
■ P. baton + P. vicrama
■ P. barbagiae
■ P. panoptes
■ P. panoptes + P. abencerragus
■ P. baton + P. panoptes
■ P. baton + P. abencerragus

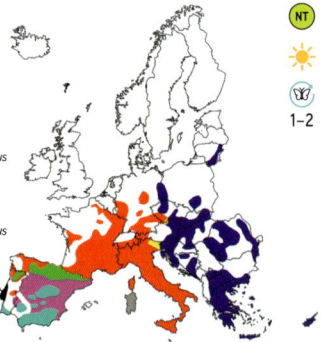

NT

1–2

Did you know?

The Eastern Baton Blue replaces the Baton Blue in Eastern Europe. In the narrow contact zone, only the examination of the genitalia allows for the reliable differentiation of these two vicariant species.

	IMAGOS		LARVAE	
Food	✿	Food	✿	
Behaviour of males		Caterpillar location		
Dispersion		Chrysalis location		

LYCAENIDAE

BAVIUS BLUE *PSEUDOPHILOTES BAVIUS*

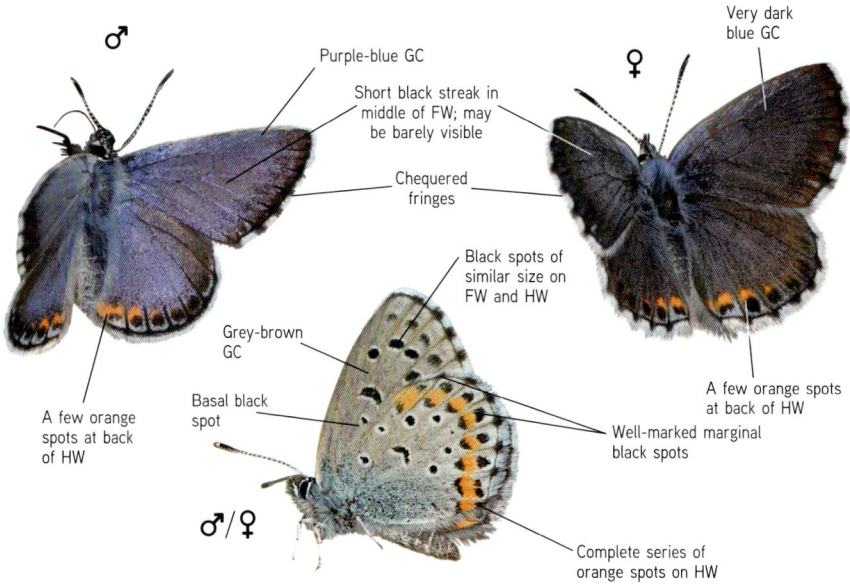

♂

Purple-blue GC

Short black streak in middle of FW; may be barely visible

Chequered fringes

Very dark blue GC

♀

Black spots of similar size on FW and HW

Grey-brown GC

Basal black spot

A few orange spots at back of HW

A few orange spots at back of HW

Well-marked marginal black spots

♂/♀

Complete series of orange spots on HW

Wingspan: 24–30 mm

Habitat: Dry grasslands and stony meadows within scrubby areas.

Hibernating stage: Pupa.

Elevational range: Up to 1,500 m.

Egg-laying: Eggs are laid singly on LHP flower buds.

Flight period: From April to June.

Host plants: Lamiaceae in genus *Salvia*, including *S. nutans*, *S. verbenaca*, *S. verticillata*, *S. officinalis*, *S. nemorosa*, and *S. transsylvanica*.

Diversity and systematics: European populations belong to different subspecies distinct from the nominate subspecies. Subspecies *hungaricus* flies in Transylvania. Subspecies *macedonicus* populates Macedonia and northern Greece. Subspecies *casimiri* is found in the Peloponnese, and subspecies *egea* flies in Dobruja.

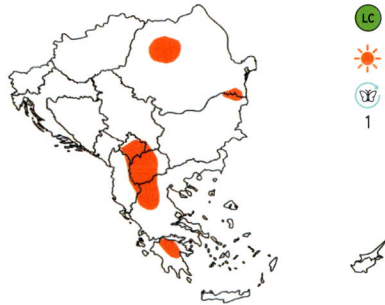

IMAGOS		LARVAE		
Food		Food		
Behaviour of males		Caterpillar location		
Dispersion		Chrysalis location		

Did you know?

Caterpillars of the Bavius Blue can be either pink or green. The pink ones are remarkably camouflaged when resting on the calyces of the host plant, while the green ones blend in more effectively on the leaves.

279

LYCAENIDAE

CHEQUERED BLUE *SCOLITANTIDES ORION*

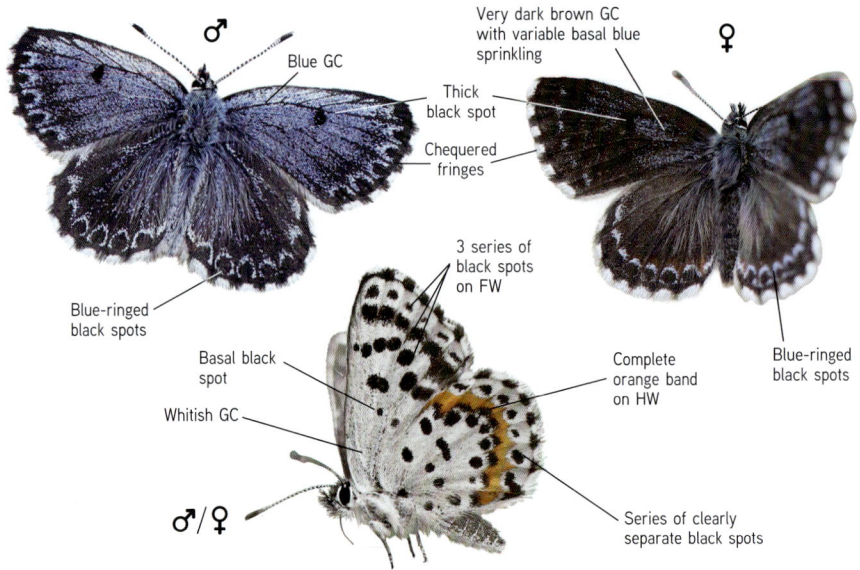

♂

Blue GC

Very dark brown GC
with variable basal blue
sprinkling

♀

Thick
black spot

Chequered
fringes

Blue-ringed
black spots

3 series of
black spots
on FW

Basal black
spot

Complete
orange band
on HW

Blue-ringed
black spots

Whitish GC

♂/♀

Series of clearly
separate black spots

Wingspan: 20–30 mm

Habitat: Rocky environments at pioneer successional stages where the LHPs grow, such as quarries, scree, sunny road edges, and cliff bases.

Hibernating stage: Pupa.

Elevational range: Up to 2,000 m (mostly below 1,000 m).

Egg-laying: Eggs are laid singly on LHP leaves.

Flight period: From April to August.

Host plants: Crassulaceae, including *Hylotelephium telephium*, *H. ewersii*, *H. maximum*, *Petrosedum sediforme*, *Phedimus aizoon*, *S. album*, *S. acre*, and *S. hispanicum*.

Diversity and systematics: Most European populations belong to the nominate subspecies. Subspecies *parvula* and *rosarioi* fly in Catalonia and northern Spain, respectively. Subspecies *ultraornata* is found in Scandinavia. Subspecies *micrometioche* flies in Italy.

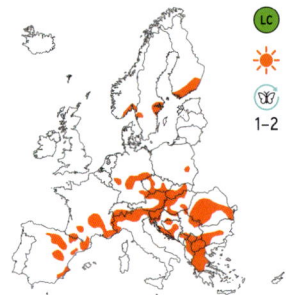

LC

1–2

Did you know?

The Chequered Blue benefits from disturbances that expose the bedrock on which its host plants grow. Its favourable habitats are inherently temporary and fragmented; its dispersal is crucial for the maintenance of its metapopulations.

IMAGOS			LARVAE		
Food			Food		
Behaviour of males			Caterpillar location		
Dispersion			Chrysalis location		

LYCAENIDAE

GREEN-UNDERSIDE BLUE *GLAUCOPSYCHE ALEXIS*

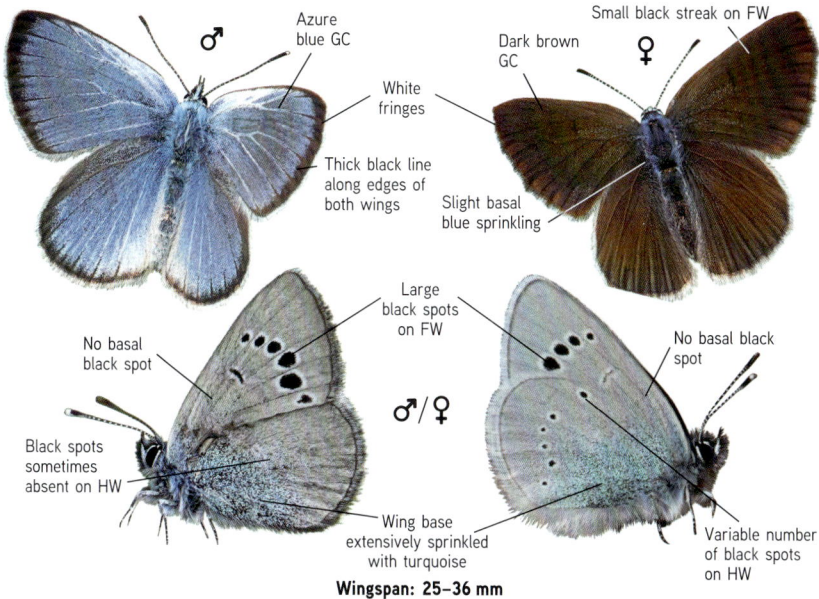

Azure blue GC

♂

White fringes

Thick black line along edges of both wings

Dark brown GC

Small black streak on FW

♀

Slight basal blue sprinkling

Large black spots on FW

No basal black spot

Black spots sometimes absent on HW

♂/♀

No basal black spot

Wing base extensively sprinkled with turquoise

Variable number of black spots on HW

Wingspan: 25–36 mm

Habitat: Open and scrubby environments, dry grasslands, bushy meadows, heaths, and edges.

Hibernating stage: Pupa.

Elevational range: Up to 2,000 m.

Egg-laying: Eggs are laid singly on LHP inflorescences.

Flight period: From March to July.

Host plants: A wide variety of legumes, including *Onobrychis viciifolia, O. ebenoides, O. alba, O. humilis, O. montana, O. saxatilis, O. supina, Medicago sativa, Securigera varia, Vicia cracca, V. sepium, V. tenuifolia, V. villosa, Melilotus albus, M. elegans, M. officinalis, Lathyrus niger, L. pratensis, Lotus corniculatus, L. dorycnium, Bituminaria bituminosa, Galega officinalis, Anthyllis vulneraria, Astragalus glycyphyllos, A. onobrychis, Genista acanthoclada, G. cinerea, G. florida, G. germanica, G. tinctoria, Hedysarum boveanum,* and *Spartium junceum.*

Diversity and systematics: Many subspecies have been described, including *pauperella, melconi,* and *velada,* which fly in Spain. Subspecies *mironi* is found in Greece. Subspecies *subpauper* flies in France, while subspecies *latina* flies in Italy.

- ■ G. alexis
- ■ G. alexis + G. melanops
- ■ G. melanops
- ■ G. paphos

Did you know?

The Green-underside Blue is part of the extensive group of species threatened by pastoral abandonment, which leads to the loss of the grasslands it thrives in.

IMAGOS		LARVAE	
Food	🌸🛖💧	Food	🌸🍃
Behaviour of males	🦋	Caterpillar location	🌿🌱🐜
Dispersion	💫	Chrysalis location	🪵

LYCAENIDAE

BLACK-EYED BLUE *GLAUCOPSYCHE MELANOPS*

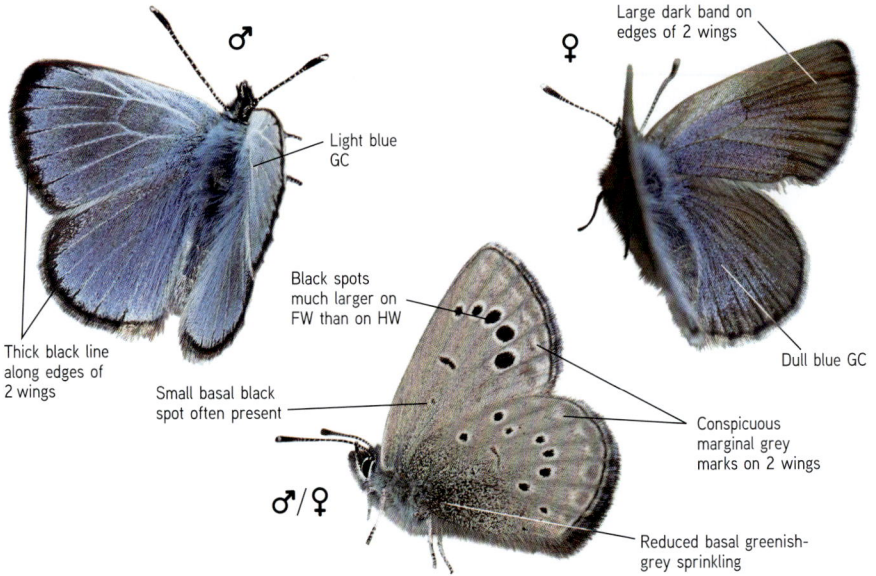

♂

Large dark band on edges of 2 wings

♀

Light blue GC

Black spots much larger on FW than on HW

Thick black line along edges of 2 wings

Dull blue GC

Small basal black spot often present

Conspicuous marginal grey marks on 2 wings

♂/♀

Reduced basal greenish-grey sprinkling

Wingspan: 22–32 mm

Habitat: Dry grasslands, garrigues, and low-growing maquis.

Hibernating stage: Pupa.

Elevational range: Up to 2,000 m.

Egg-laying: Eggs are laid singly on LHP inflorescences.

Flight period: From March to May.

Host plants: Legumes, including *Lotus dorycnium*, *L. hispidus*, *Genista cinerea*, *G. hirsuta*, *Ononis atlantica*, *Spartium junceum*, *Adenocarpus anagyrifolius*, and *Anthyllis cytisoides*.

Diversity and systematics: Many subspecies have been described in the Iberian Peninsula. Subspecies *algirica* flies in southern Spain. Subspecies *williamsi* is found in Spain and Portugal. Subspecies *diversa*, *bamba*, *cantabra*, *arcasi*, *justoi*, and *loechenis* also fly in Spain.

G. alexis
G. melanops
G. alexis + G. melanops
G. paphos

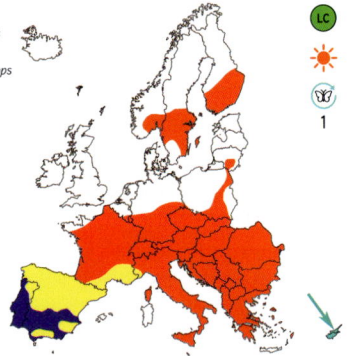

LC

1

IMAGOS		LARVAE	
Food		Food	
Behaviour of males		Caterpillar location	
Dispersion		Chrysalis location	

Did you know?

The species scientific name, *melanops*, means "black eyes" and refers to the large, round black spots that this blue displays under the forewing.

LYCAENIDAE

PAPHOS BLUE *GLAUCOPSYCHE PAPHOS*

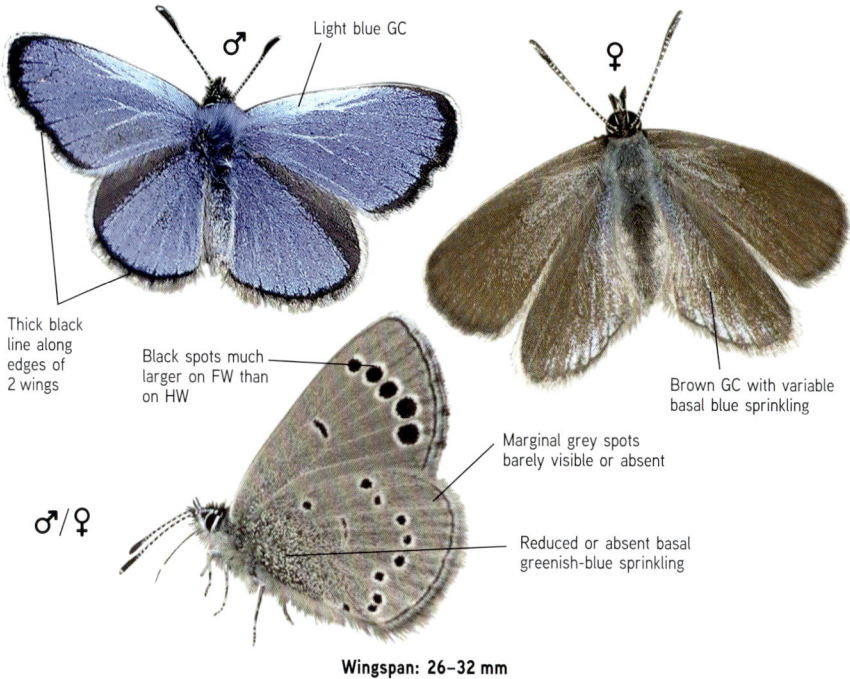

♂   Light blue GC

♀

Thick black line along edges of 2 wings

Black spots much larger on FW than on HW

Brown GC with variable basal blue sprinkling

Marginal grey spots barely visible or absent

♂/♀

Reduced or absent basal greenish-blue sprinkling

Wingspan: 26–32 mm

Habitat: Garrigues.

Hibernating stage: Pupa.

Elevational range: Up to 1,500 m.

Egg-laying: Eggs are laid singly on LHP inflorescences.

Flight period: From February to July.

Host plants: *Genista fasselata* (Fabaceae).

Diversity and systematics: There are no notable subspecies for this blue, which is endemic to Cyprus.

G. alexis
G. melanops
G. alexis + G. melanops
G. paphos

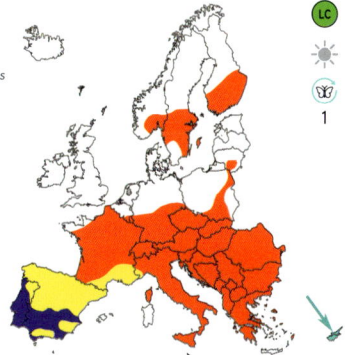

LC

1

IMAGOS		LARVAE	
Food	✰	Food	✰
Behaviour of males		Caterpillar location	
Dispersion: unknown		Chrysalis location	

Did you know?

The caterpillars are tended by *Tapinoma simrothi* ants. These ants also guard the pupa.

LYCAENIDAE

IOLAS BLUE/ORANIAN BLUE
IOLANA IOLAS/IOLANA DEBILITATA

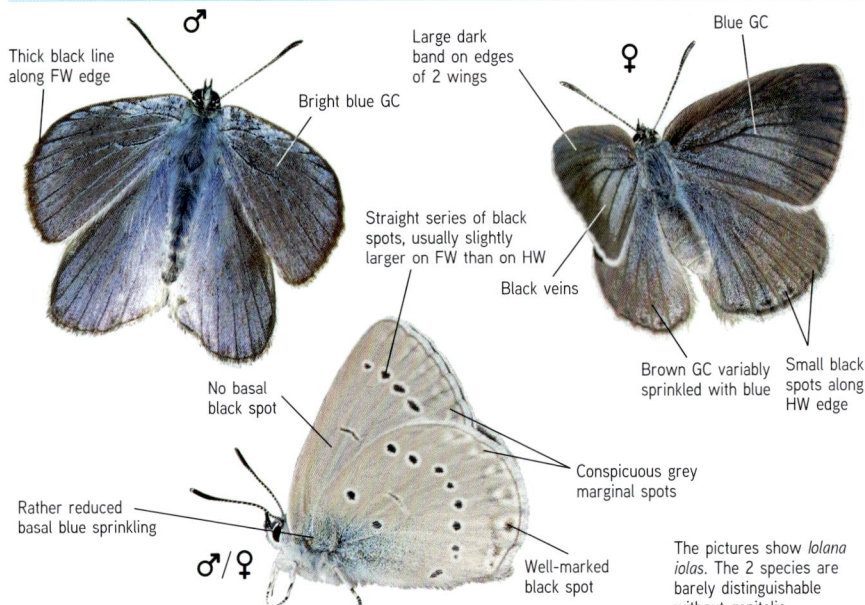

♂

Thick black line along FW edge

Bright blue GC

Large dark band on edges of 2 wings

Blue GC

♀

Straight series of black spots, usually slightly larger on FW than on HW

Black veins

No basal black spot

Rather reduced basal blue sprinkling

♂/♀

Conspicuous grey marginal spots

Brown GC variably sprinkled with blue

Small black spots along HW edge

Well-marked black spot

The pictures show *Iolas iolas*. The 2 species are barely distinguishable without genitalia examination.

Wingspan: 36–42 mm

Habitat: Warm, scrubby edges, clear woodlands, and thickets where the LHP grows.

Hibernating stage: Pupa.

Elevational range: Up to 1,500 m.

Egg-laying: Eggs are laid singly on LHP flower calyces.

Flight period: From April to July.

Host plants: Woody legumes in genus *Colutea*: *C. arborescens* for *Iolana iolas*, and *C. atlantica* and *C. arborescens* for *I. debilitata*.

Diversity and systematics: The status of the Oranian Blue is debated. It is sometimes considered a subspecies of the Iolas Blue, with which it differs little morphologically (the genitalia differ). Regarding the Iolas Blue, the nominate subspecies forms the eastern and southeastern populations in the European range. According to a recent study, subspecies *wulschlegeli* (flying in Switzerland, northern Italy, and southern France) and subspecies *protogenes* (from southern France) are synonymized. *Iolana debilitata* flies in Spain (subspecies *farriolsi* with some degree of variation).

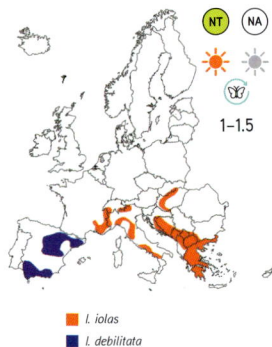

NT NA

1–1.5

■ *I. iolas*
■ *I. debilitata*

IMAGOS		LARVAE	
Food		Food	
Behaviour of males		Caterpillar location	
Dispersion		Chrysalis location	

Did you know?

The Iolas Blue spends the entire larval stage (excluding the pupa) inside the swollen pods of the Bladder-senna.

LYCAENIDAE

MAZARINE BLUE *CYANIRIS SEMIARGUS*

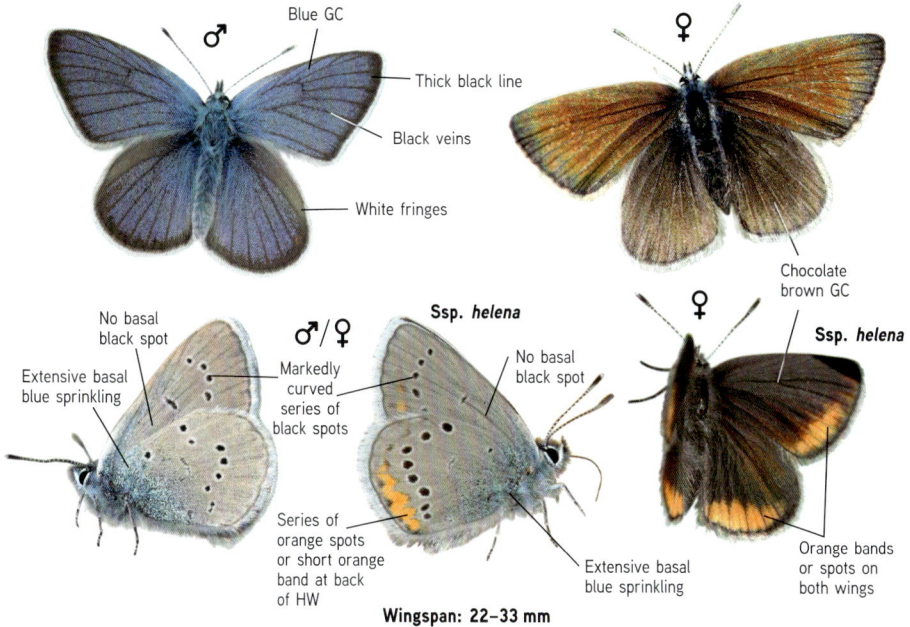

♂ Blue GC

Thick black line

Black veins

White fringes

♀

Chocolate brown GC

No basal black spot

Extensive basal blue sprinkling

♂/♀

Markedly curved series of black spots

Ssp. *helena*

No basal black spot

Ssp. *helena*

Series of orange spots or short orange band at back of HW

Extensive basal blue sprinkling

Orange bands or spots on both wings

Wingspan: 22–33 mm

Habitat: Mesophilic meadows and subalpine grasslands.

Hibernating stage: Caterpillar.

Elevational range: Up to 2,500 m.

Egg-laying: Eggs are laid singly on LHP inflorescences.

Flight period: From April to October.

Host plants: Herbaceous legumes, mainly clovers, like *Trifolium pratense, T. repens, T. badium, T. ochroleucon, T. medium, T. alpestre, T. physodes, T. pignantii,* and *T. heldreichianum*. Also *Onobrychis viciifolia, Anthyllis vulneraria, A. montana,* and *Lotus corniculatus.* Locally reported on *Armeria alpina, A. canescens, A. maritima, A. ruscinonensis,* and *A. velutina* (Plumbaginaceae).

Diversity and systematics: Most European populations belong to the nominate subspecies. Subspecies *helena* flies in southern Greece. Subspecies *parnassia* inhabits the north. Subspecies *savoiensis* is found in the Alps. Subspecies *transiens* and *tartessus* fly in the central-west and south of Spain, respectively.

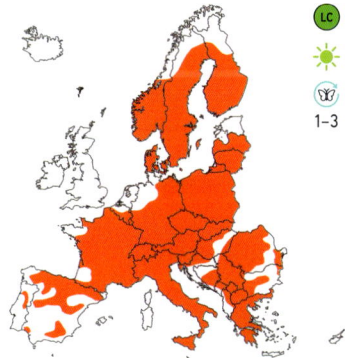

LC

1–3

Did you know?

The Mazarine Blue disappeared from England in the early 20th century, possibly due to gradual changes in agricultural practices leading to the early cutting of meadows for hay production.

IMAGOS				LARVAE			
Food				Food			
Behaviour of males				Caterpillar location			
Dispersion				Chrysalis location			

LYCAENIDAE

PONTIC BLUE *NEOLYSANDRA COELESTINA*

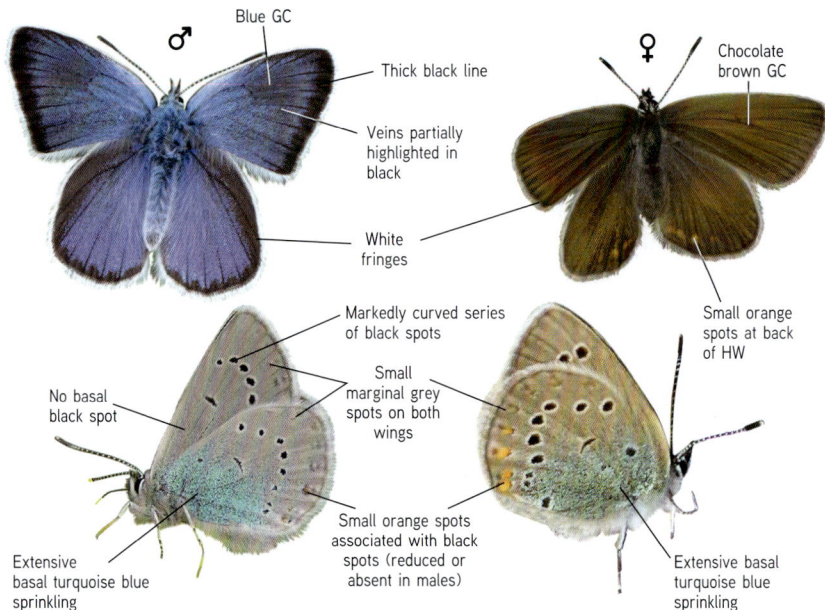

♂ Blue GC

Thick black line

Veins partially highlighted in black

White fringes

♀ Chocolate brown GC

Markedly curved series of black spots

Small marginal grey spots on both wings

No basal black spot

Small orange spots at back of HW

Extensive basal turquoise blue sprinkling

Small orange spots associated with black spots (reduced or absent in males)

Extensive basal turquoise blue sprinkling

Wingspan: 22–26 mm

Habitat: Stony, steppic slopes.

Hibernating stage: Caterpillar.

Elevational range: Between 500 and 2,000 m.

Egg-laying: Eggs are laid singly on the LHP.

Flight period: From May to June.

Host plants: *Vicia dalmatica* and *V. tenuifolia* (Fabaceae).

Diversity and systematics: European populations belong to subspecies *hera*.

LC

1

	IMAGOS		LARVAE		Did you know?
Food		Food			Due to the requirements of its LHPs, the Pontic Blue is a calcicolous species.
Behaviour of males		Caterpillar location			
Dispersion		Chrysalis location			

LYCAENIDAE

PROVENÇAL SHORT-TAILED BLUE *CUPIDO ALCETAS*

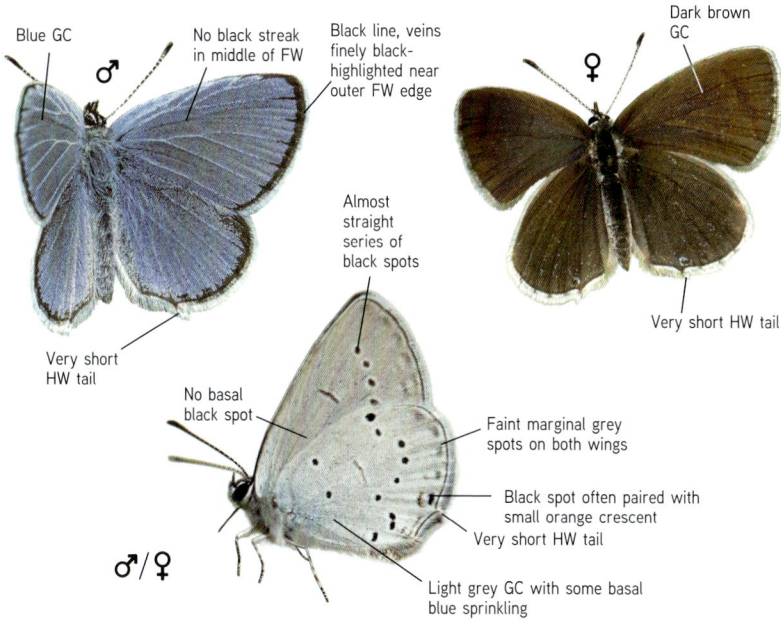

Blue GC

♂

No black streak in middle of FW

Black line, veins finely black-highlighted near outer FW edge

Dark brown GC

♀

Almost straight series of black spots

Very short HW tail

Very short HW tail

No basal black spot

♂/♀

Faint marginal grey spots on both wings

Black spot often paired with small orange crescent

Very short HW tail

Light grey GC with some basal blue sprinkling

Wingspan: 26–32 mm

Habitat: Mesophilic and damp meadows, grassy woodland clearings and edges, sometimes in dryer grasslands.

Hibernating stage: Caterpillar.

Elevational range: Up to 1,500 m (more abundant at lower elevations).

Egg-laying: Eggs are laid singly on LHP inflorescences.

Flight period: From April to October.

Host plants: Small herbaceous legumes, such as *Medicago lupulina, M. minima, Securigera varia, Vicia sativa, V. cracca, V. dumetorum, Lotus corniculatus, Trifolium pratense, Lathyrus latifolius, Galega officinalis,* and *Colutea arborescens.*

Diversity and systematics: European populations belong to the nominate subspecies.

- C. alcetas
- C. decolarata
- C. alcetas + C. decolarata

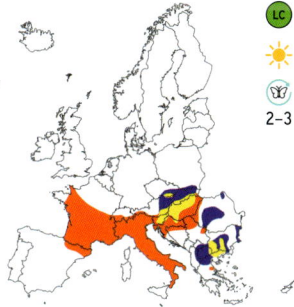

LC

2-3

Did you know?

Caterpillars of the *Cupido* genus overwinter as mature larvae. Therefore, they do not feed in spring between their emergence from diapause and their pupation.

IMAGOS		LARVAE	
Food		Food	
Behaviour of males		Caterpillar location	
Dispersion		Chrysalis location	

EASTERN SHORT-TAILED BLUE *CUPIDO DECOLORATA*

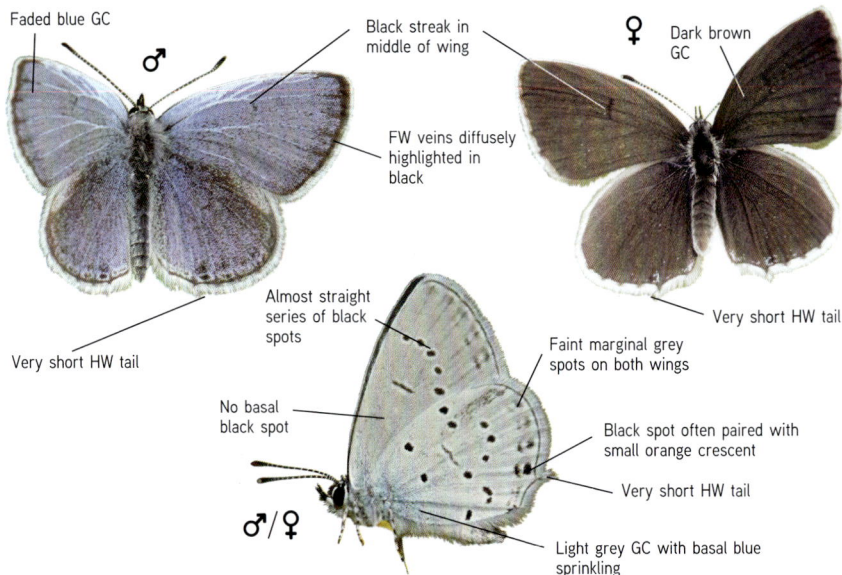

Faded blue GC

♂

Black streak in middle of wing

♀

Dark brown GC

FW veins diffusely highlighted in black

Almost straight series of black spots

Faint marginal grey spots on both wings

Very short HW tail

Very short HW tail

No basal black spot

Black spot often paired with small orange crescent

♂/♀

Very short HW tail

Light grey GC with basal blue sprinkling

Wingspan: 24–26 mm

Habitat: Flower-rich mesophilic meadows and woodland clearings.

Hibernating stage: Caterpillar.

Elevational range: Up to 1,000 m.

Egg-laying: Eggs are laid singly on LHP inflorescences.

Flight period: From May to September.

Host plants: Legumes in genus *Medicago* – above all, *M. lupulina* and *M. sativa*.

Diversity and systematics: There are no notable subspecies for this Central European blue, which has rather localized populations.

■ *C. alcetas*
■ *C. decolorata*
■ *C. alcetas*
   + *C. decolorata*

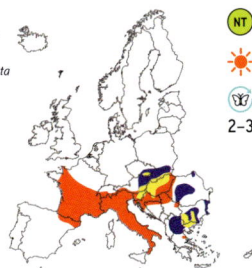

NT

2–3

Did you know?

The scientific name of the species refers to the blue colour of the male wings, which is less pronounced than in the Provençal Short-tailed Blue. However, wear can diminish this difference, and the distinction between the two species can be challenging in Central Europe, where they may fly together.

IMAGOS			LARVAE	
Food	🌼		Food	🌼
Behaviour of males			Caterpillar location	
Dispersion			Chrysalis location	

LYCAENIDAE

SMALL BLUE/CARSWELL'S SMALL BLUE   *CUPIDO MINIMUS/C. CARSWELLI*

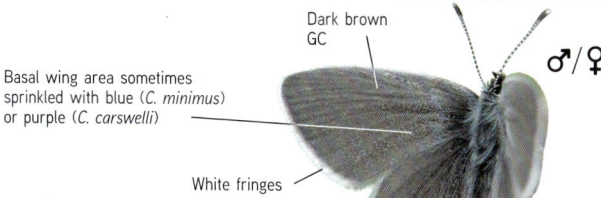

Dark brown
GC

♂/♀

Basal wing area sometimes
sprinkled with blue (*C. minimus*)
or purple (*C. carswelli*)

White fringes

Cupido minimus

Cupido carswelli

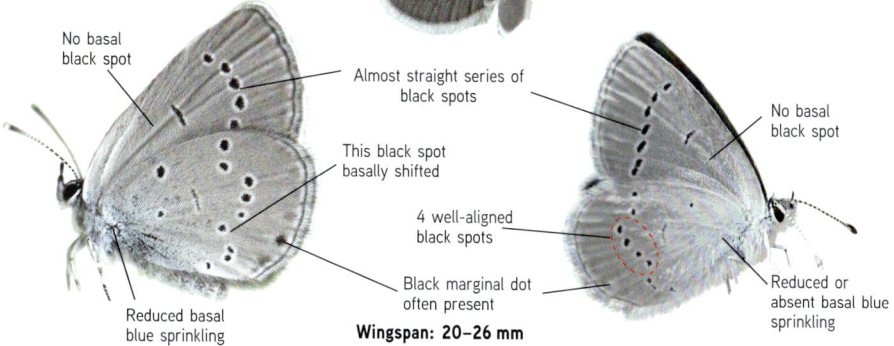

No basal
black spot

Almost straight series of
black spots

No basal
black spot

This black spot
basally shifted

4 well-aligned
black spots

Reduced or
absent basal blue
sprinkling

Black marginal dot
often present

Reduced basal
blue sprinkling

Wingspan: 20–26 mm

Habitat: Dry grasslands and mesophilic meadows for *Cupido minimus*. Dry and stony Mediterranean montane grasslands for *C. carswelli*.

Hibernating stage: Caterpillar.

Elevational range: Up to 2,500 m for *Cupido minimus*; between 1,000 and 1,800 m for *C. carswelli*.

Egg-laying: Eggs are laid singly on LHP inflorescences.

Flight period: From April to June for *Cupido carswelli*; until September for *C. minimus*.

Host plants: *Cupido minimus* mainly uses *Anthyllis vulneraria*, but also *Astragalus alpinus, A. australis, A. cicer, A. glycyphyllos, A. penduliflorus, Colutea arborescens, Coronilla juncea, Oxytropis campestris, O. halleri, O. montana,* and *Onobrychis supina.* For *C. carswelli, Anthyllis vulneraria.*

Diversity and systematics: Most European *Cupido minimus* populations belong to the nominate subspecies. Populations in Sicily form subspecies *trinacriae.* Subspecies *noguerae* and *latecaerulea* are described from the Sierra Nevada and Italy, respectively. Subspecies *alsoides* flies at high altitudes in the Alps. There is no notable subspecies for *C. carswelli.*

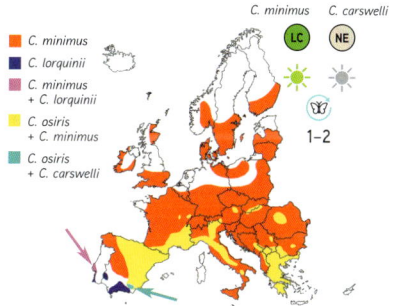

C. minimus   C. carswelli

- 🟧 *C. minimus*
- 🟦 *C. lorquinii*
- 🟪 *C. minimus + C. lorquinii*
- 🟨 *C. osiris + C. minimus*
- 🟩 *C. osiris + C. carswelli*

LC   NE

1–2

Did you know?

The species status of Carswell's Small Blue is debated; some consider it a subspecies of the Small Blue. The pupae are different; that of Carswell's Small Blue is closer to that of Lorquin's Blue (*Cupido lorquinii*). A phylogenetic study also concluded that it is more closely related to the latter.

IMAGOS			LARVAE	
Food	🌼 🐚 💧		Food	🌼
Behaviour of males	🌱		Caterpillar location	🌾 🐜
Dispersion	🦋		Chrysalis location	🪨

LYCAENIDAE

OSIRIS BLUE *CUPIDO OSIRIS*

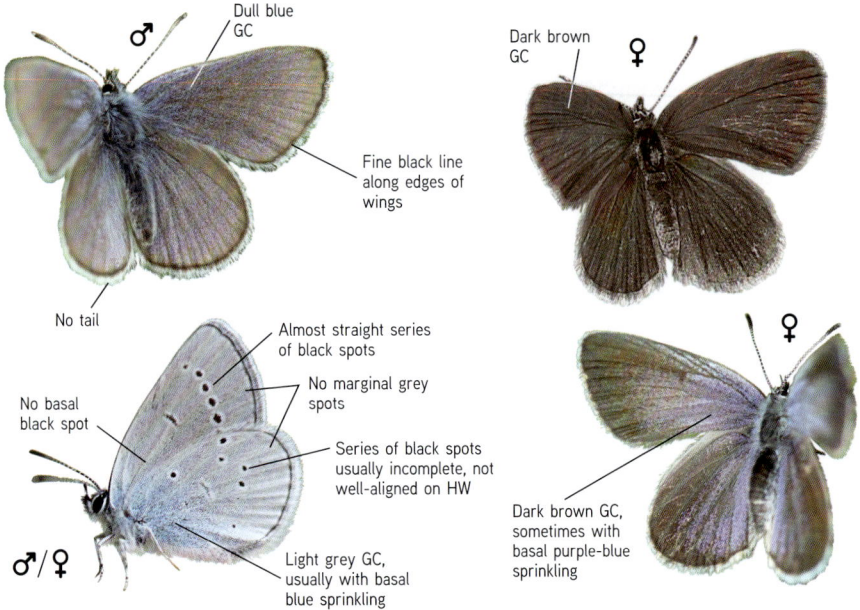

♂ Dull blue GC

Dark brown GC ♀

Fine black line along edges of wings

No tail

Almost straight series of black spots

No basal black spot

No marginal grey spots

Series of black spots usually incomplete, not well-aligned on HW

♂/♀

Light grey GC, usually with basal blue sprinkling

♀

Dark brown GC, sometimes with basal purple-blue sprinkling

Wingspan: 24–30 mm

Habitat: Mediterranean and montane dry grasslands; Common Sainfoin hay meadows.

Hibernating stage: Caterpillar.

Elevational range: Up to 2,500 m.

Egg-laying: Eggs are laid singly on LHP inflorescences.

Flight period: From April to September.

Host plants: Legumes, including *Onobrychis viciifolia, O. montana, O. saxatilis, O. supina, O. pindicola, O. alba, O. arenaria, O. ebenoides, Colutea arborescens*, and *Lathyrus linifolius*.

Diversity and systematics: Most populations belong to the nominate subspecies. Subspecies *pseudolorquinii* flies in Spain. Subspecies *saportae* inhabits the southeast of France and Italy. Subspecies *bernardiana* is found in the northern Alps, the Jura, and part of Burgundy.

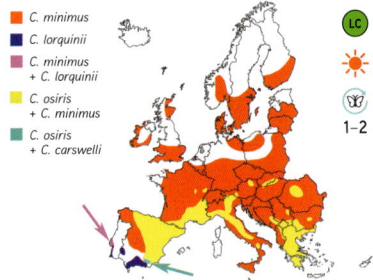

- C. minimus
- C. lorquinii
- C. minimus + C. lorquinii
- C. osiris + C. minimus
- C. osiris + C. carswelli

LC

1–2

Did you know?

The Osiris Blue has significantly declined and disappeared from several regions in the northern part of its range in France or Germany. It is thus undergoing the same fate as many species dependent on dry grasslands, which were once maintained through extensive grazing.

IMAGOS		LARVAE	
Food		Food	
Behaviour of males		Caterpillar location	
Dispersion		Chrysalis location	

LYCAENIDAE

LORQUIN'S BLUE *CUPIDO LORQUINII*

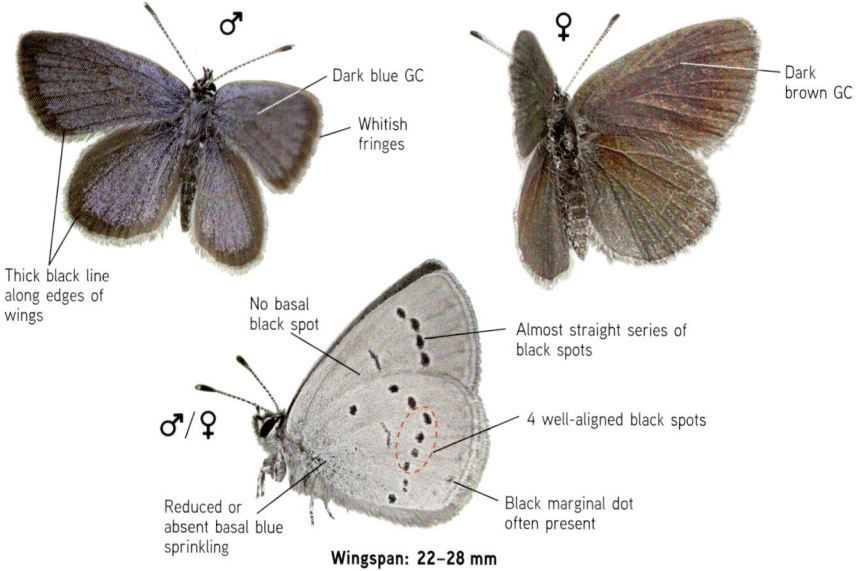

♂

Dark blue GC

Whitish fringes

Thick black line along edges of wings

♀

Dark brown GC

No basal black spot

Almost straight series of black spots

♂/♀

4 well-aligned black spots

Reduced or absent basal blue sprinkling

Black marginal dot often present

Wingspan: 22–28 mm

Habitat: Dry grasslands and scrubby, rocky slopes.

Hibernating stage: Caterpillar.

Elevational range: Up to 2,000 m.

Egg-laying: Eggs are laid singly on LHP inflorescences.

Flight period: From April to June.

Host plants: Legumes in genus *Anthyllis*, mainly *A. vulneraria*.

Diversity and systematics: There are no notable subspecies for this blue, which is present in the Iberian Peninsula and North Africa. *Cupido carswelli* could be a subspecies of *C. lorquinii*.

- C. minimus
- C. lorquinii
- C. minimus + C. lorquinii
- C. osiris + C. minimus
- C. osiris + C. carswelli

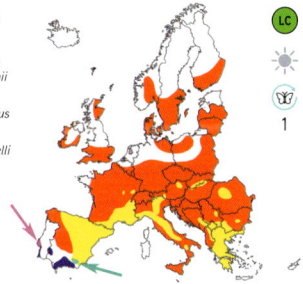

LC

1

Did you know?

In 2019, a study demonstrated that *Cupido carswelli* was genetically indistinguishable from *C. lorquinii*, although it was generally considered to be closer to *C. minimus*. The authors interpreted the difference in colour on the male forewings to be the result of a reproductive character displacement linked to sympatry with *C. osiris*. Thus, the brown males of *C. carswelli* would avoid costly hybridization with *C. osiris* females.

IMAGOS		LARVAE	
Food		Food	
Behaviour of males		Caterpillar location	
Dispersion		Chrysalis location	

LYCAENIDAE

SHORT-TAILED BLUE *CUPIDO ARGIADES*

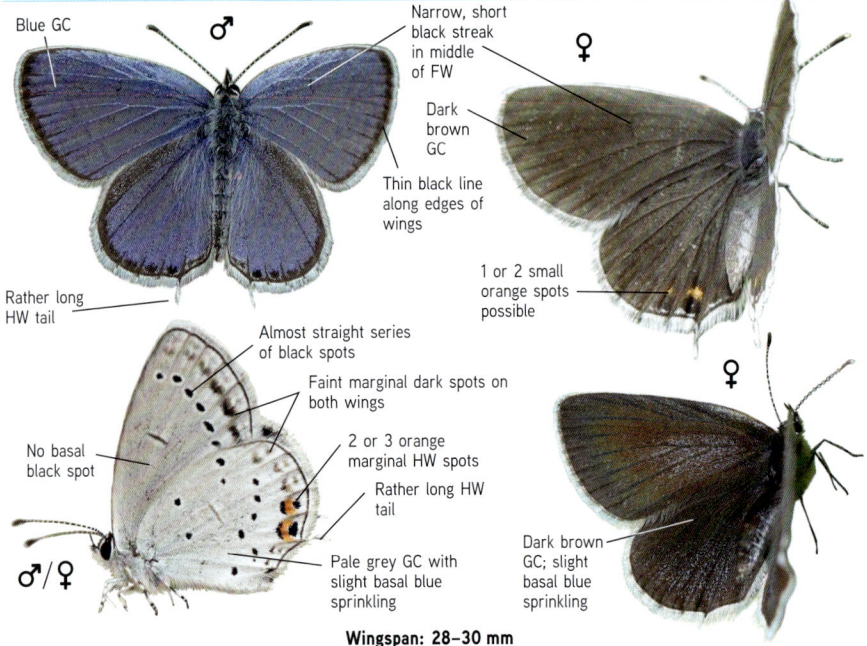

Blue GC

♂

Narrow, short black streak in middle of FW

♀

Dark brown GC

Thin black line along edges of wings

1 or 2 small orange spots possible

Rather long HW tail

Almost straight series of black spots

Faint marginal dark spots on both wings

No basal black spot

2 or 3 orange marginal HW spots

Rather long HW tail

♂/♀

Pale grey GC with slight basal blue sprinkling

♀

Dark brown GC; slight basal blue sprinkling

Wingspan: 28–30 mm

Habitat: Mesophilic or moderately damp meadows, clearings, and edges; grassy roadsides and ditches.

Hibernating stage: Caterpillar.

Elevational range: Up to 1,000 m.

Egg-laying: Eggs are laid singly on LHP inflorescences.

Flight period: From April to September.

Host plants: Numerous, mostly herbaceous legumes, including *Trifolium pratense*, *T. campestre*, *T. repens*, *Lotus corniculatus*, *L. pedunculatus*, *Lathyrus pratensis*, *L. latifolius*, *Medicago lupulina*, *M. sativa*, *M. minima*, *M. falcata*, *Melilotus albus*, *M. officinalis*, *Vicia cracca*, *V. sativa*, *V. villosa*, *Securigera varia*, *Ulex minor*, and *U. gallii*. Also reported on *Erica ciliaris* (Ericaceae).

Diversity and systematics: European populations of this blue, widespread across Asia, belong to the nominate subspecies.

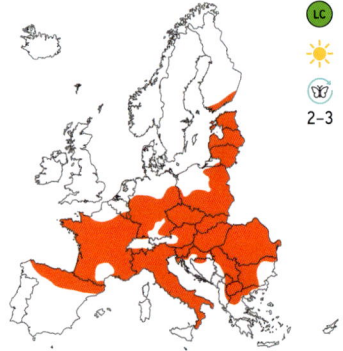

LC

2-3

IMAGOS		LARVAE	
Food		Food	
Behaviour of males		Caterpillar location	
Dispersion		Chrysalis location	

Did you know?

The Short-tailed Blue can colonize rural gardens as long as they are not mowed too frequently during the growing season, allowing its very common host plants to thrive.

LYCAENIDAE

LARGE BLUE *PHENGARIS ARION*

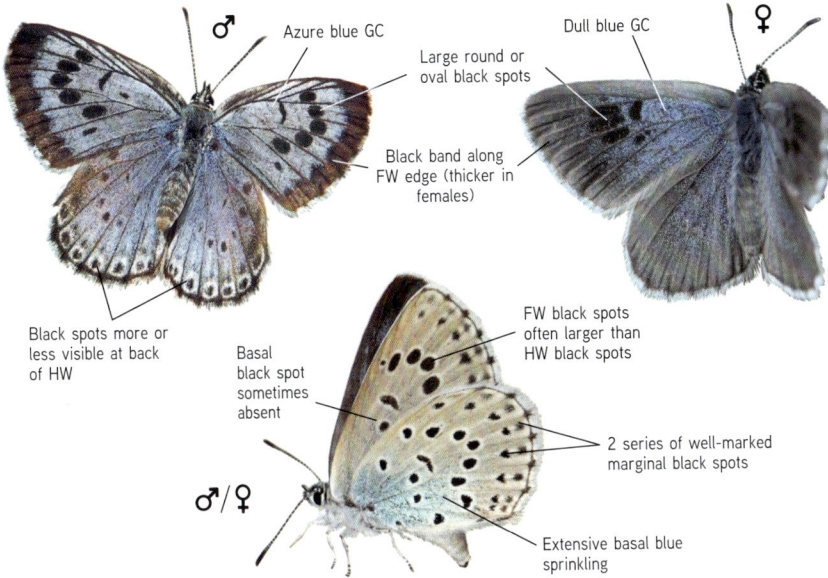

♂ Azure blue GC

Large round or oval black spots

Dull blue GC ♀

Black band along FW edge (thicker in females)

Black spots more or less visible at back of HW

Basal black spot sometimes absent

FW black spots often larger than HW black spots

2 series of well-marked marginal black spots

♂/♀

Extensive basal blue sprinkling

Wingspan: 29–39 mm

Habitat: Flower-rich, thermophilic grasslands and meadows; also montane areas.

Hibernating stage: Caterpillar.

Elevational range: Up to 2,500 m.

Egg-laying: Eggs are laid singly on LHP inflorescences.

Flight period: From May to August.

Host plants: Lamiaceae, including *Clinopodium vulgare*, *Origanum vulgare*, *Prunella hyssopifolia*, *Thymus leucotrichus*, *T. longicaulis*, *T. oenipontanus*, *T. praecox*, *T. pulegioides*, *T. serpyllum*, and *T. sibthorpii*.

Diversity and systematics: Most European populations belong to the nominate subspecies. Among the numerous described subspecies, *ligurica* flies from southeastern France to Italy. Subspecies *eutyphron* went extinct from the south of England, and subspecies *buholzeri* is found in Switzerland.

EN

1

Did you know?

After having disappeared from England in 1979, the Large Blue was successfully reintroduced. Efforts focus on both habitat conditions that favour the adults and the presence of *Myrmica sabuleti* ants, upon which the species critically depends.

IMAGOS		LARVAE	
Food	✿	Food	✿
Behaviour of males	🦋	Caterpillar location	
Dispersion	🦋	Chrysalis location	

SCARCE LARGE BLUE *PHENGARIS TELEIUS*

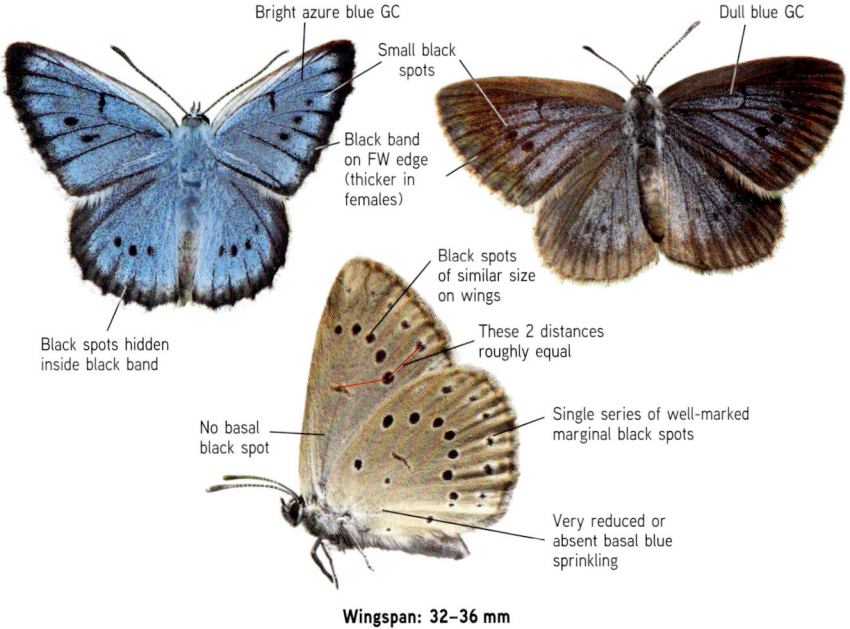

Bright azure blue GC

Small black spots

Dull blue GC

Black band on FW edge (thicker in females)

Black spots of similar size on wings

Black spots hidden inside black band

These 2 distances roughly equal

No basal black spot

Single series of well-marked marginal black spots

Very reduced or absent basal blue sprinkling

Wingspan: 32–36 mm

Habitat: Damp meadows and bog surroundings.

Hibernating stage: Caterpillar.

Elevational range: Up to 1,500 m.

Egg-laying: Eggs are laid singly or in a few units on LHP inflorescences.

Flight period: From June to August.

Host plants: *Sanguisorba officinalis* (Rosaceae).

Diversity and systematics: Most European populations belong to the nominate subspecies. Subspecies *macromelanica* flies in Italy, and subspecies *discoobsoleta* is described from Germany.

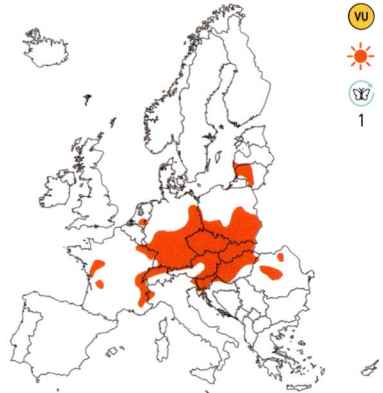

IMAGOS		LARVAE	
Food		Food	
Behaviour of males		Caterpillar location	
Dispersion		Chrysalis location	

Did you know?

Wetland drainage for agricultural purposes is a significant threat to the Scarce Large Blue, leading to a substantial decline in its European populations.

LYCAENIDAE

ALCON BLUE   *PHENGARIS ALCON*

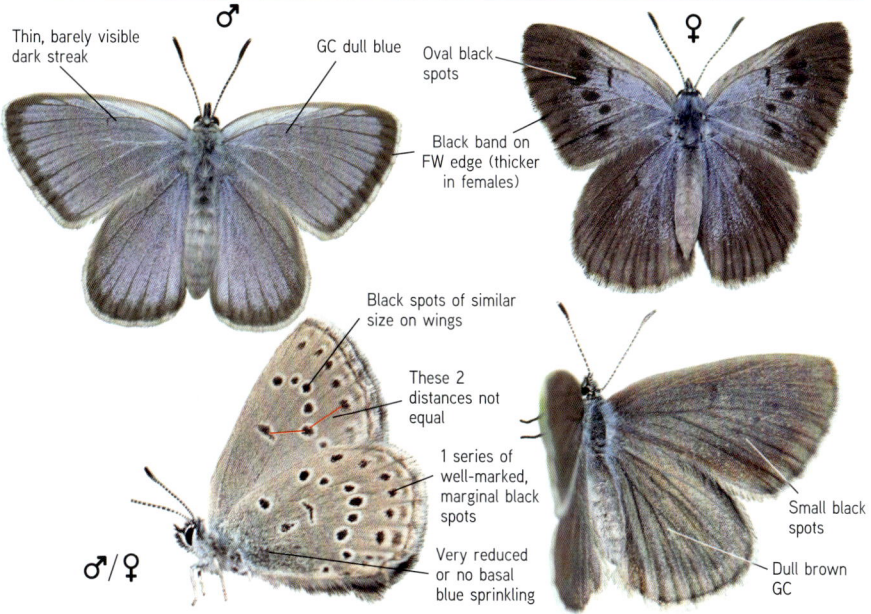

♂

Thin, barely visible dark streak

GC dull blue

♀

Oval black spots

Black band on FW edge (thicker in females)

Black spots of similar size on wings

These 2 distances not equal

1 series of well-marked, marginal black spots

Very reduced or no basal blue sprinkling

♂/♀

Small black spots

Dull brown GC

Wingspan: 34–38 mm

Habitat: Grasslands and thermophilic meadows for the *rebeli* ecotype. Damp meadows and heaths for the *alcon* ecotype.

Hibernating stage: Caterpillar.

Elevational range: Up to 2,500 m.

Egg-laying: Eggs are laid singly or in a few units, mainly on LHP inflorescences (sometimes also on leaves).

Flight period: From June to August.

Host plants: Gentianaceae, especially *Gentiana pneumonanthe* and *G. asclepiadea* for the *alcon* ecotype; *G. cruciata* and *G. lutea* for the *rebeli* ecotype.

Diversity and systematics: There are about ten subspecies described for this blue, which is widely distributed in the Palaearctic. The ecotypes *alcon* and *rebeli* do not form monophyletic groups and therefore do not correspond to distinct species or subspecies.

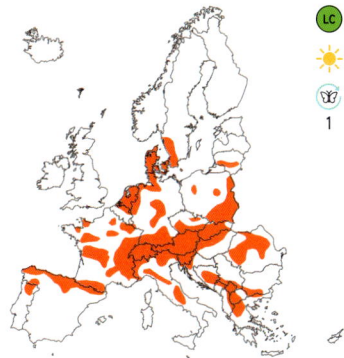

LC

1

Did you know?

Caterpillars of the Alcon Blue stridulate and thereby imitate the sounds produced by the queens of the *Myrmica* ants they parasitize. Workers thus treat them as such, feeding and protecting them accordingly.

IMAGOS			LARVAE		
Food			Food		
Behaviour of males			Caterpillar location		
Dispersion			Chrysalis location		

LYCAENIDAE

DUSKY LARGE BLUE *PHENGARIS NAUSITHOUS*

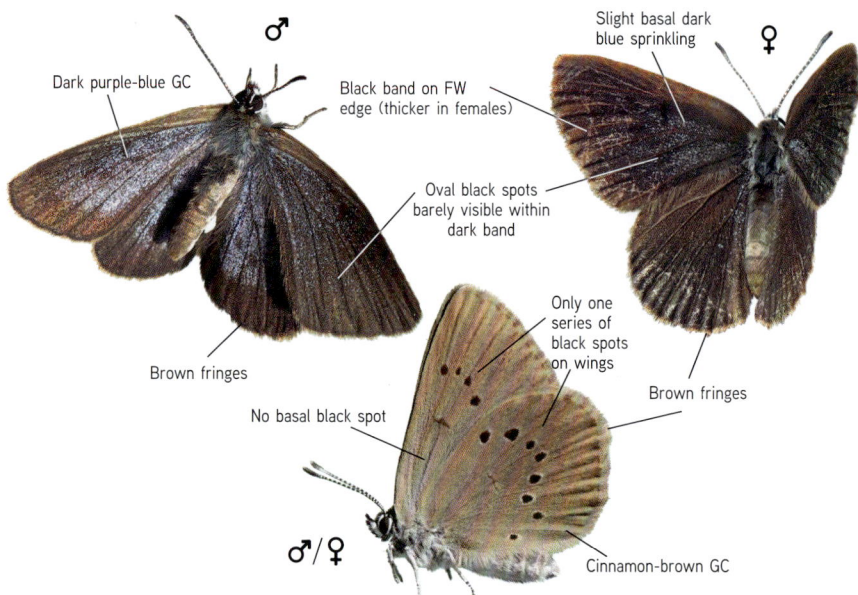

♂

Dark purple-blue GC

Black band on FW edge (thicker in females)

Slight basal dark blue sprinkling

♀

Oval black spots barely visible within dark band

Brown fringes

Only one series of black spots on wings

No basal black spot

Brown fringes

♂/♀

Cinnamon-brown GC

Wingspan: 34–36 mm

Habitat: Damp meadows and bog surroundings where the LHP grows.

Hibernating stage: Caterpillar.

Elevational range: Up to 1,500 m.

Egg-laying: Eggs are laid singly on LHP inflorescences.

Flight period: From June to August.

Host plants: *Sanguisorba officinalis* (Rosaceae).

Diversity and systematics: European populations belong to the nominate subspecies.

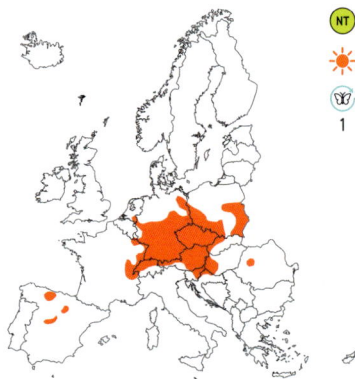

NT

1

IMAGOS		LARVAE	
Food	☆	Food	☆
Behaviour of males		Caterpillar location	
Dispersion		Chrysalis location	

Did you know?

Adults are closely associated with the LHP, on which they mainly forage and perch most frequently. The Dusky Large Blue is a parasite of *Myrmica rubra* ants.

HOLLY BLUE *CELASTRINA ARGIOLUS*

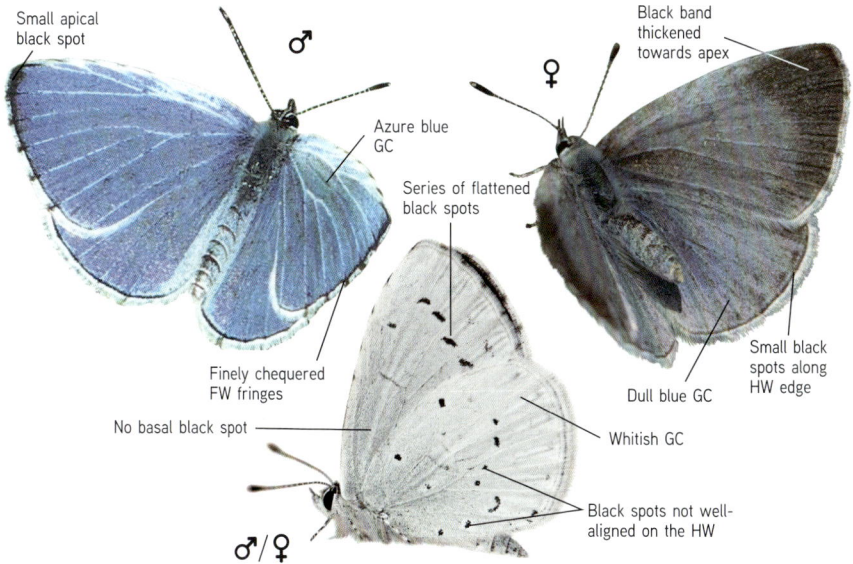

Small apical
black spot

♂

Black band
thickened
towards apex

♀

Azure blue
GC

Series of flattened
black spots

Finely chequered
FW fringes

No basal black spot

Small black
spots along
HW edge

Dull blue GC

Whitish GC

Black spots not well-
aligned on the HW

♂/♀

Wingspan: 21–32 mm

Habitat: Forest edges and clearings, hedgerows; rather common in urban parks and gardens with bushy areas.

Hibernating stage: Pupa.

Elevational range: Up to 2,500 m (mostly below 1,000 m).

Egg-laying: Eggs are laid singly on LHP inflorescences.

Flight period: From March to September.

Host plants: Probably the most polyphagous Lycaenid, capable of using about 60 plant species in no less than 19 families! These include *Ilex aquifolium*, *Cornus* spp., *Hedera helix*, *Calluna vulgaris*, *Rhamnus* spp., *Frangula alnus*, *Lythrum salicaria*, *Rubus* spp., *Euonymus europaeus*, numerous legumes in genera *Genista*, *Cytisus*, *Dorycnium*, *Ulex*, *Vicia*, *Medicago*, *Melilotus*, and *Astragalus*. Also *Alnus glutinosa*, *Ligustrum vulgare*, *Buddleia davidii*, *Clematis vitalba*, and *Humulus lupulus*.

Diversity and systematics: Most European populations belong to the nominate subspecies. Subspecies *canicularis* flies in Southern Europe. Subspecies *grisescens* is described from the Netherlands, and subspecies *britanna* flies in the British Isles.

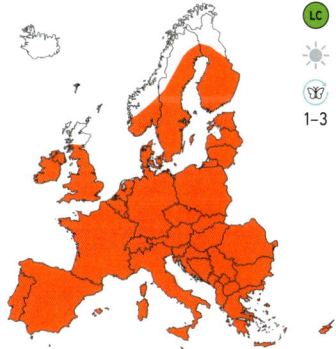

LC

1–3

Did you know?

The Holly Blue is often the first blue to emerge. Its fast and relatively high flight is characteristic. It has adapted well to anthropized environments, notably due to the presence of ivy.

IMAGOS		LARVAE	
Food	🌼 🌿 💧	Food	🌼 🌿
Behaviour of males	🦋	Caterpillar location	🌿 🌳 🌾 🐜
Dispersion		Chrysalis location	🌿

LYCAENIDAE

ALPINE BLUE *AGRIADES ORBITULUS*

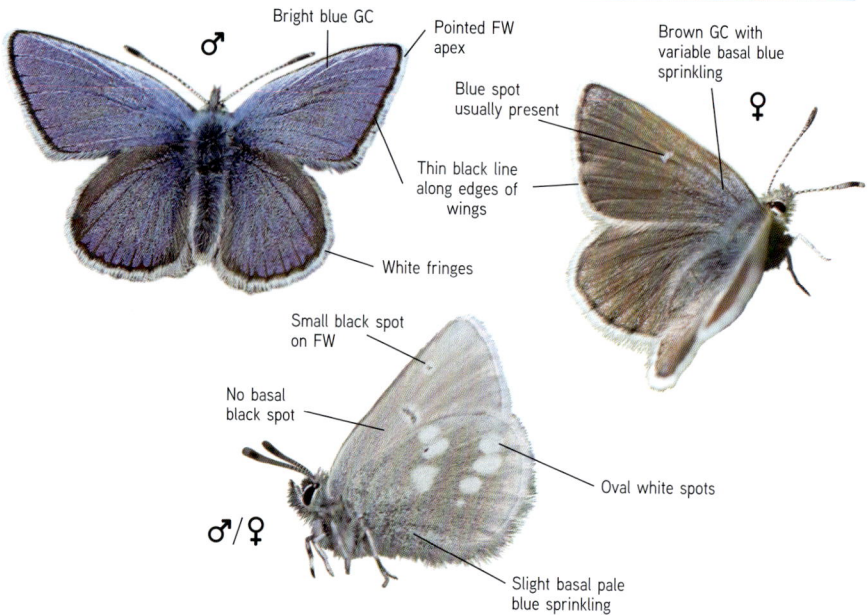

Bright blue GC

Pointed FW apex

Blue spot usually present

Thin black line along edges of wings

White fringes

Brown GC with variable basal blue sprinkling

♂

♀

Small black spot on FW

No basal black spot

Oval white spots

Slight basal pale blue sprinkling

♂/♀

Wingspan: 24–28 mm

Habitat: Subalpine and alpine grasslands and meadows, especially in the vicinity of mountain streams.

Hibernating stage: Caterpillar.

Elevational range: Between 1,000 and 3,000 m.

Egg-laying: Eggs are laid singly on LHP leaflets.

Flight period: From June to August.

Host plants: Small herbaceous legumes, such as *Astragalus alpinus*, *A. australis*, *A. norvegicus*, and *A. penduliflorus*. Also *Hedysarum hedysaroides* and some *Oxytropis*, like *O. campestris* and *O. montana*.

Diversity and systematics: Although it has a markedly disjunct range in Europe, Alpine Blue populations belong to the nominate subspecies.

LC

1

IMAGOS		LARVAE	
Food		Food	
Behaviour of males		Caterpillar location	
Dispersion		Chrysalis location	

Did you know?

Males often perch on bare spots, such as rocks. Their very fast flight makes them difficult to follow when they are startled.

LYCAENIDAE

GAVARNIE BLUE *AGRIADES PYRENAICUS*

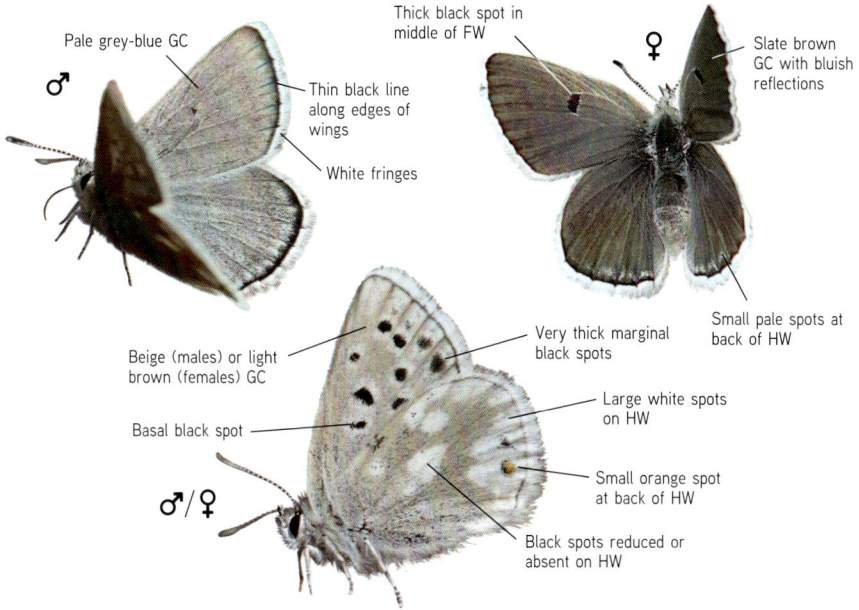

Pale grey-blue GC

♂

Thick black spot in middle of FW

Thin black line along edges of wings

White fringes

♀

Slate brown GC with bluish reflections

Small pale spots at back of HW

Beige (males) or light brown (females) GC

Basal black spot

♂/♀

Very thick marginal black spots

Large white spots on HW

Small orange spot at back of HW

Black spots reduced or absent on HW

Wingspan: 22–28 mm

Habitat: Stony, often south-facing alpine and subalpine grasslands.

Hibernating stage: Caterpillar.

Elevational range: Between 1,500 and 3,000 m.

Egg-laying: Eggs are laid singly on LHP leaves.

Flight period: From June to August.

Host plants: *Androsace villosa* (Primulaceae).

Diversity and systematics: Pyrenean populations belong to the nominate subspecies. Populations from the Cantabrian Mountains form subspecies *asturiensis*.

- A. glandon
- A. zullichi
- A. pyrenaicus
- A. glandon + A. pyrenaicus
- A. dardanus
- A. aquilo

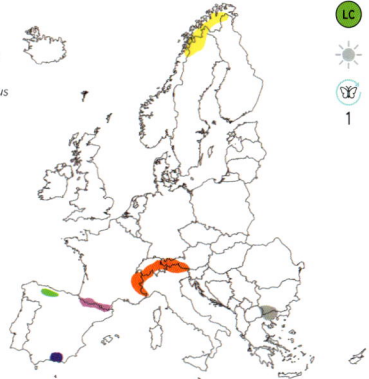

LC

1

IMAGOS		LARVAE	
Food		Food	
Behaviour of males		Caterpillar location	
Dispersion		Chrysalis location	

Did you know?

Adults, especially males, are often easier to find when they are sipping water and mineral salts from damp soils rather than in the breeding habitats.

LYCAENIDAE

GLANDON BLUE *AGRIADES GLANDON*

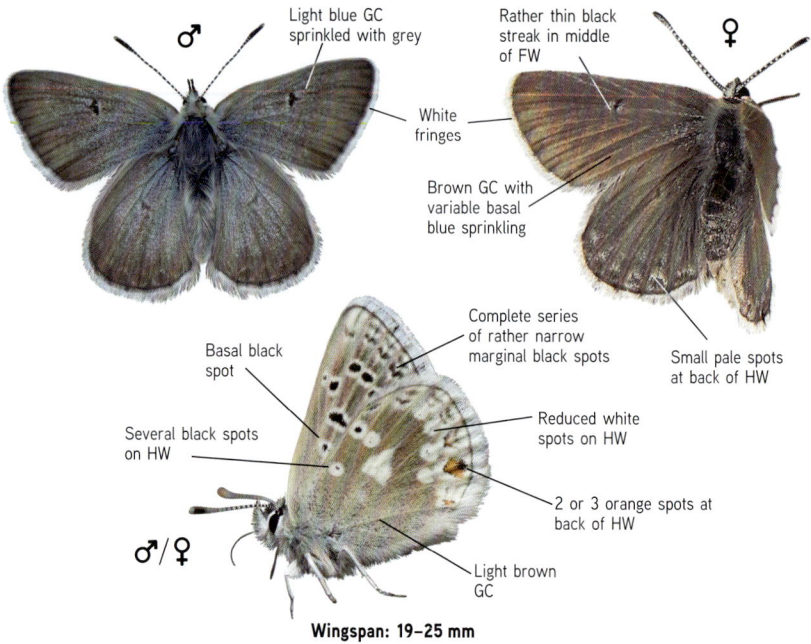

♂

Light blue GC
sprinkled with grey

Rather thin black
streak in middle
of FW

♀

White
fringes

Brown GC with
variable basal
blue sprinkling

Complete series
of rather narrow
marginal black spots

Basal black
spot

Small pale spots
at back of HW

Several black spots
on HW

Reduced white
spots on HW

2 or 3 orange spots at
back of HW

♂/♀

Light brown
GC

Wingspan: 19–25 mm

Habitat: Subalpine and alpine low-growing meadows and grasslands.

Hibernating stage: Caterpillar.

Elevational range: Between 1,500 and 2,600 m.

Egg-laying: Eggs are laid singly on LHP leaves.

Flight period: From June to August.

Host plants: Primulaceae in genus *Androsace*, especially *A. vitaliana, A. obtusifolia, A. chamaejasme, A. lactea, A. laggeri*, and *A. villosa*. Perhaps also on *Soldanella pusilla* and *S. alpina*, as well as on the legume *Oxytropis campestris*.

Diversity and systematics: Most alpine populations belong to the nominate subspecies. Subspecies *oberthueri* flies in the Pyrenees. Subspecies *centrohelvetica* is described from the Swiss Alps.

- ■ *A. glandon*
- ■ *A. zullichi*
- ■ *A. pyrenaicus*
- ■ *A. glandon + A. pyrenaicus*
- ■ *A. dardanus*
- ■ *A. aquilo*

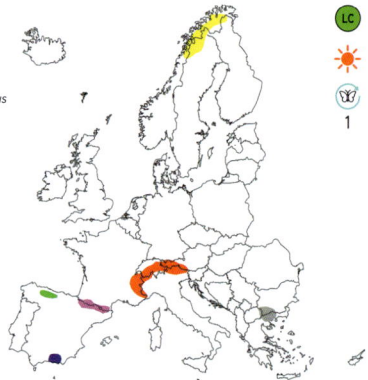

LC

1

Did you know?

The use of snowbells by the caterpillars is uncertain. Egg-laying has been observed on these iconic alpine plants, but the success of larval development has not been confirmed.

IMAGOS		LARVAE	
Food	🌼 💧	Food	🌼 🌿
Behaviour of males	🦋	Caterpillar location	🌱
Dispersion		Chrysalis location	

LYCAENIDAE

ARCTIC BLUE *AGRIADES AQUILO*

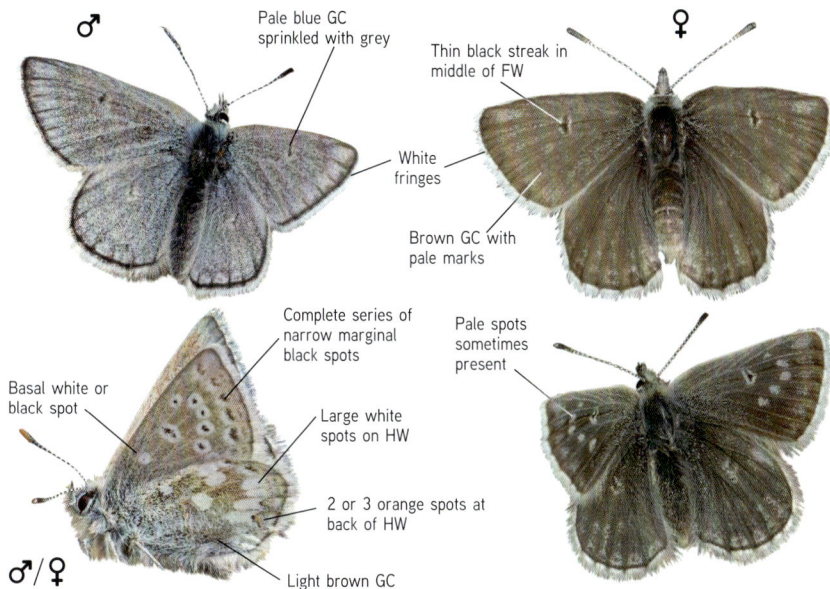

♂

Pale blue GC sprinkled with grey

♀

Thin black streak in middle of FW

White fringes

Brown GC with pale marks

Complete series of narrow marginal black spots

Pale spots sometimes present

Basal white or black spot

Large white spots on HW

♂/♀

2 or 3 orange spots at back of HW

Light brown GC

Wingspan: 19–25 mm

Habitat: Stony slopes with low-growing vegetation.

Hibernating stage: Caterpillar.

Elevational range: Up to 1,000 m.

Egg-laying: Eggs are probably laid singly on LHP leaves.

Flight period: From June to August.

Host plants: *Saxifraga aizoides* and *S. oppositifolia* (Saxifragaceae).

Diversity and systematics: There is no notable subspecies for this arctic species, which is sometimes considered a subspecies of *Agriades glandon*.

- A. glandon
- A. zullichi
- A. pyrenaicus
- A. glandon + A. pyrenaicus
- A. dardanus
- A. aquilo

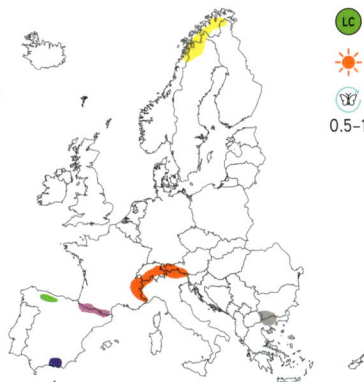

LC

0.5–1

IMAGOS		LARVAE	
Food	☆	Food	☆ 🌿
Behaviour of males		Caterpillar location	🌱
Dispersion		Chrysalis location	

Did you know?

The Arctic Blue was long considered a subspecies of the Glandon Blue. However, their LHPs belong to different families.

LYCAENIDAE

BOSNIAN BLUE *AGRIADES DARDANUS*

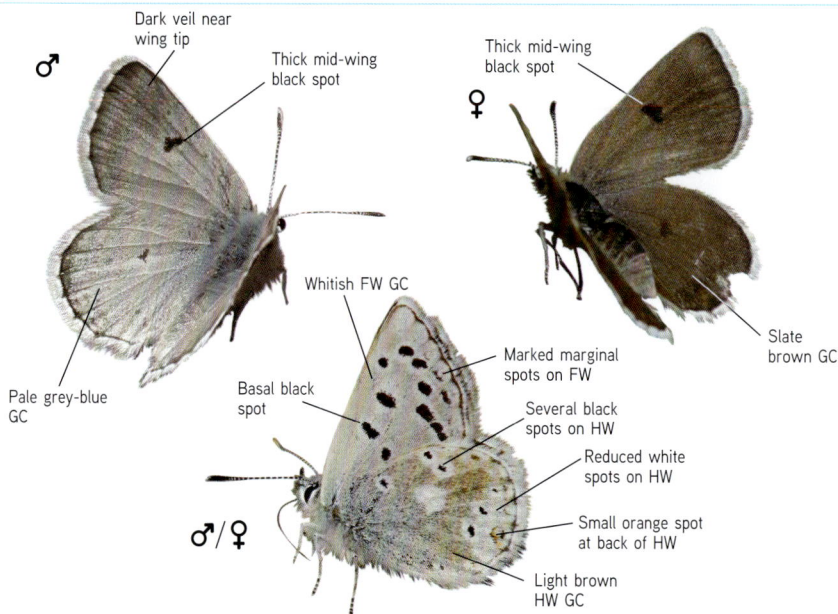

♂

Dark veil near wing tip

Thick mid-wing black spot

♀

Thick mid-wing black spot

Slate brown GC

Pale grey-blue GC

Whitish FW GC

Basal black spot

Marked marginal spots on FW

Several black spots on HW

Reduced white spots on HW

Small orange spot at back of HW

♂/♀

Light brown HW GC

Wingspan: 22–28 mm

Habitat: Stony but flower-rich subalpine and alpine grasslands.

Hibernating stage: Caterpillar.

Elevational range: Between 1,200 and 2,200 m.

Egg-laying: Eggs are laid singly on LHP leaves.

Flight period: From June to August.

Host plants: Primulaceae in genus *Androsace*, such as *A. villosa* and *A. albana*.

Diversity and systematics: Opinions on the species status of the Bosnian Blue have not reached a consensus. It is sometimes considered a subspecies of the Gavarnie Blue, despite the clear allopatric situation.

- A. glandon
- A. zullichi
- A. pyrenaicus
- A. glandon + A. pyrenaicus
- A. dardanus
- A. aquilo

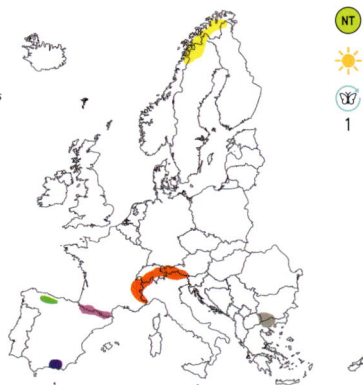

NT

1

IMAGOS		LARVAE	
Food		Food	
Behaviour of males		Caterpillar location	
Dispersion		Chrysalis location	

Did you know?

Males frequently gather on hilltops. Adults often feed on thyme inflorescences.

ZULLICH'S BLUE *AGRIADES ZULLICHI*

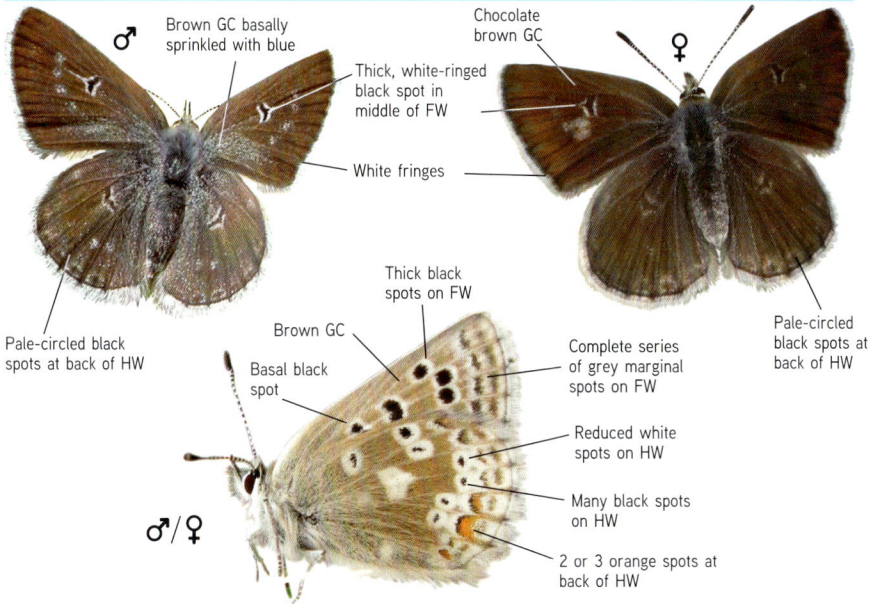

♂

Brown GC basally sprinkled with blue

Chocolate brown GC

♀

Thick, white-ringed black spot in middle of FW

White fringes

Thick black spots on FW

Brown GC

Pale-circled black spots at back of HW

Basal black spot

Complete series of grey marginal spots on FW

Pale-circled black spots at back of HW

Reduced white spots on HW

♂/♀

Many black spots on HW

2 or 3 orange spots at back of HW

Wingspan: 20–25 mm

Habitat: Dry, sparsely vegetated hilltops and slopes.

Hibernating stage: Caterpillar.

Elevational range: Between 2,500 and 3,000 m.

Egg-laying: Eggs are laid singly on LHP leaves.

Flight period: From June to August.

Host plants: *Androsace vitaliana* (Primulaceae).

Diversity and systematics: Zullich's Blue was once considered a subspecies of the Glandon Blue. It is endemic to the Sierra Nevada.

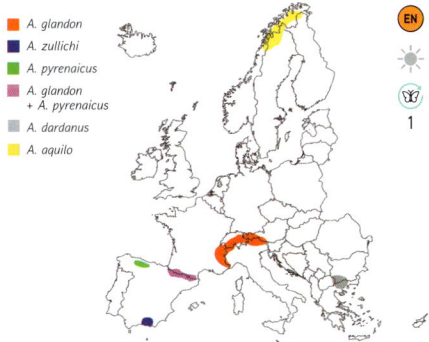

■ A. glandon
■ A. zullichi
■ A. pyrenaicus
■ A. glandon + A. pyrenaicus
■ A. dardanus
■ A. aquilo

EN

1

IMAGOS		LARVAE	
Food	✿	Food	✿ 🌿
Behaviour of males	🦋	Caterpillar location	🐛 🌱
Dispersion	🕸	Chrysalis location	🪨

Did you know?

Adults obtain nectar extensively from kidney vetches as well as from thymes. Urbanization of mountain slopes, excessive grazing, and climate warming are the greatest threats to this species, which has a very restricted range.

SILVERY ARGUS *ARICIA NICIAS*

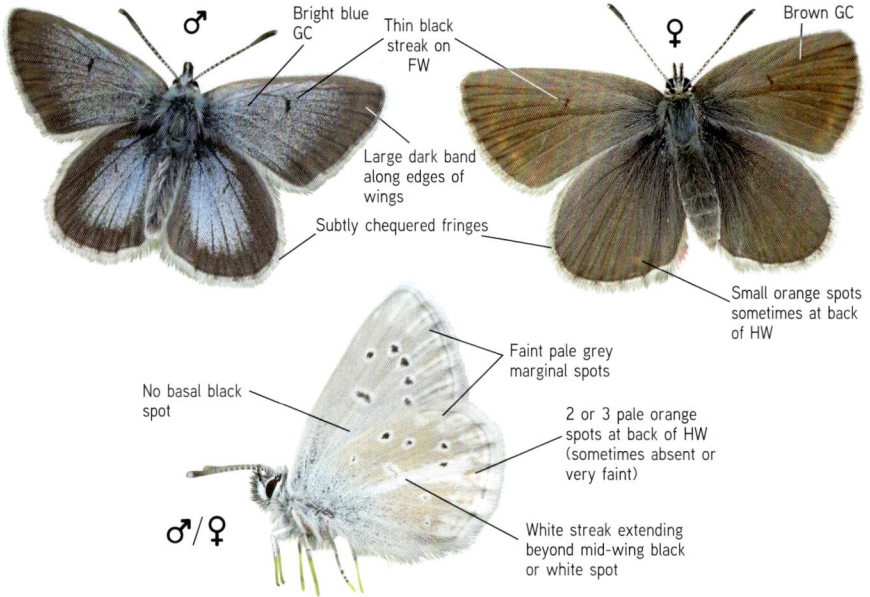

♂ Bright blue GC

Thin black streak on FW

♀ Brown GC

Large dark band along edges of wings

Subtly chequered fringes

Small orange spots sometimes at back of HW

No basal black spot

Faint pale grey marginal spots

2 or 3 pale orange spots at back of HW (sometimes absent or very faint)

♂/♀

White streak extending beyond mid-wing black or white spot

Wingspan: 23–28 mm

Habitat: Montane and subalpine, often north-facing megaphorbs and meadows.

Hibernating stage: Caterpillar.

Elevational range: Between 1,000 and 2,600 m.

Egg-laying: Eggs are laid singly or in a few units on LHP dried leaves and flowers.

Flight period: July and August.

Host plants: Geraniaceae, mainly *Geranium sylvaticum*, *G. pratense*, and *G. rivulare*.

Diversity and systematics: The nominate subspecies flies in the Western Alps. Subspecies *scandicus* is found in Scandinavia. Subspecies *agraphomena* and *ferenigra* fly in Italy. Subspecies *caerulea* is described from Tyrol, and subspecies *judithi* flies in Catalonia.

LC

1

Did you know?

Under captive breeding conditions, the Geranium Bronze can lay eggs on wild geraniums, such as *Geranium sylvaticum*, in the absence of its usual LHPs. The larvae develop quite well. Therefore, it could potentially become a new competitor against the Silvery Argus at its lowest elevations.

IMAGOS		LARVAE	
Food		Food	
Behaviour of males		Caterpillar location	
Dispersion		Chrysalis location	

LYCAENIDAE

BROWN ARGUS *ARICIA AGESTIS*

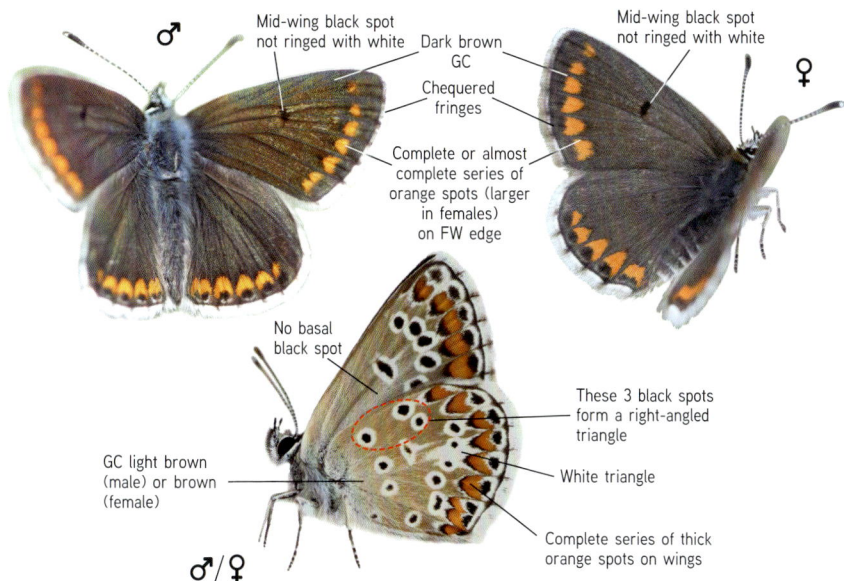

♂

Mid-wing black spot not ringed with white

Dark brown GC

Chequered fringes

Complete or almost complete series of orange spots (larger in females) on FW edge

Mid-wing black spot not ringed with white

♀

No basal black spot

These 3 black spots form a right-angled triangle

GC light brown (male) or brown (female)

White triangle

Complete series of thick orange spots on wings

♂/♀

Wingspan: 22–28 mm

Habitat: Dry grasslands, low-growing meadows, heaths, fixed dunes, parks, and gardens.

Hibernating stage: Caterpillar.

Elevational range: Up to 1,700 m.

Egg-laying: Eggs are laid singly on LHP leaves and flowers.

Flight period: From April to October.

Host plants: Geraniaceae, including *Erodium cicutarium*, *E. acaule*, *E. chium*, *E. ciconium*, *E. malacoides*, *Geranium*

molle, *G. dissectum*, *G. sanguineum*, *G. pratense*, *G. palustre*, *G. columbinum*, *G. asphodeloides*, *G. phaeum*, *G. purpureum*, *G. pusillum*, *G. pyrenaicum*, *G. rotundifolium*, *G. sylvaticum*, and *G. tuberosum*. Cistaceae, mainly *Helianthemum nummularium*, *H. apenninum*, and *Tuberaria guttata*. Sometimes on *Lotus corniculatus* and *Medicago* spp. (Fabaceae).

Diversity and systematics: Most European populations belong to the nominate subspecies. Corsican and Sicilian populations form subspecies *calida*.

- A. agestis
- A. cramera
- A. montensis + A. cramera
- A. artaxerxes + A. agestis
- A. montensis + A. agestis
- A. cramera + A. agestis

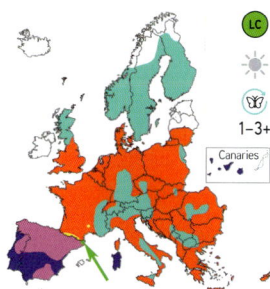

LC

1–3+

Canaries

Did you know?

In England, the range of the Brown Argus has significantly expanded northward within the past 20 years, probably due to climate warming. This expansion has been accompanied by the more frequent use of Geraniaceae as LHPs instead of rockroses.

IMAGOS		LARVAE	
Food		Food	
Behaviour of males		Caterpillar location	
Dispersion		Chrysalis location	

305

LYCAENIDAE

SOUTHERN BROWN ARGUS *ARICIA CRAMERA*

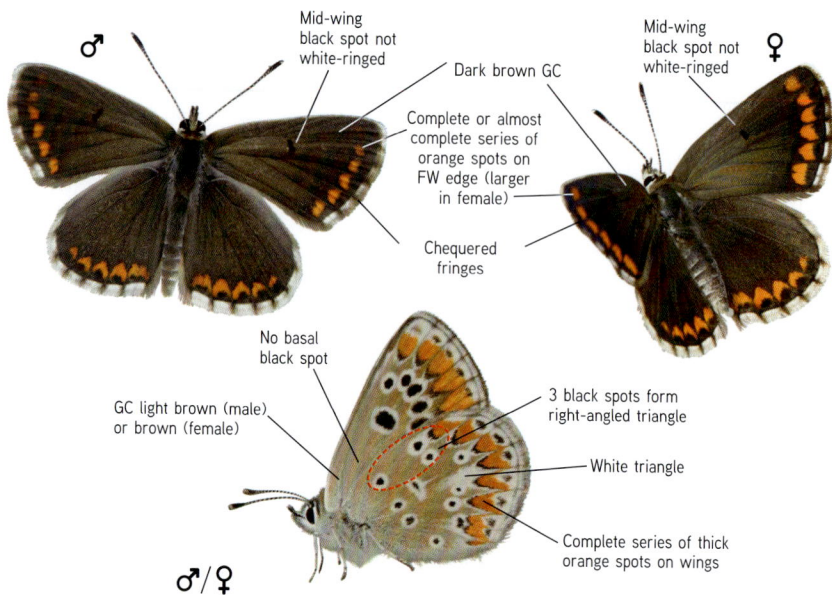

♂

Mid-wing black spot not white-ringed

Dark brown GC

Complete or almost complete series of orange spots on FW edge (larger in female)

Chequered fringes

♀

Mid-wing black spot not white-ringed

No basal black spot

GC light brown (male) or brown (female)

3 black spots form right-angled triangle

White triangle

Complete series of thick orange spots on wings

♂/♀

Wingspan: 22–28 mm

Habitat: Dry grasslands, low-growing meadows, wastelands, and flower-rich Mediterranean edges.

Hibernating stage: Egg, caterpillar, pupa, or adult in the Canaries; caterpillar in the Iberian Peninsula.

Elevational range: Up to 2,000 m.

Egg-laying: Eggs are laid singly on LHP leaves.

Flight period: Year-round in the Canaries; from April to October in the Iberian Peninsula.

Host plants: Geraniaceae, including *Erodium cicutarium*, *E. ciconium*, *E. botrys*, *E. malacoides*, *E. moschatum*, and *Geranium dissectum*. Cistaceae, like *Tuberaria guttata*, *Helianthemum nummularium*, and *H. hirtum*. Also reported on *Erigeron sumatrensis* (Asteraceae).

Diversity and systematics: There are no notable subspecies. *Aricia cramera* was previously considered a subspecies of *A. agestis*.

- ■ A. agestis
- ■ A. cramera
- ■ A. montensis + A. cramera
- ■ A. artaxerxes + A. agestis
- ■ A. montensis + A. agestis
- ■ A. cramera + A. agestis

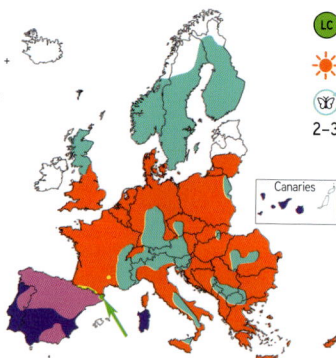

LC

2–3

Canaries

IMAGOS		LARVAE	
Food		Food	
Behaviour of males		Caterpillar location	
Dispersion		Chrysalis location	

Did you know?

Adults feed on nectar from a variety of flowers, including everlastings, wild garlics, and lavenders.

LYCAENIDAE

NORTHERN BROWN ARGUS *ARICIA ARTAXERXES*

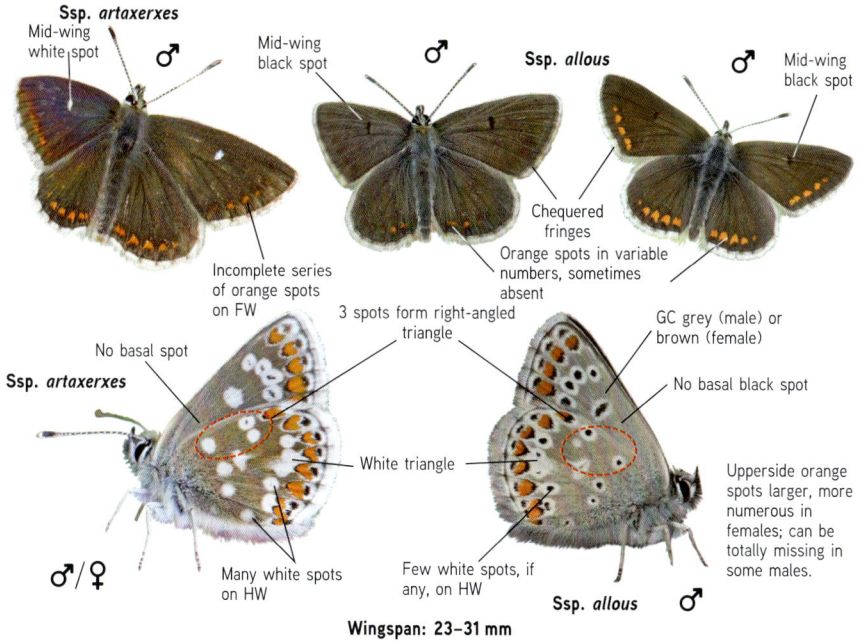

Ssp. *artaxerxes*
Mid-wing white spot ♂

Mid-wing black spot ♂

Ssp. *allous*

Mid-wing black spot ♂

Chequered fringes
Orange spots in variable numbers, sometimes absent

Incomplete series of orange spots on FW

3 spots form right-angled triangle

GC grey (male) or brown (female)

No basal spot

Ssp. *artaxerxes*

No basal black spot

White triangle

Upperside orange spots larger, more numerous in females; can be totally missing in some males.

♂/♀

Many white spots on HW

Few white spots, if any, on HW

Ssp. *allous* ♂

Wingspan: 23–31 mm

Habitat: Subalpine dry grasslands and meadows.

Hibernating stage: Caterpillars.

Elevational range: Up to 500 m in the UK; between 1,500 and 2,500 m on the continent.

Egg-laying: Eggs are laid singly on LHP leaves.

Flight period: From June to September.

Host plants: Mainly Cistaceae, including *Helianthemum nummularium* and *H. oelandicum*. Also on some Geraniaceae, like *Geranium sanguineum*, *G. sylvaticum*, *G. subcaulescens*, and *Erodium* spp.

Diversity and systematics: The nominate subspecies flies in Scotland. Subspecies *salmacis* is found in England. Alpine and southern European populations belong to subspecies *allous*. Subspecies *issekutzi* is described from Romania. Nordic populations would belong to subspecies *vandalica*.

- A. agestis
- A. cramera
- A. montensis + A. cramera
- A. artaxerxes + A. agestis
- A. montensis + A. agestis
- A. cramera + A. agestis

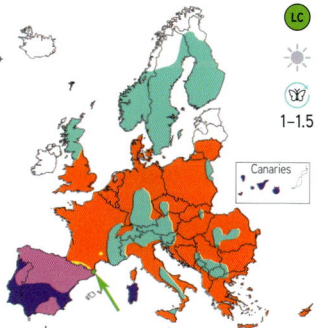

LC

1–1.5

Canaries

IMAGOS		LARVAE	
Food		Food	
Behaviour of males		Caterpillar location	
Dispersion		Chrysalis location	

Did you know?

Northern Brown Argus caterpillars are tended by ants of genera *Lasius* and *Formica*.

LYCAENIDAE

SOUTHERN MOUNTAIN ARGUS *ARICIA MONTENSIS*

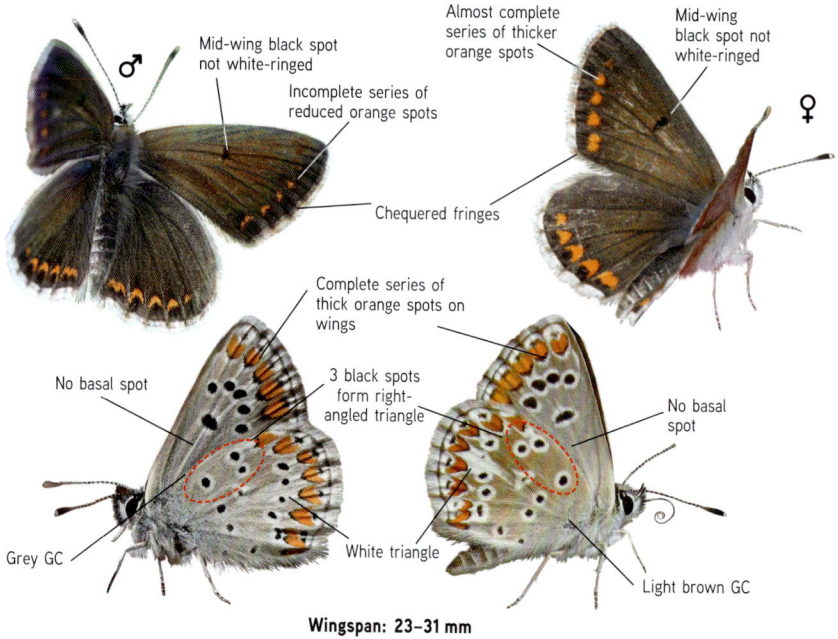

♂ Mid-wing black spot not white-ringed

Incomplete series of reduced orange spots

Almost complete series of thicker orange spots

Mid-wing black spot not white-ringed ♀

Chequered fringes

Complete series of thick orange spots on wings

No basal spot

3 black spots form right-angled triangle

No basal spot

Grey GC

White triangle

Light brown GC

Wingspan: 23–31 mm

Habitat: Dry grasslands on sunny, rocky slopes.

Hibernating stage: Caterpillar.

Elevational range: Between 1,000 and 2,200 m.

Egg-laying: Eggs are laid singly on LHP leaves.

Flight period: From June to September.

Host plants: *Helianthemum nummularium* (Cistaceae) and Geraniaceae, including *Erodium cicutarium* and *Geranium* spp.

Diversity and systematics: *Aricia montensis* was once considered a subspecies of *Aricia artaxerxes*. However, it is genetically distinct.

- ■ A. agestis
- ■ A. cramera
- ■ A. montensis + A. cramera
- ■ A. artaxerxes + A. agestis
- ■ A. montensis + A. agestis
- ■ A. cramera + A. agestis

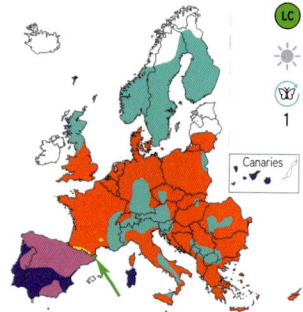

Canaries

LC

1

Did you know?

The Southern Mountain Argus is difficult to distinguish from the Brown Argus, with which it is sometimes sympatric. Early spring records rule out the former, which is generally slightly larger than the latter.

IMAGOS		LARVAE	
Food		Food	
Behaviour of males		Caterpillar location	
Dispersion		Chrysalis location	

LYCAENIDAE

SPANISH ARGUS *ARICIA MORRONENSIS*

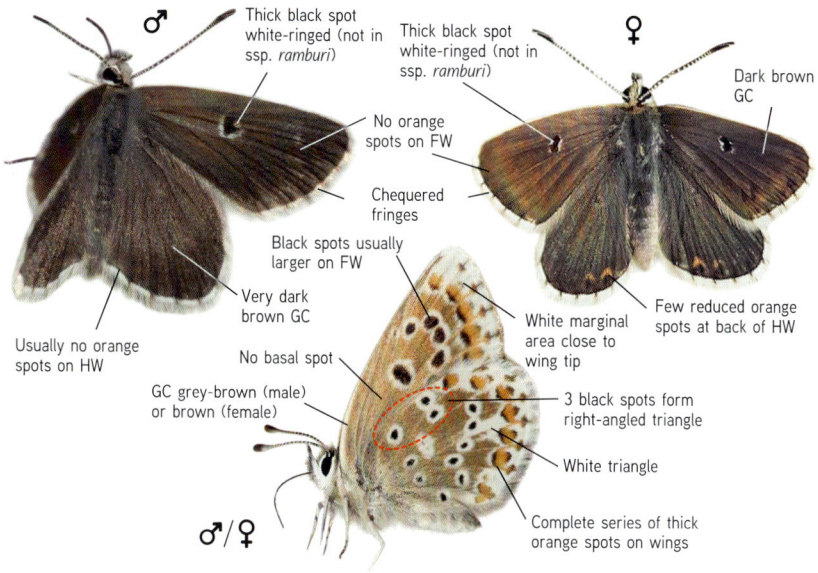

♂

Thick black spot white-ringed (not in ssp. *ramburi*)

Thick black spot white-ringed (not in ssp. *ramburi*)

♀

Dark brown GC

No orange spots on FW

Chequered fringes

Black spots usually larger on FW

Very dark brown GC

Usually no orange spots on HW

Few reduced orange spots at back of HW

White marginal area close to wing tip

No basal spot

GC grey-brown (male) or brown (female)

3 black spots form right-angled triangle

White triangle

♂/♀

Complete series of thick orange spots on wings

Wingspan: 26–30 mm

Habitat: Rocky slopes, sunny and flower-rich scree.

Hibernating stage: Caterpillar.

Elevational range: Between 1,000 and 3,000 m.

Egg-laying: Eggs are laid singly on LHP leaves.

Flight period: From June to August.

Host plants: Geraniaceae, especially *Erodium glandulosum*, *E. carvifolium*, *E. castellanum*, *E. cazorlanum*, *E. celtibericum*, *E. cheilanthifolium*, *E. daucoides*, *E. paui*, and *E. saxatile*.

Diversity and systematics: The nominate subspecies populates the Sierra Espuña. Subspecies *ramburi* inhabits the Sierra Nevada. Subspecies *boudranei* and *ordesae* fly in the Central Pyrenees and Catalonia, respectively. Subspecies *hasselbarthi* is found in Castile and León. Subspecies *chapmani* is found in Galicia.

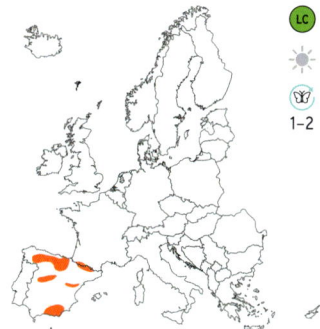

LC

1–2

Did you know?

The often steep and rocky habitats of the Spanish Argus correspond to the ecological requirements of its host plants and make it difficult to access for lepidopterists, who may risk a dramatic fall!

IMAGOS		LARVAE	
Food	✿	Food	🍃
Behaviour of males		Caterpillar location	
Dispersion		Chrysalis location	

LYCAENIDAE

BLUE ARGUS *ARICIA ANTEROS*

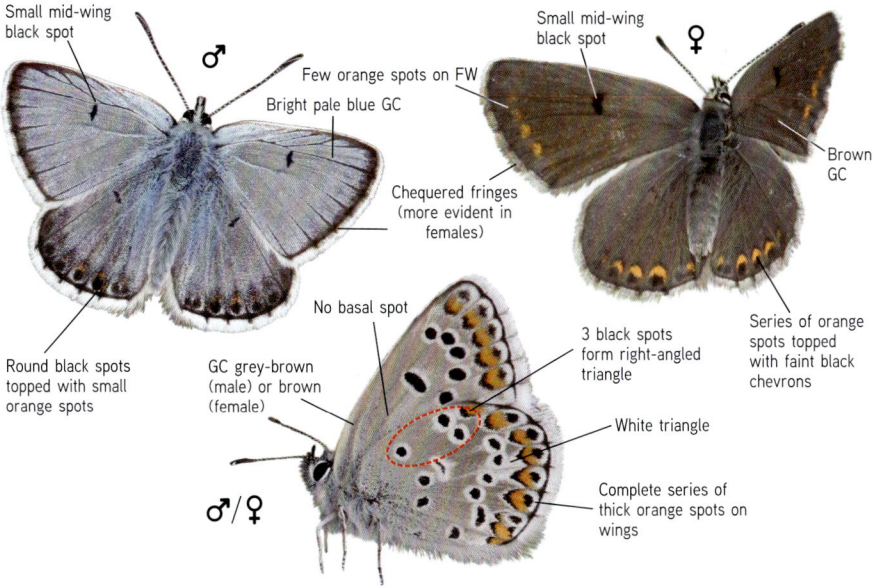

Small mid-wing black spot

♂

Few orange spots on FW

Bright pale blue GC

Small mid-wing black spot

♀

Brown GC

Chequered fringes (more evident in females)

No basal spot

Round black spots topped with small orange spots

GC grey-brown (male) or brown (female)

3 black spots form right-angled triangle

Series of orange spots topped with faint black chevrons

White triangle

♂/♀

Complete series of thick orange spots on wings

Wingspan: 24–32 mm

Habitat: Grassy, flower-rich clearings, subalpine calcareous grasslands.

Hibernating stage: Caterpillar.

Elevational range: Up to 2,500 m (mainly below 2,000 m).

Egg-laying: Eggs are laid singly on LHP leaves.

Flight period: From May to September.

Host plants: Geraniaceae in genera *Erodium*, like *E. chrysanthum*, and *Geranium*, such as *G. asphodeloides*, *G. sanguineum*, *G. macrorhizum*, *G. pyrenaicum*, and *G. subcaulescens*.

Diversity and systematics: European populations belong to the nominate subspecies.

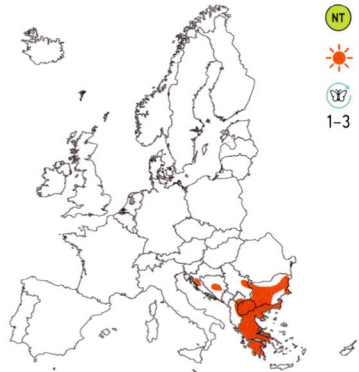

NT

1–3

IMAGOS		LARVAE	
Food		Food	
Behaviour of males		Caterpillar location	
Dispersion		Chrysalis location	

Did you know?

The very bright light blue colour of the males, similar or slightly paler than that of the Eros Blue, allows them to be distinguished at first glance from other blues.

LYCAENIDAE

ADONIS BLUE *LYSANDRA BELLARGUS*

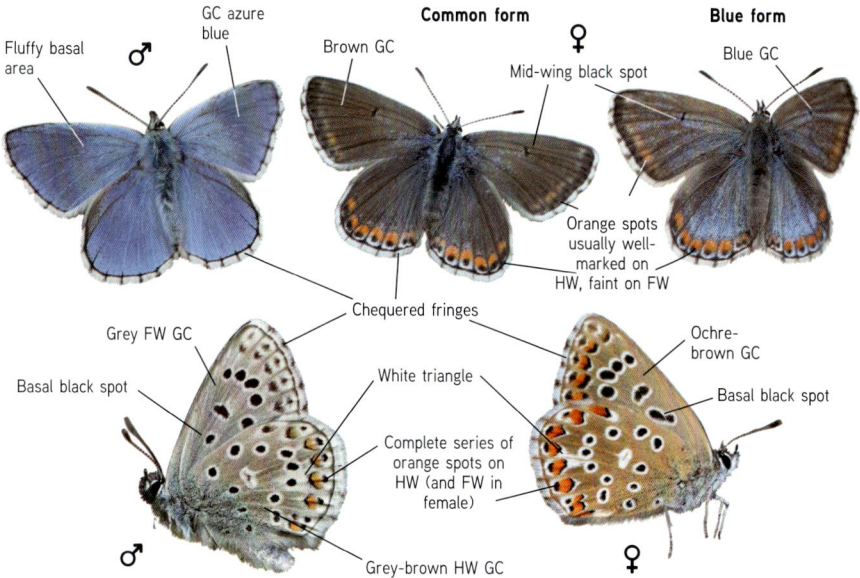

Common form

Blue form

Fluffy basal area

♂

GC azure blue

Brown GC

♀

Mid-wing black spot

Blue GC

Blue form

Orange spots usually well-marked on HW, faint on FW

Grey FW GC

Chequered fringes

Ochre-brown GC

Basal black spot

White triangle

Basal black spot

Complete series of orange spots on HW (and FW in female)

♂

Grey-brown HW GC

♀

Wingspan: 28–34 mm

Habitat: Dry grasslands and low-growing meadows. The Adonis Blue is a rather calcicolous species, although it can also thrive on volcanic or shale substrates.

Hibernating stage: Caterpillar.

Elevational range: Up to 2,000 m.

Egg-laying: Eggs are laid singly on LHP leaflets.

Flight period: From April to October.

Host plants: Legumes, including *Hippocrepis comosa*, *H. glauca*, and *H. scabra*; sometimes also *Securigera varia*, *Dorycnopsis gerardi*, and *Lotus corniculatus*.

Diversity and systematics: Several dozen subspecies have been described for this blue, which is widely distributed in the Palaearctic. Numerous forms are also reported, demonstrating a high degree of intraspecific polymorphism.

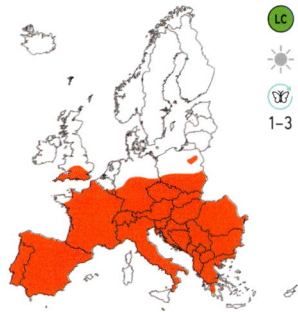

LC

1–3

Did you know?

In spring, males and females prefer flowers with nectar that is, respectively, rich in sucrose and rich in amino acids. The former favour the energy supply for their flight, while the latter prioritize egg production.

IMAGOS		LARVAE	
Food	🌸🐞💧	Food	🍃
Behaviour of males		Caterpillar location	
Dispersion		Chrysalis location	

LYCAENIDAE

AZURE CHALKHILL BLUE *LYSANDRA CAELESTISSIMA*

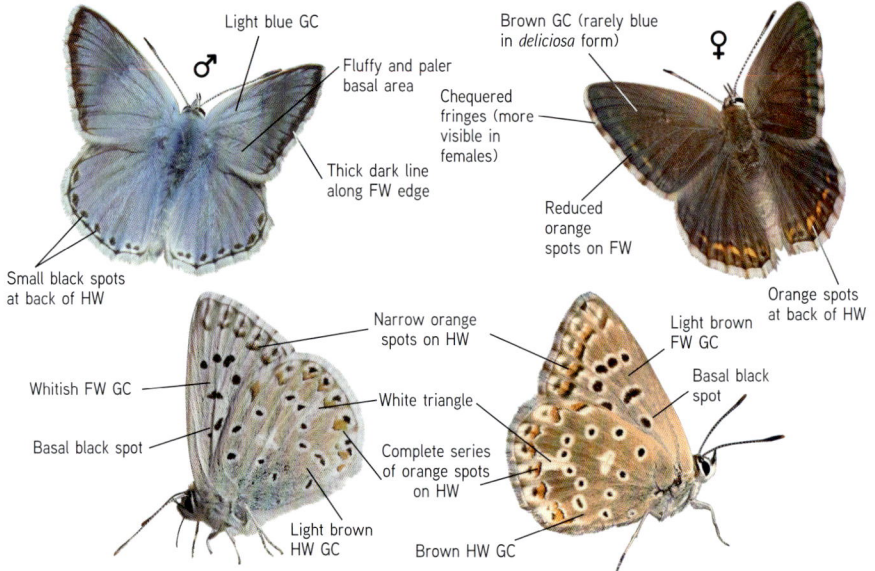

Light blue GC

♂

Fluffy and paler basal area

Brown GC (rarely blue in *deliciosa* form)

♀

Chequered fringes (more visible in females)

Thick dark line along FW edge

Reduced orange spots on FW

Small black spots at back of HW

Orange spots at back of HW

Narrow orange spots on HW

Light brown FW GC

Whitish FW GC

Basal black spot

White triangle

Basal black spot

Complete series of orange spots on HW

Light brown HW GC

Brown HW GC

Wingspan: 30–36 mm

Habitat: Montane, sheltered dry grasslands and clearings.

Hibernating stage: Egg or young caterpillar.

Elevational range: Between 1,000 and 1,800 m.

Egg-laying: Eggs are laid singly on LHP leaflets.

Flight period: July and August.

Host plants: Mainly *Hippocrepis comosa* (Fabaceae).

Diversity and systematics: The species status of *Lysandra caelestissima* remains a matter of debate. It is still sometimes considered a subspecies of *L. coridon*.

L. coridon
L. gennargenti
L. hispana
L. hispana + *L. coridon*
L. hispana + *L. caelestissima*

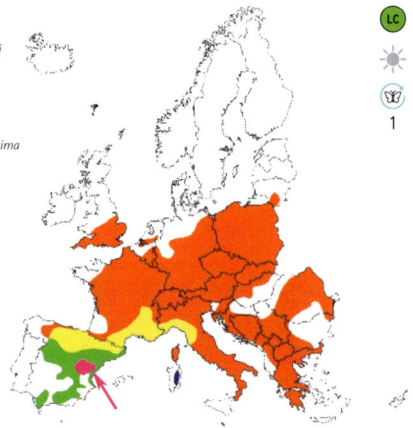

LC

1

IMAGOS			LARVAE		
Food			Food		
Behaviour of males			Caterpillar location		
Dispersion: unknown			Chrysalis location		

Did you know?

Adults relish the nectar of the eryngos, on which they are easily observed.

312

LYCAENIDAE

CHALKHILL BLUE/SARDINIAN CHALKHILL BLUE
LYSANDRA CORIDON/L. GENNARGENTI

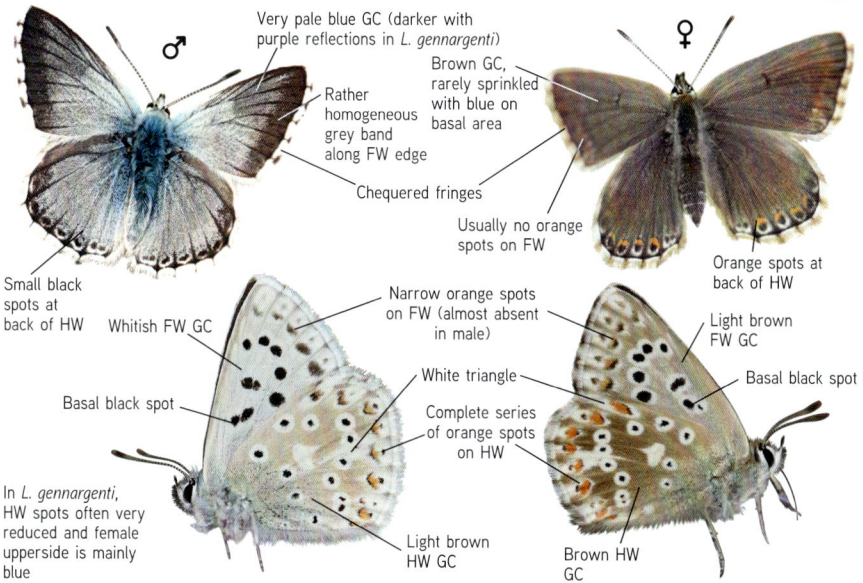

♂

Very pale blue GC (darker with purple reflections in *L. gennargenti*)

Rather homogeneous grey band along FW edge

Chequered fringes

Small black spots at back of HW

Whitish FW GC

Basal black spot

In *L. gennargenti*, HW spots often very reduced and female upperside is mainly blue

♀

Brown GC, rarely sprinkled with blue on basal area

Usually no orange spots on FW

Orange spots at back of HW

Narrow orange spots on FW (almost absent in male)

Light brown FW GC

White triangle

Basal black spot

Complete series of orange spots on HW

Light brown HW GC

Brown HW GC

Wingspan: 30–36 mm

Habitat: Calcareous or shale grasslands, low-growing meadows, and flower-rich heaths.

Hibernating stage: Caterpillar inside the egg.

Elevational range: Up to 2,500 m for *Lysandra coridon*, between 800 and 1,300 m for *L. gennargenti*.

Egg-laying: Eggs are laid singly on LHP leaflets and stems or in their surroundings.

Flight period: From July to September.

Host plants: Legumes, including *Hippocrepis comosa*, *H. conradiae*, *H. glauca*, *Astragalus glycyphyllos*, *Coronilla minima*, and *Securigera varia*.

Diversity and systematics: Numerous subspecies have been described for *Lysandra coridon*. *L. gennargenti* is sometimes considered one of them. The number of forms is also very significant.

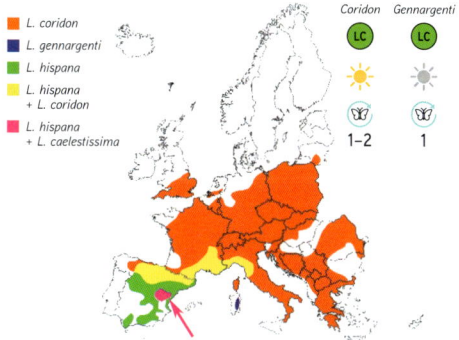

L. coridon
L. gennargenti
L. hispana
L. hispana + L. coridon
L. hispana + L. caelestissima

Coridon   Gennargenti
LC   LC

1-2   1

Did you know?

The sweet glandular secretion produced by Chalkhill Blue caterpillars contains sucrose, glucose, and no less than 14 amino acids, a real delight for the associated ants!

IMAGOS		LARVAE	
Food		Food	
Behaviour of males		Caterpillar location	
Dispersion		Chrysalis location	

LYCAENIDAE

PROVENCE CHALKHILL BLUE *LYSANDRA HISPANA*

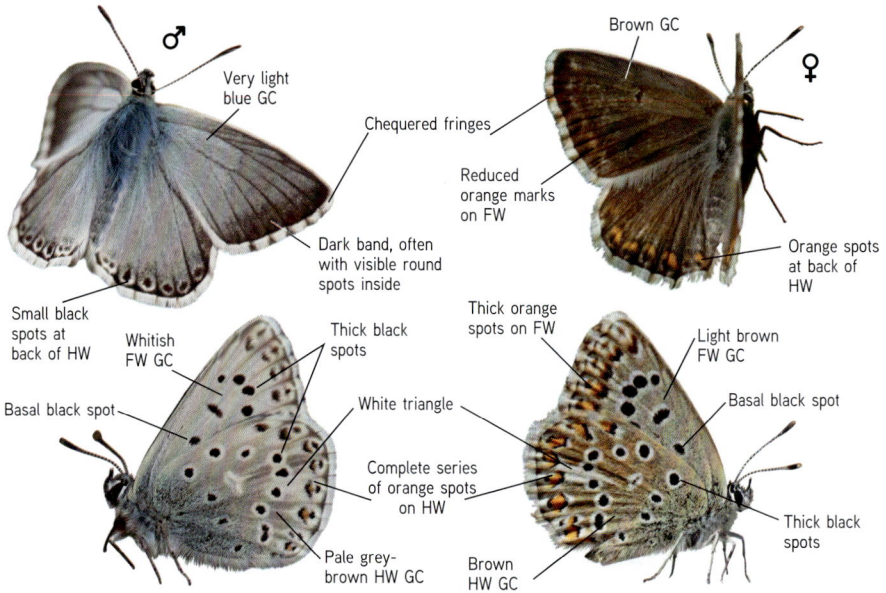

♂

Very light blue GC

Chequered fringes

Brown GC

♀

Reduced orange marks on FW

Dark band, often with visible round spots inside

Orange spots at back of HW

Small black spots at back of HW

Whitish FW GC

Thick black spots

Thick orange spots on FW

Light brown FW GC

Basal black spot

White triangle

Basal black spot

Complete series of orange spots on HW

Pale grey-brown HW GC

Brown HW GC

Thick black spots

Wingspan: 32–36 mm

Habitat: Calcareous grasslands, low-growing meadows, and garrigues.

Hibernating stage: Egg.

Elevational range: Up to 1,000 m.

Egg-laying: Eggs are laid singly on LHP leaflets.

Flight period: From April to October.

Host plants: Legumes, mainly *Hippocrepis comosa*, *H. glauca*, *H. scabra*, and *Dorycnopsis gerardi*.

Diversity and systematics: Several subspecies have been described, with little difference from the nominate subspecies. The Spanish subspecies *semperi* and *gudarensis* fly in the surroundings of Alicante and the province of Teruel, respectively.

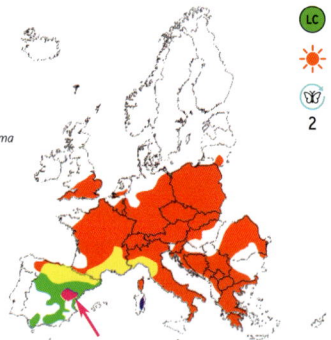

- ■ *L. coridon*
- ■ *L. gennargenti*
- ■ *L. hispana*
- ■ *L. hispana* + *L. coridon*
- ■ *L. hispana* + *L. caelestissima*

LC

2

Did you know?

The Provence Chalkhill Blue often flies sympatrically with the Chalkhill Blue. Distinguishing between the two species can be challenging, but early observations (before early June) are always Provence Chalkhill Blues.

	IMAGOS		LARVAE	
Food		Food		
Behaviour of males		Caterpillar location		
Dispersion		Chrysalis location		

LYCAENIDAE

SPANISH CHALKHILL BLUE *LYSANDRA ALBICANS*

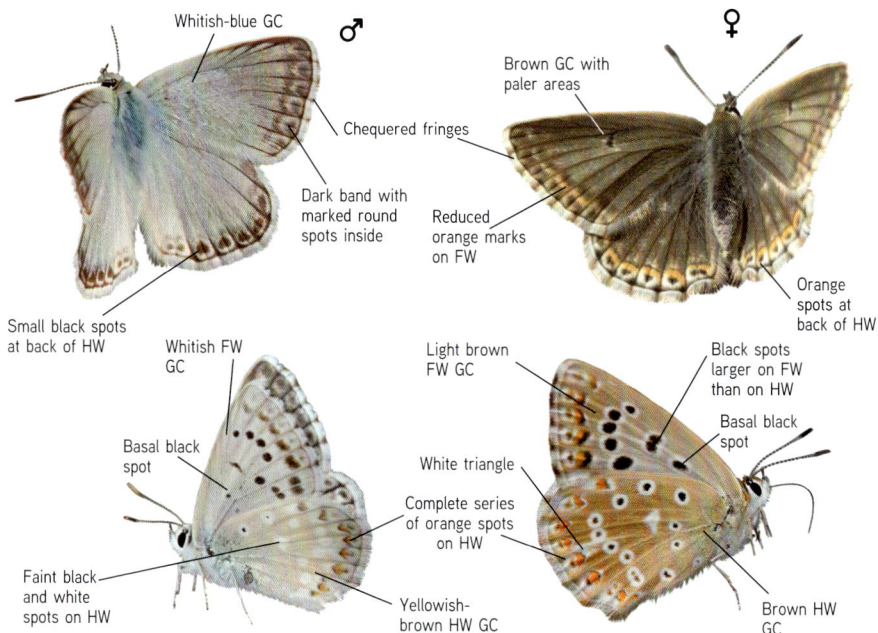

Whitish-blue GC
♂

♀
Brown GC with paler areas

Chequered fringes

Dark band with marked round spots inside

Reduced orange marks on FW

Orange spots at back of HW

Small black spots at back of HW

Whitish FW GC

Light brown FW GC

Black spots larger on FW than on HW

Basal black spot

Basal black spot

White triangle

Complete series of orange spots on HW

Faint black and white spots on HW

Yellowish-brown HW GC

Brown HW GC

Wingspan: 36–42 mm

Habitat: Arid, calcareous rocky slopes with sparse vegetation.

Hibernating stage: Egg.

Elevational range: Up to 1,500 m.

Egg-laying: Eggs are laid singly on LHP leaflets.

Flight period: From June to August.

Host plants: Mainly *Hippocrepis comosa* and *H. scabra* (Fabaceae).

Diversity and systematics: Most Spanish populations belong to the nominate subspecies. Subspecies *bolivari* and *arragonensis* fly in the Spanish provinces of Madrid and Teruel, respectively.

LC

1

IMAGOS		LARVAE	
Food		Food	
Behaviour of males		Caterpillar location	
Dispersion		Chrysalis location	

Did you know?

The very pale colouration of the males makes them easily distinguishable from other species in the same genus, such as the Provence Chalkhill Blue and the Chalkhill Blue.

315

LYCAENIDAE

CRETAN ARGUS *KRETANIA PSYLORITA*

♂/♀

Brown GC

Orange spots
becoming faint
towards wing tip

Reduced, often faint
black spots

No basal
black spot

White
fringes

Marked orange
spots at back
of HW

Thin, reduced
orange spots

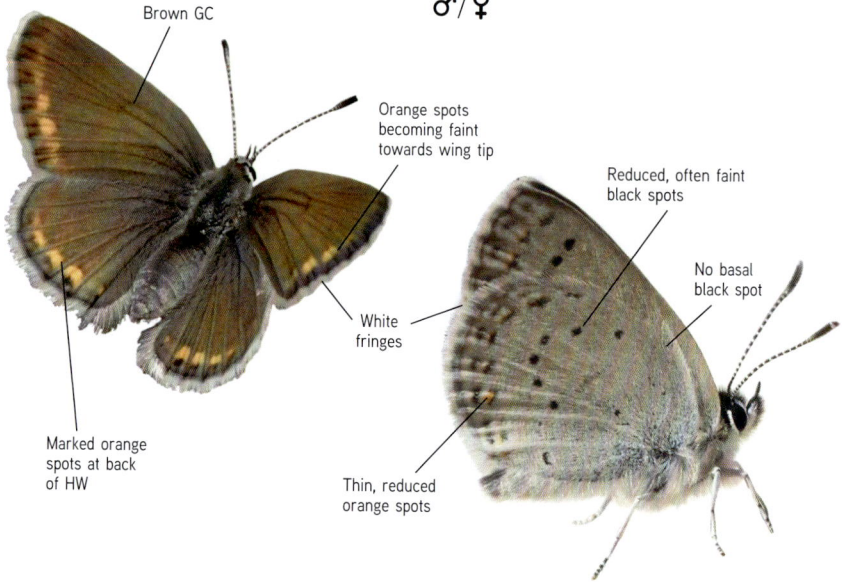

Wingspan: 23–26 mm

Habitat: Low-growing, stony garrigue.

Hibernating stage: Not known.

Elevational range: Between 1,100 and 2,200 m.

Egg-laying: Eggs are laid singly on the LHP.

Flight period: From May to July.

Host plants: Legumes, including *Astragalus creticus*.

Diversity and systematics: There are no notable subspecies for this Cretan endemic.

LC

1

Did you know?

Adults are active early in the morning and primarily fly around the LHP, on which they frequently perch. The LHP makes up the majority of the very sparse vegetation that grows in Cretan Argus habitat.

IMAGOS		LARVAE	
Food		Food: unknown	
Behaviour of males		Caterpillar location	
Dispersion		Chrysalis location	

LYCAENIDAE

ZEPHYR BLUE/PELOPONNESE BLUE
KRETANIA SEPHIRUS/K. BRETHERTONI

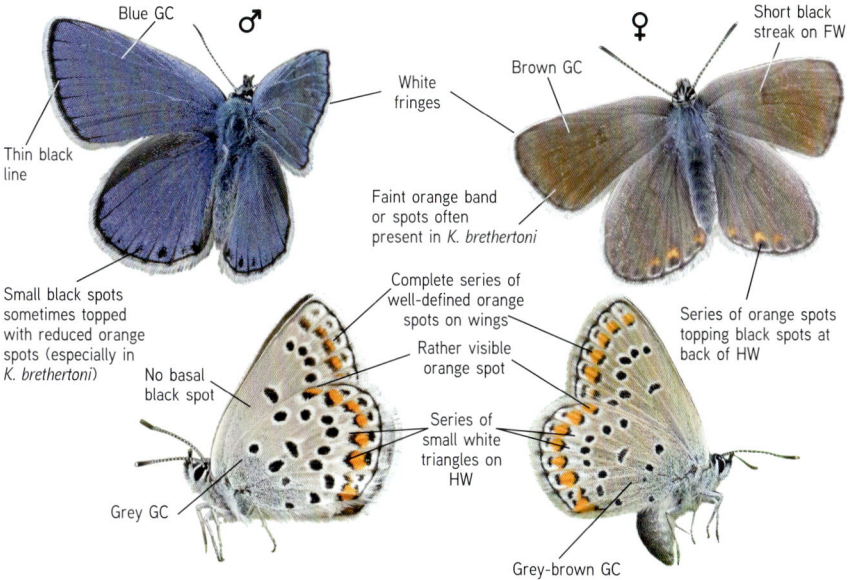

Blue GC ♂

Thin black line

White fringes

Brown GC ♀

Short black streak on FW

Small black spots sometimes topped with reduced orange spots (especially in *K. brethertoni*)

No basal black spot

Faint orange band or spots often present in *K. brethertoni*

Complete series of well-defined orange spots on wings

Rather visible orange spot

Series of small white triangles on HW

Series of orange spots topping black spots at back of HW

Grey GC

Grey-brown GC

Wingspan: 28–34 mm

Habitat: Dry grasslands and rocky or sandy grassy areas.

Hibernating stage: Caterpillar.

Elevational range: Between 500 and 2,000 m.

Egg-laying: Eggs are laid singly on LHP leaflets.

Flight period: From May to August.

Host plants: Legumes in genus *Astragalus*, mainly *A. exscapus* and *A. dasyanthus* for *Kretania sephirus*, and *A. angustifolius* and *A. parnassi* for *K. brethertoni*.

Diversity and systematics: European populations of *Kretania sephirus* belong to the nominate subspecies. The species status of *K. brethertoni* is debated: it can also be considered a subspecies of *K. sephirus*.

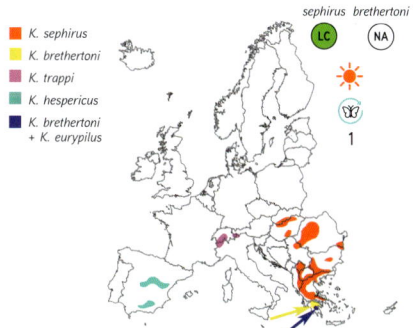

- *K. sephirus*
- *K. brethertoni*
- *K. trappi*
- *K. hespericus*
- *K. brethertoni* + *K. eurypilus*

sephirus brethertoni
LC NA

1

Did you know?

Kretania sephirus and *K. brethertoni* are morphologically very similar. However, their ranges are distinct, the latter being confined to the Peloponnese, which eliminates any confusion.

IMAGOS		LARVAE	
Food		Food	
Behaviour of males		Caterpillar location	
Dispersion		Chrysalis location	

ALPINE ZEPHYR BLUE *KRETANIA TRAPPI*

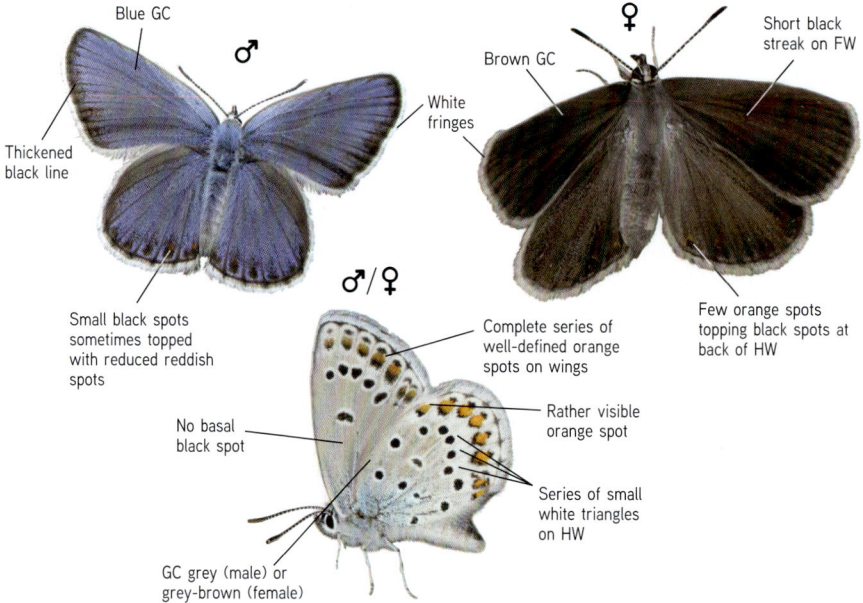

Blue GC

♂

Thickened
black line

White
fringes

♀

Brown GC

Short black
streak on FW

Few orange spots
topping black spots at
back of HW

♂/♀

Small black spots
sometimes topped
with reduced reddish
spots

Complete series of
well-defined orange
spots on wings

Rather visible
orange spot

No basal
black spot

Series of small
white triangles
on HW

GC grey (male) or
grey-brown (female)

Wingspan: 28–34 mm

Habitat: Dry, montane grasslands and pine forest clearings, sandy banks.

Hibernating stage: Caterpillar.

Elevational range: Between 1,000 and 2,000 m.

Egg-laying: Eggs are laid singly on LHP leaflets.

Flight period: From June to August.

Host plants: Legumes in genus *Astragalus*, especially *A. exscapus*, *A. alopecurus*, and *A. centroalpinus*.

Diversity and systematics: There are no notable subspecies for this blue, which is endemic to the Central Alps.

K. sephirus
K. brethertoni
K. trappi
K. hespericus
K. brethertoni + K. eurypilus

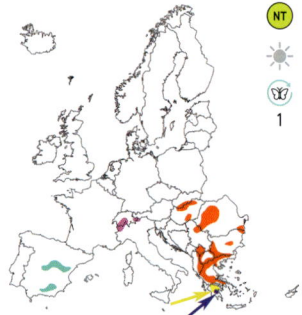

NT

1

Did you know?

The alpine Zephyr Blue is frequently observed sipping water and mineral salts from damp, sandy soils. Checking butterfly gatherings is the simplest way to find it in its habitat.

IMAGOS		LARVAE	
Food		Food	
Behaviour of males		Caterpillar location	
Dispersion		Chrysalis location	

LYCAENIDAE

EASTERN BROWN ARGUS *KRETANIA EURYPILUS*

Brown GC

♂/♀

Complete series
of well-defined
orange spots
on wings

GC grey (male)
or grey-brown
(female)

White
fringes

Rather visible
orange spot

No basal
black spot

Series of small
white triangles
on HW

Small orange spots
at back of HW

Some shiny blue
scales possible here

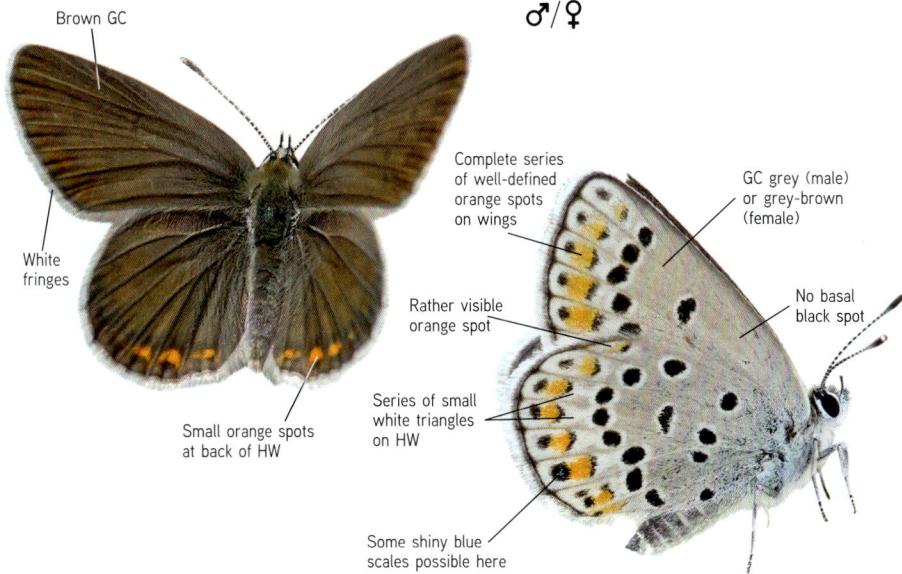

Wingspan: 28–31 mm

Habitat: Rocky subalpine grasslands.

Hibernating stage: Caterpillar.

Elevational range: Between 1,500 and 2,200 m.

Egg-laying: Eggs are laid singly on LHP leaflets.

Flight period: From May to August.

Host plants: Mainly *Astragalus rumelicus* and *A. creticus* (Fabaceae).

Diversity and systematics: European populations belong to subspecies *pelopides*.

■ *K. sephirus*
■ *K. brethertoni*
■ *K. trappi*
■ *K. hespericus*
■ *K. brethertoni*
  + K. eurypilus

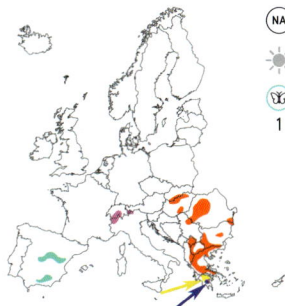

NA

1

Did you know?

The Eastern Brown Argus is
one of the few butterflies in the
Polyommatinae subfamily that
does not exhibit marked sexual
dimorphism. Its identification
in the field relies heavily on
examining the underside, as the
females of many other species
have similar upperside wing
patterns.

IMAGOS		LARVAE	
Food	☆ ◌	Food	🍃
Behaviour of males		Caterpillar location	🌱 🐜
Dispersion		Chrysalis location	

LYCAENIDAE

SPANISH ZEPHYR BLUE *KRETANIA HESPERICUS*

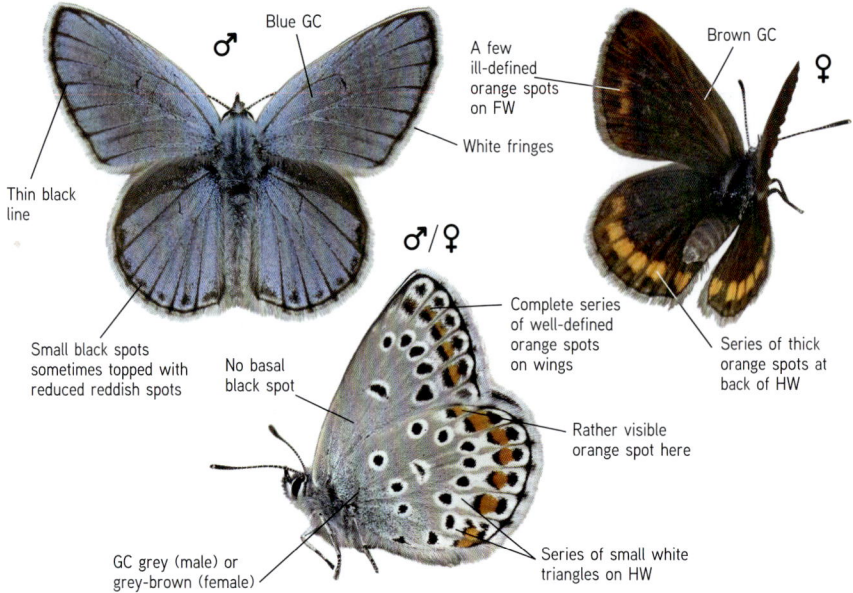

♂ Blue GC

A few ill-defined orange spots on FW

Brown GC

♀

White fringes

Thin black line

♂/♀

Small black spots sometimes topped with reduced reddish spots

No basal black spot

Complete series of well-defined orange spots on wings

Series of thick orange spots at back of HW

Rather visible orange spot here

GC grey (male) or grey-brown (female)

Series of small white triangles on HW

Wingspan: 28–32 mm

Habitat: Dry, scrubby slopes.

Hibernating stage: Caterpillar.

Elevational range: Between 500 and 1,500 m.

Egg-laying: Eggs are laid singly on LHP leaflets.

Flight period: From April to July.

Host plants: Legumes in genus *Astragalus*, especially *A. alopecuroides*, *A. clusianus*, *A. monspessulanus*, *A. nevadensis*, *A. sempervirens*, and *A. turolensis.*

Diversity and systematics: There are no notable subspecies for this blue, which is endemic to Spain.

- ■ *K. sephirus*
- □ *K. brethertoni*
- ■ *K. trappi*
- ■ *K. hespericus*
- ■ *K. brethertoni* + *K. eurypilus*

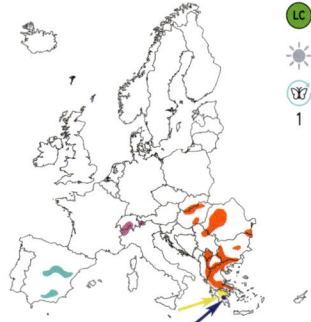

LC

1

Did you know?

With *Kretania trappi*, *K. sephirus*, and *K. brethertoni*, *K. hespericus* forms a complex of cryptic species that were split about a decade ago after being grouped under the name *K. pylaon*. The latter species is present in Ukraine and Russia.

IMAGOS		LARVAE	
Food		Food	
Behaviour of males		Caterpillar location	
Dispersion		Chrysalis location	

REVERDIN'S BLUE *PLEBEJUS ARGYROGNOMON*

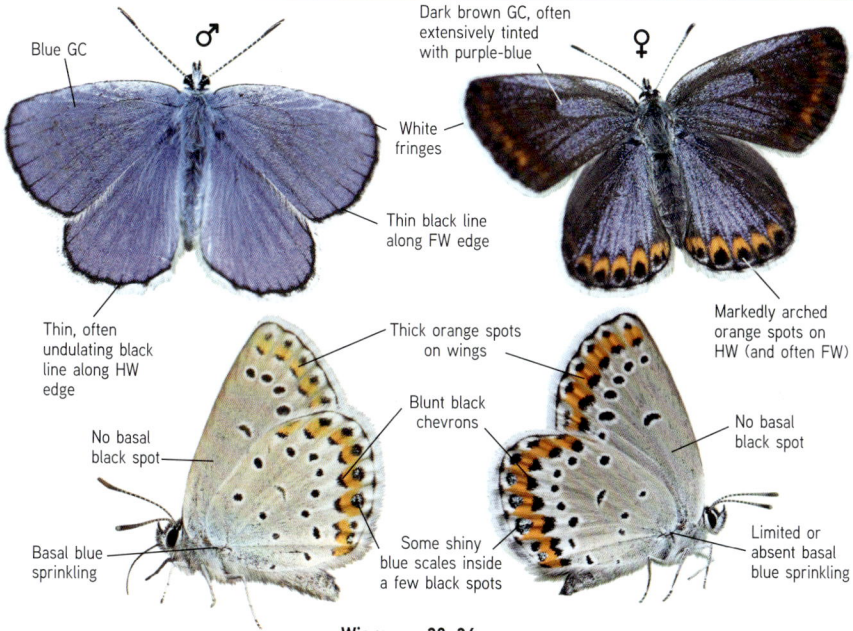

Blue GC

♂

Dark brown GC, often extensively tinted with purple-blue

♀

White fringes

Thin black line along FW edge

Thin, often undulating black line along HW edge

No basal black spot

Basal blue sprinkling

Thick orange spots on wings

Blunt black chevrons

Some shiny blue scales inside a few black spots

Markedly arched orange spots on HW (and often FW)

No basal black spot

Limited or absent basal blue sprinkling

Wingspan: 28–34 mm

Habitat: Flower-rich, mesophilic meadows and grasslands, edges, and roadsides.

Hibernating stage: Egg.

Elevational range: Up to 2,000 m (more abundant at lower elevations).

Egg-laying: Eggs are laid singly on LHP leaflets and stems.

Flight period: From May to August.

Host plants: Legumes, including *Securigera varia*, *Astragalus glycyphyllos*, *A. brachylobus*, *A. danicus*, *Hippocrepis comosa*, *Lotus corniculatus*, *Melitotus officinalis*, and *Onobrychis viciifolia*.

Diversity and systematics: Most European populations belong to the nominate subspecies. Subspecies *letitia* inhabits Italy up to southeastern France. Other subspecies have been described, but their boundaries need confirmation.

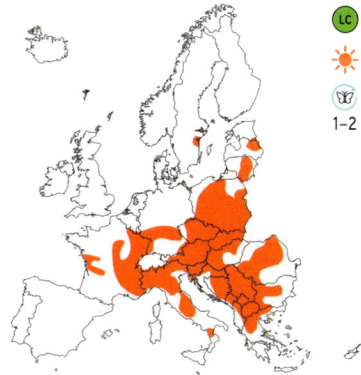

LC

1–2

	IMAGOS		LARVAE	
Food	🌸		Food	🌿
Behaviour of males	🦋		Caterpillar location	🌱 🐜
Dispersion			Chrysalis location	🪨 🌱 🐜

Did you know?

Due to its affinity for extensively managed environments, Reverdin's Blue is facing the pressures of both agricultural intensification and pastoral abandonment.

LYCAENIDAE

THE SILVER-STUDDED BLUE *PLEBEJUS ARGUS*

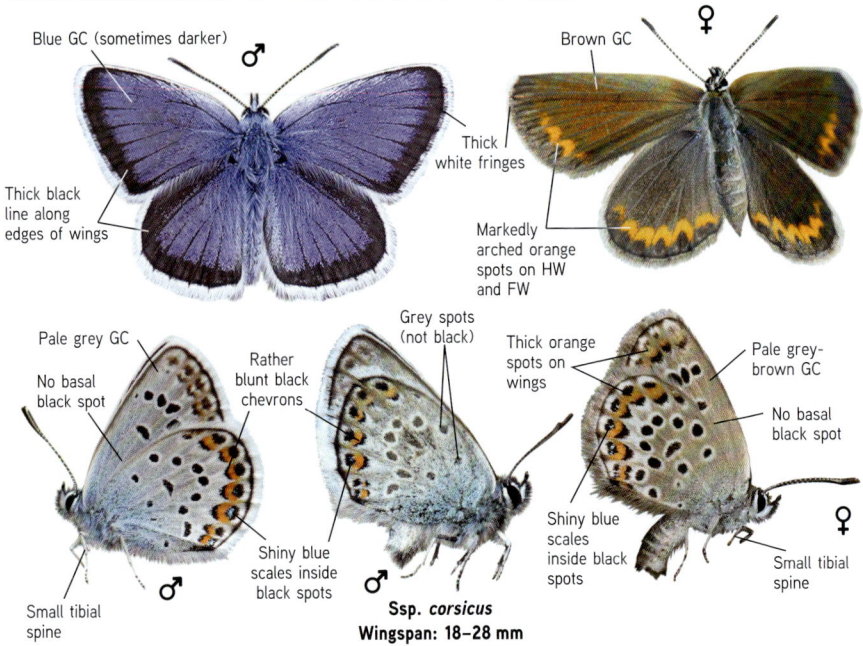

Blue GC (sometimes darker) ♂

Brown GC ♀

Thick white fringes

Thick black line along edges of wings

Markedly arched orange spots on HW and FW

Pale grey GC

Grey spots (not black)

Thick orange spots on wings

Pale grey-brown GC

No basal black spot

Rather blunt black chevrons

No basal black spot

Shiny blue scales inside black spots ♂

Shiny blue scales inside black spots

Small tibial spine ♀

Small tibial spine ♂

Ssp. *corsicus*
Wingspan: 18–28 mm

Habitat: Grasslands, heaths (including bog surroundings), meadows, and clearings.

Hibernating stage: Caterpillar inside the egg.

Elevational range: Up to 2,500 m.

Egg-laying: Eggs are laid singly on LHP leaves and stems.

Flight period: From May to August.

Host plants: A wide variety of legumes, including *Lotus corniculatus*, *L. dorycnium*, *L. tenuis*, *Securigera varia*, *Onobrychis montana*, *O. supina*, *O. viciifolia*, *Hippocrepis comosa*, *Genista anglica*, *G. salzmannii*, *G. sagittalis*, *Ononis arvensis*,

O. spinosa, *Ulex europaeus*, *U. minor*, *U. gallii*, *Cytisus scoparius*, *Medicago lupulina*, *M. sativa*, and *Colutea arborescens*. Also on some Ericacae, such as *Arctostaphylos uva-ursi*, *Calluna vulgaris*, *E. cinerea*, *Erica tetralix*, *Vaccinium myrtillus*, and *V. uliginosum*. Some Cistaceae, like *Cistus calycinus*, *C. halimifolius*, *C. libanotis*, *Helianthemum nummularium*, *H. canum*, *H. oelandicum*, and *Halimium halimifolium*. *Limonium vulgare* (Plumbaginaceae).

Diversity and systematics: Several dozen subspecies have been described for this blue, which is widespread across Eurasia.

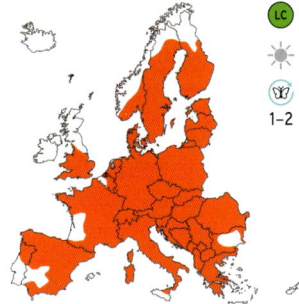

LC

1–2

IMAGOS			LARVAE				
Food			Food				
Behaviour of males			Caterpillar location				
Dispersion			Chrysalis location				

Did you know?

The Silver-studded Blue is closely associated with the presence of ants of genus *Lasius*. For instance, females lay their eggs on plants near ant colonies, facilitating encounters between the caterpillars and their bodyguards.

LYCAENIDAE

IDAS BLUE *PLEBEJUS IDAS*

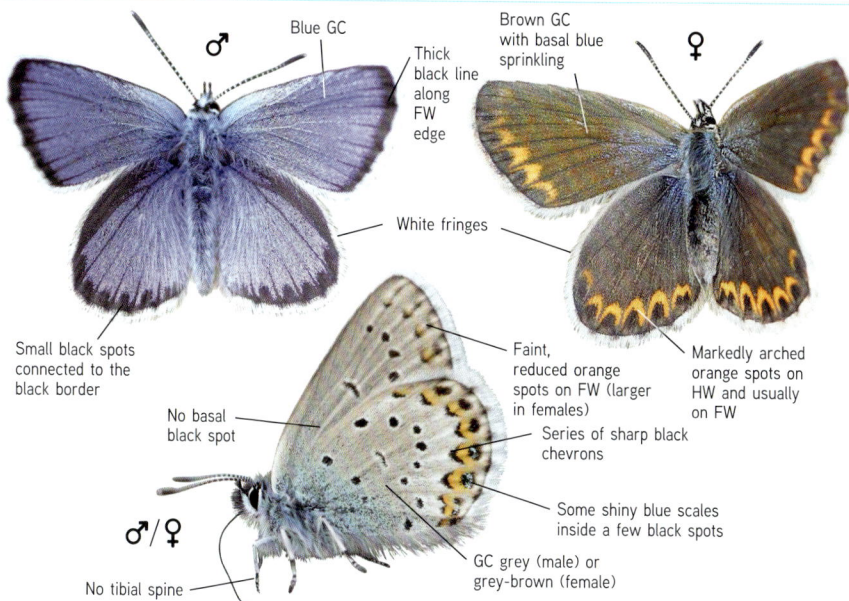

♂

Blue GC

Thick black line along FW edge

Brown GC with basal blue sprinkling

♀

White fringes

Small black spots connected to the black border

No basal black spot

Faint, reduced orange spots on FW (larger in females)

Markedly arched orange spots on HW and usually on FW

Series of sharp black chevrons

Some shiny blue scales inside a few black spots

♂/♀

No tibial spine

GC grey (male) or grey-brown (female)

Wingspan: 18–30 mm

Habitat: Sandy grasslands, meadows, heaths, and edges.

Hibernating stage: Egg.

Elevational range: Up to 2,500 m.

Egg-laying: Eggs are laid singly on LHP stems and leaves.

Flight period: From May to September.

Host plants: Numerous legumes, including *Astragalus depressus, A. glycyphyllos, A. monspessulanus, Cercis siliquastrum, Chamaecytisus albus, C. eriocarpus, Colutea arborescens, Cytisus balansae, C. scoparius, C. villosus, Genista tinctoria, G. aspalathoides, G. pilosa, G. corsica, G. tinctoria, G. germanica, Laburnum anagyroides,* *Lotus corniculatus, L. dorycnium, L. maritimus, L. tetragonolobus, Medicago falcata, M. lupulina, M. sativa, Melitotus albus, M. officinalis, Onobrychis montana, O. saxatilis, O. viciifolia, Ononis spinosa, Trifolium campestre, T. pratense, T. repens, Securigera varia, Ulex minor, U. europaeus,* and *Anthyllis vulneraria.* Some Ericaceae, like *Calluna vulgaris, Empetrum nigrum, Erica tetralix,* and *Vaccinium uliginosum.* Also on *Helianthemum nummularium* and *H. oelandicum* (Cistaceae).

Diversity and systematics: Numerous subspecies have been described for this blue, which is widespread across Eurasia and North America.

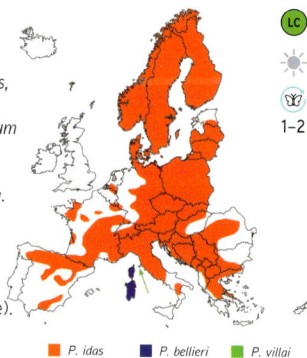

LC

1–2

■ *P. idas*   ■ *P. bellieri*   ■ *P. villai*

Did you know?

Females lay their eggs near ant colonies (genera *Lasius* and *Formica*), which will guard the caterpillars. The metamorphosis takes place within the ant nest.

IMAGOS		LARVAE	
Food	✿ 💧	Food	🍃
Behaviour of males	🦋	Caterpillar location	🌱 🌿 🐜
Dispersion	🦋	Chrysalis location	🪨 🍂 🐜

LYCAENIDAE

BELLIER'S BLUE/ELBA BLUE *PLEBEJUS BELLIERI/P. VILLAI*

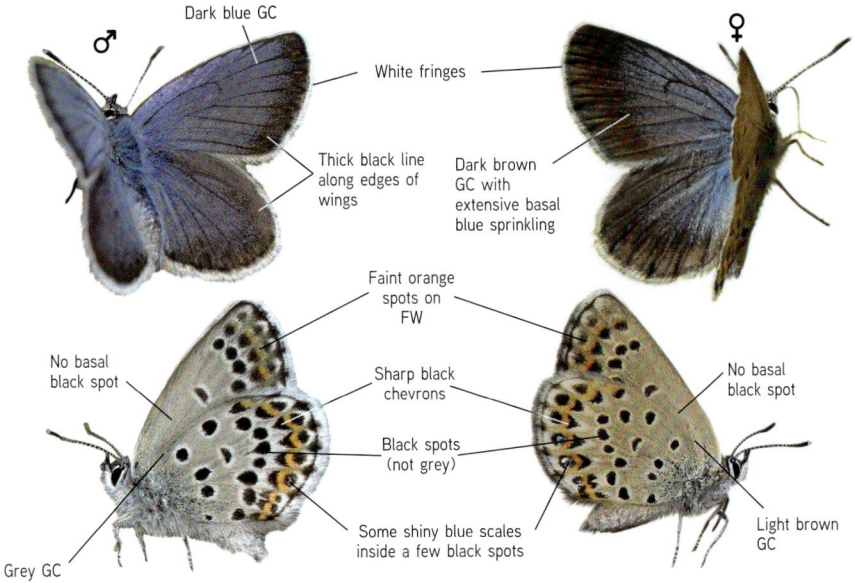

♂

Dark blue GC

White fringes

Thick black line along edges of wings

Dark brown GC with extensive basal blue sprinkling

♀

Faint orange spots on FW

No basal black spot

Sharp black chevrons

Black spots (not grey)

No basal black spot

Some shiny blue scales inside a few black spots

Light brown GC

Grey GC

Wingspan: 20–26 mm

Habitat: Garrigues, maquis, and Mediterranean clearings.

Hibernating stage: Egg.

Elevational range: Up to 1,500 m (below 1,000 m for *Plebejus villai*).

Egg-laying: Eggs are laid singly on the LHP.

Flight period: From June to August.

Host plants: Legumes in genus *Genista*, especially *G. corsica* and *G. salzmanni*. Also on *Anthyllis hermanniae* and *Hippocrepis conradiae*.

Diversity and systematics: There are no notable subspecies for *Plebejus bellieri*, once considered a subspecies of *P. idas*. Some authors still maintain this status for *P. villai*.

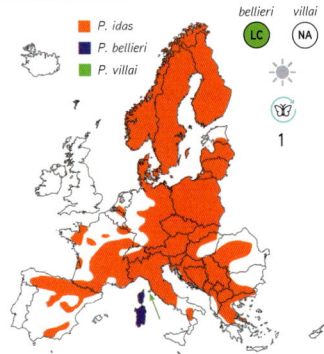

- P. idas
- P. bellieri
- P. villai

bellieri — LC
villai — NA

Did you know?

There is no risk of confusion between these blues and the Corsican Silver-studded Blue, due to well-defined black spots in the former and faded grey ones in the latter.

IMAGOS		LARVAE		
Food		Food		
Behaviour of males		Caterpillar location		
Dispersion		Chrysalis location		

LYCAENIDAE

CRANBERRY BLUE *AGRIADES OPTILETE*

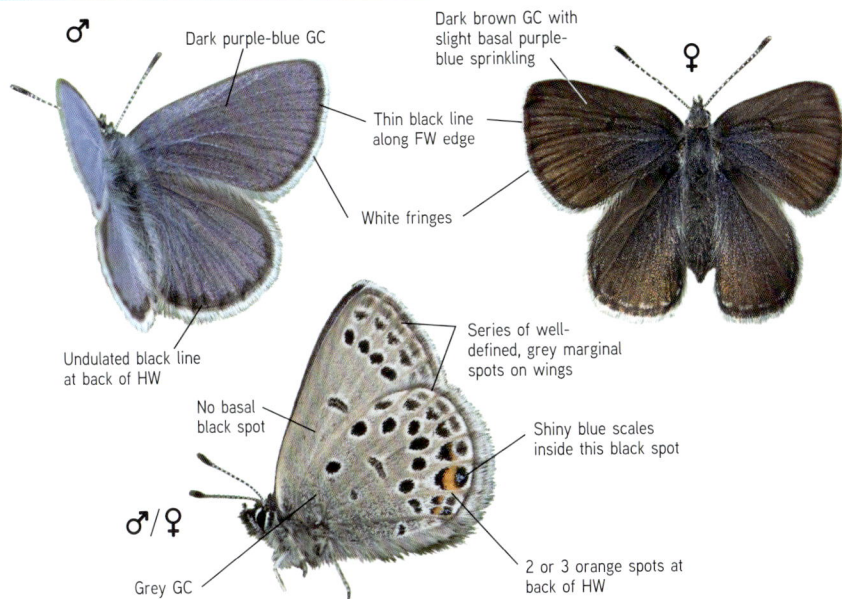

♂ Dark purple-blue GC

Dark brown GC with slight basal purple-blue sprinkling

♀

Thin black line along FW edge

White fringes

Undulated black line at back of HW

Series of well-defined, grey marginal spots on wings

No basal black spot

Shiny blue scales inside this black spot

♂/♀

Grey GC

2 or 3 orange spots at back of HW

Wingspan: 21–29 mm

Habitat: Bogs and subalpine Ericaeae-dominated heaths.

Hibernating stage: Caterpillar.

Elevational range: Up to 2,800 m (above 1,500 m in the Alps).

Egg-laying: Eggs are laid singly on LHP leaves.

Flight period: From June to August.

Host plants: Ericaeae, including *Vaccinium uliginosum*, *V. myrtillus*, *V. vitis-idaea*, *Oxycoccus palustris*, *Andromeda polifolia*, and *Erica tetralix*.

Diversity and systematics: Most European populations belong to the nominate subspecies. Subspecies *cyparissus* is present in the northern parts of Europe – for example, in Lapland.

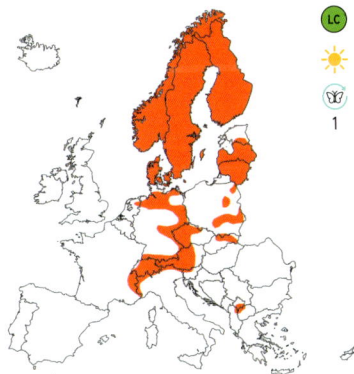

LC

1

	IMAGOS		LARVAE	
Food		Food	
Behaviour of males		Caterpillar location	
Dispersion		Chrysalis location	

Did you know?

The Cranberry Blue is often a companion species of the Moorland Clouded Yellow (*Colias palaeno*), with which it shares its main host plant, the Bog Blueberry.

325

LYCAENIDAE

LOEW'S BLUE *PLEBEJIDEA LOEWII*

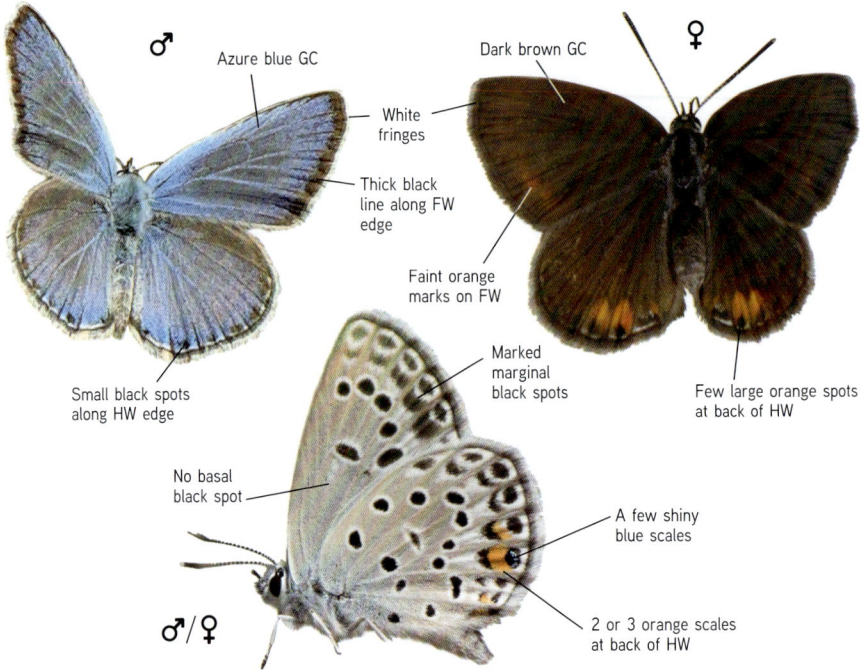

♂

Azure blue GC

White
fringes

Thick black
line along FW
edge

Faint orange
marks on FW

Small black spots
along HW edge

No basal
black spot

Dark brown GC

♀

Marked
marginal
black spots

Few large orange spots
at back of HW

A few shiny
blue scales

♂ / ♀

2 or 3 orange scales
at back of HW

Wingspan: 27–30 mm

Habitat: Stony garrigues.

Hibernating stage: Caterpillar inside the egg.

Elevational range: Up to 1,000 m in Europe.

Egg-laying: Eggs are laid singly on LHP leaves and stems.

Flight period: From May to June.

Host plants: Legumes in genus *Astragalus*.

Diversity and systematics: European populations of this blue, widespread across the Near East, belong to the nominate subspecies.

NA

1

IMAGOS		LARVAE	
Food	🌼 💧	Food	🌼 🍃 🌿
Behaviour of males	🦋 🦋	Caterpillar location	🌿
Dispersion	🔲	Chrysalis location	🍂

Did you know?

Loew's Blue reaches the western limit of its range in the Aegean Islands.

LYCAENIDAE

GERANIUM ARGUS   *EUMEDONIA EUMEDON*

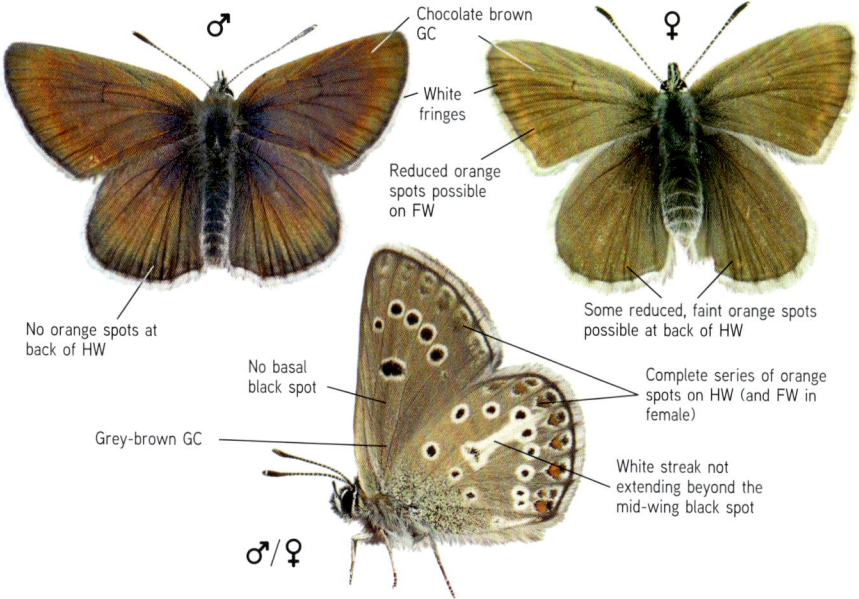

♂

Chocolate brown GC

White fringes

Reduced orange spots possible on FW

♀

No orange spots at back of HW

No basal black spot

Grey-brown GC

♂/♀

Some reduced, faint orange spots possible at back of HW

Complete series of orange spots on HW (and FW in female)

White streak not extending beyond the mid-wing black spot

Wingspan: 23–32 mm

Habitat: Hay meadows, megaphorbs, edges, and clearings.

Hibernating stage: Caterpillar.

Elevational range: Up to 2,400 m (mainly above 800 m outside Scandinavia).

Egg-laying: Eggs are laid singly or in a few units on the LHP ovaries.

Flight period: From May to August.

Host plants: Geraniaceae, including *Geranium sylvaticum*, *G. sanguineum*, *G. palustre*, *G. purpureum*, *G. phaeum*, *G. pyrenaicum*, *G. subargenteum*, *G. tuberosum*, *G. versicolor*, *G. dolomiticum*, *G. cinereum*, *G. pratense*, *Erodium foetidum*, *E. glandulosum*, *E. hartvigianum*, and *E. saxatile*.

Diversity and systematics: More than a dozen subspecies have been described for Europe, which reflects how fragmented the range of the species is.

IMAGOS		LARVAE	
Food	🌸	Food	🌸 🍃
Behaviour of males	🦋	Caterpillar location	🌿 🐜
Dispersion	🦋	Chrysalis location	🐛

Did you know?

The Geranium Argus is closely associated with its LHP, which adults primarily feed on and seldom stray far from.

MELEAGER'S BLUE *POLYOMMATUS DAPHNIS*

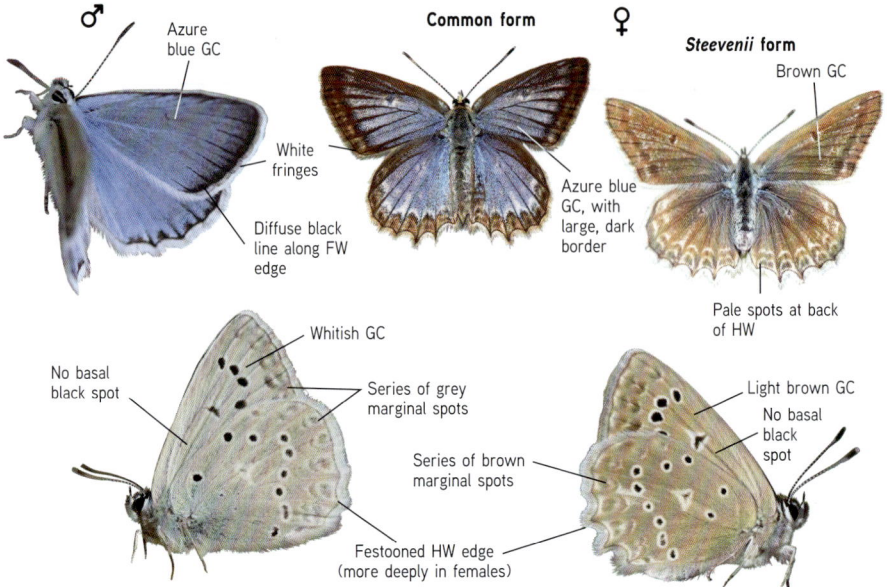

♂

Azure blue GC

Common form

♀

Steevenii form

Brown GC

White fringes

Diffuse black line along FW edge

Azure blue GC, with large, dark border

Pale spots at back of HW

Whitish GC

No basal black spot

Series of grey marginal spots

Series of brown marginal spots

Light brown GC

No basal black spot

Festooned HW edge (more deeply in females)

Wingspan: 32–38 mm

Habitat: Stony, bushy, dry grasslands, low-growing meadows, edges, and clearings.

Hibernating stage: Egg or very young caterpillar.

Elevational range: Up to 2,000 m.

Egg-laying: Eggs are laid singly on LHP leaves or on dry adjacent vegetation.

Flight period: From June to August.

Host plants: Legumes, mainly *Securigera varia*. Also on *Astragalus glycyphyllos*, *A. depressus*, *A. cylleneus*, *A. monspessulanus*, *A. onobrychis*, *A. sirinicus*, *Hedysarum candidum*, *Hippocrepis comosa*, *Lathyrus niger*, and *Onobrychis viciifolia*. Reported on *Thymus serpyllum* (Lamiaceae).

Diversity and systematics: Most European populations belong to the nominate subspecies. Subspecies *marteniana* flies in the Iberian Peninsula.

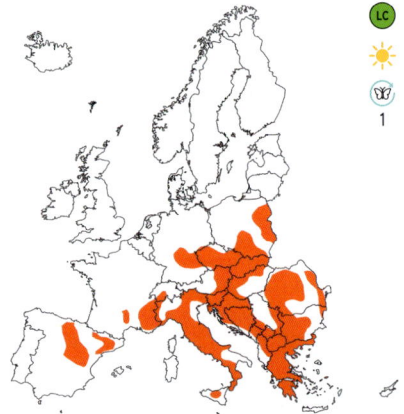

LC

1

IMAGOS		LARVAE	
Food	🌸 💧	Food	🌿 🌱
Behaviour of males		Caterpillar location	
Dispersion		Chrysalis location	

Did you know?

Meleager's Blue can rarely hybridize with the Chalkhill Blue where both species fly together.

328

COMMON BLUE *POLYOMMATUS ICARUS*

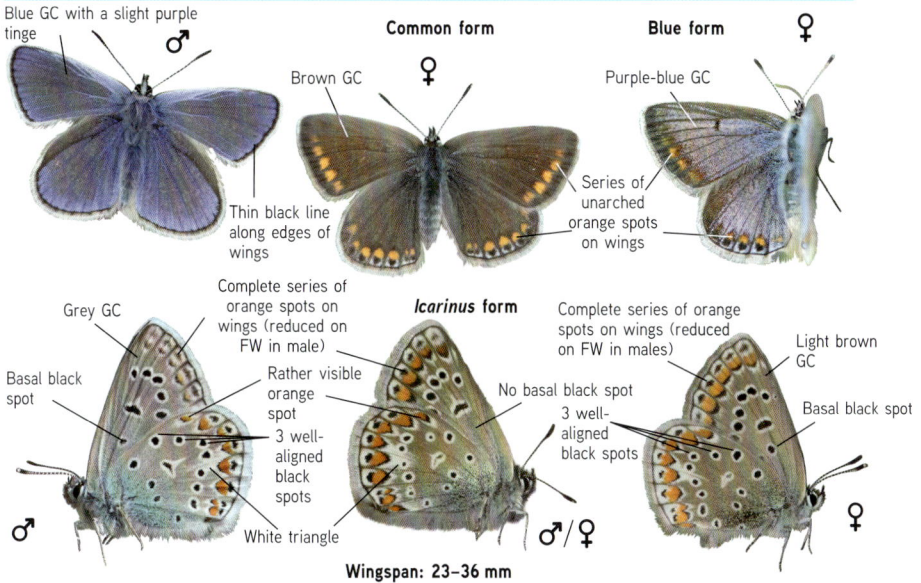

Blue GC with a slight purple tinge ♂

Common form ♀

Brown GC

Blue form ♀

Purple-blue GC

Thin black line along edges of wings

Series of unarched orange spots on wings

Grey GC

Complete series of orange spots on wings (reduced on FW in male)

Icarinus form

Complete series of orange spots on wings (reduced on FW in males)

Light brown GC

Basal black spot

Rather visible orange spot

No basal black spot

Basal black spot

3 well-aligned black spots

3 well-aligned black spots

♂

White triangle

♂/♀

♀

Wingspan: 23–36 mm

Habitat: Grasslands, meadows, and wastelands, even in very anthropized areas (parks and gardens).

Hibernating stage: Caterpillar.

Elevational range: Up to 3,000 m.

Egg-laying: Eggs are laid singly or in a few units on LHP leaves and flowers.

Flight period: From March to November.

Host plants: A wide variety of legumes, including *Astragalus alopecuroides, A. cylleneus, A. glycyphyllos, A. monspessulanus, A. sirinicus, Cytisus scoparius, Genista hispanica, G. pilosa, G. tinctoria, Hippocrepis comosa, Lathyrus oleraceus, Lotus angustissimus, L. corniculatus, L. dorycnium, L. glareosus, L. hirsutus, L. ornithopodioides, L. pedunculatus,* *Medicago arabica, M. disciformis, M. falcata, M. littorialis, M. lupulina, M. minima, M. polymorpha, M. sativa, M. truncatula, Melilotus albus, M. officinalis, M. indicus, Onobrychis caput-galli, O. supina, O. viciifolia, Ononis repens, O. arvensis, Oxytropis campestris, Securigera varia, Trifolium arvense, T. campestre, T. dubium, T. fragiferum, T. montanum, T. nigrescens, T. ochroleucon, T. parnassi, T. repens, T. scabrum, Ulex europaeus, U. parviflorus,* and *Vicia hirsuta.* Also on *Helianthemum nummularium* (Cistaceae).

Diversity and systematics: Most European populations belong to the nominate subspecies. Subspecies *boalensis* flies in Spain. Subspecies *mariscolore* is found in Ireland, and subspecies *flavocinctata* is described from Corsica.

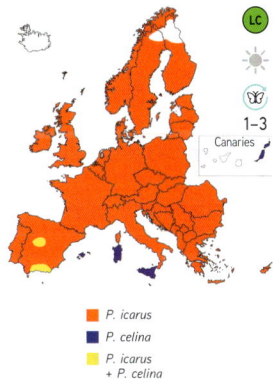

LC

1–3
Canaries

■ *P. icarus*
■ *P. celina*
□ *P. icarus*
   + *P. celina*

Did you know?

The Common Blue is the most widespread and commonly encountered Lycaenid butterfly. Being such a generalist at the larval stage, it tolerates the disturbances of urban environments quite well.

IMAGOS		LARVAE	
Food		Food	
Behaviour of males		Caterpillar location	
Dispersion		Chrysalis location	

LYCAENIDAE

SOUTHERN COMMON BLUE *POLYOMMATUS CELINA*

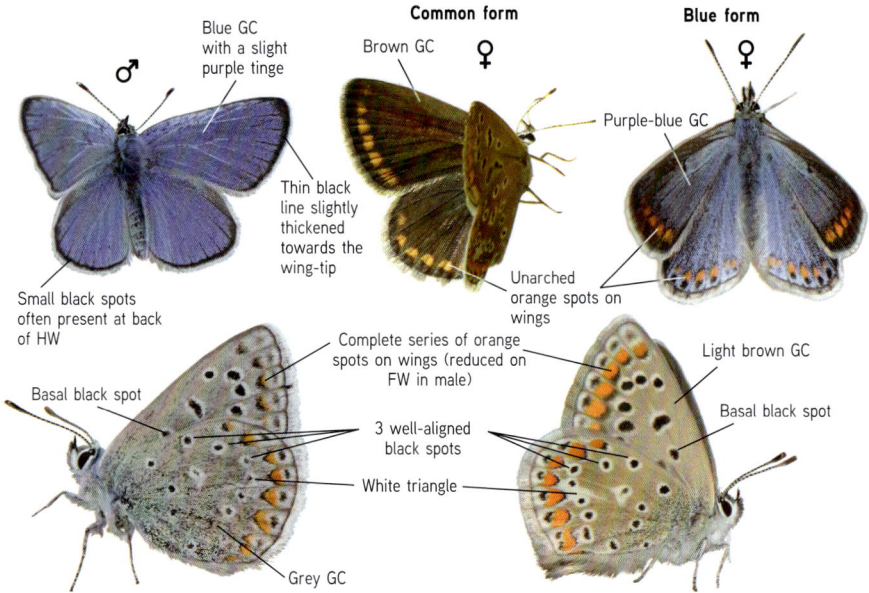

Common form

Blue form

♂ Blue GC with a slight purple tinge

Brown GC ♀

♀

Purple-blue GC

Thin black line slightly thickened towards the wing-tip

Small black spots often present at back of HW

Unarched orange spots on wings

Complete series of orange spots on wings (reduced on FW in male)

Light brown GC

Basal black spot

3 well-aligned black spots

Basal black spot

White triangle

Grey GC

Wingspan: 21–33 mm

Habitat: Open habitats, such as grasslands, meadows, grassy banks, and more arid environments.

Hibernating stage: Caterpillar in the Iberian Peninsula; all stages in the Canary Islands.

Elevational range: Up to 2,000 m.

Egg-laying: Eggs are laid singly on LHP leaflets.

Flight period: From March to October in Western Europe, year-round in the Canary Islands.

Host plants: Legumes, including *Lotus lancerottensis*, *Medicago minima*, *M. polymorpha*, *M. sativa*, *Coronilla* spp., *Melilotus* spp., *Trifolium campestre*, and *T. fragiferum*.

Diversity and systematics: European populations belong to the nominate subspecies.

■ *P. icarus*
■ *P. celina*
■ *P. icarus* + *P. celina*

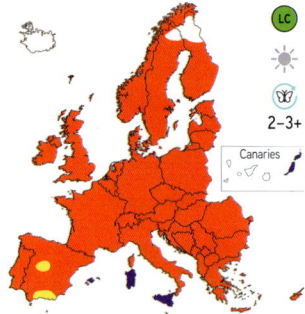

LC

2–3+

Canaries

Did you know?

The Southern Common Blue is morphologically indistinguishable (even by genitalia examination) from the Common Blue, which it replaces in the Canary Islands, Sicily, Sardinia, and the Balearic Islands, but with which it could fly in the Iberian Peninsula.

IMAGOS		LARVAE	
Food		Food	
Behaviour of males		Caterpillar location	
Dispersion: unknown		Chrysalis location	

LYCAENIDAE

CHAPMAN'S BLUE *POLYOMMATUS THERSITES*

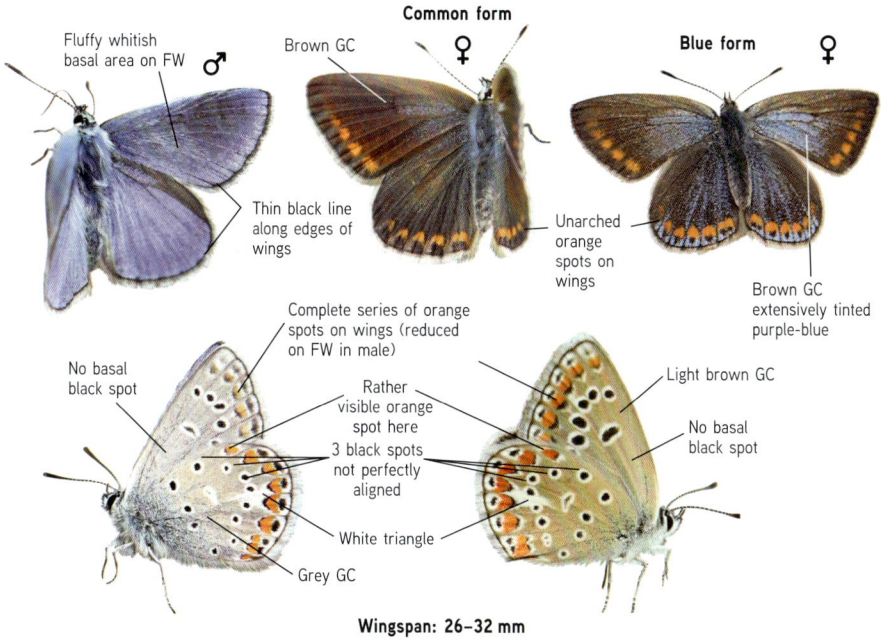

Common form

Fluffy whitish basal area on FW ♂

Brown GC ♀

Blue form ♀

Thin black line along edges of wings

Unarched orange spots on wings

Brown GC extensively tinted purple-blue

Complete series of orange spots on wings (reduced on FW in male)

No basal black spot

Rather visible orange spot here

Light brown GC

3 black spots not perfectly aligned

No basal black spot

White triangle

Grey GC

Wingspan: 26–32 mm

Habitat: Dry, calcareous grasslands and mesophilic meadows at higher altitude; grassy edges.

Hibernating stage: Caterpillar.

Elevational range: Up to 2,000 m.

Egg-laying: Eggs are laid singly on LHP leaflets.

Flight period: From April to October.

Host plants: Legumes in genus *Onobrychis*, including *O. viciifolia, O. arenaria, O. saxatilis, O. supina, O. alba, O. humilis, O. pindicola, O. pallasii, O. aequidentata,* and *O. caput-galli.* Also on *Hedysarum tauricum* and *Sulla coronaria.*

Diversity and systematics: European populations of this blue, widespread in Asia and the Near East, belong to the nominate subspecies.

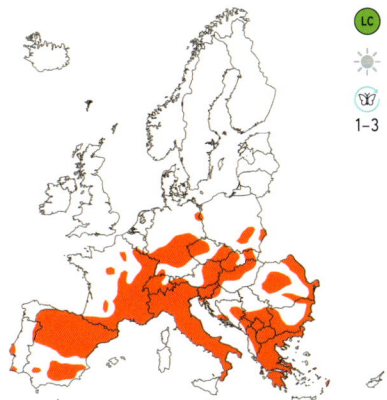

LC

1–3

IMAGOS		LARVAE	
Food	✿	Food	🍃
Behaviour of males		Caterpillar location	
Dispersion		Chrysalis location	

Did you know?

The caterpillars consume the parenchyma of the LHP leaflets without attacking the veins, leaving a distinctive pattern that signals their presence.

331

ESCHER'S BLUE *POLYOMMATUS ESCHERI*

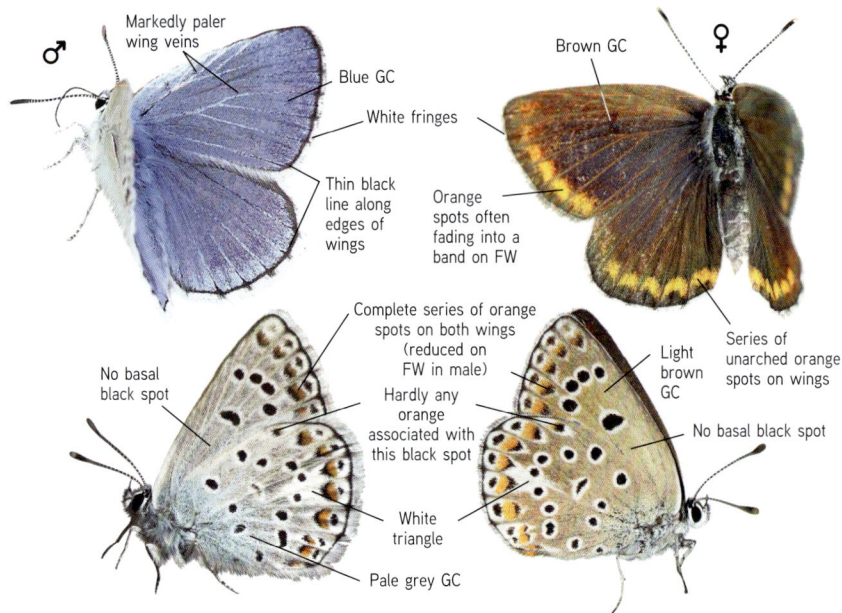

♂ Markedly paler wing veins

Blue GC

White fringes

Thin black line along edges of wings

Brown GC ♀

Orange spots often fading into a band on FW

Complete series of orange spots on both wings (reduced on FW in male)

No basal black spot

Hardly any orange associated with this black spot

Light brown GC

Series of unarched orange spots on wings

No basal black spot

White triangle

Pale grey GC

Wingspan: 24–32 mm

Habitat: Rocky dry grasslands and subalpine meadows.

Hibernating stage: Caterpillar.

Elevational range: Up to 2,500 m (mainly below 1,500 m).

Egg-laying: Eggs are laid singly on LHP leaflets.

Flight period: From May to August.

Host plants: Legumes of genus *Astragalus*, mainly *A. monspessulanus*, *A. sempervirens*, *A. exscapus*, *A. incanus*, and *A. spuneri*. Also reported on *Oxytropis helvetica*.

Diversity and systematics: Subspecies *roseonitens* flies in the south of Spain. Subspecies *helenae* is found in western France, while the nominate subspecies populates the south. Subspecies *balestrei* flies in the Maritime Alps. Subspecies *dalmatia* is described from the Balkans. Subspecies *parnassica* flies in Greece, while subspecies *splendens* is found in Italy.

LC

1

Did you know?

Males are frequently observed sucking water and minerals from damp soils. Females, on the other hand, seldom stop to do so, preferring to forage on flowers.

IMAGOS		LARVAE	
Food	🌸 💧	Food	🌸 🍃
Behaviour of males		Caterpillar location	
Dispersion		Chrysalis location	

EROS BLUE *POLYOMMATUS EROS*

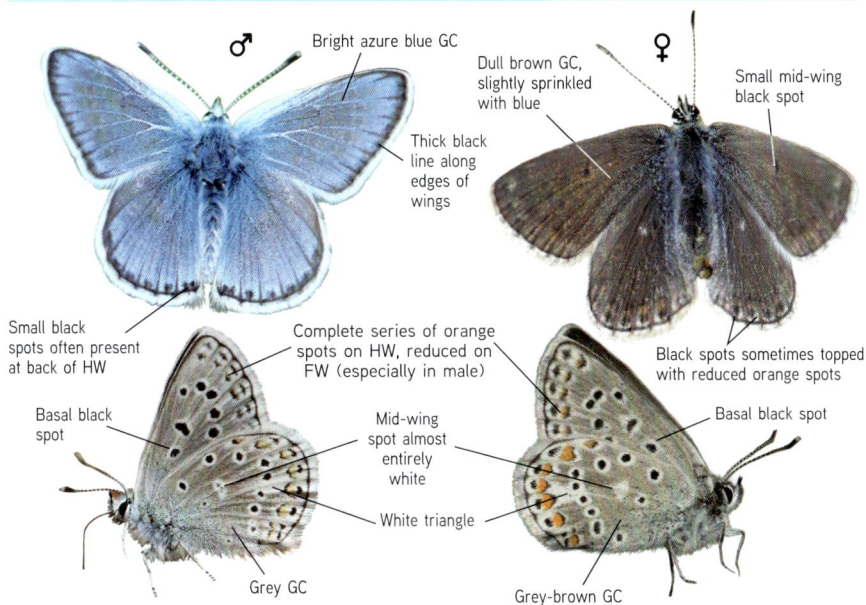

♂ Bright azure blue GC

♀ Dull brown GC, slightly sprinkled with blue

Small mid-wing black spot

Thick black line along edges of wings

Small black spots often present at back of HW

Complete series of orange spots on HW, reduced on FW (especially in male)

Black spots sometimes topped with reduced orange spots

Basal black spot

Mid-wing spot almost entirely white

Basal black spot

White triangle

Grey GC

Grey-brown GC

Wingspan: 26–36 mm

Habitat: Subalpine and alpine grasslands.

Hibernating stage: Caterpillar.

Elevational range: Between 1,200 and 2,700 m.

Egg-laying: Eggs are laid singly on LHP leaflets.

Flight period: From July to September.

Host plants: Small legumes in genus *Oxytropis*, especially *O. campestris*, *O. fetida*, *O. halleri*, *O. helvetica*, *O. montana*, *O. neglecta*, and *O. sordida*. Also on *Astragalus danicus*, *A. leontinus*, *A. levieri*, *A. sempervirens*, *A. taygeteus*, *Onobrychis montana*, *Chamaecytisus hirsutus*, *C. ruthenicus*, *Genista depressa*, and *Lotus corniculatus*.

Diversity and systematics: The nominate subspecies flies in the Alps and the Pyrenees. Subspecies *italica* populates central Italy. Subspecies *eroides* forms the Balkan populations, and subspecies *menelaos* inhabits the Peloponnese. Subspecies *silvester* flies in Poland, while subspecies *boisduvalii* is found in the Czech Republic.

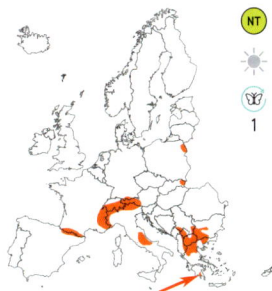

NT

1

Did you know?

The fragmented range of the Eros Blue had formerly justified elevating two of its subspecies, *Polyommatus eros menelaos* in the Peloponnese and *P. eros eroides* in the Balkans, to the species level. However, genetic studies argue against the split.

IMAGOS		LARVAE	
Food		Food	
Behaviour of males		Caterpillar location	
Dispersion		Chrysalis location	

LYCAENIDAE

THE AMANDA'S BLUE *POLYOMMATUS AMANDUS*

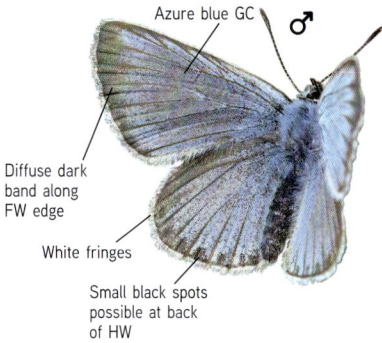

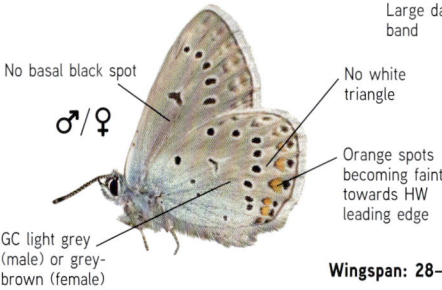

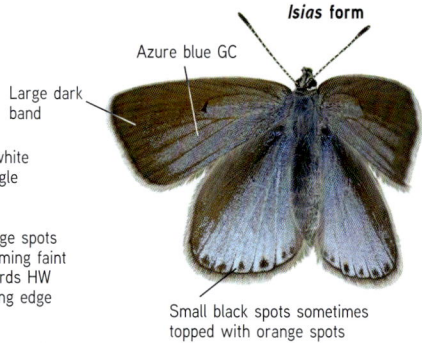

Azure blue GC ♂

Diffuse dark band along FW edge

White fringes

Small black spots possible at back of HW

♀ Common form

White fringes

Few orange spots on HW (very faint or absent on FW)

Isias form

Azure blue GC

Large dark band

No basal black spot

♂/♀

No white triangle

Orange spots becoming faint towards HW leading edge

GC light grey (male) or grey-brown (female)

Small black spots sometimes topped with orange spots

Wingspan: 28–37 mm

Habitat: Grasslands, mesophilic meadows, and bushy or woody edges where the LHPs grow.

Hibernating stage: Caterpillar.

Elevational range: Up to 2,500 m.

Egg-laying: Eggs are laid singly on LHP leaflets.

Flight period: From May to July.

Host plants: Legumes – above all, *Vicia cracca*, but also *V. cassubica*, *V. onobrychioides*, *V. tenuifolia*, *V. sibthorpii*, *V. tetrasperma*, and *V. villosa*. Also on *Lathyrus pratensis*, *L. sylvestris*, *Medicago sativa*, and *Securigera varia*.

Diversity and systematics: Most European populations belong to the nominate subspecies.

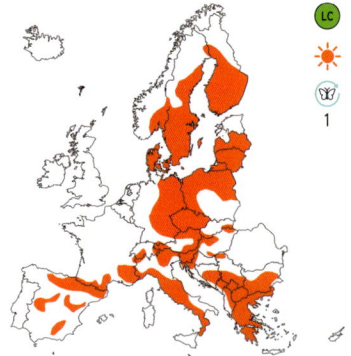

LC

1

Did you know?

The scientific name of Amanda's Blue translates to "kind-hearted". Males particularly enjoy sucking water and minerals from damp soils ... or from the naturalist's skin!

IMAGOS		LARVAE	
Food	🌼 💧	Food	🍃
Behaviour of males		Caterpillar location	
Dispersion		Chrysalis location	

TURQUOISE BLUE *POLYOMMATUS DORYLAS*

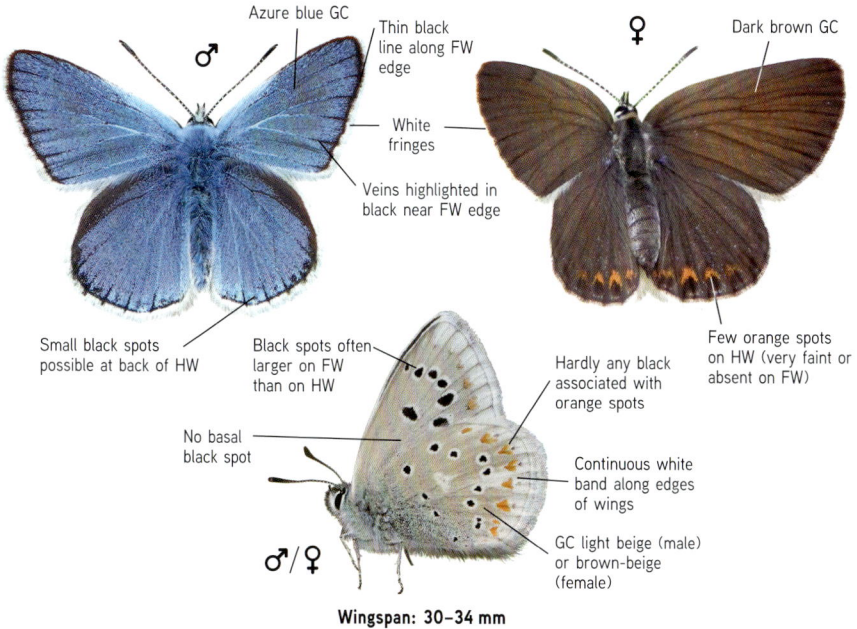

Azure blue GC

♂

Thin black
line along FW
edge

♀

Dark brown GC

White
fringes

Veins highlighted in
black near FW edge

Small black spots
possible at back of HW

Black spots often
larger on FW
than on HW

Hardly any black
associated with
orange spots

Few orange spots
on HW (very faint or
absent on FW)

No basal
black spot

Continuous white
band along edges
of wings

♂/♀

GC light beige (male)
or brown-beige
(female)

Wingspan: 30–34 mm

Habitat: Dry grasslands, including at high elevations.

Hibernating stage: Caterpillar.

Elevational range: Up to 2,500 m.

Egg-laying: Eggs are laid singly on LHP leaflets.

Flight period: From May to August.

Host plants: Legumes of genus *Anthyllis*, mainly *A. vulneraria*, and sometimes *A. montana* and *Astragalus glycyphyllos*. Reported on *Thymus serpyllum* (Lamiaceae).

Diversity and systematics: Most European populations belong to the nominate subspecies. Subspecies *castilla* has been described from Spain, subspecies *magna* from Romania.

■ P. dorylas
■ P. golgus
■ P. sagratrox

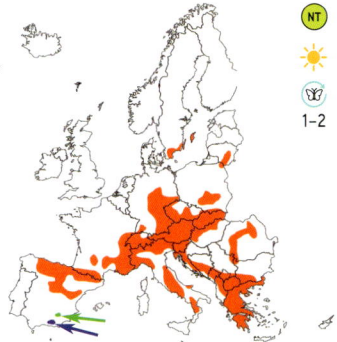

NT

1–2

Did you know?

The Turquoise Blue belongs to a group of species associated with dry grasslands (often calcareous), which are currently suffering from pastoral abandonment. As a result, it has disappeared from many non-Mediterranean and mountainous regions.

IMAGOS		LARVAE	
Food		Food	
Behaviour of males		Caterpillar location	
Dispersion		Chrysalis location	

LYCAENIDAE

NEVADA BLUE/SAGRA BLUE
POLYOMMATUS GOLGUS/P. SAGRATROX

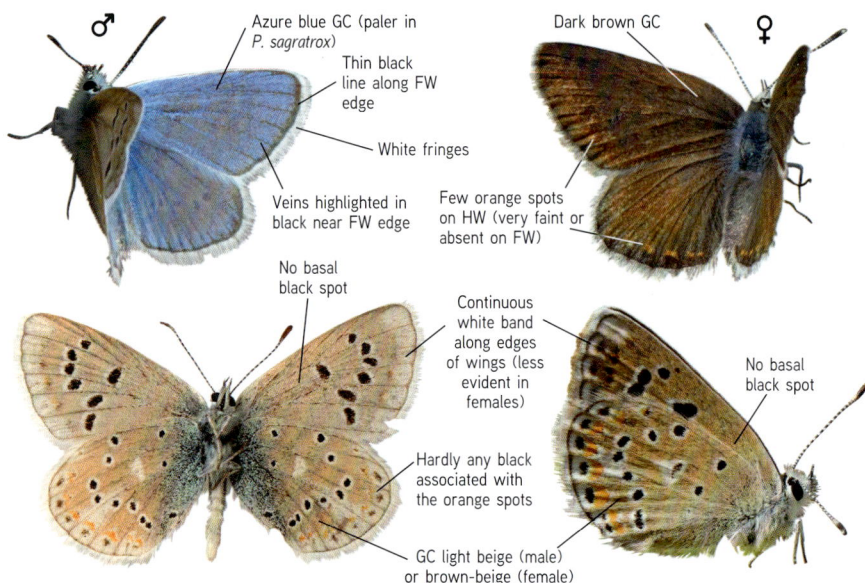

♂

Azure blue GC (paler in *P. sagratrox*)

Thin black line along FW edge

White fringes

Veins highlighted in black near FW edge

Few orange spots on HW (very faint or absent on FW)

Dark brown GC

♀

No basal black spot

Continuous white band along edges of wings (less evident in females)

Hardly any black associated with the orange spots

No basal black spot

GC light beige (male) or brown-beige (female)

Wingspan: 26–30 mm

Habitat: Sparsely vegetated, north-facing slopes and summits on schists, both dominated by dwarf junipers for *Polyommatus golgus*. Black pine woodland clearings and dolomitic slopes with cushion-like vegetation dominated by the legume *Erinacea anthyllis* for *P. sagratrox*.

Hibernating stage: Caterpillar.

Elevational range: Between 2,100 and 2,800 m for *Polyommatus golgus*. From 1,800 to 2,400 m for *P. sagratrox*.

Egg-laying: Eggs are laid singly on LHP leaflets.

Flight period: From the end of June to July.

Host plants: Above all, *Anthyllis vulneraria* and sometimes *Lotus corniculatus* (Fabaceae).

Diversity and systematics: The species status of *Polyommatus sagratrox* is debated. Some authors consider it a subspecies of *P. golgus*.

■ P. dorylas
■ P. golgus
■ P. sagratrox

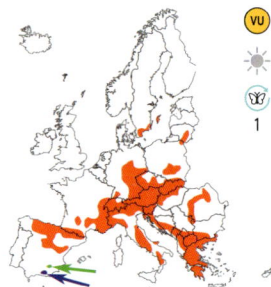

VU

1

Did you know?

These blues have some of the smallest ranges among butterflies in continental Europe. Overgrazing, trampling, and the development of tourism infrastructures represent significant threats to their populations.

	IMAGOS				LARVAE			
Food				Food				
Behaviour of males				Caterpillar location				
Dispersion				Chrysalis location				

MOTHER-OF-PEARL BLUE   *POLYOMMATUS NIVESCENS*

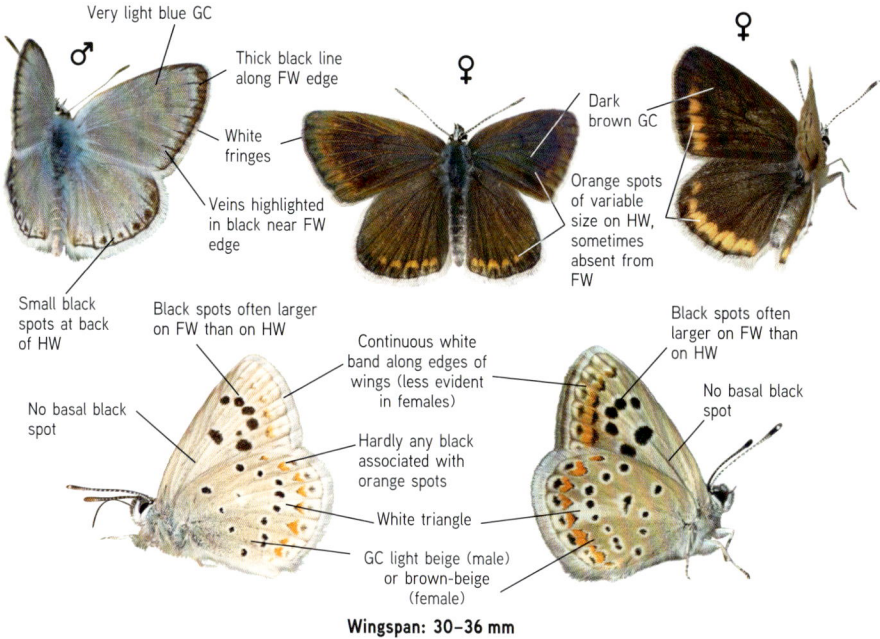

♂
Very light blue GC
Thick black line along FW edge
White fringes
Veins highlighted in black near FW edge
Small black spots at back of HW

♀
Dark brown GC
Orange spots of variable size on HW, sometimes absent from FW

♀

Black spots often larger on FW than on HW
No basal black spot
Continuous white band along edges of wings (less evident in females)
Hardly any black associated with orange spots
White triangle
GC light beige (male) or brown-beige (female)

Black spots often larger on FW than on HW
No basal black spot

Wingspan: 30–36 mm

Habitat: Stony and bushy grasslands.
Hibernating stage: Caterpillar.
Elevational range: Between 1,000 and 2,000 m.
Egg-laying: Eggs are laid singly on LHP leaflets.
Flight period: From May to August.
Host plants: Mainly *Anthyllis vulneraria* (Fabaceae).
Diversity and systematics: There are no notable subspecies for this Spanish endemic.

NT
1

Did you know?

The Mother-of-Pearl Blue is one of the European species most threatened by climate change in the 21st century. Models predict a near disappearance of its favourable habitats.

IMAGOS		LARVAE	
Food		Food	
Behaviour of males		Caterpillar location	
Dispersion		Chrysalis location	

CHELMOS BLUE *POLYOMMATUS IPHIGENIA*

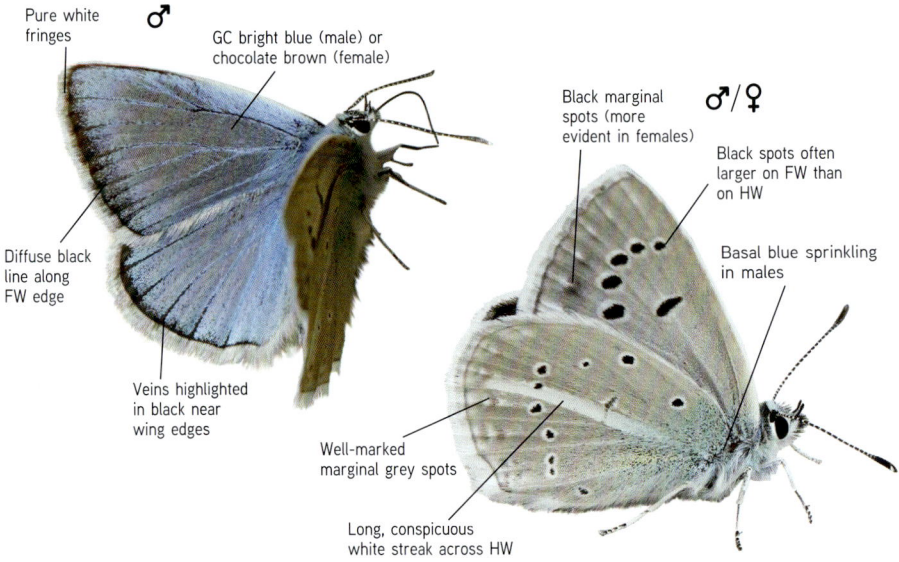

Pure white fringes ♂

GC bright blue (male) or chocolate brown (female)

Black marginal spots (more evident in females) ♂/♀

Black spots often larger on FW than on HW

Basal blue sprinkling in males

Diffuse black line along FW edge

Veins highlighted in black near wing edges

Well-marked marginal grey spots

Long, conspicuous white streak across HW

Wingspan: 28–32 mm

Habitat: Flower-rich, stony grasslands.

Hibernating stage: Caterpillar.

Elevational range: Between 1,000 and 1,800 m.

Egg-laying: Eggs are laid singly on the LHP.

Flight period: From June to August.

Host plants: Legumes, mainly *Onobrychis alba*.

Diversity and systematics: European populations belong to subspecies *nonacriensis*.

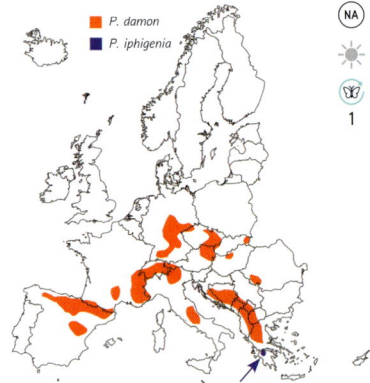

■ *P. damon*
■ *P. iphigenia*

NA

1

IMAGOS		LARVAE	
Food		Food	
Behaviour of males		Caterpillar location	
Dispersion		Chrysalis location	

Did you know?

The Turquoise Blue is present in Europe only in the region of Mount Chelmos, Greece, where it is rare and all too often targeted by collectors, who care little about the future of its populations.

338

FURRY BLUE *POLYOMMATUS DOLUS*

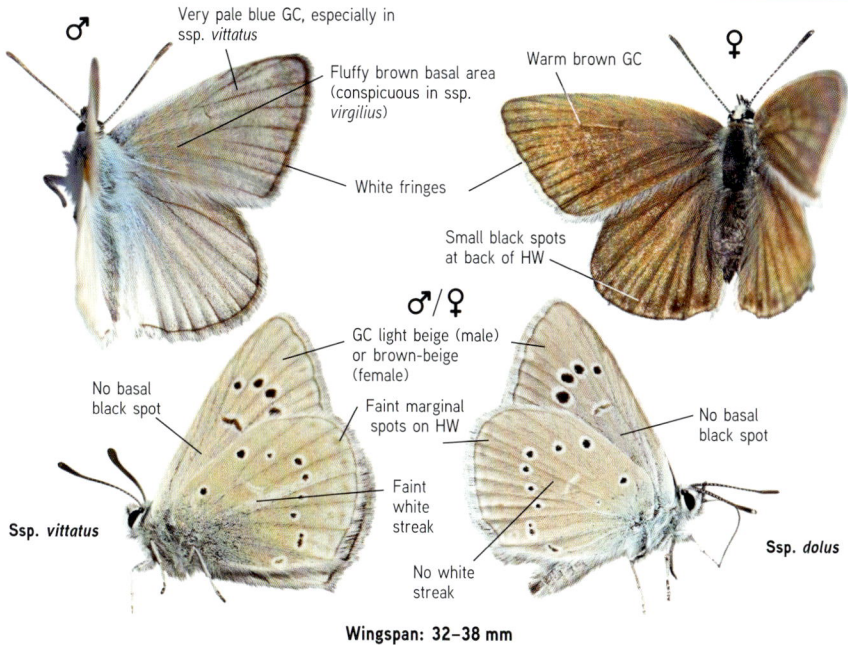

♂ Very pale blue GC, especially in ssp. *vittatus*

Fluffy brown basal area (conspicuous in ssp. *virgilius*)

Warm brown GC   ♀

White fringes

Small black spots at back of HW

♂/♀

GC light beige (male) or brown-beige (female)

No basal black spot

Faint marginal spots on HW

No basal black spot

Faint white streak

Ssp. *vittatus*

Ssp. *dolus*

No white streak

Wingspan: 32–38 mm

Habitat: Grassy, flower-rich grasslands, Mediterranean edges and clearings.

Hibernating stage: Caterpillar.

Elevational range: Up to 1,500 m.

Egg-laying: Eggs are laid singly on LHP inflorescences.

Flight period: From June to August.

Host plants: Legumes of genus *Onobrychis*, including *O. viciifolia*, *O. saxatilis*, and *O. supina*.

Diversity and systematics: The nominate subspecies populates southeastern France. Subspecies *vittatus* flies in the French Cévennes. Subspecies *virgilius* forms populations in central Italy and is sometimes considered a distinct species, while subspecies *paravirgilius* is also described from the Sorrentine Peninsula in Italy.

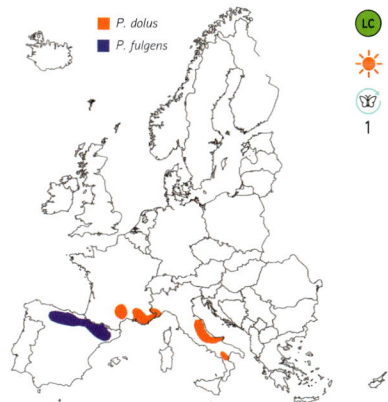

■ *P. dolus*
■ *P. fulgens*

LC

1

	IMAGOS			LARVAE	
Food	✿		Food	✿ 🌿	
Behaviour of males			Caterpillar location		
Dispersion			Chrysalis location		

Did you know?

Furry Blues spend the night in common roosting sites. These small groups are usually found in the grassiest areas of their habitat.

LYCAENIDAE

CATALONIAN FURRY BLUE *POLYOMMATUS FULGENS*

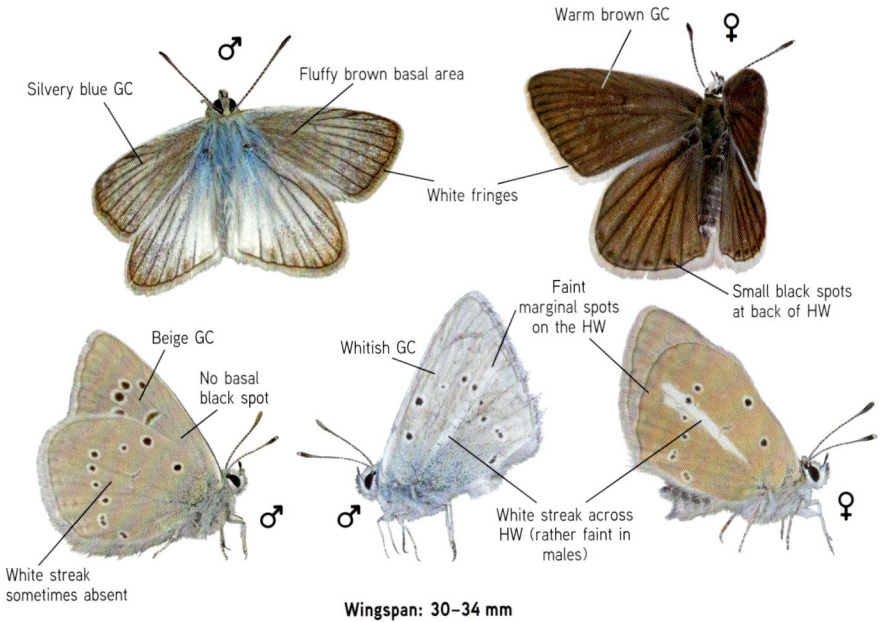

♂
Silvery blue GC
Fluffy brown basal area

Warm brown GC
♀

White fringes

Beige GC
No basal black spot
♂

Whitish GC
♂

Faint marginal spots on the HW

Small black spots at back of HW

White streak across HW (rather faint in males)
♀

White streak sometimes absent

Wingspan: 30–34 mm

Habitat: Grassy and scrubby grasslands, Mediterranean woodland clearings and edges.

Hibernating stage: Caterpillar.

Elevational range: Between 500 and 1,200 m.

Egg-laying: Eggs are laid singly on the LHP.

Flight period: From June to August.

Host plants: Legumes of genus *Onobrychis*, especially *O. viciifolia*.

Diversity and systematics: The nominate subspecies flies in Catalonia. Subspecies *ainsae* populates the southern Pyrenees, and subspecies *pseudovirgilius* is found in the Burgos region.

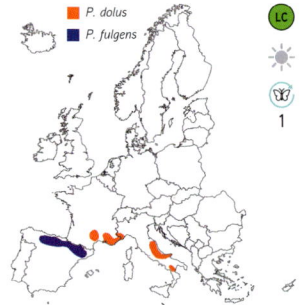

■ *P. dolus*
■ *P. fulgens*

LC

1

Did you know?

The Catalonian Furry Blue was previously considered a subspecies of the Furry Blue, to which it is closely related. Subspecies *ainsae* was considered a distinct species.

IMAGOS			LARVAE	
Food			Food	
Behaviour of males			Caterpillar location	
Dispersion			Chrysalis location	

DAMON BLUE *POLYOMMATUS DAMON*

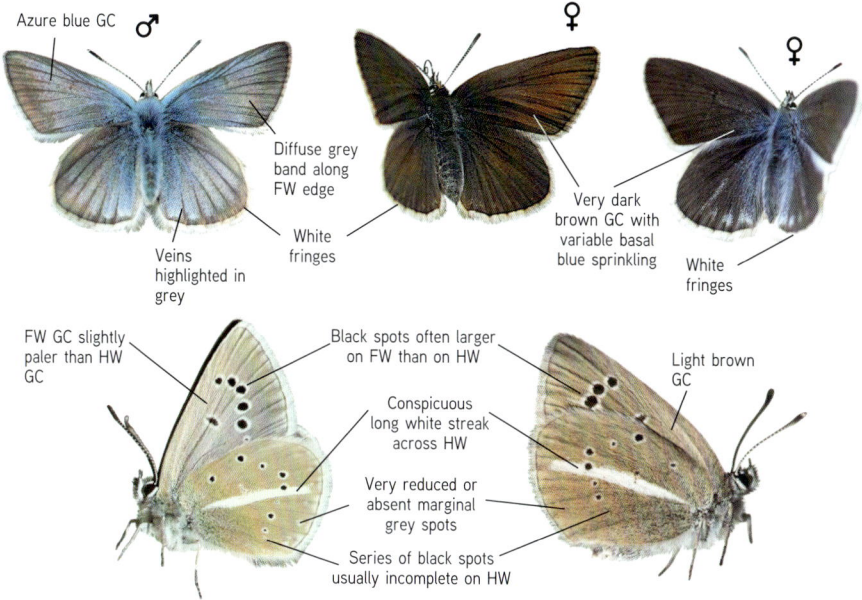

Azure blue GC ♂

♀

♀

Diffuse grey band along FW edge

White fringes

Veins highlighted in grey

Very dark brown GC with variable basal blue sprinkling

White fringes

FW GC slightly paler than HW GC

Black spots often larger on FW than on HW

Conspicuous long white streak across HW

Very reduced or absent marginal grey spots

Series of black spots usually incomplete on HW

Light brown GC

Wingspan: 30–34 mm

Habitat: Grasslands, meadows, and flower-rich montane edges.

Hibernating stage: Young caterpillar or caterpillar inside the egg.

Elevational range: Between 500 and 2,200 m.

Egg-laying: Eggs are laid singly on LHP dry parts or on nearby vegetation.

Flight period: From July to September.

Host plants: Legumes in genus *Onobrychis*, especially *O. viciifolia*, *O. montana*, *O. alba*, and *O. arenaria*.

Diversity and systematics: Most European populations belong to the nominate subspecies. Subspecies *noguerae* inhabits Spanish Catalonia. Subspecies *ferreti* flies in the northern Alps, while subspecies *ultramarina* resides in the Central Alps. Subspecies *centralitalicus* is found in Italy.

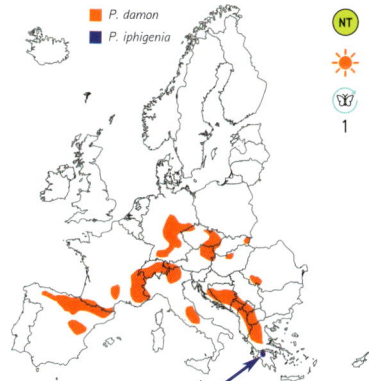

■ *P. damon*
■ *P. iphigenia*

NT

1

IMAGOS		LARVAE	
Food		Food	
Behaviour of males		Caterpillar location	
Dispersion		Chrysalis location	

Did you know?

Adults are highly dependent on flowers and forage extensively on Fabaceae and Lamiaceae (especially thymes and lavenders), as well as thistles.

LYCAENIDAE

ANOMALOUS BLUE *POLYOMMATUS ADMETUS*

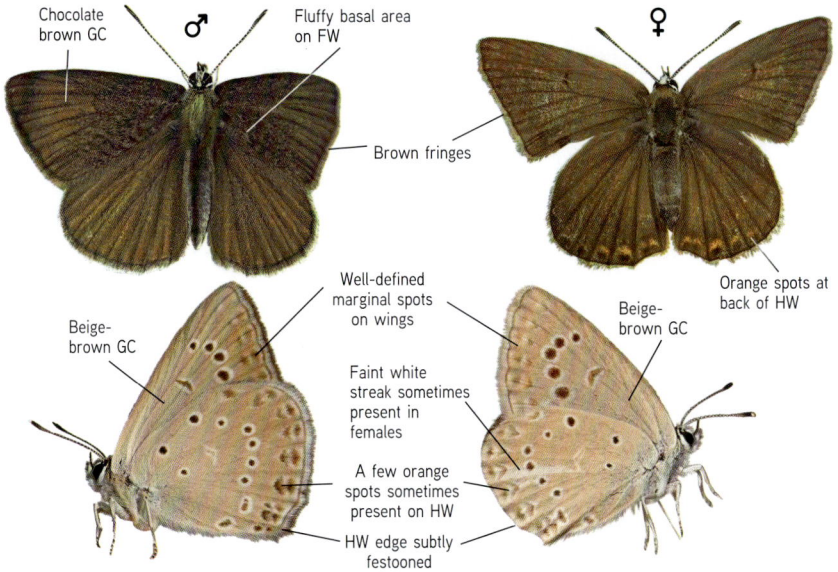

Chocolate brown GC

♂

Fluffy basal area on FW

♀

Brown fringes

Well-defined marginal spots on wings

Beige-brown GC

Beige-brown GC

Orange spots at back of HW

Faint white streak sometimes present in females

A few orange spots sometimes present on HW

HW edge subtly festooned

Wingspan: 30–38 mm

Habitat: Stony grasslands and scrubby arid and flower-rich areas.

Hibernating stage: Caterpillar inside the egg.

Elevational range: Up to 1,800 m.

Egg-laying: Eggs are laid singly on LHP inflorescences.

Flight period: From June to August.

Host plants: Legumes of genus *Onobrychis*, mainly *O. aequidentata, O. alba, O. arenaria, O. viciifolia, O. caput-galli,* and *O. ebenoides.*

Diversity and systematics: European populations belong to the nominate subspecies.

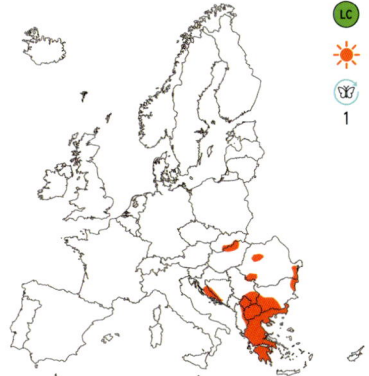

IMAGOS		LARVAE	
Food		Food	
Behaviour of males		Caterpillar location	
Dispersion		Chrysalis location	

Did you know?

Anomalous Blue populations are localized, but their numbers are often significant. Males are particularly attracted to damp soils.

342

LYCAENIDAE

RIPART'S ANOMALOUS BLUE *POLYOMMATUS RIPARTII*

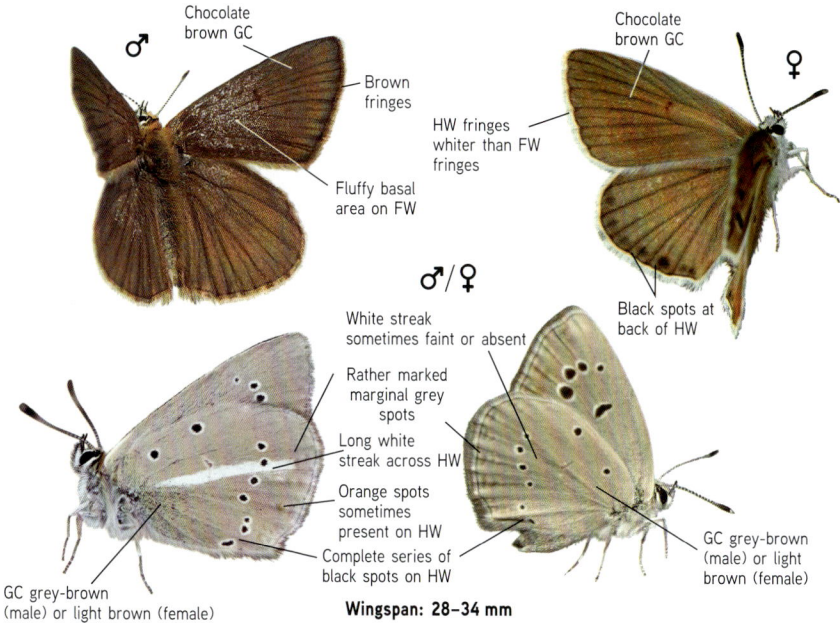

♂ Chocolate brown GC

Brown fringes

HW fringes whiter than FW fringes

Fluffy basal area on FW

♀ Chocolate brown GC

Black spots at back of HW

♂/♀

White streak sometimes faint or absent

Rather marked marginal grey spots

Long white streak across HW

Orange spots sometimes present on HW

Complete series of black spots on HW

GC grey-brown (male) or light brown (female)

GC grey-brown (male) or light brown (female)

Wingspan: 28–34 mm

Habitat: Grasslands, meadows, and dry, scrubby areas.

Hibernating stage: Caterpillar.

Elevational range: Up to 2,000 m.

Egg-laying: Eggs are laid singly on LHP inflorescences.

Flight period: From June to September.

Host plants: Legumes of genus *Onobrychis*, including *O. viciifolia*, *O. supina*, *O. saxatilis*, *O. montana*, *O. caput-galli*, *O. ebenoides*, and *O. alba*.

Diversity and systematics: Subspecies *agenjoi* flies in Catalonia. Subspecies *galloi* inhabits southern Italy, while subspecies *exuberans* is present only in the Susa Valley. Subspecies *pelopi* forms the Peloponnese populations. Some of these subspecies were once considered separate species.

- ■ P. ripartii
- ■ P. fabressei
- ■ P. violetae
- ■ P. humedasae

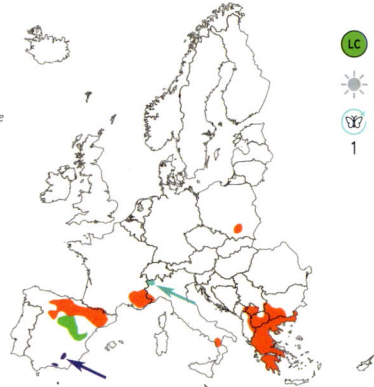

LC

1

Did you know?

The pupa of Ripart's Anomalous Blue has a stridulatory organ that allows it to produce sounds, which could be used to recruit ants in case of danger.

IMAGOS		LARVAE	
Food	✿ ◌	Food	✿ 🍃
Behaviour of males		Caterpillar location	
Dispersion		Chrysalis location	

LYCAENIDAE

GRECIAN ANOMALOUS BLUE/TIMFRISTOS ANOMALOUS BLUE
POLYOMMATUS AROANIENSIS/P. TIMFRISTOS

The distinction between *P. aroaniensis* and *P. timfristos* can only be made through molecular analysis (and, now, localization). *P. timfristos* is, in fact, challenging to differentiate from *P. ripartii*, with which it may fly. The marginal spots on the hindwing's underside are generally slightly more pronounced in *P. ripartii*. The individuals presented here are all *P. aroaniensis* and illustrate the variability of its underside.

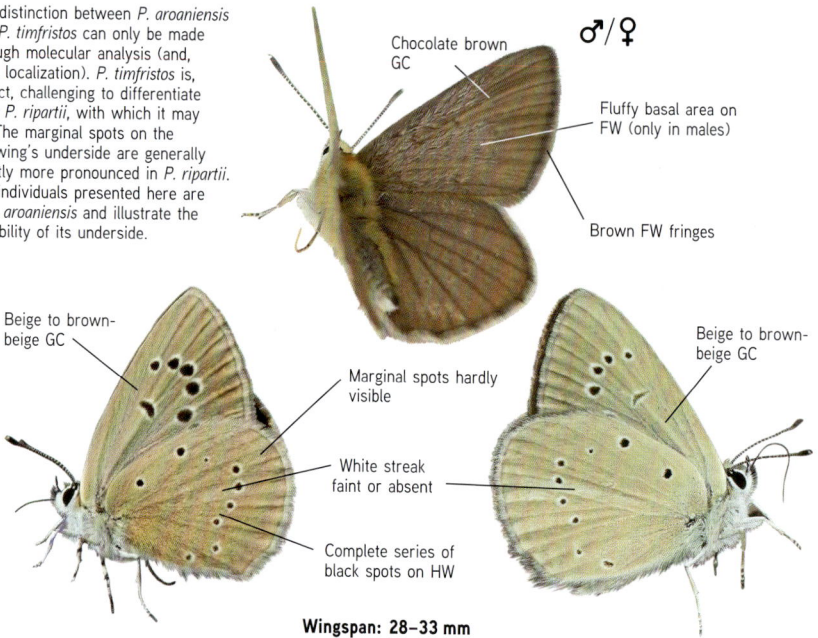

♂/♀

Chocolate brown GC

Fluffy basal area on FW (only in males)

Brown FW fringes

Beige to brown-beige GC

Marginal spots hardly visible

White streak faint or absent

Complete series of black spots on HW

Beige to brown-beige GC

Wingspan: 28–33 mm

Habitat: Arid slopes with steppic vegetation and scrub for *Polyommatus aroaniensis*, dry grasslands and meadows for *P. timfristos*.

Hibernating stage: Caterpillar.

Elevational range: Up to 2,000 m for *Polyommatus aroaniensis*, between 1,000 and 1,800 m for *P. timfristos*.

Egg-laying: Eggs are laid singly on LHP inflorescences.

Flight period: From June to August.

Host plants: Legumes of genus *Onobrychis*, including *O. alba*, *O. arenaria*, and *O. ebenoides*.

Diversity and systematics: *Polyommatus timfristos* was described in 2016 based on a genetic study focusing on anomalous blues. The populations in question were previously classified as belonging to *P. aroaniensis*.

aroaniensis timfristos
LC NA

■ P. aroaniensis
■ P. timfristos
■ P. nepho-
   -hiptamenos
■ P. orphicus
■ P. orphicus
   + P. nepho-
   -hiptamenos
■ P. lurae

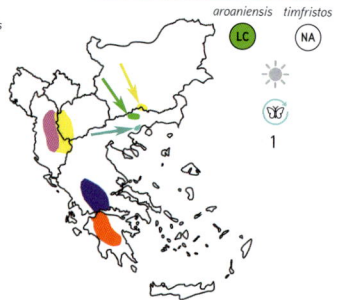

1

Did you know?

The systematics of the anomalous blues is complex and reflects a recent evolutionary divergence, the exact boundaries of which have not been fully resolved. The trend is towards a split into several young species.

IMAGOS			LARVAE		
Food			Food		
Behaviour of males			Caterpillar location		
Dispersion			Chrysalis location		

LYCAENIDAE

HIGGINS'S ANOMALOUS BLUE   *POLYOMMATUS NEPHOHIPTAMENOS*

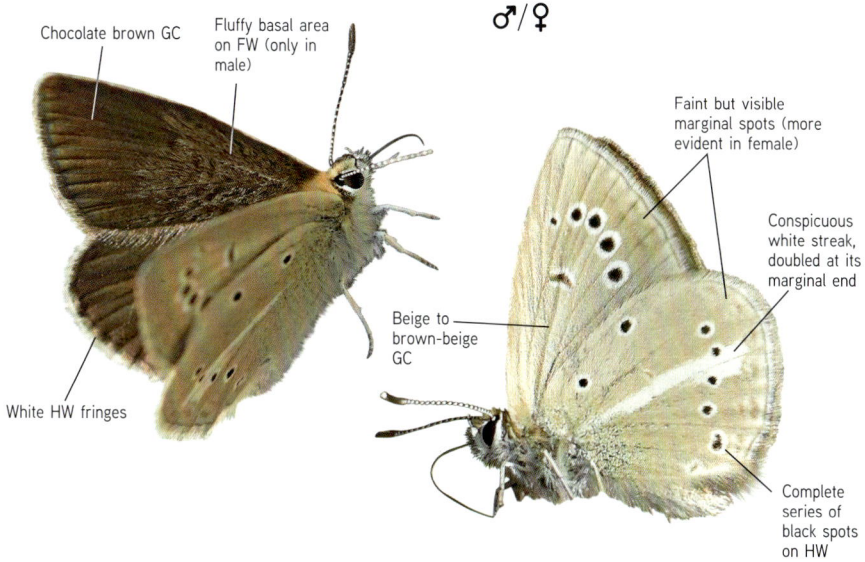

♂/♀

Chocolate brown GC

Fluffy basal area on FW (only in male)

Faint but visible marginal spots (more evident in female)

Conspicuous white streak, doubled at its marginal end

Beige to brown-beige GC

White HW fringes

Complete series of black spots on HW

Wingspan: 28–33 mm

Habitat: Dry subalpine grasslands and meadows.

Hibernating stage: Caterpillar.

Elevational range: Between 1,500 and 2,100 m.

Egg-laying: Eggs are laid singly on the LHP.

Flight period: July and August.

Host plants: *Onobrychis montana* and *O. alba* (Fabaceae).

Diversity and systematics: There are no notable subspecies for this anomalous blue, which can be found in only a few mountain ranges in northern Greece and Bulgaria.

- P. aroaniensis
- P. timfristos
- P. nepho--hiptamenos
- P. orphicus
- P. orphicus + P. nepho--hiptamenos
- P. lurae

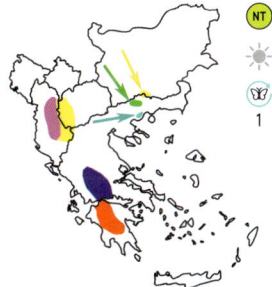

NT

1

IMAGOS		LARVAE	
Food		Food	
Behaviour of males		Caterpillar location	
Dispersion: unknown		Chrysalis location	

Did you know?

Higgins's Anomalous Blue is not easy to differentiate from Ripart's Anomalous Blue, with which it may fly locally. The colour of the fringes (whiter in the Higgins's Anomalous Blue) is the most distinctive criterion, but it is challenging to appreciate in the field.

KOLEV'S ANOMALOUS BLUE/LURA ANOMALOUS BLUE
POLYOMMATUS ORPHICUS/P. LURAE

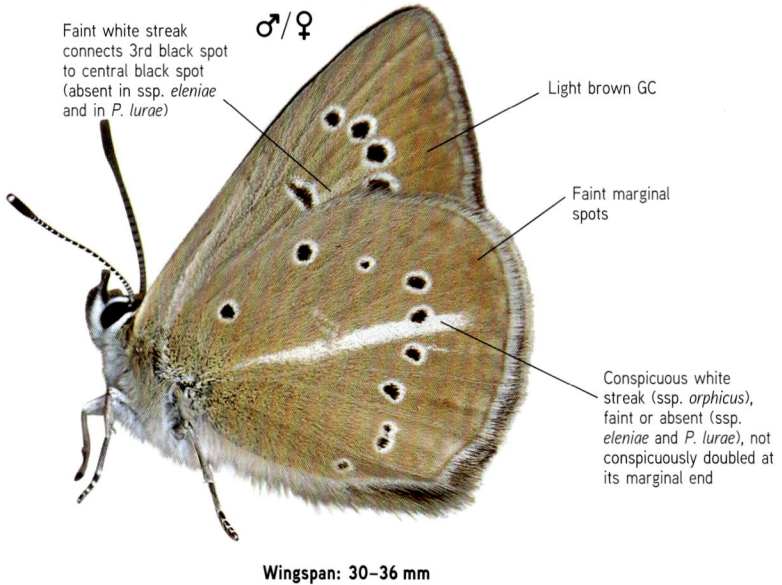

♂/♀

Faint white streak connects 3rd black spot to central black spot (absent in ssp. *eleniae* and in *P. lurae*)

Light brown GC

Faint marginal spots

Conspicuous white streak (ssp. *orphicus*), faint or absent (ssp. *eleniae* and *P. lurae*), not conspicuously doubled at its marginal end

Wingspan: 30–36 mm

Habitat: Dry, scrubby grasslands on an ophiolitic substrate for *Polyommatus lurae*; on limestone for *P. orphicus*.

Hibernating stage: Caterpillar.

Elevational range: Between 500 and 1,600 m (above 900 m for *Polyommatus lurae*).

Egg-laying: Eggs are laid singly on the LHP.

Flight period: From June to September.

Host plants: *Onobrychis alba* (Fabaceae) for *Polyommatus orphicus* and probably also for *P. lurae*.

Diversity and systematics: For *Polyommatus orphicus*, the nominate subspecies flies in the Rhodope Mountains. Subspecies *eleniae*, which is a subject of debate, is endemic to the region of Mount Falakron. The western Balkan populations have uncertain affinities.

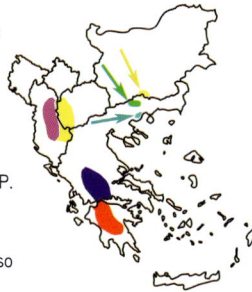

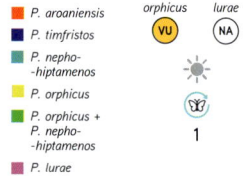

- *P. aroaniensis*
- *P. timfristos*
- *P. nepho-hiptamenos*
- *P. orphicus*
- *P. orphicus + P. nepho-hiptamenos*
- *P. lurae*

orphicus — VU
lurae — NA

1

Did you know?

Subspecies *eleniae* and *orphicus* were initially considered separate species (*orphicus* as a subspecies of *Polyommatus dantchenkoi*) before being grouped under the name *P. orphicus* based on genetic and karyotypic data, despite their morphological differences. *P. lurae* was discovered and described in 2022. It is possible that the two species hybridize in eastern Albania.

IMAGOS			LARVAE		
Food			Food		
Behaviour of males			Caterpillar location		
Dispersion			Chrysalis location		

LYCAENIDAE

ANDALUSIAN ANOMALOUS BLUE *POLYOMMATUS VIOLETAE*

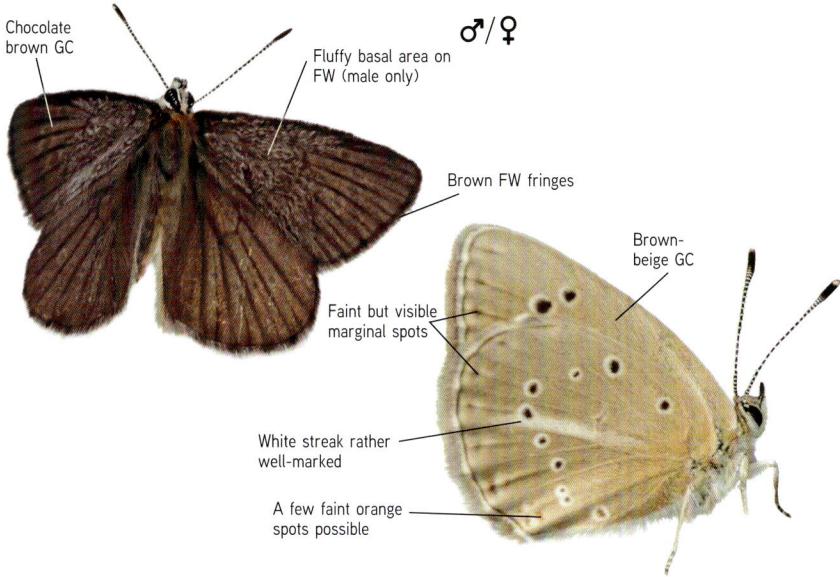

♂/♀

Chocolate brown GC

Fluffy basal area on FW (male only)

Brown FW fringes

Brown-beige GC

Faint but visible marginal spots

White streak rather well-marked

A few faint orange spots possible

Wingspan: 28–34 mm

Habitat: Montane and subalpine stony grasslands and clearings.

Hibernating stage: Caterpillar.

Elevational range: Between 1,200 and 1,800 m.

Egg-laying: Eggs are laid singly on LHP inflorescences.

Flight period: July and August.

Host plants: *Onobrychis argentea* and *O. humilis* (Fabaceae).

Diversity and systematics: Most populations belong to the nominate subspecies. Subspecies *subbaeticus* populates the Sagra mountain chain.

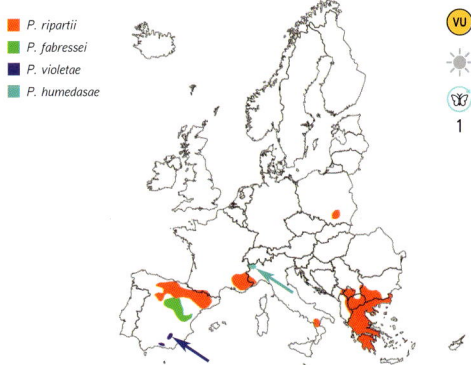

■ *P. ripartii*
■ *P. fabressei*
■ *P. violetae*
■ *P. humedasae*

VU

1

Did you know?

The Andalusian Anomalous Blue was considered a subspecies of Ripart's Anomalous Blue, to which it bears a strong resemblance, but they do not share the same range.

IMAGOS		LARVAE	
Food	🌸 💧	Food	🌸 🍃
Behaviour of males		Caterpillar location	
Dispersion		Chrysalis location	

LYCAENIDAE

OBERTHÜR'S ANOMALOUS BLUE *POLYOMMATUS FABRESSEI*

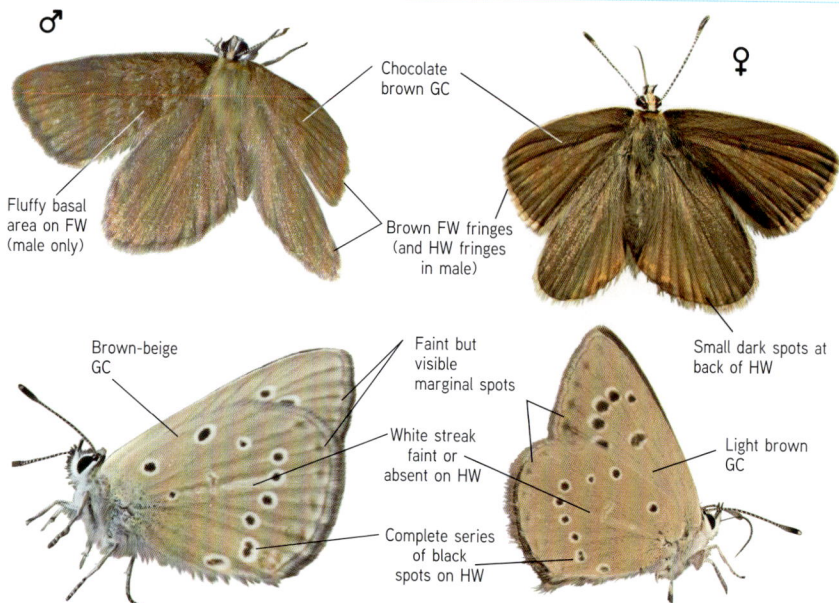

♂

Chocolate brown GC

♀

Fluffy basal area on FW (male only)

Brown FW fringes (and HW fringes in male)

Brown-beige GC

Faint but visible marginal spots

Small dark spots at back of HW

White streak faint or absent on HW

Light brown GC

Complete series of black spots on HW

Wingspan: 28–33 mm

Habitat: Dry grasslands and garrigue, Mediterranean pine woodland clearings.

Hibernating stage: Egg or young caterpillar.

Elevational range: Between 750 and 1,500 m.

Egg-laying: Eggs are laid singly on LHP inflorescences.

Flight period: From June to August.

Host plants: Legumes of genus *Onobrychis*, like *O. argentea* and *O. viciifolia*.

Diversity and systematics: There are no notable subspecies for this anomalous blue, which is endemic to central Spain.

- P. ripartii
- P. fabressei
- P. violetae
- P. humedasae

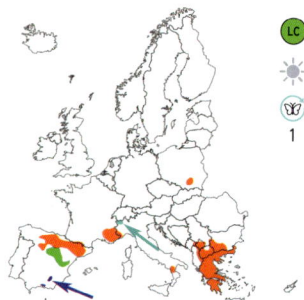

LC

1

Did you know?

Adults regularly forage on the flowers of lavenders, scabiouses, and thistles. They seldom fly with *Polyommatus ripartii*, from which they can be distinguished by the faint intensity or even absence of the white streak on the underside of their hindwing.

IMAGOS		LARVAE	
Food		Food	
Behaviour of males		Caterpillar location	
Dispersion		Chrysalis location	

LYCAENIDAE

PIEDMONT ANOMALOUS BLUE *POLYOMMATUS HUMEDASAE*

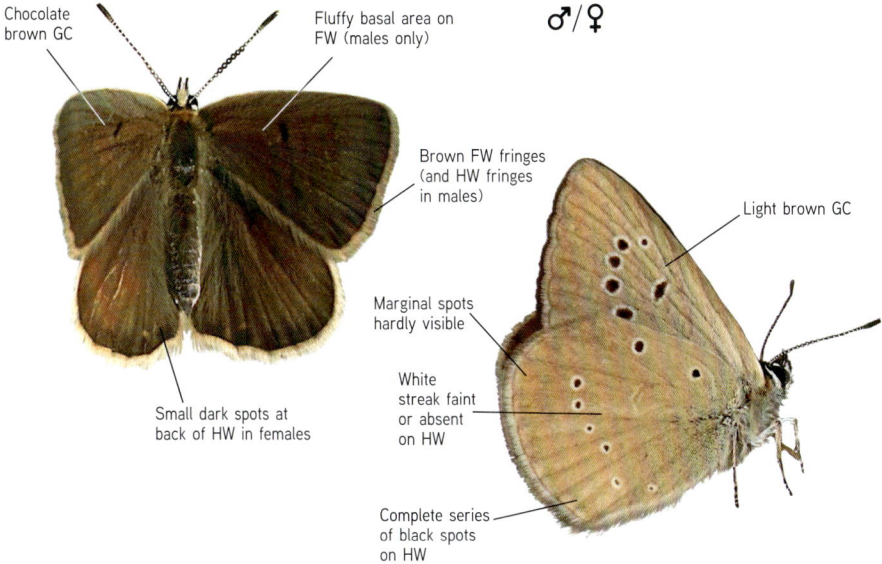

Chocolate brown GC

Fluffy basal area on FW (males only)

♂/♀

Brown FW fringes (and HW fringes in males)

Light brown GC

Marginal spots hardly visible

White streak faint or absent on HW

Small dark spots at back of HW in females

Complete series of black spots on HW

Wingspan: 28–33 mm

Habitat: Rocky grasslands and heaths.

Hibernating stage: Caterpillar.

Elevational range: Between 800 and 1,500 m.

Egg-laying: Eggs are laid singly on LHP inflorescences.

Flight period: July and August.

Host plants: Legumes of genus *Onobrychis*, including *O. montana* and *O. viciifolia*.

Diversity and systematics: There are no described subspecies for this anomalous blue, which is endemic to the Aosta Valley in Italy.

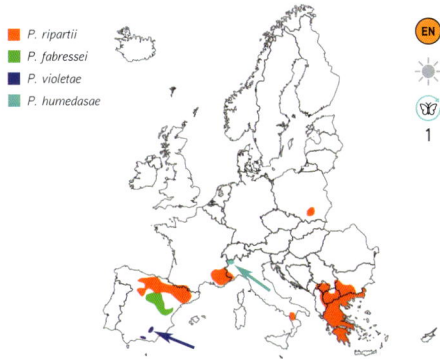

■ *P. ripartii*
■ *P. fabressei*
■ *P. violetae*
■ *P. humedasae*

EN

1

Did you know?

The Piedmont Anomalous Blue inhabits a range of a few square kilometers, where it forms only five populations. It is among the most endangered species in Europe.

IMAGOS		LARVAE	
Food	☆	Food	☆
Behaviour of males		Caterpillar location	
Dispersion		Chrysalis location	

RIODINIDAE

DUKE OF BURGUNDY *HAMEARIS LUCINA*

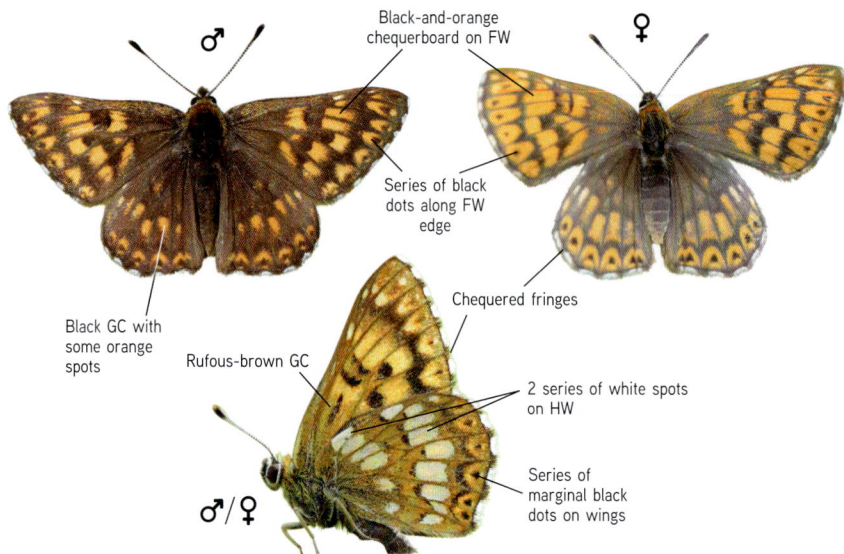

♂

Black-and-orange chequerboard on FW

♀

Series of black dots along FW edge

Black GC with some orange spots

Rufous-brown GC

Chequered fringes

2 series of white spots on HW

Series of marginal black dots on wings

♂/♀

Wingspan: 29–34 mm

Habitat: Bushy meadows and grasslands, shrub edges, fruticose areas, hedges, clearings, and forest clearcuts.

Hibernating stage: Pupa.

Elevational range: Up to 2,000 m.

Egg-laying: Eggs are laid singly or in a few units on LHP leaves.

Flight period: From April to September, usually before July.

Host plants: Primulaceae, mainly *Primula veris*, *P. elatior*, and *P. vulgaris*. Laying has also been observed on *Lysimachia nummularium* and *L. nemorum*.

Diversity and systematics: There are no notable subspecies for the only European Riodinid.

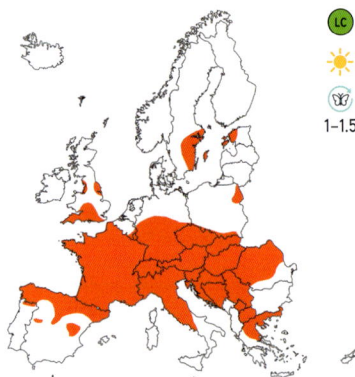

LC

1–1.5

IMAGOS		LARVAE	
Food		Food	
Behaviour of males		Caterpillar location	
Dispersion		Chrysalis location	

Did you know?

Riodinids are widely distributed in low latitudes. Some species display spectacular colours and forms, unlike our local Duke of Burgundy!

THE NON-SATYRINE NYMPHALIDS
(79 SPECIES)

SUBFAMILIES	GENERA	NUMBER OF SPECIES	MAIN LARVAL HOST-PLANT FAMILIES
Libytheinae	*Libythea*	1	Ulmaceae and Rosaceae
Charaxinae	*Charaxes*	1	Ericaceae, Lauraceae, Santalaceae, and Annonaceae
Nymphalinae	*Aglais, Araschnia, Hypolimnas, Nymphalis, Polygonia,* and *Vanessa*	15	Urticaceae, Ulmaceae, Asteraceae, Boraginaceae, Plantaginaceae, Malvaceae, Salicaceae, Ulmaceae, Rosaceae, Betulaceae, Ribesiaceae, Cannabaceae, Amaranthaceae, Convolvulaceae, and Portulacaceae
Limenitidinae	*Limenitis* and *Neptis*	5	Caprifoliaceae, Rosaceae, Fabaceae, and Salicaceae
Apaturinae	*Apatura*	3	Salicaceae
Danainae	*Danaus*	2	Asclepiadaceae
Heliconiinae	*Argynnis, Boloria, Brenthis, Fabriciana,* and *Speyeria*	26	Violaceae, Polygonaceae, Rosaceae, Ericaceae, Salicaceae, Fabaceae, and Plantaginaceae
Melitaeinae	*Euphydryas* and *Melitaea*	26	Dipsacaceae, Gentianaceae, Caprifoliaceae, Plantaginaceae, Asteraceae, Oleaceae, Scrophulariaceae, and Valerianaceae

The Nymphalids constitute the largest butterfly family, with approximately 6,000 species described to date. Two-thirds of European species belong to the Satyrine subfamily, while the remaining third is distributed among eight smaller subfamilies, often found in forested, shrubby, or edge habitats (Apaturines, Charaxines, Nymphalines, Limenitidines, Libytheines, and some Heliconiines). Nymphalids are distinctive for having only two pairs of readily visible legs; the front pair are greatly reduced and not visible without a detailed examination of the insect. Monarchs (Danaines) and certain admirals (Nymphalines) undertake journeys of several thousand kilometers, accomplishing some of the longest-known migratory routes among butterflies. Their caterpillars exhibit a wide variety of adaptations, including camouflage, aposematism, fleshy protuberances, and nocturnal feeding behaviours, that allow them to escape predators and parasitoids.

Aglais io

Apatura ilia

Boloria dia

Limenitis reducta

Polygonia c-album

Danaus plexippus

Euphydryas desfontainii

Melitaea diamina

NETTLE-TREE BUTTERFLY   *LIBYTHEA CELTIS*

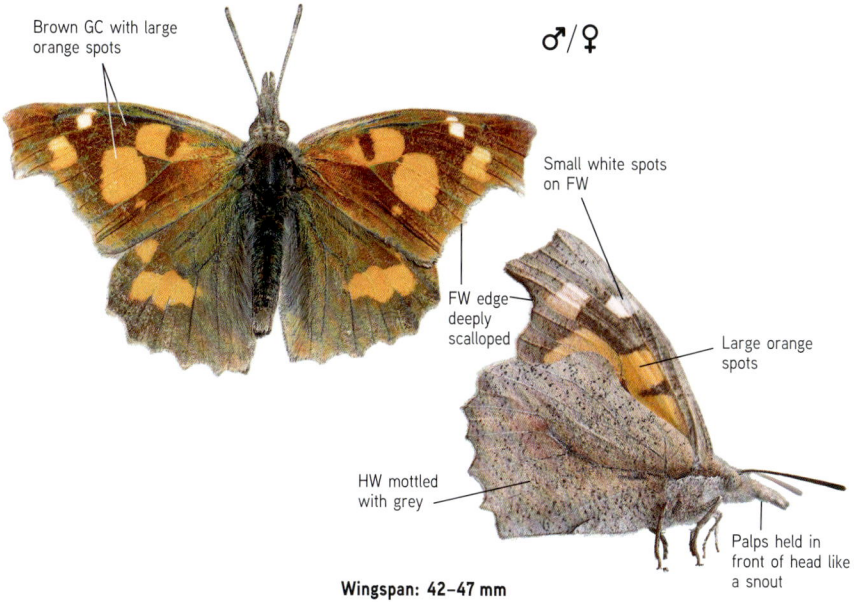

Brown GC with large
orange spots

♂/♀

Small white spots
on FW

FW edge
deeply
scalloped

Large orange
spots

HW mottled
with grey

Palps held in
front of head like
a snout

Wingspan: 42–47 mm

Habitat: Bushy Mediterranean habitats, parks, gardens, and alleys planted with nettle-trees.

Hibernating stage: Adult.

Elevational range: Up to 1,700 m.

Egg-laying: Eggs are laid singly on LHP petioles, stems, and leaf buds.

Flight period: From March to October.

Host plants: Mainly nettle-trees, like *Celtis australis*, *C. occidentalis*, and *C. tournefortii* (Ulmaceae). Laying has been reported on *Prunus avium* (Rosaceae), *Morus alba* (Moraceae), and *Arbutus unedo* (Ericaceae).

Diversity and systematics: European populations belong to the nominate subspecies.

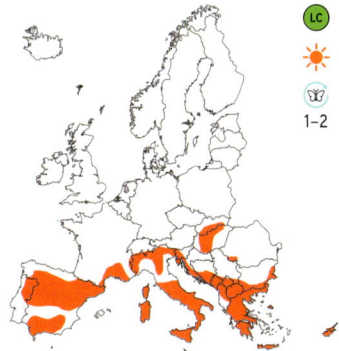

LC

1–2

Did you know?

Adult Nettle-tree Butterflies often undertake migratory movements towards the north or higher elevations, where they spend the summer before descending back towards breeding areas in early autumn.

IMAGOS		LARVAE	
Food	🌼 💧	Food	🍃
Behaviour of males		Caterpillar location	🌳
Dispersion		Chrysalis location	🌳

NYMPHALIDAE

TWO-TAILED PASHA *CHARAXES JASIUS*

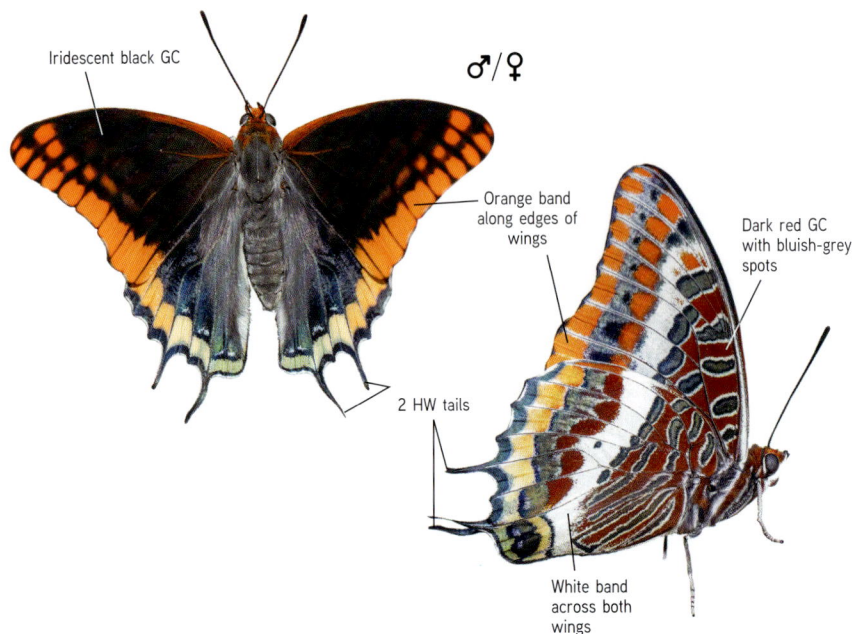

Iridescent black GC

♂/♀

Orange band
along edges of
wings

Dark red GC
with bluish-grey
spots

2 HW tails

White band
across both
wings

Wingspan: 76–83 mm

Habitat: Maquis, high-growing garrigue. Can also be seen in well-vegetated villages.

Hibernating stage: Caterpillar.

Elevational range: Up to 1,500 m (mostly below 1,000 m).

Egg-laying: Eggs are laid singly or in a few units on LHP leaves.

Flight period: From March to October.

Host plants: Mainly *Arbutus unedo* and *A. andrachne* (Ericaceae). Sometimes also *Vaccinium corymbosum* (Ericaceae), *Laurus nobilis* (Lauraceae), *Osyris lanceolata* (Santalaceae), *Citrus* spp. (Rutaceae), and *Annona cherimola* (Annonaceae).

Diversity and systematics: European populations belong to the nominate subspecies.

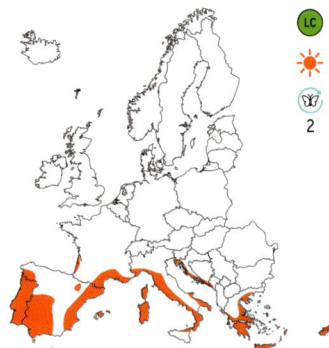

LC

2

IMAGOS			LARVAE	
Food	🍎 💩 💧		Food	🍃
Behaviour of males			Caterpillar location	🌳
Dispersion			Chrysalis location	🌳 🌳

Did you know?

Genus *Charaxes* includes many African species, of which only the Two-tailed Pasha has colonized Mediterranean Europe.

NYMPHALIDAE

PAINTED LADY *VANESSA CARDUI*

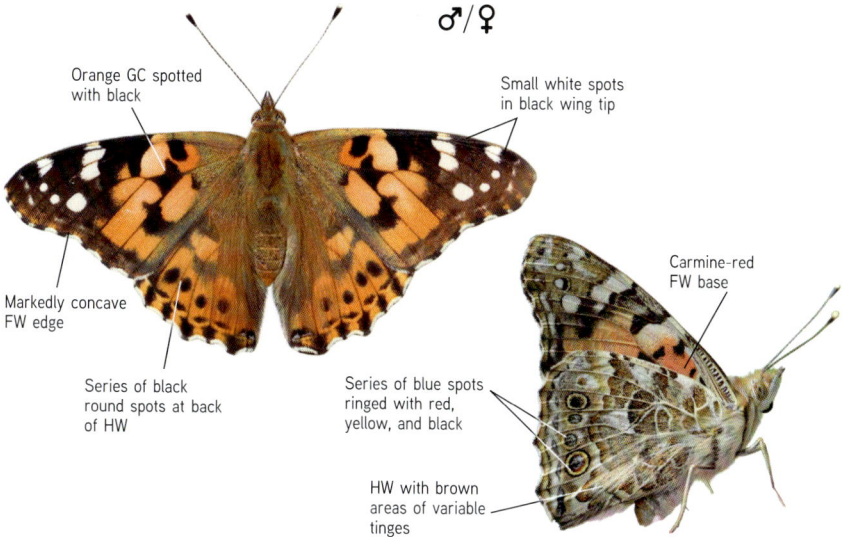

♂/♀

Orange GC spotted with black

Small white spots in black wing tip

Carmine-red FW base

Markedly concave FW edge

Series of black round spots at back of HW

Series of blue spots ringed with red, yellow, and black

HW with brown areas of variable tinges

Wingspan: 46–62 mm

Habitat: A wide variety of open habitats, like grasslands, meadows, garrigues, and maquis. Also in flower-rich parks and gardens.

Hibernating stage: The Painted Lady can't usually survive cold European winters. It colonizes Europe every year from its African overwintering areas.

Elevational range: Up to 3,000 m.

Egg-laying: Eggs are laid singly or in a few units on LHP leaves.

Flight period: Year-round in the Canary Islands; variably between March and November on the continent, depending on the latitude.

Host plants: Numerous Asteraceae in genera *Achillea, Arctium, Artemisia, Carduus, Carlina, Centaurea, Cirsium, Chrysanthemum,* *Cichorium, Cinara, Echinops, Filago, Galactites, Helichrysum, Helminthotheca, Leontopodium, Logfia, Omalotheca, Onopordum, Pulicaria, Silybum,* and *Tussilago.* Apiaceae, like *Anthriscus sylvestris* and *Heracleum spondylium*; Boraginaceae of genera *Borago, Cynoglossum, Echium,* and *Symphytum*; Malvaceae of genera *Malva, Alcea,* and *Althaea*; Urticaceae, like *Urtica dioica, U. urens, Parietaria judaica,* and *Plantago lanceolata* (Plantaginaceae). This remarkable polyphagy allows the Painted Lady to breed in different habitats along its migratory pathway.

Diversity and systematics: Many forms described, but no subspecies for this almost cosmopolitan Nymphalid.

LC

1–3

Canaries

Madeira

Azores

IMAGOS		LARVAE	
Food		Food	
Behaviour of males		Caterpillar location	
Dispersion		Chrysalis location	

Did you know?

The Painted Lady is an equally impressive migratory species as the Monarch in North America. Some individuals arriving on European coasts originate from the Intertropical Convergence Zone.

NYMPHALIDAE

AMERICAN PAINTED LADY *VANESSA VIRGINIENSIS*

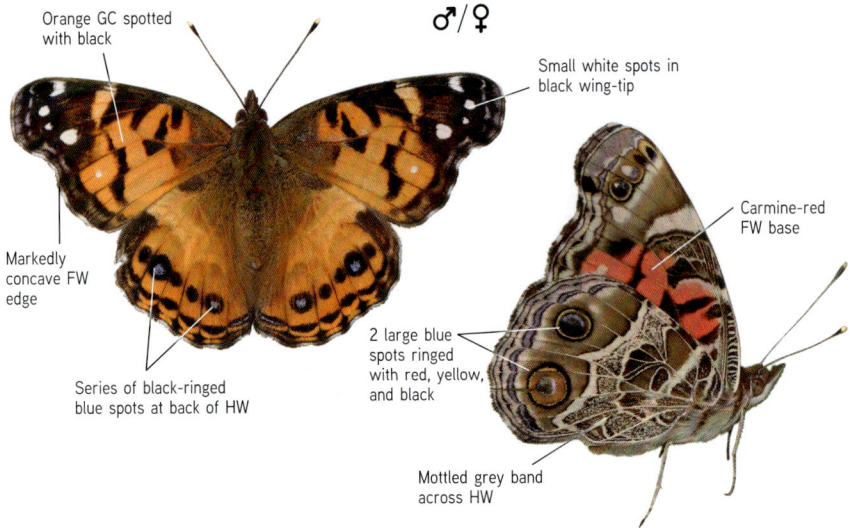

Orange GC spotted with black

♂/♀

Small white spots in black wing-tip

Carmine-red FW base

Markedly concave FW edge

2 large blue spots ringed with red, yellow, and black

Series of black-ringed blue spots at back of HW

Mottled grey band across HW

Wingspan: 40–50 mm

Habitat: Flower-rich, open habitats such as crop surroundings, wastelands, dunes, parks, and gardens.

Hibernating stage: Caterpillar.

Elevational range: Up to 1,500 m (mostly at low elevations).

Egg-laying: Eggs are laid singly on LHP leaves.

Flight period: Almost year-round in the Canary Islands.

Host plants: Asteraceae in genus *Gnaphalium*, including *G. luteoalbum* and *G. italicum*. Also on *Filago gallica*, *Antennaria* spp., and *Arctium* spp.

Diversity and systematics: There are no notable subspecies for this Nymphalid that originates from North America.

NA

3+

Canaries

Did you know?

The American Painted Lady is gradually colonizing the Iberian Peninsula from Portugal, where it has established itself permanently. Small populations now exist in Spain. Individuals observed on non-Mediterranean coasts are likely strays, presumably arrived from North America by boat.

IMAGOS		LARVAE	
Food	☆	Food	🍃
Behaviour of males		Caterpillar location	🌿
Dispersion		Chrysalis location	🌿 🌳

356

NYMPHALIDAE

RED ADMIRAL *VANESSA ATALANTA*

♂/♀

Small white spots in black wing-tip

Black GC

Markedly concave FW edge

Large white spot beneath wing tip

Narrow red band across FW

Narrow red-orange band across FW

Red-orange band with small blue spots inside at the back of the HW

Brown HW GC with dark undulated lines

Wingspan: 46–66 mm

Habitat: Flower-rich meadows, clearings, forest edges, parks, and gardens.

Hibernating stage: Adult without entering diapause in regions where winter survival is possible, but also various larval stages where the species manages to breed during winter.

Elevational range: Up to 3,000 m.

Egg-laying: Eggs are laid singly on LHP leaves.

Flight period: Almost year-round in Mediterranean regions. The duration of the winter absence varies elsewhere according to latitude and elevation.

Host plants: Urticaceae, above all *Urtica dioica*, but also *U. atrovirens*, *U. membranacea*, *U. pilulifera*, *U. urens*, *Parietaria judaica*, and *P. officinalis*.

Diversity and systematics: European populations belong to the nominate subspecies.

LC

1–3+

Canaries

Madeira

Azores

IMAGOS						LARVAE	
Food	✿	🍎	◊		♧	◊	Food	🍃
Behaviour of males							Caterpillar location	🌿
Dispersion							Chrysalis location	🌿

Did you know?

Red Admirals from the northern and central parts of Europe migrate towards Mediterranean regions during autumn. Their offspring then recolonize the continent the following spring.

CANARY RED ADMIRAL *VANESSA VULCANIA*

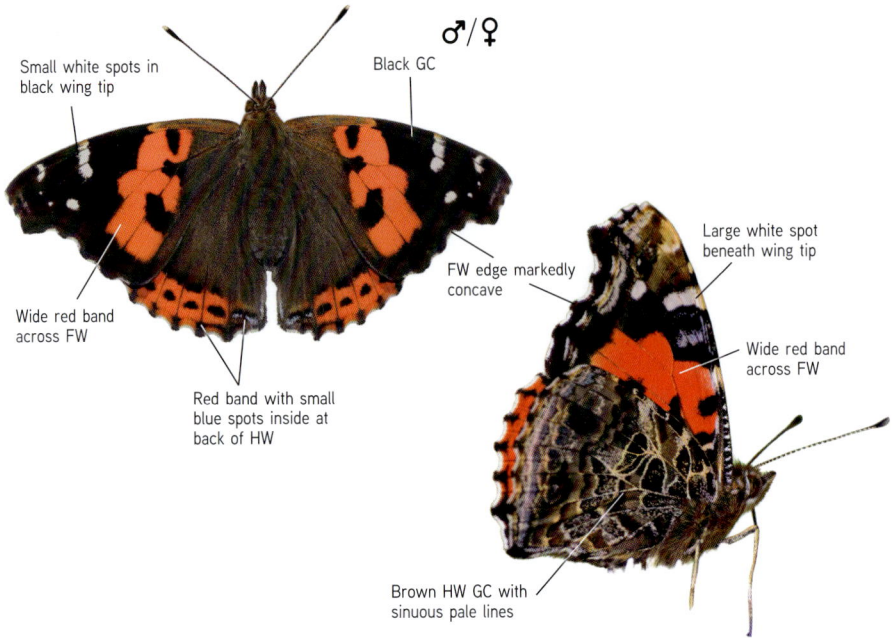

♂/♀

Small white spots in black wing tip

Black GC

Large white spot beneath wing tip

FW edge markedly concave

Wide red band across FW

Wide red band across FW

Red band with small blue spots inside at back of HW

Brown HW GC with sinuous pale lines

Wingspan: 54–60 mm

Habitat: Laurel forest, but also more anthropized areas such as parks and gardens or banana plantations.

Hibernating stage: Egg, caterpillar, pupa, or adult.

Elevational range: Up to 1,500 m.

Egg-laying: Eggs are laid singly or in a few units on LHP leaves.

Flight period: Year-round.

Host plants: Urticaceae, including *Urtica morifolia* and *U. membranacea*.

Diversity and systematics: There are no notable subspecies of this admiral, which is endemic to the Canary Islands and Madeira.

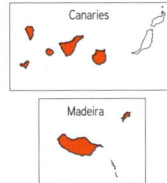

Canaries

Madeira

LC

3+

Did you know?

Vanessa vulcania is phylogenetically close to *V. indica*, a red admiral inhabiting southern Asia, and was once even considered a subspecies of the latter. Its strong dispersal abilities have enabled this distant colonization from the continent, and they possibly also explain the occasional mentions of the species in continental Europe.

IMAGOS			LARVAE	
Food			Food	
Behaviour of males			Caterpillar location	
Dispersion			Chrysalis location	

NYMPHALIDAE

CAMBERWELL BEAUTY *NYMPHALIS ANTIOPA*

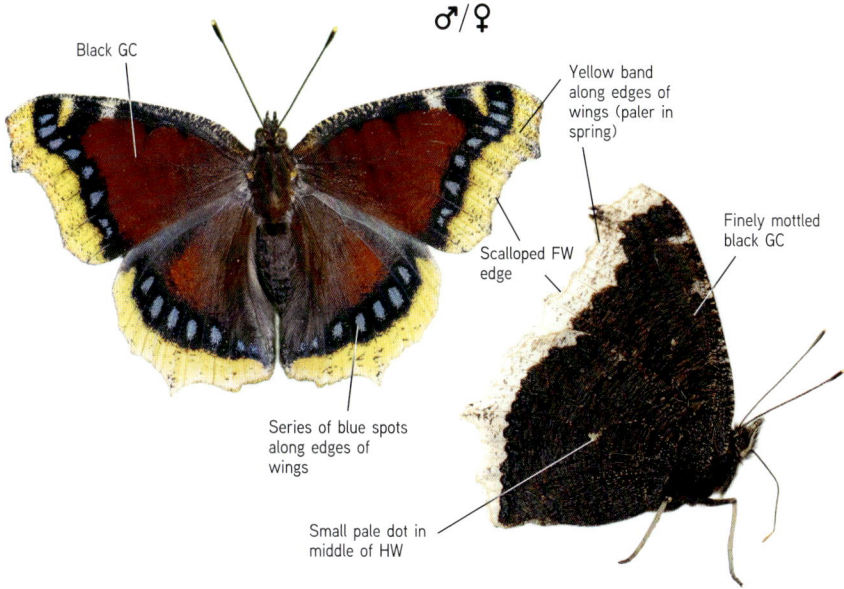

♂/♀

Black GC

Yellow band along edges of wings (paler in spring)

Finely mottled black GC

Scalloped FW edge

Series of blue spots along edges of wings

Small pale dot in middle of HW

Wingspan: 50–76 mm

Habitat: Bushy riparian areas, bogs, and damp, deciduous forests.

Hibernating stage: Adult.

Elevational range: Up to 2,000 m (mainly below 1,500 m).

Egg-laying: Eggs are laid in clusters of several dozens around LHP branches.

Flight period: From March to November.

Host plants: Salicaceae, including *Salix caprea*, *S. alba*, *S. cinerea*, *S. aurita*, *S. atrocinerea*, *S. eleagnos*, *S. pentandra*, *S. purpurea*, *S. triandra*, *S. viminalis*, *Populus tremula*, *P. alba*, and *P. nigra*. Betulaceae, like *Alnus glutinosa*, *Betulus pendula*, and *B. pubescens*. Ulmaceae, including *Ulmus glabra* and *U. minor*.

Diversity and systematics: European populations belong to the nominate subspecies.

LC

1

IMAGOS		LARVAE	
Food	🍎 💧 🐛 ✨ 🗑 💧	Food	🍃
Behaviour of males		Caterpillar location	
Dispersion		Chrysalis location	

Did you know?

The Camberwell Beauty is not very attracted to flowers. It is much more keen on sap or fermented fruits, from which it shamelessly indulges in alcohol.

NYMPHALIDAE

PEACOCK *AGLAIS IO*

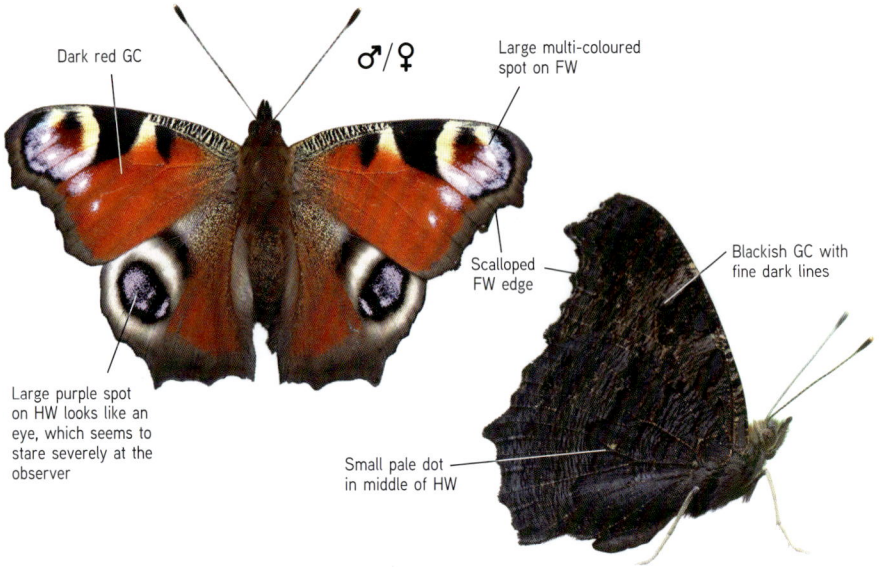

Dark red GC

♂/♀

Large multi-coloured spot on FW

Scalloped FW edge

Large purple spot on HW looks like an eye, which seems to stare severely at the observer

Blackish GC with fine dark lines

Small pale dot in middle of HW

Wingspan: 45–62 mm

Habitat: Wastelands, hedgerows, forest edges, parks, and gardens.

Hibernating stage: Adult.

Elevational range: Up to 2,500 m (mostly below 1,500 m).

Egg-laying: Eggs are laid in batches of several dozens on LHP leaves.

Flight period: From February to October.

Host plants: Above all *Urtica dioica* (Urticaceae). Sometimes also *U. urens*, *U. pilulifera*, *Parietaria judaica*, and *Humulus lupulus* (Cannabaceae).

Diversity and systematics: European populations belong to the nominate subspecies.

LC

1–3

Did you know?

The Peacock alternately uses the camouflage provided by its underside and the both aposematic and frightening colours of its upperside to evade predators. It can even produce ultrasonic sounds through wingbeats to deter rodents when perched.

IMAGOS				LARVAE	
Food				Food	
Behaviour of males				Caterpillar location	
Dispersion				Chrysalis location	

NYMPHALIDAE

SMALL TORTOISESHELL *AGLAIS URTICAE*

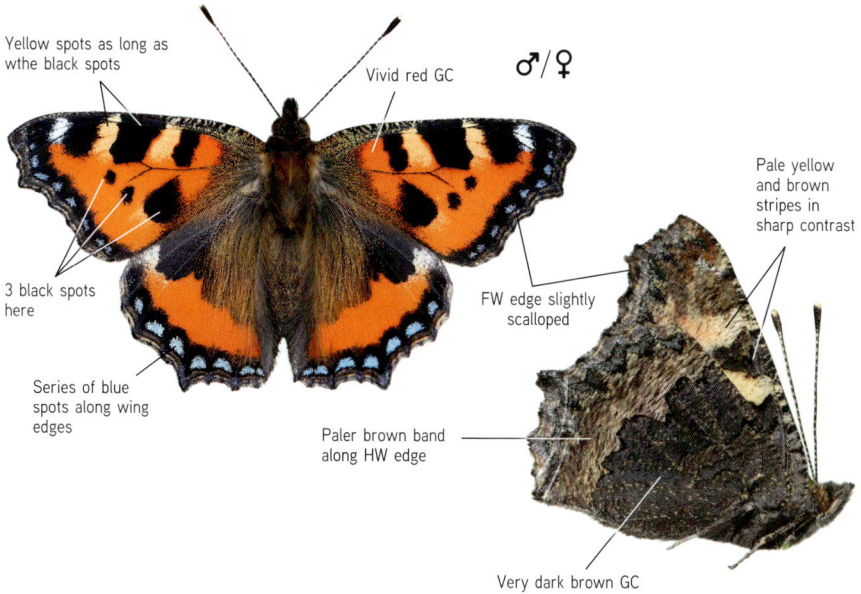

Yellow spots as long as wthe black spots

Vivid red GC

♂ / ♀

Pale yellow and brown stripes in sharp contrast

3 black spots here

Series of blue spots along wing edges

FW edge slightly scalloped

Paler brown band along HW edge

Very dark brown GC

Wingspan: 40–53 mm

Habitat: Flower-rich grasslands and meadows, edges, parks, and gardens.

Hibernating stage: Adult.

Elevational range: Up to 3,000 m.

Egg-laying: Eggs are laid in batches of several dozens on LHP leaves.

Flight period: From February to November.

Host plants: Urticaceae, above all *Urtica dioica*. Also reported on *U. urens* and *Humulus lupulus* (Cannabaceae).

Diversity and systematics: Most European populations belong to the nominate subspecies. Subspecies *polaris* and *turcica* (considered simple forms by some authors) fly in the extreme north and southeast of Europe, respectively.

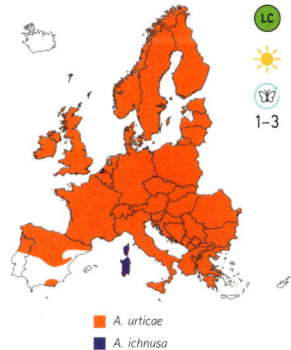

LC

1–3

■ A. urticae
■ A. ichnusa

IMAGOS				LARVAE	
Food	☆	🍎	💩	💧	Food	🍃
Behaviour of males					Caterpillar location	🌿
Dispersion					Chrysalis location	🌿

Did you know?

Populations of Small Tortoiseshells pay a heavy toll to their parasitoids, which largely explains variations in its abundance from year to year.

NYMPHALIDAE

CORSICAN SMALL TORTOISESHELL *AGLAIS ICHNUSA*

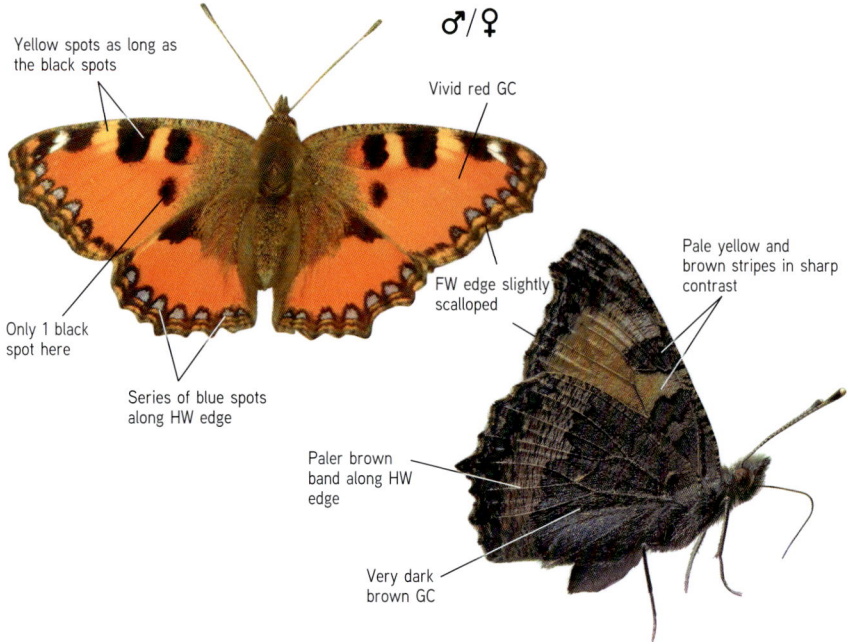

♂/♀

Yellow spots as long as
the black spots

Vivid red GC

Pale yellow and
brown stripes in sharp
contrast

Only 1 black
spot here

FW edge slightly
scalloped

Series of blue spots
along HW edge

Paler brown
band along HW
edge

Very dark
brown GC

Wingspan: 40–52 mm

Habitat: Montane grasslands and edges.

Hibernating stage: Adult.

Elevational range: Between 500 and 1,500 m.

Egg-laying: Eggs are laid in batches of several dozens on LHP leaves.

Flight period: From March to October.

Host plants: Urticaceae, including *Urtica atrovirens*, *U. pilulifera*, and *U. dioica*.

Diversity and systematics: The Corsican Small Tortoiseshell is often considered a subspecies of the Small Tortoiseshell (*Aglais urticae*). Corsican and Sardinian populations do not appear to be very differentiated.

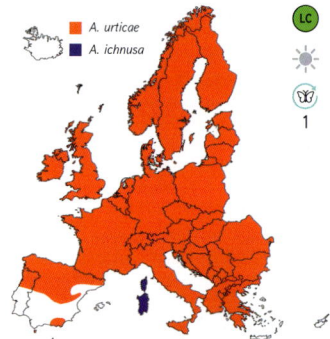

A. urticae
A. ichnusa

LC

1

IMAGOS			LARVAE	
Food			Food	
Behaviour of males			Caterpillar location	
Dispersion: unknown			Chrysalis location	

Did you know?

Unlike its continental counterpart, which is rather ubiquitous, the Corsican Small Tortoiseshell is much less abundant and more of a mountain species.

LARGE TORTOISESHELL *NYMPHALIS POLYCHLOROS*

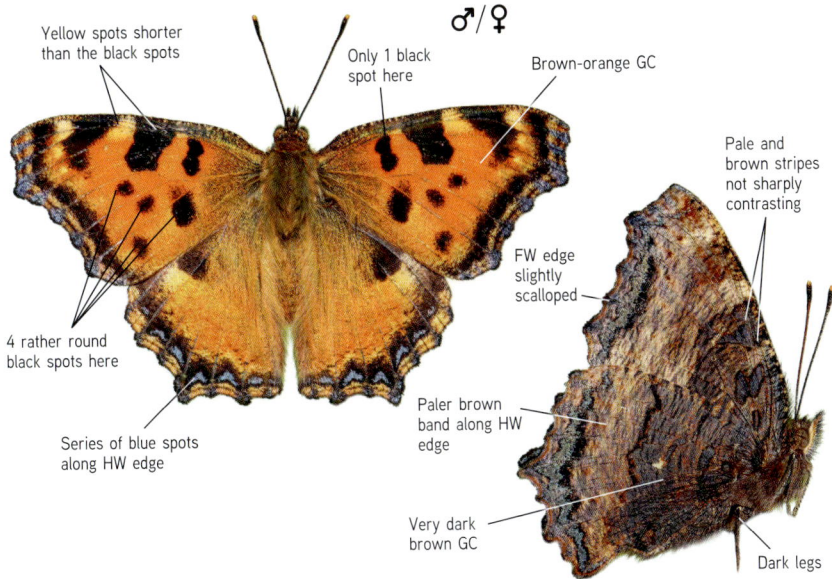

♂/♀

Yellow spots shorter than the black spots

Only 1 black spot here

Brown-orange GC

Pale and brown stripes not sharply contrasting

FW edge slightly scalloped

4 rather round black spots here

Series of blue spots along HW edge

Paler brown band along HW edge

Very dark brown GC

Dark legs

Wingspan: 56–68 mm

Habitat: Clear woodlands (especially in a wetland context), forest roadsides and edges, hedgerows, orchards, parks, and gardens.

Hibernating stage: Adult.

Elevational range: Up to 2,000 m (mainly below 1,000 m).

Egg-laying: Eggs are laid in clusters of several dozens around LHP branches.

Flight period: From February to April and then between June and October.

Host plants: Salicaceae, including *Salix caprea, S. cinerea, S. aurita, S. atrocinerea, S. babylonica,* *S. viminalis, S. purpurea, S. eleagnos, S. pedicellata, Populus nigra, P. alba, P. tremula,* and *P. deltoides.* Ulmaceae, including *Ulmus campestris, U. minor, U. americana, U. laevis,* and *U. glabra.* Rosaceae, including *Aria edulis, Prunus avium, P. cerasus, P. domestica, P. padus, Pyrus bourgaeana, P. communis, P. spinosa, Torminalis glaberrima, Crataegus monogyna, C. laevigata.*

Diversity and systematics: Most European populations belong to the nominate subspecies. Subspecies *erythromelas,* widely distributed in North Africa, could fly in Andalusia.

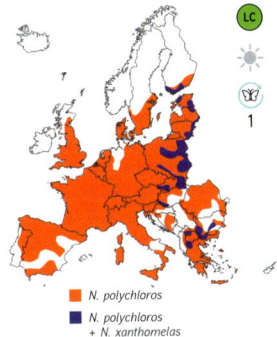

LC

1

■ *N. polychloros*
■ *N. polychloros* + *N. xanthomelas*

Did you know?

Like all Nymphalids that overwinter as adults, the Large Tortoiseshell can find refuge in buildings (barns, ruins, *etc.*) and natural cavities (hollow trees, rocky crevices, *etc.*).

IMAGOS					LARVAE	
Food	☆	🍎	💧	⌂	Food	🍃
Behaviour of males	👑				Caterpillar location	🌳
Dispersion					Chrysalis location	🌳

NYMPHALIDAE

YELLOW-LEGGED TORTOISESHELL *NYMPHALIS XANTHOMELAS*

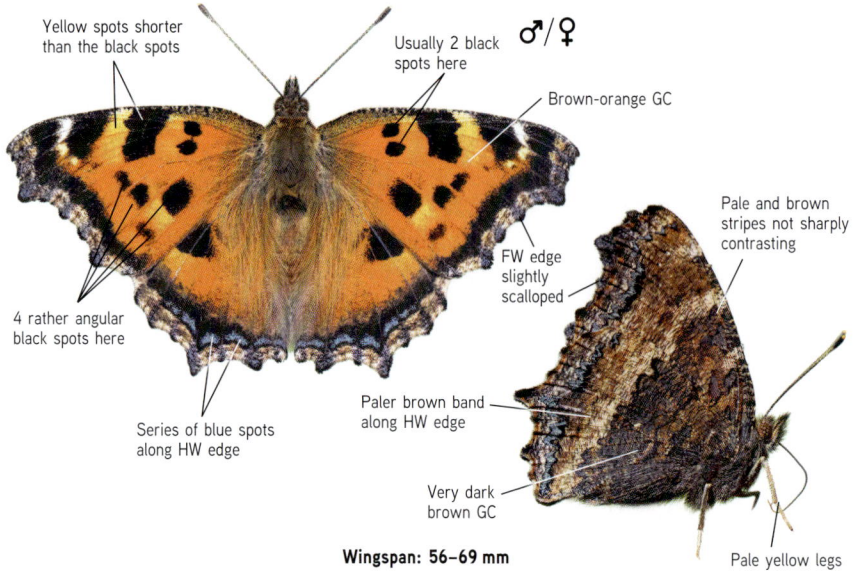

Yellow spots shorter than the black spots

Usually 2 black spots here ♂/♀

Brown-orange GC

Pale and brown stripes not sharply contrasting

FW edge slightly scalloped

4 rather angular black spots here

Series of blue spots along HW edge

Paler brown band along HW edge

Very dark brown GC

Pale yellow legs

Wingspan: 56–69 mm

Habitat: Damp or riparian woodlands.

Hibernating stage: Adult.

Elevational range: Up to 1,000 m.

Egg-laying: Eggs are laid in clusters of several dozens around LHP branches.

Flight period: From April to September.

Host plants: Salicaceae, including *Salix alba*, *S. atrocinerea*, *S. caprea*, *S. cinerea*, *S. reticulata*, and *S. phylicifolia*, *Populus nigra*, and *P. tremula*. Ulmaceae of genera *Ulmus* and *Celtis*.

Diversity and systematics: European populations of this Nymphalid, which is widespread across Asia, belong to the nominate subspecies.

■ N. polychloros
■ N. polychloros + N. xanthomelas

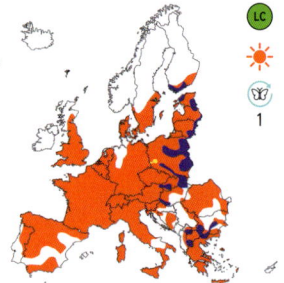

LC

1

Did you know?

Massive summer outbreaks of the Yellow-legged Tortoiseshell have been observed over the past decades beyond the northern and western limits of its range. To date, the biogeographical consequences of these events remain limited, as these individuals mostly fail to breed the following year.

IMAGOS			LARVAE	
Food			Food	
Behaviour of males			Caterpillar location	
Dispersion			Chrysalis location	

NYMPHALIDAE

COMMA *POLYGONIA C-ALBUM*

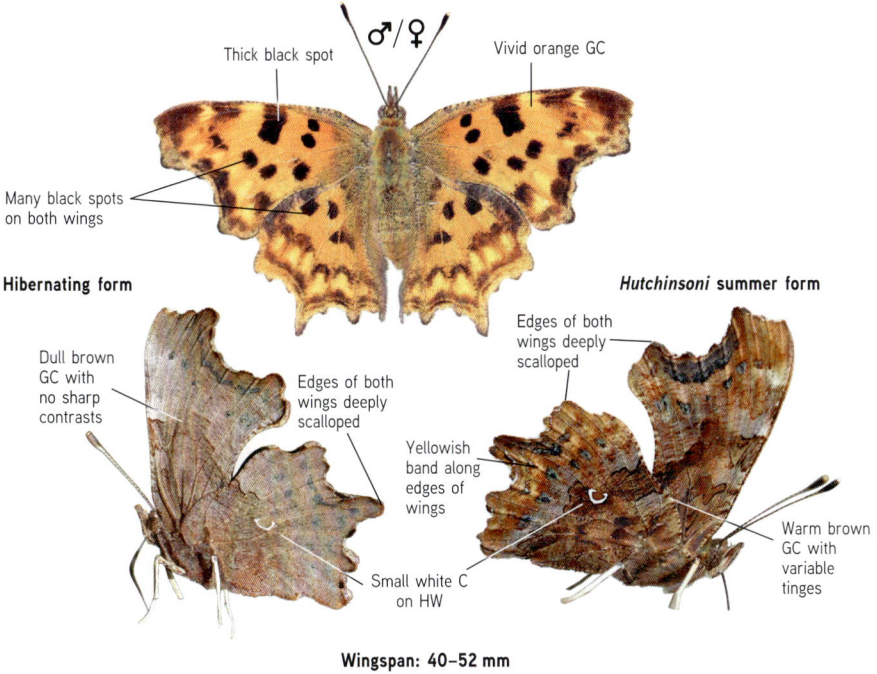

♂/♀

Thick black spot

Vivid orange GC

Many black spots on both wings

Hibernating form

Hutchinsoni summer form

Dull brown GC with no sharp contrasts

Edges of both wings deeply scalloped

Edges of both wings deeply scalloped

Yellowish band along edges of wings

Small white C on HW

Warm brown GC with variable tinges

Wingspan: 40–52 mm

Habitat: Clearings, bushy edges, and meadows, hedgerows (even in parks and gardens).

Hibernating stage: Adult usually, but occasionally the pupa.

Elevational range: Up to 2,000 m.

Egg-laying: Eggs are laid singly or in a few units on LHP leaves.

Flight period: From February to November.

Host plants: Urticaceae, including *Urtica dioica*, *U. membranacea*,

U. pilulifera, and *U. urens*. Salicaceae, including *Salix capraea*, *S. atrocinerea*, *S. alba*, and *S. cinerea*. Ulmaceae, like *Ulmus minor*, *U. laevis*, and *U. glabra*. Betulaceae, such as *Betula pubescens* and *Coryllus avellana*. Grossulariaceae, including *Ribes rubrum*, *R. nigrum*, and *R. uva-crispa*.

Diversity and systematics: European populations of this Nymphalid, which is widespread across Asia, belong to the nominate subspecies.

■ *P. c-album*
■ *P. egea*
■ *P. c-album + P. egea*

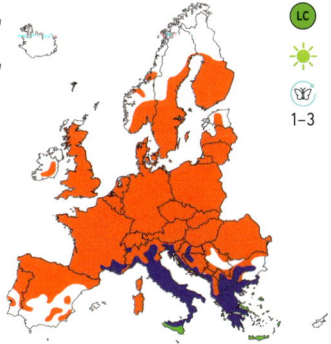

LC

1–3

Did you know?

The Comma has expanded its range due to the current climate change, especially in England, where its populations are well monitored.

IMAGOS					LARVAE		
Food	☆	💩	🐛	💧 💧	Food	🍃	
Behaviour of males					Caterpillar location		
Dispersion					Chrysalis location		

NYMPHALIDAE

SOUTHERN COMMA *POLYGONIA EGEA*

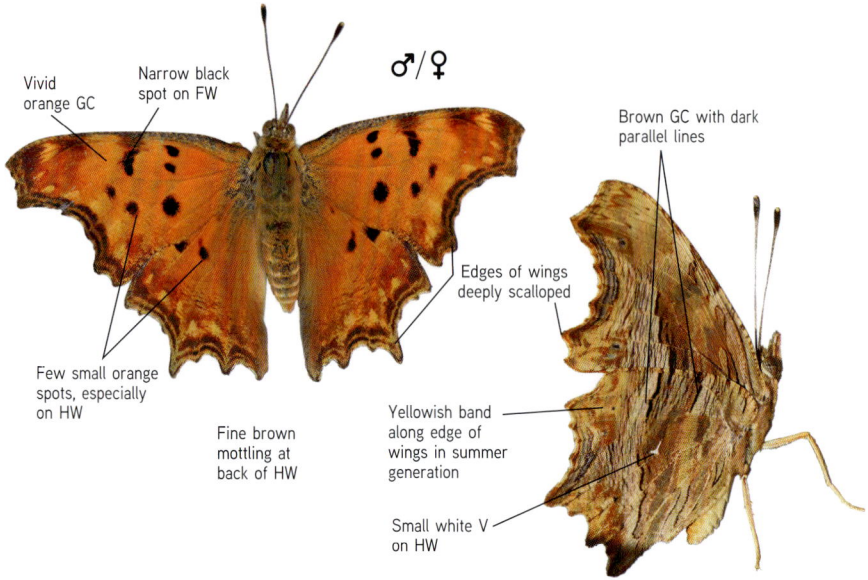

♂/♀

Vivid orange GC

Narrow black spot on FW

Brown GC with dark parallel lines

Edges of wings deeply scalloped

Few small orange spots, especially on HW

Fine brown mottling at back of HW

Yellowish band along edge of wings in summer generation

Small white V on HW

Wingspan: 44–46 mm

Habitat: Rocky Mediterranean habitats, especially those linked to human settlements, such as old walls and ruins where the LHP grows.

Hibernating stage: Adult.

Elevational range: Up to 1,500 m (mostly below 1,000 m).

Egg-laying: Eggs are laid singly or in a few units on LHP leaves.

Flight period: From March to October.

Host plants: Urticaceae, mainly *Parietaria judaica*, but also *P. officinalis* and *Urtica dioica*. Reported on *Ulmus glabra* (Ulmaceae).

Diversity and systematics: European populations belong to the nominate subspecies.

■ P. c-album
■ P. egea
■ P. c-album + P. egea

LC

2–3

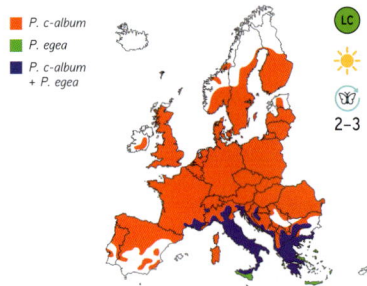

Did you know?

The Southern Comma is still relatively common in the eastern Mediterranean Basin, where it still finds old walls largely invaded by its host plant. However, it has become extremely rare in France, where relentless and unnecessary weeding poses a threat to its last populations.

IMAGOS			LARVAE		
Food			Food		
Behaviour of males			Caterpillar location		
Dispersion			Chrysalis location		

FALSE COMMA *NYMPHALIS VAUALBUM*

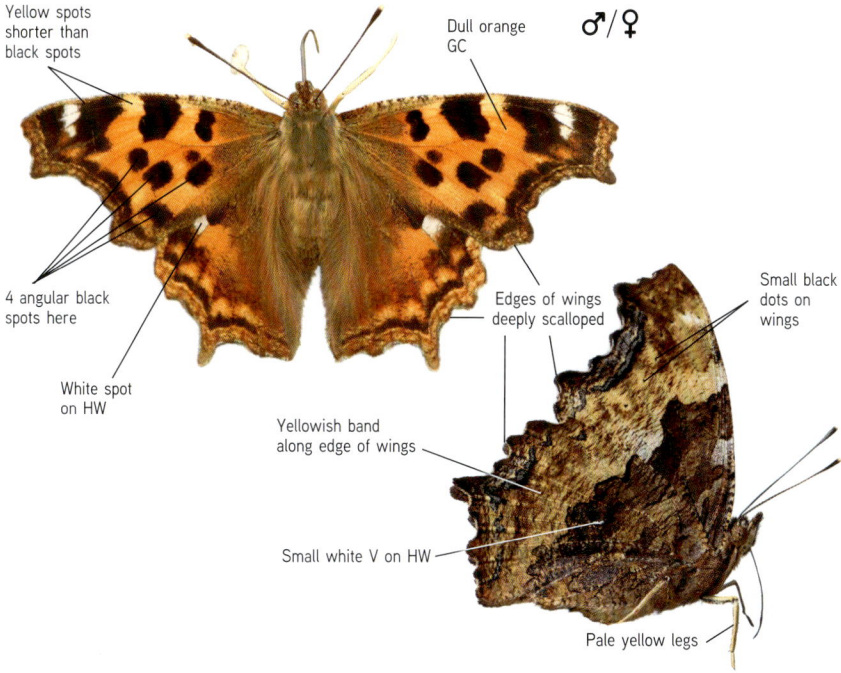

Yellow spots shorter than black spots

Dull orange GC

♂/♀

4 angular black spots here

White spot on HW

Edges of wings deeply scalloped

Small black dots on wings

Yellowish band along edge of wings

Small white V on HW

Pale yellow legs

Wingspan: 58–68 mm

Habitat: Deciduous and riparian forest clearings and edges.

Hibernating stage: Adult.

Elevational range: Up to 1,500 m.

Egg-laying: Eggs are laid in clusters of several dozens around LHP branches.

Flight period: March after overwintering, then between June and September.

Host plants: Salicaceae, especially *Salix × fragilis*, *S. cinerea*, and *Populus tremula*. Ulmaceae, including *Ulmus glabra*. Betulaceae, including *Betula pubescens*. *Fagus sylvatica* (Fagaceae). *Humulus lupulus* (Cannabaceae). *Malus domestica* (Rosaceae).

Diversity and systematics: European populations belong to the nominate subspecies.

IMAGOS			LARVAE	
Food			Food	
Behaviour of males			Caterpillar location	
Dispersion			Chrysalis location	

Did you know?

The False Comma requires cold winters, which explains the tendency for its already quite continental range to shift eastward in the context of current climate warming.

NYMPHALIDAE

MAP *ARASCHNIA LEVANA*

♂/♀

Spring form *levana*

Intermediate form *porima*

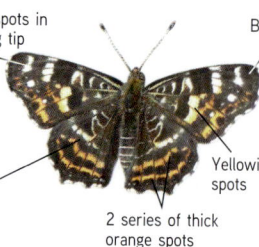

Summer form *prorsa*

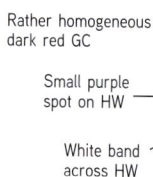

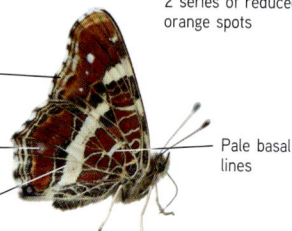

Small white spots in black wing tip

Black GC

White spots

Orange GC with black spots

Basal yellow lines

Yellowish spots

2 series of reduced orange spots

2 series of thick orange spots

Concave FW edge

Rather homogeneous dark red GC

Large purple area on both wings

Small purple spot on HW

Pale basal lines

Greyish band across HW

White band across HW

Wingspan: 28–39 mm

Habitat: Woodland clearings and forest roadsides, bocage meadows.

Hibernating stage: Pupa.

Elevational range: Up to 1,500 m (mostly at lower elevations).

Egg-laying: Eggs are laid in columns of about ten, suspended from LHP leaves.

Flight period: From April to September.

Host plants: Urticaceae, including *Urtica dioica* and *U. urens*. Also on *Humulus lupulus* (Cannabaceae).

Diversity and systematics: European populations of the Map, which is widespread across Asia, belong to the nominate subspecies.

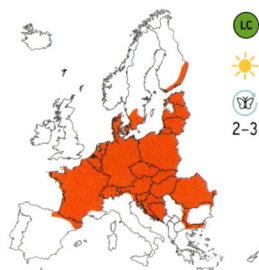

LC

2–3

Did you know?

The spectacular seasonal dimorphism of the Map is controlled by the photoperiod experienced by the larva when it pupates. A long day length inhibits diapause and leads to the *prorsa* form, while a short day length allows for diapause and results in the *levana* form.

IMAGOS		LARVAE	
Food	✿ ♨ ◊	Food	🍃
Behaviour of males		Caterpillar location	🌱
Dispersion		Chrysalis location	🌱

NYMPHALIDAE

WHITE ADMIRAL   *LIMENITIS CAMILLA*

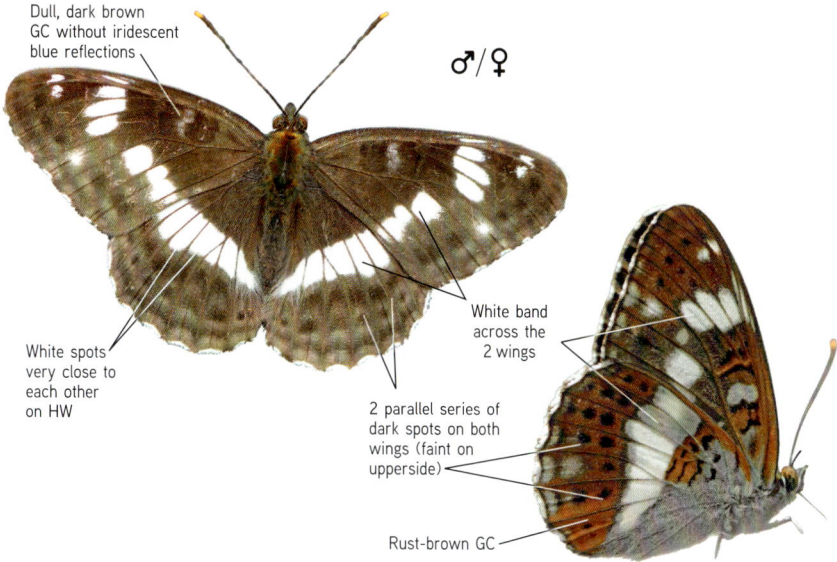

Dull, dark brown GC without iridescent blue reflections

♂/♀

White band across the 2 wings

White spots very close to each other on HW

2 parallel series of dark spots on both wings (faint on upperside)

Rust-brown GC

Wingspan: 52–60 mm

Habitat: Woodland clearings and forest alleys, sunny understorey patches, and riparian forests.

Hibernating stage: Caterpillar.

Elevational range: Up to 1,500 m (mostly at lower elevations).

Egg-laying: Eggs are laid singly on LHP leaves.

Flight period: From June to September.

Host plants: Caprifoliaceae of genus *Lonicera*, including *L. xylosteum*, *L. periclymenum*, *L. caprifolium*, *L. nigra*, and *L. tatarica*. Also reported on *Symphoricarpos albus*.

Diversity and systematics: Most European populations belong to the nominate subspecies. Subspecies *latealba* flies in France, except in the Alps, where subspecies *xylostei* is found.

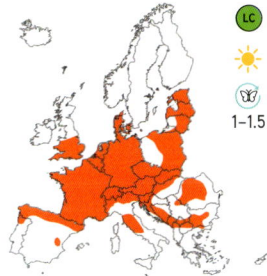

LC

1–1.5

Did you know?

The caterpillar builds itself a winter retreat using a leaf of its host plant. It can do so in several ways: by folding the leaf in half, by cutting it near the base and closing what is left, or by cutting a portion of the leaf and folding it against the remaining part.

IMAGOS				LARVAE	
Food				Food	
Behaviour of males				Caterpillar location	
Dispersion				Chrysalis location	

NYMPHALIDAE

SOUTHERN WHITE ADMIRAL   *LIMENITIS REDUCTA*

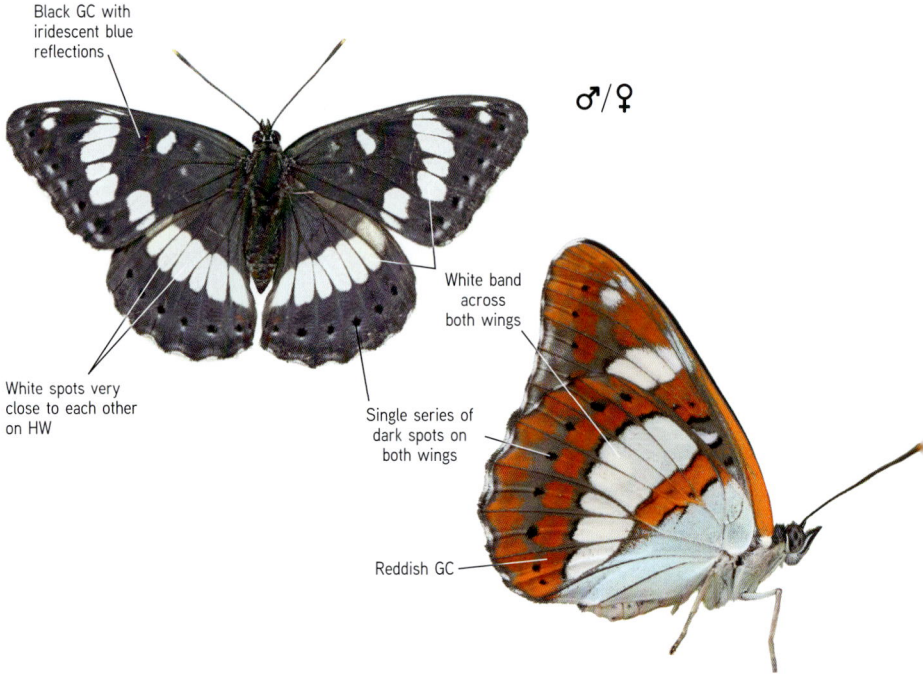

Black GC with iridescent blue reflections

♂/♀

White band across both wings

White spots very close to each other on HW

Single series of dark spots on both wings

Reddish GC

Wingspan: 46–54 mm

Habitat: Garrigue and scrubby areas, sunny forest paths and clearings, hedgerows, parks, and gardens.

Hibernating stage: Caterpillar.

Elevational range: Up to 1,500 m (mostly at lower elevations).

Egg-laying: Eggs are laid singly on LHP leaves.

Flight period: From April to October.

Host plants: Caprifoliaceae of genus *Lonicera*, including *L. xylosteum*, *L. etrusca*, *L. implexa*, *L. caprifolium*, *L. japonica*, *L. alpigena*, and *L. periclymenum*. Also on *Symphoricarpos albus*.

Diversity and systematics: Populations in southeastern Europe belong to subspecies *herculeana*. Subspecies *prodiga* flies in Western Europe. The remaining European populations belong to the nominate subspecies.

LC

1–3

IMAGOS						LARVAE	
Food						Food	
Behaviour of males						Caterpillar location	
Dispersion						Chrysalis location	

Did you know?

The Southern White Admiral frequently feeds on the inflorescences of Oregano. It regularly visits aromatic plantations in gardens.

370

NYMPHALIDAE

HUNGARIAN GLIDER *NEPTIS RIVULARIS*

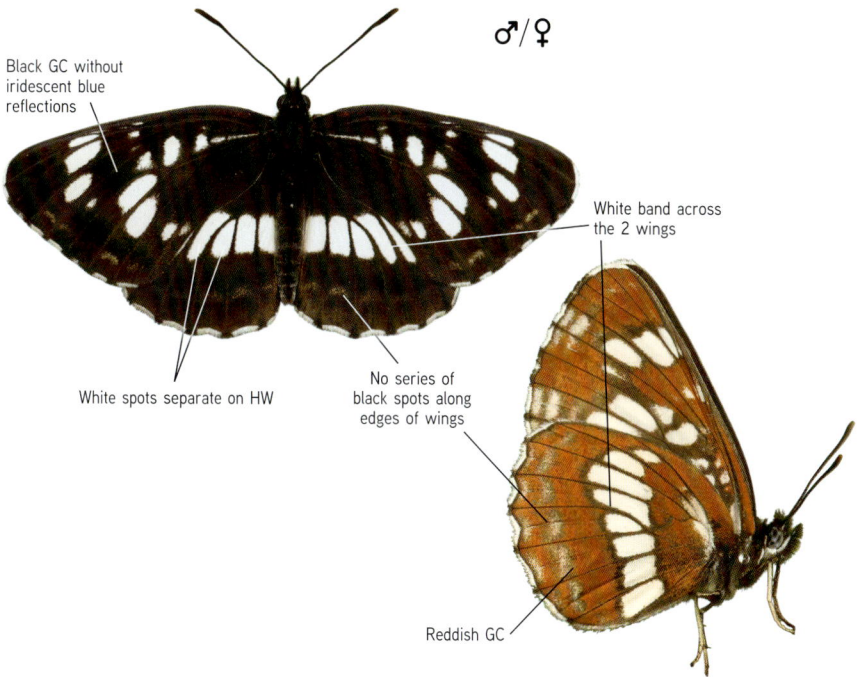

♂/♀

Black GC without iridescent blue reflections

White band across the 2 wings

White spots separate on HW

No series of black spots along edges of wings

Reddish GC

Wingspan: 50–54 mm

Habitat: Clearings, edges, and open understorey of damp forests.

Hibernating stage: Caterpillar.

Elevational range: Between 500 and 1,500 m.

Egg-laying: Eggs are laid singly on LHP leaves.

Flight period: From May to August.

Host plants: Typical megaphorbs in the Rosaceae family, including *Aruncus dioicus, Filipendula ulmaria, Spiraea chamaedryfolia, S. hypericifolia,* and *S. salicifolia.*

Diversity and systematics: European populations belong to the nominate subspecies.

LC

1

IMAGOS		LARVAE	
Food	✿ 💧	Food	🍃
Behaviour of males		Caterpillar location	🌿
Dispersion		Chrysalis location	🌿

Did you know?

The Hungarian Glider can adapt to densely urbanized environments as long as it finds spiraea bushes planted for ornamental purposes.

NYMPHALIDAE

COMMON GLIDER *NEPTIS SAPPHO*

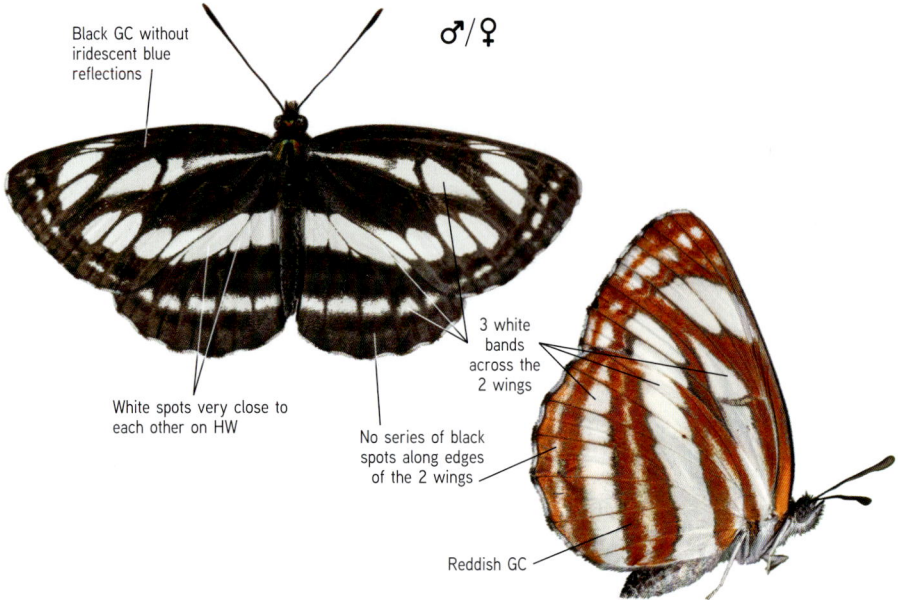

Black GC without iridescent blue reflections

♂/♀

3 white bands across the 2 wings

White spots very close to each other on HW

No series of black spots along edges of the 2 wings

Reddish GC

Wingspan: 50–58 mm

Habitat: Open woodlands, forest paths, and edges of moist deciduous forests, especially along watercourses.

Hibernating stage: Caterpillar.

Elevational range: Up to 1,500 m.

Egg-laying: Eggs are laid singly on LHP leaves.

Flight period: From May to September.

Host plants: Legumes of genus *Lathyrus*, including *L. vernus* and *L. niger*. Has also adapted to the consumption of *Robinia pseudoacacia*.

Diversity and systematics: European populations of this glider, which is widespread across Asia, belong to the nominate subspecies.

Did you know?

The recent adaptation of caterpillars to consume Black Locust leaves could provide the Common Glider with significant ecological opportunities. It prefers to lay eggs on young trees, not exceeding a few meters in height, in places where this plant grows densely.

IMAGOS			LARVAE		
Food			Food		
Behaviour of males			Caterpillar location		
Dispersion			Chrysalis location		

NYMPHALIDAE

POPLAR ADMIRAL *LIMENITIS POPULI*

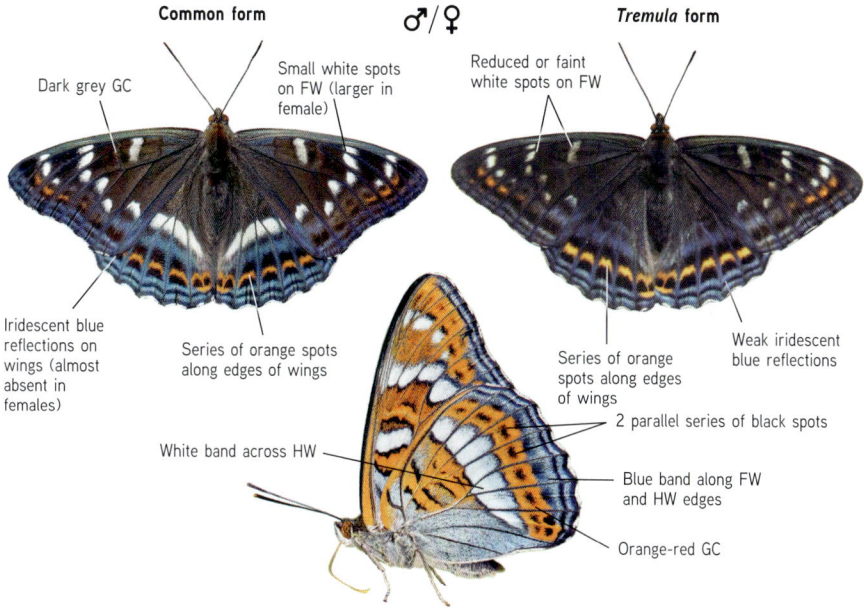

Common form   ♂/♀   *Tremula* form

Dark grey GC

Small white spots on FW (larger in female)

Reduced or faint white spots on FW

Iridescent blue reflections on wings (almost absent in females)

Series of orange spots along edges of wings

Series of orange spots along edges of wings

Weak iridescent blue reflections

2 parallel series of black spots

White band across HW

Blue band along FW and HW edges

Orange-red GC

Wingspan: 57–83 mm

Habitat: Edges, clearings, and pathways of deciduous forests, including riparian and alluvial forests.

Hibernating stage: Caterpillar.

Elevational range: Up to 1,500 m.

Egg-laying: Eggs are laid singly on LHP leaves.

Flight period: From May to August.

Host plants: Mainly *Populus tremula*, sometimes also *P. nigra* and *P. alba*.

Diversity and systematics: Most European populations of the Poplar Admiral, also widespread in Asia, belong to the nominate subspecies. Subspecies *bucovinensis* is described from the Carpathian Mountains.

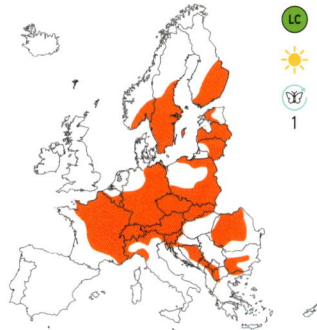

LC

1

Did you know?

Unfortunately, this magnificent butterfly is more frequently observed dead on the asphalt following a collision with a windshield than alive, soaring gracefully above forest pathways.

IMAGOS		LARVAE	
Food		Food	
Behaviour of males		Caterpillar location	
Dispersion		Chrysalis location	

NYMPHALIDAE

PURPLE EMPEROR *APATURA IRIS*

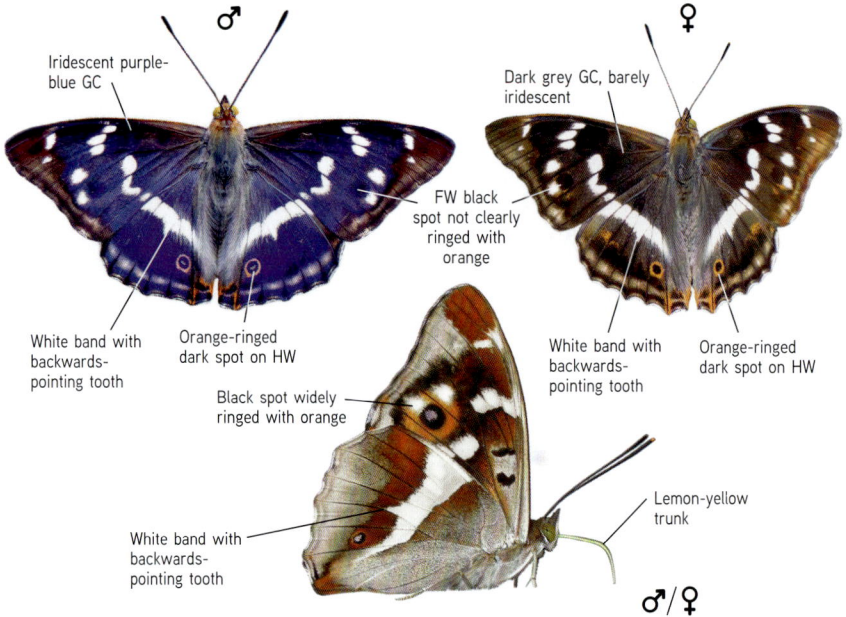

♂

Iridescent purple-blue GC

♀

Dark grey GC, barely iridescent

FW black spot not clearly ringed with orange

White band with backwards-pointing tooth

Orange-ringed dark spot on HW

White band with backwards-pointing tooth

Orange-ringed dark spot on HW

Black spot widely ringed with orange

Lemon-yellow trunk

White band with backwards-pointing tooth

♂/♀

Wingspan: 60–75 mm

Habitat: Edges, clearings, and pathways of deciduous forests; more rarely, conifer woodlands as long as host plants are present.

Hibernating stage: Caterpillar.

Elevational range: Up to 1,500 m.

Egg-laying: Eggs are laid singly on LHP leaves.

Flight period: From June to August.

Host plants: Salicaceae, including *Salix caprea*, *S. alba*, *S. atrocinerea*, *S. appendiculata*, *S. aurita*, *S. cinerea*, *S. fragilis*, and *S. purpurea*. Also on *Populus tremula*, *P. nigra*, and *P. balsamifera*.

Diversity and systematics: The Purple Emperor is widely distributed in Asia. Its European populations belong to the nominate subspecies.

LC

1

Did you know?

The emperors provide spectacular examples of iridescence among European butterflies. Their colour is due to the microstructure of their scales, which produce constructive interferences (blue colour) or destructive interferences (dark colour), depending on the viewing angle.

IMAGOS		LARVAE	
Food	🔶 🐛 🍯 ✳️ 💧	Food	🍃
Behaviour of males		Caterpillar location	
Dispersion		Chrysalis location	

NYMPHALIDAE

LESSER PURPLE EMPEROR *APATURA ILIA*

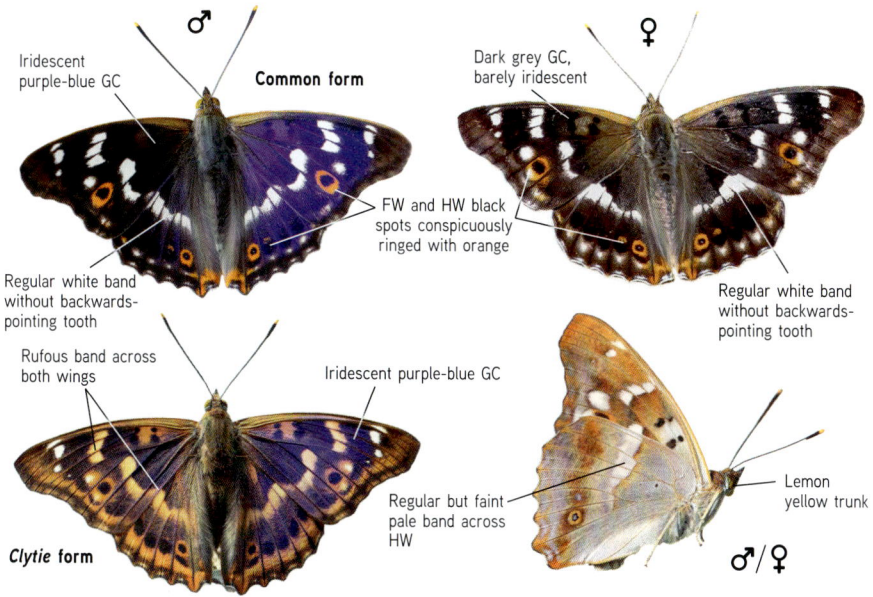

♂

Iridescent purple-blue GC

Common form

♀

Dark grey GC, barely iridescent

FW and HW black spots conspicuously ringed with orange

Regular white band without backwards-pointing tooth

Regular white band without backwards-pointing tooth

Rufous band across both wings

Iridescent purple-blue GC

Clytie form

Regular but faint pale band across HW

Lemon yellow trunk

♂/♀

Wingspan: 64–72 mm

Habitat: Edges, clearings, and pathways of riparian forests or narrow riparian zones where the host plants grow.

Hibernating stage: Caterpillar.

Elevational range: Up to 1,300 m.

Egg-laying: Eggs are laid singly on LHP leaves.

Flight period: From May to October.

Host plants: Salicaceae, mainly *Populus tremula*, but also *P. nigra*, *P. alba*, and *P. trichocarpa*, and sometimes willows like *Salix × fragilis*, *S. alba*, *S. atrocinerea*, *S. caprea*, *S. rosmarinifolia*, and *S. viminalis*.

Diversity and systematics: The Lesser Purple Emperor is widely distributed in Asia. Its European populations belong to the nominate subspecies, of which numerous forms have been described.

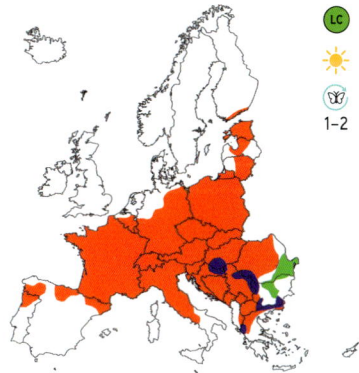

- A. ilia
- A. metis
- A. ilia + A. metis

LC

1–2

Did you know?

Lesser Purple Emperors greatly enjoy sipping sweat from the skin of the naturalist, who willingly allows this harassment by such magnificent butterflies.

IMAGOS		LARVAE	
Food		Food	
Behaviour of males		Caterpillar location	
Dispersion		Chrysalis location	

NYMPHALIDAE

FREYER'S PURPLE EMPEROR *APATURA METIS*

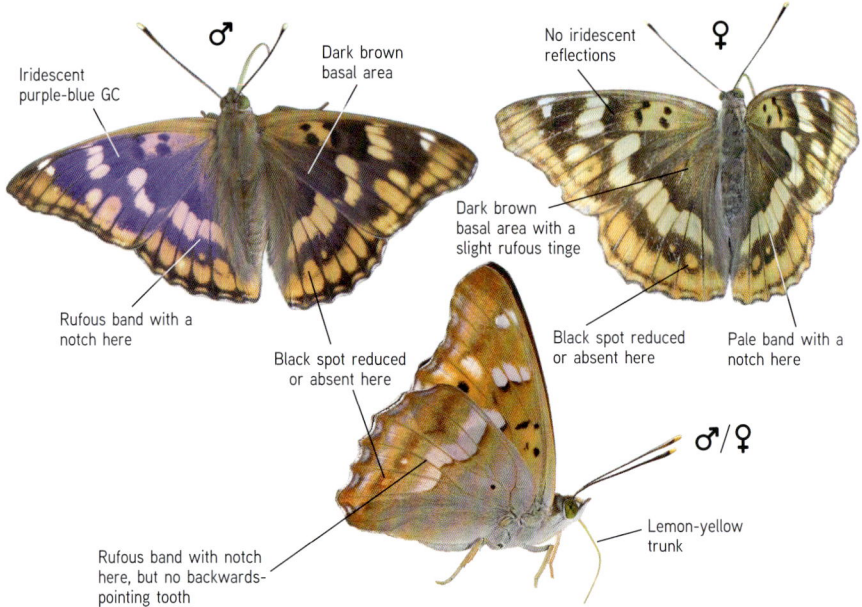

♂

Iridescent purple-blue GC

Dark brown basal area

No iridescent reflections

♀

Dark brown basal area with a slight rufous tinge

Rufous band with a notch here

Black spot reduced or absent here

Black spot reduced or absent here

Pale band with a notch here

♂/♀

Rufous band with notch here, but no backwards-pointing tooth

Lemon-yellow trunk

Wingspan: 60–64 mm

Habitat: Riparian woodlands.

Hibernating stage: Caterpillar.

Elevational range: Up to 700 m.

Egg-laying: Eggs are laid singly on LHP leaves.

Flight period: From May to September.

Host plants: Salicaceae, above all *Salix alba*.

Diversity and systematics: European populations belong to subspecies *balcanica*.

- *A. ilia*
- *A. metis*
- *A. ilia + A. metis*

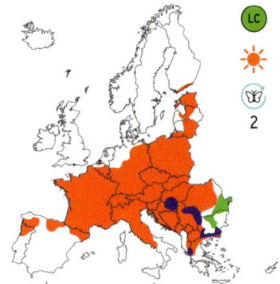

LC

2

Did you know?

Freyer's Purple Emperor generally flies not far from watercourses, where males inspect the foliage of old White Willows, encounter females, or drink on humid banks. This species can be confused only with the *clytie* form of the Lesser Purple Emperor.

IMAGOS		LARVAE	
Food		Food	
Behaviour of males		Caterpillar location	
Dispersion		Chrysalis location	

NYMPHALIDAE

MONARCH *DANAUS PLEXIPPUS*

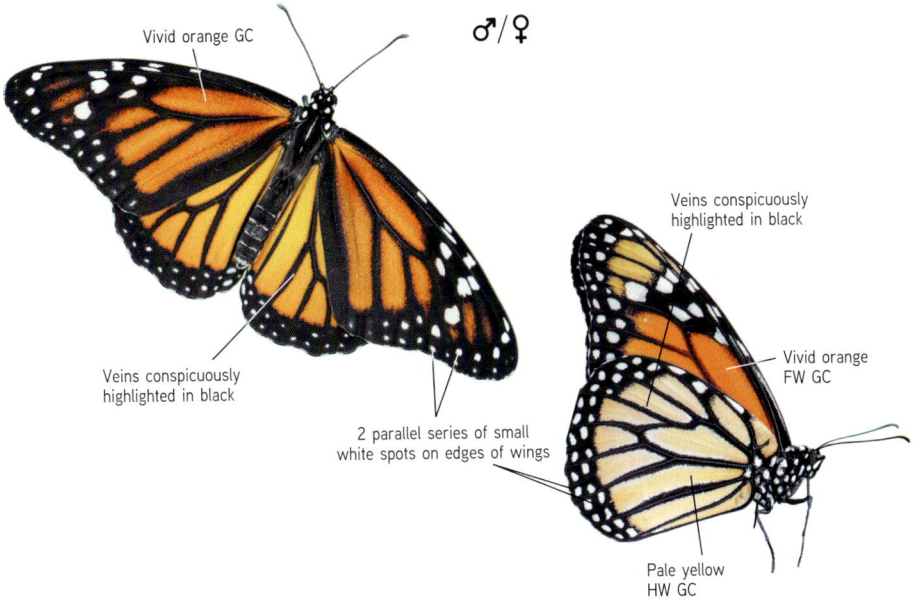

Vivid orange GC

♂/♀

Veins conspicuously highlighted in black

Veins conspicuously highlighted in black

Vivid orange FW GC

2 parallel series of small white spots on edges of wings

Pale yellow HW GC

Wingspan: 89–102 mm

Habitat: Ruderal places, wastelands, and gardens where its nonindigenous LHPs have been planted or established spontaneously.

Hibernating stage: Egg, caterpillar, pupa, or adult.

Elevational range: Up to 500 m.

Egg-laying: Eggs are laid singly on LHP leaves and inflorescences.

Flight period: Year-round.

Host plants: Asclepiadaceae, including *Asclepias curassavica*, *Gomphocarpus fruticosus*, and *Cynanchum acutum*.

Diversity and systematics: European populations, established in the Canary Islands, Madeira, the Azores, and the Southern Iberian Peninsula, belong to the nominate subspecies.

NA

3+

Canaries

Madeira

Azores

Did you know?

In the European areas where it is established, presumably through the arrival of a few strays, the famous migratory behaviour of the species has been lost – a beneficial evolutionary regression, considering the geographical location of these populations.

IMAGOS		LARVAE	
Food		Food	
Behaviour of males		Caterpillar location	
Dispersion		Chrysalis location	

NYMPHALIDAE

PLAIN TIGER *DANAUS CHRYSIPPUS*

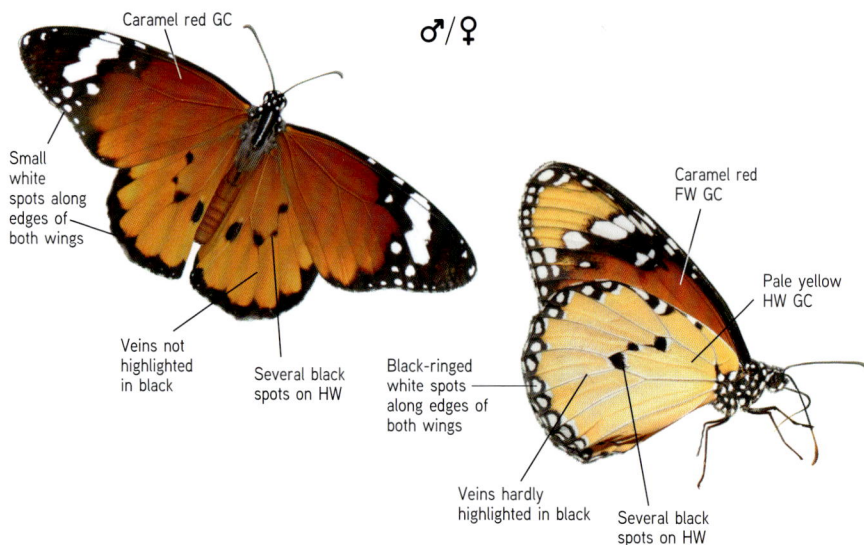

♂/♀

Caramel red GC

Small white spots along edges of both wings

Veins not highlighted in black

Several black spots on HW

Caramel red FW GC

Pale yellow HW GC

Black-ringed white spots along edges of both wings

Veins hardly highlighted in black

Several black spots on HW

Wingspan: 60–80 mm

Habitat: Crop surroundings, Mediterranean wastelands, parks, and gardens.

Hibernating stage: Egg, caterpillar, pupa, or adult.

Elevational range: Up to 500 m.

Egg-laying: Eggs are laid singly on LHP leaves.

Flight period: Year-round.

Host plants: Asclepiadaceae, especially *Asclepias curassavica*, *Araujia sericifera*, *Apteranthes burchardii*, *Gomphocarpus fruticosus*, *G. physocarpus*, *Caralluma* spp., *Cynanchum acutum*, and *Ceropegia* spp.

Diversity and systematics: European populations belong to the nominate subspecies.

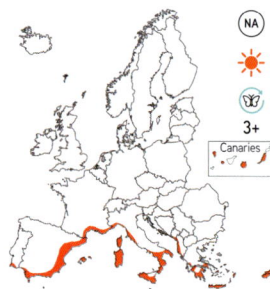

NA

3+

Canaries

Did you know?

Like those of the Monarch, the caterpillars and adult stages of the Plain Tiger are particularly toxic to potential predators. These toxins are extracted from the latex of the host plants; the caterpillar accumulates them as it develops.

IMAGOS		LARVAE	
Food		Food	
Behaviour of males		Caterpillar location	
Dispersion		Chrysalis location	

NYMPHALIDAE

DANAID EGGFLY *HYPOLIMNAS MISIPPUS*

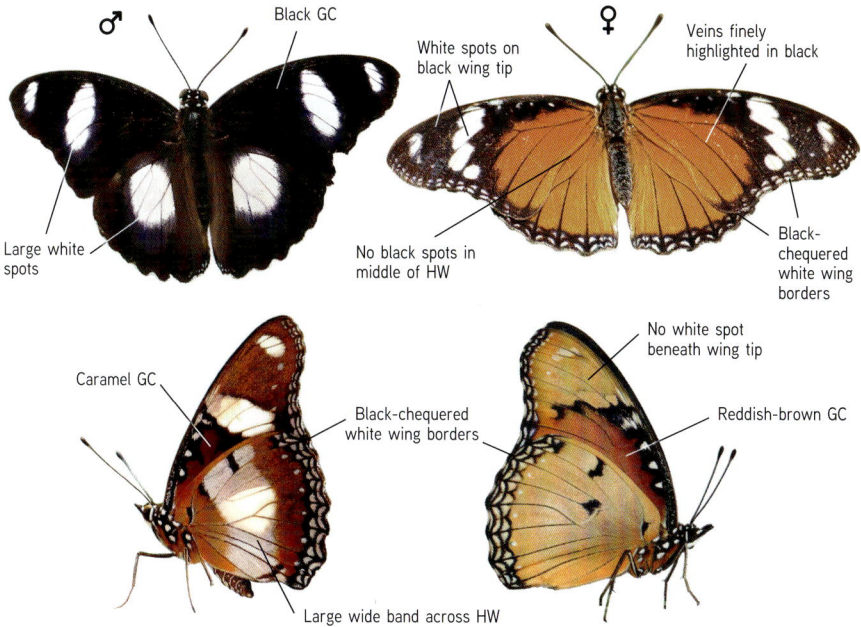

♂ — Black GC

White spots on black wing tip

♀ — Veins finely highlighted in black

Large white spots

No black spots in middle of HW

Black-chequered white wing borders

Caramel GC

Black-chequered white wing borders

No white spot beneath wing tip

Reddish-brown GC

Large wide band across HW

Wingspan: 60–80 mm

Habitat: Coastal areas (including gardens) where migratory strays arrive.

Hibernating stage: Egg, caterpillar, pupa, or adult.

Elevational range: Up to 500 m.

Egg-laying: Eggs are laid singly or in a few units on LHP leaves.

Flight period: Year-round in its usual breeding range. Migrants mostly arrive during autumn and winter.

Host plants: Rather polyphagous in its usual range. Uses *Amaranthus* spp. (Amaranthaceae), *Sedum* spp. (Crassulaceae), *Ipomea* spp. (Convolvulaceae), *Hibiscus* spp. (Malvaceae), and *Portulaca* spp. (Portulacaceae).

Diversity and systematics: There are no notable subspecies for this widely distributed, large migratory species otherwise found in South America, Africa, and southern Asia.

NA

3+

Did you know?

The Danaid Eggfly does not seem to breed consistently in Europe. Some stray migrants from Africa arrive annually in the Canary Islands or Madeira, and occasionally in the Azores. The female is a Batesian mimic of the Plain Tiger.

IMAGOS			LARVAE		
Food			Food		
Behaviour of males			Caterpillar location		
Dispersion			Chrysalis location		

NYMPHALIDAE

QUEEN OF SPAIN FRITILLARY *ISSORIA LATHONIA*

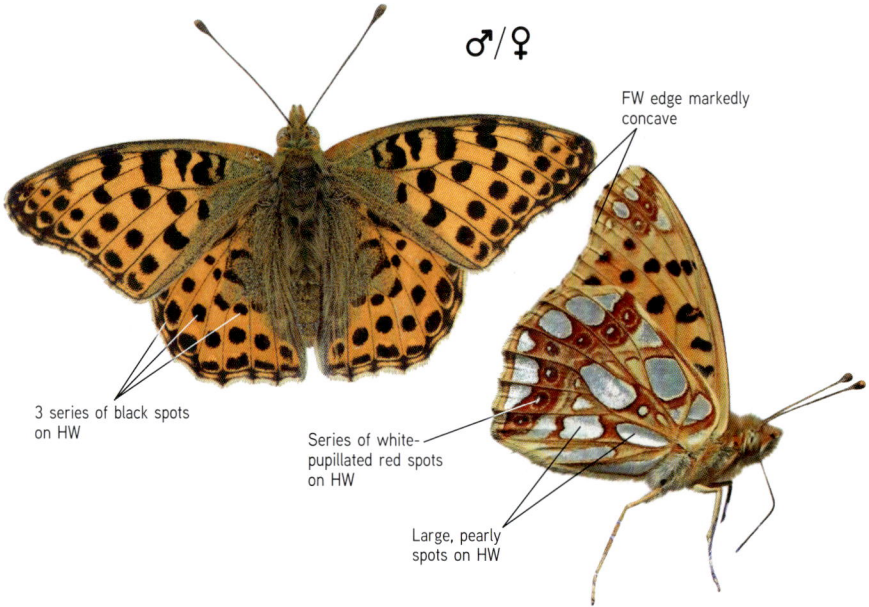

♂/♀

FW edge markedly concave

3 series of black spots on HW

Series of white-pupillated red spots on HW

Large, pearly spots on HW

Wingspan: 34–45 mm

Habitat: Grasslands, meadows, wastelands, crop surroundings, and grassy roadsides.

Hibernating stage: Caterpillar, pupa, or adult.

Elevational range: Up to 3,000 m.

Egg-laying: Eggs are laid singly on LHP leaves.

Flight period: From February to November.

Host plants: Numerous Violaceae, including *Viola arvensis, V. cornuta, V. dacica, V. eximia, V. tricolor, V. hirta, V. hispida, V. kitaibeliana, V. lutea, V. odorata, V. phitosiana, V. reichenbachiana, V. riviniana, V. rupestris,* and *V. calaminaria.*

Diversity and systematics: European populations belong to the nominate subspecies.

LC

2-3+

Did you know?

Unlike most fritillaries, the Queen of Spain Fritillary has adapted relatively well to human-induced changes in its environment. Its significant dispersal abilities likely help as it colonizes favourable locations within ecologically disrupted areas.

IMAGOS		LARVAE	
Food		Food	
Behaviour of males		Caterpillar location	
Dispersion		Chrysalis location	

SILVER-WASHED FRITILLARY *ARGYNNIS PAPHIA*

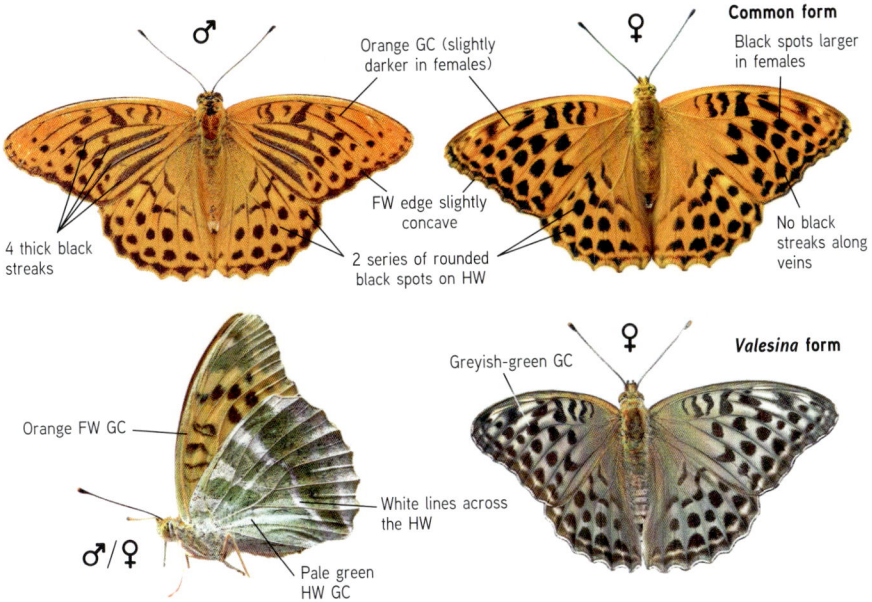

♂

Orange GC (slightly
darker in females)

♀

Common form

Black spots larger
in females

FW edge slightly
concave

No black
streaks along
veins

4 thick black
streaks

2 series of rounded
black spots on HW

Greyish-green GC

♀

Valesina form

Orange FW GC

White lines across
the HW

♂/♀

Pale green
HW GC

Wingspan: 55–66 mm

Habitat: Clearings, edges, and sunny, flower-rich forest pathways. Meadows in the vicinity of woodlands. Also visits parks and gardens.

Hibernating stage: Caterpillar.

Elevational range: Up to 2,000 m.

Egg-laying: Eggs are laid singly on the trunks of trees growing near favourable areas for the LHPs.

Flight period: From May to October.

Host plants: Violaceae, including *Viola reichenbachiana*, *V. alba*, *V. arvensis*, *V. canina*, *V. hirta*, *V. palustris*, *V. riviniana*, *V. odorata*, and *V. tricolor*. Also reported on *Filipendula ulmaria* (Rosaceae).

Diversity and systematics: Most European populations belong to the nominate subspecies. Subspecies *immaculata* is found in the Tyrrhenian Islands. Numerous other forms have been described.

- ■ A. paphia
- ■ A. pandora
- ■ A. paphia + A. pandora
- ■ A. paphia + A. laodice
- ■ A. paphia + A. pandora + laodice

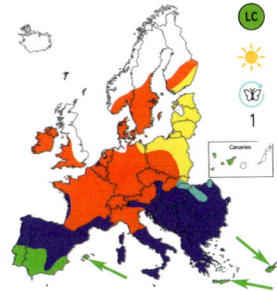

LC

1

Did you know?

The Silver-washed Fritillary is a regular visitor to the inflorescences of the famous "butterfly bush" (*Buddleia davidii*) that often grows invasively on the edges of forests and on which it can linger for a long while.

IMAGOS		LARVAE	
Food	✿ 🐛 💩 ◊	Food	🍃
Behaviour of males		Caterpillar location	
Dispersion		Chrysalis location	

CARDINAL *ARGYNNIS PANDORA*

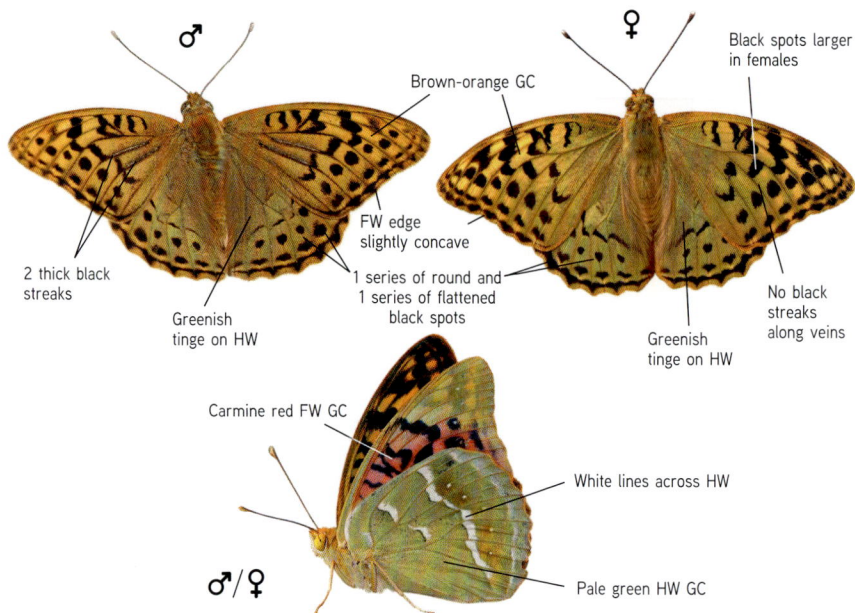

♂

♀

Black spots larger in females

Brown-orange GC

FW edge slightly concave

2 thick black streaks

1 series of round and 1 series of flattened black spots

Greenish tinge on HW

No black streaks along veins

Greenish tinge on HW

Carmine red FW GC

White lines across HW

♂/♀

Pale green HW GC

Wingspan: 64–80 mm

Habitat: Clearings, edges, sunny flower-rich forest pathways, sparse woodlands, and olive groves.

Hibernating stage: Caterpillar, usually inside the egg.

Elevational range: Up to 1,500 m.

Egg-laying: Eggs are laid singly on leaves of the LHP or on nearby leaf litter.

Flight period: From April to October.

Host plants: Violaceae, including *Viola alba*, *V. arvensis*, *V. corsica*, *V. cheiranthifolia*, *V. kitaibeliana*, and *V. tricolor*.

Diversity and systematics: Most European populations belong to the nominate subspecies. Populations in the Canary Islands belong to subspecies *seitzi*. Subspecies *cyrnea* is found in Corsica and on the island of Elba.

- 🟧 A. paphia
- 🟩 A. pandora
- 🟦 A. paphia + A. pandora
- 🟨 A. paphia + A. laodice
- 🟩 A. paphia + A. pandora + laodice

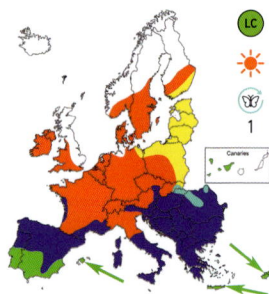

LC

1

Did you know?

The Cardinal owes its common name to the red colour on the underside of its forewing, reminiscent of the attire of Roman Catholic ecclesiastic officials. Adults require highly flowered environments to support their high metabolic activity during flight.

IMAGOS		LARVAE	
Food	🌼 🐝 💧	Food	🍃
Behaviour of males		Caterpillar location	🌿
Dispersion		Chrysalis location	🌿

PALLAS' FRITILLARY *ARGYNNIS LAODICE*

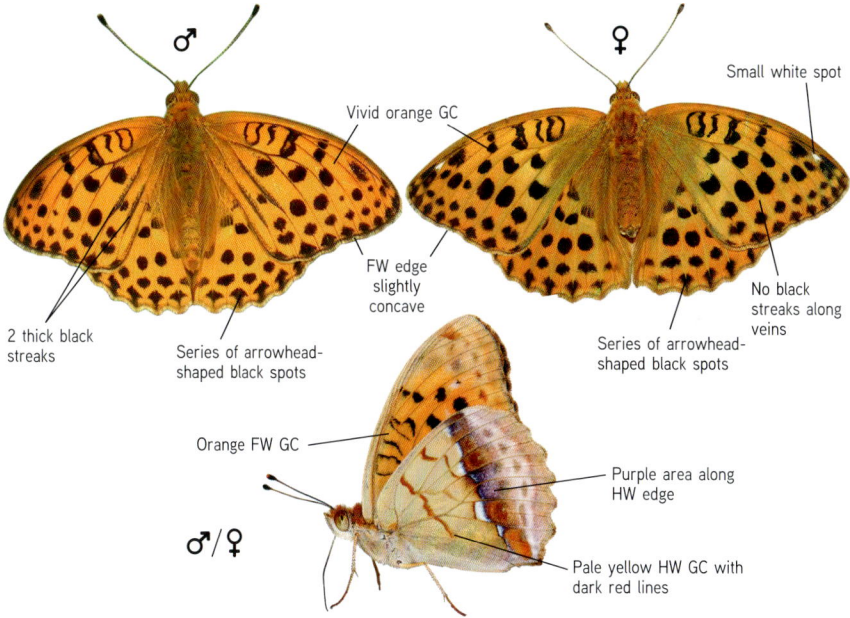

♂

♀

Vivid orange GC

Small white spot

FW edge
slightly
concave

2 thick black
streaks

Series of arrowhead-
shaped black spots

No black
streaks along
veins

Series of arrowhead-
shaped black spots

Orange FW GC

Purple area along
HW edge

♂/♀

Pale yellow HW GC with
dark red lines

Wingspan: 50–60 mm

Habitat: Large woodland clearings, megaphorbs, edges, and damp, flowered understories.

Hibernating stage: Caterpillar.

Elevational range: Up to 500 m.

Egg-laying: Eggs are laid singly on LHP leaves

Flight period: July and August.

Host plants: Violaceae, above all *Viola palustris* and *V. canina*.

Diversity and systematics: European populations belong to the nominate subspecies.

- ■ A. paphia
- ■ A. pandora
- ■ A. paphia + A. pandora
- ■ A. paphia + A. laodice
- ■ A. paphia + A. pandora + laodice

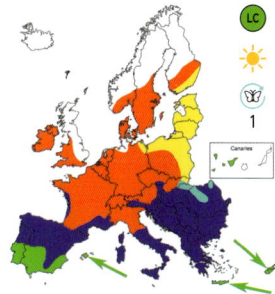

LC

1

Did you know?

Adults are particularly attracted to the inflorescences of brambles. Pallas' Fritillary reaches the western limit of its range in northeastern Germany, while it is widespread across Asia.

IMAGOS		LARVAE	
Food		Food	
Behaviour of males		Caterpillar location	
Dispersion		Chrysalis location	

NYMPHALIDAE

CORSICAN FRITILLARY *FABRICIANA ELISA*

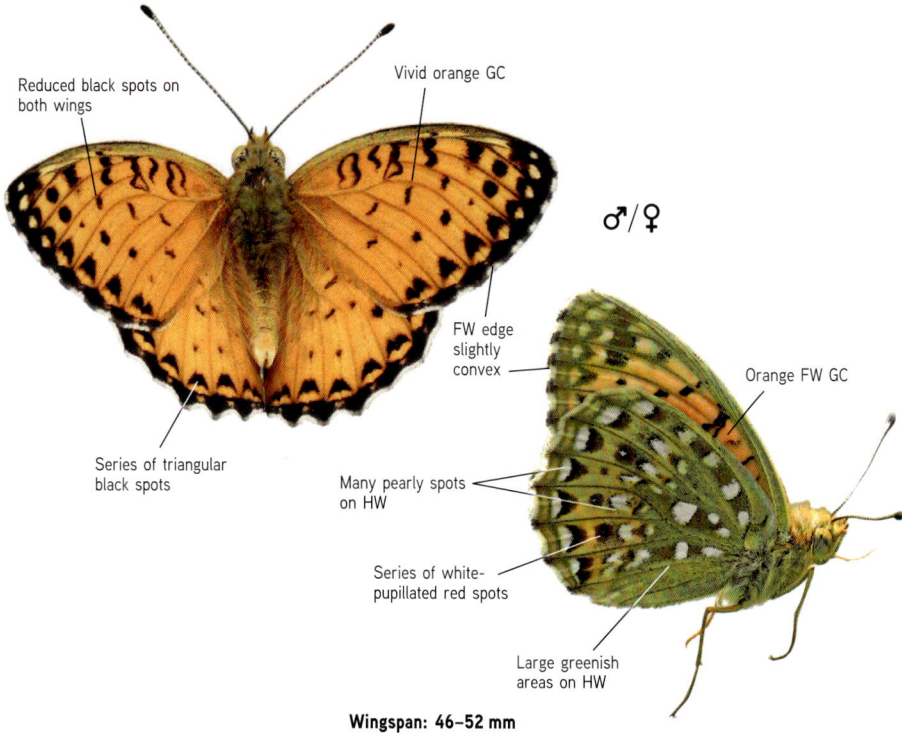

Reduced black spots on both wings

Vivid orange GC

♂/♀

FW edge slightly convex

Orange FW GC

Series of triangular black spots

Many pearly spots on HW

Series of white-pupillated red spots

Large greenish areas on HW

Wingspan: 46–52 mm

Habitat: Bushy grasslands, maquis, and Mediterranean clearings.

Hibernating stage: Caterpillar inside the egg.

Elevational range: Between 500 and 2,000 m.

Egg-laying: Eggs are laid singly.

Flight period: From June to August.

Host plants: *Viola corsica* (Violaceae), among others.

Diversity and systematics: There are no notable subspecies for this fritillary, which is endemic to Corsica and Sardinia.

IMAGOS		LARVAE	
Food	✿	Food	🍃
Behaviour of males		Caterpillar location	
Dispersion		Chrysalis location	

Did you know?

Like other large fritillaries, the caterpillar of the Corsican Fritillary builds itself a shelter using the leaves of its host plant, within which it pupates.

NYMPHALIDAE

DARK GREEN FRITILLARY *SPEYERIA AGLAJA*

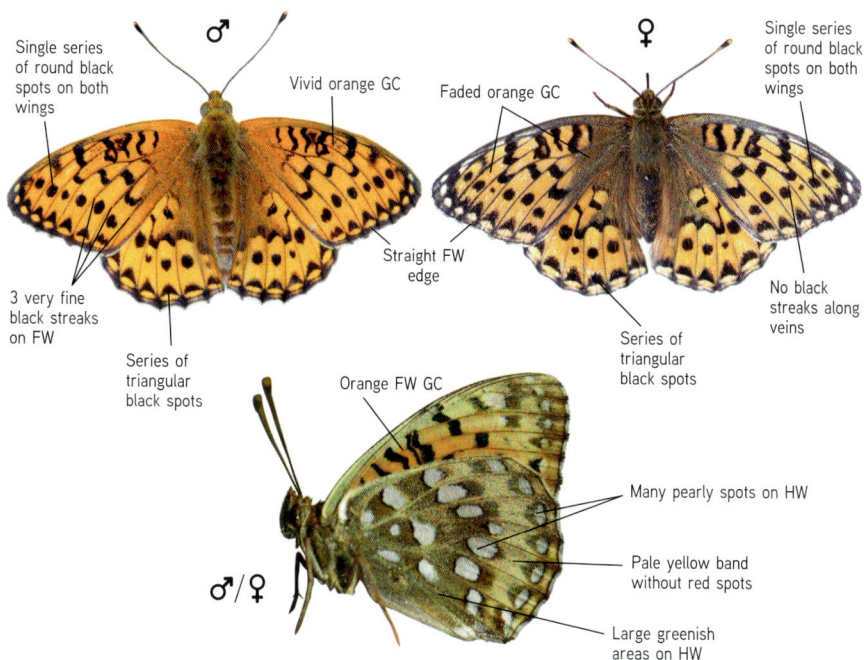

♂

Single series of round black spots on both wings

Vivid orange GC

Faded orange GC

♀

Single series of round black spots on both wings

Straight FW edge

3 very fine black streaks on FW

Series of triangular black spots

No black streaks along veins

Series of triangular black spots

Orange FW GC

♂/♀

Many pearly spots on HW

Pale yellow band without red spots

Large greenish areas on HW

Wingspan: 44–61 mm

Habitat: Clearings, edges, and sunny, flower-rich forest pathways. Hay or damp meadows in the vicinity of woodlands.

Hibernating stage: Caterpillar.

Elevational range: Up to 2,500 m.

Egg-laying: Eggs are laid singly or in a few units, often on dry LHP leaves.

Flight period: From May to September.

Host plants: Violaceae, including *Viola aetholica, V. calcarata,* *V. canina, V. elatior, V. lutea, V. odorata, V. palustris, V. hirta, V. reichenbachiana, V. riviniana, V. rupestris,* and *V. tricolor.* Occasionally on *Bistorta officinalis* (Polygonaceae).

Diversity and systematics: Numerous forms and aberrations are described. Most European populations belong to the nominate subspecies. Subspecies *scotica* flies in Scotland, while subspecies *boreas* lives in the Far North.

LC

1

Did you know?

The Dark Green Fritillary is threatened by the development of monoculture forestry, especially dense conifer plantations.

IMAGOS		LARVAE	
Food	✿ ♨ ◊	Food	◊
Behaviour of males		Caterpillar location	
Dispersion		Chrysalis location	

NYMPHALIDAE

HIGH BROWN FRITILLARY *FABRICIANA ADIPPE*

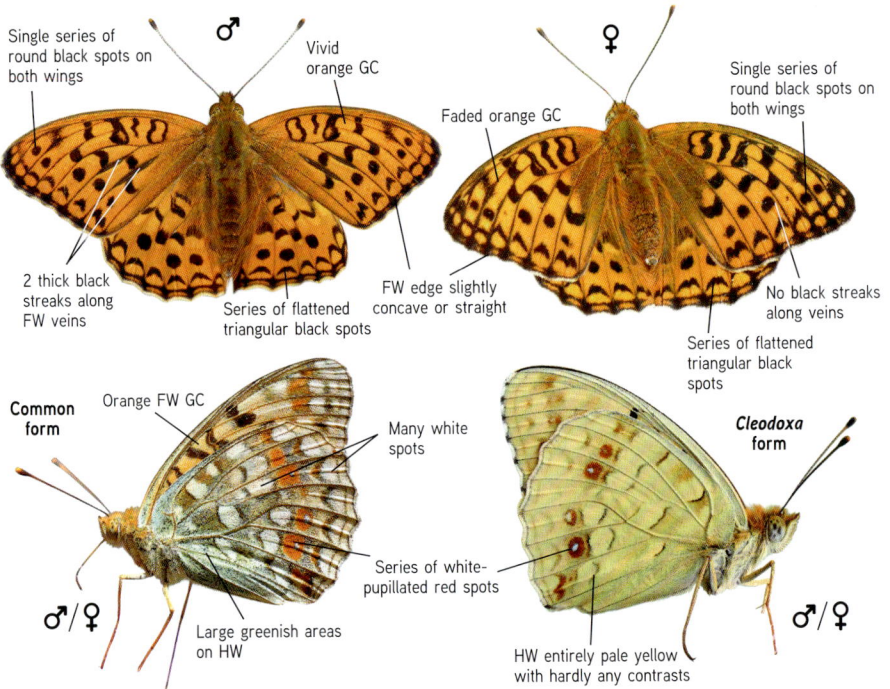

♂

Single series of round black spots on both wings

Vivid orange GC

♀

Single series of round black spots on both wings

Faded orange GC

2 thick black streaks along FW veins

FW edge slightly concave or straight

Series of flattened triangular black spots

No black streaks along veins

Series of flattened triangular black spots

Common form

Orange FW GC

Many white spots

Cleodoxa form

♂/♀

Series of white-pupillated red spots

Large greenish areas on HW

HW entirely pale yellow with hardly any contrasts

♂/♀

Wingspan: 46–58 mm

Habitat: Flower-rich clearings and hay meadows included in a forest mosaic.

Hibernating stage: Caterpillar inside the egg.

Elevational range: Up to 2,000 m.

Egg-laying: Eggs are laid singly on dry LHP leaves or on the trunks of nearby trees.

Flight period: From May to September.

Host plants: Violaceae, including *Viola canina, V. hirta, V. riviniana, V. reichenbachiana, V. odorata, V. lactea,* and *V. tricolor.*

Diversity and systematics: Numerous subspecies have been described. Subspecies *chlorodippe* flies in the Iberian Peninsula, while subspecies *norvegica* inhabits Northern Europe. Subspecies *vulgaris* is found in England and northern France.

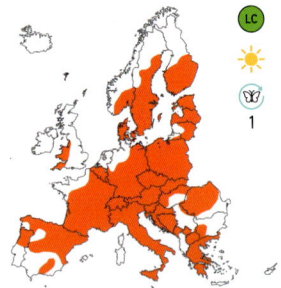

LC

1

Did you know?

Hay meadows in a forest context are disappearing, posing a threat to the High Brown Fritillary as well as other species, such as the Scarce Fritillary.

IMAGOS		LARVAE	
Food		Food	
Behaviour of males		Caterpillar location	
Dispersion		Chrysalis location	

386

NYMPHALIDAE

NIOBE FRITILLARY *FABRICIANA NIOBE*

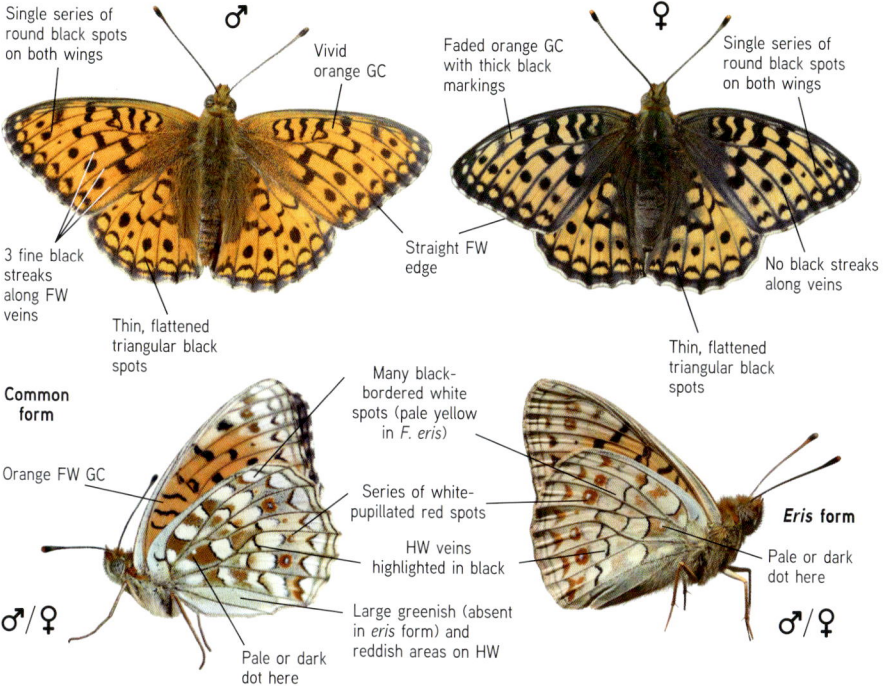

♂

Single series of round black spots on both wings

Vivid orange GC

Faded orange GC with thick black markings

♀

Single series of round black spots on both wings

3 fine black streaks along FW veins

Straight FW edge

No black streaks along veins

Thin, flattened triangular black spots

Thin, flattened triangular black spots

Common form

Orange FW GC

Many black-bordered white spots (pale yellow in *F. eris*)

Series of white-pupillated red spots

HW veins highlighted in black

Eris form

Pale or dark dot here

♂/♀

Large greenish (absent in *eris* form) and reddish areas on HW

Pale or dark dot here

♂/♀

Wingspan: 40–54 mm

Habitat: Hay and subalpine meadows, flowery edges and clearings, bushy grasslands.

Hibernating stage: Caterpillar inside the egg.

Elevational range: Up to 2,400 m.

Egg-laying: Eggs are laid singly or in a few units in areas favourable to the LHP.

Flight period: From May to August.

Host plants: Violaceae, including *Viola alba*, *V. arvensis*, *V. canina*, *V. eximia*, *V. hirta*, *V. lutea*, *V. odorata*, *V. palustris*, *V. riviniana*, *V. reichenbachiana*, *V. rupestris*, and *V. tricolor*.

Diversity and systematics: Numerous subspecies and forms are described. Subspecies *gigantea* flies in southeastern Europe. Subspecies *altonevadensis* inhabits the southern part of the Iberian Peninsula.

LC

1

Did you know?

Like other large fritillaries, the Niobe Fritillary has significantly declined in the northern part of its range, falling victim to agricultural intensification and habitat artificialization.

IMAGOS		LARVAE	
Food		Food	
Behaviour of males		Caterpillar location	
Dispersion		Chrysalis location	

NYMPHALIDAE

MARBLED FRITILLARY *BRENTHIS DAPHNE*

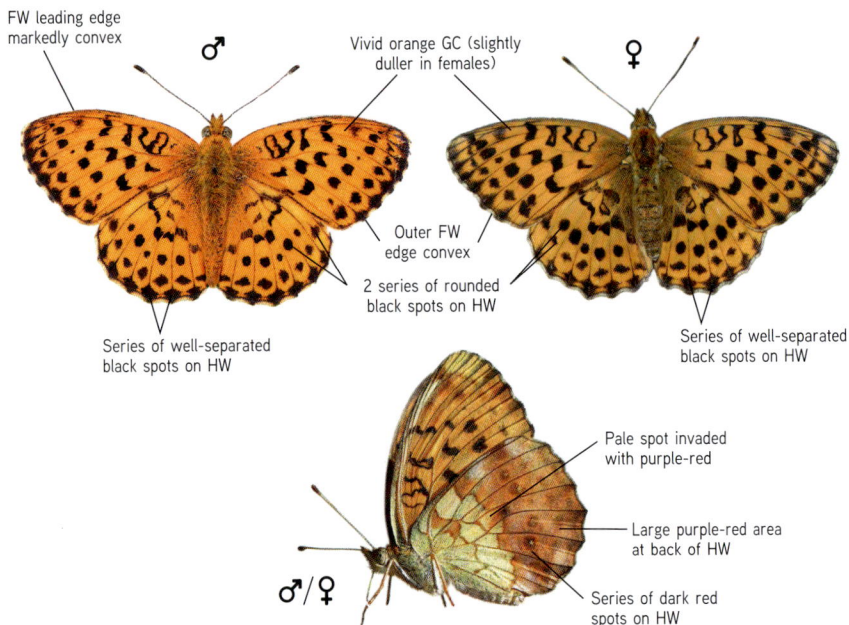

FW leading edge markedly convex

♂

Vivid orange GC (slightly duller in females)

♀

Outer FW edge convex

2 series of rounded black spots on HW

Series of well-separated black spots on HW

Series of well-separated black spots on HW

♂/♀

Pale spot invaded with purple-red

Large purple-red area at back of HW

Series of dark red spots on HW

Wingspan: 42–52 mm

Habitat: Shrub edges, hedgerows, riparian forests, and well-sunlit forest pathways.

Hibernating stage: Caterpillar inside the egg.

Elevational range: Up to 1,800 m.

Egg-laying: Eggs are laid singly on LHP leaves and inflorescences.

Flight period: From May to August.

Host plants: Rosaceae of genus *Rubus*, mainly *R. fruticosus*, *R. caesius*, *R. idaeus*, *R. aetnicus*, *R. canescens*, *R. commutatus*, *R. occidentalis*, and *R. ulmifolius*. Sometimes also on *Filipendula ulmaria*.

Diversity and systematics: Most European populations belong to the nominate subspecies. Subspecies *japygia* flies in southern Italy.

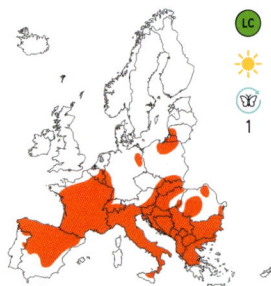

	IMAGOS			LARVAE	
Food			Food		
Behaviour of males			Caterpillar location		
Dispersion			Chrysalis location		

Did you know?

Adult Marbled Fritillaries frantically forage on the inflorescences of their host plants, where they are sometimes found in large numbers. They also regularly visit the "butterfly bush" (*Buddleia davidii*).

388

NYMPHALIDAE

TWIN-SPOT FRITILLARY *BRENTHIS HECATE*

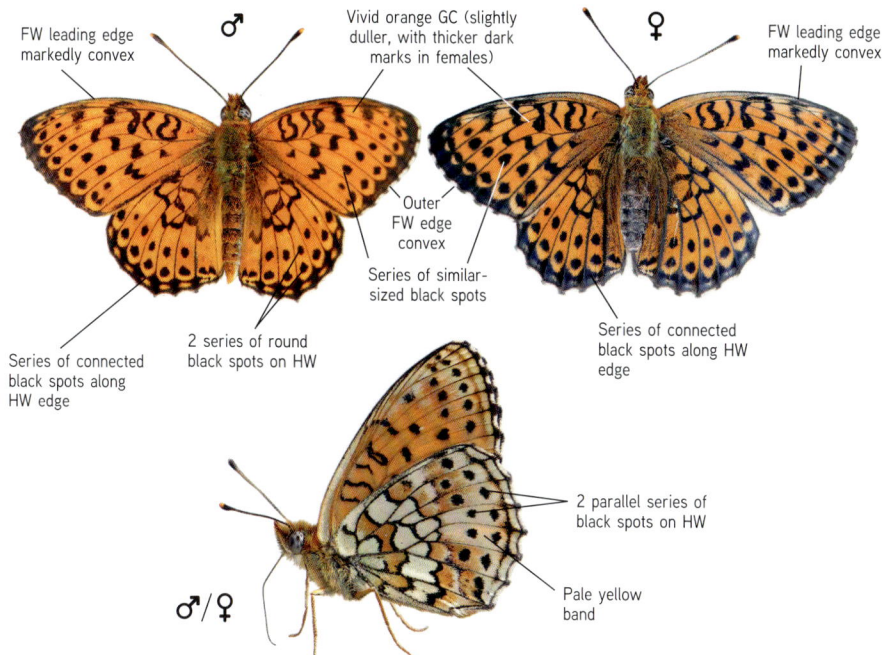

FW leading edge markedly convex

♂

Vivid orange GC (slightly duller, with thicker dark marks in females)

♀

FW leading edge markedly convex

Outer FW edge convex

Series of similar-sized black spots

Series of connected black spots along HW edge

2 series of round black spots on HW

Series of connected black spots along HW edge

Series of connected black spots along HW edge

2 parallel series of black spots on HW

♂/♀

Pale yellow band

Wingspan: 36–44 mm

Habitat: Bushy dry grasslands and meadows, abandoned pastures in the vicinity of woodlands.

Hibernating stage: Caterpillar inside the egg.

Elevational range: Up to 1,500 m.

Egg-laying: Eggs are laid singly on LHP stems or on nearby litter.

Flight period: From April to July.

Host plants: Mainly *Filipendula vulgaris*, *F. ulmaria*, and *Spiraea* *crenata* (Rosaceae). *Dorycnium* spp. in the Mediterranean region.

Diversity and systematics: Most European populations belong to the nominate subspecies. Subspecies *rubecula* forms the populations in the northern Iberian Peninsula, while subspecies *aigina* is described from Andalusia. Subspecies *triburniana* flies in the Balkans.

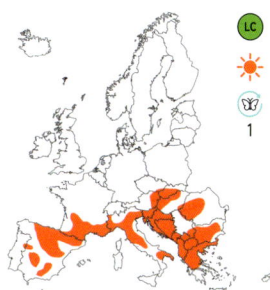

LC

1

IMAGOS		LARVAE	
Food		Food	
Behaviour of males		Caterpillar location	
Dispersion		Chrysalis location	

Did you know?

The Twin-spot Fritillary caterpillar is identified by its feeding habits. It eats leaflets on both sides at the base of the LHP leaf, but only on one side towards its tip.

389

NYMPHALIDAE

LESSER MARBLED FRITILLARY *BRENTHIS INO*

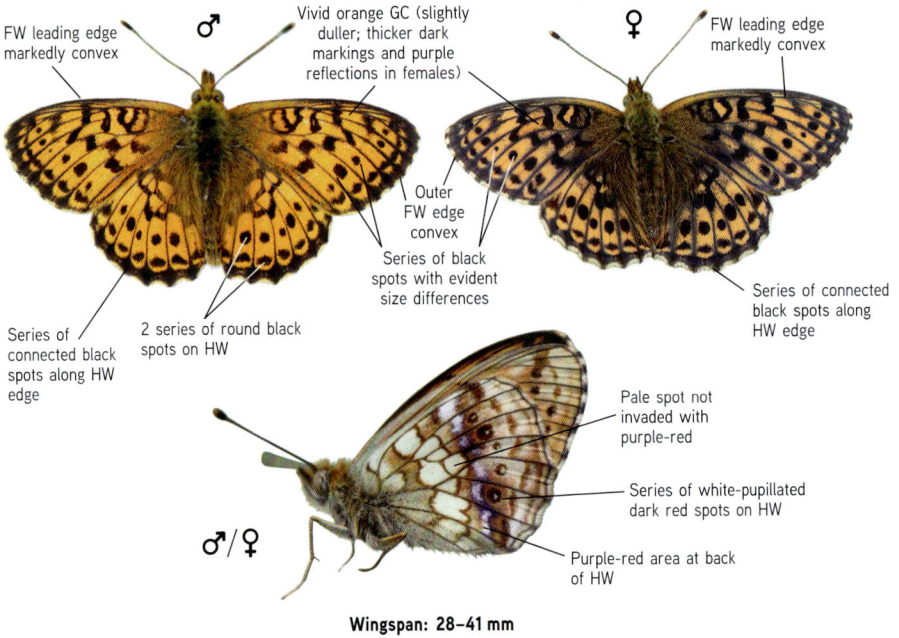

♂

♀

♂/♀

FW leading edge markedly convex

Vivid orange GC (slightly duller; thicker dark markings and purple reflections in females)

FW leading edge markedly convex

Outer FW edge convex

Series of black spots with evident size differences

Series of connected black spots along HW edge

Series of connected black spots along HW edge

2 series of round black spots on HW

Pale spot not invaded with purple-red

Series of white-pupillated dark red spots on HW

Purple-red area at back of HW

Wingspan: 28–41 mm

Habitat: Damp, bushy meadows and edges, megaphorbs, bog surroundings, and montane hay meadows.

Hibernating stage: Caterpillar inside the egg.

Elevational range: Up to 2,000 m.

Egg-laying: Eggs are laid singly on LHP leaves or at their base.

Flight period: From June to August.

Host plants: Rosaceae, including *Filipendula ulmaria, F. vulgaris, Sanguisorba minor, S. officinalis, Potentilla erecta, Comarum palustre, Aruncus dioicus, Rubus chamaemorus,* and *R. idaeus.*

Diversity and systematics: Most European populations belong to the nominate subspecies. Subspecies *erilda* flies in the Iberian Peninsula.

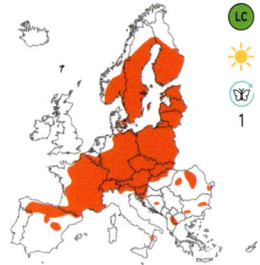

LC

1

Did you know?

The habitats of the Marsh Fritillary are inherently very fragmented. It manages to form small, locally abundant populations. Nevertheless, wet meadows are gradually disappearing from our landscapes, posing a threat to their typical butterfly communities.

IMAGOS		LARVAE	
Food		Food	
Behaviour of males		Caterpillar location	
Dispersion		Chrysalis location	

WEAVER'S FRITILLARY   *BOLORIA DIA*

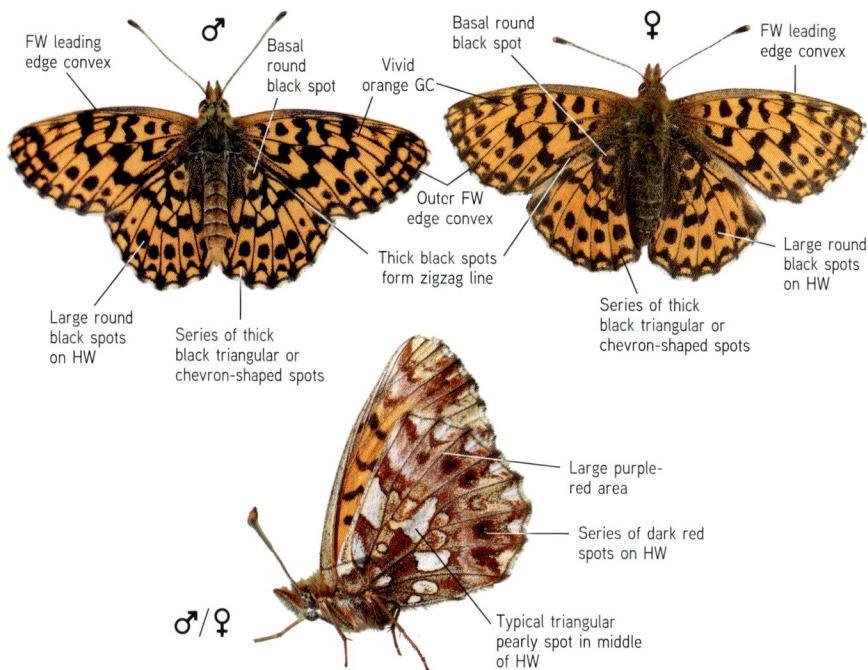

♂
FW leading edge convex
Basal round black spot
Vivid orange GC
Basal round black spot
♀
FW leading edge convex

Outer FW edge convex

Thick black spots form zigzag line

Large round black spots on HW

Large round black spots on HW

Series of thick black triangular or chevron-shaped spots

Series of thick black triangular or chevron-shaped spots

Large purple-red area

Series of dark red spots on HW

♂/♀

Typical triangular pearly spot in middle of HW

Wingspan: 32–34 mm

Habitat: Bushy, dry grasslands and meadows; forest clearings, edges, and sunny paths. Also in parks and gardens if they are not too strictly maintained.

Hibernating stage: Caterpillar.

Elevational range: Up to 1,500 m.

Egg-laying: Eggs are laid singly on LHP leaves and flowers, as well as on other nearby vegetation.

Flight period: From March to September.

Host plants: Violaceae, including *Viola arvensis*, *V. lutea*, *V. hirta*, *V. tricolor*, *V. canina*, *V. riviniana*, *V. reichenbachiana*, *V. pumila*, *V. rupestris*, and *V. odorata*. Also reported on *Potentilla reptans* and *Rubus idaeus* (Rosaceae).

Diversity and systematics: European populations belong to the nominate subspecies.

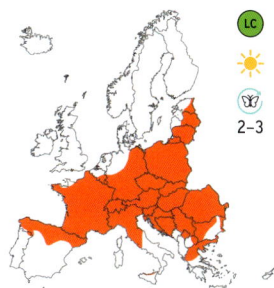

LC

2–3

IMAGOS		LARVAE	
Food		Food	
Behaviour of males		Caterpillar location	
Dispersion		Chrysalis location	

Did you know?

Weaver's Fritillary is the first species of genus *Boloria* to appear in spring and also the most widely distributed and resilient to anthropogenic pressures.

NYMPHALIDAE

THE TITANIA'S FRITILLARY *BOLORIA TITANIA*

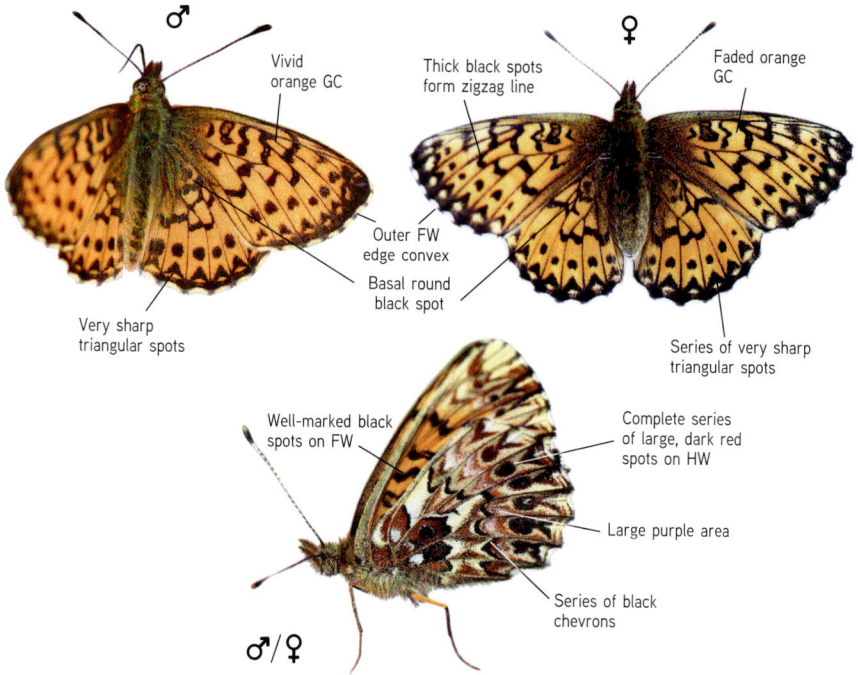

♂

Vivid orange GC

♀

Thick black spots form zigzag line

Faded orange GC

Outer FW edge convex

Basal round black spot

Very sharp triangular spots

Series of very sharp triangular spots

Well-marked black spots on FW

Complete series of large, dark red spots on HW

Large purple area

Series of black chevrons

♂/♀

Wingspan: 31–44 mm

Habitat: Flower-rich forest edges and clearings, damp meadows.

Hibernating stage: Caterpillar.

Elevational range: Between 500 and 2,000 m.

Egg-laying: Eggs are laid singly on LHP leaves as well as on other nearby vegetation.

Flight period: From June to August.

Host plants: *Bistorta officinalis* (Polygonaceae) and some Violaceae, like *Viola biflora, V. canina, V. riviniana,* and *V. reichenbachiana.*

Diversity and systematics: The nominate subspecies flies in the Southern Alps. Populations from the rest of the massif, the Baltic countries, and the Balkans belong to subspecies *cypris*. Subspecies *lemagneni* inhabits the French Massif Central.

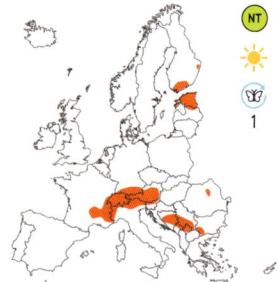

NT

1

IMAGOS		LARVAE	
Food	✿	Food	🍃
Behaviour of males	🦋	Caterpillar location	🌿
Dispersion	ꙮ	Chrysalis location	🌿

Did you know?

Females sometimes lay their eggs on the needles of conifers growing in areas favourable to the host plants.

PEARL-BORDERED FRITILLARY *BOLORIA EUPHROSYNE*

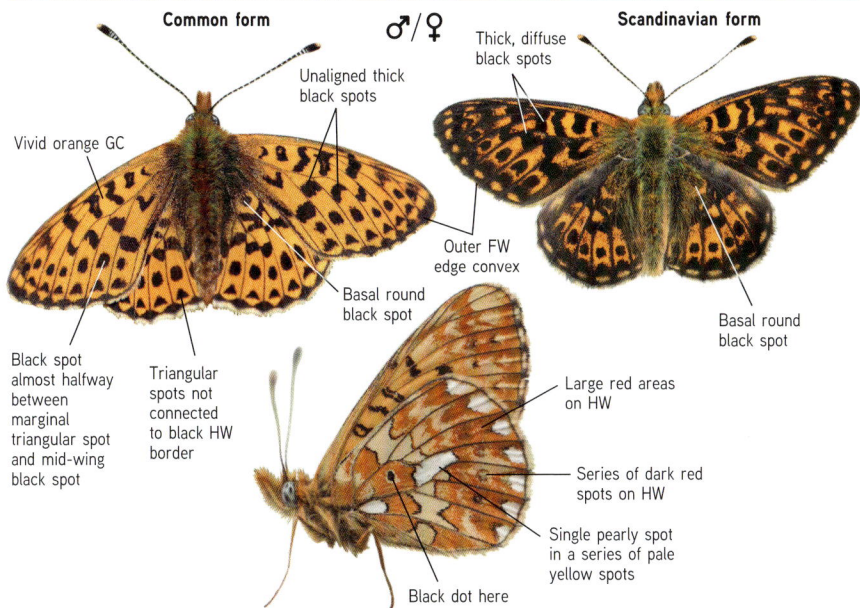

Common form

♂/♀

Scandinavian form

Thick, diffuse black spots

Unaligned thick black spots

Vivid orange GC

Outer FW edge convex

Basal round black spot

Basal round black spot

Black spot almost halfway between marginal triangular spot and mid-wing black spot

Triangular spots not connected to black HW border

Large red areas on HW

Series of dark red spots on HW

Single pearly spot in a series of pale yellow spots

Black dot here

Wingspan: 31–42 mm

Habitat: Flower-rich forest edges, clearings, and paths. Megaphorbs and damp meadows in a forested context. Also in garrigue, maquis, and subalpine heaths.

Hibernating stage: Caterpillar.

Elevational range: Up to 2,000 m.

Egg-laying: Eggs are laid singly on LHP leaves as well as on other nearby vegetation.

Flight period: From April to September.

Host plants: Violaceae, including *Viola arvensis*, *V. cenisia*, *V. elatior*, *V. eximia*, *V. hirta*, *V. lutea*, *V. riviniana*, *V. odorata*, *V. reichenbachiana*, *V. canina*, *V. biflora*, *V. tricolor*, and *V. palustris*. Sometimes on *Vaccinium uliginosum* (Ericaceae).

Diversity and systematics: The many subspecies that have been described do not differ much from the nominate subspecies.

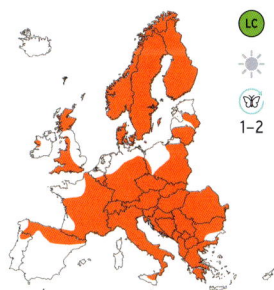

LC

1–2

Did you know?

Males patrol their territory of a few hundred square meters with incessant back-and-forth movements interrupted by short breaks. In forested environments, they often forage on geraniums to fuel their movements.

IMAGOS		LARVAE	
Food	✿	Food	🍃
Behaviour of males		Caterpillar location	
Dispersion		Chrysalis location	

NYMPHALIDAE

SMALL PEARL-BORDERED FRITILLARY *BOLORIA SELENE*

♂/♀

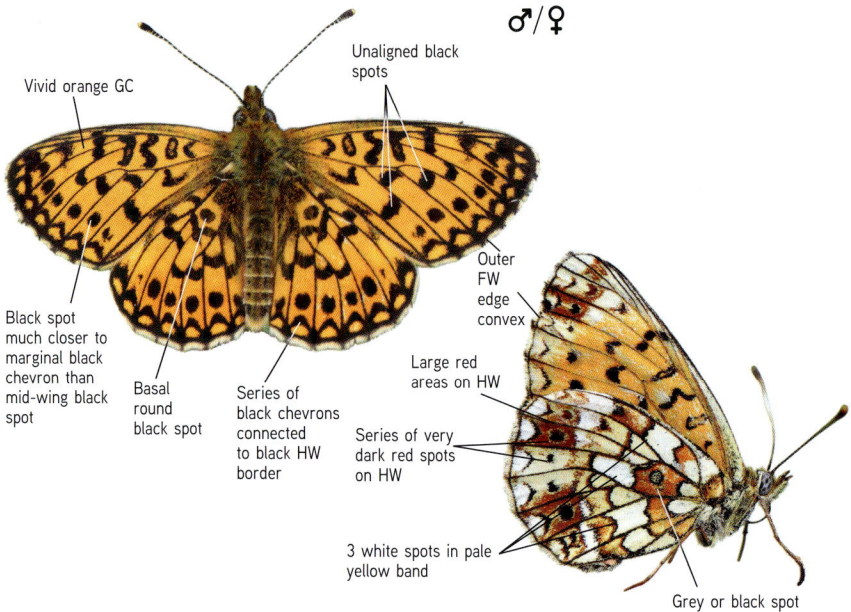

Vivid orange GC

Unaligned black spots

Black spot much closer to marginal black chevron than mid-wing black spot

Basal round black spot

Series of black chevrons connected to black HW border

Outer FW edge convex

Large red areas on HW

Series of very dark red spots on HW

3 white spots in pale yellow band

Grey or black spot

Wingspan: 31–40 mm

Habitat: Damp meadows and clearings, bogs, and megaphorbs.

Hibernating stage: Caterpillar.

Elevational range: Up to 2,000 m.

Egg-laying: Eggs are laid singly on the LHP or an adjacent plant.

Flight period: From May to August.

Host plants: Violaceae, including *Viola palustris, V. canina, V. odorata, V. lutea, V. hirta, V. uliginosa, V. reichenbachiana, V. stipularis*, and *V. riviniana*.

Diversity and systematics: Most European populations belong to the nominate subspecies. Subspecies *hela* flies in northern Scandinavia. Subspecies *insularum* inhabits Scotland.

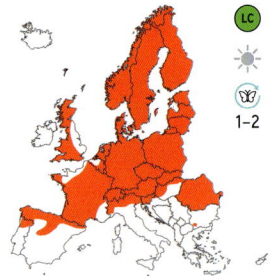

1–2

IMAGOS		LARVAE	
Food	🌸 💧	Food	🍃
Behaviour of males	🦋	Caterpillar location	🌿
Dispersion		Chrysalis location	🌿

Did you know?

The caterpillars take shelter under the leaves of the LHP and even in the underlying vegetation layer. They may take advantage of a burst of sunlight and expose themselves to warm up after a rain shower.

NYMPHALIDAE

THOR'S FRITILLARY *BOLORIA THORE*

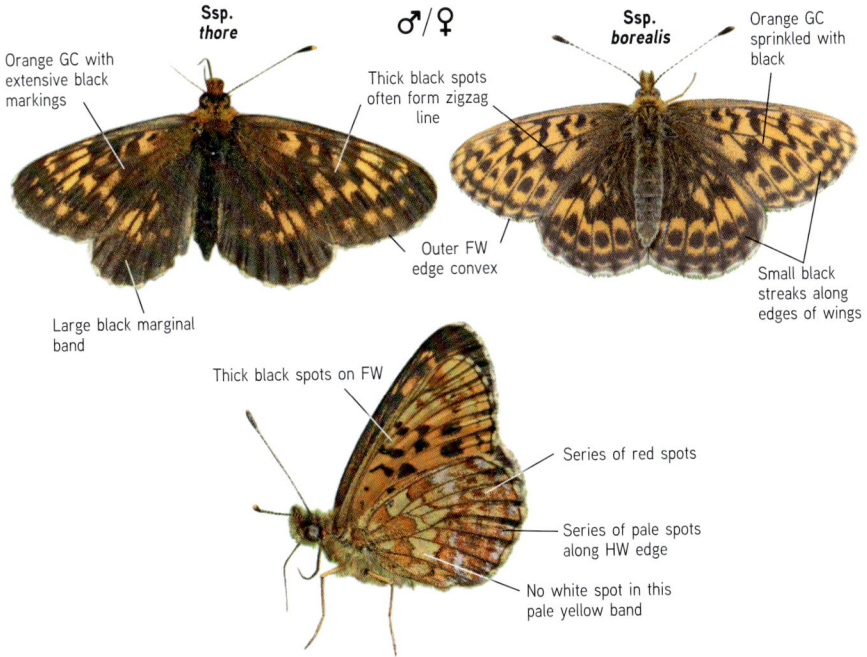

Ssp. *thore*

♂/♀

Ssp. *borealis*

Orange GC with extensive black markings

Thick black spots often form zigzag line

Orange GC sprinkled with black

Large black marginal band

Outer FW edge convex

Small black streaks along edges of wings

Thick black spots on FW

Series of red spots

Series of pale spots along HW edge

No white spot in this pale yellow band

Wingspan: 36–47 mm

Habitat: Flower-rich montane and boreal, often north-facing forest clearings,

Hibernating stage: Caterpillar.

Elevational range: Up to 1,800 m (in montane areas outside Scandinavia).

Egg-laying: Eggs are laid singly on the LHP or other nearby vegetation.

Flight period: From June to August.

Host plants: Violaceae, above all *Viola biflora*, but also *V. canina* and *V. palustris*. Reported on *Veronica longifolia* (Plantaginaceae) and *Bistorta vivipara* (Polygonaceae).

Diversity and systematics: Alpine populations belong to the nominate subspecies. Subspecies *borealis* forms Scandinavian populations.

IMAGOS		LARVAE	
Food	✿	Food	🍃
Behaviour of males	🦋	Caterpillar location	🌾
Dispersion	⊛	Chrysalis location	🌾

Did you know?

Avalanches, disturbances that locally contribute to opening up montane forest environments, create new habitats favourable to Thor's Fritillary.

NYMPHALIDAE

BOG FRITILLARY *BOLORIA EUNOMIA*

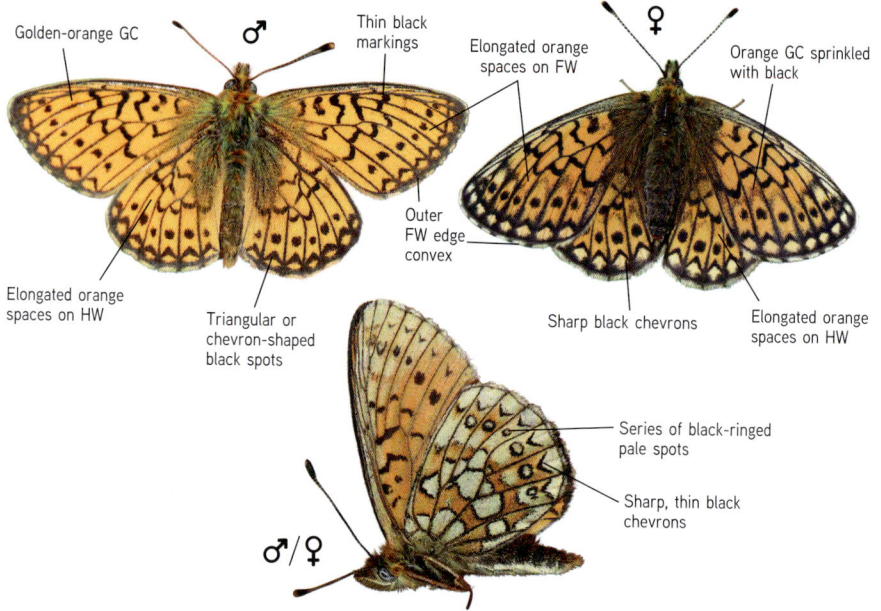

Golden-orange GC

♂

Thin black markings

Elongated orange spaces on FW

♀

Orange GC sprinkled with black

Outer FW edge convex

Elongated orange spaces on HW

Triangular or chevron-shaped black spots

Sharp black chevrons

Elongated orange spaces on HW

Series of black-ringed pale spots

Sharp, thin black chevrons

♂/♀

Wingspan: 31–40 mm

Habitat: Damp meadows and bog surroundings where the LHP is abundant.

Hibernating stage: Caterpillar.

Elevational range: Up to 2,000 m.

Egg-laying: Eggs are laid singly or in small batches on LHP leaves.

Flight period: From May to August.

Host plants: Above all, *Bistorta officinalis* (Polygonaceae). Also on *B. vivipara* in Northern Europe. Some Eastern European populations

may feed on *Viola palustris* and *V. odorata* (Violaceae), *Vaccinium oxycoccos*, *V. uliginosum*, and *Andromeda polifolia* (Ericaceae) or *Salix aurita* (Salicaceae).

Diversity and systematics: Subspecies *ossianus* flies in eastern Scandinavia and the Baltic countries. Subspecies *ceretanensis* inhabits the Eastern Pyrenees. The nominate subspecies populates Central Europe.

LC

1

IMAGOS		LARVAE	
Food	✲	Food	🍃
Behaviour of males	🦋	Caterpillar location	🌿
Dispersion	🦋	Chrysalis location	🌿

Did you know?

In the 1970s, the Bog Fritillary was intentionally introduced to the Morvan massif in the French region of Burgundy. The current presence and expansion of the species are evidence of the success of this conservation plan.

NYMPHALIDAE

SHEPHERD'S FRITILLARY *BOLORIA PALES*

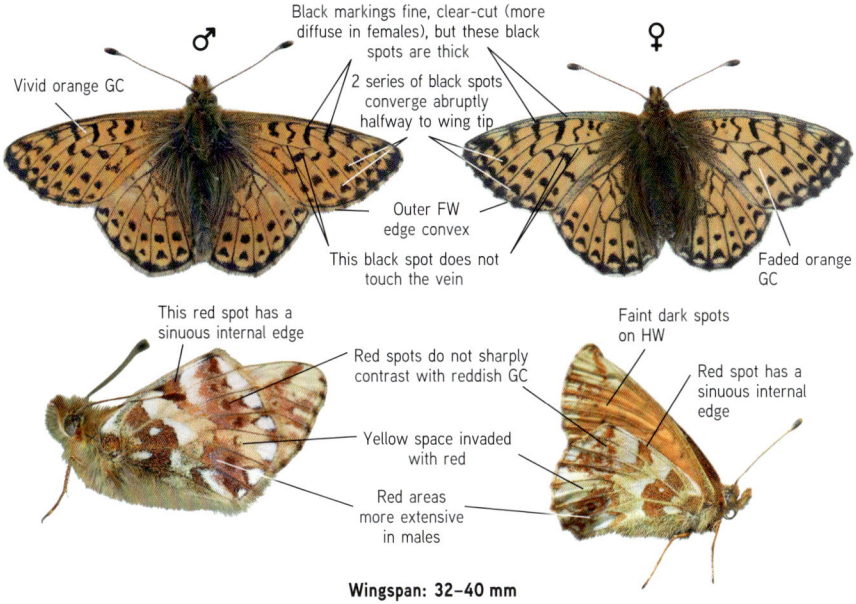

♂

Vivid orange GC

Black markings fine, clear-cut (more diffuse in females), but these black spots are thick

2 series of black spots converge abruptly halfway to wing tip

Outer FW edge convex

This black spot does not touch the vein

♀

Faded orange GC

This red spot has a sinuous internal edge

Red spots do not sharply contrast with reddish GC

Yellow space invaded with red

Red areas more extensive in males

Faint dark spots on HW

Red spot has a sinuous internal edge

Wingspan: 32–40 mm

Habitat: Subalpine and alpine grasslands, meadows, and scree.

Hibernating stage: Caterpillar.

Elevational range: Between 1,500 and 2,800 m.

Egg-laying: Eggs are laid singly on LHP leaves.

Flight period: From June to September.

Host plants: Violaceae, including *Viola biflora*, *V. cenisia*, *V. cornuta*, and *V. calcarata*. Also on *Plantago alpina* (Plantaginaceae), *Salix reticulata* (Salicaceae), *Dryas octopetala* (Rosaceae), *Bistorta vivipara* (Polygonaceae), and *Valeriana* spp. (Valerianaceae).

Diversity and systematics: The nominate subspecies flies in the Eastern Alps. Subspecies *palustris* inhabits the Western and Central Alps. Subspecies *pyrenesmiscens* forms the Pyrenean and Iberian populations. Subspecies *medioitalica* flies in central Italy, and subspecies *carpathomeridionalis* is present in Romania. Subspecies *contempta* forms the Balkan populations. Subspecies *tatrensis* flies in Slovakia.

- ■ B. pales
- ■ B. napaea
- ■ B. graeca
- ■ B. pales + B. napaea
- ■ B. pales + B. graeca
- ■ B. pales + B. graeca + B. napaea

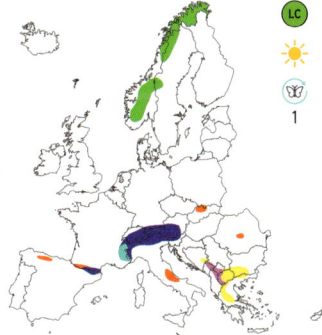

LC

1

Did you know?

Similar to the caterpillars, which are polyphagous, the adults are generalist flower feeders. They forage on the most abundant flowers in the butterfly's habitat.

IMAGOS		LARVAE	
Food		Food	
Behaviour of males		Caterpillar location	
Dispersion		Chrysalis location	

MOUNTAIN FRITILLARY *BOLORIA NAPAEA*

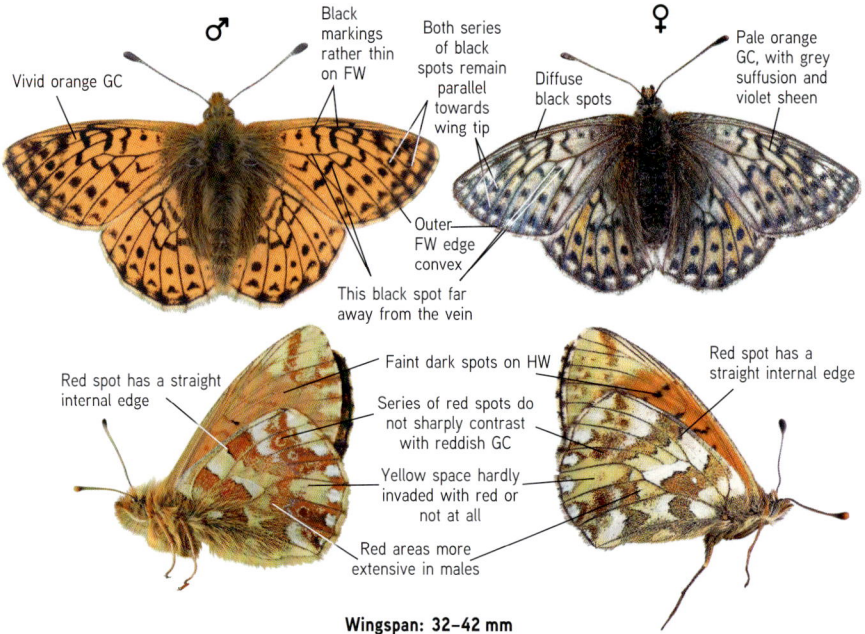

♂ | ♀

Black markings rather thin on FW

Both series of black spots remain parallel towards wing tip

Vivid orange GC

Diffuse black spots

Pale orange GC, with grey suffusion and violet sheen

Outer FW edge convex

This black spot far away from the vein

Red spot has a straight internal edge

Faint dark spots on HW

Red spot has a straight internal edge

Series of red spots do not sharply contrast with reddish GC

Yellow space hardly invaded with red or not at all

Red areas more extensive in males

Wingspan: 32–42 mm

Habitat: Subalpine, flower-rich, and rather damp meadows, usually close to the treeline.

Hibernating stage: Caterpillar.

Elevational range: Between 1,500 and 2,000 m.

Egg-laying: Eggs are laid singly on LHP leaves.

Flight period: From June to August.

Host plants: Above all, *Bistorta vivipara* and *B. officinalis* (Polygonaceae), but also some Violaceae, such as *Viola biflora*, *V. canina*, *V. tricolor*, and *V. calcarata*.

Diversity and systematics: The nominate subspecies flies in the Alps. Subspecies *frigida* inhabits Scandinavia, while subspecies *pyreneorientalis* is found in the Eastern Pyrenees.

- B. pales
- B. napaea
- B. graeca
- B. pales + B. napaea
- B. pales + B. graeca
- B. pales + B. graeca + B. napaea

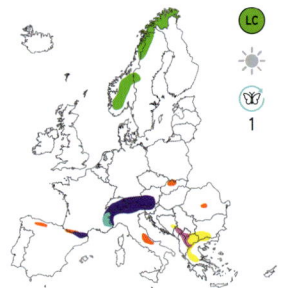

LC

1

Did you know?

The Mountain Fritillary is difficult to distinguish from Shepherd's Fritillary. However, it flies at slightly lower altitudes and in more damp and wooded environments (as indicated by the etymology of its scientific name, *napaea*, from the Greek word *napaios*, which means "who lives in wooded valleys").

IMAGOS		LARVAE	
Food		Food	
Behaviour of males		Caterpillar location	
Dispersion		Chrysalis location	

NYMPHALIDAE

BALKAN FRITILLARY *BOLORIA GRAECA*

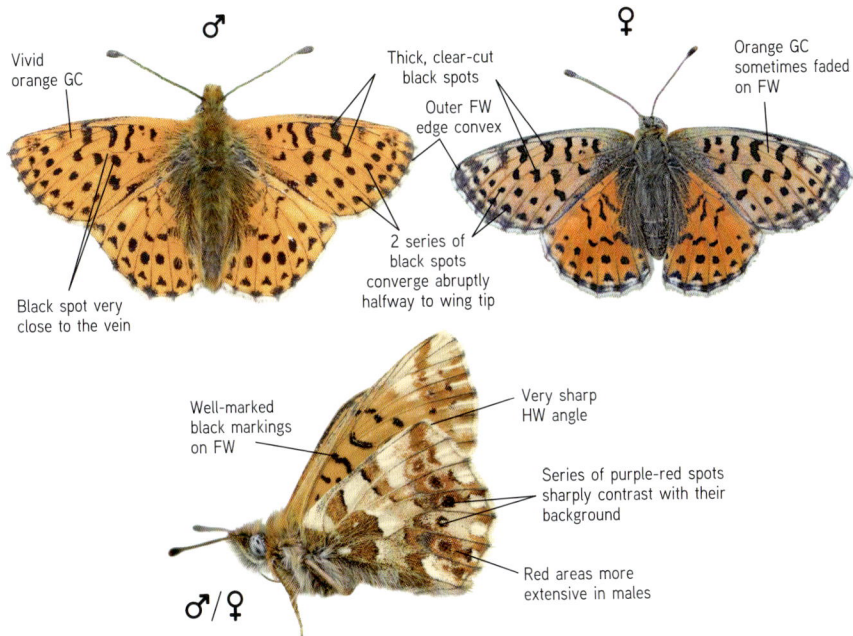

♂   ♀

Vivid orange GC

Thick, clear-cut black spots

Outer FW edge convex

Orange GC sometimes faded on FW

2 series of black spots converge abruptly halfway to wing tip

Black spot very close to the vein

Well-marked black markings on FW

Very sharp HW angle

Series of purple-red spots sharply contrast with their background

Red areas more extensive in males

♂/♀

Wingspan: 32–40 mm

Habitat: Montane and subalpine flower-rich grasslands, meadows, and clearings.

Hibernating stage: Caterpillar.

Elevational range: Between 900 and 2,600 m.

Egg-laying: Eggs are laid singly on the LHP leaves or on other nearby vegetation.

Flight period: From May to September.

Host plants: Violaceae, including *Viola calcarata*, *V. eximia*, *V. perinensis*, and *V. tricolor*.

Diversity and systematics: The nominate subspecies flies in the Balkans. Subspecies *tendensis* flies in the Western Alps.

- B. pales
- B. napaea
- B. graeca
- B. pales + B. napaea
- B. pales + B. graeca
- B. pales + B. graeca B. napaea

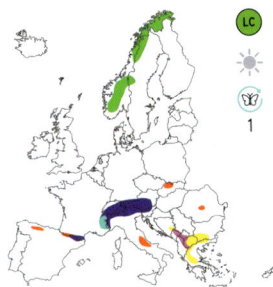

LC

1

IMAGOS		LARVAE	
Food		Food	
Behaviour of males		Caterpillar location	
Dispersion		Chrysalis location	

Did you know?

The range of the Balkan Fritillary is distinctly disjointed, reflecting the postglacial history of the species. It is more abundant in the Balkan part of its range.

399

NYMPHALIDAE

CRANBERRY FRITILLARY *BOLORIA AQUILONARIS*

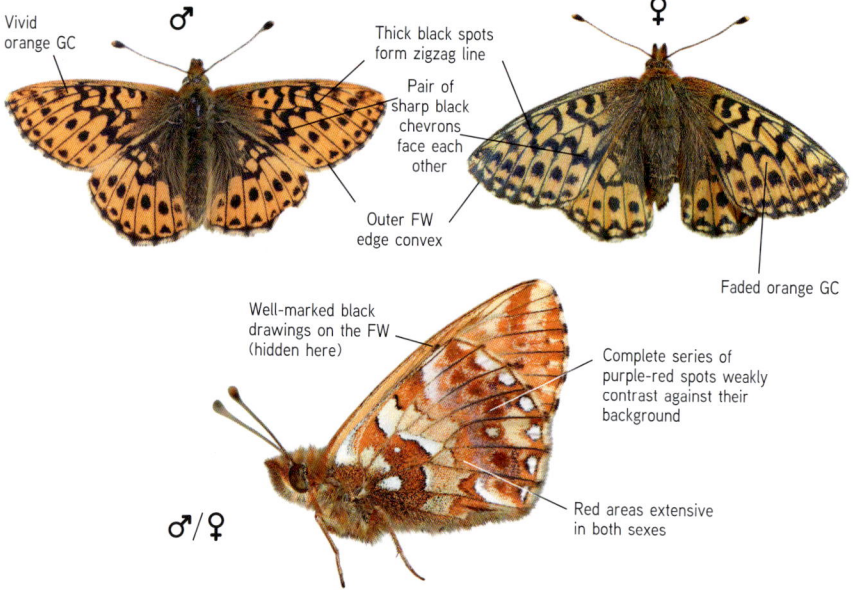

♂

Vivid orange GC

Thick black spots form zigzag line

Pair of sharp black chevrons face each other

Outer FW edge convex

♀

Faded orange GC

Well-marked black drawings on the FW (hidden here)

♂/♀

Complete series of purple-red spots weakly contrast against their background

Red areas extensive in both sexes

Wingspan: 32–40 mm

Habitat: Peat bogs and their heath surroundings, usually in a forested context.

Hibernating stage: Caterpillar.

Elevational range: Up to 2,000 m.

Egg-laying: Eggs are laid singly on LHP leaves or sometimes on a nearby plant.

Flight period: From June to August.

Host plants: Ericaceae, mainly *Vaccinium oxycoccos* and sometimes *Andromeda polifolia*. Also reported on the Violaceae, like *Viola palustris* and *V. canina*, and the Polygonaceae, like *Bistorta officinalis*.

Diversity and systematics: European populations belong to the nominate subspecies.

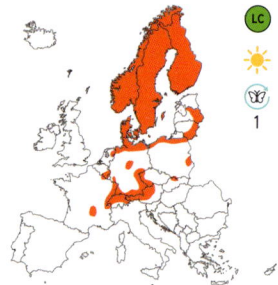

LC

1

Did you know?

The Cranberry Fritillary is threatened with extinction in the southern part of its range, where its preferred habitats have undergone agricultural intensification and where climate change is leading to a gradual drying of peat bogs.

IMAGOS		LARVAE		
Food		Food		
Behaviour of males		Caterpillar location		
Dispersion		Chrysalis location		

NYMPHALIDAE

POLAR FRITILLARY   *BOLORIA POLARIS*

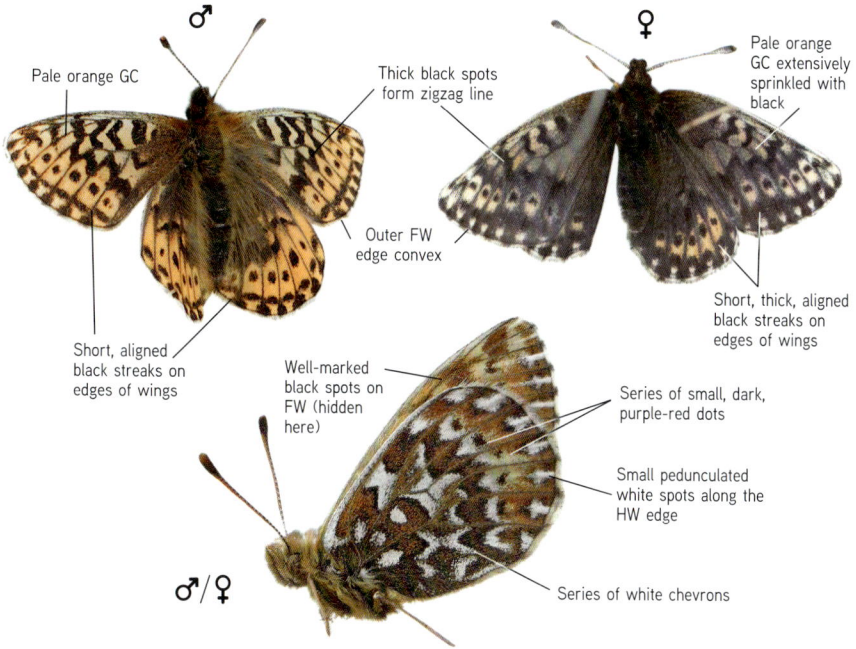

♂

Pale orange GC

Thick black spots form zigzag line

Outer FW edge convex

Short, aligned black streaks on edges of wings

♀

Pale orange GC extensively sprinkled with black

Short, thick, aligned black streaks on edges of wings

♂/♀

Well-marked black spots on FW (hidden here)

Series of small, dark, purple-red dots

Small pedunculated white spots along the HW edge

Series of white chevrons

Wingspan: 34–44 mm

Habitat: Stony arctic grasslands and meadows.

Hibernating stage: Overwinters twice as a caterpillar.

Elevational range: Between 800 and 1,400 m.

Egg-laying: Eggs are laid singly or in a few units on the LHP.

Flight period: From May to August (mainly June).

Host plants: *Dryas octopetala* (Rosaceae) and some Ericaceae, like *Vaccinium uliginosum* and *Cassiope tetragona*.

Diversity and systematics: European populations of this fritillary, also found in Greenland and North America, belong to the nominate subspecies.

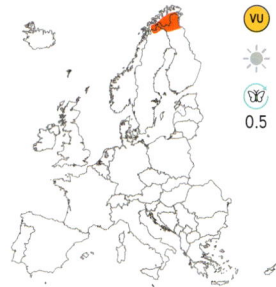

VU

0.5

IMAGOS		LARVAE	
Food		Food	
Behaviour of males		Caterpillar location	
Dispersion		Chrysalis location	

Did you know?

Emergences can be extremely rare during particularly cold years, because of a third overwintering in the pupal stage.

NYMPHALIDAE

ARCTIC FRITILLARY *BOLORIA CHARICLEA*

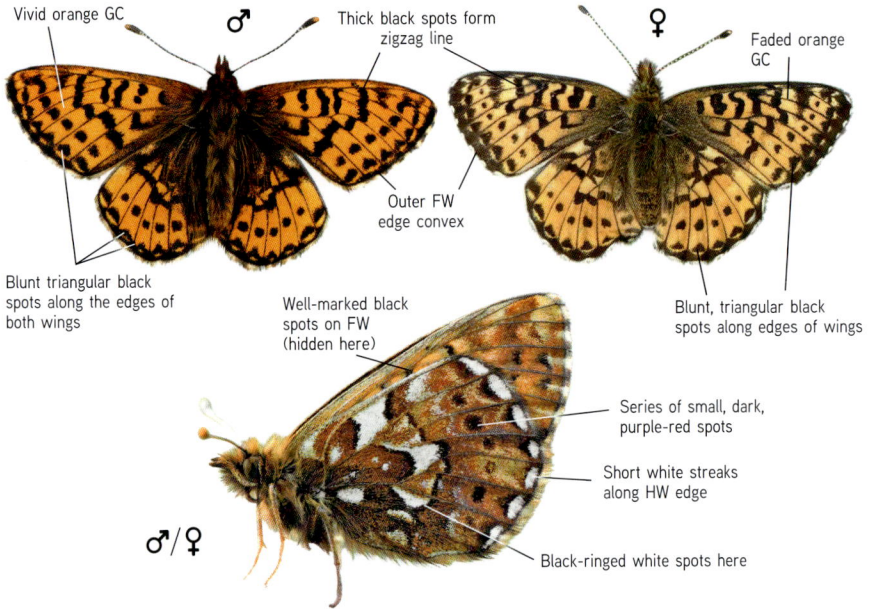

Vivid orange GC

♂

Thick black spots form zigzag line

♀

Faded orange GC

Outer FW edge convex

Blunt triangular black spots along the edges of both wings

Well-marked black spots on FW (hidden here)

Blunt, triangular black spots along edges of wings

Series of small, dark, purple-red spots

Short white streaks along HW edge

♂/♀

Black-ringed white spots here

Wingspan: 32–42 mm

Habitat: Sparsely vegetated stony grasslands in the tundra.

Hibernating stage: Overwinters twice as a caterpillar.

Elevational range: Between 500 and 1,400 m.

Egg-laying: Eggs are laid singly.

Flight period: From June to August.

Host plants: Not well known in Europe, but probably *Cassiope tetragona* (Ericaceae), perhaps also *Dryas octopetala* (Rosaceae) and *Betula nana* (Betulaceae).

Diversity and systematics: European populations of this fritillary, which is distributed all around the Arctic Circle, belong to the nominate subspecies.

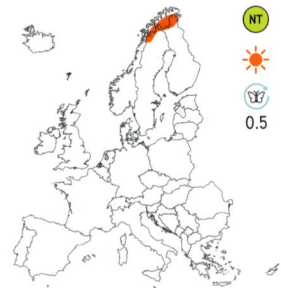

NT

0.5

IMAGOS		LARVAE	
Food		Food	
Behaviour of males		Caterpillar location	
Dispersion		Chrysalis location	

Did you know?

Due to the extremely low temperatures in its habitats, the caterpillar fails to complete its development within one year and undergoes a second hibernation.

NYMPHALIDAE

FREIJA'S FRITILLARY *BOLORIA FREIJA*

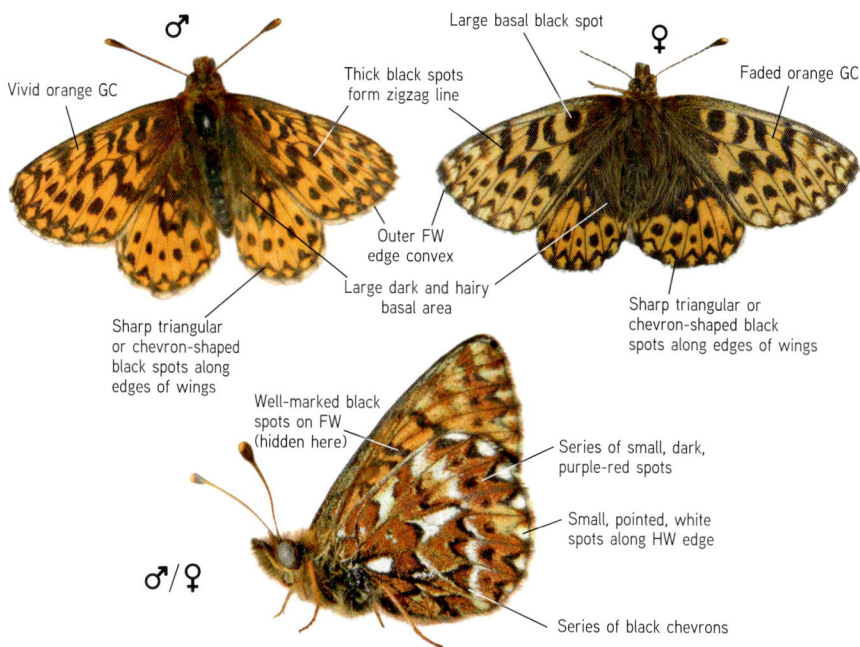

♂

Vivid orange GC

Large basal black spot

Thick black spots
form zigzag line

♀

Faded orange GC

Outer FW
edge convex

Large dark and hairy
basal area

Sharp triangular
or chevron-shaped
black spots along
edges of wings

Sharp triangular or
chevron-shaped black
spots along edges of wings

Well-marked black
spots on FW
(hidden here)

Series of small, dark,
purple-red spots

Small, pointed, white
spots along HW edge

♂/♀

Series of black chevrons

Wingspan: 29–41 mm

Habitat: Damp tundra, bogs, and clear boreal birch and pine woodlands.

Hibernating stage: Overwinters twice as a caterpillar.

Elevational range: Up to 1,000 m.

Egg-laying: Eggs are laid singly on LHP leaves or on a nearby plant.

Flight period: From May to July.

Host plants: Ericaceae, including *Vaccinium uliginosum*, *V. oxycoccos*, *Arctostaphylos uva-ursi*, *Arctous alpina*, and *Empetrum nigrum*. Also on *Rubus chamaemorus*.

Diversity and systematics: European populations of this fritillary, which is distributed all around the Arctic Circle, belong to the nominate subspecies.

LC

0.5

Did you know?

Despite the high latitudes of its range, Freija's Fritillary emerges as early as mid-spring (May), among the very first butterflies to be seen there.

IMAGOS		LARVAE	
Food		Food	
Behaviour of males		Caterpillar location	
Dispersion		Chrysalis location	

NYMPHALIDAE

FRIGGA'S FRITILLARY *BOLORIA FRIGGA*

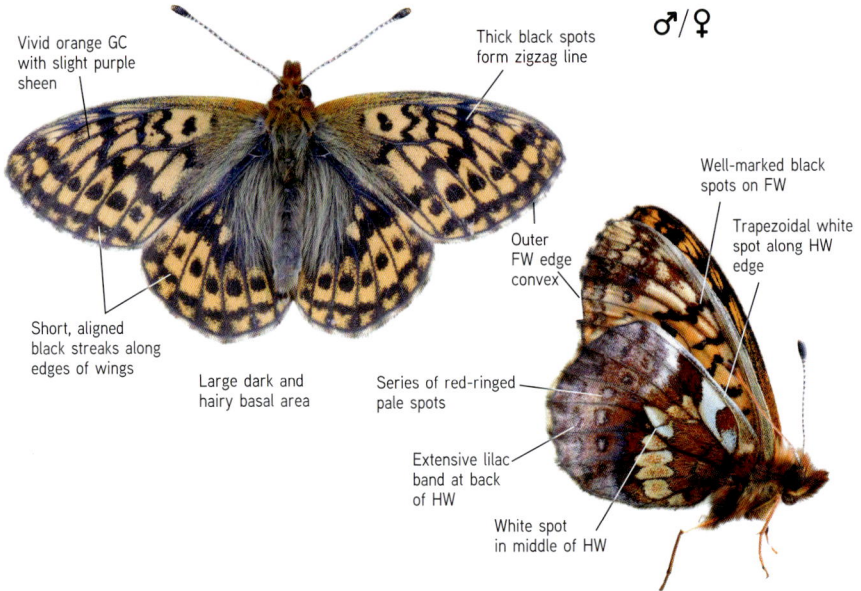

♂/♀

Vivid orange GC with slight purple sheen

Thick black spots form zigzag line

Well-marked black spots on FW

Trapezoidal white spot along HW edge

Outer FW edge convex

Short, aligned black streaks along edges of wings

Large dark and hairy basal area

Series of red-ringed pale spots

Extensive lilac band at back of HW

White spot in middle of HW

Wingspan: 35–48 mm

Habitat: Bogs and damp boreal forests.

Hibernating stage: Overwinters twice as a caterpillar.

Elevational range: Up to 600 m.

Egg-laying: Eggs are laid singly on LHP leaves or nearby.

Flight period: June and July.

Host plants: *Rubus chamaemorus* (Rosaceae), as well as some Ericaceae, like *Andromeda polifolia*.

Diversity and systematics: European populations of this fritillary, which is also present in North America, belong to the nominate subspecies.

LC
0.5

Did you know?

In boreal environments, butterfly flight periods are often very short. Frigga's Fritillary is no exception, often visible for only two to three weeks between June and July.

IMAGOS		LARVAE	
Food	✿	Food	🍃
Behaviour of males	🦋	Caterpillar location	🌱🌳
Dispersion	🦋	Chrysalis location	🌱🌳

NYMPHALIDAE

DUSKY-WINGED FRITILLARY *BOLORIA IMPROBA*

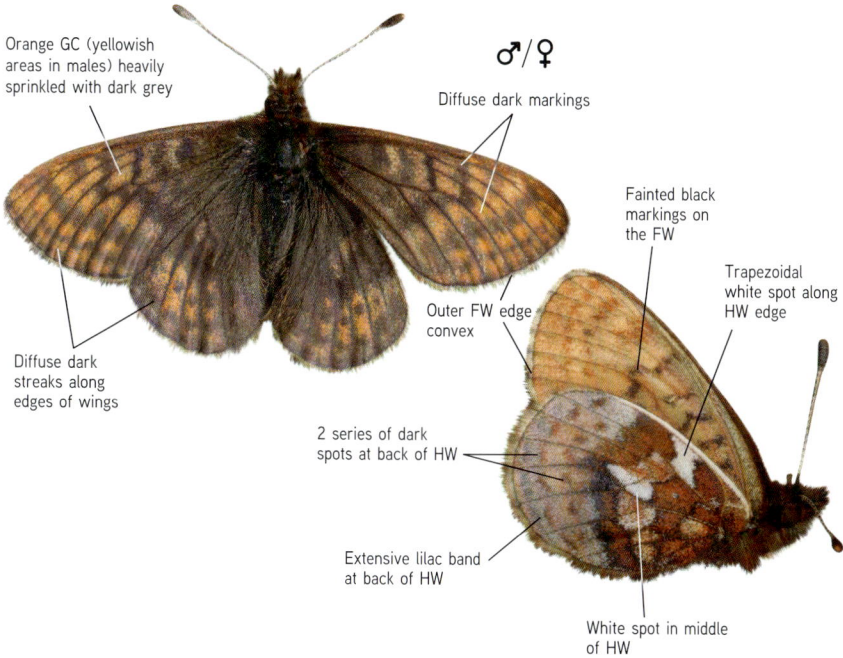

♂/♀

Orange GC (yellowish areas in males) heavily sprinkled with dark grey

Diffuse dark markings

Fainted black markings on the FW

Trapezoidal white spot along HW edge

Outer FW edge convex

Diffuse dark streaks along edges of wings

2 series of dark spots at back of HW

Extensive lilac band at back of HW

White spot in middle of HW

Wingspan: 29–36 mm

Habitat: Stony, sparsely vegetated, and low-growing montane boreal grasslands.

Hibernating stage: Overwinters at least twice as a caterpillar.

Elevational range: Between 500 and 1,000 m.

Egg-laying: Eggs are laid singly on LHP leaves or nearby.

Flight period: From June to August.

Host plants: Dwarf Salicaeae, such as *Salix reticulata*, *S. herbacea*, and *S. arctica*. Also reported on *Bistorta vivipara* (Polygonaceae).

Diversity and systematics: European populations belong to the nominate subspecies.

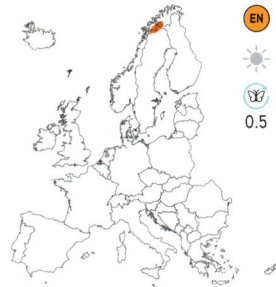

EN

0.5

Did you know?

Development lasts for at least two years in this fritillary of very high latitudes. The adults feed on cushion-like flowers, such as *Silene acaulis*, known as Moss Campion or Cushion Pink, which make up the majority of the flora in its habitat.

IMAGOS		LARVAE	
Food	☆	Food	🌿
Behaviour of males	🦋	Caterpillar location	🌿
Dispersion		Chrysalis location	

NYMPHALIDAE

MARSH FRITILLARY *EUPHYDRYAS AURINIA*

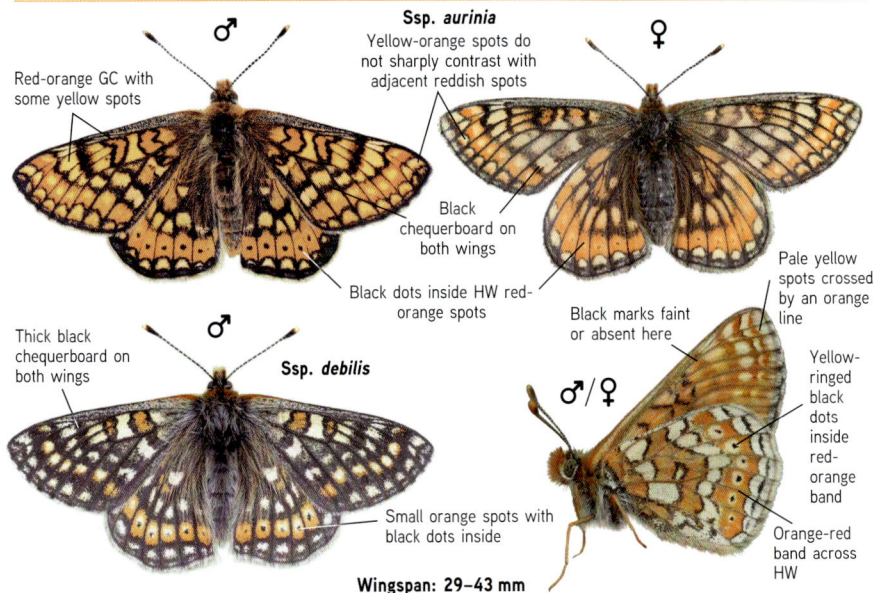

♂

Red-orange GC with some yellow spots

Ssp. *aurinia*
Yellow-orange spots do not sharply contrast with adjacent reddish spots

♀

Black chequerboard on both wings

Black dots inside HW red-orange spots

Pale yellow spots crossed by an orange line

Thick black chequerboard on both wings

♂

Ssp. *debilis*

Black marks faint or absent here

♂/♀

Yellow-ringed black dots inside red-orange band

Small orange spots with black dots inside

Orange-red band across HW

Wingspan: 29–43 mm

Habitat: A wide variety of open habitats, including damp meadows, hay meadows, subalpine grasslands, garrigues, and dry grasslands.

Hibernating stage: Caterpillar.

Elevational range: Up to 2,500 m.

Egg-laying: Eggs are laid in batches of several dozens on LHP leaves.

Flight period: From May to August.

Host plants: Caprifoliaceae, including *Succisa pratensis*, *Scabiosa columbaria*, *S. atropurpurea*, *S. ochroleuca*, *Knautia arvensis*, *K. dipsacifolia*, *Dipsacus fullonum*, *D. sativus*, *Cephalaria leucantha*, *Valeriana dioica*, *V. angustifolia*, *V. excelsa*, *V. officinalis*, and *V. rubra*. Also on honeysuckles, such as *Lonicera periclymenum*,

L. etrusca, *L. caprifolium*, *L. implexa*, and *L. xylosteum*. Gentianaceae, such as *Gentiana cruciata*, *G. asclepiadea*, *G. acaulis*, *G. lutea*, *G. punctata*, *G. clusii*, and *G. alpina*. Plantaginaceae, like *Plantago lanceolata* and *P. media*.

Diversity and systematics: Most European populations belong to the nominate subspecies. Subspecies *provincialis* flies in southern France, northern Italy, and along the Dalmatian coast. Subspecies *debilis* and *glaciegenita* fly at high altitudes in the Alps. Subspecies *pyrenesdebilis* inhabits the Eastern Pyrenees. Subspecies *bulgarica* flies in the Balkans, while subspecies *hibernica* and *anglicana* make up the Irish and English populations, respectively.

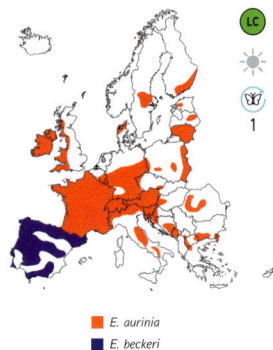

LC

1

■ *E. aurinia*
■ *E. beckeri*

Did you know?

The Marsh Fritillary suffers heavy pressure from parasitoid wasps. The caterpillars are preyed upon by numerous species from genera *Cotesia*, *Ichneumon*, *Apechthis*, *Apanteles*, and *Pteromalus*.

IMAGOS		LARVAE	
Food	✿	Food	🍃
Behaviour of males		Caterpillar location	
Dispersion		Chrysalis location	

NYMPHALIDAE

BECKER'S FRITILLARY *EUPHYDRYAS BECKERI*

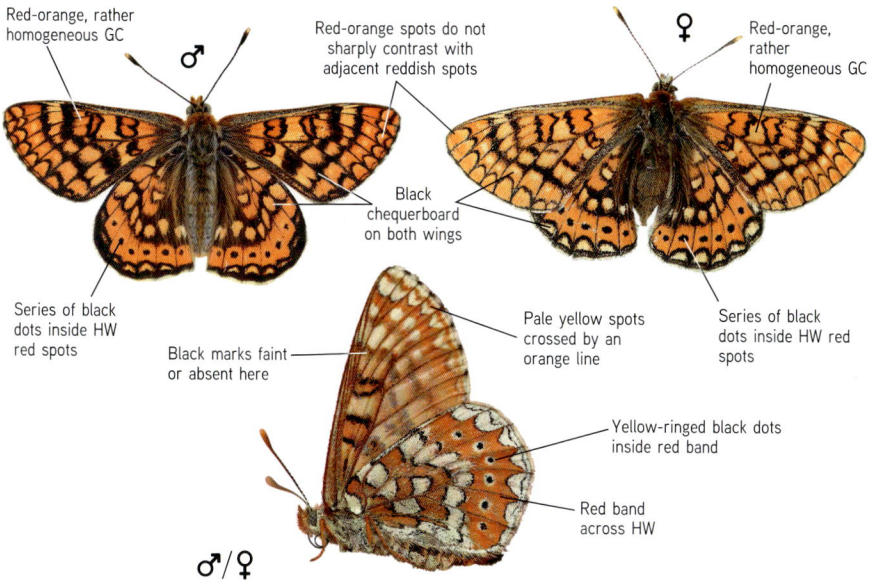

Red-orange, rather homogeneous GC

♂

Red-orange spots do not sharply contrast with adjacent reddish spots

♀

Red-orange, rather homogeneous GC

Black chequerboard on both wings

Series of black dots inside HW red spots

Black marks faint or absent here

Pale yellow spots crossed by an orange line

Series of black dots inside HW red spots

Yellow-ringed black dots inside red band

Red band across HW

♂/♀

Wingspan: 32–50 mm

Habitat: Garrigues, bushy dry grasslands, and flower-rich Mediterranean edges.

Hibernating stage: Caterpillar.

Elevational range: Up to 1,000 m.

Egg-laying: Eggs are laid in batches of several dozens on LHP leaves.

Flight period: April to June.

Host plants: Caprifoliaceae of genus *Lonicera*.

Diversity and systematics: Becker's Fritillary is still sometimes considered a subspecies of the Marsh Fritillary.

■ *E. aurinia*
■ *E. beckeri*

NA

1

Did you know?

Becker's Fritillary is present in the Iberian Peninsula, reaching the French Eastern Pyrenees. Maghreb populations have uncertain affinities and could belong either to Becker's Fritillary or to a new species.

IMAGOS		LARVAE	
Food		Food	
Behaviour of males		Caterpillar location	
Dispersion		Chrysalis location	

NYMPHALIDAE

SPANISH FRITILLARY *EUPHYDRYAS DESFONTAINII*

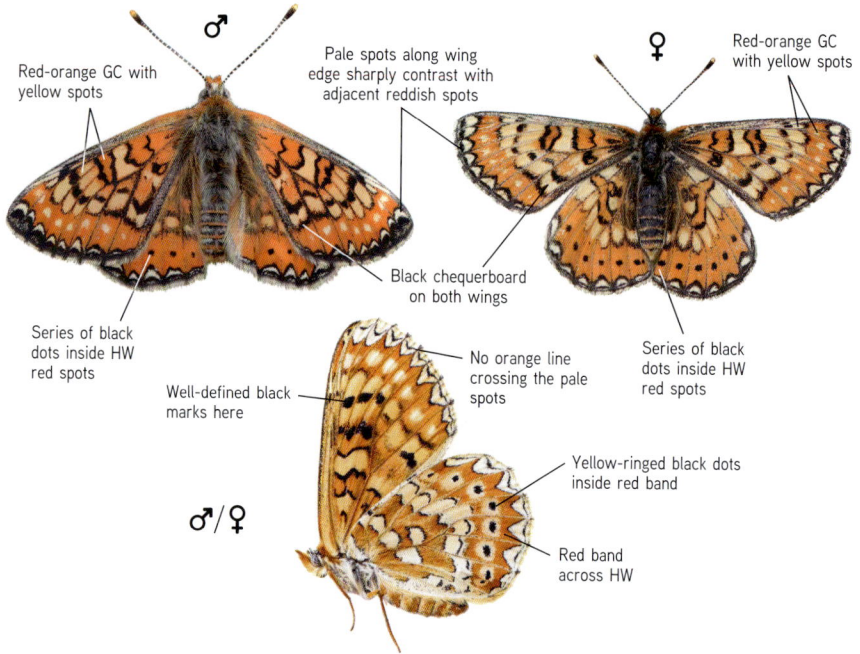

♂

Red-orange GC with yellow spots

Pale spots along wing edge sharply contrast with adjacent reddish spots

♀

Red-orange GC with yellow spots

Black chequerboard on both wings

Series of black dots inside HW red spots

Series of black dots inside HW red spots

No orange line crossing the pale spots

Well-defined black marks here

♂/♀

Yellow-ringed black dots inside red band

Red band across HW

Wingspan: 40–52 mm

Habitat: Garrigues and dry, stony grasslands.

Hibernating stage: Caterpillar.

Elevational range: Between 500 and 1,500 m.

Egg-laying: Eggs are laid in batches of several dozens on LHP leaves.

Flight period: From April to June.

Host plants: Caprifoliaceae, including *Cephalaria leucantha*, *Dipsacus comosus*, *D. fullonum*, *Knautia arvensis*, and *Scabiosa* spp.

Diversity and systematics: The nominate subspecies flies in North Africa. Several subspecies have been described for the Iberian Peninsula. Among them, subspecies *baetica* extends to the French Eastern Pyrenees.

NT

1

Did you know?

The day of the Spanish Fritillary is divided into two periods. The morning is dedicated to feeding and sunbathing, while the afternoon is spent searching for a mate and laying eggs.

IMAGOS			LARVAE	
Food	🌸		Food	🍃
Behaviour of males			Caterpillar location	🌿
Dispersion			Chrysalis location	🌿

NYMPHALIDAE

CYNTHIA'S FRITILLARY *EUPHYDRYAS CYNTHIA*

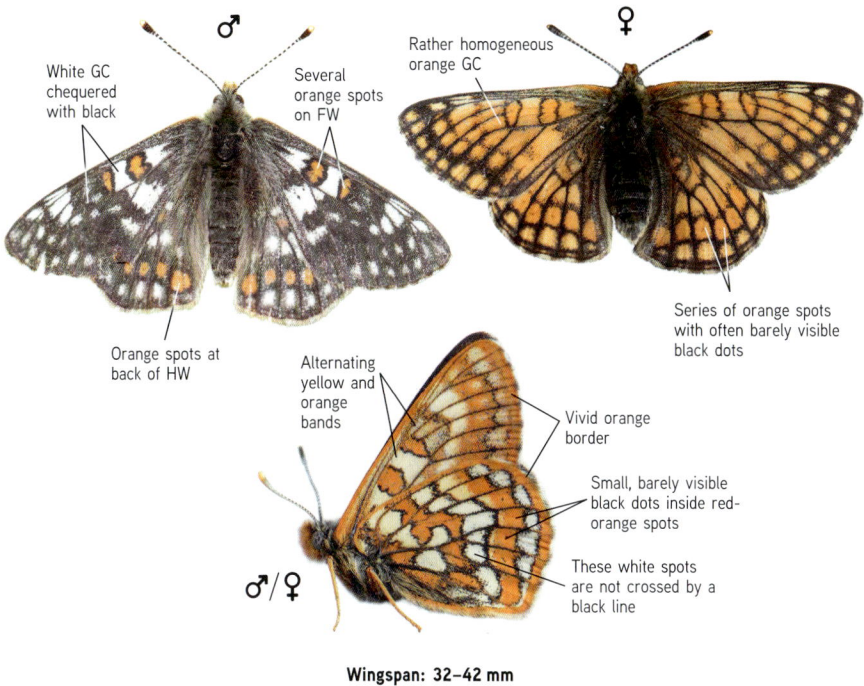

♂

♀

White GC chequered with black

Several orange spots on FW

Rather homogeneous orange GC

Orange spots at back of HW

Alternating yellow and orange bands

Series of orange spots with often barely visible black dots

Vivid orange border

Small, barely visible black dots inside red-orange spots

♂/♀

These white spots are not crossed by a black line

Wingspan: 32–42 mm

Habitat: Subalpine and alpine meadows and grasslands.

Hibernating stage: Overwinters twice as a caterpillar.

Elevational range: Between 900 and 3,000 m.

Egg-laying: Eggs are laid in batches of several dozens on LHP leaves.

Flight period: From June to August.

Host plants: Mainly *Plantago alpina*, on which laying occurs, but also other herbaceous plants in spring, such as *P. lanceolata*, *Viola allionii*, *Globularia cordifolia*, *Rhinanthus minor*, *Pedicularis tuberosa*, *P. rostratospicata*, and *Bartsia alpina*.

Diversity and systematics: Numerous subspecies have been described, reflecting the fragmentation of the range and the low dispersal capacity of this fritillary. The nominate subspecies flies in the Alps, while subspecies *leonhardi* inhabits the Rila mountains in Bulgaria.

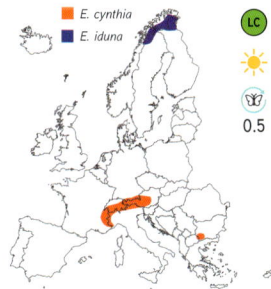

■ *E. cynthia*
■ *E. iduna*

LC

0.5

Did you know?

Caterpillars of Cynthia's Fritillary accumulate toxic glycosides present in their host plants. Hungry insectivorous birds kill them but are reluctant to consume them.

IMAGOS		LARVAE	
Food	✿	Food	🍃
Behaviour of males		Caterpillar location	
Dispersion		Chrysalis location	

LAPLAND FRITILLARY *EUPHYDRYAS IDUNA*

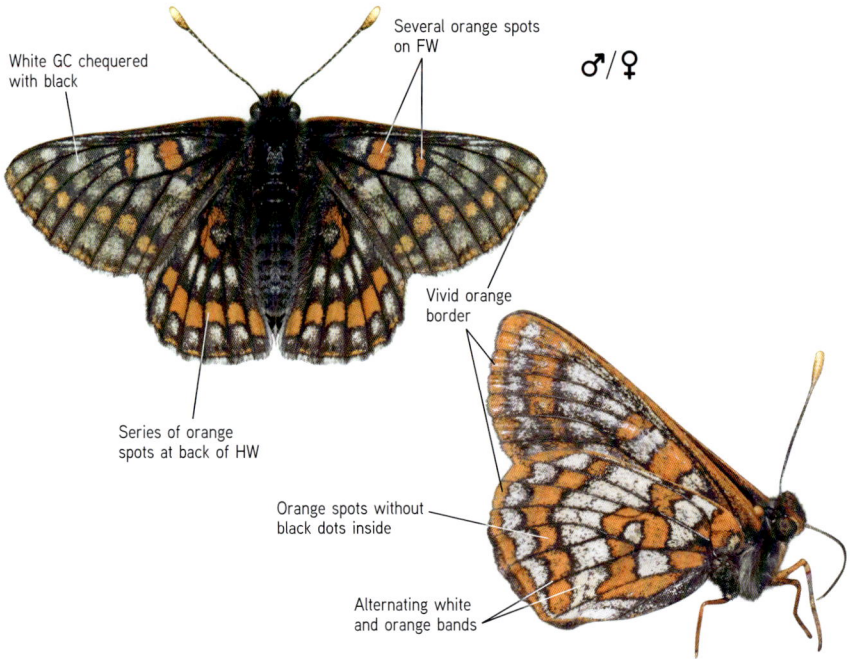

White GC chequered with black

Several orange spots on FW

♂/♀

Vivid orange border

Series of orange spots at back of HW

Orange spots without black dots inside

Alternating white and orange bands

Wingspan: 32–45 mm

Habitat: Flower-rich tundra heaths, bogs, and grasslands.

Hibernating stage: Overwinters twice as a caterpillar.

Elevational range: Up to 1,000 m.

Egg-laying: Eggs are laid in batches of several dozens on LHP leaves.

Flight period: June and July.

Host plants: Plantaginaceae, like *Plantago alpina*, *Veronica alpina*, and *V. fruticans.* Orobanchaceae, such as *Pedicularis hirsuta* and *Bartsia alpina*.

Diversity and systematics: European populations belong to the nominate subspecies.

■ *E. cynthia*
■ *E. iduna*

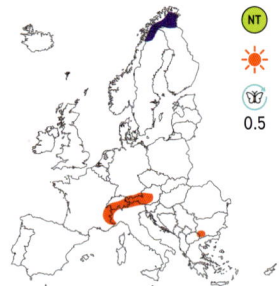

NT

0.5

IMAGOS			LARVAE		
Food			Food		
Behaviour of males			Caterpillar location		
Dispersion			Chrysalis location		

Did you know?

The Lapland Fritillary is one of the first butterflies to appear in the boreal spring. It flies for only one or two weeks.

SCARCE FRITILLARY/ITALIAN SCARCE FRITILLARY
EUPHYDRYAS MATURNA/EUPHYDRYAS ITALICA

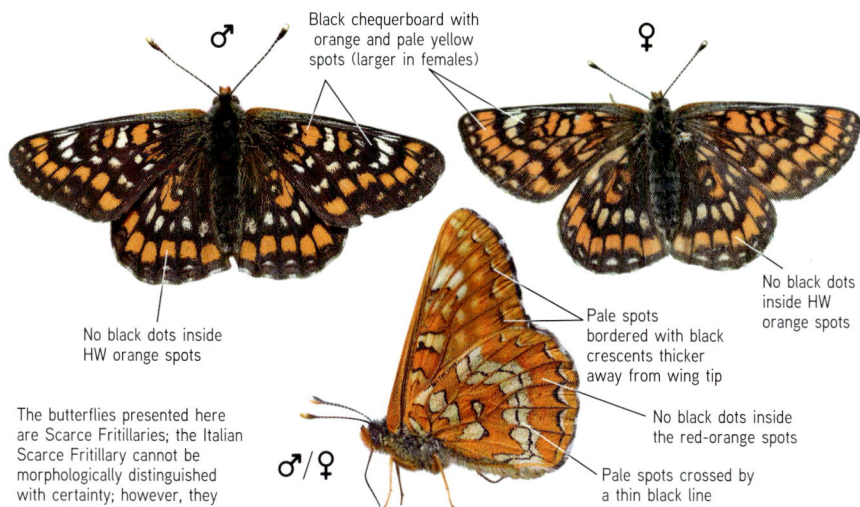

♂

Black chequerboard with orange and pale yellow spots (larger in females)

♀

No black dots inside HW orange spots

No black dots inside HW orange spots

Pale spots bordered with black crescents thicker away from wing tip

The butterflies presented here are Scarce Fritillaries; the Italian Scarce Fritillary cannot be morphologically distinguished with certainty; however, they do not fly together.

♂/♀

No black dots inside the red-orange spots

Pale spots crossed by a thin black line

Wingspan: 33–46 mm

Habitat: Flower-rich meadows, clearings, and edges in a woodland context.

Hibernating stage: Caterpillar.

Elevational range: Up to 600 m for the Scarce Fritillary; around 1,000 m for the Italian Scarce Fritillary.

Egg-laying: Eggs are laid in batches of several dozens on LHP leaves.

Flight period: From May to July for the Scarce Fritillary; June for the Italian Scarce Fritillary.

Host plants: Above all, *Fraxinus excelsior* (Oleaceae). In spring, other woody plants, such as *Ligustrum vulgare, Lonicera periclymenum, L. xylosteum, Betula pubescens, Fagus sylvatica, Viburnum lantana, V. opulus, Fraxinus angustifolia, F. ornus,* *Syringa vulgaris, Salix caprea, S. cinerea,* and *Populus tremula,* and some herbaceous plants like *Plantago lanceolata, Veronica chamaedrys, V. hederifolia, V. longifolia, Succisa pratensis, Dipsacus fullonum, D. sativus, Valeriana dioica, V. montana, V. excelsa, V. officinalis, Melampyrum nemorosum, M. pratense,* and *M. sylvaticum.*

Diversity and systematics: European populations belong to the nominate subspecies. The Italian Scarce Fritillary was described in 2015. Its genitalia are identical to those of the Scarce Fritillary, but molecular phylogeny clearly distinguishes it (surprisingly, it appears to be closer to the Lapland Fritillary).

maturna italica

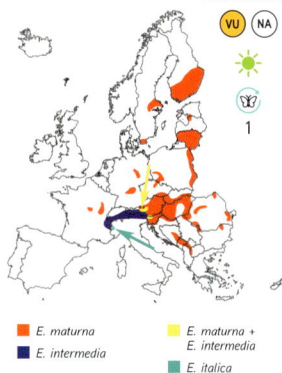

VU | NA

1

■ *E. maturna*
■ *E. intermedia*

□ *E. maturna + E. intermedia*
■ *E. italica*

Did you know?

The Scarce Fritillary has significantly declined due to the considerable loss of its favourable habitats, within a context of agricultural intensification and changes in forest management.

IMAGOS			LARVAE		
Food			Food		
Behaviour of males			Caterpillar location		
Dispersion			Chrysalis location		

NYMPHALIDAE

ASIAN FRITILLARY *EUPHYDRYAS INTERMEDIA*

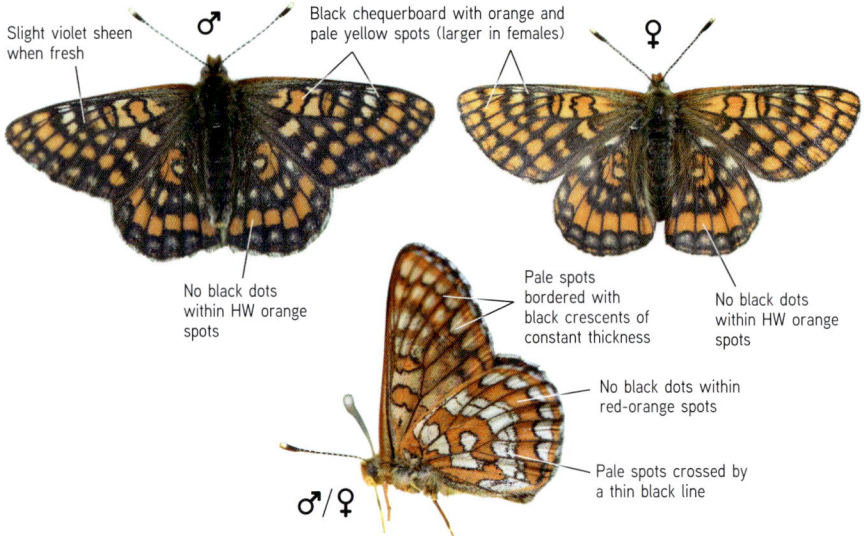

♂

Slight violet sheen when fresh

Black chequerboard with orange and pale yellow spots (larger in females)

♀

No black dots within HW orange spots

Pale spots bordered with black crescents of constant thickness

No black dots within HW orange spots

No black dots within red-orange spots

Pale spots crossed by a thin black line

♂/♀

Wingspan: 38–42 mm

Habitat: Subalpine heathlands, bushy meadows, and megaphorbs, most often within coniferous forests.

Hibernating stage: Overwinters twice as a caterpillar.

Elevational range: Between 1,500 and 2,400 m.

Egg-laying: Eggs are laid in batches of several dozens on LHP leaves.

Flight period: From June to August.

Host plants: *Lonicera caerulea* (Caprifoliaceae).

Diversity and systematics: European populations belong to subspecies *wolfensbergeri*.

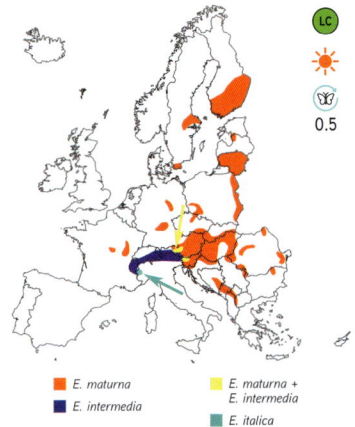

LC

0.5

■ E. maturna
■ E. intermedia
■ E. maturna + E. intermedia
■ E. italica

IMAGOS		LARVAE	
Food		Food	
Behaviour of males		Caterpillar location	
Dispersion		Chrysalis location	

Did you know?

Adults are fond of nectar from Asteraceae, especially that of adenostyles, hawkweeds, and *Arnica* spp.

NYMPHALIDAE

HEATH FRITILLARY *MELITAEA ATHALIA*

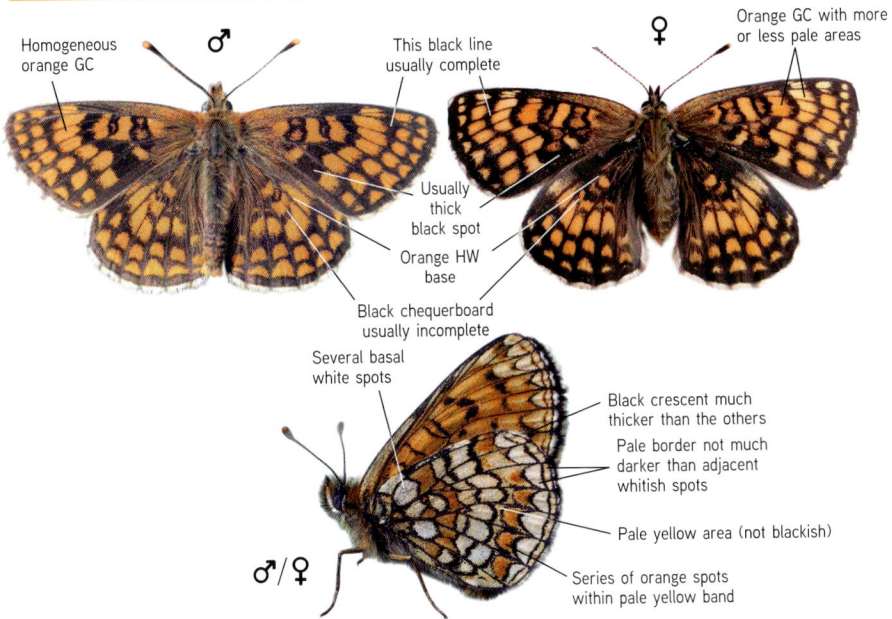

Homogeneous orange GC ♂

This black line usually complete

♀ Orange GC with more or less pale areas

Usually thick black spot

Orange HW base

Black chequerboard usually incomplete

Several basal white spots

Black crescent much thicker than the others

Pale border not much darker than adjacent whitish spots

Pale yellow area (not blackish)

♂/♀

Series of orange spots within pale yellow band

Wingspan: 31–40 mm

Habitat: Mesophilic and damp meadows, clearings, and edges. Also in parks and gardens that are not strictly maintained.

Hibernating stage: Caterpillar.

Elevational range: Up to 2,000 m.

Egg-laying: Eggs are laid in batches of several dozens on LHP leaves.

Flight period: From May to September.

Host plants: Orobanchaceae, including *Melampyrum arvense*, *M. pratense*, *M. nemorosum*, *M. sylvaticum*, and *Rhinanthus minor*. Plantaginaceae, such as *Digitalis ferruginea*, *D. purpurea*, *D. lutea*, *D. grandiflora*, *Linaria vulgaris*, *Euphrasia* spp., *Plantago lanceolata*, *P. major*, *P. media*, *P. alpina*, *P. atrata*, *Veronica chamaedrys*, *V. hederifolia*, *V. montana*, *V. officinalis*, *V. serpyllifolia*, and *V. spicata*.

Diversity and systematics: More than 30 subspecies have been described, their differences largely overshadowed by the variability of the nominate subspecies.

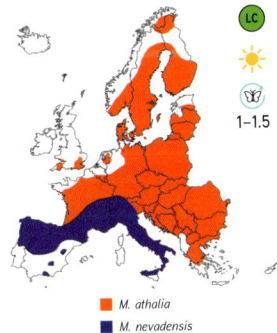

LC

1–1.5

■ M. athalia
■ M. nevadensis

Did you know?

The caterpillars pay a heavy toll to parasitoid wasps in genera *Ichneumon* and *Cotesia*, against which defensive iridoid compounds accumulated by the caterpillars from their host plants do not provide protection.

IMAGOS		LARVAE	
Food		Food	
Behaviour of males		Caterpillar location	
Dispersion		Chrysalis location	

NYMPHALIDAE

SOUTHERN HEATH FRITILLARY *MELITAEA NEVADENSIS (= CELADUSSA)*

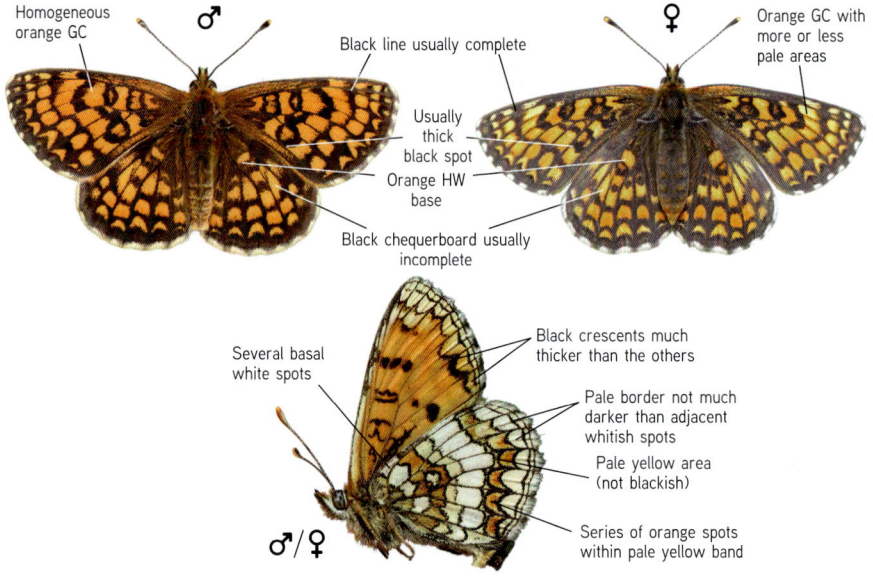

♂ Homogeneous orange GC

♀ Orange GC with more or less pale areas

Black line usually complete

Usually thick black spot

Orange HW base

Black chequerboard usually incomplete

Several basal white spots

Black crescents much thicker than the others

Pale border not much darker than adjacent whitish spots

Pale yellow area (not blackish)

Series of orange spots within pale yellow band

♂/♀

Wingspan: 31–40 mm

Habitat: Grasslands, meadows, wastelands, edges, and clearings. Also in parks and gardens that are not strictly maintained.

Hibernating stage: Caterpillar.

Elevational range: Up to 2,500 m.

Egg-laying: Eggs are laid in batches of several dozens on LHP leaves.

Flight period: From May to August.

Host plants: Plantaginaceae, including *Plantago lanceolata*, *P. albicans*, *P. alpina*, *P. media*, *P. subulata*, *Linaria* *vulgaris*, *L. repens*, *Digitalis ferruginea*, *D. grandiflora*, *D. lutea*, *D. purpurea*, *Veronica arvensis*, *V. chamaedrys*, *V. montana*, *V. officinalis*, and *V. teucrium*. Orobanchaceae, like *Melampyrum arvense*, *M. nemorosum*, *M. pratense*, and *M. sylvaticum*.

Diversity and systematics: The nominate subspecies flies in the Sierra Nevada. The remaining populations might belong to subspecies *celadussa*. However, there is not yet a general consensus on the taxonomy of the species.

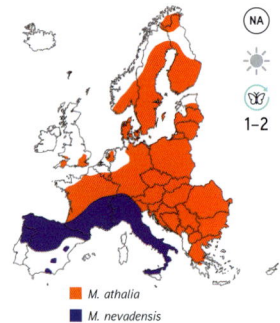

NA

1–2

■ *M. athalia*
■ *M. nevadensis*

Did you know?

The Southern Heath Fritillary and the Heath Fritillary can be distinguished with certainty only through examination of their genitalia. The former was previously considered a subspecies of the latter.

IMAGOS		LARVAE	
Food		Food	
Behaviour of males		Caterpillar location	
Dispersion		Chrysalis location	

NYMPHALIDAE

PROVENÇAL FRITILLARY *MELITAEA DEIONE*

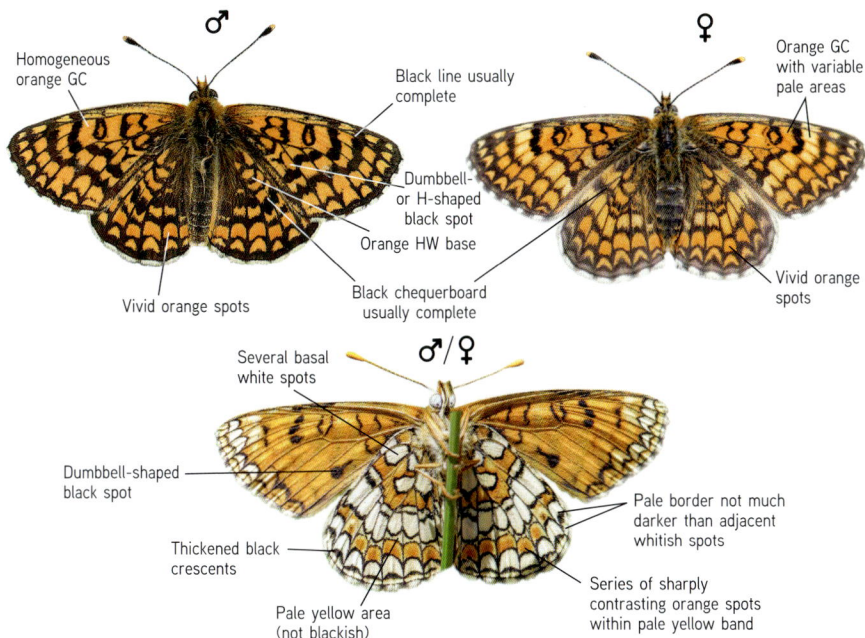

♂

Homogeneous orange GC

Black line usually complete

Dumbbell- or H-shaped black spot

Orange HW base

Vivid orange spots

Black chequerboard usually complete

♀

Orange GC with variable pale areas

Vivid orange spots

♂/♀

Several basal white spots

Dumbbell-shaped black spot

Thickened black crescents

Pale yellow area (not blackish)

Pale border not much darker than adjacent whitish spots

Series of sharply contrasting orange spots within pale yellow band

Wingspan: 32–46 mm

Habitat: Dry grasslands, stony slopes, and sunny edges. Also the vicinity of old walls where some LHPs grow.

Hibernating stage: Caterpillar.

Elevational range: Up to 1,500 m.

Egg-laying: Eggs are laid in batches of several dozens on LHP leaves.

Flight period: From April to September.

Host plants: Plantaginaceae, including *Linaria angustissima*,

L. alpina, L. purpurea, L. repens, L. vulgaris, Cymbalaria muralis, Antirrhinum graniticum, A. hispanicum, A. latifolium, A. majus, A. sempervirens, Digitalis purpurea, D. lutea, Plantago lanceolata, Misopates orontium, Chaenorrhinum minus, and *C. rubrifolium*. Also on *Valeriana rubra* (Caprifoliaceae).

Diversity and systematics: About a dozen subspecies have been described, most from the Iberian Peninsula.

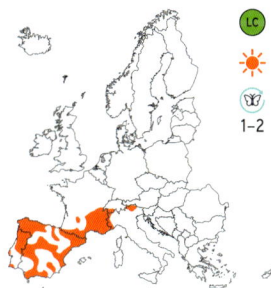

LC

1–2

Did you know?

The Provençal Fritillary is often confused with the Southern Heath Fritillary. Examination of all the typical criteria of an individual – and, if possible, the genitalia – is strongly recommended if one is to identify it with certainty.

IMAGOS		LARVAE	
Food		Food	
Behaviour of males		Caterpillar location	
Dispersion		Chrysalis location	

415

NYMPHALIDAE

NICKERL'S FRITILLARY *MELITAEA AURELIA*

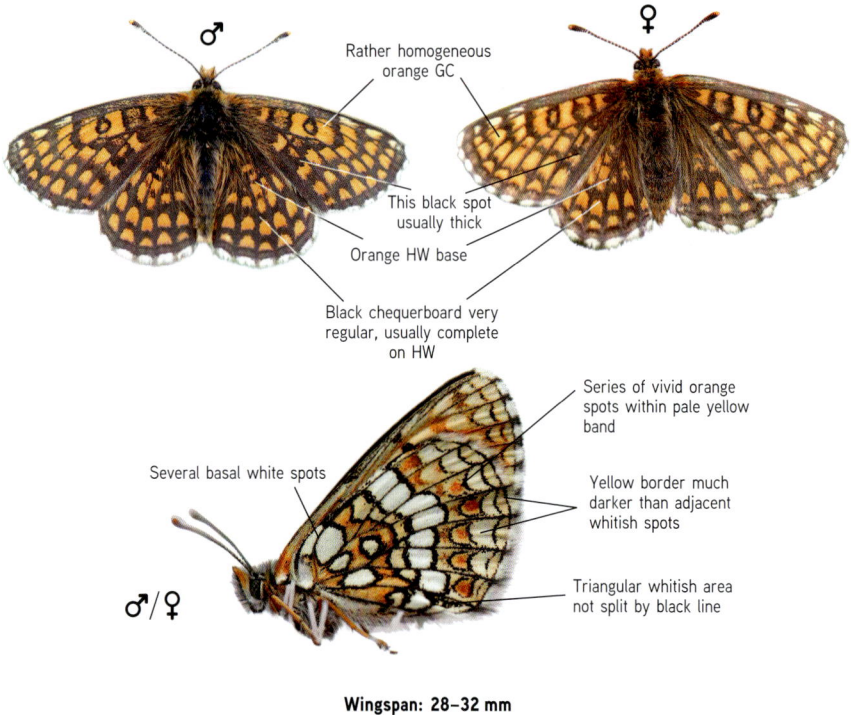

♂

♀

Rather homogeneous orange GC

This black spot usually thick

Orange HW base

Black chequerboard very regular, usually complete on HW

Series of vivid orange spots within pale yellow band

Several basal white spots

Yellow border much darker than adjacent whitish spots

♂/♀

Triangular whitish area not split by black line

Wingspan: 28–32 mm

Habitat: Flower-rich grasslands and hay meadows.

Hibernating stage: Caterpillar.

Elevational range: Up to 1,500 m.

Egg-laying: Eggs are laid in batches of several dozens on LHP leaves.

Flight period: June and July.

Host plants: Plantaginaceae, including *Plantago lanceolata, P. media,* and *Veronica austriaca.* Orobanchaceae, including *Melampyrum pratense* and *Rhinanthus minor.*

Diversity and systematics: Almost 20 subspecies have been described; they differ only slightly from the nominate subspecies.

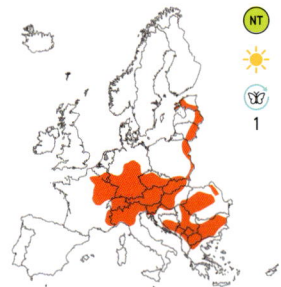

NT

1

Did you know?

Nickerl's Fritillary is distinguished from similar species by its small size and low-level flight over vegetation. Its populations are highly fragmented.

IMAGOS		LARVAE	
Food		Food	
Behaviour of males		Caterpillar location	
Dispersion		Chrysalis location	

NYMPHALIDAE

ASSMANN'S FRITILLARY *MELITAEA BRITOMARTIS*

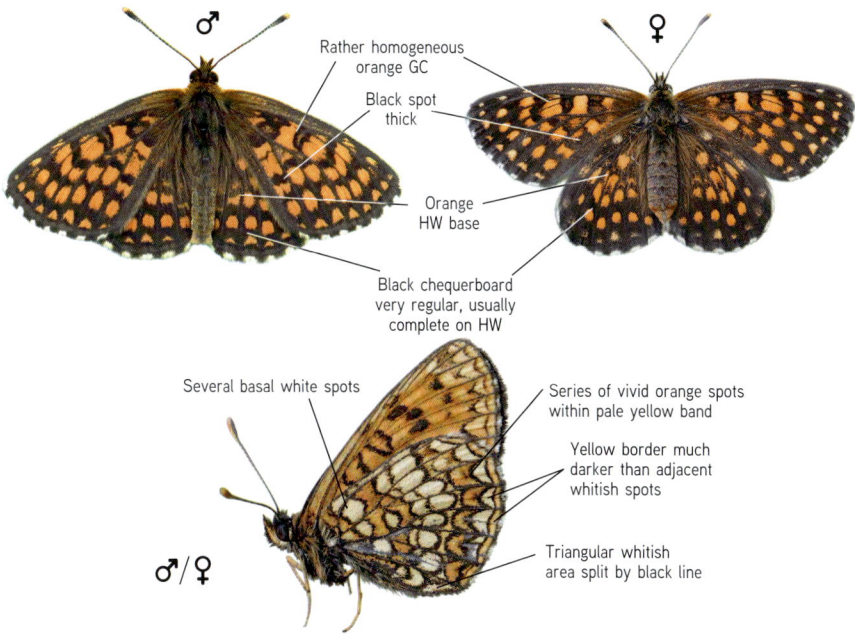

♂

Rather homogeneous
orange GC

Black spot
thick

♀

Orange
HW base

Black chequerboard
very regular, usually
complete on HW

Several basal white spots

Series of vivid orange spots
within pale yellow band

Yellow border much
darker than adjacent
whitish spots

♂/♀

Triangular whitish
area split by black line

Wingspan: 30–36 mm

Habitat: Flower-rich grasslands and low-growing meadows.

Hibernating stage: Caterpillar.

Elevational range: Up to 1,000 m.

Egg-laying: Eggs are laid in batches of several dozens on LHP leaves.

Flight period: From May to August.

Host plants: Plantaginaceae, including *Veronica teucrium*, *V. chamaedrys*, *V. austriaca*, *V. spicata*, *V. officinalis*, *Plantago lanceolata*, and *P. media*. Orobanchaceae, including *Rhinantus minor*.

Diversity and systematics: Most European populations belong to the nominate subspecies. A few poorly distinguished subspecies have been described from Hungary and Bulgaria.

NT

1

Did you know?

Assmann's Fritillary does not tolerate excessive grazing or too frequent mowing of the meadows it inhabits. The intensification of agricultural practices is therefore highly detrimental to it.

IMAGOS		LARVAE	
Food		Food	
Behaviour of males		Caterpillar location	
Dispersion		Chrysalis location	

THE FALSE HEATH FRITILLARY *MELITAEA DIAMINA*

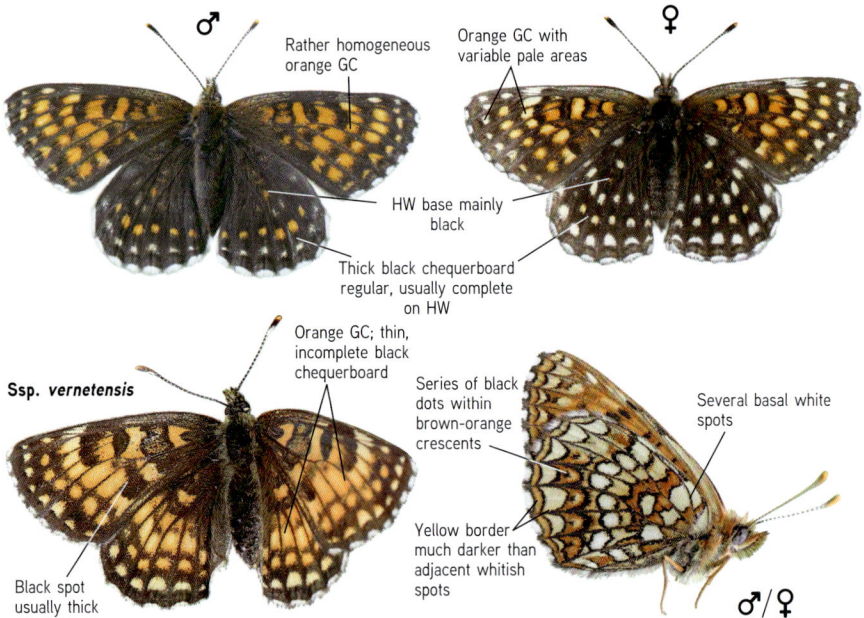

♂

Rather homogeneous orange GC

♀

Orange GC with variable pale areas

HW base mainly black

Thick black chequerboard regular, usually complete on HW

Ssp. *vernetensis*

Orange GC; thin, incomplete black chequerboard

Series of black dots within brown-orange crescents

Several basal white spots

Yellow border much darker than adjacent whitish spots

♂/♀

Black spot usually thick

Wingspan: 31–40 mm

Habitat: Hay and damp meadows, flower-rich clearings, and bog surroundings.

Hibernating stage: Caterpillar.

Elevational range: Up to 2,500 m.

Egg-laying: Eggs are laid in batches of several dozens on LHP leaves.

Flight period: From April to September.

Host plants: Caprifoliaceae, including *Valeriana dioica*, *V. officinalis*, *V. tripteris*, *V. excelsa*, *V. montana*, and *V. wallrothii*. Plantaginaceae, like *Plantago lanceolata* and *Veronica chamaedrys*. Orobanchaceae, such as *Melampyrum nemorosum* and *M. pratense*. *Bistorta officinalis* (Polygonaceae).

Diversity and systematics: About 20 subspecies are described, often poorly distinguished from the rather variable nominate subspecies. Subspecies *vernetensis* flies in the Pyrenees, while subspecies *codinai* inhabits Catalonia.

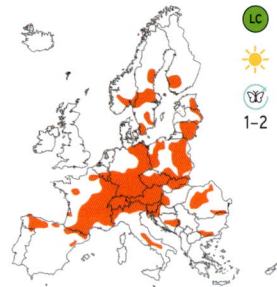

LC

1–2

Did you know?

The False Heath Fritillary is declining in the western part of its range due to the loss of its habitats in the context of overly intensive agriculture.

IMAGOS			LARVAE		
Food			Food		
Behaviour of males			Caterpillar location		
Dispersion			Chrysalis location		

MEADOW FRITILLARY *MELITAEA PARTHENOIDES*

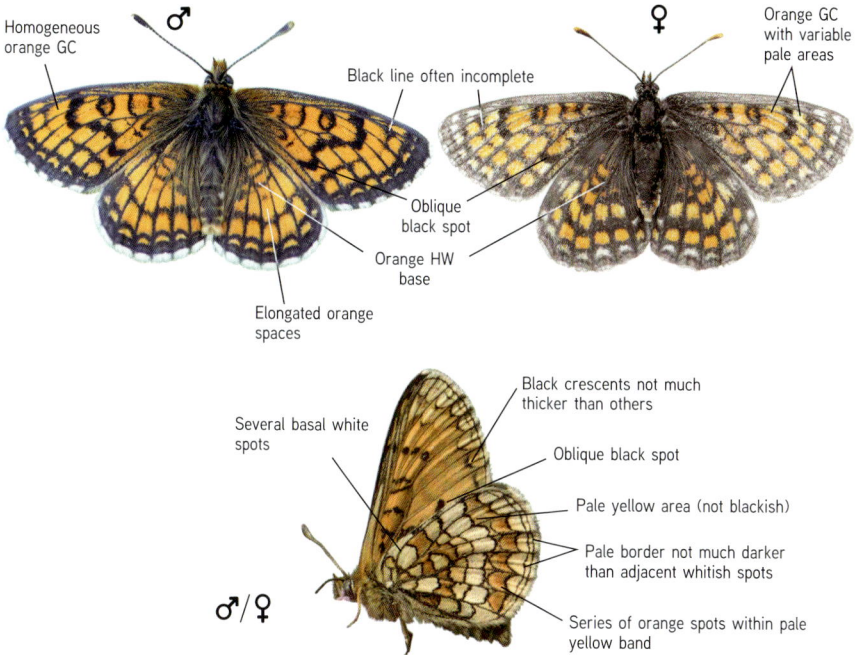

Homogeneous orange GC

♂

Black line often incomplete

♀

Orange GC with variable pale areas

Oblique black spot

Orange HW base

Elongated orange spaces

Black crescents not much thicker than others

Several basal white spots

Oblique black spot

Pale yellow area (not blackish)

Pale border not much darker than adjacent whitish spots

♂/♀

Series of orange spots within pale yellow band

Wingspan: 30–36 mm

Habitat: Mesophilic or somewhat damper meadows, sunny grasslands.

Hibernating stage: Caterpillar.

Elevational range: Up to 2,500 m.

Egg-laying: Eggs are laid in batches of several dozens on LHP leaves.

Flight period: From May to September.

Host plants: Plantaginaceae, mainly *Plantago lanceolata, P. major, P. media, P. alpina,* and *Verbascum lychnitis.* Asteraceae, including *Centaurea jacea* and *C. scabiosa.*

Diversity and systematics: About a dozen subspecies have been described, though some authors consider several as mere forms.

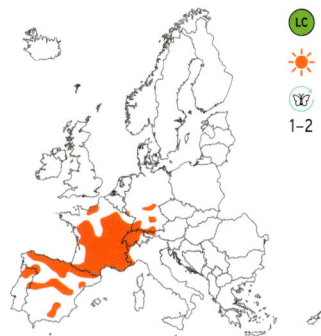

LC

1–2

	IMAGOS			LARVAE	
Food	🌟 💩 💧		Food	🍃	
Behaviour of males	🦋		Caterpillar location	🌿	
Dispersion	🦋		Chrysalis location	🌿	

Did you know?

The caterpillars of the Meadow Fritillary are often victims of the parasitoid wasp *Cotesia melitaearum.*

NYMPHALIDAE

GRISONS FRITILLARY *MELITAEA VARIA*

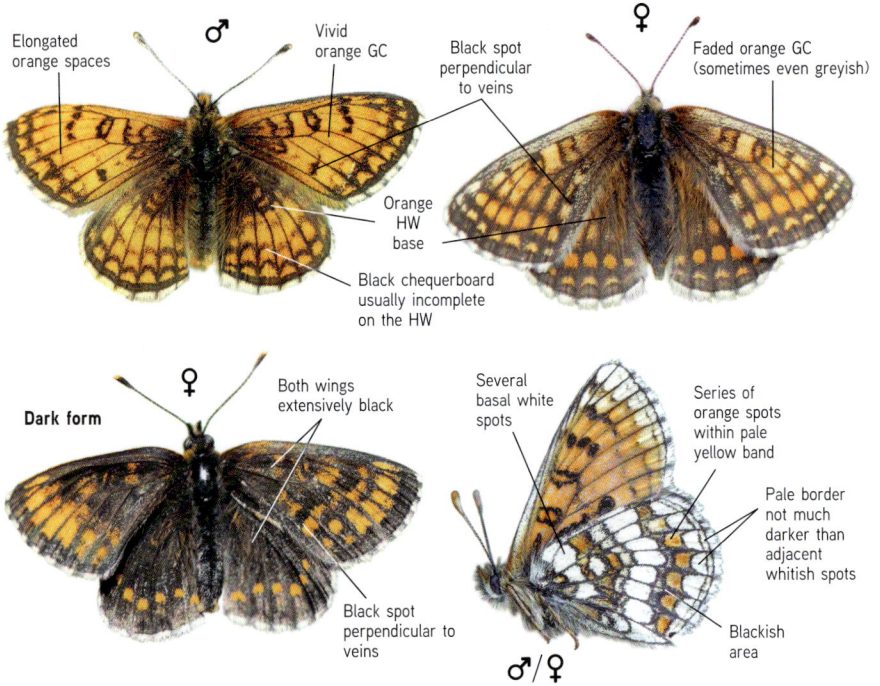

♂

Elongated orange spaces

Vivid orange GC

Black spot perpendicular to veins

♀

Faded orange GC (sometimes even greyish)

Orange HW base

Black chequerboard usually incomplete on the HW

Dark form ♀

Both wings extensively black

Several basal white spots

Series of orange spots within pale yellow band

Pale border not much darker than adjacent whitish spots

Black spot perpendicular to veins

Blackish area

♂/♀

Wingspan: 30–38 mm

Habitat: Subalpine and alpine grasslands and meadows, often sheltered.
Hibernating stage: Usually overwinters twice as a caterpillar.
Elevational range: Between 1,200 and 2,700 m.
Egg-laying: Eggs are laid in batches of several dozens on LHP leaves.
Flight period: From June to August.
Host plants: Plantaginaceae, including *Plantago alpina*. In spring, also on *Achillea* spp., *Gentiana acaulis*, and *G. verna*.
Diversity and systematics: Several subspecies have been described, especially in the Southern Alps (*variabella*, *barnumi*, and *turiniensis*). Subspecies *varissima* flies in Italy. Subspecies *gilbon* is found in the Swiss Jura. Subspecies *piana* populates the Italian Piedmont.

LC

0.5–1

IMAGOS			LARVAE		
Food			Food		
Behaviour of males			Caterpillar location		
Dispersion			Chrysalis location		

Did you know?

The scientific name of the Grisons Fritillary has been very well chosen. Its upperside is indeed outstandingly variable.

420

LITTLE FRITILLARY *MELITAEA ASTERIA*

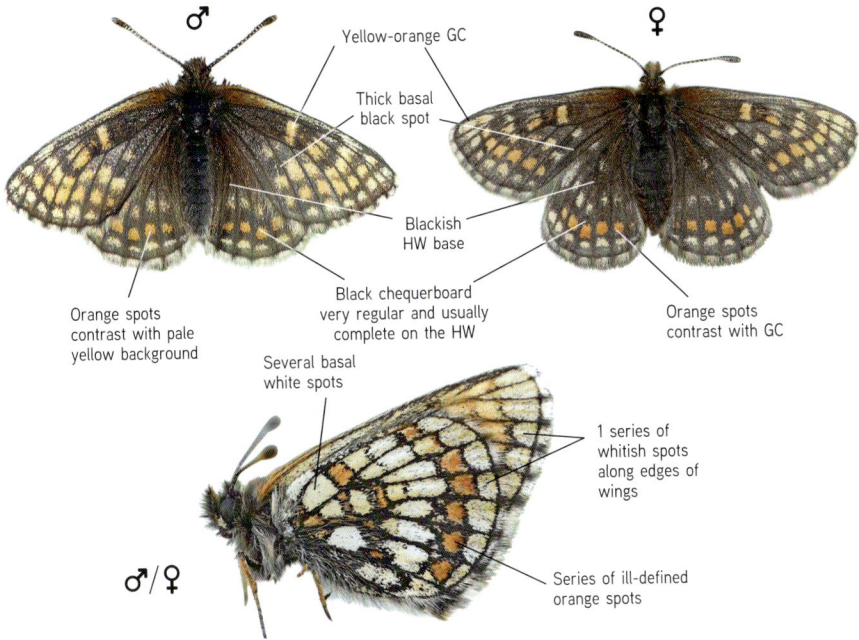

♂

Yellow-orange GC

Thick basal black spot

♀

Blackish HW base

Orange spots contrast with pale yellow background

Black chequerboard very regular and usually complete on the HW

Orange spots contrast with GC

Several basal white spots

1 series of whitish spots along edges of wings

♂/♀

Series of ill-defined orange spots

Wingspan: 28–30 mm

Habitat: Low-growing alpine grasslands.

Hibernating stage: Overwinters twice as a caterpillar.

Elevational range: Between 2,000 and 3,000 m.

Egg-laying: Eggs are laid in batches of several dozens on LHP leaves.

Flight period: From June to August.

Host plants: Plantaginaceae, including *Plantago alpina* and *Veronica bellidioides*. Also on *Bartsia alpina* and *Pedicularis tuberosa* (Orobanchaceae).

Diversity and systematics: The nominate subspecies forms most populations. Subspecies *mevania* is described from Carinthia.

LC

0.5

Did you know?

The Little Fritillary is the smallest species in the *Melitaea* genus flying in Europe. Its populations are very localized, but its numbers are often significant.

IMAGOS		LARVAE	
Food		Food	
Behaviour of males		Caterpillar location	
Dispersion		Chrysalis location	

NYMPHALIDAE

SPOTTED FRITILLARY *MELITAEA DIDYMA*

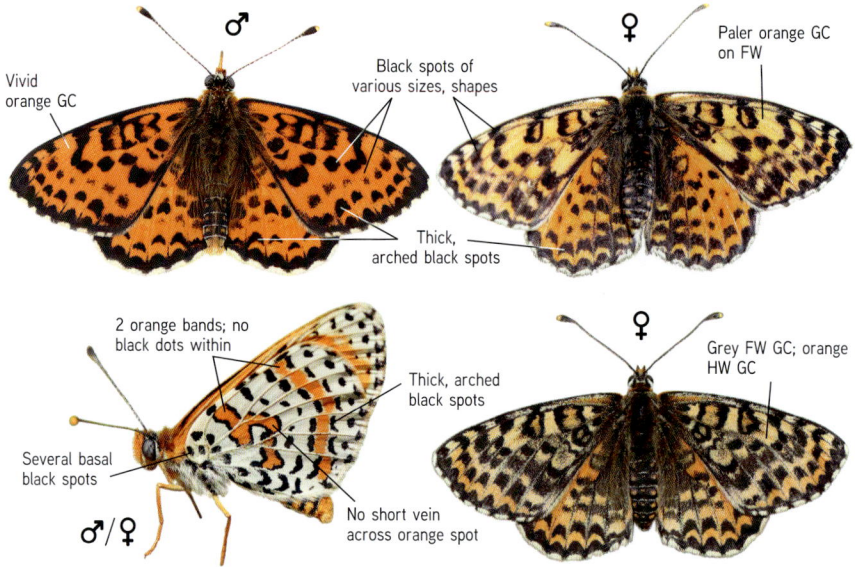

♂

Vivid orange GC

Black spots of various sizes, shapes

♀

Paler orange GC on FW

Thick, arched black spots

2 orange bands; no black dots within

Thick, arched black spots

♀

Grey FW GC; orange HW GC

Several basal black spots

♂/♀

No short vein across orange spot

Wingspan: 30–44 mm

Habitat: Dry grasslands, meadows, clearings and warm edges.

Hibernating stage: Caterpillar.

Elevational range: Up to 2,500 m.

Egg-laying: Eggs are laid in batches of several dozens on LHP leaves.

Flight period: From May to September.

Host plants: A wide variety of herbaceous plants, including some Plantaginaceae, like *Plantago lanceolata, P. media, P. major, P. amplexicaulis, P. bellardii, P. coronopus, P. subulata, Linaria alpina, L. genistifolia, L. peloponnesiaca, L. repens, L. vulgaris, Antirrhinum majus, Cymbalaria muralis, Digitalis grandiflora, D. purpurea, Globularia*

bisnagarica, Veronica chamaedrys, and *V. teucrium.* Also on some Scrophulariaceae, including *Digitalis* spp., *Linaria* spp., *Rhinanthus* spp., *Verbascum* spp.; some Asteraceae, including *Centaurea* spp. and *Achillea millefolium;* some Orobanchaceae, like *Melampyrum arvense, Odontites lanceolatus, O. luteus, Rhinanthus halophilus,* and *R. major.* Lamiaceae, such as *Galeopsis angustifolia, Melittis melissophyllum,* and *Stachys recta.* Caprifoliaceae, including *Valeriana montana* and *V. officinalis.*

Diversity and systematics: Several dozen subspecies have been described. The variability of wing patterns is highly significant in this species, as is that of its mitochondrial genome.

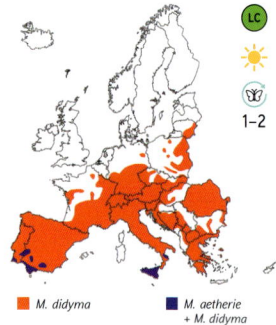

LC

1–2

■ *M. didyma*   ■ *M. aetherie + M. didyma*

Did you know?

The Spotted Fritillary, still rather common in the southern part of its range, nevertheless belongs to the group of threatened species affected by agricultural intensification and the decline of extensive grazing. The latter contributes to the maintenance of dry grasslands and flower-rich meadows.

IMAGOS		LARVAE	
Food	✿	Food	✿ 🍃
Behaviour of males		Caterpillar location	
Dispersion		Chrysalis location	

NYMPHALIDAE

LESSER SPOTTED FRITILLARY/SAGARRA'S FRITILLARY
MELITAEA TRIVIA/M. IGNASITI

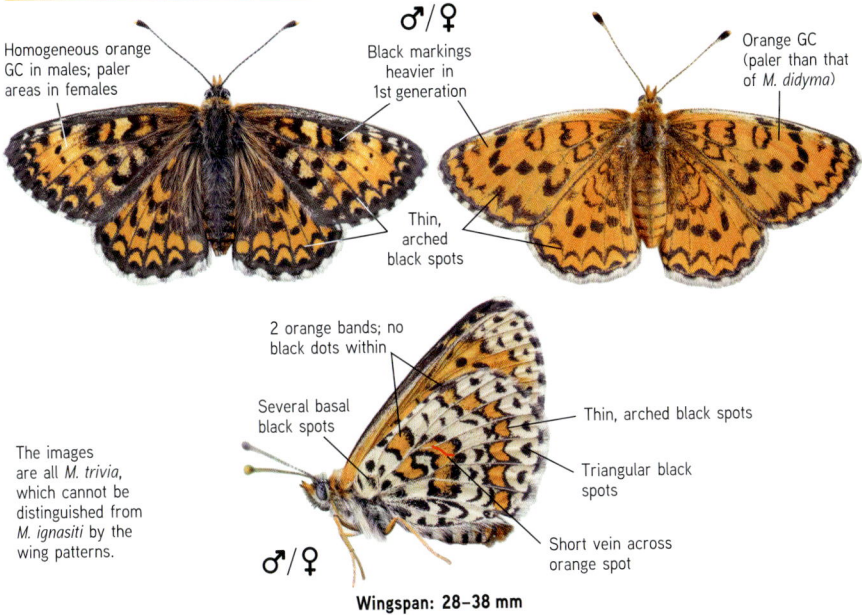

♂/♀

Homogeneous orange GC in males; paler areas in females

Black markings heavier in 1st generation

Orange GC (paler than that of *M. didyma*)

Thin, arched black spots

2 orange bands; no black dots within

Several basal black spots

Thin, arched black spots

The images are all *M. trivia*, which cannot be distinguished from *M. ignasiti* by the wing patterns.

Triangular black spots

Short vein across orange spot

♂/♀

Wingspan: 28–38 mm

Habitat: Dry grasslands, meadows, Mediterranean wastelands, and garrigue for *Melitaea trivia*. Sunny dry grasslands for *M. ignasiti*.

Hibernating stage: Caterpillar.

Elevational range: Up to 1,800 m.

Egg-laying: Eggs are laid in batches of several dozens on LHP leaves.

Flight period: From March to October.

Host plants: Scrophulariaceae of genus *Verbascum*, including *V. chaixii*, *V. epixanthinum*, *V. longifolium*, *V. nigrum*, *V. phlomoides*, *V. phoeniceum*, *V. pulverulentum*, *V. sinuatum*, *V. thapsus*, *V. undulatum*, and *V. lychnitis*.

Diversity and systematics: For *Melitaea trivia*, most European populations belong to the nominate subspecies; subspecies *lathon* and *stemmleri* are found in the Balkans. For *M. ignasiti*, subspecies *salamancaensis* is described from the Spanish region of Salamanca.

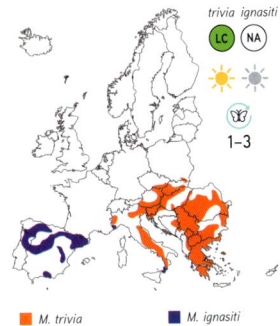

trivia ignasiti

LC NA

1–3

■ *M. trivia*   ■ *M. ignasiti*

Did you know?

The status of *Melitaea ignasiti* is a subject of debate: is it a subspecies of *M. trivia* or a distinct species? Male genitalia are distinct (although intermediate individuals exist), and populations are clearly allopatric, but their ecology differs very little.

IMAGOS		LARVAE	
Food		Food	
Behaviour of males		Caterpillar location	
Dispersion		Chrysalis location	

NYMPHALIDAE

AETHERIE FRITILLARY   *MELITAEA AETHERIE*

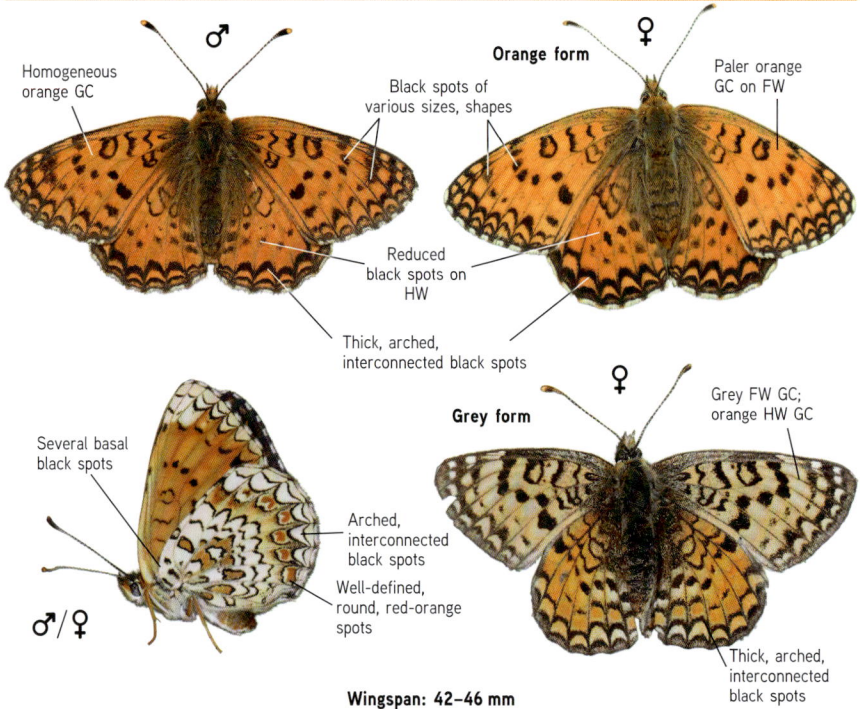

♂

Homogeneous orange GC

Orange form ♀

Black spots of various sizes, shapes

Paler orange GC on FW

Reduced black spots on HW

Thick, arched, interconnected black spots

♀

Several basal black spots

Grey form

Grey FW GC; orange HW GC

Arched, interconnected black spots

Well-defined, round, red-orange spots

♂/♀

Thick, arched, interconnected black spots

Wingspan: 42–46 mm

Habitat: Extensively grazed meadows, grassy wastelands, crop surroundings, and garrigues.

Hibernating stage: Caterpillar.

Elevational range: Up to 1,100 m.

Egg-laying: Eggs are laid in batches of several dozens on LHP leaves.

Flight period: From April to July (until September in Sicily, where a second generation occurs).

Host plants: Asteraceae, including *Centaurea jacea, C. calcitrapa, C. carratracensis, C. nigrescens, Cynara cardunculus, Carthamus caeruleus, Cirsium arvense,* and *C. vulgare.*

Diversity and systematics: The nominate subspecies flies in the Iberian Peninsula. The Italian populations constitute subspecies *perlini.*

■ M. didyma
■ M. aetherie + M. didyma

LC

☀
🦋
1–2

Did you know?

Habitats favourable to the Aetherie Fritillary are threatened by human activities. A number have been converted into golf courses along the Spanish coasts.

IMAGOS		LARVAE	
Food	🌼 💧	Food	🌿
Behaviour of males		Caterpillar location	🌱
Dispersion		Chrysalis location	🌱

GLANVILLE FRITILLARY *MELITAEA CINXIA*

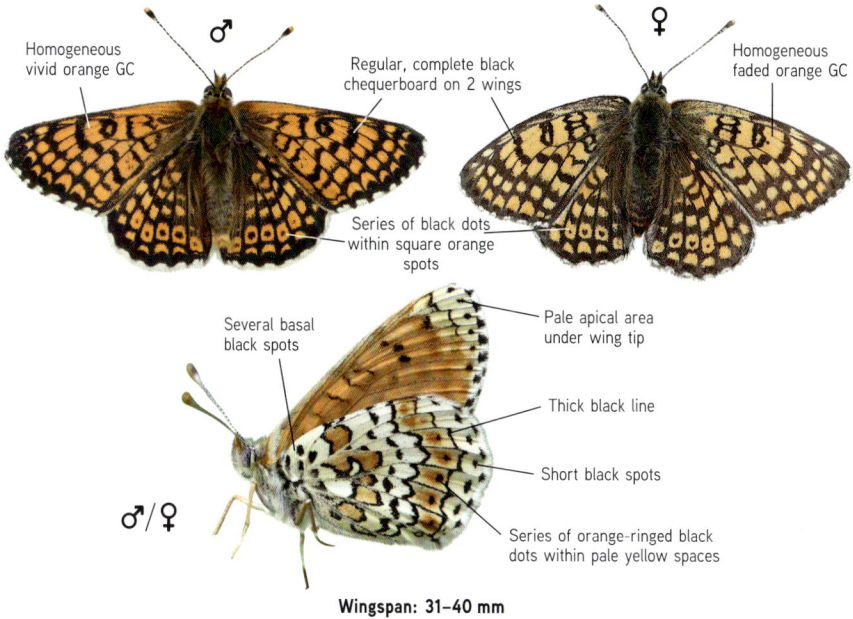

♂

Homogeneous
vivid orange GC

Regular, complete black
chequerboard on 2 wings

♀

Homogeneous
faded orange GC

Series of black dots
within square orange
spots

Several basal
black spots

Pale apical area
under wing tip

Thick black line

Short black spots

♂/♀

Series of orange-ringed black
dots within pale yellow spaces

Wingspan: 31–40 mm

Habitat: Grasslands, meadows, roadsides, parks, and gardens.

Hibernating stage: Caterpillar.

Elevational range: Up to 2,500 m.

Egg-laying: Eggs are laid in batches of several dozens on LHP leaves.

Flight period: From March to September.

Host plants: Plantaginaceae, including *Plantago lanceolata*, *P. major*, *P. alpina*, *P. coronopus*, *P. media*, *P. maritima*, *P. subulata*, *Veronica chamaedrys*, *V. incana*, *V. longifolia*, *V. officinalis*, *V. serpyllifolia*, *V. spicata*, *V. teucrium*, and *V. urticifolia*. Scrophulariaceae in the *Linaria* genus. Asteraceae, including *Centaurea deustiformis*, *C. jacea*, and *Pilosella officinarum*.

Diversity and systematics: Numerous subspecies and forms have been described. However, the majority of European populations belong to the nominate subspecies.

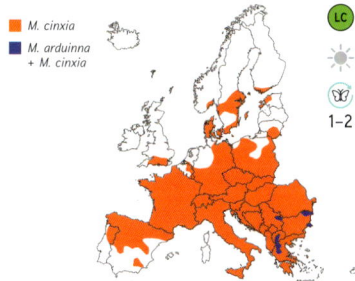

- M. cinxia
- M. arduinna + M. cinxia

LC

1–2

Did you know?

Populations of the Glanville Fritillary in the Åland archipelago, off the coast of Finland, have served as a study model for the functioning of metapopulations for over 30 years. Hundreds of meadows are monitored each year in this scientific context.

IMAGOS			LARVAE		
Food			Food		
Behaviour of males			Caterpillar location		
Dispersion			Chrysalis location		

FREYER'S FRITILLARY *MELITAEA ARDUINNA*

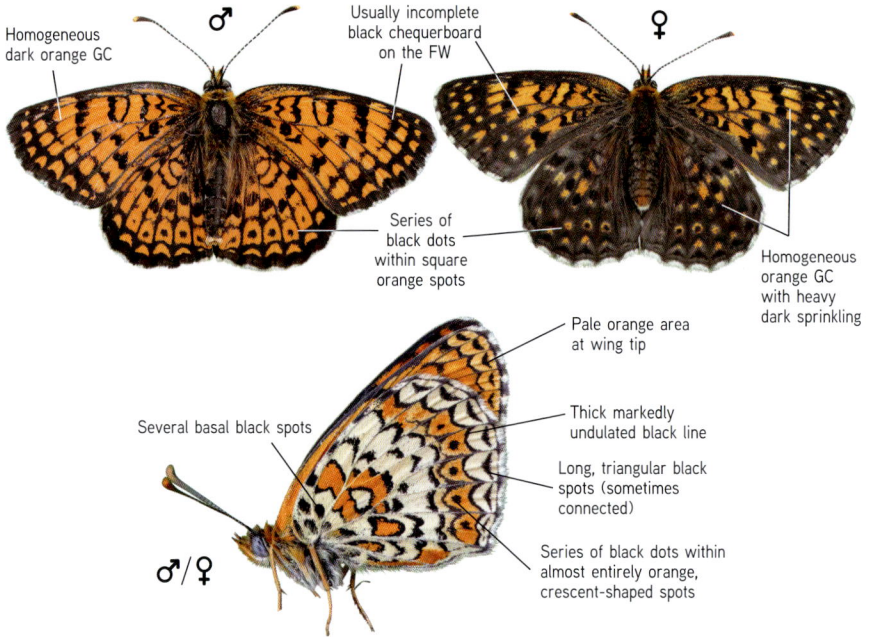

♂

Homogeneous dark orange GC

Usually incomplete black chequerboard on the FW

♀

Series of black dots within square orange spots

Homogeneous orange GC with heavy dark sprinkling

Pale orange area at wing tip

Several basal black spots

Thick markedly undulated black line

Long, triangular black spots (sometimes connected)

♂/♀

Series of black dots within almost entirely orange, crescent-shaped spots

Wingspan: 42–46 mm

Habitat: Extensively grazed grasslands and meadows.

Hibernating stage: Caterpillar.

Elevational range: Up to 1,500 m.

Egg-laying: Eggs are laid in batches of several dozens on LHP leaves.

Flight period: From May to August.

Host plants: Asteraceae of genus *Centaurea*, including *C. affinis*, *C. nemecii*, and *C. phrygia*.

Diversity and systematics: European populations belong to subspecies *rhodopensis*.

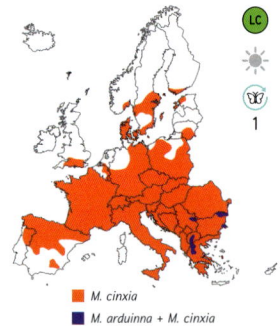

■ *M. cinxia*
■ *M. arduinna* + *M. cinxia*

IMAGOS		LARVAE	
Food		Food	
Behaviour of males		Caterpillar location	
Dispersion		Chrysalis location	

Did you know?

The caterpillars of Freyer's Fritillary live collectively in a silken shelter woven around the larval host plant. They disperse at maturity to pupate.

426

NYMPHALIDAE

KNAPWEED FRITILLARY *MELITAEA PHOEBE*

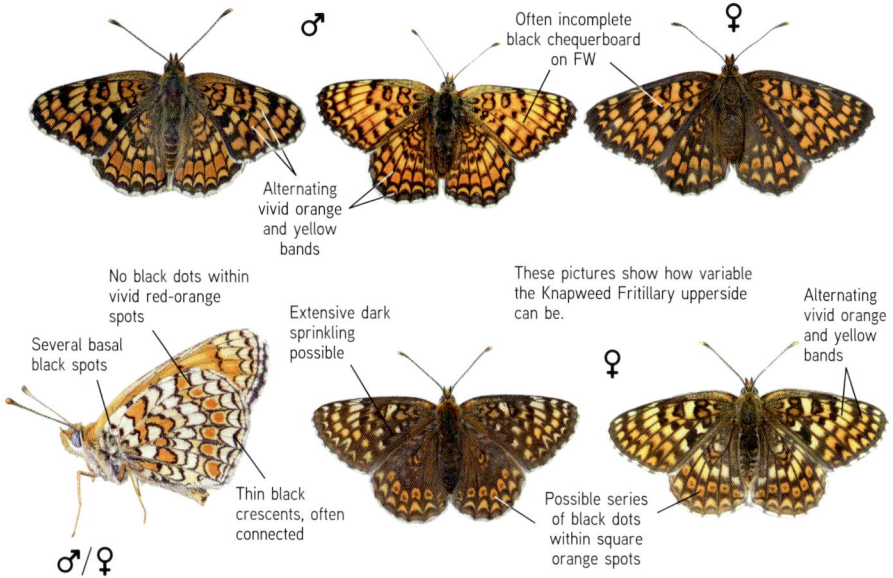

♂

Often incomplete black chequerboard on FW

♀

Alternating vivid orange and yellow bands

No black dots within vivid red-orange spots

These pictures show how variable the Knapweed Fritillary upperside can be.

Alternating vivid orange and yellow bands

Extensive dark sprinkling possible

Several basal black spots

♀

♂/♀

Thin black crescents, often connected

Possible series of black dots within square orange spots

Wingspan: 39–50 mm

Habitat: Warm grasslands and meadows, garrigues, and stony, flower-rich slopes.

Hibernating stage: Caterpillar.

Elevational range: Up to 2,500 m.

Egg-laying: Eggs are laid in batches of several dozens on LHP leaves.

Flight period: From April to September.

Host plants: Asteraceae, including *Arctium lappa, Carduus nigrescens, C. nutans, Carlina acaulis, Centaurea calcitrapa, C. collina, C. decipiens, C. grisebachii, C. jacea, C. nigra, C. nigrescens, C. ornata, C. paniculata, C. pectinata, C. phrygia, C. scabiosa,* *C. graeca, Cirsium acaule, C. arvense, C. dissectum, C. eriophorum, C. palustre, C. pannonicum, C. tuberosum, C. vulgare, Cynara cardunculus, Leuzea uniflora, Onopordum acanthium,* and *Serratula tinctoria.* Plantaginaceae, such as *Plantago lanceolata* and *P. afra.* Caprifoliaceae, including *Scabiosa columbaria.*

Diversity and systematics: Most European populations belong to the nominate subspecies, which exhibits significant variability (numerous, less robust subspecies have been described). Subspecies *occitanica* inhabits the Iberian Peninsula up to the Eastern Pyrenees.

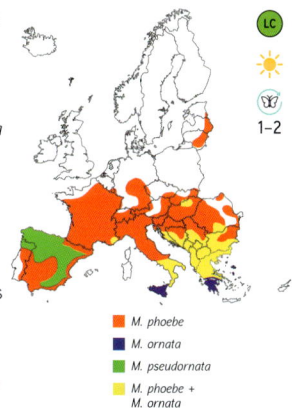

LC

1–2

■ M. phoebe
■ M. ornata
■ M. pseudornata
■ M. phoebe + M. ornata

IMAGOS			LARVAE	
Food			Food	
Behaviour of males			Caterpillar location	
Dispersion			Chrysalis location	

Did you know?

The Knapweed Fritillary requires well-flowered environments. Too frequent mowing does not allow for development of the larvae, which feed on usually unpopular weeds.

NYMPHALIDAE

EASTERN KNAPWEED FRITILLARY/IBERIAN KNAPWEED FRITILLARY
MELITAEA ORNATA/M. PSEUDORNATA

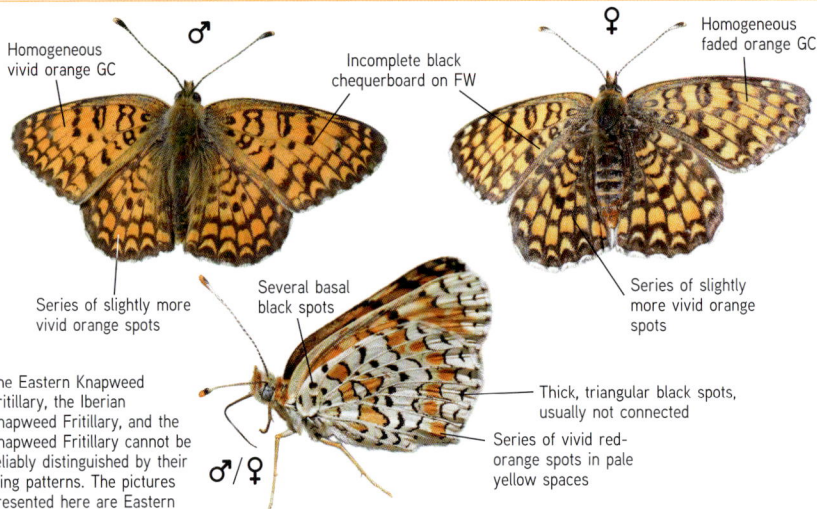

♂

Homogeneous vivid orange GC

Incomplete black chequerboard on FW

♀

Homogeneous faded orange GC

Series of slightly more vivid orange spots

Several basal black spots

Series of slightly more vivid orange spots

The Eastern Knapweed Fritillary, the Iberian Knapweed Fritillary, and the Knapweed Fritillary cannot be reliably distinguished by their wing patterns. The pictures presented here are Eastern Knapweed Fritillaries.

♂/♀

Thick, triangular black spots, usually not connected

Series of vivid red-orange spots in pale yellow spaces

Wingspan: 38–45 mm

Habitat: Open and bushy thermophilic habitats.

Hibernating stage: Caterpillar.

Elevational range: Up to 1,000 m for *Melitaea ornata*; between 500 and 1,500 m for *M. pseudornata*.

Egg-laying: Eggs are laid in batches of several dozens on LHP leaves.

Flight period: From April to July for *Melitaea ornata*; between May and August for *M. pseudornata*.

Host plants: For *Melitaea ornata*, Asteraceae, including *Carduus collinus, C. nutans, C. pycnocephalus, Centaurea achaia, C. busambarensis, C. calcitrapa, C. deusta, C. grisebachii, C. nigrescens, C. raphanina, C. salonitana, C. scabiosa, C. solstitialis, C. urvillei, Cirsium arvense, C. pannonicum, C. pyrenaicum, C. vulgare, Cynara cardunculus, Jurinea cretacea, Onopordum*

bracteatum, O. illyricum, Psephellus marschallianus, and *Serratula coronata.* For *M. pseudornata*, Asteraceae, including *Carduus platypus, Carduncellus hispanicus, Centaurea jacea, Cirsium vulgare, C. pyrenaicum, C. acaulon, Onopordum acanthium,* and *O. illyricum.*

Diversity and systematics: *Melitaea ornata* systematics remains subject to debate. The nominate subspecies is believed not to occur in Europe, where only subspecies *telona* is found on certain Aegean islands, *ogygia* in the Balkans, *emipunica* in Italy, Sicily, and Provence, and *kovacsi* in Central Europe. The Iberian Knapweed Fritillary, initially considered a subspecies of the Eastern Knapweed Fritillary, was proposed as a separate species in 2022 based on molecular, phenological, and genital data.

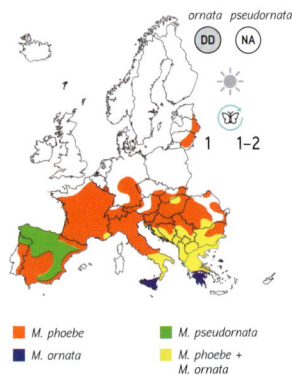

ornata   pseudornata

DD   NA

1   1–2

| ■ M. phoebe | ■ M. pseudornata |
| ■ M. ornata | ■ M. phoebe + M. ornata |

Did you know?

The caterpillars of the Eastern Knapweed Fritillary are distinguished from those of the Knapweed Fritillary by the reddish colour of their cephalic capsule when they are mature. They then resemble those of the Glanville Fritillary, but their prolegs are brownish rather than red.

IMAGOS		LARVAE	
Food	🌼 💧	Food	🌿
Behaviour of males		Caterpillar location	🌱
Dispersion		Chrysalis location	🌱

THE SATYRINES
(149 SPECIES)

TRIBES	GENERA	NUMBER OF SPECIES	MAIN LARVAL HOST-PLANT FAMILIES
Elymnini	*Kirinia, Lasiommata, Lopinga,* and *Pararge*	10	Poaceae, Cyperaceae, and Juncaceae
Coenonymphini	*Coenonympha*	16	Poaceae and Cyperaceae
Maniolini	*Aphantopus, Hyponephele, Maniola,* and *Pyronia*	13	Poaceae and Cyperaceae
Melanargini	*Melanargia*	8	Poaceae
Ypthimini	*Ypthima*	1	Poaceae
Erebini	*Erebia* and *Proterebia*	52	Poaceae, Cyperaceae, and Juncaceae
Satyrini	*Arethusana, Brintesia, Chazara, Hipparchia, Minois, Oeneis, Pseudochazara,* and *Satyrus*	49	Poaceae and Cyperaceae

Satyrines represent nearly half of Nymphalid diversity globally and two-thirds of Nymphalids in Europe. This subfamily primarily exploits monocotyledons, whose leaves are consumed by the caterpillars. Most species exhibit white-pupillated black spots on the forewing and/or hindwing, whose role might be to divert predators' attention to the less vulnerable parts of the animal. Many species display their underside only when at rest (Coenonymphini and Satyrini), providing effective camouflage on mineral substrates. Satyrines are found in a wide variety of open, semi-open, and forested environments in Mediterranean, temperate, and high-altitude regions, as well as in the Arctic. The significant diversification of the Erebini and Satyrini tribes is closely linked to climatic variations in Alpine, Iberian, and Balkan mountainous regions. Satyrine caterpillars are predominantly green or brown, with lighter stripes; they rely mainly on camouflage and nocturnal feeding to evade predators.

Aphantopus hyperantus

Coenonympha tullia

Erebia euryale

Hipparchia semele

Chazara briseis

Melanargia galathea

Pararge aegeria

Pyronia tithonus

SATYRINES

LATTICE BROWN *KIRINIA ROXELANA*

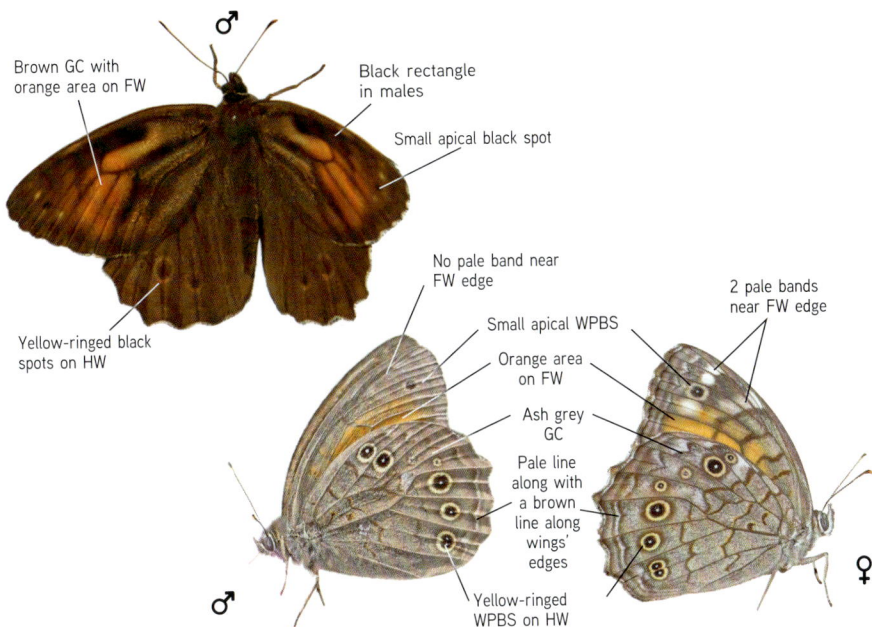

♂

Brown GC with orange area on FW

Black rectangle in males

Small apical black spot

Yellow-ringed black spots on HW

No pale band near FW edge

Small apical WPBS

2 pale bands near FW edge

Orange area on FW

Ash grey GC

Pale line along with a brown line along wings' edges

Yellow-ringed WPBS on HW

♂

♀

Wingspan: 58–62 mm

Habitat: Bushy and warm rocky slopes, clear woodlands, and olive groves.

Hibernating stage: Caterpillar.

Elevational range: Up to 1,800 m.

Egg-laying: Eggs are laid singly on the bark of trees or bushes.

Flight period: From April to September.

Host plants: Grasses, including *Anthoxanthum odoratum*, *Lolium perenne*, *Milium effusum*, *Briza* spp., *Bromus* spp., *Poa annua*, *P. pratensis*, *P. trivialis*, and *Alopecurus* spp.

Diversity and systematics: There are no notable subspecies.

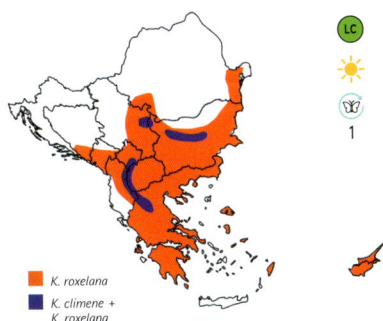

■ *K. roxelana*
■ *K. climene* + *K. roxelana*

LC

1

	IMAGOS			LARVAE	
Food			Food		
Behaviour of males			Caterpillar location		
Dispersion			Chrysalis location		

Did you know?

Lattice Browns prefer the shade of the forest canopy, especially in the early afternoon when it is very hot in their Mediterranean habitats.

LESSER LATTICE BROWN *KIRINIA CLIMENE*

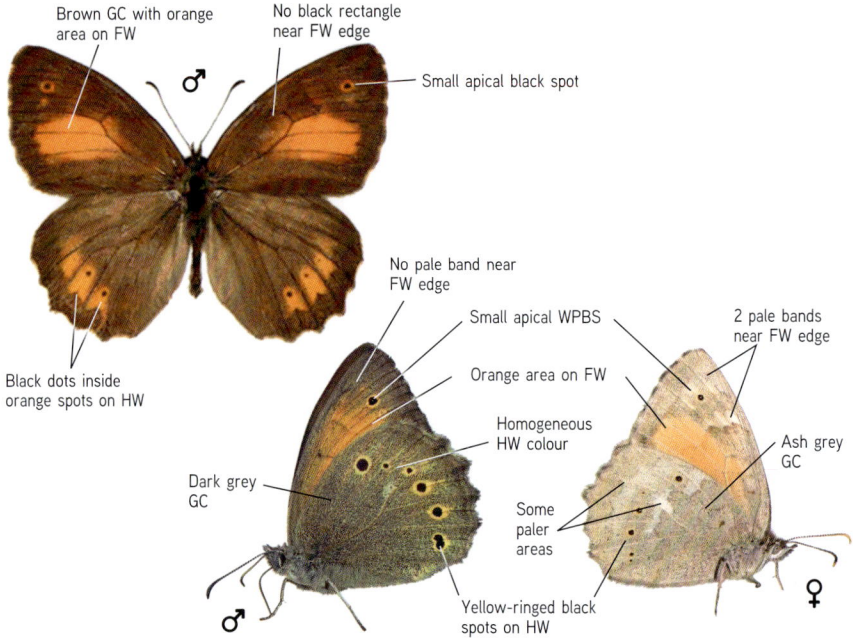

Brown GC with orange area on FW

No black rectangle near FW edge

♂

Small apical black spot

No pale band near FW edge

Small apical WPBS

2 pale bands near FW edge

Orange area on FW

Homogeneous HW colour

Ash grey GC

Black dots inside orange spots on HW

Dark grey GC

Some paler areas

♂

Yellow-ringed black spots on HW

♀

Wingspan: 46–48 mm

Habitat: Mesophilic clearings, grassy woodlands.

Hibernating stage: Caterpillar.

Elevational range: Up to 1,600 m.

Egg-laying: Eggs are dropped in vegetation.

Flight period: From June to August.

Host plants: Grasses, especially *Poa annua* and *P. nemoralis.*

Diversity and systematics: European populations belong to the nominate subspecies.

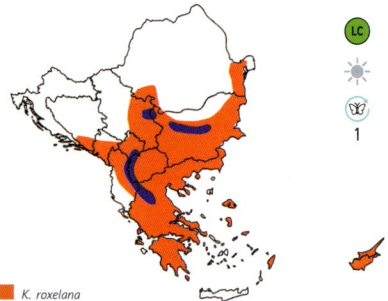

LC

1

■ *K. roxelana*
■ *K. climene + K. roxelana*

IMAGOS		LARVAE	
Food		Food	
Behaviour of males		Caterpillar location	
Dispersion		Chrysalis location	

Did you know?

Unlike the majority of butterfly eggs, those of the Lesser Lattice Brown lack adhesive secretions that would keep them attached to a substrate.

SATYRINAE

WALL BROWN *LASIOMMATA MEGERA*

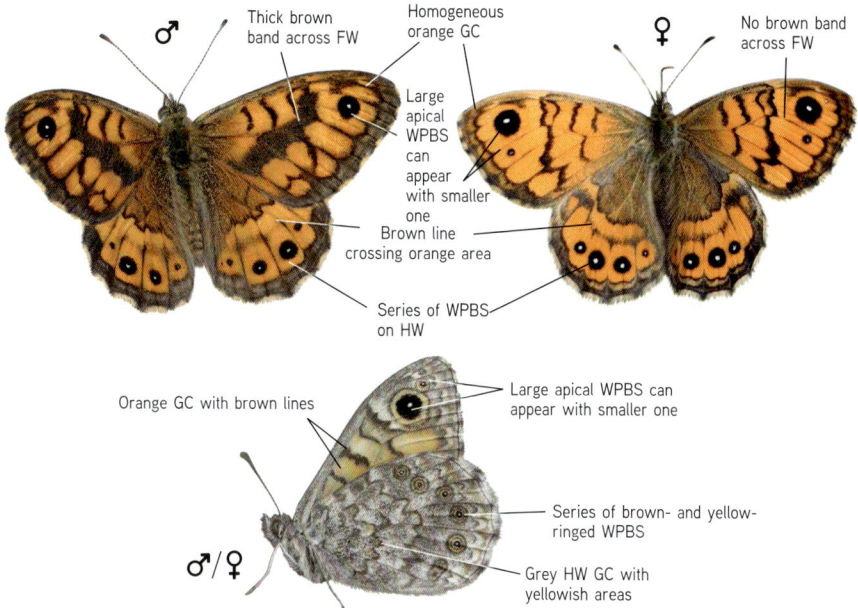

♂

Thick brown
band across FW

Homogeneous
orange GC

♀

No brown band
across FW

Large
apical
WPBS
can
appear
with smaller
one

Brown line
crossing orange area

Series of WPBS
on HW

Orange GC with brown lines

Large apical WPBS can
appear with smaller one

♂/♀

Series of brown- and yellow-
ringed WPBS

Grey HW GC with
yellowish areas

Wingspan: 38–47 mm

Habitat: Rocky and sunny grasslands, slopes, and ridges. Low-growing meadows and fallow lands with old walls.

Hibernating stage: Caterpillar.

Elevational range: Up to 1,500 m.

Egg-laying: Eggs are laid singly or in a few units on LHP leaves and stems.

Flight period: From February to November.

Host plants: A wide variety of grasses, including *Poa annua, P. pratensis, P. bulbosa, Festuca ovina, F. rubra, Lolium arundinaceum, L. perenne, Bromus erectus, B. sterilis, B. hordeaceus, Corynephorus canescens, Cynodon dactylon, Cynosurus cristatus, Dactylis glomerata, Danthonia decumbens, Elymus repens, Holcus lanatus, Brachypodium phoenicoides, B. pinnatum, B. retusum, B. sylvaticum, Oloptum miliaceum, Stipa pennata, Avenella flexuosa, Aegilops geniculata, Agrostis capillaris, A. gigantea,* and *A. stolonifera.*

Diversity and systematics: There are no notable subspecies for this species, which is widespread across the Palaearctic.

LC

2–3

■ *L. megera*
■ *L. paramegaera*

Did you know?

Males choose bare areas or rocks to monitor their territory. Thus the Wall Brown does not favour overly grassy areas and tolerates the fertilization of meadows and lawns very poorly.

IMAGOS			LARVAE		
Food			Food		
Behaviour of males			Caterpillar location		
Dispersion			Chrysalis location		

SATYRINAE

CORSICAN WALL BROWN *LASIOMMATA PARAMEGAERA*

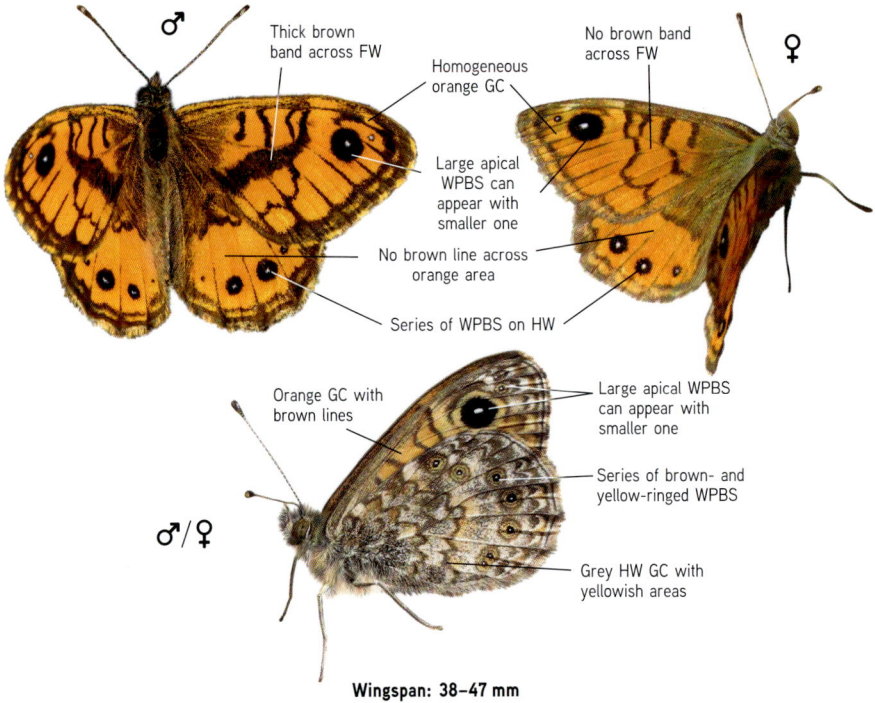

♂

Thick brown band across FW

Homogeneous orange GC

Large apical WPBS can appear with smaller one

No brown line across orange area

Series of WPBS on HW

No brown band across FW

♀

♂/♀

Orange GC with brown lines

Large apical WPBS can appear with smaller one

Series of brown- and yellow-ringed WPBS

Grey HW GC with yellowish areas

Wingspan: 38–47 mm

Habitat: Grasslands, garrigues, and sunny, rocky slopes with bare areas.
Hibernating stage: Caterpillar.
Elevational range: Up to 1,500 m.
Egg-laying: Eggs are laid singly on LHP leaves.
Flight period: From April to October.
Host plants: Grasses, including *Brachypodium retusum*, *B. ramosum*, *B. distachyon*, *Lolium arundinaceum*, and *Festuca* spp.
Diversity and systematics: There is a debate about the *Lasiommata* populations in the Balearic Islands. According to some authors, they belong to *L. megera*, while others suggest they are related to *L. paramegaera*, thus forming the *intermedia* subspecies.

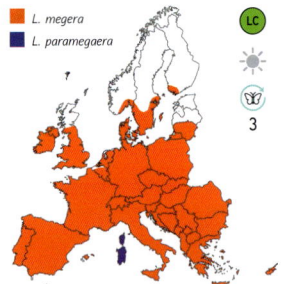

■ *L. megera*
■ *L. paramegaera*

LC

3

IMAGOS		LARVAE	
Food		Food	
Behaviour of males		Caterpillar location	
Dispersion		Chrysalis location	

Did you know?

Formerly considered a subspecies of *Lasiommata megera*, scientists now agree that *L. paramegaera* is separated based on its distinct genitalia.

LARGE WALL BROWN *LASIOMMATA MAERA*

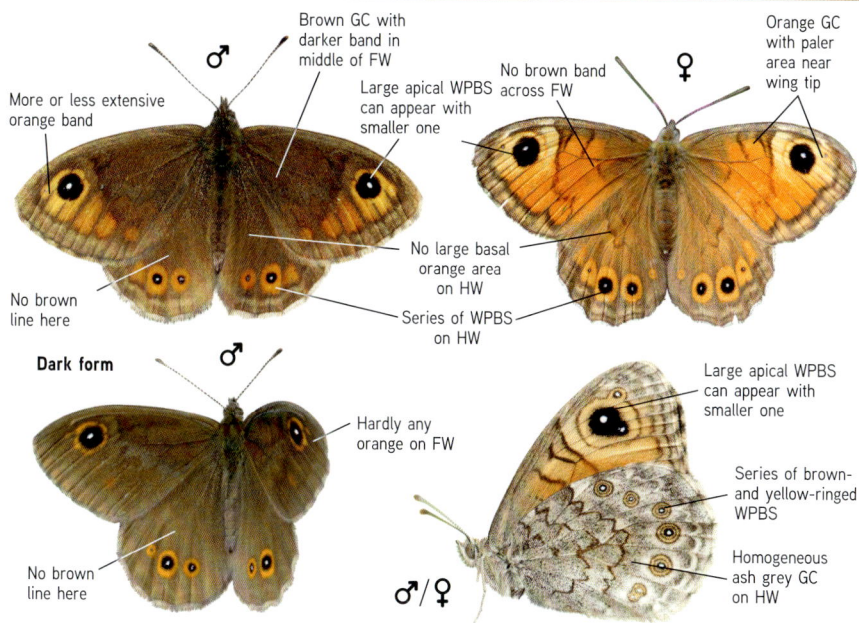

♂

More or less extensive orange band

Brown GC with darker band in middle of FW

Large apical WPBS can appear with smaller one

No brown band across FW

♀

Orange GC with paler area near wing tip

No large basal orange area on HW

No brown line here

Series of WPBS on HW

Dark form ♂

Hardly any orange on FW

No brown line here

♂/♀

Large apical WPBS can appear with smaller one

Series of brown- and yellow-ringed WPBS

Homogeneous ash grey GC on HW

Wingspan: 40–51 mm

Habitat: Flower-rich meadows and grasslands, rocky slopes, sunny forest edges, fallow lands, parks, and gardens with old walls.

Hibernating stage: Caterpillar.

Elevational range: Up to 2,500 m.

Egg-laying: Eggs are laid singly on LHP leaves and stems.

Flight period: From May to October.

Host plants: Numerous grasses, including *Brachypodium phoenicoides, B. pinnatum, Calamagrostis arundinacea, C. epigejos, C. varia, Elymus repens, Festuca ovina, F. rubra, Helictochloa pratensis, Holcus* spp., *Hordelymus europaeus, Hordeum marinum, H. murinum, Poa annua, P. bulbosa, P. pratensis, Nardus stricta, Bromus erectus, B. sterilis, Phleum pratense,* and *Melica* spp. Also reported on *Luzula luzuloides* (Juncaceae).

Diversity and systematics: Most European populations belong to the nominate subspecies. Subspecies *adrasta* inhabits Southern Europe. Subspecies *nevadensis* is endemic to the Sierra Nevada. Subspecies *herdonia* flies in the Alps, and subspecies *sicula* is described from Sicily.

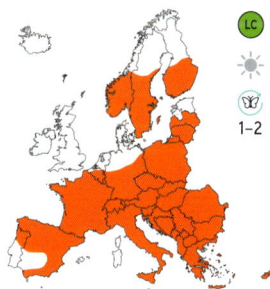

LC

1–2

Did you know?

The genus name *Lasiommata* comes from the Greek *lasios*, meaning "hairy", and *ommatos*, meaning "eye". *Lasiommata* species indeed have hairs on their compound eyes.

IMAGOS		LARVAE	
Food		Food	
Behaviour of males		Caterpillar location	
Dispersion		Chrysalis location	

SATYRINAE

NORTHERN WALL BROWN *LASIOMMATA PETROPOLITANA*

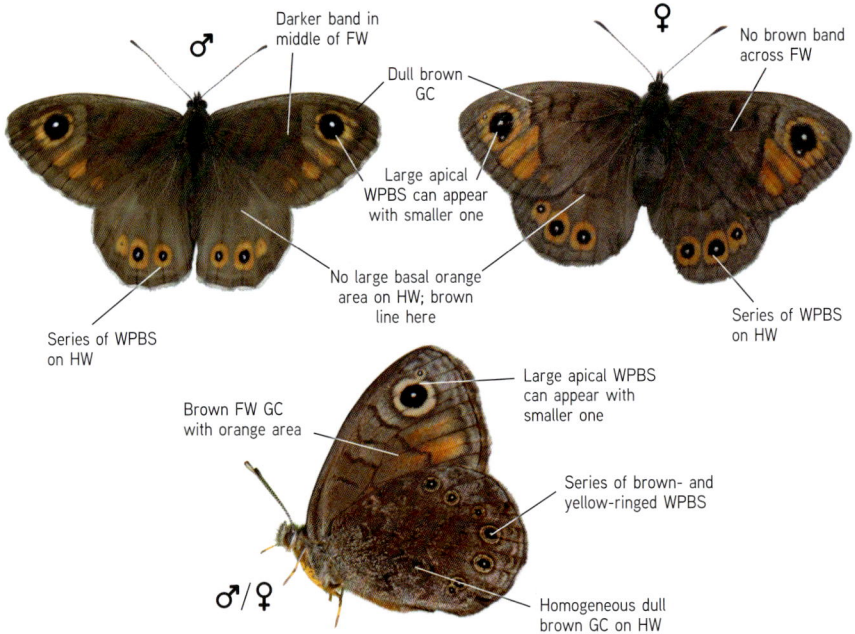

♂ — Darker band in middle of FW

Dull brown GC

♀ — No brown band across FW

Large apical WPBS can appear with smaller one

No large basal orange area on HW; brown line here

Series of WPBS on HW

Series of WPBS on HW

Brown FW GC with orange area

Large apical WPBS can appear with smaller one

Series of brown- and yellow-ringed WPBS

♂/♀

Homogeneous dull brown GC on HW

Wingspan: 33–41 mm

Habitat: Forest clearings and edges, clear woodlands.

Hibernating stage: Caterpillar or pupa.

Elevational range: Between 500 and 2,300 m.

Egg-laying: Eggs are laid singly on LHP leaves.

Flight period: From April to August.

Host plants: Grasses, including *Festuca ovina*, *F. rubra*, *Calamagrostis epigejos*, *Lolium arundinaceum*, *Melica nutans*, and *Dactylis glomerata*.

Diversity and systematics: The nominate subspecies forms Northern European populations. Subspecies *calidia* flies in the Alps and the Central Pyrenees. Subspecies *gabriellae* is described from the Ariege Pyrenees.

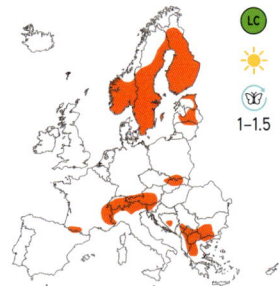

LC

1–1.5

IMAGOS		LARVAE	
Food		Food	
Behaviour of males		Caterpillar location	
Dispersion		Chrysalis location	

Did you know?

The scientific name *petropolitana* refers to the city of Saint Petersburg, where the specimen used for the description of the species originated.

436

CANARY SPECKLED WOOD   *PARARGE XIPHIOIDES*

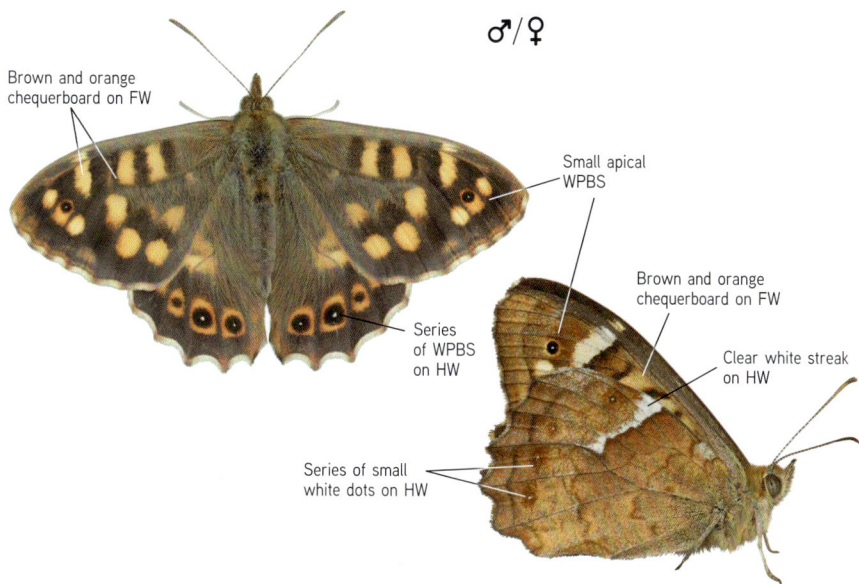

♂/♀

Brown and orange chequerboard on FW

Small apical WPBS

Brown and orange chequerboard on FW

Series of WPBS on HW

Clear white streak on HW

Series of small white dots on HW

Wingspan: 36–38 mm

Habitat: Forest edges, clear woodlands, bushy areas, parks, and gardens.

Hibernating stage: Egg, caterpillar, pupa, or adult.

Elevational range: Up to 2,000 m.

Egg-laying: Eggs are laid singly or in a few units on LHP leaves.

Flight period: Year-round.

Host plants: Grasses, including *Brachypodium sylvaticum*, *B. pinnatum*, *B. arbusculum*, *Dactylis glomerata*, *Agrostis capillaris*, and *Oryzopsis miliacea*. Sedges, like *Carex divulsa*. *Luzula forsteri* (Juncaceae).

Diversity and systematics: There are no notable subspecies for this species, which is endemic to the Canary Islands.

■ *P. aegeria*
■ *P. xiphioides*
■ *P. xiphia* + *P. aegeria*

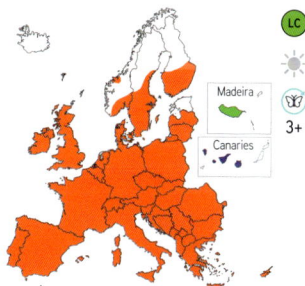

Madeira
Canaries

LC

3+

Did you know?

The Canary Speckled Wood is the only species of the *Pararge* genus present in the Canary Islands; therefore, there is no risk of confusion. It diverged from the Speckled Wood, its sister species, approximately 3 million years ago.

IMAGOS		LARVAE	
Food	✿ 🐛 ◊	Food	🍃
Behaviour of males		Caterpillar location	
Dispersion: unknown		Chrysalis location	

SPECKLED WOOD *PARARGE AEGERIA*

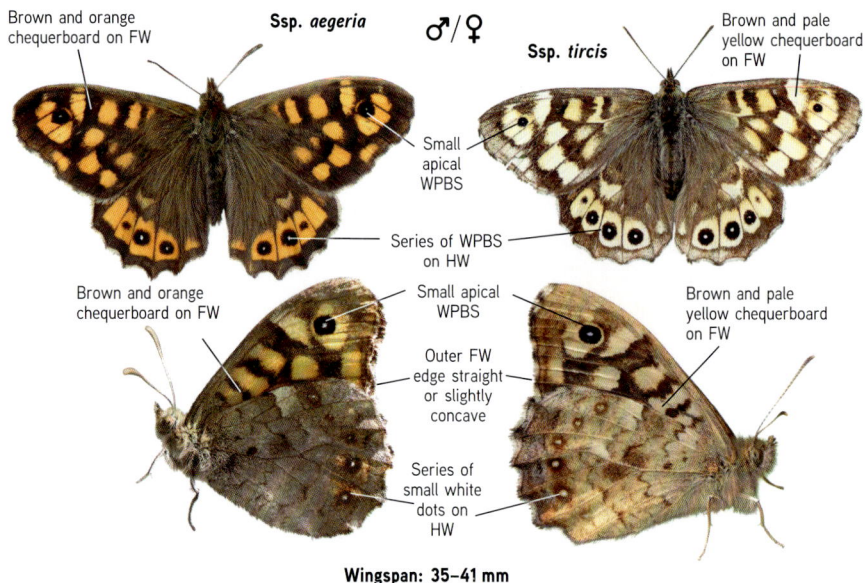

Brown and orange chequerboard on FW

Ssp. *aegeria*

♂/♀

Ssp. *tircis*

Brown and pale yellow chequerboard on FW

Small apical WPBS

Series of WPBS on HW

Brown and orange chequerboard on FW

Small apical WPBS

Outer FW edge straight or slightly concave

Series of small white dots on HW

Brown and pale yellow chequerboard on FW

Wingspan: 35–41 mm

Habitat: Forest paths, clear woodlands, sunny edges, hedgerows, parks, and gardens with trees and bushes.

Hibernating stage: Caterpillar or pupa.

Elevational range: Up to 2,000 m.

Egg-laying: Eggs are laid singly or in a few units on LHP leaves.

Flight period: From March to October in temperate regions; almost year-round in the Mediterranean area.

Host plants: Many grasses, including *Agrostis gigantea*, *A. stolonifera*, *Arrhenatherum elatius*, *Avena sterilis*, *Brachypodium pinnatum*, *B. sylvaticum*, *Calamagrostis arundinacea*, *C. epigejos*, *Cynodon dactylon*, *Dactylis glomerata*, *Deschampsia cespitosa*, *Elymus caninus*, *E. repens*, *Festuca* spp., *Glyceria notata*, *Holcus lanatus*, *Lolium giganteum*, *Melica nutans*, *M. uniflora*, *Milium effusum*, *Molinia caerulea*, *Oloptum miliaceum*, *Poa annua*, *P. bulbosa*, *P. nemoralis*, *P. pratensis*, and *P. trivialis*. Also on sedges, like *Carex sylvatica*.

Diversity and systematics: Populations in the southern half of Europe belong to the nominate subspecies, while those in the northern half belong to subspecies *tircis*.

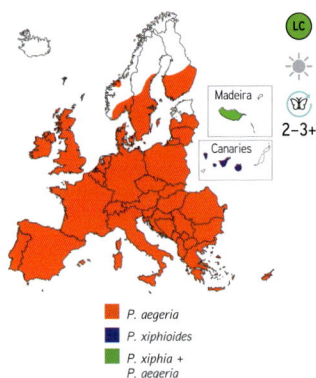

LC

Madeira

Canaries

2–3+

■ *P. aegeria*
■ *P. xiphioides*
■ *P. xiphia +*
P. aegeria

IMAGOS		LARVAE	
Food		Food	
Behaviour of males		Caterpillar location	
Dispersion		Chrysalis location	

Did you know?

Males claim sunny patches in the undergrowth, from which they watch for the passage of females. The larger the sunny patch, the more dominant the males.

SATYRINAE

MADEIRAN SPECKLED WOOD *PARARGE XIPHIA*

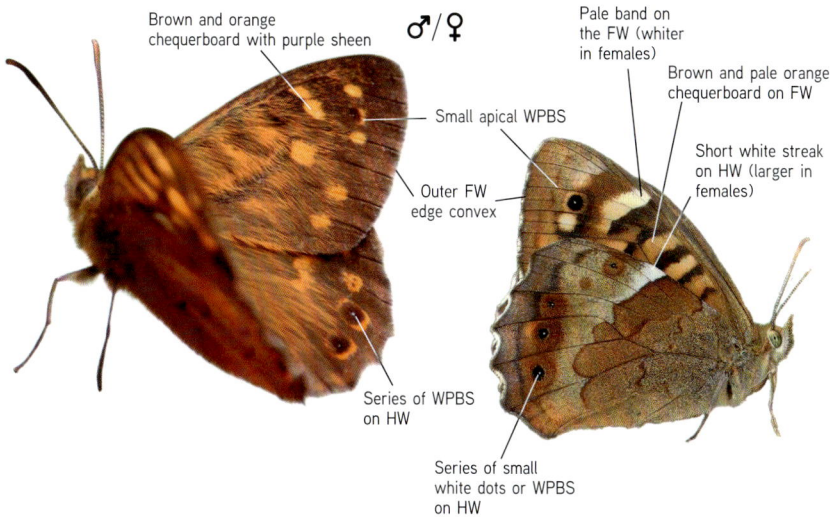

Brown and orange chequerboard with purple sheen

♂/♀

Pale band on the FW (whiter in females)

Brown and pale orange chequerboard on FW

Small apical WPBS

Short white streak on HW (larger in females)

Outer FW edge convex

Series of WPBS on HW

Series of small white dots or WPBS on HW

Wingspan: 44–47 mm

Habitat: Forest edges and clearings, especially in laurel forests.

Hibernating stage: Egg, caterpillar, pupa, or adult.

Elevational range: Up to 1,000 m.

Egg-laying: Eggs are laid singly or in a few units on LHP leaves.

Flight period: Year-round.

Host plants: Grasses, like *Brachypodium sylvaticum*, *Holcus lanatus*, *Poa trivialis*, and *Festuca donax*.

Diversity and systematics: This species, endemic to Madeira, has no notable subspecies.

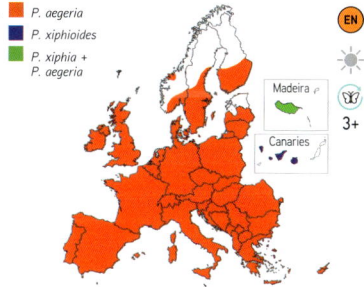

- ■ *P. aegeria*
- ■ *P. xiphioides*
- ■ *P. xiphia + P. aegeria*

EN

3+

Madeira

Canaries

Did you know?

The Madeiran Speckled Wood coexists with the Speckled Wood, which has been introduced to Madeira. The exotic species tolerates anthropogenic disturbances such as agricultural intensification, urbanization, and forest management better than its endemic cousin, which is threatened with extinction.

IMAGOS			LARVAE		
Food			Food		
Behaviour of males			Caterpillar location		
Dispersion: unknown			Chrysalis location		

SATYRINAE

GATEKEEPER *PYRONIA TITHONUS*

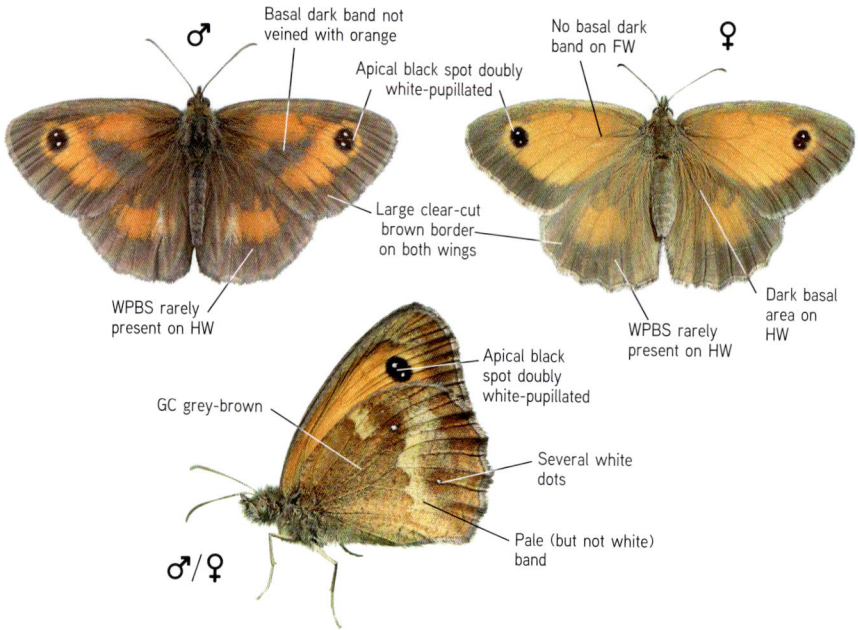

♂

Basal dark band not veined with orange

Apical black spot doubly white-pupillated

Large clear-cut brown border on both wings

WPBS rarely present on HW

♀

No basal dark band on FW

Dark basal area on HW

WPBS rarely present on HW

GC grey-brown

Apical black spot doubly white-pupillated

Several white dots

Pale (but not white) band

♂/♀

Wingspan: 34–38 mm

Habitat: Bocage, bushy grasslands, meadows and edges, wastelands, parks, and gardens.

Hibernating stage: Caterpillar.

Elevational range: Up to 2,300 m (mainly below 1,000 m).

Egg-laying: Eggs are laid singly on LHP leaves and stems.

Flight period: From May to September.

Host plants: Numerous grasses, including *Dactylis glomerata*, *Brachypodium phoenicoides*, *B. pinnatum*, *Bromus erectus*, *Cynosurus cristatus*, *Deschampsia cespitosa*, *Festuca ovina*, *F. rubra*, *Poa annua*, *P. compressa*, *P. nemoralis*, *P. pratensis*, *P. trivialis*, *Lolium giganteum*, *L. perenne*, *L. pratense*, *Avenella flexuosa*, *Agrostis canina*, *A. capillaris*, *A. vinealis*, *Alopecurus pratensis*, *Elymus repens*, and *Calamagrostis* spp. Also on *Carex caryophyllea* (Cyperaceae).

Diversity and systematics: Most European populations belong to the nominate subspecies, with numerous forms described. Subspecies *decolorata* is described from Andalusia.

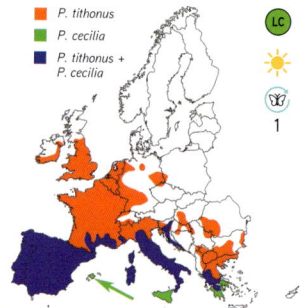

■ P. tithonus
■ P. cecilia
■ P. tithonus + P. cecilia

LC

1

Did you know?

Adults can gather in large numbers on mint, thistle, and oregano inflorescences; the nectar is so addictive to them that observation is very easy.

IMAGOS		LARVAE	
Food	🌸	Food	🍃
Behaviour of males		Caterpillar location	
Dispersion		Chrysalis location	

SOUTHERN GATEKEEPER *PYRONIA CECILIA*

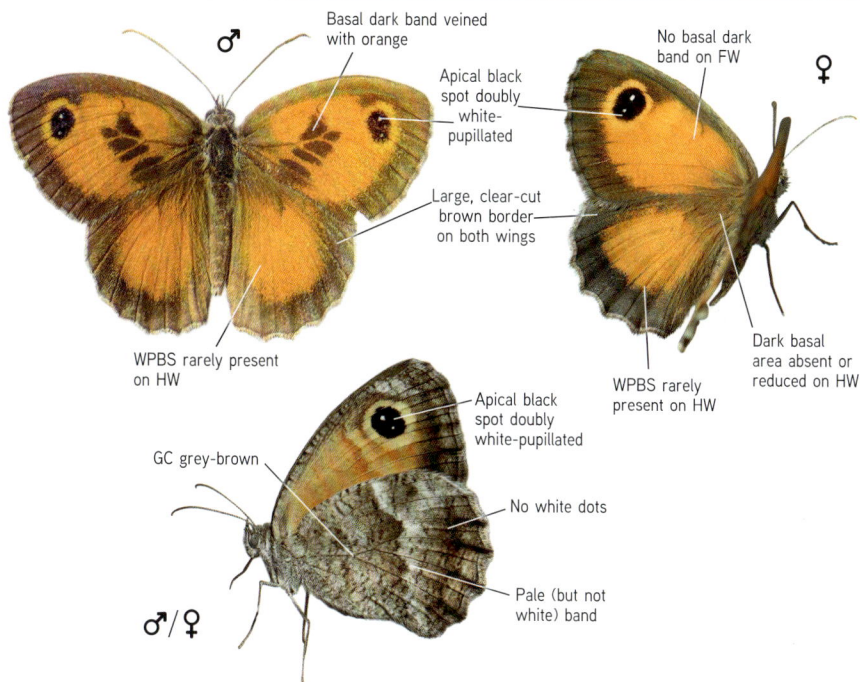

♂ Basal dark band veined with orange

Apical black spot doubly white-pupillated

No basal dark band on FW ♀

Large, clear-cut brown border on both wings

WPBS rarely present on HW

Dark basal area absent or reduced on HW

WPBS rarely present on HW

Apical black spot doubly white-pupillated

GC grey-brown

No white dots

Pale (but not white) band

♂/♀

Wingspan: 30–32 mm

Habitat: Mediterranean grasslands, wastelands, and clearings.

Hibernating stage: Caterpillar.

Elevational range: Up to 2,300 m (mainly below 1,000 m).

Egg-laying: Eggs are laid singly or in a few units on LHP leaves and stems.

Flight period: From June to August.

Host plants: Grasses, including *Brachypodium retusum*, *B. pinnatum*, *B. phoenicoides*, *B. sylvaticum*, *Poa annua*, *P. nemoralis*, *Festuca ovina*, *Dactylis glomerata*, and *Agrostis capillaris*.

Diversity and systematics: There are no notable subspecies.

■ P. tithonus
■ P. cecilia
■ P. tithonus + P. cecilia

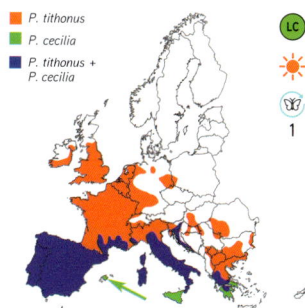

Did you know?

Like Gatekeepers, Southern Gatekeepers are usually found in groups within their favourable habitats.

IMAGOS		LARVAE	
Food		Food	
Behaviour of males		Caterpillar location	
Dispersion		Chrysalis location	

SATYRINAE

SPANISH GATEKEEPER *PYRONIA BATHSEBA*

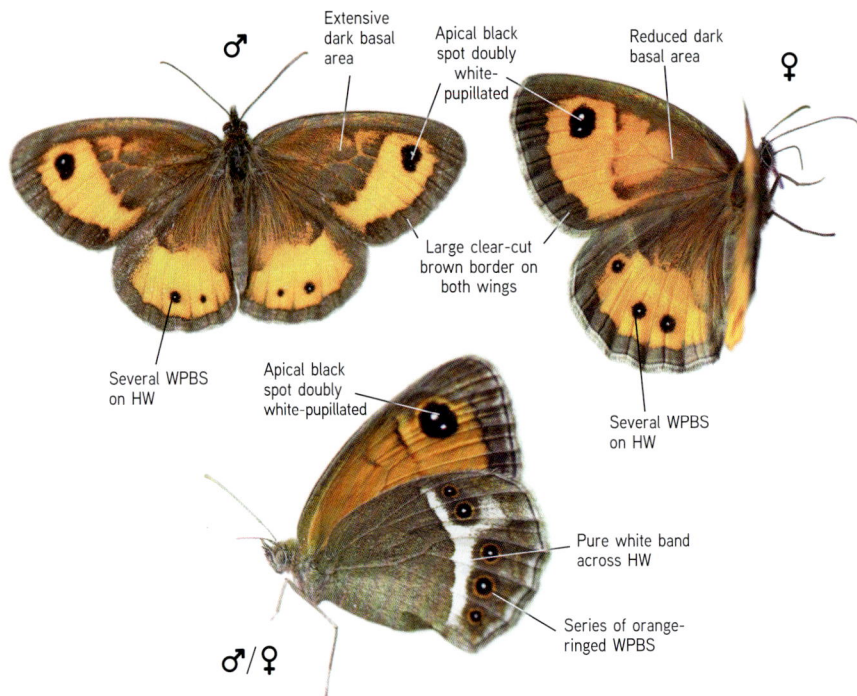

♂

Extensive dark basal area

Apical black spot doubly white-pupillated

Reduced dark basal area

♀

Large clear-cut brown border on both wings

Several WPBS on HW

Apical black spot doubly white-pupillated

Several WPBS on HW

Pure white band across HW

Series of orange-ringed WPBS

♂/♀

Wingspan: 36–38 mm

Habitat: Dry, bushy grasslands and Mediterranean wastelands.

Hibernating stage: Caterpillar.

Elevational range: Up to 1,700 m (mainly below 1,000 m).

Egg-laying: Eggs are laid singly on LHP leaves and stems.

Flight period: From April to August.

Host plants: Poaceae, including *Brachypodium retusum*, *B. phoenicoides*, and *Poa trivialis*.

Diversity and systematics: There are no notable subspecies.

LC

1

IMAGOS		LARVAE	
Food	✿	Food	🌿
Behaviour of males		Caterpillar location	
Dispersion		Chrysalis location	

Did you know?

The Spanish Gatekeeper is particularly sensitive to Mediterranean fires when frequent and are man-made.

ORIENTAL MEADOW BROWN   *HYPONEPHELE LUPINA*

♂/♀

1 apical WPBS (2nd one, often masked, in females)

Orange GC with grey-brown border

Mottled grey GC with ill-defined paler band

Markedly festooned HW edge

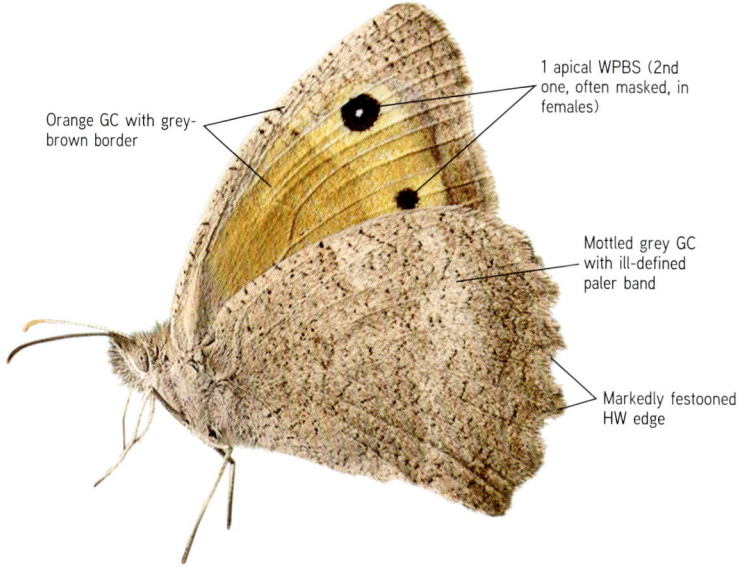

Wingspan: 42–48 mm

Habitat: Dry, bushy, stony grasslands.

Hibernating stage: Caterpillar.

Elevational range: Up to 2,000 m.

Egg-laying: Eggs are laid singly on dry plants or underneath stones.

Flight period: From May to October.

Host plants: Grasses, including *Achnatherum parviflorum, Aegilops geniculata, Bromus erectus, Stipa offneri, S. pennata, Festuca ovina, F. rubra,* and *Poa annua.*

Diversity and systematics: Most European populations belong to the nominate subspecies. Subspecies *mauritanica* flies in southern Spain. Subspecies *rhamnusia* is described from Sicily, while *cypriaca* is endemic to Cyprus.

IMAGOS		LARVAE	
Food	🌼 🐚 💧	Food	🍃
Behaviour of males		Caterpillar location	
Dispersion		Chrysalis location	

Did you know?

The scientific name *lupina*, which refers to the wolf, was probably adopted because of the grey colour of the underside, the only side that the Oriental Meadow Brown spontaneously displays.

SATYRINAE

DUSKY MEADOW BROWN *HYPONEPHELE LYCAON*

♂/♀

Orange GC with grey-brown border

1 apical WPBS (2nd one, often masked, in females)

Mottled grey GC with ill-defined paler band usually more visible than in Oriental Meadow Brown

Slightly festooned HW edge

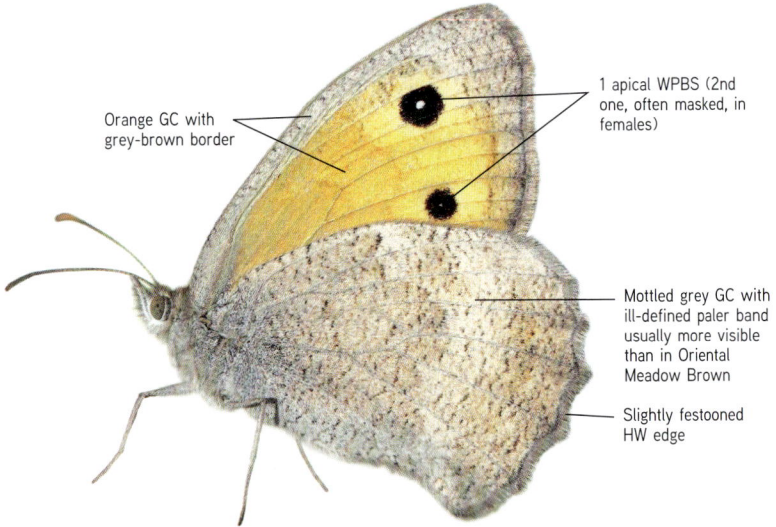

Wingspan: 34–42 mm

Habitat: Dry and warm, stony or sandy, sparsely vegetated grasslands and clearings.

Hibernating stage: Caterpillar.

Elevational range: Up to 2,000 m.

Egg-laying: Eggs are laid singly on dry plants.

Flight period: From May to September.

Host plants: Grasses, including *Brachypodium pinnatum*, *Bromus erectus*, *Festuca ovina*, *F. rubra*, and *Stipa pennata*.

Diversity and systematics: The nominate subspecies flies in Eastern and Central Europe. Subspecies *anacausta* inhabits Italy and Sicily. Subspecies *microphthalma* is found in the Iberian Peninsula. Subspecies *nikokles* flies in the Alps.

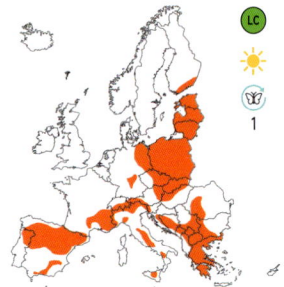

LC

1

IMAGOS			LARVAE	
Food			Food	
Behaviour of males			Caterpillar location	
Dispersion			Chrysalis location	

Did you know?

The Dusky Meadow Brown is declining, mainly due to the loss of dry grasslands as farmlands are abandoned.

SATYRINAE

MEADOW BROWN *MANIOLA JURTINA*

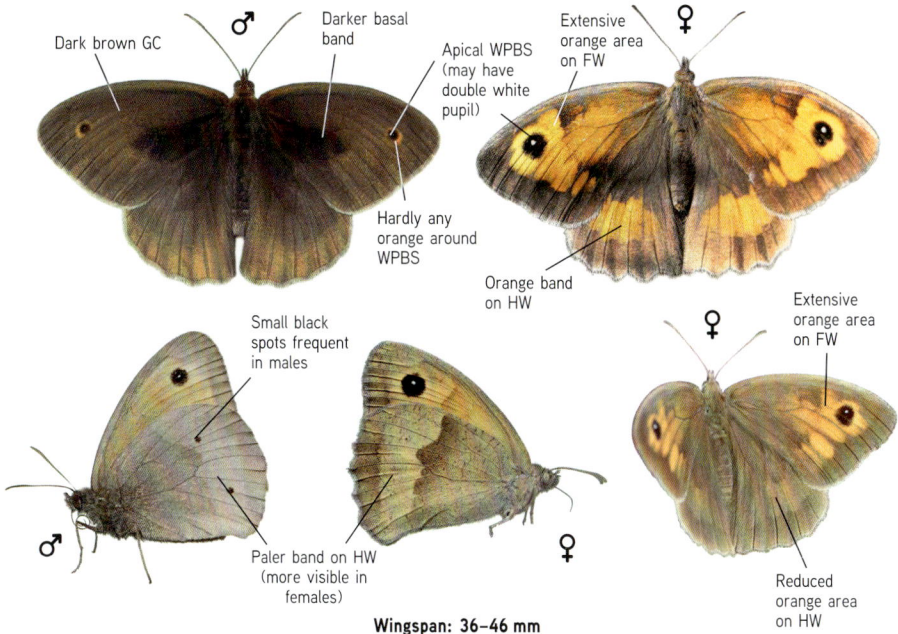

♂ Dark brown GC

Darker basal band

Apical WPBS (may have double white pupil)

Extensive orange area on FW ♀

Hardly any orange around WPBS

Orange band on HW

Small black spots frequent in males

♀ Extensive orange area on FW

♂ Paler band on HW (more visible in females)

♀ Reduced orange area on HW

Wingspan: 36–46 mm

Habitat: Meadows, clearings, roadsides, wastelands, parks, and gardens.

Hibernating stage: Caterpillar.

Elevational range: Up to 2,000 m.

Egg-laying: Eggs are laid singly on LHP leaves or nearby.

Flight period: From April to October.

Host plants: Numerous grasses, including *Agrostis capillaris*, *A. canina*, *A. stolonifera*, *Alopecurus pratensis*, *Anthoxanthum odoratum*, *Avenula pubescens*, *Brachypodium phoenicoides*, *B. pinnatum*, *B. sylvaticum*, *Cynosurus cristatus*, *Elymus repens*, *Festuca ovina*, *F. rubra*, *Dactylis glomerata*, *Danthonia decumbens*, *Lolium perenne*, *L. arundinaceum*, *L. pratense*, *Poa annua*, *P. pratensis*, *P. trivialis*, and *Bromus erectus*. Sedges, like *Carex pilulifera*.

Diversity and systematics: The nominate subspecies populates the Canary Islands and Sicily. Subspecies *janira* forms most European populations. Subspecies *hispulla* flies in southwestern Europe. Subspecies *phormia* is present in Italy and the Balkans. Subspecies *iernes* flies in Ireland.

■ M. jurtina
■ M. jurtina + M. nurag
■ M. cypricola

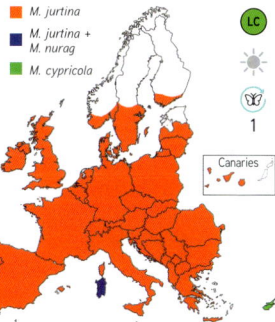

Canaries

Did you know?

Females sometimes simply drop their eggs into vegetation. The fact that the caterpillars eat so many different grasses ensures that they can easily find a suitable host plant.

IMAGOS			LARVAE	
Food			Food	
Behaviour of males			Caterpillar location	
Dispersion			Chrysalis location	

SATYRINAE

SARDINIAN MEADOW BROWN *MANIOLA NURAG*

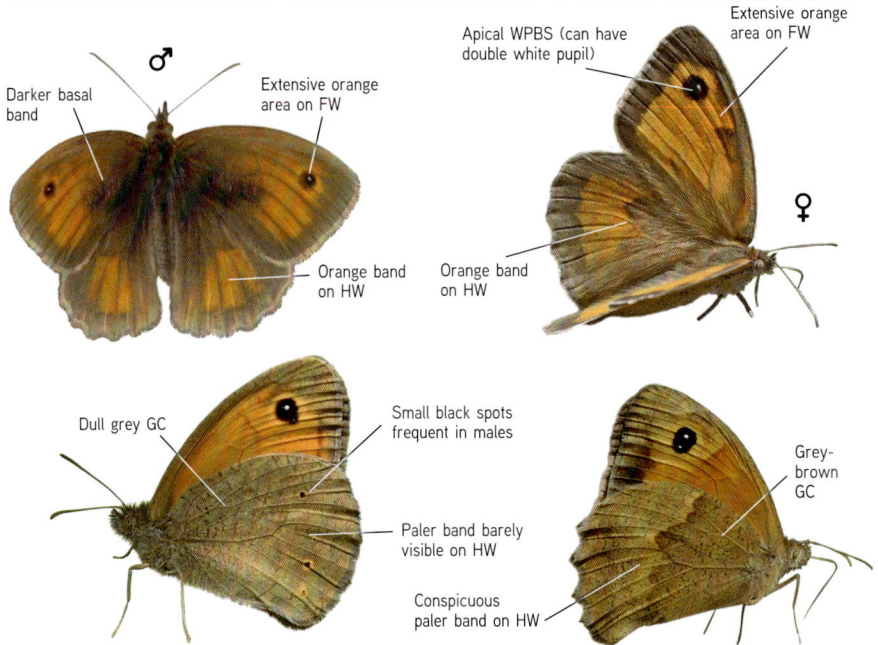

♂

Darker basal band

Extensive orange area on FW

Orange band on HW

Extensive orange area on FW

Apical WPBS (can have double white pupil)

Orange band on HW

♀

Dull grey GC

Small black spots frequent in males

Paler band barely visible on HW

Conspicuous paler band on HW

Grey-brown GC

Wingspan: 36–40 mm

Habitat: Flower-rich, rocky grasslands and bushy slopes.

Hibernating stage: Caterpillar.

Elevational range: Between 500 and 1,500 m.

Egg-laying: Eggs are laid singly on LHP leaves.

Flight period: From May to August.

Host plants: Grasses, including *Festuca morisiana*.

Diversity and systematics: This Sardinian endemic has no notable subspecies.

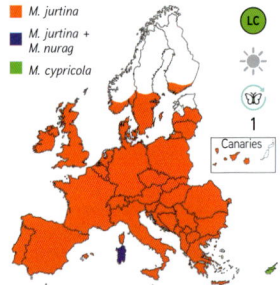

■ M. jurtina
■ M. jurtina + M. nurag
■ M. cypricola

LC

1

Canaries

IMAGOS		LARVAE	
Food	🌸	Food	🍃
Behaviour of males		Caterpillar location	
Dispersion		Chrysalis location	

Did you know?

The Meadow Brown and the Sardinian Meadow Brown are both present in Sardinia. The former is confined to lower altitudes, while the latter is more commonly found in montane areas.

CYPRUS MEADOW BROWN *MANIOLA CYPRICOLA*

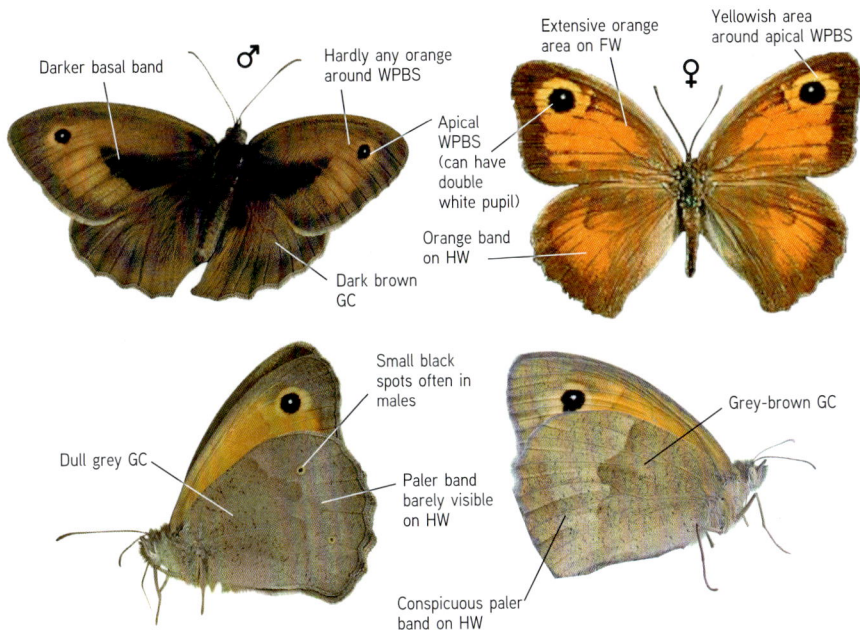

Darker basal band

♂

Hardly any orange around WPBS

Apical WPBS (can have double white pupil)

Orange band on HW

Dark brown GC

Extensive orange area on FW

Yellowish area around apical WPBS

♀

Small black spots often in males

Dull grey GC

Paler band barely visible on HW

Grey-brown GC

Conspicuous paler band on HW

Wingspan: 35–46 mm

Habitat: Grassy, open habitats and clear woodlands.

Hibernating stage: Caterpillar.

Elevational range: Up to 2,000 m.

Egg-laying: Eggs are laid singly on LHP leaves or on nearby vegetation.

Flight period: From April to July.

Host plants: Grasses.

Diversity and systematics: There are no notable subspecies.

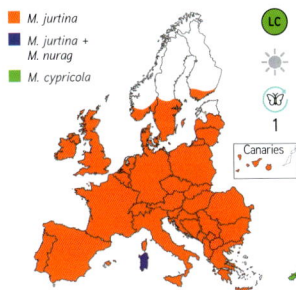

■ M. jurtina
■ M. jurtina + M. nurag
■ M. cypricola

LC

Canaries

1

IMAGOS		LARVAE		
Food		Food		
Behaviour of males		Caterpillar location		
Dispersion		Chrysalis location		

Did you know?

Some authors consider the Cyprus Meadow Brown a subspecies of the Aegean Meadow Brown. It is the only one that flies on Cyprus.

SATYRINAE

AEGEAN MEADOW BROWN *MANIOLA TELMESSIA*

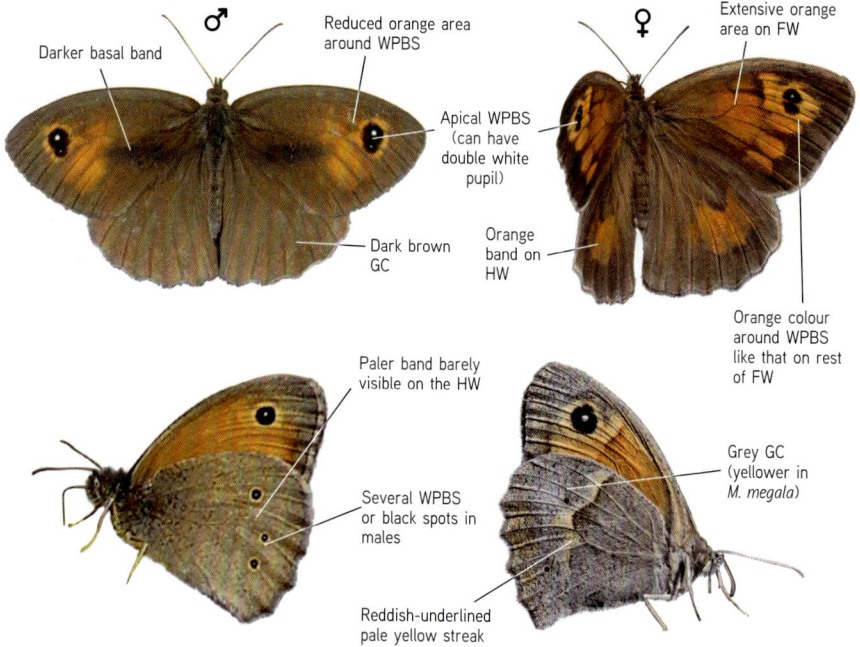

♂

Darker basal band

Reduced orange area around WPBS

Apical WPBS (can have double white pupil)

Dark brown GC

♀

Extensive orange area on FW

Orange band on HW

Orange colour around WPBS like that on rest of FW

Paler band barely visible on the HW

Several WPBS or black spots in males

Reddish-underlined pale yellow streak

Grey GC (yellower in *M. megala*)

Wingspan: 35–46 mm

Habitat: Dry grasslands, garrigues, and clear woodlands.

Hibernating stage: Caterpillar.

Elevational range: Up to 1,000 m.

Egg-laying: Eggs are laid singly on LHP leaves or dropped in vegetation.

Flight period: From May to October.

Host plants: Grasses, including *Brachypodium phoenicoides*, *B. retusum*, *B. sylvaticum*, and *Poa trivialis*.

Diversity and systematics: European populations belong to the nominate subspecies.

- ■ *M. halicarnassus*
- ■ *M. telmessia*
- ■ *M. chia*
- ■ *M. megala* + *M. telmessia*
- ■ *M. jurtina*

LC

1

IMAGOS		LARVAE	
Food		Food	
Behaviour of males		Caterpillar location	
Dispersion		Chrysalis location	

Did you know?

Adults spend the summer in more wooded areas in order to escape the typical seasonal drought.

SATYRINAE

TURKISH MEADOW BROWN/THOMSON'S MEADOW BROWN
MANIOLA MEGALA/MANIOLA HALICARNASSUS

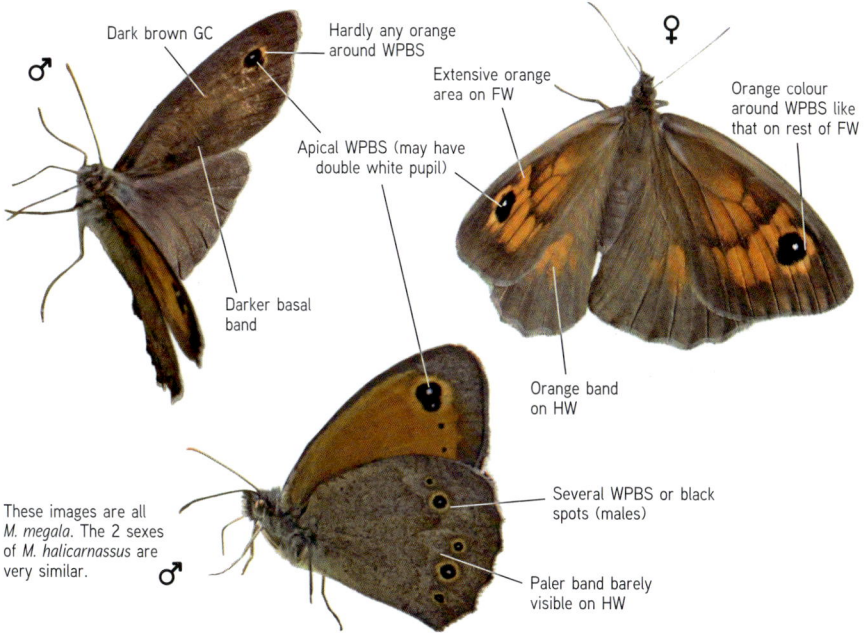

♂

Dark brown GC

Hardly any orange around WPBS

♀

Extensive orange area on FW

Apical WPBS (may have double white pupil)

Orange colour around WPBS like that on rest of FW

Darker basal band

Orange band on HW

These images are all *M. megala*. The 2 sexes of *M. halicarnassus* are very similar. ♂

Several WPBS or black spots (males)

Paler band barely visible on HW

Wingspan: 36–47 mm

Habitat: Grassy and flower-rich open habitats, edges, clear woodlands.

Hibernating stage: Caterpillar.

Elevational range: Up to 500 m for *Maniola halicarnassus*; 1,000 m for *M. megala*.

Egg-laying: Eggs are laid singly on LHP leaves.

Flight period: From May to September.

Host plants: Grasses.

Diversity and systematics: There are no notable subspecies for *Maniola megala* and *M. halicarnassus*.

- M. halicarnassus
- M. telmessia
- M. chia
- M. megala + M. telmessia
- M. jurtina

megala   halicarnassus
NT   LC

1

Did you know?

The Turkish Meadow Brown flies alongside the Aegean Meadow Brown on the island of Lesbos. Distinguishing between them is challenging without examining the genitalia. Thomson's Meadow Brown is present in Europe only on the island of Nissiros, where it is the only meadow brown.

IMAGOS		LARVAE	
Food		Food	
Behaviour of males		Caterpillar location	
Dispersion		Chrysalis location	

CHIOS MEADOW BROWN *MANIOLA CHIA*

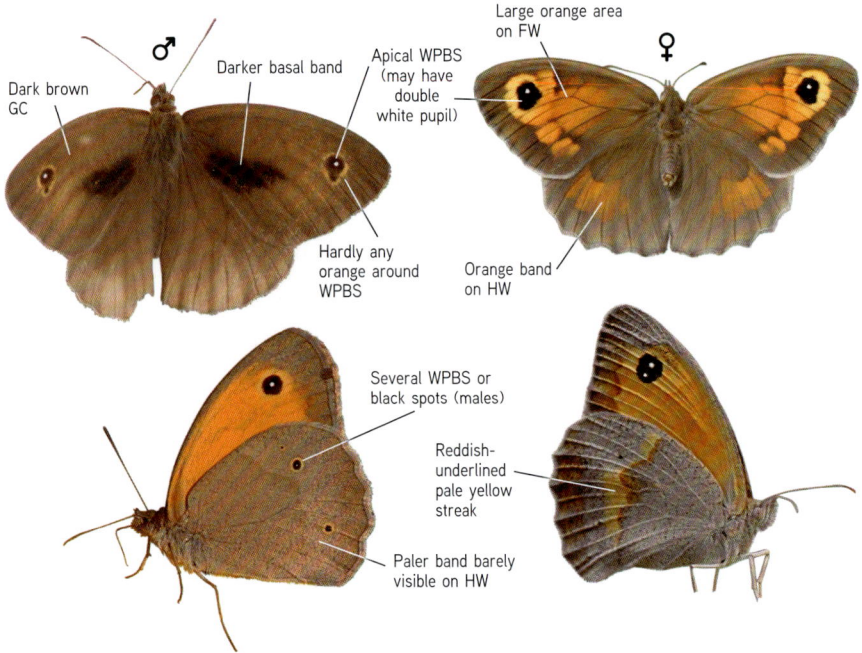

♂
Dark brown GC
Darker basal band
Apical WPBS (may have double white pupil)
Hardly any orange around WPBS

♀
Large orange area on FW
Orange band on HW

Several WPBS or black spots (males)
Reddish-underlined pale yellow streak
Paler band barely visible on HW

Wingspan: 36–46 mm

Habitat: Grassy open and semi-open habitats, including anthropized areas.

Hibernating stage: Caterpillar.

Elevational range: Up to 500 m.

Egg-laying: Eggs are laid singly on LHP leaves.

Flight period: From May to September.

Host plants: Grasses.

Diversity and systematics: There are no notable subspecies.

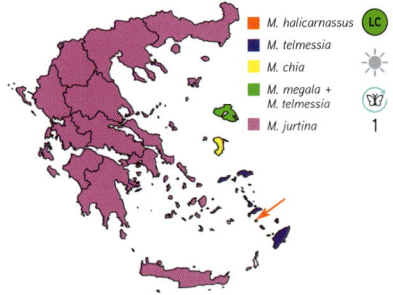

M. halicarnassus LC
M. telmessia
M. chia
M. megala + M. telmessia
M. jurtina
1

IMAGOS	LARVAE
Food	Food
Behaviour of males	Caterpillar location
Dispersion	Chrysalis location

Did you know?

The Chios Meadow Brown is sometimes considered a subspecies of the Meadow Brown. It is the only meadow brown species on the islands of Chios and Inousses, where it is thus easily identified.

SATYRINAE

SCARCE HEATH *COENONYMPHA HERO*

♂ / ♀

Small apical
WPBS

Rufous
brown GC

FW and HW
bordered by orange
line and silvery line

Small white
streak

Series of orange-
ringed WPBS

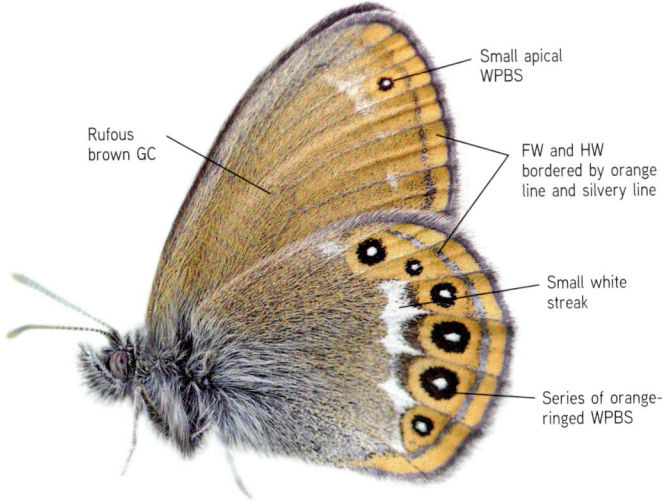

Wingspan: 28–32 mm

Habitat: Damp meadows and bushy heaths, especially in the vicinity of peat bogs.

Hibernating stage: Caterpillar.

Elevational range: Up to 1,000 m.

Egg-laying: Eggs are laid singly on LHP leaves.

Flight period: From May to July.

Host plants: Sedges, such as *Carex brizoides* and *C. remota*. Grasses, including *Calamagrostis epigejos*, *Deschampsia cespitosa*, *Elymus caninus*, *Hordelymus europaeus*, *Leymus arenarius*, *Molinia caerulea*, and *Poa annua*.

Diversity and systematics: European populations of this widely distributed Eurasian heath belong to the nominate subspecies.

Did you know?

The Scarce Heath is rapidly declining in Europe, especially in the western part of its range, where it faces habitat loss. The colonization of these habitats by the Pearly Heath can lead to hybridization between the two species, which poses an additional threat to the Scarce Heath.

IMAGOS		LARVAE	
Food	🌼	Food	🍃
Behaviour of males	🦋	Caterpillar location	🌿
Dispersion		Chrysalis location	🌿

SATYRINAE

SMALL HEATH   *COENONYMPHA PAMPHILUS*

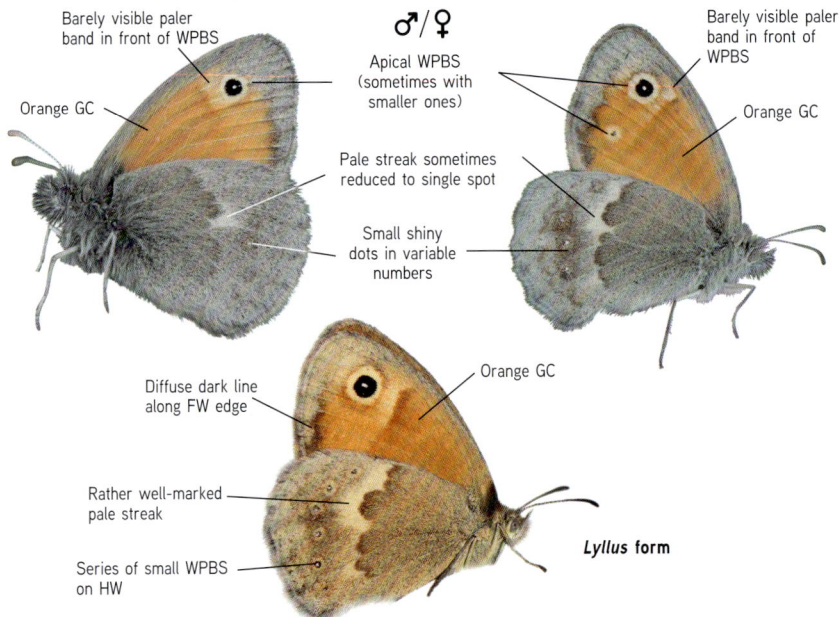

♂/♀

Barely visible paler band in front of WPBS

Orange GC

Apical WPBS (sometimes with smaller ones)

Pale streak sometimes reduced to single spot

Small shiny dots in variable numbers

Barely visible paler band in front of WPBS

Orange GC

Diffuse dark line along FW edge

Orange GC

Rather well-marked pale streak

Series of small WPBS on HW

Lyllus form

Wingspan: 22–33 mm

Habitat: Grasslands and meadows, including parks and gardens (tolerates anthropized habitats rather well).

Hibernating stage: Caterpillar.

Elevational range: Up to 2,500 m.

Egg-laying: Eggs are laid singly or in rows of a few units on LHP leaves.

Flight period: From March to November.

Host plants: Numerous grasses, including *Poa annua, P. nemoralis, P. pratensis, Brachypodium pinnatum, B. phoenicoides, Festuca ovina,*

F. rubra, Corynephorus canescens, Agrostis capillaris, A. stolonifera, A. vinealis, and *Anthoxanthum odoratum. Carex leporina* (Cyperaceae).

Diversity and systematics: Most European populations belong to the nominate subspecies. Several island subspecies are described (*e.g., sicula* in Sicily, *rhoumensis* for the Isle of Rùm in Scotland). The status of the taxon *lyllus* is debated: most authors say it is a simple form or a southern subspecies, while a few others consider it a separate species.

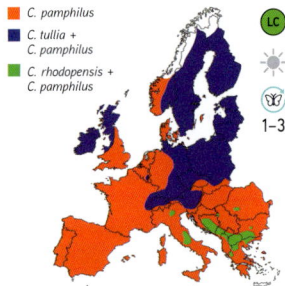

- C. pamphilus
- C. tullia + C. pamphilus
- C. rhodopensis + C. pamphilus

LC

1–3

Did you know?

Males form leks on the ground, occupying positions not far from each other within a few tens of square meters. They await the passage of females and regularly engage in short aerial skirmishes.

IMAGOS		LARVAE	
Food		Food	
Behaviour of males		Caterpillar location	
Dispersion		Chrysalis location	

SATYRINAE

LARGE HEATH   *COENONYMPHA TULLIA*

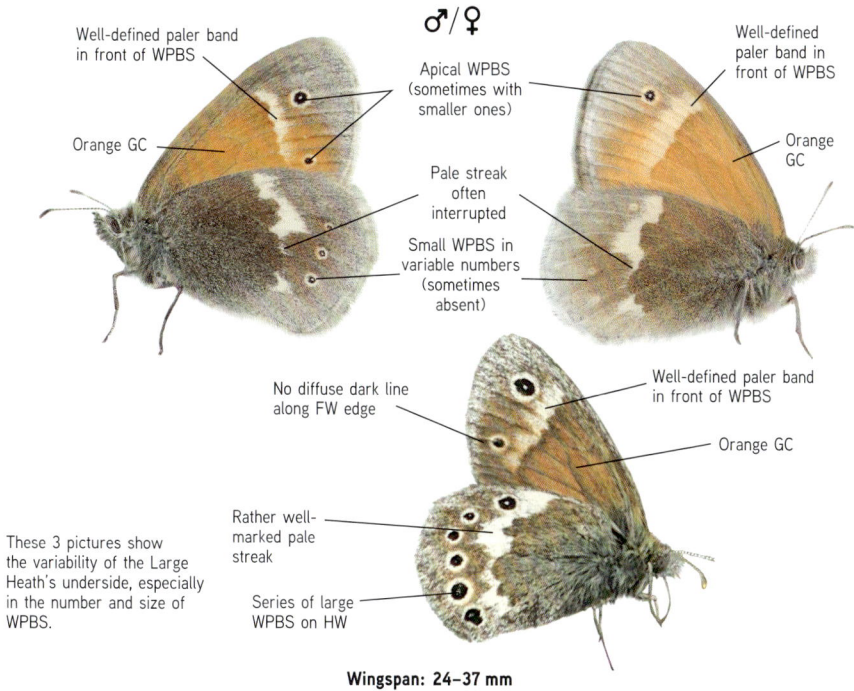

♂/♀

Well-defined paler band in front of WPBS

Orange GC

Apical WPBS (sometimes with smaller ones)

Pale streak often interrupted

Small WPBS in variable numbers (sometimes absent)

Well-defined paler band in front of WPBS

Orange GC

No diffuse dark line along FW edge

Well-defined paler band in front of WPBS

Orange GC

Rather well-marked pale streak

Series of large WPBS on HW

These 3 pictures show the variability of the Large Heath's underside, especially in the number and size of WPBS.

Wingspan: 24–37 mm

Habitat: Damp meadows and heaths, peat bog surroundings.

Hibernating stage: Caterpillar.

Elevational range: Up to 1,200 m.

Egg-laying: Eggs are laid singly on LHP leaves and stems or nearby.

Flight period: From June to August.

Host plants: Sedges, like *Eriophorum vaginatum*, *Carex canescens*, *C. diandra*, *C. rostrata*, *C. limosa*, and *Rhynchospora alba*. Grasses, such as *Molinia caerulea*, *Sesleria caerulea*, *Nardus stricta*, *Danthonia decumbens*, and *Deschampsia flexuosa*. *Juncus articulatus* (Juncaceae).

Diversity and systematics: Most European populations belong to subspecies *davus*. Subspecies *scotica* flies in northern Scotland, while subspecies *polydama* is present in the rest of the United Kingdom, except for the northwest. Subspecies *demophile* inhabits the extreme north of Europe.

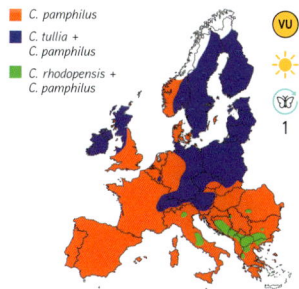

■ *C. pamphilus*
■ *C. tullia* + *C. pamphilus*
■ *C. rhodopensis* + *C. pamphilus*

VU

1

Did you know?

The Large Heath is declining rapidly in the western part of its range due to the loss of the wetland habitats it breeds in.

IMAGOS		LARVAE	
Food	✿	Food	🍃
Behaviour of males	🦋	Caterpillar location	🌿
Dispersion	🦋	Chrysalis location	🌿

SATYRINAE

EASTERN LARGE HEATH *COENONYMPHA RHODOPENSIS*

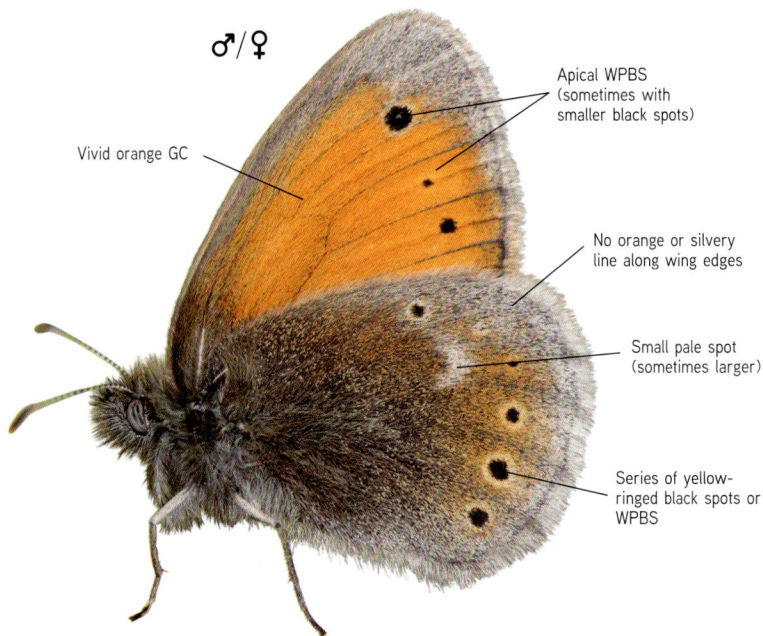

♂/♀

Apical WPBS
(sometimes with
smaller black spots)

Vivid orange GC

No orange or silvery
line along wing edges

Small pale spot
(sometimes larger)

Series of yellow-
ringed black spots or
WPBS

Wingspan: 32–34 mm

Habitat: Montane and subalpine meadows and grasslands, damp clearings.

Hibernating stage: Caterpillar.

Elevational range: Between 1,000 and 2,500 m.

Egg-laying: Eggs are laid singly on LHP leaves and stems.

Flight period: From June to August.

Host plants: Grasses, including *Festuca* spp. and *Sesleria albicans*. Sedges, like *Rhynchospora* spp., *Eriophorum* spp., and *Carex* spp.

Diversity and systematics: There are no notable subspecies for this heath, which is endemic to southeastern Europe.

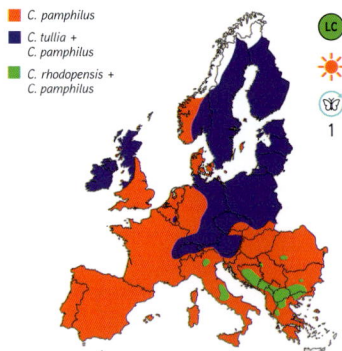

■ *C. pamphilus*
■ *C. tullia* + *C. pamphilus*
■ *C. rhodopensis* + *C. pamphilus*

IMAGOS		LARVAE	
Food	✿	Food	🍃
Behaviour of males	🌼 🦋	Caterpillar location	🌿
Dispersion	🦋	Chrysalis location	🌿

Did you know?

The Eastern Large Heath was once considered a subspecies of the Large Heath.

454

SATYRINAE

CHESTNUT HEATH *COENONYMPHA GLYCERION*

Ssp. *glycerion*

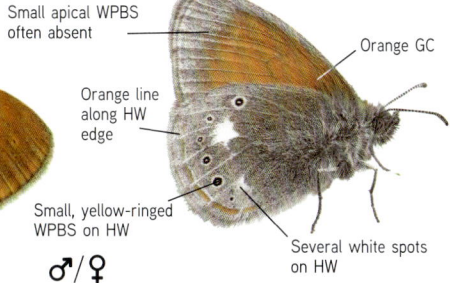

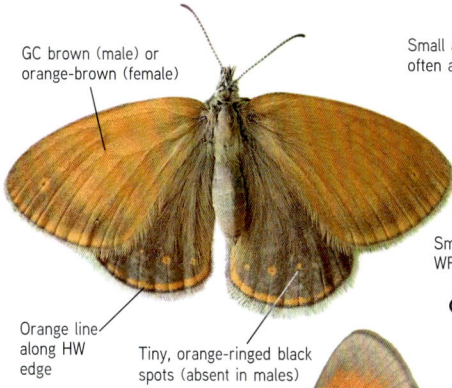

GC brown (male) or orange-brown (female)

Small apical WPBS often absent

Orange GC

Orange line along HW edge

Orange line along HW edge

Small, yellow-ringed WPBS on HW

Several white spots on HW

♂/♀

Tiny, orange-ringed black spots (absent in males)

Ssp. *bertolis*

Series of large, yellow-ringed WPBS on HW

White streak

No WPBS on HW

Faint orange line

Thick orange line along HW edge

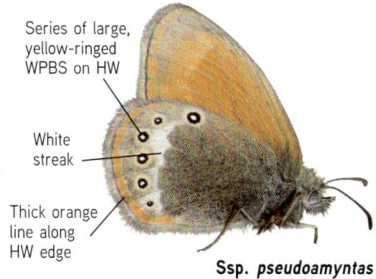

Ssp. *pseudoamyntas*

Wingspan: 25–31 mm

Habitat: Mesophilic and damp meadows, grasslands, grassy forest clearings and edges.

Hibernating stage: Caterpillar.

Elevational range: Up to 2,500 m.

Egg-laying: Eggs are laid singly or in a few units on LHP leaves.

Flight period: From June to August.

Host plants: Numerous grasses, including *Festuca ovina*, *F. rubra*, *Melica ciliata*, *Brachypodium pinnatum*, *B. sylvaticum*, *Bromus erectus*, *Briza media*, *Cynosurus cristatus*, *Deschampsia* spp., *Phleum pratense*, *Poa trivialis*, and *Molinia caerulea*.

Diversity and systematics: The nominate subspecies forms most European populations. Subspecies *bertolis* flies at high elevations in the Alps. Subspecies *pseudoamyntas* inhabits the Eastern Pyrenees and could originate from hybridization between *Coenonympha glycerion* and *C. iphioides*.

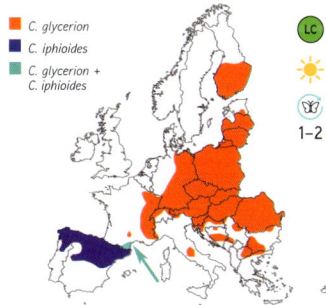

■ *C. glycerion*
■ *C. iphioides*
■ *C. glycerion* + *C. iphioides*

LC

1–2

Did you know?

The Chestnut Heath is typically associated with extensive agriculture that preserves the meadows and grasslands it needs to breed. As a result, it is declining outside the mountainous parts of its range.

IMAGOS		LARVAE	
Food		Food	
Behaviour of males		Caterpillar location	
Dispersion		Chrysalis location	

SATYRINAE

SPANISH HEATH *COENONYMPHA IPHIOIDES*

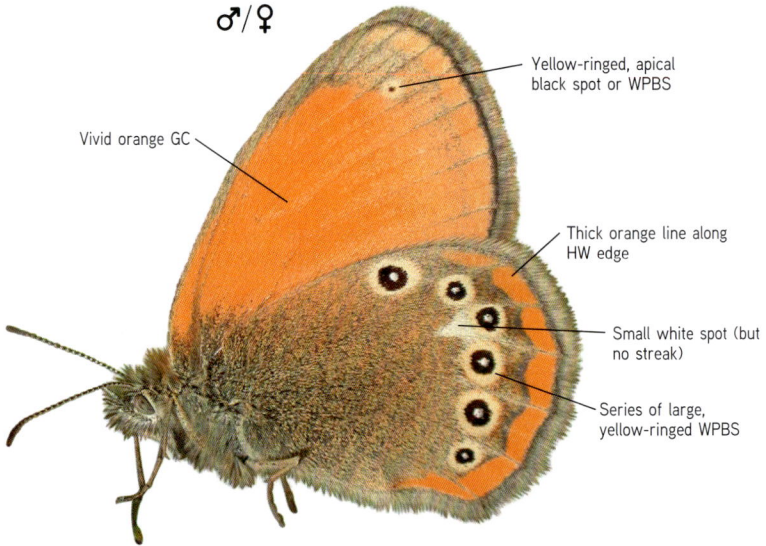

♂/♀

Yellow-ringed, apical black spot or WPBS

Vivid orange GC

Thick orange line along HW edge

Small white spot (but no streak)

Series of large, yellow-ringed WPBS

Wingspan: 25–34 mm

Habitat: Grasslands and grassy wastelands.

Hibernating stage: Caterpillar.

Elevational range: Between 500 and 1,500 m.

Egg-laying: Eggs are laid singly on LHP leaves and stems.

Flight period: From June to August.

Host plants: Grasses, including *Bromus erectus*, *Briza media*, *Cynosaurus cristatus*, and *Brachypodium* spp.

Diversity and systematics: Subspecies *escudensis* flies in the Spanish province of Santander. Subspecies *pearsoni* is found in the province of Cuenca.

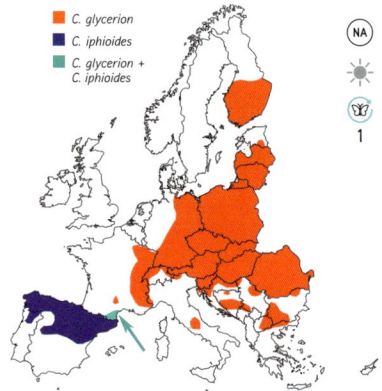

■ C. glycerion
■ C. iphioides
■ C. glycerion + C. iphioides

NA

1

IMAGOS		LARVAE	
Food	✿	Food	🍃
Behaviour of males	🦋	Caterpillar location	🌿
Dispersion	🦋	Chrysalis location	🌿

Did you know?

The status of the Spanish Heath is controversial: it is still often considered a subspecies of the Chestnut Heath, although phylogenetic studies have shown that it is not its sister species, which argues in favour of species status.

SATYRINAE

DUSKY HEATH   *COENONYMPHA DORUS*

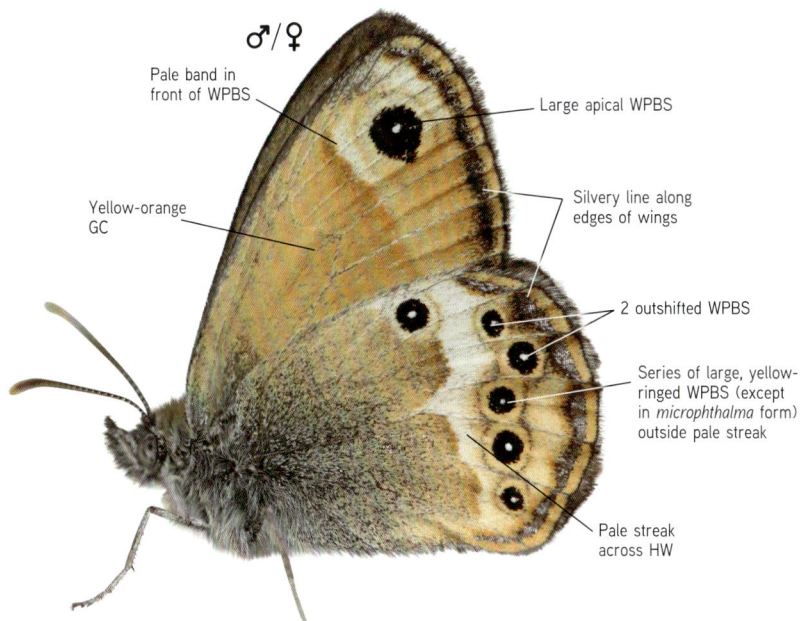

♂/♀

- Pale band in front of WPBS
- Large apical WPBS
- Yellow-orange GC
- Silvery line along edges of wings
- 2 outshifted WPBS
- Series of large, yellow-ringed WPBS (except in *microphthalma* form) outside pale streak
- Pale streak across HW

Wingspan: 28–34 mm

Habitat: Bushy, dry grasslands, stony slopes, and garrigues.

Hibernating stage: Caterpillar.

Elevational range: Up to 1,700 m.

Egg-laying: Eggs are laid singly on LHP leaves and stems.

Flight period: From June to August.

Host plants: Grasses, including *Festuca ovina*, *Brachypodium pinnatum*, *B. retusum*, *Agrostis canina*, *Aegilops geniculata*, *Poa nemoralis*, and *Stipa offneri*. *Carex halleriana* (Cyperaceae).

Diversity and systematics: Most populations belong to the nominate subspecies. Subspecies *bieli* flies in the western Iberian Peninsula, while subspecies *andalusica* is found in the Sierra d'Alfacar.

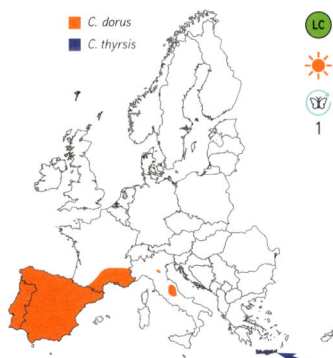

■ *C. dorus*
■ *C. thyrsis*

LC

1

Did you know?

The Dusky Heath is often discovered by chance because it takes off at one's feet. Adults rarely fly and often perch on the ground among stones.

IMAGOS			LARVAE		
Food			Food		
Behaviour of males			Caterpillar location		
Dispersion			Chrysalis location		

457

SATYRINAE

CRETAN SMALL HEATH   *COENONYMPHA THYRSIS*

♂/♀

Pale band in front of WPBS

Yellow-orange GC

Large apical WPBS

Silvery line along edges of wings

Dark marginal area

Series of large, yellow-ringed WPBS outside pale streak

Pale streak across HW

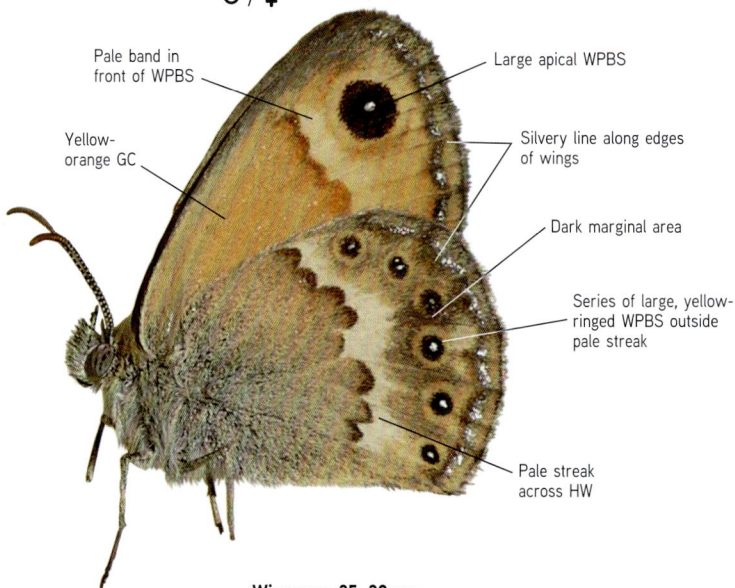

Wingspan: 25–39 mm

Habitat: Grassy, stony, open, and semi-open habitats.

Hibernating stage: Caterpillar.

Elevational range: Up to 2,000 m.

Egg-laying: Eggs are laid singly on LHP leaves and stems.

Flight period: From April to October.

Host plants: Grasses, including *Poa* spp.

Diversity and systematics: There are no notable subspecies for this species that is endemic to Crete.

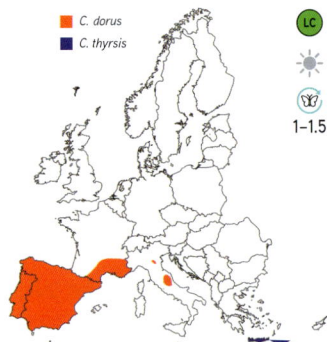

■ *C. dorus*
■ *C. thyrsis*

LC

1–1.5

Did you know?

The behaviour of the Cretan Small Heath is similar to that of the Dusky Heath. It spends a lot of time on the ground or on rocks. Adults enjoy the nectar of Lamiaceae.

IMAGOS			LARVAE	
Food	🌸		Food	🍃
Behaviour of males	🌱	🦋	Caterpillar location	🌿
Dispersion	🦋		Chrysalis location	🌿

SATYRINAE

CORSICAN HEATH *COENONYMPHA CORINNA*

♂/♀

Apical WPBS usually present

Silvery line along FW and HW edges

Variable number of WPBS on HW

White streak across HW

Wingspan: 28–30 mm

Habitat: Dry grasslands, warm bushy areas, and clear woodlands.

Hibernating stage: Caterpillar.

Elevational range: Up to 2,000 m.

Egg-laying: Eggs are laid singly on LHP leaves and stems.

Flight period: From May to September.

Host plants: Grasses, including *Brachypodium ramosum, B. retusum, Festuca morisiana,* and *Deschampsia cespitosa.* Carex distachya (Cyperaceae).

Diversity and systematics: Populations from Elba and Tuscany form the *elbana* subspecies, which is considered a distinct species by some authors.

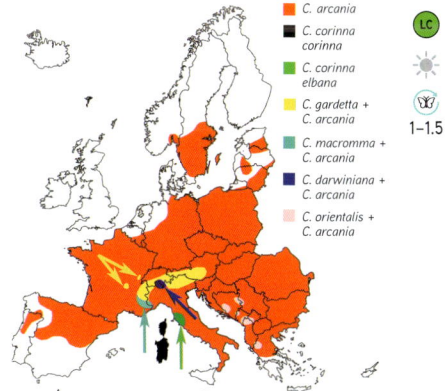

C. arcania
C. corinna corinna
C. corinna elbana
C. gardetta + C. arcania
C. macromma + C. arcania
C. darwiniana + C. arcania
C. orientalis + C. arcania

LC

1–1.5

IMAGOS		LARVAE	
Food		Food	
Behaviour of males		Caterpillar location	
Dispersion		Chrysalis location	

Did you know?

In Corsica, Corsican Heaths have fewer white-pupillated black spots on the hindwing when they live at higher altitudes.

SATYRINAE

PEARLY HEATH *COENONYMPHA ARCANIA*

♂/♀

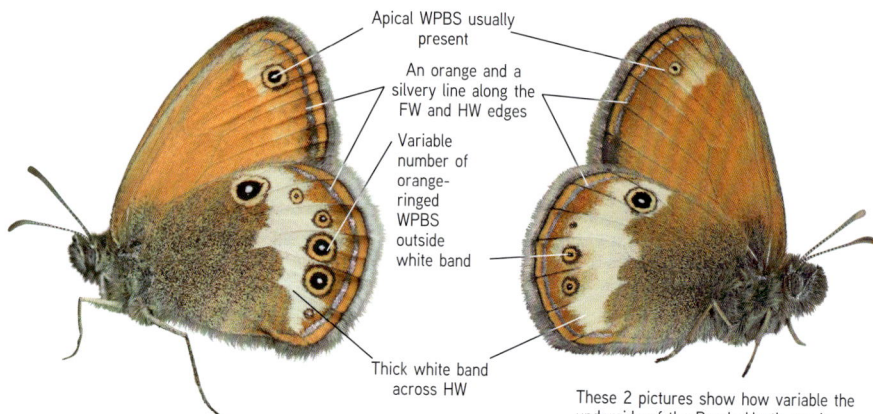

Apical WPBS usually present

An orange and a silvery line along the FW and HW edges

Variable number of orange-ringed WPBS outside white band

Thick white band across HW

These 2 pictures show how variable the underside of the Pearly Heath can be, especially regarding the number and size of the WPBS.

Wingspan: 34–40 mm

Habitat: Bushy grasslands and meadows, clearings, and scrubby edges.

Hibernating stage: Caterpillar.

Elevational range: Up to 2,000 m.

Egg-laying: Eggs are laid singly on LHP leaves and stems.

Flight period: From May to September.

Host plants: Numerous grasses, including *Brachypodium pinnatum*, *Festuca ovina*, *F. rubra*, *Agrostis vinealis*, *Holcus lanatus*, *Danthonia decumbens*, *Melica ciliata*, *M. nutans*, *M. minuta*, *M. uniflora*, *Poa* spp., and *Holcus* spp. Also on *Carex brizoides* and *C. pilulifera* (Cyperaceae).

Diversity and systematics: The nominate subspecies flies in Northern Europe. Subspecies *clorinda* inhabits the Iberian Peninsula. Subspecies *cephalus* flies in Western Europe. Subspecies *balestrei* is found in the southwestern Alps.

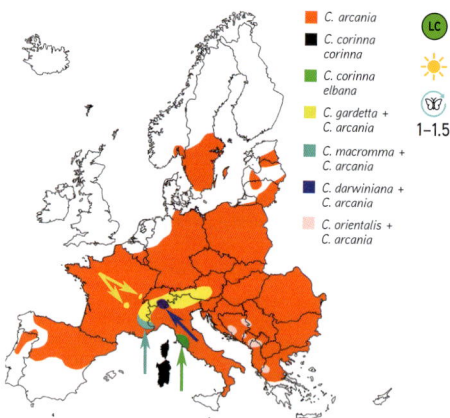

- C. arcania
- C. corinna corinna
- C. corinna elbana
- C. gardetta + C. arcania
- C. macromma + C. arcania
- C. darwiniana + C. arcania
- C. orientalis + C. arcania

LC

1–1.5

IMAGOS		LARVAE	
Food		Food	
Behaviour of males		Caterpillar location	
Dispersion		Chrysalis location	

Did you know?

Pearly Heaths gather to spend the night in communal roosts in clearings and bushes.

460

SATYRINAE

DARWIN'S HEATH/PIEDMONT HEATH
COENONYMPHA DARWINIANA/C. MACROMMA

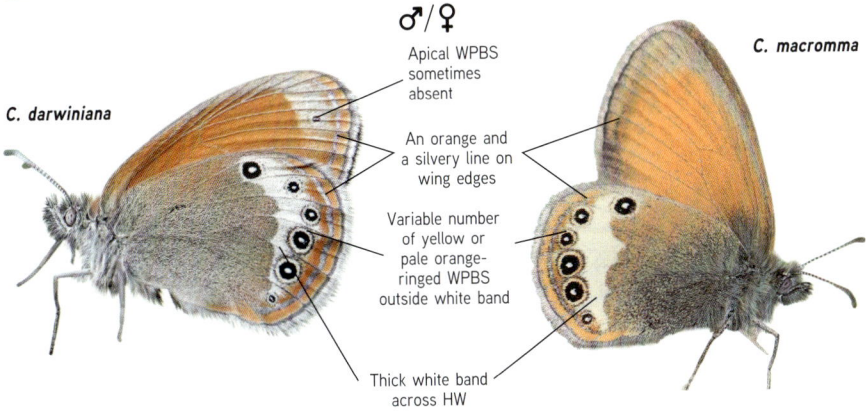

♂/♀

C. macromma

C. darwiniana

Apical WPBS sometimes absent

An orange and a silvery line on wing edges

Variable number of yellow or pale orange-ringed WPBS outside white band

Thick white band across HW

Wingspan: 31–34 mm

Habitat: Subalpine and alpine meadows and clearings.

Hibernating stage: Caterpillar.

Elevational range: Between 1,500 and 2,500 m.

Egg-laying: Eggs are laid singly on LHP dry parts.

Flight period: From June to August.

Host plants: Grasses, including *Festuca* spp., *Poa angustifolia*, and *Agrostis capillaris*.

Diversity and systematics: There are no notable subspecies of these two alpine species.

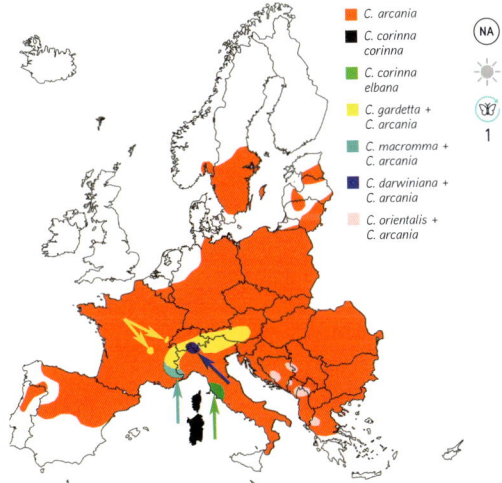

■ C. arcania
■ C. corinna corinna
■ C. corinna elbana
■ C. gardetta + C. arcania
■ C. macromma + C. arcania
■ C. darwiniana + C. arcania
■ C. orientalis + C. arcania

NA

1

Did you know?

Genetic analyses indicate that Darwin's Heath and the Piedmont Heath likely result from two independent events of speciation through hybridization between the Pearly Heath and the Alpine Heath.

IMAGOS			LARVAE	
Food			Food	
Behaviour of males			Caterpillar location	
Dispersion			Chrysalis location	

ALPINE HEATH *COENONYMPHA GARDETTA*

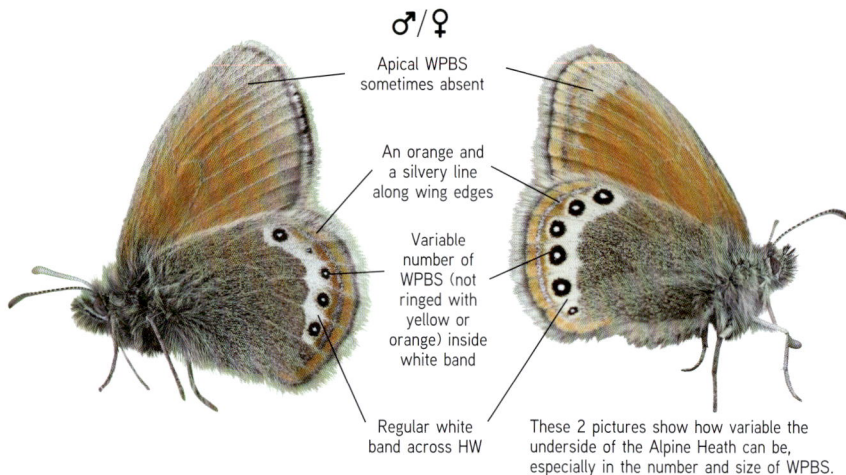

♂/♀

Apical WPBS sometimes absent

An orange and a silvery line along wing edges

Variable number of WPBS (not ringed with yellow or orange) inside white band

Regular white band across HW

These 2 pictures show how variable the underside of the Alpine Heath can be, especially in the number and size of WPBS.

Wingspan: 30–32 mm

Habitat: Subalpine and alpine grasslands and meadows.

Hibernating stage: Caterpillar.

Elevational range: Between 1,700 and 2,500 m.

Egg-laying: Eggs are laid singly on LHP leaves and stems.

Flight period: From June to September.

Host plants: Grasses, including *Festuca* spp., *Poa angustifolia*, and *Agrostis capillaris*.

Diversity and systematics: The nominate subspecies flies in the Alps. Subspecies *lecerfi* forms the populations of the French Massif Central.

- C. arcania
- C. corinna corinna
- C. corinna elbana
- C. gardetta + C. arcania
- C. macromma + C. arcania
- C. darwiniana + C. arcania
- C. orientalis + C. arcania

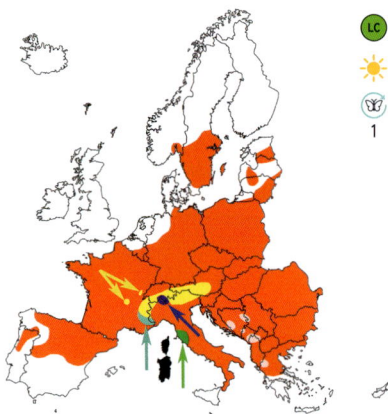

LC

1

IMAGOS		LARVAE	
Food		Food	
Behaviour of males		Caterpillar location	
Dispersion		Chrysalis location	

Did you know?

Adults are generalist nectar feeders in their high-altitude breeding habitats.

SATYRINAE

BALKAN HEATH   *COENONYMPHA ORIENTALIS*

♂/♀

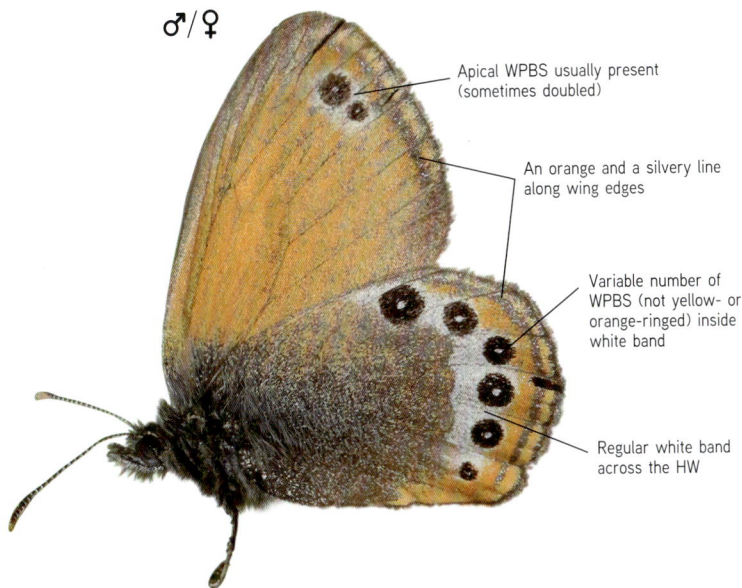

- Apical WPBS usually present (sometimes doubled)
- An orange and a silvery line along wing edges
- Variable number of WPBS (not yellow- or orange-ringed) inside white band
- Regular white band across the HW

Wingspan: 29–32 mm

Habitat: Bushy, flower-rich slopes, clearings, and edges.

Hibernating stage: Caterpillar.

Elevational range: Between 500 and 2,000 m.

Egg-laying: Eggs are laid singly on LHP leaves and stems.

Flight period: From June to August.

Host plants: Grasses, such as *Brachypodium sylvaticum* and *Festuca ovina*.

Diversity and systematics: There are no notable subspecies.

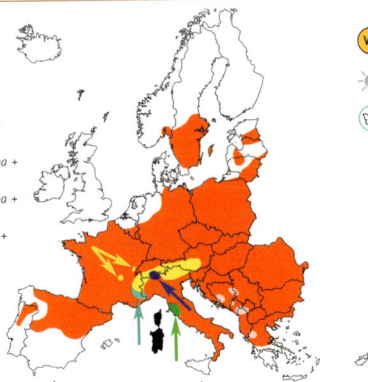

- *C. arcania*
- *C. corinna corinna*
- *C. corinna elbana*
- *C. gardetta + C. arcania*
- *C. macromma + C. arcania*
- *C. darwiniana + C. arcania*
- *C. orientalis + C. arcania*

VU
1

Did you know?

Coenonympha orientalis, sometimes considered a subspecies of *C. gardetta* and at other times a subspecies of *C. leander*, has been separated from them based on molecular studies.

IMAGOS		LARVAE	
Food	🌼	Food	🍃
Behaviour of males	🦋 🦋	Caterpillar location	🌾
Dispersion	🦋	Chrysalis location	🌾

SATYRINAE

RUSSIAN HEATH *COENONYMPHA LEANDER*

♂/♀

Apical WPBS

Vivid orange GC

An orange and a silvery line along wing edges

No white band or spot on HW

Series of yellow-ringed WPBS on HW

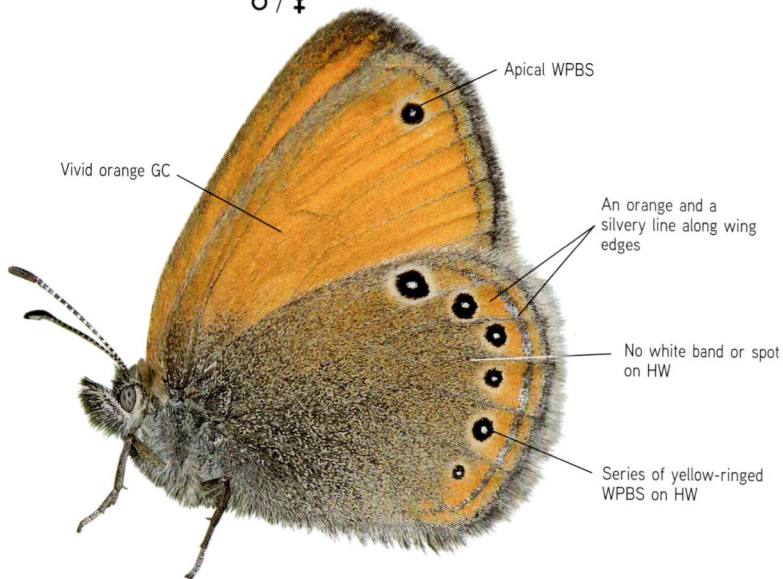

Wingspan: 32–34 mm

Habitat: Grasslands, low-growing meadows, and grassy clearings.

Hibernating stage: Caterpillar.

Elevational range: Up to 2,000 m.

Egg-laying: Eggs are laid singly on LHP leaves.

Flight period: From May to August.

Host plants: Grasses, like *Festuca ovina* and *Brachypodium sylvaticum*.

Diversity and systematics: European populations of this heath belong to the nominate subspecies.

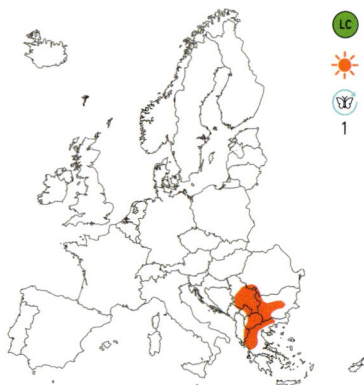

IMAGOS		LARVAE	
Food		Food	
Behaviour of males		Caterpillar location	
Dispersion		Chrysalis location	

Did you know?

Like other heaths, the Russian Heath generally flies close to the ground. However, it can perch relatively high in shrubs and trees.

SATYRINAE

FALSE RINGLET   *COENONYMPHA OEDIPPUS*

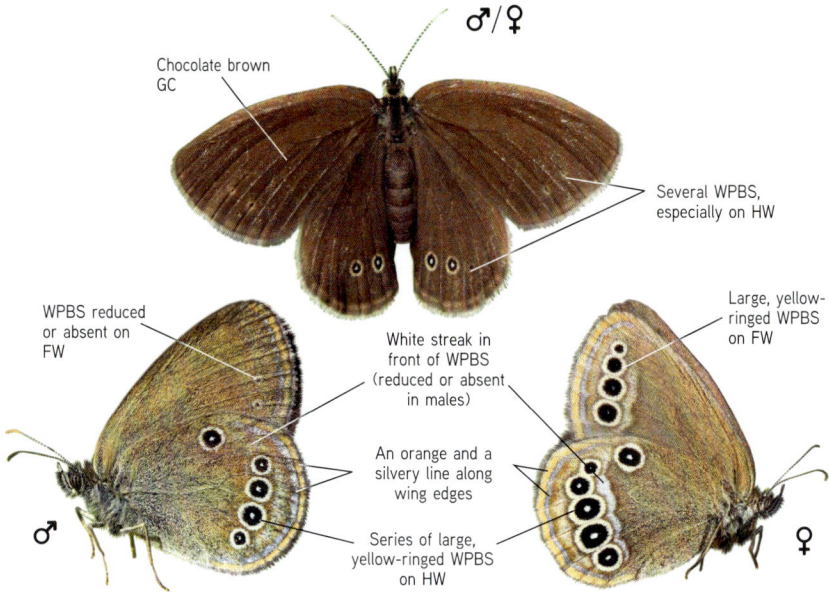

♂/♀

Chocolate brown GC

Several WPBS, especially on HW

WPBS reduced or absent on FW

White streak in front of WPBS (reduced or absent in males)

Large, yellow-ringed WPBS on FW

An orange and a silvery line along wing edges

♂

Series of large, yellow-ringed WPBS on HW

♀

Wingspan: 34–42 mm

Habitat: Damp meadows, clearings, and heaths.

Hibernating stage: Caterpillar.

Elevational range: Up to 800 m.

Egg-laying: Eggs are laid singly on LHP leaves.

Flight period: From June to August.

Host plants: Grasses, including *Molinia caerulea, Poa annua, P. palustris, P. pratensis, Deschampsia cespitosa*, and *Festuca rupicola.* Sedges, including *Carex acuta, C. davalliana, C. hostiana, C. humilis, C. panicea, C. remota, C. tomentosa, Eriophorum angustifolium*, and *Schoenus* spp.

Diversity and systematics: European populations belong to the nominate subspecies.

EN

1

Did you know?

The False Ringlet is one of the most endangered butterflies in Europe. The drainage of wetlands for agricultural purposes and the related loss of open habitats are gradually causing the disappearance of its breeding sites.

IMAGOS		LARVAE	
Food	✿	Food	🍃
Behaviour of males	🦋	Caterpillar location	🌿
Dispersion	⊛	Chrysalis location	🌿

SATYRINAE

RINGLET *APHANTOPUS HYPERANTUS*

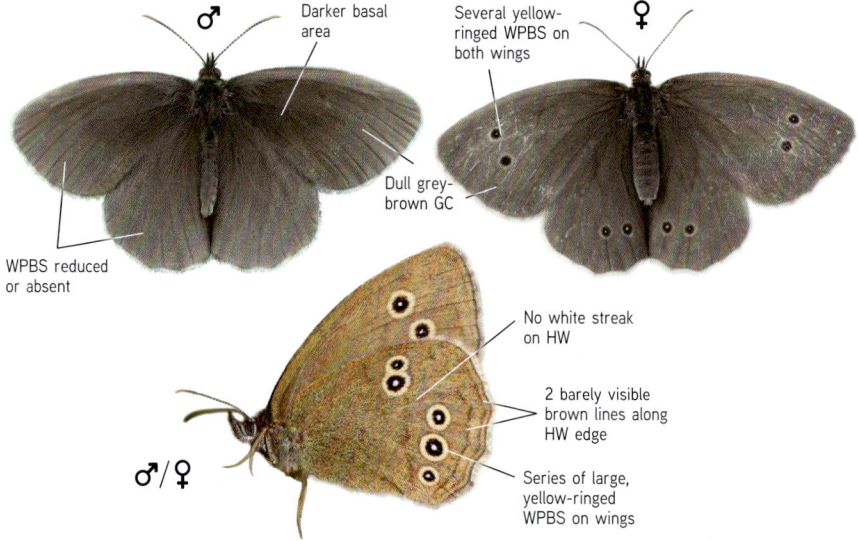

♂ Darker basal area

Several yellow-ringed WPBS on both wings ♀

Dull grey-brown GC

WPBS reduced or absent

♂/♀

No white streak on HW

2 barely visible brown lines along HW edge

Series of large, yellow-ringed WPBS on wings

Wingspan: 30–42 mm

Habitat: Mesophilic or damp meadows and clearings, megaphorbs, and peat bog surroundings.

Hibernating stage: Caterpillar.

Elevational range: Up to 1,500 m.

Egg-laying: Eggs are laid singly in vegetation.

Flight period: From June to August.

Host plants: A wide range of grasses, including *Agrostis capillaris*, *A. stolonifera*, *Alopecurus pratensis*, *Calamagrostis epigejos*, *Cynosurus cristatus*, *Dactylis glomerata*, *Deschampsia flexuosa*, *Elymus repens*, *Festuca ovina*, *F. rubra*, *Arrhenatherum elatius*, *Bromus erectus*, *Holcus lanatus*, *H. mollis*, *Brachypodium* spp., *Poa annua*, *P. pratensis*, *Milium effusum*, *Molinia caerulea*, *Phalaris arundinacea*, *Phleum pratense*. Sedges, like *Carex brizoides*, *C. fritschii*, *C. hirta*, *C. nigra*, *C. panicea*, and *C. remota*.

Diversity and systematics: European populations belong to the nominate subspecies.

LC
1

IMAGOS		LARVAE	
Food		Food	
Behaviour of males		Caterpillar location	
Dispersion		Chrysalis location	

Did you know?

Adults use forest edges and trails to disperse and colonize open breeding habitats. They tend to avoid crossing woodland areas.

SATYRINAE

WOODLAND BROWN *LOPINGA ACHINE*

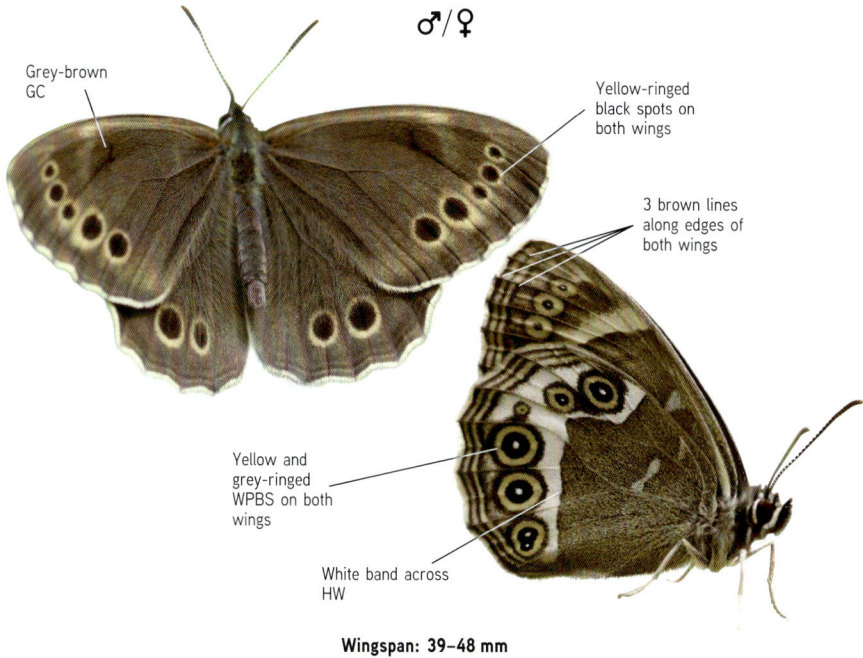

♂/♀

Grey-brown GC

Yellow-ringed black spots on both wings

3 brown lines along edges of both wings

Yellow and grey-ringed WPBS on both wings

White band across HW

Wingspan: 39–48 mm

Habitat: Grassy clearings and edges, clear woodlands.

Hibernating stage: Caterpillar.

Elevational range: Up to 1,500 m.

Egg-laying: Eggs are laid singly on LHP leaves.

Flight period: From May to July.

Host plants: Sedges of genus *Carex*, including *C. brizoides*, *C. alba*, *C. flacca*, *C. fritschii*, *C. michelii*, *C. montana*, and *C. sylvatica*. Grasses, including *Brachypodium pinnatum*, *B. sylvaticum*, *Calamagrostis arundinacea*, *Dactylis glomerata*, *Deschampsia cespitosa*, *Elymus canina*, *Festuca rubra*, *Poa annua*, *P. nemoralis*, *P. trivialis*, and *P. pratensis*. Also on *Luzula pilosa* (Juncaceae).

Diversity and systematics: Populations in northwestern Europe (including France) belong to subspecies *saltator*, while others are in the nominate subspecies.

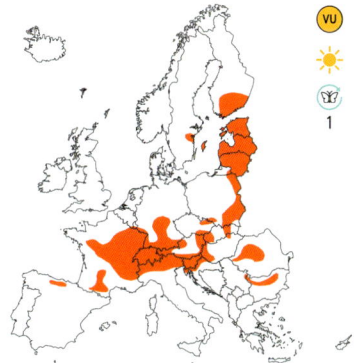

VU

1

IMAGOS		LARVAE	
Food	🌼 💩 🌿 💧 💧	Food	🌿
Behaviour of males	🦋 🦋	Caterpillar location	🌱 🌿
Dispersion	⊙	Chrysalis location	🌿

Did you know?

The overgrowth of deciduous forest clearings threatens the Woodland Brown, which has significantly declined over the last decades.

SATYRINAE

MARBLED WHITE *MELANARGIA GALATHEA*

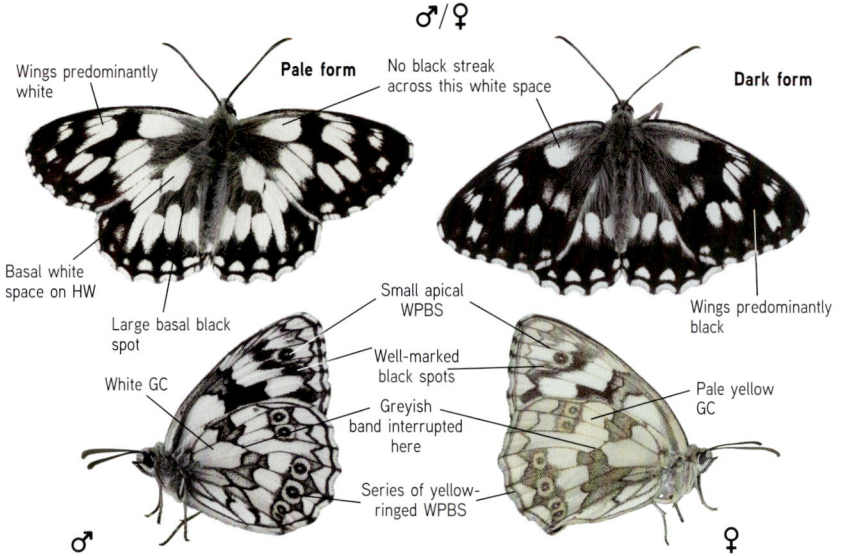

♂/♀

Pale form

Wings predominantly white

No black streak across this white space

Dark form

Basal white space on HW

Large basal black spot

White GC

Small apical WPBS

Well-marked black spots

Greyish band interrupted here

Series of yellow-ringed WPBS

Wings predominantly black

Pale yellow GC

♂

♀

Wingspan: 45–50 mm

Habitat: Grasslands, meadows, wastelands, and grassy edges.

Hibernating stage: Caterpillar.

Elevational range: Up to 2,500 m.

Egg-laying: Eggs are dropped in vegetation.

Flight period: From May to September.

Host plants: Grasses, including *Agrostis capillaris*, *Anthoxanthum odoratum*, *Arrhenatherum elatius*, *Avenula pubescens*, *Brachypodium pinnatum*, *B. sylvaticum*, *Bromus erectus*, *Calamagrostis arenaria*, *Cynosurus cristatus*, *Dactylis glomerata*, *Festuca liviensis*, *F. ovina*, *F. rubra*, *Helictochloa pratensis*, *Holcus lanatus*, *Ammophila arenaria*, *Phleum pratense*, *Poa annua*, and *P. trivialis*.

Diversity and systematics: The nominate subspecies flies in Germany and neighbouring regions. Subspecies *procida* inhabits southwestern Europe. Subspecies *serena* forms the British and western French populations. Subspecies *paludosa* is described from Camargue, in southern France. Subspecies *satnia* flies in the Balkans.

- M. galathea
- M. larissa + M. galathea
- M. lachesis
- M. russiae + M. galathea
- M. russiae + M. lachesis
- M. russiae + M. lachesis
- M. russiae + M. lachesis + M. galathea
- M. larissa + M. russiae + M. galathea
- M. larissa

LC

1

Did you know?

Marbled Whites tend to be darker at higher elevations. Such colourations may support the metabolic activity of mountainous populations, as they allow them to absorb heat from the environment more efficiently.

IMAGOS		LARVAE	
Food		Food	
Behaviour of males		Caterpillar location	
Dispersion		Chrysalis location	

SATYRINAE

BALKAN MARBLED WHITE   *MELANARGIA LARISSA*

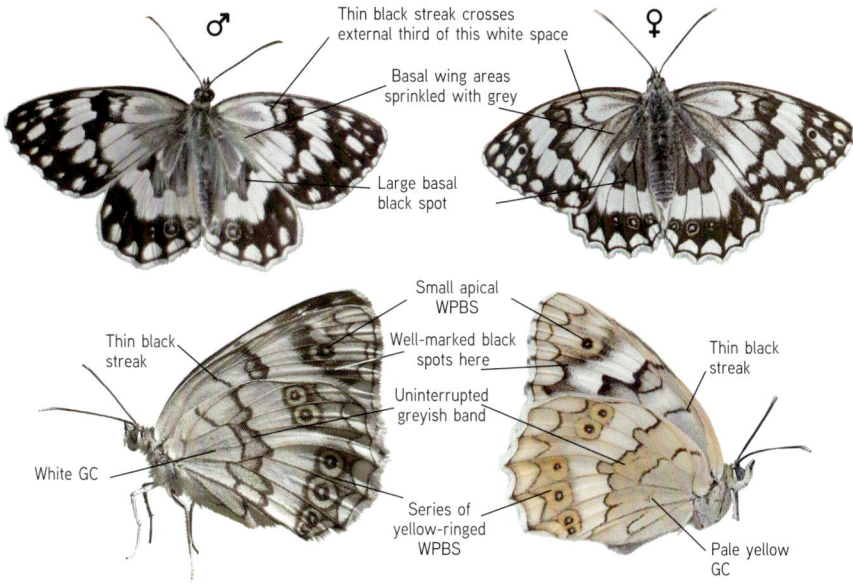

♂
Thin black streak crosses external third of this white space
Basal wing areas sprinkled with grey

♀

Large basal black spot

Small apical WPBS
Thin black streak
Well-marked black spots here
Uninterrupted greyish band
Thin black streak

White GC

Series of yellow-ringed WPBS

Pale yellow GC

Wingspan: 50–60 mm

Habitat: Dry, rocky slopes with a few trees and bushes.

Hibernating stage: Caterpillar

Elevational range: Up to 2,500 m.

Egg-laying: Eggs are dropped in vegetation.

Flight period: From May to September.

Host plants: Grasses, including *Poa annua* and *P. pratensis*.

Diversity and systematics: European populations belong to the nominate subspecies.

- M. galathea
- M. larissa + M. galathea
- M. lachesis
- M. russiae + M. galathea
- M. russiae + M. lachesis
- M. russiae + M. lachesis
- M. russiae + M. lachesis + M. galathea
- M. larissa + M. russiae + M. galathea
- M. larissa

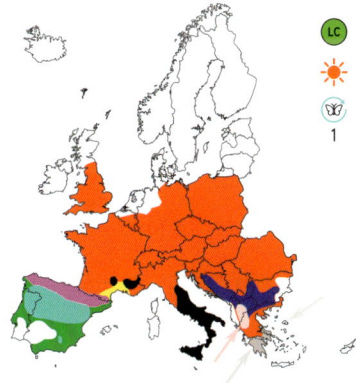

LC

1

Did you know?

The eggs of most marbled white species do not adhere to their substrate, as they lack an adhesive substance.

IMAGOS		LARVAE	
Food		Food	
Behaviour of males		Caterpillar location	
Dispersion		Chrysalis location	

SATYRINAE

IBERIAN MARBLED WHITE *MELANARGIA LACHESIS*

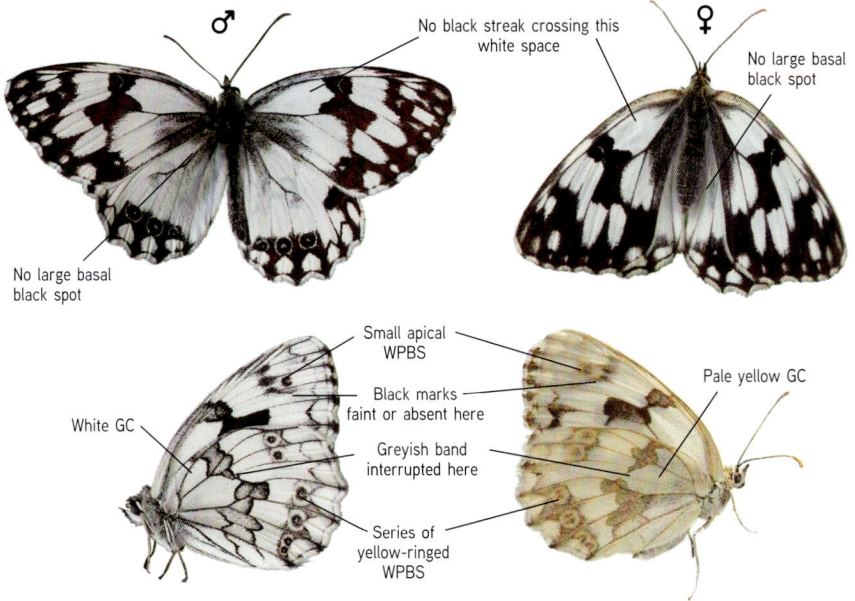

♂

♀

No black streak crossing this white space

No large basal black spot

No large basal black spot

Small apical WPBS

Pale yellow GC

White GC

Black marks faint or absent here

Greyish band interrupted here

Series of yellow-ringed WPBS

Wingspan: 45–53 mm

Habitat: Mediterranean dry grasslands, garrigues, and bushy fallow lands.

Hibernating stage: Caterpillar.

Elevational range: Up to 1,800 m.

Egg-laying: Eggs are dropped in vegetation.

Flight period: From June to August.

Host plants: Grasses, including *Brachypodium phoenicoides*, *B. pinnatum*, *Bromus erectus*, *Elymus repens*, *Festuca elegans*, *F. pseudeskia*, *Poa trivialis*, *Dactylis glomerata,* and *Phleum pratense*.

Diversity and systematics: This southwestern European endemic has no notable subspecies.

- M. galathea
- M. larissa + M. galathea
- M. lachesis
- M. russiae + M. galathea
- M. russiae + M. lachesis
- M. russiae + M. lachesis
- M. russiae + M. lachesis + M. galathea
- M. larissa + M. russiae + M. galathea
- M. larissa

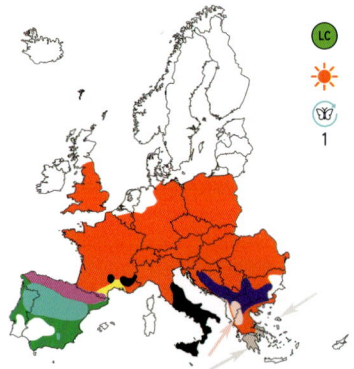

LC

1

IMAGOS		LARVAE	
Food		Food	
Behaviour of males		Caterpillar location	
Dispersion		Chrysalis location	

Did you know?

Caterpillars of the Iberian Marbled White hatch in the summer, go directly into aestivation, and resume their activity and growth only in the autumn.

ESPER'S MARBLED WHITE *MELANARGIA RUSSIAE*

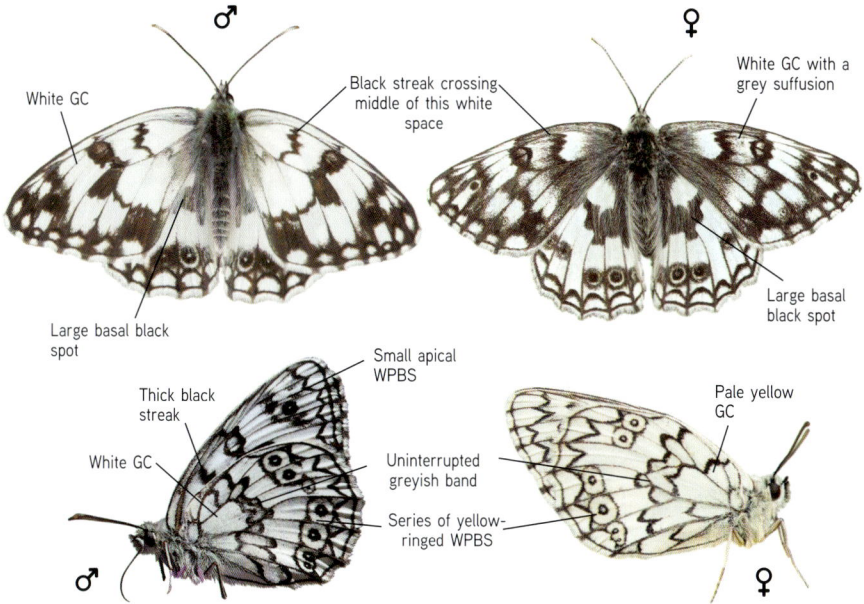

♂ ♀

White GC

Black streak crossing middle of this white space

White GC with a grey suffusion

Large basal black spot

Large basal black spot

Small apical WPBS

Thick black streak

White GC

Uninterrupted greyish band

Series of yellow-ringed WPBS

Pale yellow GC

♂ ♀

Wingspan: 50–60 mm

Habitat: Grasslands and mesoxerophilic meadows with few bushes.

Hibernating stage: Caterpillar.

Elevational range: Between 500 and 2,500 m (mainly below 2,000 m).

Egg-laying: Eggs are laid singly on LHP leaves and stems.

Flight period: From June to August.

Host plants: Grasses, including *Agrostis capillaris*, *Bromus erectus*, *Brachypodium* spp., *Celtica gigantea*, *Lamarckia aurea*, *Stipa pennata*, *Poa annua*, and *Dactylis glomerata*.

Diversity and systematics: Subspecies *cleanthe* flies in the Iberian Peninsula and France, while subspecies *japygia* forms the rest of the European populations.

■ *M. galathea*
■ *M. larissa* + *M. galathea*
■ *M. lachesis*
■ *M. russiae* + *M. galathea*
■ *M. russiae* + *M. lachesis*
■ *M. russiae* + *M. lachesis*
■ *M. larissa* + *M. lachesis* + *M. galathea*
■ *M. larissa* + *M. russiae* + *M. galathea*
□ *M. larissa*

LC

1

Did you know?

Esper's Marbled White forms disjointed populations in Western Europe, and its range extends widely in Asia. The nominate subspecies is indeed described from Russia.

IMAGOS		LARVAE	
Food	☆	Food	🍃
Behaviour of males		Caterpillar location	
Dispersion		Chrysalis location	

SATYRINAE

THE WESTERN MARBLED WHITE *MELANARGIA OCCITANICA*

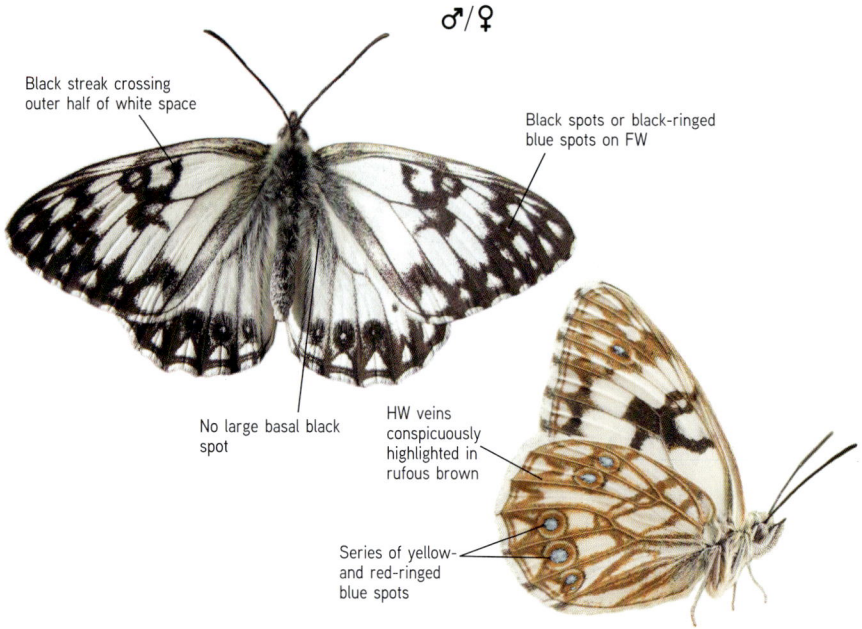

♂/♀

Black streak crossing outer half of white space

Black spots or black-ringed blue spots on FW

No large basal black spot

HW veins conspicuously highlighted in rufous brown

Series of yellow- and red-ringed blue spots

Wingspan: 46–56 mm

Habitat: Stony dry grasslands and garrigues.

Hibernating stage: Caterpillar.

Elevational range: Up to 1,500 m.

Egg-laying: Eggs are laid singly on LHP dry parts.

Flight period: From April to June.

Host plants: Grasses, including *Brachypodium phoenicoides*, *B. pinnatum*, *B. retusum*, *Festuca ovina*, *Dactylis glomerata*, *Phleum pratense*, *Stipa lagascae*, *S. offneri*, and *Cynodon dactylon*.

Diversity and systematics: European populations belong to the nominate subspecies.

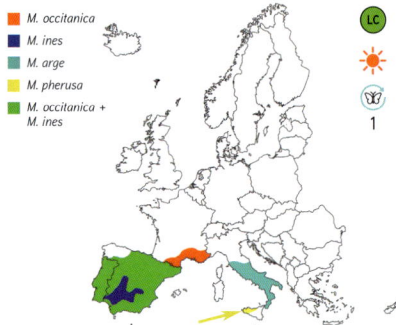

- 🟧 *M. occitanica*
- 🟦 *M. ines*
- 🟩 *M. arge*
- 🟨 *M. pherusa*
- 🟩 *M. occitanica + M. ines*

LC

1

Did you know?

The loss of the Western Marbled White's favourable Mediterranean habitats and their use for agricultural or urban purposes locally threaten this butterfly.

IMAGOS		LARVAE	
Food	☆	Food	🍃
Behaviour of males		Caterpillar location	
Dispersion		Chrysalis location	

SATYRINAE

ITALIAN MARBLED WHITE   *MELANARGIA ARGE*

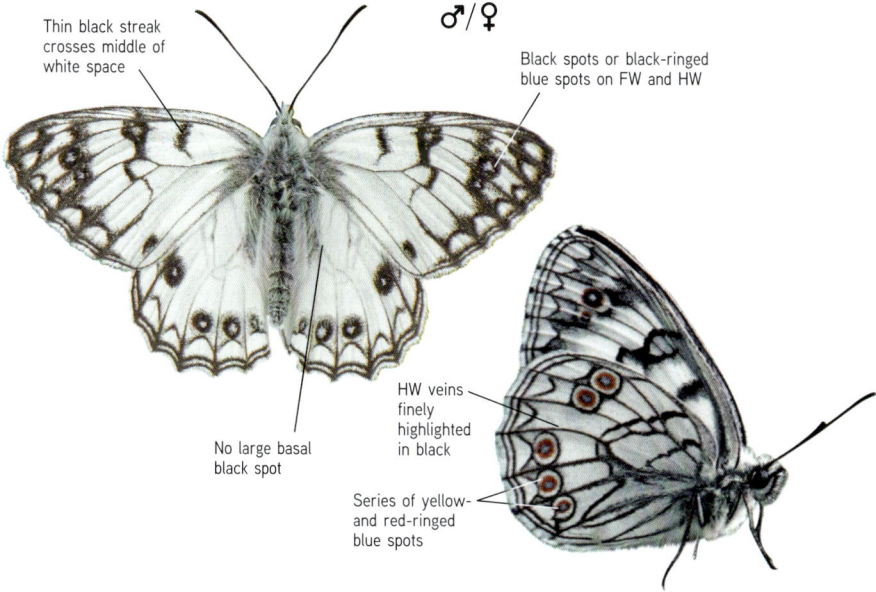

♂/♀

Thin black streak crosses middle of white space

Black spots or black-ringed blue spots on FW and HW

No large basal black spot

HW veins finely highlighted in black

Series of yellow- and red-ringed blue spots

Wingspan: 50–56 mm

Habitat: Stony and grassy slopes.

Hibernating stage: Caterpillar.

Elevational range: Between 500 and 2,000 m.

Egg-laying: Eggs are laid singly on LHP dry parts.

Flight period: May and June.

Host plants: Grasses, including *Ampelodesmos mauritanicus*, *Brachypodium distachyon*, *B. retusum*, and *Stipa pennata*.

Diversity and systematics: There are no notable subspecies.

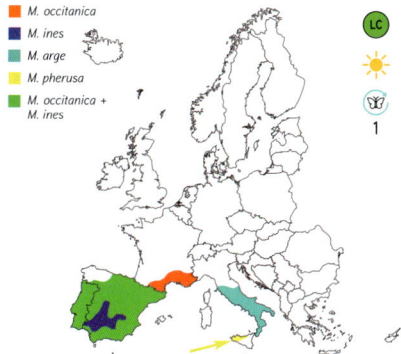

- M. occitanica
- M. ines
- M. arge
- M. pherusa
- M. occitanica + M. ines

LC

1

Did you know?

Populations of the Italian Marbled White are fragmented and localized. Overgrazing and too frequent Mediterranean fires pose threats to this species.

IMAGOS		LARVAE	
Food		Food	
Behaviour of males		Caterpillar location	
Dispersion		Chrysalis location	

SATYRINAE

SPANISH MARBLED WHITE *MELANARGIA INES*

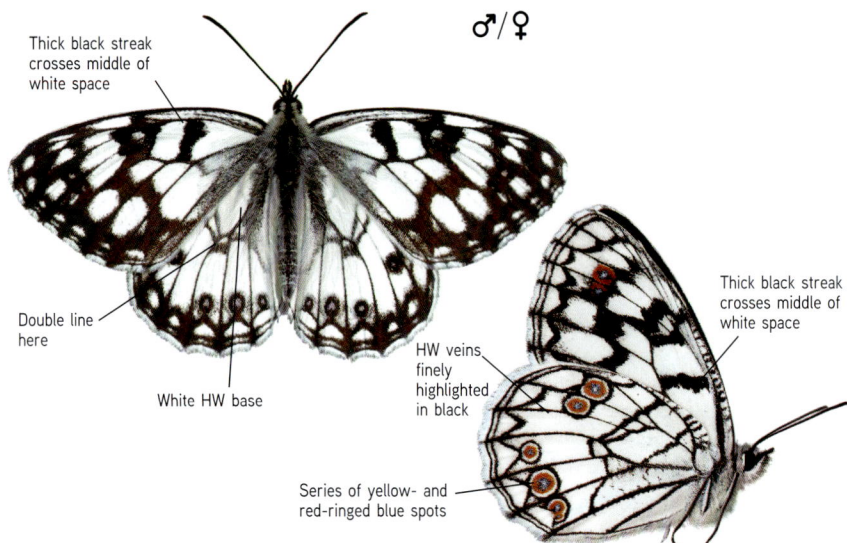

♂/♀

Thick black streak crosses middle of white space

Double line here

White HW base

Thick black streak crosses middle of white space

HW veins finely highlighted in black

Series of yellow- and red-ringed blue spots

Wingspan: 46–50 mm

Habitat: Steppic and dry grasslands, garrigues, and warm, stony slopes.

Hibernating stage: Caterpillar.

Elevational range: Up to 2,500 m.

Egg-laying: Eggs are laid singly on LHP leaves and stems.

Flight period: From March to June.

Host plants: Grasses, including *Achnatherum parviflorum*, *Bromus madritensis*, *Dactylis glomerata*, *Stipa lagascae*, and *Brachypodium pinnatum*.

Diversity and systematics: European populations belong to the nominate subspecies.

- ■ M. occitanica
- ■ M. ines
- ■ M. arge
- ■ M. pherusa
- ■ M. occitanica + M. ines

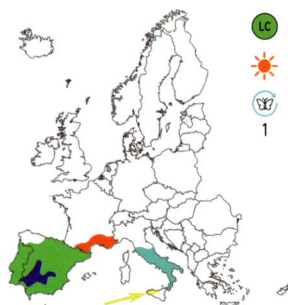

LC

1

Did you know?

During the last glacial maximum, the Spanish Marbled White sought refuge in the Maghreb, from which it rapidly recolonized the Iberian Peninsula. This rapid northward spread resulted in low genetic diversity among European populations.

IMAGOS		LARVAE	
Food		Food	
Behaviour of males		Caterpillar location	
Dispersion		Chrysalis location	

SATYRINAE

THE SICILIAN MARBLED WHITE *MELANARGIA PHERUSA*

♂/♀

Thick black streak crosses middle of white space

Thick black streak crosses middle of white space

No black line here

HW veins highlighted in grey

No large basal black spot

Series of BPBS sometimes absent

Yellow- and red-ringed blue spots faint or absent

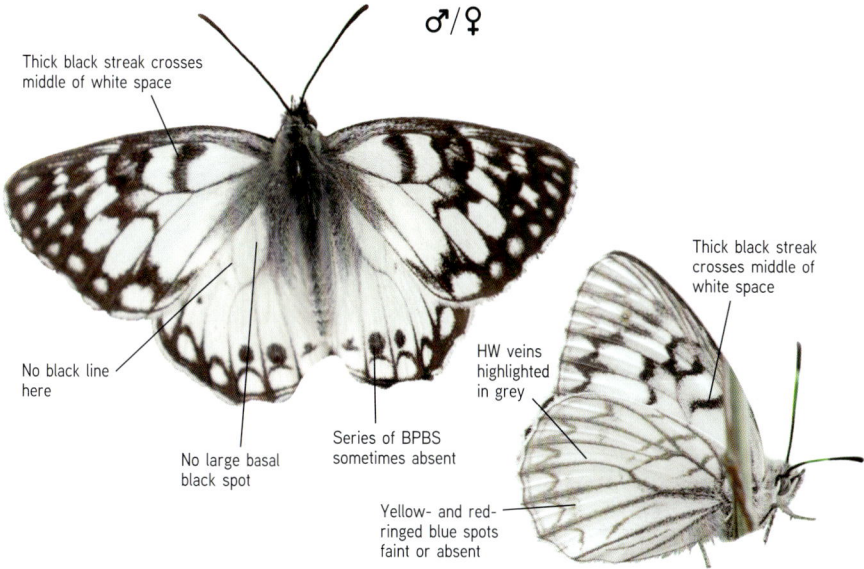

Wingspan: 46–50 mm

Habitat: Rocky, grassy habitats.

Hibernating stage: Caterpillar.

Elevational range: Between 500 and 1,000 m.

Egg-laying: Eggs are laid singly on LHP leaves and stems.

Flight period: From April to June.

Host plants: Grasses, mainly *Brachypodium pinnatum*, *Hyparrhenia hirta*, and *Lygeum spartum*.

Diversity and systematics: There are no notable subspecies.

■ *M. occitanica*
■ *M. ines*
■ *M. arge*
■ *M. pherusa*
■ *M. occitanica + M. ines*

LC

1

IMAGOS		LARVAE	
Food	✷	Food	🍃
Behaviour of males	🦋	Caterpillar location	🌿
Dispersion	🦋	Chrysalis location	🪨 🌿

Did you know?

Like other species of the *Melanargia* genus, the Sicilian Marbled White spends a considerable amount of time gathering nectar from the inflorescences of numerous plants, especially those in the Asteraceae family.

ALPINE GRAYLING *OENEIS GLACIALIS*

♂/♀

Chequered fringes

Tawny FW GC

1 apical WPBS; another (larger in females) often hidden under HW

1 small, barely visible WPBS (larger in females)

Grey, heavily mottled HW GC

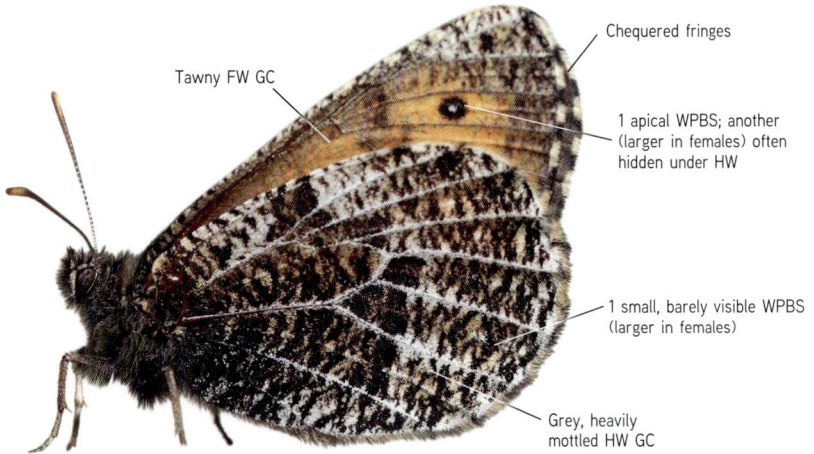

Wingspan: 50–56 mm

Habitat: Subalpine and alpine grasslands and meadows with bare areas, such as rocks or scree.

Hibernating stage: Overwinters twice as a caterpillar.

Elevational range: Between 1,500 and 3,000 m.

Egg-laying: Eggs are laid singly on LHP dry parts.

Flight period: From June to August.

Host plants: Grasses of genus *Festuca*, including *F. ovina*, *F. laevigata*, and *F. marginata*.

Diversity and systematics: There are no notable subspecies.

- ■ *O. norna*
- ■ *O. jutta*
- ■ *O. bore + O. norna*
- ■ *O. norna + O. jutta*
- ▢ *O. glacialis*

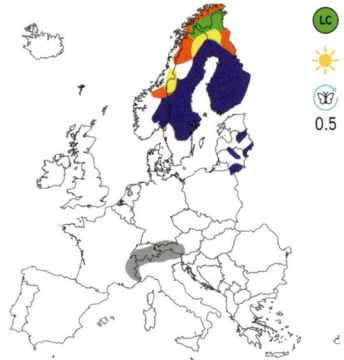

LC

0.5

Did you know?

Males fairly regularly perch on stones to monitor their territory. They display strong aggressiveness against passing butterflies, including individuals of other species.

IMAGOS			LARVAE		
Food	☆ 💩 💧		Food	🍃	
Behaviour of males			Caterpillar location	🌱	
Dispersion			Chrysalis location		🌱

SATYRINAE

BALTIC GRAYLING *OENEIS JUTTA*

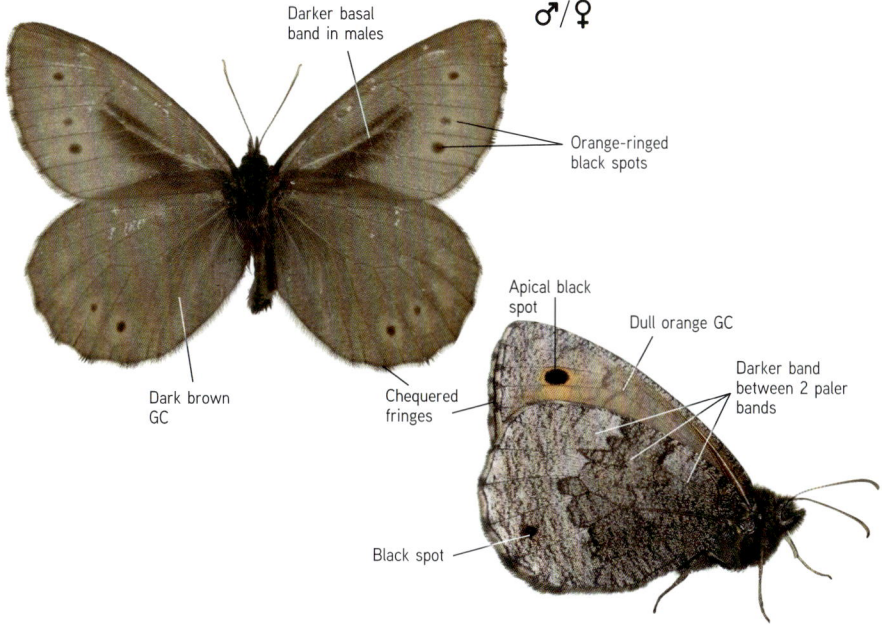

♂/♀

Darker basal
band in males

Orange-ringed
black spots

Apical black
spot

Dull orange GC

Darker band
between 2 paler
bands

Dark brown
GC

Chequered
fringes

Black spot

Wingspan: 45–58 mm

Habitat: Swampy and boggy pine woodlands.

Hibernating stage: Overwinters twice as a caterpillar.

Elevational range: Up to 1,000 m.

Egg-laying: Eggs are laid singly or in a few units on LHP leaves.

Flight period: From May to July.

Host plants: Sedges, including *Eriophorum vaginatum*, *Carex* spp., and *Scirpus caespitosus*. Grasses, mainly *Molinia caerulea*.

Diversity and systematics: European populations belong to the nominate subspecies.

- ▪ *O. norna*
- ▪ *O. jutta*
- ▪ *O. bore +*
  O. norna
- ▪ *O. norna +*
  O. jutta
- ▪ *O. glacialis*

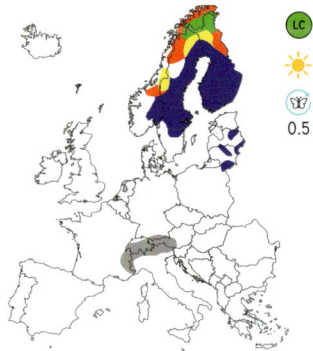

LC

0.5

IMAGOS		LARVAE	
Food	☆	Food	🍃
Behaviour of males		Caterpillar location	🌱
Dispersion		Chrysalis location	🌱

Did you know?

Adults most often perch on the trunks of pines. They frequently take nectar from the flowers of Marsh Labrador Tea (*Rhododendron tomentosum*).

SATYRINAE

ARCTIC GRAYLING *OENEIS BORE*

♂/♀

Tawny FW GC

No apical black spot

Chequered fringes

Black-underlined narrow pale band

Pale veins

No black spot here

Grey, heavily mottled HW GC

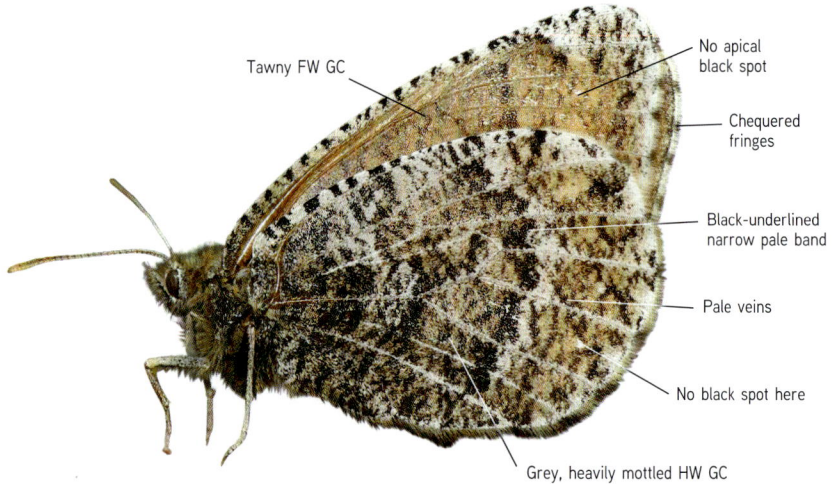

Wingspan: 36–48 mm

Habitat: Tundra and low-growing, stony grasslands.

Hibernating stage: Overwinters twice as a caterpillar.

Elevational range: Up to 1,000 m.

Egg-laying: Eggs are laid singly on LHP leaves and stems.

Flight period: June and July.

Host plants: Grasses of genera *Festuca* (including *F. ovina*) and *Nardus*.

Diversity and systematics: European populations belong to the nominate subspecies.

O. norna
O. jutta
O. bore + O. norna
O. norna + O. jutta
O. glacialis

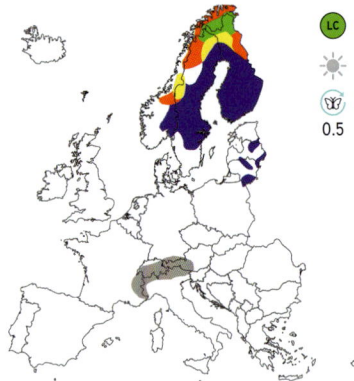

LC

0.5

IMAGOS		LARVAE	
Food	🌼 💧	Food	🌿
Behaviour of males		Caterpillar location	
Dispersion		Chrysalis location	

Did you know?

Like many other arctic species, the Arctic Grayling can also be found in North America.

478

NORSE GRAYLING *OENEIS NORNA*

♂/♀

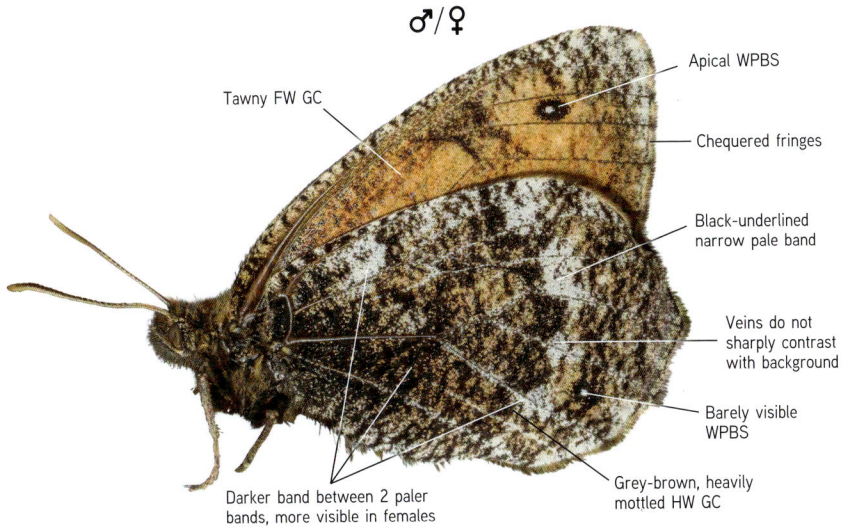

- Tawny FW GC
- Apical WPBS
- Chequered fringes
- Black-underlined narrow pale band
- Veins do not sharply contrast with background
- Barely visible WPBS
- Grey-brown, heavily mottled HW GC
- Darker band between 2 paler bands, more visible in females

Wingspan: 36–54 mm

Habitat: Tundra grasslands and damp heaths, boreal birch forests.

Hibernating stage: Overwinters twice as a caterpillar.

Elevational range: Up to 800 m.

Egg-laying: Eggs are laid singly on LHP leaves and stems.

Flight period: June and July.

Host plants: Grasses, including *Poa alpina*, *Phleum pratense*, and *Nardus stricta*. Sedges of genus *Carex*.

Diversity and systematics: European populations belong to the nominate subspecies.

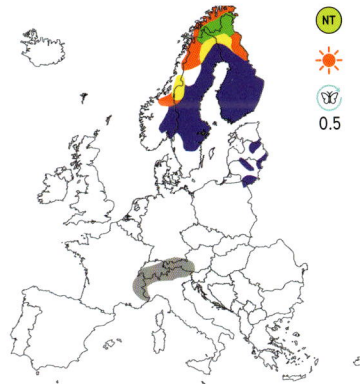

- O. norna
- O. jutta
- O. bore + O. norna
- O. norna + O. jutta
- O. glacialis

NT

0.5

	IMAGOS			LARVAE	
Food			Food		
Behaviour of males			Caterpillar location		
Dispersion			Chrysalis location		

Did you know?

Adults most often perch on tree trunks or stones, a typical behaviour among butterflies of genus *Oeneis*.

SATYRINAE

BLACK SATYR *SATYRUS ACTAEA*

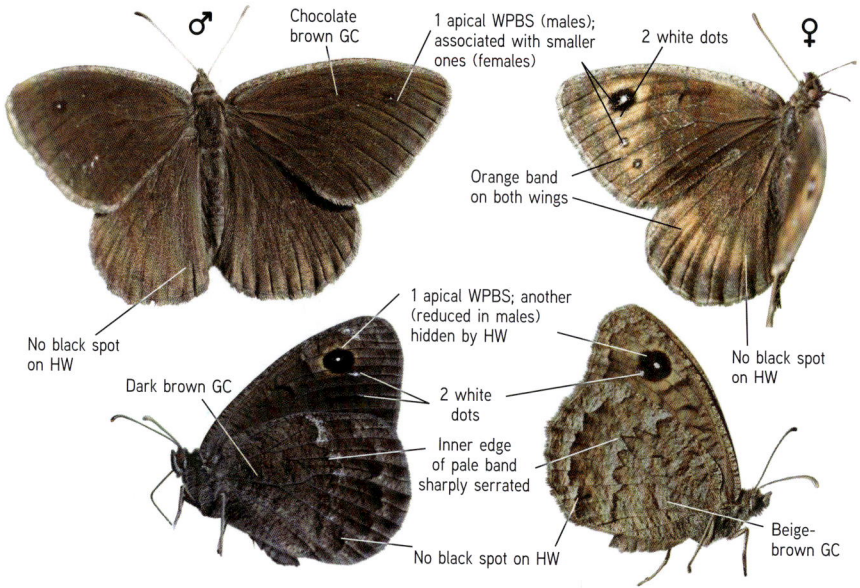

♂ Chocolate brown GC

1 apical WPBS (males); associated with smaller ones (females)

2 white dots

♀

Orange band on both wings

No black spot on HW

1 apical WPBS; another (reduced in males) hidden by HW

Dark brown GC

2 white dots

Inner edge of pale band sharply serrated

No black spot on HW

No black spot on HW

Beige-brown GC

Wingspan: 50–60 mm

Habitat: Dry grasslands, garrigues, and stony slopes.

Hibernating stage: Caterpillar.

Elevational range: Up to 2,000 m.

Egg-laying: Eggs are laid singly on LHP leaves and stems.

Flight period: From June to August.

Host plants: Grasses, including *Festuca iberica, F. ovina, F. pseudeskia, F. trichophylla, Brachypodium pinnatum, Dactylis* spp., *Deschampsia cespitosa, Bromus* spp., *Lolium* spp., *Stipa capillata, S. offneri,* and *S. pennata.*

Diversity and systematics: There are no notable subspecies, although many forms have been described.

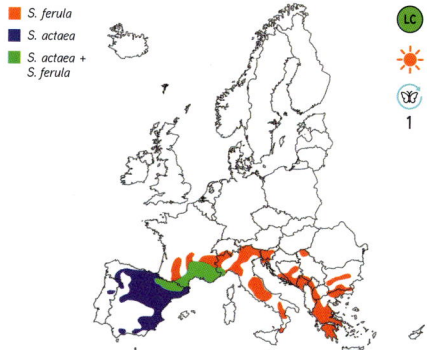

■ S. ferula
■ S. actaea
■ S. actaea + S. ferula

LC

1

Did you know?

Agricultural intensification contributes to the decline of the Black Satyr in the lowland areas of its range.

IMAGOS		LARVAE	
Food		Food	
Behaviour of males		Caterpillar location	
Dispersion		Chrysalis location	

SATYRINAE

GREAT SOOTY SATYR *SATYRUS FERULA*

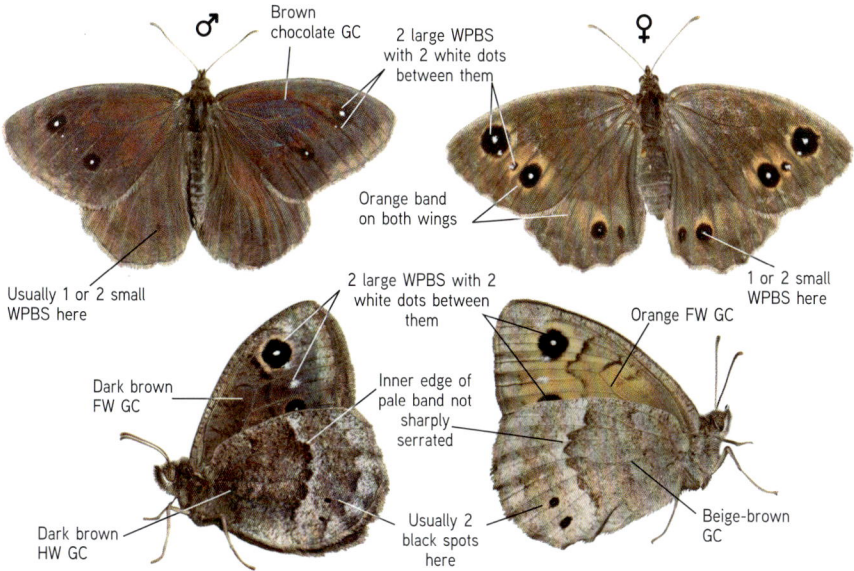

♂

Brown chocolate GC

2 large WPBS with 2 white dots between them

♀

Orange band on both wings

Usually 1 or 2 small WPBS here

2 large WPBS with 2 white dots between them

Orange FW GC

1 or 2 small WPBS here

Dark brown FW GC

Inner edge of pale band not sharply serrated

Dark brown HW GC

Usually 2 black spots here

Beige-brown GC

Wingspan: 50–60 mm

Habitat: Dry, bushy grasslands, sunny rocky slopes and clearings.

Hibernating stage: Caterpillar.

Elevational range: Up to 2,000 m.

Egg-laying: Eggs are laid singly or in a few units on LHP leaves.

Flight period: From June to September.

Host plants: Grasses, including *Festuca ovina*, *F. liviensis*, *Bromus erectus*, *Deschampsia cespitosa*, *Helictochloa pratensis*, *Stipa capillata*, and *S. pennata*.

Diversity and systematics: Most European populations belong to the nominate subspecies. Subspecies *penketia* and *serva* are, respectively, described from Taygetos and Dalmatia.

■ S. ferula
■ S. actaea
■ S. actaea + S. ferula

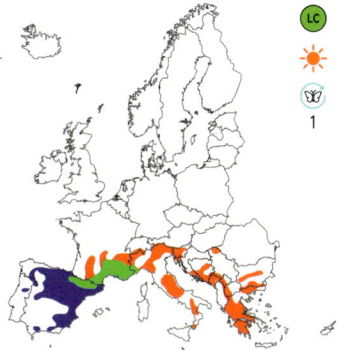

LC

1

IMAGOS			LARVAE		
Food			Food		
Behaviour of males			Caterpillar location		
Dispersion			Chrysalis location		

Did you know?

Pastoral abandonment and the conversion of habitats favourable to the Large Sooty Satyr into vineyards are the main threats to this species, especially in the northern part of its range.

SATYRINAE

DRYAD *MINOIS DRYAS*

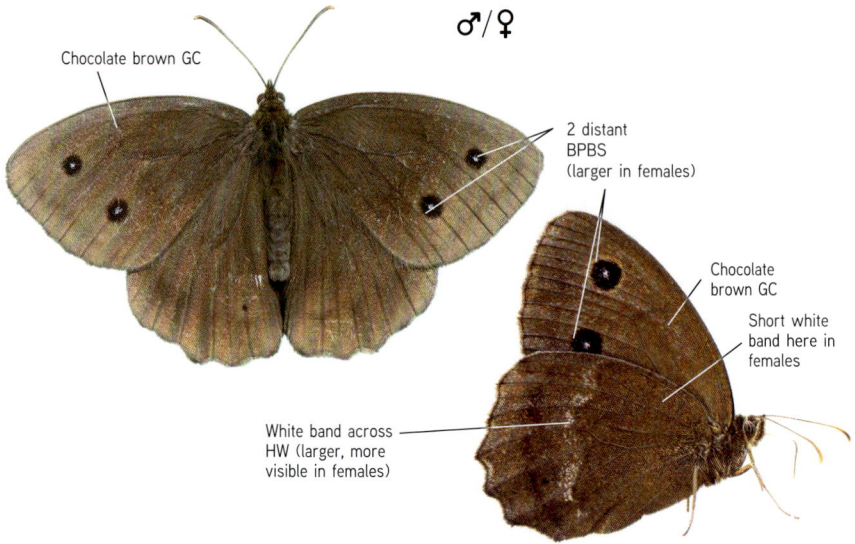

♂/♀

Chocolate brown GC

2 distant BPBS (larger in females)

Chocolate brown GC

Short white band here in females

White band across HW (larger, more visible in females)

Wingspan: 54–70 mm

Habitat: Damp meadows, bushy grasslands and clearings, forest edges, and clear woodlands.

Hibernating stage: Caterpillar.

Elevational range: Up to 1,500 m.

Egg-laying: Eggs are dropped in vegetation.

Flight period: From June to September.

Host plants: Grasses, including *Arrhenatherum elatius*, *Avena fatua*, *Avenula pubescens*, *Brachypodium pinnatum*, *Briza media*, *Bromus erectus*, *Calamagrostis epigejos*, *C. varia*, *Molinia caerulea*, *Festuca ovina*, *F. rubra*, *Koeleria macrantha*, *Lolium arundinaceum*, *L. perenne*, *Dactylis glomerata*, and *Phragmites australis*. Sedges, like *Carex acuta*, *C. acutiformis*, *C. alba*, *C. caryophyllea*, and *C. panicea*.

Diversity and systematics: European populations belong to the nominate subspecies.

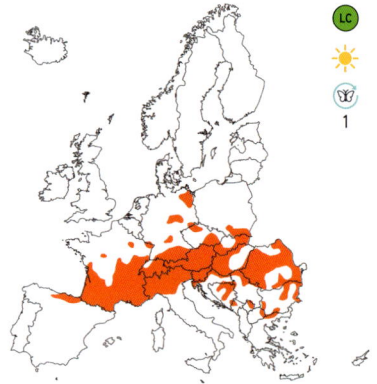

LC

1

IMAGOS		LARVAE	
Food		Food	
Behaviour of males		Caterpillar location	
Dispersion		Chrysalis location	

Did you know?

Adults are fond of taking nectar from the inflorescences of Oregano and scabiouses. Populations tend to fragment due to the loss of suitable, extensively managed habitats.

482

SATYRINAE

GREAT BANDED GRAYLING *BRINTESIA CIRCE*

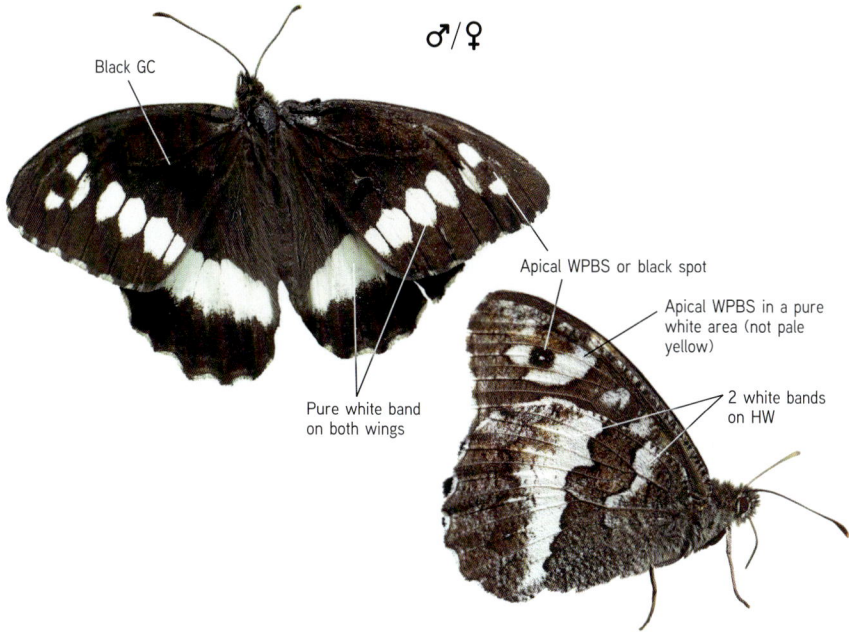

♂/♀

Black GC

Apical WPBS or black spot

Apical WPBS in a pure white area (not pale yellow)

Pure white band on both wings

2 white bands on HW

Wingspan: 66–80 mm

Habitat: Grasslands and meadows in the vicinity of woodlands, flower-rich clearings and edges, clear woodlands.

Hibernating stage: Caterpillar.

Elevational range: Up to 2,000 m.

Egg-laying: Eggs are dropped in vegetation.

Flight period: From May to October.

Host plants: Grasses, including *Bromus erectus, B. sterilis, Brachypodium pinnatum, B. phoenicoides, B. retusum, B. sylvaticum, Festuca ovina, F. rubra, F. elegans, F. nigrescens, Anthoxanthum odoratum, Arrhenatherum elatius, Lolium perenne, L. arundinaceum, Phleum pratense, Poa pratensis, Celtica gigantea, Danthonia decumbens, Deschampsia flexuosa,* and *Elymus repens.* Also reported on *Carex* (Cyperaceae).

Diversity and systematics: European populations belong to the nominate subspecies.

LC

1

IMAGOS		LARVAE	
Food	🌟 💧 🍎 💩 💧	Food	🌿
Behaviour of males		Caterpillar location	🐛 🌾
Dispersion		Chrysalis location	

Did you know?

The Great Banded Grayling is tending to expand its range northward, probably because of climate warming.

SATYRINAE

AFRICAN RINGLET *YPTHIMA ASTEROPE*

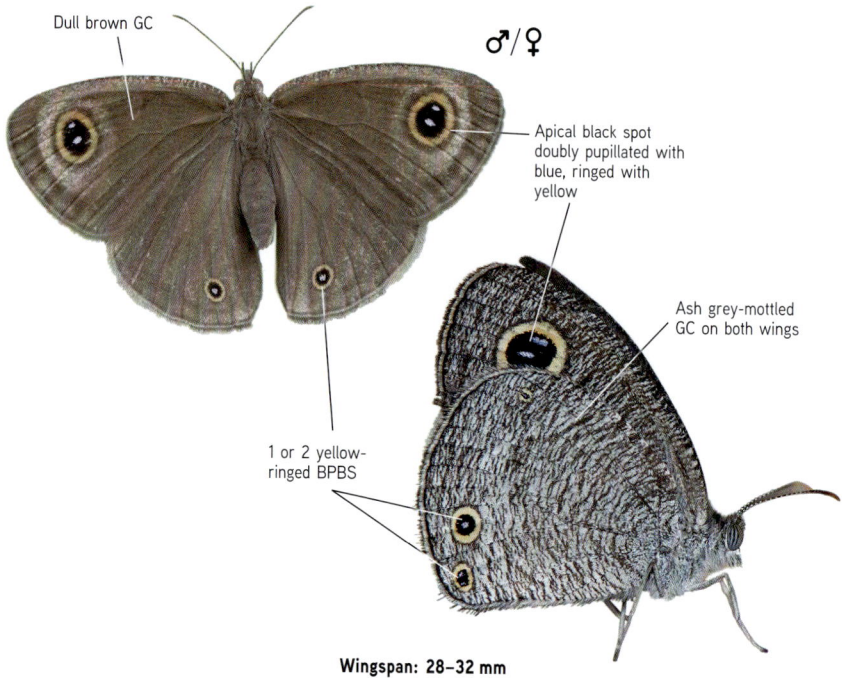

Dull brown GC

♂/♀

Apical black spot doubly pupillated with blue, ringed with yellow

Ash grey-mottled GC on both wings

1 or 2 yellow-ringed BPBS

Wingspan: 28–32 mm

Habitat: Warm habitats, such as arid rocky slopes, garrigues, and dried riverbeds.

Hibernating stage: Caterpillar.

Elevational range: Up to 500 m.

Egg-laying: Eggs are laid singly on LHP leaves.

Flight period: From March to November.

Host plants: Grasses such as *Hyparrhenia hirta*.

Diversity and systematics: European populations belong to the nominate subspecies.

NA

3

IMAGOS		LARVAE	
Food		Food	
Behaviour of males		Caterpillar location	
Dispersion		Chrysalis location	

Did you know?

Genus *Ypthima* is primarily composed of tropical African and South Asian species. The African Ringlet is its only representative in Europe; its populations are very localized in Cyprus and on a few Aegean islands.

SATYRINAE

DALMATIAN RINGLET   *PROTEREBIA AFRA*

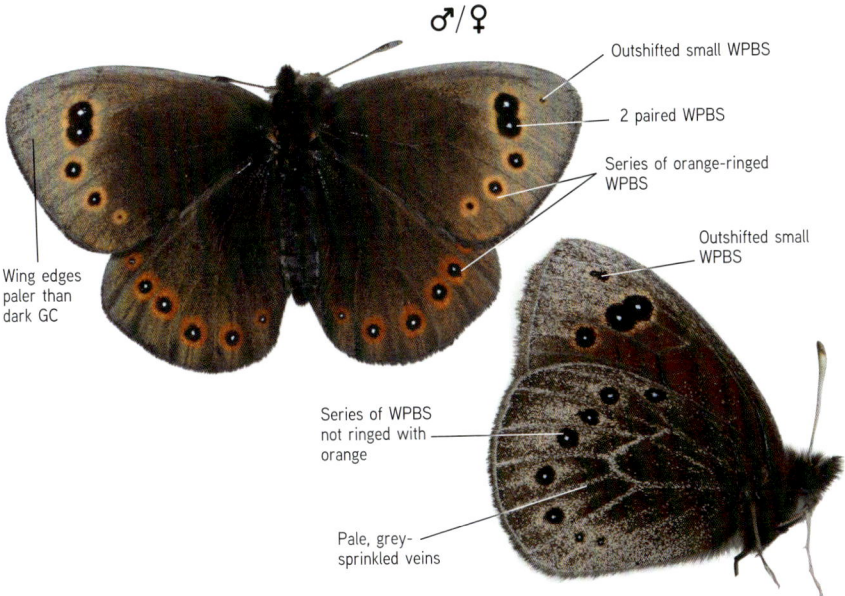

♂/♀

Outshifted small WPBS

2 paired WPBS

Series of orange-ringed WPBS

Outshifted small WPBS

Wing edges paler than dark GC

Series of WPBS not ringed with orange

Pale, grey-sprinkled veins

Wingspan: 44–48 mm

Habitat: Stony and often grazed dry grasslands with a few bushes.

Hibernating stage: Caterpillar.

Elevational range: Up to 1,300 m.

Egg-laying: Eggs are dropped in vegetation.

Flight period: From April to June.

Host plants: Grasses, like *Festuca ovina*.

Diversity and systematics: European populations belong to subspecies *dalmata*.

IMAGOS			LARVAE		
Food			Food		
Behaviour of males			Caterpillar location		
Dispersion			Chrysalis location		

Did you know?

Eggs of the Dalmatian Ringlet do not adhere to the LHP. They settle in the middle of a tuft of leaves. The caterpillars enter a slowed-down state in summer and resume their activity during autumn.

SATYRINAE

MOUNTAIN RINGLET *EREBIA EPIPHRON*

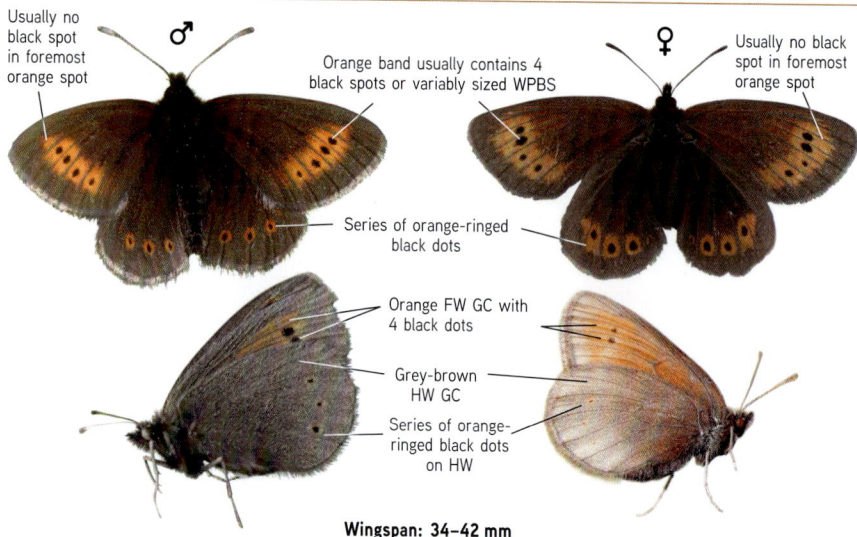

♂

Usually no black spot in foremost orange spot

Orange band usually contains 4 black spots or variably sized WPBS

♀

Usually no black spot in foremost orange spot

Series of orange-ringed black dots

Orange FW GC with 4 black dots

Grey-brown HW GC

Series of orange-ringed black dots on HW

Wingspan: 34–42 mm

Habitat: Mesophilic or damper montane and subalpine grasslands, meadows, heaths, and clearings, often in a sheltered context.

Hibernating stage: Caterpillar (often twice).

Elevational range: Between 500 and 2,500 m.

Egg-laying: Eggs are laid singly on LHP leaves and stems.

Flight period: From June to August.

Host plants: Grasses, including *Festuca ovina, F. airoides, F. rubra, F. quadriflora, F. valesiaca, F. violacea, Poa annua, Aira praecox, Avenella flexuosa, Deschampsia cespitosa, Danthonia decumbens,* and *Nardus stricta.* Also reported on *Carex pilulifera* and *Eleocharis palustris* (Cyperaceae).

Diversity and systematics: The nominate subspecies flies in Germany. Subspecies *mackeri* forms populations in the Vosges massif. Subspecies *aetheria* inhabits the Alps. Subspecies *mnemon* and *scotica* fly in England and Scotland, respectively. Subspecies *amplevittata* is present in Italy (Tuscany). Subspecies *pyrenaica* and *orientpyrenaica* populate the Central and Eastern Pyrenees, respectively. Subspecies *silesiana* flies in the Czech Republic. Subspecies *transylvanica* is found in Romania. Subspecies *valdeonica* is described from Spain, and subspecies *roosi* from the Balkans.

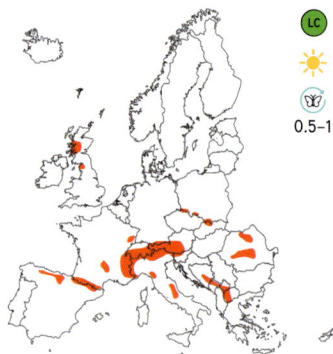

LC

0.5–1

Did you know?

The particularly complex systematics and significant morphological variability of the Mountain Ringlet suggest a fragmented range during glacial and postglacial periods, leading to numerous genetic isolations.

IMAGOS		LARVAE	
Food		Food	
Behaviour of males		Caterpillar location	
Dispersion		Chrysalis location	

SATYRINAE

RÄTZER'S RINGLET *EREBIA CHRISTI*

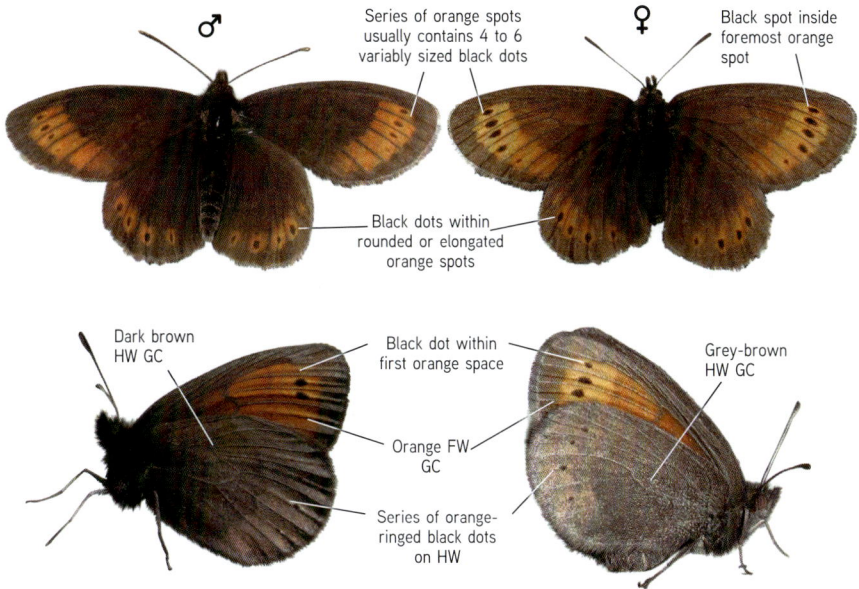

♂

Series of orange spots usually contains 4 to 6 variably sized black dots

♀

Black spot inside foremost orange spot

Black dots within rounded or elongated orange spots

Dark brown HW GC

Black dot within first orange space

Grey-brown HW GC

Orange FW GC

Series of orange-ringed black dots on HW

Wingspan: 36–40 mm

Habitat: Steep, rocky slopes that are grassy with a few larch trees.

Hibernating stage: Overwinters twice as a caterpillar.

Elevational range: Between 1,400 and 2,300 m.

Egg-laying: Eggs are laid singly on LHP leaves and stems.

Flight period: From June to August.

Host plants: *Festuca ovina* (Poaceae).

Diversity and systematics: There are no notable subspecies.

VU

0.5

IMAGOS		LARVAE	
Food		Food	
Behaviour of males		Caterpillar location	
Dispersion		Chrysalis location	

Did you know?

Rätzer's Ringlet is the species in genus *Erebia* with the most restricted range in Europe. It flies only on the southern slope of the Simplon Pass in a small area lying between Switzerland and Italy.

SATYRINAE

LESSER MOUNTAIN RINGLET *EREBIA MELAMPUS*

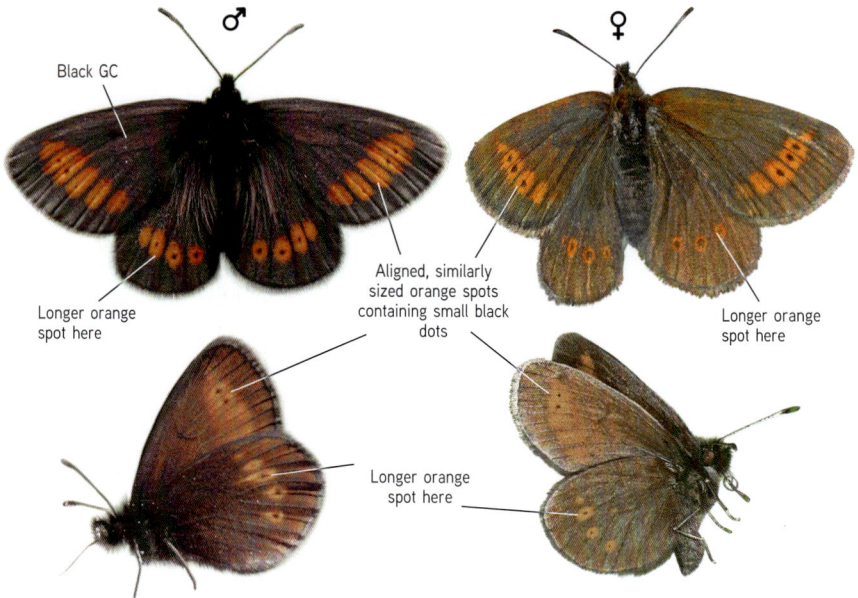

♂

Black GC

Longer orange
spot here

Aligned, similarly
sized orange spots
containing small black
dots

♀

Longer orange
spot here

Longer orange
spot here

Wingspan: 30–36 mm

Habitat: Montane and subalpine mesophilic or damp meadows, edges, and clearings.

Hibernating stage: Caterpillar.

Elevational range: From 1,000 to 2,500 m.

Egg-laying: Eggs are laid singly on LHP leaves.

Flight period: From July to September.

Host plants: Grasses, including *Festuca ovina*, *F. rubra*, *F. violacea*, *Poa annua*, *P. nemoralis*, and *Anthoxanthum odoratum*.

Diversity and systematics: There are no notable subspecies.

■ E. melampus
■ E. sudetica
■ E. melampus + E. sudetica

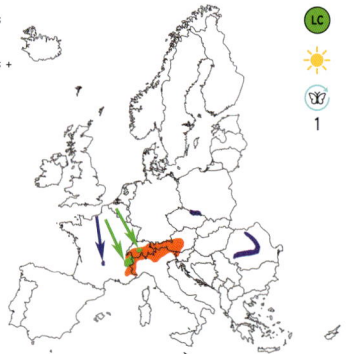

LC

1

IMAGOS		LARVAE	
Food		Food	
Behaviour of males		Caterpillar location	
Dispersion		Chrysalis location	

Did you know?

The Lesser Mountain Ringlet does not like dry environments. It is therefore more abundant in the Northern and Central Alps than in the southern part of the massif.

SUDETEN RINGLET *EREBIA SUDETICA*

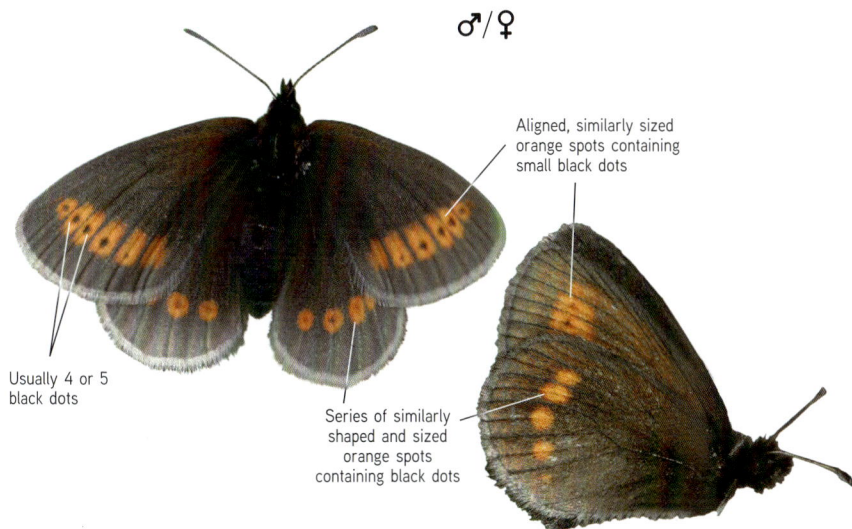

♂/♀

Aligned, similarly sized orange spots containing small black dots

Usually 4 or 5 black dots

Series of similarly shaped and sized orange spots containing black dots

Wingspan: 27–30 mm

Habitat: Montane and subalpine mesophilic or damp meadows, edges, and clearings.

Hibernating stage: Caterpillar.

Elevational range: Between 1,000 and 2,000 m.

Egg-laying: Eggs are laid singly on LHP leaves.

Flight period: From July to September.

Host plants: Grasses, including *Anthoxanthum odoratum*, *Poa annua*, and *Festuca rubra*.

Diversity and systematics: The nominate subspecies flies in the Czech Republic. Subspecies *inalpina* populates Switzerland and Savoie. Subspecies *belledonnae* forms populations in the alpine Belledonne massif, while subspecies *liorana* is found in the French Massif Central. Romanian populations belong to subspecies *radnaensis*.

■ E. melampus
■ E. sudetica
■ E. melampus + E. sudetica

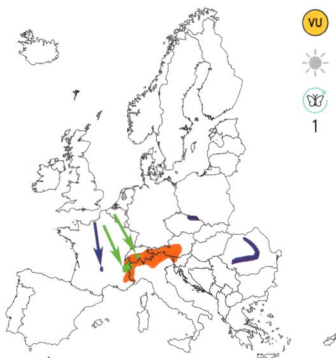

VU

1

Did you know?

The Sudeten Ringlet is ecologically and morphologically similar to the Lesser Mountain Ringlet. In regions where their ranges overlap, they likely mutually exclude each other.

IMAGOS		LARVAE	
Food	✿	Food	🌿
Behaviour of males	🦋	Caterpillar location	🌾
Dispersion	✿	Chrysalis location	🌾

SATYRINAE

YELLOW-SPOTTED RINGLET/WHITE-SPOTTED RINGLET/VOSGES RINGLET
EREBIA MANTO/E. BUBASTIS/E. VOGESIACA

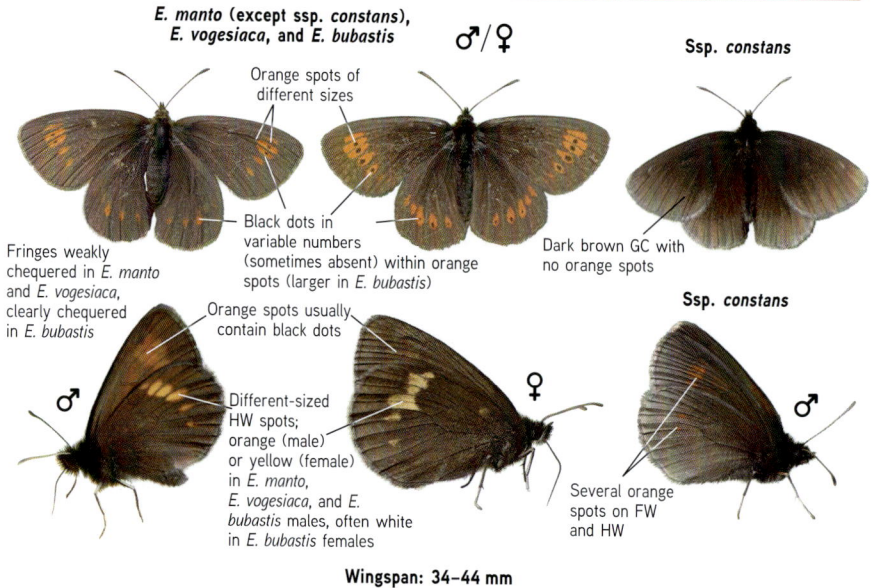

E. manto (except ssp. *constans*),
E. vogesiaca, and *E. bubastis* ♂/♀

Ssp. *constans*

Orange spots of different sizes

Black dots in variable numbers (sometimes absent) within orange spots (larger in *E. bubastis*)

Fringes weakly chequered in *E. manto* and *E. vogesiaca*, clearly chequered in *E. bubastis*

Dark brown GC with no orange spots

Ssp. *constans*

Orange spots usually contain black dots

Different-sized HW spots; orange (male) or yellow (female) in *E. manto*, *E. vogesiaca*, and *E. bubastis* males, often white in *E. bubastis* females

Several orange spots on FW and HW

Wingspan: 34–44 mm

Habitat: Mesophilic montane and subalpine meadows, clearings, and edges.

Hibernating stage: Egg or caterpillar during the first overwintering, caterpillar for the second.

Elevational range: Between 1,000 and 2,000 m.

Egg-laying: Eggs are laid singly on LHP leaves and stems.

Flight period: From June to September.

Host plants: Grasses, including *Festuca rubra*, *F. ovina*, *F. eskia*, *Poa alpina*, *P. nemoralis*, *Anthoxanthum odoratum*, and *Phleum* spp. Sedges, like *Carex ferruginea* and *C. flacca*.

Diversity and systematics: Most alpine populations belong to subspecies *manto*. *Erebia vogesiaca* populates the Vosges massif and probably the Jura. Subspecies *constans* flies in the French Massif Central, the Pyrenees, and the Cantabrian Mountains. Subspecies *osmanica* and *praeclara* live in the Balkans and Central Europe, respectively. For *E. bubastis*, the nominate, *willieni*, and *valmaritima* subspecies fly in Switzerland, the northern French Alps, and southern Italian Alps, respectively.

	E. manto manto
	E. m. constans
	E. vogesiaca
	E. m. praeclara
	E. bubastis
	E. b. trajanus
	E. m. osmanica

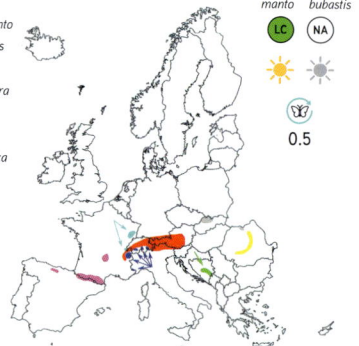

manto bubastis
LC NA

0.5

Did you know?

The Yellow-spotted, White-spotted, and Vosges Ringlets can only be distinguished through genitalia examination. The Vosges Ringlet has recently reached species status and is particularly threatened by climate change.

IMAGOS		LARVAE	
Food	🌼	Food	🍃
Behaviour of males		Caterpillar location	
Dispersion		Chrysalis location	

ERIPHYLE RINGLET *EREBIA ERIPHYLE*

♂/♀

Aligned, similarly sized orange spots contain small black dots

Orange spot markedly longer than the others

Few black dots within FW orange spots

No black dots within HW orange spots

Orange spot markedly longer than the others

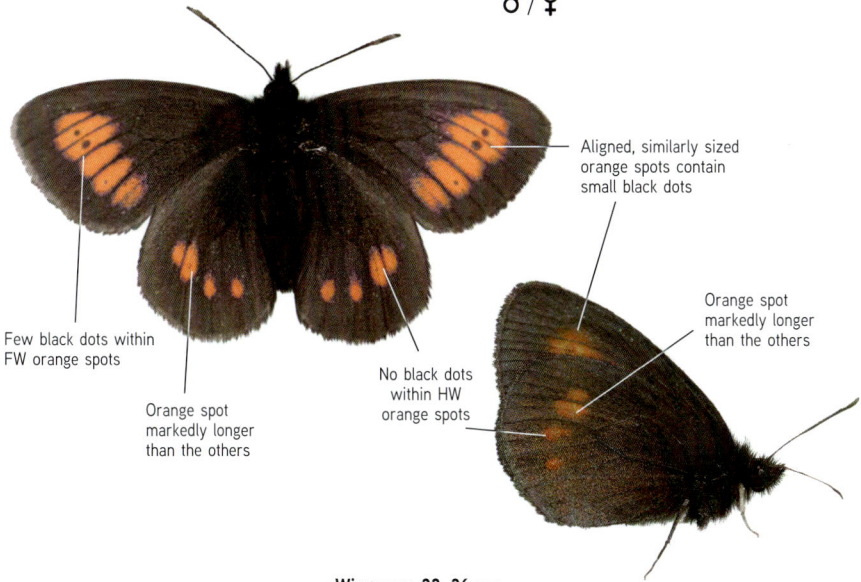

Wingspan: 32–36 mm

Habitat: Subalpine megaphorbs in the green alder zone, often on north-facing slopes.

Hibernating stage: Overwinters twice as a caterpillar (usually inside the egg for the first winter).

Elevational range: Between 1,500 and 2,500 m.

Egg-laying: Eggs are laid singly on LHP leaves and stems.

Flight period: From June to August.

Host plants: Grasses, including *Anthoxanthum odoratum* and *Deschampsia cespitosa. Carex ferruginea* (Cyperaceae).

Diversity and systematics: The nominate subspecies constitutes most populations. Subspecies *tristis* flies in Austria.

LC

0.5

Did you know?

The presence of the Eriphyle Ringlet in France is not confirmed. However, it does fly in the Swiss Alps not far from the border. Therefore, one should look for it in the nearby Savoie . . . and be aware of the Yellow-spotted Ringlet, to which it bears a strong resemblance.

IMAGOS		LARVAE	
Food	☆	Food	🍃
Behaviour of males		Caterpillar location	
Dispersion		Chrysalis location	

YELLOW-BANDED RINGLET *EREBIA FLAVOFASCIATA*

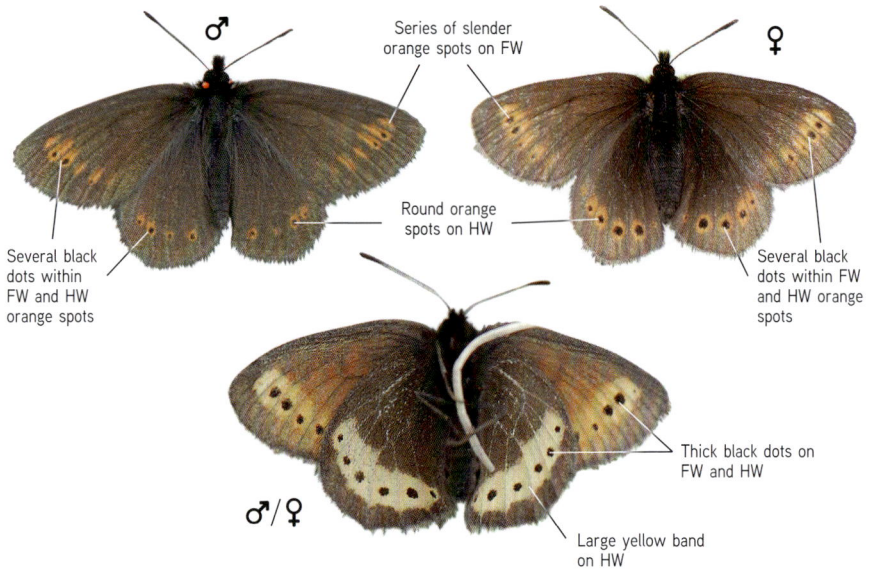

♂

Series of slender
orange spots on FW

♀

Round orange
spots on HW

Several black
dots within
FW and HW
orange spots

Several black
dots within FW
and HW orange
spots

♂/♀

Thick black dots on
FW and HW

Large yellow band
on HW

Wingspan: 34–36 mm

Habitat: Sunny subalpine and alpine meadows.

Hibernating stage: Overwinters twice as a caterpillar.

Elevational range: Between 1,600 and 2,600 m.

Egg-laying: Eggs are laid singly on LHP leaves and stems.

Flight period: From June to August.

Host plants: Grasses, including *Festuca rubra*, *F. ovina*, *F. violacea*, *Lolium* spp., *Dactylis* spp., and *Poa* spp.

Diversity and systematics: Most populations belong to the nominate subspecies. Subspecies *thiemei* is described from the Swiss Engadine region.

NT

0.5

IMAGOS		LARVAE	
Food		Food	
Behaviour of males		Caterpillar location	
Dispersion		Chrysalis location	

Did you know?

Adult butterflies often feed on the inflorescences of wild thyme and large Asteraceae flowers.

BLIND RINGLET   *EREBIA PHARTE*

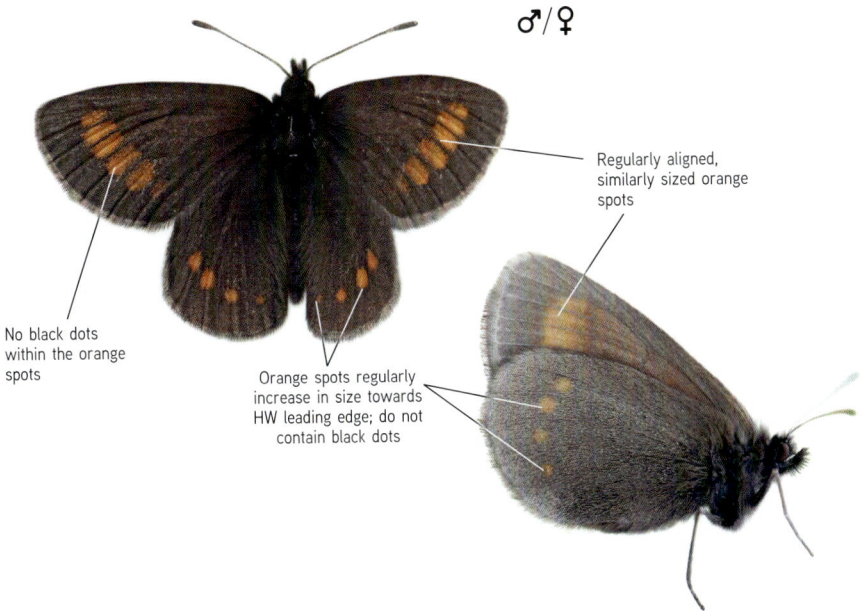

♂/♀

Regularly aligned, similarly sized orange spots

No black dots within the orange spots

Orange spots regularly increase in size towards HW leading edge; do not contain black dots

Wingspan: 32–40 mm

Habitat: Damp or mesophilic meadows, heaths, and clearings.

Hibernating stage: Overwinters twice as a caterpillar.

Elevational range: Between 1,200 and 2,300 m.

Egg-laying: Eggs are laid singly on LHP leaves and stems.

Flight period: July and August.

Host plants: Grasses, including *Nardus stricta*, *Festuca ovina*, *F. rubra*, and *F. quadriflora*. Sedges, such as *Carex flacca* and *C. ferruginea*.

Diversity and systematics: There are no notable subspecies. Several forms have been described.

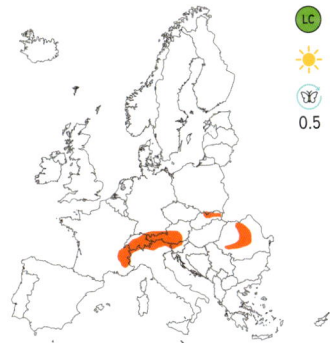

LC

0.5

IMAGOS		LARVAE	
Food	☆	Food	🍃
Behaviour of males		Caterpillar location	
Dispersion		Chrysalis location	

Did you know?

The term "blind" in the common name of this ringlet refers to the typical absence of black dots within the orange spots on the wings.

SATYRINAE

WHITE SPECK RINGLET *EREBIA CLAUDINA*

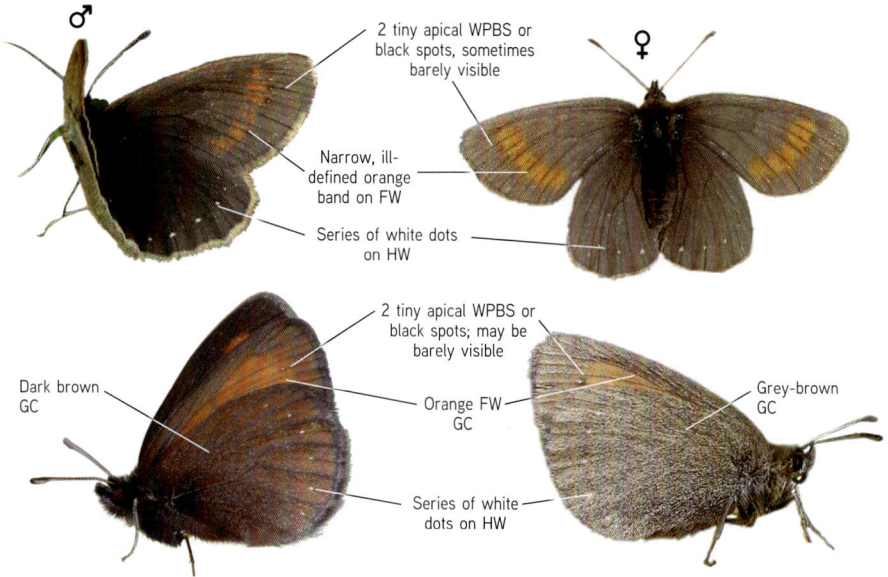

♂

2 tiny apical WPBS or black spots, sometimes barely visible

♀

Narrow, ill-defined orange band on FW

Series of white dots on HW

2 tiny apical WPBS or black spots; may be barely visible

Dark brown GC

Orange FW GC

Grey-brown GC

Series of white dots on HW

Wingspan: 34–36 mm

Habitat: Mesophilic, flower-rich subalpine and alpine meadows around the treeline.

Hibernating stage: Overwinters twice as a caterpillar.

Elevational range: Between 1,400 and 2,300 m.

Egg-laying: Eggs are dropped in vegetation or on the ground.

Flight period: From June to August.

Host plants: Grasses, including *Festuca quadriflora*, *Poa* spp., and *Deschampsia cespitosa*.

Diversity and systematics: There are no notable subspecies.

NT

0.5

IMAGOS		LARVAE	
Food		Food	
Behaviour of males		Caterpillar location	
Dispersion		Chrysalis location	

Did you know?

Adult butterflies often feed on the inflorescences of yellow Asteraceae and thymes.

DEWY RINGLET/FALSE DEWY RINGLET
EREBIA PANDROSE/E. STHENNYO

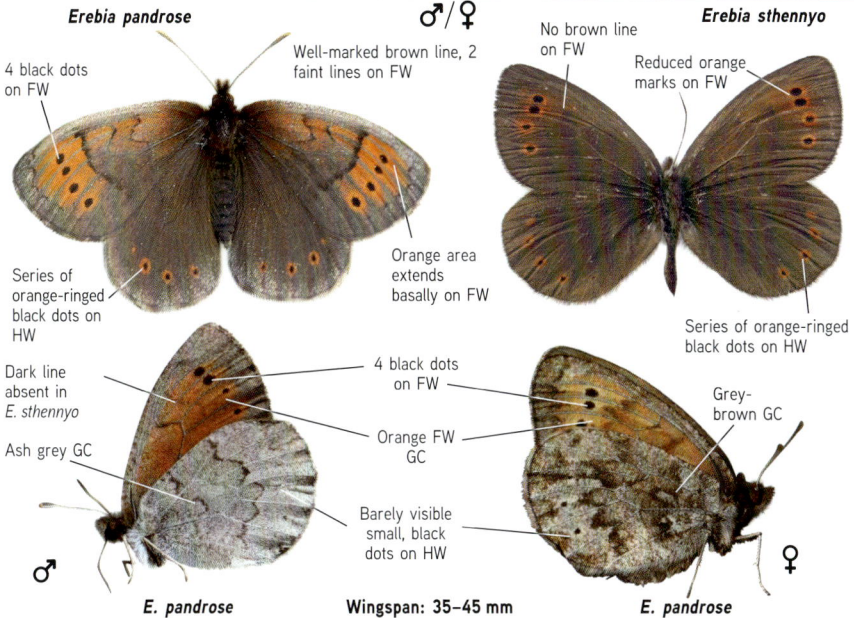

Erebia pandrose ♂/♀ **Erebia sthennyo**

4 black dots on FW

Well-marked brown line, 2 faint lines on FW

No brown line on FW

Reduced orange marks on FW

Series of orange-ringed black dots on HW

Orange area extends basally on FW

Series of orange-ringed black dots on HW

Dark line absent in *E. sthennyo*

Ash grey GC

4 black dots on FW

Orange FW GC

Grey-brown GC

Barely visible small, black dots on HW

♂

♀

E. pandrose **Wingspan: 35–45 mm** **E. pandrose**

Habitat: Subalpine and alpine stony slopes, grasslands, and low-growing meadows.

Hibernating stage: Overwinters twice as a caterpillar.

Elevational range: Up to 3,000 m in mountain regions (but also at low elevations in Scandinavia).

Egg-laying: Eggs are laid singly on the ground, without adherence, for *Erebia pandrose* and on LHP leaves and stems for *E. sthennyo*.

Flight period: From June to August.

Host plants: Grasses, including *Festuca alpina, F. ovina, F. pallens, F. quadriflora, F. violacea, Nardus stricta, Poa* spp., *Sesleria albicans,* and *S. caerulea.*

Diversity and systematics: For *Erebia pandrose,* the nominate subspecies flies in the Alps, while subspecies *lappona* is found in Scandinavia. Subspecies *roberti* and *sibiniaca* populate the Carpathians. Subspecies *gracilis* is present in the Pyrenees, and subspecies *sevoensis* populates the Apennines. Subspecies *ambicolorata* is described from Bulgaria.

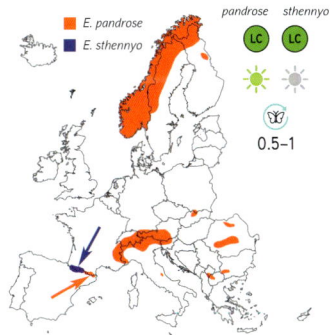

■ *E. pandrose*
■ *E. sthennyo*

pandrose   sthennyo

LC   LC

0.5–1

Did you know?

The status of the False Dewy Ringlet is not universally agreed upon. It can also be considered a subspecies of the Dewy Ringlet, especially since intermediate forms between the two taxa have been discovered in the Alps.

IMAGOS		LARVAE	
Food		Food	
Behaviour of males		Caterpillar location	
Dispersion		Chrysalis location	

SATYRINAE

MNESTRA'S RINGLET *EREBIA MNESTRA*

♂/♀

Basal black area not veined with orange (males)

2 tiny apical WPBS sometimes absent

Large orange band on outer half of FW

Series of orange spots contain no WPBS

Orange FW GC

2 small apical WPBS

Orange FW GC

No WPBS on HW

Dark brown homogeneous GC

Grey-brown GC, with slightly paler outer HW half

♀

♂

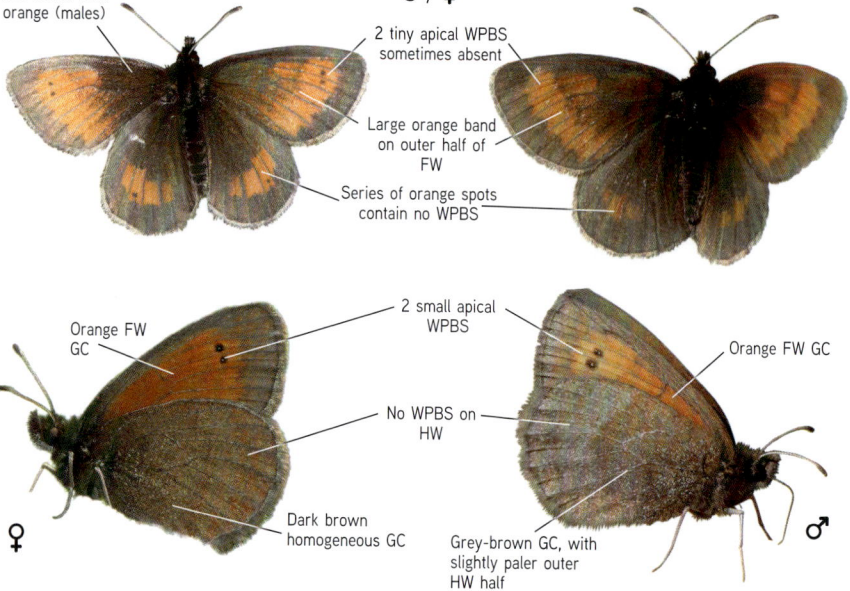

Wingspan: 34–38 mm

Habitat: Subalpine and alpine grasslands, low-growing meadows, and heaths.

Hibernating stage: Overwinters twice as a caterpillar.

Elevational range: From 1,500 to 2,600 m.

Egg-laying: Eggs are laid singly on LHP dry parts.

Flight period: From June to August.

Host plants: Grasses, including *Festuca ovina*, *F. cinerea*, *F. varia*, *F. violacea*, *Patzkea paniculata*, *Sesleria albicans*, and *S. caerulea*.

Diversity and systematics: There are no notable subspecies.

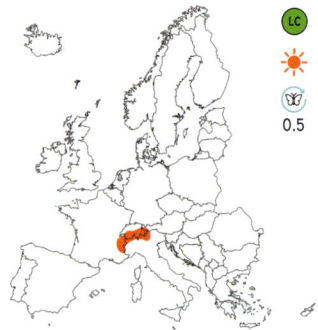

LC

0.5

IMAGOS		LARVAE	
Food		Food	
Behaviour of males		Caterpillar location	
Dispersion		Chrysalis location	

Did you know?

Mnestra's Ringlet closely resembles the False Mnestra Ringlet, which tends to fly in the southwestern Alps. Adults particularly enjoy the nectar of Asteraceae flowers.

SATYRINAE

FALSE MNESTRA RINGLET *EREBIA AETHIOPELLUS*

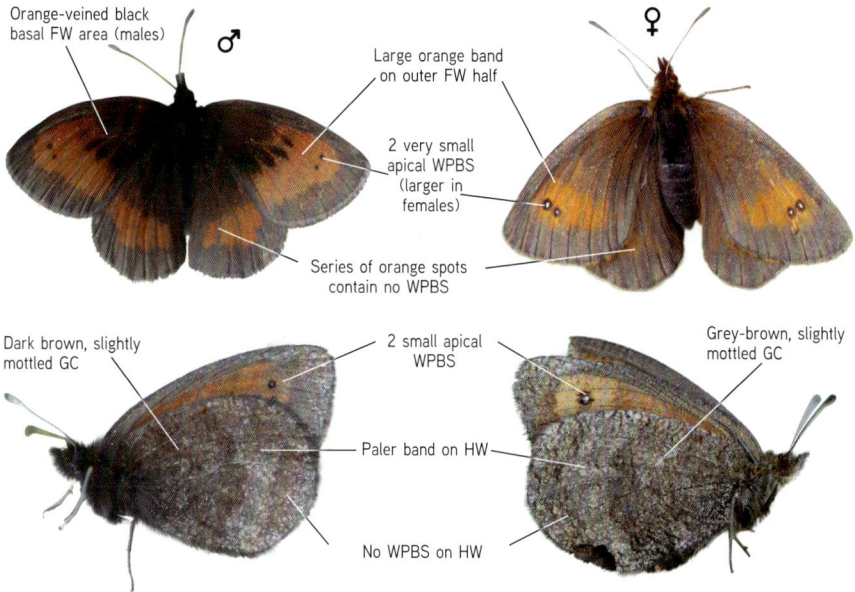

Orange-veined black
basal FW area (males) ♂

Large orange band
on outer FW half ♀

2 very small
apical WPBS
(larger in
females)

Series of orange spots
contain no WPBS

Dark brown, slightly
mottled GC

2 small apical
WPBS

Grey-brown, slightly
mottled GC

Paler band on HW

No WPBS on HW

Wingspan: 36–40 mm

Habitat: Subalpine and alpine rather dry, stony grasslands.

Hibernating stage: Caterpillar.

Elevational range: Between 1,800 and 2,800 m.

Egg-laying: Eggs are laid singly on LHP dry parts or nearby.

Flight period: From June to August.

Host plants: Grasses, including *Festuca quadriflora* and *Patzkea paniculata*.

Diversity and systematics: There are no notable subspecies.

LC

1

Did you know?

The scientific name *aethiopellus* means "small *aethiops*" and refers to the relatively reduced size of the False Mnestra Ringlet compared with other ringlet species.

IMAGOS		LARVAE	
Food		Food	
Behaviour of males		Caterpillar location	
Dispersion		Chrysalis location	

SATYRINAE

SOOTY RINGLET *EREBIA PLUTO*

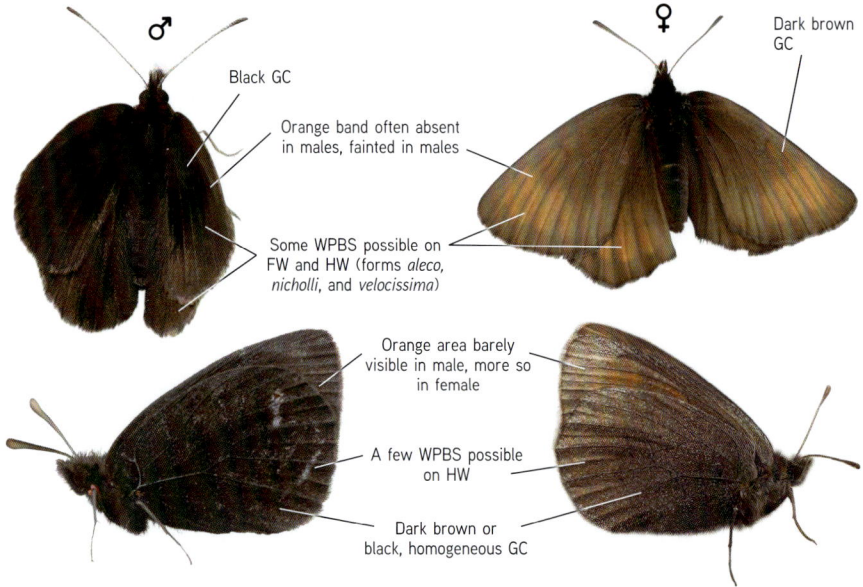

♂

Black GC

Orange band often absent in males, fainted in males

Some WPBS possible on FW and HW (forms *aleco*, *nicholli*, and *velocissima*)

♀

Dark brown GC

Orange area barely visible in male, more so in female

A few WPBS possible on HW

Dark brown or black, homogeneous GC

Wingspan: 40–50 mm

Habitat: Alpine sparsely vegetated moraines and scree.

Hibernating stage: Overwinters twice as a caterpillar.

Elevational range: Between 2,000 and 3,300 m.

Egg-laying: Eggs are laid singly underneath stones.

Flight period: From June to August.

Host plants: Grasses, including *Festuca rubra*, *F. quadriflora*, *F. pseudodura*, *F. halleri*, *Poa alpina*, *P. minor*, *P. annua*, *Sesleria albicans*, and *S. caerulea*.

Diversity and systematics: Several forms are described, varying by the presence of WPBS. There are no notable subspecies.

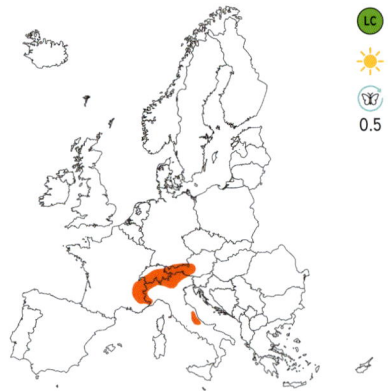

LC

0.5

IMAGOS		LARVAE	
Food		Food	
Behaviour of males		Caterpillar location	
Dispersion		Chrysalis location	

Did you know?

The retreat of glaciers due to climate warming provides ecological opportunities for the Sooty Ringlet, which can colonize these new pioneer habitats.

SATYRINAE

SILKY RINGLET *EREBIA GORGE*

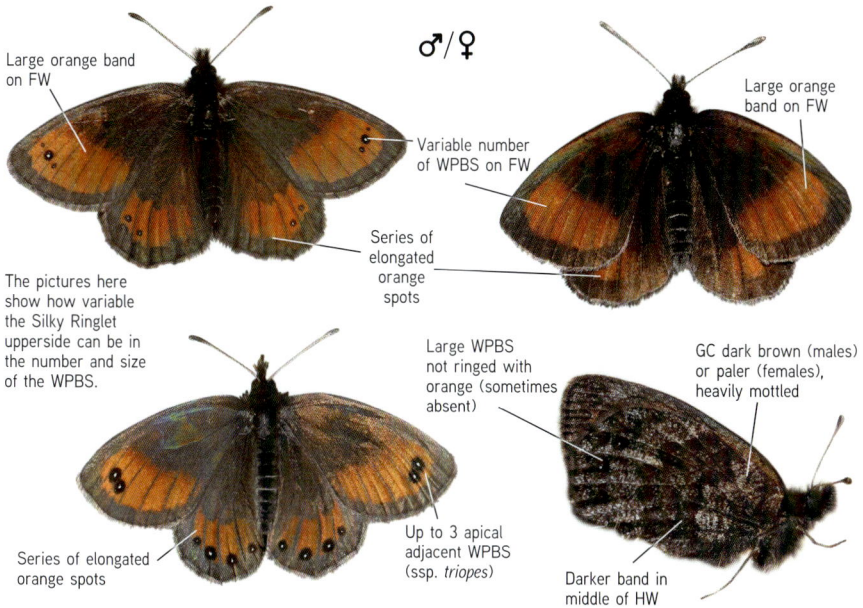

♂/♀

Large orange band on FW

Variable number of WPBS on FW

Large orange band on FW

Series of elongated orange spots

The pictures here show how variable the Silky Ringlet upperside can be in the number and size of the WPBS.

Large WPBS not ringed with orange (sometimes absent)

GC dark brown (males) or paler (females), heavily mottled

Series of elongated orange spots

Up to 3 apical adjacent WPBS (ssp. *triopes*)

Darker band in middle of HW

Wingspan: 34–40 mm

Habitat: Stony slopes, scree, and sparsely vegetated dry grasslands.

Hibernating stage: Overwinters twice as a caterpillar.

Elevational range: Between 1,600 and 3,000 m.

Egg-laying: Eggs are laid singly underneath stones.

Flight period: From June to August.

Host plants: Grasses, including *Festuca quadriflora, F. airoides, F. alpina, F. violacea, F. halleri, Poa minor, P. annua,* *P. alpina, Sesleria albicans,* and *S. caerulea.*

Diversity and systematics: The nominate subspecies flies from the French Alps to the west of Austria alongside subspecies *erynis.* Subspecies *triopes* is present in the southern Swiss Alps and adjacent Italy. Subspecies *ramondi* inhabits the Pyrenees alongside the nominate subspecies. Subspecies *albanica* and *pirinica* are described from the Balkans. Numerous forms are also referenced, illustrating the great variability of the species.

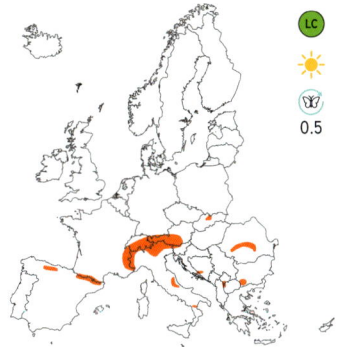

LC

0.5

Did you know?

The behaviour of adult Silky Ringlets is strongly influenced by the wind, which often blows strongly in the species' high-altitude habitats. They often take shelter behind stones and fly close to the ground, where the wind is less forceful.

IMAGOS		LARVAE	
Food	🌼 💧	Food	🌿
Behaviour of males	🦋	Caterpillar location	🐛 🌾
Dispersion	Ⓦ	Chrysalis location	🪱

NICHOLL'S RINGLET *EREBIA RHODOPENSIS*

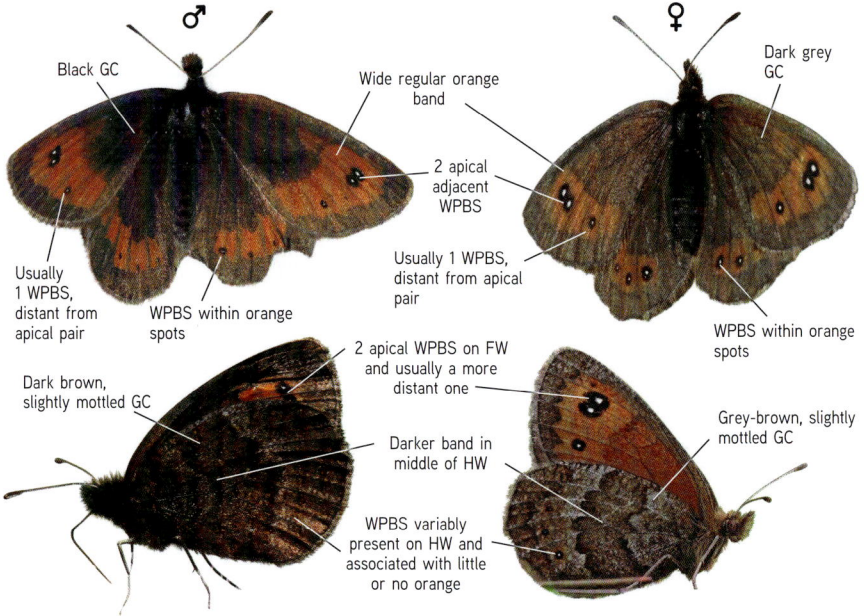

♂ ♀

Black GC

Wide regular orange band

Dark grey GC

2 apical adjacent WPBS

Usually 1 WPBS, distant from apical pair

WPBS within orange spots

Usually 1 WPBS, distant from apical pair

WPBS within orange spots

2 apical WPBS on FW and usually a more distant one

Dark brown, slightly mottled GC

Darker band in middle of HW

Grey-brown, slightly mottled GC

WPBS variably present on HW and associated with little or no orange

Wingspan: 35–38 mm

Habitat: Subalpine and alpine sunny grasslands, above the treeline.

Hibernating stage: Overwinters twice as a caterpillar.

Elevational range: Between 1,700 and 2,600 m.

Egg-laying: Eggs are laid singly on LHP leaves and stems.

Flight period: July and August.

Host plants: Grasses, including *Poa* spp.

Diversity and systematics: There are no notable subspecies.

0.5

IMAGOS		LARVAE	
Food	☆	Food	🍃
Behaviour of males	🦋	Caterpillar location	🌿
Dispersion	🦋	Chrysalis location	🌱

Did you know?

The various aspects of the larval life of Nicholl's Ringlet are known only from captive rearing. The exact identity of the host plants in the wild remains to be determined.

WATER RINGLET   *EREBIA PRONOE*

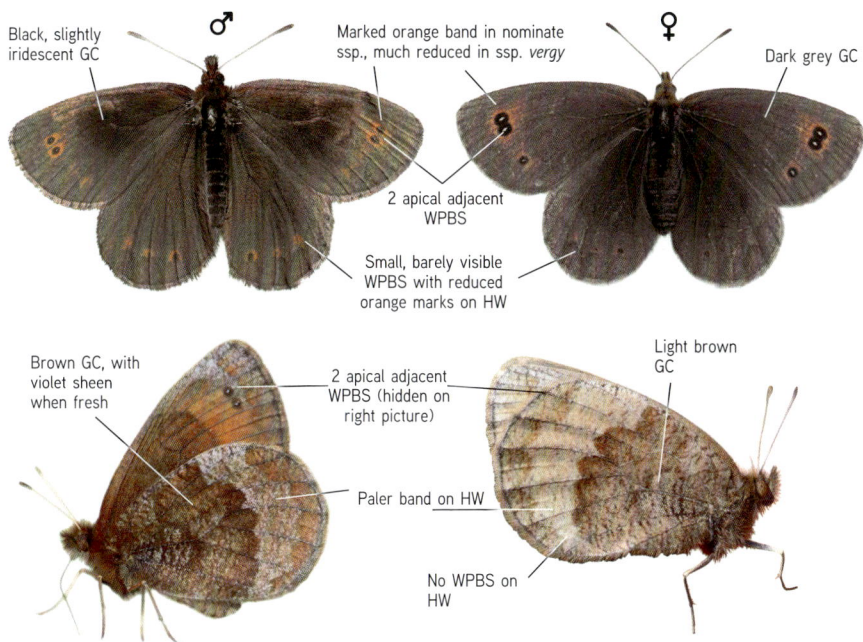

♂

Black, slightly iridescent GC

Marked orange band in nominate ssp., much reduced in ssp. *vergy*

♀

Dark grey GC

2 apical adjacent WPBS

Small, barely visible WPBS with reduced orange marks on HW

Brown GC, with violet sheen when fresh

2 apical adjacent WPBS (hidden on right picture)

Paler band on HW

No WPBS on HW

Light brown GC

Wingspan: 42–50 mm

Habitat: Montane and subalpine meadows and clearings, often on calcareous substrates.

Hibernating stage: Caterpillar.

Elevational range: Between 900 and 2,300 m.

Egg-laying: Eggs are laid singly on LHP dry leaves and stems.

Flight period: From June to September.

Host plants: Grasses, mainly *Festuca ovina, F. quadriflora, F. rubra, Poa spp, Anthoxanthum odoratum*, and *Sesleria albicans*.

Diversity and systematics: The nominate subspecies flies in the Central Alps. Subspecies *vergy* inhabits the Western Alps and the Jura. Subspecies *glottis* forms populations in the Pyrenees and Spain. Subspecies *fruhstorferi* is described from the Balkans, and subspecies *regalis* flies in Romania. Subspecies *gardeina* flies in western Austria while subspecies *psathura* is found in Swiss Wallis and is sometimes considered a different species.

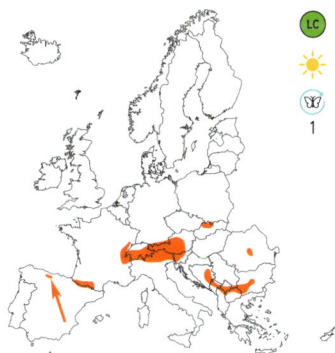

LC

1

IMAGOS			LARVAE		
Food			Food		
Behaviour of males			Caterpillar location		
Dispersion			Chrysalis location		

Did you know?

The Water Ringlet can hybridize with the Mountain Ringlet in the Pyrenees. A genetic analysis confirmed their hybrid origin.

SATYRINAE

COMMON BRASSY RINGLET/WESTERN BRASSY RINGLET/FREYER'S BRASSY RINGLET
EREBIA CASSIOIDES/E. ARVERNENSIS/E. NELEUS

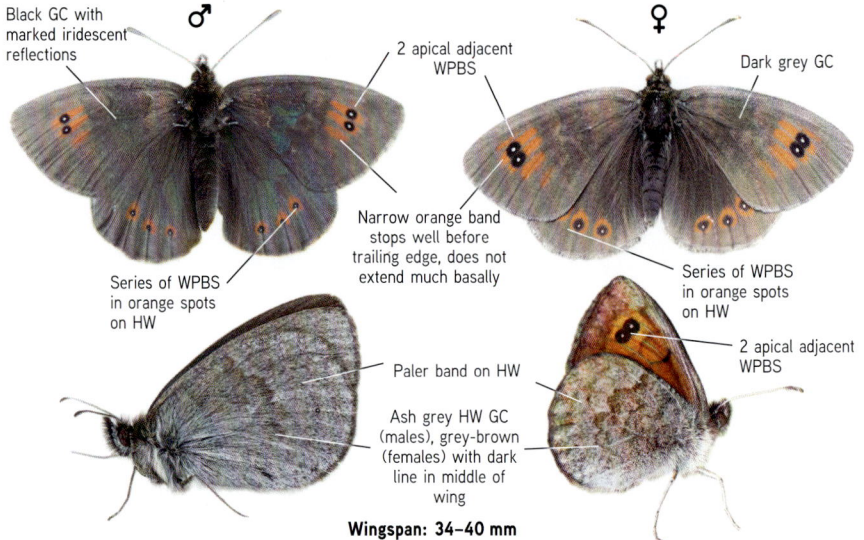

♂

Black GC with marked iridescent reflections

2 apical adjacent WPBS

♀

Dark grey GC

Narrow orange band stops well before trailing edge, does not extend much basally

Series of WPBS in orange spots on HW

Series of WPBS in orange spots on HW

2 apical adjacent WPBS

Paler band on HW

Ash grey HW GC (males), grey-brown (females) with dark line in middle of wing

Wingspan: 34–40 mm

Habitat: Subalpine and alpine low-growing grasslands and meadows.

Hibernating stage: Caterpillar.

Elevational range: Between 1,600 and 2,700 m.

Egg-laying: Eggs are laid singly on LHP dry leaves and stems.

Flight period: From June to September.

Host plants: Grasses, like *Festuca rubra*, *F. ovina*, *F. violacea*, *Nardus stricta*, and *Sesleria* spp.

Diversity and systematics: The systematics of this species group is complex. *Erebia arvernensis* was previously considered a subspecies of *E. cassioides*. *E. neleus* comprises a set of former Balkan subspecies of *E. cassioides*.

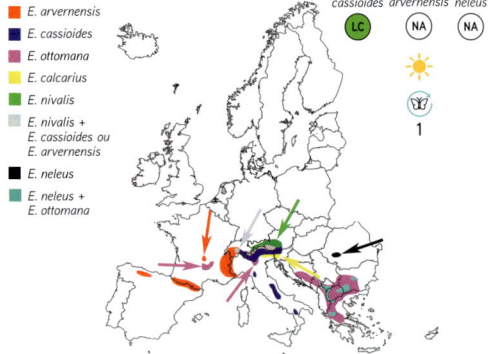

- E. arvernensis
- E. cassioides
- E. ottomana
- E. calcarius
- E. nivalis
- E. nivalis + E. cassioides ou E. arvernensis
- E. neleus
- E. neleus + E. ottomana

cassioides arvernensis neleus

LC   NA   NA

1

Did you know?

These three ringlets can be distinguished only by genetics, geography, and sometimes by genitalia examination. *Erebia arvernensis* inhabits the Pyrenees, the French Massif Central, and the Western Alps. *E. cassioides* forms populations in the central alpine region, and *E. neleus* inhabits the Balkans.

IMAGOS		LARVAE	
Food		Food	
Behaviour of males		Caterpillar location	
Dispersion		Chrysalis location	

OTTOMAN BRASSY RINGLET *EREBIA OTTOMANA*

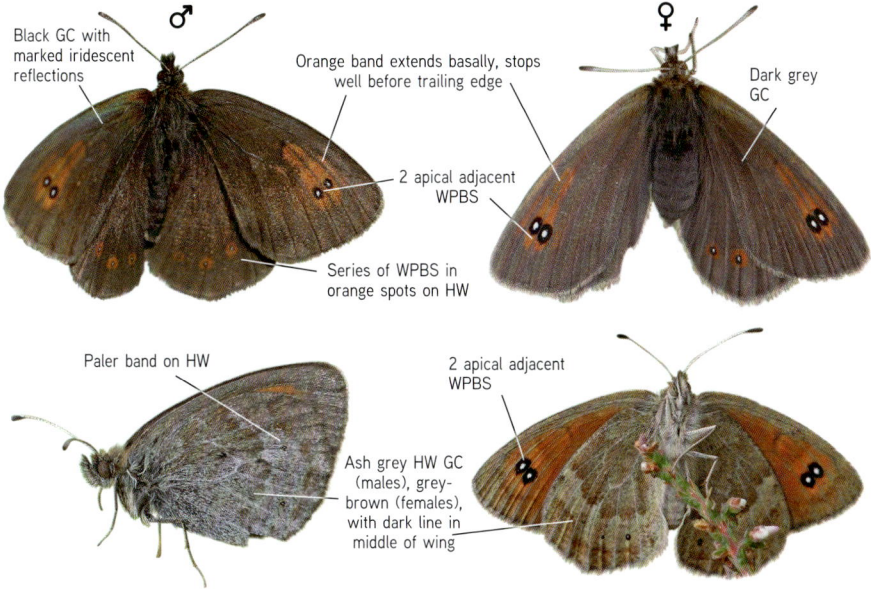

♂

Black GC with marked iridescent reflections

Orange band extends basally, stops well before trailing edge

2 apical adjacent WPBS

Series of WPBS in orange spots on HW

♀

Dark grey GC

Paler band on HW

2 apical adjacent WPBS

Ash grey HW GC (males), grey-brown (females), with dark line in middle of wing

Wingspan: 34–44 mm

Habitat: Montane, subalpine, and alpine meadows often near edges.

Hibernating stage: Caterpillar.

Elevational range: Between 1,200 and 2,500 m.

Egg-laying: Eggs are laid singly on LHP dry leaves and stems.

Flight period: From June to September.

Host plants: Grasses, such as *Festuca ovina, F. alpina, F. lemanii, F. nigrescens, F. rubra, Patzkea paniculata,* and *Nardus stricta*.

Diversity and systematics: Subspecies *tardenota* forms the French populations. Subspecies *benacensis* is localized in northern Italy. Subspecies *balcanica* flies in the Balkans. The nominate subspecies is described from Turkey.

- E. arvernensis
- E. cassioides
- E. ottomana
- E. calcarius
- E. nivalis
- E. nivalis + E. cassioides ou E. arvernensis
- E. neleus
- E. neleus + E. ottomana

LC

1

Did you know?

The Ottoman Brassy Ringlet is difficult to distinguish from the Western Brassy Ringlet without examining the genitalia. However, the two species aren't known to fly together.

IMAGOS		LARVAE	
Food	☆	Food	🍃
Behaviour of males		Caterpillar location	🌾
Dispersion		Chrysalis location	

SATYRINAE

DE LESSE'S BRASSY RINGLET *EREBIA NIVALIS*

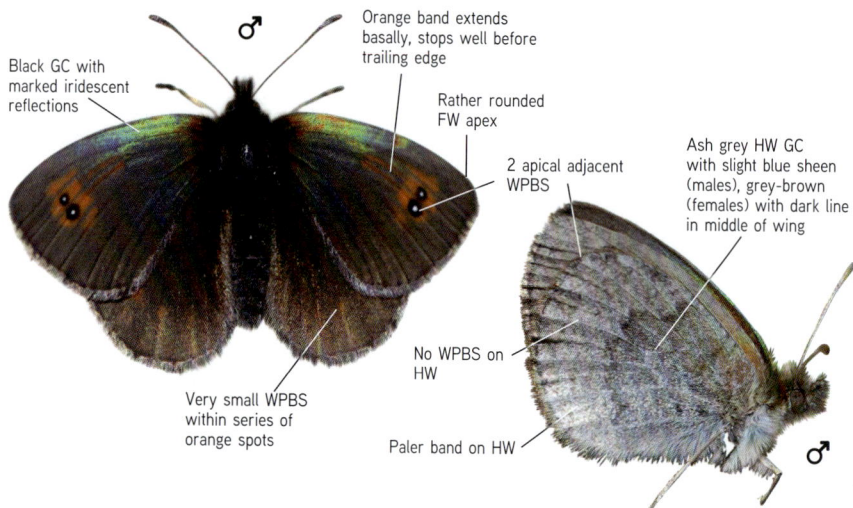

♂

Black GC with marked iridescent reflections

Orange band extends basally, stops well before trailing edge

Rather rounded FW apex

2 apical adjacent WPBS

Ash grey HW GC with slight blue sheen (males), grey-brown (females) with dark line in middle of wing

No WPBS on HW

Very small WPBS within series of orange spots

Paler band on HW

♂

Wingspan: 30–34 mm

Habitat: Alpine low-growing grasslands, moraines, and scree.

Hibernating stage: Overwinters twice as a caterpillar.

Elevational range: Between 2,000 and 2,800 m.

Egg-laying: Eggs are laid singly on LHP leaves and stems.

Flight period: July and August.

Host plants: Grasses, including *Festuca quadriflora*, *F. violacea*, and *Nardus stricta*.

Diversity and systematics: The nominate and *campestris* subspecies fly in Austria from the Grossglockner region to the west and to the east, respectively. Subspecies *warreniana* is described from Switzerland. The Swiss and Austrian populations are allopatric as well as genetically and ecologically distinct.

- E. arvernensis
- E. cassioides
- E. ottomana
- E. calcarius
- E. nivalis
- E. nivalis + E. cassioides ou E. arvernensis
- E. neleus
- E. neleus + E. ottomana

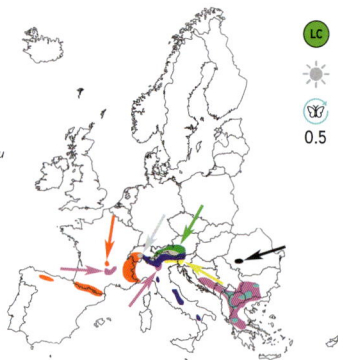

LC

0.5

Did you know?

Upon close inspection, the orange area on the forewing of De Lesse's Brassy Ringlet resembles a sideways-lying elephant head, with the adjacent WPBS appearing as its eyes. The Ottoman Brassy Ringlet displays a similar pattern.

IMAGOS		LARVAE	
Food	☆	Food	🍃
Behaviour of males	🦋	Caterpillar location	🌿
Dispersion		Chrysalis location	

SATYRINAE

SWISS BRASSY RINGLET   *EREBIA TYNDARUS*

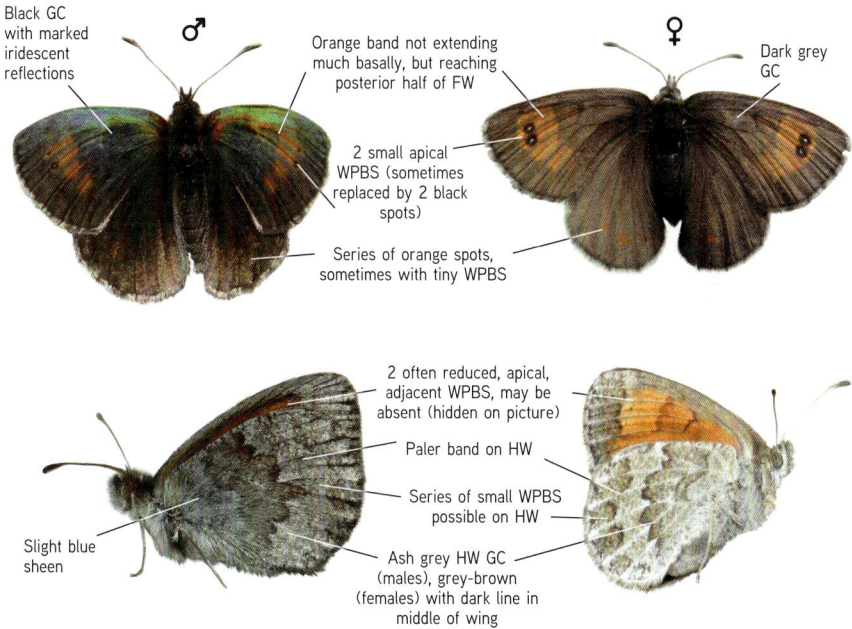

♂

Black GC with marked iridescent reflections

Orange band not extending much basally, but reaching posterior half of FW

2 small apical WPBS (sometimes replaced by 2 black spots)

Series of orange spots, sometimes with tiny WPBS

♀

Dark grey GC

2 often reduced, apical, adjacent WPBS, may be absent (hidden on picture)

Paler band on HW

Series of small WPBS possible on HW

Slight blue sheen

Ash grey HW GC (males), grey-brown (females) with dark line in middle of wing

Wingspan: 34–36 mm

Habitat: Subalpine and alpine grasslands and meadows, rocky slopes, moraines, and scree.

Hibernating stage: Caterpillar.

Elevational range: Between 1,500 and 2,900 m.

Egg-laying: Eggs are laid singly on LHP leaves and stems.

Flight period: From June to September.

Host plants: Grasses, including *Nardus stricta*, *Festuca quadriflora*, *F. halleri*, *F. ovina*, *F. violacea*, *F. varia*, *Poa annua*, and *Anthoxanthum odoratum*.

Diversity and systematics: There are no notable subspecies.

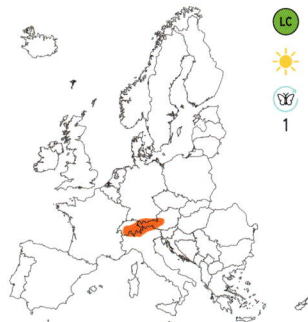

IMAGOS		LARVAE	
Food	✿	Food	🍃
Behaviour of males	🦋	Caterpillar location	🌾
Dispersion	🦋	Chrysalis location	🌾

Did you know?

The Swiss Brassy Ringlet lends its scientific name to a species complex that results from a recent evolutionary radiation. The degree of reproductive isolation among these young taxa is variable.

SATYRINAE

LORKOVIC'S BRASSY RINGLET *EREBIA CALCARIUS*

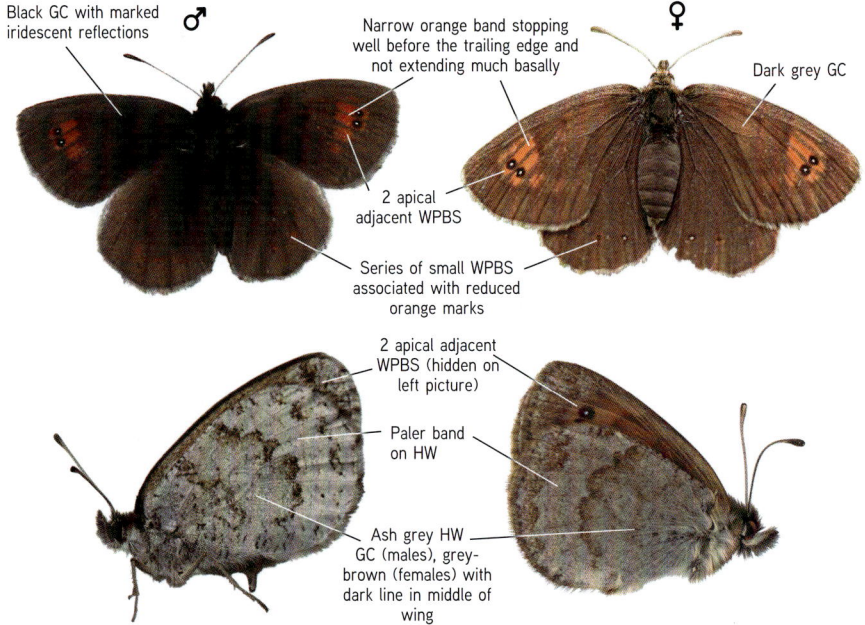

♂ Black GC with marked iridescent reflections

♀ Narrow orange band stopping well before the trailing edge and not extending much basally

Dark grey GC

2 apical adjacent WPBS

Series of small WPBS associated with reduced orange marks

2 apical adjacent WPBS (hidden on left picture)

Paler band on HW

Ash grey HW GC (males), grey-brown (females) with dark line in middle of wing

Wingspan: 36–40 mm

Habitat: Subalpine and alpine meadows on rocky slopes.

Hibernating stage: Caterpillar.

Elevational range: Between 1,400 and 2,500 m.

Egg-laying: Eggs are laid singly on LHP dry leaves and stems.

Flight period: July and August.

Host plants: Grasses of genus *Festuca*, like *F. ovina*, but also *Nardus stricta* and *Sesleria caerulea*.

Diversity and systematics: The nominate subspecies flies in Slovenia. Subspecies *cavallus* is described from the Italian Alps.

- ■ E. arvernensis
- ■ E. cassioides
- ■ E. ottomana
- ■ E. calcarius
- ■ E. nivalis
- ■ E. nivalis + E. cassioides ou E. arvernensis
- ■ E. neleus
- ■ E. neleus + E. ottomana

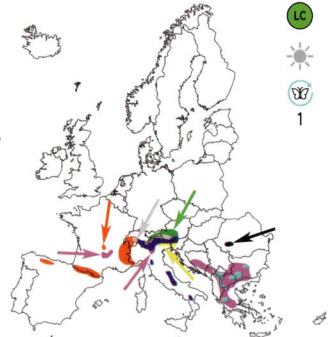

LC

1

IMAGOS		LARVAE	
Food		Food	
Behaviour of males		Caterpillar location	
Dispersion		Chrysalis location	

Did you know?

Lorkovic's Brassy Ringlet is endemic to some Slovenian, Austrian, and Italian mountain ranges.

PYRENEES BRASSY RINGLET/SPANISH BRASSY RINGLET
EREBIA RONDOUI/E. HISPANIA

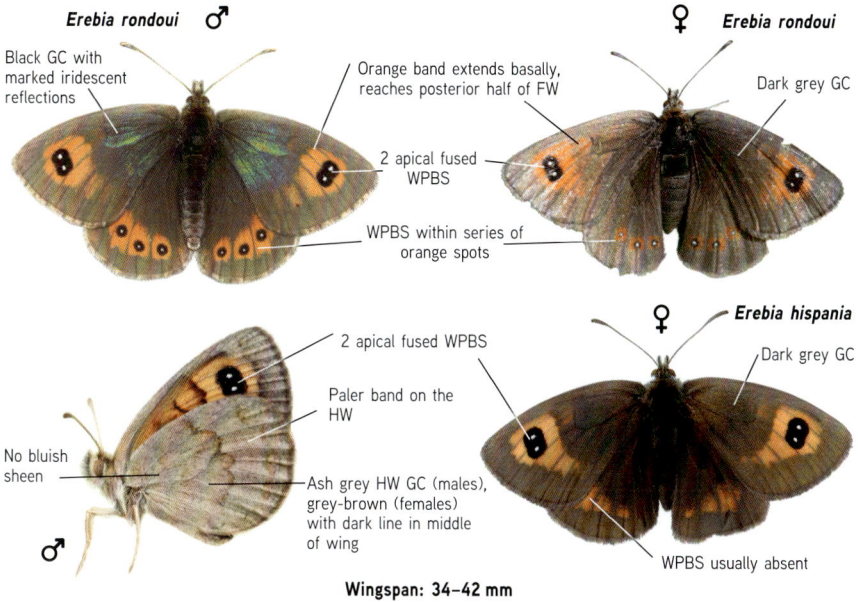

Erebia rondoui ♂

Black GC with marked iridescent reflections

Orange band extends basally, reaches posterior half of FW

2 apical fused WPBS

WPBS within series of orange spots

♀ **Erebia rondoui**

Dark grey GC

2 apical fused WPBS

Paler band on the HW

No bluish sheen

Ash grey HW GC (males), grey-brown (females) with dark line in middle of wing

♂

♀ **Erebia hispania**

Dark grey GC

WPBS usually absent

Wingspan: 34–42 mm

Habitat: Montane and subalpine low-growing and stony grasslands (often scattered with dwarf junipers for *Erebia hispania*).

Hibernating stage: Caterpillar.

Elevational range: Between 1,000 and 2,500 m for *Erebia rondoui*; up to 2,900 m for *E. hispania*.

Egg-laying: Eggs are laid singly on LHP dry leaves and stems.

Flight period: From June to August.

Host plants: Grasses, like *Festuca ovina* and *Nardus stricta*.

Diversity and systematics: For *Erebia rondoui*, the nominate subspecies flies in the Western and Central Pyrenees. Subspecies *goya* inhabits the Eastern Pyrenees and Andorra. For *E. hispania*, there is no notable subspecies.

■ *E. hispania*
■ *E. rondoui*

LC

1

	IMAGOS		LARVAE	
Food		Food		
Behaviour of males		Caterpillar location		
Dispersion		Chrysalis location		

Did you know?

The colour of the caterpillar provides a fairly reliable indication of the adult's gender. Future females have a body of a more vivid green colour compared with the future males, whose larval bodies are greenish-grey.

SATYRINAE

PIEDMONT RINGLET *EREBIA MEOLANS*

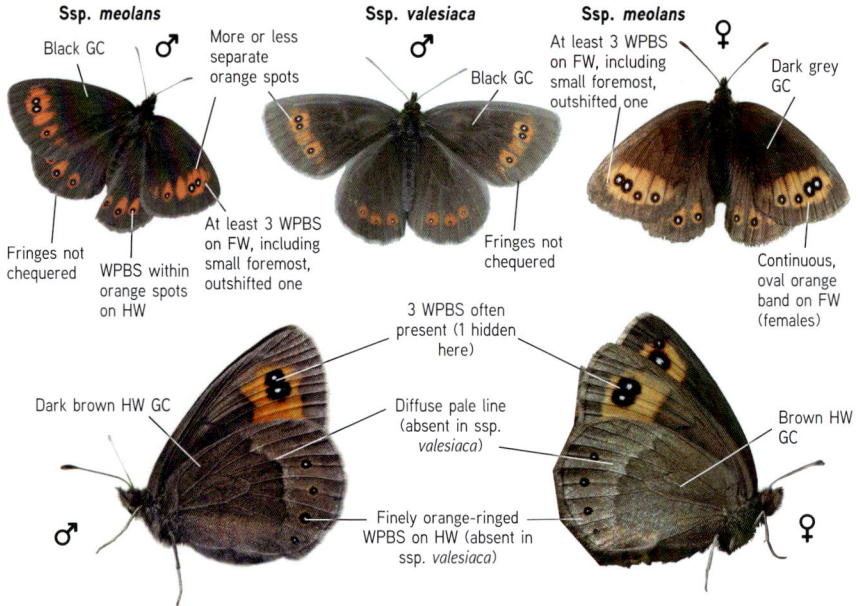

Ssp. *meolans* ♂
- Black GC
- More or less separate orange spots
- Fringes not chequered
- WPBS within orange spots on HW
- At least 3 WPBS on FW, including small foremost, outshifted one

Ssp. *valesiaca* ♂
- Black GC
- Fringes not chequered
- At least 3 WPBS on FW, including small foremost, outshifted one

Ssp. *meolans* ♀
- At least 3 WPBS on FW, including small foremost, outshifted one
- Dark grey GC
- Continuous, oval orange band on FW (females)

- 3 WPBS often present (1 hidden here)
- Dark brown HW GC
- Diffuse pale line (absent in ssp. *valesiaca*)
- Finely orange-ringed WPBS on HW (absent in ssp. *valesiaca*)
- Brown HW GC

♂   ♀

Wingspan: 38–54 mm

Habitat: Rocky forest edges and clearings, grasslands, and meadows usually in a woodland context.

Hibernating stage: Caterpillar.

Elevational range: Up to 2,500 m.

Egg-laying: Eggs are laid singly on LHP leaves and dry stems.

Flight period: From May to August.

Host plants: Grasses, including *Festuca ovina*, *F. rubra*, *F. violacea*, *F. iberica*, *F. trichophylla*, *Lolium arundinaceum*, *Deschampsia cespitosa*, *Nardus stricta*, *Poa annua*, *Agrostis capillaris*, *Avenella flexuosa*, and *Danthonia decumbens*. Sedges, like *Carex pilulifera*.

Diversity and systematics: Most European populations belong to the nominate subspecies. Subspecies *gavarnica* flies in the Pyrenees. Subspecies *bejarensis* inhabits central Spain. Subspecies *stygne* flies from the Vosges to the Central Alps. Subspecies *valesiaca* is present in the Valais, the Grisons, southern Germany, and Savoie.

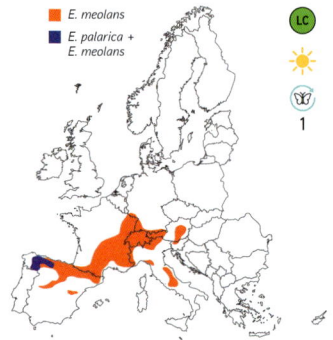

■ E. meolans
■ E. palarica + E. meolans

LC
1

IMAGOS			LARVAE		
Food			Food		
Behaviour of males			Caterpillar location		
Dispersion			Chrysalis location		

Did you know?

As one of the few ringlets to inhabit low elevations, the Piedmont Ringlet faces anthropogenic pressures from agricultural and forestry activities, as well as urbanization.

SATYRINAE

CHAPMAN'S RINGLET *EREBIA PALARICA*

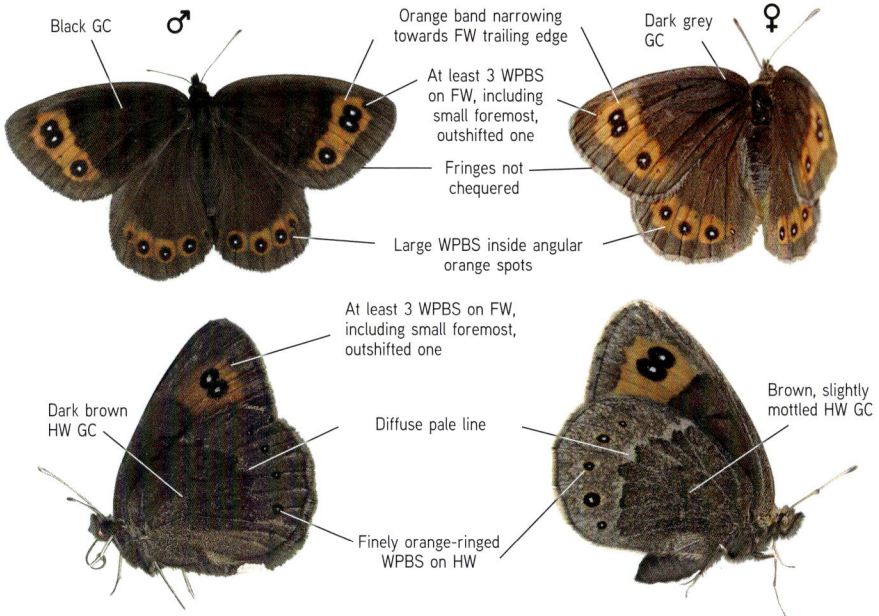

Black GC ♂

Orange band narrowing towards FW trailing edge

Dark grey GC ♀

At least 3 WPBS on FW, including small foremost, outshifted one

Fringes not chequered

Large WPBS inside angular orange spots

At least 3 WPBS on FW, including small foremost, outshifted one

Dark brown HW GC

Diffuse pale line

Brown, slightly mottled HW GC

Finely orange-ringed WPBS on HW

Wingspan: 56–60 mm

Habitat: Grasslands and meadows with bushes (especially brooms), often on siliceous substrates.

Hibernating stage: Caterpillar.

Elevational range: Between 800 and 2,000 m (mainly between 1,000 and 1,600 m).

Egg-laying: Eggs are laid singly or in a few units on LHP leaves and stems.

Flight period: From June to September.

Host plants: Grasses in genus *Festuca*.

Diversity and systematics: The westernmost populations (Serra de Queixa) belong to subspecies *castroviejoi*, which is genetically distinct from the nominate subspecies populations found in the rest of the range.

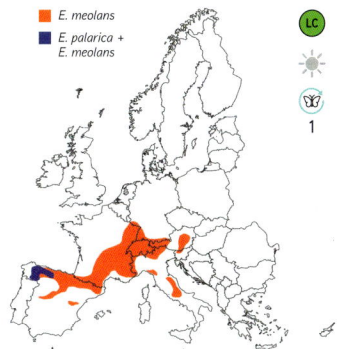

- ■ E. meolans
- ■ E. palarica + E. meolans

LC

1

IMAGOS		LARVAE	
Food		Food	
Behaviour of males		Caterpillar location	
Dispersion		Chrysalis location	

Did you know?

Chapman's Ringlet is the largest European ringlet. Its significant size is the main criterion distinguishing it from the Piedmont Ringlet, with which it shares its range.

SATYRINAE

STYRIAN RINGLET *EREBIA STIRIA*

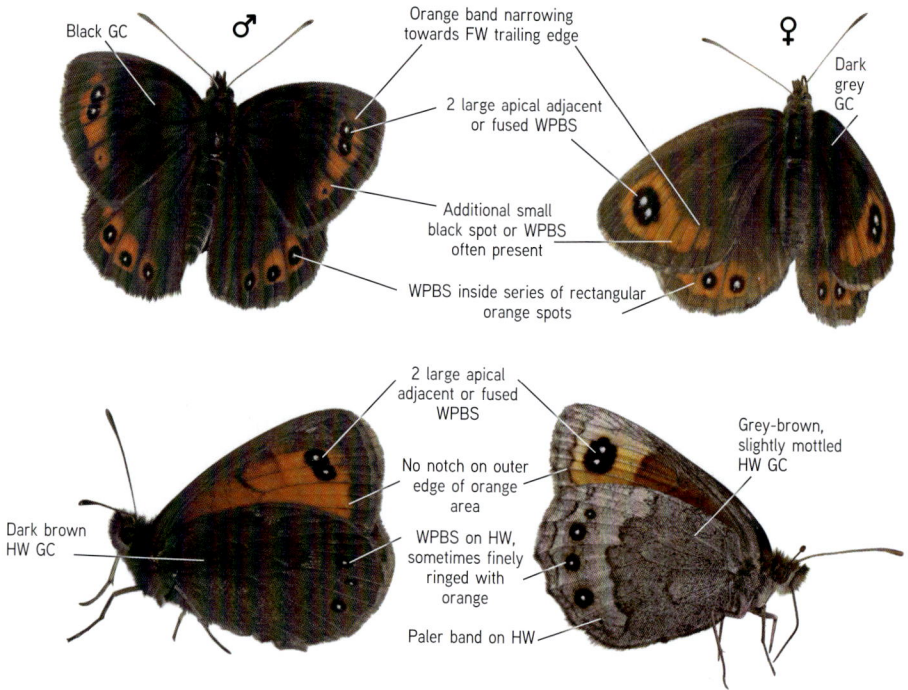

♂

Black GC

Orange band narrowing towards FW trailing edge

2 large apical adjacent or fused WPBS

Additional small black spot or WPBS often present

WPBS inside series of rectangular orange spots

♀

Dark grey GC

2 large apical adjacent or fused WPBS

No notch on outer edge of orange area

WPBS on HW, sometimes finely ringed with orange

Paler band on HW

Dark brown HW GC

Grey-brown, slightly mottled HW GC

Wingspan: 46–52 mm

Habitat: Grassy rocky slopes near forest edges.

Hibernating stage: Caterpillar.

Elevational range: Between 700 and 1,800 m.

Egg-laying: Eggs are laid singly on dry vegetation or on stones.

Flight period: From July to September.

Host plants: Grasses, including *Sesleria caerulea* and *Poa alpina*. Probably sedges, such as *Carex mucronata*.

Diversity and systematics: There are no notable subspecies.

IMAGOS		LARVAE	
Food		Food	
Behaviour of males		Caterpillar location	
Dispersion		Chrysalis location	

Did you know?

The Styrian Ringlet has sometimes been considered a subspecies of the Stygian Ringlet.

SATYRINAE

STYGIAN RINGLET *EREBIA STYX*

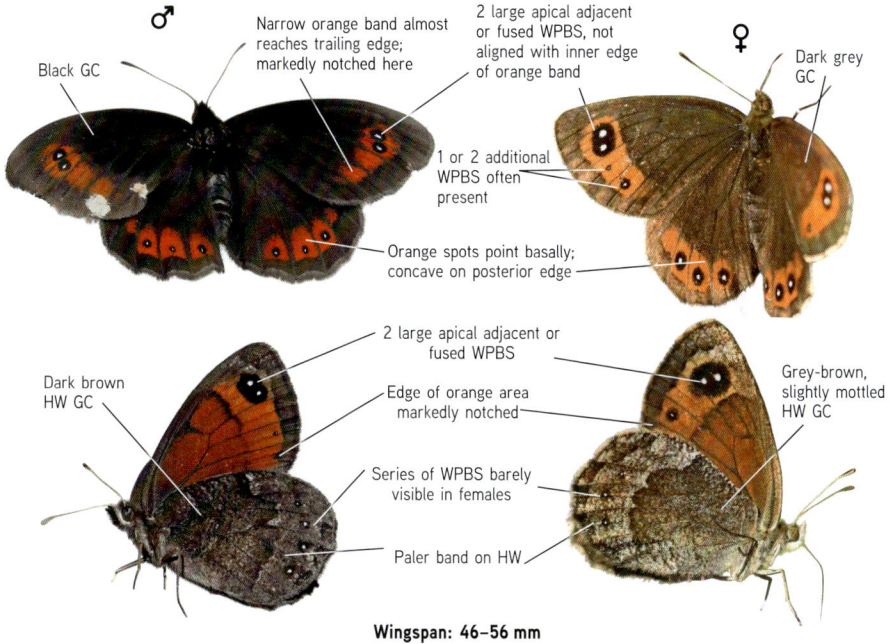

♂

Black GC

Narrow orange band almost reaches trailing edge; markedly notched here

2 large apical adjacent or fused WPBS, not aligned with inner edge of orange band

♀

Dark grey GC

1 or 2 additional WPBS often present

Orange spots point basally; concave on posterior edge

Dark brown HW GC

2 large apical adjacent or fused WPBS

Edge of orange area markedly notched

Series of WPBS barely visible in females

Paler band on HW

Grey-brown, slightly mottled HW GC

Wingspan: 46–56 mm

Habitat: Grassy, rocky slopes or scree with a few Swiss Pines.

Hibernating stage: Caterpillars (sometimes twice).

Elevational range: Between 500 and 2,500 m (mainly above 1,500 m).

Egg-laying: Eggs are laid singly on dry vegetation or on stones.

Flight period: From June to September.

Host plants: Grasses, including *Molinia caerulea*, *Poa annua*, *Sesleria albicans*, and *S. caerulea*. Probably sedges, such as *Carex mucronata*.

Diversity and systematics: The nominate subspecies flies in the Central Alps. Subspecies *reichlini* inhabits the Bavarian Alps. Subspecies *triglites* forms populations in northeastern Italy, and subspecies *trentae* is found in the Julian Alps.

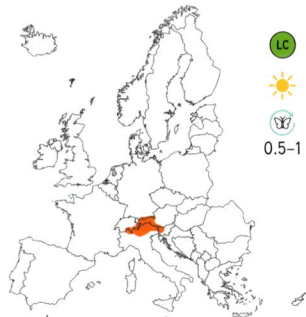

LC

0.5–1

Did you know?

The Stygian Ringlet can be confused with the Styrian and Marbled Ringlets. The shape of the orange area on the forewing and the arrangement of the WPBS in relation to the edge of this orange area usually allow them to be differentiated.

IMAGOS		LARVAE	
Food	🟊	Food	🍃
Behaviour of males	🦋	Caterpillar location	🌿
Dispersion		Chrysalis location	

SATYRINAE

MARBLED RINGLET *EREBIA MONTANA*

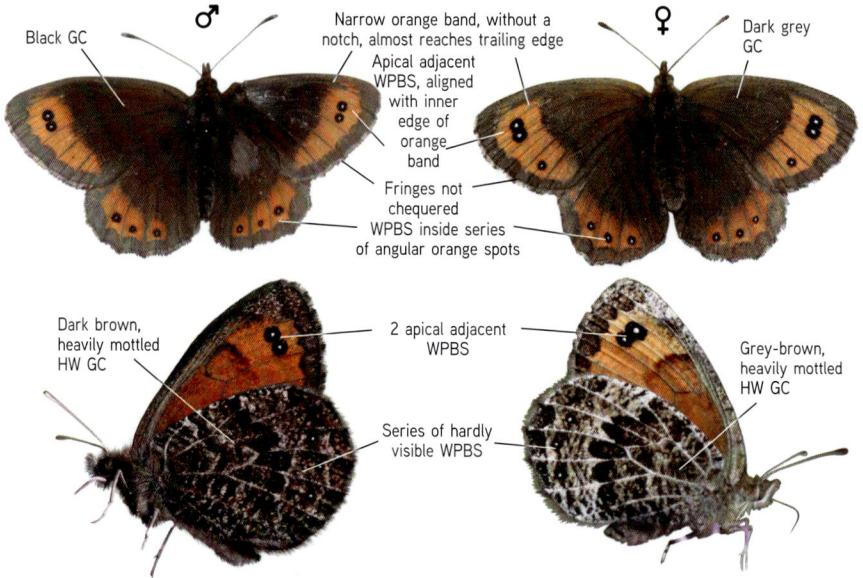

♂

Black GC

Narrow orange band, without a notch, almost reaches trailing edge

Apical adjacent WPBS, aligned with inner edge of orange band

Fringes not chequered

WPBS inside series of angular orange spots

♀

Dark grey GC

Dark brown, heavily mottled HW GC

2 apical adjacent WPBS

Series of hardly visible WPBS

Grey-brown, heavily mottled HW GC

Wingspan: 44–50 mm

Habitat: Stony dry grasslands, rocky forest edges near the treeline, and vegetated scree.

Hibernating stage: Caterpillar, sometimes twice.

Elevational range: Between 900 and 2,500 m.

Egg-laying: Eggs are laid singly on LHP dry leaves and stems.

Flight period: From June to September.

Host plants: Grasses, including *Festuca ovina, F. alpina, F. rubra, F. quadriflora, F. vallesiaca, F. varia, Helictochloa versicolor,* and *Nardus stricta.*

Diversity and systematics: There are no notable subspecies.

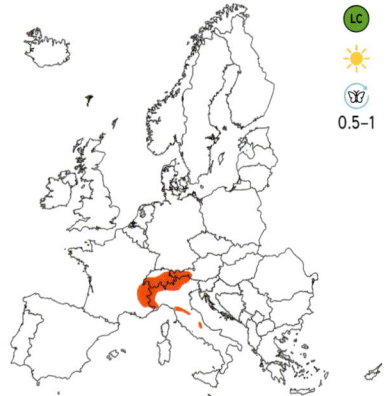

LC

0.5–1

IMAGOS		LARVAE	
Food		Food	
Behaviour of males		Caterpillar location	
Dispersion		Chrysalis location	

Did you know?

The Marbled Fritillary flies for so long because the caterpillars develop over periods of highly variable duration.

SATYRINAE

SCOTCH ARGUS *EREBIA AETHIOPS*

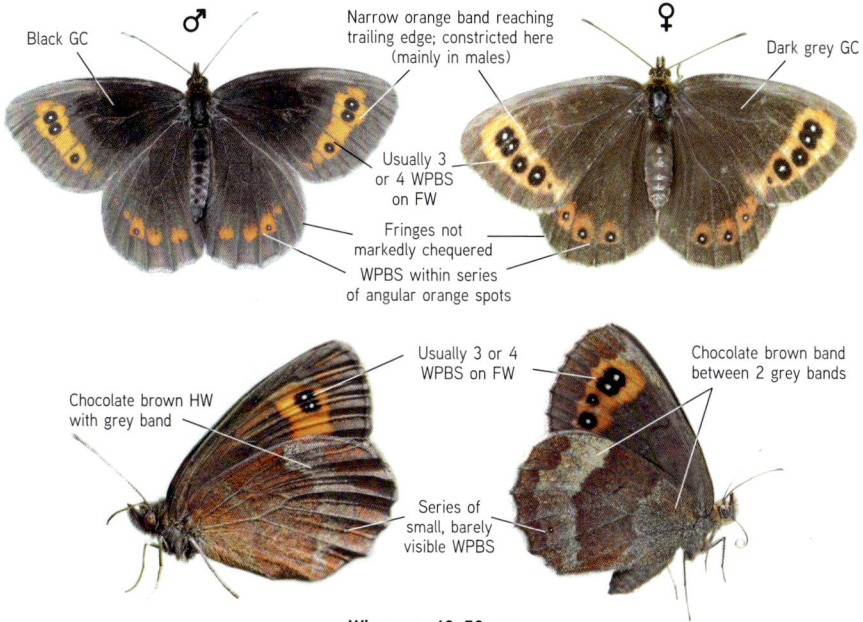

♂   ♀

Black GC

Narrow orange band reaching trailing edge; constricted here (mainly in males)

Dark grey GC

Usually 3 or 4 WPBS on FW

Fringes not markedly chequered

WPBS within series of angular orange spots

Chocolate brown HW with grey band

Usually 3 or 4 WPBS on FW

Chocolate brown band between 2 grey bands

Series of small, barely visible WPBS

Wingspan: 42–52 mm

Habitat: Meadows in the vicinity of forests; grassy, flower-rich clearings, sunny forest paths, and clear woodlands.

Hibernating stage: Caterpillar.

Elevational range: Up to 2,000 m.

Egg-laying: Eggs are laid singly on LHP leaves and stems.

Flight period: From June to September.

Host plants: Grasses, including *Aira praecox*, *Agrostis canina*, *Brachypodium sylvaticum*, *B. pinnatum*, *Briza media*, *Bromus erectus*, *Calamagrostis epigejos*, *Poa annua*, *P. trivialis*, *Phleum pratense*, *Dactylis glomerata*, *Anthoxanthum odoratum*, *Festuca ovina*, *F. rubra*, and *Sesleria caerulea*. Sedges, like *Carex ferruginea*, *C. nigra*, and *C. sempervirens*. *Luzula nivea* (Juncaceae).

Diversity and systematics: Most European populations belong to the nominate subspecies. Subspecies *peneplana* is described from Belgium. Subspecies *caledonia* flies in Scotland.

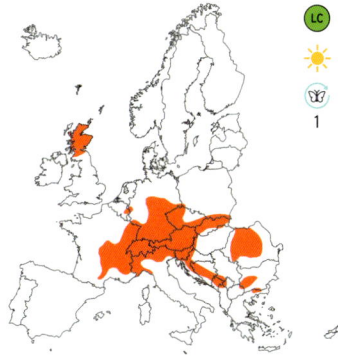

LC

1

IMAGOS		LARVAE	
Food		Food	
Behaviour of males		Caterpillar location	
Dispersion		Chrysalis location	

Did you know?

The Scotch Argus is one of the few *Erebia* species that can be found in lowlands, although it is more abundant in montane areas.

SATYRINAE

LARCHE RINGLET *EREBIA SCIPIO*

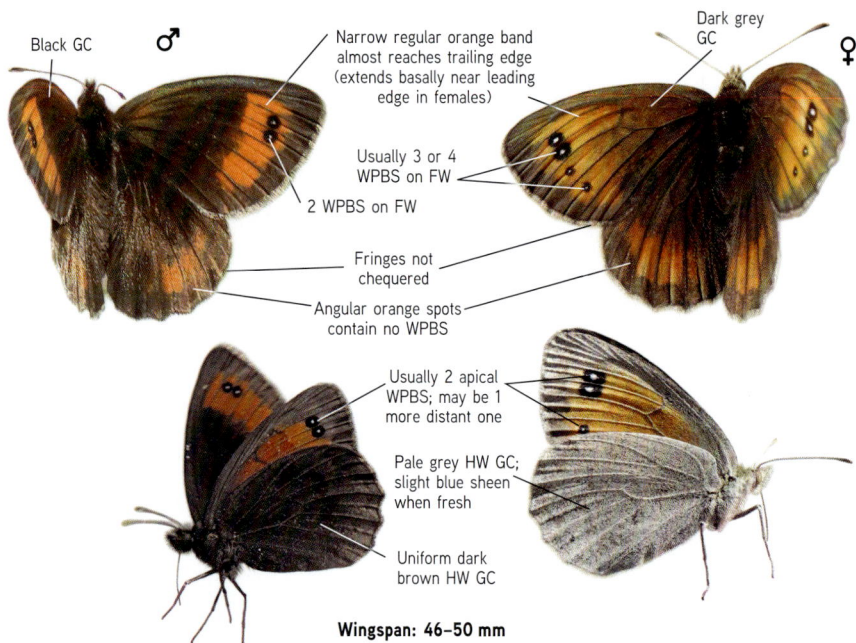

Black GC ♂

Narrow regular orange band almost reaches trailing edge (extends basally near leading edge in females)

Dark grey GC ♀

Usually 3 or 4 WPBS on FW

2 WPBS on FW

Fringes not chequered

Angular orange spots contain no WPBS

Usually 2 apical WPBS; may be 1 more distant one

Pale grey HW GC; slight blue sheen when fresh

Uniform dark brown HW GC

Wingspan: 46–50 mm

Habitat: Moraines, scree, and rocky slopes. On calcareous substrates.

Hibernating stage: Caterpillar, usually twice.

Elevational range: Between 1,500 and 2,500 m.

Egg-laying: Eggs are laid singly underneath stones or at the base of the LHP tuft.

Flight period: July and August.

Host plants: Grasses, mainly *Helictotrichon sedenense* and *H. setaceum.*

Diversity and systematics: There are no notable subspecies.

LC

0.5–1

IMAGOS		LARVAE	
Food	☆	Food	🌿
Behaviour of males	🦋	Caterpillar location	🌱
Dispersion	⊛	Chrysalis location	🪨

Did you know?

The Larche Ringlet is often challenging to access, given the unstable environments it inhabits. Adults primarily feed on the nectar of alpine thistles and carline flower inflorescences.

AUTUMN RINGLET *EREBIA NEORIDAS*

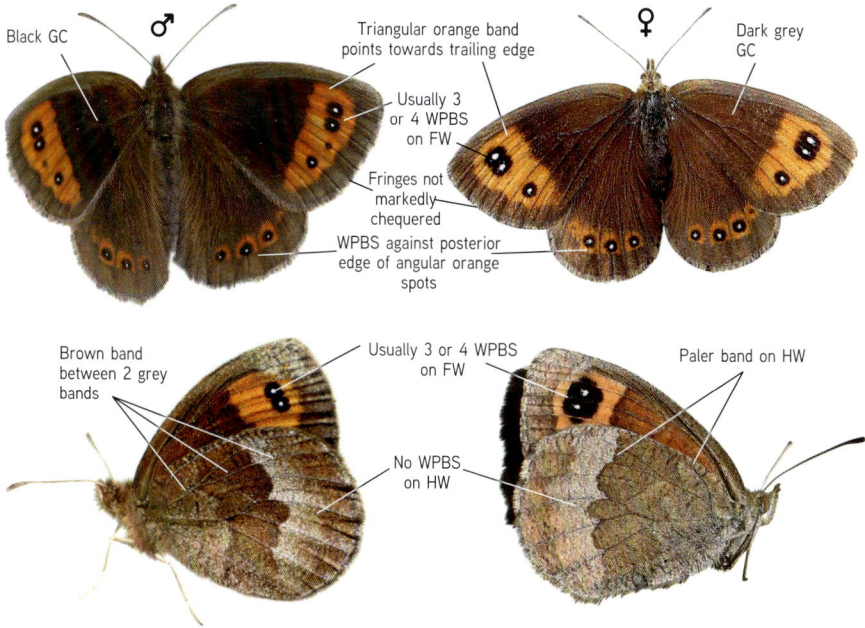

♂

- Black GC
- Triangular orange band points towards trailing edge
- Usually 3 or 4 WPBS on FW
- Fringes not markedly chequered
- WPBS against posterior edge of angular orange spots

♀

- Dark grey GC

- Brown band between 2 grey bands
- Usually 3 or 4 WPBS on FW
- No WPBS on HW
- Paler band on HW

Wingspan: 36–46 mm

Habitat: Bushy and stony grasslands, dry clearings.

Hibernating stage: Caterpillar.

Elevational range: Between 500 and 2,000 m.

Egg-laying: Eggs are dropped in vegetation or laid singly on LHP leaves and stems.

Flight period: From August to October.

Host plants: Grasses, including *Festuca ovina*, *F. liviensis*, *Poa annua*, *P. pratensis*, *P. alpina*, *Calamagrostis epigejos*, and *Digitaria sanguinalis*.

Diversity and systematics: Most populations belong to the nominate subspecies. Subspecies *sibyllina* inhabits central Italy.

IMAGOS			LARVAE	
Food			Food	
Behaviour of males			Caterpillar location	
Dispersion			Chrysalis location	

Did you know?

The decline of pastoralism comes at a cost to the Autumn Ringlet, as its favoured habitats are being lost.

515

SATYRINAE

SPRING RINGLET *EREBIA EPISTYGNE*

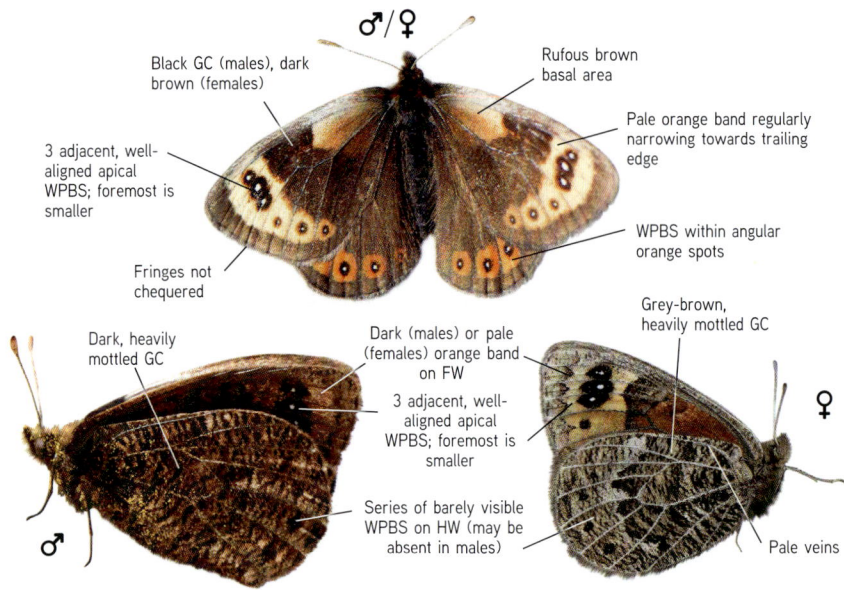

♂/♀

Black GC (males), dark brown (females)

Rufous brown basal area

Pale orange band regularly narrowing towards trailing edge

3 adjacent, well-aligned apical WPBS; foremost is smaller

WPBS within angular orange spots

Fringes not chequered

Grey-brown, heavily mottled GC

Dark, heavily mottled GC

Dark (males) or pale (females) orange band on FW

3 adjacent, well-aligned apical WPBS; foremost is smaller

♀

♂

Series of barely visible WPBS on HW (may be absent in males)

Pale veins

Wingspan: 44–50 mm

Habitat: Stony, dry, sparsely vegetated grasslands.

Hibernating stage: Caterpillar.

Elevational range: Between 500 and 1,500 m.

Egg-laying: Eggs are laid singly on LHP tussocks.

Flight period: From February to May.

Host plants: Grasses, mainly *Festuca ovina*, *F. rubra*, *F. cinerea*, *F. filiformis*, *F. marginata*, *Poa annua*, and *P. pratensis*.

Diversity and systematics: There are no notable subspecies.

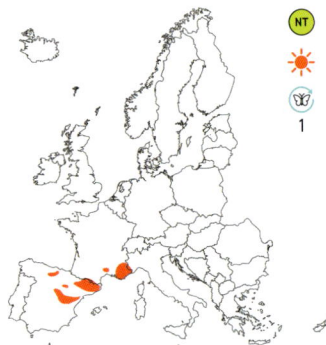

NT

1

Did you know?

Males generally fly for a few dozen seconds before landing very briefly and then resuming their patrol. Photographers are often frustrated by the Spring Ringlet unless they find it before its first morning flight.

IMAGOS		LARVAE	
Food	🌸	Food	🍃
Behaviour of males		Caterpillar location	
Dispersion		Chrysalis location	

DE PRUNNER'S RINGLET *EREBIA TRIARIUS*

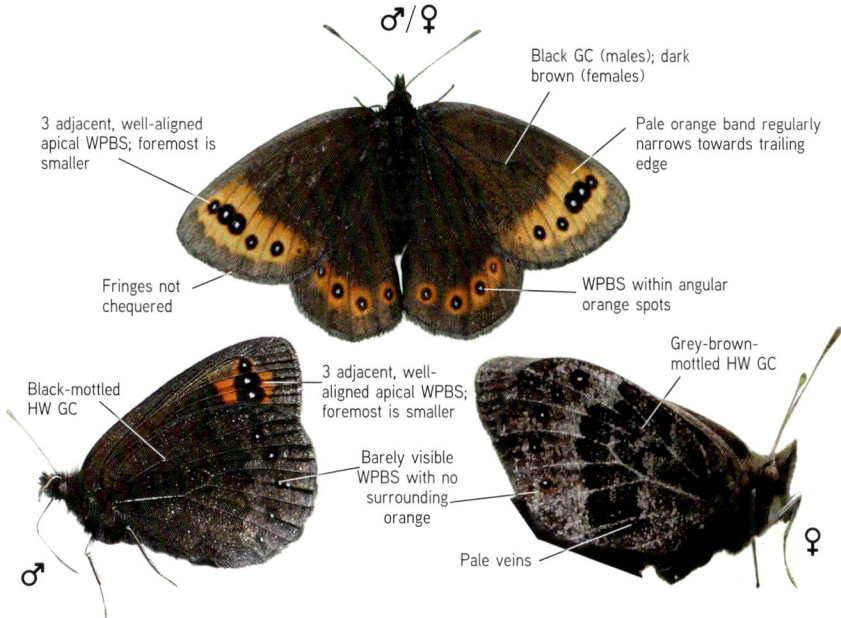

♂/♀

Black GC (males); dark brown (females)

3 adjacent, well-aligned apical WPBS; foremost is smaller

Pale orange band regularly narrows towards trailing edge

Fringes not chequered

WPBS within angular orange spots

Grey-brown-mottled HW GC

Black-mottled HW GC

3 adjacent, well-aligned apical WPBS; foremost is smaller

Barely visible WPBS with no surrounding orange

Pale veins

♂

♀

Wingspan: 44–50 mm

Habitat: Dry grasslands with bare areas, clear woodlands, and rocky clearings.

Hibernating stage: Caterpillar.

Elevational range: From 400 to 2,400 m.

Egg-laying: Eggs are laid singly on the dry parts of the LHP or on nearby litter.

Flight period: From April to July.

Host plants: Grasses, including *Festuca ovina*, *F. varia*, *F. valesiaca*, *F. heterophyllea*, *Poa pratensis*, *P. alpina*, and *Stipa pennata*.

Diversity and systematics: Most populations belong to the nominate subspecies. Subspecies *hispanica* inhabits central Spain. Subspecies *evias* is found in the Pyrenees.

IMAGOS		LARVAE	
Food		Food	
Behaviour of males		Caterpillar location	
Dispersion		Chrysalis location	

Did you know?

Along with the Spring Ringlet, De Prunner's Ringlet is the earliest *Erebia* on the wing. Both inhabit dry environments that strongly constrain their larval development.

SATYRINAE

GAVARNIE RINGLET *EREBIA GORGONE*

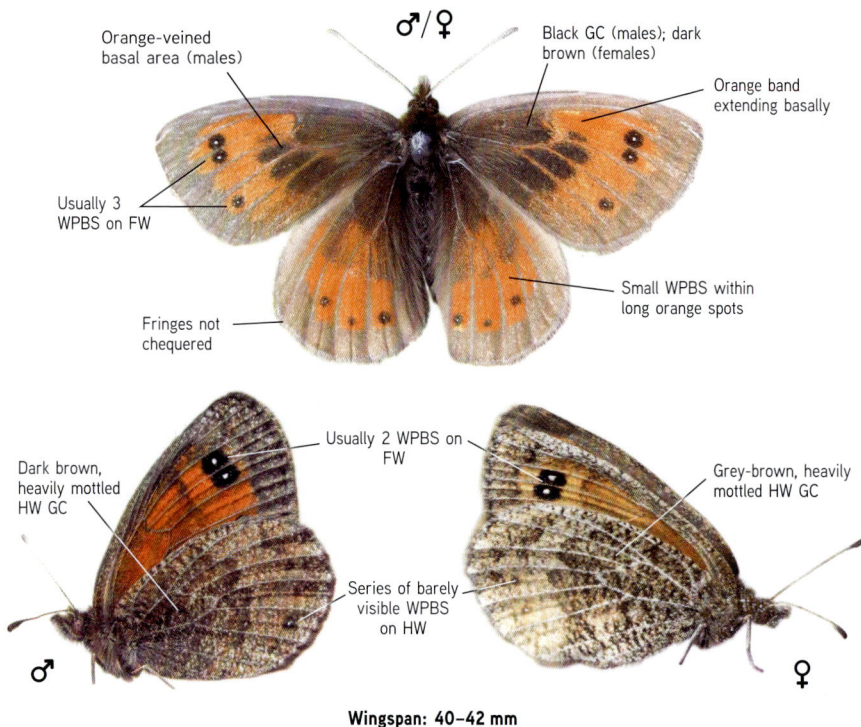

♂/♀

Orange-veined basal area (males)

Black GC (males); dark brown (females)

Orange band extending basally

Usually 3 WPBS on FW

Small WPBS within long orange spots

Fringes not chequered

Dark brown, heavily mottled HW GC

Usually 2 WPBS on FW

Grey-brown, heavily mottled HW GC

Series of barely visible WPBS on HW

♂

♀

Wingspan: 40–42 mm

Habitat: Subalpine grasslands and vegetated scree.

Hibernating stage: Caterpillar.

Elevational range: Between 1,500 and 2,500 m.

Egg-laying: Eggs are laid singly on LHP dry leaves and stems.

Flight period: July and August.

Host plants: Grasses. Caterpillars feed on *Festuca ovina* when reared in captivity.

Diversity and systematics: There are no notable subspecies.

LC

1

IMAGOS		LARVAE	
Food	🌼 💧	Food	🍃
Behaviour of males	🦋	Caterpillar location	🐛 🌾
Dispersion		Chrysalis location	🌾

Did you know?

Adults are fond of the nectar of Asteraceae. The species can do well in areas with extensive grazing.

ZAPATER'S RINGLET *EREBIA ZAPATERI*

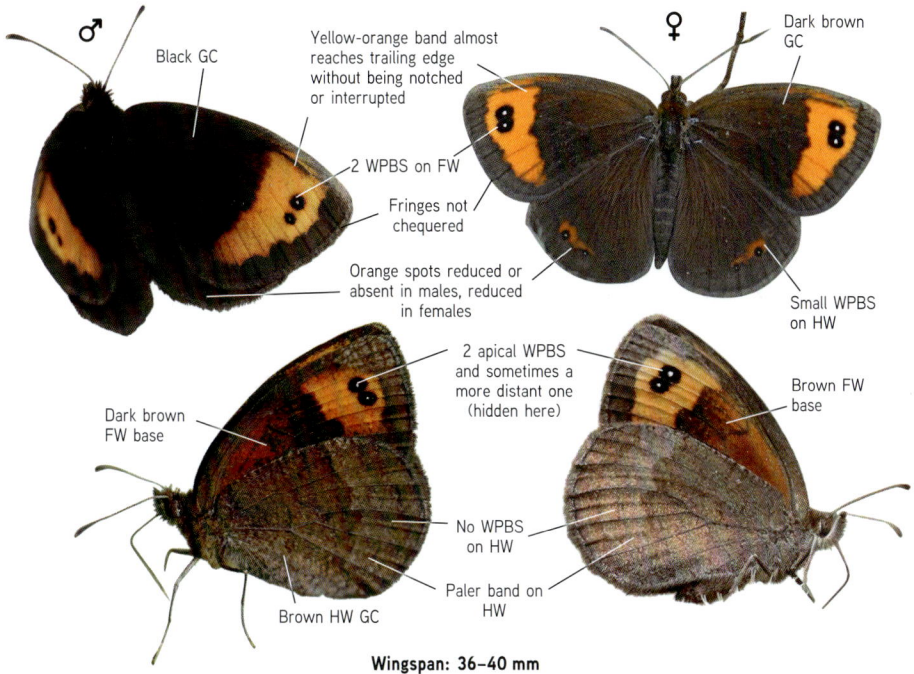

♂

Black GC

Yellow-orange band almost
reaches trailing edge
without being notched
or interrupted

2 WPBS on FW

Fringes not
chequered

Orange spots reduced or
absent in males, reduced
in females

♀

Dark brown
GC

Small WPBS
on HW

Dark brown
FW base

2 apical WPBS
and sometimes a
more distant one
(hidden here)

Brown FW
base

No WPBS
on HW

Paler band on
HW

Brown HW GC

Wingspan: 36–40 mm

Habitat: Grassy pine woodlands, clearings, and dry grasslands near edges.

Hibernating stage: Caterpillar.

Elevational range: Between 1,000 and 1,700 m.

Egg-laying: Eggs are laid singly at the base of the LHP tuft.

Flight period: From July to September.

Host plants: Grasses, including *Festuca ovina*, *Brachypodium retusum*, *B. pinnatum*, and *Nardus stricta*.

Diversity and systematics: There are no notable subspecies.

LC

1

IMAGOS		LARVAE	
Food		Food	
Behaviour of males		Caterpillar location	
Dispersion		Chrysalis location	

Did you know?

Dependent on open environments within a woodland context, Zapater's Ringlet is affected by the abandonment of extensive pastoral activities, which is causing the gradual loss of its Mediterranean habitats.

ARRAN BROWN *EREBIA LIGEA*

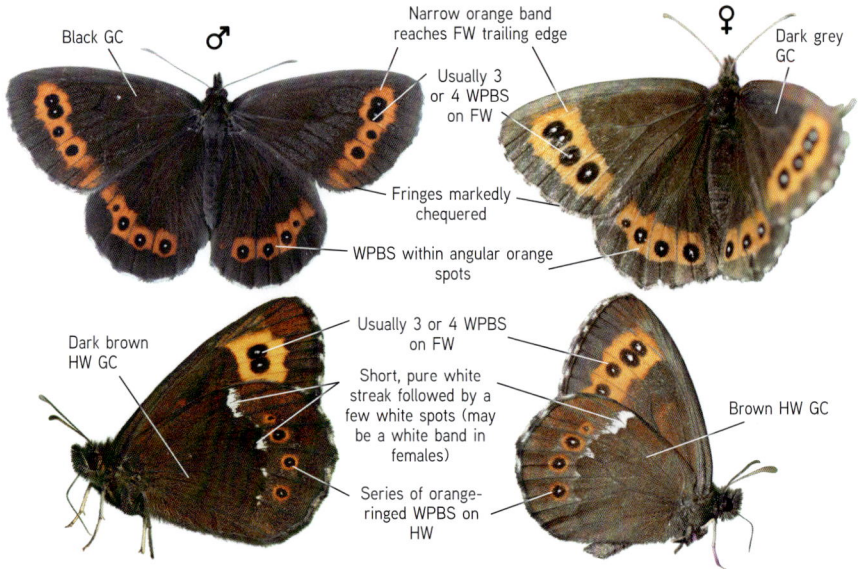

Black GC

♂

Narrow orange band reaches FW trailing edge

Usually 3 or 4 WPBS on FW

♀

Dark grey GC

Fringes markedly chequered

WPBS within angular orange spots

Dark brown HW GC

Usually 3 or 4 WPBS on FW

Short, pure white streak followed by a few white spots (may be a white band in females)

Series of orange-ringed WPBS on HW

Brown HW GC

Wingspan: 36–46 mm

Habitat: Grassy, flower-rich environments within a forest context (mainly coniferous), such as clearings, edges, and clear woodlands.

Hibernating stage: Young caterpillar inside the egg for the first winter; caterpillar for the second overwintering.

Elevational range: Up to 2,000 m.

Egg-laying: Eggs are laid singly on LHP leaves and stems.

Flight period: From June to August.

Host plants: Grasses, including *Festuca rubra, Aira praecox, Deschampsia cespitosa, Dactylis glomerata, Danthonia decumbens, Digitaria sanguinalis, Bromus erectus, Molinia caerulea, Milium effusum, Sesleria caerulea, S. albicans,* and *Melica nutans.* Sedges, such as *Carex pilulifera, C. sylvatica, C. remota,* and *C. strigosa.* Also on *Luzula sylvatica* (Juncaceae).

Diversity and systematics: The nominate subspecies is described from Sweden. Subspecies *dovrensis* flies in Scandinavia. Subspecies *carthusianorum* forms Western European populations. Several forms have also been described.

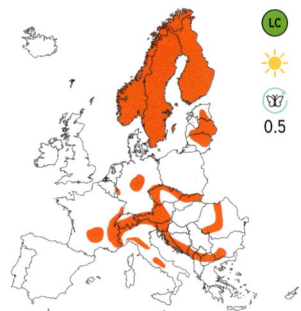

LC

0.5

IMAGOS		LARVAE	
Food		Food	
Behaviour of males		Caterpillar location	
Dispersion		Chrysalis location	

Did you know?

The Arran Brown is one of the most common and widespread species in genus *Erebia*. Adults can gather in groups of dozens, especially to drink water from damp paths.

SATYRINAE

LARGE RINGLET *EREBIA EURYALE*

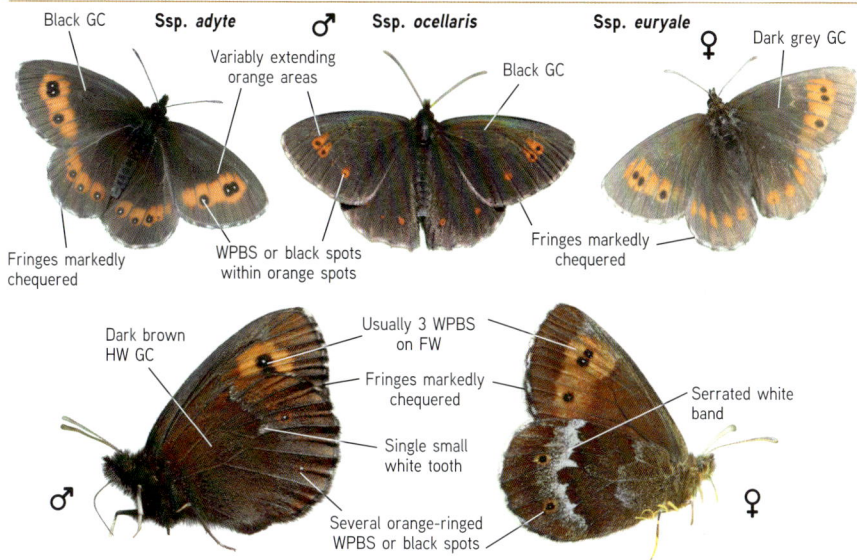

Black GC — **Ssp. adyte** ♂ **Ssp. ocellaris** **Ssp. euryale** ♀ Dark grey GC

Variably extending orange areas

Black GC

Fringes markedly chequered

WPBS or black spots within orange spots

Fringes markedly chequered

Dark brown HW GC

Usually 3 WPBS on FW

Fringes markedly chequered

Single small white tooth

Serrated white band

Several orange-ringed WPBS or black spots

♂ ♀

Wingspan: 42–46 mm

Habitat: Montane and subalpine grasslands, heaths, clearings, forest edges, and clear woodlands.

Hibernating stage: Young caterpillar inside the egg for the first winter; caterpillar for the second.

Elevational range: Between 500 and 2,500 m.

Egg-laying: Eggs are dropped in vegetation.

Flight period: From June to August.

Host plants: Grasses, including *Anthoxanthum odoratum, Avenella flexuosa, Briza media, Bromus erectus, Calamagrostis varia, Dactylis glomerata, Danthonia decumbens, Deschampsia cespitosa, Festuca airoides, F. alpina, F. ovina, F. rubra, Milium effusum, Molinia caerulea, Nardus stricta, Poa alpina, P. nemoralis, Sesleria albicans,* and *S. caerulea.* Sedges, such as *Carex ferruginea, C. flacca,* and *C. sempervirens.* Also on *Luzula luzuloides* (Juncaceae).

Diversity and systematics: Many subspecies : nominate (Sudeten mountains), *adyte* (Western and Southern Alps), *isarica* (Northern Alps), *phoreta* (French Massif Central and Pyrenees), *tramelana* (Jura), *ocellaris* (Southern Austria and Northern Italy). *Kunzi* (Eastern Italy) separated from *adyte* by *pseudoadyte*.

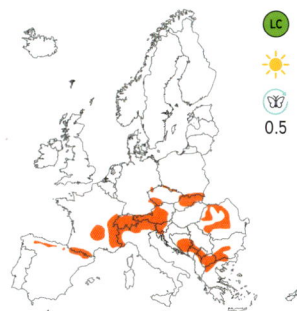

LC

0.5

IMAGOS			LARVAE		
Food			Food		
Behaviour of males			Caterpillar location		
Dispersion			Chrysalis location		

Did you know?

Adults can gather in large numbers on thistle inflorescences and on mammal dung. Subspecies *adyte* and *isarica* are locally sympatric but have asynchronous phenologies.

521

LEFÈBVRE'S RINGLET *EREBIA LEFEBVREI*

Orange band reduced (nominate ssp.) or absent (ssp. *pyrenaea*)

Black GC with iridescent reflections

Number, size of WPBS variable (many, large in nominate ssp.; fewer, smaller in ssp. *pyrenaea*)

Dark brown GC

Fringes not chequered

Large WPBS with hardly any orange (nominate subspecies) or no WPBS (ssp. *pyrenaea*)

Rather uniform black GC

2 or 3 WPBS on FW (hidden here)

Paler band on HW

Brown, slightly mottled GC

WPBS with no orange (nominate ssp.) or no WPBS (ssp. *pyrenaea*)

Wingspan: 40–48 mm

Habitat: Moraines and sparsely vegetated scree.

Hibernating stage: Overwinters twice as a caterpillar.

Elevational range: Between 1,700 and 2,700 m.

Egg-laying: Eggs are laid underneath stones or at the base of LHP tussocks.

Flight period: Between June and August.

Host plants: Grasses like *Festuca gautieri*.

Diversity and systematics: The nominate subspecies flies in the Western and Central Pyrenees. Subspecies *pyrenaea* inhabits the Eastern Pyrenees and Catalonia. Subspecies *astur* forms populations in the Picos de Europa. Subspecies *demandensis* is endemic to the Sierra de la Demanda.

■ *E. melas*
■ *E. lefebvrei*

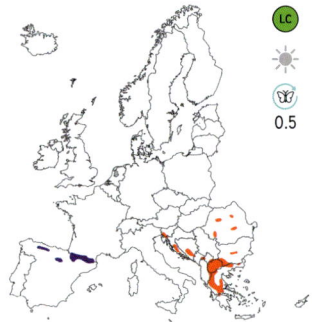

0.5

Did you know?

Photographing Lefèbvre's Ringlet requires agility and perseverance as it must be followed along vertiginous scree slopes. However, it stops from time to time to feed on an Asteraceae or a thyme inflorescence.

IMAGOS		LARVAE	
Food		Food	
Behaviour of males		Caterpillar location	
Dispersion		Chrysalis location	

BLACK RINGLET *EREBIA MELAS*

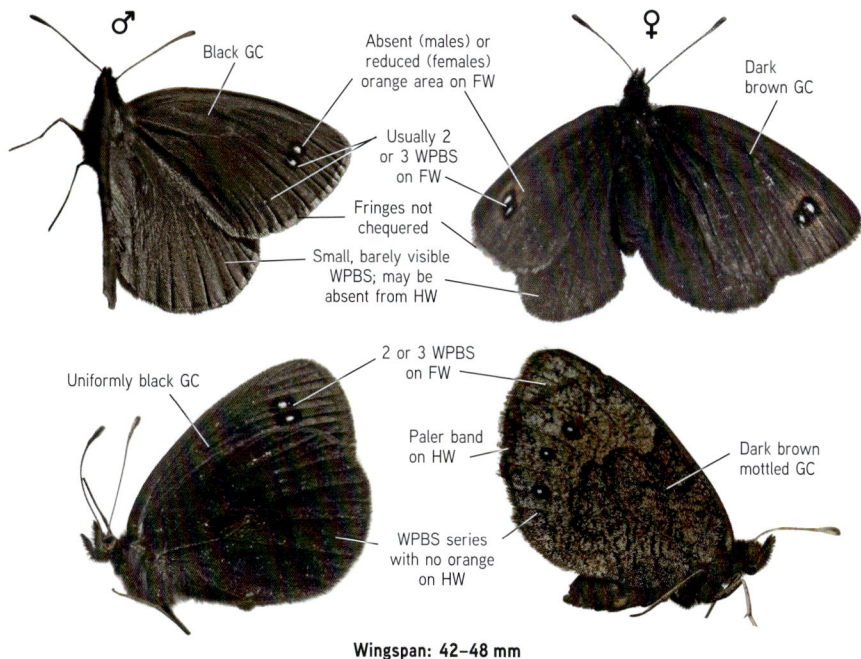

♂

Black GC

Absent (males) or reduced (females) orange area on FW

Usually 2 or 3 WPBS on FW

Fringes not chequered

Small, barely visible WPBS; may be absent from HW

♀

Dark brown GC

Uniformly black GC

2 or 3 WPBS on FW

Paler band on HW

WPBS series with no orange on HW

Dark brown mottled GC

Wingspan: 42–48 mm

Habitat: Rocky slopes with sparse and low-growing vegetation, limestone cliffs, and escarpments.

Hibernating stage: Caterpillar.

Elevational range: Between 500 and 2,800 m depending on the mountain range.

Egg-laying: Eggs are laid singly at the base of LHP tussocks, in the surrounding vegetation, or on stones.

Flight period: From June to September.

Host plants: Grasses, like *Festuca ovina*, *F. graeca*, and *F. olympica*.

Diversity and systematics: The nominate subspecies is described from Romania. Subspecies *schawerdae* inhabits the southern Balkans. Subspecies *runcensis* flies in the Carpathians. Subspecies *leonhardi* populates Croatia and Slovenia. Subspecies *acoris* and *koenigiella* are present in Bulgaria and Romania, respectively.

■ E. melas
■ E. lefebvrei

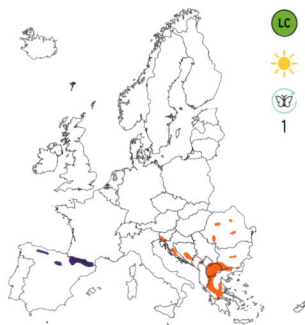

LC

1

Did you know?

The Black Ringlet closely resembles Lefèbvre's Ringlet, to which it is closely related. There is no risk of confusion, however, as their ranges are clearly distinct.

IMAGOS		LARVAE	
Food		Food	
Behaviour of males		Caterpillar location	
Dispersion		Chrysalis location	

WOODLAND RINGLET/ARCTIC WOODLAND RINGLET
EREBIA MEDUSA/E. POLARIS

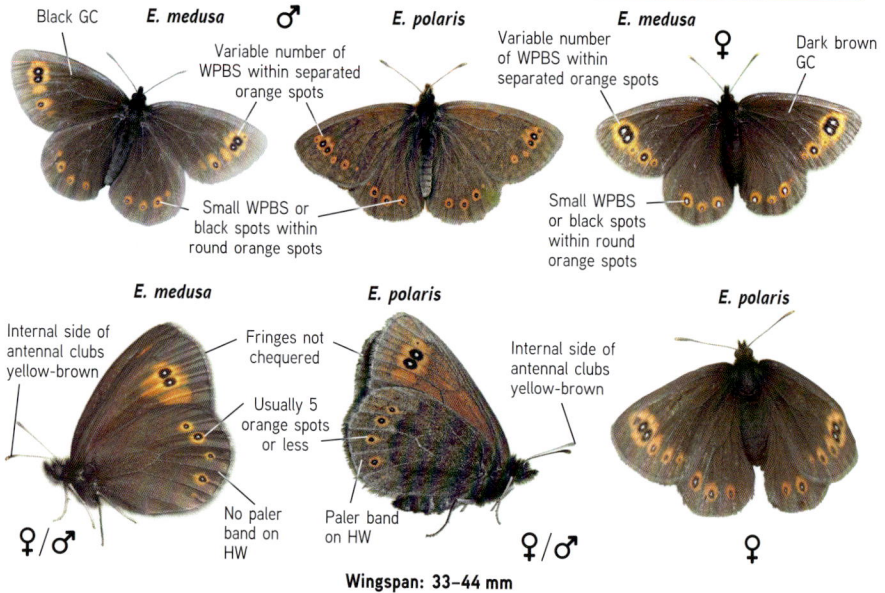

E. medusa ♂ — Black GC — Variable number of WPBS within separated orange spots — Small WPBS or black spots within round orange spots

E. polaris — Variable number of WPBS within separated orange spots

E. medusa ♀ — Dark brown GC — Small WPBS or black spots within round orange spots

E. medusa ♀/♂ — Internal side of antennal clubs yellow-brown — Fringes not chequered — Usually 5 orange spots or less — No paler band on HW

E. polaris ♀/♂ — Internal side of antennal clubs yellow-brown — Paler band on HW

E. polaris ♀

Wingspan: 33–44 mm

Habitat: Hay meadows, damp meadows, and megaphorbs in the vicinity of forests, clearings.

Hibernating stage: Caterpillar (sometimes twice).

Elevational range: Up to 2,500 m for *Erebia medusa*; below 500 m for *E. polaris*.

Egg-laying: Eggs are laid singly on LHP leaves and stems.

Flight period: From May to August for *Erebia medusa*, July and August for *E. polaris*.

Host plants: Grasses, including *Festuca rubra*, *F. ovina*, *Bromus erectus*, *Brachypodium pinnatum*, *Digitaria sanguinalis*, *Deschampsia flexuosa*, *Milium effusum*, *Molinia caerulea*, *Nardus stricta*, *Panicum miliaceum*, *Poa annua*, and *P. palustris*. Sedges, such as *Carex nigra* and *C. pilulifera*.

Diversity and systematics: For *Erebia medusa*, most European populations belong to the nominate subspecies. Subspecies *brigobanna* flies in Switzerland and France, excluding Jura and Alsace. Subspecies *euphrasia* is described from Bulgaria, and subspecies *psodea* from Hungary. For *E. polaris*, European populations belong to the nominate subspecies.

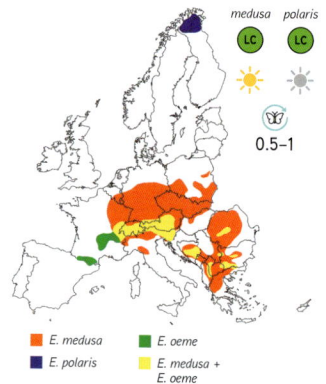

medusa polaris — LC LC — 0.5–1

- E. medusa (orange)
- E. polaris (dark blue)
- E. oeme (green)
- E. medusa + E. oeme (yellow)

IMAGOS		LARVAE	
Food		Food	
Behaviour of males		Caterpillar location	
Dispersion		Chrysalis location	

Did you know?

The flight of the Woodland and Arctic Woodland Ringlets is slow and undulating above vegetation. They stop frequently to feed, making them easily recognizable.

BRIGHT-EYED RINGLET *EREBIA OEME*

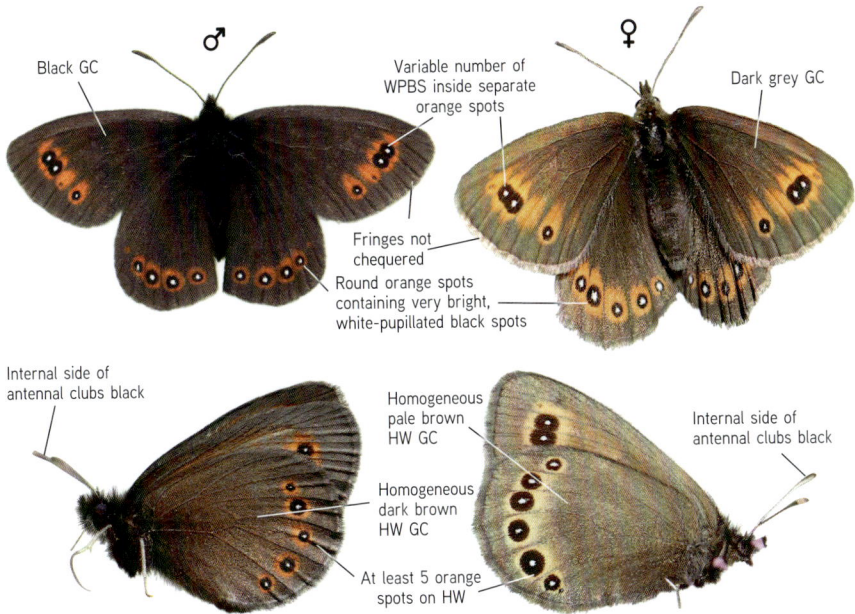

♂

Black GC

Variable number of WPBS inside separate orange spots

♀

Dark grey GC

Fringes not chequered

Round orange spots containing very bright, white-pupillated black spots

Internal side of antennal clubs black

Homogeneous pale brown HW GC

Homogeneous dark brown HW GC

Internal side of antennal clubs black

At least 5 orange spots on HW

Wingspan: 38–46 mm

Habitat: Damp meadows, hay meadows, flower-rich megaphorbs, woodland clearings, and subalpine meadows.

Hibernating stage: Caterpillar (sometimes twice).

Elevational range: Between 500 and 2,500 m (mainly above 1,000 m).

Egg-laying: Eggs are dropped in vegetation.

Flight period: From June to August.

Host plants: Sedges, including *Carex ferruginea*, *C. flacca*, and *C. sempervirens*. Grasses, such as *Briza media*, *Poa alpina*, *P. nemoralis*, *P. pratensis*, *Molinia caerulea*, *Festuca rubra*, and *Holcus mollis*.

Diversity and systematics: European populations belong to the nominate subspecies. Some forms (*pacula*, *lugens*, *zagora*) are nevertheless considered subspecies by some authors.

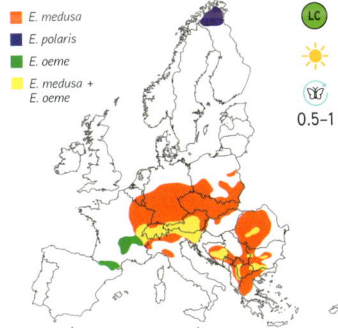

- ■ E. medusa
- ■ E. polaris
- ■ E. oeme
- ■ E. medusa + E. oeme

LC

0.5–1

IMAGOS			LARVAE		
Food			Food		
Behaviour of males			Caterpillar location		
Dispersion			Chrysalis location		

Did you know?

The Bright-eyed Ringlet is threatened by agricultural intensification at low elevations, but also by anthropization in mountainous areas.

SATYRINAE

BULGARIAN RINGLET *EREBIA ORIENTALIS*

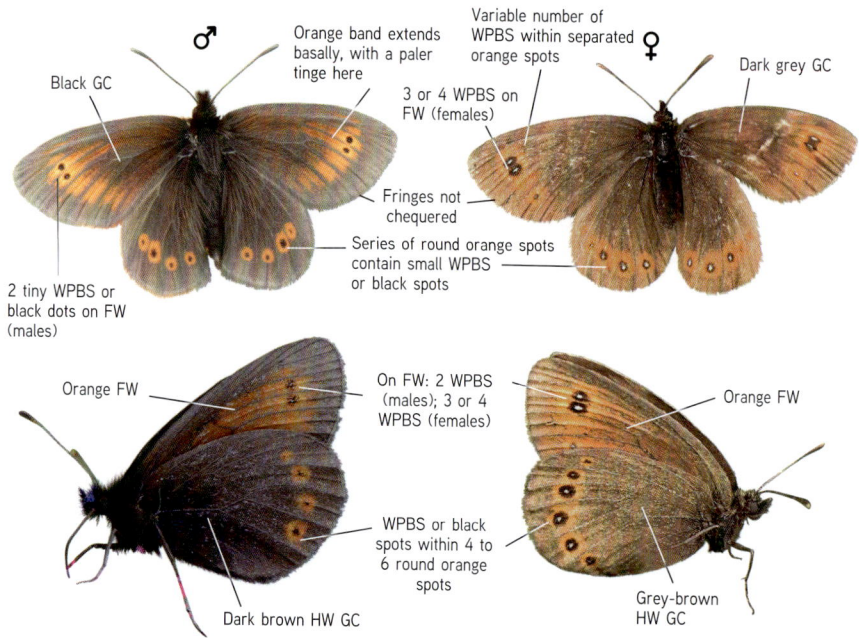

♂

Black GC

Orange band extends basally, with a paler tinge here

Variable number of WPBS within separated orange spots

♀

Dark grey GC

3 or 4 WPBS on FW (females)

Fringes not chequered

Series of round orange spots contain small WPBS or black spots

2 tiny WPBS or black dots on FW (males)

Orange FW

On FW: 2 WPBS (males); 3 or 4 WPBS (females)

Orange FW

WPBS or black spots within 4 to 6 round orange spots

Dark brown HW GC

Grey-brown HW GC

Wingspan: 29–32 mm

Habitat: Subalpine and alpine grasslands, meadows, and heaths.

Hibernating stage: Caterpillar.

Elevational range: Between 1,800 and 2,600 m.

Egg-laying: Eggs are laid singly on LHP leaves and stems.

Flight period: From June to August.

Host plants: Grasses.

Diversity and systematics: There are no notable subspecies. It was formerly considered a subspecies of the Mountain Ringlet.

LC

1

Did you know?

The Bulgarian Ringlet diverged from the Mountain Ringlet relatively recently (around 1.5 million years ago). Its genetic diversity is low, suggesting that it undergoes an inbreeding phase due to its small populations.

IMAGOS		LARVAE	
Food		Food	
Behaviour of males		Caterpillar location	
Dispersion		Chrysalis location	

ALMOND-EYED RINGLET *EREBIA ALBERGANUS*

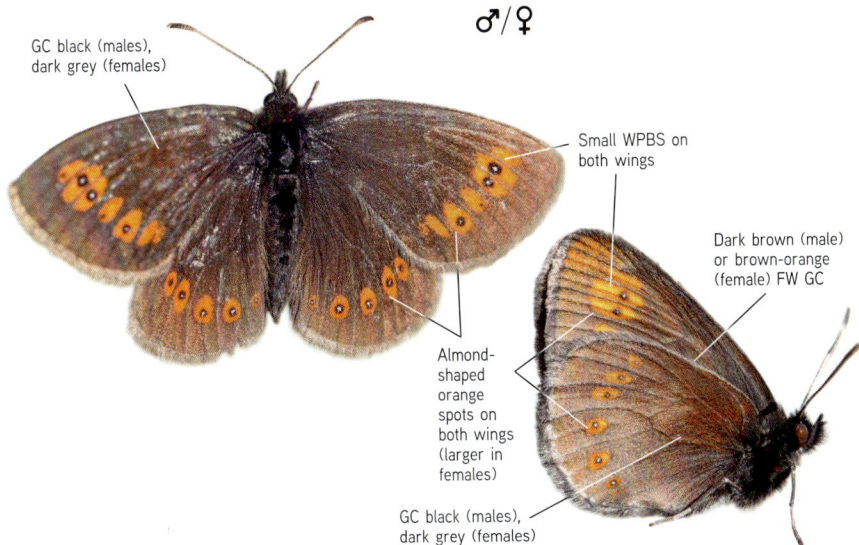

♂/♀

GC black (males), dark grey (females)

Small WPBS on both wings

Dark brown (male) or brown-orange (female) FW GC

Almond-shaped orange spots on both wings (larger in females)

GC black (males), dark grey (females)

Wingspan: 40–46 mm

Habitat: Montane and subalpine bushy grasslands and meadows often sheltered by forest edges.

Hibernating stage: Caterpillar.

Elevational range: Between 800 and 2,400 m (mainly below 2,000 m).

Egg-laying: Eggs are laid singly in vegetation, particularly on inflorescences.

Flight period: From June to August.

Host plants: Grasses, mainly *Festuca ovina*, *Anthoxanthum odoratum*, and *Poa annua*.

Diversity and systematics: Most populations belong to the nominate subspecies. Subspecies *phorcys* is described from Bulgaria. The presence of *E. alberganus* in Northern Spain relied only on some mislabelled collection specimens which were used to describe two (obviously virtual) subspecies in the 1970s.

LC

1

Did you know?

The highly disjointed range of the Almond-eyed Ringlet reflects its glacial history, as evidenced by genetic studies showing that Balkan populations and, later, those from the Apennines diverged from the Alpine population.

IMAGOS		LARVAE	
Food		Food	
Behaviour of males		Caterpillar location	
Dispersion		Chrysalis location	

SATYRINAE

ARCTIC RINGLET *EREBIA DISA*

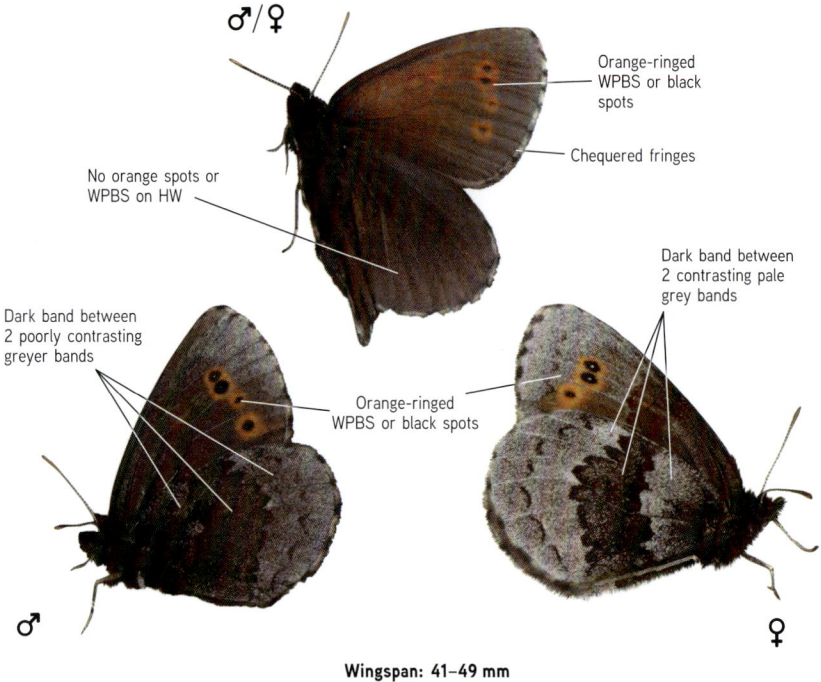

♂/♀

Orange-ringed WPBS or black spots

Chequered fringes

No orange spots or WPBS on HW

Dark band between 2 contrasting pale grey bands

Dark band between 2 poorly contrasting greyer bands

Orange-ringed WPBS or black spots

♂

♀

Wingspan: 41–49 mm

Habitat: Tundra peat bogs.

Hibernating stage: Overwinters twice as a caterpillar.

Elevational range: Up to 500 m.

Egg-laying: Eggs are laid singly or by a few units on LHP dry parts.

Flight period: June and July.

Host plants: Sedges of genus *Carex* and probably also *Eriophorum*.

Diversity and systematics: European populations belong to the nominate subspecies.

- E. embla
- E. disa
- E. embla + E. disa

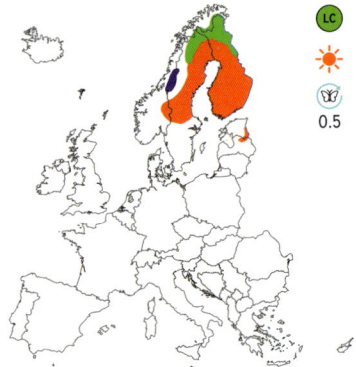

LC

0.5

IMAGOS		LARVAE	
Food		Food	
Behaviour of males		Caterpillar location	
Dispersion		Chrysalis location	

Did you know?

The Arctic Ringlet is distributed all around the Arctic, not only in Europe.

SATYRINAE

LAPLAND RINGLET *EREBIA EMBLA*

♂/♀

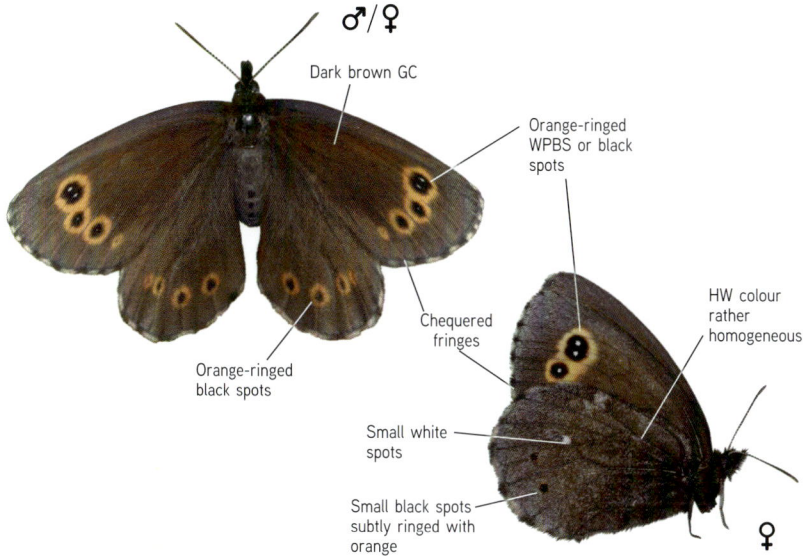

Dark brown GC

Orange-ringed WPBS or black spots

Chequered fringes

Orange-ringed black spots

HW colour rather homogeneous

Small white spots

Small black spots subtly ringed with orange

♀

Wingspan: 42–51 mm

Habitat: Edges of boreal pine woodlands associated with peat bogs.

Hibernating stage: Overwinters twice as a caterpillar.

Elevational range: Up to 500 m.

Egg-laying: Eggs are laid singly on LHP leaves and stems.

Flight period: June and July.

Host plants: Sedges of genera *Carex* and *Eriophorum*. Grasses, like *Deschampsia setacea* and *D. cespitosa*.

Diversity and systematics: European populations belong to the nominate subspecies.

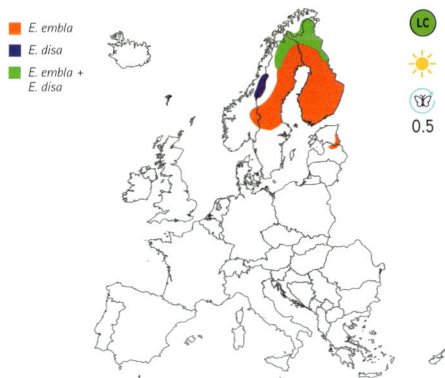

- ■ *E. embla*
- ■ *E. disa*
- ■ *E. embla* + *E. disa*

LC

0.5

IMAGOS			LARVAE		
Food			Food		
Behaviour of males			Caterpillar location		
Dispersion			Chrysalis location		

Did you know?

Lapland Ringlets have the habit of landing on tree trunks. They also spend the night there.

NEVADA GRAYLING *PSEUDOCHAZARA WILLIAMSI*

♂/♀

Pale yellow FW GC

2 large WPBS on FW (1 hidden here) with no white spots between them

Undulating dark line

Narrow whitish band

Small black spot

Grey HW GC with dark lines

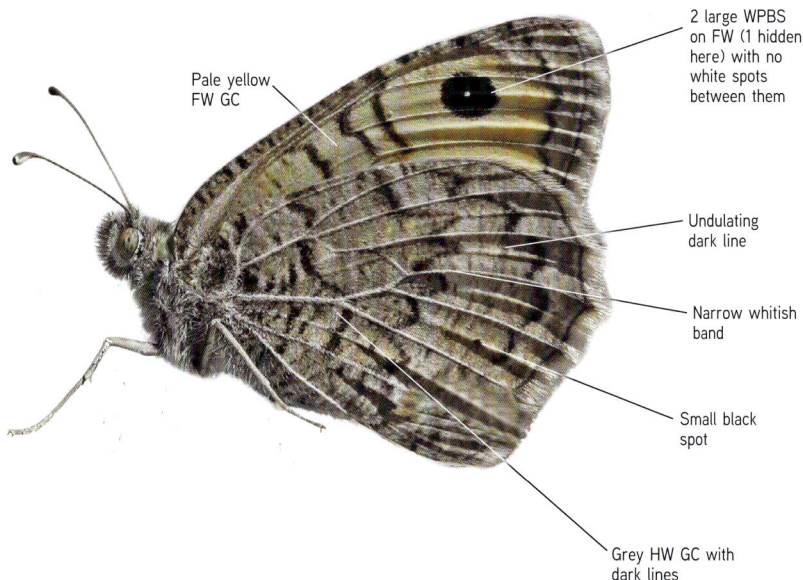

Wingspan: 43–52 mm

Habitat: Stony and sparsely vegetated grasslands and heaths on summits.

Hibernating stage: Caterpillar.

Elevational range: Between 2,000 and 2,700 m.

Egg-laying: Eggs are laid singly.

Flight period: From June to August.

Host plants: *Festuca indigesta* (Poaceae).

Diversity and systematics: Several ecotypes have been described, corresponding to different mountain ranges. *Williamsi* flies in the Sierra Nevada. *Augustini* populates the Sierra de Gador. *Reverchoni* forms the populations of the Sierra de la Sagra, and *aislada* is found in the Sierra de Maria.

LC

1

Did you know?

The various ecotypes of the Nevada Grayling differ slightly in their background colour. This could result from a local adaptation to the geological substrate colour, as their concealment while on the ground relies entirely on camouflage.

IMAGOS		LARVAE	
Food		Food	
Behaviour of males		Caterpillar location	
Dispersion		Chrysalis location	

BALKAN WHITE-BANDED GRAYLING/WHITE-BANDED GRAYLING
PSEUDOCHAZARA AMALTHEA/P. ANTHELEA

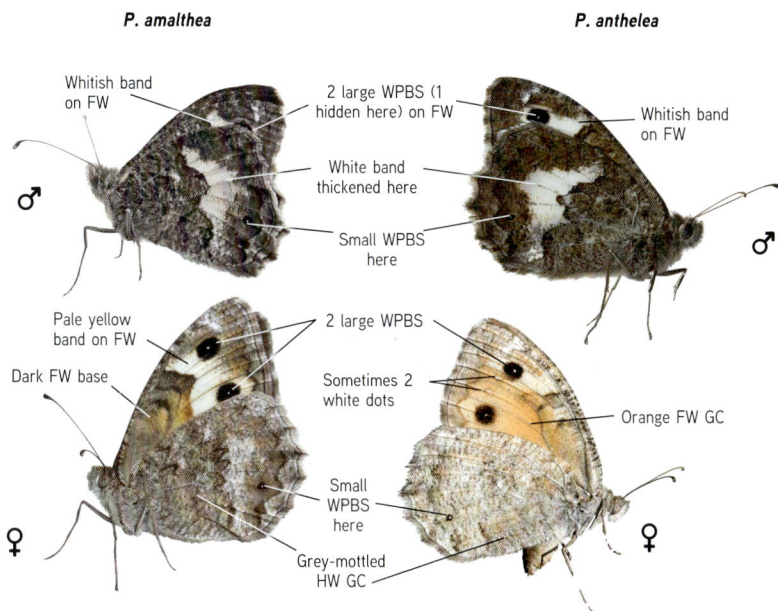

P. amalthea

P. anthelea

Whitish band on FW

2 large WPBS (1 hidden here) on FW

Whitish band on FW

White band thickened here

Small WPBS here

♂

♂

Pale yellow band on FW

2 large WPBS

Dark FW base

Sometimes 2 white dots

Orange FW GC

Small WPBS here

Grey-mottled HW GC

♀

♀

Wingspan: 49–55 mm

Habitat: Dry, stony slopes with sparse, grassy vegetation.

Hibernating stage: Caterpillar.

Elevational range: Between 500 and 2,000 m.

Egg-laying: Eggs are laid singly.

Flight period: From June to September.

Host plants: Grasses of genus *Festuca*.

Diversity and systematics: *Pseudochazara amalthea* is sometimes considered a subspecies of *P. anthelea*. The latter flies only in the Aegean Islands and on Cyprus.

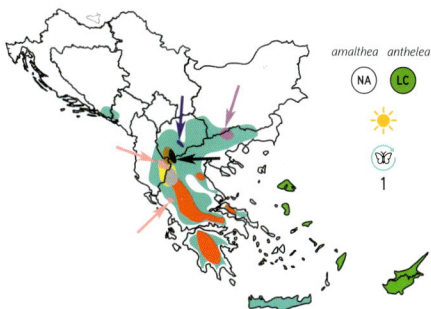

amalthea anthelea

NA   LC

1

- 🟩 *P. amalthea*
- 🟩 *P. anthelea*
- 🟥 *P. graeca + P. amalthea*
- 🟪 *P. orestes + P. amalthea*
- 🟦 *P. cingovskii + P. amalthea*

- 🟫 *P. geyeri + P. amalthea*
- ⬛ *P. geyeri + P. graeca + P. amalthea*
- 🟨 *P. tisiphone + P. amalthea*
- ⬜ *P. tisiphone + P. graeca + P. amalthea*
- 🟧 *P. tisiphone + P. amymone + P. amalthea*

IMAGOS		LARVAE	
Food	✿ 💧	Food	🍃
Behaviour of males		Caterpillar location	🐛 🌿
Dispersion		Chrysalis location	🍂

Did you know?

Egg-laying primarily occurs after the summer season, which is less favourable for caterpillar development in the arid Mediterranean environments these two species inhabit.

BROWN'S GRAYLING   *PSEUDOCHAZARA AMYMONE*

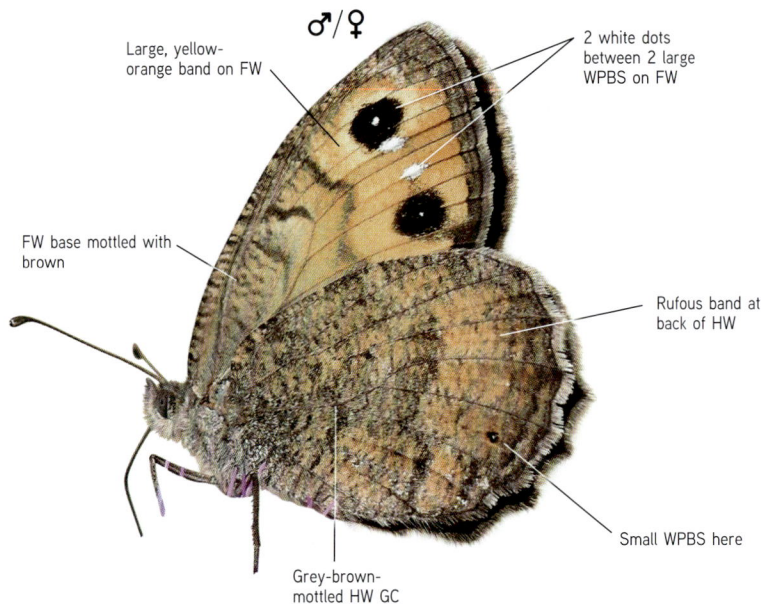

♂ / ♀

Large, yellow-orange band on FW

2 white dots between 2 large WPBS on FW

FW base mottled with brown

Rufous band at back of HW

Small WPBS here

Grey-brown-mottled HW GC

Wingspan: 52–54 mm

Habitat: Sparsely vegetated scree and grassy, stony slopes on ophiolithic substrates.

Hibernating stage: Caterpillar.

Elevational range: Between 500 and 1,400 m.

Egg-laying: Eggs are laid singly.

Flight period: July and August.

Host plants: Grasses. The caterpillars accept *Festuca ovina* and *Dactylis glomerata* when they are reared in captivity.

Diversity and systematics: There are no notable subspecies. It is sometimes considered a subspecies of *Pseudochazara mamurra*, a species whose closest populations are found in Turkey.

EN

1

- ■ *P. amalthea*
- ■ *P. anthelea*
- ■ *P. graeca + P. amalthea*
- ■ *P. orestes + P. amalthea*
- ■ *P. cingovskii + P. amalthea*
- ■ *P. geyeri + P. amalthea*
- ■ *P. geyeri + P. graeca + P. amalthea*
- ■ *P. tisiphone + P. amalthea*
- ■ *P. tisiphone + P. graeca + P. amalthea*
- ■ *P. tisiphone + P. amymone + P. amalthea*

IMAGOS		LARVAE	
Food	🌟 💧	Food	🍃
Behaviour of males		Caterpillar location	
Dispersion: unknown		Chrysalis location	

Did you know?

The rare sites where Brown's Grayling flies were not disclosed upon its discovery in 1976, in an attempt to prevent it from falling victim to collectors. However, this effort was in vain. The price of a pinned butterfly at that time could reach around 1,000 euros.

DARK GRAYLING *PSEUDOCHAZARA TISIPHONE*

♂/♀

2 white dots between 2 large WPBS on FW

Pale orange FW GC

Grey-brown-mottled HW GC

No conspicuous darker area along HW edge

No marked pale band here

No black spot here

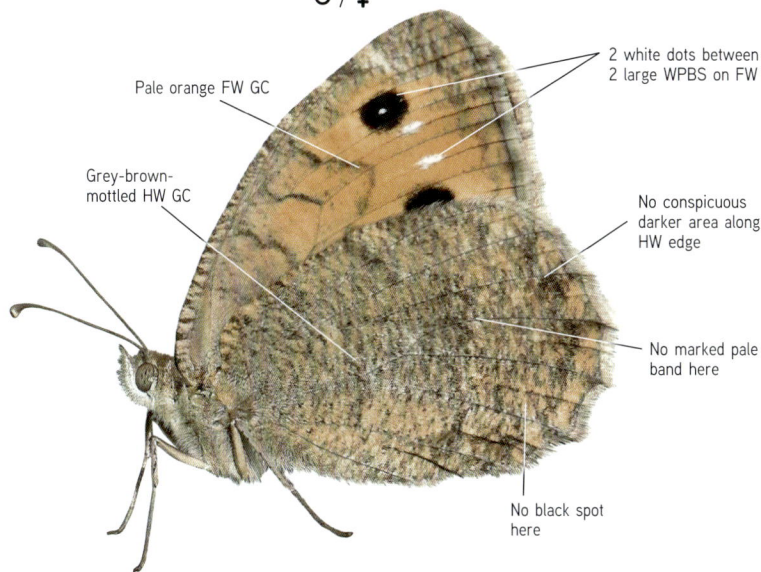

Wingspan: 46–56 mm

Habitat: Rocky, arid, sparsely vegetated montane slopes.

Hibernating stage: Caterpillar.

Elevational range: Between 600 and 1,900 m.

Egg-laying: Eggs are laid singly.

Flight period: From June to September.

Host plants: Grasses, like *Festuca ovina*.

Diversity and systematics: There are no notable subspecies.

LC

1

- P. amalthea
- P. anthelea
- P. graeca + P. amalthea
- P. orestes + P. amalthea
- P. cingovskii + P. amalthea
- P. geyeri + P. amalthea
- P. geyeri + P. graeca + P. amalthea
- P. tisiphone + P. amalthea
- P. tisiphone + P. graeca + P. amalthea
- P. tisiphone + P. amymone + P. amalthea

IMAGOS			LARVAE		
Food			Food		
Behaviour of males			Caterpillar location		
Dispersion			Chrysalis location		

Did you know?

The Dark Grayling was previously considered a subspecies of *Pseudochazara mniszechii* (a species that is absent from Europe). Phylogenetic studies have shown that this classification was incorrect due to a closer relationship with an Asian grayling, *P. hippolyte*.

SATYRINAE

DILS' GRAYLING *PSEUDOCHAZARA ORESTES*

♂/♀

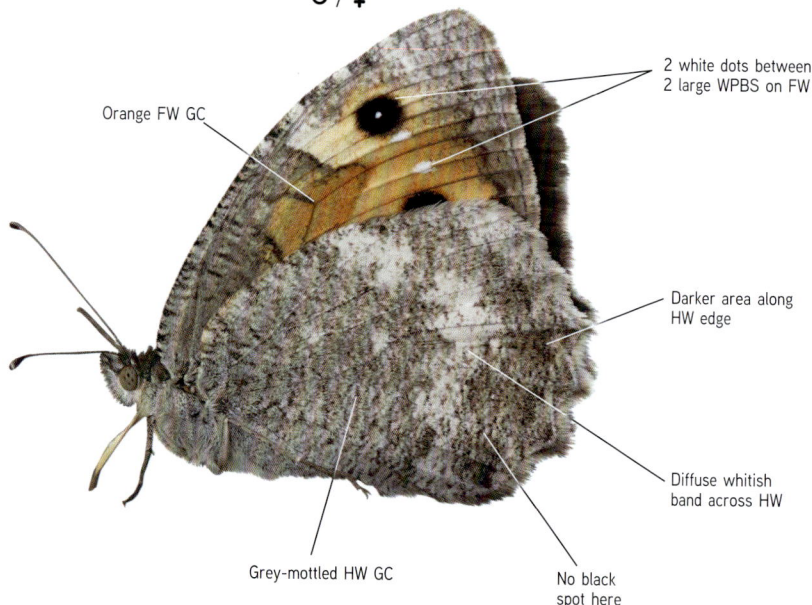

Orange FW GC

2 white dots between 2 large WPBS on FW

Darker area along HW edge

Diffuse whitish band across HW

Grey-mottled HW GC

No black spot here

Wingspan: 49–55 mm

Habitat: Warm and dry, bushy escarpments, clear woodlands. On calcareous substrates.

Hibernating stage: Caterpillar.

Elevational range: Between 800 and 1,900 m.

Egg-laying: Eggs are laid singly on LHP dry parts.

Flight period: June and July.

Host plants: Grasses.

Diversity and systematics: There are no notable subspecies.

VU

1

P. amalthea	P. geyeri + P. amalthea
P. anthelea	P. geyeri + P. graeca + P. amalthea
P. graeca + P. amalthea	P. tisiphone + P. amalthea
P. orestes + P. amalthea	P. tisiphone + P. graeca + P. amalthea
P. cingovskii + P. amalthea	P. tisiphone + P. amymone + P. amalthea

Did you know?

Because of its restricted range, a small region in southern Bulgaria and northern Greece, Dils' Grayling cannot be confused with any other species of the *Pseudochazara* genus.

IMAGOS		LARVAE	
Food		Food	
Behaviour of males		Caterpillar location	
Dispersion		Chrysalis location	

GRECIAN GRAYLING *PSEUDOCHAZARA GRAECA*

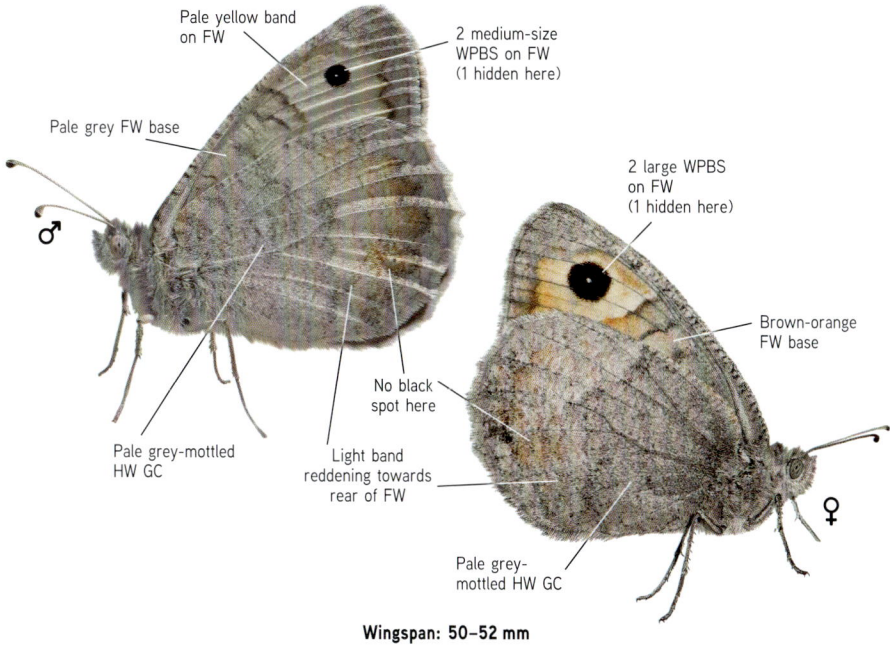

Pale yellow band on FW

2 medium-size WPBS on FW (1 hidden here)

Pale grey FW base

2 large WPBS on FW (1 hidden here)

♂

Brown-orange FW base

No black spot here

Pale grey-mottled HW GC

Light band reddening towards rear of FW

♀

Pale grey-mottled HW GC

Wingspan: 50–52 mm

Habitat: Arid, stony, and often grazed grasslands.

Hibernating stage: Caterpillar.

Elevational range: Between 800 and 2,300 m.

Egg-laying: Eggs are laid singly on LHP leaves and stems.

Flight period: From June to September.

Host plants: Grasses, like *Festuca* spp.

Diversity and systematics: Subspecies *coutsisi* flies in northwestern Greece. The remaining populations belong to the nominate subspecies.

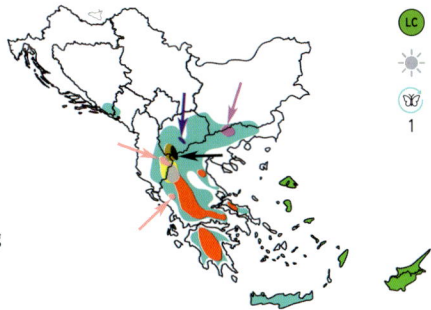

LC

1

- ▇ *P. amalthea*
- ▇ *P. anthelea*
- ▇ *P. graeca + P. amalthea*
- ▇ *P. orestes + P. amalthea*
- ▇ *P. cingovskii + P. amalthea*
- ▇ *P. geyeri + P. amalthea*
- ▇ *P. geyeri + P. graeca + P. amalthea*
- ▇ *P. tisiphone + P. amalthea*
- ▇ *P. tisiphone + P. graeca + P. amalthea*
- ▇ *P. tisiphone + P. amymone + P. amalthea*

IMAGOS			LARVAE	
Food			Food	
Behaviour of males			Caterpillar location	
Dispersion			Chrysalis location	

Did you know?

Adult butterflies primarily feed on Asteraceae flowers, such as thistles and carlines.

SATYRINAE

MACEDONIAN GRAYLING *PSEUDOCHAZARA CINGOVSKII*

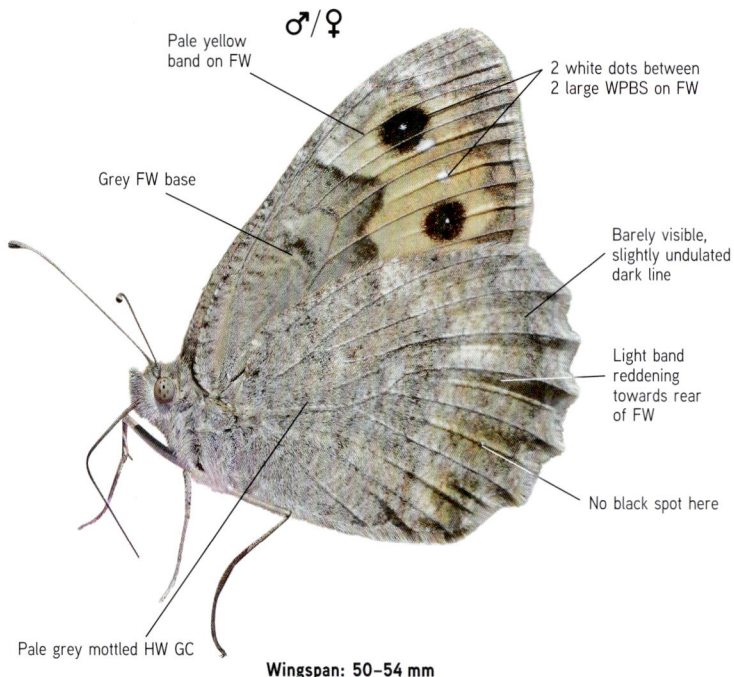

♂/♀

Pale yellow band on FW

2 white dots between 2 large WPBS on FW

Grey FW base

Barely visible, slightly undulated dark line

Light band reddening towards rear of FW

No black spot here

Pale grey mottled HW GC

Wingspan: 50–54 mm

Habitat: Arid, sparsely vegetated calcareous grasslands.

Hibernating stage: Caterpillar.

Elevational range: Between 1,000 and 1,200 m.

Egg-laying: Eggs are laid singly.

Flight period: July and August.

Host plants: Grasses of genus *Festuca*.

Diversity and systematics: There are no notable subspecies.

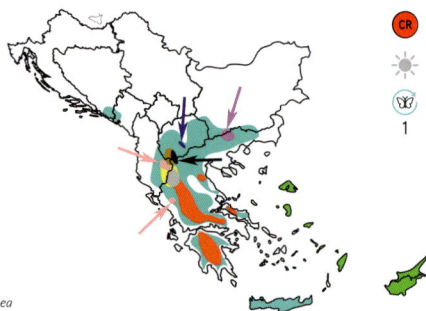

CR

1

- ■ *P. amalthea*
- ■ *P. anthelea*
- ■ *P. graeca + P. amalthea*
- ■ *P. orestes + P. amalthea*
- ■ *P. cingovskii + P. amalthea*
- ■ *P. geyeri + P. amalthea*
- ■ *P. geyeri + P. graeca + P. amalthea*
- ■ *P. tisiphone + P. amalthea*
- ■ *P. tisiphone + P. graeca + P. amalthea*
- ■ *P. tisiphone + P. amymone + P. amalthea*

IMAGOS		LARVAE	
Food	✦	Food	🍃
Behaviour of males	🦋 🦋	Caterpillar location	🐛 🌿
Dispersion	🦋	Chrysalis location	🪨

Did you know?

The range of the Macedonian Grayling barely reaches 10 square kilometers. It is particularly threatened by habitat destruction due to mining activities and is hindered by its limited dispersal ability.

GREY ASIAN GRAYLING *PSEUDOCHAZARA GEYERI*

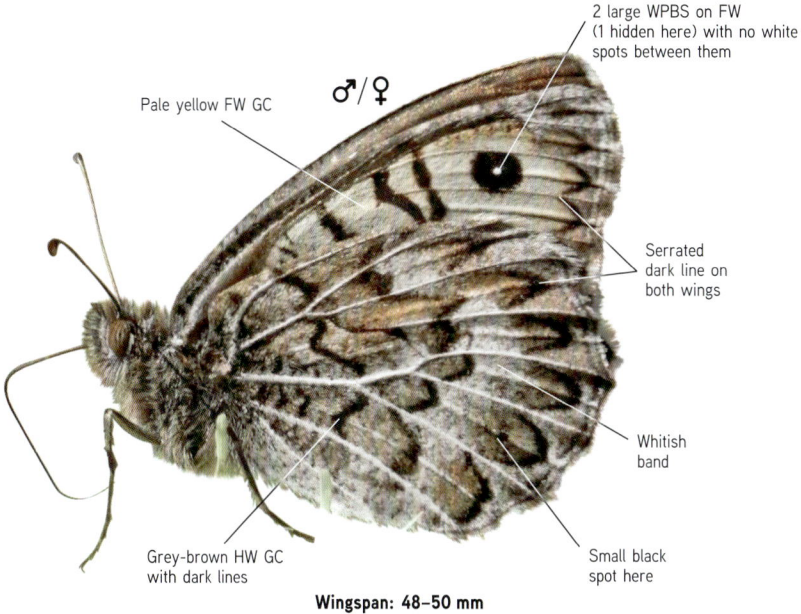

♂/♀

- Pale yellow FW GC
- 2 large WPBS on FW (1 hidden here) with no white spots between them
- Serrated dark line on both wings
- Whitish band
- Grey-brown HW GC with dark lines
- Small black spot here

Wingspan: 48–50 mm

Habitat: Montane and subalpine dry, stony grasslands.

Hibernating stage: Caterpillar.

Elevational range: Between 1,200 and 1,700 m.

Egg-laying: Eggs are laid singly.

Flight period: July and August.

Host plants: Grasses. The caterpillars will eat *Festuca ovina* when reared in captivity.

Diversity and systematics: European populations belong to subspecies *occidentalis*.

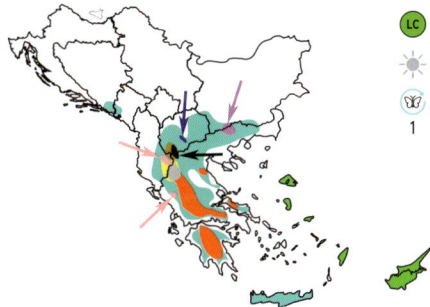

- P. amalthea
- P. anthelea
- P. graeca + P. amalthea
- P. orestes + P. amalthea
- P. cingovskii + P. amalthea
- P. geyeri + P. amalthea
- P. geyeri + P. graeca + P. amalthea
- P. tisiphone + P. amalthea
- P. tisiphone + P. graeca + P. amalthea
- P. tisiphone + P. amymone + P. amalthea

Did you know?

Adults frequently forage on the inflorescences of *Eryngium* thistles. The background colour of the *occidentalis* subspecies is lighter than that of the nominate subspecies, likely a result of a local adaptation to the colour of the limestone environments it inhabits.

IMAGOS			LARVAE		
Food			Food		
Behaviour of males			Caterpillar location		
Dispersion			Chrysalis location		

HERMIT *CHAZARA BRISEIS*

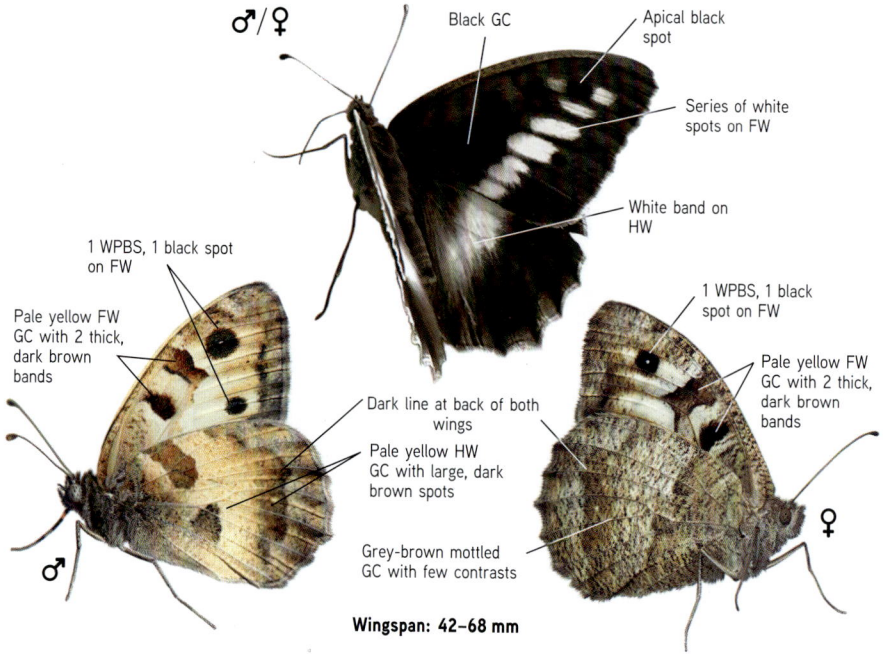

♂/♀

Black GC

Apical black spot

Series of white spots on FW

White band on HW

1 WPBS, 1 black spot on FW

Pale yellow FW GC with 2 thick, dark brown bands

1 WPBS, 1 black spot on FW

Pale yellow FW GC with 2 thick, dark brown bands

Dark line at back of both wings

Pale yellow HW GC with large, dark brown spots

Grey-brown mottled GC with few contrasts

♀

♂

Wingspan: 42–68 mm

Habitat: Rocky, dry grasslands and grassy escarpments with bare areas.

Hibernating stage: Caterpillar.

Elevational range: Up to 2,500 m.

Egg-laying: Eggs are laid singly on dry parts of the LHP or in nearby vegetation.

Flight period: From June to October.

Host plants: Grasses, including *Festuca ovina, F. pallens, F. rubra, Sesleria caerulea, S. albicans, Brachypodium pinnatum, B. phoenicoides, Bromus erectus, Achnatherum parviflorum, Stipa capillata,* and *S. pennata.* Also reported *on Carex leporina* (Cyperaceae).

Diversity and systematics: The nominate subspecies flies in Central Europe. Subspecies *meridionalis* inhabits the southern part of Europe, and subspecies *ianthe* forms populations in the southeast of the European continent. Subspecies *martinae* is present in the Eastern Pyrenees. Cypriot populations belong to subspecies *larnacana.*

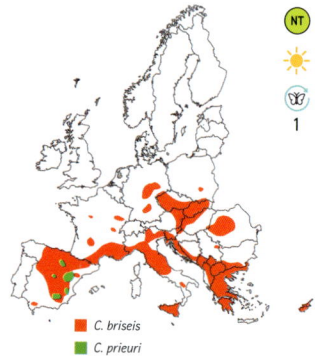

■ C. briseis
■ C. prieuri

NT

1

Did you know?

The Hermit is one of the most endangered butterflies in non-Mediterranean Europe, due to pastoral abandonment and grassland fertilization.

IMAGOS				LARVAE	
Food				Food	
Behaviour of males				Caterpillar location	
Dispersion				Chrysalis location	

SATYRINAE

SOUTHERN HERMIT *CHAZARA PRIEURI*

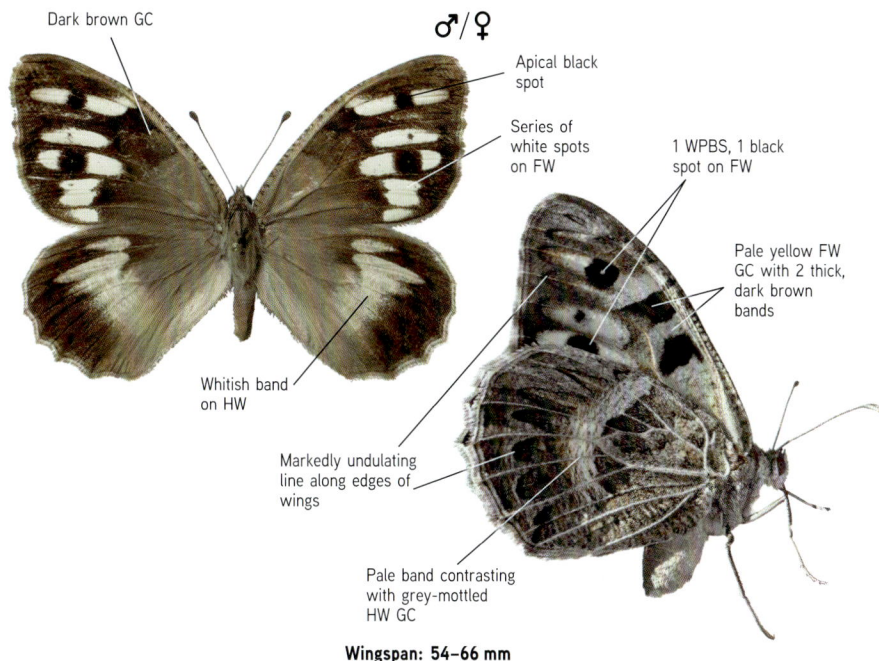

Dark brown GC

♂/♀

Apical black spot

Series of white spots on FW

1 WPBS, 1 black spot on FW

Pale yellow FW GC with 2 thick, dark brown bands

Whitish band on HW

Markedly undulating line along edges of wings

Pale band contrasting with grey-mottled HW GC

Wingspan: 54–66 mm

Habitat: Very arid and stony grasslands with a few bushes.

Hibernating stage: Caterpillar.

Elevational range: Between 600 and 2,000 m.

Egg-laying: Eggs are laid singly.

Flight period: Between June and August.

Host plants: Mainly *Lygeum spartum* (Poaceae).

Diversity and systematics: European populations belong to subspecies *iberica*.

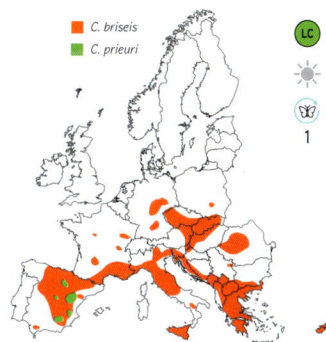

■ *C. briseis*
■ *C. prieuri*

LC

1

Did you know?

In their very hot and dry habitats, the adults are active primarily in the morning and late afternoon; during the hottest hours, they shelter in the shade of bushes.

IMAGOS			LARVAE	
Food			Food	
Behaviour of males			Caterpillar location	
Dispersion			Chrysalis location	

Introduction to *Hipparchia* Graylings

European graylings form a group of 15 Satyrine species within genus *Hipparchia*. These butterflies of Mediterranean origin generally inhabit warm, dry, and open environments, including bare areas, where males like to perch when they are guarding their territory.

Identification is highly complex due to wing patterns that are almost identical, with few exceptions, reflecting a recent evolutionary radiation that likely began less than 10 million years ago. Traditionally, graylings were classified into two groups based on the shape of their genitalia. The Balkan Grayling (*H. senthes*), Madeiran Grayling (*H. maderensis*), Italian Grayling (*H. neapolitana*), and Sicilian Grayling (*H. blachieri*) were considered close to the Mediterranean Southern Grayling (*H. aristaeus*), while the Karpathos Grayling (*H. christenseni*), Ponza Grayling (*H. sbordonii*), Eolian Grayling (*H. leighebi*), Cretan Grayling (*H. cretica*), Cyprus Grayling (*H. cypriensis*), and Delattin's Grayling (*H. volgensis*) were rather associated with the Grayling (*H. semele*), the most widely distributed species in the group.

General phylogenetic studies published by Dapporto *et al.* in 2019 and Wiemers *et al.* in 2020 have not definitively established the relationships between the different species of this radiation. The figure below, produced from Wiemers *et al.*'s data, illustrates these uncertainties. Traditional concepts based on genitalia studies are represented by dashed rectangles and are seemingly in contradiction with the phylogeny, whose corresponding nodes are, however, not very robust. Future studies will likely clarify this systematic complexity, emphasizing that it primarily involves a set of rather recent divergences.

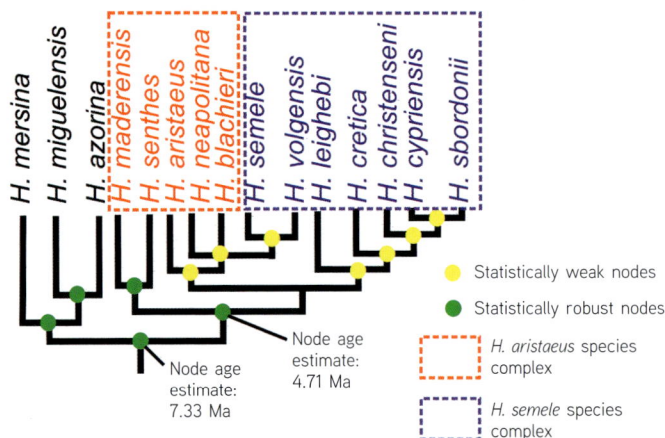

Phylogeny of the *Hipparchia* graylings drawn from the study by Wiemers *et al.* (2020). Several critical nodes are not robustly supported by the data. The apparent contradiction between this phylogeny and traditional concepts (enclosed in dashed rectangles) should thus be considered with caution for now.

GRAYLING *HIPPARCHIA SEMELE*

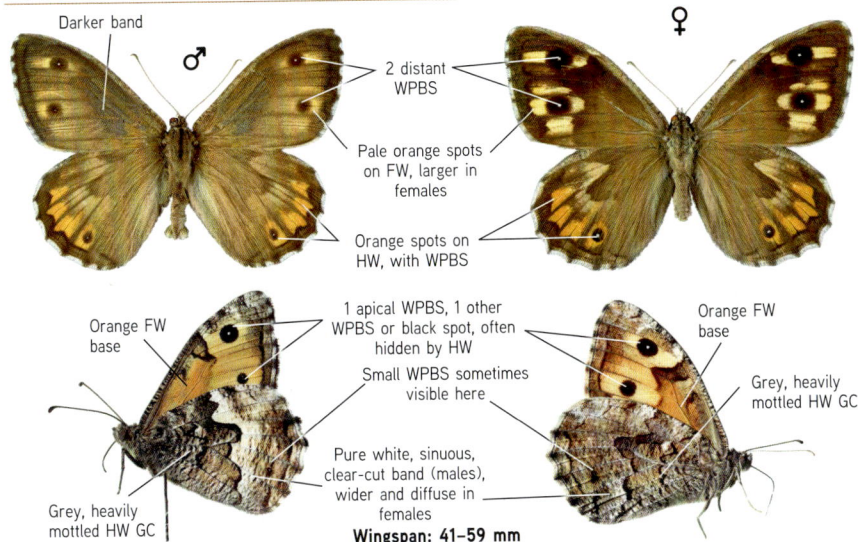

Darker band ♂

2 distant WPBS ♀

Pale orange spots on FW, larger in females

Orange spots on HW, with WPBS

Orange FW base

1 apical WPBS, 1 other WPBS or black spot, often hidden by HW

Small WPBS sometimes visible here

Orange FW base

Grey, heavily mottled HW GC

Pure white, sinuous, clear-cut band (males), wider and diffuse in females

Grey, heavily mottled HW GC

Wingspan: 41–59 mm

Habitat: Grasslands and dry heaths, stabilized dunes, rocky slopes, and open Mediterranean woodlands. The Grayling requires bare spots for perching.

Hibernating stage: Caterpillar.

Elevational range: Up to 2,000 m.

Egg-laying: Eggs are laid singly on LHP leaves and stems or on nearby vegetation.

Flight period: From June to October.

Host plants: Grasses, including *Festuca ovina, F. rubra, Ammophila arenaria, Achnatherum parviflorum, Brachypodium pinnatum, B. phoenicoides, B. retusum, Aira caryophyllea, A. praecox, Arrhenatherum elatius, Alpagrostis setacea, Avenella flexuosa, Calamagrostis arenaria, Corynephorus canescens, Deschampsia cespitosa, Elymus repens, Festuca elegans, F. rubra, F. ovina, Koeleria pyramidata, Bromus erectus, Briza media, Lolium perenne, Phleum phleoides, Poa annua, Sesleria albicans, Stipa lagascae, S. offneri, S. pennata, Agrostis vinealis,* and *A. capillaris.* Sedges, such as *Carex leporina* and *C. pilulifera.*

Diversity and systematics: The nominate subspecies is described from Sweden and flies in the northern half of Europe. Subspecies *cadmus* inhabits the southern part of the continent. Subspecies *scota, thyone, atlantica,* and *clarensis* fly in Scotland, Wales, the Hebrides, and Ireland, respectively. Subspecies *wilkinsoni* forms the Sicilian populations. Numerous forms are also described.

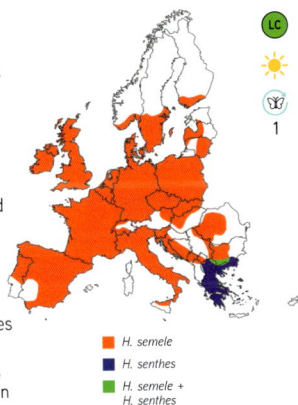

LC

1

■ *H. semele*
■ *H. senthes*
■ *H. semele + H. senthes*

Did you know?

The Grayling is the most widely distributed species in genus *Hipparchia* in Europe. However, it is declining due to habitat anthropization and pastoral abandonment, leading to the loss of dry grasslands outside the Mediterranean region.

IMAGOS		LARVAE	
Food		Food	
Behaviour of males		Caterpillar location	
Dispersion		Chrysalis location	

SATYRINAE

BALKAN GRAYLING *HIPPARCHIA SENTHES*

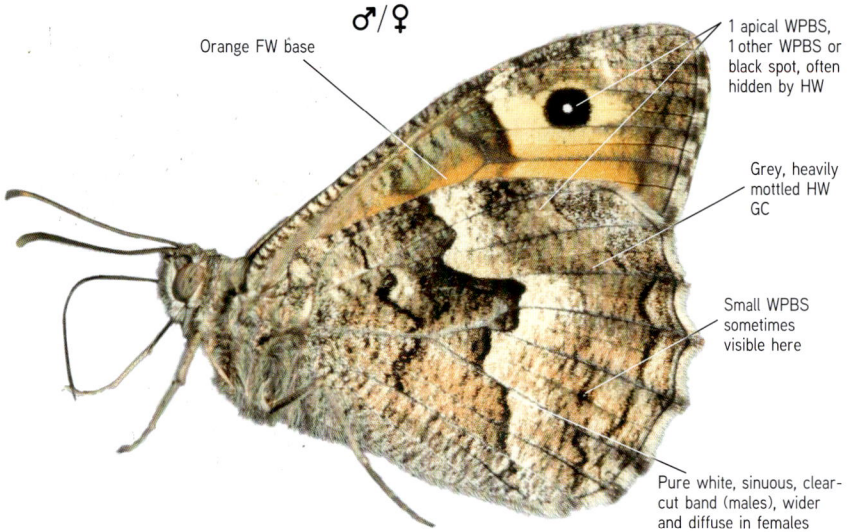

♂/♀

Orange FW base

1 apical WPBS,
1 other WPBS or
black spot, often
hidden by HW

Grey, heavily
mottled HW
GC

Small WPBS
sometimes
visible here

Pure white, sinuous, clear-
cut band (males), wider
and diffuse in females

Wingspan: 50–54 mm

Habitat: Dry grasslands, garrigues, and stony slopes.

Hibernating stage: Caterpillar.

Elevational range: Up to 2,200 m.

Egg-laying: Eggs are laid singly on LHP leaves and stems.

Flight period: From May to September.

Host plants: Grasses, especially *Brachypodium retusum*.

Diversity and systematics: There are no notable subspecies.

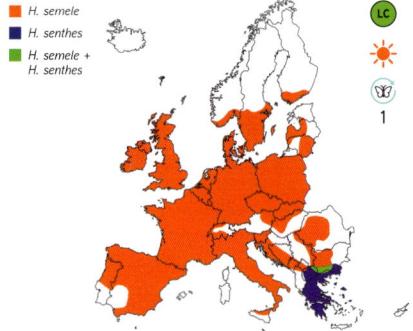

■ *H. semele*
■ *H. senthes*
■ *H. semele +*
  H. senthes

LC

1

Did you know?

Hipparchia senthes has been considered a subspecies of *H. aristaeus*. It can be confused with *H. semele* in the northern Balkans and with *H. volgensis* elsewhere. The examination of the genitalia is necessary for certainty.

IMAGOS		LARVAE	
Food		Food	
Behaviour of males		Caterpillar location	
Dispersion		Chrysalis location	

SATYRINAE

DELATTIN'S GRAYLING *HIPPARCHIA VOLGENSIS*

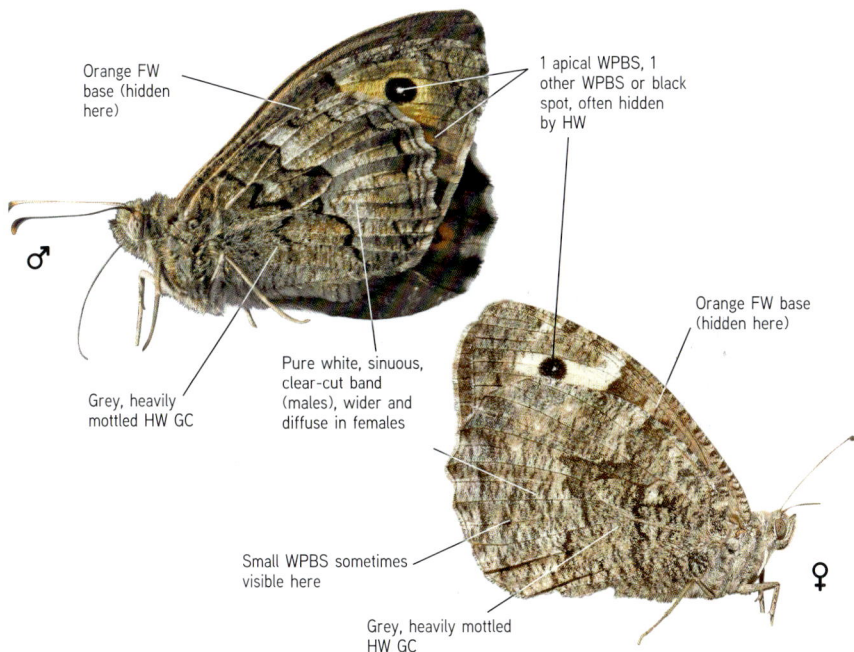

Orange FW base (hidden here)

1 apical WPBS, 1 other WPBS or black spot, often hidden by HW

Orange FW base (hidden here)

♂

Grey, heavily mottled HW GC

Pure white, sinuous, clear-cut band (males), wider and diffuse in females

Small WPBS sometimes visible here

Grey, heavily mottled HW GC

♀

Wingspan: 49–58 mm

Habitat: Dry grasslands, stony slopes, and clear woodlands.

Hibernating stage: Caterpillar.

Elevational range: Up to 1,500 m.

Egg-laying: Eggs are laid singly on LHP leaves and stems.

Flight period: From May to September.

Host plants: Grasses, including *Elymus repens*.

Diversity and systematics: The Balkans are populated by subspecies *delattini* (in the north) and *muelleri* (more in the south).

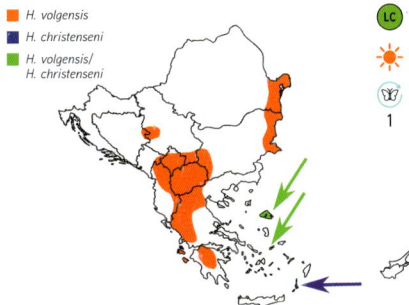

- ■ *H. volgensis*
- ■ *H. christenseni*
- ■ *H. volgensis/ H. christenseni*

LC

1

	IMAGOS		LARVAE
Food	☆ ◌	Food	◖
Behaviour of males		Caterpillar location	
Dispersion		Chrysalis location	

Did you know?

Delattin's Grayling can be distinguished from the Grayling only through genitalia examination.

543

SATYRINAE

KARPATHOS GRAYLING *HIPPARCHIA CHRISTENSENI*

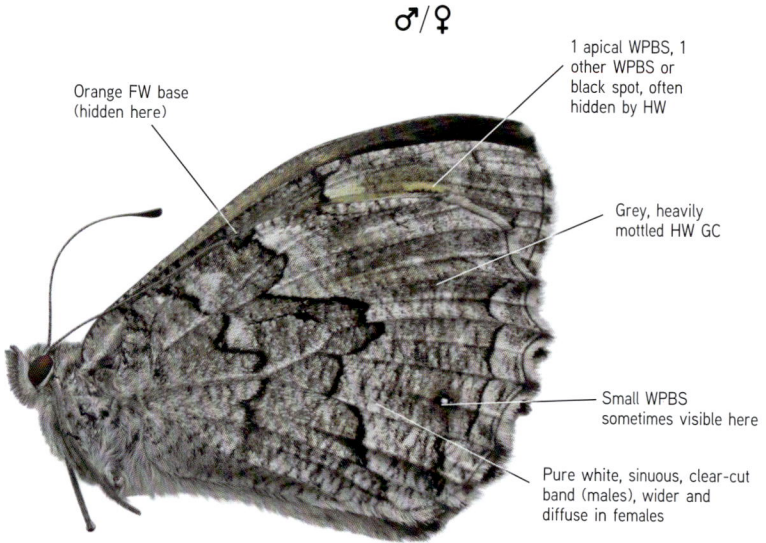

♂/♀

Orange FW base
(hidden here)

1 apical WPBS, 1
other WPBS or
black spot, often
hidden by HW

Grey, heavily
mottled HW GC

Small WPBS
sometimes visible here

Pure white, sinuous, clear-cut
band (males), wider and
diffuse in females

Wingspan: 41–59 mm

Habitat: Stony and bushy slopes, clear pine woodlands.
Hibernating stage: Caterpillar.
Elevational range: Up to 800 m.
Egg-laying: Eggs are laid singly on LHP leaves and stems.
Flight period: From June to September.
Host plants: Grasses.
Diversity and systematics: There are no notable subspecies.

- ■ H. volgensis
- ■ H. christenseni
- ■ H. volgensis/
  H. christenseni

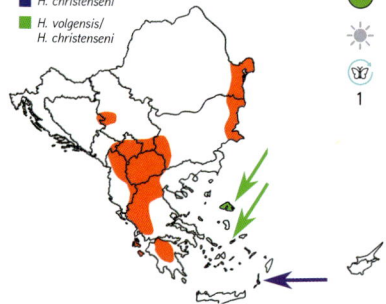

LC

1

Did you know?

The Karpathos Grayling is
endemic to the island of
Karpathos, where it is the only
grayling species. Graylings from
the islands of Lesbos and Icaria
are part of the species complex
formed by the Karpathos and
Delattin's Graylings.

IMAGOS		LARVAE	
Food		Food	
Behaviour of males		Caterpillar location	
Dispersion		Chrysalis location	

SATYRINAE

SAMOS GRAYLING *HIPPARCHIA MERSINA*

♂/♀

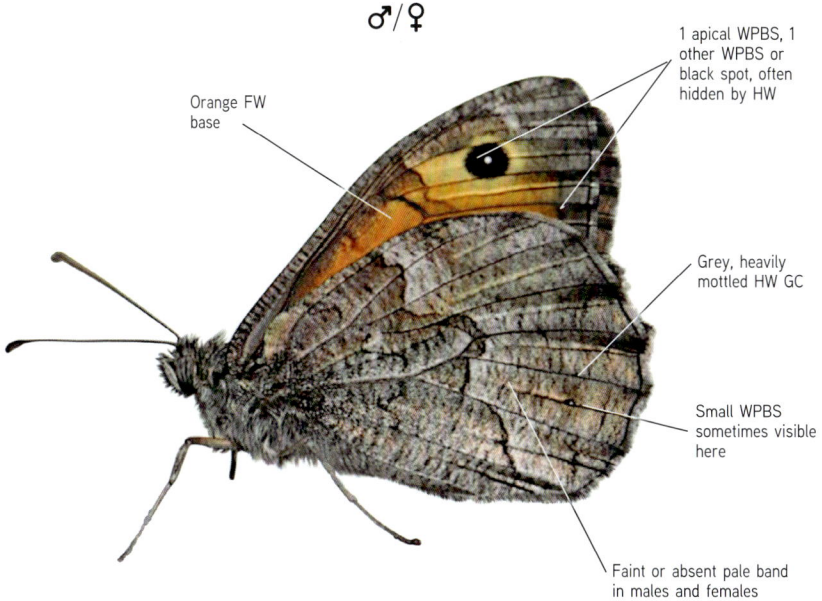

Orange FW base

1 apical WPBS, 1 other WPBS or black spot, often hidden by HW

Grey, heavily mottled HW GC

Small WPBS sometimes visible here

Faint or absent pale band in males and females

Wingspan: 41–59 mm

Habitat: Dry clearings, including at high elevations near the treeline.

Hibernating stage: Caterpillar.

Elevational range: Up to 2,000 m.

Egg-laying: Eggs are laid singly on LHP leaves and stems.

Flight period: From May to July.

Host plants: Grasses.

Diversity and systematics: There are no notable subspecies.

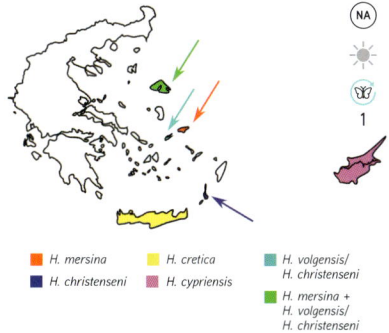

■ H. mersina	■ H. cretica	■ H. volgensis/
■ H. christenseni	■ H. cypriensis	H. christenseni
		■ H. mersina + H. volgensis/ H. christenseni

Did you know?

This grayling is found only on the islands of Samos and Lesbos. It coexists on the former with the Balkan Grayling and on the latter with graylings in the species complex formed by the Karpathos and Delattin's Graylings.

IMAGOS		LARVAE	
Food	☆ 💩 💧	Food	🍃
Behaviour of males	🌷 🌼	Caterpillar location	🐛 🌾
Dispersion	🦋	Chrysalis location	🐚

CRETAN GRAYLING *HIPPARCHIA CRETICA*

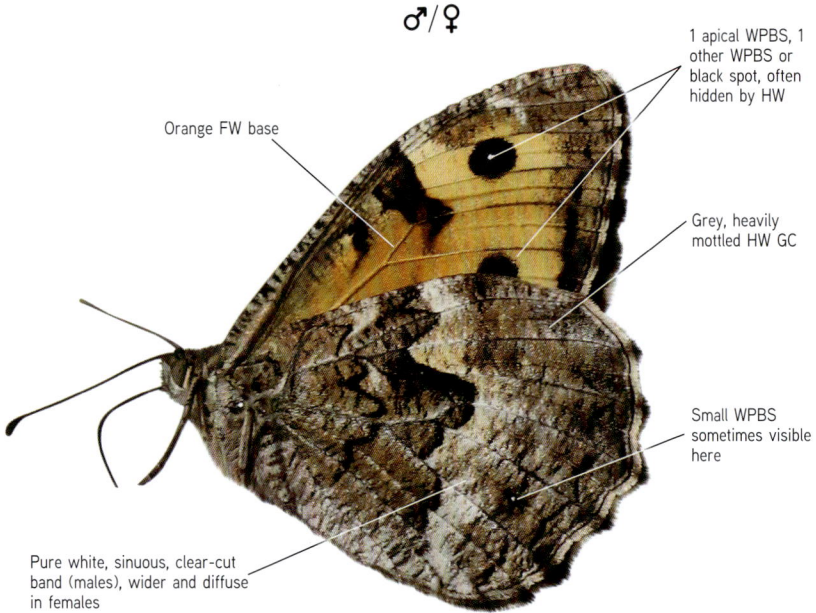

♂/♀

Orange FW base

1 apical WPBS, 1 other WPBS or black spot, often hidden by HW

Grey, heavily mottled HW GC

Small WPBS sometimes visible here

Pure white, sinuous, clear-cut band (males), wider and diffuse in females

Wingspan: 52–60 mm

Habitat: Garrigues and dry, rocky slopes.
Hibernating stage: Caterpillar.
Elevational range: Up to 1,500 m.
Egg-laying: Eggs are laid singly on LHP leaves and stems.
Flight period: From May to October.
Host plants: Grasses.
Diversity and systematics: There are no notable subspecies.

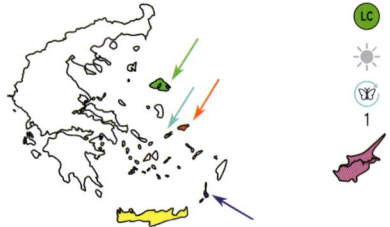

| ■ H. mersina | ■ H. cretica | ■ H. volgensis/ H. christenseni |
| ■ H. christenseni | ■ H. cypriensis | ■ H. mersina + H. volgensis/ H. christenseni |

IMAGOS			LARVAE	
Food			Food	
Behaviour of males			Caterpillar location	
Dispersion			Chrysalis location	

Did you know?

The Cretan Grayling is the only grayling present in Crete, where it cannot be confused with other species.

546

SATYRINAE

CYPRUS GRAYLING   *HIPPARCHIA CYPRIENSIS*

♂/♀

1 apical WPBS,
1 other WPBS
or black spot,
often hidden
by HW

Orange FW base

Grey, heavily
mottled HW GC

Small WPBS
sometimes
visible here

Pure white sinuous, clear-cut
band (males), wider and diffuse
in females

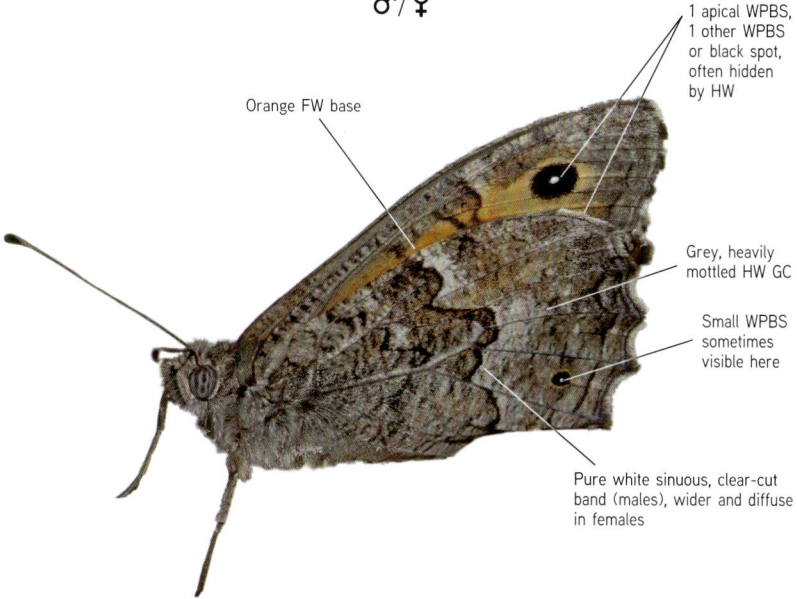

Wingspan: 46–63 mm

Habitat: Grasslands, garrigues, stony slopes, and clear woodlands.

Hibernating stage: Caterpillar.

Elevational range: Up to 1,500 m.

Egg-laying: Eggs are laid singly on LHP leaves and stems.

Flight period: From May to November.

Host plants: Grasses.

Diversity and systematics: *Hipparchia cypriensis* has sometimes been considered a subspecies of the Eastern Grayling, *H. pellucida* which flies in Crimea.

LC

1

| ■ H. mersina | ■ H. cretica | ■ H. volgensis/ H. christenseni |
| ■ H. christenseni | ■ H. cypriensis | ■ H. mersina + H. volgensis/ H. christenseni |

IMAGOS			LARVAE		
Food			Food		
Behaviour of males			Caterpillar location		
Dispersion			Chrysalis location		

Did you know?

In summer, the Cyprus Grayling stays in the mountains to escape the excessive heat. In autumn, it descends to lowlands to breed.

SATYRINAE

MADEIRAN GRAYLING *HIPPARCHIA MADERENSIS*

♂/♀

1 apical WPBS, 1 other WPBS or black spot, often hidden by HW

Orange FW base (hidden here)

Dark grey, heavily mottled HW GC

Small WPBS sometimes visible here

Pure white, sinuous, clear-cut band (males), wider and diffuse in females

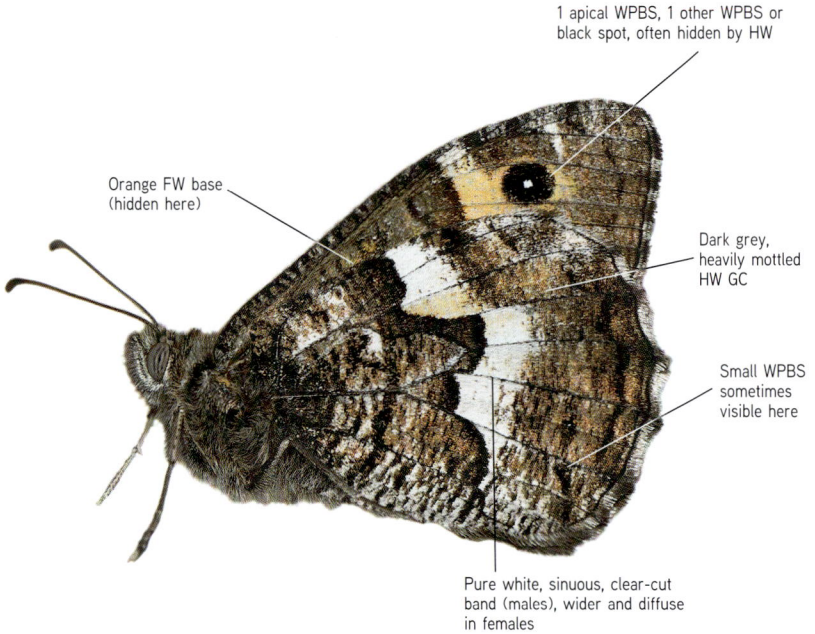

Wingspan: 40–48 mm

Habitat: Grazed grasslands, grassy and stony slopes.

Hibernating stage: Caterpillar.

Elevational range: Between 800 and 1,800 m.

Egg-laying: Eggs are laid singly on LHP leaves and stems.

Flight period: From June to September.

Host plants: Grasses, like *Aira praecox*, *A. caryophyllea*, and *Agrostis* spp.

Diversity and systematics: There are no notable subspecies.

Madeira

LC

1

IMAGOS			LARVAE		
Food			Food		
Behaviour of males			Caterpillar location		
Dispersion: unknown			Chrysalis location		

Did you know?

The Madeiran Grayling is sometimes considered a subspecies of the Southern Grayling, *Hipparchia aristaeus*.

SOUTHERN GRAYLING *HIPPARCHIA ARISTAEUS*

♂/♀

- 1 apical WPBS, 1 other WPBS or black spot, often hidden by HW
- Orange FW base
- Grey, heavily mottled HW GC
- Small WPBS sometimes visible here
- Pure white, sinuous, clear-cut band (males), wider and diffuse in females

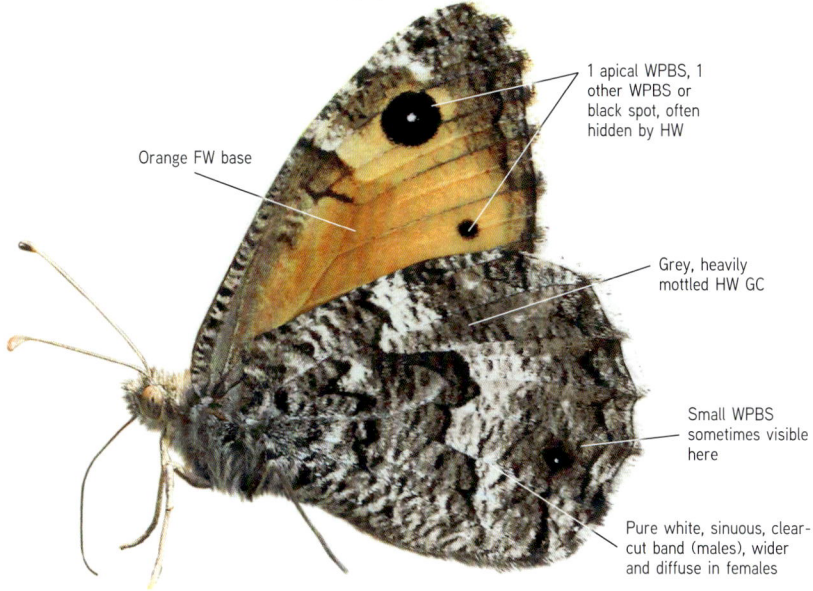

Wingspan: 50–54 mm

Habitat: Dry grasslands, garrigues, maquis, and clear woodlands.

Hibernating stage: Caterpillar.

Elevational range: Up to 2,000 m.

Egg-laying: Eggs are laid singly on LHP leaves and stems.

Flight period: From June to October.

Host plants: Grasses, including *Brachypodium retusum*, *Festuca morisiana*, and *Poa balbisii*.

Diversity and systematics: There are no notable subspecies.

- ■ H. aristaeus
- ■ H. blachieri + H. semele
- ■ H. neapolitana + H. semele
- ■ H. sbordonii
- ■ H. leighebi

LC
1

Did you know?

The Southern Grayling is macroscopically indistinguishable from the allopatric Italian and Sicilian Graylings, with which it also shares the morphology of its genitalia. Their divergence likely dates back to less than 1 million years ago.

IMAGOS		LARVAE	
Food		Food	
Behaviour of males		Caterpillar location	
Dispersion		Chrysalis location	

SATYRINAE

ITALIAN GRAYLING   *HIPPARCHIA NEAPOLITANA*

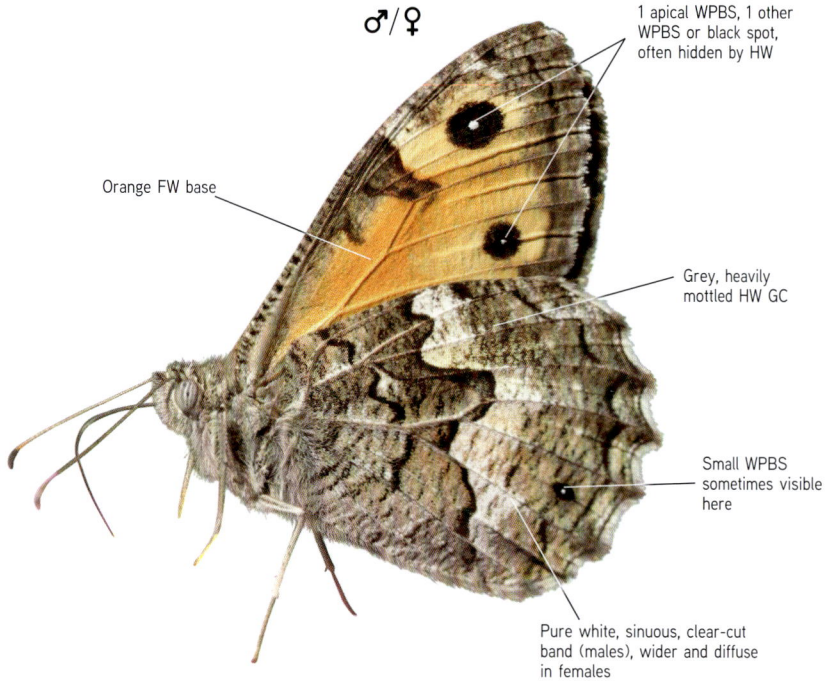

♂/♀

1 apical WPBS, 1 other WPBS or black spot, often hidden by HW

Orange FW base

Grey, heavily mottled HW GC

Small WPBS sometimes visible here

Pure white, sinuous, clear-cut band (males), wider and diffuse in females

Wingspan: 50–54 mm

Habitat: Dry grassy and bushy areas.

Hibernating stage: Caterpillar.

Elevational range: Up to 1,300 m.

Egg-laying: Eggs are laid singly on LHP leaves and stems.

Flight period: From July to September.

Host plants: Grasses, including *Festuca circummediterranea*, *F. jeanpertii*, *Brachypodium distachyon*, and *Poa* spp.

Diversity and systematics: There are no notable subspecies. *Hipparchia blachieri* is sometimes considered a subspecies of *H. neapolitana*.

- *H. aristaeus*
- *H. blachieri* + *H. semele*
- *H. neapolitana* + *H. semele*
- *H. sbordonii*
- *H. leighebi*

LC

1

IMAGOS		LARVAE	
Food		Food	
Behaviour of males		Caterpillar location	
Dispersion		Chrysalis location	

Did you know?

The Italian Grayling cannot be distinguished with certainty from the Grayling, with which it flies, except through detailed genitalia examination.

SATYRINAE

SICILIAN GRAYLING *HIPPARCHIA BLACHIERI*

♂/♀

Orange FW base

1 apical WPBS, 1 other WPBS or black spot, often hidden by HW

Grey, heavily mottled HW GC

Small WPBS sometimes visible here

Pure white, sinuous, clear-cut band (males), wider and diffuse in females

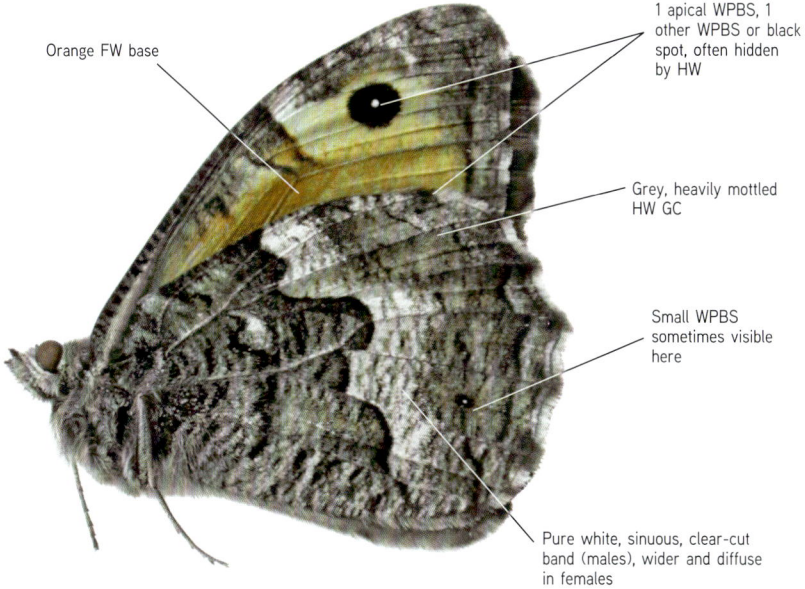

Wingspan: 50–54 mm

Habitat: Dry grasslands and garrigues.

Hibernating stage: Caterpillar.

Elevational range: Up to 2,000 m.

Egg-laying: Eggs are laid singly on LHP leaves and stems.

Flight period: From May to October.

Host plants: Grasses.

Diversity and systematics: The nominate subspecies flies in Sicily. Subspecies *vallettai* inhabits Malta.

- ■ H. aristaeus
- ■ H. blachieri + H. semele
- ■ H. neapolitana + H. semele
- ■ H. sbordonii
- ■ H. leighebi

LC

1

IMAGOS		LARVAE	
Food		Food	
Behaviour of males		Caterpillar location	
Dispersion		Chrysalis location	

Did you know?

Hipparchia blachieri is sometimes considered a subspecies of *H. neapolitana*. It can be confused with *H. semele*, which also flies in Sicily and southern Italy.

SATYRINAE

PONZA GRAYLING *HIPPARCHIA SBORDONII*

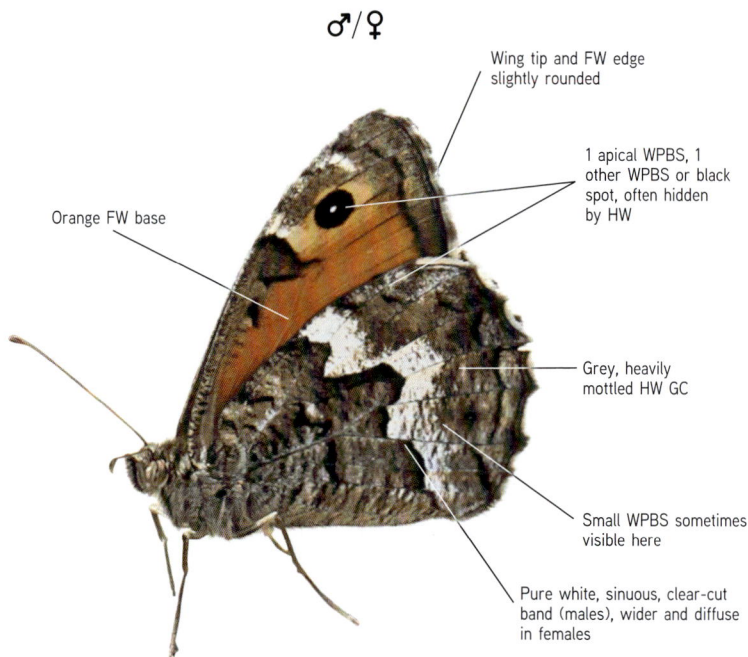

♂/♀

Wing tip and FW edge slightly rounded

1 apical WPBS, 1 other WPBS or black spot, often hidden by HW

Orange FW base

Grey, heavily mottled HW GC

Small WPBS sometimes visible here

Pure white, sinuous, clear-cut band (males), wider and diffuse in females

Wingspan: 50–54 mm

Habitat: Bushy and grassy areas.

Hibernating stage: Caterpillar.

Elevational range: Below 500 m.

Egg-laying: Eggs are laid singly on LHP leaves and stems.

Flight period: June and July.

Host plants: Grasses, like *Festuca* spp., *Brachypodium retusum*, and *Poa* spp.

Diversity and systematics: There are no notable subspecies.

■ H. aristaeus
■ H. blachieri + H. semele
■ H. neapolitana + H. semele
■ H. sbordonii
■ H. leighebi

EN

1

IMAGOS		LARVAE	
Food		Food	
Behaviour of males		Caterpillar location	
Dispersion		Chrysalis location	

Did you know?

The Ponza Grayling is endemic to the Pontine Islands (including the island of Ponza) and is the only grayling in this region; it cannot be confused with others.

EOLIAN GRAYLING *HIPPARCHIA LEIGHEBI*

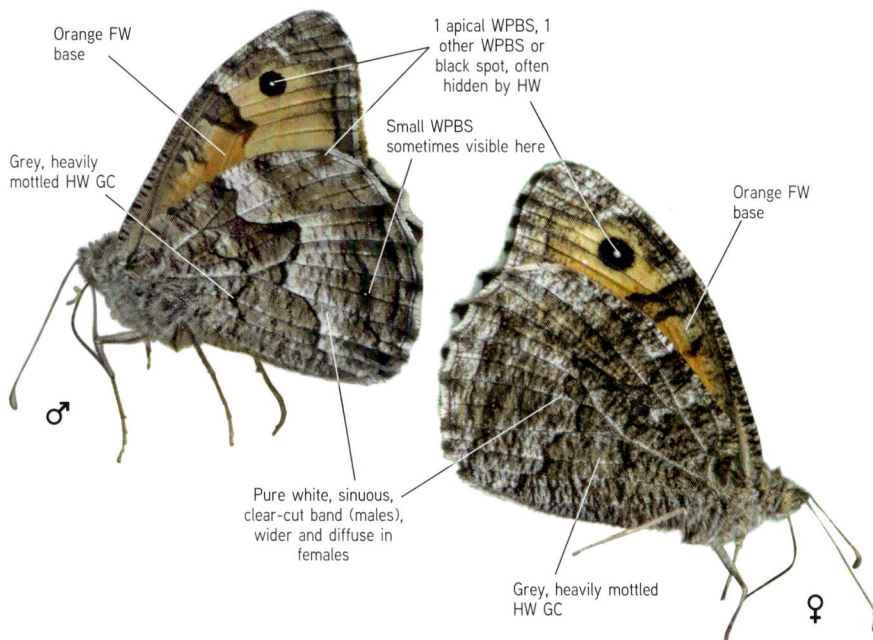

Orange FW base

1 apical WPBS, 1 other WPBS or black spot, often hidden by HW

Small WPBS sometimes visible here

Grey, heavily mottled HW GC

Orange FW base

♂

Pure white, sinuous, clear-cut band (males), wider and diffuse in females

Grey, heavily mottled HW GC

♀

Wingspan: 50–54 mm

Habitat: Rocky areas.

Hibernating stage: Caterpillar.

Elevational range: Up to 500 m.

Egg-laying: Eggs are laid singly on LHP leaves and stems.

Flight period: From June to August.

Host plants: Grasses, such as *Festuca* spp. and *Agrostis stolonifera*.

Diversity and systematics: *Hipparchia leighebi* is sometimes considered a subspecies of *H. semele*.

- H. aristaeus
- H. blachieri + H. semele
- H. neapolitana + H. semele
- H. sbordonii
- H. leighebi

NT

1

IMAGOS		LARVAE	
Food		Food	
Behaviour of males		Caterpillar location	
Dispersion		Chrysalis location	

Did you know?

The Eolian Grayling is the only grayling present on the Aeolian Islands and therefore cannot be confused with other species.

CORSICAN GRAYLING *HIPPARCHIA NEOMIRIS*

♂/♀

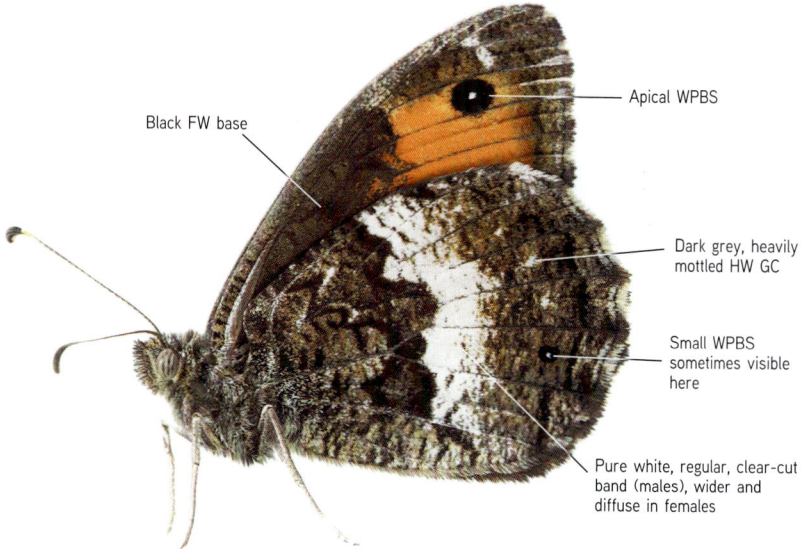

Black FW base

Apical WPBS

Dark grey, heavily mottled HW GC

Small WPBS sometimes visible here

Pure white, regular, clear-cut band (males), wider and diffuse in females

Wingspan: 46–50 mm

Habitat: Dry grasslands and heaths, rocky slopes, and clear pine woodlands.

Hibernating stage: Caterpillar.

Elevational range: Up to 2,000 m.

Egg-laying: Eggs are dropped in vegetation or laid singly on LHP leaves and stems.

Flight period: From June to August.

Host plants: Grasses, like *Festuca morisiana*, *Poa balbisii*, and *Brachypodium* spp.

Diversity and systematics: There are no notable subspecies.

IMAGOS			LARVAE		
Food			Food		
Behaviour of males			Caterpillar location		
Dispersion			Chrysalis location		

Did you know?

In sheep-grazed areas, the caterpillars are often found on grasses growing near shrubs, which provide some protection against grazing pressure.

AZORES GRAYLING/LE CERF'S GRAYLING
HIPPARCHIA AZORINA/H. MIGUELENSIS

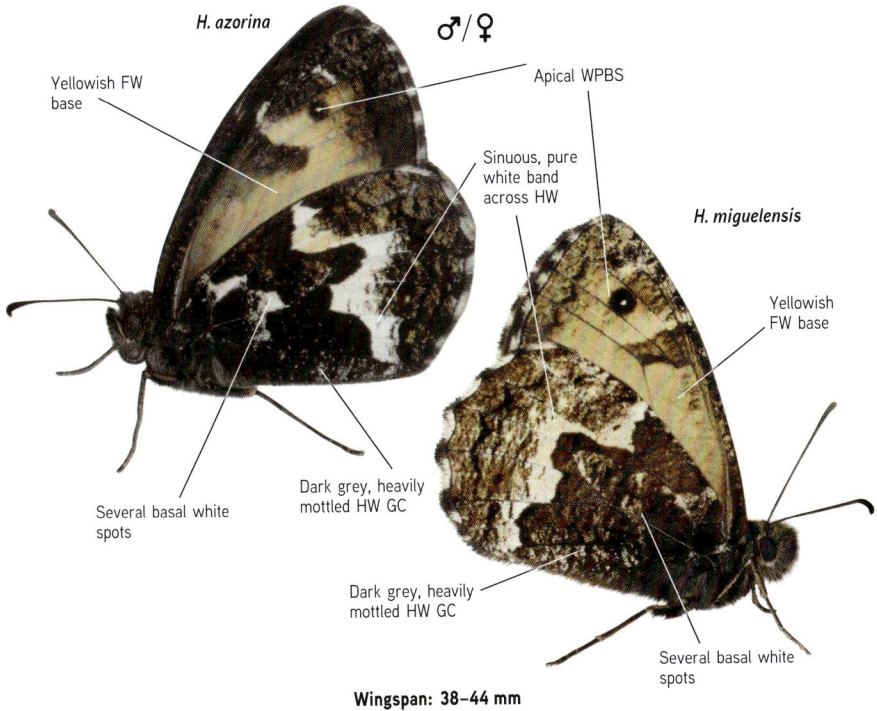

H. azorina

♂/♀

Yellowish FW base

Apical WPBS

Sinuous, pure white band across HW

H. miguelensis

Yellowish FW base

Several basal white spots

Dark grey, heavily mottled HW GC

Dark grey, heavily mottled HW GC

Several basal white spots

Wingspan: 38–44 mm

Habitat: Bushy grasslands and low-growing heaths.

Hibernating stage: Caterpillar.

Elevational range: Up to 2,000 m for *Hipparchia azorensis*, 1,000 m for *H. miguelensis*.

Egg-laying: Eggs are laid singly on LHP leaves and stems.

Flight period: From May to October.

Host plants: Grasses, including *Festuca jubata*.

Diversity and systematics: *Hipparchia miguelensis* is sometimes considered a subspecies of *H. azorina*, whose nominate subspecies flies on the islands of Pico, Faial, São Jorge, and Terceira. Subspecies *occidentalis* inhabits the islands of Flores and Corvo.

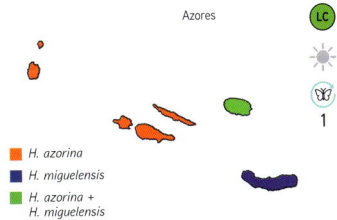

Azores

LC

■ *H. azorina*
■ *H. miguelensis*
■ *H. azorina* + *H. miguelensis*

1

Did you know?

These two grayling species are the most differentiated among the other graylings in terms of their background colour. One phylogeny also suggests that their divergence is among the oldest in the group.

IMAGOS		LARVAE	
Food	☆	Food	🍃
Behaviour of males	🦋	Caterpillar location	🌱
Dispersion: unknown		Chrysalis location	

TREE GRAYLING   *HIPPARCHIA STATILINUS*

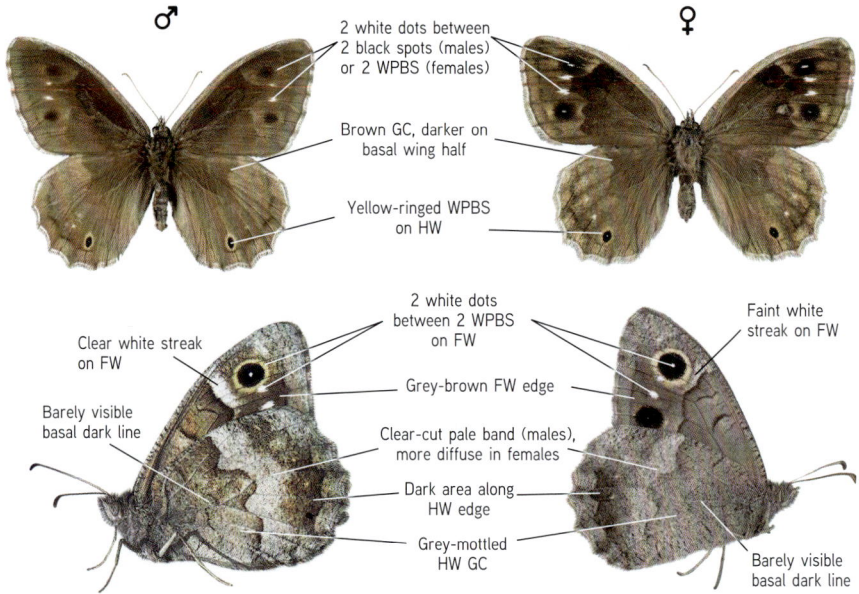

♂

♀

2 white dots between 2 black spots (males) or 2 WPBS (females)

Brown GC, darker on basal wing half

Yellow-ringed WPBS on HW

2 white dots between 2 WPBS on FW

Clear white streak on FW

Grey-brown FW edge

Faint white streak on FW

Barely visible basal dark line

Clear-cut pale band (males), more diffuse in females

Dark area along HW edge

Grey-mottled HW GC

Barely visible basal dark line

Wingspan: 44–46 mm

Habitat: Dry grasslands with bare areas, rocky thickets, heaths, and backdunes.

Hibernating stage: Caterpillar.

Elevational range: Up to 1,500 m.

Egg-laying: Eggs are laid singly on LHP dry tussocks or stones.

Flight period: From June to October.

Host plants: Grasses, including *Brachypodium distachyon*, *B. phoenicoides*, *B. retusum*, *Bromus erectus*, *B. secalinus*, *B. sterilis*, *Achnatherum parviflorum*, *Agrostis vinealis*, *Calamagrostis epigejos*, *Corynephorus canescens*, *Festuca ovina*, *F. rubra*, *Dactylis glomerata*, *Danthonia decumbens*, *Helictochloa gervaisii*, *Koeleria vallesiana*, *Molinia caerulea*, *Nardus tricta*, *Poa annua*, *Stipa lagascae*, *S. offneri*, and *S. pennata*. Sedges, such as *Carex pilulifera* and *C. halleriana*.

Diversity and systematics: The nominate subspecies lives in Germany. Subspecies *allionia*, *apennina* and *martianii* fly in Southern Europe, central Italy, and Sicily, respectively.

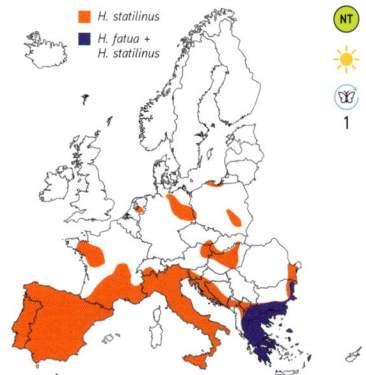

■ *H. statilinus*
■ *H. fatua* + *H. statilinus*

NT

1

IMAGOS			LARVAE	
Food	🌼 ☁ 💧		Food	🍃
Behaviour of males			Caterpillar location	🐛 🌿
Dispersion			Chrysalis location	

Did you know?

Easy to observe when it moves because of its large size, the Tree Grayling is much harder to spot when it is perched, owing to its particularly cryptic grey coat.

FREYER'S GRAYLING *HIPPARCHIA FATUA*

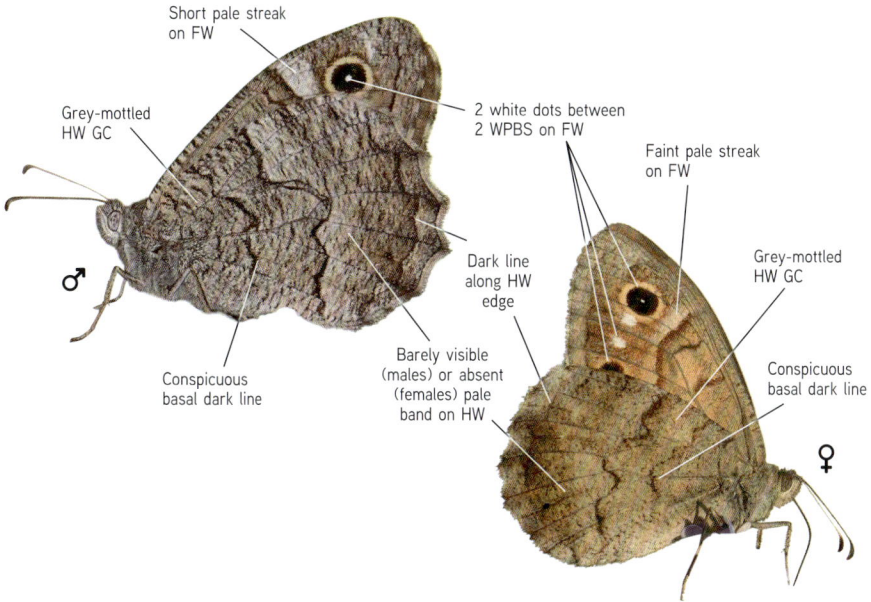

Short pale streak on FW

Grey-mottled HW GC

2 white dots between 2 WPBS on FW

Faint pale streak on FW

Grey-mottled HW GC

♂

Dark line along HW edge

Conspicuous basal dark line

Barely visible (males) or absent (females) pale band on HW

Conspicuous basal dark line

♀

Wingspan: 50–65 mm

Habitat: Dry, thermophilic grassy areas, often within clear pine woodlands.

Hibernating stage: Caterpillar.

Elevational range: Up to 1,500 m (mainly at low elevations).

Egg-laying: Eggs are laid singly on LHP dry tussocks or stones.

Flight period: From June to October.

Host plants: Grasses, like *Poa annua* and *Festuca* spp.

Diversity and systematics: European populations belong to the nominative subspecies.

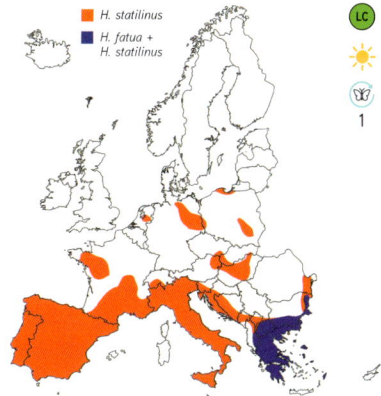

H. statilinus

H. fatua + H. statilinus

LC

1

IMAGOS		LARVAE	
Food	🍎🍯✿♨💧	Food	🍃
Behaviour of males		Caterpillar location	
Dispersion		Chrysalis location	

Did you know?

Freyer's Graylings aren't very keen on floral nectar. They particularly enjoy the juice of rotting fruits and the sap from wounded trees.

SATYRINAE

STRIPED GRAYLING   *HIPPARCHIA FIDIA*

♂/♀

Grey-brown GC

2 white dots between 2 yellow-ringed WPBS on FW

Grey GC on both wings

2 white dots between 2 black spots or WPBS on FW

Pure white band underlined by a black chevron

Small black spot or WPBS here

Wingspan: 56–62 mm

Habitat: Stony, dry grasslands, garrigues, and clear pine woodlands.

Hibernating stage: Caterpillar, without entering diapause.

Elevational range: Up to 2,000 m.

Egg-laying: Eggs are laid singly on LHP dry tussocks or on stones.

Flight period: From June to October.

Host plants: Grasses, especially *Achnatherum parviflorum*, *Brachypodium pinnatum*, *B. phoenicoides*, *B. retusum*, *Stipa offneri*, *Oloptum miliaceum*, *Piptatherum* spp., *Poa annua*, and *Festuca ovina*.

Diversity and systematics: European populations belong to subspecies *velleia*.

IMAGOS			LARVAE		
Food			Food		
Behaviour of males			Caterpillar location		
Dispersion			Chrysalis location		

Did you know?

The caterpillar exhibits the typical behaviour of Satyrine larvae: it is diurnal at the beginning of its development, then becomes nocturnal, changing colour from green to brown.

TENERIFE GRAYLING/GRAN CANARIA GRAYLING
HIPPARCHIA WYSSII/H. TAMADABAE

TILOS GRAYLING/GOMERA GRAYLING/HIERRO GRAYLING
H. TILOSI/H. GOMERA/H. BACCHUS

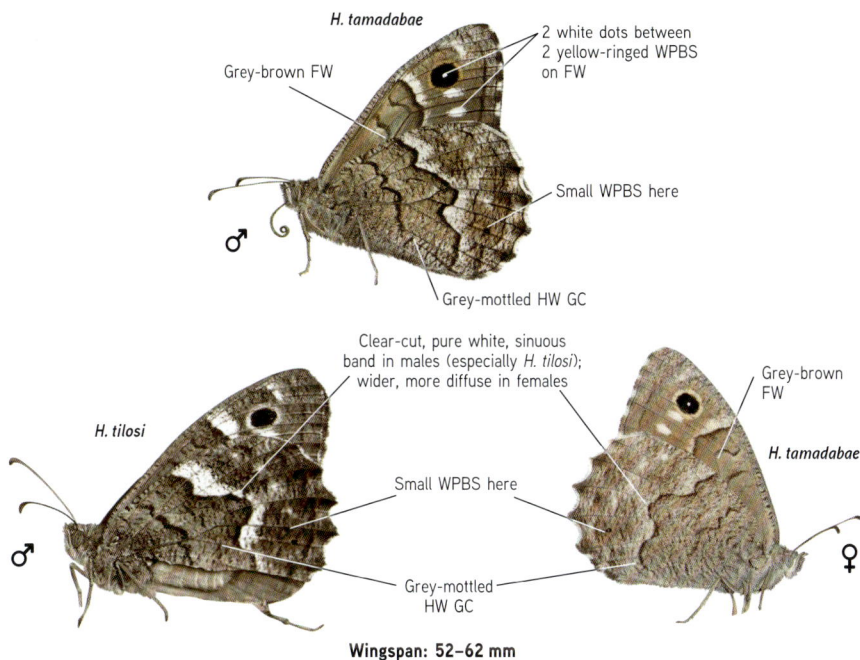

H. tamadabae

Grey-brown FW

2 white dots between 2 yellow-ringed WPBS on FW

Small WPBS here

Grey-mottled HW GC

♂

Clear-cut, pure white, sinuous band in males (especially *H. tilosi*); wider, more diffuse in females

H. tilosi

♂

Small WPBS here

Grey-mottled HW GC

Grey-brown FW

H. tamadabae

♀

Wingspan: 52–62 mm

Habitat: Dry, rocky gullies with pines and bushy heaths.

Hibernating stage: Caterpillar (without entering diapause at lower elevations).

Elevational range: Up to 2,000 m.

Egg-laying: Eggs are laid singly on LHP leaves and stems.

Flight period: From March to November, depending on the elevation.

Host plants: Grasses, including *Dactylis glomerata*.

Diversity and systematics: These five grayling species are often considered subspecies of *Hipparchia wyssii*.

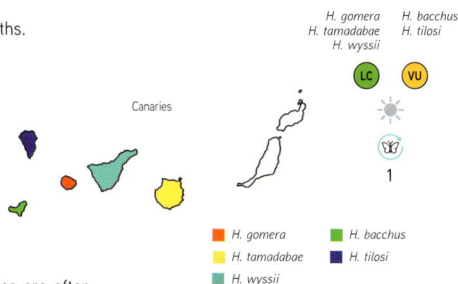

Canaries

H. gomera   H. bacchus
H. tamadabae   H. tilosi
H. wyssii

LC   VU

1

■ H. gomera   ■ H. bacchus
■ H. tamadabae   ■ H. tilosi
■ H. wyssii

IMAGOS		LARVAE	
Food		Food	
Behaviour of males		Caterpillar location	
Dispersion: unknown		Chrysalis location	

Did you know?

These five Canarian grayling species inhabit different islands of the archipelago. Therefore, they cannot be confused.

WOODLAND GRAYLING *HIPPARCHIA FAGI*

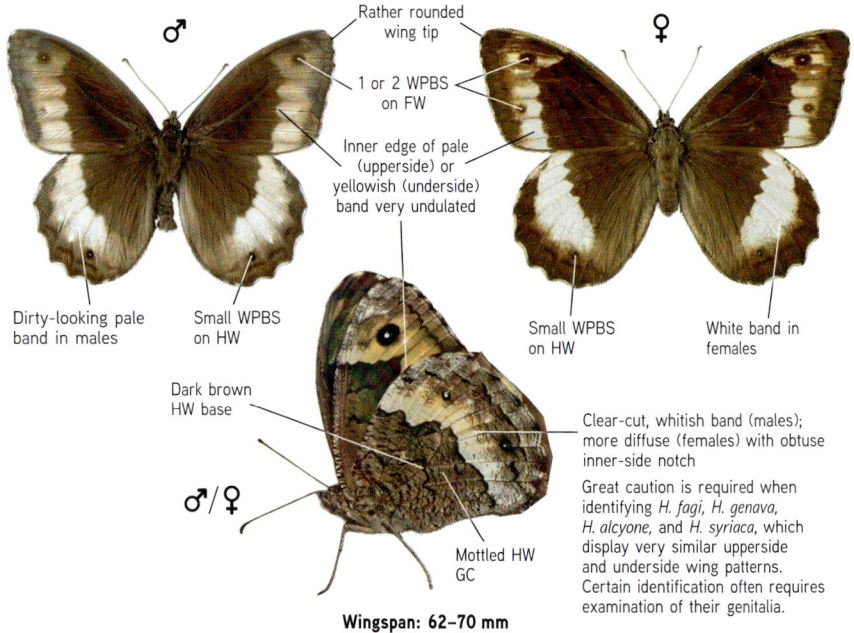

♂

Rather rounded
wing tip

♀

1 or 2 WPBS
on FW

Inner edge of pale
(upperside) or
yellowish (underside)
band very undulated

Dirty-looking pale
band in males

Small WPBS
on HW

Small WPBS
on HW

White band in
females

Dark brown
HW base

♂/♀

Clear-cut, whitish band (males);
more diffuse (females) with obtuse
inner-side notch

Great caution is required when
identifying *H. fagi, H. genava,
H. alcyone,* and *H. syriaca,* which
display very similar upperside
and underside wing patterns.
Certain identification often requires
examination of their genitalia.

Mottled HW
GC

Wingspan: 62–70 mm

Habitat: Warm, grassy forest edges and clearings,
bushy dry grasslands.

Hibernating stage: Caterpillar.

Elevational range: Up to 2,000 m.

Egg-laying: Eggs are laid singly on LHP dry tussocks
or on stones.

Flight period: From June to September.

Host plants: Grasses, including *Brachypodium
phoenicoides, B. pinnatum,* and *B. retusum, Festuca
ovina, F. rubra, Dactylis glomerata, Helictochloa
pratensis, Holcus lanatus, H. mollis, Lolium
arundinaceum, Poa pratensis,* and *Bromus erectus.*

Diversity and systematics: European populations
belong to the nominate subspecies.

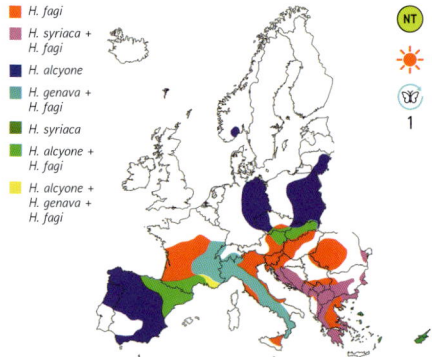

H. fagi
*H. syriaca +
H. fagi*
H. alcyone
*H. genava +
H. fagi*
H. syriaca
*H. alcyone +
H. fagi*
*H. alcyone +
H. genava +
H. fagi*

NT

1

	IMAGOS		LARVAE	
Food			Food	
Behaviour of males			Caterpillar location	
Dispersion			Chrysalis location	

Did you know?

Forest management, particularly
the dense planting of
conifers, poses a threat to the
Woodland Grayling, which has
significantly declined in the non-
Mediterranean part of its range.

SATYRINAE

EASTERN ROCK GRAYLING *HIPPARCHIA SYRIACA*

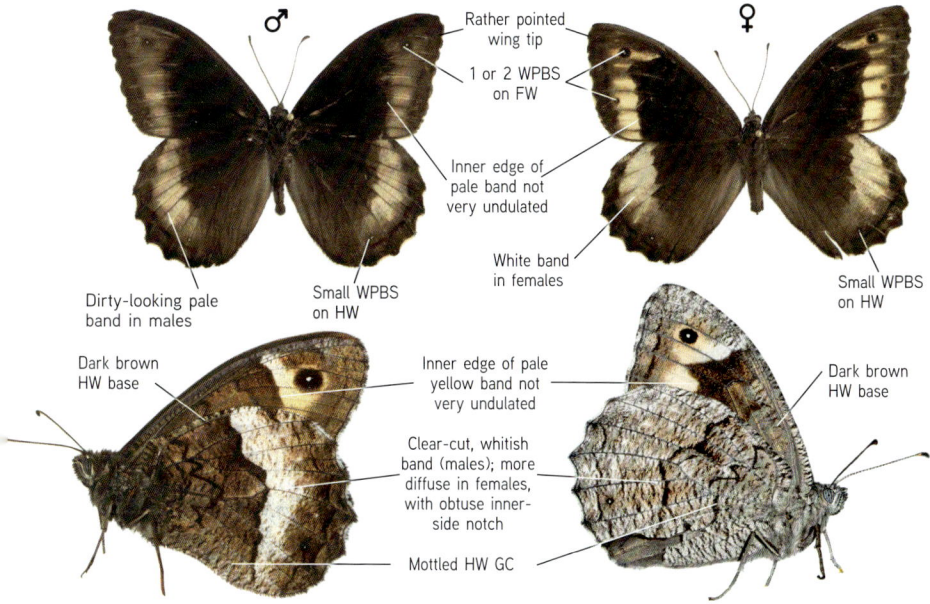

♂   Rather pointed wing tip

1 or 2 WPBS on FW

Inner edge of pale band not very undulated

White band in females

♀

Dirty-looking pale band in males

Small WPBS on HW

Small WPBS on HW

Dark brown HW base

Inner edge of pale yellow band not very undulated

Clear-cut, whitish band (males); more diffuse in females, with obtuse inner-side notch

Dark brown HW base

Mottled HW GC

Wingspan: 62–68 mm

Habitat: Bushy areas and clear woodlands.

Hibernating stage: Caterpillar.

Elevational range: Up to 2,000 m.

Egg-laying: Eggs are laid singly on LHP dry tussocks or on branches of garrigue bushes.

Flight period: From May to November.

Host plants: Grasses, including *Brachypodium* spp. and *Holcus* spp.

Diversity and systematics: Most European populations belong to the nominate subspecies. Subspecies *cypriaca* is endemic to Cyprus; it is the only rock grayling to fly in the Aegean Islands.

- H. fagi
- H. syriaca + H. fagi
- H. alcyone
- H. genava + H. fagi
- H. syriaca
- H. alcyone + H. fagi
- H. alcyone + H. genava + H. fagi

LC

1

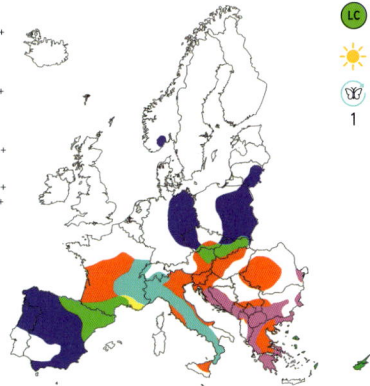

IMAGOS		LARVAE	
Food		Food	
Behaviour of males		Caterpillar location	
Dispersion		Chrysalis location	

Did you know?

Egg-laying often takes place in early autumn, after the hot season, which is a challenging period in the Mediterranean region.

SATYRINAE

ROCK GRAYLING *HIPPARCHIA ALCYONE*

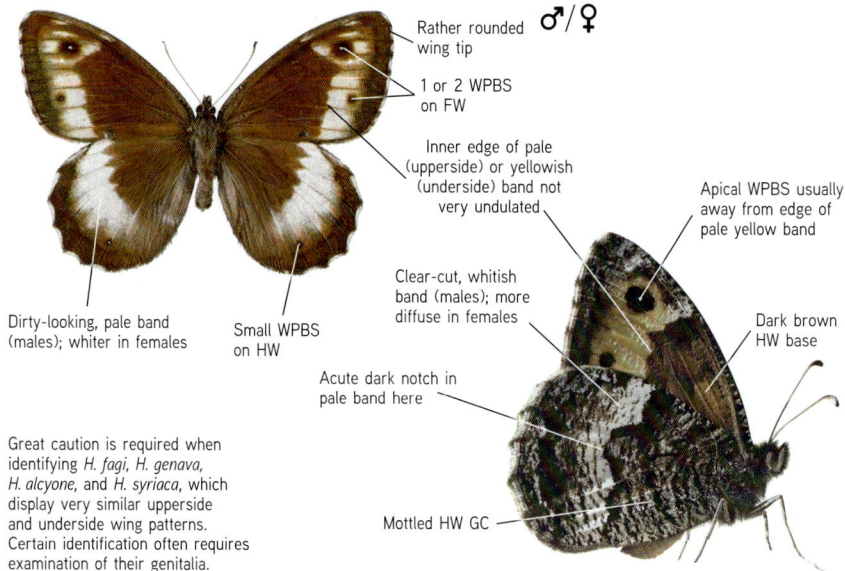

♂/♀

Rather rounded wing tip

1 or 2 WPBS on FW

Inner edge of pale (upperside) or yellowish (underside) band not very undulated

Apical WPBS usually away from edge of pale yellow band

Clear-cut, whitish band (males); more diffuse in females

Dark brown HW base

Dirty-looking, pale band (males); whiter in females

Small WPBS on HW

Acute dark notch in pale band here

Great caution is required when identifying *H. fagi*, *H. genava*, *H. alcyone*, and *H. syriaca*, which display very similar upperside and underside wing patterns. Certain identification often requires examination of their genitalia.

Mottled HW GC

Wingspan: 56–66 mm

Habitat: Stony, dry grasslands, rocky escarpments, and clear woodlands.

Hibernating stage: Caterpillar.

Elevational range: Up to 1,800 m.

Egg-laying: Eggs are laid singly on LHP dry tussocks or on stones.

Flight period: From June to September.

Host plants: Grasses, including *Arrhenatherum elatius*, *Festuca ovina*, *F. rubra*, *F. ampla*, *Lolium arundinaceum*, *Patzkea paniculata*, *Bromus erectus*, *Brachypodium pinnatum*, *B. phoenicoides*, *B. retusum*, and *B. sylvaticum*.

Diversity and systematics: The nominate subspecies populates Central Europe. Subspecies *vandalusica* flies in Spain and in the Eastern Pyrenees. Subspecies *pyrenaea* forms populations in the Central Pyrenees. Subspecies *norvegica* is found in southern Norway.

- ■ *H. fagi*
- ■ *H. syriaca +* *H. fagi*
- ■ *H. alcyone*
- ■ *H. genava +* *H. fagi*
- ■ *H. syriaca*
- ■ *H. alcyone +* *H. fagi*
- ■ *H. alcyone +* *H. genava +* *H. fagi*

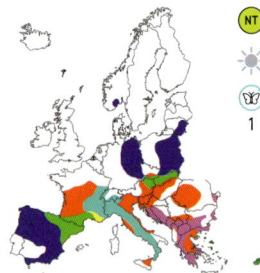

NT

1

Did you know?

A controversy exists regarding the scientific name of the Rock Grayling. The name *hermione*, still used by some authors, was proposed by Linnaeus for a probably different group of butterflies. The name *alcyone*, more commonly accepted today, was proposed by Ignaz Schiffermüller, a prominent Austrian entomologist.

IMAGOS		LARVAE	
Food	✿ 🐜 💧	Food	🌱
Behaviour of males		Caterpillar location	🌿
Dispersion		Chrysalis location	

562

LESSER ROCK GRAYLING *HIPPARCHIA GENAVA*

♂/♀

Great caution is required when identifying *H. fagi*, *H. genava*, *H. alcyone*, and *H. syriaca*, which display very similar upperside and underside wing patterns. Certain identification often requires examination of their genitalia.

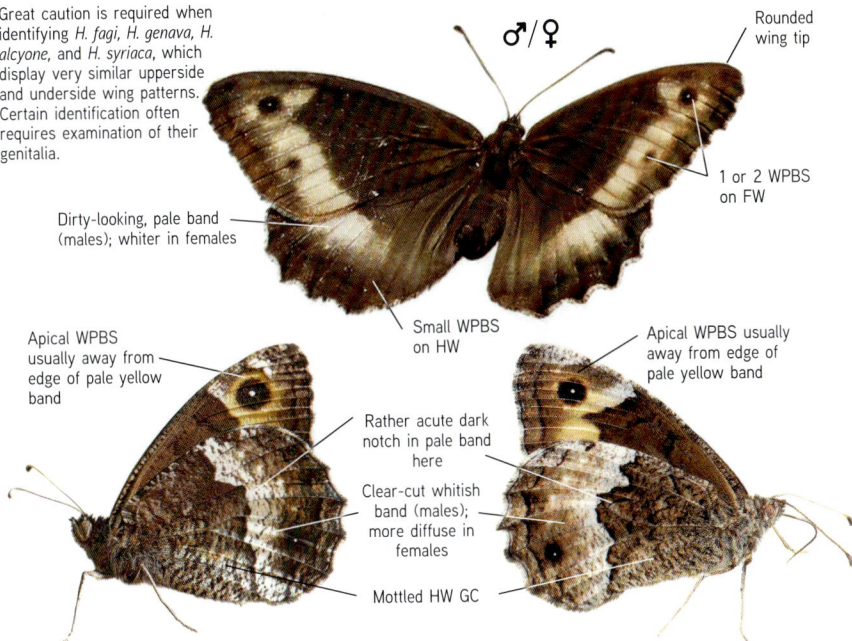

Rounded wing tip

1 or 2 WPBS on FW

Dirty-looking, pale band (males); whiter in females

Small WPBS on HW

Apical WPBS usually away from edge of pale yellow band

Apical WPBS usually away from edge of pale yellow band

Rather acute dark notch in pale band here

Clear-cut whitish band (males); more diffuse in females

Mottled HW GC

Wingspan: 55–66 mm

Habitat: Dry edges, clear woodlands, rocky escarpments, and scree.

Hibernating stage: Caterpillar.

Elevational range: Up to 2,000 m.

Egg-laying: Eggs are laid singly on dry tussocks of the LHP or on stones.

Flight period: From June to August.

Host plants: Grasses.

Diversity and systematics: The nominate subspecies is described from Switzerland. Subspecies *latevittata* forms populations in Italy south of the Alps. Subspecies *odilo* populates the central and eastern parts of France.

- H. fagi
- H. syriaca + H. fagi
- H. alcyone
- H. genava + H. fagi
- H. syriaca
- H. alcyone + H. fagi
- H. alcyone + H. genava + H. fagi

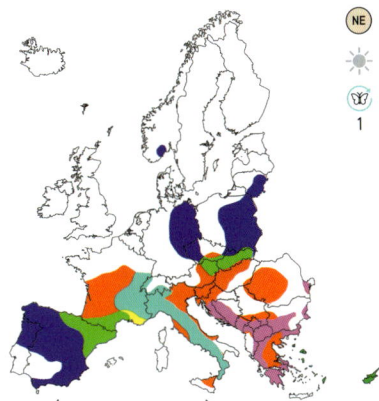

NE

1

IMAGOS			LARVAE	
Food			Food	
Behaviour of males			Caterpillar location	
Dispersion: unknown			Chrysalis location	

Did you know?

Hipparchia genava was formerly included in the taxon *H. hermione*, now usually considered invalid.

FALSE GRAYLING   *ARETHUSANA ARETHUSA*

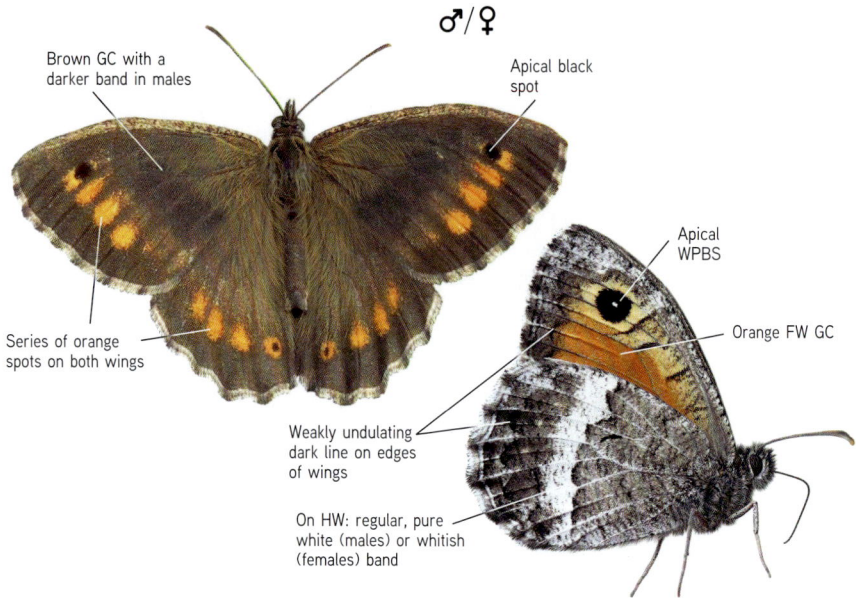

♂/♀

Brown GC with a darker band in males

Apical black spot

Apical WPBS

Orange FW GC

Series of orange spots on both wings

Weakly undulating dark line on edges of wings

On HW: regular, pure white (males) or whitish (females) band

Wingspan: 38–44 mm

Habitat: Sparsely vegetated, dry grasslands and heaths, clear Mediterranean woodlands.

Hibernating stage: Caterpillar.

Elevational range: Up to 1,800 m.

Egg-laying: Eggs are dropped in vegetation.

Flight period: From July to September.

Host plants: Grasses, including *Festuca ovina*, *F. rubra*, *Bromus erectus*, *Brachypodium phoenicoides*, *B. pinnatum*, *Lolium* spp., *Poa* spp., *Dactylis glomerata*, *Corynephorus canescens*, *Cynosurus cristatus*, and *Danthonia decumbens*.

Diversity and systematics: The nominate subspecies flies in Central Europe and the Balkans. Subspecies *variegata* flies in the western part of the range, and subspecies *galathia* in the Iberian Peninsula.

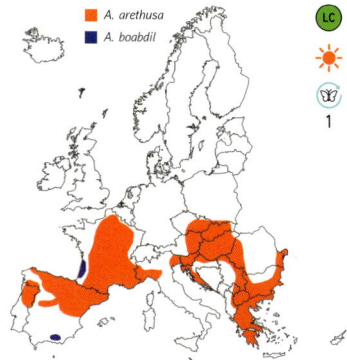

■ A. arethusa
■ A. boabdil

LC

1

Did you know?

The False Grayling is among the thermophilic species that are declining in the non-Mediterranean part of their range due to the loss of habitats once extensively grazed by sheep.

IMAGOS			LARVAE		
Food			Food		
Behaviour of males			Caterpillar location		
Dispersion			Chrysalis location		

SOUTHERN FALSE GRAYLING *ARETHUSANA BOABDIL*

♂/♀

Orange FW GC

Apical WPBS

Markedly
undulating dark line
on edges of wings

On HW: regular, pure white (males)
or whitish (females) band

Wingspan: 37–49 mm

Habitat: Dry, stony grasslands and sandy heaths.

Hibernating stage: Caterpillar.

Elevational range: Up to 1,700 m.

Egg-laying: Eggs are dropped in vegetation.

Flight period: From June to September.

Host plants: Grasses of genera *Festuca* and *Brachypodium*.

Diversity and systematics: The nominate subspecies flies in southern Spain. Subspecies *dentata* is found in the southwest of France, where the extent of its distribution and its potential sympatry with the False Grayling are currently being investigated.

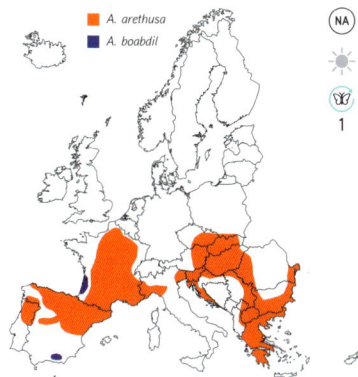

■ A. arethusa
■ A. boabdil

NA
1

Did you know?

The status of the Southern False Grayling remains controversial, as some authors still consider it a subspecies of the False Grayling.

IMAGOS		LARVAE	
Food		Food	
Behaviour of males		Caterpillar location	
Dispersion		Chrysalis location	

Introduction to the Use of Genitalia to Identify a Butterfly

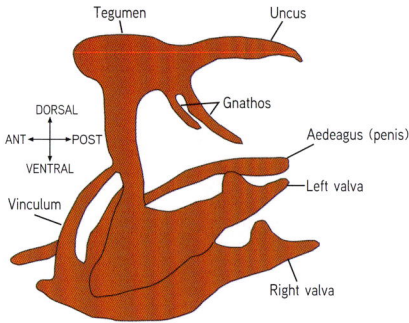

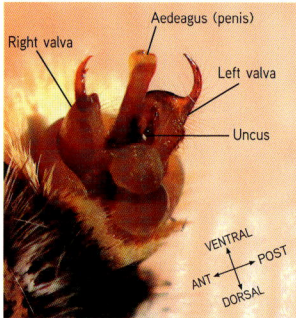

Diagram of the genitalia of a male Southern Grayling (*Hipparchia aristaeus*) in a lateral view and a photograph of the genitalia of a male Southern Heath Fritillary (*Melitaea nevadensis*) under examination. Gently pressing the rear of the abdomen between the thumb and index finger allows the hardened pieces, which exhibit a typical caramel-brown colour, to stand out.

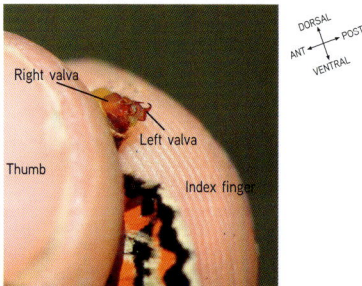

Here is how a butterfly, in this case a Spotted Fritillary (*Melitaea didyma*), can be handled to examine its genitalia.

Most European species can be distinguished by external morphological features related to their wings or visible parts of their body. Others that are very similar can be differentiated based on biogeography when they live in very distinct regions. However, for a few dozen species, reliable identification can be achieved only upon examination of their genitalia. Differences in the shape of these structures often lead to the description of new species, even if their wings are identical. During mating, male genitalia interlock with those of the female, like a key in a lock. Lack of correspondence in the shapes of these hardened parts can hinder mating or diminish its efficiency and contribute to reproductive isolation between individuals belonging to distinct populations – an important step in the emergence of separate lineages that can later be classified as species. It is possible to observe butterfly genitalia in a harmless manner so that the individual can be released safely. The examination is carried out on males, as their genital structures are prominent when the posterior end of the abdomen is gently pressed between the thumb and index finger. The genitalia can then be observed through a field lens (preferably one that provides a magnification of 10 or higher) and be photographed with a good macro lens. For many species, noticeable differences are visible in the shape of valva, particularly at their posterior end or on their dorsal edge. In others, the shape and length of the uncus are determining factors. However, reliable identification of several species in the genera *Pyrgus* and *Carcharodus* requires sacrificing the individual and dissecting its genitalia. Subsequently, these parts are mounted on a thin slide after a preparation that gets rid of the fleshy parts and retains only the hardened armatures. I advocate for this type of deadly sampling to be reserved for scientific studies aiming at a better understanding of that particular species and the spreading of this knowledge to a wider audience.

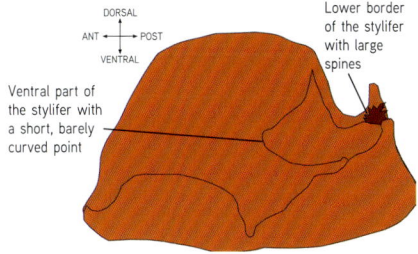

C. tripolina (internal view of the right valva)

PAPILIONIDAE
(dissection not required)

Muschampia floccifera and M. orientalis

Zerynthia polyxena and Z. cassandra

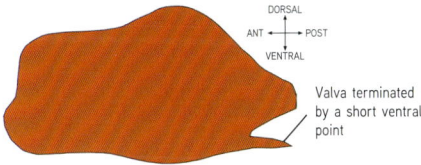

Z. polyxena (valva only)

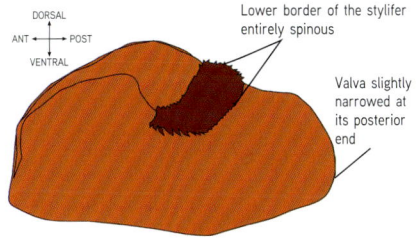

Z. cassandra (valva only)

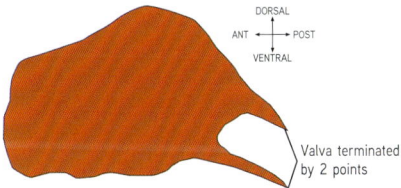

M. floccifera (internal view of the right valva)

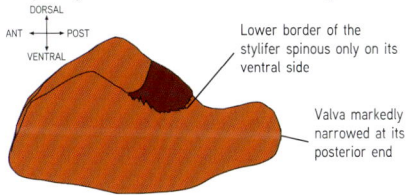

M. orientalis (internal view of the right valva)

HESPERIIDAE
(dissection is required)

Muschampia baeticus and M. stauderi

Carcharodus alceae and C. tripolina

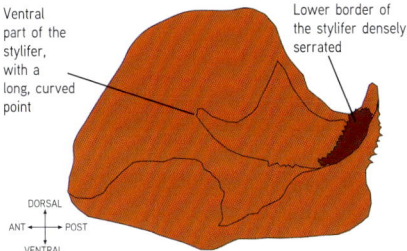

C. alceae (internal view of the right valva)

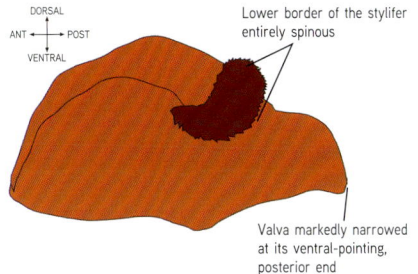

M. baeticus (internal view of the right valva)

DORSAL
ANT ← → POST
VENTRAL

Ventral side of the stylifer lower border not fully spined

Valva markedly narrowed at its posterior end

M. stauderi (internal view of the right valva)

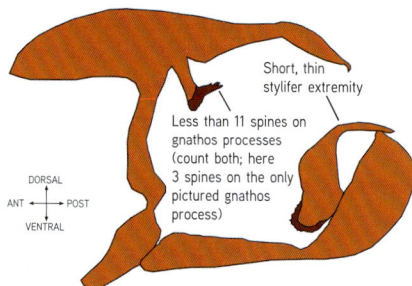

Pyrgus carlinae and P. cirsii

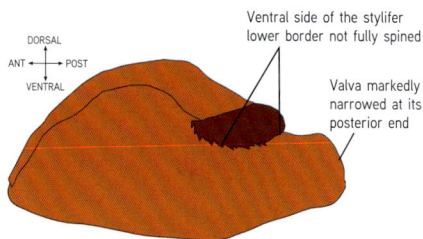

Short, thin stylifer extremity

Less than 11 spines on gnathos processes (count both; here 3 spines on the only pictured gnathos process)

DORSAL
ANT ← → POST
VENTRAL

P. carlinae (complete armatures without aedeagus)

Pyrgus malvae and P. malvoides

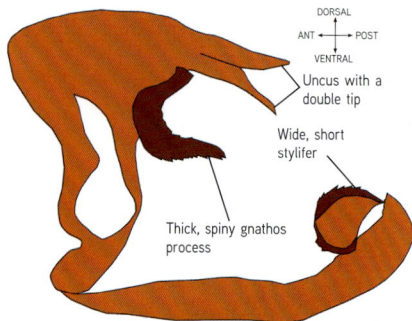

DORSAL
ANT ← → POST
VENTRAL

Uncus with a double tip

Wide, short stylifer

Thick, spiny gnathos process

P. malvae (complete armatures without aedeagus)

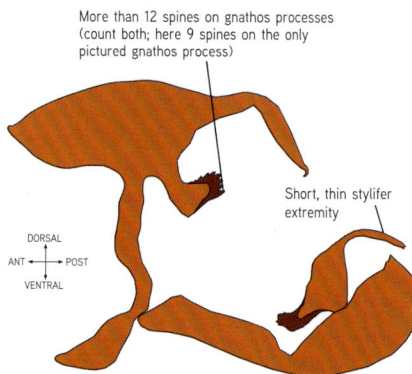

More than 12 spines on gnathos processes (count both; here 9 spines on the only pictured gnathos process)

DORSAL
ANT ← → POST
VENTRAL

Short, thin stylifer extremity

P. cirsii (complete armatures without aedeagus)

Pyrgus carthami and P. sidae

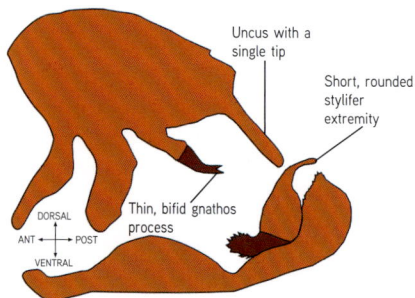

Uncus with a single tip

Short, rounded stylifer extremity

Thin, bifid gnathos process

DORSAL
ANT ← → POST
VENTRAL

P. malvoides (complete armatures without aedeagus)

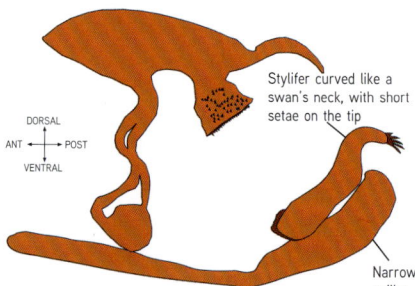

DORSAL
ANT ← → POST
VENTRAL

Stylifer curved like a swan's neck, with short setae on the tip

Narrow cuiller

P. carthami (complete armatures without aedeagus)

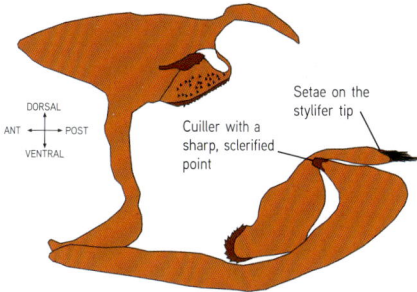

P. sidae (complete armatures without aedeagus)

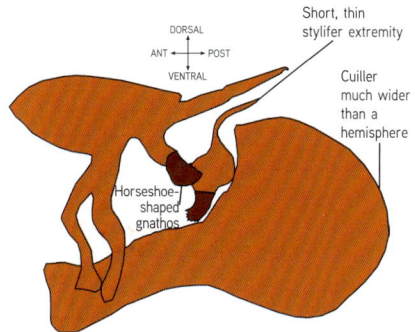

Pyrgus alveus, P. armoricanus, P. foulquieri, and P. warrenensis

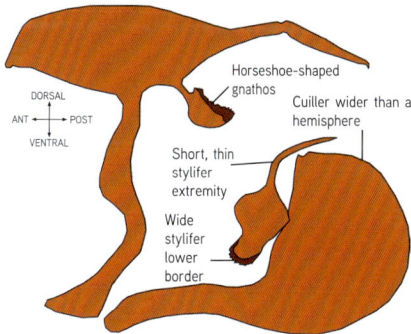

P. foulquieri (complete armatures without aedeagus)

P. alveus (complete armatures without aedeagus)

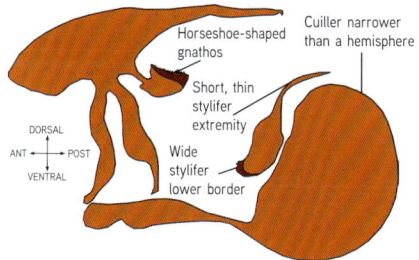

P. warrenensis (complete armatures without aedeagus)

Pyrgus andromedae, P. cacaliae, P. onopordi, and P. serratulae

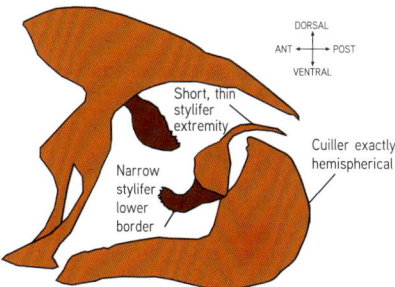

P. armoricanus (complete armatures without aedeagus)

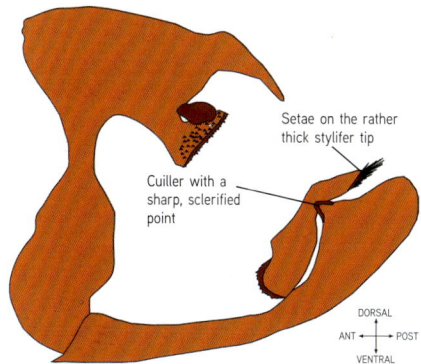

P. andromedae (complete armatures without aedeagus)

Cuiller with a finely spinous, angular dorsal border

Rather thick stylifer tip with dense setae

DORSAL
ANT — POST
VENTRAL

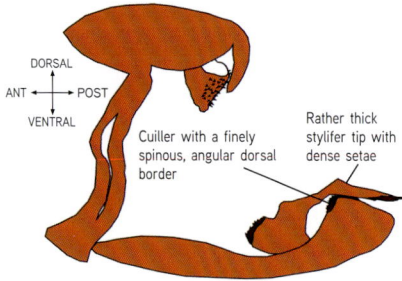

P. cacaliae (complete armatures without aedeagus)

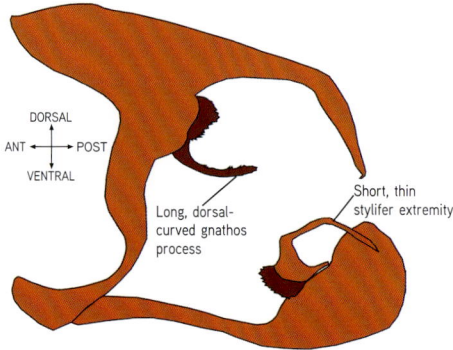

DORSAL
ANT — POST
VENTRAL

Long, dorsal-curved gnathos process

Short, thin stylifer extremity

P. onopordi (complete armatures without aedeagus)

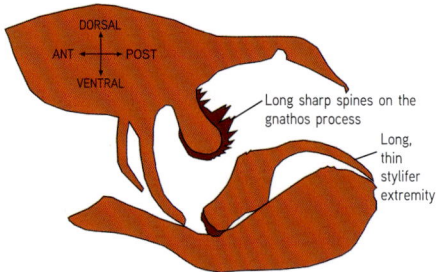

DORSAL
ANT — POST
VENTRAL

Long sharp spines on the gnathos process

Long, thin stylifer extremity

P. serratulae (complete armatures without aedeagus)

PIERIDAE
(dissection not required)

Colias alfacariensis, C. erate, and *C. hyale*

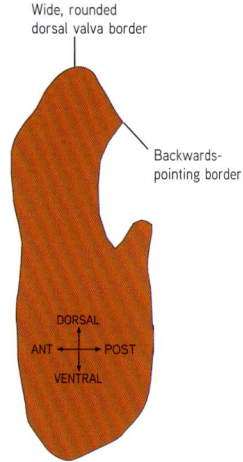

Wide, rounded dorsal valva border

Backwards-pointing border

DORSAL
ANT — POST
VENTRAL

C. alfacariensis (valva only)

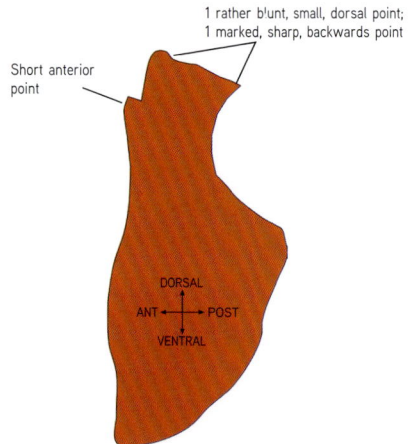

1 rather blunt, small, dorsal point; 1 marked, sharp, backwards point

Short anterior point

DORSAL
ANT — POST
VENTRAL

C. erate (valva only)

Narrow, rounded
dorsal valva border

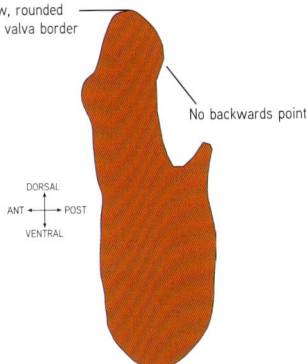

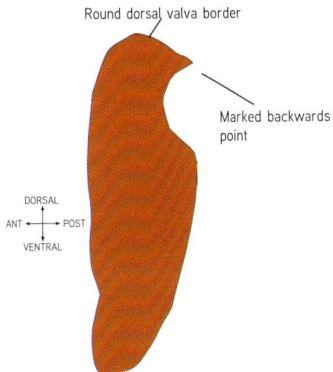

No backwards point

DORSAL
ANT ← → POST
VENTRAL

C. hyale (valva only)

Pieris napi and P. balcana

Slightly angular
distal valva border

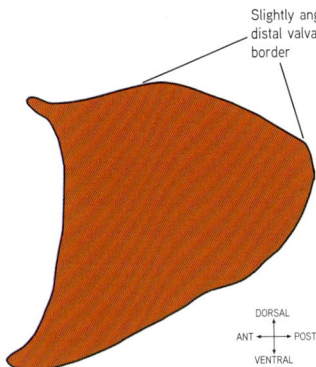

DORSAL
ANT ← → POST
VENTRAL

P. napi (valva only)

Colias crocea and C. myrmidone

1 dorsal, rounded point and a small,
sharp backwards point

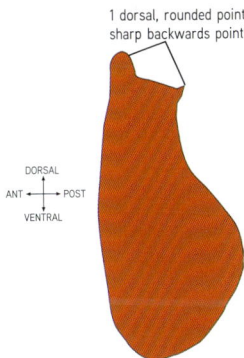

DORSAL
ANT ← → POST
VENTRAL

C. crocea (valva only)

Rather rounded
distal valva border

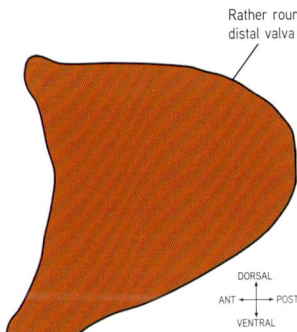

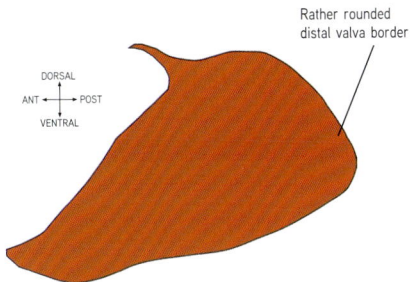

DORSAL
ANT ← → POST
VENTRAL

P. balcana (valva only)

Round dorsal valva border

Marked backwards
point

DORSAL
ANT ← → POST
VENTRAL

C. myrmidone (valva only)

Pontia daplidice and P. edusa

Rather rounded
distal valva border

DORSAL
ANT ← → POST
VENTRAL

P. daplidice (valva only)

571

Rather pointed
distal valva border

DORSAL
ANT ← → POST
VENTRAL

P. edusa (valva only)

LYCAENIDAE

(Direct observation is difficult given the small
size of these butterflies)

Pseudophilotes baton and P. vicrama

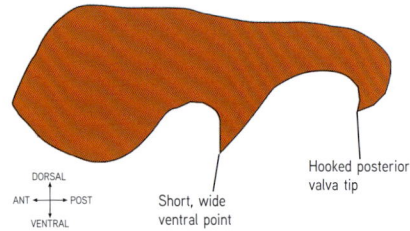

Hooked posterior
valva tip

Short, wide
ventral point

DORSAL
ANT ← → POST
VENTRAL

P. baton (valva only)

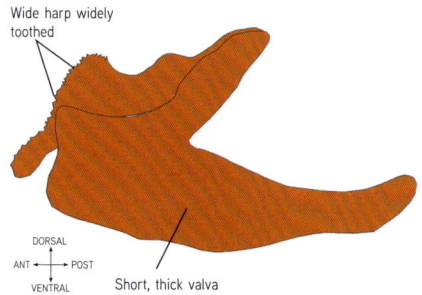

Round posterior
valva tip

DORSAL
ANT ← → POST
VENTRAL

Long, slender ventral point

P. vicrama (valva only)

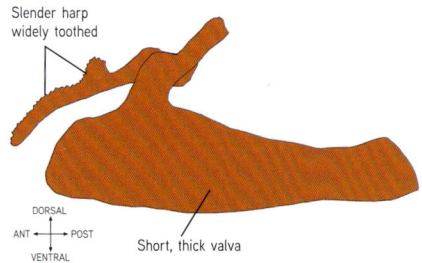

NYMPHALIDAE

Except Satyrinae
(dissection not required)

Boloria graeca, B. napaea, and B. pales

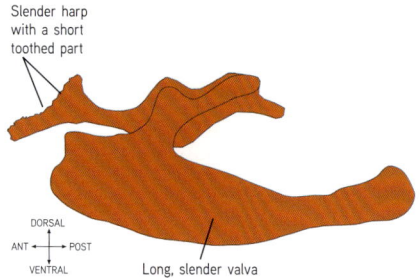

Slender harp
with a short
toothed part

DORSAL
ANT ← → POST
VENTRAL

Long, slender valva

B. graeca (valva and stylifer only)

Wide harp widely
toothed

DORSAL
ANT ← → POST
VENTRAL

Short, thick valva

B. napaea (valva and stylifer only)

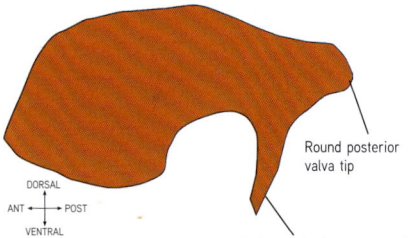

Slender harp
widely toothed

DORSAL
ANT ← → POST
VENTRAL

Short, thick valva

B. pales (valva and stylifer only)

Melitaea aetherie, M. didyma, M. trivia, and M. ignasiti

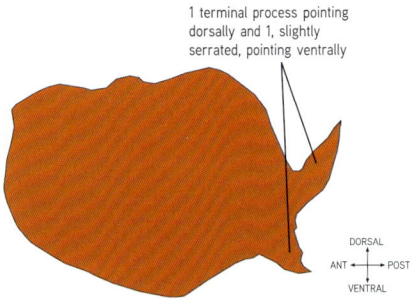

1 terminal process pointing dorsally and 1, slightly serrated, pointing ventrally

DORSAL
ANT ← → POST
VENTRAL

M. aetherie (valva only)

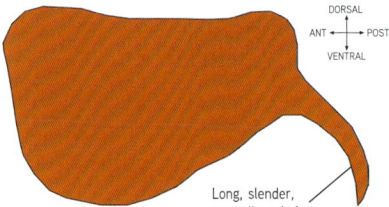

DORSAL
ANT ← → POST
VENTRAL

Long, slender, ventrally pointing terminal process

M. didyma (valva only)

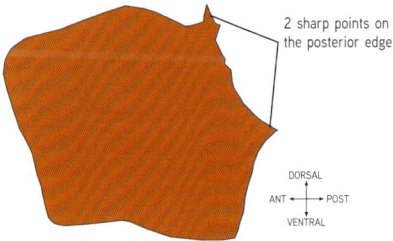

2 sharp points on the posterior edge

DORSAL
ANT ← → POST
VENTRAL

M. ignasiti (valva only)

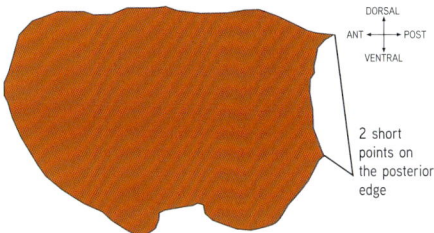

DORSAL
ANT ← → POST
VENTRAL

2 short points on the posterior edge

M. trivia (valva only)

Melitaea arduinna and M. cinxia

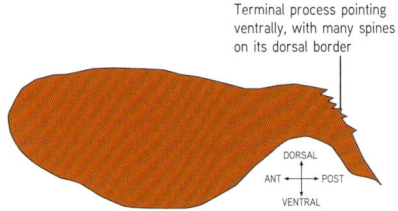

Terminal process pointing ventrally, with many spines on its dorsal border

DORSAL
ANT ← → POST
VENTRAL

M. arduinna (valva only)

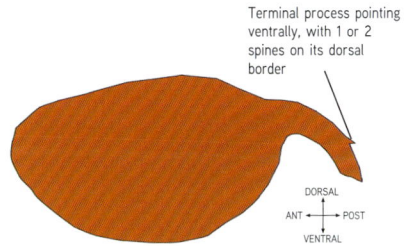

Terminal process pointing ventrally, with 1 or 2 spines on its dorsal border

DORSAL
ANT ← → POST
VENTRAL

M. cinxia (valva only)

Melitaea ornata and M. phoebe

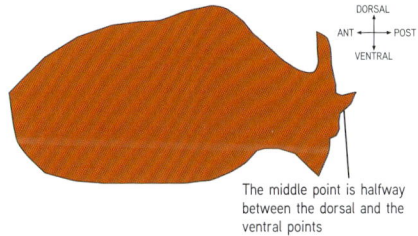

DORSAL
ANT ← → POST
VENTRAL

The middle point is halfway between the dorsal and the ventral points

M. ornata (valva only)

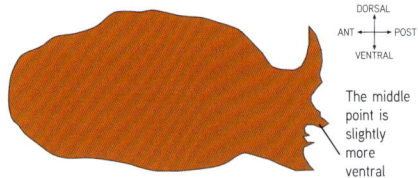

DORSAL
ANT ← → POST
VENTRAL

The middle point is slightly more ventral

M. phoebe (valva only)

The differences between both species' genitalia are very subtle and have been evidenced by statistical analyses rather than direct observation.

Melitaea asteria, M. athalia, M. aurelia,
M. britomartis, M. deione, M. diamina,
M. nevadensis, M. parthenoides, and M. varia

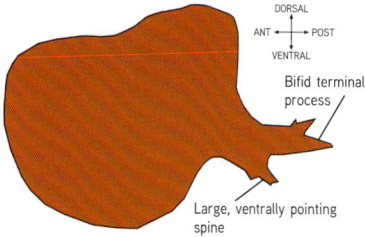

DORSAL
ANT ← → POST
VENTRAL

Bifid terminal process

Large, ventrally pointing spine

M. athalia (valva only)

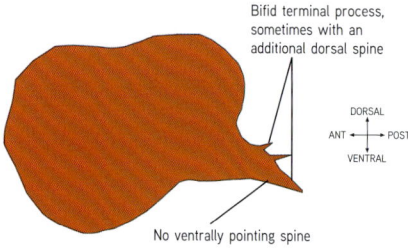

Bifid terminal process, sometimes with an additional dorsal spine

DORSAL
ANT ← → POST
VENTRAL

No ventrally pointing spine

M. nevadensis (valva only)

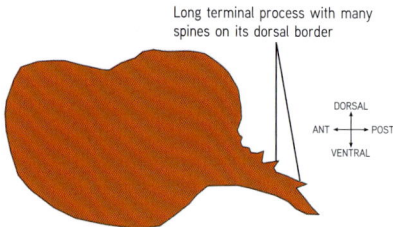

Long terminal process with many spines on its dorsal border

DORSAL
ANT ← → POST
VENTRAL

M. deione (valva only)

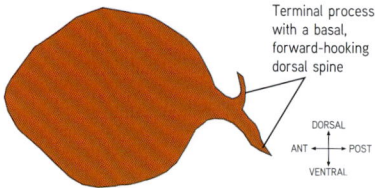

Terminal process with a basal, forward-hooking dorsal spine

DORSAL
ANT ← → POST
VENTRAL

M. diamina (valva only)

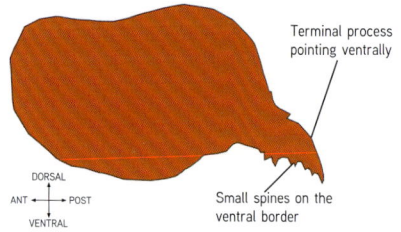

Terminal process pointing ventrally

DORSAL
ANT ← → POST
VENTRAL

Small spines on the ventral border

M. parthenoides (valva only)

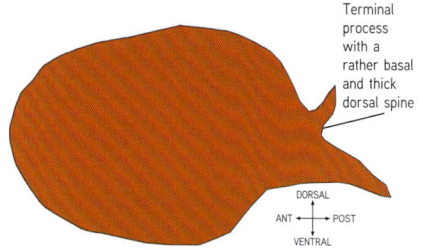

Terminal process with a rather basal and thick dorsal spine

DORSAL
ANT ← → POST
VENTRAL

M. varia (valva only)

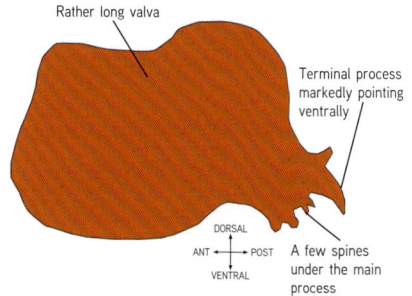

Rather long valva

Terminal process markedly pointing ventrally

DORSAL
ANT ← → POST
VENTRAL

A few spines under the main process

M. aurelia (valva only)

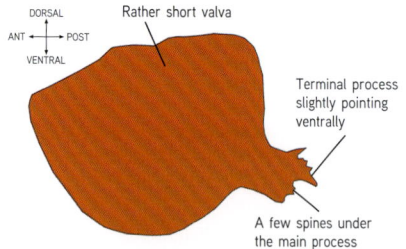

DORSAL
ANT ← → POST
VENTRAL

Rather short valva

Terminal process slightly pointing ventrally

A few spines under the main process

M. britomartis (valva only)

Thick, dorsally pointing spine

DORSAL
ANT ← → POST
VENTRAL

Terminal process points ventrally

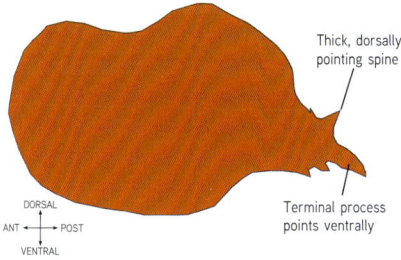

M. asteria (valva only)

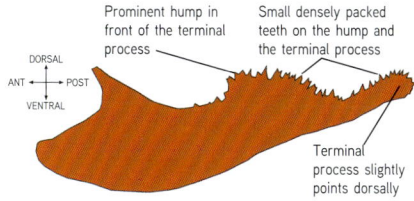

NYMPHALIDAE SATYRINAE
(direct observation usually possible but sometimes difficult)

Erebia bubastis, E. christi, E. claudina, E. epiphron, E. eriphyle, E. flavofasciata, E. manto, E. melampus, E. pharte, and E. sudetica

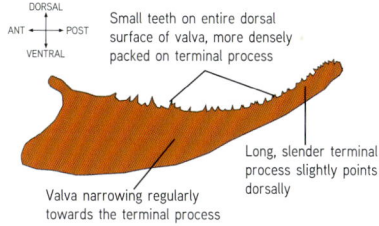

Prominent hump with a few large teeth in front of the terminal process

DORSAL
ANT ← → POST
VENTRAL

Slender terminal process with few spines (less in *E. vogesiaca*)

E. bubastis (valva only)

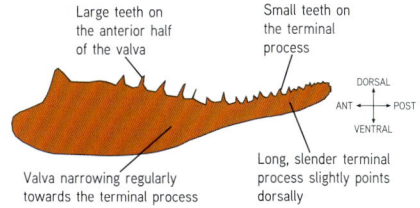

Ill-defined hump with rather small teeth in front of terminal process

DORSAL
ANT ← → POST
VENTRAL

Slender terminal process with a variable number of spines

E. manto (valva only)

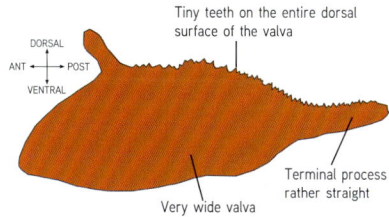

Large teeth on entire dorsal surface of valva, more densely packed on terminal process

DORSAL
ANT ← → POST
VENTRAL

Wide valva

Terminal process slightly points dorsally

E. pharte (valva only)

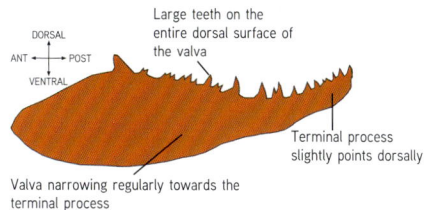

Prominent hump in front of the terminal process

Small densely packed teeth on the hump and the terminal process

DORSAL
ANT ← → POST
VENTRAL

Terminal process slightly points dorsally

E. eriphyle (valva only)

DORSAL
ANT ← → POST
VENTRAL

Small teeth on entire dorsal surface of valva, more densely packed on terminal process

Long, slender terminal process slightly points dorsally

Valva narrowing regularly towards the terminal process

E. melampus (valva only)

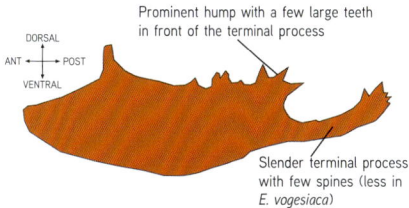

Large teeth on the anterior half of the valva

Small teeth on the terminal process

DORSAL
ANT ← → POST
VENTRAL

Valva narrowing regularly towards the terminal process

Long, slender terminal process slightly points dorsally

E. sudetica (valva only)

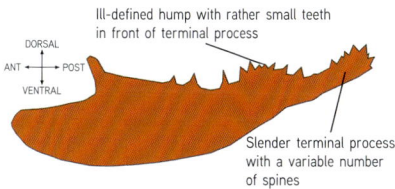

Tiny teeth on the entire dorsal surface of the valva

DORSAL
ANT ← → POST
VENTRAL

Very wide valva

Terminal process rather straight

E. epiphron (valva only)

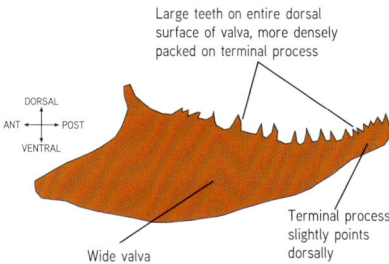

Large teeth on the entire dorsal surface of the valva

DORSAL
ANT ← → POST
VENTRAL

Valva narrowing regularly towards the terminal process

Terminal process slightly points dorsally

E. christi (valva only)

Small teeth on entire dorsal surface of valva

DORSAL
ANT ← → POST
VENTRAL

Terminal process rather straight

Valva width decreases regularly towards terminal process

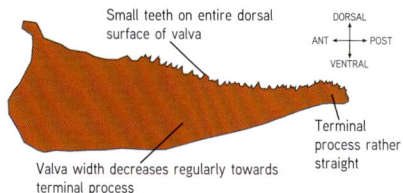

E. flavofasciata (valva only)

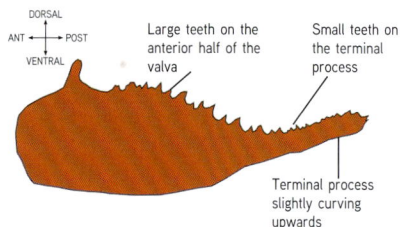

DORSAL
ANT ← → POST
VENTRAL

Large teeth on the anterior half of the valva

Small teeth on the terminal process

Terminal process slightly curving upwards

E. claudina (valva only)

Long, slender valva

DORSAL
ANT ← → POST
VENTRAL

1 to 5 teeth on the long, slender terminal process

E. calcarius (valva only)

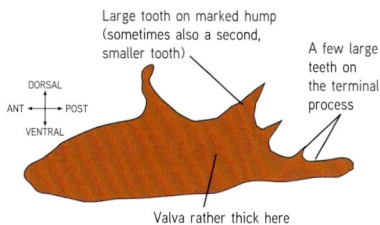

Large tooth on marked hump (sometimes also a second, smaller tooth)

DORSAL
ANT ← → POST
VENTRAL

A few large teeth on the terminal process

Valva rather thick here

E. nivalis (valva only)

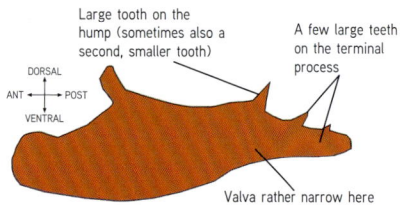

Large tooth on the hump (sometimes also a second, smaller tooth)

DORSAL
ANT ← → POST
VENTRAL

A few large teeth on the terminal process

Valva rather narrow here

E. tyndarus (valva only)

> **Erebia arvernensis, E. cassioides, E. calcarius, E. nivalis, E. ottomana, and E. tyndarus**

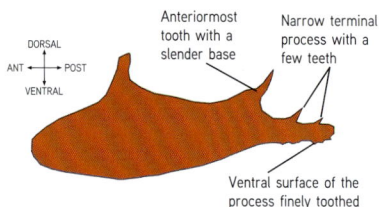

Anteriormost tooth with a slender base

DORSAL
ANT ← → POST
VENTRAL

Narrow terminal process with a few teeth

Ventral surface of the process finely toothed

E. arvernensis (valva only)

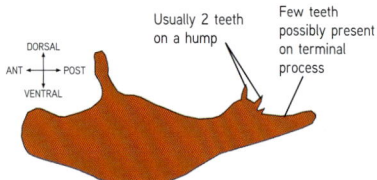

> **Erebia aethiops, E. euryale, E. ligea, E. montana, E. neoridas, E. scipio, E. stiria, and E. styx**

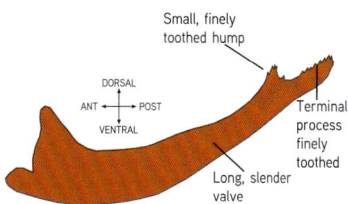

Usually 2 teeth on a hump

DORSAL
ANT ← → POST
VENTRAL

Few teeth possibly present on terminal process

E. ottomana (valva only)

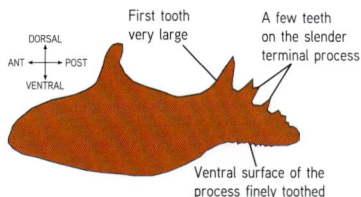

Small, finely toothed hump

DORSAL
ANT ← → POST
VENTRAL

Terminal process finely toothed

Long, slender valve

E. aethiops (valva only)

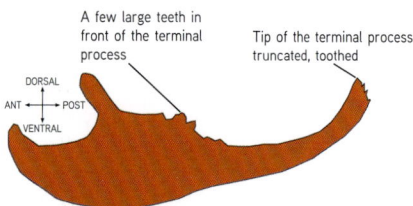

First tooth very large

DORSAL
ANT ← → POST
VENTRAL

A few teeth on the slender terminal process

Ventral surface of the process finely toothed

E. cassioides (valva only)

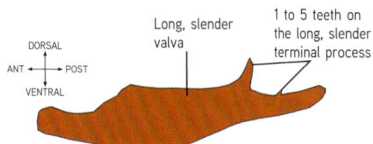

A few large teeth in front of the terminal process

DORSAL
ANT ← → POST
VENTRAL

Tip of the terminal process truncated, toothed

E. neoridas (valva only)

576

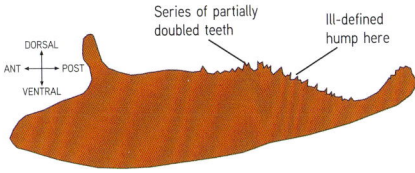

Series of partially doubled teeth

Ill-defined hump here

DORSAL
ANT POST
VENTRAL

E. euryale (valva only)

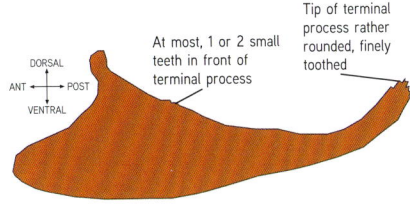

At most, 1 or 2 small teeth in front of terminal process

Tip of terminal process rather rounded, finely toothed

DORSAL
ANT POST
VENTRAL

E. styx (valva only)

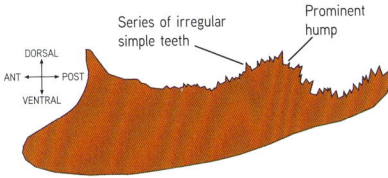

Series of irregular simple teeth

Prominent hump

DORSAL
ANT POST
VENTRAL

E. ligea (valva only)

Erebia aethiopellus, E. gorge, E. mnestra, and E. pluto

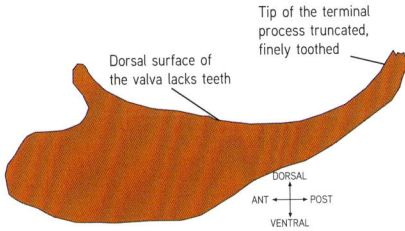

Tip of the terminal process truncated, finely toothed

Dorsal surface of the valva lacks teeth

DORSAL
ANT POST
VENTRAL

E. montana (valva only)

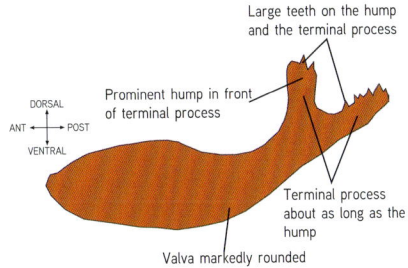

Large teeth on the hump and the terminal process

Prominent hump in front of terminal process

Terminal process about as long as the hump

Valva markedly rounded

DORSAL
ANT POST
VENTRAL

E. aethiopellus (valva only)

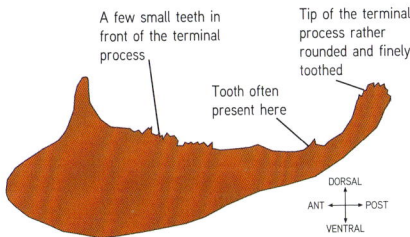

A few small teeth in front of the terminal process

Tip of the terminal process rather rounded and finely toothed

Tooth often present here

DORSAL
ANT POST
VENTRAL

E. scipio (valva only)

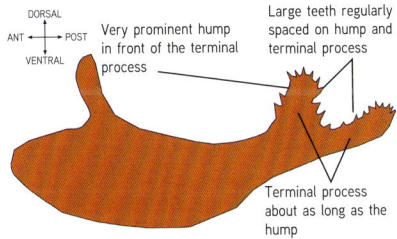

Very prominent hump in front of the terminal process

Large teeth regularly spaced on hump and terminal process

Terminal process about as long as the hump

DORSAL
ANT POST
VENTRAL

E. mnestra (valva only)

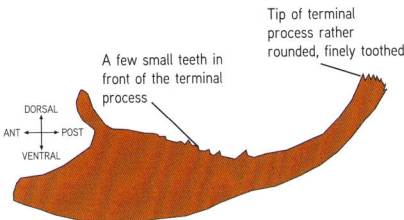

A few small teeth in front of the terminal process

Tip of terminal process rather rounded, finely toothed

DORSAL
ANT POST
VENTRAL

E. stiria (valva only)

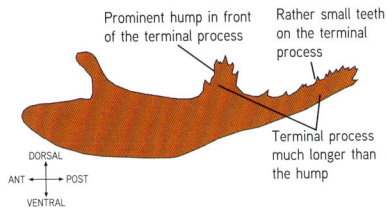

Prominent hump in front of the terminal process

Rather small teeth on the terminal process

Terminal process much longer than the hump

DORSAL
ANT POST
VENTRAL

E. gorge (valva only)

Prominent hump in front of terminal process

Large teeth on hump and base of terminal process

DORSAL
ANT ← → POST
VENTRAL

Terminal process about as long as hump

E. pluto (valva only)

2 humps bearing big teeth in front of terminal process

Tip of the terminal process truncated, finely toothed

DORSAL
ANT ← → POST
VENTRAL

Terminal process curving upwards

E. lefebvrei (valva only)

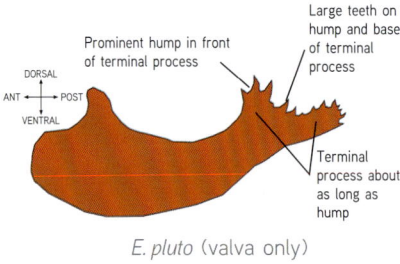

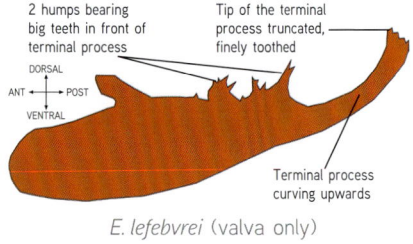

Erebia gorgone, E. lefebvrei, E. meolans, and E. triarius

Tip of terminal process wide, truncated, finely toothed

DORSAL
ANT ← → POST
VENTRAL

Short terminal process markedly curving upwards

E. meolans (valva only)

Erebia alberganus, E. medusa, E. oeme, and E. pronoe

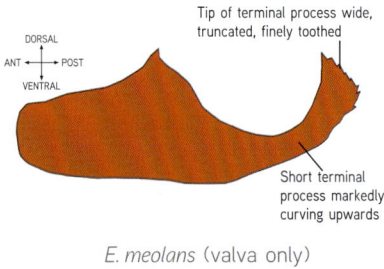

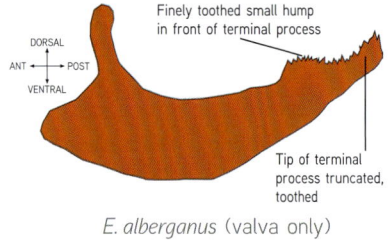

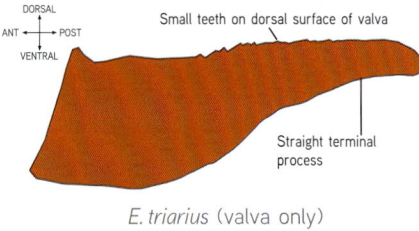

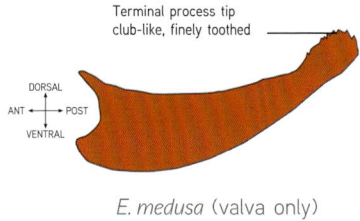

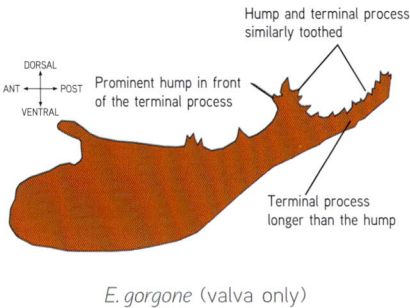

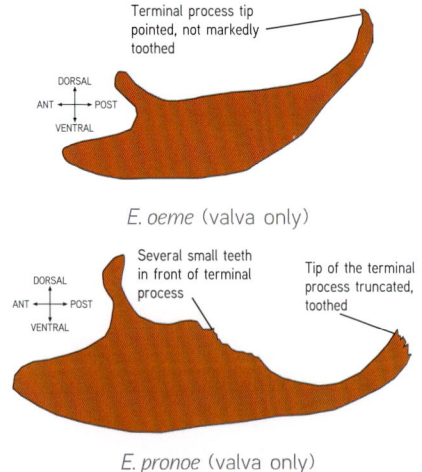

Finely toothed small hump in front of terminal process

DORSAL
ANT ← → POST
VENTRAL

Tip of terminal process truncated, toothed

E. alberganus (valva only)

DORSAL
ANT ← → POST
VENTRAL

Small teeth on dorsal surface of valva

Straight terminal process

E. triarius (valva only)

Terminal process tip club-like, finely toothed

DORSAL
ANT ← → POST
VENTRAL

E. medusa (valva only)

Hump and terminal process similarly toothed

DORSAL
ANT ← → POST
VENTRAL

Prominent hump in front of the terminal process

Terminal process longer than the hump

E. gorgone (valva only)

Terminal process tip pointed, not markedly toothed

DORSAL
ANT ← → POST
VENTRAL

E. oeme (valva only)

Several small teeth in front of terminal process

Tip of the terminal process truncated, toothed

DORSAL
ANT ← → POST
VENTRAL

E. pronoe (valva only)

Hipparchia alcyone, H. genava, H. fagi, and H. syriaca

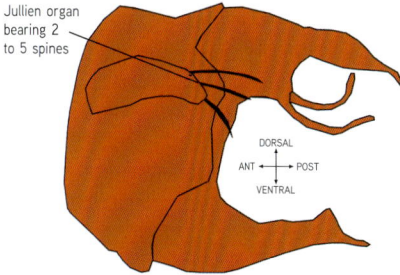

Jullien organ bearing 2 to 5 spines

DORSAL
ANT ← → POST
VENTRAL

H. fagi (complete armatures without aedeagus)

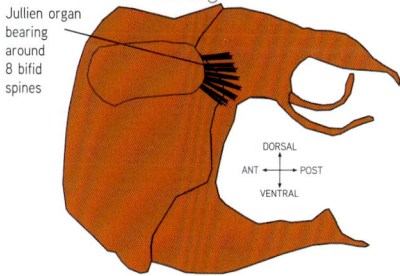

Jullien organ bearing around 8 bifid spines

DORSAL
ANT ← → POST
VENTRAL

H. syriaca (complete armatures without aedeagus)

Jullien organ bearing 15 to 25 spines

DORSAL
ANT ← → POST
VENTRAL

H. alcyone (complete armatures without aedeagus)

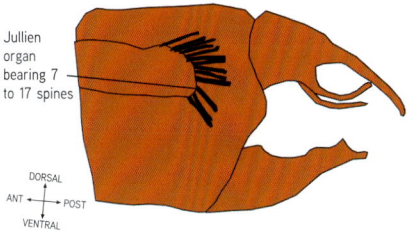

Jullien organ bearing 7 to 17 spines

DORSAL
ANT ← → POST
VENTRAL

H. genava (complete armatures without aedeagus)

Hipparchia aristaeus, H. mersina, H. semele, H. senthes, and H. volgensis

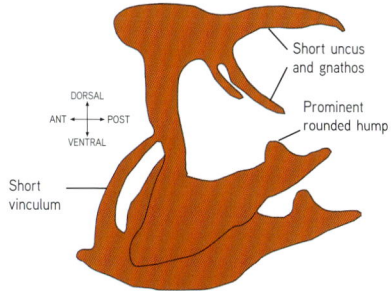

Short uncus and gnathos

Prominent rounded hump

DORSAL
ANT ← → POST
VENTRAL

Short vinculum

H. aristaeus (complete armatures without aedeagus)

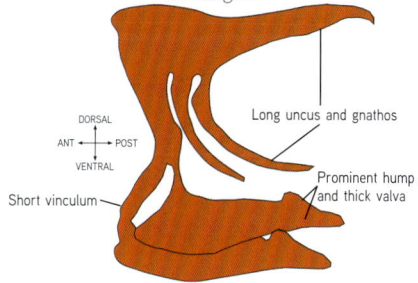

Long uncus and gnathos

Prominent hump and thick valva

DORSAL
ANT ← → POST
VENTRAL

Short vinculum

H. semele (complete armatures without aedeagus)

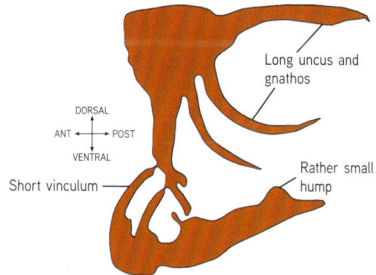

Long uncus and gnathos

Rather small hump

DORSAL
ANT ← → POST
VENTRAL

Short vinculum

H. mersina (complete armatures without aedeagus)

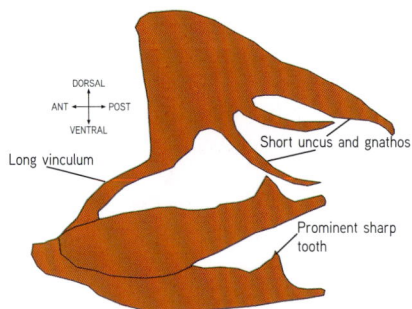

H. senthes (complete armatures without aedeagus)

Long vinculum

Short uncus and gnathos

Prominent sharp tooth

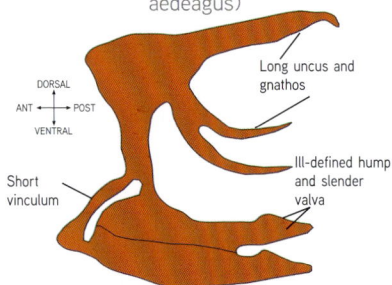

H. volgensis (complete armatures without aedeagus)

Long uncus and gnathos

Short vinculum

Ill-defined hump and slender valva

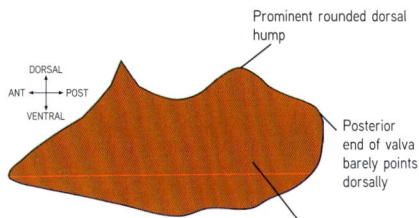

M. nurag (valva only)

Prominent rounded dorsal hump

Posterior end of valva barely points dorsally

Slender valva

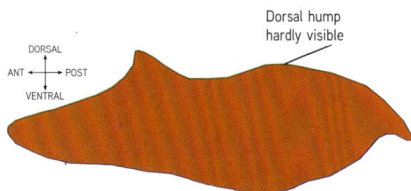

M. megala (valva only)

Dorsal hump hardly visible

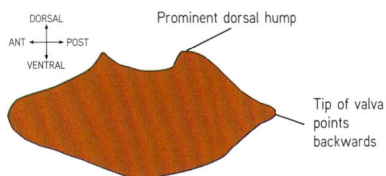

M. telmessia (valva only)

Prominent dorsal hump

Tip of valva points backwards

The genitalia of *H. blachieri, H. maderensis,* and *H. neapolitana* are similar to those of *H. aristaeus.* The genitalia of *H. christenseni* are similar to those of *H. volgensis.* The genitalia of *H. cretica, H. leighebi,* and *H. sbordonii* are similar to those of *H. semele.*

Maniola jurtina, M. megala, M. nurag, and M. telmessia

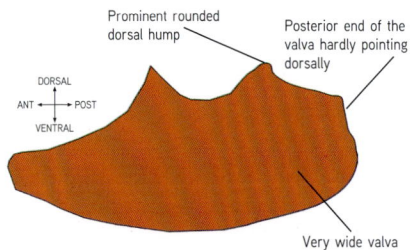

Prominent rounded dorsal hump

Posterior end of the valva hardly pointing dorsally

Very wide valva

M. jurtina (valva only)

Introduction
to Caterpillar Identification

This guide provides a key to identifying the caterpillars of approximately three-quarters of European butterfly species. As with identifying an adult butterfly, identifying a caterpillar requires a methodical approach. The first step is to ensure that it is indeed a butterfly caterpillar and not that of a moth or sawfly larva. Unfortunately, the probability of that is quite low because all Lepidoptera (and some Hymenoptera) produce caterpillar-shaped larvae. This means that, in addition to the three pairs of thoracic legs, two to five pairs of fleshy lobes, called prolegs, are present under the abdomen. However, 95% of Lepidoptera species aren't butterflies, which suggests that a randomly encountered caterpillar is far more likely to belong to another group.

While there may not be criteria to definitively distinguish a butterfly caterpillar, it is possible to eliminate many caterpillars not belonging to this group based on morphological features (*e.g.*, counting the number of prolegs). Nevertheless, some Noctuid caterpillars closely resemble butterfly caterpillars. The identification key following this introduction starts by eliminating caterpillars from various non-butterfly Lepidoptera groups before subdividing butterfly caterpillars into broad morphological classes that may match a taxonomic family (*e.g.*, for skippers and blues) or not.

Just as morphology is not the only information useful for identifying an adult butterfly, caterpillar determination also relies on critical complementary parameters. It is crucial to identify the plant on which the caterpillar is found, or at least its family. Caterpillars of different species can be indistinguishable or challenging to determine based on morphological criteria but may use very distinct host plants. A leaf-shaped icon between the names of two species indicates that they can be distinguished based on this dietary preference. Referring to species monographs and the section on larval host plants is necessary to resolve such identifications. This information supplements the distribution ranges of the two species, which may not overlap.

During postembryonic development, a caterpillar often undergoes radical colour changes. They can transform a cryptic pattern into an evident aposematic (warning) appearance, as seen in some swallowtails, for example. This guide focuses on the morphological diversity of mature caterpillars, as, for many species, they are the most likely to be found due to their larger size. Frequent colour changes, such as the transition from green to brown, are indicated by an explicit icon. Additionally, some species (especially *Melanargia* Satyrines) exhibit colour polymorphism in mature caterpillars, which are either brown or green. A dedicated icon is used here as well to specify this intraspecific colour diversity.

The reader will also notice that the names of species with very similar or identical caterpillars are associated with the same picture (the name of the species matching the picture is specified in bold). When it is possible to distinguish them, the labels specify the differences to focus on.

However, many species have macroscopically identical caterpillars, while the adults are more easily distinguishable. These similarities are not surprising. Caterpillar patterns (colour, characteristics of any fleshy protuberances) reflect a biological evolutionary process. The primary challenges of postembryonic larval development are survival and the accumulation of nutrient stores in preparation for the adult stage. The characters used for determination are thus primarily associated with the caterpillar's survival. Commonly observed green colourations ensure that the animal will blend in with herbaceous vegetation or the foliage of trees and shrubs. Brown colours conceal it against bark. Conversely, the very bright and sharply contrasting colours of some caterpillars, which potential predators learn to recognize and avoid, are correlated with the accumulation of toxic compounds extracted from their host plants.

There are a limited number of ways to be green or brown, or even to display colours that contrast significantly with the surrounding environment. Within a given taxonomic group, caterpillars with similar lifestyles are probably likely not to have diverged much morphologically because natural selection has stabilized these patterns, increasing the probability of survival until emergence. The same applies to fleshy outgrowths (scoli) that cover the entire body of some caterpillars. The presence of these protuberances can significantly hinder the oviposition (egg-laying behaviour) of parasitoid wasps and flies, especially if the caterpillar wriggles when it senses their presence. Scoli are present in both certain Nymphalids and, convergently, in Papilionids of the Zerynthia genus.

Some of the differences between adults of distinct species are also interpreted as the result of natural selection increasing

The caterpillar of the Swallowtail (Papilio machaon) undergoes a radical colour change during its development. Initially black with a white spot on its back (top), it closely resembles a bird dropping, which is consistent with its small size. During successive moults, it gradually acquires a highly visible aposematic appearance (bottom right) while accumulating toxic compounds from its Apiaceae host plants. The transition occurs through some intermediate stages (bottom left).

The scoli present on the surface of the body of this Southern Festoon caterpillar (Zerynthia polyxena, Papilionidae, left) and this Spotted Fritillary caterpillar (Melitaea didyma, Nymphalidae, right) limit the probability of their being parasitized, which would ultimately be fatal. The presence of these structures in these phylogenetically very distant species reflects a similar environmental context that might have independently selected twice for this morphological trait.

the survival rate. However, in adults, there are also morphological characteristics that differ in relation to reproductive success (recognition among individuals of the same species, sexual selection). These drivers of differentiation are absent in caterpillars, which do not play a direct role in breeding. This likely contributes to making them more similar than adults and significantly complicates their identification.

KEY TO CATERPILLARS

1/17 More than 5 pairs of prolegs

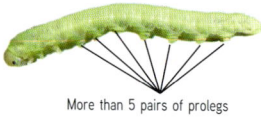

More than 5 pairs of prolegs

SAWFLIES LARVAE (TENTHREDINIDAE HYMENOPTERANS)

2/17 Fewer than 5 pairs of prolegs (often only 2)

2 pairs of prolegs

GEOMETRID OR NOCTUID CATERPILLARS

3/17 [5 pairs of prolegs] AND [stout body and head not clearly distinct from the body] AND [black spots on a yellow or pale green GC] OR [brown or pink colour with dense hair tufts on the body]

Reduced head hidden by prothorax

Pale green GC with small black spots

Reduced head hidden by prothorax

Yellow GC with large black spots

Pinkish-brown GC

Dense hair tufts

Stout body

Reduced head hidden by prothorax

New Forest Burnet Moth   **Six-spot Burnet Moth**   **Green Forester**

ZYGAENID CATERPILLARS

4/17 [5 pairs of prolegs] AND [a posterior dorsal tail or pointed outgrowth]

No other dorsal outgrowth

Posterior tail

No other dorsal outgrowth

Posterior tail

No other dorsal outgrowth

Posterior tail

Privet Hawk-moth   **Spurge Hawk-moth**   **Elephant Hawk-moth**

SPHINGID OR NOCTUID CATERPILLARS

5/17 [5 pairs of prolegs] AND [2 posterior tails]

Pair of tail-shaped anal prolegs

Puss Moth

NOTODONTID CATERPILLARS

6/17 [5 pairs of prolegs] AND [very angular posterior abdominal end] AND [no outgrowths on dorsal surface]

No fleshy outgrowth on the dorsal surface

Angular posterior abdominal end

Sprawler

NOTODONTID OR NOCTUID CATERPILLARS

KEY TO CATERPILLARS

7/17 [5 pairs of prolegs] AND [body very hairy; colours exactly match those of picture below]

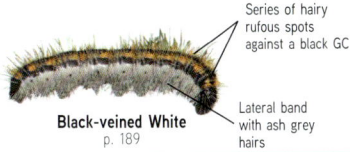

Series of hairy rufous spots against a black GC

Black-veined White
p. 189

Lateral band with ash grey hairs

8/17 [5 pairs of prolegs] AND [body very hairy; colours do not match those of picture shown in block 7]

High hair density

Lackey Moth

Fox Moth

Hairs sometimes in dense tufts

Knot Grass Moth

Hairs sometimes in dense tufts

Pale Tussock

Hairs sometimes very long

Garden Tiger Moth

LASIOCAMPID, EREBID, AND NOCTUID CATERPILLARS

9/17 [5 pairs of prolegs] AND [bright green GC with small orange or yellow outgrowths bristling with black hairs]

EMPEROR MOTHS CATERPILLARS (SATURNIDS)

10/17 [5 pairs of prolegs] AND [whitish or brownish GC with a vitreous aspect] AND [prothorax of same width as the head]

NOCTUID, COSSID, HEPIALID, AND SESIID CATERPILLARS

11/17 [5 pairs of prolegs] AND [GC with large black and yellow motifs exactly matching one of these 5 pictures]

Black tentacles branching along the body

Dorsal and lateral series of yellow spots separated by small white spots

Alder Moth

Body alternatively ringed with yellow-orange and black

Cinnabar Moth

White and yellow dorsal lines

Many hairs inserted on small outgrowths

Scarlet Tiger Moth

Yellow rings forming a grid pattern with the yellow longitudinal lines

Buff-tip

White-ringed lateral black spots

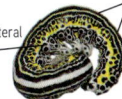

Apopestes spectrum

585

KEY TO CATERPILLARS

12/17 [5 pairs of prolegs] AND [prothorax markedly constricted; looks like a neck between the head and the abdomen]

Prothorax thinner than the head and often of a different colour

Prothorax thinner than the head and often of a different colour

HESPERID CATERPILLARS → **Page 588**

13/17 [5 pairs of prolegs] AND [body stout, rather flattened with reduced head hidden under prothorax] AND [no large black spots]

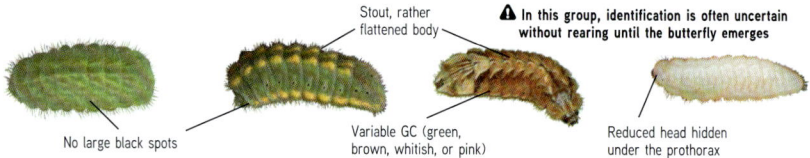

Stout, rather flattened body

⚠ In this group, identification is often uncertain without rearing until the butterfly emerges

No large black spots

Variable GC (green, brown, whitish, or pink)

Reduced head hidden under the prothorax

LYCAENID AND RIODINID CATERPILLARS → **Page 590 (block 1/6 and following)**

14/17 [5 pairs of prolegs] AND [body covered with fleshy outgrowths] OR [several long, fleshy outgrowths or tentacles on the dorsal surface] OR [2 fleshy horns on the head]

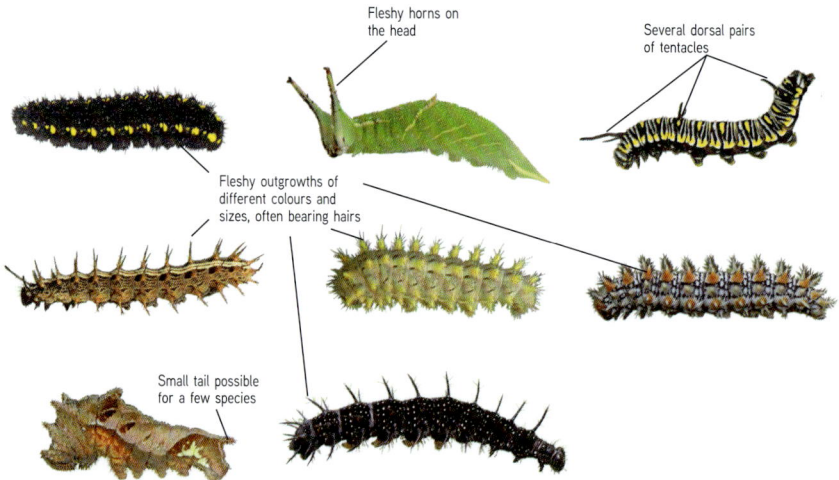

Fleshy horns on the head

Several dorsal pairs of tentacles

Fleshy outgrowths of different colours and sizes, often bearing hairs

Small tail possible for a few species

NYMPHALID (EXCLUDING SATYRINES) AND PAPILIONID CATERPILLARS → **Page 595**

KEY TO CATERPILLARS

15/17 [5 pairs of prolegs] AND [no fleshy outgrowths on the body] AND [numerous black or dark brown spots on the entire body]

Green, white, yellow, or dark grey GC

Many black spots of variable sizes on the entire body

PIERID AND PAPILIONID CATERPILLARS → Page 600

⚠ Some moth caterpillars in genera *Cucullia* and *Calophasia* (Noctuids) are very similar to the butterfly caterpillars shown in this block. The caterpillar to be identified should be compared with the pictures on this line.

Striped Lychnis   *Shargacucullia caninae*   Toadflax Moth

NOCTUID CATERPILLARS

16/17 [5 pairs of prolegs] AND [no fleshy outgrowths on the body] AND [GC green] AND [black spots absent (spiracles can be black)]

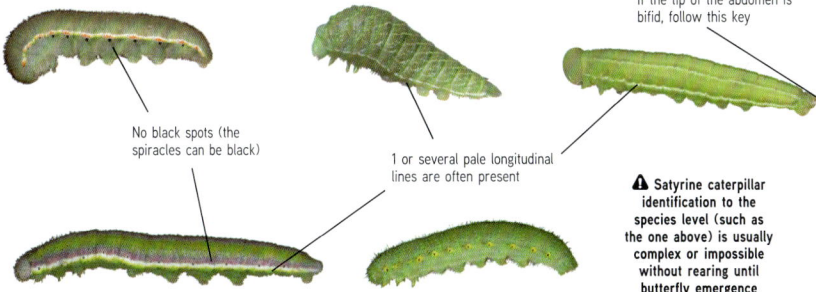

If the tip of the abdomen is bifid, follow this key

No black spots (the spiracles can be black)

1 or several pale longitudinal lines are often present

⚠ Satyrine caterpillar identification to the species level (such as the one above) is usually complex or impossible without rearing until butterfly emergence

PIERID, SATYRINE, AND SWALLOWTAIL CATERPILLARS → Page 601 (block 1/7 and following)

17/17 [5 pairs of prolegs] AND [no fleshy outgrowths on the body] AND [GC brown or beige] AND [posterior tip of the abdomen bifid]

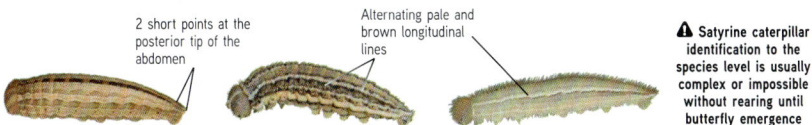

2 short points at the posterior tip of the abdomen

Alternating pale and brown longitudinal lines

⚠ Satyrine caterpillar identification to the species level is usually complex or impossible without rearing until butterfly emergence

SATYRINE CATERPILLARS → Page 604

KEY TO CATERPILLARS

1.1 [Head dark-coloured] AND [no well-defined pale longitudinal line along the body]

Several pale marks on both sides of the head

1 pale band on each side of the head

No pale mark across the head

Dingy Skipper p. 145
Inky Skipper p. 146

Large Skipper
p. 143

Grizzled Skipper p. 175
Southern Grizzled Skipper p. 176

1.2 Greenish head not entirely crossed by pale or dark lines

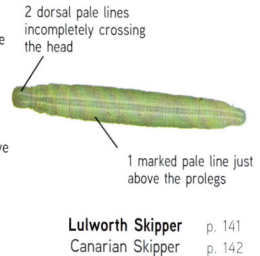

No pale line across the head

No pale line across the head

Marked lateral pale line

2 dorsal pale lines incompletely crossing the head

1 marked lateral pale line just above the prolegs

No pale line just above the prolegs

1 marked pale line just above the prolegs

Small Skipper p. 140
Levantine Skipper p. 138

Chequered Skipper p. 135
Northern Chequered Skipper p. 136

Lulworth Skipper p. 141
Canarian Skipper p. 142

1.3 Greenish head entirely crossed by yellow or brown lines

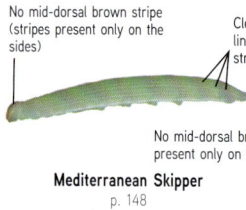

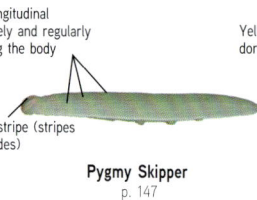

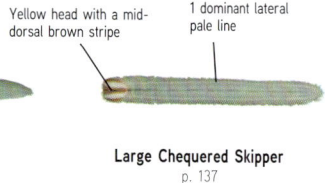

No mid-dorsal brown stripe (stripes present only on the sides)

Clear longitudinal lines finely and regularly streaking the body

Yellow head with a mid-dorsal brown stripe

1 dominant lateral pale line

No mid-dorsal brown stripe (stripes present only on the sides)

Mediterranean Skipper
p. 148

Pygmy Skipper
p. 147

Large Chequered Skipper
p. 137

No mid-dorsal brown stripe (stripes present only on the sides)

1 dominant lateral pale line

Essex Skipper
p. 139

KEY TO CATERPILLARS

2.1 GC whitish or grey and body bearing many long hairs

Small dorsal and lateral black spots

GC rather whitish

Small dorsal and lateral black spots

GC rather pale yellowish

Small dorsal and lateral black spots

GC whitish or greyish

Rather large black spots

GC pale yellowish

Tuft Marbled Skipper p. 153
Oriental Marbled Skipper p. 154

Southern Marbled Skipper p. 155
False Marbled Skipper p. 156

Sage Skipper
p. 158

Marbled Skipper
p. 157

2.2 [GC grey with short hairs] AND [prothorax orange or black and yellow]

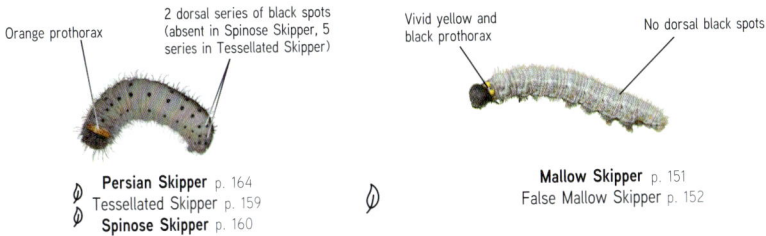

Orange prothorax

2 dorsal series of black spots (absent in Spinose Skipper, 5 series in Tessellated Skipper)

Vivid yellow and black prothorax

No dorsal black spots

Persian Skipper p. 164
Tessellated Skipper p. 159
Spinose Skipper p. 160

Mallow Skipper p. 151
False Mallow Skipper p. 152

2.3 [GC grey brown or dark brown with very short hairs or glabrous] AND [prothorax grey and brown]

No longitudinal pale lines

GC grey-brown, barely mottled

Pale longitudinal lines ill-defined

GC brown mottled with beige

Pale longitudinal lines ill-defined

Short but visible hairs

Hairs hardly visible

Silver-spotted Skipper
p. 144

Oberthür's Grizzled Skipper, Olive Skipper pp. 171 and 172
Large Grizzled Skipper, Foulquier's Grizzled Skipper pp. 173 and 174
Dusky Grizzled Skipper, Safflower Skipper pp. 168 and 165
Rosy Grizzled Skipper, Yellow-banded Skipper, Warren's Skipper pp. 180, 166, and 170

2.4 [GC black with 2 yellow continuous or dotted dorsal stripes] AND [prothorax orange]

2 continuous dorsal yellow lines (thicker in Spanish Red-underwing Skipper)

2 dotted stripes

Red-underwing Skipper p. 161
Spanish Red-underwing Skipper p. 161

Hungarian Skipper p. 162

KEY TO CATERPILLARS

GC whitish, grey, brown, or black] AND [head dark]

2.5 [GC whitish to pale brown with short hairs] AND [prothorax brown and beige]

Safflower Skipper
p. 165

Carline Skipper
p. 177

Cinquefoil Skipper p. 178
Sandy Grizzled Skipper p. 179

⚠ Caterpillars in genus
Pyrgus are very hard
to distinguish, often use
similar host plants

Large Grizzled Skipper
p. 173

Grizzled Skipper p. 176
Southern Grizzled Skipper p. 175

1/6 **[GC green without pink line] AND [pale marks, if any, ill-defined]**

⚠ Copper caterpillars are very similar and often use the
same Polygonaceae host plants. They are very difficult to
distinguish without being reared until the butterfly emerges.

Pale markings
visible

Rather marked mid-dorsal line
surrounded by a paler area

Rather marked mid-
dorsal line

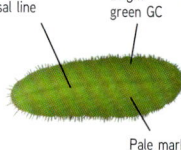

Bright
green GC

Mid-dorsal line and
pale markings barely
visible

Pale markings
visible

Glaucous
green GC

Violet Copper
p. 241

Large Copper
p. 237

Purple-edged Copper p. 233
Balkan Copper p. 234
Pontic Blue p. 286

Mid-dorsal line
and pale markings
barely visible

Pale green
GC

Mid-dorsal line and
pale markings barely
visible

Pale green
GC

Pale green
GC

Mid-dorsal line and pale
markings barely visible

Purple-shot Copper p. 240
Lesser Fiery Copper p. 238

Scarce Copper p. 235
Grecian Copper p. 236

Sooty Copper p. 243
Iberian Sooty Copper p. 244

Greyish
green GC

Mid-dorsal line
and pale markings
barely visible

Dorsal and
lateral series of
pink hairs

Bluish-green GC

2 dorsal and 2 lateral
series of pink hairs

Yellowish lateral
spots (or line in
Chapman's Green
Hairstreak)

Turquoise Blue p. 335

Ilex Hairstreak p. 257

False Ilex Hairsteak p. 258

Chapman's Green Hairstreak p. 248

KEY TO CATERPILLARS

GC green with a pink lateral line

2.1 [Lateral pink lines well-defined] AND [1 mid-dorsal vivid pink line surrounded by white spots]

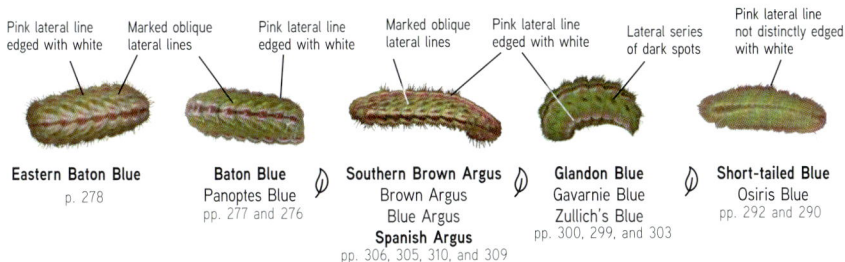

Pink lateral line edged with white

Marked oblique lateral lines

Pink lateral line edged with white

Marked oblique lateral lines

Pink lateral line edged with white

Lateral series of dark spots

Pink lateral line not distinctly edged with white

Eastern Baton Blue
p. 278

Baton Blue
Panoptes Blue
pp. 277 and 276

Southern Brown Argus
Brown Argus
Blue Argus
Spanish Argus
pp. 306, 305, 310, and 309

Glandon Blue
Gavarnie Blue
Zullich's Blue
pp. 300, 299, and 303

Short-tailed Blue
Osiris Blue
pp. 292 and 290

2.2 [Lateral pink lines well-defined] AND [1 mid-dorsal dark green line surrounded by white or yellow spots]

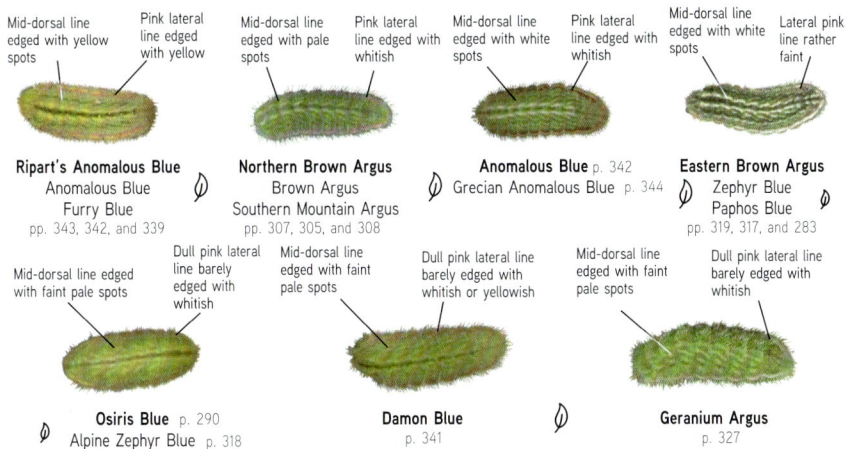

Mid-dorsal line edged with yellow spots

Pink lateral line edged with yellow

Mid-dorsal line edged with pale spots

Pink lateral line edged with whitish

Mid-dorsal line edged with white spots

Pink lateral line edged with whitish

Mid-dorsal line edged with white spots

Lateral pink line rather faint

Ripart's Anomalous Blue
Anomalous Blue
Furry Blue
pp. 343, 342, and 339

Northern Brown Argus
Brown Argus
Southern Mountain Argus
pp. 307, 305, and 308

Anomalous Blue p. 342
Grecian Anomalous Blue p. 344

Eastern Brown Argus
Zephyr Blue
Paphos Blue
pp. 319, 317, and 283

Mid-dorsal line edged with faint pale spots

Dull pink lateral line barely edged with whitish

Mid-dorsal line edged with faint pale spots

Dull pink lateral line barely edged with whitish or yellowish

Mid-dorsal line edged with faint pale spots

Dull pink lateral line barely edged with whitish

Osiris Blue p. 290
Alpine Zephyr Blue p. 318

Damon Blue
p. 341

Geranium Argus
p. 327

2.3 Lateral pink lines ill-defined, incomplete, or diffuse

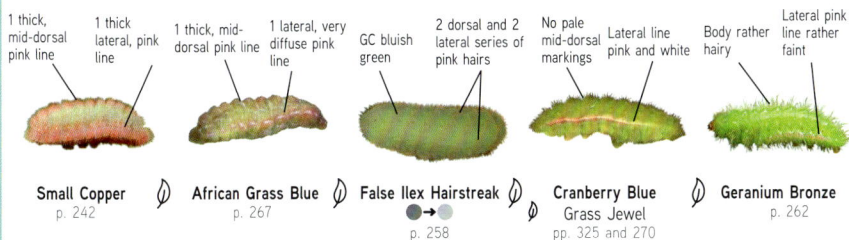

1 thick, mid-dorsal pink line

1 thick lateral, pink line

1 thick, mid-dorsal pink line

1 lateral, very diffuse pink line

GC bluish green

2 dorsal and 2 lateral series of pink hairs

No pale mid-dorsal markings

Lateral line pink and white

Body rather hairy

Lateral pink line rather faint

Small Copper
p. 242

African Grass Blue
p. 267

False Ilex Hairstreak
●→◐◯
p. 258

Cranberry Blue
Grass Jewel
pp. 325 and 270

Geranium Bronze
p. 262

591

KEY TO CATERPILLARS

[GC green] AND [very visible yellow or whitish markings]

3.1 [1 complete brown or very dark pink mid-dorsal line] OR [1 pale mid-dorsal line underlined with pink on its foremost part]

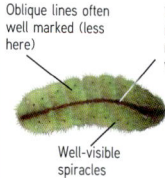

Oblique lines often well marked (less here)

Very dark pink mid-dorsal stripe not distinctly edged with white

Brown mid-dorsal stripe distinctly edged with white

Pale mid-dorsal stripe underlined with pink only in its foremost part

Pinkish mid-dorsal stripe edged with whitish

GC mainly pale green or pink with faint oblique lines

Well-visible spiracles

Well-marked pale oblique lines

Chequered Blue p. 280

Silver-studded Blue p. 322
Idas Blue p. 323
Bellier's Blue p. 324

Little Tiger Blue
Common Tiger Blue pp. 271 and 272

Long-tailed Blue p. 263

3.2 [1 mid-dorsal green stripe edged with vivid yellow spots] AND [1 lateral, vivid yellow line]

⚠ Caterpillars in genus *Lysandra* are very difficult to distinguish and use similar host plants

No yellow oblique lines

No yellow oblique lines

No yellow oblique lines

Thin but visible oblique lines

Adonis Blue p. 311

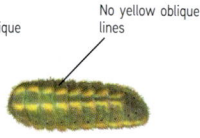

Provence Chalkhill Blue p. 314
Spanish Chalkhill Blue p. 315

Chalkhill Blue p. 313
Azure Chalkhill Blue p. 312
Sardinian Chalkhill Blue p. 313

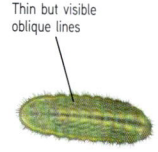

Meleager's Blue p. 328

3.3 [1 mid-dorsal green stripe edged with yellowish-green spots] AND [1 faint lateral yellowish-green line] AND [ill-defined pale, oblique lines]

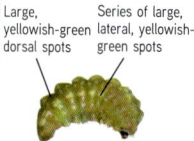

Large, yellowish-green dorsal spots

Series of large, lateral, yellowish-green spots

Large, triangular, yellowish-green dorsal spots

Thin, dotted, yellowish-green dorsal spots

No small mid-dorsal pink spots

Thin, dotted, yellowish-green dorsal spots

No small mid-dorsal pink spots

Small mid-dorsal pink spots

Thin, dotted, yellowish-green dorsal spots

Bright Babul Blue p. 266

Green Hairstreak p. 247

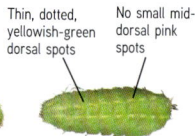

Sloe Hairstreak
●➔● p. 254

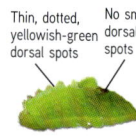

Blue-spot Hairstreak
●➔● p. 253

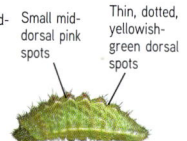

Black Hairstreak
Orange-banded H'streak pp. 256 and 260

3.4 [1 mid-dorsal green stripe edged with yellowish-green spots] AND [1 faint, lateral, yellowish-green line] AND [well-defined, pale, oblique lines]

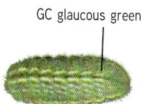

GC glaucous green

GC glaucous green

GC bright green

Chapman's Blue p. 331

Escher's Blue
Canary Blue pp. 332 and 261

Geranium Argus
●➔● p. 304

KEY TO CATERPILLARS

3/6 [GC green] AND [very visible yellow or whitish markings]

3.5 [1 mid-dorsal green stripe edged with whitish spots] AND [1 well-marked, whitish lateral line] AND [well-defined pale, oblique lines]

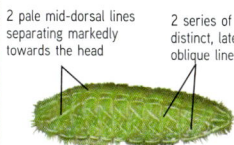

2 pale mid-dorsal lines separating markedly towards the head

2 series of thin, distinct, lateral, oblique lines

2 pale mid-dorsal lines not separating markedly towards the head

Rather thick lateral, oblique lines

Green, mid-dorsal stripe much darker than the GC

Green, mid-dorsal stripe much darker than the GC

Mid-dorsal stripe edged with large pale spots

Brown Hairstreak
●→●
p. 251

Idas Blue p. 323
Bellier's Blue p. 324
Reverdin's Blue p. 321

Black-eyed Blue p. 282
Green-underside Blue p. 281

3.6 [1 mid-dorsal green stripe, edged with whitish spots] AND [1 ill-defined whitish lateral line] AND [poorly marked pale oblique lines]

Common Blue p. 329
Southern Common Blue p. 330
Loew's Blue p. 326

Eros Blue p. 333
Nevada Blue p. 336
Sagra Blue p. 336

Amanda's Blue
p. 334

Provençal Short-tailed Blue
Eastern Short-tailed Blue
pp. 287 and 288

⚠ Polyommatine caterpillars are very similar and often feed on the same host plants (especially legumes), which makes them very difficult to distinguish without rearing until the butterfly emerges.

Mazarine Blue
p. 285

Reverdin's Blue
p. 321

Alpine Blue
p. 298

4/6 **GC light brown or brown**

GC brown mottled with black

Dark mid-dorsal stripe within a pale brown area

GC brown barely mottled

Dark mid-dorsal stripe within a pale brown area

Pale oblique lines

Dark mid-dorsal stripe edged with pale lines and widening markedly towards the head

Spanish Purple Hairstreak
p. 259

Purple Hairstreak
p. 252

Lang's Short-tailed Blue
p. 264

Dark mid-dorsal stripe edged with pale lines

Lateral dark stripe possible

Body bearing long hairs

Series of mid-dorsal black spots

Silver-studded Blue p. 322

Duke of Burgundy p. 350

593

KEY TO CATERPILLARS

GC pale or vivid pink

5.1 Pale markings in poor contrast with the GC

⚠ The caterpillars of these 4 species spend most of their development inside an ant nest

Pink, mid-dorsal stripe edged with pale spots

GC mainly pink

GC mainly pink

GC mainly pink

Pink mid-dorsal stripe edged with pale spots

GC pale pink or greenish pink with faint, pale, oblique lines

Large Blue
p. 293

Dusky Large Blue
Alcon Blue
pp. 296 and 295

Scarce Large Blue
p. 294

Long-tailed Blue
p. 263

5.2 Pale markings in sharp contrast with the GC

Dorsal surface markedly humped

Marked dark and white oblique lines

Dorsal crests often bearing yellow spots

Marked dark and white oblique lines

Dark mid-dorsal stripe edged with white lines

Dark pink, mid-dorsal stripe edged with large white spots

Provence Hairstreak
p. 245

Bavius Blue
p. 279

Holly Blue
p. 297

CG whitish or pale yellow

6.1 Dorsal dark markings in sharp contrast with the GC

Pale, mid-dorsal stripe edged with small dark spots

Dark oblique lines

Green, mid-dorsal stripe dotted with pink spots

Dark, mid-dorsal stripe

Dark oblique lines

White-letter Hairstreak ●➔●
p. 255

Canary Blue
p. 261

Green-underside Blue
p. 281

6.2 Dorsal markings absent or in poor contrast with the GC

Dorsally weakly flattened body

Dorsally flattened body

Iolas Blue p. 284
Nogel's Hairstreak p. 246

Small Blue
p. 289

KEY TO CATERPILLARS

1/13 [GC black] AND [vivid yellow or yellow orange lines, spots or fleshy outgrowths]

1.1 [Small black fleshy outgrowths] AND [2 dorsal lines of vivid yellow or yellow-orange spots]

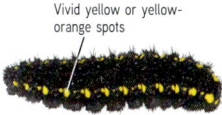

Vivid yellow or yellow-orange spots

GC sometimes more contrasted with black spots on a brown background

Bright yellow spots

Apollo
p. 120

Clouded Apollo
p. 122

Small Apollo
p. 121

1.2 [Long, dorsal, black, fleshy outgrowths] AND [1 or 2 vivid yellow mid-dorsal lines]

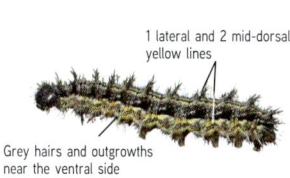

1 lateral and 2 mid-dorsal yellow lines

1 mid-dorsal series of large, vivid yellow spots

1 lateral series of vivid yellow spots

1 mid-dorsal series of large, vivid yellow spots

1 lateral series of vivid yellow spots

Grey hairs and outgrowths near the ventral side

Small Tortoiseshell p. 361
Corsican Small Tortoiseshell p. 362

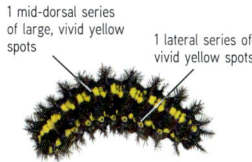

Asian Fritillary
p. 412

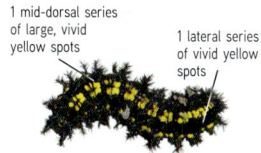

Scarce Fritillary p. 411
Italian Scarce Fritillary p. 411

1.3 [Long, dorsal, black, fleshy outgrowths] AND [no mid-dorsal yellow line or spots]

1 lateral series of yellow, crescent-shaped spots

Prolegs brown or reddish

Lateral series of reddish, fleshy outgrowths

Body regularly ringed with yellow

Series of abdominal white spots

Body regularly ringed with yellow

1 lateral series of vivid yellow spots

Red Admiral
p. 357

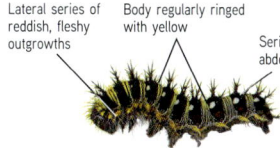

American Painted Lady
p. 356

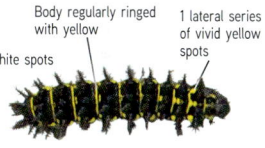

Cynthia's Fritillary
p. 409

1.4 Dorsal fleshy outgrowths long and yellow

2 mid-dorsal yellow lines

Long, yellow, fleshy outgrowths

Densely haired body

Dorsal stripe mottled with yellow

Black dorsal surface

Tip of the fleshy outgrowths black

Dark body with black spots (and several yellow-orange spots in Thor's Fritillary)

2 black horns on the head

Prolegs brown or reddish

1 lateral series of yellow, crescent-shaped spots

Whitish area above the prolegs

Prolegs brown or reddish

Painted Lady
p. 355

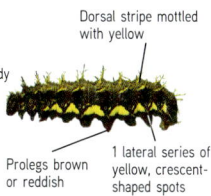

Canary Red Admiral
Red Admiral
pp. 358 and 357

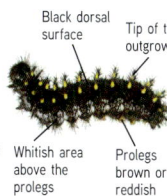

Pearl-bordered Fritillary
p. 393

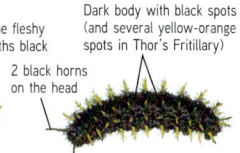

Titania's Fritillary p. 392
Thor's Fritillary p. 395

KEY TO CATERPILLARS

2/13 [GC black] AND [black dorsal fleshy outgrowths] AND [series of red spots]

2 dorsal and 1 lateral series of red spots

Long, black outgrowths

Long, black outgrowths

1 dorsal series of red spots on each side

Black outgrowths rather small

1 lateral series of red spots just above the prolegs

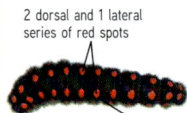

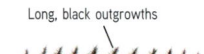

False Apollo
p. 123

Dark Green Fritillary
p. 385

Camberwell Beauty
p. 359

3/13 [GC black] AND [body covered with black, fleshy outgrowths] AND [lateral series of white spots]

Body regularly mottled with small white dots

Long, black outgrowths

White spots concentrated in a lateral and a dorsal band

Outgrowths rather short and hairy

White spots (sometimes reduced) concentrated in a lateral and a dorsal band

Red head

Small white spots (often barely visible) concentrated along abdominal rings

Black head

Black head

Outgrowths rather short and hairy

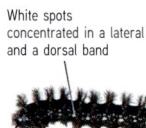

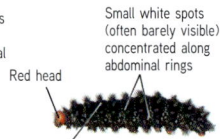

Peacock
p. 360

Spanish Fritillary
p. 408

Marsh Fritillary
Becker's Fritillary
pp. 406 and 407

Glanville Fritillary
p. 425

4/13 [GC rather dark] AND [body covered with pale grey, fleshy outgrowths]

Dorsal surface brown with darker areas

2 close yellow mid-dorsal lines interrupted by browner marks

Dorsal surface mainly dark

2 dorsal series of red spots (2 mid-dorsal yellow lines in Pallas' Fritillary and 1 in Corsican Fritillary)

Dorsal surface mainly dark (browner in Pallas' Fritillary)

Head becomes red in mature caterpillars (stays black in Knapweed Fritillary)

Frequent whitish dorsal area

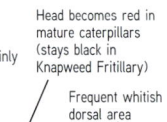

Shepherd's Fritillary
Balkan Fritillary
pp. 397 and 399

Mountain Fritillary
Balkan Fritillary
pp. 398 and 399

Cardinal p. 382
Pallas' Fritillary p. 383
Corsican Fritillary p. 384

Spanish Knapweed Fritillary p. 428
Eastern Knapweed Fritillary p. 428
Knapweed Fritillary p. 427

Dark body largely tinged with rufous brown

1 mid-dorsal reddish line

Body finely ringed with black

Series of paired lateral black spots

Body ringed with yellow and black

Dark head

Orange head

Orange head

Dark head

Numerous hairs

Pale yellow lateral band underlined with black

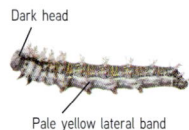

Niobe Fritillary
p. 387

Southern Comma
p. 366

Painted Lady
p. 355

Painted Lady
p. 355

KEY TO CATERPILLARS

[GC black] AND [dorsal, dark fleshy outgrowths] AND [1 lateral rufous band]

Black head

Frequent whitish dorsal area

Head becomes red in mature caterpillars

Frequent whitish dorsal area

Almost no white, if any, on dorsal surface

Rufous hairy lateral band just above the prolegs

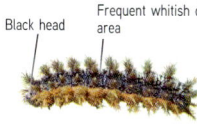

Knapweed Fritillary
p. 427

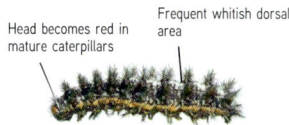

Eastern Knapweed Fritillary p. 428
Spanish Knapweed Fritillary p. 428

Freyer's Fritillary p. 426
Aetherie Fritillary p. 424

[Body stout with grey GC, mottled with white and black] AND [body covered with orange or pale, fleshy outgrowths]

6.1 Outgrowths orange with a pale tip

Body ringed with small white spots, giving impression of grey GC

Body ringed with very small white spots, giving impression of very dark GC, especially in Little and Grisons Fritillaries

False Heath Fritillary
p. 418

Southern Heath Fritillary p. 414
Heath Fritillary p. 413

Meadow Fritillary p. 419
Provence Fritillary p. 415
Nickerl's Fritillary p. 416
Little Fritillary p. 421
Grisons Fritillary p. 420

Blackish GC mottled with white spots

Black head (red in Eastern and Spanish Knapweed Fritillaries mature caterpillars)

White lateral band above prolegs

2 black horns on the head

Outgrowths rather long

Paler dorsal region

2 much longer outgrowths on prothorax

Dark body with black spots (and several yellow-orange spots in Thor's Fritillary)

Weaver's Fritillary
p. 391

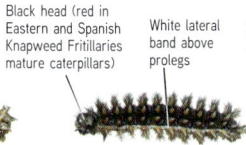

Knapweed Fritillary
Eastern Knapweed Fritillary
Spanish Knapweed Fritillary
pp. 427 and 428

Map
p. 368

Small Pearl-bordered Fritillary
Thor's Fritillary
pp. 394 and 395

6.2 Outgrowths mainly whitish (or with a reduced basal orange area)

⚠ Body of Queen of Spain Fritillary can also be grey and black

Light grey GC

Outgrowths similar with a reduced basal orange colour

Outgrowths rather long and almost entirely pale

Light grey GC

GC dark grey

Long orange and pale outgrowths in alternating series

Pure white mid-dorsal stripe

Outgrowths rather short with an orange base

Black head

Reddish head

Reddish head

Reddish head mottled with dark spots

Assmann's Fritillary
p. 417

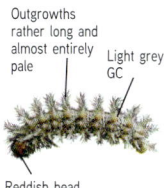

Lesser Spotted Fritillary p. 423
Sagarra's Fritillary p. 423

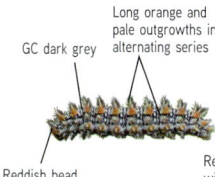

Spotted Fritillary
p. 422

Queen of Spain Fritillary
p. 380

KEY TO CATERPILLARS

7/13 — GC black; body covered with orange or vivid red, fleshy outgrowths

No horns on the head

GC mottled with tiny yellow spots

2 horns on the head

Dark body with black spots (and several yellow-orange spots in Thor's Fritillary)

Pale outgrowths with a vivid red tip

Little black streaks (dots in Southern Festoon)

Rufous, branched outgrowths

Rufous stripe above the prolegs

Series of yellow, crescent-shaped spots just above prolegs

Body somewhat hairy

Red Admiral p. 357

Titania's Fritillary p. 392
Thor's Fritillary p. 395

Spanish Festoon p. 124
Southern Festoon p. 125

Large Tortoiseshell p. 363
Yellow-legged Tortoiseshell p. 364

8/13 — [1 mid-dorsal pure white stripe (sometimes incomplete)] AND [body at least partially covered with orange, fleshy outgrowths]

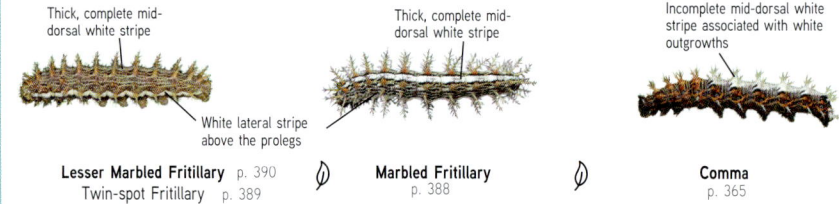

Thick, complete mid-dorsal white stripe

White lateral stripe above the prolegs

Thick, complete mid-dorsal white stripe

Incomplete mid-dorsal white stripe associated with white outgrowths

Lesser Marbled Fritillary p. 390
Twin-spot Fritillary p. 389

Marbled Fritillary p. 388

Comma p. 365

9/13 — [GC reddish or reddish-brown] AND [body covered with orange, fleshy outgrowths]

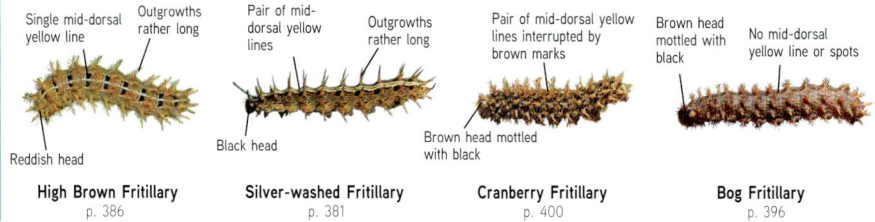

Single mid-dorsal yellow line

Outgrowths rather long

Reddish head

Pair of mid-dorsal yellow lines

Outgrowths rather long

Black head

Pair of mid-dorsal yellow lines interrupted by brown marks

Brown head mottled with black

Brown head mottled with black

No mid-dorsal yellow line or spots

High Brown Fritillary p. 386

Silver-washed Fritillary p. 381

Cranberry Fritillary p. 400

Bog Fritillary p. 396

10/13 — [Pale GC (sometimes with dark bands)] AND [body covered with yellow or vivid orange, fleshy outgrowths]

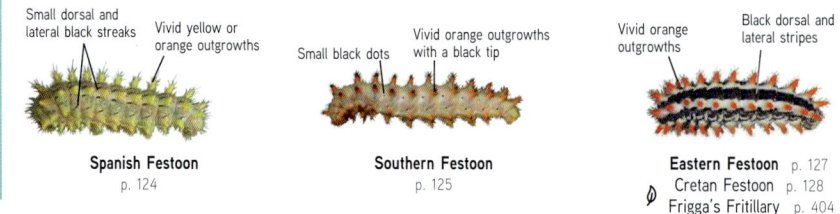

Small dorsal and lateral black streaks

Vivid yellow or orange outgrowths

Small black dots

Vivid orange outgrowths with a black tip

Vivid orange outgrowths

Black dorsal and lateral stripes

Spanish Festoon p. 124

Southern Festoon p. 125

Eastern Festoon p. 127
Cretan Festoon p. 128
Frigga's Fritillary p. 404

598

KEY TO CATERPILLARS

11/13 [Body ringed with yellow, white, and black] AND [several dorsal pairs of long, black tentacles]

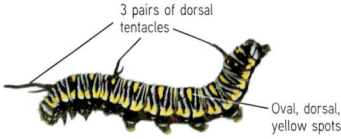

3 pairs of dorsal tentacles

Oval, dorsal, yellow spots

2 pairs of dorsal tentacles

Body ringed with yellow, black, and white

Plain Tiger
p. 378

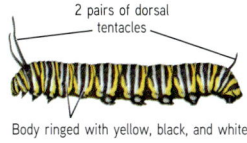

Monarch
p. 377

12/13 [1 or 2 pairs of fleshy horns on the head] AND [no prominent outgrowth on the rest of the body]

No dark streak in front of the horns

Black streak often present in front of the horns

2 pairs of horns on the head

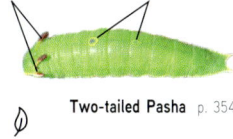

Dorsal yellow-ringed blue spots

Purple Emperor
●→●
p. 374

Lesser Purple Emperor p. 375
Freyer's Purple Emperor p. 376
●→●

Two-tailed Pasha p. 354

13/13 Only 2 series of several dorsal outgrowths

13.1 No dorsal outgrowth at the end of the abdomen

Rather slender outgrowths

No grey area on the abdomen

Brown area on the back

Rather thick outgrowths

Thick thoracic outgrowths

Grey area

2 reduced abdominal outgrowths

White Admiral p. 369
●→●

Southern White Admiral p. 370
●→●

Poplar Admiral p. 373
●→●

13.2 1 dorsal outgrowth at the end of the abdomen

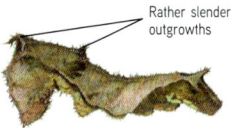

Rather slender outgrowths

Rather slender outgrowths

Rufous area above the prolegs

Common Glider
p. 372

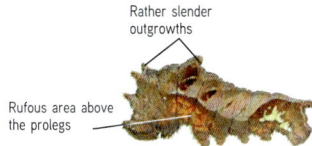

Hungarian Glider
p. 371

KEY TO CATERPILLARS

1/5 [1 white lateral stripe] AND [1 yellow mid-dorsal stripe] OR [1 series of yellow or orange rings]

Large yellow dorsal stripe between 2 grey stripes

Body alternately ringed with yellow and grey

Body alternately ringed with vivid orange and grey

Yellow-orange head

Provence Orange-tip
p. 184

Lederer's Sooty Orange-tip
p. 187

Small Bath White
p. 208

2/5 [No white lateral stripe] AND [grey mid-dorsal stripe surrounded by 2 continuous yellow stripes]

White areas within the lateral yellow stripe

Few white areas within the lateral yellow stripe

⚠ These 3 caterpillars are very difficult to distinguish. The Eastern Dappled White caterpillar becomes lilac-grey in the last larval instar, while the Western Dappled White caterpillar becomes purple-pink.

Eastern Dappled White
p. 215

Western Dappled White
p. 214

Mountain Dappled White
p. 216

3/5 [No white lateral stripe] AND [grey, mid-dorsal stripe surrounded by 2 series of yellow spots] OR [yellow mid-dorsal stripe surrounded by 2 series of black spots of different sizes]

Pair of yellow spots on head

Yellow spots within pale lateral stripe

Pair of yellow spots on head

Distinct dorsal yellow spots

Variably sized black spots

Mid-dorsal yellow stripe

Bath White p. 206
Eastern Bath White p. 207

Peak White
p. 209

Large White p. 222
Canary Islands Large White p. 221

4/5 [No lateral white stripe] AND [body covered with a mosaic of black and orange spots on a green or white GC] AND [a fleshy bifid organ protruding from the head when the caterpillar is disturbed]

Green GC (black and white in earlier instars)

White GC

Green GC

Vivid orange spots above the prolegs

No vivid orange spots above the prolegs (faint orange spots possible)

Mosaic of orange, black, and blue spots

Swallowtail p. 132
● → ○

Southern Swallowtail
p. 129

Corsican Swallowtail p. 133
● → ○

KEY TO CATERPILLARS

5/5 [Green GC] AND [at least 2 dorsal or latero-dorsal series of black or dark brown spots]

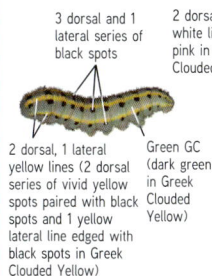

3 dorsal and 1 lateral series of black spots

2 dorsal, 1 lateral white lines (tinged with pink in Pale Arctic Clouded Yellow)

Black spots under each white line (faint in Pale Arctic Clouded Yellow)

2 dorsal white lines (and 1 lateral in Spring Ringlet)

Dark mid-dorsal line

Small orange spots

Series of dark brown spots in variable numbers

2 dorsal, 1 lateral yellow lines (2 dorsal series of vivid yellow spots paired with black spots and 1 yellow lateral line edged with black spots in Greek Clouded Yellow)

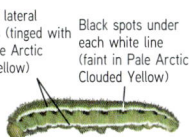

Green GC (dark green in Greek Clouded Yellow)

1 series of small dark streaks above each white line (absent or faint in Yellow-banded and Spring Ringlets)

2 short points at end of abdomen

Pale mid-dorsal and oblique lines

Berger's Clouded p. 190
Yellow
Greek Clouded p. 198
Yellow

Northern Clouded p. 201
Yellow
Pale Arctic Clouded p. 195
Yellow

Silky Ringlet p. 499
Spring Ringlet p. 516
Yellow-banded Ringlet p. 492
De Prunner's Ringlet p. 517

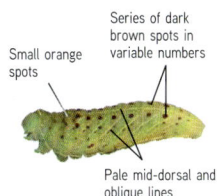

Iberian Scarce p. 131
Swallowtail
Scarce Swallowtail p. 130

1/7 [1 lateral white line containing small pink and sometimes yellow spots] OR [1 continuously yellow lateral line]

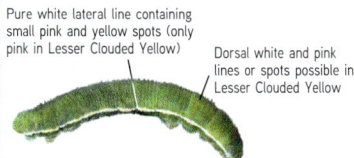

Pure white lateral line containing small pink and yellow spots (only pink in Lesser Clouded Yellow)

Dorsal white and pink lines or spots possible in Lesser Clouded Yellow

Pure white lateral line containing small pink and yellow spots (only pink in Lesser Clouded Yellow)

Some Eastern Pale Clouded Yellow caterpillars do not have black spots beneath the white line and thus can barely be distinguished from Pale Clouded Yellow caterpillars

Danube Clouded Yellow p. 199
Lesser Clouded Yellow p. 197

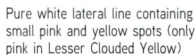

Pale Clouded Yellow p. 191
Lesser Clouded Yellow p. 197
Eastern Pale Clouded Yellow p. 192

Pure white lateral line containing small pink and yellow spots

Pure white lateral line containing small pink and yellow spots

Small black spots beneath white line (may be absent in Eastern Pale Clouded Yellow)

Thick, yellow, lateral line tinged with white

Clouded Yellow
p. 196

Eastern Pale Clouded Yellow
p. 192

Moorland Clouded Yellow
p. 193

2/7 1 white lateral line containing small yellow spots

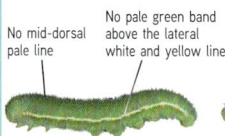

No mid-dorsal pale line

No pale green band above the lateral white and yellow line

2 faint pale dorsal lines

No pale green band above the lateral white and yellow line

2 faint pale dorsal lines

Green head with yellow marks

Paler green band above the white and yellow lateral line

Mountain Clouded Yellow
p. 194

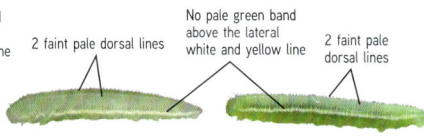

Eastern Wood White p. 228
Fenton's Wood White p. 230

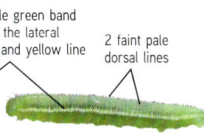

Wood White p. 229
Réal's Wood White p. 229
Cryptic Wood White p. 229

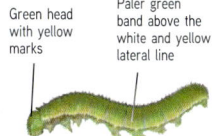

Nettle-tree
Butterfly
p. 353

KEY TO CATERPILLARS

3/7 [1 continuously white lateral line] AND [no other lateral line along this one]

Lateral white line barely diffusing dorsally

Lateral white line barely diffusing dorsally

Lateral white line often tinged with yellow and barely diffusing dorsally

Powdered Brimstone
p. 203

Brimstone
p. 202

Cleopatra p. 204
Canarian Brimstones p. 205
Madeiran Brimstone p. 205

Lateral white line largely diffusing dorsally (more clearly defined in Eastern Orange-tip and with yellow spots in Grüner's Orange-tip)

Thin, ill-defined pale lateral line

Greyish-green GC

Small orange dots

Pale oblique lines

Thin, pale lateral line

Thin, sometimes ill-defined white lateral line

Bright green GC

Body rather hairy

Orange-tip p. 182
Grüner's Orange-tip p. 183
Eastern Orange-tip p. 185

Greenish Black-tip p. 212
Eastern Greenish Black-tip p. 210
Spanish Greenish Black-tip p. 211

Scarce Swallowtail p. 130
Iberian Scarce p. 131
Swallowtail

Meadow p. 445
Brown
●→●

4/7 [1 continuously white lateral line] AND [another lilac, grey, or black line just above or beneath this one]

Clear white line associated with pale pink line (faint or greyish in Corsican Dappled White)

No grey dorsal stripe

Clear white line associated with a thick pink line

Dorsal grey stripe

Faint white lateral line underlined by ill-defined grey stripe

Greyish-green GC

Black line just above the white line

Small, yellow-orange outgrowths

Portuguese Dappled White p. 217
Corsican Dappled White p. 213

Green-striped White
Canarian Green-striped Whites
pp. 218 and 219

Desert Orange-tip
p. 186

African Migrant
p. 188

5/7 [No continuous lateral line] AND [spiracles ringed with vivid yellow]

Pale brown spiracles ringed with yellow

No mid-dorsal yellow line

Black spiracles ringed with yellow

No mid-dorsal yellow line

Pale spiracles variably ringed with yellow

Mid-dorsal yellow line

Pale spiracles variably ringed with yellow

Mid-dorsal yellow line

No small yellow spots between spiracles

No small yellow spots between spiracles

Small yellow spots between spiracles

Small yellow spots between spiracles

Mountain Small White
p. 225

Green-veined White p. 226
Balkan Green-veined White p. 226
Mountain Green-veined White p. 227

Small White p. 223
Krueper's Small White p. 220

Southern Small White p. 224

KEY TO CATERPILLARS

[Abdomen ending in 2 small points] AND [several pale lateral lines, the most conspicuous one just above the prolegs]

⚠ *Coenonympha* caterpillars are typical yet very hard or impossible to determine at the species level. These 3 pictures are here to show the variability of the intensity and thickness of their lateral lines.

Head entirely green — Pale line (can be pinkish in Scarce Heath) — Small whitish or pinkish points

Head entirely green — Small whitish or pinkish points

Head entirely green — Small whitish or pinkish points

Chestnut Heath p. 455
Spanish Heath p. 456
Russian Heath p. 464
Scarce Heath p. 451
Dusky Heath p. 457
Corsican Heath p. 459

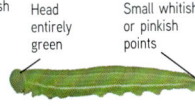

Pearly Heath p. 460
Balkan Heath p. 463
Darwin's Heath p. 461
Piedmont Heath p. 461
Alpine Heath/Cretan
Small Heath pp. 462 and 458

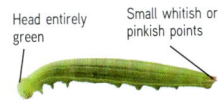

Small Heath p. 452
Eastern Large
Heath p. 454
False Ringlet p. 465
Large Heath p. 453

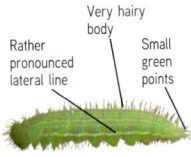

Very hairy body — Rather pronounced lateral line — Small green points

Very hairy body — Ill-defined lateral line — Small green points

Head crossed by 2 brown stripes edged with yellow — Pale, pinkish-brown lateral line above prolegs — Small pinkish points

Head entirely green — Small green or whitish points

Wall Brown p. 433
Corsican Wall Brown p. 434
Northern Wall Brown p. 436

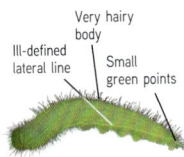

Large Wall Brown
p. 435

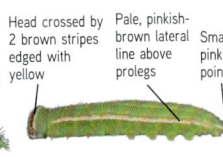

Dusky Meadow Brown
p. 444
Oriental Meadow Brown
p. 443

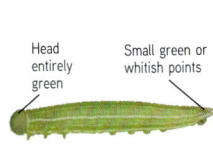

Mountain Ringlet p. 486
Lesser Mountain Ringlet p. 488
Blind Ringlet p. 493
Bulgarian Ringlet p. 526
Sudeten Ringlet p. 489

[Abdomen ending in 2 small points] AND [several equivalent pale lateral lines; the most conspicuous one may be close to the dorsal area]

Brown head bearing 2 small dorsal outgrowths (Marbled White and Balkan M. White), more prominent (Iberian M. White) or in a frontal position (Western and Spanish M. Whites) — Small brownish points

Green head bears 2 prominent outgrowths at the top — Small brownish points

Green head (with 2 forward points and 2 pale dorsal lines in Lattice and Lesser Lattice Browns) — Small whitish points

Marbled white p. 468
Balkan Marbled White p. 469
Iberian Marbled White p. 470
Western Marbled White p. 472
Italian Marbled White p. 473
Spanish Marbled White p. 474

Esper's Marbled White
p. 471

Speckled Wood p. 438
Canary Speckled Wood p. 437
Madeiran Speckled Wood p. 439
Lattice Brown p. 431
Lesser Lattice Brown p. 432

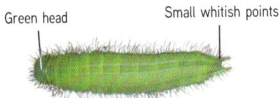

Green head — Small whitish points

Dark green or brown mid-dorsal line — Brown head — Small whitish points

Woodland Brown
p. 467

Piedmont Ringlet p. 508
Almond-eyed Ringlet p. 527
Woodland Ringlet p. 524
Mnestra's Ringlet p. 496
Gavarnie Ringlet p. 518

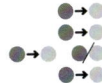

603

KEY TO CATERPILLARS

At least 4 dark brown stripes across the head

1.1   At least 1 mid-dorsal or lateral, dotted, brown stripe

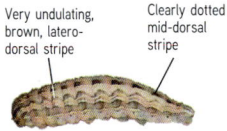

Very undulating, brown, latero-dorsal stripe

Clearly dotted mid-dorsal stripe

Slightly undulating brown, latero-dorsal stripe

Clearly dotted mid-dorsal stripe

Straight latero-dorsal brown stripe

Clearly dotted mid-dorsal stripe

White-banded Grayling   p. 531
Balkan White-banded Grayling   p. 531

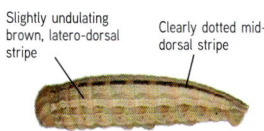

Grecian Grayling   p. 535
Brown's Grayling   p. 532
Dils' Grayling   p. 534

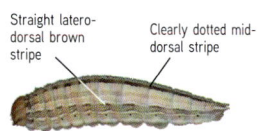

Hermit
p. 538

Dotted, rather faint, mid-dorsal stripe (absent behind head in Woodland and Eastern Rock Graylings, faint but visible in Rock and Lesser Rock Graylings)

Brown lateral stripes rather faint against beige GC

Dark mid-dorsal stripe interrupted by paler areas

Straight, latero-dorsal, dark brown stripe

Dark mid-dorsal stripe interrupted by paler areas

Dotted but very faint mid-dorsal stripe

Straight, latero-dorsal, dark brown stripe

Incomplete, dotted, lateral stripe

Woodland Grayling   p. 560
Rock Grayling   p. 562
Lesser Rock Grayling   p. 563
Eastern Rock Grayling   p. 561

Grayling
p. 541

Alpine Grayling   p. 476
Baltic Grayling   p. 477
Arctic Grayling   p. 478
Norse Grayling   p. 479

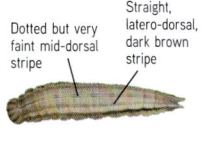

Dryad
p. 482

1.2   No dorsal or lateral dotted brown stripe

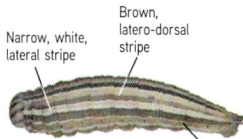

Narrow, white, lateral stripe

Brown, latero-dorsal stripe

Thick, white lateral stripe

Brown, latero-dorsal stripe

White, latero-dorsal stripe

2 similar brown stripes above the prolegs

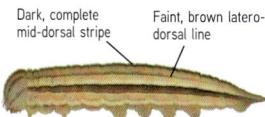

Great Sooty Satyr   p. 481
Black Satyr   p. 480

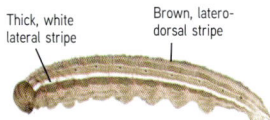

Great-banded Grayling
p. 483

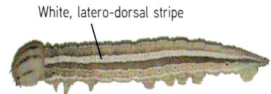

False Grayling   p. 564
Southern False Grayling   p. 565

Dark, complete mid-dorsal stripe

Faint, brown latero-dorsal line

Faint, incomplete mid-dorsal stripe

Faint, brown, latero-dorsal line

Dark, complete mid-dorsal stripe

Faint, brown, latero-dorsal line

Striped Grayling
p. 558

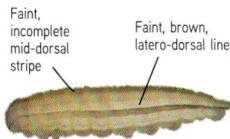

Tree Grayling
p. 556

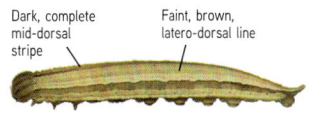

Canarian Graylings
p. 559

KEY TO CATERPILLARS

[Head not striped] OR [only 2 brown stripes on head]

2.1 [1 dotted, lateral, brown line] AND [rather faint lateral stripes]

Dark mid-dorsal stripe faint towards head

Series of brown spots faint towards head

Dark mid-dorsal stripe may be faint towards head

1 series of dark spots above prolegs, 1 latero-dorsal series of dark spots (more visible in False Mnestra Ringlet)

Dark mid-dorsal stripe paler towards head

Thin, almost continuous lateral brown line

Dark mid-dorsal stripe paler towards head

Thin, almost continuous lateral brown line

No dark spots above prolegs

Dewy Ringlet
False Dewy Ringlet   p. 495

Arran Brown   p. 520
False Mnestra Ringlet   p. 497
Autumn Ringlet   p. 515

Yellow-spotted Ringlet   p. 490
Water Ringlet   p. 501
Zapater's Ringlet   p. 519

Scotch Argus   p. 513

2.2 [1 dotted lateral brown line] AND [conspicuous lateral stripes]

Small, prominent frontal outgrowths

Dark areas at front of head

Conspicuous yellowish band above the prolegs

Bright-eyed Ringlet   p. 525
Eriphyle Ringlet   p. 491
White Speck Ringlet   p. 494

Common Brassy Ringlet   p. 502
Western Brassy Ringlet   p. 502
Lorkovic's Brassy Ringlet   p. 506
Ottoman Brassy Ringlet   p. 503
De Lesse's Brassy Ringlet   p. 504
Swiss Brassy Ringlet   p. 505

Large Ringlet   p. 521
Styrian Ringlet   p. 510

2.3 No dotted lateral line

Brown head bears 2 small frontal outgrowths

Brown head bears 2 small outgrowths at the top (Marbled and Balkan Marbled Whites); more prominent in Iberian Marbled White

Brown head with no outgrowths

Faint lateral stripes

Western Marbled White
Spanish Marbled White   p. 472 et 474

Marbled White   p. 468
Balkan Marbled White   p. 469
Iberian Marbled White   p. 470
Italian Marbled White   p. 473

Woodland Ringlet   p. 524
Larche Ringlet   p. 514

1 dark brown stripe edged with pale brown on each side of the head

Thick brown stripe edged with 2 paler stripes

1 dark brown stripe edged with pale brown on each side of the head

Thick brown stripe edged with 2 paler stripes

Ringlet
p. 466

Gatekeeper   p. 440
Spanish Gatekeeper   p. 442
Southern Gatekeeper   p. 441

Introduction to the Biology of Butterfly Eggs and Oviposition

The life of a butterfly begins with the fertilization of eggs stored in the abdomen of a female, who typically produces several dozens of them throughout her life. For nearly 90% of European butterflies, these eggs are laid on the host plants of the caterpillars. In the remaining 10%, eggs may be deposited in environments favourable to the presence of these host plants. Some species, such as several Satyrines, do not associate egg-laying with adhesive secretions and may lay their eggs under stones or release them in the vegetation. Upon hatching, caterpillars must then find their food source (usually rather common and abundant plants, such as grasses). Eggs can be laid on different plant organs. The majority of European species (62%) deposit their eggs on the host plant foliage, favouring either the upper or lower leaf surface. Others, such as certain Lycaenids, prefer to lay their eggs on floral parts, particularly the flower calyx (20%), or on stems and branches (about 9%). Rarely, eggs may be laid on dead parts of the host plant (6%). Oviposition (egg-laying behaviour) has been extensively studied in butterflies due to its significant economic implications for species that may damage cultivated plants. Ecologists and evolutionary biologists have also paid special attention to oviposition because it occurs within a complex set of constraints. Females explore their environment in search of an ideal site that offers the best survival chances for its eggs and emerging caterpillars. However, dispersal associated with this quest for the perfect location increases the risk for the female to die from predation, accidents, or unfavourable weather events. The choice of an egg-laying site thus represents a trade-off between these different pressures and may not always be optimal. Some species (around 10%) lay their eggs in groups of several dozens called batches, while most scatter them individually or in small groups of a few units. Putting all eggs in one basket, so to speak, may have the advantage of diluting predation risk and showcasing aposematic (warning) colours in young caterpillars or promoting cooperation in building a common shelter. Eggs located towards the top of the mass can also protect those below from drying out. Nevertheless, large egg batches can also increase the risk of intense competition among caterpillars for food resources. Species that lay eggs in clusters often use densely aggregated host plants, such as nettles by *Aglais* species, or large plants, as seen in *Nymphalis* species exploiting willows.

Butterfly eggs contain energetic stores necessary for embryo development, primarily a yolk located at the centre of the egg. The young caterpillar forms inside, gradually consuming these reserves, which vary in composition among species. Such stores are accumulated during the female's larval stages as well as acquired during her adult life. The caterpillar may remain inside the egg during winter. The embryo and its stores are wrapped in a proteinaceous envelope called the chorion, which often constitutes the newly hatched caterpillar's first meal. The chorion's structure forms regular patterns that vary depending on the species and are very useful for identification. Important features include ribs, which are ridges connecting the apical and basal poles of the egg. The number and intensity of these ribs also differ among species within a family. The overall egg shape is also a criterion for reliably identifying a butterfly family and sometimes even a genus. Species-level determination often requires examining the eggs by scanning electron microscopy, a technique that goes far beyond the scope of this guide, which simply presents the major egg types as they can be observed with a field magnifying lens or on a good macrophotograph.

KEY TO THE MAIN EGG TYPES

1/10 Eggs laid in batches of several dozen eggs

Oval-shaped eggs laid in a single layer, not on Rosaceae

Large White

Oval eggs laid in a single layer on Rosaceae

Black-veined White

Globular eggs with non-spiny ribs

Genera *Euphydryas* and *Melitaea*

Globular green eggs, ribs spiking at apical pole

Genus *Aglais*

Eggs laid in columns under the LHP leaf

Map

Single-layer batch around LHP stems

Genus *Nymphalis*

2/10 Spherical, smooth eggs laid singly or in very small numbers (a few units)

On Apiaceae and Rutaceae

Swallowtail or Corsican Swallowtail

On a few particular Apiaceae

Southern Swallowtail

On woody Rosaceae

Genus *Iphiclides*

On Primulaceae or Aristolochiaceae

Duke of Burgundy and genus *Zerynthia*

3/10 Elongated eggs, bordered by fine ribs, laid singly or in very small numbers (a few units)

Very slender eggs

On legumes

On Rhamnaceae

Slightly thicker eggs that become orange in most species

Genera *Leptidea* and *Colias*

Genus *Gonepteryx*

Genera *Pieris* (except *P. brassicae*, *P. cheiranthi*), *Anthocharis*, *Euchloe*, *Iberochloe*, *Pontia*, *Colotis*, and *Zegris*

KEY TO THE MAIN EGG TYPES

4/10 Globular, slightly ovoid eggs with very pronounced ribs spiking at the apex, laid singly or in very small numbers (a few units)

Around 10 ribs

Around 10 ribs

Around 15 ribs

Genus *Polygonia*

Genus *Vanessa* (Red Admiral on left and Painted Lady on right)

5/10 Globular eggs, slightly ovoid or flattened at the top, without ribs or with ribs not spiking at the apex, laid singly or in very small numbers (a few units)

Depressed apex, brown circular band

Covered in bristles, adorned with hexagons

Fine, reticulated ornamentation

Visible ribs, small apical ornamentations

Genera *Erebia*, *Hipparchia*, *Coenonympha*, *Satyrus*, *Pyronia*, *Maniola*, *Hyponephele*, and *Melanargia* (in part)

Two-tailed Pasha

Genus *Limenitis*

Genera *Pararge, Lasiommata, Lopinga,* and *Melanargia* (in part)

6/10 Conical eggs with marked ribs, laid singly or in very small numbers (a few units)

Ovoid, conical egg on Asclepiadaceae

More or less truncated, conical eggs; ribs spike at apex in genus *Brenthis*

Monarch or Plain Tiger

Genera *Argynnis, Boloria, Brenthis, Fabriciana,* and *Speyeria*

7/10 Eggs forming a highly flattened cone with more or less pronounced ribs, laid singly or in very small numbers (a few units)

Ribs fine, pronounced

Slightly pronounced ribs

Pinkish colour; thick, very pronounced ribs

Genera *Spialia* and *Erynnis*

Genera *Pyrgus* and *Heteropterus*

Genera *Carcharodus* and *Muschampia*

KEY TO THE MAIN EGG TYPES

8/10 Eggs with a swollen disc shape and coarse ornamentation, laid singly or in very small numbers (a few units)

Large, polygonal pits cover the entire egg surface

Aligned circular pits in radiating patterns

Most species in genus *Lycaena* (here Small, Purple-edged, and Violet Coppers)

Large Copper

9/10 Eggs with a depressed or flattened disc shape and fine or absent ornamentation, laid singly or in very small numbers (a few units)

Smooth egg surface

Large, triangular ornamentations

Genus *Thymelicus*

Genus *Lysandra* (here Provence Chalkhill Blue and Chalkhill Blue)

Very small polygonal ornamentations

Most other Lycaenid genera, except *Satyrium, Thecla, Laeosopis,* and *Neozephyrus* (here Common, Holly, Alpine, and Chequered Blues)

10/10 Eggs with a depressed or flattened disc shape and fine or absent ornamentation, laid singly or in very small numbers (a few units) on tree or bush stems or buds

Small polygonal ornamentations

Egg surface covered with small well-defined holes.

Egg with a very flattened disc shape

Black, Blue-spot, Sloe, Ilex, and False Ilex Hairstreaks

Brown and Purple Hairstreaks

White-letter Hairstreak

Bibliography

BOOKS

Browning P.R.G. *Butterflies of the Iberian Peninsula.* Self-edited work (2019), 302 pp.

Essayan R., Jugan D., Mora F., Ruffoni A., and Collectif Bourgogne Nature. *Atlas des papillons de jour et zygènes de Bourgogne et Franche-Comté.* Éditions Bourgogne Nature (2013), 494 pp.

Gergely P. *Butterflies of Central Europe and Britain, a Photographic Guide.* Self-edited work (2021), 64 pp.

Haahtela T., Saarinen K., Ojalainen P., and Aarnio H. *Guide photo des papillons d'Europe.* Éditions Delachaux et Niestlé (2017), 384 pp.

Lafranchis T. *Les Papillons de jour de France, Belgique et Luxemboug et leurs chenilles.* Éditions Biotope (2000), 448 pp.

Lafranchis T. *Papillons d'Europe.* Éditions Diatheo (2007), 380 pp.

Lafranchis T. *Papillons de France: Guide de détermination des papillons diurnes.* Éditions Diatheo (2016), 351 pp.

Lafranchis T., Jutzeler D., Guillosson J.-Y., Kan P., and Kan B. *La vie des papillons. Écologie, biologie et comportement des Rhopalocères de France.* Éditions Diatheo (2015), 752 pp. + CD ROM.

Leraut P. *Papillons de jour d'Europe et des contrées voisines.* Éditions NAP (2016), 1,100 pp.

Moussus J. P., Lorin T., and Cooper A. *Guide pratique des papillons de jour.* Tous les Papilionoidea de France métropolitaine. Éditions Delachaux et Niestlé (2022), 416 pp.

Pamperis L. N. *The Butterflies of Greece.* New Maps Distribution of Species 3.3', New Map 3.4' New Chart 4.15', and New Chart 4.16'. Online (2019), 250 pp.

Settele J., Kudrna O., Harpke A., Kuhn I., van Swaay C., Verovnik R., Warren M., Wiemers M., Hanspach J., Hickler T., Kuhn E., van Halder I., Veling K., Vliegenthart A., Wynhof I., and Schweiger O. *Climatic Risk Atlas of European Butterflies.* Éditions Pensoft Publishers (2008), 710 pp.

Tolman T. and Lewington R. *Guide des papillons d'Europe et d'Afrique du Nord.* Éditions Delachaux et Niestlé (2010), 320 pp.

Tolman T. and Lewington R. *Guide Delachaux des papillons de France.* Éditions Delachaux et Niestlé (2015), 224 pp.

GENERAL ARTICLES

Clarke H. E. "A Provisional Checklist of European Butterfly Larval Foodplants". *Nota Lepidopterologica* (2022), **45**, 139–167.

Dapporto L. et al. "Integrating Three Comprehensive Data Sets Shows That Mitochondrial DNA Variation Is Linked to Species Traits and Paleogeographic Events in European Butterflies". *Molecular Ecology Resources* (2019), **19**, 1623–1636.

Dupont P., Demerges D., Drouet E., and Luquet G. C. "Révision systématique, taxinomique et nomenclaturale des Rhopalocera et des Zygaenidae de France métropolitaine. Conséquences sur l'acquisition et la gestion des données d'inventaire". Rapport MMNHN-SPN (2013), **19**, 201 pp.

Lafranchis T. "Notes on the Biology of Some Butterflies in Greece (Lepidoptera: Papilionoidea)". *Entomologist's Gazette* (2019), **70**.

Middleton-Welling J. et al. "A New Comprehensive Trait Database of European and Maghreb Butterflies, Papilionoidea". *Scientific Data* (2020), **7**, 351.

Schweiger O. et al. "CLIMBER: Climatic Niche Characteristics of the Butterflies in Europe". *ZooKeys* (2014), **367**, 65–84.

Shaw M. R., Stefanescu C., and van Nouhuis S. "Parasitoids of European Butterflies", *in Ecology of Butterflies in Europe*, eds. Settele J., Shreeve T., Konvicka M., and Van Dyck H. *Cambridge University Press* (2009), 130–156.

Wiemers M. et al. "An Updated Checklist of the European Butterflies (Lepidoptera, Papilionoidea)". *ZooKeys* (2018), **811**, 9–45.

Wiemers M. et al. "A Complete Time-Calibrated Multi-Gene Phylogeny of the European Butterflies". *ZooKeys* (2020), **938**, 97–124.

INTRODUCTION

Dapporto L. "Speciation in Mediterranean Refugia and Post-Glacial Expansion of *Zerynthia polyxena* (Lepidoptera, Papilionidae)". *Journal of Zoological Systematics and Evolutionary Research* (2010), **48**, 229–237.

Essens T. et al. "Ecological Determinants of Butterfly Vulnerability Across the European Continent". *Journal of Insect Conservation* (2017), **21**, 439–450.

Maes D. et al. "Integrating National Red Lists for Prioritising Conservation Actions for European Butterflies". *Journal of Insect Conservation* (2019), **23**.

MacArthur R. et al. *The Theory of Island Biogeography*. Princeton University Press (1967), 203 pp.

Schmitt T. "Molecular Biogeography of Europe: Pleistocene Cycles and Postglacial Trends". *Frontiers in Zoology* (2007), **4**, 11.

Schmitt T. "Biogeographical and Evolutionary Importance of the European High Mountain Systems". *Frontiers in Zoology* (2009), **6**, 9.

Schmitt T. "Molecular Biogeography of the High Mountain Systems of Europe: An Overview", *in High Mountain Conservation in a Changing World*, eds. Catalan J., Ninot J. M., and Merce Aniz M. Springer (CC-BY). (2017), 413 pp.

Schmitt T. et al. "Extra-Mediterranean Refugia: The Rule and Not the Exception?" *Frontiers in Zoology* (2012), **9**, 22.

Schmitt T. et al. "Effects of Recent and Past Climatic Shifts on the Genetic Structure of the High Mountain Yellow-spotted Ringlet Butterfly *Erebia manto* (Lepidoptera, Satyrinae): A Conservation Problem". *Global Change Biology* (2014), **20**, 2045–2061.

Schmitt T. et al. "Species Radiation in the Alps: Multiple Range Shifts Caused Diversification in Ringlet Butterflies in the European High Mountains". *Organisms Diversity and Evolution* (2016), **16**, 791–808.

Van Swaay C. et al. "Biotope Use and Trends of European Butterflies". *Journal of Insect Conservation* (2006), **10**, 189–209.

Van Swaay C. et al. "European Red List of Butterfies". *Luxembourg: Publications Office of the European Union* (2010).

Wiemers M. "The Butterflies of the Canary Islands: A Survey on Their Distribution, Biology and Ecology (Lepidoptera: Papilionoidea and Hesperioidea)". *Linneana Belgica* (1995), **2**, 63–118.

Zinetti F. et al. "When the Rule Becomes the Exception. No Evidence of Gene Flow between Two *Zerynthia* Cryptic Butterflies Suggests the Emergence of a New Model Group". *PLoS ONE* (2013), **8** (6), e65746.

SKIPPERS

Albrecht M. et al. "Observations on the Ecology and Habitat of *Carcharodus stauderi* Reverdin, 1913 on the Greek Island of Kalymnos (Lepidoptera: Hesperiidae)". *Nachrichten des Entomologischen Vereins Apollo* (2013), **34**, 1–8.

Cock M.J.W. "Observations on the Biology of *Pelopidas thrax* (Hübner) (Lepidoptera: Hesperiidae: Hesperiinae) in the Hajar Mountains, Oman". *Tribulus* (2009), **18**, 42–49.

Costache E. et al. "The Distribution of the Hesperiidae (Lepidoptera) Family in Romania". *Entomologica Romanica* (2019), **23**, 27–48.

Cuvelier S. "*Pelopidas thrax*, a New Species for the Island of Kós and an Update of Its Distribution in Greece (Lepidoptera: Hesperioidea and Papilionoidea)". *Phegea* (2009), **37**.

Cuvelier S. et al. "Notes and Recent Observations Concerning *Borbo borbonica* (Lepidoptera: Hesperiidae) in Andalucía (Spain)". *Phegea* (2015), **43** (3).

De Jong R. "Notes on the Genus *Thymelicus* Hübner (Lepidoptera, Hesperiidae)". *Nota Lepidopterologica* (1984), **7**, 148–163.

Dinca V. et al. "The Distribution, Ecology and Conservation Status of the Spinose Skipper *Muschampia Cribrellum* (Eversmann, 1841) at the Western Limit of Its Range in Europe (Hesperiidae)". *Nota Lepidopterologica* (2010), **33**, 39–57.

Eeles P. "A Study of the Life Cycle of the Chequered Skipper Butterfly *Carterocephalus palaemon* (Pallas)" [Online] (2016). Available at www.dispar.org/reference.php?id=119.

Fenberg F. B. et al. "Exploring the Universal Ecological Responses to Climate Change in a Univoltine Butterfly". *Journal of Animal Ecology* (2016), **85**, 739–748.

Hernandez Roldan J. et al. "Natural History, Immature Stage Morphology, and Taxonomic Status of the Threatened Skipper *Pyrgus cinarae* (Rambur, 1839) in the Iberian Peninsula (Lepidoptera: Hesperiidae)". *Nota Lepidopterologica* (2012), **35**, 3–18.

Hernandez Roldan J. et al. "Integrative Analyses Unveil Speciation Linked to Host Plant Shift in *Spialia* Butterflies". *Molecular Ecology* (2016), **25**. 10.1111/mec.13756.

Hernandez Roldan J. et al. "Natural History and Immature Stage Morphology of *Spialia* Swinhoe, 1912 in the Iberian Peninsula (Lepidoptera: Hesperiidae)". *Nota Lepidopterologica* (2018), **41**, 1–22.

Hinojosa J. et al. "Overlooked Cryptic Diversity in *Muschampia* (Lepidoptera: Hesperiidae) Adds Two Species to the European Butterfly Fauna". *Zoological Journal of the Linnean Society* (2021). 0.1093/zoolinnean/zlaa171.

Hoejgaard K. et al. "Rediscovering *Muschampia tessellum* ([Hübner, [1803]) (Lep.: Hesperiidae) in Bulgaria with Additional Notes on *M. cribrellum* (Eversmann, 1814) from the Eastern Balkan (Stara Planina) Mountains". *Entomologist's Record and Journal of Variation* (2011), **123**, 147–150.

Lafranchis T. "Biologie, écologie et répartition d'*Erynnis marloyi* (Boisduval, 1834) en Grece (Lepidoptera: Hesperiidae)". *Linneana Belgica* (2003), **19**, 135–139.

Lawson C. et al. "The Status and Conservation of the Silver-spotted Skipper *Hesperia comma* in South-East England 2000–2009". University of Exeter, Exeter, UK (2013).

Munoz Sariot M. G. "Ciclo biológico, morfología de los estadios preimaginales y nuevos datos sobre la distribución de *Borbo borbonica zelleri* (Lederer, 1855) (Lepidoptera: Hesperiidae) en la provincia de Cádiz, Espana". *Revista gaditana de Entomología* (2013), **4**, 137–158.

Obregon R. et al. "Updating Distribution of *Borbo Borbonica* (Boisduval, 1833) in Southern Iberian Peninsula (Lepidoptera, Hesperiidae): Potential and Future Distribution Models". *North-Western Journal of Zoology* (2016), **2**, 205–212.

Popovic M. et al. "On the Extremely Rich Butterfly Fauna (Lepidoptera: Rhopalocera) of the South-Eastern Foothills of Stara Planina Mts in Serbia". *Phegea* (2013), **41**.

Popović M. et al. "First Records of *Pyrgus cinarae* (Lepidoptera: Hesperiidae) in Serbia". *Acta Entomologica Serbica* (2014), **19**, 45–51.

Rakosy L. "*Carcharodus orientalis* Reverdin, 1913 und *Melitaea (punica) telona* Fruhstorfer, 1908 (Lepidoptera: Hesperiidae, Nymphalidae) in der Fauna Rumaniens". *Entomologica Romanica* (2001), **5**, 45–49.

Willis S. et al. "Assisted Colonization in a Changing Climate: A Test-study Using Two U.K. Butterflies". *Conservation Letters* (2009), **2**, 46–52.

Zhang J. et al. "A Genomic Perspective on the Taxonomy of the Subtribe *Carcharodina* (Lepidoptera: Hesperiidae: Carcharodini)". *Zootaxa* (2020), **4748**, 182–194.

PAPILIONIDS

Coutsis J. G. et al. "Differences in the Male and Female Genitalia Between *Iphiclides podalirius* and *Iphiclides feisthamelii*, Further Supporting Species Status for the Latter (Lepidoptera: Papilionidae)". *Phegea* (2011), **39**.

Ghesini S. et al. "A Successful Habitat Patch Creation for *Zerynthia Cassandra*". *Bulletin of Insectology* (2019), **72**, 261–266.

Lafranchis T. "Biologie et écologie en Grece de la Diane *Zerynthia polyxena* (Denis and Schiffermüller, 1775) (Lepidoptera, Papilionidae)". (2013).

Lafranchis T. et al. "Le contact *Iphiclides feisthamelii – I. podalirius* Statut de ces deux taxons". *Revue de l'Association roussillonnaise d'entomologie* (2015), **24**, 3–24.

Lukhtanov V. A. et al. "A Taxonomic Structure and Wing Pattern Evolution in the *Parnassius mnemosyne* Species Complex (Lepidoptera, Papilionidae)". *Insects* (2023), **14**.

Slancarova J. *et al.* "Co-occurrence of Three Aristolochia-feeding Papilionids (*Archon apollinus*, *Zerynthia polyxena* and *Zerynthia cerisy*) in Greek Thrace". *Journal of Natural History* (2015), **49**, 1825–1848.

PIERIDS

Benton E. *et al.* "Observations on *Euchloe bazae* Fabiano, 1993 (Lepidoptera: Pieridae) in Southern Spain, April 1998". *Entomologist's Gazette* (2000), **51**, 53–55.

Gascoigne-Pees M. *et al.* "The Distribution, Life Cycle, Ecology and Present Status of *Leptidea morsei* (Fenton 1882) in Slovenia with Additional Observations from Romania (Lepidoptera: Pieridae)". *Nachrichten des entomologischen Vereins Apollo.* (2008), **N.F.: 29**, 113–121.

Gutierrez D. *et al.* "Climate Conditions and Resource Availability Drive Return Elevational Migrations in a Single-Brooded Insect". *Oecologia* (2014), **175**, 861–873.

John E. *et al.* "A Review of Mediterranean Records of *Catopsilia florella* (Lepidoptera: Pieridae, Coliadinae), with Notes on the Spring 2019 Arrival in Cyprus of This Afrotropical Migrant". *Phegea* (2019), **47**.

Marhoul P. *et al.* "Action Plan for the Conservation of the Danube Clouded Yellow *Colias myrmidone* in the European Union". European Commission (2012).

Sairot M.G.M. "Descripción del huevo y estadios larvarios de Elphinstonia Bazae (Fabiano, 1993) (Lepidoptera: Pieridae)". *Boletín de la Sociedad Entomológica Aragonesa.* (2016), **59**, 207–211.

Sala-Garcia J. *et al.* "Phylogeography and diversification of the *Pieris napi* species group in the Western Palaearctic". *bioRxiv* 2025.01.31.634921

Warnock N. "The Ecology and Conservation of *Leptidea reali* (Real's Wood White) in Northern Ireland". Msc Ecological Management and Conservation Biology. Queen's University Belfast (2008).

LYCAENIDS

Abbes K. *et al.* "The Pomegranate Butterfly *Deudorix livia* (Lepidoptera: Lycaenidae): An Emerging Pest on Dates in Tunisia". *EPPO Bulletin* (2020), **50**.

Anastassiu H. T. *et al.* "*Polyommatus* (*Neolysandra*) *coelestina* from Central Greece (Lepidoptera: Lycaenidae)". *Phegea* (2004), **32**, 153–155.

Arranz J.C.V. *et al.* "Primeros registros de *Lycaena bleusei* Oberthür, 1884 en las provincias de Burgos y León (Castilla y León: Espana) (Lepidoptera: Lycaenidae)". *Arquivos Entomologicos Gallegos* (2016), **16**, 217–224.

Benyamini D. *et al.* "The Biology of the Cyprus Endemic Blue *Glaucopsyche paphos* Chapman, 1920 (Lepidoptera: Lycaenidae, Polyommatinae)". *Entomologist's Gazette* (2018), **69**, 151–165.

Buckley J. *et al.* "Evidence for Evolutionary Change Associated with the Recent Range Expansion of the British Butterfly, *Aricia agestis*, in Response to Climate Change". *Molecular Ecology* (2011), **21**, 267–280.

Bury J. *et al.* "New Data on the Biology of Ten Lycaenid Butterflies (Lepidoptera: Lycaenidae) of the Genera *Tomares* Rambur, 1840, *Pseudophilotes* Beuret, 1958, *Polyommatus* Latreille, 1804, and *Plebejus* Kluk, 1780 from the Crimea and Their Attending Ants (Hymenoptera: Formicidae)". *Acta Entomologica Silesiana* (2015), **23**, 1–16.

Crişan A. *et al.* "The Protected Transylvanian Blue (*Pseudophilotes bavius hungarica*): New Information on the Morphology and Biology". *Nota Lepidopterologica* (2011), **34**, 163–168.

De Freina J. J. "Zoogeographische, ökologische und taxonomische Studie zu den Zwillingsarten *Chilades trochylus* Freyer, 1845 und *Chilades putli* Kollar, 1848 (Lepidoptera: Lycaenidae, Lycaeninae, Polyommatini)". *Nachrichten des entomologischen Vereins Apollo* (2014), **34**, 145–160.

Diringer Y. "Chronique d'élevage 3: L'élevage des coridon espagnols: *Polyommatus* (*Lysandra*) *albicans* (HERRICH-SCHÄFFER, 1852) et *Polyommatus* (*Lysandra*) *caelestissima* (VERITY, 1921) (Lepidoptera: Lycaenidae)". *Lépidoptères – Revue des Lépidoptéristes de France* (2010), **19**, 50–59.

Diringer Y. "L'élevage du cuivré turc, *Lycaena candens* (Herrich-Schäffer, 1844) (Lepidoptera: Lycaenidae)". *Revue des Lépidoptéristes de France* (2020), **29**, 49–56.

Dumont D. "Revision du genre *Iolana* Bethune-Baker, 1914 (Lepidoptera: Lycaenidae)". *Linneana Belgica* (2004), **19**, 332–358.

Fernandez R. et al. "*Polyommatus (Agrodiaetus) fabressei* (Oberthur, 1910) y *P. (A.) ripartii* (Freyer, 1830) en el centro de la Península Ibérica. Provincia de Guadalajara (Espana). Distribución geográfica y aspectos de su morfología, ecología y biología. (Lepidoptera: Lycaenidae)". *SHILAP Revisita de Lepidopterologia* (2019), **47**, 449–468.

Fiedler K. et al. "Oviposition Behaviour in *Lycaena thetis* Klug (Lepidoptera: Lycaenidae)". *Nota Lepidopterologica* (1994), **17**, 25–29.

Fischer K. et al. "Partial Biennialism in Alpine *Lycaena Hippothoe* (Lycaenidae: Lycaenini)?" *Nota Lepidopterologica* (2001), **24**, 73–76.

Fischer K. et al. "Sexual Differences in Lifehistory Traits in the Butterfly *Lycaena tityrus*: A Comparison Between Direct and Diapause Development". *Entomologia Experimentalis et Applicata* (2001), **100**, 325–330.

Galanos C. "Bionomics of *Freyeria trochylus* (Freyer, 1844) and *Zizeeria karsandra* (Moore, 1865) (Lepidoptera, Lycaenidae) on Rodos Island, Greece". *Nota Lepidopterologica* (2020), **43**, 139–150.

Gascoigne-Pees M. "The Life Cycle and Ecology of *Azanus ubaldus* (Stoll, 1782) (Lepidoptera: Lycaenidae) on Gran Canaria". **67**, 153–163.

Gil-T. F. "*Polyommatus (Plebicula) sagratrox* (Aistleitner, 1986) ecología, morfología comparada de sus estadios preimaginales con los de *Polyommatus (Plebicula) golgus* (Hübner, 1813), taxonomía y nuevos argumentos para su validez específica (Lepidoptera, Lycaenidae)". *Boletín de la SEA* (2003), **33**, 219–227.

Grill A. et al. "Confirmation du status specifique de *Polyommatus gennargenti* (Leigheb, 1987) de Sardaigne comparé a *Polyommatus coridon* (Poda, 1761) de la région de Schaffhousen (CH) par élevage parrallele (Lepidoptera: Lycaenidae) 1re partie". *Linneana Belgica* (2003), **19**, 109–118.

Haaland C. "Abundances and Movement of the Scarce Copper Butterfly (*Lycaena virgaureae*) on Future Building Sites at a Settlement Fringe in Southern Sweden". *Journal of Insect Conservation* (2015), **19**, 255–264.

Hinojosa J. et al. "Rapid Colour Shift by Reproductive Character Displacement in *Cupido* Butterflies". *Molecular Ecology* (2020), **29**, 1–14.

Ignatov A. et al. "*Chilades trochylus* (Freyer, [1845]) (Lep.: Lycaenidae) Confirmed for the Bulgaria Fauna and Doubt Cast on Earlier Records of This and Other Species". *Entomologist's Record and Journal of Variation* (2013), **125**, 119–122.

John E. et al. "*Chilades galba* (Lederer, 1855) and *Aporia crataegi* (Linnaeus, 1758): Significant Contributions to the Cyprus Butterfly Recording Scheme, April / May 2008". *Atalanta* (2008), **39**, 165–171.

Kan P. et al. "La vie secrete de *Laeosopis evippus* (HÜBNER, 1793) (Lepidoptera: Lycaenidae)". *Revue des Lépidoptéristes de France* (2009), **18**, 90–97.

Koren T. "New Data about the Distribution of Anomalous Blue *Polyommatus admetus* (Esper, 1783) (Lepidoptera: Lycaenidae) in Croatia". *Acta entomologica Serbica* (2010), **15**, 221–226.

Koren T. et al. "New Records of Grecian Copper, *Lycaena ottomana* (Lefebvre, 1830) (Lep.: Lycaenidae) in Croatia". *Entomologist's Record and Journal of Variation.* (2012), **124**, 215–223.

Larsen T. et al. "Notes on the Ecology, Biology and Taxonomy of *Apharitis acamas* (Klug) (Lepidoptera: Lycaenidae)". *Entomologist's Gazette* (1982), **33**, 163–168.

Leigheb G. et al. "*Kretania psylorita* Freyer (Lepidoptera, Lycaenidae). Discovery of a New Locality in Crete". *Nota Lepidopterologica* (1990), **13**, 242–245.

Leigheb G. et al. "Observations on the Biology and Distribution of *Pseudophilotes barbagiae* (Lycaenidae, Polyommatini)". *Nota Lepidopterologica* (1998), **21**, 66–73.

Martins R.F.R. "On the Evolutionary History of the Iberian Sooty Copper Butterflies". *Mestrado em Biologia Evolutiva e do Desenvolvimento*, Universidade et Lisboa (2011).

Montiel C. et al. "Nota: Nuevas citas de *Scolitantides (Pseudophilotes) abencerragus* (Pierret, 1837) en la provincia de Jaén, Andalucía (Espana) (Lepidoptera: Lycaenidae)". *Arquivos Entomolóxicos* (2015), **14**, 281–284.

Munguira M. L. et al. "Species Recovery Plan for the Zullichi's Blue (*Agriades zullichi*)". *Butterfly Conservation Europe* (2015).

Munguira M. L. et al. "Species Recovery Plan for the Sierra Nevada Blue *Polyommatus (Plebicula) golgus*". *Butterfly Conservation Europe* (2015).

Nazari V. et al. "Co-Evolution of *Iolana* Blues with Their Host Plants and the Higher Phylogeny of Subtribe *Scolitantidina* (Lepidoptera, Lycaenidae)". *Diversity* (2024), **16**.

Obregon R. et al. "Biología, ecología y modelo de distribución de las especies del género *Pseudophilotes* Beuret, 1958 en Andalucía (Sur de Espana) (Lepidoptera: Lycaenidae)". *SHILAP Revisita de Lepidopterologia* (2014), **42**, 501–515.

Parmentier L. et al. "Integrative Analysis Reveals Cryptic Speciation Linked to Habitat Differentiation within Albanian Populations of the Anomalous Blues (Lepidoptera, Lycaenidae, *Polyommatus* Latreille, 1804)". *CompCytogen* (2022), **16**, 211–242.

Quacchia A. et al. "Can the Geranium Bronze, *Cacyreus marshalli*, Become a Threat for European Biodiversity?" *Biodiversity and Conservation* (2008), **17**, 1429–1437.

Rakosy L. et al. "Rediscovering *Tomares nogelii dobrogensis* Caradja, 1895 in Romania". *Entomologica Romanica* (2016), **19**, 13–16.

Sanetra M. et al. "Behaviour and Morphology of an Aphytophagous Lycaenid Caterpillar: *Cigaritis* (*Apharitis*) *acamas* Klug, 1834 (Lepidoptera: Lycaenidae)". *Nota Lepidopterologica* (1996), **18**, 57–76.

Sanudo-Restrepo C. et al. "Biogeography and Systematics of *Aricia* Butterflies (Lepidoptera, Lycaenidae)". *Molecular Phylogenetics and Evolution* (2012), **66**, 369–379.

Seguna A. et al. "On the Occurrence of the *Azanus ubaldus* (Stoll, 1782) in the Maltese Islands (Lepidoptera: Lycaenidae)". *SHILAP Revisita de Lepidopterologia* (2017), **45**, 213–216.

Tolman T. "Concerning the Biology and Conservation of *Polyommatus* (*Agrodiaetus*) *iphigenia* (Herrich–Schäffer, [1847]) in Greece (Lepidoptera: Lycaenidae)". *Phegea* (1995), **23**, 113–117.

Tot I. et al. "Little Tiger Blue, *Tarucus balkanicus* (Freyer, 1845) – A New Butterfly Species in the Fauna of Serbia (Lepidoptera: Lycaenidae)". *Acta Entomologica Serbica* (2021), **26**, 1–4.

Verovnik R. "The Presence of *Plebeius pyrenaicus dardanus* (Freyer, 1845) (Lepidoptera: Lycaenidae) on Mt Čvrsnica in Bosnia and Herzegovina, with Notes on the Butterfly Fauna of this Mountain". *Entomologist's Gazette* (2004), **55**, 29–34.

Verovnik R. et al. "Contribution to the Knowledge of the Butterfly Fauna of the Republic of Macedonia (Lepidoptera: Papilionoidea, and Hesperioidea)". *Acta Entomologica Slovenica* (2010), **18**, 31–46.

Vicente-Arranz J. C. et al. "Geographic Distribution, Biology, Habitat and Conservation of *Thecla betulae* (Linnaeus 1758), in the Central Mountain System (Iberian Peninsula) (Lepidoptera: Lycaenidae)". *SHILAP Revista de Lepidopterologia* (2013), **41**, 541–557.

Vishnevskaya M. et al. "Karyosystematics and Molecular Taxonomy of the Anomalous Blue Butterflies (Lepidoptera, Lycaenidae) from the Balkan Peninsula". *Comparative Cytogenetics* (2016), **10**, 1–85.

NYMPHALIDS

Albre J. et al. "Taxonomic Notes on the Species of the *Erebia tyndarus* Group (Lepidoptera, Nymphalidae, Satyrinae)". *Revue des Lépidoptéristes de France* (2008), **17**, 12–28.

Augustijnen H. et al. "Living on the Edge: Genomic and Ecological Delineation of Cryptic Lineages in the High-elevation Specialist *Erebia nivalis*". *Insect Conservation and Diversity* (2024), **17**, 526–542.

Back W. et al. "Eine neue Art der Gattung *Euphydryas* Scudder, 1872 aus Nordwest-Italien". *Atalanta* (2015), **46,** 111–116.

Bouaouina S. et al. "Asynchronous Life Cycles Contribute to Reproductive Isolation Between Two Alpine Butterflies". *Evolution Letters* (2023), **7**, 436–446.

Brunton C.F.A. et al. "Altitude-dependent Variation in Wing Pattern in the Corsican Butterfly *Coenonympha corinna* Hubner (Satyridae)". *Biological Journal of the Linnean Society* (1991), **42**, 367–378.

Bury J. "Common Glider – *Neptis sappho* (Pallas, 1771) (Lepidoptera: Nymphalidae) in South-eastern Poland: Another Case of Oversight or

Rapid Range Expansion of a Species Considered Extinct?" *Annals of the Upper Silesian Museum in Bytom Entomology* (2020), **29**, 1–20.

Capblancq T. *et al.* "Hybridization Promotes Speciation in *Coenonympha* Butterflies". *Molecular Ecology* (2015), **24**, 6209–6222.

Capblancq T. *et al.* "Speciation with Gene Flow: Evidence from a Complex of Alpine Butterflies (*Coenonympha*, Satyridae)". *Ecology and Evolution* (2019), **9**, 6444–6457.

Colosimo G. "Inferring Phylogeny of the Genus *Maniola* (Lepidoptera, Nymphalidae, Satyrinae) through COI Barcode Sequence". These, Université de Rome "Tor Vergata" (2008).

Cupedo F. *et al.* "The Intraspecific Structure of the Yellow-spotted Ringlet *Erebia manto* (Denis and Schiffermüller [1775]), with Special Reference to the *Bubastis* Group: An Integration of Morphology, Allozyme and mtDNA Data (Lepidoptera, Nymphalidae, Satyrinae)". *Nota Lepidopterologica* (2020), **43**, 43–60.

Cupedo F. *et al.* "Mitochondrial DNA-based Phylogeography of the Large Ringlet *Erebia euryale* (Esper, 1805) Suggests Recurrent Alpine-Carpathian Disjunctions during Pleistocene (Nymphalidae, Satyrinae)". *Nota Lepidopterologica* (2022), **45**, 65–86.

Dapporto L. *et al.* "The Thorny Subject of Insular Endemic Taxonomy: Morphometrics Reveal No Evidence of Speciation between *Coenonympha corinna* and *Coenonympha elbana* Butterflies (Lepidoptera: Nymphalidae)". *Zootaxa* (2008), **1755**, 47–56.

Dincă V. *et al.* "The Conundrum of Species Delimitation: A Genomic Perspective on a Mitogenetically Super-variable Butterfly". *Proceedings of the Royal Society B* (2019), **286**, 20191311.

Eeles P. "The Hibernaculum Habits of the White Admiral Butterfly *Limenitis camilla* (Linnaeus)" [online] (2016). Available on www.dispar.org/reference. php?id=120.

Fernandez-Rubio F. *et al.* "Taxonomic Situation of the Species of the Genus *Pararge* Hübner, 1819 – *P. aegeria*, *P. xiphia*, and *P. xiphioides* (Lepidoptera: Satyridae) in the Macaronesian Islands". *Bol. Mus. Mun. Funchal* (1995), **47**, 39–50.

Gascoigne-Pees M. *et al.* "Notes on the Lifecycle of *Melitaea arduinna* (Esper, 1783) ("Freyer's Fritillary") (Lepidoptera: Nymphalidae)

with Further Records from SE Serbia". *Nachrichten des entomologischen Vereins Apollo* (2012), **33**, 9–14.

Gascoigne-Pees M. *et al.* "The Lifecycle of *Nymphalis vaualbum* ([Denis and Schiffermüller], 1775) in Serbia, Including New Records and a Review of Its Present Status in Europe (Lepidoptera: Nymphalidae)". *Nachrichten des entomologischen Vereins Apollo* (2014), **35**, 77–96.

Gascoigne-Pees M. *et al.* "The Lifecycle and Ecology of *Pseudochazara amymone* (Brown, 1976) (Lepidoptera: Nymphalidae, Satyrinae)". *Nachrichten des entomologischen Vereins Apollo* (2014), **35**, 129–138.

Gil-T F. "Compared Morphology and Distribution of the Taxa Described of *Pseudochazara williamsi* (Romei, 1927) [= "*Pseudochazara hippolyte*" Esper from Spain] Are They Valid Subspecies or Only the Result of Phenotypic Plasticity (Ecological Forms)?" *Atalanta* (2017), **48**, 188–196.

Gordon I. J. *et al.* "Pupal Diapause in the Diadem Butterfly, *Hypolimnas misippus* (Lepidoptera: Nymphalidae)". *Journal of East African Natural History* (2014), **103**, 69–72.

Habel J. C. *et al.* "Biogeographical Dynamics of the Spanish Marbled White *Melanargia ines* (Lepidoptera: Satyridae) in the Western Mediterranean: Does the Atlanto-Mediterranean Refuge Exist?". *Biological Journal of the Linnean Society* (2011), **104**, 828–837.

Hinojosa J. C. *et al.* "*Erebia epiphron* and *Erebia orientalis*: Sibling Butterfly Species with Contrasting Histories". *Biological Journal of the Linnean Society* (2018), **20**, 1–11.

Hinojosa J. C. *et al.* "Integrative Taxonomy Reveals a New *Melitaea* (Lepidoptera: Nymphalidae) Species Widely Distributed in the Iberian Peninsula". *Insect Systematics and Diversity* (2022), **6**, 1–9.

John E. and Parker R. "Dispersal of *Hipparchia cypriensis* (Holik, 1949) (Lepidoptera: Nymphalidae, Satyridae) in Cyprus, with Notes on Its Ecology and Life-history". *Entomologist's Gazette* (2002), **53**, 3–18.

Jospin A. *et al.* "Genomic Evidence for Three Distinct Species in the *Erebia manto* Complex in Central Europe (Lepidoptera, Nymphalidae)". *Conservation Genetics* (2023), **24**, 293–304.

Jutzeler D. *et al.* "Biology of *Neptis sappho* (PALLAS, 1771) Based on the Monograph by Timpe and Timpe (1993) and Its Actual Distribution and Conservation Status in Austria, Italy and Slovenia (Lepidoptera: Nymphalidae)". *Linneana Belgica* (2000), **17**, 315–332.

Jutzeler D. *et al.* "*Melitaea aetherie* (HUBNER, 1826) de Sicile et d'Afrique du Nord: Nouvelles données écologiques, géonémiques et taxinomiques induites par un élevage de la souche sicilienne (*Lepidoptera: Nymphalidae*)". *Linneana Belgica* (2004), **19**, 361–374.

Jutzeler D. *et al.* "Biologie, répartition, histoire nomenclaturale et taxinomie d'*Erebia aethiopellus* HOFFMANNSEG (1806) (*Lepidoptera: Nymphalidae, Satyrinae*)". *Linneana Belgica* (2005), **20**, 75–87.

Jutzeler D. *et al.* "Essai d'appréciation du statut taxinomique de *Coenonympha* (*Glycerion*) *iphioides* STAUDINGER (1870) résultant d'un élevage provenant de la province espagnole de Burgos avec rappel des formes locales décrites (*Lepidoptera: Nymphalidae, Satyrinae*)". *Linneana Belgica* (2006), **20**, 215–228.

Konvicka M. *et al.* "Early-spring Floods Decrease the Survival of Hibernating Larvae of a Wetland-inhabiting Population of *Neptis rivularis* (Lepidoptera: Nymphalidae)". *Acta Zoologica Academiae Scientiarum Hungaricae* (2002), **48**, 79–88.

Korb S. K. *et al.* "Cluster Biodiversity as a Multidimensional Structure Evolution Strategy: Checkerspot Butterflies of the Group *Euphydryas aurinia* (Rottemburg, 1775) (Lepidoptera: Nymphalidae)". *Systematic Entomology* (2016), **41**, 441–457.

Koren T. "The Lattice Brown, *Kirinia roxelana* (Cramer, 1777) (Lepidoptera: Nymphalidae), Rediscovered in Croatia after More Than a Century". *Natura Croatica* (2015), **24**, 317–321.

Louy D. *et al.* "Out of the Alps: The Biogeography of a Disjunctly Distributed Mountain Butterfly, the Almond-Eyed Ringlet *Erebia alberganus* (Lepidoptera, Satyrinae)". *Journal of Heredity* (2014), **105**, 28–38.

Lukhtanov V. *et al.* "Taxonomic Rearrangement of the *Erebia tyndarus* Species Group (Lepidoptera, Nymphalidae, Satyrinae) Based on an Analysis of *COI* Barcodes, Morphology, and Geographic Distribution". *Folia Biologica (Kraków)* (2019), **67**, 149–157.

Mazel R. *et al.* "Le complexe *Coenonympha glycerion – iphioides*: Un modele de spéciation par hybridation?" *Revue de l'Association roussillonnaise d'entomologie* (2015), **24**, 135–153.

Merit X. *et al.* "Contribution a la connaissance de la faune lépidoptérique du val d'Ossola (Piémont, Italie): 6. – Nouvelles localités de *Neptis rivularis* (Scopoli, 1763) (Lepidoptera: Nymphalidae)". *Revue des lépidoptéristes de France* (2016), **25**, 97–99.

Mutanen M. *et al.* "Allopatry as a Gordian Knot for Taxonomists: Patterns of DNA Barcode Divergence in Arctic-Alpine Lepidoptera". *PLoS ONE* (2012), **7**, e47214.

Predrag J. "*Melitaea arduinna* (Lepidoptera: Nymphalidae): A New Species for Serbia". *Phegea* (2011), **39**, 8–11.

Russell P. *et al.* "The Use of the Pre-imaginal Stages of the Macaronesian *Hipparchia* Species in the Clarification of the Numbers and Ranks of the Taxa Present in Madeira and the Azores Archipelago (*Lepidoptera: Nymphalidae, Satyrinae*). Part 2.2: The Populations of the Central Azores Islands of Terceira, Sao Jorge and Pico". *Linneana Belgica* (2007), **20**, 45–54.

Russell P. *et al.* "The Use of the Pre-imaginal Stages of the Macaronesian *Hipparchia* Species in the Clarification of the Numbers and Ranks of the Taxa Present in Madeira and the Azores Archipelago (*Lepidoptera: Nymphalidae, Satyrinae*). Part 3: The Populations of the Western Azores Islands of Flores and Corvo and General Conclusions". *Linneana Belgica* (2007), **20**, 55–67.

Schmitt T. *et al.* "Upslope Movements and Large Scale Expansions: The Taxonomy and Biogeography of the *Coenonympha arcania – C. darwiniana – C. gardetta* Butterfly Species Complex". *Zoological Journal of the Linnean Society* (2010), **159**, 890–904.

Swengel S. R. *et al.* "Jutta Arctic (*Oeneis jutta*) (Lepidoptera: Nymphalidae) Populations in Central and Northern Wisconsin: Localized Butterfly Populations in a Naturally Fragmented Landscape". *Great Lakes Entomologist* (2013), **46**, 174–192.

Takats K. *et al.* "Partial mtCOI-sequences of Balkanic Species of *Pseudochazara* (Lepidoptera: Nymphalidae, Satyrinae) Reveal Three Well-differentiated Lineages". *Entomologica Romanica* (2015), **19**, 21–40.

Torrado-Blanco L. *et al.* "Phylogeography of the Iberian Endemic Butterfly *Erebia palarica*

Chapman, 1905 (Lepidoptera: Nymphalidae): An Integrative Approach". *Insect Conservation and Diversity* (2024), **17**, 651–675.

Verovnik R. et al. "Wanted! Dead or Alive: The Tale of the Brown's Grayling (*Pseudochazara amymone*)". *Journal of Insect Conservation* (2014), **18**, 675–682.

Vieira V. "*Vanessa virginiensis* (Drury, 1773) in the Azores Islands (Lepidoptera: Nymphalidae)".

SHILAP Revisita de Lepidopterologia (2017), **45**, 75–81.

Weingartner E. et al. "Speciation in *Pararge* (Satyrinae: Nymphalidae) Butterflies – North Africa Is the Source of Ancestral Populations of All Pararge Species". *Systematic Entomology* (2006), **31**, 621–632.

GENITALIA

Anastassiu H. et al. "*Maniola Megala* (Lepidoptera: Nymphalidae, Satyrinae) from the Greek Island of Lésvos: A Historical Review of Past Relevant Publications, and an Illustration and Description of Its Male and Female Genitalia". *Phegea* (2016), **44**.

Coutsis J. G. "The Male and Female Genital Structures of Skippers Currently Placed in the Genus *Carcharodus* Hübner [1819], and Their Taxonomic Significance (Lepidoptera: Hesperiidae, Pyrginae)". *Phegea* (2016), **44**.

Coutsis J. G. et al. "The True Identity of Butterflies Originally Recorded as *Hipparchia* (*Parahipparchia*) *Pellucida* (Stauder, 1923) from the Eastern Aegean Greek Islands of Lézvos and Ikaría (Lepidoptera: Nymphalidae, Satyrinae)". *Phegea* (2018), **46**, 106–109.

Cuvelier S. et al. "New Data Regarding the Butterflies (Lepidoptera: Rhopalocera) of Romania, with Additional Comments (General Distribution in Romania, Habitat Preferences, Threats and Protection) for Ten Localized Romanian Species". *Phegea* (2007), **35**, 93–115.

Delmas S. "Aide a l'identification des *Pyrgus* de France. Premiere partie: Illustration des *genitalia* mâles (Lepidoptera, Hesperiidae)". *Oreina* (2018), **42**, 11–18.

Delmas S. "Aide a l'identification des *Pyrgus* de France. Deuxieme partie: Illustration des *genitalia* femelles (Lepidoptera, Hesperiidae)". *Oreina* (2018), **43**, 13–21.

Dinca V. E. et al. "Complete DNA Barcode Reference Library for a Country's Butterfly Fauna Reveals High Performance for Temperate Europe". *Proceedings of the Royal Society B* (2011), **278**, 347–355.

Eckweiler W. "New Discoveries of *Pseudochazara mamurra amymone* (Brown, 1976) (Lepidoptera: Nymphalidae, Satyrinae)".

Nachrichten des entomologischen Vereins Apollo (2012), **33**, 1–4.

Grill A. et al. "The Shape of Endemics: Notes on Male and Female *Genitalia* in the Genus *Maniola* (Schrank, 1801), (Lepidoptera, Nymphalidae, Satyrinae)". *Contributions to Zoology* (2004), **73**, 293–303.

Jakšić P. "*Melitaea arduinna* (Lepidoptera: Nymphalidae): A New Species for Serbia". *Phegea* (2011), **39**, 8–11.

Macia R. et al. "Designació del lectotipus de *Melitaea ignasiti* (Sagarra, 1926) (Lepidoptera: Nymphalidae: Nymphalinae)". *Butlletí de la Institució Catalana d'Història Natural* (2015), **79**, 141–143.

Nazari V. et al. "Molecular Systematics and Phylogeny of the 'Marbled Whites' (Lepidoptera: Nymphalidae, Satyrinae, *Melanargia* Meigen)". *Systematic Entomology* (2009).

Olivier A. et al. "Taxonomy and Geographical Variation of *Hipparchia mersina* (Staudinger, 1871) with Notes on Its Ecology and Phenology (Lepidoptera: Nymphalidae Satyrinae)". *Phegea* (1989), **17**, 169–221.

Olivier A. et al. "A Revision of the Superspecies *Hipparchia azorina* and of the *Hipparchia aristaeus* Group (Nymphalidae: Satyrinae)". *Nota Lepidopterologica* (1997), **20**, 150–292.

Palmi P. "Farfalle Italiane", www.farfalleitalia.it, accessed in 2022 and 2023.

Takats K. et al. "Partial MtCOI-sequences of Balkanic Species of *Pseudochazara* (Lepidoptera: Nymphalidae, Satyrinae) Reveal Three Well-differentiated Lineages". *Entomologica Romanica* (2015), **19**, 21–40.

www.lepinet.fr: A reference for every lepidopterist. It is the most comprehensive database on butterflies and moths in France, including information on host plants, photographs, and a regularly updated distribution map. In French.

inpn.mnhn.fr: The website of the French National Inventory of Natural Heritage is very useful for distribution maps and taxonomy. In French.

www.eurobutterflies.com: Matt Rowlings offers a comprehensive website with numerous photographs of European butterfly species, helpful comments for their identification, and details on their ecology. In English.

www.lepido.ch: The Lepido.ch group, founded by Michel and Vincent Baudraz, provides numerous resources on the butterflies found in Switzerland, many of which are also present in other European countries. Visitors will find online identification keys, photographs, distribution maps, as well as summaries by habitat type and phenology. In French.

www.pyrgus.de: The absolutely outstanding website of Wolfgang Wagner offers numerous photographs of all stages of development of European butterflies and moths, their habitats, and ecological descriptions. The majority of caterpillar photographs presented in this guide are from this great Lepidoptera enthusiast. In English and German.

diatheo.weebly.com: The website of Tristan Lafranchis and his collaborators, who are among the top French specialists in Lepidoptera, provides updated information, precise distribution maps, articles, videos, and comprehensive bibliographies for French species. In French.

www.european-lepidopteres.fr: The website of Yoann and Jean-Louis Pelouard, dedicated to European Lepidoptera, provides extensive photographic galleries of adults and developmental stages (eggs, caterpillars, and chrysalises). The site also offers visually informative identification sheets, as well as videos and detailed thematic articles on butterfly biology. In French.

www.farfalleitalia.it: Paolo Palmi's website covers species seen in Italy. Beyond photographs of all species and detailed descriptions, this site also presents the genitalia of numerous species with dedicated comments. Many were used to produce the genitalia drawings presented in this guide. In Italian.

lepidoptera.eu: This website, created by Christopher Jonko, offers comprehensive content for numerous European Lepidoptera species. The species presentation is highly visual, combining photographs and diagrams for aid in understanding their ecology. The content is translated into many languages.

www.filming-varwild.com: Pieter and Brigitte Kan, along with the collective they have gathered, offer a website dedicated to the life cycle of French butterflies in Provence. The content is rich, with numerous videos and information concerning the life relationships, particularly with parasitoids, of the butterflies. In French and English.

www.guypadfield.com: Guy Padfield has uploaded his photographs of numerous French and Swiss species, accompanied by comments on their ecology. In English.

www.lepiforum.de: A website founded by a collective primarily composed of German lepidopterists and presided over by Erwin Rennwald. It provides a wealth of information, very up-to-date, concerning the identification criteria of European species, and their ecology, systematics, and taxonomy. In German.

www.lavieb-aile.com: Jean-Yves Cordier's blog offers comprehensive summaries on zoonymy, which is the origin of the names of many butterfly species. In French.

www.biofotoquiz.ch: This site, managed by the Aargau Nature Museum, Naturama, is an ideal place to practise identifying European butterflies during the non-flight season. Numerous quizzes with varying levels of difficulty are provided at the end of the test. In German, French, English, and Italian.

www.vigienature.fr: Vigie Nature is a participatory observatory of French biodiversity that offers various protocols for collecting data, which will then be analyzed by researchers at the National Natural History Museum. Regarding butterflies, the Operation Papillons, the Temporal Monitoring of French Butterflies, and the PROPAGE protocol allow everyone, according to their skills and available time, to participate in this extensive monitoring of French biodiversity. In French.

www.faune-france.org: A national portal that allows everyone to enter their observations online and geolocate them. These observations contribute to a massive database. The data, accessible to all, is a good way to prepare for an outing and participate in a collective effort to monitor our French biodiversity. In both French and English.

https://ftp.funet.fi/index/Tree_of_life/insecta/lepidoptera/ditrysia/papilionoidea/: Markku Savela's website is dedicated to the taxonomy and systematics of animals, plants, and fungi. It contains a catalogue of all described subspecies and forms for a vast number of species worldwide; the section dedicated to butterflies is particularly rich. In English.

www.ufz.de/european-butterflies: This is the website of the Helmholtz Centre for Environmental Research, located in Germany. Researchers from this team, including Martin Wiemers, Alexander Harpke, Oliver Shweiger, and Josef Settele, coordinate the LepiDiv project, which publishes distribution maps and bioclimatic data for all European species. In German and English.

https://www.vlinderstichting.nl/butterfly-conservation-europe: Butterfly Conservation Europe is a partnership organization focused on halting and reversing the decline of butterflies, moths, and their habitats throughout Europe. The board members are renowned lepidopterists; the organization supports numerous conservation projects and produces valuable information about European butterflies. In English.

Photographic Credits

M: male, F: female, R: upperside, V: underside, C: caterpillar, O: egg

Piotr Abraszek: *Argynnis laodice* FR, *Colias caucasica* FR and FV, *Polygonia egea* R and V.

Antonia Aga: *Maniola chia* MR, FR, MV, and FV.

ajott (CC BY 4.0): *Deudorix livia* V.

Firos AK (CC BY-SA 4.0): *Zizeeria karssandra* MR.

Jerome Albre (CC BY-SA 2.0): *Agriades glandon* V, *Boloria dia* C, *Brintesia circe* C, *Charaxes jasius* C, *Cupido argiades* FR, *Erebia neoridas* FR, *Euphydryas aurinia* C, *Melanargia occitanica* R, *Thymelicus lineola* C, and *Zerynthia rumina* C.

Alex: *Vanessa cardui* C (public domain).

Alonto (CC BY-SA 4.0): *Deudorix livia* R.

Alpsdake (CC BY-SA 3.0): *Lampides boeticus* MR and FR, and *Nymphalis vaualbum* R.

Alvesgaspar (CC BY-SA 3.0): *Carcharodus tripolina* R.

Paul Asman and Jill Lenoble (CC-BY 2.0): *Euphydryas cynthia* C.

Milind Bakhare (CC-BY-SA 4.0): *Azanus jesous* MR and V, and *Ypthima asterope* R.

Mathieu Bally: *Euchloe simplonia* V.

Diana Balogh: *Brenthis daphne* C, *Erynnis tages* C, and *Melitaea trivia* C.

Yves Bas (CC BY 4.0): *Eumedonia eumedon* FR and *Lasiommata paramegaera* FR.

Vincent Baudraz: *Erebia christi* MR, FR, MV, and FV, and *Erebia tyndarus* MV.

Friedrich Bohringer: *Colias hyale* MV (CC BY-SA 3.0 AT) and *Polyommatus icarus icarinus* V (CC BY-SA 2.5).

Sonke Bonde (CC0): *Plebejea loewii* MR.

Thomas Bresson (CC BY 2.0): *Danaus chrysippus* V.

Paul D. Brock: *Arethusana boabdil* V.

Juan Pablo Cancela (CC BY-SA 3.0): *Polyommatus violetae* V.

Pedro Candela Gallego: *Argynnis pandora* MR, *Aricia morronensis* MR and V, *Erebia palarica* FR, and FV, *Gonepteryx rhamni* FR, *Laeosopis roboris* FR, *Lycaena alciphron gordius* FR, *Lysandra albicans* FR, *Lysandra bellargus* FR, *Melanargia russiae* FV, *Melitaea parthenoides* V, *Polyommatus amandus* FR, *Pseudophilotes panoptes* MR, *Pyrgus onopordi* MR, and *Satyrus actaea* FR.

Pedro José Castellano Reloba: *Boloria euphrosyne* V, *Colotis evagore* MV and FV, *Erebia rondoui* V, *Euphydryas desfontainii* V, *Lasiommata maera* V, and *Melanargia occitanica* V.

Caleb Catto (CC BY-SA 4.0): *Boloria chariclea* FR.

Zeynel Cebeci (CC BY-SA 4.0): *Anthocharis damone* FR, *Boloria graeca* FR, *Euchloe ausonia* V, *Fabriciana adippe* V, *Freyeria trochylus* V, *Gegenes pumilio* FR and V, *Hipparchia mersina* V, *Iolana iolas* C, *Kirinia climene* V, *Leptidea sinapis printemps* V, *Lycaenae thersamon* V (x2), *Lycaena thetis* V, *Muschampia proto* V, *Muschampia tessellum* R, *Neolysandra coelestina* MR, *Pieris ergane* V, *Plebejidea loewii* V, *Pseudochazara anthelea* FV, *Pyrgus cinarae* R and V, *Tarucus balkanicus* V, *Turanana taygetica* MR and V, and *Zizeeria karsandra* V.

Jose Antonio Chanivet Mendez: *Muschampia baeticus* R, *Melanargia ines* MR, and *Melitaea aetherie* MR and FR.

Yannick Chittaro: *Boloria aquilonaris* FR, *Boloria pales* FV, *Erebia epistygne* R, *Erebia eriphyle* V, *Erebia flavofasciata* MR, FR, and V, *Erebia nivalis* MV, *Erebia pandrose* R, *Erebia triarius* MV, *Euphydryas cynthia* V, *Hipparchia genava* MV and FV, *Melitaea asteria* MR, *Melitaea phoebe* FR, *Melitaea varia* FR, *Nymphalis antiopa* V, *Pieris bryoniae* FR, *Plebejus argus* V, and *Pyrgus onopordi* FR.

Durzan Cirano (CC BY-SA 3.0): *Luthrodes galba* V.

Yann Coatanéa: *Melanargia pherusa* R.

Alan Cooper: *Agriades glandon* FR, *Colotis evagore* MR, *Erebia aethiopellus* FR, *Erebia claudina* MR, *Erebia gorge* V, *Erebia melampus* MR, *Erebia pharte* R, *Erebia pluto* MR and FV, *Erebia triarius* FV, *Euchloe insularis* R and V, *Euchloe simplonia* R, *Fabriciana elisa* R, *Glaucopsyche melanops* MR, *Hipparchia aristaeus* V, *Hipparchia cretica* V, *Hipparchia genava* R, *Lasiommata paramegaera* V, *Plebejus bellieri* FR and V, *Polyommatus humedasae* R and V, *Pontia callidice* FR, *Pseudophilotes barbagiae* R and V, *Pyrgus andromedae* FR, *Pyrgus foulquieri* V, and *Zerynthia cretica* V.

Andrew Cooper: *Maniola jurtina* C.

Samuele De Angelis: *Maniola cypricola* FV.

Federico Del Barba (CC0): *Erebia tyndarus* FV.

Diego Delso (CC BY-SA 3.0): *Cacyreus marshalli* R.

Didier Descouens (CC BY-SA 4.0): *Hipparchia alcyone* R, *Hipparchia fagi* MR and FR, *Hipparchia semele* FR, and *Hipparchia statilinus* MR and FR.

Markus Dumke: *Cyaniris semiargus helena* FR and V, *Erebia pluto* FR, and *Turanana taygetica* FR.

Bernard Dupont (CC BY-SA 2.0): *Aglais io* C and *Danaus chrysippus* R.

Bob Eade: *Coenonympha pamphilus* C, *Favonius quercus* MR, and *Lasiommata megera* C.

Juan Emilio (CC BY-SA 2.0): *Pontia daplidice* FR and *Vanessa vulcania* V.

ETF89: *Papilio demoleus* R.

Bernard Fransen: *Agriades aquilo* FR, *Anthocharis gruneri* MR, FR, MV, and FV, *Boloria chariclea* MR and V, *Boloria euphrosyne scandinave* R, *Boloria frigga* MR and V, *Boloria polaris* MR, *Borbo borbonica* R and V, *Erebia hispania* MR, MV, and FV, *Erebia polaris* MR and MV, *Euphydryas desfontainii* MR, *Fabriciana elisa* V, *Favria cribrellum* V, *Lycaena candens* FR, *Maniola cypricola* MR and MV, *Maniola nurag* FV, *Melanargia pherusa* V, *Melitaea aetherie* FR, *Oeneis bore* V, *Polyommatus amandus isias* FR, *Polyommatus golgus* MR, FR, MV, and FV, *Pseudophilotes bavius* MR and FR, *Tarucus balkanicus* FR, and *Turanan taygetica* FR. **Frayle** (CCO): *Fabriciana adippe* V.

Mike Friel: *Carterocephalus silvicola* V, *Colias caucasica* MV, and *Pseudochazara cingovskii* V.

Gailhampshire (CC BY 2.0): *Hesperia comma* MR and FR, *Pieris napi* MR and FR, *Polyommatus celina* FR, *Tentrhedinidé* C, and *Zerynthia rumina* C.

Judy Gallagher (CC BY 2.0): *Coloris evagore* FR, *Thymelicus lineola* FR, and *Vanessa virginiensis* R and V.

J. M. Garg (CC BY-SA 4.0): *Azanus jesous* FR.

Francoise Gasnier: *Erebia scipio* MR, FR, MV, and FV, and *Papilio alexanor* C.

Adam Gor: *Apatura ilia* MR and FR, *Apatura iris* MR and FR, *Apatura metis* V, *Archon apollinus* MR, FR, and V, *Argynnis laodice* V, *Argynnis paphia* MR and FR, *Boloria graeca* V, *Boloria napaea* FR, *Brenthis hecate* FR and V, *Muschampia orientalis* R and V, *Charaxes jasius* R and V, *Coenonympha leander* V, *Coenonympha rhodopensis* V, *Colias aurorina* FV, *Colias chrysotheme* MV and FV, *Colias erate* V, *Colias myrmidone* MV, *Danaus plexippus* R and V, *Erebia cassioides* MV and FV, *Erebia manto* MR, *Euchloe ausonia* R, *Eumedonia eumedon* MR, *Euphydryas aurinia* MR, *Gonepteryx farinosa* FV, *Hipparchia syriaca* FV, *Iolana iolas* FR and V, *Kirinia roxelana* FV, *Kretania eurypilus* R and V, *Kretania sephirus* FV, *Leptidea duponcheli* V, *Libythea celtis* R, *Limenitis populi* MR and V, *Lycaena alciphron alciphron* MR and FR, *Lycaena candens* MR, *Lycaena dispar* MR and FR, *Lycaena phlaeas forme sombre* R, *Lycaena thetis* MR and FR, *Lysandra bellargus* FV, *Melanargia larissa* MV and FV, *Melitaea arduinna* FR and V, *Melitaea phoebe* V, *Melitaea trivia* MR, FR, and V, *Neptis sappho* R and V, *Nymphalis antiopa* R, *Nymphalis polychloros* R and V, *Nymphalis vaualbum* V, *Nymphalis xanthomelas* R and V, *Polyommatus admetus* V, *Pontia chloridice* V, *Pseudochazara graeca* FV, *Pseudophilotes vicrama* V, *Pyrgus sidae* MR and V, *Pyrgus warrenensis* FR, *Spialia orbifer* R and V, *Thymelicus lineola* MR, *Yphthima asterope* V, *Zerynthia cerisy* V, and *Zerynthia polyxena* V.

Ferran Turmo Gort: *Erebia neoridas* MV, *Euchloe crameri* C, *Gegenes nostrodamus* FR, *Hipparchia fidia* R and V, *Leptidea sinapis* R, *Muschampia proto*

MR, *Pieris brassicae* FR, *Polyommatus nivescens* MR, FR, MV, and FV, *Polyommatus ripartii* V, and *Polyommatus thersites* FR.

Janet Graham (CC-BY 2.0): *Aricia agestis* C.

Edmundas Greimas (CCBY 4.0): *Hipparchia senthes* MV.

Josef Grieshuber (CC BY-SA 3.0): *Colias alfacariensis* FR, *Colias aurorina* FR, *Colias caucasica* MR, *Colias chrysotheme* MR, *Colias erate* MR and FR, *Colias myrmidone* MR and FR, and *Colias tyche* R.

Andrea Grill (CC BY 3.0): *Maniola cypricola* FR, *Maniola halicarnassus* MR and FR, and *Maniola nurag* FR.

Haeferl (CC BY-SA 3.0): *Carterocephalus palaemon* R.

Regine Hakenbeck: *Lysandra caelestissima* FR and FV, and *Polyommatus fabressei* R and V.

Jean-Pierre Hamon (CC-BY-SA 3.0): *Abraxas grossulariata* C, and *Sphinx ligustri* C.

Tamas Hapka: *Agriades dardanus* FR, *Cupido decolorata* MR, *Kretania hespericus* MR and FR, and *Kretania psylorita* V.

Hectonichus (CC BY-SA 4.0): *Colias crocea* MR, *Erebia melampus* FR and FV, *Hipparchia fagi* FV, and *Leptotes pirithous* MR.

Joan C. Hinojosa: *Euphydryas desfontainii* C (public domain).

Ryan Hodnett (CC-BY-SA 2.0): *Danaus plexippus* C.

Tamas Hudak: *Agriades optilete* FR, *Arethusana arethusa* R, *Argynnis laodice* MR, *Argynnis pandora* FR, *Argynnis paphia* FR, *Boloria napaea* FV, *Brintesia circe* R, *Celastrina argiolus* MR, *Chazara briseis* FV, *Coenonympha oedippus* R, *Colias hyale* FV, *Erebia medusa* V, *Erebia oeme* MR, *Eumedonia eumedon* V, *Glaucopsyche alexis* MR and FR, *Hipparchia statilinus* MV, *Iolana iolas* MR, *Kirinia climene* MV, *Lasiommata maera* FR, *Leptidea duponcheli estival* V, *Limenitis populi* FR, *Lycaena hippothoe* V, *Lycaena thersamon* MR and FR, *Maniola jurtina* MR, *Melitaea britomartis* MR, *Phengaris alcon* MR and FR, *Phengris arion* MR, *Phengaris nausithous* MR and FR, *Phengaris teleius* MR and FR, *Pieris brassicae* MR, *Pieris ergane* FR, *Polyommatus admetus* MR and FR, *Polyommatus daphnis* FR, *Polyommatus dorylas* MR and FR, *Pontia edusa* MR and FR, *Pseudophilotes vicrama* FR, *Satyrium w-album* V, and *Scolitantides orion* FR.

Ian Hurst: *Maniola megala* FR.

Louis Imbeau (CC BY 4.0): *Boloria freija* MR and V.

Charlie Jackson (CC BY 2.0): *Cupido lorquinii* V, *Erynnis tages* R and V, *Hipparchia volgensis* FV, *Kretania sephirus* FR and MV, *Leptidea sinapis* été V, *Melitaea ornata* FR, *Pararge aegeria* V, *Plebejus argus* MR, *Polygonia c-album printemps* V, *Polyommatus admetus* V, *Pyrgus malvoides* V, *Spialia orbifer* R,

Spialia phlomidis R and V, and *Thymelicus sylvestris* FR.

Jee and Rani Nature Photography (CC BY-SA 4.0): *Hypolimnas misippus* MV, and *Papilio demoleus* V.

Lukas Jonaitis (CC-BY 2.0): *Cerula vinula* C.

Jrcagle (CC BY 4.0): *Agriades zullichi.*

Seyfi Karaman: *Proterebia afra* V, *Satyrium ledereri* V, *Thymelicus hyrax* V, and *Tomares nogelii* V.

Katunchik (CC-BY 4.0): *Adscita statices* C.

Katya (CC BY-SA 2.0): *Leptotes pirithous* V, and *Melitaea trivia aberrant* R.

Jani Kettunen (CC0): *Carterocephalus silvicola* FR.

Nigel Kiteley: *Melanargia ines* V.

Zdravko Kolev: *Polyommatus orphicus* V.

Norbert Kondla: *Boloria polaris* V.

Oleg Kosterin (CC BY 4.0): *Apatura metis* MR and FR, *Apopestes spectrum* C, *Leptidea morsei printemps* V, and *Favria cribrellum* MR and FR.

Ioannis Koutroubakis: *Zerynthia cretica* MR.

Holger Krisp (CC-BY 3.0): *Macrothylacia rubi* C, and *Vanessa atalanta* C.

Komisuji Kūkō (CC BY-SA 4.0): *Leptidea morsei* R.

Kulacgmx.at (CC BY-SA 3.0): *Arctia caja* C, *Callimorpha dominula* C, and *Melitaea britomartis* V.

Dmitri Kulakov (CC BY 4.0): *Araschnia levana porima* R.

Tero Laakso (CC BY-SA 2.0): *Lasiommata petropolitana* V.

Salvatore Lai: *Papilio hospiton* R and V.

Ian Lawson: *Agriades dardanus* MR and V, *Aricia anteros* MR and V, *Carcahrodus tripolina* V, *Cigaritis acamas* V, *Cupido lorquinii* MR, *Erebia rhodopensis* MR and MV, *Freyeria trochylus* R, *Hipparchia volgensis* MV, *Kretania sephirus* MR, *Lysandra caelestissima* MV, *Melitaea britomartis* FR, *Melitaea ornata* V, *Polyommatus iphigenia* MR and V, *Polyommatus nivescens* FR, *Pseudochazara anthelea* MV, *Tarucus theophrastus* MR and V.

Lebrac (CC-BY-SA 3.0): *Acronicta alni* C.

Ivan Leidus (CC-BY-SA 4.0): *Saturnia pavonia* C.

Le.Loup.Gris (CC BY-SA 3.0): *Noelysandra coelestina* V.

Patrick Leopold (CC-BY-SA 3.0 de): *Hipparchia semele* C.

Xenofon Levadiotis: *Cupido decolorata* V.

Daniel Linzbauer (CC BY 4.0): *Araschnia levana* V.

Gyorgy Liptovszky: *Erebia orientalis* MV, and *Melitaea arduinna* MR.

Lsadonkey (CC BY-SA 4.0): *Chazara prieuri* R.

Lucarelli (CC BY-SA 3.0): *Ochlodes sylvanus* C, and *Zerynthia cassandra* R.

Lynk Media (CC-BY-SA 3.0): *Deleiphila elpenor* C.

John Maddocks: *Colias myrmidone* FV, *Erebia melas* MV, and *Leptidea morsei estival* V.

Vitězslav Maňak (CC BY-SA 3.0): *Colias hyale* MR, *Oeneis jutta* R, and *Pyrgus centaureae* V.

John Mann: *Erynnis marloyi* V, and *Pelopidas thrax* MR and V.

Markus (CC BY-ND 2.0): *Pelopidas thrax* FR.

Pablo Martinez-Darve Sanz: *Argynnis pandora* V, *Aricia cramera* MR, FR, V, and C, *Aricia montensis* FR, *Azanus ubaldus* MR, FR, V, and C, *Brenthis hecate* MR, *Catopsilia florella* FV, *Colias crocea* FR, *Cyclirius webbianus* MR, FR, V, and C, *Erebia gorgone* FV, *Erebia rondoui* MR and FR, *Erebia triarius* R, *Euchloe bazae* R and V, *Euchloe belemia* V, *Euchloe charlonia* R, V, and C, *Euchloe eversi* V, *Euchloe grancanariensis* R, *Euchloe tagis* V, *Gegenes nostrodamus* V, *Gonepteryx cleobule* MR, FR, MV, and FV, *Gonepteryx cleopatra* FR, *Gonepteryx rhamni* MR, *Hipparchia tamadabae* MV, FV, and C, *Hipparchia tilosi* V, *Hypolimnas misippus* FV, *Iphiclides feisthamelii* R, V, and C, *Lycaena bleusei* R and V, *Lycaena thersamon* FR, *Lysandra albicans* MR, MV, and FV, *Melanargia lachesis* FV, *Melanargia russiae* MR and FR, *Muschampia proto* FR, *Neptis rivularis* R and V, *Pararge xiphioides* R and V, *Phengaris arion* V, *Pieris cheiranthi* V, *Plebejus argus* FR, *Polyommatus celina* MR, FR, MV, and FV, *Polyommatus fulgens* MV and FV, *Polyommatus ripartii* FR, *Pontia daplidice* C, *Pseudophilotes abencerragus* FR and V, *Speyeria aglaja* MR, *Thymelicus christi* R and V, *Tomares ballus* C, *Vanessa virginiensis* C, *Vanessa vulcania* R and C, *Zegris meridionalis* MR, FR, and C, and *Zizeeria knysna* MR, FR, V, and C.

D. and N. Massie: *Aglais ichnusa* R.

David McCorquodale (CC BY-SA 4.0): *Boloria polaris* MR.

Ivan Medenica (CC-BY-SA 4.0): *Melitaea arduinna* C.

Mehmetcelik80 (CC BY-SA 4.0): *Hyponephele lupina* V.

Mario Modesto Mata (CC BY-SA 3.0): *Pyrgus cirsii* FR.

Reinhold Moller (CC-BY-SA 4.0): *Thecla betulae* FR.

Angus Molyneux: *Melanargia arge* R.

Yeray Monasterio Leon: *Melitaea pseudornata* C (x2).

Christoph Moning (CC BY 4.0): *Aricia artaxerxes* MR, *Boloria thore* V, *Cupido lorquinii* FR, *Cupido osiris* FR, *Erebia claudina* FR and FV, *Erebia euryale* MV, *Erebia gorge* R (x2), *Erebia mnestra* MR and MV, *Erebia neoridas* MV, *Erebia ottomana* MR, MV, and FV, *Erebia stiria* O, *Euchloe penia* V, *Hipparchia cypriensis* V, *Kirinia roxelana* MV, *Maniola nurag* FR, *Melitaea asteria* FR, *Melitaea phoebe* MR, *Pararge xiphia* R, *Plebejus idas* C, *Polyommatus aroaniensis* V, *Pseudochazara graeca* MV, and *Satyrus actaea* MR and FV.

Dean Morley: *Argynnis paphia* C, *Colias crocea* C, *Limenitis reducta* C, *Melanargia galathea* C (x2), *Nymphalis antiopa* C, *Pararge aegeria* C, and *Speyeria aglaja* C.
Souvik Moukherjee (CC BY-SA 4.0): *Tarucus balkanicus* MR.
Jean-Pierre Moussus: *Acronicta rumicis* C, *Aglais io* R and V, *Aglais urticae* R, V, and C, *Agriades glandon* MR and V, *Agriades optilete* MR and V, *Agriades orbitulus* MR, FR, V, and O, *Agriades pyrenaicus* MR, FR, and V, *Anthocharis cardamines* MR, FV, and C, *Anthocharis euphenoides* MR, FR, FV, C, and O, *Apatura ilia clytie* FR, *Apatura ilia* V and C, *Aphantopus hyperantus* MR, FR, and V, *Aporia crataegi* MV, FV, C, and O, *Araschnia levana levana* R, *Araschnia levana prorsa* R and V, *Arethusana arethusa* V, *Argynnis paphia* V, *Aricia agestis* MR, FR, and V, *Aricia artaxerxes* MR and MV, *Aricia montensis* MR and MV, *Aricia nicias* MR and V, *Asteroscopus shinx* C, *Boloria aquilonaris* MR and V, *Boloria dia* MR, FR, and V, *Boloria eunomia* MR and V, *Boloria euphrosyne* R, *Boloria napaea* MR and MV, *Boloria pales* MR, FR, and MV, *Boloria selene* R and V, *Boloria titania* MR, FR, and V, *Brenthis daphne* MR, FR, and V, *Brenthis ino* MR, FR, and V, *Brintesia circe* V, *Cacyreus marshalli* V, *Callophrys avis* V, *Callophrys rubi* V, *Carcharodus alceae* R and V, *Muschampia floccifera* R, *Muschampia lavatherae* R and V, *Celastrina argiolus* FR and V, *Chazara briseis* MV, *Coenonympha arcania* V (x2), *Coenonympha corinna* V, *Coenonympha dorus* V, *Coenonympha gardetta* V (x2), *Coenonympha glycerion glycerion* V (x2), *Coenonympha glycerion pseudoamyntas* V, *Coenonympha hero* V, *Coenonympha macromma* V, *Coenonympha oedippus* MV and FV, *Coenonympha pamphilus* V (x3), *Coenonympha tullia* V (x2), *Colias alfacariensis* MR, FR, and MV, *Colias crocea* MV, *Colias hyale* FR, *Colias palaeno* MR, FR, MV (x2), and FV, *Colias phicomone* V, *Cuculia lychnitis* C, *Cupido alcetas* V, *Cupido argiades* FR and V, *Cupido minimus* R and V, *Cupido osiris* MR, FR, and V, *Cyaniris semiargus* MR, FR, and V, *Erebia aethiopellus* MR, MV, and FV, *Erebia aethiops* MR, MV, and FV, *Erebia alberganus* R and V, *Erebia cassioides* MR and FR, *Erebia epiphron* MR, FR, and V, *Erebia euryale* MR (x2), FR, MV, and FV, *Erebia lefebvrei* MR and MV, *Erebia ligea* MR, FR, and V, *Erebia manto* MR (x2), FR, MV, and FV (x2), *Erebia medusa* MR and FR, *Erebia meolans* MR, FR, and FV, *Erebia mnestra* MR and FR, *Erebia montana* MR, FR, MV, and FV, *Erebia oeme* FR, MV, and FV, *Erebia pandrose* MV and FV, *Erebia pluto* MV, *Erebia pronoe* MR, FR, MV, and FV, *Erebia sudetica* R and V, *Erynnis tages* R, *Euchloe tagis* R, *Euphydryas aurinia* FR and V, *Euphydryas beckeri* MR, FR, and V, *Euphydryas cynthia* MR and FR, *Euphydryas desfontainii* FR, *Euphydryas intermedia* MR, FR, and V, *Euphydryas maturna* MR, FR, and V, *Fabriciana adippe* MR, *Fabriciana niobe* MR, FR, and V (x2), *Favonius quercus* V, *Glaucopsyche alexis* V (x2), *Glaucopsyche melanops* FR and V, *Gonepteryx cleopatra* MR and MV, *Gonepteryx rhamni* MV and FV, *Hamearis lucina* MR, FR, V, and O, *Hesperia comma* V, *Hipparchia alcyone* V, *Hipparchia neomiris* V, *Hipparchia semele* MV and FV, *Hyles euphorbiae* C, *Hyponephele lycaon* V, *Iphiclides podalirius* R, V, C, and O, *Issoria lathonia* R, *Laeosopis roboris* MR and V, *Lasiommata maera* FR, *Lasiommata megera* FR and V, *Leptidea sinapis* C and O, *Libythea celtis* V, *Limenitis camilla* R and V, *Limenitis reducta* R and V, *Lopinga achine* R and V, *Lycaena alciphron gordius* MR, *Lycaena dispar* V, *Lycaena helle* MR, FR, V, and O, *Lycaena hippothoe hippothoe* MR, *Lycaena hippothoe eurydame* MR, *Lycaena phlaeas* R, V, and O, *Lycaena tityrus* MR, FR, and FV, *Lycaena virgaureae* MR, FR, and V, *Lycia hirtaria* C, *Lysandra bellargus* MR, FR, MV, and C, *Lysandra coridon* MR, FR, MV, and FV, *Lysandra hispana* MR, FR, MV, FV, and O, *Malacosoma neustria* C, *Maniola jurtina* MR, FR, MV, and FV, *Melanargia galathea* R (x2), MV, and FV, *Melanargia lachesis* MR and MV, *Melanargia russiae* MV, *Melitaea athalia* MR, *Melitaea aurelia* MR, FR, and V, *Melitaea cinxia* MR, FR, V, and C, *Melitaea deione* MR, *Melitaea diamina diamina* MR, FR, and V, *Melitaea diamina vernetensis* MR, *Melitaea didyma* MR, FR (x2), V, and C, *Melitaea nevadensis* MR, FR, V, and C, *Melitaea parthenoides* MR and FR, *Melitaea phoebe* MR and C, *Melitaea varia* MR (x2) and V, *Minois dryas* R and V, *Ochlodes sylvanus* MR, FR, and V, *Oeneis glacialis* V, *Papilio alexanor* R, V, and O, *Papilio machaon* R, V, C, and O, *Pararge aegeria* R (x2) and V, *Parnassius apollo* MR, FR, and V, *Parnassius phoebus* R and V, *Phengaris alcon* FR and V, *Phengaris arion* FR, *Phengaris nausithous* V, *Phengaris teleius* V, *Pieris brassicae* V and C, *Pieris bryoniae* MR and V, *Pieris ergane* MR, *Pieris mannii* FR and V, *Pieris napi estival* V and O, *Pieris rapae* MR, FR, V, C, and O, *Plebejus argus* FV, *Plebejus argus corsicus* V, *Plebejus argyrognomon* MR, FR, MV, and FV, *Plebejus idas* MR and V, *Polygonia c-album* R and V, *Polyommatus amandus* MR, *Polyommatus damon* MR, FR (x2), MV, and FV, *Polyommatus daphnis* MR, FR, MV, and FV, *Polyommatus dolus* MR, FR, and V, *Polyommatus dorylas* MV, *Polyommatus eros* MR, FR, MV, and FV, *Polyommatus escheri* MR, FR, MV and FV, *Polyommatus icarus* MR, FR (x2), MV, and FV, *Polyommatus ripartii* V, *Polyommatus thersites* MR, FR, MV, and FV, *Pontia callidice* MR and V, *Pontia daplidice* MR and V, *Pseudophilotes*

baton FR and V, *Pyrgus* O, *Pyrgus alveus* MR and V, *Pyrgus armoricanus* MR, FR, and V, *Pyrgus cacaliae* MR, FR, and V, *Pyrgus carlinae* MR, FR, and V, *Pyrgus carthami* MR, FR, and V, *Pyrgus cirsii* MR and V, *Pyrgus malvoides* R, *Pyronia bathseba* MR, FR, and V, *Pyronia cecilia* FR and V, *Pyronia tithonus* MR, FR, and V, *Satyrium acaciae* V, *Satyrium esculi* V, *Satyrium pruni* V and O, *Satyrium spini* V, *Satyrus actaea* MV, *Satyrus ferula* MR, FR, MV, and FV, *Scolitantides orion* FR, V, and O, *Shargacucullia caninae* C, *Speyeria aglaja* FR and V, *Spialia sertorius* R and V, *Thymelicus acteon* V and A, *Thymelicus lineola* V, *Thymelicus sylvestris* MR and V, *Tomares ballus* V, *Vanessa atalanta* R, V, and C, *Vanessa cardui* R and V, *Zerynthia polyxena* R and C, *Zerynthia rumina* R and V, *Zygaena filipendulae* C, and *Zygaena viciae* C.

Michael Mueller (CC BY 2.0): *Erebia ligea* MV.

Natural History Museum Rotterdam, Netherlands: *Colias chrysotheme* FR, *Colias erate* FR, *Colias hecla* FR, *Colias phicomone* MR and FR, *Gonepteryx farinosa* MR and FR, *Leptidea duponcheli* R, and *Pieris cheiranthi* MR.

NSG Group (CC0): *Erebia calcarius* FR, *Erebia melas* MV, *Erebia sthennyo* R, *Hipparchia blachieri* MV, *Hipparchia christenseni* V, and *Hipparchia syriaca* MR and FR.

Secundino Ordonez Garcia: *Aricia morronensis* FR, *Lycaena vigaureae miegii* MR, *Plebejus idas* FR, *Polyommatus fulgens* MR and FR, and *Polyommatus ripartii* MR.

Guy Padfield: *Erebia gorgone* MR and MV, *Erebia meolans* MV, *Kretania trappi* MR, *Pyrgus andromedae* MR and V, *Pyrgus foulquieri* MR and FR, *Pyrgus onopordi* V, and *Pyrgus warrenensis* V.

Jose Maria Paraiso Hernandez: *Aricia montensis* FV, *Muschampia baeticus* V, *Leptotes pirithous* FR, *Pseudophilotes abencerragus* MR, *Pseudophilotes panoptes* V, *Pyrgus serratulae* V, *Pyronia cecilia* MR, and *Zegris meridionalis* V.

Peelden (CC BY-SA 4.0): *Colias erate* V (x2).

Ferran Pestana (CC BY-SA 2.0): *Danaus chrysippus* C, *Euchloe crameri* R, and *Pseudophilotes panoptes* FR.

Pascal Peyrache: *Euchloe crameri* V, *Pyrgus alveus* FR, *Pyrgus serratulae* MR and FR, and *Satyrium ilicis* V.

Olli Pihlajamaa: *Agriades aquilo* MR and V, *Boloria freija* FR, *Boloria improba* MR, *Boloria thore* FR, *Carterocephalus silvicola* MR, *Colias hecla* MV, *Colias tyche* V, *Erebia polaris* MR, and *Oeneis norna* V.

Tony Pittaway: *Lycaena ottomana* FR and V, *Lysandra caelestissima* MR, *Neolysandra coelestina* FV, and *Polyommatus fabressei* MR.

Simon Plat (CC BY 2.0): *Colias aurorina* MR, MV, and FV, and *Erynnis marloyi* R.

Pmau (CC BY-SA 4.0): *Erebia meolans* MR.

Alexandre Polyakov (CC BY-SA 4.0): *Lasiommata maera* MR.

Andrey Pomonarev (CC BY 4.0): *Melitaea britomartis* C.

Milos Popovic (CC BY-SA 4.0): Kirinia climene R, and Phengaris teleius C.

Simon Popy (CC BY 4.0): *Glaucopsyche melanops* C, and *Hipparchia leighebi* MV.

Dave Potter: *Aricia artaxerxes artaxerxes* R and V, *Cupido alcetas* FR, and *Glaucopsyche paphos* FR.

Fyodor Pudovikov (CC-BY 4.0): *Leptidea juvernica* R.

Quartl (CC BY-SA 3.0): *Anthocharis cardamines* MV, and *Pieris napi printemps* V.

Alastair Rae (CC BY-SA 2.0): *Lycaena candens* V, *Thymelicus acteon* R, and *Zerynthia cerisy* FR.

Lois Rancilhac: *Glaucopsyche paphos* V, *Hipparchia syriaca* MV, and *Leptidea duponcheli* A.

Linda and John Reinecke: *Euchloe belemia* R.

Erwin Rennwald (CC-BY-SA 3.0 de): *Erebia aethiops* C.

Eloy Revilla: *Muschampia floccifera* V.

Ghislain Riou: *Erebia epistygne* FV, and *Plebejus bellieri* MR and V.

Matt Rowlings: *Melanargia arge* V (CC BY 3.0).

William Teppo Salmela: *Lycaena phlaeas polaris* V.

Gilles San Martin (CC BY-SA 2.0): *Anthocharis cardamines* FR, *Apatura iris* V, *Araschnia levana* C, *Boloria aquilonaris* C and O, *Boloria eunomia* C and O, *Callophrys rubi* C, *Carcharodus alceae* C and O, *Carterocephalus palaemon* V, *Celastrina argiolus* O, *Charaxes jasius* O, *Cupido minimus* C, *Erebia aethiops* FR, *Euphydryas aurinia* O, *Favonius quercus* FR and C, *Gonepteryx cleopatra* FV, *Gonepteryx rhamni* C and O, *Hipparchia statilinus* MV, *Issoria lathonia* C, *Lycaena dispar* FR, *Lycaena hippothoe* FR, V, and O, *Lycaena phlaeas* C, *Lysandra coridon* O, *Nymphalis polychloros* C and O, *Pararge aegeria* O, *Polygonia c-album* C and O, *Polyommatus icarus* O, *Satyrium w-album* C, *Spialia sertorius* O, *Thecla betulae* O, *Thymelicus sylvestris* O, and *Vanessa atalanta* O.

Andreas Sanchez: *Coenonympha darwiniana* V, *Erebia epiphron* V, *Erebia eriphyle* R, *Erebia melampus* MV, *Erebia nivalis* MR, *Erebia pharte* V, *Erebia tyndarus* FR, *Euphydryas aurinia debilis* MR, *Melitaea deione* FR and V.

David Sandler (CC BY-SA 4.0): *Melitaea athalia* FR.

Dennis Sanetra (CC BY-SA 4.0): *Anthocharis damone* MR, MV, and FV.

Emmanuele Santarelli (CC BY-SA 4.0): *Pieris brassicae* O.

Carminda Santos (CC BY 4.0): *Melanargia lachesis* FR.

Ani Sarkisyan: *Colias crocea* FR.

Luca Sattin: *Hipparchia maderensis* V, and *Pararge xiphia* V.

Saydelah (CC BY 4.0): *Zizeeria karsandra* FR.

Lorie Schaull (CC-BY 2.0): *Danaus plexippus*.

Alan Schmierer: *Agriades zullichi* R, and *Pyrgus centaureae* R.

W. Schon (CC-BY-SA 3.0 de): *Aglais io*.

Katja Schultz (CC BY 2.0): *Cacyreus marshalli* C.

Charles J. Sharp (CC BY-SA 4.0): *Boloria graeca* MR, *Colias crocea* FR, *Erebia melas* MR, *Erebia rhodopensis* FR and FV, *Gegenes pumilio* MR, *Hipparchia fatua* MV, *Issoria lathonia* V, *Lasiommata megera* MR, *Limenitis reducta* V, *Lycaena tityrus* MV, *Pieris krueperi estival* V, *Polyommatus aroaniensis* V, *Pseudochazara geyeri* V, and *Thecla betulae* V.

K. B. Simoglou (CC BY-SA 4.0): *Lasiommata petropolitana* MR.

Ria en Sjaak (CC-BY-SA 4.0: *Colias hyale* C).

Mickael Skelton: *Cupido alcetas* MR, and *Polyommatus dolus* V.

Dietrich Sommerfeld (CC-BY-SA 3.0 de): *Plebejus argus* C.

Anne Sorbes: *Lycaena alciphron* V.

Hedwig Storch (CC-BY-SA 3.0): *Phalera bucephala* C.

Stu's Images (CC-BY-SA 3.0): *Tyria jacobaeae* C.

Suncana (CC BY-SA 4.0): *Catopsilia florella* MV.

Superdrac (CC BY-SA 4.0): *Araschnia levana* O.

Harald Supfle (CC-BY-SA 3.0): *Apamea monoglypha* C, *Coenonympha thyrsis* V, *Fabriciana adippe* FR, *Lasiommata petropolitana* FR, *Parnassius mnemosyne* C, and *Vanessa cardui* C and O.

Michael Sveikutis (CC BY-ND 2.0): *Kirinia roxelana* MR, *Maniola megala* MR and MV, *Maniola telmessia* FR, MV, and FV, *Melanargia larissa* MR and FR, and *Thymelicus hyrax* MR.

Roman Sykora: *Cupido decolorata* FR.

Francois-Xavier Taxil (CC BY 4.0): *Coenonympha glycerion bertolis* V, *Coenonympha iphioides* V, *Erebia epistygne* MV, and *Erebia lefebvrei* FR.

Koen Thonissen: *Pyrgus warrenensis* MR.

Alexandre Tichonov (CC BY 4.0): *Apatura iris* C.

Kevin Tolhurst: *Coenonympha tullia* V, *Erebia calcarius* MR, *Erebia orientalis* MR, *Erebia polaris* FR, *Gonepteryx farinosa* MV, *Hipparchia neapolitana* V, *Hipparchia sbordonii* V, and *Pontia chloridice* MR and FR.

Enrico Tomscke (CC BY 4.0): *Hipparchia leighebi* FV.

Uajith (CC BY-SA 4.0): *Hypolimnas misippus* MR and FR.

Ken-Ichi Ueda (CC-BY 4.0): *Vanessa cardui* C.

Ilia Ustyantsev (CC BY-SA 2.0): *Colias myrmidone* C, *Euphydryas maturna* C, *Melitaea athalia* V, *Muschampia tessellum* V, and *Satyrium pruni* C.

Jacinta Iluch Valero (CC BY-SA 2.0): *Erebia palarica* MV.

Pieter Vantieghem: *Aricia anteros* FR, *Chazara prieuri* V, *Coenonympha orientalis* V, *Erebia calcarius* MV, *Erebia claudina* MV, *Erebia lefebvrei* FV, *Erebia melas* FR, *Erebia mnestra* FV, *Erebia stiria* FV, *Erebia styx* MV, *Erebia zapateri* MR and FV, *Gegenes nostrodamus* MR, *Kretania hespericus* V, *Luthrodes galba* MR and FR, *Polyommatus fabressei* V, *Polyommatus violetae* MR, *Pseudochazara amalthea* MV and FV, *Pseudochazara orestes* V, and *Pseudochazara williamsi* V.

Ge Van't Hoff: *Satyrium ilicis* C.

Franck Vassen (CC BY 2.0): *Aporia crataegi* R, *Boloria eunomia* FR, *Heteropterus morpheus* R and V, *Lycaena hippothoe aberrant* V, *Oeneis jutta* V, *Pyrgus malvae* V, *Thymelicus lineola* A, *Thymelicus sylvestris* A, and *Zerynthia cerisy* MR.

John Vergo: *Kretania psylorita* R.

Roger Vila: *Melitaea phoebe* C.

Albert Vliegenthart (CC BY 3.0): *Pseudophilotes bavius* V.

David Vraju (CC BY-SA 4.0): *Lampides boeticus* V.

Wolfgang Wagner: *Agriades aquilo* FR, *Agriades glandon* C, *Agriades optilete* C, *Agriades orbitulus* C, *Aphantopus hyperantus* C, *Archon apollinus* C, *Arethusana arethusa* C, *Argynnis pandora* C, *Aricia artaxerxes* C, *Aricia nicias* C, *Boloria euphrosyne* C, *Boloria improba* V, *Boloria napaea* C, *Boloria pales* C, *Boloria selene* C, *Boloria titania* C, *Brenthis ino* C, *Carterocephalus palaemon* C, *Catopsilia florella* C, *Celastrina argiolus* C, *Chazara briseis* C, *Coenonympha arcania* C, *Coenonympha glycerion* C, *Colias alfacariensis* C, *Colias erate* C, *Colias hecla* C, *Colias palaeno* C, *Colias phicomone* C, *Colotis evagore* C, *Cupido alcetas* C, *Cupido argiades* C, *Cupido osiris* C, *Cyaniris semiargus* C, *Erebia arvernensis* C, *Erebia disa* MR, MV, and FV, *Erebia embla* FR and MV, *Erebia epiphron* C, *Erebia euryale* C, *Erebia gorge* C, *Erebia ligea* C, *Erebia manto* C, *Erebia medusa* C, *Erebia oeme* C, *Erebia pandrose* C, *Erebia stiria* MR, FR, and MV, *Euchloe ausonia* C, *Euchloe belemia* C, *Euchloe simplonia* C, *Eumedonia eumedon* C, *Euphydryas iduna* MR and V, *Euphydryas intermedia* C, *Fabriciana adippe* C, *Fabriciana niobe* C, *Gegenes nostrodamus* C, *Gegenes pumilio* C, *Glaucopsyche alexis* C, *Gonepteryx cleopatra* C, *Gonepteryx farinosa* C, *Hamearis lucina* C, *Hesperia comma* C, *Heteropterus morpheus* C, *Hipparchia azorina* V, *Hipparchia fagi* C, *Hipparchia fidia* C, *Hipparchia miguelensis* V, *Hipparchia statilinus*

C, *Hyponephele lycaon* C, *Iberochloe tagis* C, *Kretania eurypilus* C, *Kretania trappi* MR, FR, and V, *Laeosopis roboris* C, *Lampides boeticus* C, *Lasiommata maera* C, *Leptidea duponcheli* C, *Leptotes pirithous* C, *Libythea celtis* C, *Limenitis camilla* C, *Limenitis populi* C, *Lopinga achine* C, *Lycaena alciphron* C, *Lycaena dispar* C, *Lycaena helle* C, *Lycaena hippothoe* C, *Lycaena tityrus* C, *Lycaena virgaureae* C, *Lysandra coridon* C, *Lysandra hispana* C, *Maniola nurag* MR, *Melanargia occitanica* C, *Melanargia russiae* C, *Melitaea aetherie* V, *Melitaea diamina* C, *Melitaea parthenoides* C, *Minois dryas* C, *Muschampia baeticus* C, *Muschampia floccifera* C, *Muschampia lavatherae* C, *Muschampia proto* C, *Muschampia stauderi* R and V, *Neolysandra coelestina* FR, *Neptis rivularis* C, *Neptis sappho* C, *Oeneis glacialis* C, *Papilio hospiton* C, *Parnassius apollo* C, *Parnassius phoebus* C, *Phengaris arion* C, *Phengaris nausithous* C, *Pieris ergane* C, *Pieris krueperi printemps* MR and V, *Pieris mannii* C, *Pieris napi* C, *Plebejidea loewii* FR, *Plebejus argus* C, *Plebejus argyrognomon* C, *Polygonia egea* C, *Polyommatus admetus* C, *Polyommatus amandus* C, *Polyommatus damon* C, *Polyommatus daphnis* C, *Polyommatus dorylas* C, *Polyommatus eros* C, *Polyommatus escheri* C, *Polyommatus icarus* C, *Polyommatus ripartii* C, *Polyommatus thersites* C, *Pontia callidice* C, *Pontia chloridice* C, *Proterebia afra* R, *Pseudochazara anthelea* C, *Pseudochazara graeca* C, *Pseudophilotes baton* C, *Pseudophilotes bavius* C, *Pseudophilotes vicrama* C, *Pyrgus alveus* C, *Pyrgus armoricanus* C, *Pyrgus carlinae* C, *Pyrgus carthami* C, *Pyrgus cirsii* C, *Pyrgus malvae* C, *Pyrgus malvoides* C, *Pyrgus serratulae* C, *Satyrium acaciae* C, *Satyrium esculi* C, *Satyrus ferula* C, *Scolitantides orion* C, *Spialia orbifer* C, *Spialia phlomidis* C, *Spialia sertorius* C, *Spialia therapne* R and V, *Tarucus balkanicus* C, *Tarucus theophrastus* FR, *Thymelicus acteon* C, *Thymelicus hyrax* FR, *Thymelicus sylvestris* C, and *Zerynthia cerisy* C.
Barry Walter (CC BY 4.0): *Calophasia lunula* C.
Roger Wasley: *Cupido carswelli* V, *Erebia tyndarus* MR, *Maniola telmessia* MR, *Pieris cheiranthi* FR, and *Zerynthia cassandra* V.
Waugsberg (CC BY-SA 3.0): *Calliteara pudibunda* C.
David Williams: *Pyronia tithonus* C.
Simon de Winter: *Erebia calcarius* FR, *Erebia neoridas* FV, *Erebia orientalis* FR and FV, *Erebia styx* FR and FV, *Erebia zapateri* FR and MV, *Lycaena ottomana* MR, *Lycaena tityrus subalpinus* MR, *Maniola nurag* MV, *Melitaea asteria* MV, *Melitaea ornata* MR, *Polyommatus aroaniensis* MR, *Polyommatus nephohiptamenos* MR and V, *Pseudochazara amymone* V, and *Pseudochazara tisiphone* V.
Pete Withers: *Anthocharis euphenoides* MV, *Hipparchia fatua* FV, *Polyommatus amandus* V,

Pseudophilotes baton MR, and *Thecla betulae* MR and FR.
Julia Wittmann (CC BY 4.0): *Aricia nicias* FR, *Boloria thore* MR, *Chazara briseis* R, *Coenonympha glycerion* R, *Cupido argiades* MR, *Erebia gorge* R, *Erebia styx* MR, *Euchloe penia* R, *Melitaea phoebe* FR, *Pieris mannii* MR, *Pyrgus malvae* FR, *Satyrium spini* C, and *Thecla betulae* C.
Alan Woodward: *Glaucopsyche paphos* MR.
Worldwidewulf (CC BY 4.0): *Lycaena hippothoe* FR.
Xulescu_g (CC BY-SA 2.0): *Aglais ichnusa* V, *Melitaea phoebe* FR, *Parnassius mnemosyne* R and V, *Pontia edusa* V, *Pseudophilotes vicrama* MR, and *Pyrgus malvae* MR.
Nicola Zannino (CC BY-SA 4.0): *Lasiommata paramegaera* MR.
Kristof Zyskowski and Yulia Bereshpolova (CC BY 2.0): *Colias hecla* MR and FV.

Acknowledgements

I would like to extend special thanks to Ghislain Riou and Sylvain Delmas for their work on the genitalia of the *Pyrgus* genus, from which the diagrams presented in this guide draw significant inspiration. Ghislain Riou also provided valuable advice for this book and the *Guide pratique des papillons de jour*; I am particularly grateful to him. I would also like to thank Thibault Lorin for his help on the layout of this guide; he has been a longtime companion since the publication of the *Guide pratique des papillons de jour*. I express my gratitude and appreciation to all lepidopterists, whether amateur or professional, who, through the publication of their observations in articles or on often detailed and well-furnished websites, have significantly contributed to my synthesis effort. I would also like to thank all the photographic contributors and especially those with whom I have been able to exchange and who, through their enthusiasm, have, in their own way, supported this project: Pablo Martinez Darve Sanz, Adam Gor, Tamas Hudak, Alan Cooper, and Wolfgang Wagner. This book probably would never have come to fruition if I had not benefited from the understanding, patience, and support of my family in this endeavour, which devoured their spouse and father for several years. Kathleen, Colin, Robin, and Mélie, from the depths of my heart: thank you.

Index of Scientific Names

Aglais ichnusa 362
Aglais io 360
Aglais urticae 361
Agriades aquilo 301
Agriades dardanus 302
Agriades glandon 300
Agriades optilete 325
Agriades orbitulus 298
Agriades pyrenaicus 299
Agriades zullichi 303
Anthocharis cardamines 182
Anthocharis damone 185
Anthocharis euphenoides 184
Anthocharis gruneri 183
Apatura ilia 375
Apatura iris 374
Apatura metis 376
Aphantopus hyperantus 466
Aporia crataegi 189
Araschnia levana 368
Archon apollinus 123
Arethusana arethusa 564
Arethusana boabdil 565
Argynnis laodice 383
Argynnis pandora 382
Argynnis paphia 381
Aricia agestis 305
Aricia anteros 310
Aricia artaxerxes 307
Aricia cramera 306
Aricia montensis 308
Aricia morronensis 309
Aricia nicias 304
Azanus jesous 265
Azanus ubaldus 266

Boloria aquilonaris 400
Boloria chariclea 402
Boloria dia 391
Boloria eunomia 396
Boloria euphrosyne 393
Boloria freija 403
Boloria frigga 404
Boloria graeca 399
Boloria improba 405
Boloria napaea 398
Boloria pales 397
Boloria polaris 401
Boloria selene 394
Boloria thore 395
Boloria titania 392
Borbo borbonica 149
Brenthis daphne 388
Brenthis hecate 389
Brenthis ino 390
Brintesia circe 483

Cacyreus marshalli 262
Callophrys avis 248
Callophrys rubi 247
Carcharodus alceae 151
Carcharodus tripolina 152
Carterocephalus palaemon 135
Carterocephalus silvicola 136
Catopsilia florella 188
Celastrina argiolus 297
Charaxes jasius 354
Chazara briseis 538
Chazara prieuri 539
Cigaritis acamas 249
Coenonympha arcania 460
Coenonympha corinna 459
Coenonympha darwiniana 461
Coenonympha dorus 457
Coenonympha gardetta 462
Coenonympha glycerion 455
Coenonympha hero 451
Coenonympha iphioides 456
Coenonympha leander 464
Coenonympha macromma 461
Coenonympha oedippus 465
Coenonympha orientalis 463
Coenonympha pamphilus 452
Coenonympha rhodopensis 454
Coenonympha thyrsis 458
Coenonympha tullia 453
Colias alfacariensis 190
Colias aurorina 198
Colias caucasica 200
Colias chrysotheme 197
Colias crocea 196
Colias erate 192
Colias hecla 201
Colias hyale 191
Colias myrmidone 199
Colias palaeno 193
Colias phicomone 194
Colias tyche 195
Colotis evagore 186
Cupido alcetas 287
Cupido argiades 292
Cupido carswelli 289
Cupido decolorata 288
Cupido lorquinii 291
Cupido minimus 289
Cupido osiris 290
Cyaniris semiargus 285
Cyclyrius webbianus 261

Danaus chrysippus 378
Danaus plexippus 377
Deudorix livia 250

Erebia aethiopellus 497
Erebia aethiops 513
Erebia alberganus 527
Erebia arvernensis 502
Erebia bubastis 490
Erebia calcarius 506
Erebia cassioides 502
Erebia christi 487
Erebia claudina 494
Erebia disa 528
Erebia embla 529
Erebia epiphron 486
Erebia epistygne 516
Erebia eriphyle 491
Erebia euryale 521
Erebia flavofasciata 492
Erebia gorge 499
Erebia gorgone 518
Erebia hispania 507
Erebia lefebvrei 522
Erebia ligea 520
Erebia manto 490
Erebia medusa 524
Erebia melampus 488
Erebia melas 523
Erebia meolans 508
Erebia mnestra 496
Erebia montana 512
Erebia neleus 502
Erebia neoridas 515
Erebia nivalis 504
Erebia oeme 525
Erebia orientalis 526
Erebia ottomana 503
Erebia palarica 509
Erebia pandrose 495
Erebia pharte 493
Erebia pluto 498
Erebia polaris 524
Erebia pronoe 501
Erebia rhodopensis 500
Erebia rondoui 507
Erebia scipio 514
Erebia sthennyo 495
Erebia stiria 510
Erebia styx 511
Erebia sudetica 489
Erebia triarius 517
Erebia tyndarus 505
Erebia vogesiaca 490
Erebia zapateri 519
Erynnis marloyi 146
Erynnis tages 145
Euchloe ausonia 215
Euchloe bazae 211
Euchloe belemia 218

Index of English Names

		Page	Date	Place

	Page	Date	Place
❑ False Heath Fritillary	418		
❑ False Ilex Hairstreak	258		
❑ False Mallow Skipper	152		
❑ False Marbled Skipper	156		
❑ False Mnestra Ringlet	497		
❑ False Ringlet	465		
❑ Fenton's Wood White	230		
❑ Fiery Copper	239		
❑ Foulquier's Grizzled Skipper	174		
❑ Freija's Fritillary	403		
❑ Freyer's Fritillary	426		
❑ Freyer's Grayling	557		
❑ Freyer's Purple Emperor	376		
❑ Freyer's Brassy Ringlet	502		
❑ Frigga's Fritillary	404		
❑ Furry Blue	339		
❑ Gatekeeper	440		
❑ Gavarnie Blue	299		
❑ Gavarnie Ringlet	518		
❑ Geranium Argus	327		
❑ Geranium Bronze	262		
❑ Glandon Blue	300		
❑ Glanville Fritillary	425		
❑ Gomera Grayling	559		
❑ Gran Canaria Grayling	559		
❑ Grass Jewel	270		
❑ Grayling	541		
❑ Great Banded Grayling	483		
❑ Great Sooty Satyr	481		
❑ Grecian Anomalous Blue	344		
❑ Grecian Copper	236		
❑ Grecian Grayling	535		
❑ Greek Clouded Yellow	198		
❑ Green Hairstreak	247		
❑ Green-striped White	218		
❑ Green-underside Blue	281		
❑ Green-veined White	226		
❑ Greenish Black-tip	212		
❑ Grey Asian Grayling	537		
❑ Grisons Fritillary	420		
❑ Grizzled Skipper	175		
❑ Grüner's Orange-tip	183		
❑ Heath Fritillary	413		
❑ Hierro Grayling	559		
❑ Higgins's Anomalous Blue	345		
❑ High Brown Fritillary	386		
❑ Holly Blue	297		
❑ Hungarian Glider	371		
❑ Hungarian Skipper	162		
❑ Iberian Knapweed Fritillary	428		
❑ Iberian Marbled White	470		
❑ Iberian Scarce Swallowtail	131		
❑ Iberian Sooty Copper	244